Dedication

This book is dedicated to the memory of my father, Dennis Wiley Roberts, who passed away on October 8, 1999, at age 70, after a long struggle with cancer. In the last months of his life, he provided all of those around him with a model of courage and optimism in the face of a devastating disease.

Denise Boyd

Brief Contents

3RD
EDITION

...opment

Helen

Denis

Houston Co...

ALLYN AND BACON
Boston   London   Toronto   Sydney   Tokyo   Singapore

Executive Editor: Carolyn O. Merrill
Managing Editor: Tom Pauken
Developmental Editor: Jodi Devine
Senior Marketing Manager: Caroline Croley
Production Administrator: Elaine Ober
Editorial/Production Services: Lifland et al., Bookmakers
Text Designer: Schneck-DePippo Graphics
Formatting/Page Layout: Monotype Composition
Cover Administrator: Linda Knowles
Composition Buyer: Linda Cox
Manufacturing Buyer: Megan Cochran
Photo Researcher: Kathleen Smith

Copyright © 2002 by Allyn & Bacon
A Pearson Education Company
75 Arlington St.
Boston, MA 02116
Internet: www.abacon.com

Library of Congress Cataloging-in-Publication Data
Bee, Helen L., 1939–
   Lifespan development/Helen Bee, Denise Boyd.--3rd ed.
      p. cm.
   Includes bibliographical references and index.
   ISBN 0-321-04522-X
   1. Developmental psychology. I. Boyd, Denise. II. Title.

BF713.B435 2001
155--dc21   2001022691

Printed in the United States of America
10 9 8 7 6 5 4 3 2 1   RRDW   04 03 02 01 00

List of Features

Contents

U N I T III MIDDLE CHILDHOOD AND ADOLESCENCE

8 Physical and Cognitive Development in Middle Childhood   216

9 Social and Personality Development in Middle Childhood   246

To the Student

Before you begin your study of human development across the lifespan, it is important that you know what an incredibly complex field it is. To convey this complexity, textbooks must include a great deal of information. Thus, studying human development may be one of the most information-intensive learning experiences of your academic career. Fortunately, this book includes a number of features that will help you manage and sort out all this information.

How to Work with This Book

A textbook isn't like a magazine or a novel. You should keep in mind that the goal of working with a textbook is to understand and remember the information in it. To work with this book most effectively, take advantage of its structural and pedagogical features.

- *Chapter Outlines.* Before you read each chapter, read over the outline at its beginning. More information will stick in your mind if you have an idea of what to expect.

- *Preview Questions.* The introduction to each chapter ends with a list of questions to keep in mind as you read. Be sure to read the questions before continuing with the rest of the chapter. Like the chapter outline, the questions create a set of mental "hooks" on which to hang the information in the chapter.

- *Headings and Subheadings.* The preview questions correspond to the chapter's major headings. Think of these headings and their subheadings as a way of dividing the information that follows them into categories. Thinking of the information in this way will create a network of information in your mind that will make it easier to recall information when you are tested. Taking notes on your reading and arranging them according to the book's headings will help even more. To give yourself the best chance of creating these information networks, stop reading between major sections, reflect back on what you have read, and review your written notes.

- *Before Going On.* To help you review, the book includes a feature called Before Going On at the end of each major section. You should stop reading and try to answer the questions in this feature when you come to it. If you can't answer the questions, go back and review the section. You will know what parts of the text to review because each question corresponds to a subheading. Once you've completed this process, take a break before you begin another major section.

- *Marginal Glossary.* Key terms are defined in the margin near where they are first used in the text. As you come to each boldface term in the text, stop and read its definition in the margin. Then go back and reread the sentence that introduced the key term.

- *Critical Thinking Questions.* These questions encourage you to relate material in the book to your own experiences. They can also help you remember the information in the text, because linking new information to things you already know is a highly effective memory strategy.

- *Make the Connection.* Each chapter includes a question titled Make the Connection. Thinking about these questions will help you integrate information across chapters.

- *Themed Essays.* There are four kinds of themed essays throughout the book. **No Easy Answers** help you understand the complexities involved in trying to apply developmental theories and research to real life problems. **Development in the Information Age** essays will inform you about how various information media have affected perceptions of development and how such media may influence the developmental process itself. **Research Reports** recount the findings of important studies, and essays entitled **The Real World** offer practical advice on parenting, teaching, caregiving, and other aspects of daily life to which developmental psychology is relevant.

- *Policy Questions.* Discussions of social policy issues relevant to human development appear at the end of each unit. For example, the Policy Question at the end of Unit I addresses proposals to prosecute women for using drugs during pregnancy. These discussions will provide you with insight into how the findings of developmental research may be used to influence policy changes in the real world. They may also serve as starting points for group discussions and research projects.

- *Key Terms.* Key terms are listed alphabetically at the end of each chapter, in addition to being defined in the margin. When you finish a chapter, try to recall the definition of each term. Page numbers are listed for all the terms, so you can easily look back in the chapter if you can't remember a definition.

- *Chapter Summaries.* Looking over the chapter summary can also help you assess how much of the information you remember.

The task of understanding and remembering the information in a developmental psychology textbook may seem overwhelming. However, when you finish reading this book, you will have a better understanding of yourself and of other people. So, all your hard work will be well worth the effort.

Denise Boyd

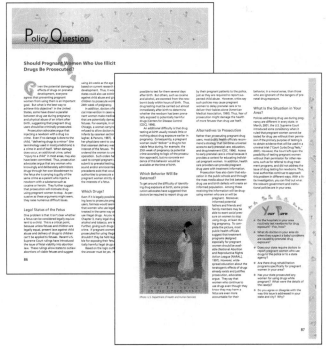

To the Instructor

The most obvious change from the second to the third edition of *Lifespan Development* is the addition of a second author. After a long and distinguished career, Helen Bee retired from writing and suggested that the publisher contract with a second author who would be solely responsible for the third edition. I was delighted to be offered the opportunity to take on this project.

My interest in the project stemmed from two sources: First, I have been teaching developmental psychology for 14 years, and writing a textbook has been one of my long-standing professional goals. Second, I particularly like Helen Bee's books and was enthusiastic about having the opportunity to build on her work. I have always thought that her books do an excellent job of conveying the idea that the answers to most questions about human development begin with the words "It depends," and I have tried to retain this feature of her writing throughout the third edition. Thus, one of my aims in preparing the third edition of *Lifespan Development* was to present the basic facts of development and, at the same time, to make readers aware of alternative interpretations of those facts.

Goals

The goals of the third edition are the same as those articulated by Helen Bee in the first and second:

- To find that difficult but essential balance of theory, research, and practical application
- To make the study of human development relevant not just for psychologists but also for students in the many other fields in which this information is needed, including nursing, medicine, social work, education, and home economics
- To keep all discussions as current as humanly possible, so that students can encounter the very latest thinking and the most recent research
- To write in as personal and direct a way as possible, so that the book is more like a conversation than a traditional text, without sacrificing either theoretical clarity or rigor of research

Changes and Additions in the Third Edition

In addition to updating theories and research presented in the second edition, the third edition of *Lifespan Development* includes the following changes:

● ***Organization*** ● Chapters 4 and 5 from the second edition (Infant Physical and Perceptual Development and Infant Cognitive Development) have been consolidated into a single chapter in this edition (Chapter 4, Physical and Cognitive Development in Infancy). This change has resulted in a book that has 18 rather than 19 chapters. The chapters are organized into five units:

Unit I: Foundations (Chapters 1–3)

Unit II: Infancy and Early Childhood (Chapters 4–7)

Unit III: Middle Childhood and Adolescence (Chapters 8–11)
Unit IV: Early and Middle Adulthood (Chapters 12–15)
Unit V: Late Adulthood and the End of Life (Chapters 16–18)

In addition, some topics have been moved from one chapter to another, or are discussed in connection with a different age period; the structure of some of the chapters has also been changed. The List of Features on page v should be helpful in locating the kinds of information included in most lifespan development texts.

Another organizational change is that the second edition's boxed material on culture has been integrated into the text, with new cultural information added. I adopted this approach because one of my goals for this revision was to include more information on culture and diversity than had been included in the first two editions. Integrating all discussions of culture into the body of the text provided more consistency.

● *History of Developmental Psychology* ● Chapter 1 (Basic Concepts and Methods) includes a new section on the history of developmental psychology. This section discusses the roles and contributions of women and minorities in the study of human development.

● *Streamlined Presentation of Research Methods* ● I have made a substantial effort to present research information as clearly and concisely as possible.

● *Evaluation of Theories* ● Chapter 2 (Theories of Development) cautions students against thinking of theories as either "true" or "false." Instead, students are urged to compare theories as developmentalists do, in terms of their underlying epistemological assumptions and overall usefulness (heuristic value, ability to be tested, and so on).

● *Biological Theories* ● Biological theories are given greater emphasis in this edition. For example, Chapter 2 includes a section on biological theories. The discussion of Piaget's sensorimotor stage in Chapter 4 touches on recent theories that object permanence may be inborn rather than learned. Chapter 13 discusses evolutionary theories of mate selection, and Chapter 16 includes an extensive examination of biological theories of aging.

● *Information-Processing and Other Cognitive Theories* ● Newer cognitive theories are discussed more extensively in the third edition than in the previous editions. For example, there is a fuller explanation of the memory system in Chapter 2. In addition, information-processing alternatives to Piaget's stages are presented in Chapters 6, 8, and 10. Social-cognitive theories of social and personality development are also more thoroughly discussed.

● *Pregnancy and Prenatal Development* ● The third edition of *Lifespan Development* significantly expands the coverage of prenatal development, reflecting rapidly expanding knowledge about this period of development. The coverage of pregnancy includes a discussion of the pregnant woman's experience and a comprehensive table outlining the major events, discomforts, prenatal care priorities, and possible complications for each trimester. A similar table outlines fetal development. In addition, the text provides a week-by-week description of the major milestones of prenatal development. There is also a new section on prenatal behavior.

● **Brain Development** ●   Each chapter on physical and cognitive development now includes a section on the brain and nervous system, which discusses how changes in the brain may be related to behavior. My goal in including this information for every age period was to convey the idea that the brain changes with age and that it influences, or is influenced by, behavior throughout the lifespan.

● **Health and Wellness** ●   Each chapter on physical development includes a section that discusses the major concerns and health care needs of that age period.

● **Mental Health** ●   The third edition of *Lifespan Development* expands on the coverage of atypical development presented in the second edition. New topics include attention deficit hyperactivity disorder (Chapter 8) and personality disorders (Chapter 12).

● **Moral Development** ●   In the first and second editions, moral development was included in the chapter on adolescent cognitive development. In this edition, moral development is discussed in both Chapter 9 (Social and Personality Development in Middle Childhood) and Chapter 11 (Social and Personality Development in Adolescence). I also expanded the coverage of moral development to include emotions and behavior as well as cognition.

● **Education** ●   The chapters on cognitive development in early childhood, middle childhood, adolescence, and early adulthood (Chapters 6, 8, 10, and 12, respectively) contain a great deal of new information about schooling and education. The early childhood chapter includes information on the psychological foundations of literacy learning. The middle childhood chapter includes expanded discussions of literacy learning, schooling and cognitive development, and children with disabilities, as well as new information about homeschooling. The adolescence chapter discusses emerging research on the transitions from elementary to middle school and middle school to high school. In addition, this chapter expands the second edition's coverage of the issue of teen employment. The early adulthood chapter offers extensive discussion of issues surrounding post-secondary education.

● **Social Policy** ●   A Policy Question feature follows each unit in the third edition. The features discuss the following questions:

Unit I: Should Pregnant Women Who Use Illicit Drugs Be Prosecuted?

Unit II: "Deadbeat Dads": Irresponsible Parents or Political Scapegoats?

Unit III: Has Test-Based Reform Improved Schools in the United States?

Unit IV: What Types of Couples Should Be Sanctioned by Society?

Unit V: Do People Have a Right to Die?

The first goal of these discussions is to acquaint students with a few social and political issues related to topics discussed in the text. The second goal is to encourage students to find out how these issues are being dealt with where they live. Each Policy Question feature ends with a list of suggestions that should help students find out more about the issue. My hope is that students will gain an understanding of the implications of developmental psychology for social policy as well as of the impact of social policies on human development.

Pedagogy

The third edition of *Lifespan Development* includes several important pedagogical features.

- *Marginal Glossary:* Each boldface term mentioned in the text is defined in the margin. This feature is new to the third edition.

- *Before Going On:* Another new feature appears at the end of each major section. Before Going On encourages students to stop reading and test their recall of various pieces of information before moving on.

- *Make the Connection:* Another feature new to the third edition is Make the Connection, a question that encourages students to look back at previously discussed theories or data and relate them to information in the current chapter.

- *Critical Thinking:* Critical Thinking questions throughout each chapter focus on relationships between the information in the text and students' personal experiences.

- *Key Terms:* All boldface terms in a chapter are also listed at the end of the chapter in alphabetical order with page references.

- *Chapter Summaries:* Each chapter ends with a summary organized by major chapter headings, with each point under each heading corresponding to a specific subheading in the chapter. This organization allows students to assess systematically how well they remember the chapter material and to know exactly where to look back in the chapter for information they may want to review.

Themed Essays

The third edition of *Lifespan Development* includes four kinds of thought-provoking themed essays.

No Easy Answers   The *No Easy Answers* essays, which are new to this edition, introduce students to the idea that there are many questions for which developmental psychologists cannot provide definitive answers. For example, the essay in Chapter 3 deals with the issue of pregnancy in women with epilepsy. A woman with epilepsy must decide between two risks: possible birth defects in her baby caused by her anticonvulsant medication or the many complications that can accompany epileptic seizures during pregnancy. Either path she chooses carries risk. Developmentalists can't tell a woman with epilepsy that if she does *x, y,* or *z*, her baby will turn out fine.

I developed these discussions in response to my own students' continuing difficulty in understanding that psychology is not a science that can offer straightforward recipes for perfect behavioral outcomes. My hope is that, by reading these discussions, students will become more sensitive to the complexity of human development and more tolerant of the ambiguities inherent in the behavioral and social sciences.

Development in the Information Age   The *Development in the Information Age* essays are also new to the third edition. In the first three chapters, these discussions focus students' attention on how various information media have shaped the public's understanding of development. For example, *Development in the Information Age* in Chapter 3 discusses how the news media sensationalize multiple births and, as a result, often obscure the real risks inherent in multiple pregnancies. In subsequent chapters, *Development in the Information Age* essays present ideas and research about how information technology may shape development itself. For example, the essay in Chapter 4 considers what babies actually learn from television, and the one in Chapter 14 deals with Internet addiction.

● **Research Report** ● *Research Reports* provide detailed accounts of specific research studies. For example, Chapter 16 discusses the New England Centenarian Study, a project aimed at discovering the variables that predict extreme longevity. Many of the *Research Reports* appeared in the first and second editions.

● **The Real World** ● A popular feature in the first and second editions, *The Real World* essays explore practical applications of developmental theory and research. The focus of each of these essays has been indicated by the addition of one of five subheadings: Parenting, Teaching, Caregiving, Aging, or Working. For example, the essay in Chapter 2 is titled *The Real World: Parenting,* and it suggests how a parent might use learning principles to shape a child's behavior. The subheadings let students know what kind of practical information they can expect in each essay.

Supplements for the Instructor

● **Instructor's Manual** ● The *Instructors' Manual* has been thoroughly revised by Karen Saenz of Houston Community College. Each chapter includes the following sections:

● What's New, highlighting the changes to the third edition
● Chapter Preview
● Learning Goals
● Extensive and detailed Teaching Notes, which include the Learning Objectives, cross-referenced in the student *Study Guide*
● Lecture Enhancement notes
● Instructor Resources, including suggested videos, Transparency and Handout Masters, and references to the full-color transparency acetates found in the Allyn & Bacon Human Development Transparency Set

● **Test Bank** ● Prepared by Pat Lefler Teeple of Lexington Community College, the *Test Bank* is composed of approximately 2,000 fully referenced multiple-choice, true/false, short-answer, matching, and essay questions. This supplement is also available on CD-ROM from your local Allyn & Bacon sales representative.

● **Video** ● A completely new Allyn & Bacon Interactive Video is available to accompany the third edition of *Lifespan Development.* The videos highlights important high-interest topics across the lifespan. Ask your local sales representative how to obtain a copy.

● **Transparencies** ● An extensive set of full-color transparencies is available through your sales representative.

Supplements for the Student

● **Study Guide** ● The *Study Guide* for the third edition of *Lifespan Development* has been revised by Karen Saenz. It offers students a rich and highly structured learning tool. Each chapter of the *Study Guide* includes the following sections:

- Overview of the chapter
- Learning Goals
- Guided Study Questions, which form the bulk of the *Study Guide*, including Learning Objectives cross-referenced in the *Instructor's Manual*
- Critical Reflection Exercises
- Practice Questions, similar in format to those found in the *Test Bank* and accompanied by an answer key
- Research Projects, updated and moved here from the *Instructor's Manual* for the second edition.

Practice Tests   Prepared by Pat Lefler Teeple (who also wrote the *Test Bank*, to ensure consistency), 20 multiple-choice items per chapter plus an answer key will assist students in preparing for course exams. These questions are different from those found in the *Study Guide*. The Practice Tests are available with the purchase of a new book, if requested by the instructor.

Web Site   The Allyn & Bacon Human Development SuperSite, www.abacon.com/development, offers a wide range of resources to both instructors and students. Students will find Practice Tests specific to the third edition of *Lifespan Development*, plus an array of learning activities, flashcards, research studies and summaries, video clips with questions, and annotated links to research. The site can be accessed through a PIN code available with the purchase of a new book.

Acknowledgments

No one ever accomplishes much of anything alone. Therefore, I would like to thank a number of people for providing me with the support I needed to complete this project. First and foremost, my husband, Jerry Boyd, my sons Matt and Chris Boyd, my daughter Marianne Meece, my son-in-law Michael Meece, and my mother, Bobbie Roberts, have served as my most important cheerleaders. Likewise, a number of people in my church and neighborhood "families" were instrumental in helping me accomplish this goal.

My colleagues at Houston Community College–Central (Madeleine Wright, Genevieve Stevens, David Gersh, and Saundra Boyd) acted as sounding boards for various ideas and supported me through some personally challenging events that happened to coincide with the writing of this book. I would also like to acknowledge and thank my department chair, Feleccia Moore-Davis, and Academic Dean Cheryl Peters for encouraging me and for allowing me a great deal of flexibility in my teaching responsibilities so that I could complete this project on time.

I also must thank several people at Allyn & Bacon for their help. First, I am indebted to Rebecca Dudley Pascal for encouraging me to get involved in textbook writing. Thanks also to Carolyn Merrill, who was instrumental in my being offered the opportunity to prepare the third edition of this book. The entire project was supervised by Jeff Lasser, who provided many ideas and words of encouragement over 16 months. To all three, I express my thanks for educating me about the process of turning an idea into a textbook. The knowledge I acquired from them about textbook writing and marketing has resulted in a book that is far better than I ever could have produced on my own.

Of course, developmental editors are essential to the process. I am indebted to Jodi Devine for pointing out digressions, improving the logical order of the topics in several chapters, and correcting numerous typos and grammatical errors. I also deeply appreciate her cogent summaries of reviewers' comments.

Finally, I would like to thank the many colleagues who served as reviewers for their thought-provoking comments and criticisms as well as their willingness to take time out of their busy schedules to help me improve this book.

Jeffrey Arnett
University of Maryland

Cynthia Avens
Daytona Beach Community College

Barbara E. Baker
Nashville State Tech

Laura Hess Brown
State University of New York at Oswego

Barbara DeFilippo
Lane Community College

Julie Felender
Fullerton College

Loren Ford
Clackamas Community College

Kathleen V. Fox
Salisbury State University

Lynn Haller
Morehead State University

Debra L. Hollister
Valencia Community College

Scott L. Horton
University of Southern Maine

Suzy Horton
Mesa Community College

John S. Klein
Castleton State College

David D. Kurz
Delmar College

Billie Laney
Central Texas Community College

April Mansfield
Long Beach City College

James E. Oliver
Henry Ford Community College

Regina K. Peters
Hawkeye Community College

Paul Roodin
State University of New York at Oswego

Lynn Shelley
Westfield State College

Kevin Sumrall
Montgomery College

Bradley M. Waite
Central Connecticut State University

Eugene H. Wong
California State University–
San Bernardino

Virginia V. Wood
University of Texas–Brownsville

Denise Boyd

Lifespan Development

CHAPTER 1

Basic Concepts and Methods

Spencer Grant, PhotoEdit

We are all observers of human development. For example, at family gatherings like the one pictured, we comment on the changes we notice in our relatives:

He's grown so much since the last time I saw him.

She's turned into such a beautiful young lady.

His hair's turning gray—the hair he has left, that is.

Grandma seems more frail than last year.

At the same time, we notice the things about people that appear to remain the same:

Aunt Frieda's as bossy as ever.

I don't understand how someone could go through so much and still be so cheerful, but he's always had a lot of faith.

We also view people in light of the expectations of our culture for their age group:

Is he going to college after he graduates this year?

I wonder when those two are going to start a family of their own. They've been married for 3 years now.

We even theorize about why our relatives behave the way they do:

They've never tried to control that child. No wonder he's such a brat.

She was born with a mean streak.

Scientists who study human development do precisely the same things. Their goal, however, is to produce observations and explanations that can be applied to as wide a range of human beings and in as many contexts as possible. To accomplish this goal, they study both change and stability. In addition, they examine the impact of cultural expectations on individual development. They make predictions about development and use scientific methods to test them. Finally, most hope that their findings can be used to positively influence the development of individual human beings.

In this chapter, you will learn how the science of developmental psychology came into being. You will also learn how modern psychologists differ from the early pioneers with respect to a variety of issues. In addition, when you finish reading the chapter, you will be acquainted with the research designs and methods used by developmentalists. While you read, keep the following questions in mind:

- What were the contributions of early philosophers and behavioral scientists to developmental psychology?

- How do today's psychologists think about issues that have to do with nature versus nurture and age-related change?

- What research designs and methods do developmentalists use to study change across the human lifespan?

The Scientific Study of Human Development

The field of **developmental psychology** is the scientific study of age-related changes in behavior, thinking, emotion, and personality. Long before the scientific method was used to study development, though, philosophers offered a variety of explanations for differences they observed in individuals of different ages. Their ideas continue to influence the field today, and many Western beliefs about human development are based on them.

Philosophical Roots

Philosophers who attempted to explain human development were especially interested in understanding why babies, who seem to start life so similarly, grow up to be adults who differ widely in intelligence, personality, and other characteristics. Of particular concern to most was the problem of explaining how and why some people grow up to be productive citizens while others become threats to the community. Expressed more simply, why do some of us grow up to be "good" and others "bad"?

In one way or another, most philosophers have approached this question by trying to determine whether factors inside people (such as intelligence) or outside of them (such as family environment) make them good or bad. Three ideas about the interaction of internal and external factors have been especially important in Western thinking about human development.

For centuries, the Christian doctrine of *original sin* has influenced European and American views on human development. This doctrine teaches that all humans are born with a selfish nature because of the sin of Adam and Eve in the Garden of Eden. Even when people do good works, this doctrine says, they do so for selfish reasons. For example, a man may give money to charity so others will admire him. According to this doctrine, to become capable of doing good works for pure motives, people must experience spiritual rebirth. After rebirth, individuals are in touch with the Holy Spirit, which helps them learn how to behave morally through prayer and Bible study. However, throughout life, even those who have experienced rebirth must confront the constant temptation to follow the inclinations of their sinful nature. Thus, from this perspective, differences in "goodness" and "badness" are the result of different degrees of success in overcoming one's sinful nature. In other words, interactions between an inborn, internal characteristic—the original sin nature—and an external influence—the Holy Spirit—produce differences in development.

The ideas of 18th-century Swiss philosopher Jean-Jacques Rousseau have also influenced Western views of human development. Rousseau claimed that all humans have *innate goodness*. This view asserts that all human beings are naturally good and seek out experiences that help them grow (Ozman & Craver, 1986). Rousseau believed that just as an acorn contains everything necessary to make an oak tree, children have within themselves everything they need to grow up to be competent and moral adults. Like acorns, children need only nutrition and protection to reach their full potential. For Rousseau, the goal of human development is to achieve one's inborn potential. "Good" behavior results from growing up in an environment that doesn't interfere with the individual's attempts to do so. In contrast, "bad" behavior is learned from others or happens when a person experiences frustration in his efforts to express the innate goodness with which he was born. Therefore, like the original sin view, the innate goodness perspective suggests that development involves a struggle between internal and external factors.

developmental psychology the scientific study of age-related changes in behavior, thinking, emotion, and personality

In contrast to both of these perspectives, 17th-century English philosopher John Locke proposed that the mind of a child is a *blank slate*. Locke said, "I imagine the minds of children as easily turned, this or that way, as water" (Ozman & Craver, 1986, p. 62). The blank slate view suggests that adults can mold children into whatever they want them to be. Therefore, differences among adults can be explained in terms of differences in their childhood environments. Thus, from this perspective, development—whether its results are good or bad—takes place because of external, environmental factors acting on a person, whose only relevant internal characteristic is the capacity to respond.

Critical Thinking

Other cultures and religions have different ways of viewing the process of development. How do the original sin, innate goodness, and blank slate views compare to your own beliefs? How do you think your own culture and religion have contributed to these beliefs?

The Study of Human Development Becomes a Science

Philosophy can provide a framework for ideas about human development. However, in the 19th century, people who wanted to better understand development began to turn to science. By 1930, the foundations of modern developmental psychology had been established (see Table 1.1).

Charles Darwin and other evolutionists believed they could understand the development of the human species by studying child development. Many, including Darwin, kept detailed records of their own children's early development (called *baby biographies*), in the hope of finding evidence to support the theory of evolution (Charlesworth, 1992). These were the first organized studies of human development.

Darwin's theory of evolution is the source of many important ideas in modern developmental psychology. For example, the concept of developmental stages comes from evolutionary theory. However, critics of baby biographies claimed that studying children for the purpose of proving a theory might cause observers to misinterpret or ignore important information.

G. Stanley Hall of Clark University wanted to find more objective ways to study development. He used questionnaires and interviews to study large numbers of children. His 1891 article titled "The Contents of Children's Minds on Entering School" represented the first scientific study of child development (White, 1992).

TABLE 1.1   Milestones in the History of Developmental Psychology

1875–1900	Darwin and others publish baby biographies based on evolutionary theory.
1891	Hall publishes first scientific study of children.
1890–1900	Freud begins publishing and lecturing in Europe about his psychosexual theory.
1904	Hall publishes book on adolescence.
1909	Freud lectures in the United States.
1913	Watson publishes his behaviorist theory.
1925	Gesell publishes his views on maturation.
1921–1930	Piaget publishes several books about his theory of cognitive development.

IN COURT

The Real World

The Leopold and Loeb Trial

Freud's theory has influenced Western culture as well as developmental psychology. For example, the use of psychological theories to defend people accused of crimes made its debut in United States courtrooms when one of the most famous attorneys in legal history, Clarence Darrow, used Freud's theory to defend two young men against a murder charge during the 1920s (Higdon, 1975; Weinberg & Weinberg, 1980). Eighteen-year-old Nathan Leopold and 19-year-old Richard Loeb confessed to murdering 13-year-old Bobby Franks to prove that they were intelligent enough to commit the perfect crime. After the boys' arrest, the Leopold and Loeb families hired Darrow to save the pair from the death penalty.

Darrow had written about his belief that judges and juries might look favorably on defendants in death penalty cases if lawyers could persuade them, based on Freud's theory, that various traumatic experiences in early childhood had caused the defendants to become violent and antisocial (Darrow, 1922). It's important to note here that, for Darrow, this kind of defense was not merely a courtroom gimmick to provoke sympathy. Rather, he sincerely believed that it was immoral to put murderers to death for crimes he believed had their roots in

traumatic childhood experiences. Specifically, Darrow claimed:

> It seems to me to be clear that there is really no such thing as crime. . . . Man is in no sense the maker of himself and has no more power than any other machine to escape the law of cause and effect. He does as he must. Therefore, there is no such thing as moral responsibility in the sense in which the expression is normally used. (Darrow, 1922, pp. 274–275)

Darrow hired several psychoanalysts to testify at the trial. They asserted that Leopold and Loeb had been neglected by their busy parents. As a result, they said, the two were emotionally equivalent to young children and, thus, should not be blamed for their crime.

(*Photo:* CORBIS)

Live radio broadcasts from the courthouse kept the enthralled American public up to date on the trial's events. Newspapers offered Sigmund Freud thousands of dollars to comment on the case, but he refused. Editorial writers expressed outrage at the idea that two murderers could escape justice by blaming their parents. At the end of the trial, the judge sided with Darrow and sentenced the two young men to life in prison.

As Darrow predicted, the psychoanalytic defense has been effective with judges and juries. However, most psychologists disagree with the simplistic way in which Freud's theory is often used to explain criminal behavior, because human development is far too complex to be explained by a single theory. Examination of any person's background may help us better understand him or her, but most of Freud's predictions about the link between childhood experiences and abnormal behavior in adulthood have turned out to be unfounded (Eysenck, 1985; Eysenck & Wilson, 1973). Most individuals who suffer trauma in childhood grow up to be normal, healthy, productive adults. Consequently, most developmentalists reject the notion that childhood trauma or poor parenting should be used as an excuse for criminal behavior.

Hall agreed with Darwin that the milestones of childhood were similar to those that had taken place in the development of the human species. He thought that developmentalists should identify **norms**, average ages at which milestones are reached. Norms, Hall said, could be used to learn about the evolution of the species as well as to track the development of individual children.

In 1904, Hall published *Adolescence: Its Psychology and Its Relations to Physiology, Anthropology, Sociology, Sex, Crime, Religion and Education*. This book introduced the idea that adolescence is a unique developmental period. Hall also arranged for Sigmund Freud, a Viennese physician who was unknown in the United States at the time, to lecture at Clark University in 1909, thereby introducing Americans to one of the most important theories in developmental psychology (see The Real World).

norms average ages at which developmental milestones are reached

By the time Freud accepted Hall's invitation to lecture in the United States, he had been studying hysterical disorders for more than 20 years. Hysterical disorders are physical problems, like blindness, for which doctors can't find a medical cause. Freud thought that these problems were caused by experiences patients couldn't remember. He hypnotized patients to help them remember, and he studied the dreams they reported. He also asked patients to tell him everything they could remember about specific periods of their lives, without censoring anything. These methods led to the development of modern psychotherapy.

Many of Freud's patients had memories of sexual feelings and behavior in childhood. This led Freud to believe that sexual feelings are important in personality development. Based on his patients' childhood memories, Freud proposed stages of personality development, which you will read about later in this book.

When Freud began publishing his theory in the early 1890s, people were shocked by it. Eventually, his views changed the way people thought about sexuality and the role of early childhood experiences in development. In addition, his theory introduced many new ideas, such as the existence of the unconscious mind. For these reasons, Freud's theory continues to be influential in modern developmental psychology (Emde, 1992).

Psychologist John Watson offered ideas about child development very different from those of Hall and Freud. Watson coined a new term, **behaviorism,** to refer to his point of view (Watson, 1913). Behaviorism defines development in terms of behavior changes caused by environmental influences. Watson believed that, through manipulation of the environment, children could be trained to be or do anything (Jones, 1924; Watson, 1930). As Watson put it,

> Give me a dozen healthy infants, well-formed, and my own specified world to
> bring them up in and I'll guarantee to take any one at random and train him to
> become any type of specialist I might select—doctor, lawyer, merchant,-chief,
> and yes, even beggarman and thief, regardless of his talents, penchants, abilities,
> vocations, and race of his ancestors. (1930, p. 104)

In a famous study known as the "Little Albert" experiment, Watson conditioned a baby boy to fear white rats (Watson & Rayner, 1920). As the baby played with a rat, Watson made banging sounds that frightened him. Over time, the baby came to associate the rat with the noises. He cried and tried to escape from the room whenever the rat was present. Based on the Little Albert study and several others, Watson claimed that all developmental changes are the result of learning (Watson, 1928).

Watson's views came to dominate American developmental psychology almost as soon as he published them. He also wrote popular books and magazine articles on child-rearing (see Development in the Information Age). Although Watson's theories are considered extreme by modern developmental psychologists, when they were first introduced they helped developmentalists better understand the role of environmental influences in development. Thus, Watson's ideas led to the development of modern learning theories, and the learning principles Watson used in the Little Albert experiment continue to be important in the treatment of children's fears.

Arnold Gesell studied and wrote about development in the same era as Watson, but his views were very different. Gesell's research suggested the existence of a genetically programmed sequential pattern of change (Gesell, 1925; Thelen & Adolph, 1992). Gesell used the term **maturation** to describe such a pattern of changes. He thought that maturationally determined development occurred regardless of practice, training, or effort. For example, infants don't have to be taught how to walk—they begin to do so on their own once they reach a certain age. Because of his strong belief that many important developmental changes are determined by maturation, Gesell spent decades studying children and developing norms. He pioneered the use of movie cameras and one-way observation devices to study children's behavior. Gesell's findings became the basis for many tests that are used today to determine whether individual children are developing normally.

MAKE THE CONNECTION

Review philosopher John Locke's blank slate idea. How does Watson's view, quoted in the text, compare to it?

behaviorism the view that defines development in terms of behavior changes caused by environmental influences

maturation the gradual unfolding of genetically programmed sequential patterns of change

in the Information Age

Child-Rearing Experts

Most of the 20th century can be characterized as part of the "information age," a period when various methods of mass communication—newspapers, magazines, radio, movies, television, audio and video recordings, the Internet—have exposed people at every level of society to an enormous and continuously growing amount of information. Throughout this book, Development in the Information Age features will acquaint you with many of the ways in which the information age has influenced development.

One consequence of the mass dissemination of information has been that "expert" advice on child-rearing has strongly influenced the beliefs and practices of parents in the industrialized world. This trend seems to have begun early in the 20th century, when popular magazines began to publish articles on child-rearing that referred to the theories of Sigmund Freud and other psychologists (Torrey, 1992). Soon, child-rearing books authored by experts became best-sellers. These articles and books recommended "scientific" approaches to child-rearing. No longer were grandparents or other older adults to be viewed as experts on

bringing up children. Instead, young parents were encouraged to turn to pediatricians and psychologists.

John Watson was one of the first information-age child-rearing experts. During the 1920s and 1930s, he wrote a number of influential books and articles about child-rearing based on his belief that American parenting traditions caused children to grow up to be emotionally weak. Watson advised parents:

> Never hug and kiss them, never let them sit in your lap. If you must, kiss them once on the forehead when they say good night. Shake hands with them in the morning. Give them a pat on the head if they have made an extraordinarily good job of a difficult task. (1928, pp. 81–82)

In addition to condemning physical affection, Watson favored an orderly approach to infant care involving rigid feeding schedules. Watson's writings were enormously popular, perhaps because his advice fit with the way life in the United States was changing at the time. People's work schedules were increasingly defined by the clock rather than by the cycles of daylight and darkness and the change of seasons. Thus, it became more common for babies to be fed on a timed schedule rather than when they were actually hun-

gry. Thanks to Watson, parents could take comfort in the idea that the new practice, often necessitated by their movement from agricultural to industrial work, was better for their babies.

Watson's popularity ebbed as the radically different ideas of Dr. Benjamin Spock, author of the classic book *Baby and Child Care,* became predominant in the 1950s. In contrast to Watson, Spock urged parents to openly display affection toward children. Based on Freud's ideas about the possible impact of early childhood emotional trauma on later personality development, Spock also warned parents against engaging in too much conflict with children over weaning or toilet-training. He emphasized the need to wait until children were ready, on their own, to take on such challenges.

Today, Watson's ideas are viewed as emotionally cold and excessively rigid by pediatricians, psychologists, and parents alike. Similarly, many view Dr. Spock's recommendations as overly indulgent. Nevertheless, young parents in the United States still have a tendency to look to experts, whose recommendations are now abundantly available in every information medium, for advice and reassurance.

One of the most influential theories in the history of developmental psychology is that of Swiss developmentalist Jean Piaget (Thomas, 1996). At 10, Piaget published his first scientific article, on sparrows. By the time he was 21, he had published more than 20 scientific articles and had received a PhD in natural science from the University of Geneva. In 1918, he went to Paris to work on an intelligence testing project. While in Paris, his wife gave birth to their first child, Jacqueline. Piaget and his wife, who was also trained as a scientist, made detailed notes about Jacqueline's development.

Piaget became a professor at the University of Geneva in 1921 and spent the next 6 decades studying the development of logical thinking in children, until his death in 1980. His studies convinced him that logical thinking develops in four stages between birth and adolescence. At first, infants explore the world using their senses and motor abilities. Through their actions, they develop basic concepts of time and space. Next, young children develop the ability to use symbols (primarily words) to think and communicate. Once they become proficient in the use of symbols, around age 6 or 7, children are ready to develop the skills needed for logical thinking. They spend the next 5 to 6 years using these skills to solve problems in the everyday world. Finally, in the teenage years, individuals develop the capacity to apply logic to abstract and hypothetical problems.

Because of the popularity of Watson's views, psychologists in the United States paid little attention to Piaget's work. During the late 1950s, however, American developmentalists "discovered" Piaget. From then on, developmental psychologists in the United States began to focus on children's thinking more than on how environmental stimuli influence their behavior.

The stages Piaget described and the theory he proposed to explain them became the foundation of modern cognitive-developmental psychology. Consequently, you will be reading a great deal more about them in later chapters. Although many developmentalists disagree with Piaget's theoretical explanations, a vast body of research, including numerous cross-cultural studies, supports the existence of the sequence of cognitive development that Piaget observed in his research (Mishra, 1997).

Women and Minorities in Developmental Psychology

As you may have noticed, this brief summary of developmental psychology's historical roots makes almost no reference to women. However, it is important to remember that many of the most influential men in the field could not have achieved their goals without the help of their wives. Valentine Chatenay Piaget and Rosalie Rayner Watson, for example, contributed to some of the pioneering research studies that came to be identified with their husbands' names. However, until relatively recently, women's position in most societies was such that even a woman who was a scientist in her own right would be regarded primarily as her husband's helper.

Despite discrimination, several women managed to earn degrees in psychology and to establish themselves as successful researchers during the early days of psychology (Milar, 2000). One of their most important contributions was to challenge the widespread belief that women were less capable than men of academic learning. In fact, many eminent psychologists of the early 20th century, including G. Stanley Hall, claimed that advanced education diminished women's reproductive capacity. Therefore, Hall and others argued, in order to protect the human species from extinction, it was critical to exclude women from colleges and graduate schools. Female psychologists of the era, such as Mary Whiton Calkins, Kate Gordon, and Helen Bradford Thompson, produced research findings that refuted the views of Hall and those who agreed with him (Milar, 2000).

Like women, minorities were barred from many colleges and graduate schools during psychology's early days. Nevertheless, in 1920, Francis Sumner became the first African American to receive a doctoral degree in psychology (Guthrie, 1998). During Sumner's tenure as chair of the psychology department at Howard University—a historically black institution in Washington, DC—the department became the center of research challenging popular notions about intelligence and other traits in minority populations. Similarly, the first Hispanic American to receive a PhD in psychology, George Sanchez, was instrumental in making psychologists and others aware of cultural bias in intelligence tests and other kinds of tests during the 1930s (American Psychological Association, 1997).

Today, more women than men receive degrees in psychology at both the undergraduate and graduate levels (APA, 1997). Moreover, many of the field's most highly respected researchers are women. The late Mary Ainsworth, for example, whose work you will encounter in Chapter 5, established the theoretical and empirical framework through which developmentalists continue to view infant-caregiver relations. Further,

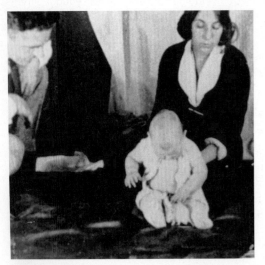

Rosalie Rayner Watson was a psychologist and an important contributor to her husband's theories and research studies. However, in the early days of psychology, female psychologists seldom received credit for their accomplishments because of societal attitudes toward women. (*Photo:* Archives of the History of American Psychology)

African American psychologists Kenneth and Mamie Phipps Clark conducted research on black children's self-esteem that continues to influence the way developmentalists think about racial identity. Their research was also a factor in the United States Supreme Court's decision to outlaw school segregation in the mid-1950s (Guthrie, 1998).

Before going on

- Summarize the original sin, innate goodness, and blank slate views of human development.

- List the contributions of Darwin, Hall, Freud, Watson, and Piaget to developmental psychology.

- Describe the position of women and minorities in the field of developmental psychology during the field's formative years.

Modern Developmental Psychology

Developmental psychology has changed considerably since the early days. For one thing, developmentalists have come to understand that inborn characteristics interact with environmental factors in complex ways. For another, the pioneers thought of change almost exclusively in terms of norms, whereas today's developmentalists view norms as representing only one way to measure change. Finally, the term *development* now encompasses the entire human lifespan rather than just childhood and adolescence.

Nature versus Nurture

You may have noticed that some early developmentalists, such as Watson and Gesell, thought of change as resulting from *either* forces outside the person (Watson's learning) *or* forces inside the person (Gesell's maturation). The debate about the relative contributions of biological processes and experiential factors is known as the **nature-nurture controversy**. In struggling with this important issue, psychologists have moved away from either/or approaches like those of Watson and Gesell toward more subtle ways of looking at both types of influences.

One of the newer ideas on the nature side is the concept of *inborn biases*. The basic notion is that children are born with tendencies to respond in certain ways. Some of these inborn biases are shared by virtually all children. For instance, from the earliest days of life, babies seem to listen more to the beginnings and ends of sentences than to the middle (Slobin, 1985b). Babies also come equipped with a set of apparently instinctive behaviors that entice others to care for them, including crying, snuggling, and, very soon after birth, smiling.

Other inborn biases may vary from one individual to another. Even in the early days of life, for example, some infants are relatively easy to soothe when they become

nature-nurture controversy the debate about the relative contributions of biological process and experiential factors to development

distressed, while others are more difficult to manage. Whether these inborn patterns are coded in the genes, are created by variations in the prenatal environment, or arise through some combination of the two, the basic point is that a baby is not a blank slate at birth. Babies seem to start life prepared to seek out and react to particular kinds of experiences.

Thinking on the nurture side of the issue is also more complex than in the past. For example, modern developmentalists have accepted the concept of *internal models of experience*. There are two key elements to this concept. The first is the idea that the effect of some experience depends not on any objective properties of the experience but rather on the individual's *interpretation* of it, the meaning the individual attaches to that experience. For instance, suppose a friend says to you, "Your new haircut looks great; it's a lot nicer when it's short like that." Your friend intends to pay you a compliment, but you also hear an implied criticism ("Your hair used to look awful"), so your reactions, your feelings, and even your relationship with your friend are affected by how you interpret the comment—not by what your friend meant or by the objective qualities of the remark.

The second key element of the internal models concept is that interpretations of experience are not random or governed by temporary moods but rather are organized into *models,* which can be thought of as organized sets of assumptions or expectations about oneself or others. For example, if you regularly hear criticism in other people's comments, you may have an internal model whose basic assumption is something like this: "I usually do things wrong, so other people criticize me."

Another important facet of current thinking about environmental influences is a growing emphasis on the importance of looking beyond a child's immediate family for explanations of development. According to this view, we must understand the *ecology,* or the *context,* in which the child is growing: his neighborhood and school, the occupations of his parents and their level of satisfaction in these occupations, his parents' relationships with each other and their own families, and so on (e.g., Bronfenbrenner, 1979, 1989). For example, a child growing up in a poverty-stricken, inner-city neighborhood, where drugs and violence are a part of everyday life, is coping with a set of problems radically different from those of a child in a relatively safe and more affluent neighborhood.

A good example of research that examines such a larger system of influences is Gerald Patterson's work on the origins of delinquency (Patterson, Capaldi, & Bank, 1991; Patterson, DeBarsyshe, & Ramsey, 1989). His studies show that parents who use poor discipline techniques and poor monitoring are more likely to have non-compliant children. Once established, such a behavior pattern has repercussions in other areas of the child's life, leading to both rejection by peers and difficulty in school. These problems, in turn, are likely to push the young person toward delinquency (Dishion, Patterson, Stoolmiller, & Skinner, 1991; Vuchinich, Bank, & Patterson, 1992). So a pattern that began in the family is maintained and exacerbated by interactions with peers and with the school system. Figure 1.1 shows Patterson's conception of how these various components fit together. Clearly, such models enhance our understanding of how the environment influences development.

A similarly interactionist model is implicit in the ideas of *vulnerability* and *resilience* (Garmezy, 1993; Garmezy & Rutter, 1983; Masten, Best, & Garmezy, 1990; Moen & Erickson, 1995; Rutter, 1987; Werner, 1995). According to this view, each child is born with certain vulnerabilities, such as a tendency toward emotional irritability or alcoholism, a physical abnormality, an allergy, or whatever. Each child is also born with some protective factors, such as high intelligence, good physical coordination, an easy temperament, or a lovely smile, that tend to make her more resilient in the face of stress. These vulnerabilities and protective factors then interact with the child's environment so that the same environment can have quite different effects, depending on the qualities the child brings to the interaction.

The combination of a highly vulnerable child and a poor or unsupportive environment produces by far the most negative outcomes (Horowitz, 1990). Either of these two negative conditions alone—a vulnerable child or a poor environment—can be overcome. A resilient child in a poor environment may do quite

If the concept of internal models is correct, then what matters about this team's victory is not the experience of success itself but rather how each girl interprets it. (*Photo:* Frank Siteman/ Tony Stone)

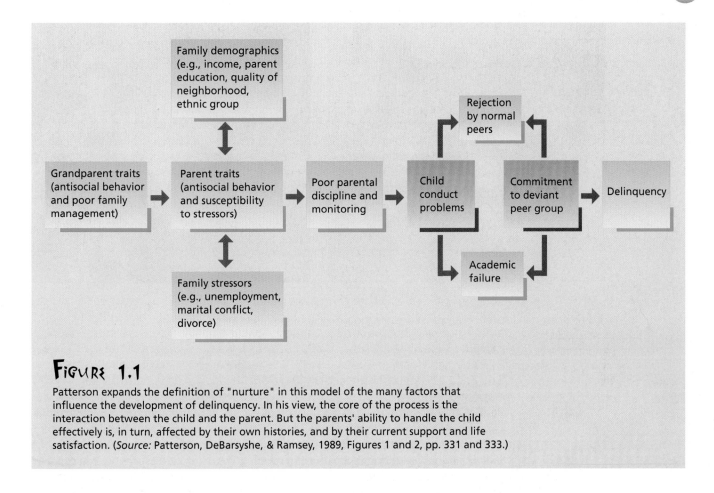

FIGURE 1.1

Patterson expands the definition of "nurture" in this model of the many factors that influence the development of delinquency. In his view, the core of the process is the interaction between the child and the parent. But the parents' ability to handle the child effectively is, in turn, affected by their own histories, and by their current support and life satisfaction. (*Source:* Patterson, DeBarsyshe, & Ramsey, 1989, Figures 1 and 2, pp. 331 and 333.)

well, since she can find and take advantage of all the stimulation and opportunities available; similarly, a vulnerable child may do quite well in a highly supportive environment in which parents help the child overcome or cope with her vulnerabilities. The "double whammy"—being a vulnerable child in a poor environment—leads to really poor outcomes for the child.

Universals, Contexts, and Individual Differences

In addition to their views on individuals and the enviroment, modern developmental psychologists' views on change itself are more complex than those of the field's pioneers. They study three very different types of age-related change. *Universal changes* are common to every individual in a species and are linked to specific ages. Some universal changes happen because we are all biological organisms subject to a genetically programmed maturing process. The infant who shifts from crawling to walking and the older adult whose skin becomes progressively more wrinkled are following a plan that is an intrinsic part of the physical body, most likely something in the genetic code itself.

However, some changes are universal because of shared experiences. A social clock also shapes all (or most) lives into shared patterns of change (Helson, Mitchell, & Moane, 1984). In each culture, the **social clock,** or a set of *age norms,* defines a sequence of normal life experiences, such as the right time to start school, the appropriate timing of marriage and childbearing, and the expected time of retirement.

Age norms can lead to **ageism**—a set of prejudicial attitudes about older adults, analogous to sexism or racism (Palmore, 1990). In U.S. culture, for example, older adults are very often perceived as incompetent. As a result, many are

social clock a set of age norms that defines a sequence of life experiences that is considered normal in a given culture and that all individuals in that culture are expected to follow

ageism a prejudicial view of older adults that characterizes them in negative ways

The biological clock obviously constrains the social clock to some extent at least. Virtually every culture emphasizes family formation in early adulthood because that is, in fact, the optimal biological time for childbearing. (*Photos:* Alan Oddie, PhotoEdit; Stephanie Maze, Woodfin Camp and Associates)

denied opportunities to work because employers believe that they are incapable of carrying out required job functions. Thus, social expectations about the appropriate age for retirement work together with ageism to shape individual lives, resulting in a pattern in which most people retire or significantly reduce their working hours in later adulthood.

Group-specific changes are shared by all individuals who grow up together in a particular group. One of the most important groups to which we all belong is our culture. The term *culture* has no commonly agreed-on definition, but in essence it describes some system of meanings and customs, including values, attitudes, goals, laws, beliefs, moral guidelines, and physical artifacts of various kinds, such as tools, forms of dwellings, and the like. Furthermore, to be called a culture, a system of meanings and customs must be shared by some identifiable group, whether that group is a subsection of some population or a larger unit, and must be transmitted from one generation of that group to the next (Betancourt & Lopez, 1993; Cole, 1992). Culture shapes not only the development of individuals, but also our ideas about what normal development is.

For example, researchers interested in middle and late adulthood often study retirement: why people retire, how retirement affects their health, and so on. But their findings do not apply to older adults in nonindustrialized cultures, where adults gradually shift from one kind of work to another as they get older rather than giving up work altogether and entering a new phase of life called "retirement." Consequently, developmentalists must be aware that retirement-related phenomena do not constitute universal changes. Instead, they represent developmental experiences that are culturally specific.

Equally important as a source of variation in life experience are historical forces, which affect each generation somewhat differently. Social scientists use the word **cohort** to describe groups of individuals who are born within some fairly narrow span of years and thus share the same historical experiences at the same times in their lives. Within any given culture, successive cohorts may have quite different life experiences (see Research Report).

Critical Thinking

How do expectations of 20-year-olds differ from expectations of 70-year-olds in your culture?

cohort a group of individuals who share the same historical experiences at the same times in their lives

Research Report

Children and Adolescents in the Great Depression: An Example of a Cohort Effect

Research involving children and adolescents who grew up during the Great Depression of the 1930s illustrates that the same historical event can have different effects on adjacent cohorts (Elder, 1974; 1978; Elder, Liker, & Cross, 1984). Glen Elder and his colleagues used several hundred participants who were born either in 1920 or in 1928 and who were also participants in the Berkeley/Oakland Growth Study, a long-term study of groups of participants from childhood through late adulthood. Those in the 1920 group were in their teens during the Depression; those born in 1928 were still young children during the worst economic times.

In each cohort, researchers compared participants whose families had lost more than 35% of their pre-Depression income with those whose economic condition was better. They found that economic hardship was largely beneficial to the cohort born in 1920, who were teenagers when the Depression struck full force, while it was generally detrimental to the cohort born in 1928. Most of those whose families experienced the worst economic hardship were pushed into assuming adult responsibilities prematurely. Many worked at odd jobs, earning money that was vitally important to the family's welfare. They felt needed by their families, and as adults, they had a strong work ethic and commitment to family.

Those who were born in 1928 had a very different Depression experience. Their families frequently suffered a loss of cohesion and warmth. The consequences were generally negative for the children, especially the boys. They were less hopeful and less confident than their less economically stressed peers; in adolescence, they did less well in school and completed fewer years of education; as adults, they were less ambitious and less successful.

These two cohorts were only 8 years apart, yet their experiences were strikingly different because of the timing of a key environmental event in their lives.

Individual differences are changes resulting from unique, unshared events. One clearly unshared event in each person's life is conception; the combination of genes each individual receives at conception is unique. Thus, genetic differences—including physical characteristics such as body type and hair color as well as genetic disorders—represent one category of individual differences. Characteristics influenced by both heredity and environment, such as intelligence and personality, constitute another class of individual differences.

Other individual differences are the result of the timing of a developmental event. Child development theorists have adopted the concept of a **critical period.** The idea is that there may be specific periods in development when an organism is especially sensitive to the presence (or absence) of some particular kind of experience.

Most knowledge about critical periods comes from animal research. For baby ducks, for instance, the first 15 hours or so after hatching is a critical period for the development of a following response. Newly hatched ducklings will follow any duck or any other moving object that happens to be around them at that critical time. If nothing is moving at that critical point, they don't develop any following response at all (Hess, 1972).

The broader concept of a *sensitive period* is more common in the study of human development. A **sensitive period** is a span of months or years during which a child may be particularly responsive to specific forms of experience or particularly influenced by their absence. For example, the period from 6 to 12 months of age may be a sensitive period for the formation of parent-infant attachment.

In studies of adults, one important concept related to timing has been the idea of *on-time* and *off-time* events (Neugarten, 1979). The idea is that experiences occurring at the expected times for an individual's culture or cohort will pose fewer difficulties for her than will off-time experiences. Thus, being widowed at 30 is more likely to produce serious life disruption or forms of pathology such as depression than would being widowed at 70.

critical period a specific period in development when an organism is especially sensitive to the presence (or absence) of some particular kind of experience

sensitive period a span of months or years during which a child may be particularly responsive to specific forms of experience or particularly influenced by their absence

Atypical development is another kind of individual change. **Atypical development** (also known as *abnormal behavior, psychopathology, pathological behavior,* and *maladaptive development*) refers to deviation from a typical, or "normal," developmental pathway in a direction that is harmful to an individual. Examples of atypical development include mental retardation, mental illness, and behavioral problems such as extreme aggressiveness in children and compulsive gambling in adults.

The Lifespan Perspective

Until quite recently, psychologists thought of adulthood as a long period of stability followed by a short span of unstable years immediately preceding death. This view has changed because, for one thing, it has become common for adults to go through major life changes, such as divorce and career shifts. As a result, several theorists whose ideas you will encounter later in this book have proposed stage models of development that include adult phases.

Another important factor that has affected developmental perspectives on adulthood is the significant increase in life expectancy that has occurred in the industrialized world. At the beginning of the 20th century, Americans' life expectancy at birth was only 49 years. By the century's end, the expected lifespan of someone born in the United States was about 76 years. As a result, older adults now constitute a larger proportion of the U.S. population than ever before. In fact, adults over the age of 100 are one of the most rapidly growing age groups in the industrialized world. Thus, the characteristics and needs of older adults are increasingly influencing many disciplines, including developmental psychology.

As interest in the entire lifespan has grown, developmental psychology has become more interdisciplinary. Psychologists, who are primarily interested in individuals, have learned that research in other sciences can greatly enhance their understanding of human development. Anthropologists provide information about culture, and sociologists explain the influence of race, socioeconomic status, and other social factors on individual development. Advances in biology are especially critical to an understanding of the physiological foundations of human behavior.

The changes outlined above have led to the adoption of a lifespan perspective. The **lifespan perspective** maintains that important changes occur during every period of development and that these changes must be interpreted in terms of the cultures and contexts in which they occur (Baltes, Reese, & Lipsitt, 1980). Thus, understanding change in adulthood has become just as important as understanding change in childhood, and input from many disciplines is necessary to fully explain human development.

atypical development development that deviates from the typical developmental pathway in a way that is harmful to the individual

lifespan perspective the current view of developmentalists that changes happen throughout the entire human lifespan and that changes must be interpreted in light of the culture and context in which they occur; thus, interdisciplinary research is critical to understanding human development

Before going on

● How do modern developmental psychologists view the two sides of the nature-nurture controversy?

● What are the three kinds of change modern developmentalists study?

● What is the lifespan perspective?

Research Designs and Methods

The easiest way to understand research methods is to look at a specific question and the alternative ways we might answer it. For example, older adults frequently complain that they have more trouble remembering people's names than they did when they were younger. Suppose we wanted to find out whether memory really declines with age. How would we go about answering this question?

Relating Goals to Methods

Developmental psychology uses the scientific method to achieve four goals: to describe, to explain, to predict, and to influence human development from conception to death. To describe development is simply to state what happens. A descriptive statement such as "Older adults make more memory errors than young and middle-aged adults" is an example of this first goal of developmental psychology. To meet this goal, all we would have to do is measure memory function in adults of various ages.

Explaining development involves telling why a particular event occurs. To generate explanations, developmentalists rely on *theories*—sets of statements that propose general principles of development. Students often say that they hate reading about theories; what they want are the facts. However, theories are important because they help us look at facts from different perspectives. For example, "Older adults make more memory mistakes because of changes in the brain that happen as people get older" is a statement that attempts to explain the fact of age-related memory decline from a biological perspective. Alternatively, we could explain memory decline from an experiential perspective and hypothesize that memory function declines with age because older adults don't get as much memory practice as younger adults do.

Useful theories produce predictions, or *hypotheses,* that researchers can test, such as "If changes in the brain cause declines in memory function, then elderly adults whose brains show the most change should also make the greatest number of memory errors." To test this hypothesis about changes in the brain and memory, we would have to measure some aspects of brain structure or function as well as memory function. Then we would have to find a way to relate one to the other. Alternatively, we could test the experiential explanation by comparing the memories of older adults who presumably get the most memory practice, such as those who are still working, to the memories of those who get less practice. If the working adults do better on tests of memory, the experiential perspective gains support. Moreover, if both the biological and the experiential hypotheses are supported by research, we have far more insight into age-related memory decline than we would have from either kind of hypothesis alone. In this way, theories add tremendous depth to psychologists' understanding of the facts of human development and provide them with information they can use to influence development.

Let's say, for example, that an older adult is diagnosed with a condition that can affect the brain, such as high blood pressure. If we know that brain function and memory are related, we can use tests of memory to make judgments about how much the person's medical condition may have already influenced his brain. At the same time, because we know that experience affects memory as well, we may be able to provide him with training that will help prevent memory problems from developing of worsening (see No Easy Answers).

No Easy Answers

It Depends . . .

Using research to improve people's lives is an important goal of developmental psychology. In most cases, however, applying research to developmental problems isn't as simple as it might seem. Thus, one of the most important things you can learn about developmental psychology is that the answers to many of the practical questions people ask about development begin with "It depends."

For example, when a parent discovers her son has been molested by a neighbor, she wants to know how the abuse will affect him in the future. But developmental psychologists don't have a concrete answer. They can tell the mother that the overwhelming majority of traumatized children show no long-term effects. They can also analyze the child and his particular situation and make an educated guess about what *might* happen in the future. In other words, the long-term outcomes depend on a variety of variables: how long the abuse lasted, at what age it began, the child's personality, the way the parents handled the situation when they learned of the abuse, and so on.

To further complicate matters, all of the relevant variables interact with one another. For example, counseling might benefit an outgoing child but be ineffective for a shy child who tends to keep his feelings to himself. Conversely, art therapy, a strategy that encourages children to express their feelings in drawings, might be effective with a shy child but have little impact on one who is outgoing. Because of such complexities, developmentalists can't tell the mother what she wants to hear: that if she follows a certain formula, her child will turn out fine.

Throughout this book, you will encounter discussions of how research can be applied to developmental problems in No Easy Answers features. These should give you a better appreciation of the intricate ways in which variables interact in human development. You will also learn that these intricacies often frustrate efforts to use psychology to find solutions to everyday problems.

Studying Age-Related Changes

When a researcher sets out to study age-related change, she has basically three choices: (1) Study different groups of people of different ages, using what is called a **cross-sectional design;** (2) study the same people over a period of time, using a **longitudinal design;** (3) combine cross-sectional and longitudinal designs in some fashion, in a **sequential design.**

● *Cross-Sectional Designs* ●   To study memory cross-sectionally, we might select groups of people of various ages, such as groups of 25-, 35-, 45-, 55-, 65-, 75-, and 85-year-olds. Figure 1.2 shows the results of just such a study, in which adults of different ages listened to a list of letters being read to them, one letter per second, and then had to repeat the letters back in the order given. You can see that performance was distinctly worse for the 60- and 70-year-olds, a pattern found in a great many memory studies (Salthouse, 1991).

Because these findings fit our hypothesis, it is tempting to conclude that memory ability declines with age, but we cannot say this conclusively based on the cross-sectional data, because these adults differ not only in age, but in cohort. The differences in memory might reflect, for example, differences in education and not changes linked to age or development. Furthermore, cross-sectional studies cannot tell us anything about sequences of change with age or about the consistency of individual behavior over time, because each participant is tested

Critical Thinking

Suppose a cross-sectional study of sex-role attitudes reveals that adults between ages 20 and 50 have the most egalitarian attitudes, while teenagers and adults over 50 have more traditional attitudes. How might cohort differences influence your interpretation of these results?

cross-sectional design a research design in which groups of different ages are compared

longitudinal design a research design in which people in a single group are studied at different times in their lives

sequential design a research design that combines cross-sectional and longitudinal examinations of development

only once. Still, cross-sectional research is very useful because it can be done relatively quickly and can reveal possible age differences or age changes.

● *Longitudinal Designs* ● Longitudinal designs seem to solve the problems presented by cross-sectional designs, because they follow the same individuals over a period of time. For example, to examine our hypothesis on memory decline, we could test a group first at age 25, then at 35, again at 45, and so on. Such studies allow psychologists to look at sequences of change and at individual consistency or inconsistency over time. And because longitudinal studies compare performance by the same people at different ages, they get around the obvious cohort problem.

A few well-known longitudinal studies have followed groups of children into adulthood or groups of adults from early to late adult life. The Berkeley/Oakland Growth Study is one of the most famous of these long-term studies (see Figure 1.3) (Eichorn, Clausen, Haan, Honzik, & Mussen, 1981). The Grant study of Harvard men is perhaps equally famous (Vaillant, 1977). This study followed several hundred men from age 18 until they were in their 60s. Such studies are extremely important in developmental psychology, so you'll be reading more about them in later chapters.

Despite their importance, longitudinal designs have several major difficulties. One problem is that longitudinal studies typically involve giving each participant the same tests over and over again. Over time, people learn how to take the tests. Such *practice effects* may distort the measurement of any underlying developmental changes.

Another significant problem is that not everyone sticks with the program. Some participants drop out; others die or move away. As a general rule, the healthiest and best educated are most likely to stick it out, and that fact biases the results, particularly if the study covers the final decades of life. Each succeeding set of test results comes from proportionately more and more healthy adults, which may make it look as if there is less change, or less decline, than actually exists.

Longitudinal studies also don't really get around the cohort problem. For example, both the Grant study and the Berkeley/Oakland Growth Study observed and tested participants born in the same decade (1918–1928). Even if both studies showed the same pattern of change with age, we wouldn't know whether the pattern was unique to that cohort or reflected more basic developmental changes that would be observed in other cultures and other cohorts.

● *Sequential Designs* ● One way to avoid the shortcomings of both cross-sectional and longitudinal designs is to use a sequential design. To study our memory hypothesis using a sequential design, we would begin with at least two age groups. One group might include 25- to 30-year-olds, and the other 30- to 35-year-olds. We would then test each group

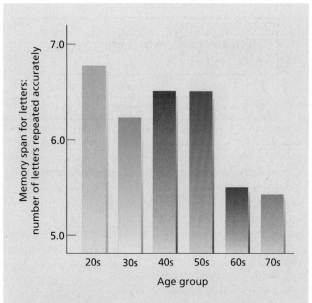

FIGURE 1.2

In this study, adults of various ages listened to an experimenter reading a series of letters, one letter per second. The participant's task was to try to repeat back the list in the order it had been read. The scores shown here are the average number of letters each age group could repeat back. (*Source:* Botwinick & Storandt, 1974.)

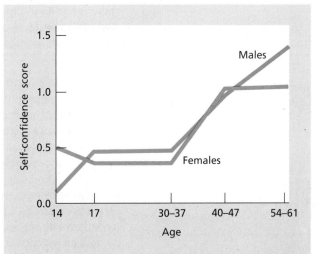

FIGURE 1.3

These results are from a famous study in Berkeley and Oakland, California, of a group of participants born either in 1920 or in 1928. They were tested frequently in childhood and adolescence, as well as three times in adulthood. Here you can see the sharp rise in self-confidence that occurred for both men and women in this group in their 30s — a pattern that *may* reflect a shared personality change, triggered by the common experiences of the social clock. (*Source:* Haan, Millsap, & Hartka, 1986, Figure 1, p. 228.)

		Age at testing point 1	Age at testing point 2	Age at testing point 3
Group	A	30 to 35	35 to 40	40 to 45
	B	25 to 30	30 to 35	35 to 40

FIGURE 1.4

This grid represents a design for a sequential study of memory function.

several times over a number of years as illustrated in Figure 1.4. In a sequential study, each testing point beyond the initial one allows researchers to make two types of comparisons. Age-group comparisons provide them with the same kind of information as a cross-sectional study. Comparison of each group to itself at an earlier testing point allows the researchers to collect longitudinal evidence at the same time.

Sequential designs also allow for comparisons of cohorts. For example, notice in Figure 1.4 that Group A is 30 to 35 years old at Testing Point 1, and Group B is 30 to 35 years old at Testing Point 2. Likewise, Group A is 35 to 40 at point 2, and their counterparts in Group B are this age at point 3. If same-age comparisons of the two groups reveal that their memory performance is different, researchers have evidence that, for some reason, the two cohorts differ. Conversely, if the groups perform similarly, investigators can conclude that their respective performances represent developmental characteristics rather than cohort effects. Moreover, if both groups demonstrate similar age-related patterns of change over time, researchers can conclude that the developmental pattern is not specific to any particular cohort. Finding the same developmental pattern in two cohorts provides psychologists with stronger evidence than either cross-sectional or longitudinal data alone.

Identifying Relationships between Variables

After deciding what design to use, the researcher interested in age and memory ability must decide how to go about finding relationships between *variables*. To developmentalists, variables are characteristics that vary from person to person, such as physical size, intelligence, and personality. When two or more variables vary together, there is some kind of relationship between them. The hypothesis that memory declines with age involves two variables, memory and age, and suggests a relationship between them. There are several ways of identifying such relationships.

● *Case Studies and Naturalistic Observation* ●   **Case studies** are in-depth examinations of single individuals. To test the hypothesis about memory and age, we could use a case study comparing one individual's scores on tests of memory in early and late adulthood. Such a study might tell us a lot about the stability or instability of memory in the individual studied, but we wouldn't know if our findings applied to others.

Still, case studies are extremely useful in making decisions about individuals. For example, to find out whether a child is mentally retarded, a psychologist would conduct an extensive case study involving tests, interviews of the child's parents, behavioral observations, and so on. Case studies are also frequently the basis of important hypotheses about unusual developmental events, such as head injuries and strokes.

When psychologists use **naturalistic observation** as a research method, they observe people in their normal environments. For instance, to find out more about memory in older adults, a researcher could observe them in their homes or workplaces. Such studies provide developmentalists with information about psychological processes in everyday contexts.

The weakness of naturalistic observation, however, is *observer bias*. For example, if the researcher who is observing older adults is convinced that most of them have poor memories, he is likely to ignore any behavior that goes against this view. Because of observer bias, naturalistic observation studies often use "blind" observers who don't know what the research is about. In most cases, for the sake of accuracy, researchers use two or more observers so that the observations of each observer can be checked against those of the other(s).

case study an in-depth examination of a single individual

naturalistic observation the process of studying people in their normal environments

Like case studies, naturalistic observation studies are limited in the extent to which the results can be generalized. In addition, naturalistic observation studies are very time-consuming. They must be repeated in a variety of settings so that researchers can be sure people's behavior reflects development and not the influences of a specific environment.

● *Correlations* ●   A **correlation** is a relationship between two variables that can be expressed as a number ranging from −1.00 to +1.00. A zero correlation indicates that there is no relationship between those variables. A positive correlation means that high scores on one variable are usually accompanied by high scores on the other. The closer a positive correlation is to +1.00, the stronger the relationship between the variables. Two variables that change in opposite directions result in a negative correlation, and the nearer the correlation to −1.00, the more strongly the two are connected.

To understand positive and negative correlations, think about the relationship between temperature and the use of air conditioners and heaters. Temperature and air conditioner use are positively correlated. As the temperature climbs, the number of air conditioners in use goes up. Conversely, temperature and heater use are negatively correlated. As the temperature decreases, the number of heaters in use goes up.

If we wanted to know whether age is related to memory, we could use a correlation. All that would be necessary would be to administer memory tests to adults of varying ages and calculate the correlation between test scores and ages. If there is a positive correlation between age and the number of memory errors people make—if older people make more errors—then we could say that our hypothesis has been supported. Conversely, if there is a negative correlation—if older people make fewer errors—then we would have to conclude that our hypothesis has not been supported.

Useful as they are, though, correlations have a major limitation: They do not indicate *causal* relationships. For example, even a high positive correlation between memory errors and age would only tell us that memory performance and age are connected in some way. It wouldn't tell us what caused the connection. It might be that younger adults understand the test instructions better. In order to identify a cause, we have to carry out experiments.

Critical Thinking

Researchers have found a positive correlation between a mother's age at the birth of her child and the child's later IQ: Very young mothers have children with lower IQs. How many different explanations of this correlation can you think of?

● *Experiments* ●   An **experiment** is a study that tests a causal hypothesis. Suppose, for example, that we think age differences in memory are caused by older adults' failure to use memory techniques such as repeating a list mentally in order to remember it. We could test this hypothesis by providing memory technique training to one group of older adults and no training to another group. If the trained adults got higher scores on memory tests than they did before training, and the no-training group showed no change, we could claim support for our hypothesis.

A key feature of an experiment is that participants are assigned *randomly* to one of two or more groups. In other words, chance determines which group each participant is placed in. When participants are randomly assigned to groups, the groups have equal amounts of variation with respect to characteristics such as intelligence, personality traits, height, weight, health status, and so on. Consequently, none of these variables can affect the outcome of the experiment.

Participants in the **experimental group** receive the treatment the experimenter thinks will produce a particular effect, while those in the **control group** receive either no special treatment or a neutral treatment. The presumed causal element in the

correlation a relationship between two variables that can be expressed as a number ranging from −1.00 to +1.00

experiment a study that tests a causal hypothesis

experimental group the group in an experiment that receives the treatment the experimenter thinks will produce a particular effect

control group the group in an experiment that receives either no special treatment or a neutral treatment

experiment is called the **independent variable,** and the characteristic or behavior that the independent variable is expected to affect is called the **dependent variable.**

In a memory technique training experiment like the one suggested above, the group that receives the memory training is the experimental group, and the one that receives no instruction is the control group. Memory technique training is the variable that we, the experimenters, think will cause differences in memory function, so it is the independent variable. Performance on memory tests is the variable we are using to measure the effect of the memory technique training. Therefore, performance on memory tests is the dependent variable.

Experiments are essential for understanding many aspects of development. But two special problems in studying child or adult development limit the use of experiments: First, many of the questions researchers want to answer have to do with the effects of particular unpleasant or stressful experiences on individuals—abuse, prenatal influences of alcohol or tobacco, low birth weight, poverty, unemployment, widowhood. For obvious ethical reasons, researchers cannot manipulate these variables. For example, they cannot ask one set of pregnant women to have two alcoholic drinks a day and others to have none. To study the effects of such experiences, they must rely on nonexperimental methods, such as correlations.

Second, the independent variable developmentalists are often most interested in is age itself, and researchers cannot assign participants randomly to age groups. They can compare 4-year-olds and 6-year-olds in their approach to some particular task, such as searching for a lost object, but the children differ in a host of ways other than their ages. Older children have had more and different experiences. Thus, unlike psychologists studying other aspects of behavior, developmental psychologists cannot systematically manipulate many of the variables they are most interested in.

To get around this problem, researchers can use any one of a series of strategies, sometimes called *quasi-experiments*, in which they compare groups without assigning the participants randomly. Cross-sectional studies are a form of quasi-experiment. So are studies in which researchers compare members of naturally occurring groups that differ in some dimension of interest, such as children whose parents choose to place them in day-care programs and children whose parents keep them at home.

Such comparisons have built-in problems, because groups that differ in one way are likely to differ in other ways as well. Parents who place their children in day care are likely to be poorer, to be single parents, and to have different values or religious backgrounds compared with parents who keep their children at home. If researchers find that the two groups of children differ in some fashion, is it because they have spent their days in different environments or because of these other differences in their families? Researchers can make such comparisons a bit easier if they select comparison groups that are matched on those variables the researchers think might matter, such as income, marital status, or religion. But a quasi-experiment, by its very nature, will always yield more ambiguous results than will a fully controlled experiment.

Cross-Cultural Research

Increasingly common in developmental psychology are studies comparing cultures or contexts, a task that researchers approach in several ways. One method of study, borrowed from the field of anthropology, is **ethnography**. The ethnographic method creates a detailed description of a single culture or context based on extensive observation. Often the observer lives in the culture or context for a period of time, perhaps as long as several years. Each ethnographic study is intended to stand alone, although it is sometimes possible to combine information from several different studies to see whether similar developmental patterns exist in the various cultures or contexts.

Alternatively, investigators may attempt to compare two or more cultures directly, by testing children or adults in each of the cultures with the same or comparable measures. Sometimes this involves comparing groups from different countries.

independent variable the presumed causal element in an experiment

dependent variable the characteristic or behavior that is expected to be affected by the independent variable

ethnography a detailed description of a single culture or context

Sometimes the comparisons are between subcultures within the same country; for example, increasingly common in the United States is research involving comparisons of children or adults living in different ethnic groups or communities, such as African Americans, Hispanic Americans, Asian Americans, and European Americans.

Cross-cultural research is important to developmental psychology for two reasons. First, developmentalists want to identify universal changes, that is, predictable events or processes experienced by individuals in all cultures. Developmentalists don't want to make a general statement about development—such as "Memory declines with age"—if the phenomenon in question happens only in certain cultures. Without cross-cultural research, it is impossible to know whether studies involving North Americans and Europeans apply to people in other parts of the world.

Second, one of the goals of developmental psychology is to produce findings that can be used to improve people's lives. Cross-cultural research is critical to this goal as well. For example, developmentalists know that children in cultures that emphasize the community more than the individual are more cooperative than children in more individualistic cultures. However, to use this information to help all children learn to cooperate, they need to know exactly how adults in such cultures teach their children to be cooperative. Cross-cultural research helps developmentalists identify specific variables that explain cultural differences.

Research Ethics

Research ethics are the guidelines researchers follow to protect the rights of animals used in research and humans who participate in studies. Ethical guidelines are published by professional organizations such as the American Psychological Association, the American Educational Research Association, and the Society for Research in Child Development. Universities, private foundations, and government agencies have review committees that make sure all research sponsored by the institution is ethical. Guidelines for animal research include the requirement that animals be protected from unnecessary pain and suffering. Further, researchers must demonstrate that the potential benefits of their studies to either human or animal populations will be greater than any potential harm to animal subjects.

Ethical standards for research involving human participants address the following major concerns:

● *Protection from Harm* ●   It is unethical to do research that may cause participants permanent physical or psychological harm. Moreover, if the possibility of temporary harm exists, researchers must provide participants with some way of repairing the damage. For example, if the study will remind subjects of unpleasant experiences, like rape, researchers must provide them with counseling.

● *Informed Consent* ●   Researchers must inform participants of any possible harm and have them sign a consent form stating that they are aware of the risks of participating. In order for children to participate in studies, their parents must give permission after the researcher has informed them of possible risks. Children older than 7 must also give their own consent. If the research takes place in a school or day-care center, an administrator representing the institution must consent. In addition, both children and adults have the right to discontinue participation in a study at any time. Researchers are obligated to explain this right to children in language they can understand.

● *Confidentiality* ●   Participants have the right to confidentiality. Researchers must keep the identities of participants confidential and must report their data in such a way that no particular piece of information can be associated with any specific

research ethics the guidelines researchers follow to protect the rights of animals used in research and humans who participate in studies

participant. The exception to confidentiality is when children reveal to researchers that they have been abused in any way by an adult. In most states, all citizens are required to report suspected cases of child abuse.

● **Knowledge of Results** ●   Participants, their parents, and the administrators of institutions in which research takes place have a right to a written summary of a study's results.

● **Deception** ●   If deception has been a necessary part of a study, participants have the right to be informed about the deception as soon as the study is over.

Before going on

- Discuss the pros and cons of cross-sectional, longitudinal, and sequential research designs.

- How do developmentalists use case studies, naturalistic observation, correlations, and experiments to identify relationships between variables?

- Why is cross-cultural research important to developmental psychology?

- List the ethical standards used by researchers to protect the rights of research participants.

A Final Word

Even if you never conduct research yourself, you will still find the information you have just read about research methods useful. For example, many students respond to research results by saying either "I agree with that study" or "I don't agree with that study." A better approach is to learn to use your knowledge of research methods to become a "critical consumer" of research.

For example, suppose you read a newspaper report of a study "proving" that putting infants in day care causes behavior problems later in childhood. After reading this chapter, you should know that only an experiment can produce such proof. To demonstrate that day care causes behavior problems, researchers would have to randomly assign infants to day-care and home-care groups. You should be aware that such a study would be unethical and, therefore, impossible. Thus, a newspaper report may claim that a study showing a *correlation* between day care and behavior problems demonstrates that one *causes* the other—but you, the critical consumer, should know better.

As you read the remaining chapters of this book, keep in mind that research findings, whether reported in the newspaper or in psychology textbooks, should never be thought of as authoritative statements that can't be questioned. However, neither are they ordinary opinions that call for a response of "I agree" or "I disagree." The appropriate response to research results is critical thinking based on solid knowledge of both the possibilities and limitations of psychological research.

Summary

The Study of Human Development

- The philosophical concepts of original sin, innate goodness, and the blank slate have influenced Western ideas about human development.

- Darwin studied child development to gain insight into evolution. G. Stanley Hall published the first scientific study of children, introduced the concepts of norms and adolescence, and brought Freud to America. Freud based his psychoanalytic theory on sexual themes in the childhood memories of his emotionally disturbed patients. Watson convinced American psychologists and parents that most changes in childhood are due to learning. Piaget identified stages of cognitive development.

- Although women and minorities were excluded from many colleges and universities in psychology's early days, many overcame this barrier to make important contributions to the field.

Modern Developmental Psychology

- Historically, developmentalists have argued about nature versus nurture, but now they believe that every developmental change is a product of both.

- Modern developmental psychologists study three kinds of changes: universal, group-specific, and individual.

- Today's developmentalists recognize that change happens throughout the lifespan.

Research Designs and Methods

- Developmental psychologists use scientific methods to describe, explain, and predict age-related changes and individual differences. Most also want to use research results to improve people's lives.

- In cross-sectional studies, separate age groups are each tested once. In longitudinal designs, the same individuals are tested repeatedly over time. Sequential designs combine cross-sectional and longitudinal comparisons.

- Case studies and naturalistic observation provide a lot of important information, but it usually isn't generalizable to other individuals or groups. Correlational studies measure relationships between variables. They can be done quickly, and the information they yield is more generalizable than that from case studies or naturalistic observation. To test causal hypotheses, it is necessary to use experimental designs in which participants are assigned randomly to experimental or control groups.

- Cross-cultural research helps developmentalists identify universal factors and cultural variables that affect development.

- Ethical principles governing psychological research include protection from harm, informed consent, confidentiality, knowledge of results, and protection from deception.

Key Terms

ageism (p. 11)

atypical development (p. 14)

behaviorism (p. 6)

case study (p. 18)

cohort (p. 12)

control group (p. 19)

correlation (p. 19)

critical period (p. 13)

cross-sectional design (p. 16)

dependent variable (p. 20)

developmental psychology (p. 3)

ethnography (p. 20)

experiment (p. 19)

experimental group (p. 19)

independent variable (p. 20)

lifespan perspective (p. 14)

longitudinal design (p. 16)

maturation (p. 6)

naturalistic observation (p. 18)

nature-nurture controversy (p. 9)

norms (p. 5)

research ethics (p. 21)

sensitive period (p. 13)

sequential design (p. 16)

social clock (p. 11)

Theories of Development

David J. Sams, Stock Boston

Every parent knows it's a constant struggle to keep babies from putting everything in their mouths. Whether it's an attractive toy or a dead insect they encounter while crawling across the living room floor, infants seem to be driven to use their mouths to explore. Have you ever wondered why? An inborn drive to explore the environment may be responsible, or babies may find the physical sensation of mouthing an object as highly pleasurable. Perhaps babies use their mouths more than toddlers and preschoolers do because they don't yet have the ability to fully control other parts of their bodies. Clearly, there are many possible explanations.

As you learned in Chapter 1, developmental psychologists use theories to formulate *hypotheses,* or testable answers, to such "why" questions. For this reason, you'll be reading about theories in every chapter of this book. To help you make sense of all these theories, this chapter will introduce you to three influential families of theories that have quite different ways of answering questions about development. Theories in these families will come up again and again as you make your way through this book. This chapter will also acquaint you with a few current theoretical trends in the field of developmental psychology, and you will learn how developmental psychologists compare theories. As you read, keep the following questions in mind:

- How do the theories of Freud and Erikson explain developmental change?
- How do the theories of Pavlov, Skinner, and Bandura explain developmental change?
- How do Piaget's theory and the information-processing approach explain developmental change?
- What kinds of theories have recently captured the attention of developmental psychologists?
- What criteria do psychologists use to compare one theory to another?

Psychoanalytic Theories

One theoretical approach to explaining babies' fascination with mouthing objects might suggest that infants derive more physical pleasure from mouthing objects than from manipulating them with other parts of their bodies. Such an approach would most likely belong to the family of **psychoanalytic theories,** a school of thought that originated with Sigmund Freud. Psychoanalytic theorists believe that developmental change happens because internal drives and emotions influence behavior.

Freud's Psychosexual Theory

One of Freud's most distinctive concepts is the idea that behavior is governed by both conscious and unconscious processes. The most basic of these unconscious processes is an internal drive for physical pleasure that Freud called the **libido.** He believed the libido to be the motivating force behind most behavior.

psychoanalytic theories theories proposing that developmental change happens because of the influence of internal drives and emotions on behavior

libido in Freud's theory, an instinctual drive for physical pleasure present at birth and forming the motivating force behind virtually all human behavior

TABLE 2.1   Common Defense Mechanisms

Mechanism	Definition	Example
Denial	Behaving as if a problem doesn't exist	A pregnant woman fails to get prenatal care because she convinces herself she can't possibly be pregnant, even though she has all the symptoms.
Repression	Pushing the memory of something unpleasant into the unconscious	A child "forgets" about a troublesome bully on the bus as soon as he gets safely home from school every day.
Projection	Seeing one's own behavior or beliefs in others, whether they are actually present or not	A woman complains about her boss to a co-worker and comes away from the conversation believing that the co-worker shares her dislike of the boss, even though the co-worker made no comment on what she said.
Regression	Behaving in a way that is inappropriate for one's age	A toilet-trained 2-year-old starts wetting the bed every night after a new baby arrives.
Displacement	Directing emotion to an object (or a person) other than the one that provoked it	An elderly adult suffers a stroke, becomes physically impaired, and expresses her frustration through verbal abuse of the hospital staff.
Rationalization	Creating an explanation to justify an action or to deal with a disappointment	A man stealing money from his employer says to himself "They won't give me a raise, so I deserve whatever I can take."

id in Freud's theory, the part of the personality that comprises a person's basic sexual and aggressive impulses; it contains the libido and motivates a person to seek pleasure and avoid pain

ego according to Freud, the thinking element of personality

superego Freud's term for the part of personality that is the moral judge

defense mechanisms strategies for reducing anxiety, such as repression, denial, or projection, proposed by Freud

Freud also argued that personality has three parts. The **id** contains the libido and operates at an unconscious level; the id is a person's basic sexual and aggressive impulses, which are present at birth. The **ego,** the conscious, thinking part of personality, develops in the first 2 to 3 years of life. One of the ego's jobs is to keep the needs of the id satisfied. For instance, when a person is hungry, it is the id that demands food immediately, and the ego is supposed to find a way to obtain it. The **superego,** the portion of the personality that acts as a moral judge, contains the rules of society and develops near the end of early childhood, at about age 6. Once the superego develops, the ego's task becomes more complex. It must satisfy the id without violating the superego's rules.

The ego is responsible for keeping the three components of personality in balance. According to Freud, a person experiences tension when any of the three components is in conflict with another. For example, if a person is hungry, the id may motivate her to do anything to find food, but the ego—her conscious self—may be unable to find any. Alternatively, food may be available, but the ego may have to violate one of the superego's moral rules to get it. In such cases, the ego may generate **defense mechanisms,** ways of thinking about a situation that reduce anxiety (see Table 2.1 and No Easy Answers). Without defense mechanisms, Freud thought, the degree of tension within the personality would become intolerable, leading to mental illness or suicide.

No Easy Answers

The Repressed Memory Controversy

Though they are removed from consciousness by the defense mechanisms of denial and repression, Freud claimed, traumatic events suffered in childhood, such as sexual abuse, lie smoldering in the unconscious. While hidden away, they cause distress in the personality and may even lead to serious mental illness. Consequently, Freud thought that the goal of psychotherapy was to uncover such events and help individuals learn to cope with them.

Memory researchers have investigated Freud's claim that childhood trauma is often forgotten in this way. It turns out that a few people who were crime victims or who were abused by their parents as children do forget the events for long periods of time, just as Freud predicted. However, most victims have vivid memories of traumatic events, even though they may forget minor details (Baddeley, 1998; Lindsay & Read, 1994). Moreover, those who commit crimes or abuse children are more likely to forget the incidents than are the victims (Taylor & Kopelman, 1984).

Memory experts also point out that therapists who directly suggest the possibility of repressed memories risk creating false memories in their clients' minds (Ceci & Bruck, 1993). However, repression does sometimes occur, and discovery of a repressed memory does sometimes improve a person's mental health. Thus, mental health professionals face a dilemma. Should they ignore the possibility of a repressed memory or risk creating a false one?

Therapists address the dilemma by obtaining training in techniques that can bring out repressed memories but don't directly suggest that such memories exist. For example, when clients believe they have recalled a repressed event, therapists help them look for concrete evidence. In the end, however, both therapist and client should recognize that they must often rely on flawed human judgment to decide whether a "recovered" memory was really repressed or was invented in the client's mind.

Freud proposed a series of **psychosexual stages** through which a child moves in a fixed sequence determined by maturation (see Table 2.2, page 28). In each stage, the libido is centered on a different part of the body. In the infant, the mouth is the focus of the drive for physical pleasure; the stage is therefore called the *oral stage*. As maturation progresses, the libido becomes focused on the anus (hence, the *anal stage*), and later on the genitals (the *phallic stage* and eventually the *genital stage*).

Optimum development, according to Freud, requires an environment that will satisfy the unique needs of each period. For example, the infant needs sufficient opportunity for oral stimulation. An inadequate early environment will result in *fixation*, characterized by behaviors that reflect unresolved problems and unmet needs. Thus, as you might guess from looking at the list of stages in Table 2.2, emphasis on the formative role of early experiences is a hallmark of psychoanalytic theories.

Freud's most controversial idea about early childhood is his assertion that children experience sexual attraction to the opposite-sex parent during the phallic stage (ages 3 to 6). Freud borrowed names for this conflict from Greek literature. Oedipus was a male character who was involved in a romantic relationship with his mother. Electra was a female character who had a similar relationship with her father. During the phallic stage boys are supposed to have such an intense desire to possess their mothers that they often fantasize about killing their fathers. Freud referred to these feelings as the *Oedipus complex*. In Freud's view, the boy responds to the anxiety generated by these conflicting feelings with a defense mechanism called *identification*. In other words, he attempts to match his own behavior to that of his father. According to Freud, by trying to make himself as much like his father as possible, the boy not only reduces what he perceives as the chance of an attack from the father, but also acquires masculine behavior patterns.

A parallel process is supposed to occur in girls; Freud named it the *Electra complex*. A girl experiences the same kind of attraction to her father as a boy does toward his mother. Likewise, she sees her mother as a rival for her father's attentions and has some fear of her mother. Like the boy, she resolves the problem by identifying with the same-sex parent.

psychosexual stages Freud's five stages of personality development through which children move in a fixed sequence determined by maturation; the libido is centered in a different body part in each stage

TABLE 2.2 Freud's Psychosexual Stages

Stage	Approximate Ages	Focus of Libido	Major Developmental Task	Some Characteristics of Adults Fixated at This Stage
Oral	Birth to 1 year	Mouth, lips, tongue	Weaning	Oral behavior, such as smoking and overeating; passivity and gullibility
Anal	1 to 3 years	Anus	Toilet training	Orderliness, obstinacy or messiness, disorganization
Phallic	3 to 6 years	Genitals	Resolving Oedipus/Electra complex	Vanity, recklessness, sexual dysfunction or deviancy
Latency*	6 to 12 years	None	Developing defense mechanisms; identifying with same-sex peers	None
Genital	12+	Genitals	Achieving mature sexual intimacy	Adults who have successfully integrated earlier stages should emerge with sincere interest in others and mature sexuality.

*Freud thought that the latency period is not really a psychosexual stage, because libido is not focused on the body during this period; therefore, fixation is impossible.

Erikson's Psychosocial Theory

Apart from Freud, Erik Erikson is the psychoanalytic theorist who has had the greatest influence on the study of development (Erikson, 1950, 1959, 1980b, 1982; Erikson, Erikson, & Kivnick, 1986; Evans, 1969). Erikson thought development resulted from the interaction between internal drives and cultural demands; thus, his theory refers to **psycho*social*** stages rather than to psycho*sexual* ones. Furthermore, Erikson thought that development continued through the entire lifespan.

In Erikson's view, to achieve a healthy personality, an individual must successfully resolve a crisis at each of the eight stages of development, as summarized in Table 2.3. Each crisis is defined by a pair of opposing possibilities, such as trust versus mistrust or integrity versus despair. Successful resolution of a crisis results in the development of the characteristic on the positive side of the dichotomy. A healthy resolution, however, does not mean moving totally to the positive side. For example, an infant needs to have experienced some mistrust in order to learn to identify people who are not trustworthy. But healthy development requires a favorable ratio of positive to negative. Of the eight stages described in Table 2.3, four have been the focus of the greatest amount of theorizing and research: trust in infancy, identity in adolescence, intimacy in early adulthood, and generativity in middle adulthood.

psychosocial stages Erikson's eight stages, or crises, of personality development in which inner instincts interact with outer cultural and social demands to shape personality

TABLE 2.3   Erikson's Psychosocial Stages

Approximate Ages	Stage	Positive Characteristics Gained and Typical Activities
Birth to 1 year	Trust versus mistrust	Hope; trust in primary caregiver and in one's own ability to make things happen (secure attachment to caregiver is key)
1 to 3	Autonomy versus shame and doubt	Will; new physical skills lead to demand for more choices, most often seen as saying "no" to caregivers; child learns self-care skills such as toileting
3 to 6	Initiative versus guilt	Purpose; ability to organize activities around some goal; more assertiveness and aggressiveness (Oedipus conflict with parent of same sex may lead to guilt)
6 to 12	Industry versus inferiority	Competence; cultural skills and norms, including school skills and tool use (failure to master these leads to sense of inferiority)
12 to 18	Identity versus role confusion	Fidelity; adaptation of sense of self to pubertal changes, consideration of future choices, achievement of a more mature sexual identity, and search for new values
18 to 30	Intimacy versus isolation	Love; person develops intimate relationships beyond adolescent love; many become parents
30 to old age	Generativity versus stagnation	Care; people rear children, focus on occupational achievement or creativity, and train the next generation; turn outward from the self toward others
old age	Integrity versus despair	Wisdom; person conducts a life review, integrates earlier stages and comes to terms with basic identity; develops self-acceptance

Erikson believed that the behavior of the major caregiver (usually the mother) is critical to the child's resolution of the first life crisis: *trust versus mistrust*. To ensure successful resolution of this crisis, the caregiver must be consistently loving and must respond to the child predictably and reliably. Infants whose early care has been erratic or harsh may develop mistrust. In either case, the child carries this aspect of personality throughout her development, and it affects the resolution of later tasks.

Erikson's description of the central adolescent dilemma, *identity versus role confusion*, has been particularly influential. He argued that, in order to arrive at a mature sexual and occupational identity, every adolescent must examine his identity and the roles he must occupy. He must achieve an integrated sense of self, of what he wants to do and be, and of his appropriate sexual role. The risk is that the adolescent will suffer from confusion arising from the profusion of roles opening up to him at this age.

Critical Thinking

In which of Erikson's psychosocial stages would you place yourself? Does Erikson's description of it correspond to the challenges and concerns you are confronting?

In the first of the three adult stages, the young adult builds on the identity established in adolescence to confront the crisis of *intimacy versus isolation.* Erikson defined intimacy as "the ability to fuse your identity with someone else's without fear that you're going to lose something yourself" (Erikson, in Evans, 1969). Many young people, Erikson thought, make the mistake of thinking they will find their identity in a relationship, but in his view it is only those who have already formed (or are well on the way to forming) a clear identity who can successfully enter this fusion of identities that he called *intimacy.* Young adults whose identities are weak or unformed will remain in shallow relationships and will experience a sense of isolation or loneliness.

The middle adulthood crisis is *generativity versus stagnation,* which is "primarily the concern in establishing and guiding the next generation" (Erikson, 1963, p. 267). The rearing of children is the most obvious way to achieve a sense of generativity, but it is not the only way. Doing creative work, giving service to an organization or to society, or serving as a mentor to younger colleagues can help the midlife adult achieve a sense of generativity. Failing that, the self-absorbed, nongenerative adult may feel a sense of stagnation.

The key idea underlying Erikson's theory is that each new crisis is thrust on the developing person because of changes in social demands that accompany changes in age. The fourth stage of industry versus inferiority, for example, begins when the child starts school and must learn to read and write. The child can't stay in elementary school until she does so. If she doesn't, she is pushed forward into middle school and high school, carrying the unresolved crisis with her as excess baggage. Thus, the childhood crises set the stage for those of adolescence and adulthood.

Evaluation of Psychoanalytic Theories

Psychoanalytic theories such as Freud's and Erikson's, summarized in Table 2.4, have several attractive aspects. Most centrally, they highlight the importance of the child's earliest relationships with caregivers. Furthermore, they suggest that the child's needs change

TABLE 2.4   Psychoanalytic Theories

Theory	Main Idea	Evaluation	
		Strengths	**Weaknesses**
Freud's Psychosexual Theory	Personality develops in five stages from birth to adolescence; in each stage, the need for physical pleasure is focused on a different part of the body.	Emphasizes importance of experiences in infancy and early childhood; provides psychological explanations for mental illness	Sexual feelings are not as important in personality development as Freud claimed.
Erikson's Psychosocial Theory	Personality develops through eight life crises across the entire lifespan; a person finishes each crisis with either a good or a poor resolution.	Helps explain the role of culture in personality development; important in lifespan psychology; useful description of major themes of personality development at different ages	Describing each period in terms of a single crisis is probably an oversimplification.

with age, so that parents and other caregivers must constantly adapt to the changing child. One of the implications of this is that we should not think of "good parenting" as an unchanging quality. Some people may be very good at meeting the needs of an infant but less capable of dealing with teenagers' identity struggles. The child's eventual personality, and her overall mental health, thus depend on the interaction pattern that develops in a particular family. The idea of changing needs is an extremely attractive element of these theories, because more and more of the research in developmental psychology is moving developmentalists toward just such a conception of the process.

Psychoanalytic theory has also given psychologists a number of helpful concepts, such as the unconscious, the ego, and identity, which have become a part of everyday language as well as theory. Moreover, psychologists are taking a fresh look at Freud's ideas about the importance of defense mechanisms in coping with anxiety (Cramer, 2000). Freud is also usually credited with the invention of psychotherapy, which is still practiced today. An additional strength of the psychoanalytic perspective is the emphasis on continued development during adulthood found in Erikson's theory. His ideas have provided a framework for a great deal of new research and theorizing about adult development.

The major weakness of psychoanalytic theories is the fuzziness of many of their concepts. For example, how could researchers detect the presence of the id, ego, superego, and so on? Without more precise definitions, it is extremely difficult to test these theories, despite their provocative explanations of development.

The Humanistic Alternative

In addition to criticizing the fuzziness of some psychoanalytic concepts, psychologists have also taken issue with the psychoanalytic emphasis on atypical development. Some have proposed alternative theories that focus on the positive aspects of development while accepting the psychoanalytic assumption that behavior is motivated by internal drives and emotions. These *humanistic theories,* begin with the optimistic assumption that the most important internal drive is each individual's motivation to achieve his full potential. The key figure in the humanistic tradition is Abraham Maslow (1968, 1970a, 1970b, 1971), who used the term *self-actualization* to describe this ultimate goal of human life.

Maslow's greatest interest was in the development of motives, or needs, which he divided into two subsets: deficiency motives and being motives. *Deficiency motives* involve drives to maintain physical or emotional homeostasis (inner balance), such as the drive to get enough to eat or drink, the sexual drive, or even the drive to obtain sufficient love or respect from others. *Being motives* involve the desire to understand, to give to others, and to grow—that is, to achieve self-actualization. In general, the satisfaction of deficiency motives prevents or cures illness or re-creates homeostasis. In contrast, the satisfaction of being motives produces a general sense of well-being. The distinction is like the "difference between fending off threat or attack, and positive triumph and achievement" (Maslow, 1968, p. 32).

Maslow described these various needs or motives in his famous needs hierarchy, shown in Figure 2.1 (page 32). He argued that the various needs must be met in order from the bottom up. For example, only when physiological needs are met do safety needs come to the fore; only when love and esteem needs are met can the need for self-actualization become dominant. For that reason, Maslow thought that being motives were likely to be significant only in adulthood, and only in those individuals who had found stable ways to satisfy both love and esteem needs. In this sense, Maslow's theory sounds very similar to Erikson's stages of intimacy and generativity.

Another humanistic psychologist, Carl Rogers, talked about the capacity of each individual to become a "fully functioning person," without guilt or seriously distorting defenses (Rogers, 1961). In this idea, we see an assumption that it is never too late—not only can adults overcome early conditioning or the residue of unresolved dilemmas, but they are motivated to try to do just that.

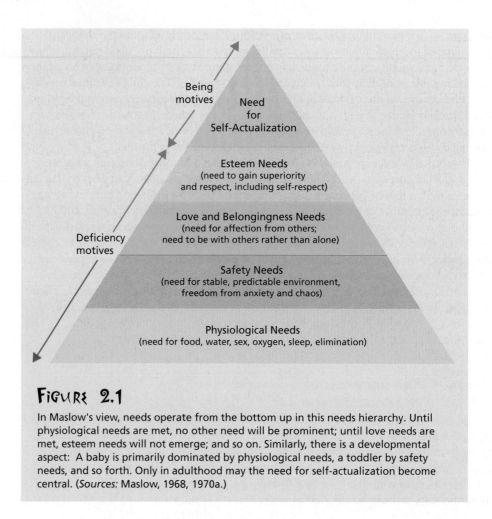

FIGURE 2.1

In Maslow's view, needs operate from the bottom up in this needs hierarchy. Until physiological needs are met, no other need will be prominent; until love needs are met, esteem needs will not emerge; and so on. Similarly, there is a developmental aspect: A baby is primarily dominated by physiological needs, a toddler by safety needs, and so forth. Only in adulthood may the need for self-actualization become central. (*Sources:* Maslow, 1968, 1970a.)

The inherent optimism in humanistic theories makes them very appealing. However, as is true of psychoanalytic theories, humanistic models like Maslow's are stated in broad, rather imprecise terms. They have appealed to a great many people because they seem to resonate with some aspects of everyday experience. But they are difficult to test empirically because the propositions are not stated clearly enough.

Before going on

- In Freud's view, how do the id, ego, and superego work together to keep the personality functioning?

- How do Erikson's stages differ from Freud's?

- Name at least two strengths and two weaknesses of psychoanalytic theory.

- What are the major ideas of Maslow's and Rogers's humanistic theories?

Learning Theories

In general, **learning theories** assert that development results from an accumulation of experiences. Thus, in contrast to psychoanalysts, learning theorists would say that infants repeat the behavior of putting objects in their mouths because they find the sensations it produces rewarding. Alternatively, when they put something in their mouths that tastes bad, infants learn not to mouth such an object again.

Pavlov's Classical Conditioning

Classical conditioning is the acquisition of new signals for existing responses. Each incidence of learning begins with a biologically programmed stimulus-response connection, or *reflex*. For example, salivation happens naturally when you put food in your mouth. In classical conditioning terms, the food is the *unconditioned (unlearned, natural) stimulus*; salivating is an *unconditioned (unlearned, natural) response*.

Stimuli presented just before or at the same time as the unconditioned stimulus are those that are likely to be associated with it. For example, most foods have odors, and to get to your mouth, food has to pass near your nose. Thus, you usually smell food before you taste it. Food odors eventually become *conditioned (learned) stimuli* that elicit salivation. In effect, they act as a signal to your salivary glands that food is coming. Once the connection between food odors and salivation is established, smelling food triggers the salivation response even when you do not actually eat the food. When a response occurs reliably in connection with a conditioned stimulus in this way, it is known as a *conditioned (learned) response*.

Classical conditioning is of interest in the study of development because of the role it plays in the acquisition of emotional responses. For example, things or people present when you feel good will become conditioned stimuli for pleasant feelings, while those associated with uncomfortable feelings may become conditioned stimuli for a sense of unease. Classical conditioning is especially important in infancy. Because a child's mother or father is present so often when nice things happen, such as when the child feels warm, comfortable, and cuddled, the mother and father usually serve as conditioned stimuli for pleasant feelings, a fact that makes it possible for the parents' presence to comfort a child.

Skinner's Operant Conditioning

Another type of learning is **operant conditioning,** a term coined by B. F. Skinner, the most famous proponent of this theory (Skinner, 1953, 1980). Operant conditioning involves learning to repeat or stop behaviors because of the consequences they bring about. **Reinforcement** is anything that follows a behavior and causes it to be repeated. **Punishment** is anything that follows a behavior and causes it to stop.

A *positive reinforcement* is a consequence (usually involving something pleasant) that follows a behavior and increases the chances that the behavior will occur again. Some kinds of pleasant consequences, such as attention, serve as reinforcers for most people most of the time. But strictly speaking, a reinforcement is defined by its effect; we don't know something is reinforcing unless we see that its presence increases the probability of some behavior.

Negative reinforcement occurs when an individual learns to perform a specific behavior in order to cause something unpleasant to stop. For example, coughing is an

learning theories theories that assert that development results from an accumulation of experiences

classical conditioning learning that results from the association of stimuli

operant conditioning learning to repeat or stop behaviors because of their consequences

reinforcement anything that follows a behavior and causes it to be repeated

punishment anything that follows a behavior and causes it to stop

Laboratory research involving animals was important in the development of Skinner's operant conditioning theory. (*Photo:* Ken Hayman, Black Star)

unpleasant experience for most of us, and taking a dose of cough medicine usually stops it. As a result, when we begin coughing, we reach for the cough syrup. The behavior of swallowing a spoonful of cough syrup is reinforced by the cessation of coughing. In other words, we make the unpleasant experience of coughing go away when we engage in the behavior of swallowing cough syrup. Thus, the behavior of taking cough syrup is learned through negative reinforcement.

Critical Thinking

Describe instances in your everyday life when your behavior is affected by classical or operant conditioning or when you use these principles to affect others' behavior.

Definitions and simple examples of positive and negative reinforcement may be misleading when it comes to understanding how the two operate in real-life contexts. For example, most people understand that paying attention to a preschooler's whining is likely to increase it, an example of positive reinforcement. However, parents learn to attend to whining preschoolers because whining is irritating, and responding to it usually makes it stop. In other words, like taking cough syrup for an annoying cough, the parents' behavior of responding to whining is negatively reinforced by its consequence—namely, that the child *stops* whining.

In contrast to both kinds of reinforcement, punishment stops a behavior. Sometimes punishments involve eliminating nice things, taking away TV privileges, for example. However, punishment may also involve unpleasant things such as scolding. Like reinforcement, however, punishment is defined by its effect. Consequences that do not stop behavior can't be properly called punishments.

An alternative way to stop an unwanted behavior is **extinction,** which is the gradual elimination of a behavior through repeated nonreinforcement. If a teacher succeeds in eliminating a student's undesirable behavior by ignoring it, the behavior is said to have been *extinguished.*

Such examples illustrate the complex manner in which reinforcements and punishments operate in the real world. In laboratory settings, operant conditioning researchers usually work with only one participant or animal subject at a time; they needn't worry about the social consequences of behaviors or consequences. They can also control the situation so that a particular behavior is reinforced every time it occurs. In the real world, *partial reinforcement*—reinforcement of a behavior on some occasions but not others—is more common (see The Real World). Studies of partial reinforcement show that people take longer to learn a new behavior under partial reinforcement conditions; once established, however, such behaviors are very resistant to extinction.

Shaping is the reinforcement of intermediate steps until an individual learns a complex behavior. For example, you wouldn't start learning to play tennis by challenging a skilled player to a match. Instead, you would first learn to hold the racquet properly. Next, you would learn the basic strokes and practice hitting balls hit or thrown to you by an instructor. Next, you would learn to serve. Finally, you would put all your skills together and play an actual match. All along the way, you would be encouraged by the sense of satisfaction gained from accomplishing each step toward the goal.

extinction the gradual elimination of a behavior through repeated nonreinforcement

shaping the reinforcement of intermediate steps until an individual learns a complex behavior

observational learning, or **modeling** learning that results from seeing a model reinforced or punished for a behavior

Bandura's Social-Cognitive Theory

Learning theorist Albert Bandura, whose ideas are more influential among developmental psychologists than those of the conditioning theorists, argues that learning does not always require reinforcement (1977a, 1982a, 1989). Learning may also occur as a result of watching someone else perform some action and experience reinforcement or punishment. Learning of this type, called **observational learning,** or **modeling,** is involved in a wide range of behaviors. Children learn to hit by watching

PARENTING
The Real World

Learning Principles in Real Life

Virtually all parents try to reinforce some behaviors in their children by praising them or giving them attention. And most try to discourage unwanted behaviors through punishment. But it is easy to misapply learning principles or to create unintended consequences if you have not fully understood all the mechanisms involved.

For example, you want your children to stop climbing on a chair, so you scold them. You are conscientious and knowledgeable, and you carefully time your scolding and stop scolding when they stop climbing, so that the scolding operates as a negative reinforcer—but nothing works. They keep on leaving muddy footprints on your favorite chair. Why? Perhaps the children enjoy climbing on the chair, so the climbing is intrinsically reinforcing to them and outweighs the unpleasantness of your scolding. One way to deal with this might be to provide something else for them to climb on.

Another example: Suppose your 3-year-old son repeatedly demands your attention while you are fixing dinner. Because you don't want to reinforce this behavior, you ignore him the first six or eight times he calls you or tugs at your clothes. But after the ninth or tenth repetition, with his voice getting whinier each time, you can't stand it any longer and finally say something like "All right! What do you want?" Since you have ignored most of his demands, you might think you have not been reinforcing them. But what you have actually done is create a partial reinforcement schedule. You have rewarded only every tenth demand, and psychologists have established that this pattern of reinforcement helps create behavior that is very hard to extinguish. So your son may continue to be overly demanding for a very long time.

If such situations are familiar to you, it may pay to keep careful records for a while, noting each incident and your response. Then see whether you can figure out which principles are really at work and how you might change the pattern.

other people in real life and on television. Adults learn job skills by observing or being shown them by others.

Bandura also calls attention to a class of reinforcements called *intrinsic reinforcements*. These are reinforcements within an individual, such as the pleasure a child feels when she figures out how to draw a star. Bandura has gone a long way toward

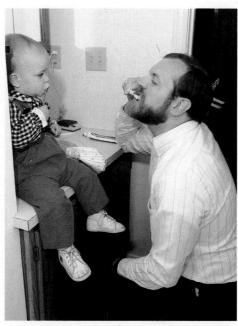

Modeling is an important source of learning for both children and adults. What behaviors have you learned by watching and copying others? (*Photos:* Kathy Sloane, 1992, Photo Researchers; Richard Sobel, Stock Boston)

bridging the gap between learning theories and other approaches by emphasizing cognitive (mental) elements in learning.

Furthermore, what a person learns from observing others is influenced by processes such as attention and memory. Maturation is important as well: A 4-year-old probably won't learn geometry from watching his high-school-age sister do her homework. Bandura also suggests that what an observer learns from a particular model is influenced by his own goals, expectations about what kinds of consequences are likely if he adopts the model's behavior, and judgments of his own performance.

Evaluation of Learning Theories

Several implications of learning theories, summarized in Table 2.5, are worth emphasizing. First, learning theories can explain both consistency and change in behavior. If a child is friendly and smiling both at home and at school, learning theorists would explain the child's behavior by saying that the child is being reinforced for that behavior in both settings. It is equally possible to explain why a child is happy at home but miserable at school. We need only hypothesize that the home environment reinforces cheerful behavior but the school setting does not.

Learning theorists also tend to be optimistic about the possibility of change. Children's behavior can change if the reinforcement system, or their beliefs about themselves, change. So, problem behavior can be modified.

TABLE 2.5   Learning Theories

Theory	Main Idea	Evaluation	
		Strengths	**Weaknesses**
Pavlov's Classical Conditioning	Learning happens when neutral stimuli become so strongly associated with natural stimuli that they elicit the same response.	Useful in explaining how emotional responses such as phobias are learned	Explanation of behavior change is too limited to serve as comprehensive theory of human development
Skinner's Operant Conditioning Theory	Development involves behavior changes that are shaped by reinforcement and punishment.	Basis of many useful strategies for managing and changing human behavior	Humans are not as passive as Skinner claimed; the theory ignores hereditary and cognitive, emotional, and social factors in development
Bandura's Social-Cognitive Theory	People learn from models; what they learn from a model depends on how they interpret the situation cognitively and emotionally.	Helps explain how models influence behavior; explains more about development than other learning theories because of addition of cognitive and emotional factors	Does not provide an overall picture of development

The great strength of learning theories is that they seem to give an accurate picture of the way in which many behaviors are learned. It is clear that both children and adults learn through conditioning and modeling. Furthermore, Bandura's addition of mental elements to learning theory adds further strength, since it allows an integration of learning models and other approaches.

However, the learning theorists' approach is not really developmental; it doesn't tell us much about change with age, either in childhood or adulthood. Even Bandura's variation on learning theory does not tell us whether there are any changes with age in what a child can learn from modeling. Thus, learning theories help developmentalists understand how specific behaviors are acquired but do not contribute to an understanding of age-related change.

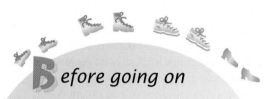

Before going on

- What is classical conditioning?

- How does operant conditioning cause learning?

- What concepts does Bandura add to learning theories to make them more useful?

- What are the strengths and weaknesses of learning theories as an explanation of human development?

Cognitive Theories

The group of theories known as **cognitive theories** emphasize mental aspects of development such as logic and memory. A cognitive theorist might propose that babies use their senses, including the sense of taste, to build mental pictures of the world around them. Thus, infants mouth everything in their environment until they have learned all they can from this behavior, then they move on to a more mature way of interacting with the world.

Piaget's Cognitive-Developmental Theory

For Jean Piaget, as you should remember from Chapter 1, the central question of interest in developmental psychology was "How does thinking develop?" (Piaget, 1952, 1970, 1977; Piaget & Inhelder, 1969). He was struck by the fact that all children seem to go through the same sequence of discoveries about their world, making the same mistakes and arriving at the same solutions. For example, all 3- and 4-year-olds seem to think that if water is poured from a short, wide glass into a taller, narrower one, there is then more water, because the water level is higher in the narrow glass than it was in the wide glass. In contrast, most 7-year-olds realize that the

cognitive theories theories that emphasize mental processes in development, such as logic and memory

Piaget based many of his ideas on naturalistic observations of children of different ages on playgrounds and in schools. (*Photo:* Judith Behling Ford)

Using Piaget's terminology, we would say this infant is assimilating the object to her grasping scheme. What scheme is being accommodated at the same time as she adapts her grasping scheme? (*Photo:* Stone)

amount of water has not changed. To explain such age differences, Piaget proposed several concepts that continue to guide developmental research.

A pivotal idea in Piaget's model is that of a **scheme,** an internal cognitive structure that provides an individual with a procedure to follow in a specific circumstance. For example, when you pick up a ball, you use your picking-up scheme. To throw it to someone, you use your looking scheme, your aiming scheme, and your throwing scheme. Piaget proposed that each of us begins life with a small repertoire of sensory and motor schemes, such as looking, tasting, touching, hearing, and reaching. As we use each scheme, it becomes better adapted to the world; in other words, it works better.

We possess mental schemes as well, most of which develop in childhood and adolescence. Mental schemes allow us to use symbols and think logically. Piaget proposed three processes to explain how children get from built-in schemes such as looking and touching to the complex mental schemes used in childhood, adolescence, and adulthood.

Assimilation is the process of using schemes to make sense of experiences. Piaget would say that a baby who grasps a toy is *assimilating* it to his grasping scheme. The complementary process is **accommodation,** which involves changing the scheme as a result of some new information acquired through assimilation. When the baby grasps a square object for the first time, he will accommodate his grasping scheme; so the next time he reaches for a square object, his hand will be more appropriately bent to grasp it. Thus, the process of accommodation is the key to developmental change. Through accommodation, we improve our skills and reorganize our ways of thinking.

Equilibration is the process of balancing assimilation and accommodation to create schemes that fit the environment. To illustrate, think about infants' tendency to put things in their mouths. In Piaget's terms, they assimilate objects to their mouthing scheme. As they mouth each one, their mouthing scheme changes to include the instructions "*Do* mouth this" or "*Don't* mouth this." The accommodation is based on mouthing experiences. A pacifier feels good in the mouth, but a dead insect has an unpleasant texture. So, eventually, the mouthing scheme says it's okay to put a pacifier in the mouth, but it's not okay to mouth a dead insect. In this way, an infant's mouthing scheme attains a better fit with the real world.

Piaget's research suggested to him that logical thinking evolves in four stages. During the *sensorimotor stage,* from birth to 18 months, infants use their sensory and motor schemes to act on the world around them. In the *preoperational stage,* from 18 months to about age 6, youngsters acquire symbolic schemes, such as language and fantasy, that they use in thinking and communicating. Next comes the *concrete operational stage,* during which 6- to 12-year-olds begin to think logically and become capable of solving problems such as the one illustrated in Figure 2.2. The last phase is the *formal operational stage,* in which adolescents learn to think logically about abstract ideas and hypothetical situations.

Table 2.6 describes these stages more fully; you will read about each of them in detail later in the book. For now, it is important to understand that in Piaget's view, each stage grows out of the one that precedes it, and each involves a major restructuring of the child's way of thinking. It's also important to know that research has

Critical Thinking

Describe three or four examples of assimilation and accommodation in your everyday life.

confirmed Piaget's belief that the sequence of the stages is fixed. However, children progress through them at different rates. In addition, some individuals do not attain the formal operational stage in adolescence or even in adulthood. Consequently, the ages associated with the stages are approximations.

Information-Processing Theory

The goal of **information-processing theory** is to explain how the mind manages information (Klahr, 1992). Information-processing theorists use the computer as a model of human thinking. Consequently, they often use computer terms, like *hardware* and *software,* to talk about human cognitive processes. In addition, they experiment with programs designed to enable computers to think as humans do.

Theorizing about and studying memory processes are central to information-processing theory. This theory breaks memory down into subprocesses of encoding, storage, and retrieval. *Encoding* is organizing information to be stored in memory. For example, you may be encoding the information in this chapter by relating it to your own childhood. *Storage* is keeping information, and *retrieval* is getting information out of memory.

Most memory research assumes that the human memory is made up of multiple components. The idea is that information

FIGURE 2.2

In one of the problems Piaget devised, a child is shown two clay balls of equal size and asked if they both contain the same amount of clay. Next, the researcher rolls one ball into a sausage shape and asks the child if the two shapes still contain the same amount of clay. A preoperational child will say that one now contains more clay than the other and will base his answer on their appearance: "The sausage has more because it's longer now." A concrete operational thinker will say that the two still contain the same amount of material because no clay was added or taken away from either. (*Photo:* Will Hart)

TABLE 2.6   Piaget's Cognitive-Developmental Stages

Approximate Ages	Stage	Description
Birth to 18 months	Sensorimotor	The baby understands the world through her senses and her motor actions; she begins to use simple symbols, such as single words and pretend play, near the end of this period.
18 months to 6 years	Preoperational	By age 2, the child can use symbols both to think and to communicate; he develops the abilities to take others' points of view, classify objects, and use simple logic by the end of this stage.
6 to 12	Concrete operational	The child's logic takes a great leap forward with the development of new internal operations, such as conservation and class inclusion, but is still tied to the known world; by the end of the period, he can reason about simple "what if" questions.
12+	Formal operational	The child begins to manipulate ideas as well as objects; she thinks hypothetically and, by adulthood, can easily manage a variety of "what if" questions; she greatly improves her ability to organize ideas and objects mentally.

scheme in Piaget's theory, an internal cognitive structure that provides an individual with a procedure to use in a specific circumstance

assimilation the process of using a scheme to make sense of an event or experience

accommodation changing a scheme as a result of some new information

equilibration the process of balancing assimilation and accommodation to create schemes that fit the environment

information-processing theory a theoretical perspective that uses the computer as a model to explain how the mind manages information

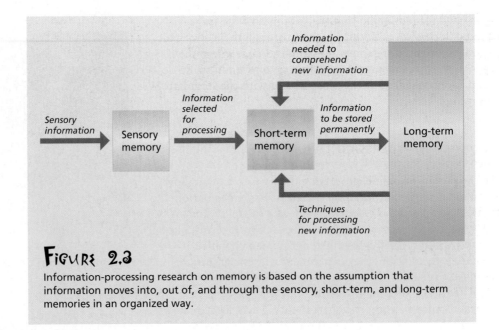

FIGURE 2.3

Information-processing research on memory is based on the assumption that information moves into, out of, and through the sensory, short-term, and long-term memories in an organized way.

moves through these components in an organized way (see Figure 2.3). The process of understanding a spoken word serves as a good example.

First, you hear the word when the sounds enter your *sensory memory*. Your experiences with language allow you to recognize the pattern of sounds as a word. Next, the word moves into your *short-term memory*, the component of the memory system where all information is processed. Thus, short-term memory is often called *working memory*. Knowledge of the word's meaning is then called up out of *long-term memory*, the component of the system where information is permanently stored, and placed in short-term memory, where it is linked to the word's sounds to enable you to understand it.

Each memory component manages information differently. Information flows through the sensory memory in a constant stream. Bits of information that are not attended to drop out quickly. The short-term memory is extremely limited in capacity—it can contain only about seven items at a time. However, information can be retained in short-term memory as long as it is processed in some way—as you do when you repeat your grocery list to yourself on the way to the store.

Long-term memory is unlimited in capacity, and information is often stored in terms of meaningful associations. For example, suppose you read a sentence such as "Bill wrote a letter to his brother." When you think about the sentence later, you might mistakenly recall that it contained the word *pen*. This happens because information about the process of writing and the tools used to do it are stored together in long-term memory.

Some developmentalists have used information-processing theory to explain Piaget's stages. Their theories are called **neo-Piagetian theories** because they expand on Piaget's theory rather than contradict it (Case, 1985; 1997). According to neo-Piagetians, older children and adults can solve complex problems like those in Piaget's research because they can hold more pieces of information in their short-term memories at the same time than younger children can. To solve the problem in Figure 2.2, for example, a child must be able to think about the appearance of the two balls of clay before one was rolled into a sausage shape and their appearance afterward in her working memory at the same time. She must also think about how the transformation was carried out. Neo-Piagetians maintain that children are incapable of performing all of this mental work in short-term memory until after age 6 or 7 (Case, 1985; 1997).

neo-Piagetian theory an approach that uses information-processing principles to explain the developmental stages indentified by Piaget

Besides age differences, there are individual differences in information-processing. For example, some people use more efficient strategies for remembering and solving problems than others. Differences in prior knowledge also affect memory. For example, if you have already taken a psychology course, you are likely to have an easier time remembering and understanding what you read in this book. In a sense, prior knowledge gives you a set of mental "hooks" on which to hang new information about psychology.

Evaluation of Cognitive Theories

Research based on cognitive theories, especially the work of Piaget, has demonstrated that simplistic views, such as those of the conditioning theorists, cannot explain the development of the complex phenomenon that is logical thinking. Moreover, Piaget's research findings have been replicated in virtually every culture and in every cohort of children since his work was first published in the 1920s. Thus, not only did he formulate a theory that forced psychologists to think about child development in a new way, he also provided a set of findings that were impossible to ignore and difficult to explain. In addition, he developed innovative methods of studying children's thinking that continue to be important today (see Research Report).

Research Report

Piaget's Clever Research

Piaget not only proposed a novel and provocative theory, he also devised creative strategies for testing children's understanding. Probably the most famous of all Piaget's clever techniques is his method for studying *conservation*, the understanding that matter does not change in quantity when its appearance changes. As shown in Figure 2.2, Piaget began with two balls of clay of equal size; he showed them to a child and let the child hold and manipulate them until she agreed that they had the same amount of clay. Then in full view of the child, Piaget rolled one of the balls into a sausage shape. Then he asked the child whether there was still the same amount of clay in the sausage and the ball or whether one had more. Children of 4 and 5 consistently said that the ball contained more clay; children of 6 and 7 consistently said that the shapes still had the same amount. Thus, the older children understood that the quantity of clay was conserved even though its appearance changed.

In another study, Piaget explored children's understanding that objects can belong to multiple categories. (For example, Fido is both a dog and an animal; a high chair is both a chair and furniture.) Piaget usually studied this by having children first create their own classes and subclasses, and then asking them questions about these. One 5-year-old child, for example, played with a set of flowers and had made two heaps, one large group of primroses and a smaller group of other mixed flowers. Piaget then had this conversation with the child (Piaget & Inhelder, 1959, p. 108):

Piaget: If I make a bouquet of all the primroses and you make one of all the flowers, which will be bigger?

Child: Yours.

Piaget: If I gather all the primroses in a meadow, will any flowers remain?

Child: Yes.

The child understood that there are other flowers than primroses but did not yet understand that all primroses are flowers, that the smaller, subordinate class is included in the larger class. Piaget's term for this concept was *class inclusion.*

In these conversations with children, Piaget was always trying to understand how the child thought, rather than trying to see whether the child could come up with the right answer. So he used an investigative method in which he followed the child's lead, asking probing questions or creating special exploratory tests to try to discover the child's logic. In the early days of Piaget's work, many American researchers were critical of this method, since Piaget did not ask precisely the same questions of each child. Still, the results were so striking, and so surprising, that they couldn't be ignored. And when stricter research techniques were devised, more often than not the investigators confirmed Piaget's observations.

Nevertheless, Piaget turned out to be wrong about some of the ages at which children develop particular skills. As you will see in later chapters, researchers have found that children develop some intellectual skills at earlier ages than Piaget's findings suggested. Furthermore, Piaget was probably wrong about the generality of the stages themselves. Most 8-year-olds, for example, show concrete operational thinking on some tasks but not on others, and they are more likely to show complex thinking on familiar than on unfamiliar tasks. Thus, the whole process seems to be a great deal less stagelike than Piaget proposed.

Information-processing theory has helped to clarify some of the cognitive processes underlying Piaget's findings. Furthermore, it has greatly enhanced developmentalists' understanding of human memory. For example, information-processing research on the inaccuracies often found in eyewitness testimony is influencing the way police officers, prosecutors, and attorneys interview witnesses (Wells et al., 2000). Thus, information-processing theory is currently one of the most important psychological theories because of its adaptability to explaining and studying specific cognitive tasks such as how eyewitnesses remember what they have seen.

Critics of information-processing theory point out that human thinking is more complex than that of a computer. They also correctly point out that much information-processing research involves artificial memory tasks such as learning lists of words. Therefore, say critics, research based on the information-processing approach doesn't always accurately describe how memory works in the real world.

Piagetians claim that information-processing theory emphasizes explanations of single cognitive tasks at the expense of a comprehensive picture of development. Finally, critics of both cognitive theories say that they ignore the role of emotions in development. The cognitive theories are summarized in Table 2.7.

TABLE 2.7   Cognitive Theories

Theory	Main Idea	Evaluation	
		Strengths	**Weaknesses**
Piaget's Theory of Cognitive Development	Reasoning develops in four universal stages from birth through adolescence; in each stage, the child builds a different kind of scheme.	Helps explain how children of different ages think about and act on the world	Stage concept may cause adults to underestimate children's reasoning abilities; there may be additional stages in adulthood
Information-Processing Theory	The computer is used as a model for human cognitive functioning; encoding, storage, and retrieval processes change with age, causing changes in memory function; these changes happen because of both brain maturation and practice.	Helps explain how much information people of different ages can manage at one time and how they process it; provides a useful framework for studying individual differences in people of the same age	Human information processing is much more complex than that of a computer; the theory doesn't provide an overall picture of development

Before going on

● What did Piaget discover about the development of logical thinking in children, and how did he explain it?

● What is the focus of information-processing theory?

● List some contributions and criticisms of cognitive theories.

Current Trends

A number of theories have generated interest among developmentalists in recent years because of their potential for explaining biological and cultural influences on development.

Biological Theories

Theories that propose links between physiological processes and development represent one of the most important current trends in developmental psychology. Some biological theories explain universal changes, while others address individual differences.

● *Nativism, Ethology, and Sociobiology* ● **Nativism** is the view that humans possess unique genetic traits that will be manifested in all members of the species, regardless of differences in their environments. Nativist theory is supported when developmentalists identify behaviors that appear early in life, develop in almost all individuals in every culture, and do not exist in other species. For example, all healthy children learn language early in life without any specific instruction from adults, and, to date, scientists have found no evidence of grammatical language in nonhuman species.

Critics of nativism claim that it underestimates the impact of the environment. For example, it is true that children learn all languages in the same way. However, environmental factors, including characteristics of different languages, affect the rate at which children learn language.

Ethology emphasizes genetically determined survival behaviors that are assumed to have evolved through natural selection. For example, nests are necessary for the survival of young birds. Therefore, ethologists say, evolution has equipped birds with nest-building genes.

Similarly, ethologists believe that emotional relationships are necessary to the survival of human infants (Bowlby, 1969, 1980). They claim that evolution has produced genes that cause humans to form these relationships. For example, most people feel irritated when they hear a newborn crying. Ethologists say the baby is

nativism the view that human beings possess unique genetic traits that will be manifested in all members of the species, regardless of differences in environments

ethology a perspective on development that emphasizes genetically determined survival behaviors presumed to have evolved through natural selection

Ethologists assert that the first 2 years of life are a critical period for the establishment of relationships between infants and caregivers. (*Photo:* Stone)

genetically programmed to cry in a certain way, and adults are genetically programmed to get irritated when they hear it. The caretaker responds to a crying baby's needs in order to remove the irritating stimulus of the noise. As the caretaker and infant interact, an emotional bond is created between them. Thus, genes for crying in an irritating manner increase infants' chances of survival.

Like other biological theorists, ethologists are criticized for placing too much emphasis on heredity. Critics say that ethological theories are difficult to test. How could a researcher test the idea that infants attach to caregivers because attachment has survival value? Some argue that ethology ignores the human tendency to invent cultural solutions for problems that go far beyond any genetic programming we may have inherited.

Sociobiology is the study of society using the methods and concepts of biological science. When applied to human development, sociobiology emphasizes genes that aid group survival. Sociobiologists claim individual humans have the best chance for survival when they live in groups. Therefore, they claim, evolution has provided humans with genetic programming that helps us cooperate.

To support their views, sociobiologists look for social rules and behaviors that exist in all cultures. For example, every society has laws against murder. Sociobiologists believe that humans are genetically programmed to create rules based on respect for other people's lives. Evolution has selected these genes, they claim, because people need to respect each other's lives and to be able to cooperate.

Sociobiology is criticized on much the same grounds as ethology is. Critics say that societies have similar rules because, over many generations, people have learned which rules work. When social rules no longer work, say critics, people invent new ones. Both the new rules and the reasons for them are passed on from one generation to the next through language, not genes.

● *Behavior Genetics* ●   **Behavior genetics** focuses on the effect of heredity on individual differences. Traits or behaviors are believed to be influenced by genes when those of related people, such as children and their parents, are more similar than those of unrelated people. Behavior geneticists have shown that heredity affects a broad range of traits and behaviors, including intelligence, shyness, and aggressiveness.

Furthermore, hereditary traits are fairly stable across the lifespan. For example, longitudinal studies have found that children who are hard to get along with have more difficulties in adult life. One important study examined the life histories of 284 children born in the 1920s (Caspi & Elder, 1988; Caspi, Elder, & Bem, 1987, 1988). Among the participants were a number who had been rated "ill-tempered" as children. It turned out that men who had been ill-tempered boys had life pathways very different from those of their good-tempered peers. They completed fewer years of school, had lower-status jobs (as shown in Figure 2.4), achieved lower rank when they served in the military, and were twice as likely to be divorced by age 40.

Still, such studies often show that environments determine how apparently hereditary traits affect an individual's development, and to what extent. For instance, Figure 2.4 suggests that only those ill-tempered boys who ended up in low-status occupations changed jobs often in adulthood. Ill-tempered boys who attained jobs with higher status had stable careers.

Critics of behavior genetics cite such findings as evidence that psychological characteristics aren't completely determined by a person's genetic heritage. Individual behavior is *always* a product of both heredity and environment, as the data on ill-tempered men in high- and low-status jobs suggest. Still, behavior genetics helps scientists understand that humans are born with certain response patterns that shape

sociobiology the study of society using the methods and concepts of biology; when used by developmentalists, an approach that emphasizes genes that aid group survival

behavior genetics the study of the role of heredity in individual differences

socio-cultural theory Vygotsky's view that complex forms of thinking have their origins in social interactions rather than in an individual's private explorations

ecological theory Bronfenbrenner's theory that explains development in terms of relationships between individuals and their environments, or interconnected *contexts*

their reactions to the world. And because we carry those same response patterns with us through our lives, these inherited characteristics contribute to a basic continuity over time.

Vygotsky's Socio-Cultural Theory

Following the Bolshevik revolution of 1917, the new Soviet government hired Russian psychologist Lev Vygotsky, among others, to create a school system that would serve the ends of the new communist regime (Vygotsky, 1978). Although influenced by Freud, Pavlov, and Piaget, Vygotsky devised a theory of child development that was unique. His death in 1938 and the historical events that followed—World War II and the Cold War—resulted in his work remaining largely unknown outside the Soviet Union for decades. Recently, however, developmentalists have become interested in his views on the influence of cultural forces on individual development (Thomas, 1996).

Vygotsky's **socio-cultural theory** asserts that complex forms of thinking have their origins in social interactions rather than in the child's private explorations, as Piaget thought. According to Vygotsky, children's learning of new cognitive skills is guided by an adult (or a more skilled child, such as an older sibling), who structures the child's learning experience, a process Vygotsky called *scaffolding*. To create an appropriate scaffold, the adult must gain and keep the child's attention, model the best strategy, and adapt the whole process to the child's developmental level, or *zone of proximal development* (Landry, Garner, Swank, & Baldwin, 1996; Rogoff, 1990).

Vygotsky used this term to signify tasks that are too hard for the child to do alone but that he can manage with guidance. For example, parents of a beginning reader provide a scaffold when they help him sound out new words.

Critical Thinking

How is scaffolding involved when a parent helps a child with homework?

Vygotsky's ideas have important educational applications. Like Piaget's, Vygotsky's theory suggests the importance of opportunities for active exploration. But assisted discovery would play a greater role in a Vygotskian than in a Piagetian classroom; the teacher would provide the scaffolding for children's discovery, through questions, demonstrations, and explanations (Tharp & Gallimore, 1988). To be effective, the assisted discovery processes would have to be within the zone of proximal development of each child.

Bronfenbrenner's Ecological Theory

Another approach gaining interest in developmental psychology is Bronfenbrenner's **ecological theory,** which explains development in terms of relationships between people and their environments, or *contexts,* as Bronfenbrenner calls them (Bronfenbrenner,

FIGURE 2.4

In this study, men who had been ill-tempered as boys changed jobs more often in adult life than did those who had been more even-tempered — but only if the men were in low-status, low-autonomy jobs. Studies demonstrating such consistencies across the lifespan are important to both behavior geneticists and their critics. (*Source:* Caspi & Elder, 1988, Figure 6.3, p.128.)

Developmental psychologist Lev Vygotsky hypothesized that social interactions among children are critical to both cognitive and social development. (*Photo:* David Young-Wolff, PhotoEdit)

1979, 1993). Bronfenbrenner attempts to classify all the individual and contextual variables that affect development and to specify how they interact.

According to Bronfenbrenner, the contexts of development are like circles within circles (see Figure 2.5). The outermost circle, the *macrosystem* (or the cultural context), contains the values and beliefs of the culture in which a child is growing up. For example, a society's beliefs about the importance of education exist in the cultural context.

The next level, the *exosystem* (the socioeconomic context), includes the institutions of the culture that affect children's development indirectly. For example, funding for education exists in the socioeconomic context. The citizens of a specific nation may strongly believe that all children should be educated (cultural context), but their ability to provide universal education may be limited by the country's wealth (socioeconomic context).

The *microsystem* (or the immediate context) includes those variables to which people are exposed directly, such as their families, schools, religious institutions, and neighborhoods. The *mesosystem* is made up of the interconnections between these components. For example, the specific school a child attends and her own family are part of the microsystem. Her parents' involvement in her school and the response of the school to their involvement are part of the mesosystem. Thus, the culture a child is born into may strongly value quality education. Moreover, her nation's economy may provide ample funds for schooling. However, her own education will be more strongly affected by the particular school she attends and the connections, or lack thereof, between her school and her family. Thus, the child's immediate context may be either consistent with the cultural and socioeconomic contexts or at odds with them.

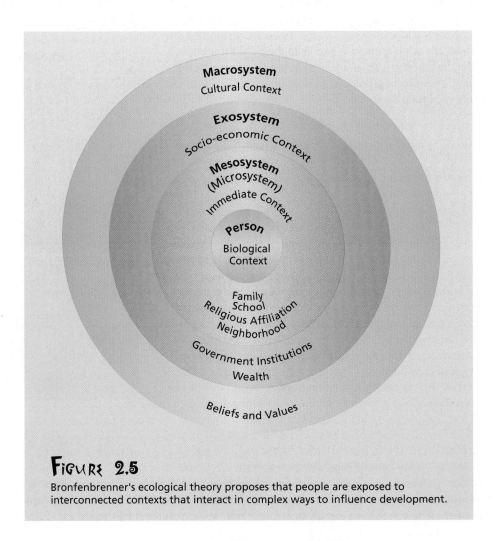

Figure 2.5

Bronfenbrenner's ecological theory proposes that people are exposed to interconnected contexts that interact in complex ways to influence development.

Finally, the child's genetic makeup and developmental stage—her *biological context*—also influence her development. For example, a student who hasn't mastered the skill of reading isn't likely to benefit from an enriched literature program. Thus, her culture, the socioeconomic situation, the school she attends, and her own family may all be geared toward providing a quality education. However, her ability to benefit from it will be determined by the degree to which her education fits her individual needs.

Ecological theory provides a way of thinking about development that captures the complexity of individual and contextual variables. To date, its greatest contribution to developmental psychology has been its emphasis on the need for research examining interactions among these variables (Thomas, 1996). For example, ecological theory has helped developmentalists understand that studies of infant day care can't just compare infants in day care to infants in home care. Such studies must also consider family variables, such as parents' educational level, and day-care variables, such as the ratio of caretakers to infants. Since the 1980s, an increasing number of such studies have appeared.

MAKE THE CONNECTION

Like the learning theories you read about earlier in the chapter, Bronfenbrenner's ecological theory emphasizes environmental factors. But what are some of the important differences between learning theories and Bronfenbrenner's perspective?

Before going on

- What kind of behaviors interest proponents of nativism, ethology, sociobiology, and behavior genetics?

- How did Vygotsky use the concepts of scaffolding and the zone of proximal development to explain cognitive development?

- What is the main idea of Bronfenbrenner's ecological theory?

Comparing Theories

After learning about theories, students usually want to know which one is right. However, developmentalists don't think of theories in terms of right or wrong but, instead, compare theories on the basis of their assumptions and how useful they are in promoting understanding of development.

Assumptions about Development

When we say that a theory assumes something about development, we mean that it holds some general perspective to be true. We can think of a theory's assumptions in terms of its answers to three questions about development.

One question addresses the *active or passive* issue: *Is a person active in shaping his own development, or is he a passive recipient of environmental influences?* Theories that claim a person's actions on the environment are the most important determinants of development are on the active side. Cognitive theories, for example, typically view development this way. In contrast, theories on the passive side, such as those of

Pavlov and Skinner, maintain that development results from the environment acting on the individual.

As you learned in Chapter 1, the *nature versus nurture* question—*How do nature and nurture interact to produce development?*—is one of the most important in developmental psychology. All developmental theories, while admitting that both nature and nurture are involved in development, make assumptions about their relative importance. Theories claiming that biology contributes more to development than environment are on the nature side of the question. Those that view environmental influences as most important are on the nurture side. Other theories assume that nature and nurture are equally important, and that it is impossible to say which contributes more to development.

Developmental theories also disagree on the *stability versus change* issue. Here, the question is *Does development happen continuously or in stages?* Theories that do not refer to stages assert that development is a stable, continuous process. Stage theories, on the other hand, emphasize change more than stability. They claim that development happens in leaps from lower to higher steps.

For the three major families of theories you have read about in this chapter, Table 2.8 lists the assumptions each makes regarding these issues. Because each theory is based on different assumptions, each takes a different approach to studying development. Consequently, research derived from each theory tells us something different about development. Moreover, a theory's assumptions shape the way it is applied in the real world.

Critical Thinking

How do the biological theories, Vygotsky's socio-cultural theory, and Bronfenbrenner's ecological theory answer the three questions about development?

For example, a teacher who approached instruction from the cognitive perspective would create a classroom in which children could experiment to some degree on their own. He would also recognize that children differ in ability, interests, developmental level, and other internal characteristics. He would believe that structuring the educational environment is important, but would assume that what each student ultimately learns will be determined by his own actions on the environment.

Alternatively, a teacher who adopted the learning perspective would guide and reinforce children's learning very carefully. Such a teacher would place little importance on ability differences among children. Instead, she would try to accomplish the same instructional goals for all children through proper manipulation of the environment.

TABLE 2.8   How Theories Answer Three Questions about Development

Theories	Active or Passive?	Nature or Nurture?	Stability or Change?
Psychoanalytic Theories			
Psychosexual Theory	Passive	Nature	Change (stages)
Psychosocial Theory	Passive	Both	Change
Learning Theories			
Classical Conditioning	Passive	Nurture	Stability (no stages)
Operant Conditioning	Passive	Nurture	Stability
Social-Cognitive Theory	Active	Nurture	Stability
Cognitive Theories			
Cognitive Developmental Theory	Active	Both	Change
Information-Processing Theory	Active	Both	Both

Usefulness

Developmentalists also compare theories with respect to their usefulness. You should be aware that there is a fair amount of disagreement among psychologists on exactly how useful each theory is. Nevertheless, there are a few general criteria most psychologists use to evaluate the usefulness of a theory.

One way to evaluate usefulness is to assess a theory's ability to generate predictions that can be tested using scientific methods. For example, as you learned earlier in this chapter, one criticism of Freud's theory is that many of his claims are difficult to test. In contrast, when Piaget claimed that most children can solve concrete operational problems by age 7, he made an assertion that is easily tested. Thus, Piaget's theory is viewed by many developmentalists as more useful in this sense than Freud's. Vygotsky, learning theorists, and information-processing theorists also proposed many testable ideas. By contrast, according to some developmental psychologists, current biological and ecological theories are weak because they are difficult to test (Thomas, 1996).

Another criterion by which to judge the usefulness of a theory is its *heuristic* value, the degree to which it stimulates thinking and research. In terms of heuristic value, Freud's and Piaget's theories earn equally high marks. Both are responsible for an enormous amount of theorizing and research on human development, often by psychologists who strongly disagree with them. In fact, all of the theories in this chapter are important heuristically.

Yet another way of evaluating a theory's usefulness, though, is in terms of practical value. In other words, a theory may be deemed useful if it provides solutions to problems. Based on this criterion, the learning and information-processing theories seem to stand out because they provide tools that can be used to influence behavior. A person who suffers from anxiety attacks, for example, can learn to use biofeedback, a technique derived from conditioning theories, to manage anxiety. Similarly, a student who needs to learn to study more effectively can get help from study skills courses based on information-processing research.

Ultimately, of course, no matter how many testable hypotheses or practical techniques a theory produces, it has little or no usefulness to developmentalists if it doesn't explain the basic facts of development. Based on this criterion, learning theories, especially classical and operant conditioning, are regarded by many developmentalists as somewhat less useful than other perspectives (Thomas, 1996). Although they explain how specific behaviors may be learned, they cannot account for the complexity of human development, which can't be reduced to connections between stimuli and responses or between behaviors and reinforcers.

As you can see, the point of comparing theories is not to conclude which one is true. Instead, such comparisons help to reveal the unique contribution each can make to a comprehensive understanding of human development.

efore going on

- What assumptions do the three families of theories make about development?

- On what criteria do developmentalists compare the usefulness of theories?

A Final Word

Y ou may be a bit bleary-eyed after all this discussion of theory. Even when theories are simplified and contrasted, as in Table 2.8, the theoretical issues may not seem real if you have not delved into actual data. However, it will be almost impossible to assimilate and integrate all the data you will be reading about in later chapters without having some theoretical models to which to relate them. You'll find it very helpful to keep the contrasting models in mind as you move through the rest of the book. So hang in there—these ideas will help you create some order out of a vast array of facts.

Summary

Psychoanalytic Theories

- Freud emphasized that behavior is governed by both conscious and unconscious motives and that the personality develops in steps: The id is present at birth; the ego and the superego develop in childhood. Freud also proposed psychosexual stages: the oral, anal, phallic, latency, and genital stages.

- Erikson emphasized social forces more than unconscious drives as motives for development. He proposed that personality develops in eight psychosocial stages over the course of the lifespan: trust versus mistrust; autonomy versus shame and doubt; initiative versus guilt; industry versus inferiority; identity versus role confusion; intimacy versus isolation; generativity versus stagnation; and integrity versus despair.

- Psychoanalytic concepts, such as the unconscious and identity, have contributed to psychologists' understanding of development. However, these theories propose many ideas that are difficult to test.

- Humanistic theorist Abraham Maslow suggested that individuals are motivated to fulfill inner needs in order to ultimately attain self-actualization.

Learning Theories

- Classical conditioning—learning through association of stimuli—helps explain the acquisition of emotional responses.

- Operant conditioning involves learning to repeat or stop behaviors because of their consequences. However,

consequences often affect behavior in complex ways in the real world.

- Bandura's social-cognitive theory places more emphasis on mental elements than other learning theories and assumes a more active role for the individual.

- Learning theories provide useful explanations of how behaviors are acquired but fall short of a truly comprehensive picture of human development.

Cognitive Theories

- Piaget focused on the development of logical thinking. He discovered that such thinking develops across four childhood and adolescent stages: the sensorimotor, preoperational, concrete operational, and formal operational stages. He proposed that movement from one stage to another is the result of changes in mental frameworks called *schemes.*

- Information-processing theory uses the computer as a model to explain intellectual processes such as memory and problem-solving. It suggests that there are both age differences and individual differences in the efficiency with which humans use their information-processing systems.

- Research has confirmed the sequence of skill development Piaget proposed but suggests that young children are more capable of logical thinking than he believed. Information-processing theory has been important in explaining Piaget's findings and memory processes.

Current Trends

- Biological theories such as nativism, ethology, sociobiology, and behavior genetics have gained popularity as developmentalists have sought to better understand the role of physiological processes in development.
- Vygotsky's socio-cultural theory has become important to developmentalists' attempts to explain how culture affects development.
- Bronfenbrenner's ecological theory has helped developmental psychologists categorize environmental factors and think about the ways in which they influence individuals.

Comparing Theories

- Theories vary in how they answer three basic questions about development: Are individuals active or passive in their own development? How do nature and nurture interact to produce development? Does development happen continuously or in stages?
- Useful theories allow psychologists to devise hypotheses to test their validity, are heuristically valuable, provide practical solutions to problems, and explain the facts of development.

Key Terms

accommodation (p. 38)

assimilation (p. 38)

behavior genetics (p. 44)

classical conditioning (p. 33)

cognitive theories (p. 37)

defense mechanisms (p. 26)

ecological theory (p. 44)

ego (p. 26)

equilibration (p. 38)

ethology (p. 43)

extinction (p. 34)

id (p. 26)

information-processing theory (p. 39)

learning theories (p. 33)

libido (p. 25)

nativism (p. 43)

neo-Piagetian theory (p. 40)

observational learning, modeling (p. 34)

operant conditioning (p. 33)

psychoanalytic theories (p. 25)

psychosexual stages (p. 27)

psychosocial stages (p. 28)

punishment (p. 33)

reinforcement (p. 33)

scheme (p. 38)

shaping (p. 34)

sociobiology (p. 44)

socio-cultural theory (p. 44)

superego (p. 26)

CHAPTER 3

Prenatal Development and Birth

David Young-Wolff, PhotoEdit

Like any good story, human development has a beginning, a middle, and an end. Genes and chromosomes passed on to the new individual at the moment of conception and the prenatal environment of the first months set the stage for all that is to follow. From conception to birth, prenatal development follows a truly amazing course that begins with a single cell and ends with a crying, but curious, newborn making his or her debut in the outside world.

Throughout pregnancy, most parents speculate about the baby's inherited characteristics, confident that all will be well. ("Will she be tall like her father?" "Will he be musically talented like his mother?") However, for those few parents-to-be whose babies are affected by a variety of agents that can cause birth defects or whose children are born too soon or too small, pregnancy and birth can bring more anxiety than joy. However, it's important to keep in mind that, in many of these cases, there are ways of limiting the damage.

In this chapter, you will learn about the beginning of the developmental process: conception, prenatal development, and birth. As you read, keep the following questions in mind:

- How does conception happen, and what rules govern the transmission of genetic traits from parent to child?

- What are the milestones of pregnancy and prenatal development? How does prenatal development for males and females differ? What have researchers learned about prenatal behavior?

- What are the potential negative effects of genetic disorders, chromosomal errors, diseases, drugs, and other factors on prenatal development?

- What are the stages in the birth process, from labor to delivery? What choices do parents in the industrialized world have to make regarding birth? What can go wrong during birth?

Conception and Genetics

The first step in the development of an individual human being happens at conception, when each of us receives a combination of genes that will shape our experiences throughout the rest of our lives.

The Process of Conception

● **Conception** ● Ordinarily, a woman produces one *ovum* (egg cell) per month from one of her two ovaries, roughly midway between menstrual periods. If the ovum is not fertilized, it travels from the ovary down the *fallopian tube* toward the *uterus,* where it gradually disintegrates and is expelled as part of the menstrual fluid. However, if a couple has intercourse during the crucial few days when the ovum is in the fallopian tube, one of the millions of sperm ejaculated as part of each male orgasm may travel the full distance through the woman's vagina, cervix, uterus, and fallopian tube and penetrate the wall of the ovum.

As you probably know, every cell in the human body contains 23 pairs of **chromosomes,** or strings of genetic material. However, sperm and ovum, collectively called **gametes,** contain 23 single (unpaired) chromosomes.

At conception, chromosomes in the ovum and the sperm combine to form 23 pairs in an entirely new cell called a **zygote.** Twenty-two of these pairs of chromosomes, called *autosomes,* contain most of the genetic information for the new individual. The twenty-third pair, the *sex chromosomes,* determine the sex. One of the two sex chromosomes, the *X chromosome,* is one of the largest chromosomes in the body and carries a large number of genes. The other, the *Y chromosome,* is quite small and contains only a few genes. Zygotes containing two X chromosomes develop into females, and those containing one X and one Y chromosome develop into males. Since the cells in a woman's body contain only X chromosomes, all her ova carry X chromosomes. Half of a man's sperm contain X chromosomes; the other half contain Y chromosomes. Consequently, the sex of the new individual is determined by the sex chromosome in the sperm.

Chromosomes are composed of molecules of **deoxyribonucleic acid (DNA).** Each chromosome can be further subdivided into segments, called **genes,** each of which influences a particular feature or developmental pattern. A gene controlling some specific characteristic always appears in the same place (the *locus*) on the same chromosome in every individual of the same species. For example, the locus of the gene that determines whether a person's blood is type A, B, or O is on chromosome 9.

● *Twins* ● In most cases, human infants are conceived and born one at a time. However, in about 4 out of every 100 births, more than one baby is born, usually twins. Roughly two-thirds of twins are *fraternal twins,* or twins that come from two sets of ova and sperm. Such twins, also called *dizygotic twins* (meaning that they originate from two zygotes), are no more alike genetically than any other pair of siblings, and need not even be of the same sex.

The remaining one-third of twins are *identical twins* (*monozygotic,* or arising from one zygote). Identical twins result when a single zygote, for unknown reasons, separates into two parts, each of which develops into a separate individual. Because identical twins develop from the same zygote, they have identical genes. Research involving identical twins is one of the major investigative strategies in the field of behavior genetics (see the Research Report).

Over the past 10 years, the annual number of multiple births has increased about 30% in the United States. Furthermore, births of triplets, quadruplets, and quintuplets have increased almost 400% (National Center for Health Statistics [NCHS], 1999). One reason for the increase is that the number of women over 35 giving birth for the first time has grown. As women get older, they are more likely to conceive fraternal twins. Another reason for the increased frequency of multiple births is the growing number of women who are using fertility drugs. These drugs stimulate the ovaries in ways that may result in the simultaneous production of more than one ovum.

chromosomes strings of genetic material in the nuclei of cells

gametes cells that unite at conception (ova in females; sperm in males)

zygote single cell created when sperm and ovum unite

deoxyribonucleic acid (DNA) chemical material that makes up chromosomes and genes

genes pieces of genetic material that control or influence traits

● *Assisted Reproductive Techniques* ● Fertility drugs are one of many *assisted reproductive techniques (ART)* available to couples who have trouble conceiving. Another is *in vitro fertilization* (IVF), popularly known as the "test-tube baby" method. (*In vitro* is Latin for "in glass.") This technique involves uniting an ovum and a sperm in a laboratory dish and implanting the resulting embryo in a woman's uterus. The egg can come from the woman who will carry the child or from a donor. Likewise, sperm can be from the woman's partner or a donor.

Typically, IVF laboratories create numerous embryos, which are then frozen, or *cryopreserved,* prior to being implanted. Cryopreservation increases the likelihood that implantation of an IVF embryo will result in a live birth (Schieve et al., 1999).

Research Report

Twins in Genetic Research

Researchers interested in the role of heredity in human development have been comparing identical and fraternal twins since the earliest days of developmental psychology. The logic is this: If identical twins (whose genes are exactly the same) who are raised apart are more similar than fraternal twins or non-twin siblings (whose genes are similar, but not identical) who are raised together, heredity must be important in the trait being studied. For example, the numbers below are correlations based on several studies of twins' intelligence test scores (Bouchard & McGue, 1981, p. 1056, Fig. 1). Recall from Chapter 1 that the closer to 1.00 a correlation is, the stronger the relationship.

Identical twins reared together	.85
Identical twins reared apart	.67
Fraternal twins reared together	.58
Non-twin siblings reared apart	.24

As you can see, intelligence test scores are more strongly correlated in identical twins than in fraternal twins or non-twin siblings, even when the identical twins are raised in different families. Such findings are taken to be evidence for the heritability of intelligence.

Developmentalists have also studied emotional characteristics in identical and fraternal twins. For example, researchers in Sweden examined 99 pairs of identical twins and 229 pairs of fraternal twins reared apart, and then compared these to twins reared together (Bergeman et al., 1993). Identical twins, whether raised together or apart, were found to be more similar than fraternal twins on measures of emotionality, activity, and sociability.

Taken together, the findings of these studies point to strong genetic components in both intelligence and emotional characteristics. However, what these studies reveal about environment may be even more significant. If psycho-

logical characteristics such as intelligence, emotionality, activity, and sociability were determined solely by heredity, identical twins would be *exactly* alike, and researchers would find correlations of +1.00. The correlations twin researchers have found are less than +1.00, even for identical twins who grow up in the same home. Moreover, the correlations for identical twins raised apart are lower than those for identical twins raised together.

To see the point more clearly, think about blood type. An individual's blood type *is* determined by the genes. Thus, identical twins always have the same blood type; that is, there is a correlation of +1.00, a perfect correlation, between the blood types of identical twins. Identical twin studies offer strong evidence that psychological traits, though clearly influenced by heredity, are not determined by the genes to the same extent as physical traits such as blood type.

Developmentalists have addressed concerns about the possible effects of cryopreservation on children's development in several studies. Both comparative (IVF infants and children versus non-IVF ones) and longitudinal studies have failed to find any significant effects of the procedure (Levy-Schiff et al., 1998; van Balen, 1998).

However, IVF is not a highly successful procedure. For one thing, the older a woman is, the lower the probability that she will be able to achieve a successful IVF pregnancy. Roughly 35% of 20- to 29-year-old women undergoing IVF achieve a live birth, but only about 13% of IVF procedures involving women over age 40 are successful (Schieve et al., 1999). The failure of IVF treatment can lead to depression (Weaver, Clifford, Hay, & Robinson, 1997). Even with successful IVF procedures, women sometimes remain emotionally detached from their fetuses for fear of losing them. However, once an IVF baby is born, some studies suggest that parents are more likely to express emotional warmth toward her or him than parents who conceive naturally (Eugster & Vingerhoets, 1999).

Multiple births are more frequent among women who become pregnant using IVF because doctors typically implant several embryos at once in order to increase the likelihood of at least one live birth. In order to reduce the chance of multiple births (which can place both mother and babies at risk), most European nations limit the number of embryos that can be simultaneously implanted to three (Schieve et al., 1999). In the United States, however, it is not uncommon for three or more, sometimes as many as six or seven, embryos to be implanted at once. Consequently, 20% of IVF pregnancies result in twins, and another 2% yield triplets (Schieve et al., 1999).

Another technique, *artificial insemination,* is both more successful and less likely to result in multiple births. In artificial insemination, sperm are injected directly into a woman's uterus, usually during the part of her menstrual cycle when she is most likely to conceive. The procedure can employ the sperm of a woman's partner or that of a donor. This method is most often used by couples in which the male partner has a low sperm count or by fertile women who want to conceive without a male partner. However, like blood transfusions, artificial insemination procedures carry some risk of infection.

Assisted reproductive techniques are somewhat controversial. For example, donated ova and sperm are usually provided by anonymous donors. Consequently, it is impossible to determine the genetic heritage of children conceived with donated ova or sperm. Furthermore, a few divorce cases have included disputes over the ownership of cryopreserved embryos. Thus, while probably everyone is thankful for the array of techniques available to help infertile couples, these have raised a number of serious concerns.

Genotypes, Phenotypes, and Patterns of Inheritance

At conception, the genes from the father contained in the sperm and those from the mother in the ovum combine to create a unique genetic blueprint—the **genotype**—that characterizes the new individual. The **phenotype** is the individual's whole set of actual characteristics. One way to remember the distinction is that the phenotype can be identified by directly observing the individual. For example, you can easily see that a woman has brown eyes, which are part of her phenotype. Her genotype, though, can't be so easily determined. In many cases, you have to know her parents' and offsprings' eye color to find out whether she carries genes for another eye color, because complex rules govern the way genotypes influence phenotypes.

genotype the unique genetic blueprint of each individual

phenotype an individual's particular set of observed characteristics

dominant-recessive pattern pattern of inheritance in which a single dominant gene influences a person's phenotype but two recessive genes are necessary to produce an associated trait

● *Dominant and Recessive Genes* ● The simplest genetic rule is the **dominant-recessive pattern,** in which a single dominant gene strongly influences phenotype. (Table 3.1 lists several normal phenotypical traits and indicates whether they arise from dominant or recessive genes.) People whose chromosomes carry either two dominant or two recessive genes are referred to as *homozygous.* Those with one dominant and one recessive gene are said to be *heterozygous.*

TABLE 3.1   Genetic Sources of Normal Traits

Dominant Genes	Recessive Genes	Polygenic (many genes)
Freckles	Flat feet	Height
Coarse hair	Thin lips	Body type
Dimples	Rh-negative blood	Eye color
Curly hair	Fine hair	Skin color
Nearsightedness	Red hair	Personality
Broad lips	Blond hair	
Rh-positive blood	Type O blood	
Types A and B blood		
Dark hair		

(*Source:* Tortora & Grabowski, 1993.)

If a child receives a single dominant gene for a trait from one parent, the child's phenotype will include the trait determined by that gene. In contrast, a child's phenotype will include a recessive trait only if she inherits a recessive gene from both parents. For example, geneticists have found that the curliness of hair is controlled by a single pair of genes (see Figure 3.1, page 58). The gene for curly hair is dominant; therefore, if a man has curly hair, his genotype includes at least one gene for curly hair and half of his sperm carry this gene. Conversely, straight hair is recessive, so a straight-haired man's genotype must include two straight-hair genes for his phenotype to include straight hair. Geneticists also know that the only kind of hair type a straight-haired father can pass on to his children is straight hair, because all his sperm carry recessive, straight-hair genes.

Critical Thinking

Think about your hair type and that of your siblings. What does your hair suggest about your parents' genotypes?

In addition, human geneticists have learned that both dominant and recessive genes differ in *expressivity*, meaning that the degree to which any gene influences phenotypes varies from person to person. For example, all individuals who have the gene for curly hair don't have equally curly hair. So, even when a child receives a dominant gene for curly hair from her father, the amount and type of curl in her hair probably won't be exactly the same as his.

Blood type is also determined by a dominant-recessive pattern of inheritance. Because a person must have two recessive genes to have type O blood, the genotype of every person who has this type is clear. However, the genotype of people with type A or B blood is not obvious because types A and B are dominant. Thus, when a person's phenotype includes either type A or type B blood, one of the person's blood type genes must be for that type, but the other could be for some other type. However, if a type A father and a type B mother produce a child with type O, each of them carries a gene for type O, because the child must receive one such gene from each parent to have the type O phenotype.

Figure 3.2 (page 59) illustrates the possible blood types of the offspring of a heterozygous type A father and a heterozygous type B mother. Notice that type AB is one of the possible phenotypes. This can happen because the genes for types A and B are *co-dominant* when they are together; each exerts an equal influence on the phenotype. As you can see, even the simplest pattern of inheritance can get fairly complicated.

● *Polygenic and Multi-Factorial Inheritance* ●   With **polygenic inheritance,** many genes influence the phenotype. There are many polygenic traits in which the dominant-recessive pattern is also at work. For example, geneticists believe that children get three genes for skin color from each parent (Tortora & Grabowski, 1993). Dark skin is dominant over light skin, but the skin colors also blend together. Thus, when one parent is dark-skinned and the other is fair-skinned, the child will have skin that is somewhere between the two. The dark-skinned parent's dominant genes will ensure that the child will be darker than the fair parent, but the fair-skinned parent's genes will prevent the child from having skin as dark as that of the dark-skinned parent.

Eye color is another polygenic trait with a dominant-recessive pattern (Tortora & Grabowski, 1993). Scientists don't know for sure how many genes influence eye color. They do know, however, that these genes don't cause specific colors. Instead, they cause the colored part of the eye to be dark or light. Dark colors (black, brown, hazel, and green) are dominant over light colors (blue and gray). However, blended colors are also possible. People whose chromosomes carry a combination of genes for green, blue, and gray eyes can have blue-gray, green-blue, or blue-green eyes. Likewise, genes that cause different shades of brown can combine their effects to make children's eye color phenotypes different from those of their brown-eyed parents.

polygenic inheritance pattern of inheritance in which many genes influence a trait

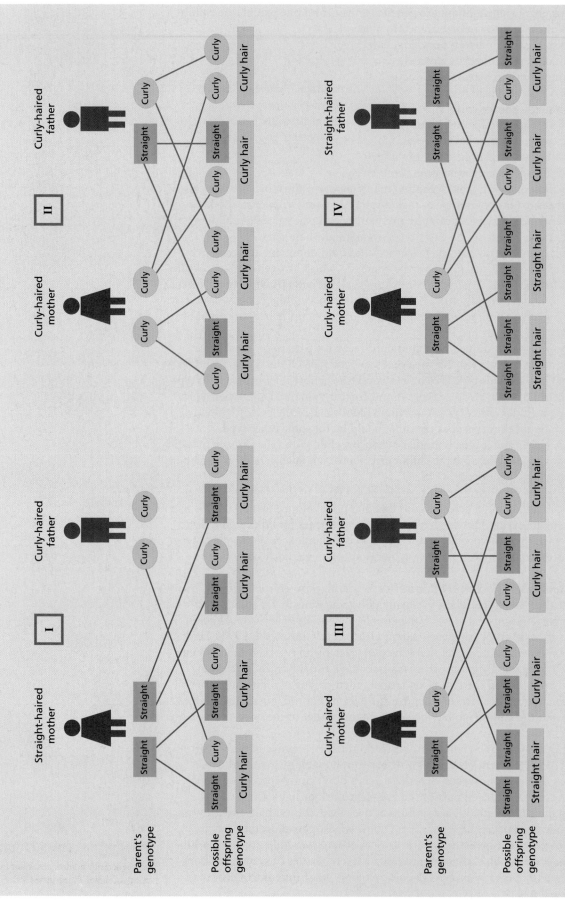

Figure 3.1
Examples of how the recessive gene for straight hair passes from parents to children.

Many genes influence height, and they are not subject to a dominant-recessive pattern of inheritance. Most geneticists believe that each height gene has a small influence over a child's size (Tanner, 1990). Thus, a child's height will be the sum of the effects of all of these genes.

Height, like most polygenic traits, is also a result of **multi-factorial inheritance**—that is, it is affected by both genes and environment. For this reason, doctors use a child's height as a measure of his general health (Sulkes, 1998; Tanner, 1990). If a child is ill, poorly nourished, or emotionally neglected, he may be smaller than others his age. Thus, when a child is shorter than 97% of his agemates, doctors try to determine if he is short because of his genes or because something is causing him to grow poorly (Tanner, 1990).

● *Mitochondrial Inheritance* ●   Scientists have discovered some additional principles of genetic inheritance. In *mitochondrial inheritance,* children inherit genes that are carried in structures called *mitochondria* which are found in the fluid that surrounds the nucleus of the ovum before it is fertilized. Consequently, mitochondrial genes are passed only from mother to child. Geneticists have learned that several serious disorders, including some types of blindness, are transmitted in this way. In most such cases, the mother herself is unaffected by the harmful genes (Amato, 1998).

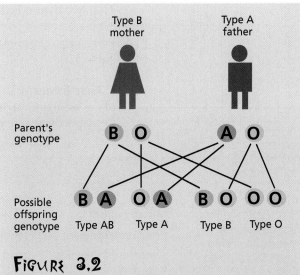

FIGURE 3.2
Possible blood types of offspring of a type B heterozygote and a type A heterozygote.

Before going on

● Explain the process by which gametes from a woman and a man unite to form a zygote. What are the characteristics of the new cell?

● Explain the dominant-recessive, polygenic, multi-factorial, and mitochondrial patterns of inheritance.

Pregnancy and Prenatal Development

P regnancy is a physical condition in which a woman's body is nurturing a developing embryo or fetus. *Prenatal development,* or *gestation,* is the process that transforms a zygote into a newborn. Thus, the process that ends with the birth of a baby involves two sets of experiences: those of the pregnant woman, and those of the developing zygote, embryo, and fetus.

multi-factorial inheritance inheritance affected by both genes and the environment

The Mother's Experience

Pregnancy is customarily divided into *trimesters*, three periods of 3 months each (see Table 3.2).

● *First Trimester* ● Pregnancy begins when the zygote implants itself in the lining of the woman's uterus (also called the *womb*). The zygote then sends out chemical messages that cause the woman's menstrual periods to stop. Some of these chemicals

TABLE 3.2 Pregnancy Summary

Trimester	Events	Discomforts	Prenatal Care	Serious Problems
First trimester: From first day of last menstrual period (LMP) to 12 weeks	Missed period Breast enlargement Abdominal thickening	Nausea Frequent urination Breast soreness Insomnia Fatigue	Confirmation of pregnancy Calculation of due date Blood and urine tests (and other tests if needed) Monthly doctor visits to monitor vital functions, uterine growth, weight gain, sugar and protein in urine	Ectopic pregnancy Abnormal urine or blood tests Increased blood pressure Malnutrition Bleeding Miscarriage
Second trimester: From 12 weeks after LMP to 24 weeks after LMP	Weight gain "Showing" Fetal movements felt Increased appetite	Varicose veins Frequent urination	Monthly doctor visits continue Ultrasound to measure fetal growth and locate placenta	Gestational diabetes Excessive weight gain Increased blood pressure Rh incompatibility of mother and fetus Miscarriage 13 to 20 weeks Premature labor 21+ weeks
Third trimester: From 25 weeks after LMP to beginning of labor	Weight gain Breast discharge	Swelling of extremities Indigestion Hemorrhoids Insomnia Diminished sex drive Difficulty moving around Hot flashes Fatigue Backache Leg cramps Stretch marks False labor	Weekly visits beginning at 32nd week Ultrasound to assess position of fetus Treatment of Rh incompatibility if needed Pelvic exams to check for cervical dilation	Increased blood pressure Bleeding Premature labor Bladder infection

(*Sources:* Hobbs & Ferth, 1993; Kliegman, 1998; Tortora, & Grabowski, 1993.)

are excreted in her urine, making it possible to diagnose pregnancy within a few days after conception. Other chemicals cause physical changes, such as breast enlargement.

The *cervix* (the narrow, lower portion of the uterus, which extends into the vagina) thickens and secretes mucus that serves as a barrier to protect the developing embryo from harmful organisms that might enter the womb through the vagina. The uterus begins to shift position and put pressure on the woman's bladder, causing her to urinate more often. This and other symptoms, like fatigue and breast tenderness, may interfere with sleep. Another common early symptom of pregnancy is *morning sickness*—feelings of nausea, often accompanied by vomiting, that usually occur in the morning.

Prenatal care during the first trimester is critical to prevent birth defects, because all of the baby's organs form during the first 8 weeks. Early prenatal care can identify maternal conditions, such as sexually transmitted diseases, that may threaten prenatal development. Doctors and nurses can also urge women to abstain from drugs and alcohol early in prenatal development, when such behavior changes may prevent birth defects.

Early prenatal care can also be important to the pregnant woman's health. For example, a small number of zygotes implant in one of the fallopian tubes instead of in the uterus, a condition called *ectopic pregnancy*. Early surgical removal of the zygote is critical to the woman's future ability to have children.

About 15% of pregnancies end in miscarriage, or *spontaneous abortion*. From the woman's point of view, an early miscarriage is similar to a menstrual period, although feelings of discomfort and blood loss are usually greater. Medical care is always necessary after a miscarriage because the woman's body may fail to completely expel the embryo.

● **Second Trimester** ●   During the second trimester of pregnancy, from the end of week 12 through week 24, morning sickness usually disappears, resulting in increases in appetite. The pregnant woman gains weight, and the uterus expands to accommodate a fetus that is growing rapidly. Consequently, the woman begins to "show" sometime during the second trimester. She also begins to feel the fetus's movements, usually at some point between the 16th and 18th weeks.

At monthly clinic visits, doctors monitor both the mother's and the baby's vital functions and keep track of the growth of the baby in the womb. Ultrasound tests are usually performed, and the sex of the baby can be determined after about the 13th week. Monthly urine tests check for *gestational diabetes,* a kind of diabetes that happens only during pregnancy. Women who have any kind of diabetes, including gestational diabetes, have to be carefully monitored during the second trimester because their babies may grow too rapidly, leading to premature labor or a baby that is too large for vaginal delivery.

The risk of miscarriage drops in the second trimester. However, a few fetuses die between the 13th and 20th weeks of pregnancy. In addition, premature labor after the 21st week can result in delivery of a living, but extremely small, baby. A small percentage of such infants survive, but most have significant health problems.

● **Third Trimester** ●   At 25 weeks, the pregnant woman enters her third trimester. Weight gain and abdominal enlargement are the main experiences of this period. In addition, the woman's breasts may begin to secrete a substance called *colostrum* in preparation for nursing.

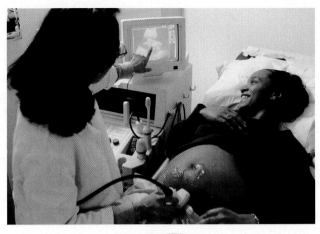

During the second trimester of pregnancy, ultrasound tests allow doctors to identify the fetus's sex, to diagnose fetal deformities and growth problems, and to determine the fetus's position in the uterus. (*Photo:* PhotoDisc, Inc.)

Supportive partners, friends, and relatives can help third-trimester mothers-to-be maintain positive attitudes and balance negative emotions that often accompany their feelings of physical awkwardness against the anticipated joy of birth. (*Photo:* Michael Newman, PhotoEdit)

Most women begin to feel more emotionally connected to the fetus during the third trimester. Individual differences in fetal behavior, such as hiccupping or thumb-sucking, sometimes become obvious during the last weeks of pregnancy. These behaviors may be observed during ultrasound tests that produce increasingly clear images of the fetus. In addition, most women notice that the fetus has regular periods of activity and rest.

Monthly prenatal doctor visits continue in the third trimester until week 32, when most women begin visiting the doctor's office or clinic once a week. Monitoring of blood pressure is especially important, as some women develop a life-threatening condition called *toxemia of pregnancy* during the third trimester. This condition is signaled by a sudden increase in blood pressure and can cause a pregnant woman to have a stroke.

Critical Thinking

Why do you think most women become emotionally attached to the fetus during the third trimester?

Prenatal Development

In contrast to the trimesters of pregnancy, the three stages of prenatal development are defined by specific developmental milestones and are not of equal length. Moreover, the entire process follows two developmental patterns you can see at work in the photographs in Table 3.3. With the **cephalocaudal pattern,** development proceeds from the head down. For example, the brain is formed before the reproductive organs. With the **proximodistal pattern,** development happens in an orderly way from the center of the body outward to the extremities. In other words, structures closer to the center of the body, such as the rib cage, develop before the fingers and toes.

● *The Germinal Stage* ● The first 2 weeks of gestation, from conception to implantation, constitute the **germinal stage.** During this stage, cells specialize into those that will become the fetus's body and those that will become the structures needed to support its development. Over the first 2 days, the single-celled zygote becomes four-celled as it drifts down the fallopian tube. On the 3rd day, cell division begins to happen rapidly, and by the 4th day, the zygote contains dozens of cells.

On day 5, the cells become a hollow, fluid-filled ball called a *blastocyst.* Inside the blastocyst, cells that will eventually become the embryo begin to clump together. On day 6 or 7, the blastocyst comes into contact with the uterine wall, and by the 12th day, it is completely buried in the uterine tissue. Some of the cells of the blastocyst's outer wall combine with cells of the uterine lining to begin creating the **placenta,** an organ that allows oxygen, nutrients, and other substances to be transferred between the mother's and baby's blood. The placenta's specialized structures bring the mother's and baby's blood close to one another without allowing them to mix.

Like the zygote, the placenta secretes chemical messages (hormones) that stop the mother's menstrual periods and keep the placenta connected to the uterus. Other placental hormones allow the bones of the woman's pelvis to become more flexible, induce breast changes, and increase the mother's metabolism rate. At the same time, the blastocyst's inner cells begin to specialize. One group of cells will become the **umbilical cord,** the organ that connects the embryo to the placenta. Vessels in the umbilical cord carry blood from the baby to the mother and back again. Other cells will form the *yolk sac,* a structure that produces blood cells until the embryo's blood-cell-producing organs are formed. Still others will become the **amnion,** a fluid-filled sac in which the baby floats until just before it is born. By the 12th day, the cells that will become the embryo's body are also formed.

cephalocaudal pattern growth that proceeds from the head downward

proximodistal pattern growth that proceeds from the middle of the body outward

germinal stage the first stage of prenatal development, beginning at conception and ending at implantation (approximately 2 weeks)

placenta specialized organ that allows substances to be transferred from mother to embryo and from embryo to mother, without their blood mixing

umbilical cord organ that connects the embryo to the placenta

amnion fluid-filled sac in which the fetus floats until just before it is born

TABLE 3.3   Milestones in Prenatal Development

Stage/Time Frame	Milestones	
Germinal Stage Day 1: Conception	Sperm and ovum unite, forming a zygote containing genetic instructions for the development of a new and unique human being. *Photo:* P. Motta & J. Van Blerkom, Photo Researchers	
Days 10 to 14: Implantation	The zygote burrows into the lining of the uterus. Specialized cells that will become the placenta, umbilical cord, and embryo are already formed. *Photo:* Lennart Nilsson/Albert Bonniers Forlag AB	
Embryonic Stage Weeks 3 to 8: Organogenesis	All of the embryo's organ systems form during the 6-week period following implantation. *Photo:* Petit Format/Nestle/Science Source Library, Photo Researchers	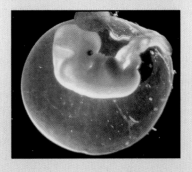

Fetal Stage

Weeks 9 to 38: Growth and Organ Refinement

The fetus grows from 1 inch long and $\frac{1}{4}$ ounce to a length of about 20 inches and a weight of 7–9 pounds. By week 12, most fetuses can be identified as male or female. Changes in the brain and lungs make viability possible by week 24; optimum development requires an additional 14 to 16 weeks in the womb. Most neurons form by week 28, and connections among them begin to develop shortly thereafter. In the last 8 weeks, the fetus can hear and smell, is sensitive to touch, and responds to light. Learning is also possible.

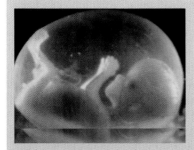
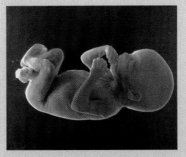

Photo: Petit Format/Nestle/Science Source Library, Photo Researchers

Photo: James Stevenson/Science Photo Library, Photo Researchers

Photo: Petit Format/Nestle/Science Source, Photo Researchers

(*Sources:* Kliegman, 1998; Tortora & Grabowski, 1993.)

● *The Embryonic Stage* ● The **embryonic stage** begins at implantation, approximately 2 weeks after conception, and continues until the end of week 8. By the time many women first suspect a pregnancy, usually 3 weeks after conception, the embryo's cells are starting to specialize and come together to form the foundations of all the body's organs. For example, the cells of the nervous system, the **neurons,** form a structure called the *neural tube,* from which the brain and spinal cord will develop. A primitive heart and the forerunners of the kidneys also develop during week 3, along with three sacs that will become the digestive system.

In week 4, the end of the embryo's neural tube swells to form the brain. Spots that will become the eyes appear on the embryo's head, and its heart begins to beat. The backbone and ribs become visible as bone and muscle cells move into place. The face starts to take shape, and the endocrine system begins to develop.

By week 5, the embryo is about $\frac{1}{4}$ inch long, 10,000 times larger than the zygote. Its arms and legs are developing rapidly. Five fingers are visible on its hands. Its eyes have corneas and lenses, and its lungs are beginning to develop.

In week 6, the embryo's brain begins to produce patterns of electrical activity. It moves in response to stimuli, and the **gonads,** or sex glands (ovaries in females and testes in males), develop. At first, the gonads of male and female embryos are identical. However, between the 4th and 6th weeks, genes on the Y chromosome cause the male embryo to produce the male hormone *testosterone.* The testosterone causes the gonads to become testes. In the absence of testosterone, the gonads develop into ovaries.

During week 7, a male embryo begins to develop a penis. Also, by this time, both male and female embryos begin to move spontaneously (Joseph, 2000). They have visible skeletons and fully developed limbs. The bones are beginning to harden and the muscles are maturing; by this point, the embryo can maintain a semi-upright posture. The eyelids seal shut to protect the developing eyes. The ears are completely formed, and x-rays can detect tooth buds in the jawbones.

During the last week of the embryonic stage, week 8, the liver and spleen begin to function. These organs allow the embryo to make and filter its own blood cells. Its heart is well developed and efficiently pumps blood to every part of the body. The embryo's movements increase as the electrical activity in its brain becomes more organized. Connections between the brain and the rest of the body are also well established. The embryo's digestive and urinary systems are functioning. By the end of week 8, **organogenesis,** the technical term for organ development, is complete.

● *The Fetal Stage* ● The final phase is the **fetal stage,** beginning at the end of week 8 and continuing until birth. The fetus grows from a weight of about $\frac{1}{4}$ ounce and a length of 1 inch to a baby weighing about 7 pounds and having a length of about 20 inches, who is ready to be born. In addition, this stage involves refinements of the organ systems, especially the lungs and brain, that are essential to life outside the womb.

During week 9, the fetus develops fingerprints and will try to grasp objects that come into contact with the palms of its hands. By week 11, the muscles in its face respond reflexively to stimuli in ways that look like facial expressions. The 9-week fetus also swallows amniotic fluid and urinates. Neurons are rapidly multiplying in the fetus's brain, spinal cord, and peripheral nervous system.

By the end of week 12, the facial profile of the fetus is almost identical to that of a full-term baby. The genitals are clearly visible, making it possible to identify the sex of a fetus using ultrasound. The fetus has definable, though irregular, periods of activity and rest. The lungs rhythmically expand and contract as the fetus "breathes" amniotic fluid through the nose.

Hair follicles begin to form in the 13th week. The fetus also begins to be able to hear its mother's voice and loud, external noises between the 13th and 15th weeks. Major brain structures are beginning to take shape, as the **glial cells** needed to support the neurons develop. By the 16th week, the umbilical cord is transporting 300 quarts of fluid per day. The fetus is 8–10 inches long and weighs about 6 ounces.

embryonic stage the second stage of prenatal development, from week 2 through week 8, during which the embryo's organ systems form

neurons specialized cells of the nervous system

gonads sex glands (ovaries in females; testes in males)

organogenesis process of organ development

fetal stage the third stage of prenatal development, from week 9 to birth, during which growth and organ refinement take place

glial cells specialized cells in the brain that support neurons

In approximately week 17 or week 18, the mother begins to feel the fetus moving. The heartbeat can be detected with a stethoscope, and the fetus grows an additional 2 inches. A fine hair, *lanugo,* covers the body, and some fetuses already have hair on the head.

In the 19th and 20th weeks, the fetus becomes much more responsive to stimuli. For example, when a light is introduced into the womb, the fetus covers its eyes with its hands (Nilsson & Hamberger, 1990). The fetus also develops eyebrows and fingernails. By week 20, the mother's family members or friends may be able to hear the baby's heartbeat by pressing an ear against her rapidly enlarging abdomen.

By week 21, the fetus is covered with an oily, cheese-like substance, *vernix,* that protects its skin from harsh chemicals in the amniotic fluid. At approximately week 22, the lungs begin producing a substance called *surfactant,* which is necessary for the exchange of oxygen and carbon dioxide in the blood.

By the end of week 23, a small number of babies have attained **viability,** the ability to live outside the womb (Moore & Persaud, 1993). However, most babies born this early die, and those who do survive struggle for many months. Remaining in the womb just 1 week longer, until the end of week 24, greatly increases a baby's chances of survival. The extra week probably allows time for lung function to become more efficient. In addition, most brain structures are completely developed by the end of the 24th week. For these reasons, most experts accept 24 weeks as the average age of viability.

At the end of week 25, the fetus is 14–15 inches long and weighs 2 pounds. It recognizes its mother's voice, and its eyelids reopen sometime between weeks 26 and 27. The 28-week-old fetus has regular periods of rest and activity. A fetus born at this time has a good chance of survival, though most babies born this early have significant health problems.

As week 29 begins, the fetus is growing very rapidly. Neurons in the brain are beginning to form connections, a process that will continue across the entire lifespan (see Figure 3.3). The fetus is 16–17 inches long and weighs 4 pounds. In weeks 30 and 31, it begins to acquire antibodies from the mother's blood that will provide protection against many illnesses for several weeks after birth. By week 32, the fetus is getting very crowded in the uterus and is beginning to put on layers of fat in preparation for life outside the womb.

In weeks 33 and 34, the approximately 18-inch-long, 6-pound fetus starts to get ready for birth. The fetus reverses position so its head, which had been toward the top of the uterus, is at the bottom of the uterus; the womb is now so crowded that the fetus has to remain in one position (the "fetal" position) all the time. Important changes that will allow the baby to breathe efficiently after birth take place in the lungs. By week 35, the fetus is spending more and more time at rest (DiPietro, Hodgson, Costigan, & Johnson, 1996).

By the time the fetus reaches week 36, it has virtually a 100% chance of survival. All organs are fully functional. *Engagement*—the movement of the head into the lower neck of the uterus—happens at the end of the 36th week. At 37 weeks, the fetus is considered full-term. Most are 19–21 inches long and weigh 6–9 pounds. At this point, pressure from the baby's head on the cervix may cause it to begin to open. In addition, the placenta may begin to deteriorate in preparation for expulsion from the uterus following the baby's birth.

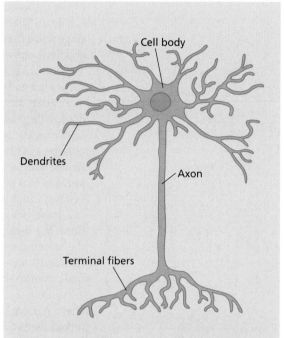

FIGURE 3.3

The structure of a single developed neuron. The cell bodies are the first to be developed, primarily between weeks 12 and 24. Axons and dendrites develop later, especially during the final 12 weeks, and continue to increase in size and complexity for several years after birth.

Sex Differences

Because prenatal development is strongly influenced by maturational codes that are the same for both males and females, there are only a few sex differences in prenatal development. One fairly well-documented difference is that male fetuses, on average, are more

viability ability of the fetus to survive outside the womb

physically active (DiPietro, Hodgson, Costigan, & Johnson, 1996; DiPietro, Hodgson, Costigan, Hilton, & Johnson, 1996). Further, activity level is fairly stable from the fetal stage through childhood (Accardo et al., 1997). This means that the sex differences in children's activity level you'll read about in later chapters probably begin in the womb.

Sometime between 4 and 8 weeks after conception, the male embryo begins to secrete the male hormone *testosterone*. If this hormone is not secreted or is secreted in inadequate amounts, the embryo will be "demasculinized," even to the extent of developing female genitalia. Female embryos do not appear to secrete any equivalent hormone. However, the presence of male hormone at the critical time (from a drug the mother takes or from a genetic disease called *congenital adrenal hyperplasia*) acts to "masculinize" the female fetus, sometimes resulting in genitalia that appear to be male. Some research even suggests that prenatal masculinization of female fetuses leads to "tomboyish" childhood behavior, such as rough-and-tumble play (Collaer & Hines, 1995).

In addition, male fetuses secrete small amounts of testosterone into the amniotic fluid. If a male shares the womb with a female fraternal twin, she is likely to swallow the secreted testosterone. Although the research is fairly new, studies suggest that these girls have some neurological characteristics that are more similar to the average male than to the average female (McFadden, 1998).

Subtle sex differences in prenatal brain development probably contribute to different patterns of growth hormone secretions in adolescence as well. Researchers have linked prenatal hormones to sex differences in the dominance of the right and left hemispheres of the brain, physical aggression, and connections between brain and motor patterns (Pressman et al., 1998; Todd, Swarzenski, Rossi, & Visconti, 1995).

Developmentalists aren't sure why, but female fetuses appear to be more sensitive to external stimulation and to advance more rapidly in skeletal development (Groome et al., 1999; Tanner, 1990). Female infants are about 1–2 weeks ahead in bone development at birth, even though newborn boys are typically longer and heavier. Female superiority in skeletal development persists through childhood and early adolescence, causing girls to acquire many coordinated movements and motor skills, especially those involving the hands and wrists, earlier than boys. The gap between the sexes gets wider every year until the mid-teens, when boys catch up and surpass girls in general physical coordination.

Boys are more vulnerable to all kinds of prenatal problems. Many more boys than girls are conceived—from 120 to 150 male embryos to every 100 female ones—but more of the males are spontaneously aborted. At birth, there are about 105 boys for every 100 girls. Boys are also more likely to have birth defects (Tanner, 1990).

Prenatal Behavior

Centuries before scientists began to study prenatal development, pregnant women noticed fetal responses to music and other sounds. However, in recent years, developmentalists have learned a great deal about how such stimuli affect the fetus. For one thing, researchers have discovered that the fetus responds to sounds and vibrations with heart rate changes, head turns, and body movements as early as the 25th week of gestation (Joseph, 2000).

Research also suggests that the fetus can distinguish between familiar and novel stimuli by the 32nd or 33rd week (Sandman, Wadhwa, Hetrick, Porto, & Peeke, 1997). In one study, pregnant women recited a short children's rhyme out loud each day from week 33 through week 37. In week 38 researchers played a recording of either the rhyme the mother had been reciting or a different rhyme and measured the fetal heart rate. Fetal heart rates dropped during the familiar rhyme, but not during the unfamiliar rhyme, suggesting that the fetuses had learned the sound patterns of the rhyme recited by their mothers (DeCasper, Lecaneut, Busnel, Granier-DeFerre, & Maugeais, 1994). The ability to learn in this way seems to emerge between 24 and 38 weeks, along with changes in the nervous system that allow the fetal brain to gain greater control of physical movements (Pressman et al., 1998).

Evidence for fetal learning also comes from studies in which newborns appear to remember stimuli to which they were exposed prenatally: their mother's heartbeats, the odor of the amniotic fluid, and stories or pieces of music they heard in the womb (Righetti, 1996; Schaal, Marlier, & Soussignan, 1998). For example, in a classic study of prenatal learning, pregnant women read Dr. Seuss's classic children's story *The Cat in the Hat* out loud each day for the final 6 weeks of their pregnancies. After the infants were born, they were allowed to suck on special pacifiers that turned a variety of sounds off and on. Each kind of sound required a special type of sucking. Researchers found that the babies quickly adapted their sucking patterns in order to listen to the familiar story, but did not increase their sucking in order to listen to an unfamiliar story (DeCasper & Spence, 1986). In other words, babies preferred the sound of the story they had heard *in utero* (in the womb).

Developmentalists are trying to find out how, or whether, prenatal learning affects later development. In one study, pregnant women wore waistbands equipped with speakers through which they exposed their fetuses to an average of 70 hours of classical music between 28 weeks and birth (Lafuente et al., 1997). By age 6 months, the babies who had heard the music were more advanced than control infants in many motor and cognitive skills. Of course, the exact meaning of this result is difficult to assess, but it does suggest that the prenatal sensory environment may be important in later development.

Stable individual differences in behavior are also identifiable in fetuses. You have already read about the sex difference in activity level. As is true of most sex differences, however, the range of individual differences within each gender is far greater than the difference in *average* activity levels between male and female fetuses. Longitudinal studies have shown that very active fetuses, both males and females, tend to become children who are very active. Moreover, these children are more likely to be labeled "hyperactive" by parents and teachers. In contrast, fetuses who are less active than average are more likely to be mentally retarded (Accardo et al., 1997).

Before going on

- Describe a woman's experiences during the three trimesters of pregnancy.

- Outline the milestones of the germinal, embryonic, and fetal stages of prenatal development.

- How do male and female fetuses differ?

- What do developmentalists know about prenatal behavior?

Problems in Prenatal Development

Prenatal development is not immune to outside influences, as you'll see in this section. Keep in mind that most of the problems you'll read about are very rare, many are preventable, and many need not have permanent consequences for the child.

Genetic Disorders

Many disorders appear to be transmitted through the operation of dominant and recessive genes (see Table 3.4). *Autosomal disorders* are caused by genes located on the autosomes (chromosomes other than sex chromosomes). The genes that cause *sex-linked* disorders are found on the X chromosome.

● *Autosomal Disorders* ●   Most disorders caused by recessive genes are diagnosed in infancy or early childhood. For example, a recessive gene causes a baby to have problems digesting the amino acid phenylalanine. Toxins build up in the baby's brain and cause mental retardation. This condition, called *phenylketonuria (PKU),* is found in about 1 in every 10,000 babies (Nicholson, 1998). If a baby consumes no foods containing phenylalanine, however, he will not become mentally retarded. Milk is one of the foods PKU babies can't have, so early diagnosis is critical. For this reason, most states require all babies to be tested for PKU soon after birth.

Like many recessive disorders, PKU is associated with ethnicity. Caucasian babies are more likely to have the disorder than infants in other groups. Similarly, West African and African American infants are more likely to suffer from *sickle-cell disease,* a recessive disorder that causes red blood cell deformities (Scott, 1998). In sickle-cell disease, the blood can't carry enough oxygen to keep the body's tissues healthy. Few children with sickle-cell disease live past the age of 20, and most who survive to adulthood die before they are 40 (Scott, 1998).

Almost one-half of West Africans have either sickle-cell disease or *sickle-cell trait* (Amato, 1998). Persons with sickle-cell trait carry a single recessive gene for sickle-cell disease, which causes a few of their red blood cells to be abnormal. Thus, doctors can identify carriers of the sickle-cell gene by testing their blood for sickle-cell trait. Once potential parents know they carry the gene, they can make informed decisions about future childbearing. In the United States, about 1 in 650 African Americans has sickle-cell disease, and 1 in 8 has sickle-cell trait. The disease and trait also occur more frequently in Americans of Mediterranean, Caribbean, Indian, Arab, and Latin American ancestry than in those of European ancestry (Wong, 1993).

About 1 in every 3,000 babies born to Jewish couples of Eastern European ancestry suffers from another recessive disorder, *Tay-Sachs disease.* By the time she is 1 to 2 years old, a Tay-Sachs baby is likely to be severely mentally retarded and blind. Very few survive past the age of 3 (Painter & Bergman, 1998).

TABLE 3.4   Some Genetic Disorders

Autosomal Dominant Disorders	Autosomal Recessive Disorders	Sex-Linked Recessive Disorders
Huntington's disease	Phenylketonuria	Hemophilia
High blood pressure	Sickle-cell disease	Fragile-X syndrome
Extra fingers	Cystic fibrosis	Red-green color blindness
Migraine headaches	Tay-Sachs disease	Missing front teeth
Schizophrenia	Kidney cysts in infants	Night blindness
	Albinism	Some types of muscular dystrophy
		Some types of diabetes

(*Sources:* Amato, 1998; Tortora & Grabowski, 1993.)

Disorders caused by dominant genes, such as *Huntington's disease,* are usually not diagnosed until adulthood (Amato, 1998). This disorder causes the brain to deteriorate and affects both psychological and motor functions. Until recently, children of Huntington's disease sufferers had to wait until they became ill themselves to know for sure that they carried the gene. There is now a blood test to identify the Huntington's gene. Thus, people who have a parent with this disease can now make better decisions about their own child-bearing, as well as prepare themselves to live with a serious disorder when they get older.

● **Sex-Linked Disorders** ● Most sex-linked disorders are caused by recessive genes (see Figure 3.4). One fairly common sex-linked recessive disorder is *red-green color blindness.* People with this disorder have difficulty distinguishing between the colors red and green when these colors are adjacent. About 1 in 800 men and 1 in 400 women have this disorder. Most learn ways of compensating for the disorder and thus live perfectly normal lives.

A more serious sex-linked recessive disorder is *hemophilia.* The blood of people with hemophilia lacks the chemical components that cause blood to clot. Thus, when a person with hemophilia bleeds, the bleeding doesn't stop naturally. Approximately 1 in 5,000 baby boys is born with this disorder, which is almost unknown in girls (Scott, 1998).

About 1 in every 1,500 males and 1 in every 2,500 females have a sex-linked disorder called *fragile-X syndrome* (Amato, 1998). A person with this disorder has an X chromosome with a "fragile," or damaged, spot. Fragile-X syndrome can cause mental retardation that becomes progressively worse as a child gets older (Adesman, 1996). In fact, experts estimate that 5–7% of all retarded males have fragile-X syndrome (Zigler & Hodapp, 1991).

FIGURE 3.4

Compare this pattern of sex-linked transmission of a recessive disease (hemophilia) with the pattern shown in Figure 3.2.

Chromosomal Errors

A variety of problems can be caused when a child has too many or too few chromosomes, a condition referred to as a *chromosomal error,* or *chromosomal anomaly.* Like genetic disorders, these are distinguished by whether they involve autosomes or sex chromosomes.

● **Trisomies** ● A *trisomy* is a condition in which a child has three copies of a specific autosome. The most common is *trisomy 21,* or *Down syndrome,* in which the child has three copies of chromosome 21. Roughly 1 in every 800–1,000 infants is born with this abnormality (Nightingale & Goodman, 1990). These children are mentally retarded and have distinctive facial features, smaller brains, and often other physical abnormalities such as heart defects (Haier et al., 1995).

The risk of bearing a child with trisomy 21 is greatest for mothers over 35. Among women aged 35–39, the incidence of Down syndrome is about 1 in 280 births. Among those over 45, it is as high as 1 in 50 births (D'Alton & DeCherney, 1993).

Scientists have identified children with trisomies in the 13th and 18th pairs of chromosomes as well (Amato, 1998). These disorders have more severe effects than

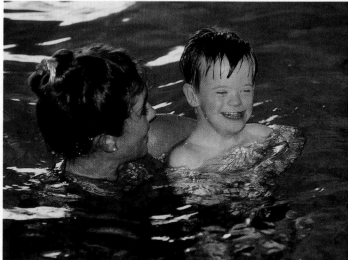

This child shows the distinctive facial features of a child with Down syndrome. (*Photo:* Mark Richards, PhotoEdit)

trisomy 21. Few trisomy 13 or trisomy 18 children live past the age of 1 year. As with trisomy 21, the chances of having a child with one of these disorders increase with a woman's age.

● *Sex-Chromosome Anomalies* ● A second class of anomalies is associated with the sex chromosomes. The most common is an XXY pattern, called *Klinefelter's syndrome,* that occurs in 1 or 2 out of every 1,000 males (Amato, 1998). Affected boys usually look normal but have underdeveloped testes and, as adults, very low sperm production. Most are not mentally retarded, but many have language and learning disabilities. At puberty, these boys experience both male and female changes. For example, their penises enlarge and their breasts develop.

A single-X pattern (X0), called *Turner's syndrome,* may also occur. Individuals with Turner's syndrome are anatomically female but show stunted growth and are usually sterile. Without hormone therapy, they do not menstruate or develop breasts at puberty. About one-fourth have serious heart defects (Amato, 1998). These girls also show an imbalance in their cognitive skills: They often perform particularly poorly on tests that measure spatial ability but usually perform at or above normal levels on tests of verbal skill (Golombok & Fivush, 1994).

Neither Kleinfelter's nor Turner's syndrome is associated with the mother's age. However, older mothers are more likely to produce normal-appearing girls with an extra X chromosome and boys with an extra Y chromosome (Amato, 1998). Females with an XXX pattern, about 1 in every 1,000 female births, are usually of normal size but develop more slowly than their peers (Amato, 1998). Many, though not all, have poor verbal abilities, score low on intelligence tests, and do more poorly in school than other groups with sex chromosome anomalies (Bender, Harmon, Linden, & Robinson, 1995).

Approximately 1 in 1,000 boys has an extra Y chromosome. Most are taller than average and have large teeth. They usually experience normal puberty, and they have no difficulty fathering children (Amato, 1998). Developmentalists now know that it is only a myth that an extra Y chromosome causes below-average intelligence and high aggression (Tortora & Grabowski, 1993).

Teratogens: Maternal Diseases

Deviations in prenatal development can result from exposure to **teratogens,** substances that cause damage to an embryo or fetus. The general rule is that each organ system is most vulnerable to harm when it is developing most rapidly (Moore & Persaud, 1993). Because most organ systems develop most rapidly during the first 8 weeks of gestation, this is the period when exposure to teratogens carries the greatest risk. Because of space limitations, we will discuss only a few of the most significant teratogens. Table 3.5 lists several others.

Several viruses pass through the placental filters and attack the embryo or fetus directly. For example, *rubella,* or *German measles,* causes a short-lived mild reaction in adults but may be deadly to a fetus. Most infants exposed to rubella in the first 4–5 weeks show some abnormality, compared with only about 10% of those exposed in the final 6 months of pregnancy (Moore & Persaud, 1993). Deafness, cataracts, and heart defects are the most common abnormalities.

HIV, the virus that causes AIDS, is one of many sexually transmitted organisms that can be passed directly from mother to fetus. The virus may cross the placenta and enter the fetus's bloodstream, or the infant may contract the virus in the birth canal during delivery.

Only about a quarter of infants born to HIV-infected mothers become infected, although scientists don't yet know how to predict which infants will contract the virus (Abrams et al., 1995; Annunziato & Frenkel, 1993). Transmission appears to

teratogens substances such as viruses and drugs that can cause birth defects

TABLE 3.5   Some Important Teratogens and Their Effects

Teratogens	Possible Effects on Fetus
Maternal Diseases	
Cancer	Fetal or placental tumor
Toxoplasmosis	Brain swelling, spinal abnormalities
Chicken pox	Scars, eye damage
Parvovirus	Anemia
Hepatitis B	Hepatitis
Chlamydia	Conjunctivitis, pneumonia
Tuberculosis	Pneumonia or tuberculosis
Drugs	
Inhalants	Problems similar to those of fetal alcohol syndrome; premature labor
Accutane/Vitamin A	Facial, ear, heart deformities
Streptomycin	Deafness
Penicillin	Skin disorders
Tetracycline	Tooth deformities
Diet pills	Low birth weight

(*Sources:* Amato, 1998; Kliegman, 1998.)

be more likely when the mother has AIDS than when she is HIV-positive but not yet ill (Abrams et al., 1995). In addition, HIV-positive pregnant women who take the drug AZT have a markedly lower risk of transmitting the disease to their children—as low as 8% (Prince, 1998).

Infants who acquire HIV from their mothers typically become ill within the first 2 years of life (Prince, 1998). The virus weakens children's immune systems, allowing a host of other infectious agents, such as the bacteria that cause pneumonia and meningitis, to attack their bodies. Even children who remain symptom-free must restrict their exposure to viruses and bacteria. For example, HIV-positive children cannot be immunized with vaccines that utilize live viruses, such as the polio vaccine (Prince, 1998).

Other sexually transmitted diseases (STDs), including *syphilis, genital herpes, gonorrhea,* and *cytomegalovirus,* cause a variety of birth defects. Unlike most teratogens, the bacterium that causes syphilis is most harmful during the last 26 weeks of prenatal development and causes eye, ear, and brain defects. Genital herpes is usually passed from mother to infant during birth. One-third of infected babies die, and another 25–30% suffer blindness or brain damage. Thus, doctors usually deliver the babies of women who have herpes surgically. Gonorrhea, which can cause the infant to be blind, is also usually transmitted during birth. For this reason, doctors usually treat the eyes of newborns with a special ointment that prevents damage from gonorrhea.

Critical Thinking

Given the new findings about the benefits of AZT, do you think all pregnant women should be required to be tested for HIV infection so that those who test positive can be given AZT?

A much less well-known sexually transmitted virus is *cytomegalovirus (CMV),* which is in the herpes group. As many as 60% of *all* women carry CMV, but most have no recognizable symptoms. Of babies whose mothers are infected with CMV, 1–2% become infected prenatally. When the mother's disease is in an active phase, the transmission rate is more like 40–50% (Blackman, 1990). About 2,500 babies born each year in the United States display symptoms of CMV and have a variety of serious problems, including deafness, central nervous system damage, and mental retardation (Blackman, 1990).

Teratogens: Drugs

Sorting out the effects of drugs (prescription and nonprescription, legal and illegal) on prenatal development has proven to be an immensely challenging task because many pregnant women take multiple drugs. Other factors, such as maternal stress, lack of social support, or poverty and poor prenatal care, also often accompany illegal drug use (Johnson, Nusbaum, Bejarano, & Rosen, 1999). Nevertheless, there are several drugs that seem to affect infant development, independent of other variables.

● *Smoking* ● Infants of mothers who smoke are on average about half a pound lighter at birth than infants of nonsmoking mothers, and lower birth weight has a variety of potential negative consequences (Floyd, Rimer, Giovino, Mullen, & Sullivan, 1993; Fourn, Ducic, & Seguin, 1999). Also, some studies suggest there are higher rates of learning and behavior problems among children whose mothers smoked heavily during pregnancy (Fergusson, Horwood, & Lynskey, 1993; Tomblin, Smith, & Zhang, 1997). However, smokers who quit early in pregnancy have the same rates of preterm or low-birth-weight infants as those who did not smoke at all (Ahlsten, Cnattingius, & Lindmark, 1993).

Children with fetal alcohol syndrome have distinctive features. (*Photo:* © 2000 George Steinmetz)

● *Drinking* ● Researchers have also documented the effects of alcohol on prenatal development. In fact, recent studies show that alcohol can even adversely affect an ovum prior to ovulation or during its journey down the fallopian tube to the uterus. Likewise, a zygote can be affected by alcohol even before it has been implanted in the uterine lining (Kaufman, 1997).

Mothers who are heavy drinkers or alcoholics are at significant risk of delivering infants with *fetal alcohol syndrome (FAS).* These children are generally smaller than normal, with smaller brains. They frequently have heart defects and hearing losses, and their faces are distinctive, with a somewhat flattened nose and often an unusually long space between nose and mouth (Church, Eldis, Blakley, & Bawle, 1997). As children, adolescents, and adults, they are shorter than normal and have smaller heads, and their intelligence test scores indicate mild mental retardation. Indeed, FAS is one of the most frequent causes of retardation in the United States, exceeding even trisomy 21 according to some studies (Streissguth et al., 1991). FAS children who are not retarded often have learning and behavior difficulties (Mattson & Riley, 1999; Mattson, Riley, Gramling, Delis, & Jones, 1998; Meyer, 1998; Uecker & Nadel, 1996). Moreover, these problems can persist into adolescence and adulthood (Kerns, Don, Mateer, & Streissguth, 1997; Olson, Feldman, Streissguth, Sampson, & Bookstein, 1998).

Recent evidence also suggests that even moderate drinking by a pregnant woman may cause her child to have learning and behavioral difficulties in childhood and adolescence (Larroque & Kaminski, 1998; Sampson et al., 1997). Binge drinking, even once during pregnancy, is also associated with a variety of problems (Olson, Sampson, Barr, Streissguth, & Bookstein, 1992; Streissguth, Barr, & Sampson, 1990). In the face of this evidence, the safest course for pregnant women is to drink no alcohol at all.

● *Marijuana and Heroin* ● Significant numbers of pregnant women the world over take various illegal drugs. The drug most frequently used is marijuana. The infants of twice-weekly marijuana smokers suffer from tremors and sleep problems. Moreover, they seem to have little interest in their surroundings for up to 2 weeks after birth (Brockington, 1996). How these early differences affect babies' later development is unknown.

Both heroin and methadone, a drug often used in treating heroin addiction, can cause miscarriage, premature labor, and early death (Brockington, 1996). Further, 60–80% of babies born to heroin- or methadone-addicted women are addicted to these drugs as well. Addicted babies have high-pitched cries and suffer from withdrawal symptoms, such as irritability, uncontrollable tremors, vomiting, convulsions, and sleep problems. These symptoms may last as long as 4 months.

The degree to which heroin and methadone affect development depends on the quality of the environment in which babies are raised. Babies who are cared for by mothers who continue to be addicted themselves usually don't do as well as those whose mothers stop using drugs or who are raised by relatives or foster families (Brockington, 1996). By age 2, most heroin- or methadone-addicted babies in good homes are developing normally.

● *Cocaine* ● Use of cocaine, in either powder or "crack" form, by pregnant women is linked to many kinds of developmental problems in their children (Chatlos, 1997). However, most cocaine-using pregnant women are poor and abuse multiple substances, making it difficult to separate the effects of cocaine from those of poverty and other drugs. Some studies suggest that cocaine alone has no long-term effects on cognitive or social development (Kilbride, Castor, Hoffman, & Fuger, 2000; Phelps, Wallace, & Bontrager, 1997; Richardson, Conroy, & Day, 1996). However, other research has demonstrated that prenatal exposure to cocaine, especially when women use it several times a week, leads to a variety of developmental problems in infants (Brown, Bakeman, Coles, Sexson, & Demi, 1998; Madison, Johnson, Seikel, Arnold, & Schultheis, 1998; Schuler & Nair, 1999). Still other studies indicate that cocaine-exposed infants' problems may seem to be minimal when the children are assessed individually in researchers' laboratories. However, in complex environments such as school classrooms, their difficulties become more apparent (Betancourt et al., 1999).

The mixed findings on prenatal exposure to cocaine probably mean that this drug interacts with other environmental factors to produce a complex set of effects. For example, a cocaine-exposed infant who receives good follow-up care and whose mother discontinues her drug use may be less likely to suffer than another who receives little or no such care and is raised by a drug-using mother. Consequently, health professionals suggest that the development of cocaine-exposed babies should be closely monitored and that interventions should be tailored to fit the individual circumstances and characteristics of each infant (Kilbride et al., 2000).

Other Maternal Influences on Prenatal Development

Other maternal characteristics that can adversely affect prenatal development include the mother's diet, her age, and her mental and physical health.

● *Diet* ●　Some specific nutrients are vital to prenatal development. One is folic acid, a B vitamin found in beans, spinach, and other foods. Inadequate amounts of this nutrient are linked to neural tube defects, such as *spina bifida* (Daly, Kirke, Molloy, Weir, & Scott, 1995). The potential negative effects of insufficient folic acid occur in the very earliest weeks of pregnancy, before a woman may know she is pregnant. So it is important for women who plan to become pregnant to obtain at least 400 micrograms of this vitamin daily, the minimum required level.

It is also important for a pregnant woman to take in sufficient overall calories and protein to prevent malnutrition. A woman who experiences malnutrition during pregnancy, particularly during the final 3 months, has an increased risk of delivering a low-birth-weight infant who will have intellectual difficulties in childhood (Mutch, Leyland, & McGee, 1993). In addition, researchers have recently identified prenatal malnutrition, along with a variety of obstetrical complications, as an important risk factor in the development of mental illnesses in adulthood (Neugebauer, Hoek, & Susser, 1999; Susser, & Lin, 1992).

The impact of maternal malnutrition appears to be greatest on the developing nervous system—a pattern found in studies of both humans and other mammals. For example, rats whose caloric intake has been substantially restricted during the fetal and early postnatal periods show a pattern described as *brain stunting,* in which both the weight and volume of the brain are reduced. They also develop fewer dendrites and show less rich synaptic formation (Pollitt & Gorman, 1994). In human studies of cases in which prenatal malnutrition has been severe enough to cause the death of the fetus or newborn, effects very similar to those seen in the rat studies have been observed. That is, these infants had smaller brains and fewer and smaller brain cells (Georgieff, 1994).

● *Age* ●　One intriguing trend in the industrialized world is that more women postpone first pregnancy until their late 20s or early 30s. By 1992, 23.5% of first births in the United States were to women over 30, more than double the rate in 1970 (U.S. Bureau of the Census, 1995). One effect of this trend, as you have already learned, is that the number multiple births each year has increased dramatically.

Mothers over 30 are at increased risk for several kinds of problems, including miscarriage, complications of pregnancy such as high blood pressure, and death during pregnancy or delivery (Berkowitz, Skovron, Lapinski, & Berkowitz, 1990; McFalls, 1990). In one large study of nearly 4,000 women in New York, all of whom had received adequate prenatal care, researchers found that women who were 35 or older during their first pregnancy were almost twice as likely as women in their 20s to suffer pregnancy complications (Berkowitz et al., 1990). These effects of age seem to be exacerbated if the mother has not had adequate prenatal care or has poor health habits. For example, the negative effects of maternal smoking on birth weight are considerably greater among women over 35 than among younger women (Wen et al., 1990).

Whether the infants born to these older mothers also face higher risks is not so clear. Infants born to older mothers appear to be only slightly more likely to weigh less than 5.5 pounds at birth, a difference that may be entirely explained by the different rates of multiple births between younger and older women (Berkowitz et al., 1990; Cnattingius, Berendes, & Forman, 1993; NCHS, 1999). Babies of older mothers are also no more likely to have birth defects—aside from the well-established risk of chromosomal anomalies such as trisomy 21 (Baird, Sadovnick, & Yee, 1991). However, researchers in Sweden, where mothers of all ages receive good prenatal care, have found higher rates of late-pregnancy miscarriage and infant mortality for older mothers, especially for first births to mothers over 35 (Cnattingius et al., 1993). Given these varying results, the experts have been unable to reach a clear conclusion about risks for babies born to older mothers.

At the other end of the age continuum, there is also disagreement about how to interpret the findings regarding very young mothers. When simply comparing the rates of problems seen in teenage mothers with those among mothers in their 20s, almost all researchers find higher rates among the teens. However, teenage mothers are also more likely to be poor and less likely to receive adequate prenatal care, so it is very hard to sort out the causal factors.

A number of researchers have found that when poverty and prenatal care are taken into account, the differences in rates of problems between teenage and older mothers disappear (e.g., McCarthy & Hardy, 1993; Osofsky, Hann, & Peebles, 1993). However, other researchers have found higher rates of adverse pregnancy outcomes even among teenage mothers with adequate incomes who remained in school and received good prenatal care (Fraser, Brockert, & Ward, 1995). Developmentalists speculate that the higher rate of problems experienced by teenagers results from some biological consequence of pregnancy in bodies whose own growth is not complete.

● *Chronic Illnesses* ● Chronic illnesses, whether emotional or physical, can also affect prenatal development. For example, long-term severe depression and other mood disorders can lead to slow fetal growth and premature labor (Weinstock, 1999). Moreover, developmentalists have learned that depressed mothers are less likely to feel attached to their fetuses. At least one study suggested that infants whose mothers do not develop a prenatal attachment to them are less socially responsive than other infants of the same age (Oates, 1998).

Conditions such as heart disease, diabetes, lupus, hormone imbalances, and epilepsy can also affect prenatal development negatively (Kliegman, 1998; McAllister et al., 1997; Sandman, Wadhwa, Chicz-DeMet, Porto, & Garite, 1999). In fact, one of the most important goals of the new specialty of *fetal-maternal medicine* is to manage the pregnancies of women who have such conditions in ways that will support the health of both mother and fetus. For example, pregnancy often makes it impossible for a diabetic woman to keep her blood sugar levels under control. In turn, erratic blood sugar levels may damage the fetus's nervous system or cause it to grow too rapidly (Allen & Kisilevsky, 1999; Kliegman, 1998). To prevent such complications, a fetal-maternal specialist must find a diet, a medication, or a combination of the two that will stabilize the mother's blood sugar but will not harm the fetus. Similarly, fetal-maternal specialists help women who have epilepsy balance their own need for anticonvulsant medication against possible harm to the fetus (see No Easy Answers).

No Easy Answers

Pregnancy, Epilepsy, and Anticonvulsant Drugs

Epilepsy is a chronic neurological disorder that causes seizures. To control the seizures, most people with epilepsy take *anticonvulsant drugs*. However, epileptic women who want to bear children face a dilemma that can be agonizing.

In about 30% of epileptics, seizures increase in both severity and frequency during pregnancy. The physical trauma associated with seizures can rupture the placenta and, in rare cases, cause fatal bleeding in the fetus's brain. However,

brain and spinal cord defects happen more frequently in fetuses exposed to anticonvulsant drugs. In addition, a recent study found an extraordinarily high rate of transsexualism among adults who had been prenatally exposed to anticonvulsants (Dessens et al., 1999).

Balancing the risks of medication against those of seizures, most physicians think it's better to try to manage the effects of the medicines through proper dosage than to risk uncontrolled seizures during pregnancy. They point out that the risks of medication and methods for minimizing them are better

known and more predictable than those of epileptic seizures (American Association of Family Physicians, 1998). However, pregnancy changes the way an epileptic woman's body responds to anticonvulsant medication. In most cases, many adjustments in dosage and type of medication are required before the right combination is found. For some women, nothing works. Therefore, even though doctors can advise them of the various probabilities, epileptic women often have to make childbearing decisions without really knowing what the outcome will be.

● ***Maternal Emotions*** ● Some psychologists have suggested that maternal emotions can affect prenatal development. Their rationale is that stressful psychological states such as anxiety and depression lead to changes in body chemistry. In a pregnant woman, these changes result in both qualitative and quantitative differences in the hormones and other chemicals to which the fetus is exposed.

As persuasive as this idea may be, the question of whether maternal emotional states such as anxiety and depression affect prenatal development remains open. For example, one study found children of mothers who reported high levels of psychological distress during pregnancy to be more emotionally negative at both 6 months and 5 years of age than children of nondistressed mothers (Martin, Noyes, Wisenbaker, & Huttunen, 1999). But critics claim that the real connection is a matter of maternal genes and/or parenting style: Emotionally negative mothers may simply be more likely to have children who are less emotionally positive than their peers.

One fairly consistent finding, however, is that the fetuses of severely distressed mothers tend to grow more slowly than others (Paarlberg, Vingerhoets, Passchier, Dekker, & van Geign, 1995). Developmentalists do not really know whether this effect results directly from emotion-related hormones or is an indirect effect of the mother's emotional state. A stressed or depressed mother may eat less, or her weakened immune system may limit her ability to fight off viruses and bacteria—either of these situations may retard fetal growth. Consequently, many psychologists suggest that providing stressed and/or depressed pregnant women with social support and counseling may lead to improvements in both maternal and fetal health (Brockington, 1996).

Fetal Assessment and Treatment

Certain tests, including *chorionic villus sampling (CVS)* and *amniocentesis,* can be used to identify chromosomal errors and many genetic disorders prior to birth (see Figure 3.5). With CVS, cells are extracted from the placenta and used in a variety of laboratory tests during the early weeks of prenatal development. With amniocentesis, which is done between weeks 14 and 16 of a woman's pregnancy, a needle is used to extract amniotic fluid containing fetal cells. Fetal cells filtered out of the fluid are then tested in a variety of ways to diagnose chromosomal and genetic disorders. In addition, *ultrasonography* has become a routine part of prenatal care in the United States because of its usefulness in monitoring fetal growth during high-risk pregnancies.

There are also many laboratory tests that use maternal blood, urine, and/or samples of amniotic fluid to help health care providers monitor fetal development. For example, the presence of a substance called *alpha-fetoprotein* in a pregnant woman's blood is associated with a number of prenatal defects, including abnormalities in the brain and spinal cord. Doctors can also use a laboratory test to assess the maturity of fetal lungs (Kliegman, 1998). This test is critical when doctors have to deliver a baby early because of the mother's health.

Fetoscopy involves insertion of a tiny camera into the womb to directly observe fetal development. Fetoscopy makes it possible for doctors to correct some kinds of defects surgically (Kliegman, 1998). Likewise, fetoscopy has made such techniques as fetal blood transfusions and bone marrow transplants possible. Specialists also use fetoscopy to take samples of blood from the umbilical cord. Laboratory tests performed on fetal blood samples can assess fetal organ function, diagnose genetic and chromosomal disorders, and detect fetal infections (D'Alton & DeCherney, 1993). For example, fetal blood tests can help doctors identify a bacterial infection that is causing a fetus to grow too slowly. Once diagnosed, the infection can be treated by injecting antibiotics into the amniotic fluid (so that they will be swallowed by the fetus) or into the umbilical cord (Kliegman, 1998).

Researchers have examined how prenatal diagnosis affects parents-to-be. Compared to parents of 1-year-olds with disabilities, who did not know about the problems

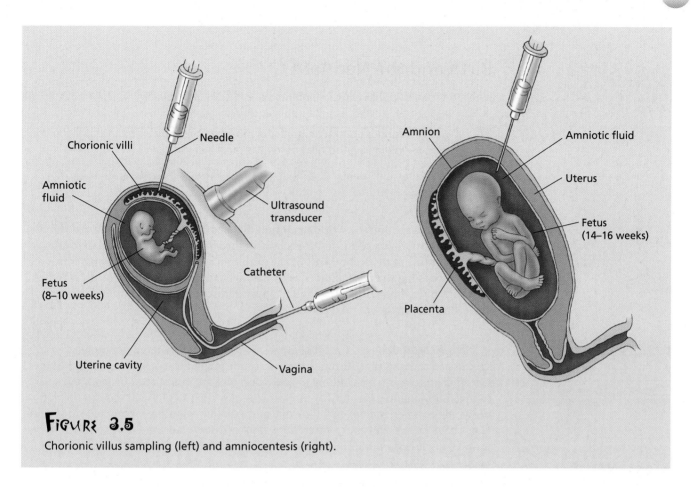

Figure 3.5

Chorionic villus sampling (left) and amniocentesis (right).

prior to birth, parents whose infants' difficulties were diagnosed prenatally report greater feelings of stress and depression (Hunfeld et al., 1999). However, specialists in fetal medicine suggest that the negative emotional effects of prenatal diagnosis can be moderated by providing parents-to-be with counseling and specific information about treatment at the time the diagnosis is made, rather than waiting until after the birth.

Before going on

- Briefly describe the genetic disorders presented in this section: PKU, sickle-cell disease, Tay-Sachs disease, Huntington's disease, red-green color blindness, hemophilia, and fragile-X syndrome.

- What is a trisomy, and which type is most common?

- Which sex chromosome anomalies are the most serious?

- List the risks associated with the teratogenic diseases.

- What are the potential adverse effects of smoking, drinking, and drug use on prenatal development?

- What additional maternal factors influence prenatal development?

Birth and the Neonate

nce gestation is complete, the fetus must be born—an event that holds some pain as well as a good deal of joy for most parents.

Birth Choices

In most places around the world, tradition dictates how babies are delivered. However, in industrialized countries, especially in the United States, hospital deliveries became routine in the second half of the 20th century. Today, however, parents in such societies have several choices as to who will attend their baby's birth, whether medication will be used to manage the physical discomforts of labor and delivery, and where the birth will take place.

● **Birth Attendants** ● *Certified nurse-midwives* are registered nurses who have specialized training that allows them to care for pregnant women and deliver babies. *Certified midwives* have training in midwifery but are not nurses. Instead, most received training in other health care professions, such as physical therapy, before becoming certified midwives. In Europe and Asia, nurse-midwives and certified midwives have been the primary caretakers of pregnant women and newborns for many years. By contrast, in the United States, physicians provide prenatal care and deliver babies for 95% of women.

● **Drugs During Labor and Delivery** ● One key decision for expectant mothers concerns whether to use drugs during labor and delivery. *Analgesics* may be given during labor to reduce pain. *Sedatives* or *tranquilizers* can be administered to reduce anxiety. *Anesthesia,* when used, is usually given later in labor to block pain, either totally (using general anesthesia) or in certain portions of the body (using local anesthesia).

Studying the causal links between drug use during labor and delivery and the baby's later behavior or development has proven to be difficult. First, it's clear that nearly all drugs given during labor pass through the placenta, enter the fetal bloodstream, and may remain there for several days. Not surprisingly, then, infants whose mothers have received any type of drug are typically slightly more sluggish, gain a little less weight, and spend more time sleeping in the first few weeks than do infants of nondrugged mothers (Maurer & Maurer, 1988).

In the developing world, tradition determines where a baby is born and who attends its birth. Hospital deliveries are common in the United States, but many hospitals offer parents the option of delivering their babies in non-surgical settings such as the birthing room pictured on the right. (*Photos:* Sean Sprague, Stock Boston; © Margaret Miller, 1992, Photo Researchers)

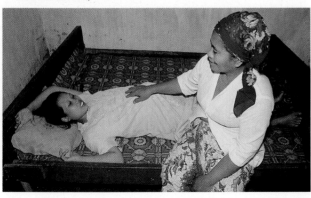

Second, there are no consistently observed effects from analgesics and tranquilizers beyond the first few days, and only hints from a few studies of long-term effects of anesthesia (Rosenblith, 1992). Given such contradictory findings, only one specific piece of advice seems warranted: If you are a new mother who received medication during childbirth, bear in mind that your baby is also drugged, and that this will affect her behavior in the first few days. If you allow for this effect and realize that it will wear off, your long-term relationship with your child is likely to be unaffected.

Nevertheless, many women choose to avoid drugs altogether. The general term *natural childbirth* is commonly used to refer to this particular choice. This approach is also often called the *Lamaze method,* after the physician who popularized the notion of natural childbirth and devised a variety of pain management techniques. In natural childbirth, women rely on psychological and behavioral methods of pain management rather than on pain-relieving drugs.

Natural childbirth involves several components. First, a woman selects someone, usually the baby's father, to serve as a labor coach. *Prepared childbirth classes* psychologically prepare the woman and her labor coach for the experience of labor and delivery. For example, they learn to use the term *contraction* instead of *pain.* Further, believing that her baby will benefit from natural childbirth provides the woman with the motivation she needs to endure labor without the aid of pain-relieving medication. Finally, relaxation and breathing techniques provide her with behavioral responses to contractions that serve to replace the negative emotions that typically result from physical discomfort. Aided by her coach, the woman focuses attention on her breathing rather than on the pain.

The Location of Birth

Another choice parents must make is where the baby is to be born. In most of the industrialized world, women deliver their babies in specialized maternity clinics. However, in the United States there are four alternatives in most communities:

- A traditional hospital maternity unit
- A birth center or birthing room located within a hospital, which provides a more homelike setting for labor and delivery and often allows family members to be present throughout
- A free-standing birth center, like a hospital birth center except that it is located apart from the hospital, with delivery typically attended by a midwife rather than (or in addition to) a physician
- The mother's home

More than 98% of babies in the United States are born in hospitals (U.S. Bureau of the Census, 1994). About 1% are born at home, and the remaining 1% are born in birthing centers. Thus, much of what researchers know about out-of-hospital births comes from studies in Europe. For example, in the Netherlands, a third of all deliveries occur at home (Eskes, 1992). Home deliveries are encouraged for uncomplicated pregnancies during which the woman has received good prenatal care. When these conditions are met, with a trained birth attendant present at delivery, the rate of delivery complications or infant problems is no higher than for hospital deliveries.

The Physical Process of Birth

Labor is typically divided into three stages. Stage 1 covers the period during which two important processes occur: dilation and effacement. The cervix (the opening at the bottom of the uterus) must open up like the lens of a camera (*dilation*) and also

MAKE THE CONNECTION

Which of the research methods you learned about in Chapter 1 would you have to use to identify causal connections between anesthetics (and other drugs administered during childbirth) and subsequent development of the child? Why have no such studies been done?

Many fathers take prenatal classes like this one so they can provide support to their partners during labor. (*Photo:* Joseph Nettis, Stock Boston)

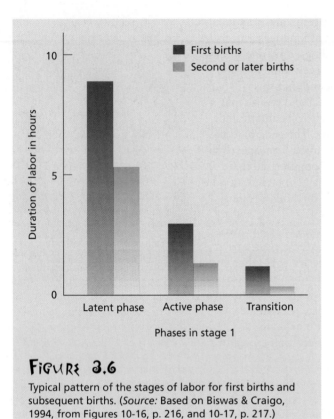

FIGURE 3.6

Typical pattern of the stages of labor for first births and subsequent births. (*Source:* Based on Biswas & Craigo, 1994, from Figures 10-16, p. 216, and 10-17, p. 217.)

flatten out (*effacement*). At the time of actual delivery, the cervix must normally be dilated to about 10 centimeters (about 4 inches).

Customarily, stage 1 is itself divided into phases. In the *early* (or *latent*) phase, contractions are relatively far apart and typically are not too uncomfortable. In the *active* phase, which begins when the cervix is 3 to 4 centimeters dilated and continues until dilation has reached 8 centimeters, contractions are closer together and more intense. The last 2 centimeters of dilation are achieved during a phase usually called *transition*. It is this phase, when contractions are closely spaced and strong, that women typically find the most painful. Fortunately, transition is also ordinarily the shortest phase.

Figure 3.6 shows the typical length of these various phases of labor for first births and later births. What the figure does not convey is the wide individual variability that exists. Among women delivering a first child, stage 1 may last as few as 3 hours or as many as 20 (Biswas & Craigo, 1994; Kilpatrick & Laros, 1989).

At the end of the transition phase, the mother will normally have the urge to help the infant emerge by "pushing." When the birth attendant (physician or midwife) is sure the cervix is fully dilated, she or he will encourage this pushing, and stage 2 of labor, the actual delivery, begins. The baby's head moves past the stretched cervix, into the birth canal, and finally out of the mother's body. Most women find this part of labor markedly less distressing than the transition phase because at this point they can assist the delivery process by pushing. Stage 2 typically lasts less than an hour and rarely takes longer than 2 hours. Stage 3, also typically quite brief, is the delivery of the placenta (also called the *afterbirth*) and other material from the uterus.

Most infants are delivered head first, facing toward the mother's spine; 3% to 4%, however, are oriented differently, either feet first or bottom first (called *breech* presentations) (Brown, Karrison, & Cibils, 1994). In the United States today, infants in breech positions are nearly all delivered through an abdominal incision (a *cesarean section*) rather than vaginally.

Though most physicians agree that a breech presentation requires a cesarean delivery, the procedure itself is somewhat controversial. Critics argue that the operation is often performed unnecessarily. In fact, concern about possible complications arising from unnecessary cesarean sections contributed to a significant decline in their frequency during the 1990s. At the beginning of the decade, almost 30% of babies in the United States were delivered by cesarean section. By 1995, the most recent year for which comprehensive statistics are available, the frequency of surgical delivery had dropped to about 21% (NCHS, 1997). Nevertheless, the cesarean delivery rate in the United States remains the highest in the world.

● *Birth Complications* ● During the process of birth, some babies go into *fetal distress,* signaled by a sudden change in heart rate. In most cases, doctors don't know why a baby experiences fetal distress. However, one cause of distress is pressure on the umbilical cord. For example, if the cord becomes lodged between the baby's head and the cervix, each contraction will push the baby's head against the cord. The collapsed blood vessels can no longer carry blood to and from the baby. When this happens, the baby experiences **anoxia,** or oxygen deprivation. Anoxia can result in death or brain damage, but doctors can prevent long-term effects by

anoxia oxygen deprivation experienced by a fetus during labor and/or delivery

PARENTING
The Real World

Singing to Your Newborn

Singing to newborns is a behavior that has been found everywhere in the world. Just as they do when speaking to a newborn or an older infant, both mothers and fathers sing to infants with a unique singing style that includes a high-pitched tone and exaggerated rhythms (Bergeson & Trehub, 1999; Trainor, Clark, Huntley, & Adams, 1997; Trehub et al., 1997). Remarkably, researchers have found that newborns as young as 2 days old can distinguish among videotaped adults who are singing to babies, to other adults, or to no audience (Masataka, 1999). These findings suggest that the characteristics of the infant-directed singing style, as well as the ability to recognize it, may be inborn.

Researchers have identified two universal categories of songs for newborns: lullabies and playsongs. Songs of even tempo that are composed of smoothly connected notes are classified as lullabies. A good example in English is "Rock-a-Bye Baby." Songs that feature sharp

disconnections between notes, often accompanied by gestures, are playsongs. The English song "The Itsy-Bitsy Spider" is such a song.

Lullabies and playsongs elicit different responses from infants. Babies respond to lullabies by turning their attention toward themselves and playing with their hands or sucking their thumbs (Rock, Trainor, & Addison, 1999). In contrast, they display externally directed responses to playsongs. Infants listening to playsongs wriggle, smile, and behave in ways that seem to encourage adults to continue singing (Rock et al., 1999). Adults seem to have an intuitive understanding of infants' responses to the two types of songs and can easily determine which type of song a videotaped baby is hearing (Rock et al., 1999). Thus, it isn't surprising that parents the world over use the two types of songs to regulate infant behavior. Lullabies help calm them, and playsongs entertain them.

However, being sung to may make important contributions to babies' development as well. One study found that

preterm newborns in a neonatal intensive care nursery who were sung to three times a day for 20 minutes over a 4-day period ate more, gained weight faster, and were discharged from the hospital earlier than infants who were not sung to (Coleman, Pratt, Stoddard, Gerstmann, & Abel, 1997). Remarkably, too, the physiological functioning of babies who were sung to (as measured by variables such as oxygen saturation levels in their bloodstreams) was superior.

Some developmentalists speculate that singing to infants is linked to language development because important milestones in singing and speech—the first songs and the first words—appear at the same time (Chen-Hafteck, 1997). Others theorize that stimulation of the part of the brain used to perceive songs may enhance intellectual development. However, the greatest effect of parents' singing and babies' reactions to it may be communication of a mutual "I love you" message that helps to establish a lasting emotional bond between parent and child (Bergeson & Trehub, 1999).

---

acting quickly to surgically deliver infants who experience distress (Handley-Derry et al., 1997).

Infants may also dislocate their shoulders or hips during birth. Some experience fractures, and in others, nerves that control facial muscles are compressed, causing temporary paralysis on one side of the face. Such complications are usually not serious and resolve themselves with little or no treatment.

If a laboring woman's blood pressure suddenly increases or decreases, a cesarean delivery may be indicated. In addition, some women's labor progresses so slowly that they remain in stage 1 for more than 24 hours. This can happen if the infant's head is in a position that prevents it from exerting enough pressure on the cervix to force it open. In such cases, surgery is indicated, because continuing labor can cause permanent damage to the mother's body.

After birth, most women require a period of a month or so to recover. During this time, the mother's body experiences a variety of hormonal changes including those required for nursing and for returning to the normal menstrual cycle. A few women experience a period of depression after giving birth (a potential problem that you will read more about in the chapters on early adulthood). However, most recover quickly, both physically and emotionally, from the ordeal of pregnancy and birth.

TABLE 3.6   The Apgar Scale

Aspect Observed	Score Assigned		
	0	**1**	**2**
Heart rate	Absent	< 100 beats per minute	> 100 beats per minute
Respiratory rate	No breathing	Weak cry and shallow breathing	Good cry and regular breathing
Muscle tone	Flaccid	Some flexion of extremities	Well flexed extremities
Response to stimulation of feet	None	Some motion	Crying
Color	Blue; pale	Body pink, extremities blue	Completely pink

(*Source:* Francis, Self, & Horowitz, 1987, pp. 731–732.)

Assessing the Neonate

A baby is referred to as a **neonate** for the first month of life. The health of babies born in hospitals and birthing centers, as well as most who are delivered at home by professional midwives, is usually assessed with the *Apgar scale* (Apgar, 1953). The baby receives a score of 0, 1, or 2 on each of five criteria, listed in Table 3.6. A maximum score of 10 is fairly unusual immediately after birth, because most infants are still somewhat blue in the fingers and toes at that stage. At a second assessment, usually 5 minutes after birth, however, 85–90% of infants score 9 or 10. Any score of 7 or better indicates that the baby is in no danger. A score of 4, 5, or 6 usually means that the baby needs help establishing normal breathing patterns; a score of 3 or below indicates a baby in critical condition.

Health professionals often use the *Brazelton Neonatal Behavioral Assessment Scale* to track a newborn's development over about the first 2 weeks following birth (Brazelton, 1984). A health professional examines the neonate's responses to stimuli, reflexes, muscle tone, alertness, cuddliness, and ability to quiet or soothe herself after being upset. Scores on this test can be helpful in identifying children who may have significant neurological problems.

Low Birth Weight

Classification of a neonate's weight is another important factor in assessment. All neonates below 2,500 grams (about 5.5 pounds) are classified as having **low birth weight (LBW)**. Most LBW infants are *preterm,* or born before the 38th week of gestation. The proportion of LBW infants is particularly high in the United States, where just over 7% of newborns weigh less than 2,500 grams (MacDorman & Atkinson, 1999). Multiple fetuses, which, as you learned earlier in the chapter, are increasing in frequency in the industrialized world, are especially likely to result in preterm birth (see Development in the Information Age).

However, it is possible for an infant to have completed 38 weeks or more of gestation and still be an LBW baby. In addition, some preterm babies weigh the right amount for their gestational age, while others are smaller than expected. These *small-for-date neonates* appear to have suffered from retarded fetal growth and, as a group, have poorer prognoses than do infants who weigh an appropriate amount for their gestational age.

neonate term for babies between birth and 1 month of age

low birth weight (LBW) newborn weight below 5.5 pounds

in the Information Age

The Youngest Celebrities

The Information Age was just beginning when Olivia Dionne, a Canadian housewife, gave birth to five identical girls in 1934. The doctor who delivered the babies notified the local newspaper, whose reporters telegraphed the information to news agencies around the world. The Dionne quintuplets became instant celebrities. Well-wishers overwhelmed them with letters and gifts. Publicity-seek-

(*Photo:* CORBIS)

ing manufacturers sent them diapers, clothes, toys, and baby food.

Today, it takes more than five babies to capture public attention. Births of quadruplets and quintuplets, though certainly not commonplace, rate only a few local headlines. However, the McCaughey septuplets, born in 1997, and the Chukwu octuplets, born in 1998, became international sensations. In fact, when the octuplets' mother was hospitalized during the last 2 months of her pregnancy, the hospital staff spent almost as much time managing the horde of reporters that hovered near the labor and delivery unit 24 hours a day as they did taking care of Nkem Chukwu, the babies' mother (Hellinghausen, 1999).

Health care professionals worry that the media attention given to

multiple births obscures the more typical outcomes of pregnancies involving multiple fetuses (McCullough, 1998). In most cases, they say, pregnancies involving more than three fetuses end in prenatal or neonatal death of all of them. They also fear that the rosy portrait of multiple births painted in the press may cause couples to seek fertility-drug treatment to deliberately pursue such births.

Reproductive specialists are also concerned about the possibility that the news media so strongly link fertility drugs with multiple births that infertile couples may forgo such treatment because they think such a birth is always the outcome. Even with fertility drugs, experts say, multiple pregnancy is still the exception rather than the rule. In addition, reproductive specialists do everything possible to avoid multiple pregnancy because of its inherent risks.

LBW infants display markedly lower levels of responsiveness at birth and in the early months of life. Those born more than 6 weeks early also often suffer from *respiratory distress syndrome* (also referred to as *hyaline membrane disease*). Their poorly developed lungs cause serious breathing difficulties. In 1990, physicians began treating this problem by administering surfactant (the chemical that makes it possible for the lungs to exchange oxygen and carbon dioxide in the blood) to preterm neonates, a therapy that has reduced the rate of death among very-low-birth-weight infants by about 30% (Corbet, Long, Schumacher, Gerdes, & Cotton, 1995; Schwartz, Anastasia, Scanlon, & Kellogg, 1994).

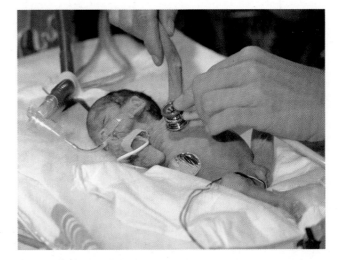

The majority of LBW babies who weigh more than 1,500 grams (about 3 pounds) and who are not small-for-date catch up to their normal peers within the first few years of life. But those below 1,500 grams remain smaller than normal and have significantly higher rates of long-term health problems, lower intelligence test scores, and more problems in school (Breslau et al., 1994; Hack et al., 1994). In fact, 40–50% of such babies show some kind of significant problem later.

An LBW neonate's general health also makes a difference. For example, LBW babies who experience bleeding in the brain immediately after birth are more likely to have later problems (Bendersky & Lewis, 1994). The economic circumstances of an LBW infant's family matter as well. Children in low-income families are more likely to suffer from long-term effects of low birth weight, such as attention prob-

LBW infants' chances of survival are better when they receive care in a neonatal intensive care unit. (*Photo:* Susan Leavines, Photo Researchers)

lems, than are those who grow up in more affluent homes (Breslau & Chilcoat, 2000).

Boys are more likely than girls to show long-term effects of low birth weight. In fact, one recent study involving more than 700 6-year-olds found a higher rate of learning disabilities and other problems in LBW boys than among their normal-birth-weight (NBW) peers (Johnson & Breslau, 2000). By contrast, LBW girls did not differ at all from their NBW counterparts. The difference between LBW and NBW boys persisted when they were examined again at age 11.

Critical Thinking

What three pieces of advice would you give a pregnant friend after reading this chapter?

Before going on

- What happens in each of the three stages of labor?

- What choices do most mothers in the United States have with respect to birth attendants, drugs to relieve pain, and birth location? What are some of the complications that can happen during birth?

- Explain how neonates are assessed, and list the risks of low birth weight.

A Final Word

Because scientists keep learning more about prenatal and birth risks, the number of warnings to pregnant women seems to grow continually. However, you should remember that *most* pregnancies are normal and largely uneventful, and most babies are healthy and normal at birth. In addition, there are specific preventive steps that any woman can take to reduce the risks for herself and her unborn child. She can be properly immunized; she can stop smoking and drinking; she can watch her diet and make sure her weight gain is sufficient; and she can get early and regular prenatal care. Keep in mind as well that many disorders can be diagnosed prenatally, making it possible to modify the infant's post-birth environment in ways that will moderate the disorder's effects.

Summary

Conception and Genetics

- At conception, the 23 chromosomes from the sperm join with the 23 chromosomes from the ovum to make up the set of 46 that will be reproduced in each cell of the new individual.

- Geneticists distinguish between the genotype (the pattern of inherited genes) and the phenotype (the individual's observable characteristics). Genes are transmitted from parents to children according to complex rules that include the dominant-recessive pattern, the polygenic pattern, and multi-factorial inheritance.

Pregnancy and Prenatal Development

- Pregnancy is divided into three approximately equal trimesters.

- Prenatal development occurs in three stages of unequal length (germinal, embryonic, fetal) that are marked by specific developmental milestones.

- During the embryonic period, an XY embryo secretes the hormone testosterone, which stimulates the growth of male genitalia and shifts the brain into a "male" pattern. Boys are more active, develop more slowly skeletally, are bigger at birth, and are more vulnerable to most forms of prenatal stress.

- The fetus is responsive to stimuli and appears to learn in the womb. Prenatal temperamental differences (for example, activity level) persist into infancy and childhood, and some aspects of the prenatal sensory environment may be important to future development.

Problems in Prenatal Development

- Genes for specific diseases can cause a variety of disorders at conception.

- Abnormal numbers of chromosomes or damage to chromosomes cause a number of serious disorders, including Down syndrome.

- Some diseases contracted by the mother may cause abnormalities or disease in the child. These include rubella, AIDS, syphilis, gonorrhea, genital herpes, and CMV.

- Drugs such as alcohol and nicotine appear to have harmful effects on the developing fetus; effects of drugs depend on the timing of exposure and the dosage.

- If the mother suffers from poor nutrition, her fetus faces increased risks of stillbirth, low birth weight, and death during the first year of life. Older mothers and very young mothers also run increased risks, as do their infants. Long-term, severe depression or chronic physical illnesses in the mother may also increase the risk of complications of pregnancy or difficulties in the infant.

- Several methods of prenatal diagnosis and treatment of birth defects or fetal abnormalities have become available in recent years.

Birth and the Neonate

- Most babies are delivered by physicians in the United States. In uncomplicated low-risk pregnancies, delivery at home or in a birthing center is as safe as hospital delivery.

- The normal birth process has three parts: dilation and effacement, delivery, and placental delivery. Most drugs given to the mother during delivery pass through to the infant's bloodstream and have short-term effects on infant responsiveness and feeding patterns.

- Doctors, nurses, and midwives use the Apgar scale to assess a neonate's health immediately after birth.

- Neonates weighing less than 2,500 grams are designated as having low birth weight. The lower the weight, the greater the risk of significant lasting problems, such as low intelligence test scores or learning disabilities.

Key Terms

amnion (p. 62)

anoxia (p. 80)

cephalocaudal pattern (p. 62)

chromosomes (p. 54)

deoxyribonucleic acid (DNA) (p. 54)

dominant-recessive pattern (p. 56)

embryonic stage (p. 64)

fetal stage (p. 64)

gametes (p. 54)

genes (p. 54)

genotype (p. 56)

germinal stage (p. 62)

glial cells (p. 64)

gonads (p. 64)

low birth weight (LBW) (p. 82)

multi-factorial inheritance (p. 59)

neonate (p. 82)

neurons (p. 64)

organogenesis (p. 64)

phenotype (p. 56)

placenta (p. 62)

polygenic inheritance (p. 57)

proximodistal pattern (p. 62)

teratogens (p. 70)

umbilical cord (p. 62)

viability (p. 65)

zygote (p. 54)

Should Pregnant Women Who Use Illicit Drugs Be Prosecuted?

Given the potential damaging effects of drugs on prenatal development, everyone agrees that preventing pregnant women from using them is an important goal. But what is the best way to achieve this objective? In the United States, some have drawn a parallel between drug use during pregnancy and physical abuse of an infant after birth, suggesting that pregnant drug users should be criminally prosecuted.

Prosecution advocates argue that injecting a newborn with a drug is a crime. Even if no damage is done to the child, "delivering drugs to a minor" (the terminology used in most jurisdictions) is a crime in and of itself. When damage does occur, an additional crime, called "injury to a child" in most areas, may also have been committed. Thus, prosecution advocates argue that any woman who knowingly and deliberately administers drugs through her own bloodstream to the fetus she is carrying is guilty of the same crime as a parent who injects a newborn with a substance such as cocaine or heroin. They further suggest that prosecution will motivate drug-using pregnant women to stop. As persuasive as these arguments might seem, they raise numerous difficult issues.

Legal Status of the Fetus

One problem is that it isn't clear whether a fetus can be considered legally equivalent to a child. This is a critical point, because unless fetuses and children are legally equal, present laws against child abuse and delivery of drugs to children can't be applied to fetuses. Recent U.S. Supreme Court rulings have introduced the issue of fetal viability into abortion law. These rulings allow states to outlaw abortions of viable fetuses and suggest

using 24 weeks as the age of viability, based on current research on prenatal development. Thus, it would seem that states could also use existing laws against child abuse and giving drugs to children to prosecute women after the 24th week of pregnancy.

In addition, doctors often seek judicial intervention in cases where pregnant women make medical decisions that are potentially damaging to their fetuses. For example, in one case in Chicago, a woman carrying triplets refused to allow doctors to deliver the infants by cesarean section (Kolder, Gallagher, & Parsons, 1987). In response, her physicians went to court and argued that cesarean delivery was in the best interest of the fetuses. The judge then ordered the woman to undergo the operation. Such orders have also been used to compel pregnant women to submit to prenatal testing, such as ultrasound and/or amniocentesis. Thus, precedents exist that would allow authorities to prosecute a drug-using pregnant woman strictly on the basis of the interests of a fetus.

Which Drugs?

Even if it is legally possible to use existing laws to prosecute pregnant drug users, fairness would seem to demand that women who use legal drugs be treated in the same way as those who use illegal drugs. As you learned in Chapter 3, many legal drugs, including alcohol and tobacco, are teratogenic. Further, giving such drugs to a child is a crime. If pregnant women are to be prosecuted for using illegal drugs, then shouldn't they be held legally responsible for exposing their fetuses to potentially harmful legal drugs as well?

Based on the logic outlined above, the answer must be yes. However, critics

of the prosecution approach point out that prosecuting pregnant women for legal drug use undermines their right under the U.S. Constitution to equal protection under the law. Adults are legally entitled to use alcohol and tobacco despite evidence that it is dangerous or unwise to do so. Thus, criminalizing such behavior only for pregnant women places them in a special class and takes away their legal status as adults.

What would be next, critics ask. Would pregnant women no longer be allowed to decide what to eat or where to go simply because they were pregnant? After all, they point out, Americans commonly consume many substances, such as coffee, that may harm a fetus. Likewise, many environmental toxins, such as lead, that are less regulated in developing countries than in the United States and thus more widespread (for example, in water supplies) can be teratogenic, so should pregnant women be prohibited from traveling to developing countries?

What Kind of Evidence Will Be Required?

If women are to be prosecuted for delivering drugs to their fetuses, as happened to one South Carolina woman in 1992 (Associated Press, July 17, 1996), how will judges and jurors know that delivery has actually occurred? It might seem that hospitals could test newborns for various drugs and that positive test results would constitute evidence of delivery. The difficulty is that, while many drugs pass through the placenta, they don't always do so in sufficient amounts to be identifiable in a newborn's blood or urine. In addition, some drugs, including marijuana, remain in the system for a long time, making it possible to test for them several days after birth. But others, such as cocaine and alcohol, are excreted from the newborn's body within hours of birth. Thus, drug testing must be carried out almost immediately after birth to determine whether the newborn has been prenatally exposed to potentially harmful drugs (Centers for Disease Control [CDC], 1996).

An additional difficulty is that drug testing at birth usually reveals little or nothing about drug exposure earlier in pregnancy. Consequently, a pregnant woman could "deliver" a drug to her viable fetus during, for example, the 25th week of pregnancy (a potential crime according to logic of the prosecution approach), but no concrete evidence of this behavior would be available at the time of birth.

Which Behavior Will Be Deterred?

To get around the difficulty of identifying drug exposure at birth, some prosecution advocates have suggested that doctors be required to report drug use by their pregnant patients to the police, just as they are required to report suspected child abuse. However, critics say such policies may cause pregnant women to delay prenatal care or to deliver their babies alone (American Medical Association, 1990). Thus, fear of prosecution might damage the health of more fetuses than drug use itself.

Alternatives to Prosecution

Rather than prosecuting pregnant drug users, most public health officials recommend a strategy that combines universal access to early prenatal care, education, and drug treatment (CDC, 1996). Access to early prenatal care is critical because it provides a context for educating individual pregnant women. In addition, health care providers can provide pregnant drug users with treatment information.

Prosecution foes also claim that education in the public schools and through the mass media about the link between drug use and birth defects will create an informed population. Among those receiving the information will be drug-using women who are or will be pregnant. Moreover, informed potential fathers and friends and family members may be able to exert social pressure on women to stop using drugs, at least during pregnancy. To complete the picture, most public health officials suggest that treatment programs designed especially for pregnant women should be available (National Abortion and Reproductive Rights Action League [NARAL], 1997). However, widespread education about the teratogenic effects of drugs already exists and justifies prosecution, advocates argue. They say that women who continue to use drugs even though they know they may harm a fetus are even more accountable for their behavior, in a moral sense, than those who are ignorant of the dangers of prenatal drug exposure.

What Is the Situation in Your Area?

Policies addressing drug use during pregnancy are different in every state. In March, 2001, the U.S. Supreme Court introduced some consistency when it ruled that pregnant women cannot be tested for drug use without their permission if the primary purpose of testing is to obtain evidence that will be used in a criminal trial ("Court Curbs Drug Tests," 2001). However, the Court left open the possibility of testing pregnant women without their permission for other reasons, such as for referral to drug treatment programs, and did not address the issue of drug testing for newborns. Thus, local authorities continue to approach this problem in different ways. With a little investigation, you can find out what the relevant government and institutional policies are in your area.

Your Turn

- Do the hospitals in your area routinely test newborns for drug exposure? If so, how?

- What do doctors in your area do when they suspect a baby's problems are caused by prenatal drug exposure?

- Does your state require doctors to report pregnant women who use drugs to the police or to a state agency?

- Are there drug rehabilitation programs specifically for pregnant women in your area?

- Has your state prosecuted any women for using drugs while pregnant? What were the details of the case(s)?

- Do you agree or disagree with the way this issue is addressed in your state and city? Why?

AN INNER VOICE

TELLS YOU NOT TO DRINK OR USE OTHER DRUGS

(*Photo:* U.S. Department of Health and Human Services)

Physical and Cognitive Development in Infancy

David Young-Wolff, PhotoEdit

One of the most fascinating features of babies' behavior is their "busy-ness." They seem to be constantly on the go, manipulating objects with their hands, looking at them, feeling them, tasting them, and making sounds with them. At times, such activities seem purposeless, but they provide just the kind of skill practice and information infants need for both physical and cognitive development. Considering the energy it takes to keep up with infants' level of activity, it's little wonder their parents seem to be exhausted much of the time (see The Real World, page 91).

In this chapter, you will read about the processes through which a relatively unskilled newborn becomes a 2-year-old who can move about efficiently, formulate goals and plans, and use words. You will also learn about important variations across individuals and groups. While you read, keep the following questions in mind:

- What changes occur in infants' bodies, and how can their health be maintained?

- How do babies think, learn, and remember?

- How does language begin to develop?

- Can individual differences in intelligence be identified in infancy, and is development different for preterm babies, boys and girls, and infants in different cultures?

Physical Changes

Babies grow 10–12 inches and triple their body weight in the first year of life. By age 2 for girls and about $2\frac{1}{2}$ for boys, toddlers are half as tall they will be as adults. This means a 2- to $2\frac{1}{2}$-year-old's adult height can be reliably predicted by doubling his or her current height. But, 2-year-olds have proportionately much larger heads than do adults—which they need to hold their nearly full-sized brains.

The Brain and the Nervous System

The body's systems grow and develop at different rates and at different times. The reproductive system, for instance, is completely formed at birth but doesn't grow or change much until puberty. In contrast, the brain and nervous system develop rapidly during the first 2 years.

Figure 4.1 (page 90) shows the main structures of the brain. At birth, the midbrain and the medulla are the most fully developed. These two parts, both in the lower part of the skull and connected to the spinal cord, regulate vital functions such as heartbeat and respiration, as well as attention, sleeping, waking, elimination, and movement of the head and neck—all actions a newborn can perform at least moderately well. The least-developed part of the brain at birth is the cortex, the convoluted gray matter that wraps around the midbrain and is involved in perception, body movement, thinking, and language.

● *Synaptic Development* ● You'll recall from Chapter 3 that all brain structures are composed of two basic types of cells: neurons and glial cells. Virtually all of a person's full complement of both types of cells are already present at birth. The developmental

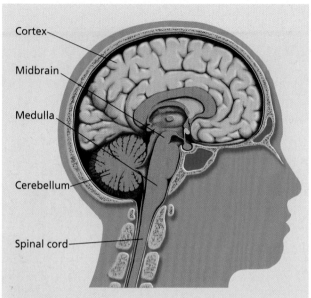

FIGURE 4.1

The medulla and the midbrain are largely developed at birth. In the first 2 years after birth it is primarily the cortex that develops, with each neuron going through an enormous growth of dendrites and a vast increase in synapses.

process after birth primarily involves the creation of **synapses,** or connections between neurons. Synapse development results from growth of both dendrites and axons (look back at Figure 3.3 on p. 65). *Synaptogenesis,* the creation of synapses, occurs rapidly in the cortex during the first 2 years after birth, resulting in a tripling of the overall weight of the brain during that period (Nowakowski, 1987). However, brain development is not entirely smooth and continuous. An initial burst of synapse formation in about the first year after birth is followed by a "pruning" of synapses in each area of the brain, as redundant pathways and connections are eliminated and the "wiring diagram" is made more efficient (Huttenlocher, 1994).

For example, early in development, each muscle cell seems to develop synaptic connections with several motor neurons (nerve cells that carry impulses to muscles) in the spinal cord. But after the pruning process has occurred, each muscle fiber is connected to only one neuron. Some neurophysiologists have suggested that the initial surge of synapse formation follows a built-in pattern (Greenough, Black, & Wallace, 1987). The organism seems to be programmed to create certain kinds of neural connections and makes an abundance of them, creating redundant pathways. According to this argument, the pruning that takes place beginning at around 18 months is a response to experience and results in selective retention of the most efficient pathways. Putting it briefly, "Experience does not create tracings on a blank tablet; rather, experience erases some of them" (Bertenthal & Campos, 1987). However, neurophysiologists point out that some synapses are formed entirely as a result of experience, and that synaptogenesis continues throughout our lives as we learn new skills.

Interestingly, pruning does not occur at the same time in all parts of the brain. For example, synapses in the portions of the brain that have to do with language comprehension and production achieve their maximum density when a child is about 3 years old. In contrast, the part of the cortex devoted to vision is maximally dense when an infant is 4 months old, and rapid pruning occurs thereafter (Huttenlocher, 1994).

One of the most intriguing points about this pattern of development is that the combination of the early surge of synaptic growth and the later pruning means that a 1-year-old actually has denser dendrites and synapses than an adult does—a piece of information that has surprised many psychologists. Even at age 4, when the early burst of pruning has occurred in all areas of the brain, a child's synaptic density is about twice that of an adult. Pruning continues in spurts throughout childhood and adolescence.

Developmentalists draw several important implications from information about neurological development. First, they conclude that a kind of "programmed plasticity" is built into the human organism. The brain has a remarkable ability to reorganize itself, to make the "wiring diagram" more efficient, and to use compensatory pathways following some injury. But this plasticity is greater in infancy than it is later. Perhaps paradoxically, the period of greatest plasticity is also the period in which the child may be most vulnerable to major deficits—just as a fetus is most vulnerable to teratogens during the time of most rapid growth of any body system. Thus, a young infant needs sufficient stimulation and order in his environment to maximize the early period of rapid growth and plasticity (de Haan, Luciana, Maslone, Matheny, & Richards, 1994). A really inadequate diet or a serious lack of stimulation in the early months may thus have subtle but long-range effects on the child's later cognitive progress.

synapses connections between neurons

PARENTING
The Real World

A Day in the Life of Two Babies

You can gain some insight into what it's like to care for an infant by examining the daily routines of two babies: 6-month-old Amanda and 9-month-old Andrew. Notice that Andrew eats less often than Amanda, plays and naps for longer periods, and sleeps through the night. Looking at these routines, you can see why, in most cases, all members of an infant's household have to accommodate their schedules at least somewhat to that of the infant.

Amanda

6:30 a.m.: Wakes up; takes bottle; diaper change; back to sleep

9:00 a.m.: Wakes up; diaper change; eats cereal and fruit; gets dressed; watches television; plays in walker until bored; moves to playpen; out of playpen onto floor; crawls and practices pulling up on furniture; chews on everything in sight

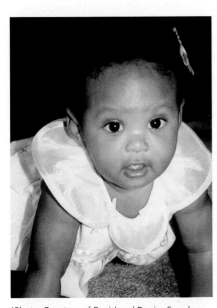

(*Photo:* Courtesy of David and Denise Sowders. Used with permission.)

10:30 a.m.: Gets fussy; takes bottle; naps for 30 minutes; wakes up; plays outside in walker

12:00 p.m.: Eats meat and vegetables; tries to drink from cup; same play routine as earlier in the day

2:00 p.m.: Takes bottle; repeats play routine

4:00 p.m.: Gets fussy; naps for 1 hour

5:30 p.m.: Eats cereal and fruit; takes bottle

6:30 p.m.: Has bath; plays in tub for 20 minutes; gets dressed for bed; watches television with older brother and sister; plays, snuggles, and jabbers with siblings, Mom, and Dad

9:00 p.m.: Takes bottle; listens to Mom read a story; goes to sleep

2:00 a.m.: Wakes up; diaper change; takes bottle

4:00 a.m.: Wakes up; diaper change; takes bottle

6:30 a.m.: Daily cycle starts again

Andrew

7:30 a.m. Wakes up; diaper change; gets dressed; eats cereal and fruit

8:30 a.m.: Watches television

9:00 a.m.: Diaper change; plays with toys

10:00 a.m.: Takes bottle; naps for 1 hour

11:00 a.m.: Wakes up; diaper change; plays with toys

11:30 a.m.: Watches television

12:00 p.m.: Eats lunch

12:30 p.m.: Diaper change; plays with toys

2:00 p.m.: Takes bottle; naps for 2 hours

(*Photo:* Courtesy of Jimmy and Kimberly Adkins. Used with permission.)

4:30 p.m.: Wakes up; diaper change; eats snack

4:45 p.m.: Plays with toys; listens to music

5:15 p.m.: Has bath; plays in tub

6:00 p.m.: Takes bottle; plays with toys

7:00 p.m.: Dinner with Mom and Dad

7:30 p.m.: Plays and watches television with Mom and Dad

9:00 p.m.: Gets dressed for bed; takes bottle

9:30 p.m.: Bedtime; usually sleeps 10 hours; sometimes wakes up in night but goes back to sleep with pacifier

7:30 a.m.: Daily cycle starts again

Second, new information about the continuation of the pruning process throughout childhood and adolescence and into adulthood has forced developmental psychologists to change their ideas about the links between brain development and behavior. If the brain is almost completely organized by age 2, as most developmentalists believed until recently, it seemed logical to assume that whatever developments occurred after that age were largely the product of experience. But researchers now know that the brain changes significantly throughout the entire human lifespan. These facts reopen all the questions about brain-behavior connections. Is there a language spurt between ages 2 and 3 because that is when the relevant portion of the brain is undergoing significant reorganization? Or does the spurt in language behavior induce changes in the brain? Researchers do not yet have enough data to answer such questions, but the theoretical climate has definitely shifted toward greater interest in the neurological underpinnings of development across the lifespan and away from the assumption that brain development is complete very early in life.

● *Myelinization* ●   Another crucial process in the development of neurons is the creation of sheaths, or coverings, around individual axons, which insulate them from one another electrically and improve their conductivity. These sheaths are made of a substance called *myelin*; the process of developing the sheath is called **myelinization**.

The sequence of myelinization follows both cephalocaudal and proximodistal patterns (these were defined in Chapter 3). Thus, nerves serving muscle cells in the hands are myelinized earlier than those serving the feet. Myelinization is most rapid during the first 2 years after birth, but it continues at a slower pace throughout childhood and adolescence. For example, the parts of the brain that govern motor movements are not fully myelinized until a child is about 6 years old (Todd, Swarzenski, Rossi, & Visconti, 1995).

Other structures take even longer to become myelinized, For example, the **reticular formation** is the part of the brain responsible for keeping your attention on what you're doing and for helping you sort out important and unimportant information. Myelinization of the reticular formation begins in infancy but continues in spurts across childhood and adolescence. In fact, the process isn't complete until a person is in her mid-20s (Spreen, Risser, & Edgell, 1995). Consequently, during the first 2 years, infants improve their ability to focus on a task. Likewise, a 12-year-old is much better at concentrating than an infant but is still fairly inefficient when compared to an adult.

myelinization a process in the development of neurons in which sheaths of a substance called myelin gradually cover individual axons and electrically insulate them from one another, which improves the conductivity of the nerve

reticular formation the part of the brain that regulates attention

adaptive reflexes reflexes such as sucking that help newborns survive; some adaptive reflexes persist throughout life

primitive reflexes reflexes controlled by primitive parts of the brain; these reflexes disappear by about 6 months of age

Reflexes, Sensory Abilities, and Behavioral States

Changes in the brain result in predictable changes in babies' reflexes, sensory capacities, and patterns of waking and sleeping. In fact, such changes, or their lack, can be important indicators of nervous system health.

● *Reflexes* ●   Humans are born with many **adaptive reflexes** that help them survive. Some, such as automatically sucking any object that enters the mouth, disappear in infancy or childhood. Others protect us against harmful stimuli over the whole lifespan. These include withdrawal from a painful stimulus and the opening and closing of the pupil of the eye in response to variations in brightness. Weak or absent adaptive reflexes in neonates suggest that the brain is not functioning properly and that the baby requires additional assessment.

The purposes of **primitive reflexes**, so called because they are controlled by the less sophisticated parts of the brain (the medulla and the midbrain), are less clear. For

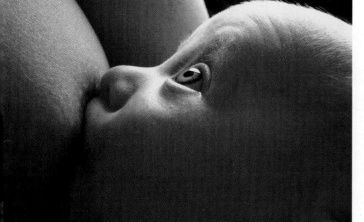

This 4-week-old baby is using the inborn adaptive reflex of sucking. (*Photo:* Stone)

example, if you make a loud noise or startle a baby in some other way, you'll see her throw her arms outward and arch her back, a pattern that is part of the *Moro*, or *startle, reflex*. Stroke the bottom of her foot and she will splay out her toes and then curl them in, a reaction called the *Babinski reflex*. By about 6 months of age, primitive reflexes begin to disappear. If such reflexes persist past about 6 months, the baby may have some kind of neurological problem.

● *Sensory Abilities* ● Visual acuity, the ability to see details from various distances, is fairly poor in newborns compared to adults. However, if objects are positioned within 8–10 inches of a baby's eyes, he can focus on them. Newborns can also track slowly moving objects with their eyes, and they learn to recognize their mothers' faces soon after birth. Moreover, researchers have recently discovered that measures of visual development in early infancy, like changes in adaptive and primitive reflexes, are correlated with mental development at 18 months (Birch, Garfield, Hoffman, Uauy, & Birch, 2000). Consequently, a slow rate of visual development in the first 4 months may mean that a baby is suffering from some kind of general developmental problem.

Newborns are pretty nearsighted, so they can focus very well at about 8 to 10 inches—just the distance between a parent's face and the baby's eyes when the baby is held for feeding. (*Photo:* Jonathan Nourok, PhotoEdit)

Babies respond to the same four categories of tastes (sweet, sour, bitter, and salty) as adults do. In addition, they can identify familiar body odors and can even discriminate their mother's smell from the smell of another woman (Porter, Making, Davis, & Christensen, 1992). Likewise, they display sensitivity to temperature by increasing physical activity in a cold room and to touch by becoming calmer when stroked and crying in protest when pricked with a needle by a nurse drawing blood for a laboratory test.

● *Behavioral States* ● Researchers have described five different states of sleep and wakefulness in neonates, referred to as **states of consciousness** and summarized in Table 4.1. Most infants move through these states in the same sequence: from deep sleep to lighter sleep and then to alert wakefulness and fussing. After they are fed, they become drowsy and drop back into deep sleep. The cycle repeats itself about every 2 hours.

Neonates sleep as much as 90% of the time, as much in the daytime as at night (Whitney & Thoman, 1994). By 6 or 8 weeks of age, the total amount of sleep per

TABLE **4.1**   The Basic States of Infant Sleep and Wakefulness

State	Characteristics
Deep sleep	Eyes closed, regular breathing, no movement except occasional startles
Active sleep	Eyes closed, irregular breathing, small twitches, no gross body movement
Quiet awake	Eyes open, no major body movement, regular breathing
Active awake	Eyes open, movements of the head, limbs, and trunk, irregular breathing
Crying, fussing	Eyes partly or entirely closed, vigorous diffuse movement with crying or fussing sounds

(*Sources:* Based on the work of Hutt, Lenard, & Prechtl, 1969; Parmelee, Wenner, & Schulz, 1964; Prechtl & Beintema, 1964.)

visual acuity the ability to see details at a distance

states of consciousness different states of sleep and wakefulness in infants

day has dropped somewhat and signs of day/night sleep rhythms (called *circadian rhythms*) become evident. Babies of this age begin to sleep through two or three 2-hour cycles in sequence without coming to full wakefulness, and are thus often said to have started to "sleep through the night." By 6 months, babies are still sleeping a bit over 14 hours per day, but sleep is more regular and predictable. Most have clear nighttime sleep patterns and nap during the day at more predictable times.

Of course, babies vary a lot around these averages. Of the 6-week-old babies in one study, there was one who slept 22 hours per day and another who slept only 8.8 hours per day (Bamford et al., 1990). (Now, *that* must have been one tired set of parents!) And some babies do not develop a long nighttime sleep period until late in the first year of life. Moreover, cultural beliefs play an important role in parents' responses to infants' sleep patterns. For example, parents in the United States typically see a newborn's erratic sleep cycle as a behavior problem that requires "fixing" through parental intervention (Harkness, 1998). As a result, they focus a great deal of attention on trying to force babies to sleep through the night. In contrast, European parents are more likely to regard newborns' patterns of sleeping as manifestations of normal development and tend to expect babies to acquire stable sleeping patterns naturally, without parental intervention, during the first 2 years.

Infants have a whole repertoire of cry sounds, with different cries for pain, anger, or hunger. The basic cry, which often signals hunger, is usually a rhythmical pattern: cry, silence, breath, cry, silence, breath, with a kind of whistling sound often accompanying the in-breath. An anger cry is typically louder and more intense, and the pain cry normally has a very abrupt onset—unlike the other two kinds of cries, which usually begin with whimpering or moaning.

Cross-cultural studies suggest that crying increases in frequency over the first 6 weeks and then tapers off (St. James-Roberts, Bowyer, Varghese, & Sawdon, 1994). Moreover, parents across a variety of cultures use very similar techniques to soothe crying infants. Most babies stop crying when they are picked up, held, and talked or sung to. Getting a baby to suck on a pacifier also usually helps. Parents sometimes worry that picking up a crying baby will lead to even more crying. But research suggests that prompt attention to a crying baby in the first 3 months actually leads to less crying later in infancy (Sulkes, 1998).

Critical Thinking

What advice would you give to parents who believe that picking up a baby when she cries will "spoil" her?

For the 15–20% of infants who develop **colic**, a pattern involving intense bouts of crying for no immediately apparent reason such as hunger or a wet diaper, totaling 3 or more hours a day, nothing seems to help. Typically, colic appears at about 2 weeks of age and then disappears spontaneously at 3–4 months. The crying is generally worst in late afternoon or early evening. Neither psychologists nor physicians know why colic begins, or why it stops without any intervention. It is a difficult pattern to live with, but the good news is that it does go away.

On average, neonates are awake and alert for a total of only 2–3 hours each day, and this time is unevenly distributed over a 24-hour period. In other words, the baby may be awake for 15 minutes at 6:00 a.m., another 30 minutes at 1:00 p.m., another 20 minutes at 4:00 p.m. and so on. Over the first 6 months, advances in neurological development enable infants to remain awake and alert for longer periods of time as their patterns of sleeping, crying, and eating become more regular.

Other Body Systems and Motor Skills

colic an infant behavior pattern involving intense daily bouts of crying, totaling 3 or more hours a day

Like behavioral states, the acquisition of motor skills also depends on brain development. Substantial changes in other body systems—bones, muscles, and so on—are required as well.

● **Bones** ●   During infancy, bones change in size, number, and composition. Increases in the lengths of the body's long bones—those in the legs and arms—underlie increases in height (Tanner, 1990). Changes in the number and density of bones in particular parts of the body are responsible for improvements in coordinated movement.

For example, at birth, the wrist contains a single mass of cartilage; by 1 year of age, the cartilage has developed into three separate bones. The progressive separation of the wrist bones is one of the factors behind gains in manipulative skills over the first 2 years. Wrist bones continue to differentiate over the next several years until eventually, in adolescence, the wrist has nine separate bones (Tanner, 1990).

The process of bone hardening, called *ossification*, occurs steadily beginning in the last weeks of prenatal development and continuing through puberty. Bones in different parts of the body harden in a sequence that follows the typical proximodistal and cephalocaudal patterns. Motor development depends on ossification to a large extent. Standing, for example, is impossible if an infant's leg bones are too soft, no matter how well developed the muscles and nervous system are.

● **Muscles** ●   The body's full complement of muscle fibers is present at birth, although the fibers are initially small and have a high ratio of water to muscle (Tanner, 1990). In addition, a newborn's muscles contain a fairly high proportion of fat. By 1 year of age, the water content of an infant's muscles is equal to that of an adult, and the ratio of fat to muscle tissue has begun to decline (Tershakovec & Stallings, 1998). Changes in muscle composition lead to increases in strength that enable 1-year-olds to walk, run, jump, climb, and so on.

● **Lungs and Heart** ●   The lungs also grow rapidly and become more efficient during the first 2 years (Kercsmar, 1998). Improvements in lung efficiency, together with the increasing strength of heart muscles, give a 2-year-old greater *stamina*, or ability to maintain activity, than a newborn. Consequently, by the end of infancy, children are capable of engaging in fairly long periods of sustained motor activity without rest (often exhausting their parents in the process!).

● **Motor Skills** ●   Changes in all of the body's systems are responsible for the impressive array of motor skills children acquire in the first 2 years. Developmentalists typically divide these skills into three rough groups: *locomotor skills*, *nonlocomotor skills*, and *manipulative skills* (Malina, 1982). Table 4.2 (page 96) summarizes developments in each of these three areas over the first 18 months; it is based primarily on two large studies, one in the United States and one in the Netherlands. The U.S. study involved 381 babies tested by their pediatricians at regular visits during the first 2 years of life (Capute et al., 1984). The Dutch study included 555 babies who had been tested repeatedly for their first 5 years (Den Ouden, Rijken, Brand, Verloove-Vanhorick, & Ruys, 1991). The milestones identified in these two studies were highly similar in sequence, as were the ages at which babies passed each test.

● **Explaining Motor Skill Development** ●   The sequence of motor skill development is virtually the same for all children, even those with serious physical or mental handicaps. Mentally retarded children, for example, move through the various motor milestones more slowly than normal children do, but they do so in the same sequence. Furthermore, motor skill development follows the cephalocaudal and proximodistal patterns. Whenever developmentalists find such consistencies, maturation of some kind seems an obvious explanation (Thelen, 1995).

However, a classic early study of children raised in Iranian orphanages demonstrated that babies who were routinely placed on their backs in cribs learned to walk eventually, but they did so about a year later than babies in less restrictive settings

The striking improvements in motor development in the early months are easy to illustrate. Between 6 and 12 months of age, babies progress from sitting alone, to crawling, to walking. (*Photos:* © Myrleen Ferguson Cate, PhotoEdit; Laura Dwight, PhotoEdit; Myrleen Ferguson, PhotoEdit)

TABLE 4.2   Milestones of Motor Development in the First 2 Years

Age (in months)	Locomotor Skills	Nonlocomotor Skills	Manipulative Skills
1	Stepping reflex	Lifts head slightly; follows slowly moving objects with eyes	Holds object if placed in hand
2–3		Lifts head up to 90-degree angle when lying on stomach	Begins to swipe at objects in sight
4–6	Rolls over, sits with support; moves on hands and knees ("creeps")	Holds head erect while in sitting position	Reaches for and grasps objects
7–9	Sits without support; crawls		Transfers objects from one hand to the other
10–12	Pulls self up and walks grasping furniture; then walks alone	Squats and stoops	Shows some signs of hand preference; grasps a spoon across palm but has poor aim when moving food to mouth
13–18	Walks backward, sideways; runs (14–20 mos.)	Rolls ball to adult	Stacks two blocks; puts objects into small container and dumps them out

(*Sources:* Capute et al., 1984; Den Ouden et al., 1991.)

(Dennis, 1960). In contrast, early studies seemed to show that extra practice in such basic skills as sitting and crawling didn't speed up babies' development at all. However, more recent research contradicts this conclusion, including one study showing that very young babies who are given more practice sitting are able to sit upright longer than those without such practice (Zelazo, Zelazo, Cohen, & Zelazo, 1993). Consequently, developmentalists are fairly certain that severely restricting a baby's movement slows down acquisition of motor skills, but they are less sure about the effects of more typical restrictions, such as keeping babies in playpens for short periods of time, or of motor skills practice.

Health and Wellness

Babies depend on the adults in their environments to help them stay healthy. Specifically, they need the right foods in the right amounts, and they need regular medical care.

● *Nutrition* ●   After several decades of extensive research in many countries, experts agree that, for most infants, breast-feeding is substantially superior nutritionally to bottle-feeding. Breast milk provides the infant with important antibodies against many kinds of diseases, especially gastrointestinal and upper respiratory infections (Cunningham, Jelliffe, & Jelliffe, 1991). Human breast milk also appears to promote the growth of the nerves and intestinal tract and to contribute to more rapid weight and size gain, and it may improve immune system functioning over the long term (Prentice, 1994). On the down side, some viruses (including HIV) can be transmitted through breast milk.

However, not all infants can be breast-fed. For example, it is physically impossible for an adoptive mother to nurse. In addition, drugs are often present in the breast milk of mothers who are substance abusers or who depend on medications to maintain their own health. Many of these drugs can negatively affect infant development. Consequently, doctors recommend that these women avoid breast-feeding. In such cases, babies who are fed high-quality infant formula, prepared according to manufacturer's instructions and properly sterilized, usually thrive on it (Tershakovec & Stallings, 1998). Moreover, social interactions between mother and child seem to be unaffected by the type of feeding.

Up until 4–6 months, babies need only breast milk or formula accompanied by appropriate supplements. For example, pediatricians usually recommend Vitamin B12 supplements for infants whose nursing mothers are vegetarians (Tershakovec & Stallings, 1998). Likewise, doctors may recommend supplemental formula feeding for infants who are growing poorly.

There is no evidence to support the belief that solid foods encourage babies to sleep through the night. In fact, early introduction of solid food can interfere with nutrition. Pediatricians usually recommend withholding solid foods until a baby is 4–6 months old. The first solids should be single-grain cereals, such as rice cereal, with added iron. Parents should introduce a baby to no more than one new food each week. By following a systematic plan, parents can easily identify food allergies (Tershakovec & Stallings, 1998).

Malnutrition in infancy can seriously impair a baby's brain because the nervous system is the most rapidly developing body system during the first 2 years of life. *Macronutrient* malnutrition results from a diet that contains too few calories. Macronutrient malnutrition is the world's leading cause of death of children under the age of 5 (Tershakovec & Stallings, 1998).

When the calorie deficit is severe, a disease called *marasmus* results. Infants with marasmus weigh less than 60% of what they should at their age, and many suffer permanent neurological damage from the disease. Most also suffer from parasitic infections that lead to chronic diarrhea. This condition makes it very difficult to treat marasmus by simply increasing an infant's intake of calories. However, a program of dietary supplementation with formula combined with intravenous feedings and treatment for parasites can reverse marasmus (Tershakovec & Stallings, 1998).

Some infants' diets contain almost enough calories, but not enough protein. Diets of this type lead to a disease called *kwashiorkor*, which is common in countries where infants are weaned too early to low-protein foods. Kwashiorkor-like symptoms are also seen in children who are chronically ill because of their bodies' inability to use the protein from the foods they eat. Like marasmus, kwashiorkor can lead to a variety of health problems as well as permanent brain damage (Tershakovec & Stallings, 1998).

Growth rate studies of poor children in the United States suggest that a small number of them suffer from macronutrient malnutrition (Tanner, 1990). In addition, a small proportion of infants have feeding problems, such as a poorly developed sucking reflex, that place them at risk for macronutrient malnutrion (Wright & Birks, 2000). However, most nutritional problems in industrialized societies involve *micronutrient malnutrition*, a deficiency of certain vitamins and/or minerals. For example, about 65% of infants and children in the United States have diets that are low enough in iron to cause anemia (Tershakovec & Stallings, 1998). Calcium deficiency, which results in poor bone health, is also becoming more common in the United States (Tershakovec & Stallings, 1998). Such deficiencies, although more common among the poor, are found in children of all economic levels.

Recent evidence suggests that micronutrient malnutrition in infancy, especially when it leads to iron-deficiency anemia, may impede both social and language development (Guesry, 1998; Josse et al., 1999). Interestingly, researchers found that supplementing anemic infants' diets with iron led to improved scores on measures of social development but not language development, suggesting that the cognitive effects of anemia may be irreversible. Consequently, most public health officials support efforts to educate parents about the micronutritional needs of infants and children.

● *Health Care and Immunizations* ●   Infants need frequent medical check-ups. Much of *well baby care* may seem routine, but it is extremely important to development. For example, during routine visits to the doctor's office or health clinic, babies' motor skills are usually assessed. An infant whose motor development is less advanced than expected for his age may require additional screening for developmental problems such as mental retardation (Sulkes, 1998).

One of the most important elements of well baby care is vaccination of the infant against a variety of diseases. Although immunizations later in childhood provide good protection, the evidence suggests that immunization is most effective when it begins in the first month of life and continues through childhood and adolescence (Umetsu, 1998). Even adults need occasional "booster" shots to maintain immunity.

As recently as 1992, only 55% of children in the United States had received the full set of immunizations—a schedule that includes three separate injections of hepatitis vaccine, four of diphtheria/tetanus/pertussis, three of influenza, three of polio, and one each of measles/rubella and varicella zoster virus vaccines (Committee on Infectious Diseases, 1996). Vaccination against hepatitis A is also recommended in some cities (Centers for Disease Control, 2000). By 1999, after intensive efforts, the U.S. vaccination rate was raised to more than 90% (CDC, 2000).

However, recent history suggests that the public can easily become complacent about immunizations (CDC, 1999). For example, declines in measles immunizations during the late 1980s and early 1990s led to epidemics of this potentially fatal disease in many urban areas (Umetsu, 1998). Thus, it is important to remember that diseases such as measles will remain rare only as long as parents are diligent in having their children immunized.

● *Illnesses in the First 2 Years* ●   In the United States, the average baby has seven respiratory illnesses in the first year of life. Interestingly, research in a number of countries shows that babies in day-care centers have about twice as many infections as those reared entirely at home, with those in small-group day care falling somewhere in between, presumably because babies cared for in group settings are exposed to a wider range of germs and viruses (Collet et al., 1994; Hurwitz, Gunn, Pinsky, & Schonberger, 1991). In general, the more people a baby is exposed to, the more often she is likely to be sick.

Neuropsychologists have suggested that the timing of respiratory illnesses that can lead to ear infections is important. Many note that infants who have chronic ear infections are more likely than their peers to have learning disabilities and language deficits during the school years. These psychologists hypothesize that, because ear infections temporarily impair hearing, they may compromise the development of brain areas that are essential for language learning during the first 2 years of life (Spreen, Risser, & Edgell, 1995). Thus, most pediatricians emphasize the need for effective hygiene practices in day-care centers, such as periodic disinfection of all toys, as well as prompt treatment of infants' respiratory infections.

● *Sudden Infant Death Syndrome* ●   Sudden infant death syndrome (SIDS), in which an apparently healthy infant dies suddenly and unexpectedly, is the leading cause of death in the United States of infants between 1 month and 1 year of age (Kercsmar, 1998). In the United States, between 2 and 3 of every 1,000 infants die from SIDS. SIDS deaths occur worldwide, although for unexplained reasons the rate

MAKE THE CONNECTION

*F*ormulate an idea about how an infant's suffering a series of ear infections might affect the social environment that supports language development. Do you think it's possible for ear infections in infancy to affect language development for social as well as neurological reasons?

sudden infant death syndrome (SIDS)
the sudden and unexpected death of an apparently healthy infant

varies quite a lot from country to country. For example, SIDS rates are particularly high in Australia and New Zealand and particularly low in Japan and Sweden (Hoffman & Hillman, 1992).

Physicians have not yet uncovered the basic cause of SIDS. But there are a few clues. For one thing, it is more common in the winter when babies may be suffering from viral infections that cause breathing difficulties. In addition, babies with a history of *apnea*—brief periods when their breathing suddenly stops—are more likely to die from SIDS (Kercsmar, 1998). Episodes of apnea may be noticed by medical personnel in the newborn nursery, or a nonbreathing baby may be discovered by her parents in time to be resuscitated. In such cases, physicians usually recommend using electronic breathing monitors that will sound an alarm if the baby stops breathing again while asleep.

SIDS is also more frequent among babies who sleep on their stomachs, especially on a soft or fluffy mattress, pillow, or comforter (Hoffman & Hillman, 1992; Ponsonby, Dwyer, Gibbons, Cochrane, & Wang, 1993). The American Academy of Pediatrics, along with physicians' organizations in many other countries, recommends that healthy infants be positioned on their sides or backs to sleep. During the first 2 years after this recommendation was introduced, there was a 12% overall drop in SIDS cases in the United States, with even more dramatic declines of as much as 50% in areas where the recommendation was widely publicized (Spiers & Guntheroth, 1994). In England, Wales, New Zealand, and Sweden, major campaigns to discourage parents from placing their babies in the prone position (on their stomachs) have also been followed by sharp drops in SIDS rates (Gilman, Cheng, Winter, & Scragg, 1995).

Autopsies of SIDS babies have revealed that their brains often show signs of delayed maturation. Myelinization seems to have been progressing at a particularly slow rate in many such infants' brains. Because myelinization depends on dietary fat intake, some researchers suggest that low-fat diets, either consumed by the mother during the final weeks of pregnancy or fed to the infant after birth, may be a factor in many SIDS deaths (Saugstad, 1997). Studies linking poverty to SIDS may also indicate that inadequate nutrition plays a role in these deaths (Bambang, Spencer, Logan, & Gill 2000).

Another important contributor is smoking by the mother during pregnancy or by anyone in the home after the child's birth. Babies exposed to such smoke are about four times as likely to die of SIDS as are babies with no smoking exposure (Klonoff-Cohen et al., 1995; Schoendorf & Kiely, 1992; Taylor & Danderson, 1995).

Before going on

- What important changes in the brain take place in infancy?

- How do babies' states of consciousness change?

- How do other body systems change during infancy, and what is the typical pattern of motor skill development in the first 2 years?

- What are the nutritional and health care needs of infants?

Cognitive Changes

Changes in cognitive skills over the first 2 years are highly consistent across environments (see Development in the Information Age). Two-year-olds are still a long way from cognitive maturity, but they have taken several important steps toward that goal.

Perception

Recent evidence suggests that very young infants can make remarkably fine discriminations among sounds, sights, and tactile sensations, and that they attend and respond to patterns.

● ***What Babies Look At*** ● From the first days of life, babies scan the world around them with their eyes—not very smoothly or skillfully, to be sure, but nonetheless regularly, even in the dark (Haith, 1980). A baby keeps moving his eyes until they come to a sharp contrast between light and dark, which typically signals the edge of some object. Having found an edge, the baby stops searching and moves his eyes back and forth across and around the edge. These looking strategies change at about 2 months of age, when attention shifts from *where* an object is to *what* an object is.

Several studies on infant perception suggest that many abilities and preferences are inborn. For example, infants appear to discriminate between attractive and unattractive faces in the same way adults do. Babies as young as 2 months will look longer at a face that adults rate as attractive than at one adults judge to be less attrac-

in the Information Age

What Do Babies Really Learn from Watching Television?

You may have noticed in The Real World feature on page 91 that television is part of both Amanda's and Andrew's daily routine. Parents often assume that exposing babies to intellectual stimulation via television, especially programs produced specifically for infants, will enhance their cognitive development. In fact, cross-cultural researchers have noted that parents in the United States are far more concerned about stimulating their babies' cognitive development

than are their counterparts in other countries (Harkness, 1998). Consequently, U.S. parents devote a considerable amount of time, energy, and money to making sure that their infants are stimulated almost all the time, and television has become an important tool in accomplishing this goal.

Studies have shown that infants and young children readily acquire the information presented in programs such as *Sesame Street* and *Blue's Clues*, especially if they watch the same program repeatedly (Crawley, Anderson, Wilder, Williams, & Santomero, 1999). However,

it also seems clear that extraordinary amounts of intellectual stimulation contribute little or nothing to basic developmental processes such as the acquisition of object permanence (Bruer, 1999). Moreover, research suggests that ordinary infant toys such as rattles and balls—and even common household items like pots and pans—are just as useful in an infant's attempts to learn about the world as TV programs or videos. Thus, many developmentalists suggest that the main thing babies learn from watching television is the behavior of watching television.

tive, without regard to the face's race, sex, or other variables (Langlois, Ritter, Roggman, & Vaughn, 1991; Langlois et al., 1987).

In addition, babies as young as 3 or 4 months attend to relationships among objects, or among features of objects. For example, suppose you show babies a series of drawings, one at a time, each of which shows a small object above a larger object of the same shape—like the ones in the top row of Figure 4.2. After seeing a series of such pictures, babies **habituate**, or decrease their attention because the stimulus has become familiar. Once habituation has occurred, you can present a picture that illustrates the opposite pattern, like the one shown at the bottom of Figure 4.2. What you will find is that babies 3 and 4 months old will show renewed interest in this different pattern; this indicates that the baby's original habituation was not to the specific stimuli but to a pattern (Caron & Caron, 1981).

Depth perception, the ability to judge how far away an object is, develops slowly over the first year. A complex visual skill, depth perception requires that the baby integrate visual information from both eyes at the same time. One reason why this skill takes a while to develop is that the baby's movements provide her with experiential information about distance and depth as she moves toward and away from objects. Thus, babies' depth perception improves as they gain motor skills. Research suggests that babies possess some degree of depth perception fairly early, as young as 3 months of age, but don't really use information from both eyes in a coordinated way until they are about 7 months old (Bornstein, 1992; Yonas & Owsley, 1987).

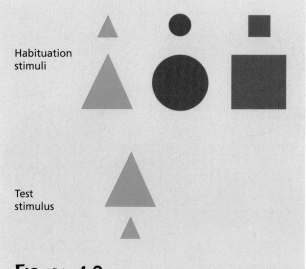

Habituation stimuli

Test stimulus

Figure 4.2

In Caron and Caron's study, babies were first habituated to a series of pictures, each of which displayed the same pattern, like those in the upper row. Then they were tested either on more of the same, or on a picture with a reverse pattern, like the one on the bottom. Babies 3 and 4 months old showed renewed interest in the test stimulus, which indicates that they noticed the pattern and saw that it had changed.

● ***Intersensory Integration and Cross-Modal Perception*** ●   If you think about the way you use perceptual information, you'll quickly realize that, ordinarily, you perceive complex combinations of sound, sight, touch, and smell. Psychologists have been interested in knowing how early an infant can integrate information from several senses, so that she knows, for example, which mouth movements go with which sounds, a skill called **intersensory integration**. As with all perceptual abilities, debate centers around the question of whether such skill is inborn or learned.

Research suggests that intersensory integration isn't completely inborn. Some studies indicate that infants younger than 4 months have some ability to coordinate sensory information. However, in most investigations, younger infants do not consistently demonstrate this skill (Lewkowicz, 1994).

By contrast, intersensory integration is common in older babies. In one study, 5-month-olds viewed two films side by side, each displaying a train moving along a track (Pickens, 1994). Next, the babies heard recordings of engine sounds of various types. In one recording, the engine sounds got gradually louder (as if the engine were coming closer); in the other, the engine sounds got gradually fainter (as if the engine were moving away). The babies looked longer at the film of a train whose movement matched the pattern of engine sounds. That is, they appeared to have some understanding of the link between the pattern of sound and the pattern of movement—knowledge they could only acquire through intersensory integration.

Moreover, intersensory integration appears to be important in infant learning. One group of researchers found that babies who habituated to a combined auditory-visual stimulus were better able to recognize a new stimulus than infants who habituated to either the auditory or the visual stimulus alone (Bahrick & Lickliter, 2000). For example, suppose you played a videotape of someone singing for one baby, played

habituate to decrease one's attention because a stimulus has become familiar

intersensory integration coordination of information from two or more senses, such as knowing which mouth movements go with which sounds

Over the first few months, babies learn to make perceptual judgments based on depth. Among other things, this helps them determine if they are near enough to an object to grasp it. (*Photo:* Laima Druskis, Stock Boston)

the videotape without the sound for another, and played an audio recording of the song for a third. Research suggests that the first baby, the one who both saw the singer and heard the song, would recognize a change in either the singer (visual stimulus) or the song (auditory stimulus) more quickly than either of the other two infants.

Evidence suggests that **cross-modal perception**, the ability to perceive something via one sense and transfer the information to another sense, is probably inborn. For example, if you give a baby a nubby round pacifier and let the baby suck on it, you can test for cross-modal perception by showing the baby pictures of a nubby sphere and a smooth sphere. If the baby looks longer at the nubby sphere, that would suggest cross-modal perception. In one study of this type, developmentalists demonstrated cross-modal perception in infants as young as 12 hours old (Kaye & Bower, 1994). Clearly, these newborns were too young to have learned to combine information from different senses.

Piaget's View of the First 2 Years

Recall from Chapter 2 that Piaget assumed that a baby *assimilates* incoming information to the limited array of schemes she is born with—looking, listening, sucking, grasping—and *accommodates* those schemes based on her experiences. He called this form of thinking *sensorimotor intelligence*. Thus, the **sensorimotor stage** is the period during which infants develop and refine sensorimotor intelligence.

● *Sensorimotor Stage* ●   In Piaget's view, the newborn is entirely tied to the immediate present, responding to whatever stimuli are available. She forgets events from one encounter to the next and does not appear to plan. This gradually changes, across six substages during the first 18 months, as the baby comes to understand that objects continue to exist even when they are out of sight (Piaget & Inhelder, 1969) (see Table 4.3).

Each substage represents a definite advance over the one that came before. Substage 2 is marked by the beginning of the coordinations between looking and listening, between reaching and looking, and between reaching and sucking that are such central features of the 2-month-old's means of exploring the world. The technique that distinguishes substage 2, *primary circular reactions*, refers to the many simple repetitive actions seen at this time, each organized around the infant's own body. For example, the baby may accidentally suck his thumb one day, find it pleasurable, and repeat the action.

In substage 3, the baby repeats some action in order to trigger a reaction outside her own body, a *secondary circular reaction*. The baby coos and Mom smiles, so the baby coos again to get Mom to smile again. These initial connections between body actions and external consequences seem to be simple, almost mechanical, links between stimuli and responses. However, in substage 4, the baby shows the beginnings of understanding causal connections, at which point she moves into exploratory high gear.

In substage 5, exploration of the environment becomes more focused, with the emergence of *tertiary circular reactions*. In this pattern, the baby doesn't merely repeat the original behavior but tries out variations. She may try out many sounds or facial expressions to see if they will trigger Mom's smile, or she may try dropping a toy from several heights to see if it makes different sounds or lands in different places. At this stage, the baby's behavior has a purposeful, experimental quality.

cross-modal perception transfer of information from one sense to another, as when an infant can recognize by feel a toy he has seen but never felt before

sensorimotor stage Piaget's first stage of development, in which infants use information from their senses and motor actions to learn about the world

TABLE 4.3   Substages of Piaget's Sensorimotor Stage

Substage	Age (in months)	Primary Technique	Characteristics
1	0–1	Reflexes	Use of built-in schemes or reflexes such as sucking or looking. Primitive schemes begin to change through very small steps of accommodation. Limited imitation, no ability to integrate information from several senses.
2	1–4	Primary circular reactions	Further accommodation of basic schemes, as the baby practices them endlessly—grasping, listening, looking, sucking. Beginning coordination of schemes from different senses, so that the baby now looks toward a sound and sucks on anything he can reach and bring to his mouth. But the baby does not yet link his body actions to results outside of his body.
3	4–8	Secondary circular reactions	The baby becomes much more aware of events outside his own body and makes them happen again in a kind of trial-and-error learning. Scientists are unsure whether babies this young understand the causal links yet, however. Imitation may occur, but only of schemes already in the baby's repertoire. Beginning understanding of the "object concept" can also be detected in this period.
4	8–12	Coordination of secondary schemes	Clear intentional means-ends behavior. The baby not only goes after what she wants, she may combine two schemes to do so, such as moving a pillow aside to reach a toy. Imitation of novel behavior occurs, as does transfer of information from one sense to the other (cross-modal perception).
5	12–18	Tertiary circular reactions	"Experimentation" begins, in which the infant tries out new ways of playing with or manipulating objects. Very active, very purposeful trial-and-error exploration.
6	18–24	Beginning of mental representation	Development of use of symbols to represent object or events. The child understands that the symbol is separate from the object. Deferred imitation can only occur after this point because it requires ability to represent internally the event to be imitated.

Nonetheless, Piaget thought that the baby still does not have mental symbols to stand for objects in this substage.

The ability to manipulate mental symbols, such as words or images, marks substage 6, which lasts from roughly 18 months to 24 months of age. This new capacity also allows the infant to generate solutions to problems simply by thinking about them, without the trial-and-error behavior typical of substage 5. For example, a 24-month-old who knows there are cookies in the cookie jar can figure out how to get one. Furthermore, she can find a way to overcome just about any obstacle placed in her path (Bauer, Schwade, Wewerka, & Delaney, 1999). Suppose, for example, parents respond to a toddler's climbing on the kitchen counter in pursuit of a cookie by moving the cookie jar to the top of the refrigerator. The toddler's response, thanks to the advances of substage 6, will likely be to find a way to climb to the top of the refrigerator. Thus, changes in cognition are probably behind the common impression of parents and other caregivers that 18- to 24-month-olds cannot be left unsupervised, even for very short periods of time.

● **The Object Concept** ●   You know that this book continues to exist even when you are unable to see it—an understanding that Piaget called **object permanence**. Piaget thought that babies acquired this understanding gradually during the sensorimotor period. According to his observations, replicated frequently by later researchers, the first sign that a baby is developing object permanence comes at about 2 months of age (in substage 2). Suppose you show a toy to a child of this age, then

object permanence the understanding that objects continue to exist when they can't be seen

put a screen in front of the toy and remove the toy. When you then remove the screen, the baby shows some indication of surprise, as if he knows that something should still be there. The child thus seems to have a rudimentary expectation about the permanence of an object. But infants of this age show no signs of searching for a toy that has fallen over the side of the crib or that has disappeared beneath a blanket or behind a screen.

In substage 3, however (at about 6–8 months), babies will look over the edge of the crib for dropped toys or on the floor for food that was spilled. (In fact, babies of this age may drive their parents nuts playing "dropsy" from the high chair.) Infants this age will also search for partially hidden objects. If you put a baby's favorite toy under a cloth but leave part of it sticking out, the infant will reach for the toy, which indicates that in some sense he "recognizes" that the whole object is there even though he can see only part of it. But if you cover the toy completely with the cloth or put it behind a screen, the infant will stop looking at it and will not reach for it, even if he has seen you put the cloth over it.

This behavior changes again between 8 and 12 months, in substage 4. Infants of this age will reach for or search for a toy that has been covered completely by a cloth or hidden by a screen. Thus, by 12 months, most infants appear to grasp the basic fact that objects continue to exist even when they are no longer visible.

● *Imitation* ●   Piaget thought that as early as the first few months of life, infants could imitate actions they could see themselves make, such as hand gestures. But he thought that they could not imitate other people's facial gestures until substage 4 (8–12 months). This second form of imitation seems to require some kind of cross-modal perception, combining the visual cues of seeing the other's face with the *kinesthetic cues* (perceptions of muscle motion) from one's own facial movements. Piaget also argued that imitation of any action that wasn't already in the child's repertoire did not occur until about 1 year, and that **deferred imitation**—a child's imitation of some action at a later time—was possible only in substage 6, since deferred imitation requires some kind of internal representation.

Challenges to Piaget's View

Some developmentalists have suggested that the ability of modern researchers to use computers and other kinds of advanced technology to measure infants' responses to object permanence problems have enabled them to identify infant capabilities that Piaget could not discover (Flavell, 1985). Others point out that Piaget may have wrongly equated the infant's lack of ability to carry out a motor behavior, such as removing a blanket from a hidden toy, with a lack of understanding of object permanence.

Whatever the reason, newer research suggests that very young babies have more understanding of object permanence than Piaget supposed. For example, in a series of studies, researchers have shown that babies as young as $3\frac{1}{2}$ or 4 months show clear signs of object permanence if a visual response rather than a reaching response is used to test it (Baillargeon, 1987, 1994; Baillargeon & DeVos, 1991; Baillargeon, Spelke, & Wasserman, 1985).

Similarly, another series of experiments demonstrated that 2- and 3-month-olds are remarkably aware of the kinds of movements objects are capable of—even when the objects are out of sight (Spelke, 1991). Infants expect objects to continue to move on their initial trajectories and show surprise if the objects appear somewhere else. They also seem to have some awareness that solid objects cannot pass through other solid objects.

Findings like these have reopened the debate about Piaget's description of the development of object permanence. More generally, they have sparked renewed discussion of the nature-versus-nurture issue (e.g., Diamond, 1991; Fischer & Bidell,

deferred imitation imitation by an infant of an action seen earlier

1991; Karmiloff-Smith, 1991). Piaget assumed that a baby came equipped with a repertoire of sensorimotor schemes, but his most fundamental theoretical proposal was that the child constructed an understanding of the world, based on experience. In contrast, recent theorizing suggests that the development of object permanence is more a process of elaboration than discovery. Newborns may have considerable awareness of objects as separate entities that follow certain rules. Certainly, all the research on the perception of patterns suggests that babies pay far more attention to relationships between events than Piaget's model supposed. Indeed, the research on babies' preferences for attractive faces suggests that there may be built-in preferences for particular patterns. Still, no one would argue that a baby comes equipped with a full-fledged knowledge of objects or a well-developed ability to experiment with the world.

With respect to imitation, Piaget's proposed sequence has been supported. Imitation of someone else's hand movement or an action with an object seems to improve steadily, starting at 1 or 2 months of age; imitation of two-part actions develops much later, perhaps around 15–18 months (Poulson, Nunes, & Warren, 1989). Yet there are two important exceptions to this general confirmation of Piaget's theory: Infants imitate some facial gestures in the first weeks of life, and deferred imitation seems to occur earlier than Piaget proposed.

Several researchers have found that newborn babies will imitate certain facial gestures, particularly tongue protrusion (Anisfeld, 1991). This seems to happen only if the model sits there with his tongue out looking at the baby for a fairly long period of time, perhaps as long as a minute. But the fact that newborns imitate at all is striking—although it is entirely consistent with the observation that quite young babies are capable of tactile/visual cross-modal perception.

Studies of deferred imitation also support Piaget. However, at least one study showed that babies as young as 9 months can defer their imitation for as long as 24 hours (Meltzoff, 1988). By 14 months, toddlers can recall and imitate someone's actions as much as 2 days later (Hanna & Meltzoff, 1993).

These findings are significant for several reasons. First, they make it clear that infants can and do learn specific behaviors through modeling, even when they have no chance to imitate the behavior immediately. In addition, these results suggest that babies may be more skillful than Piaget thought, and more abilities than he suggested may be built in from the beginning. However, the findings leave open deeper questions about the relative contributions of nature and experience to the developmental process.

Learning

From the first moments following birth, babies are capable of learning in a variety of ways.

● *Conditioning* ●   Learning of emotional responses through classical conditioning processes may begin as early as the first week of life. Thus, the mere presence of Mom or Dad or another favored person may trigger a sense of comfort or "feeling good." Such early learning may contribute to the child's attachment to the parent.

Newborns also clearly learn by operant conditioning. Both the sucking response and head turning have been successfully increased by the use of reinforcements such as sweet liquids or the sound of the mother's voice or heartbeat (Moon & Fifer, 1990). At the least, the fact that conditioning of this kind can take place means that whatever neurological wiring is needed for operant learning is present at birth. Results like these also tell developmentalists

Critical Thinking

Can you think of other examples of classically conditioned emotional responses that might develop in early infancy?

something about the sorts of reinforcements that are effective with very young children; it is surely highly significant for the whole process of mother-infant interaction that the mother's voice is an effective reinforcer for virtually all babies.

● *Habituation and Dishabituation* ●   As you learned earlier in this chapter, *habituation* is the process of getting used to a stimulus. Its opposite is **dishabituation**, or learning to respond to a familiar stimulus as if it were new. Both habituation and dishabituation are well developed by 10 weeks of age. For example, an infant will stop showing a startle reaction (Moro reflex) to a loud sound after the first few presentations, but will again show the startle reaction if the sound is changed somewhat. Such habituation and dishabituation are not voluntary processes; they are entirely automatic. But in order for them to work, the newborn must be equipped with the capacity to recognize familiar experiences. That is, she must have, or must develop, schemes of some kind.

The existence of these processes in the newborn has an added benefit for researchers: It has enabled them to figure out what an infant perceives as being "the same" or "different." If a baby is habituated to some specific stimulus, such as a sound or a picture, the experimenter can then present slight variations on the original stimulus to see the point at which dishabituation occurs. In this way, researchers have begun to get a picture of how the newborn baby or young infant experiences the world around him.

● *Schematic Learning* ●   Studies of a third type of infant learning, sometimes referred to as *schematic learning*, are based on both Piaget's theory and the information-processing approach. **Schematic learning** is the organizing of experiences into expectancies, or "known" combinations. These expectancies, often called *schemas*, are built up over many exposures to particular experiences. Once formed, they help the baby to distinguish between the familiar and the unfamiliar.

One kind of schematic learning involves categories. Research suggests that by 7 months of age, and perhaps even earlier, infants actively use categories to process information (Pauen, 2000). For example, a 7-month-old is likely to habituate to a sequence of ten animal pictures and, if the next picture is another animal, will not show surprise or look at it any longer than the first ten. If, however, researchers show the baby a picture of a human after ten animals, the baby will look surprised and gaze at the picture longer. The same thing is likely to happen if researchers show an infant several pictures of humans and then switch to an animal picture. Such findings suggest that infants build and use categories as they take in information.

Memory

Researchers have used an ingenious variation of an operant conditioning procedure to demonstrate that babies as young as 3 months of age can remember specific objects and their own actions with those objects over periods as long as a week (Bhatt & Rovee-Collier, 1996; Gerhardstein, Liu, & Rovee-Collier, 1998; Hayne & Rovee-Collier, 1995; Rovee-Collier, 1993). A researcher first hangs an attractive mobile over a baby's crib and watches to see how the baby responds, noting how often he kicks his legs while looking at the mobile. After 3 minutes of this "baseline" observation, a string is used to connect the mobile to the baby's leg, so that each time the baby kicks his leg, the mobile moves. Babies quickly learn to kick repeatedly in order to make this interesting action occur. Within 3–6 minutes, 3-month-olds double or triple their kick rates, clearly showing that learning has occurred. The researcher next tests the baby's memory of this learning by coming back some days later and hanging the same mobile over the crib but not attaching the string to the baby's foot. The crucial issue is whether the baby kicks rapidly at the mere sight of the mobile. If

dishabituation learning to respond to a familiar stimulus as if it were new

schematic learning organization of experiences into expectancies, called schemas, which enable infants to distinguish between familiar and unfamiliar stimuli

the baby remembers the previous occasion, he should kick at a higher rate than he did when he first saw the mobile, which is precisely what 3-month-old babies do, even after a delay of as long as a week.

Such findings demonstrate that the young infant is more cognitively sophisticated than developmentalists (and Piaget) had supposed. At the same time, these studies support Piaget's view that infants show systematic gains in the ability to remember over the months of infancy. Two-month-olds can remember their kicking action for only 1 day, 3-month-olds can remember for over a week, and 6-month-olds can remember longer than 2 weeks.

However, early infant memories are strongly tied to the specific context in which the original experience occurred. Even 6-month-olds do not recognize or remember the mobile if the context is changed even slightly, for example, by hanging a different cloth around the crib in which the child was originally tested. Thus, babies do remember more than Piaget believed, but their memories are highly specific. With age, their memories become less and less tied to specific cues or contexts.

Before going on

- Describe the development of the senses in the first 2 years of life.

- How do infants combine information from two or more senses?

- Outline the important milestones of Piaget's sensorimotor stage.

- What are some recent challenges offered to Piaget's explanation of infant cognitive development?

- How do infants learn through classical conditioning, operant conditioning, habituation, and schematic learning?

- Describe infants' ability to remember.

The Beginnings of Language

Most of us think of "language" as beginning when the baby uses her first words, at about 12 months of age, but all sorts of important developments precede the first words.

Theoretical Perspectives

In the late 1950s, B. F. Skinner, the scientist who formulated operant conditioning theory, suggested a *behaviorist* explanation of language development. He claimed that language development begins with babbling. While babbling, babies accidentally make sounds that somewhat resemble real words as spoken by their parents. Parents hear the word-like sounds and respond to them with praise and encouragement, which serve as reinforcers. Thus, word-like babbling becomes more frequent, while utterances that do not resemble words gradually disappear from babies' vocalizations. Skinner further hypothesized that parents and others respond to grammatical uses of words and do not respond to nongrammatical ones. As a result, correct grammar is reinforced and becomes more frequent, but incorrect grammar is extinguished through nonreinforcement.

At first glance, Skinner's theory might appear to make sense. However, systematic examination of the interactions between infants and parents reveals that adults do not reinforce babies' vocalizations in this manner. Instead, parents and others respond to *all* of a baby's vocalizations, and even sometimes imitate them—a consequence that, according to operant conditioning theory, should prolong babbling rather than lead to the development of grammatical language. Skinner's mistake was that his theory was not based on observations of language development but rather on his assumption that the principles of operant conditioning underlie all human learning and development.

Linguist Noam Chomsky strongly criticized Skinner's theory (Chomsky, 1959). The cornerstone of Chomsky's argument was the universal observation of field linguists that children make rule-governed rather than random grammatical errors when learning language. For example, almost all 3-year-old English-speaking children *over-regularize* the past tense of verbs. That is, they create the past tense for every verb by adding *-ed* to the present tense. Consequently, they say such things as, "Yesterday, we goed to the store," or "I breaked my cookie." In response to correction, they often regularize the correction itself by saying, "Yesterday we wented to the store," or "I broked my cookie."

Chomsky argued that the only possible explanation for such errors was that children acquire grammar rules before they master the exceptions to them. Further, Chomsky proposed a *nativist* explanation for language development: Children's comprehension and production of language are guided by an innate language processor that he called the **language acquisition device (LAD)**, which contains the basic grammatical structure of all human language. In effect, the LAD tells infants what characteristics of language to look for in the stream of speech to which they are exposed. For example, newborns actively segment the sounds of natural human speech into vowel and consonant categories. Chomsky identified this phenomenon as an example of the LAD's action on the phonological (sound) data contained in spoken language. Simply put, the LAD tells babies that there are two basic types of sounds—consonants and vowels—and enables them to properly divide the speech they hear into the two categories so that they can analyze and learn the sounds that are specific to the language they are hearing. Chomsky further supported the existence of the LAD with evidence compiled over hundreds of years by field linguists, which demonstrated that all human languages have the same grammatical forms. He also argued that the LAD is species-specific—that is, nonhuman species do not have one, and therefore, cannot learn grammatical language.

Speech Perception

Babies as young as 1 month can discriminate between simple speech sounds like *pa* and *ba* (Jusczyk, 1995). By 6 months old, they can discriminate between two-syllable "words" like *bada* and *baga* and can even respond to a syllable that is hidden inside a string of other syllables (as in *tibati* or *kobako*) (Fernald & Kuhl, 1987; Goodsitt, Morse, Ver Hoeve, & Cowan, 1984; Morse & Cowan, 1982). Even more remarkable, it doesn't seem to matter what voice quality is used to produce the sound. By 2 or 3 months of age, babies respond to individual sounds in the same way, whether the sounds are spoken by male or female, children's or adult voices (Marean, Werner, & Kuhl, 1992).

Also striking is the finding that babies are actually better than adults at discriminating some kinds of speech sounds. Each language uses only a subset of all possible speech sounds. Japanese, for example, does not use the *l* sound that appears in Eng-

language acquisition device (LAD) an innate language processor, theorized by Chomsky, that contains the basic grammatical structure of all human language

lish; Spanish distinguishes between the *d* and *t* sounds differently than English does. It turns out that up to about 6 months of age, babies can accurately discriminate among all sounds that appear in any language, including sounds they do not hear in the language spoken to them. At about 6 months of age, they begin to lose the ability to distinguish pairs of vowels that do not occur in the language they are hearing; by age 1, the ability to discriminate nonheard consonant contrasts begins to fade (Polka & Werker, 1994).

Sounds, Gestures, and Word Meanings

The ability to discriminate among sounds arises early but is not accompanied by much skill in producing sounds. From birth to about 1 month of age, the most common sound an infant makes is a cry, although she also produces other fussing, gurgling, and satisfied sounds. This sound repertoire expands at about 1 or 2 months, when the baby begins to make some laughing and cooing vowel sounds. Sounds like this are usually signals of pleasure and may show quite a lot of variation in tone, running up and down in volume or pitch.

Consonant sounds appear at about 6 or 7 months, frequently combined with vowel sounds to make a kind of syllable. Babies of this age seem to play with these sounds, often repeating the same sound over and over (such as *babababababa* or *dahdahdah*). This sound pattern is called *babbling*, and it makes up about half of babies' noncrying sounds from about 6 to 12 months of age (Mitchell & Kent, 1990).

Any parent can tell you that babbling is a delight to listen to. It also seems to be an important part of the preparation for spoken language. For one thing, infants' babbling gradually acquires some of what linguists call the *intonational pattern* of the language they are hearing—a process one developmental psychologist refers to as "learning the tune before the words" (Bates, O'Connell, & Shore, 1987). At the very least, infants do seem to develop at least two such "tunes" in their babbling. Babbling with a rising intonation at the end of a string of sounds seems to signal a desire for a response; a falling intonation requires no response.

A second important thing about babbling is that when babies first start babbling, they typically babble all kinds of sounds, including some that are not part of the language they are hearing. But at about 9 or 10 months, their sound repertoire gradually begins to narrow down to the set of sounds they are listening to, with the nonheard sounds dropping out (Oller, 1981). Findings like these do not prove that babbling is necessary for language development, but they certainly make it look as if babbling is part of a connected developmental process that begins at birth.

Another part of that process appears to be a kind of gestural language that develops at around 9 or 10 months. At this age, babies begin "demanding" or "asking" for things using gestures or combinations of gestures and sound. A 10-month-old baby who apparently wants you to hand her a favorite toy may stretch and reach for it, opening and closing her hand while making whining or whimpering sounds. Interestingly, infants of this age use gestures in this way whether they are exposed to spoken or sign language (see Research Report). At about the same age, babies enter into those gestural games much loved by parents: "patty-cake," "soooo big," and "wave bye-bye" (Bates et al., 1987).

Recent research has shown that babies are beginning to store individual words in their memories at around 8 months of age (Jusczyk & Hohne, 1997). By 9 or 10 months, most can understand the meanings of 20–30 words; this ability to understand words is known as **receptive language**. In the next few months, the number of words understood increases dramatically. In one investigation, researchers asked hundreds of mothers about their babies' understanding of various words. Reportedly,

These little girls probably haven't yet spoken their first words, but chances are they already understand quite a few. Receptive language usually develops before expressive language. (*Photo:* Michael Newman, PhotoEdit)

receptive language the ability to understand spoken language

Research Report

Early Gestural "Language" in the Children of Deaf Parents

For scientists who want to understand language development, deaf children of deaf parents are a particularly interesting group to study. The children do not hear oral language, but many are exposed to sign language. Do these children show the same early steps in language development as hearing children do, only using gestural language?

The answer seems to be yes. Deaf children show a kind of "sign babbling" between about 7 and 11 months of age, much as hearing children babble sounds in these same months. Then, at 8 or 9 months, deaf children begin using simple gestures, such as pointing, which is just about the age when such gestures emerge in hearing babies of hearing parents. At about 12 months of age, deaf babies seem to display their first referential signs—that is, gestures that appear to stand for some object or event—such as signaling that they want a drink by making a motion of bringing a cup to the mouth (Petitto, 1988).

Researchers have also studied an equally interesting group: hearing children of deaf parents (Folven and Bonvillian, 1991). These babies are exposed to sign language from their parents and to hearing language from their contacts with others in their world, including teachers, other relatives, playmates, and even people on television. In a small sample of nine such babies, the first sign appeared at an average age of 8 months, the first referential sign at 12.6 months, and the first spoken word at 12.2 months (Folven & Bonvillian, 1991). What is striking here is that the first referential signs and the first spoken words appear at nearly the same time, and that the spoken words appear at a completely normal time, despite the fact that these children of deaf parents hear comparatively little spoken language.

This marked similarity in the sequence and timing of the steps of early language in deaf and hearing children provides strong support for the argument that babies are somehow "primed" to learn language in some form, whether spoken or gestural.

10-month-olds understood an average of about 30 words; for 13-month-olds, the number was nearly 100 words (Fenson et al., 1994).

But how do babies separate a single word from the constant flow of speech to which they are exposed? Many linguists have proposed that a child can cope with the monumentally complex task of word learning only because he applies some built-in biases or constraints (Baldwin, 1995; Golinkoff, Mervis, & Hirsh-Pasek, 1994; Jusczyk & Hohne 1997; Markman, 1992; Waxman & Kosowski, 1990). For example, the child may have a built-in assumption that words refer to objects or actions but not both.

Learning a language's patterns of word stress may also help babies identify words. Recent research suggests that infants discriminate between stressed and unstressed syllables fairly early, around 7 months of age, and use syllable stress as a cue to identify single words (Jusczyk, Houston, & Newsome, 1999). For example, first-syllable stress, such as in the word "*mar*ket," is far more common in English than second-syllable stress, such as in the word "gar*age*." Thus, when English-learning infants hear a stressed syllable, they may assume that a new word is beginning. This strategy would help them single out a very large number of individual English words.

All of this information reveals a whole series of changes that seem to converge by 9 or 10 months: the beginning of meaningful gestures, the drift of babbling toward the heard language sounds, imitative gestural games, and the first comprehension of individual words. It is as if the child now understands something about the process of communication and is intending to communicate to adults.

The First Words

Expressive language, the ability to produce as well as understand and respond to words, typically appears at about 12 or 13 months (Fenson et al., 1994). The baby's first word is an event that parents eagerly await, but it's fairly easy to miss. A word,

expressive language the ability to produce spoken language

as linguists usually define it, is any sound or set of sounds that is used consistently to refer to some thing, action, or quality. This means that a child who uses *ba* consistently to refer to her bottle is using a word even though it isn't considered a word in English.

Often, a child's earliest words are used in specific situations and in the presence of many cues. The child may say "bow-wow" or "doggie" only in response to such promptings as "How does the doggie go?" or "What's that?" Typically, this early word learning is very slow, requiring many repetitions for each word. In the first 6 months of word usage, children may learn as few as 30 words. Most linguists have concluded that this earliest word-use phase involves learning each word as something connected to a set of specific contexts. What the child has apparently not yet grasped is that words are symbolic—that they refer to objects or events.

Very young children often combine a single word with a gesture to create a "two-word meaning" before they use two words together in their speech. For example, a child may point to his father's shoe and say "Daddy," as if to convey "Daddy's shoe" (Bates et al., 1987). In such cases, meaning is conveyed by the use of gesture and body language combined with a word. Linguists call these word-and-gesture combinations **holophrases**, and children use them frequently between 12 and 18 months of age.

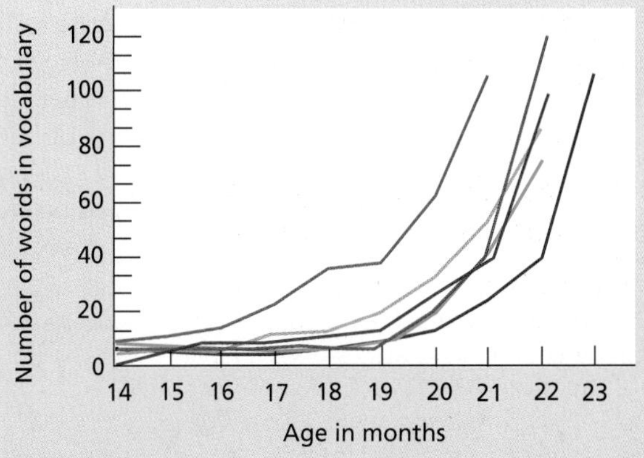

FIGURE 4.3

Each of the lines in this figure represents the vocabulary growth of one of the children studied longitudinally by Goldfield and Reznick. The six children shown here each acquired new words in the most common pattern: slow initial growth followed by a fairly rapid spurt. (*Source*: Goldfield & Reznick, 1990, Figure 3, p.177.)

Between 16 and 24 months, after the early period of very slow word learning, most children begin to add new words rapidly, as if they had figured out that things have names. Developmentalists refer to this period as the **naming explosion**. In this period, children seem to learn new words with very few repetitions, and they generalize these words to many more situations. According to one large cross-sectional study based on mothers' reports, the average 16-month-old has a speaking vocabulary of about 50 words; for a 24-month-old the total has grown to about 320 words (Fenson et al., 1994).

For most children, the naming explosion is not a steady, gradual process; instead, vocabulary "spurts" begin at about the time that the child has acquired 50 words. This pattern, observed by several researchers, is illustrated in Figure 4.3, which shows the vocabulary growth curves of six children studied longitudinally (Bloom, 1993; Goldfield & Reznick, 1990). Not all children show precisely this pattern, but a rapid increase over a period of a few months is typical.

Most observers agree that the bulk of new words learned during this early period of rapid vocabulary growth are names for things or people: "ball," "car," "milk," "doggie," "he." Action words tend to appear later (Gleitman & Gleitman, 1992). One study involving a large group of children suggested that as many as two-thirds of the words children knew by age 2 were nouns, and only 8.5% were verbs (Fenson et al., 1994). It appears that infants lack the ability to consistently associate words with actions until about 18 months of age (Casasola & Cohen, 2000). Recent cross-linguistic research also suggests that compared to Korean-speaking parents, English-speaking parents emphasize nouns more than verbs in speaking and reading to infants (Choi, 2000). Thus, the pattern of learning nouns before verbs may be influenced by the characteristics of the language being learned as well as by the behavior of mature speakers as they speak to infants. Indeed, the noun-before-verb pattern does not hold even for all English-speaking children. Some toddlers use what developmentalists call an *expressive style* (Nelson, 1973; Shore, 1995; Thal & Bates,

Critical Thinking

Think of contrasting "nature" and "nurture" explanations for expressive and referential styles.

holophrases "phrases" or "sentences" consisting of words and gestures, used by infants in the 2nd year of life

naming explosion a period between 16 and 24 months of age when most children rapidly begin to add new words to their vocabularies

1990). For these children, most early words are linked to social relationships rather than to objects. They often learn pronouns ("you," "me") early and use many more of what Nelson calls "personal-social" words, such as "no," "yes," "want," or "please." Their early vocabulary may also include some multiword strings, such as "love you" or "do it" or "go away." This is in sharp contrast to children who use a *referential style*, that is, children whose early vocabulary is made up predominantly of nouns or pronouns.

Before going on

- Briefly explain the behaviorist and nativist theories of language development.

- Describe infants' ability to perceive speech sounds.

- How do infants use sounds and gestures to communicate?

- When are the first words used, and what kinds of words do most infants learn first?

Individual and Group Differences

We've already touched on several kinds of differences among babies that affect their physical and cognitive development in the first few years: diet, feeding experience, and opportunities for exploration. Let's consider several others.

Individual Differences in Intelligence

To help identify infants with treatable problems, psychologists have developed various infant intelligence tests. These tests, including the widely used Bayley Scales of Infant Development, measure primarily sensory and motor skills (Bayley, 1969, revised 1993). For example, 3-month-old infants are challenged to reach for a dangling ring; older babies are observed as they attempt to put cubes in a cup (9 months) or build a tower of three cubes (17 months). Some more clearly cognitive items are also included; for example, uncovering a toy hidden by a cloth is a test item used with 8-month-old infants to measure an aspect of object permanence.

Bayley's test and others like it have proven to be helpful in identifying infants and toddlers with serious developmental delays (Sulkes, 1998). But as more general predictive tools for forecasting later IQ or school performance, such tests have not been nearly as useful as many had hoped. For example, the typical correlation between a Bayley test score at 12 months old and an intelligence test score at a 4 years is only about .20 to .30 (e.g., Bee et al., 1982)—hardly substantial enough to be used for predicting intellectual performance at later ages. On the whole, it appears that what is being measured on typical infant intelligence tests is not the same as what is tapped by the commonly used childhood or adult intelligence tests (Colombo, 1993).

Recent research has indicated that habituation tasks have high potential as measures of infant intelligence. For example, if a baby is shown an object or a picture over and over, how many exposures does it take before the infant stops showing interest? The speed with which such habituation/recognition takes place may reveal something about the efficiency of the baby's perceptual/cognitive system and its neurological underpinnings. And if such efficiency lies behind some of the characteristics that psychologists call "intelligence," then individual differences in rate of habituation in the early months of life may predict later intelligence test scores.

That is exactly what researchers have found in studies over the past 15 years. Babies who habituate quickly (that is, who rapidly become uninterested when shown the same object repeatedly) when they are 4 or 5 months old are likely to have higher intelligence test scores at later ages; slower infant habituation is associated with subsequent lower test scores and poorer language skills. The average correlation in studies in both the United States and England is in the range of .45 to .50 (Rose & Feldman, 1995; Slater, 1995). This is certainly not perfect correlation, but it is remarkably high compared to the correlation between conventional tests of infant intelligence and later IQ tests. Moreover, results like these underline the importance of examining information-processing skills in any effort to understand individual differences in cognitive abilities in early infancy.

Preterm and Low-Birth-Weight Infants

Infants born before 32 weeks of gestation may not have adaptive reflexes that are sufficiently developed to enable them to survive. Sucking and swallowing, for example, are extremely difficult for these tiny infants. Consequently, many preterm infants must be fed intravenously or through a tube inserted into the esophagus or stomach (Kliegman, 1998).

Once preterm infants can be fed orally, breast milk is often not the best food for them. For one thing, premature infants require diets supplemented with amino acids and fats that full-term infants' bodies can manufacture on their own (Guesry, 1998; Kliegman, 1998). In most cases, preterm babies are fed a combination of breast milk and specially formulated substitutes that contain exactly the proteins, fats, vitamins, and minerals their bodies need.

Preterm and low-birth-weight babies also move more slowly from one developmental milestone to the next. This is what researchers would expect, of course, because the preterm baby is, in fact, maturationally younger than the full-term baby. If a correction is made for the baby's gestational age, most (but not all) of the difference in physical development disappears. Parents of preterms need to keep this in mind when they compare their babies' progress with that of full-term babies. By age 2 or 3, the physically normal preterm will catch up to his peers, but in the early months he is definitely behind.

Boys and Girls

As is always true when sex differences are considered, discussions of variations in averages can obscure the fact that boys and girls develop in highly similar ways. Nevertheless, there are a few important differences between averages for male infants and those for female infants. Just as they were prenatally, girls continue to be ahead in some aspects of physical maturity during infancy. For example, the separate bones of the wrist appear earlier in girls than in boys (Tanner, 1990). This means that female infants may have a slight advantage in the development of manipulative skills such as self-feeding. In addition, boys are more likely to suffer from developmental delays, are less healthy, and have higher mortality rates (Halpern, 1997; MacDorman & Atkinson, 1999).

Typically, boys are found to be more physically active, but some investigators report no difference at all (Cossette, Malcuit, & Pomerleau, 1991). However, in both human and primate studies, male infants display a clear preference for rough-and-tumble play even during the first few months of life (Brown & Dixson, 2000; Humphreys & Smith, 1987). Likewise, differences between boys and girls in physical aggression are already evident near the end of the second year, a finding that has been replicated in studies of many cultures (Maccoby & Jacklin, 1974; Whiting & Edwards, 1988).

Most studies suggest that cognitive development is virtually identical for boys and girls in infancy, with one important exception. Girls acquire language somewhat more rapidly than boys do (Halpern, 1997). However, a Norwegian study involving approximately 200 children suggested that boys may be more cognitively vulnerable to the effects of impoverished environments. Researchers found that boys' intelligence test scores at age 5 were more strongly correlated with environmental conditions they had experienced in infancy (such as access to developmentally appropriate toys) than were the scores of girls of that age (Andersson, Sonnander, & Sommerfelt, 1998).

Racial Group Differences in Infant Mortality

In the United States, about 7 babies out of every 1,000 die before age 1 (MacDorman & Atkinson, 1999). The rate has been declining steadily for the past few decades (down from 20 per 1,000 in 1970), but the United States continues to have a higher infant mortality rate than other industrialized nations. Almost two-thirds of these infant deaths occur in the first month of life and are directly linked to either congenital anomalies or low birth weight (MacDorman & Atkinson, 1999).

There are large variations in infant mortality rates across racial groups in the United States, as shown in Figure 4.4 (MacDorman & Atkinson, 1999). Rates are lowest among Asian American infants; about 5 of every 1,000 such infants die each year. Among white babies, the rate is approximately 6 per 1,000. The groups with the highest rates of infant death are Native Americans (8.7 per 1,000), Native Hawaiians (9 per 1,000), and African Americans (13.7 per 1,000). One reason for these differences is that these infants are two to three times more likely to suffer from congenital abnormalities and low birth weight—the two leading causes of infant death in the first month of life—than babies in other groups. Furthermore, SIDS is also two to three times as common these groups.

Because babies born into poor families, regardless of race, are more likely to die than those born into families that are better off economically, some observers have suggested that poverty explains the higher rates of infant death among Native Americans (including Native Hawaiians) and African Americans, the racial groups with the highest rates of poverty. However, infant mortality rates among Hispanic groups suggest that the link between poverty and infant mortality is complex. The average infant mortality rate among Mexican American, Cuban American, and South and Central American populations is only 5.6 per 1,000 (MacDorman & Atkinson, 1999). These groups are almost as likely to be poor as African Americans and Native Americans. By contrast, Americans of Puerto Rican ancestry are no more likely to be poor than other Hispanic American groups, but the infant mortality rate in this group is 7.9 per 1,000.

Interestingly, mortality rates among the babies of immigrants of all racial groups are lower than those of U.S.-born infants. This finding also challenges the poverty explanation for racial group differences in infant mortality, because immigrant

Critical Thinking

Generate your own hypothesis to explain the finding that mortality is lower among babies whose mothers are immigrants than among those whose mothers were born in the United States. What kind of information would you need to test your hypothesis?

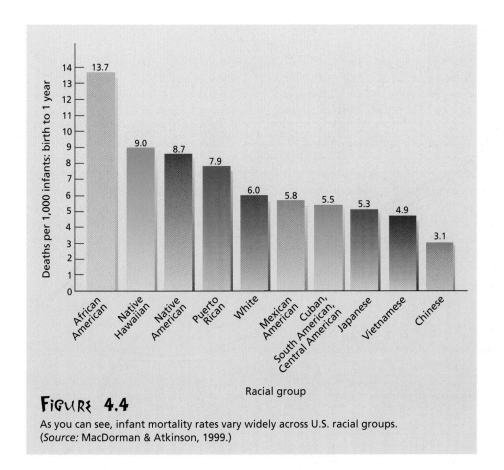

FIGURE 4.4

As you can see, infant mortality rates vary widely across U.S. racial groups. (*Source:* MacDorman & Atkinson, 1999.)

women are more likely to be poor and less likely to receive prenatal care than are women born in the United States (MacDorman & Atkinson, 1999). Many researchers suggest that lower rates of tobacco and alcohol use among women born outside the United States may be an important factor.

Another indication that complex factors influence infant mortality is the finding that, even when researchers compare only infants born to college-educated mothers, those born to African American women are more likely to die (Schoendorf, Hogue, Kleinman, & Rowley, 1992). Moreover, when only full-term, normal-weight babies are compared, infant mortality is still higher among African American infants (see Figure 4.5, page 116). Consequently, researchers believe that understanding race differences in infant mortality is critical to gaining insight into the basic causes of infant death in general. Thus, explaining group differences has become an important goal of research examining the causes of death in the first year of life.

Cross-Cultural Differences

The sequence of physical and cognitive changes described in this chapter seems to hold true for babies in all cultures, but there are some interesting differences.

● **Reflexes, Behavioral States, and Motor Skills** ● In a classic cross-cultural study, developmentalists tested white, Navaho, Chinese, and Japanese babies for the Moro reflex (Freedman, 1979). They found that when startled, the white babies showed the typical pattern, in which they reflexively extended both arms, cried vigorously and persistently, and moved their bodies in an agitated way. Navaho babies, on the other hand, showed quite a different pattern. Instead of thrusting their limbs outward, they retracted their arms and legs, rarely cried, and showed little or very brief agitation.

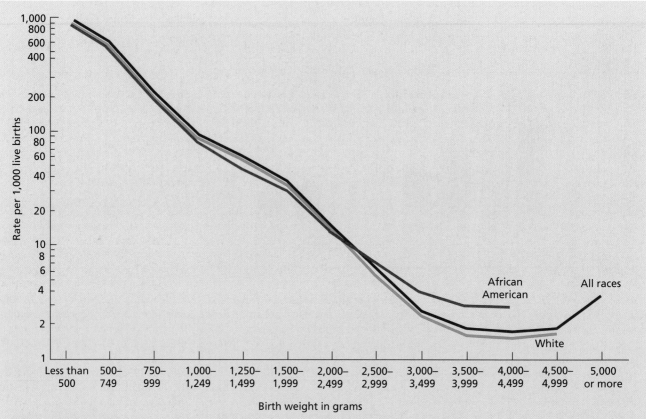

Figure 4.5

The death rate for average-size African American babies is higher than the death rate for average-size babies from other groups. Thus, the unusually high proportion of low-birth-weight infants born to African American mothers accounts for only some of the difference in infant mortality rates between African Americans and other groups. (*Source*: MacDorman & Atkinson, 1999, Figure 1, p. 6.)

Other researchers have replicated part of these results in a comparison of Chinese, Irish, and white American 4-month-olds (Kagan et al., 1994). They found that the Chinese infants were significantly less active, less irritable, and less vocal than were babies in the other two groups. The white American infants showed the strongest reactions to new sights, sounds, and smells. Similarly, Navaho babies have been found to be significantly less irritable, less excitable, and more able to quiet themselves than Euro-American babies (Chisholm, 1989).

Such differences may explain cross-cultural variations in physical growth and motor development, but researchers don't really know why infants in some groups advance more rapidly than others. For example, both African and African American infants grow somewhat faster than those in other groups, both prenatally and after birth, and they also show somewhat faster development of motor skills such as sitting and walking (Tanner, 1990). In contrast, Asian and Native American infants are smaller and somewhat slower to achieve early motor milestones than babies in other groups (Tanner, 1990).

● *Language Development* ●   Cross-cultural studies of early language development support the generalization that children learn words for people or things before they learn words for actions or other parts of speech. Vocabulary development in children who are learning two languages follows the same pattern (see No Easy Answers). Children appear to learn naming words more rapidly than other words no matter what language they are learning to speak.

No Easy Answers

One Language or Two?

Today, many people emigrate from one country to another. Thus, many children are growing up with the very real possibility of becoming bilingual. However, most children of immigrants never acquire native proficiency in their parents' language (Pease-Alvarez, 1993). Many immigrant parents believe that teaching children their language will undermine the children's future educational and economic success—even though knowing two languages is clearly a social and economic benefit for an adult. However, research suggests that there are cognitive advantages and disadvantages to growing up bilingual.

On the positive side, bilingualism seems to have no impact on early language milestones such as babbling (Oller, Cobo-Lewis, & Eilers, 1997). Infants in bilingual homes also readily discriminate between the two languages both phonologically and grammatically from the earliest days of life (Bosch & Sebastian-Galles, 1997; Koeppe, 1996). Further, learning a grammatical device, such as using -*s* to signify plurals, in one language seems to facilitate learning corresponding devices in the other language (Schlyter, 1996).

In preschool and school-age children, bilingualism is associated with a clear advantage in *metalinguistic ability*, the capacity to think about language (Bialystok, Shenfield, & Codd, 2000; Mohanty & Perregaux, 1997). In addition, most bilingual children display greater ability than monolingual children to focus attention on language tasks (Bialystok & Majumder, 1998). These two advantages enable bilingual children to more easily grasp the connection between sounds and symbols in the beginning stages of learning to read (Bialystok, 1997; Oller, Cobo-Lewis, & Eilers, 1998).

On the negative side, infants in bilingual homes reach some language milestones later than do those in monolingual homes. For example, bilingual infants' receptive and expressive vocabularies are as large as those of monolingual infants, but the words they know are divided between two languages (Patterson, 1998). Consequently, their vocabulary in either language tends to be more limited than that of monolingual infants, a difference that persists into the school years.

Research indicates that bilingual children who are equally fluent in both languages encounter few, if any, learning problems in school (Vuorenkoski, Kuure, Moilanen, & Peninkilampi, 2000). However, most children do not attain equal fluency in both languages. As a result, they tend to think more slowly in the language in which they have the lesser fluency (Chincotta & Underwood, 1997). Thus, if the language in which they are less fluent is the language they are taught in at school, they are at risk for learning problems (Anderson, 1998; Thorn & Gathercole, 1999). Therefore, parents who choose bilingualism should probably take into account whether they will be able to help their children become fluent in both langues.

Whatever the cognitive advantages or disadvantages, children who speak their immigrant parents' language appear to develop a stronger sense of attachment to their parents' culture of origin (Buriel, Perez, DeMent, Chavez, & Moran, 1998). And teaching children about parents' culture of origin seems to help them acquire the language (Wright, Taylor & Macarthur, 2000). Finally, the advantages in adulthood of being bilingual are substantial and may outweigh any disadvantages experienced in childhood. Thus, bilingual parents should weigh the various advantages and disadvantages of bilingualism and consider their long-term parenting goals, in order to reach an informed decision about the kind of linguistic environment to provide for their babies.

Before going on

- How do psychologists measure intelligence in infancy? What is the best predictor of future IQ test score?

- How do preterm babies differ from full-term infants in physical and cognitive development?

- In what ways do boys and girls develop differently in the first 2 years?

- Describe differences in infant mortality across racial groups in the United States.

- Are the milestones of physical and language development the same in all cultures?

A Final Word

n infant's lack of motor organization may lead an adult to believe that she is equally deficient intellectually. However, as you have learned in this chapter, psychologists and parents alike have seriously underestimated infants' perceptual and cognitive capacities. Recent research has forced developmentalists to consider the hypothesis that many abilities are "wired in" by nature. What isn't provided by nature, though, is the physical and social environment that is required to nurture whatever inborn capacities an infant has. Parents and other caregivers must provide infants with an environment that supports physical health and intellectual development.

Summary

Physical Changes

- Changes in the nervous system are extremely rapid in the first 2 years. In most parts of the brain, development of dendrites and synapses reaches its first peaks between 12 and 24 months, after which "pruning" of synapses occurs. Myelinization of nerve fibers also occurs rapidly in the first 2 years.

- Adaptive reflexes include such essential responses as sucking; primitive reflexes include the Moro and Babinski reflexes, which disappear within a few months. At birth, a baby's vision and other senses function, but are limited in some ways; they improve substantially across the first year. Babies move through a series of states of consciousness in a cycle that lasts about 2 hours.

- During infancy, bones increase in number and density; muscle fibers become larger and contain less water. Stamina improves as the lungs grow and the heart gets stronger. Motor skills rapidly improve in the first 2 years, as the baby moves from creeping to crawling to walking to running and becomes able to grasp objects.

- Breast-feeding has been shown to be better for a baby nutritionally. Babies need regular check-ups and a variety of immunizations. Sudden infant death syndrome is the most common cause of death in the first year.

Cognitive Changes

- In the first weeks of life, infants appear to be intent on locating objects; after about 2 months, they seem intent on identifying objects, so their method of scanning changes. Babies also show cross-modal perception as early as a few weeks of age.

- Piaget described the sensorimotor stage as a period of six substages in which an infant with a small repertoire

of basic schemes moves toward symbolic representation. The most important cognitive milestone of this stage is object permanence.

- More recent research suggests that Piaget underestimated infants' capabilities as well as the degree to which some concepts may be "wired into" the brain.

- Babies are able to learn by both classical and operant conditioning within the first few weeks of life.

- Infants as young as 3–4 months show signs of remembering specific experiences over periods as long as a few days to a week, a sign that they must have some ability to form internal representations, well before Piaget proposed they could.

The Beginnings of Language

- Behaviorist theories of language development claim that infants learn language through parental reinforcement of word-like sounds and correct grammar. Nativists point out that parents seldom reinforce babies in this way. Instead, they say, babies have an innate language processor that helps them learn the rules of language.

- Babies can discriminate among speech sounds in their first weeks. Between 6 and 12 months of age, babies lose the ability to respond to subtle differences in speech sounds to which they are not exposed.

- Babies' earliest sounds are cries, followed by cooing at about 2 months, then by babbling at about 6 months. At 9 months, babies typically use meaningful gestures and can understand a small vocabulary of spoken words.

- A baby's first spoken words, usually names for objects or people, typically occur at about 1 year, after which toddlers add words slowly for a few months and then rapidly during the naming explosion.

Individual and Group Differences

- Infant intelligence tests are not strongly correlated with later measures of intelligence. However, basic information-processing skills in infancy, such as rate of habituation at 4 months, are correlated with later intelligence test scores.
- Preterm infants lag behind their full-term peers in achieving the milestones of development, but they normally catch up within a few years.

- Girls are physically more advanced than boys and acquire language more rapidly. Most studies find boys to be more active and to prefer rough-and-tumble play.
- African American, Hawaiian American, and Native American children are more likely to die in the first year of life than those in other U.S. racial groups. Poverty seems a likely explanation, but the relationship between low income and infant mortality is complex.
- Native American and Chinese infants are less irritable than white American babies. African and African American infants develop somewhat more rapidly, Asian infants somewhat more slowly, than white babies. Early word learning seems to follow similar patterns in all cultures.

Key Terms

adaptive reflexes (p. 92)

colic (p. 94)

cross-modal perception (p. 102)

deferred imitation (p. 104)

dishabituation (p. 106)

expressive language (p. 110)

habituate (p. 101)

holophrases (p. 111)

intersensory integration (p. 101)

language acquisition device (LAD) (p. 108)

myelinization (p. 92)

naming explosion (p. 111)

object permanence (p. 103)

primitive reflexes (p. 92)

receptive language (p. 109)

reticular formation (p. 92)

schematic learning (p. 106)

sensorimotor stage (p. 102)

states of consciousness (p. 93)

sudden infant death syndrome (SIDS) (p. 98)

synapses (p. 91)

visual acuity (p. 93)

CHAPTER

5

Social and Personality Development in Infancy

DeVore, Anthro-Photo

During infancy, there is more physical closeness, or *proximity*, between parents and child than in any other period. Proximity is pleasurable for both parents and babies, but it is also practical. For one thing, a mother or father usually has to carry out other duties while simultaneously caring for a baby. Keeping young infants close by helps because they aren't sufficiently mobile to move to the parent when they need care. Once infants become mobile, they can get themselves into all kinds of trouble. Thus, with older babies, one of the goals of maintaining proximity is to protectively restrict their movements.

Practical considerations aside, caregiver-infant proximity contributes to the development of a strong emotional bond. In many parts of the world, mothers carry their babies with them most of the time in some kind of sling or wrap—as the Masai mother is doing in the photo. This system is not only practical but also keeps the caregiver and baby in close physical contact, a factor that seems to promote the development of a secure, affectionate relationship between them. In addition, physical closeness allows parents and babies to interact by exchanging smiles, frowns, or silly faces. Likewise, when parents and babies are close to each other, the parents can easily teach infants the names of objects in the environment.

In industrialized societies, a variety of devices such as strollers allow caregivers to easily transport babies just about anywhere an adult can go. You might think that a stroller would restrict contact between caregiver and infant. However, if you observe parents and their stroller-bound infants at a shopping mall or park, you will see babies taken out of their strollers to be fed and put back in for naps. You will also notice that parents wheel infants to places they think the babies will find interesting—such as a pet store window where kittens are frolicking—and converse with the babies about what they see: "Look at the kitties. Aren't they cute?" Thus, baby slings such as those used by the Masai may look very different from the industrialized world's strollers, but both help caregivers and infants form relationships.

Every culture devises ways of transporting infants that protect them and keep them close to their caregivers. (*Photo:* Stone)

Developmentalists of diverse theoretical orientations agree that the formation of a strong emotional connection to a primary caregiver early in life is critical to healthy child development and has important implications across the entire human lifespan. In this chapter, you will learn how such relationships develop. In addition, you will read about inborn biases concerning social interaction that infants bring with them into the world, as well as how their perceptions of themselves develop over the first 2 years. The chapter will also address the effects of non-parental care and a variety of other variables on infant development. As you read, keep the following questions in mind:

- What are the major theoretical perspectives that inform research on infants' social and personality development?

- How does the parent-infant relationship develop?

- Do infants come into the world with inborn traits? How do infants develop their self-concepts?

- How does non-parental care affect infant development?

- What are some important individual and group differences in infant social and personality development?

Theories of Social and Personality Development

Psychologists have used all of the theoretical perspectives you learned about in Chapter 2 to formulate hypotheses about infant social and personality development. However, the two most influential perspectives on these issues are the psychoanalytic and the ethological perspectives.

Psychoanalytic Perspectives

You may remember from Chapter 2 that Freud proposed a series of psychosexual stages that extend from birth through adolescence, during which individuals attempt to satisfy certain basic drives in different ways. In the first stage, from birth to age 2, infants derive satisfaction through the mouth. Therefore, Freud named this stage the *oral stage*. He further believed that the weaning process should be managed in such a way that the infant's need to suck is neither frustrated nor overgratified. The consequences of either, Freud claimed, would be fixation at this stage of development. As a result of fixation, the infant would carry with her into adulthood a need to use her mouth to attain physical gratification of her instinctual drives. Fixation would manifest itself, in Freud's view, in oral behaviors such as nail-biting and swearing.

Freud also emphasized the *symbiotic* relationship between the mother and young infant, in which the two behave as if they were one. He believed that the infant did not understand herself to be separate from her mother. Thus, another result of a gratifying nursing period followed by a balanced weaning process, Freud thought, was the infant's development of a sense of both attachment to and separation from the mother.

Erikson went beyond Freud's view. Nursing and weaning are important, he conceded, but they are only

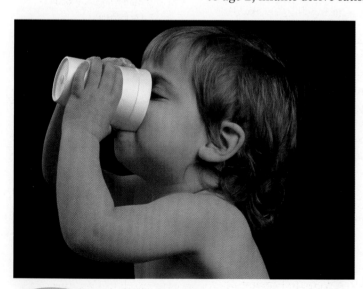

Freud asserted that infant weaning practices were central to the attachment process. (*Photo:* Felicia Martinez, PhotoEdit)

one aspect of the overall social environment. Erikson claimed that responding to the infant's other needs by talking to him, comforting him, and so on, was just as important. He proposed that the first 2 years comprise a period during which the infant learns to trust the world around him or becomes cynical about the social environment's ability to meet his needs—the *trust versus mistrust* stage.

One of the best-known studies in developmental psychology demonstrated that Erikson's view of infant development was more accurate than Freud's (Harlow & Zimmerman, 1959). In this study, infant monkeys were separated from their mothers at birth. The experimenters placed two different kinds of "surrogate" mothers in their cages. The monkeys received all their feedings from a wire mother with a nursing bottle attached. The other mother was covered with soft terrycloth. The researchers found that the monkeys approached the wire mother only when hungry. Most of the time, they cuddled against the cloth mother and ran to it whenever they were frightened or stressed. Subsequent studies with human infants correlating maternal feeding practices with infant adjustment suggested that the infant's social relationships are not based solely on either nursing or weaning practices (Schaffer & Emerson, 1964).

Ethological Perspectives

The strongest theoretical influence in modern-day studies of infant-parent relationships is an ethological approach known as **attachment theory,** based originally on the work of John Bowlby (1969, 1973, 1980, 1988a, 1988b). Bowlby argued that "the propensity to make strong emotional bonds to particular individuals [is] a basic component of human nature, already present in germinal form in the neonate" (1988a, p. 3). Such relationships have survival value, because they ensure that the infant will be nurtured. They are built and maintained by instinctive behaviors that create and sustain proximity between parent and child.

Bowlby's writings, and the equally influential writings of Mary Ainsworth, draw a distinction between different types of affectionate human relationships (Ainsworth, Blehar, Waters, & Wall, 1978). An **affectional bond** is defined as "a relatively long-enduring tie in which the partner is important as a unique individual and is interchangeable with none other. In an affectional bond, there is a desire to maintain closeness to the partner" (Bowlby, 1989, p. 711). An **attachment** is a type of affectional bond in which a person's sense of security is bound up in the relationship. When you are attached, you feel a special sense of security and comfort in the presence of the other, and you can use the other as a "safe base" from which to explore the rest of the world.

Ethologists believe that the first 2 years of life constitute a sensitive period for attachment in human infants. They claim that infants who fail to form a close relationship with a primary caregiver are at risk for future social and personality problems. Studies of infants whose life circumstances do not permit them to engage in extended contact with a single caregiver—such as children who are brought up in orphanages or who are hospitalized for long periods during infancy—seem to confirm ethologists' view (DeAngelis, 1997; Fahrenfort, Jacobs, Miedema, & Schweizer, 1996).

Harlow's ingenious research demonstrated that infant monkeys became attached to a terrycloth covered "mother" and would cling to it rather than to a wire mother that provided them with food.
(*Photo:* © Martin Rogers, Woodfin Camp and Associates)

Critical Thinking

Think about your own relationships. In Bowlby's and Ainsworth's terms, which are attachments and which are affectional bonds?

attachment theory the view that the ability and need to form an attachment relationship early in life are genetic characteristics of all human beings

affectional bond the emotional tie to an infant experienced by a parent

attachment the emotional tie to a parent experienced by an infant, from which the child derives security

No Easy Answers

Adoption and Development

Most people who adopt a child assume that if they provide enough love and support, the child will develop both cognitively and emotionally pretty much the way their biological child would. By now, you should know enough about human development to realize that it just isn't that simple. For one thing, many aspects of temperament and personality are inherited. Therefore, an adopted child is more likely than a biological child to be different from his parents in these traits, which may give rise to problems. For example, if two extremely shy parents adopt a child who is very outgoing, the parents may view the child's behavior as difficult or even "disturbed" in some way, rather than just different from theirs.

Adoptive parents also need to take into account the child's circumstances prior to the adoption in order to form a realistic set of expectations. Children adopted before the age of 6 months, who have no history of institutionalization or abuse, are generally indistinguishable from nonadopted children in security of attachment, cognitive development, and social adjustment (Kirchner, 1998). This is true whether adoptive parents and children are of the same or different races and/or nationalities (Juffer & Rosenboom, 1997). For example, in one study involving 211 teenagers adopted into Swedish families at an early age, 90% of the adoptees thought of themselves as Swedish even though

many were of non-European birth and, thus, had physical features quite different from those of most Swedish people (Cederblad, Hook, Irhammar, & Mercke, 1999). Such findings suggest that raising a low-risk adopted child differs little from raising a biological child.

However, children who are adopted later, who have histories of abuse and/or neglect, or who have lived in institutions for long periods tend to have more problems, both cognitive and emotional, than nonadopted children (Castle et al., 1999; Marcovitch, Goldberg, Gold, & Washington, 1997; O'Connor, Bredenkamp, & Rutter, 1999; Roy, Rutter, & Pickles, 2000; Verhulst & Versluis-Den Bieman, 1995). One study found that 91% of children who had been adopted after being abused, neglected, or institutionalized suffered from emotional problems even after having been in their adoptive families for an average of 9 years (Smith, Howard, & Monroe, 1998). Not surprisingly, parents of such children reported experiencing more parenting-related stress than did parents of either adoptees from more positive backgrounds or biological children (Mainemer, Gilman, & Ames, 1998). Consequently, people who adopt such children should expect that parenting them will not be easy.

However, there are a few important facts that parents who adopt high-risk children should keep in mind. First, these children are better off developmentally than their peers who remain

institutionalized or who are returned to biological parents who abused and/or neglected them (Bohman & Sigvardsson, 1990). Further, despite increased risks, the large majority of adopted children are indistinguishable from nonadopted children in social behavior and emotional functioning by the time they reach late adolescence or adulthood (Brand & Brinich, 1999; Cederblad et al., 1999).

Second, the task of raising high-risk children can be made more manageable with parent training (Juffer, Hoksbergen, Riksen-Walraven, & Kohnstamm, 1997). Thus, adoptive parents should take advantage of any training offered by the institutions through which the adoption was arranged. If none is available, they should look for training elsewhere, perhaps at a local community college.

Finally, at the first sign of difficulty, adoptive parents should seek help from a social worker or psychologist who specializes in treating children. In fact, many developmentalists recommend that agencies that place high-risk children in adoptive or long-term foster families should routinely provide them with post-adoption therapeutic services (Mainemer et al., 1998; Minty, 1999; Smith et al., 1997). Therapists can help with everyday tasks such as toilet-training and teach parents strategies for dealing with behavior that reflects severe emotional disturbance, such as self-injury.

---

reactive attachment disorder a disorder that appears to prevent a child from forming close social relationships

For example, children who are adopted after spending more than 2 years in an orphanage are more likely to suffer from a disorder known as *reactive attachment disorder* than those who are adopted in infancy (DeAngelis, 1997). Children with **reactive attachment disorder** seem to be unable to form close emotional relationships with anyone, including foster and adoptive parents. Long-term institutional care is also associated with cognitive deficits (Castle et al., 1999). Even children whose institutional care does not extend beyond the first 2 years are more likely to display developmental delays and emotional difficulties the later in infancy they are adopted (De Angelis, 1997); see No Easy Answers.

Before going on

- How do Freud's and Erikson's views of personality development in the first 2 years differ?

- What is attachment theory, and what evidence is there to suggest that the first 2 years are a critical period for forming an attachment?

MAKE THE CONNECTION

Choose one of the theoretical perspectives in Chapter 2 not discussed here and think about how it would color hypotheses about infants' social and personality development. For example, how would B. F. Skinner apply operant conditioning principles to explain the development of parent-infant relationships in the first 2 years?

Attachment

Somehow, in the midst of endless diaper changes, food preparation, baths, and periods of exhaustion that exceed anything they have ever experienced before, the overwhelming majority of parents manage to respond to their infants in ways that foster the development of a close relationship. To understand the early relationship between parent and infant, it is important to look at both sides of the equation—at the development of both the parents' bond to the child and the child's attachment to the parents.

The Parents' Attachment to the Infant

Contact between parent and infant immediately after birth does not appear to be either necessary or sufficient for the formation of a stable long-term affectional bond between either mother or father and child (Wong, 1993). What *is* essential in the formation of that bond is the opportunity for parent and infant to develop a mutual, interlocking pattern of attachment behaviors, called **synchrony**.

Synchrony is like a conversation. The baby signals his needs by crying or smiling; he responds to being held by quieting or snuggling; he looks at the parents when they look at him. The parents, in their turn, enter into the interaction with their own repertoire of caregiving behaviors. One of the most intriguing things about this process is that we all seem to know how to engage in this particular conversation and do it in very similar ways. In the presence of a young infant, most adults will automatically display a distinctive pattern of interactive behaviors, including smiling, raised eyebrows, and very wide-open eyes. And we all seem to use our voices in special ways with babies. Parents all over the world use a characteristic high-pitched and lilting voice when speaking to an infant and specific intonation patterns to signal different meanings. For example, one

Critical Thinking

Listen to yourself speak the next time you interact with a baby. Do you speak in a higher, more lilting voice? Do your intonation patterns match the ones described in the Papousek study?

synchrony a mutual, interlocking pattern of attachment behaviors shared by a parent and child

Fathers engage in physical play with infants more often than mothers do. (*Photo:* © Lynne J. Weinstein, Woodfin Camp and Associates)

study found that Chinese, German, and American mothers all tended to use a rising voice inflection when they wanted their babies to become involved in the interaction and a falling intonation when they wanted to soothe their babies (Papousek & Papousek, 1991).

Even though adults can perform all these attachment behaviors with many infants, they do not form a bond with every baby they coo at in a restaurant or the grocery store. For an adult, the critical ingredient for the formation of a bond seems to be the opportunity to develop real synchrony—to practice the conversation until the participants follow each other's lead smoothly and pleasurably. For example, research suggests that an imitative conversation style, a pattern in which mother imitates baby's vocalizations and vice versa, may be an important component of parent-infant synchrony (Masur & Rodemaker, 1999). Such interactions require time and many rehearsals, and some parents (and infants) become more skillful at them than others. In general, the smoother and more predictable the process becomes, the more satisfying it seems to be to the parents and the stronger the attachment relationship becomes. Moreover, the degree of synchrony in parent-infant interactions seems to contribute to cognitive development as well. Developmentalists have found that 6- to 8-month-old infants whose interactions with their parents are highly synchronous tend to have larger vocabularies at age 2 and higher intelligence test scores at age 3 than their counterparts whose interactions are less synchronous (Saxon, Colombo, Robinson, & Frick, 2000).

The father's bond with the infant, like the mother's, seems to depend more on the development of synchrony than on contact immediately after birth. Aiding the development of such mutuality is the fact that fathers seem to have the same repertoire of attachment behaviors as do mothers. In the early weeks of the baby's life, fathers touch, talk to, and cuddle their babies in the same ways that mothers do (Parke & Tinsley, 1981).

After the first weeks of the baby's life, however, signs of a kind of specialization of parental behaviors begin to emerge. Fathers spend more time playing with the baby, with more physical roughhousing; mothers spend more time in routine caregiving and also talk to and smile at the baby more (Walker, Messinger, Fogel, & Karns, 1992). This does not mean that fathers have a weaker affectional bond with the infant; it simply means that fathers and mothers use different attachment behaviors in interacting with their infants.

The Infant's Attachment to the Parents

Like the parent's bond to the baby, the baby's attachment emerges gradually and is based on her ability to discriminate between her parents and other people. As you learned in Chapters 3 and 4, an infant can recognize her mother's voice prior to birth. By the time the baby is a few days old, she recognizes her mother by sight and smell as well (Cernoch & Porter, 1985; Walton, Bower, & Bower, 1992). Thus, the cognitive foundation for attachment is in place within days after birth.

Bowlby suggested three phases in the development of the infant's attachment (Bowlby, 1969). Bowlby thought that in the first phase, known as *nonfocused orienting and signaling*, the baby uses a set of innate behavior patterns that orient her toward others and signal her needs. Ainsworth described these as "proximity promoting" behaviors—they bring people closer. In the newborn's repertoire, these behaviors include crying, making eye contact, clinging, cuddling, and responding to caregiving efforts by being soothed. At this stage, there is little evidence of an attachment. As Ainsworth says, "These attachment behaviors are simply emitted, rather than being directed toward any specific person" (1989, p. 710). Nonetheless, the roots of attachment are to be found in this phase. The baby is building up expectancies and schemas and fine-tuning her ability to discriminate Mom and Dad from others.

By 3 months of age, the baby enters the *focus on one or more figures phase* and begins to aim her attachment behaviors somewhat more narrowly. She may smile more at the people who regularly take care of her and may not smile readily at a stranger. Yet despite the change, Bowlby and Ainsworth have argued that the infant does not yet have a full-blown attachment. The child still favors a number of people with her "proximity promoting" behaviors, and no one person has yet become the "safe base." Children in this phase show no special anxiety at being separated from their parents and no fear of strangers.

In phase 3, *secure base behavior*, the 6-month-old changes her attachment behavior. Because the 6- to 7-month-old begins to be able to move about the world more freely by creeping and crawling, she can move toward a parent as well as enticing the parent to come to her. Her attachment behaviors therefore shift from mostly "come here" signals (proximity promoting) to what Ainsworth called "proximity seeking" behaviors—which might be thought of as "go there" behaviors. A child of this age also uses the "most important" person as a safe base from which to explore the world around her—one of the key signs that an attachment exists.

Not all infants have a single attachment figure, even at this stage. Some may show strong attachment to both parents or to a parent and another caregiver, such as a baby-sitter or a grandparent. But even these babies, when under stress, usually show a preference for one of their favored persons over the others.

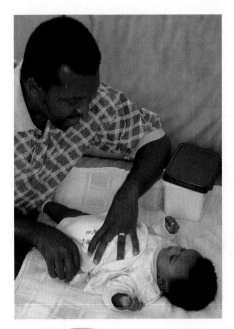

Dads like this one, who get involved with the day-to-day care of their babies, seem to develop stronger attachment relationships with their babies. (*Photo:* Laura Dwight, PhotoEdit)

● *Attachment Behaviors* ● Once the child has developed a clear attachment, at about 6 to 8 months of age, several related behaviors also begin appearing. *Stranger anxiety* and *separation anxiety*, attachment behaviors that are rare before 5 or 6 months, rise in frequency until about 12 to 16 months, and then decline. Infants express **stranger anxiety** with behaviors such as clinging to their mothers when strangers are present. **Separation anxiety** is evident when infants cry or protest being separated from the mother. The research findings are not altogether consistent, but fear of strangers apparently emerges first. Separation anxiety starts a bit later but continues to be visible for a longer period. Such an increase in fear and anxiety has been observed in children from a number of different cultures, and in both home-reared children and children in day care in the United States.

Another attachment behavior is **social referencing** (Walden, 1991). By roughly 10 months, infants use cues from the facial expressions of their attachment figures to help them figure out what to do in novel situations, such as when a stranger comes to visit. Babies this age will first look at Mom's or Dad's face to check for the adult's emotional expression. If Mom looks pleased or happy, the baby is likely to explore a new toy with more ease or to accept a stranger with less fuss. If Mom looks concerned or frightened, the baby responds to those cues and reacts to the novel situation with equivalent fear or concern.

From the age of 7 to 8 months, when strong attachments are first seen, infants prefer either the father or the mother to a stranger. When both the father and the mother are available, an infant will smile at or approach either or both, except when he is frightened or under stress. When that happens, especially between 8 and 24 months of age, the child typically turns to the mother rather than the father (Lamb, 1981).

Variations in Attachment Quality

Virtually all babies seem to go through the three phases of attachment first identified by Bowlby, but the quality of the attachments they form differs from one infant to the next.

● *Internal Models* ● In Bowlby's terminology, infants create different *internal models* of their relationships with parents and other key adults. These models include such elements as the child's confidence (or lack of it) that the attachment figure will

stranger anxiety expressions of discomfort, such as clinging to the mother, in the presence of strangers

separation anxiety expressions of discomfort, such as crying, when separated from an attachment figure

social referencing an infant's use of others' facial expressions as a guide to his or her own emotions

be available or reliable, the child's expectation of rebuff or affection, and the child's sense of assurance that the other is really a safe base for exploration. The internal model begins to be formed late in the child's first year of life and becomes increasingly elaborated and better established through the first 4 or 5 years. By age 5, most children have clear internal models of the mother (or other primary caregiver), a self model, and a model of relationships. Once formed, such models shape and explain experiences and affect memory and attention. Children notice and remember experiences that fit their models and miss or forget experiences that don't match. As Piaget might say, a child more readily *assimilates* data that fit the model. More importantly, the model affects the child's behavior: The child tends to re-create, in each new relationship, the pattern with which he is familiar.

● ***Secure and Insecure Attachments*** ●   Variations in the quality of the first attachment relationship are now almost universally described using Ainsworth's category system (Ainsworth et al., 1978). The Ainsworth system distinguishes between secure attachment and two types of insecure attachment, which psychologists assess using a procedure called the *Strange Situation*.

The Strange Situation consists of a series of eight episodes played out in a laboratory setting, typically with children between 12 and 18 months of age. The child is observed in each of the following situations:

- With the mother
- With the mother and a stranger
- Alone with the stranger
- Completely alone for a few minutes
- Reunited with the mother
- Alone again
- With the stranger again
- Reunited with the mother

Ainsworth suggested that children's reactions in these situations—particularly to the reunion episodes—showed attachment of one of three types: **secure attachment**, **insecure/avoidant attachment**, and **insecure/ambivalent attachment**. More recently, developmentalists have suggested a fourth type: **insecure/disorganized attachment** (Main & Solomon, 1990).

Whether a child cries when he is separated from his mother is not a helpful indicator of the security of his attachment. Some securely attached infants cry then, others do not: the same is true of insecurely attached infants. It is the entire pattern of the child's response to the Strange Situation that is critical, not any one response. These attachment types have been observed in studies in many different countries, and secure attachment is the most common pattern in every country.

● ***Origins of Secure and Insecure Attachments*** ●   Studies of parent-child interactions suggest that one crucial ingredient for secure attachment is *emotional availability* on the part of the primary caregiver (Biringen, 2000). An emotionally available caregiver is one who is able and willing to form an emotional attachment to the infant. For example, economically or emotionally distressed parents may be so distracted by their own problems that they can't invest emotion in the parent-infant relationship. Such parents may be able to meet the baby's physical needs but unable to respond emotionally.

Contingent responsiveness is another key ingredient of secure attachment (Isabella, 1995; Pederson & Moran, 1995; Pederson et al., 1990; Seifer, Schiller, Sameroff, Resnick, & Riordan, 1996). Parents who demonstrate contingent responsiveness are sensitive to the child's cues and respond appropriately. They smile when the baby smiles, talk to the baby when he vocalizes, pick him up when he cries, and

secure attachment a pattern of attachment in which an infant readily separates from the parent, seeks proximity when stressed, and uses the parent as a safe base for exploration

insecure/avoidant attachment a pattern of attachment in which an infant avoids contact with the parent and shows no preference for the parent over other people

insecure/ambivalent attachment a pattern of attachment in which the infant shows little exploratory behavior, is greatly upset when separated from the mother, and is not reassured by her return or efforts to comfort him

insecure/disorganized attachment a pattern of attachment in which an infant seems confused or apprehensive and shows contradictory behavior, such as moving toward the mother while looking away from her

so on (Ainsworth & Marvin, 1995). Infants of parents who display contingent responsiveness in the early months are more likely to be securely attached at age 12 months (Heinicke et al., 2000).

A low level of parental responsiveness thus appears to be an ingredient in any type of insecure attachment. However, each of the several subvarieties of insecure attachment are affected by additional distinct factors. For example, if the mother rejects the infant or regularly withdraws from contact with her, the baby is more likely to show an avoidant pattern of attachment, although the pattern also seems to occur when the mother is overly intrusive or overly stimulating toward the infant (Isabella, 1995). An ambivalent pattern is more common when the primary caregiver is inconsistently or unreliably available to the child. A disorganized/disoriented pattern seems especially likely when the child has been abused, and in families in which either parent had some unresolved trauma in his or her own childhood, such as abuse or a parent's early death (Cassidy & Berlin, 1994; Main & Hesse, 1990).

● **Stability of Attachment Classification** ● Researchers have found that the quality of a child's attachment can be either consistent or changeable. It seems that, when a child's family environment or life circumstances are reasonably consistent, the security or insecurity of her attachment also seems to remain consistent, even over many years (Hamilton, 1995; Wartner, Grossman, Fremmer-Bombik, & Suess, 1994). However, when a child's circumstances change in some major way—such as when the parents divorce or the family moves—the security of the child's attachment may change as well, either from secure to insecure, or the reverse. For example, in one important study, developmentalists followed one group of middle-class white children from age 1 to age 21 (Waters, Treboux, Crowell, Merrick, & Albersheim, 1995). Those whose attachment classification changed over this long interval had nearly all experienced some major upheaval, such as the death of a parent, physical or sexual abuse, or a serious illness.

The fact that the security of a child's attachment can change over time does not refute the notion of attachment as arising from an internal model. Bowlby suggested that for the first 2 or 3 years, the particular pattern of attachment a child shows is in some sense a property of each specific relationship. For example, studies of toddlers' attachments to mothers and fathers show that about 30% of the children are securely attached to one parent and insecurely attached to the other, with both possible combinations equally likely (Fox, Kimmerly, & Schafer, 1991). It is the quality of each relationship that determines the security of the child's attachment to that specific adult. If the relationship changes markedly, the security of attachment may change, too. But, Bowlby argued, by age 4 or 5, the internal model becomes more a property of the child, more generalized across relationships, and thus more resistant to change. At that point, the child tends to impose the model on new relationships, including relationships with teachers or peers.

Long-Term Consequences of Attachment Quality

Ainsworth's classification system has proven to be extremely helpful in predicting a remarkably wide range of other behaviors in infants, children, adolescents, and adults. Dozens of studies show that children rated as securely attached to their mothers in infancy are later more sociable, more positive in their behavior toward friends and siblings, less clinging and dependent on teachers, less aggressive and disruptive, more empathetic, and more emotionally mature in their interactions in school and other settings outside the home (e.g., Carlson & Sroufe, 1995; Jacobsen, Husa, Fendrich, Kruesi, & Ziegenhain, 1997; Leve & Fagor, 1995).

Adolescents who were rated as securely attached in infancy or who are classed as secure on the basis of interviews in adolescence are also more socially skilled, have more intimate friendships, are more likely to be rated as leaders, and have higher self-esteem and better grades (Black & McCartney, 1995; Jacobsen & Hofmann, 1997; Lieberman, Doyle, & Markiewicz, 1995; Ostoja, McCrone, Lehn, Reed, & Sroufe, 1995). Those with insecure attachments—particularly those with avoidant attachments—not only have less positive and supportive friendships in adolescence, they are also more likely to become sexually active early and to practice riskier sex (O'Beirne & Moore, 1995; Sroufe, Carlson, & Schulman, 1993; Urban, Carlson, Egeland, & Sroufe, 1991).

Quality of attachment in infancy also predicts sociability through early, middle, and late adulthood (Van Lange, DeBruin, Otten, & Joireman, 1997). Moreover, one study found a link between attachment history and sexual dysfunction in adult males (Kinzl, Mangweth, Traweger, & Biebl, 1996). In fact, that investigation found that quality of attachment in infancy predicted sexual dysfunction in adulthood better than a history of sexual abuse did.

Developmentalists have also begun to examine the question of whether an adult's internal model of attachment affects his or her parenting behaviors (Crittenden, Partridge, & Claussen, 1991). To answer this question, psychologists have devised an interview that allows them to classify the security or insecurity of an adult's attachment to his or her parents (Main & Hesse, 1990). In this interview, adults are asked about their childhood experiences and their current relationship with their parents. For example, one question asks the adult to choose five adjectives to describe her relationship with each parent and to say why she chose each adjective. On the basis of the interview, the adult's internal model of attachment is assigned to one of three categories.

Adults in the *secure/autonomous/balanced* category value attachment relations and see their early experiences as influential, but they are objective in describing both good and bad qualities of their parents. They speak coherently about early experiences and have thought about what motivated their parents' behavior. Those in the *dismissing/detached* category minimize the importance or the effects of early experiences. Many of these adults idealize their parents, perhaps even denying the existence of any negative experiences, and emphasize their own personal strengths. *Preoccupied/enmeshed* adults often talk about inconsistent or role-reversed parenting. These individuals are still engrossed in their relationships with their parents, still actively struggling to please them or still very angry at them. They are confused and ambivalent, but still engaged.

When researchers study the security of attachment displayed by the children of adults in each of these three categories, the expected patterns emerge strongly. Adults with secure attachment to their own parents are much more likely to have infants or toddlers with secure attachment. Those with dismissing attachment are more likely to have infants with avoidant attachment; adults with preoccupied attachment are more likely to have infants with ambivalent attachment. Across 20 studies, the typical finding was that three-quarters of the mother-infant pairs shared the same attachment category (van IJzendoorn, 1995). One researcher has even found marked consistency across three generations: grandmothers, young mothers, and infants (Benoit & Parker, 1994).

Clearly, a mother's (or other primary caregiver's) behavior toward her child varies as a function of her own internal model of attachment. Mothers who are themselves securely attached are more responsive and sensitive in their behavior toward their infants or young children (Hammond, Landry, Swank, & Smith, 2000; van IJzendoorn, 1995). For example, securely attached mothers are more likely to prepare their children ahead of time for an anticipated separation (Crowell & Feldman, 1988). These mothers also have less anxiety themselves about the separation and are most physically responsive to the child at reunion. Preoccupied mothers tend to be more anxious about separating from their children and to prepare them less well than secure mothers do. Dismissing mothers also prepare the child very little, but leave without difficulty and remain physically distant from their children after they are reunited.

Mothers with dismissing or preoccupied internal models also appear to interpret children's behavior very differently than the secure mothers do. For example, in one study, a mother observed her crying child through the observation window and said, "See, she isn't upset about being left." At reunion, she said to the child, "Why are you crying? I didn't leave" (Crowell & Feldman, 1991, p. 604). Thus, the mother's own internal model not only affects her actual behavior but affects the meaning she ascribes to the child's behavior, both of which will affect the child's developing model of attachment.

Examinations of the long-term consequences of quality of attachment suggest that both psychoanalysts and ethologists are correct in their assumption that the attachment relationship becomes the foundation for future social relationships. Certainly, it appears to be critical to the relationship most similar to it—the relationship an individual ultimately develops with her or his own child.

Before going on

- Describe the effects of synchrony on parent-infant relations.

- What are the three phases of attachment and the behaviors that are associated with them?

- Define the four types of attachment and discuss their origins and stability.

- What are the long-term consequences of attachment quality?

Personality, Temperament, and Self-Concept

Psychologists typically use the word **personality** to describe patterns in the way children and adults relate to the people and objects in the world around them. Individual differences in personality appear to develop throughout childhood and adolescence, based on a basic set of behavioral and emotional predispositions present at birth (McCrae, Costa, Ostendord, & Angleitner, 2000). These predispositions are usually referred to as **temperament** (Rothbart, Ahadi, & Evans, 2000).

Critical Thinking

How would you describe your own temperament as a child? Is your adult personality similar to the temperament you displayed in childhood?

Dimensions of Temperament

Psychologists who study infant temperament have yet to agree on a basic set of temperament dimensions. One influential early theory, proposed by Thomas and Chess, listed nine dimensions: activity level, rhythmicity, approach/withdrawal, adaptability to new experience, threshold of responsiveness, intensity of reaction, quality of mood

personality a pattern of responding to people and objects in the environment

temperament inborn predispositions such as activity level that form the foundations of personality

(positive or negative), distractibility, and persistence (Thomas & Chess, 1977). Thomas and Chess further proposed that variations in these nine qualities tended to cluster into three types, which they called the *easy child*, the *difficult child*, and the *slow-to-warm-up child*. In contrast, Buss and Plomin have argued for three basic temperament dimensions: activity level, emotionality, and sociability (Buss, 1989; Buss & Plomin, 1984, 1986). The questionnaire they devised to measure these three dimensions has been widely used by researchers studying infants, children, and adults.

Despite such disagreements, a few key dimensions are now appearing in lists compiled by many researchers who study infant temperament (Ahadi & Rothbart, 1994; Belsky, Hsieh, & Crnic, 1996; Kagan, 1994; Martin, Wisenbaker, & Huttunen, 1994). *Activity level* refers to an infant's tendency to either move often and vigorously or remain passive or immobile. *Approach/positive emotionality* is a tendency to move toward rather than away from people, new things, or objects, usually accompanied by positive emotion. (This dimension is similar to what Buss and Plomin call *sociability*.) *Inhibition*—a tendency to respond with fear or withdrawal to new people, new situations, new objects—is the flip side of approach. *Negative emotionality* is a tendency to respond to frustrating circumstances with anger, fussing, loudness, or irritability. Finally, *effortful control/task persistence* is an ability to stay focused, to manage attention and effort.

Origins and Stability of Temperament

Because temperamental differences appear so early in life, even during the prenatal period (see Chapter 3), it may seem that genes are entirely responsible for them. However, research suggests that both nature and nurture contribute to individual differences in temperament.

● *Heredity* ● Clear, strong evidence, both from studies of adult personality and from studies of children's temperament, supports the assertion that temperamental differences are inborn (Goldsmith, Buss, & Lemery, 1995; Rose, 1995). Studies of twins in many countries show that identical twins are more alike in their temperament than are fraternal twins (Rose, 1995). For example, one group of researchers studied 100 pairs of identical twins and 100 pairs of fraternal twins at both 14 and 20 months. At each age, the children's temperaments were rated by their mothers using the Buss and Plomin categories. In addition, each child's level of behavioral inhibition was measured by observing how the child reacted to strange toys and a strange adult in a special laboratory playroom. Did the child approach the novel toys quickly and eagerly or hang back or seem fearful? Did the child approach the strange adult or remain close to the mother? The correlations between temperament scores on all four of these dimensions were consistently higher for identical than for fraternal twins, indicating a strong genetic effect (Emde et al., 1992; Plomin et al., 1993).

Many temperament theorists take the argument a step further and trace the basic differences in behavior to variations in underlying physiological patterns (e.g., Gunnar, 1994; Rothbart, Derryberry, & Posner, 1994). For example, Jerome Kagan has suggested that differences in behavioral inhibition are based on differing thresholds for arousal in the parts of the brain that control responses to uncertainty—the amygdala and the hypothalamus (Kagan, 1994; Kagan, Reznick, & Snidman, 1990; Kagan, Snidman, & Arcus, 1993). Arousal of these parts of the brain leads to increases in muscle tension and heart rate. Shy or inhibited children are thought to have a low threshold for such a reaction. That is, they more readily become tense and alert in the presence of uncertainty, perhaps even interpreting a wider range of situations as uncertain. What we inherit, then, according to this view, is not "shyness" or some equivalent, but a tendency for the brain to react in particular ways (Davidson, 1994).

● *Environment* ●   The child's experiences play a crucial role in personality development as well. A number of temperament-environment interactions tend to strengthen built-in qualities. For one thing, people of all ages choose their experiences, a process Sandra Scarr refers to as **niche-picking** (Scarr & McCartney, 1983). Our choices reflect our temperaments. For example, highly sociable children seek out contact with others; children low on the activity dimension are more likely to choose sedentary activities such as puzzles or board games than baseball.

Similarly, temperament may affect how a child interprets a given experience—a factor that helps to account for the fact that two children in the same family may experience the family's patterns of interaction and situation quite differently. Imagine, for example, a family that moves often, such as a military family. If one child in this family has a strong built-in pattern of behavioral inhibition, the myriad changes and new experiences will trigger repetitive fear responses. This child comes to anticipate each new move with dread and is likely to interpret his family life as highly stressful. A second child in the same family, with a more strongly approach-oriented temperament, will find the many moves stimulating and energizing and is likely to think of his childhood in a much more positive light.

A third environmental factor that tends to reinforce built-in temperamental patterns is the tendency of parents and others to respond quite differently to children, depending on the children's temperaments. The sociable child, who may smile often, is likely to elicit more smiles and more positive interactions with parents, simply because she has reinforced their behavior by her positive temperament. Buss and Plomin have proposed the general argument that children in the middle range on temperament dimensions typically adapt to their environment, while those children whose temperaments are extreme—for example, extremely difficult children—force their environments to adapt to them (Buss & Plomin, 1984). Parents of difficult children, for example, may adapt to the children's negativity by punishing them more and providing them with less support and stimulation than do parents of more adaptable children (Luster, Boger, & Hannan, 1993).

However, although it is borne out by observations of children, Buss and Plomin's proposal doesn't convey the additional complexities of personality development. First of all, sensitive and responsive parents can moderate the more extreme forms of infant or child temperament. For example, a series of investigations involving a group of highly inhibited toddlers who differed in the security of their attachment to their mothers revealed that insecurely attached and inhibited toddlers showed the usual physiological responses to challenging or novel situations. In contrast, securely attached and inhibited toddlers showed no such indications of physiological arousal in the face of novelty or challenge (Colton et al., 1992; Gunnar, 1994; Nachmias, 1993). Thus, the secure attachment appears to have modified a basic physiological/temperamental style. Over time, secure attachment may shift the child's personality pattern away from extreme inhibition or shyness. Such findings suggest that, while many forces in the environment reinforce children's basic temperaments, other forces can push them toward new patterns or enable them to control temperamental extremes.

Most researchers who study temperament in infants assume that these dispositions persist through childhood and into adulthood. No one proposes that initial temperamental dispositions remain unchanged by experience. However, if temperament patterns create a kind of "bias" toward particular behaviors, there should be a fair amount of stability of temperament over time. Such stability ought to show itself in the form of at least modest correlations between measures of a given temperamental dimension at different ages.

Although the results of research are somewhat mixed, there is growing evidence of consistency in temperamental ratings over rather long periods of infancy and childhood. For example, Australian researchers studying a group of 450 children found that mothers' reports of children's irritability, cooperation/manageability, inflexibility, rhythmicity, persistence, and tendency to approach rather than avoid

niche-picking the process of selecting experiences on the basis of temperament

contact were all quite consistent from infancy through age 8 (Pedlow, Sanson, Prior, & Oberklaid, 1993). Similarly, in an American longitudinal study of a group of children from age 1 through 12, psychologists found strong consistency in parents' reports of their children's overall "difficultness" as well as approach versus withdrawal, positive versus negative mood, and activity level (Guerin & Gottfried, 1994a, 1994b). Other research suggests that temperamental differences are stable from the preschool years into adulthood (Caspi, 2000).

Researchers have also found considerable consistency at various ages in Kagan's measure of inhibition, which is based on direct observation of the child's behavior rather than on the mother's ratings of the child's temperament. In one study, for example, children who had been classified as inhibited at 4 months were less socially responsive to both adults and children at age 2 than unhibited peers (Young, Fox & Zahn-Waxler, 1999). In Kagan's own longitudinal study, half of the children who had shown high levels of crying and motor activity in response to a novel situation when they were 4 months old were still classified as highly inhibited at age 8, and three-fourths of those rated as uninhibited at 4 months remained in that category 8 years later (Kagan et al., 1993).

Thus, babies who approach the world around them with some eagerness and with a positive attitude continue to be more positive as children; babies who show a high level of behavioral inhibition are quite likely to continue to show such "shyness" at later ages. Similarly, cranky, or temperamentally difficult, babies continue to show many of the same temperamental qualities 10 years later (Kagan et al., 1993).

Temperament and Attachment

The general timing of the development of attachment behaviors is the same for virtually all children. However, the emotional intensity of the attachment relationship varies considerably from child to child. For example, infants differ widely in how much fear they show toward strangers or in novel situations. Some of this difference may reflect basic temperamental variations (Kagan, 1994). Heightened fearfulness may also be a temporary response to some upheaval or stress in the child's life, such as the family's recent move or a parent's changing jobs. Whatever the origin of such variations in fearfulness, heightened fearfulness does eventually disappear in most toddlers, typically by the middle of the second year.

Individual differences in infant temperament may also be related to security of attachment. Generally speaking, easy infants, as defined by Thomas and Chess, are more likely to be securely attached than babies in those theorists' other two categories (Goldsmith & Alansky, 1987; Seifer et al., 1996; Vaughn et al., 1992). The relationship makes sense if you think about the traits of difficult infants and slow-to-warm-up ones. Difficult infants actively resist comfort; consequently, synchrony may lead a parent to make less effort to establish a nurturing relationship with a difficult infant. Likewise, slow-to-warm-up babies are less responsive to parental behaviors directed toward them. Once again, synchrony causes the parents of these unresponsive infants to reduce the frequency of behaviors directed toward them. The result is that the kind of give-and-take relationships most easy infants experience with their parents never develop for babies who are difficult or slow-to-warm-up (Kagan, 1989).

It's important to remember, however, that a correlation is just a correlation—it is certainly not the case that all easy infants develop secure attachment or that all babies of the other two temperament categories are insecurely attached. In fact, the majority of infants in all three temperament categories are securely attached (van IJzendoorn, Goldberg, Kroonenberg, & Frenkel, 1992). In addition, if infant temperament dictated attachment quality, researchers wouldn't expect to see infants who are securely attached to one parent but insecurely attached to the other. In reality, this is a very common research finding (e.g., Goossens & van IJzendoorn, 1990).

For these reasons, developmentalists propose that it is not temperament, per se, that influences attachment. Rather, it is the **goodness-of-fit** between an infant's temperament and his or her environment (Thomas & Chess, 1977). For example, if the parents of an irritable baby boy are good at tolerating his irritability and persist in establishing a synchronous relationship with him, then his irritability doesn't lead to the development of an insecure attachment.

Self-Concept

During the same months when a baby is creating an internal model of attachment and expressing her own unique temperament, she is also developing an internal model of self. Freud suggested that the infant needed to develop a sense of separateness from her mother before she could form a sense of self. Piaget emphasized that the infant's understanding of the basic concept of object permanence was a necessary precursor for the child's attaining self-permanence. Both of these aspects of early self-development reappear in current descriptions of the emergence of the sense of self (Lewis, 1990, 1991).

Research that has examined babies' ability to recognize themselves suggests that self-awareness develops in the middle of the second year.
(*Photo:* Ray Ellis, Photo Researchers)

● **The Subjective Self** ● The child's first task is to figure out that he is separate from others and that this separate self endures over time and space. Developmentalists call this aspect of the self-concept the **subjective self,** or sometimes the *existential self,* because the key awareness seems to be "I exist." The roots of this understanding lie in the myriad everyday interactions the baby has with the objects and people in his world that lead him to understand during the first 2–3 months of life that he can have effects on things (Lewis, 1991). For example, when the child touches a mobile, it moves; when he cries, someone responds; when he smiles, his mother smiles back. Through this process, the baby separates self from everything else and a sense of "I" begins to emerge.

By the time the infant has constructed a fairly complete understanding of object permanence, at about 8–12 months, the subjective self has fully emerged. Just as he is figuring out that Mom and Dad continue to exist when they are out of sight, he is figuring out—at least in some preliminary way—that he exists separately and has some permanence.

● **The Objective Self** ● The second major task is for the toddler to come to understand that she is also an object in the world (Lewis, 1991). Just as a ball has properties—roundness, the ability to roll, a certain feel in the hand—so the "self" also has qualities or properties, such as gender, size, a name, or qualities such as shyness or boldness, coordination or clumsiness. It is this self-awareness that is the hallmark of the second aspect of identity, the **objective self,** sometimes called the **categorical self,** because once the child achieves self-awareness the process of defining the self involves placing oneself in a whole series of categories.

It has not been easy to determine just when a child has developed the initial self-awareness that delineates the formation of the objective self. The most commonly used procedure involves a mirror. First, the baby is placed in front of a mirror, just to see how she behaves. Most infants between about 9 and 12 months old will look at their own images, make faces, or try to interact with the baby in the mirror in some way. After allowing this free exploration for a time, the experimenter, while pretending to wipe the baby's face with a cloth, puts a spot of rouge on the baby's nose, and then lets the baby look in the mirror again. The crucial test of self-recognition, and thus of awareness of the self, is whether the baby reaches for the spot on her own nose, rather than the nose on the face in the mirror.

goodness-of-fit the degree to which an infant's temperament is adaptable to his or her environment, and vice versa

subjective self an infant's awareness that she or he is a separate person who endures through time and space and can act on the environment

objective (categorical) self the toddler's understanding that she or he is defined by various categories such as gender or qualities such as shyness

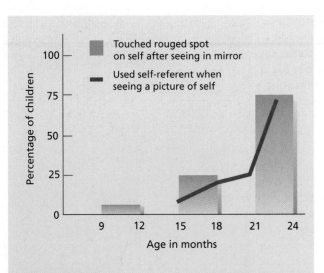

FIGURE 5.1

Mirror recognition and self-naming develop at almost exactly the same time. (*Source*: Lewis & Brooks, 1978, pp. 214-215.)

The results of a classic study using this procedure are graphed in Figure 5.1. As you can see, few of the 9- to 12-month-old children in this study touched their own noses, but three-quarters of the children aged 21 months showed that level of self-recognition, a result confirmed in a variety of other research studies, including studies in Europe (Asendorpf, Warkentin, & Baudonniere, 1996; Lewis & Brooks, 1978). Figure 5.1 also shows the rate at which children refer to themselves by name when they are shown a picture of themselves, which is another commonly used measure of self-awareness. You can see that this development occurs at almost exactly the same time as self-recognition in a mirror. Both are present by about the middle of the second year of life, a finding confirmed by other investigators (Bullock & Lutkenhaus, 1990). At this point, toddlers begin to show a newly proprietary attitude ("Mine!") toward toys or other treasured objects.

Research examining the development of self-awareness suggests that the "terrible twos" is a rather unfortunate term that can lead to misunderstanding of young children's behavior. Instead of applying negative labels to behavior that is assumed to represent willful defiance, parents and other caregivers should understood the self-oriented behavior of 2-year-olds as an outgrowth of self-awareness. Such understanding may not make it any easier to live with a 2-year-old, but it can lead to more positive interactions between parents and child.

As self-awareness develops, infants begin to refer to themselves by name and, near the end of the second year, to label themselves as boys or girls. In addition, infants recognize that they belong to the "child" category. They also use categorical terms such as "good" and "big" to describe themselves. For example, a girl might say "good girl" when she obeys her parent or "big girl" when she is successful at a task like using the toilet (Stipek, Gralinski, & Kopp, 1990).

In Bowlby's language, a child apparently creates an internal model of self, just as he creates an internal model of relationships. He first learns that he exists separately and that he has effects on the world. Then he begins to understand that he is also an object in the world, with properties including gender and age. The internal model of self, or the *self-scheme*, as it is often labeled, is not developed fully at age 2. But the toddler is already building up an image of himself, his qualities, and his abilities. Like the internal model of attachment, this self-model, or self-scheme, affects the choices the toddler makes—such as choosing to play with other children of the same gender—and influences the way he interprets experiences. Thus, the internal model is strengthened and tends to endure.

● ***The Emotional Self*** ●   Development of the *emotional self* begins when the baby learns to identify changes in emotion expressed in others' faces. Before about 2 months of age, babies seem to look mostly at the edges of adults' faces (the hairline and the chin); after 2 months, they seem to look more at the features nearer the center, particularly the eyes. At this point, infants begin to respond differently to various emotional expressions. For example, when her mother expresses happiness, a 10-week-old baby looks happy and interested and gazes at the mother. When the mother expresses sadness, the baby shows increased mouth movements or looks away. When the mother expresses anger, some babies cry; others display a "frozen" look (Haviland and Lelwica, 1987). These responses seem to be not merely imitation, but rather responses to the parent's specific emotions.

By 5–7 months, babies respond differently to strangers' faces that display different emotions as well as to voices speaking with varying emotional tones (Balaban,

1995). They can tell the difference between happy and sad voices and can distinguish happy, surprised, angry, fearful, interested, and sad faces (Soken & Pick, 1999; Walker-Andrews & Lennon, 1991). Near the end of the first year, infants react to another infant's neutral facial expression by actively trying to elicit an emotional expression from that child (Striano & Rochat, 1999). Just as adults often work at getting a baby to smile at them, babies seem to be following the same sort of script by 8–10 months of age.

As the infant's understanding of self advances, it is matched by parallel progressions in expression of emotions. At birth, infants have different facial expressions for interest, pain, and disgust, and an expression that conveys enjoyment develops very quickly. By the time a baby is 2–3 months old, adult observers can also distinguish expressions of anger and sadness, with expressions of fear appearing by 6 or 7 months (Izard et al., 1995; Izard & Harris, 1995). However, it is only in the middle of the second year of life, at about the same time that a child shows self-recognition in the mirror, that such self-conscious emotional expressions as embarrassment, pride, or shame emerge—all of which involve some aspect of self-evaluation (Lewis, Allesandri, & Sullivan, 1992; Lewis, Sullivan, Stanger, & Weiss, 1989; Mascolo & Fischer, 1995).

This baby's emotional reaction is best described as joy or delight rather than pride; her sense of self is not yet well-enough developed that she can feel pride in learning to walk. (*Photo:* Stone)

Before going on

- What is the difference between personality and temperament?

- On which dimensions of temperament do most developmentalists agree?

- Discuss the roles of heredity and environment in the formation of temperament.

- Is temperament consistent over time?

- How do the subjective self, the objective self, and the emotional self develop during the first 2 years?

Effects of Nonparental Care

In virtually every industrialized country in the world, women have entered the workforce in great numbers in the past two decades. In the United States, the change has been particularly rapid and massive: In 1970, only 18% of U.S. married women with children under age 6 were in the labor force; by the mid-1990s, 61.7% of such women (and more than half of women with children under age 1) were working outside the home at least part-time, a rate that appears to be higher than that in any other country (Cherlin, 1992a; U.S. Bureau of the Census, 1995). The younger children are, the less likely they are to receive nonparental care. However, even among U.S. infants under the age of 12 months, almost half are cared for by someone other than a parent at least part-time (National Institute of Child Health and Human Development [NICHD] Early Child Care Research

T he majority of infants in the United States now experience at least some nonparental care. (*Photo:* Lawrence Migdale, Photo Researchers)

Network, 1998). The key question for psychologists is, what effect does such nonparental care have on infants and young children?

Difficulties in Studying Nonparental Care

It might seem that the effect on infant development of this trend toward nonparental care could easily be determined by comparing babies receiving nonparental care to those cared for by their parents. However, both "nonparental care" and "parental care" are really complex interactions among numerous variables rather than single factors whose effects can be studied independently. Thus, interpretation of research on nonparental care has to take into account a variety of issues.

First, an enormous range of different care arrangements are all lumped under the general title of "nonparental care." Infants who are cared for by grandparents in their own homes as well as those who are enrolled in day-care centers receive nonparental care. In addition, infants enter these care arrangements at different ages, and they remain in them for varying lengths of time. Some have the same nonparental caregiver over many years; others shift often from one care setting to another. Moreover, nonparental care varies widely in quality.

Furthermore, even distinguishing among the various types of care arrangements does not begin to convey the numerous hybrid solutions parents arrive at in seeking alternative care for their children (Clarke-Stewart, Gruber, & Fitzgerald, 1994). For example, in one national survey, between a quarter and a third of employed mothers reported that their children were in some type of combined care, such as family day care some of the time and care by a relative part of the time (Folk & Yi, 1994). (In *family day care* a person takes care of other parents' children in her own home.) The majority of researchers have studied only children in day-care centers in the United States. It is not known whether these findings will generalize to children in family day care or to children who are given at-home care by someone other than a parent. Moreover, it's not clear whether the results of these studies apply to other cultures.

Child care arrangements seem to be becoming somewhat more homogeneous in the United States. During the early 1990s, the most common pattern—especially for infants and toddlers—was for a child to be cared for in his own home, by the father, another relative, or someone employed for that purpose. Family day care was a close second, and use of day-care centers was actually one of the least common arrangements (U.S. Bureau of the Census, 1995). However, by the mid-1990s, more than half of all 3- to 5-year-olds receiving nonparental care were enrolled in some kind of day-care center or nursery school (National Center for Education Statistics, 1998). Although home-based and family day care arrangements continue to be more common for children under age 3, enrollment of infants and toddlers in day-care facilities has also become considerably more common since the early 1990s. If this trend continues, it may become easier to study the effects of nonparental care.

However, families who place their children in nonparental care are different in a whole host of ways from those who care for their children primarily at home. How can researchers be sure that effects attributed to nonparental care are not instead the result of these other family differences? Mothers also differ in their attitudes toward the care arrangements they have made. Some mothers with children in nonparental care would far rather be at home taking care of their children; others are happy to be working. Similarly, some mothers who are at home full-time would rather be working and some are delighted to be at home. Some studies suggest that children show more positive reactions to their situations when the mother is satisfied with her situation, whether she is working or at home (e.g., DeMeis, Hock, & McBride, 1986; Greenberger & Goldberg, 1989). However, most studies of the effects of non-parental care offer no information at all about the mother's level of satisfaction with her situation.

Most of the research on nonparental versus parental care has not taken these complexities into account. Researchers have frequently compared children "in day care" with those "reared at home" and assumed that any differences between the two groups were attributable to the day-care experience. Recent studies are often better, but clear answers to even the most basic questions about the impact of nonparental care on children's development are still not available. Nonetheless, because the issue is so critical, you need to be aware of what is and is not yet known.

Effects on Cognitive Development

There is a good deal of evidence that high-quality, cognitively enriched day care has beneficial effects on many children's overall cognitive development. This effect is particularly strong for children from poor families, who show significant and lasting gains in IQ and later school performance after attending highly enriched day care throughout infancy and early childhood (Campbell & Ramey, 1994; Ramey, 1993). Even middle-class children show some cognitive benefit when they are in high-quality day care (Peisner-Feinberg, 1995).

However, the picture is not entirely rosy. Several studies in the United States point to possible negative effects of day-care experience on cognitive development in some children, perhaps middle-class children especially. For example, in one large study of over 1,000 preschoolers, researchers found that white children—but not African American children—who had entered day care in the first year of life had lower vocabulary scores than those who had entered after age 1 (Baydar & Brooks-Gunn, 1991). Conversely, in a large study of 5- and 6-year-olds, researchers found that children from poor families who began day care before age 1 had higher reading and math scores at the start of school than did children from middle-class families who entered day care in infancy (Caughy, DiPietro, & Strobino, 1994).

How can these conflicting findings be reconciled? One fairly straightforward possibility is that the crucial issue is the discrepancy between the level of stimulation the child would receive at home and the quality of the child care. When a particular day-care setting for a given child provides more enrichment than the child would have received at home, then day-care attendance has some beneficial cognitive effects; when day care is less stimulating than full-time home care would be for that child, then day care has negative effects. However, there are not yet enough well-designed, large studies to make developmentalists confident that this is the right way to conceptualize the process. Consequently, the most that can be said about the effects of non-parental care on cognitive development is that it seems to be beneficial for children from impoverished environments, but research findings are mixed with respect to middle-class children.

Effects on Peer Relations

When researchers look at the impact of day care on children's personalities, they find yet another confusing story. A number of investigators have found that most children in day care are more sociable and more popular and have better peer-play skills than their counterparts reared primarily at home (Andersson, 1989, 1992; Scarr & Eisenberg, 1993). However, at least one researcher has reported finding links between day care and behavior problems at school age (Kim, 1997). Many others find day-care attendance linked to subsequent heightened aggression with peers and lower compliance with teachers and parents.

For example, in one very well-designed large study, developmentalists found that kindergarteners who had spent the most time in day care—in infancy, toddlerhood, or the preschool years—were more aggressive and less popular with their peers at school age than were children who had been reared entirely at home or who had spent fewer years in day care (Bates et al., 1994). Interestingly, the age at which children entered nonparental care—that is, the timing of that care—was less important than the total length of time in nonparental care. Of course, a child's level of aggressiveness in elementary school is influenced by a wide variety of things, including temperament and the effectiveness of the parents' disciplinary techniques, but the fact that day care is implicated in this equation certainly sounds a cautionary note.

Confusing, isn't it? By some measures, children who have been in day care seem to be more socially competent; by other measures, they seem less so. One possible resolution is to look again at the relative quality of care at home versus day care. Some studies have found that what seems to be critical for the child's level of aggression is whether the child spends his daytime hours in an organized, well-structured situation or in a messy, unstimulating one—the unstructured and messy setting is the problem, whether it is at home or in day care (Clarke-Stewart et al., 1994; Field, 1991). If this argument holds, then it is not being in day care itself that leads to later social problems, but the quality of the child's daily experiences.

Effects on Attachment

Can an infant or toddler develop a secure attachment to her mother and father if she is repeatedly separated from them? This question has been at the center of a hot debate. Until the mid-1980s, most psychologists believed that infant day care had no negative effect on attachment. But then developmental psychologist Jay Belsky, in a series of papers and in testimony before a congressional committee, sounded an alarm (Belsky, 1985, 1992; Belsky & Rovine, 1988). Combining data from several studies, he concluded that there was a heightened risk of an insecure attachment for infants who enter day care before their first birthday.

Since that time, a number of other researchers have analyzed the combined results of large numbers of studies and confirmed Belsky's original conclusion. For example, a summary of the findings of 13 different studies involving 897 infants revealed that 35% of infants who had experienced at least 5 hours per week of nonparental care were insecurely attached, compared to 29% of the infants with exclusively maternal care (Lamb, Sternberg, & Prodromidis, 1992). In contrast, a study of more than 1,000 infants found no differences between those who were in nonparental care and those who were cared for at home, regardless of the age at which they entered outside care or how many hours per week they were cared for there (NICHD Early Child Care Research Network, 1998).

The present controversy focuses on how to interpret inconsistencies in day-care research. Some developmentalists argue that there are so many variables affecting attachment that it is impossible to draw any clear conclusion (e.g., Roggman, Langlois, Hubbs-Tait, & Rieser-Danner, 1994). For one thing, mothers who work are different in some ways from mothers who do not: More are single mothers; more find child care onerous.

Developmental psychologist Sandra Scarr, a leading day-care researcher, has suggested that the kind of day care parents choose is an extension of their own characteristics and parenting styles (Scarr, 1997). For example, poorly educated parents may choose day-care arrangements that do not emphasize infant learning. Similarly, parents whose focus is on intellectual development may not place a

Critical Thinking

How do you think the way you were cared for (at home or not, by a parent or by another adult) influenced your development?

Choosing a Day-Care Center

You may be wondering what criteria a parent can use to identify a high-quality day-care setting. Of course, it's important to realize that the "fit" between an infant and her day-care setting is what really matters. Some babies do well no matter where they are cared for or by whom. Others, perhaps those with more difficult temperaments, seem to have problems adjusting to even the best of settings. Consequently, parents can't really judge the quality of a given setting until their babies have spent some time in it. Nevertheless, there are a few general characteristics common to good-quality day-care settings (Clarke-Stewart, 1992; Howes, Phillips, & Whitebook, 1992; Scarr & Eisenberg, 1993):

- *A low teacher/child ratio.* For children younger than 2, the ratio should be no higher than 1:4; for 2- to 3-year-olds, ratios between 1:4 and 1:10 appear to be acceptable.

- *A small group size.* The smaller the number of children cared for together—whether in one room in a day-care center or in a home—the better for the child. For infants, a maximum of 6 to 8 per group appears best; for 1- to 2-year-olds, between 6 and 12 per group; for older children, groups as large as 15 or 20 appear to be acceptable.

- *A clean, colorful space, adapted to child play.* It is not essential to have lots of expensive toys, but the center must offer a variety of activities that children find engaging, organized in a way that encourages play.

- *A daily plan.* The daily curriculum should include some structure, some specific teaching, and some supervised activities. However, too much regimentation is not ideal.

- *Sensitive caregivers.* The adults in the day-care setting should be positive, involved, and responsive to the children, not merely custodial.

- *Knowledgeable caregivers.* Training in child development and infant curriculum development helps caregivers provide a day-care setting that meets criteria for good quality.

---

high priority on the emotional aspects of a particular day-care arrangement. Thus, Scarr claims, day-care effects are likely to be parenting effects in disguise.

The confusion inherent in the mixed findings on non-parental care serves to underline the importance of the quality of child care. A general conclusion that can be drawn is that good-quality care is generally linked with positive or neutral outcomes, while inconsistent or poor-quality care can be actively detrimental to the child. Beyond that, all psychologists can tell parents at this point is that the debate about the effects of nonparental care on children is still an open one (see The Real World).

Before going on

- Why is it difficult to study the effects of nonparental care on development?

- What might be the effects of nonparental care on cognitive development?

- Do children who experience nonparental care develop personalities different from those of children who are cared for at home in infancy?

- What does research suggest about the potential risks of nonparental care with respect to attachment?

Individual and Group Differences

Y ou have already learned that a parent's own internal model of attachment can influence how she or he interacts with an infant. Other variables can also affect infant social and personality development.

Caregiver Characteristics and Attachment

One caregiver variable that predicts attachment quality is age. Adolescent mothers are more likely than older mothers to describe their babies as "difficult" and to be less responsive to them (Miller, Eisenberg, Fabes, & Shell, 1996). Not surprisingly, at school age, children of teen mothers experience emotional difficulties more often than their peers. However, studies suggest that training in child development along with specific instruction on how to interpret an infant's behavior may change this pattern (Culp, Culp, Blankemeyer, & Passmark, 1998; Stockman & Budd, 1997).

Depression is another caregiver characteristic that appears to be related to attachment quality (Murray et al., 1999; Teti, Gelfand, Messinger, & Isabella, 1995). In fact, when mothers are depressed, babies's own facial expressions and behaviors suggest that they feel depressed as well. They smile less, show more sad and angry facial expressions, and seem to be less organized in motor activity and attention (Hart, Jones, Field, & Lundy, 1999).

However, not all depressed mothers interact with their babies in the same way. Some are withdrawn and detached; they look at, touch, or talk to their babies less often than nondepressed mothers do and are less affectionate toward them (Field, 1995; Hart et al., 1999). Children of such mothers are less likely to form a secure attachment with the mother. They are also at higher risk for later behavior problems, including either heightened aggression or withdrawal (Cummings & Davies, 1994; Murray et al., 1999; Teti et al., 1995). Other depressed mothers are overly involved with their infants, often interrupting and overstimulating them. Babies seem to respond to this kind of treatment by withdrawing from both their mothers and others in their environments (Hart et al., 1999). Still other depressed mothers overreact and respond angrily to babies' undesirable behaviors. Infants of these depressed mothers are more likely than others to display aggressive behavior in early childhood (O'Leary, Slep, & Reid, 1999).

Of course, there are many depressed mothers who are just as sensitive and responsive to their babies' needs as those who do not suffer from depression. Infants whose depressed mothers exhibit sensitive parenting behaviors are less likely to display long-term negative effects than are infants with less sensitive depressed mothers (NICHD Early Child Care Research Network, 1999). Further, training can increase the frequency of parents' sensitive behaviors and, as a result, lead to changes in infants' attachment status (van den Boom, 1994, 1995).

As you learned earlier in this chapter, parents who were abused in childhood may have problems forming attachments to their infants (Cassidy & Berlin, 1994; Main & Hesse, 1990). In some cases, these parents fall into the interactional pattern that they themselves experienced with their own parents—namely, an abusive relationship. This may happen when parents adapt poorly to their baby's temperament and become frustrated with their inability to manage the infant effectively.

Stressful living conditions may also contribute to the development of an abusive relationship. Infant abuse is more common in large families, in single-parent households, in families living in poverty or in extremely crowded conditions, and in families in which substance abuse is a problem (Garbarino & Sherman, 1980; Pianta, Egeland, & Erickson, 1989; Sack, Mason, & Higgins, 1985). Even these adverse conditions can be surmounted, though, if the parents have adequate emotional support, either from one another or from other adults.

Preterm and Low-Birth-Weight Infants

For the most part, preterm and low-birth-weight (LBW) babies seem to differ little in attachment pattern from full-term infants (Pederson & Moran, 1996; Wintgens et al., 1998). However, preterm and LBW infants who are very ill, especially those who hover between life and death for many weeks after birth or who have physical deformities, are at significantly greater risk for developing insecure attachments than those who are healthy. This risk arises because parents distance themselves both physically and emotionally from babies who might not live and those who are deformed (Clark & Miles, 1999; Feldman, Weller, Leckman, Kuint, & Eidelman, 1999; Moehn & Rossetti, 1996; Weiss, 1998).

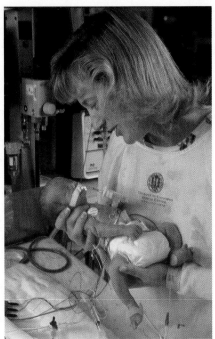

Preterm babies may be less responsive to parents than full-term infants. (*Photo:* Jonathan Nourok, PhotoEdit)

Preterm infants also may display temperamental characteristics that place them at risk for insecure attachment. For example, most are less responsive than full-term infants, and their parents more often become frustrated in attempts to engage them in synchronous social interactions (Lester, Hoffman, & Brazelton, 1985). As a result, these infants are more likely to be insecurely attached and more likely to be abused than are full-term babies (Brockington, 1996; Mangelsdorf et al., 1996).

To further complicate the picture, the insecure attachment itself is an additional risk factor for preterm and LBW infants (Heidt-Kozisek, Pipp-Siegel, Easterbrooks, & Harmon, 1997). Those who are both very ill *and* insecurely attached to parents in infancy are more likely to suffer from developmental problems later in childhood (Andersson & Sommerfelt, 1999; Wintgens et al., 1998). Consequently, health care professionals have devised training programs to help parents establish close relationships with preterm and LBW infants in the early days of their lives and throughout the preschool and grade school years (Brooks-Gunn, Klebanov, Liaw, & Spiler, 1993; McCarton et al., 1997).

Effects of Gender

It is clear that parents treat boys and girls differently beginning in infancy. Some of these differences depend on both the parent's and the baby's sex. For example, parents sing more expressively to same-sex than to opposite-sex infants (Trehub, Hill, & Kamenetsky, 1997). Likewise, mothers maintain more physical and visual contact with infant daughters than with sons (Lindahl & Heimann, 1997). Differences such as these may contribute in some way to the formation of same-sex alliances between parents and children that may be important later in childhood.

Both mothers and fathers demonstrate other kinds of variations in their interactions with boys and girls. For example, temperamental differences between boys and girls are much smaller than the differences *perceived* by parents and other adults. In one classic study, researchers found that adults viewing a videotape of an infant interpreted the baby's behavior differently depending on the gender label experimenters provided. Participants who were told the baby was a girl interpreted a particular behavior as expressing "fear." Amazingly, participants who believed the infant was a boy, labeled the same behavior "anger" (Condry & Condry, 1976). More recent research employing this technique suggests that the current cohort of adults is somewhat less likely to stereotype infant behavior in this way, although, like their counterparts in the 1970s, they attend to and comment on motor activity more when they believe an infant under observation is a boy (Pomperleau, Malcuit, Turgeon, & Cossette, 1997).

Thus, temperamental stereotyping may affect the quality of the parent-infant relationship. For example, a parent of a calm, quiet girl may view her activity level as a sign of "girlness" and respond to her behavior with acceptance and approval. At the same time, parents of a very active boy may tolerate his activity level, or even encourage it, because they regard it as evidence of masculinity. But what about parents of active girls and quiet boys? A parent whose infant girl is very active may work hard to teach her to be less active because of concerns about the sex-appropriateness of her activity level. Likewise, parents of quiet boys may push them to be more active. In the process, such parents may develop a rejecting, disapproving attitude toward their children that generalizes to all aspects of their relationships with them. In this way, stereotypically based ways of responding to infants can lead to differences in quality of attachment.

Research on another dimension of temperament—emotionality—provides another example of gender effects. Most studies have found that even in infancy, girls use gestures and language to express emotions more often than boys do (Kuebli, Butler, & Fivush, 1995). Similarly, girls are more responsive to others' facial expressions (McClure, 2000). These differences often lead to the perception that girls are more emotionally sensitive. However, studies of actual behavior reveal that boys are just as affectionate and empathetic as girls during infancy (Melson, Peet, & Sparks, 1991; Zahn-Waxler, Radke-Yarrow, Wagner, & Chapman, 1992). Nevertheless, a parent's perception of an infant's emotional sensitivity affects how the parent responds to the child. Not surprisingly, then, parents initiate conversations about emotions and emotion-provoking events more often with girls than with boys (Kuebli et al., 1995). But which comes first, girls' greater emotional expressivity or parents' greater willingness to discuss emotions with them? Likewise, are boys less expressive because parents don't frame conversations with them in ways that encourage emotional expression?

Stereotypes notwithstanding, some sex differences in social behavior are quite striking even in infancy. For example, if you observe 2-year-olds playing freely in a room stocked with a wide range of attractive toys, girls are more likely to play with dolls. Boys of this age more often choose to play with guns, toy trucks, or tools (O'Brien, 1992). Psychologists call this behavioral difference **sex-typing**, which is formally defined as the manifestation or adoption of culturally defined sex-appropriate behavior.

However, the question "which comes first?" arises here, too. Do boys and girls have different play preferences because of inborn differences or because their parents, siblings, and others encourage them to behave differently? Clearly, infants' behavior and their parents' reactions to that behavior are difficult variables to separate. Thus, most developmental psychologists believe that parents' stereotypical reactions to male and female infants contribute just as much to the development of sex differences in behavior and personality as any inborn gender-based differences (Halpern, 1997).

Critical Thinking

Make a list of your own personality characteristics. How many of them relate to your gender?

Cross-Cultural Research on Attachment

Studies in a variety of countries (e.g., Posada et al., 1995) support Ainsworth's contention that some form of "secure base behavior" occurs in every child, in every culture. But there is also some evidence suggesting that secure attachments may be more likely in certain cultures than in others. The most thorough analyses have come from some Dutch psychologists who have examined the results of 32 separate studies in eight different countries. (Table 5.1 presents the percentage of babies classified in

sex-typing the manifestation or adoption of culturally defined sex-appropriate behavior

TABLE 5.1   Cross-Cultural Comparisons of Secure and Insecure Attachments

Country	Number of Studies	Attachment Pattern (percentage of children studied)		
		Secure	Avoidant	Ambivalent
West Germany	3	56.6	35.3	8.1
Great Britain	1	75.0	22.2	2.8
The Netherlands	4	67.3	26.3	6.4
Sweden	1	74.5	21.6	3.9
Israel	2	64.4	6.8	28.8
Japan	2	67.7	5.2	25.0
China	1	50.0	25.0	25.0
United States	18	64.8	21.1	14.1
Overall average		65.0	21.3	13.7

(*Source:* Based on Table 1 of van IJzendoorn & Kroonenberg, 1988, pp. 150–151.)

each category for each country (van IJzendoorn & Kroonenberg, 1988). It is important to avoid overinterpreting the information in this table, because in most cases there are only one or two studies from a given country, normally with quite small samples. The single study from China, for example, included only 36 babies. Still, the findings are thought-provoking.

The most striking thing about these data is their consistency. In each of the eight countries, secure attachment is the most common pattern, found in more than half of all babies studied; in six of the eight countries, an avoidant pattern is the more common of the two forms of insecure attachment. Only in Israel and Japan is this pattern significantly reversed. How can developmentalists explain such differences?

One possibility is that the Strange Situation is simply not an appropriate measure of attachment security in all cultures. For example, because Japanese babies are rarely separated from their mothers in the first year of life, being left totally alone in the midst of the Strange Situation may be far more stressful for them and might result in more intense, inconsolable crying and hence a classification of ambivalent attachment. Yet when researchers look directly at toddlers' actual behavior in the Strange Situation, they find few cultural differences in such things as proximity seeking or avoidance of mother—which gives researchers more confidence that the Strange Situation is tapping similar processes among children in many cultures (Sagi, van IJzendoorn, & Koren-Karie, 1991).

It is also possible that what people mean by a "secure" or an "avoidant" pattern is different in different cultures, even if the percentages for the categories are similar. German researchers, for example, have suggested that an insecure-avoidant classification in their culture may not reflect indifference in the mother, but rather explicit training toward greater independence for the baby (Grossmann, Grossmann, Spangler, Suess, & Unzner, 1985). Research in Israel shows that the Strange Situation attachment classification predicts a baby's later social skills in much the same way as it does for U.S. babies, which suggests that the classification system is valid in both cultures (Sagi, 1990). Physically "clingy" behavior in American preschool children is related both to a history of insecure attachment and to emotional disturbance. However, in Japanese children, it is correlated with a secure attachment history and good adjustment at preschool age (Mizuta, Zahn-Waxler, Cole, & Hiruma, 1996).

Ainsworth also observed Bowlby's three phases of attachment formation among children in non-industrialized Uganda, although these children showed a more intense fear of strangers than is usually found in American samples. But in that culture, as in

American and other Western cultures, the mother is the primary caregiver. What would researchers find in a culture in which the child's early care is more communal?

To find out, developmentalists studied a group called the Efe, who forage in the forests of Zaire (Tronick, Morelli, & Ivey, 1992). The Efe live in camps, in small groups of perhaps twenty individuals, each group consisting of several extended families, often brothers and their wives. Infants in these communities are cared for communally in the early months and years of life. They are carried and held by all the adult women, and interact regularly with many different adults. If they have needs, they are tended to by whichever adult or older child is nearby; they may even be nursed by women other than the mother, although they normally sleep with the mother. The researchers reported two things of particular interest about early attachment in this group. First, Efe infants seem to use virtually any adult or older child in their group as a safe base, which suggests that they may have no single central attachment. But, beginning at about 6 months, the Efe infants nonetheless seem to insist on being with their mother more and to prefer her over other women, although other women continue to help with caregiving responsibilities. Thus, even in an extremely communal rearing arrangement, some sign of a central attachment is evident, though perhaps less dominant.

At the moment, the most plausible hypothesis is that the same factors involving mother-infant interaction contribute to secure and insecure attachments in all cultures, and that these patterns reflect similar internal models. But it will take more research in which long-term outcomes for individuals in the various categories are studied before researchers will know whether this is correct.

Before going on

- What variables might affect parents' ability to establish a good fit between their behavior and an infant's temperament?

- How do preterm and LBW infants differ from healthy babies in temperament and attachment?

- How do developmentalists explain sex differences in infants' social and personality development?

- Do infants in different cultures exhibit different attachment patterns?

A Final Word

All developmentalists agree that children create two important internal models during the first 2 years of life. The first is a model of social relationships based on quality of attachment. This model, though somewhat subject to change, influences most, if not all, of an individual's future relationships. The second is a model of self. Unlike the relationship model, however, the self-concept is only just beginning to form in infancy. As you will learn in future chapters, it undergoes significant modification throughout childhood and adolescence.

Summary

Theories of Social and Personality Development

- Freud suggested that individual differences in personality originated in the nursing and weaning practices of infants' mothers. Erikson emphasized the roles of both mothers and fathers, as well as other adults in the infant's environment, in providing for all the infant's needs, thereby instilling a sense of trust concerning the social world.

- Ethologists hypothesize that attachment is the foundation of later personality and social development. They further suggest that the first 2 years of life are a sensitive, or critical, period for the development of attachment.

Attachment

- For parents to form a strong attachment relationship with an infant, what is most crucial is the development of synchrony, a set of mutually reinforcing and interlocking behaviors that characterize most interactions between parent and infant. Fathers as well as mothers form strong bonds with their infants, but fathers show more physically playful behaviors with their children than do mothers.

- Bowlby proposed that the child's attachment to a caregiver develops in three phases, beginning with rather indiscriminate aiming of attachment behaviors toward anyone within reach, through a focus on one or more figures, and finally to "secure base behavior," beginning at about 6 months of age, which signals the presence of a clear attachment.

- Children differ in the security of their first attachments, and thus in the internal models of relationships that they develop. The secure infant uses the parent as a safe base for exploration and can be readily consoled by the parent.

- The security of the initial attachment is reasonably stable, and, later in childhood, securely attached children appear to be more socially skillful, more curious and persistent in approaching new tasks, and more mature. The internal model of attachment that individuals develop in infancy affects how they parent their own babies.

Personality, Temperament, and Self-Concept

- Temperament theorists generally agree on the following basic temperamental dimensions: activity level, approach/positive emotionality, inhibition, negative emotionality, and effortful control/task persistence.

- There is strong evidence that temperamental differences have a genetic component, and that they are at least somewhat stable over infancy and childhood.

However, temperament is not totally determined by heredity or ongoing physiological processes. A child's built-in temperament does shape the child's interactions with the world and affect others' responses to the child.

- Infant temperament may affect security of attachment. However, it is more likely that the goodness-of-fit between an infant's temperament and the ways his environment responds to him is the real basis of correlations between temperament and attachment.

- The infant also begins to develop a sense of self, including the awareness of a separate self and the understanding of self-permanence (which may be collectively called the subjective self) and awareness of herself as an object in the world (the objective self). An emotional self also develops in the first year. The range of emotions babies experience as well as their ability to make use of information about emotions, such as facial expressions, increases dramatically over the first year.

Effects of Nonparental Care

- Comparing parental to nonparental care is difficult because there are so many types of nonparental care arrangements.

- Day care often has positive effects on the cognitive development of less advantaged children, but it may have negative effects on that of more advantaged children if there is a large discrepancy between the home environment and the level of stimulation in day care.

- The impact of day care on children's social relationships is unclear. Some studies show children who spend more time in day care to be more aggressive; others show them to be more socially skillful.

- Some studies show a small difference in security of attachment between children in day care and those reared at home; others suggest that home-care and day-care children do not differ with respect to attachment.

Individual and Group Differences

- Caregiver characteristics such as age, emotional state, and a history of abuse can affect infants' attachment quality.

- Preterm and LBW infants are at greater risk for developing insecure attachments, perhaps because of their temperamental differences from full-term babies or because of frustrations parents experience in attempting to achieve synchrony with them.

- Perceived temperamental differences between boys and girls may affect attachment. Most developmentalists believe that gender differences in infant social development are affected both by biological factors and by parents' beliefs about the differences between boys and girls.

- Studies in many countries suggest that secure attachment is the most common pattern everywhere, but cultures differ in the frequency of different types of insecure attachment.

Key Terms

affectional bond (p. 123)

attachment (p. 123)

attachment theory (p. 123)

goodness-of-fit (p. 135)

insecure/ambivalent attachment (p. 128)

insecure/avoidant attachment (p. 128)

insecure/disorganized attachment (p. 128)

niche-picking (p. 133)

objective (categorical) self (p. 135)

personality (p. 131)

reactive attachment disorder (p. 124)

secure attachment (p. 128)

separation anxiety (p. 127)

sex-typing (p. 144)

social referencing (p. 127)

stranger anxiety (p. 127)

subjective self (p. 135)

synchrony (p. 125)

temperament (p. 131)

CHAPTER

6

Physical and Cognitive Development in Early Childhood

© Jacques Cheney, Woodfin Camp and Associates

Watch a 2-year-old playing near her mom or dad and you'll notice that she glances at her parent regularly, as if checking to make sure the safe base is still there.

Her play is dominated by sensory explorations of objects; she seems motivated to touch and manipulate everything in her environment. In contrast to infants, however, most 2-year-olds have added a new dimension to sensorimotor play—the idea that objects have names. Consequently, almost every object manipulation is accompanied by an important question for nearby adults: "Whazit?" (What is it?) A few years later, by about age 4, sophisticated forms of pretending, such as "dress-up," become the preferred modes of play.

Profound changes in the physical and cognitive domains underlie these shifts in play behavior. In the years from 2 to 6, the period known as *early childhood*, the child changes from a dependent toddler, able to communicate only in very primitive ways, to a remarkably competent, communicative, social creature, ready to begin school.

In this chapter, you will learn about the subtle physical changes and a number of advances in cognitive and language development that happen during early childhood. Furthermore, after reading the chapter, you should have a better understanding of the issues involved in intelligence testing. While you read, keep the following questions in mind:

- What important physical and motor changes happen during early childhood?
- How did Piaget characterize this period, and what does recent research suggest about his theory?
- How does children's language change during the early childhood years?
- What are the strengths and weaknesses of IQ tests?

Physical Changes

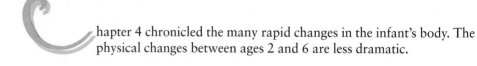

Chapter 4 chronicled the many rapid changes in the infant's body. The physical changes between ages 2 and 6 are less dramatic.

Growth and Motor Development

Changes in height and weight happen far more slowly in the preschool years than in infancy. Each year, the child adds about 2–3 inches in height and about 6 pounds in weight. At the same time, the young child makes steady progress in motor development. The changes are not as dramatic as the beginning of walking, but they enable the child to acquire skills that markedly increase his independence and exploratory ability.

Table 6.1 lists the major locomotor, nonlocomotor, and manipulative skills that emerge in these preschool years. What is most striking are the impressive gains the child makes in large-muscle skills. By age 5 or 6, children are running, jumping, hopping, galloping, climbing, and skipping. They can ride a tricycle; some can ride a two-wheeled bike. The degree of confidence with which the 5-year-old uses her body for these movements is impressive, particularly in contrast to the somewhat unsteady movements of the 18-month-old.

Manipulative skills also improve in these years, but not to the same level of confidence. Three-year-olds can indeed pick up Cheerios, and 5-year-olds can thread beads on a string. But even at age 5 or 6, children are not highly skilled at such fine-motor tasks as using a pencil or crayon or cutting accurately with scissors. When a young child uses a crayon or a pencil, he uses his whole body—the tongue is moving and the whole arm and back are involved in the writing or drawing motion. This is important for teachers to understand; it is the rare kindergartner who is really skilled at such fine-motor tasks.

TABLE 6.1   Milestones of Motor Development from Age 2 to Age 6

Age	Locomotor Skills	Nonlocomotor Skills	Manipulative Skills
18–24 months	Runs (20 months); walks well (24 months); climbs stairs with both feet on each step	Pushes and pulls boxes or wheeled toys; unscrews lid on a jar	Shows clear hand preference; stacks four to six blocks; turns pages one at a time; picks up things without overbalancing
2–3	Runs easily; climbs on furniture unaided	Hauls and shoves big toys around obstacles	Picks up small objects; throws small ball while standing
3–4	Walks upstairs one foot per step; skips on two feet; walks on tiptoe	Pedals and steers tricycle; walks in any direction pulling large toys	Catches large ball between outstretched arms; cuts paper with scissors; holds pencil between thumb and fingers
4–5	Walks up and down stairs one foot per step; stands, runs, and walks on tiptoe		Strikes ball with bat; kicks and catches ball; threads beads on a string; grasps pencil properly
5–6	Skips on alternate feet; walks on a line; slides, swings		Plays ball games well; threads needle and sews large stitches

(*Sources:* Connolly & Dalgleish; 1989; The Diagram Group, 1977; Fagard & Jacquet; 1989; Mathew & Cook, 1990; Thomas, 1990a.)

Βy age 3, most preschoolers can ride a tricycle. (*Photo: Courtesy of Erik Skagestad*)

The Brain and Nervous System

Brain growth, synapse formation, and myelinization continue in early childhood, although at a pace slower than in infancy. However, the slower rate of growth should not be taken to mean that brain development is nearly complete. Indeed, a number of important neurological milestones happen between the ages of 2 and 6. It is likely that these milestones represent the neurological underpinnings of the remarkable advances in thinking and language that occur during this period.

● *Lateralization* ● The **corpus callosum**, the brain structure through which the left and right sides of the cerebral cortex communicate, grows and matures more during the early childhood years than in any other period of life. The growth of this structure accompanies the functional specialization of the left and right hemispheres of the cerebral cortex. This process is called **lateralization**.

Figure 6.1 illustrates how brain functions are lateralized in 95% of humans, a pattern known as *left-brain dominance*. In a small proportion of the remaining 5%, the functions are reversed, a pattern called *right-brain dominance*. However, most people who are not left-brain dominant have a pattern known as *mixed dominance*, with some functions following the typical pattern and others reversed.

Neuroscientists suspect that our genes dictate which functions will be lateralized and which will not be, because some degree of lateralization is already present in the human fetus (de LaCoste, Horvath, & Woodward, 1991). For example, both fetuses and adults turn their heads in order to be able to listen to language with the right ear. Because sounds entering the right ear are routed to the left side of the brain for interpretation, such findings suggest that language is already lateralized in most fetuses. Full lateralization of language function, though, doesn't happen until near the end of the early childhood period (Spreen, Risser, & Edgell, 1995).

Critical Thinking

Ask your friends, relatives, and fellow students to estimate the age at which brain development is complete. How do you think people's assumptions about the completeness or incompleteness of brain development affect their attitudes and behavior toward children?

corpus callosum the membrane that connects the right and left hemispheres of the cerebral cortex

lateralization the process through which brain functions are divided between the two hemispheres of the cerebral cortex

hippocampus a brain structure that is important in learning

handedness a strong preference for using one hand or the other that develops between 3 and 5 years of age

● *Experience and Brain Maturation* ● It appears that the experience of learning and using language, not simply genetically programmed maturation of the brain, is the impetus behind hemispheric specialization. Young children whose language skills are the most advanced also show the strongest degree of lateralization (Mills, Coffey-Corina, & Neville, 1994). Neuroscientists have not determined whether some children advance rapidly in language acquisition *because* their brains are lateralizing at a faster pace. It seems that the reverse is just as likely to be true—namely, that some children's brains are lateralizing language function more rapidly because they are learning language faster.

Studies of deaf children who are learning sign language also suggest that experience contributes to brain development (Mills et al., 1994). These children use the same area of the brain to process sign meanings as hearing children use for spoken word meanings. Likewise, deaf children's sign vocabularies grow at about the same rate as those of children learning spoken language.

However, deaf children's processing of the grammar of sign language happens in an entirely different area of the brain from that used by hearing children to understand the structure of spoken language. In addition, deaf children acquire grammatical knowledge at a slower pace. These results suggest that some aspects of brain development are linked more to the kinds of linguistic stimuli to which the brain is exposed (in other words, to experience) than to a rigid genetic plan.

● **The Reticular Formation and the Hippocampus** ●   Myelin-ization of the neurons of the reticular formation, which you will remember from Chapter 4 is the brain structure that regulates attention and concentration, is another important milestone of early childhood brain development. Neurons in other parts of the brain, such as the *hippocampus*, are also myelinated during this period (Tanner, 1990). The **hippocampus** is involved in the transfer of information to long-term memory. Maturation of this brain structure probably accounts for improvements in memory function across the preschool years (Rolls, 2000).

● **Handedness** ●   Handedness, the tendency to rely primarily on the right or left hand, is another neurological milestone of the 2- to 6-year-old period (Tanner, 1990). Scientists used to assume that right-handedness increased among humans along with literacy. The idea was that parents and teachers encouraged children to use their right hands when teaching them how to write. In this way, right-handedness became a custom that was passed on from one genera-tion to the next through instruction.

By examining skeletons that predate the invention of writing, archaeologists have determined that the proportions of right- and left-handers were about the same in illiterate ancient populations as among modern humans (83% right-handed, 14% left-handed, and 3% ambidextrous) (Steele & Mayes, 1995). These findings suggest that the prevalence of right-handedness is likely to be the result of genetic inheritance. Moreover, geneticists at the National Cancer Institute (NCI) have recently identified a dominant gene for right-handedness, which they believe to be so common in the human population that most people receive a copy of it from both parents (Talan, 1998).

Studies relating brain lateralization to handedness suggest that a common neurological process may be involved in both. About 96% of right-handers pos-sess the typical pattern of left-brain dominance (Pujol, Deus, Losilla, & Capdevila, 1999). However, only 75% of left-handers are left-brain dominant. About 1% have complete right-brain dominance, and the rest have a mixed pattern of dominance (Pujol et al., 1999). The prevalence of mixed dominance among left-handers may explain the frequent finding of higher rates of learning disabilities and mental disorders among them (Grouios, Sakadami, Poderi, & Alevriadou, 1999; Hernandez, Camacho-Rosales, Nieto, & Barroso, 1997; Tanner, 1990).

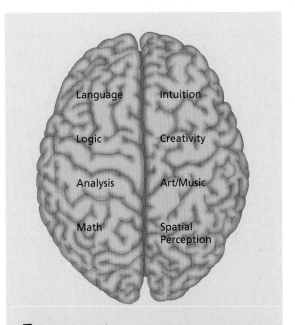

FIGURE 6.1

Brain functions are lateralized, as shown in the figure. Neurologists think that the basic outline of lateralization is genetically determined, whereas the specific timing of the lateralization of each function is determined by an interaction of genes and experiences.

Health and Wellness

Young children continue to require periodic medical check-ups as well as a variety of immunizations. Just as they do with infants, doctors monitor preschoolers' growth and motor development. At the same time, doctors and nurses often serve as parents' first source of help with children who have sensory or developmental disabilities that were not diagnosed in infancy (Sulkes, 1998).

Because children grow more slowly during the early childhood years, they may seem to eat less than when they were babies. Moreover, food aversions often develop during the preschool years. For example, a child who loved carrots as an infant may refuse to eat them at age 2 or 3. Consequently, conflicts between young children and their parents often focus on eating behavior (Wong, 1993).

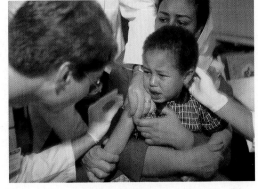

Immunizing young children against a variety of diseases is an important goal of routine health care for this age group.

(*Photo:* Corbis Sygma)

Nutritionists point out that it is important that parents not become so concerned about the quantity of food a child consumes that they cater to his preferences for sweets and other high-calorie or high-fat foods (Wong, 1993). Although obesity in early childhood is rare, many children acquire eating habits during these years that lead to later weight problems. Nutritionists recommend keeping a variety of nutritious foods on hand and allowing a child's appetite to be a good guide to how much food he should eat. Of course, this approach only works if young children's access to sweets and other attractive, but nonnutritious, foods is limited.

Parents should also keep in mind that young children eat only about half as much food as adults, and, unlike adults, many don't consume the majority of their daily calories at regular meals (Wong, 1993). Nutritionists suggest that concerned parents keep a daily record of what their children are actually eating for a week. In most cases, parents will find that children are consuming plenty of food.

In the United States, the average preschooler has four to six brief bouts of sickness each year, most often colds or the flu (Sulkes, 1998). Children who are experiencing high levels of stress or family upheaval are more likely to become ill. For example, a large nationwide study in the United States showed that children living in single-parent homes have more asthma, more headaches, and a generally higher vulnerability to illnesses of many types than do those living with both biological parents (Dawson, 1991). Figure 6.2 shows one comparison from this study, based on a "health vulnerability score" that is the sum of nine questions parents answered about their child's health. You can see in the figure that the average score in each group was well below the total possible score of 9, which implies that most children are quite healthy. But it is clear that children living in more stressful family structures have greater vulnerability to health problems—and this is true even when such other differences between the families as race, income, and mother's level of education are factored out.

Another danger for children is accidents. In any given year, about a quarter of all children under 5 in the United States have at least one accident that requires some kind of medical attention, and accidents are the major cause of death in preschool and school-age children (Starfield, 1991; U.S. Bureau of the Census, 1995). At every age, accidents are more common among boys than among girls, presumably because of their more active and daring styles of play. The majority of accidents among children in this age range—falls, cuts, accidental poisonings, and the like—occur at home. Automobile accidents are the second greatest source of injuries among preschoolers.

Abuse and Neglect

Legally, *child abuse* is defined as physical or psychological injury that results from an adult's intentional exposure of a child to potentially harmful physical stimuli, sexual acts, or neglect (Sulkes, 1998). However, it is fairly difficult to define child abuse and neglect in a practical sense. For example, if a parent allows a 2-year-old to play outdoors alone, and the child falls and breaks her arm, has the injury resulted from an accident or from neglect? Such are the dilemmas confronting medical professionals, who are bound by law to report suspected cases of abuse and neglect to authorities. Doctors and nurses are reluctant to accuse parents of abuse in such situations, but they are also concerned about protecting children from further injury (Sulkes, 1998). In addition, cultural values concerning acceptable and unacceptable treatment of children make it extremely difficult to define abuse so that it is possible to study child maltreatment cross-culturally. What is abusive in one culture may not be so regarded in another.

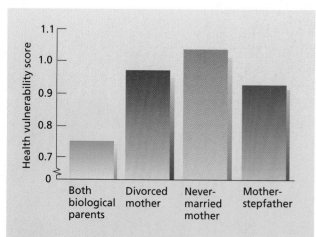

FIGURE 6.2

If we assume that single-parent and stepparent families contribute to higher stress for children (an assumption supported by research), then these results are yet another illustration of the link between higher stress and increased rates of illness. (*Source:* Dawson, 1991, from Table 3, p. 577.)

In the United States, most cases of abuse involve children between the ages of 2 and 9 (U.S. Bureau of the Census, 1997). Because of the inherent difficulties in defining abuse, it is difficult to say just how many children suffer abuse. However, research suggests that 1–5% of U.S. children are treated by medical professionals for injuries resulting from abuse every year (Sulkes, 1998; U.S. Bureau of the Census, 1997). Moreover, physicians estimate that abuse and/or neglect are responsible for about 10% of emergency room visits involving children under age 5 (Sulkes, 1998). Sadly, about 2,000 infants and children die as a result of abuse and/or neglect each year in the United States (Sulkes, 1998).

The majority of child abuse cases, about two-thirds, involve physical injuries (Sulkes, 1998). Another quarter of the cases involve sexual abuse, and about 5% are the result of neglect, such as underfeeding an infant. Other kinds of abuse include failure to obtain medical attention for an illness or injury, providing inadequate supervision, and drugging or poisoning children.

One useful model for explaining abuse classifies its causes into four broad categories: socio-cultural factors, characteristics of the child, characteristics of the abuser, and family stresses (Bittner & Newberger, 1981). The main idea of this model is that episodes of abuse are typically precipitated by everyday interactions between parents and children—for example, when a parent reprimands a young child for spilling a glass of milk. At the time of the episode, several causal factors work together to produce abusive responses in parents. Thus, what differentiates abusive from nonabusive parents, according to this model, is the presence of a number of risk factors that shape how they respond to the ordinary stresses of parenting.

Socio-cultural factors include personal or cultural values that regard physical abuse of children as morally acceptable. Parents are more likely to be abusive if they believe that there are few, in any, moral limits on what they can do to their children physically. Sociologists suggest that such beliefs stem from cultural traditions that regard children as property rather than human beings with individual rights (Mooney, Knox, & Schacht, 2000). Moreover, parents who live in communities where others share and act on these beliefs are more likely to be abusive.

Several characteristics of children or parents may set the stage for child abuse. For example, children with physical or mental disabilities or those who have difficult temperaments are more likely to be abused than others (Sulkes, 1998). Parents who are depressed, lack parenting skills and knowledge, have a history of abuse themselves, or are substance abusers are more likely to abuse or neglect their children (Emery & Laumann-Billings, 1998). In addition, mothers' live-in male partners who are not biologically related to the children in a household are more likely than biological fathers to be abusers (Daly & Wilson, 1996). Family stressors include factors such as poverty, unemployment, and interparental conflict (Sulkes, 1998). Keep in mind that no single factor produces abuse; but the presence of several of these variables in a particular family significantly increases the chances that the children will experience abuse.

Some children who are frequently or severely abused develop *post-traumatic stress disorder (PTSD)* (Kendall-Tackett, Williams, & Finkelhor, 1993; Margolin & Gordis, 2000; Morrissette, 1999; Pynoos, Steinberg, & Wraith, 1995). This disorder involves extreme levels of anxiety, flashback memories of episodes of abuse, nightmares, and other sleep disturbances. Abused children are also more likely than nonabused peers to exhibit poor school performance in middle childhood, to develop substance abuse problems in adolescence, and to exhibit slower rates of brain growth (Glaser, 2000; Malinosky-Rummell & Hansen, 1993; Rogosch, Cicchetti, & Aber, 1995).

Preventing abuse begins with education. Informing parents about the potential consequences of some physical acts, such as the link between shaking an infant and brain damage, may help. In addition, parents need to know that injuring children is a crime, even if the intention is to discipline them. Parenting classes, perhaps as a required part of high school curricula, can help inform parents or future parents about principles of child development and appropriate methods of discipline (Mooney et al., 2000).

Another approach to prevention of abuse involves identification of families at risk. Physicians, nurses, and other professionals who routinely interact with parents of infants and young children have a particularly important role to play in this kind of prevention. Parents who seem to have problems attaching to their children can sometimes be identified during medical office visits. These parents can be referred to parenting classes or to social workers for help. Similarly, parents may ask doctors or nurses how to discipline their children. Such questions provide professionals with opportunities to discuss which practices are appropriate and which are not.

Finally, children who are abused must be protected from further injury. This can be accomplished through vigorous enforcement of existing child abuse laws. As noted, health professionals must report suspected abuse. However, in most states, ordinary citizens are also legally required to report suspected abuse. And reporting is only part of the picture. Once abuse is reported, steps must be taken to protect injured children from suspected abusers.

Before going on

- What are the major milestones of growth and motor development between ages 2 and 6?

- What important changes happen in the brain during these years?

- How do young children's nutritional and health care needs differ from those of infants?

- What factors can contribute to abuse and neglect, and how does abuse affect children's development?

Cognitive Changes

The changes in thinking that happen during the early childhood years are staggering. At the beginning of the period, children are just beginning to learn how to accomplish goals. By the time they reach age 5 or 6, they are proficient at manipulating symbols and can make accurate judgments about others' thoughts, feelings, and behavior.

Piaget's Preoperational Stage

According to Piaget, the 18- to 24-month-old child begins to use symbols—images or words or actions that stand for something else—and enters the **preoperational stage**. During this stage, children become proficient at using symbols for thinking and communicating but still have difficulty thinking logically. At age 2 or 3, children begin to pretend in their play (Walker-Andrews & Kahana-Kalman, 1999). A broom may become a horse, or a block may become a train. Cross-cultural research suggests that this kind of object use by 2- to 3-year-olds in pretend play is universal (Haight et al., 1999). In fact, observing children at play can provide parents or teachers with a good idea about their levels of cognitive development (see The Real World). Young children

preoperational stage Piaget's second stage of cognitive development, during which children become proficient in the use of symbols in thinking and communicating but still have difficulty thinking logically

TEACHING The Real World

Children's Play and Cognitive Development

Careful observation of young children's play behaviors can provide preschool teachers with useful information about cognitive development, because the forms of play change in very obvious ways during the years from 1 to 6, following a sequence that closely matches Piaget's stages (Rubin, Fein, & Vandenberg, 1983).

Sensorimotor Play. A 12-month-old child spends most of her playtime exploring and manipulating objects, using all the sensorimotor schemes in her repertoire. She puts things in her mouth, shakes them, and moves them along the floor.

Constructive Play. Such exploratory play with objects does continue past 12 months, but by age 2 or so, children also begin to use objects to build or construct things, as the child in the photo is doing. Piaget hypothesized that this kind of play is the foundation of children's understanding of the rules that govern physical reality. For example, through block play, they come to understand that a tower that is broad at the top and narrow at the bottom will be unstable.

(*Photo*: PhotoDisc, Inc.)

First Pretend Play. Piaget believed that pretend play was an important indicator of a child's capacity to use symbols. The first instances of such pretending are usually simple, like pretending to drink from a toy cup. The toy is used for its actual or typical purpose (a cup is for drinking), and the actions are still oriented to the self,

but some pretending is involved. The age at which pretend play appears varies widely, but most children exhibit some pretending at around 12 months. Thus, for a while, children engage in both sensorimotor and pretend play. Typically, between 15 and 21 months, the recipient of the pretend action becomes another person or a toy, most often a doll. The child is still using objects for their usual purposes, but now she is using the toy cup with a doll instead of using it herself. Dolls are especially good toys for this kind of pretending, because it is not a very large leap from doing things to yourself to doing things to a doll. So children feed dolls imaginary food, comb their hair, and soothe them. This change signals a significant movement away from sensorimotor and toward true symbolic thinking.

(*Photo*: Courtesy of Jerry and Denise Boyd. Used with permission.)

Substitute Pretend Play. Between 2 and 3 years of age, children begin to use objects to stand for something altogether different. For example, the 30-month-old boy in the photo is using a carrot as an imaginary violin and a stick as a bow. Children this age may use a broom as a horse or make "trucks" out of blocks.

Sociodramatic Play. Sometime in the preschool years children also begin to play parts or take roles. This is really still a form of pretending, except that several children are creating a mutual pretense. For example, in playing house, as the children in the photo are doing, participants fill roles such as "mommy," "daddy," "sister," "brother,"

(*Photo*: © D. Young-Wolff, PhotoEdit)

and "baby." At first, children simply take up these roles; later, they name the various roles and may give each other explicit instructions about the right way to pretend a particular role. Most take delight in inventing and wearing costumes at this age. Here again, ages vary widely. Some 2-year-olds participate in this form of play; by age 4, virtually all children engage in some play of this type (Howes & Matheson, 1992). Interestingly, at about the same age, a great many children seem to create imaginary companions (Taylor, Cartwright, & Carlson, 1993). For many years, psychologists believed that having an imaginary companion was a sign of disturbance in a child; now, it is clear that such a creation is a normal part of the development of pretense in many children.

Rule-Governed Play. By age 5 or 6, children begin to prefer rule-governed pretending and formal games. For example, children of this age use rules such as "Whoever is smallest has to be the baby" when playing "house" and play simple games such as Red Rover and Red Light, Green Light. Younger children play these games as well, but 5- and 6-year-olds better understand their rules and will follow them for longer periods of time. Piaget suggested that older preschoolers' preference for rule-governed play indicates that they are about to make the transition to the next stage of cognitive development, *concrete operations*, in which they will acquire an understanding of rules (Piaget & Inhelder, 1969).

FIGURE 6.3

The experimental situation shown here is similar to one Piaget used to study egocentrism in children. The child is asked to pick out a picture that shows how the mountains look to her, and then to pick out a picture that shows how the mountains look to the doll.

also show signs of increasing proficiency at symbol use in their growing ability to understand models, maps, and graphic symbols such as letters (Callaghan, 1999; DeLoache, 1995).

Although young children are remarkably good at using symbols, their reasoning about the world is often flawed. For example, Piaget described the preoperational child's tendency to look at things entirely from her own point of view, a characteristic Piaget called **egocentrism** (Piaget, 1954). This term does not suggest that the young child is a self-centered egomaniac. It simply means that she assumes that everyone sees the world as she does. For example, while riding in the back seat of a car, a 3- or 4-year-old may suddenly call out "Look at that, Mom!"- not realizing that Mom can't see the object she's talking about. Moreover, the child doesn't realize that the car's motion prevents Mom from ever seeing the object in question. As a result, the youngster may become frustrated in her attempts to communicate with her mother about what she saw.

Figure 6.3 illustrates a classic experiment in which most young children demonstrate this kind of egocentrism. The child is shown a three-dimensional scene with mountains of different sizes and colors. From a set of drawings, she picks out the one that shows the scene the way she sees it. Most preschoolers can do this without much difficulty. Then the examiner asks the child to pick out the drawing that shows how someone else sees the scene, such as a doll or the examiner. At this point, most preschoolers choose the drawing that shows their own view of the mountains (Flavell, Everett, Croft, & Flavell, 1981; Gzesh & Surber, 1985).

Piaget also pointed out that the preschool-aged child's thinking is guided by the appearance of objects—a theme that still dominates the research on children of this age. In Piaget's work, this theme is evident in some of the most famous of his studies, those on conservation, which you read about in the Research Report in Chapter 2. **Conservation** is the understanding that matter can change in appearance without changing in quantity. Children rarely show any type of conservation before age 5. They think that spreading out the pennies in a row means that there are now more pennies, or that pouring water from a short, wide glass into a taller, thinner glass means that there is now more water. From their point of view, the spread-out row of pennies *looks* like more, so it must be more. Likewise, the liquid rises to a higher level in the thinner glass, so there must be more. Children younger than 5 disregard the fact that the number of pennies or the quantity of liquid has not changed.

Critical Thinking

Overcoming egocentrism is the foundation of many cognitive tasks later in life. For example, textbook authors must be able to evaluate what they write from the students' point of view. Can you think of other examples?

Challenges to Piaget's View

Studies of conservation have generally confirmed Piaget's observations (e.g., Ciancio et al., 1999; Gelman, 1972; Sophian, 1995; Wellman, 1982). Although younger children can demonstrate some understanding of conservation if the task is made very simple, most children cannot consistently solve conservation and other kinds of logical problems until at least age 5. However, evidence suggests that preschoolers are a great deal more cognitively sophisticated than Piaget thought.

egocentrism the young child's belief that everyone sees and experiences the world the way she does

conservation the understanding that matter can change in appearance without changing in quantity

● *Egocentrism and Perspective Taking* ●   Despite their egocentrism, children as young as 2 and 3 appear to have at least some ability to understand that another person sees things or experiences things differently than they do. For example, children this age adapt their speech or their play to the demands of a companion. They play differently with older and younger playmates and talk differently to a younger or handicapped child (Brownell, 1990; Guralnik & Paul-Brown, 1984).

However, such understanding is clearly not perfect at this young age. Developmental psychologist John Flavell has proposed two levels of perspective-taking ability. At level 1, the child knows that other people experience things differently. At level 2, the child develops a whole series of complex rules for figuring out precisely what the other person sees or experiences (Flavell, Green, & Flavell, 1990). At 2 and 3 years old, children have level 1 knowledge but not level 2; level 2 knowledge begins to be evident in 4- and 5-year-olds.

For example, a child of 4 or 5 understands that another person feels sad if she fails or happy if she succeeds. The preschool child also begins to figure out that unpleasant emotions occur in situations in which there is a gap between desire and reality. Sadness, for example, normally occurs when someone loses something that is valued or fails to acquire some desired object (Harris, 1989).

Studies of preschoolers' understanding of emotion have also challenged Piaget's description of the young child's egocentrism. For example, between 2 and 6, children learn to regulate or modulate their expressions of emotion to conform to others' expectations (Dunn, 1994). In addition, preschool children use emotional expressions such as crying or smiling to get things they want. These behaviors are obviously based at least in part on a growing awareness that other people judge your feelings by what they see you expressing. These behaviors wouldn't occur if children were completely incapable of looking at their own behavior from another person's perspective, as Piaget's assertions about egocentrism would suggest.

This young child is able to adapt his speech to the needs of his younger sibling, one of many indications that preschoolers are less egocentric than Piaget thought. (*Photo:* TROIS/EXPLORER, Photo Researchers, Inc.)

● *Appearance and Reality* ●   The young child's movement away from egocentrism seems to be part of a much broader change in her understanding of appearance and reality. Flavell has studied this understanding in a variety of ways (Flavell, Green, & Flavell, 1989; Flavell, Green, Wahl, & Flavell, 1987). In the most famous Flavell procedure, the experimenter shows the child a sponge that has been painted to look like a rock. Three-year-olds will say either that the object looks like a sponge and is a sponge or that it looks like a rock and is a rock. But 4- and 5-year-olds can distinguish between appearance and reality; they realize that the item looks like a rock but is a sponge (Flavell, 1986). Thus, the older children understand that the same object can be represented differently, depending on one's point of view.

Using similar materials, investigators have also asked when a child can first grasp the **false belief principle.** Individuals who understand this principle can look at a problem or situation from another person's point of view and discern what kind of information would cause that person to believe something that isn't true. For example, after a child has felt the sponge/rock and has answered questions about what it looks like and what it "really" is, a researcher can ask something like this: "John [a playmate of the child] hasn't touched this, he hasn't squeezed it. If John just sees it over here like this, what will he think it is? Will he think it's a rock or will he think it's a sponge?" (Gopnik & Astington, 1988, p. 35). Most 3-year-olds think John will believe the object is a sponge because it is a sponge. By contrast, 4- and 5-year-olds realize that, because John hasn't felt the sponge, he will have a false belief that it is a rock. Some studies show that 3-year-olds can perform more accurately if they are given a hint or clue. For example, if experimenters tell them that a "naughty" person is trying to fool John, more of them will say that he will falsely think the sponge is rock (Bowler, Briskman, & Grice, 1999). But the child of 4 or 5 more consistently understands that someone else can believe something that isn't true and act on that belief.

false belief principle an understanding that enables a child to look at a situation from another person's point of view and determine what kind of information will cause that person to have a false belief

Theories of Mind

Evidence like that described in the previous section has led a number of theorists to propose that the 4- or 5-year-old has developed a new and quite sophisticated **theory of mind**, or a set of ideas that explains other people's ideas, beliefs, desires, and behavior (e.g., Astington & Gopnik, 1991; Gopnik & Wellman, 1994; Harris, 1989).

● *Understanding Thoughts, Desires, and Beliefs* ● The theory of mind does not spring forth full-blown at age 4. Toddlers as young as 18 months have some beginning understanding of the fact that people (but not inanimate objects) operate with goals and intentions (Meltzoff, 1995). By age 3, children understand some aspects of the link between people's thinking or feeling and their behavior. For example, they know that a person who wants something will try to get it. They also know that a person may still want something even if she can't have it (Lillard & Flavell, 1992). But they do not yet understand the basic principle that each person's actions are based on her own representation of reality, which may differ from what is "really" there. For example, a person's *belief* about how popular she is has more influence on her behavior than her actual popularity. It is this new aspect of the theory of mind that clearly emerges at about 4 or 5.

Critical Thinking

Consider your own theory of mind. What assumptions do you make about the way other people's behavior is affected by their beliefs, feelings, or ideas? You operate on the basis of such a theory all the time, but can you articulate it?

Still, there is much that the 4- or 5-year-old doesn't yet grasp about other people's thinking. The child of this age understands that other people think, but does not yet understand that other people can think about him. The 4-year-old understands "I know that you know." But he does not yet fully understand that this process is reciprocal, namely, "You know that I know."

Furthermore, it is not until about age 6 that most children realize that knowledge can be derived through inference. For example, researchers in one study showed 4- and 6-year-olds two toys of different colors (Pillow, 1999). Next, they placed the toys in separate opaque containers. They then opened one of the containers and showed the toy to a puppet. When asked whether the puppet now knew which color toy was in each container, only the 6-year-olds said yes.

Understanding of the reciprocal nature of thought seems to develop between age 5 and age 7 for most children. This would seem to be a particularly important understanding, because it is probably necessary for the creation of genuinely reciprocal friendships, which begin to emerge in the elementary school years (Sullivan, Zaitchik, & Tager-Flusberg, 1994). In fact, the rate at which an individual preschooler develops a theory of mind is a good predictor of her social skills both later in early childhood and during the school years (Moore, Barresi, & Thompson, 1998; Watson, Nixon, Wilson, & Capage, 1999).

● *Influences on the Development of a Theory of Mind* ● Developmentalists have found that a child's theory of mind is correlated with his performance on Piaget's tasks as well as on more recently developed problems designed to assess egocentrism and appearance/reality (Melot & Houde, 1998; Yirmiya & Shulman, 1996). In addition, pretend play seems to contribute to theory of mind development. Shared pretense with other children, in particular, is strongly related to theory of mind (Dockett & Smith, 1995; Schwebel, Rosen, & Singer, 1999). Furthermore, children whose parents discuss emotion-provoking past events with them develop a theory of mind more rapidly than do their peers who do not have such conversations (Welch-Ross, 1997).

theory of mind a set of ideas constructed by a child or adult to explain other people's ideas, beliefs, desires, and behavior

Language skills, such as knowledge of words like *want*, *need*, *think*, or *remember*, which express feelings, desires, and thoughts—are also related to theory of mind development (Astington & Jenkins, 1995). Indeed, some level of language facility may be a necessary condition for the development of a theory of mind. Developmentalists have found that children in this age range simply do not succeed at false-belief tasks until they have reached a certain threshold of general language skill (Astington & Jenkins, 1999; Jenkins & Astington, 1996; Watson et al., 1999).

Further support for the same point comes from the finding that children with disabilities that affect language development, such as congenital deafness or mental retardation, develop a theory of mind more slowly than others (Peterson & Siegal, 1995; Sicotte & Stemberger, 1999). Research has also demonstrated that, for children with mental disabilities, progress toward a fully developed theory of mind is better predicted by language skills than by type of disability (Bauminger & Kasari, 1999; Peterson & Siegal, 1999; Yirmiya, Eriel, Shaked, & Solomonica-Levi, 1998; Yirmiya, Solomonica-Levi, Shulman, & Pilowsky, 1996).

● **Theory of Mind across Cultures** ●   Cross-cultural psychologists claim that theory of mind research in the United States and Europe may not apply to children in other cultures and have produced some preliminary evidence to support this contention (Lillard, 1998). However, research also suggests that certain aspects of theory of mind development may be universal. For example, similar sequences of theory of mind development have been found in the United States, China, Europe, and India (Flavell, Zhang, Zou, Dong, & Qi, 1983; Joshi & MacLean, 1994; Tardif & Wellman, 2000). Moreover, participation in shared pretending has been shown to contribute to theory of mind development cross-culturally (Tan-Niam, Wood, & O'Malley, 1998). Critics, however, argue that most of the societies where these results have been found are industrialized and that very different findings might emerge in studies of nonindustrialized societies.

In response to this argument, developmentalists adapted the traditional false-belief testing procedure for use with a group called the Baka, who live in Cameroon (Avis & Harris, 1991). The Baka are hunter-gatherers who live together in camps. Each child was tested in his or her own hut, using materials with which the child was completely familiar. The child watched one adult, named Mopfana (a member of the Baka), put some mango kernels into a bowl with a lid. Mopfana then left the hut, and a second adult (also a group member) told the child they were going to play a game with Mopfana: They were going to hide the kernels in a cooking pot. Then he asked the child what Mopfana was going to do when he came back. Would he look for the kernels in the bowl or in the pot? The second adult also asked the child whether Mopfana's heart would feel good or bad before he lifted the lid of the bowl and after he lifted the lid. Children between 2 and 4 years old were likely to say that Mopfana would look for the kernels in the pot or that he would be sad before he looked in the bowl; 4- and 5-year-olds were nearly always right on all three questions. Even in very different cultures, then, something similar seems to be occurring between age 3 and age 5. In these years, all children seem to develop a theory of mind.

Alternative Theories of Early Childhood Thinking

In recent years, a number of interesting theoretical approaches have attempted to explain both Piaget's original results and the more recent findings that contradict them.

● **Information-Processing Theories** ●   One set of alternative proposals is based on the information-processing model. As you may remember from Chapter 2, these theories are called *neo-Piagetian* because they expand on, rather than contradict, Piaget's views. For example, neo-Piagetian Robbie Case explains age differences in cognitive development as a function of changes in children's use of their short-term

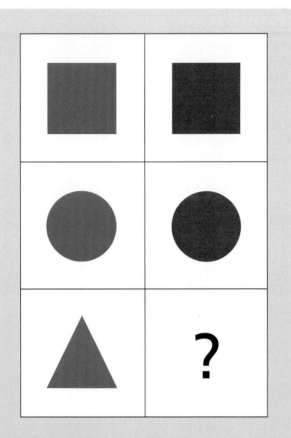

FIGURE 6.4

Neo-Piagetians have used Piaget's matrix classification task in strategy training studies with young children. Before training, most preschoolers say that a blue triangle or red circle belongs in the box with the question mark. After learning a two-step strategy in which they are taught to classify each object first by shape and then by color, children understand that a red triangle is the figure that is needed to complete the matrix.

memories (Case, 1985, 1992). Case uses the term **short-term storage space (STSS)** to refer to the child's working memory. According to Case, there is a limit on how many schemes can be attended to in STSS. He refers to the maximum number of schemes that may be put into STSS at one time as **operational efficiency**. Improvements in operational efficiency occur through both practice (doing tasks that require memory use, such as learning the alphabet) and brain maturation as the child gets older. Thus, a 7-year-old is better able to handle the processing demands of conservation tasks than is a 4-year-old because of improvements in operational efficiency of the STSS.

A good example of the function of STSS may be found by examining *matrix classification*, a task Piaget often used with both young and school-aged children (see Figure 6.4). Matrix classification requires the child to place a given stimulus in two categories at the same time. Young children fail such tasks, according to neo-Piagetian theory, because they begin by processing the stimulus according to one dimension (either shape or color) and then either fail to realize that it is necessary to re-process it along the second dimension or forget to do so.

However, researchers have trained young children to perform correctly on such problems by using a two-step strategy. The children are taught to think of a red triangle, for example, in terms of shape first and color second. Typically, instruction involves a number of training tasks in which researchers remind children repeatedly to remember to re-classify stimuli with respect to the second variable. According to Case, both children's failure prior to instruction and the type of strategy training to which they respond illustrate the constraints imposed on problem solving by the limited operational efficiency of the younger child's STSS. There is only room for one scheme at a time in the child's STSS, either shape or color. The training studies show that younger children *can* learn to perform correctly, but their approach is qualitatively different from that of older children. The older child's more efficient STSS allows her to think about shape and color at the same time and, therefore, perform successfully without any training.

Information-processing theorists also maintain that children's ability to make efficient use of their memory system is influenced by other cognitive processes. **Metamemory** is knowledge about and control of memory processes. For example, young children know that it takes longer to memorize a list of ten words than a list of five words (Kail, 1990). However, between the ages of 2 and 6, children aren't very good at coming up with strategies to apply to more difficult memory tasks. Thus, they can't perform as well as older children on tasks, like those of Piaget, that call for efficient use of the memory system.

Metacognition is knowledge about and control of thought processes. For example, a child listening to a story may realize he has forgotten the main character's name and ask the reader what it is. Both knowing that the character's name has been forgotten and knowing that the character's name will make the story easier to understand are forms of metacognition. Moreover, metacognitive processes enable the child to generate a strategy, such as asking the reader, that will solve the problem.

Children's metamemory and metacognition improve during the early childhood period. Between age 3 and age 5, for example, children figure out that in order to tell whether a sponge painted like a rock is really a sponge or a rock, a person needs to

short-term storage space (STSS) neo-Piagetian theorist Robbie Case's term for the working memory

operational efficiency a neo-Piagetian term that refers to the maximum number of schemes that can be processed in working memory at one time

metamemory knowledge about how memory works and the ability to control and reflect on one's own memory function

metacognition knowledge about how the mind thinks and the ability to control and reflect on one's own thought processes

touch or hold it. Just looking at it doesn't give someone enough information (Flavell, 1993; O'Neill, Astington, & Flavell, 1992). Thus, by about age 4 or 5, children seem to have some beginning grasp of these processes, but they still have a long way to go. As a result, their ability to solve complex problems such as those Piaget used is limited compared to that of older children.

● *Vygotsky's Socio-Cultural Theory* ●   In Chapter 2 you learned that psychologists' interest in Russian psychologist Lev Vygotsky's views on development has grown recently. Vygotsky's theory differs from both Piagetian and information-processing theory in its emphasis on the role of social factors in cognitive development. For example, two preschoolers working on a puzzle together discuss where the pieces belong. After a number of such dialogues, the participants internalize the discussion. It then becomes a model for an internal conversation the child uses to guide himself through the puzzle-solving process. In this way, Vygotsky suggested, solutions to problems are socially generated and learned. Vygotsky did not deny that individual learning takes place. Rather, he suggested that group learning processes are central to cognitive development. Consequently, from Vygotsky's perspective, social interaction is required for cognitive development (Thomas, 1996).

Chapter 2 described two important general principles of Vygotsky's theory: *the zone of proximal development* and *scaffolding*. Vygotsky also proposed specific stages of cognitive development from birth to age 7. Each stage represents a step toward the child's internalization of the ways of thinking used by the adults around him.

In the first period, called the *primitive stage*, the infant possesses mental processes that are similar to those of lower animals. He learns primarily through conditioning, until language begins to develop in the second year. At that point, he enters the *naive psychology stage*, in which he learns to use language to communicate but still does not understand its symbolic character. For example, he doesn't realize that any collection of sounds could stand for the object "chair" as long as everyone agreed—that is, if all English speakers agreed to substitute the word *blek* for *chair,* we could do so because we would all understand what *blek* meant.

Once the child begins to appreciate the symbolic function of language, near the end of the third year of life, he enters the *egocentric speech stage*. In this stage, he uses language as a guide to solving problems. In effect, he tells himself how to do things. For example, a 3-year-old walking down a flight of stairs might say "Be careful" to himself. Such a statement would be the result of his internalization of statements made to him by adults and older children.

Piaget recognized the existence and importance of egocentric speech. However, he believed that such speech disappeared as the child approached the end of the preoperational stage. In contrast, Vygotsky claimed that egocentric speech becomes completely internalized at age 6 or 7, when children enter the final period of cognitive development, the ingrowth stage. Thus, he suggested that the logical thinking Piaget ascribed to older children resulted from their internalization of speech routines they had acquired from older children and adults in the social world rather than from schemes children constructed for themselves through interaction with the physical world.

At present, there is insufficient evidence to either support or contradict most of Vygotsky's ideas (Thomas, 1996). However, some intriguing research on children's construction of theory of mind during social interactions lends weight to Vygotsky's major propositions. It seems that children in pairs and groups do produce more sophisticated ideas than individual children who work on problems alone. However, the sophistication of a group's ideas appears to depend on the presence of at least one fairly advanced individual child in the group (Tan-Niam et al., 1998). Thus, Vygotsky's theory may ignore the important contributions of individual thought to group interaction.

Before going on

- List the characteristics of children's thought during Piaget's preoperational stage.

- How has recent research challenged Piaget's view of this period?

- What is a theory of mind, and how does it develop?

- How do the information-processing and socio-cultural theories explain the changes in children's thinking that happen between age 2 and age 6?

Changes in Language

By age $2\frac{1}{2}$, the average child has a vocabulary of about 600 words; by age 5 or 6, that number has risen to roughly 15,000 words (Pinker, 1994). By age 3, most children have acquired all the basic tools needed to form sentences and make conversation (Bloom, 1991).

First Sentences

These 2- to 3-year-olds probably speak to each other in short sentences that include uninflected nouns and verbs. (*Photo:* Will Faller)

You may recall that toddlers combine single words with gestures to create *holophrases* (see Chapter 4). The first two-word sentences usually appear near the end of the second year of life. Research suggests that sentences appear when a child has reached a threshold vocabulary of around 100–200 words rather than at any particular age (Fenson et al., 1994).

The first sentences have several distinguishing features. They are short—generally two or three words—and they are simple. Nouns, verbs, and adjectives are usually included, but virtually all grammatical markers (which linguists call **inflections**) are missing. When they first use sentences, children learning English, for example, do not normally use the *-s* ending for plurals or put the *-ed* ending on verbs to make the past tense.

It is also clear that even at this earliest stage, children create sentences following rules—not adult rules, to be sure, but rules nonetheless. They focus on certain types of words and put them together in particular orders. They also manage to convey a variety of different meanings with their simple sentences. For example, young children frequently use a sentence made up of two nouns, such as "Mommy sock" or "sweater chair" (Bloom, 1973). The child who says "Mommy sock" may mean either "This is mommy's sock" or "Mommy is putting a sock on my foot" (Bloom, 1973). Thus, to understand what a child means by a two-word sentence, it is necessary to know the context in which the statement is made.

The Grammar Explosion

inflections grammatical markers attached to words to indicate tense, gender, number, and the like, such as the use of the ending *-ed* to mark the past tense of a verb in English

Just as the vocabulary explosion you read about in Chapter 4 begins slowly, so the grammar explosion of the 2- to 6-year-old period starts with several months of simple sentences such as "Mommy sock". You can get some feeling for these changes

TABLE 6.2   Examples of Daniel's Sentences at Two Ages

Early Simple Sentences (aged 21 months)	More Complex Sentences (aged 23 months)
A bottle	A little boat
Broke it	Doggies here
Here bottle	Give you the book
Hi Daddy	It's a boy
Horse doggie	It's a robot
What that?	Little box there
Kitty cat	No book
Poor Daddy	Oh cars
That monkey	That flowers
Want bottle	Where going?

(*Source:* Reprinted by permission of the publisher. Ingram, 1981, Tables 6 and 7, pp. 344–345. Copyright © 1981 by Elsevier Science Publishing Co., Inc.)

from Table 6.2, which lists some of the sentences spoken by a little boy named Daniel (Ingram, 1981). The left-hand column lists some of Daniel's sentences at about 21 months of age, when he was still using the simplest forms; the right-hand column lists some of his sentences only $2\frac{1}{2}$ months later (aged 23 months), when he had shifted into higher gear.

● *Inflections* ●   Daniel obviously did not add all the inflections at once. The sentences in the right-hand column of Table 6.2 include only a few, such as -*s* for plural. The beginning of negative constructions is apparent in "No book," and the beginning of the question form shows in "Where going?" Within each language community, children seem to add inflections and more complex word orders in fairly predictable sequences.

In a classic early study, Roger Brown found that the earliest inflection used among children learning English is typically -*ing* added to a verb, as in "I playing" or "Doggie running," expressions that are common in the speech of $2\frac{1}{2}$- to 3-year-olds (Brown, 1973). Over the next year or so come (in order) prepositions such as "on" and "in," the plural -*s* on nouns, irregular past tenses (such as "broke" or "ran"), possessives, articles ("a" and "the" in English), the -*s* added to third-person verbs such as "He wants," regular past tenses such as "played" and "wanted," and various forms of auxiliary verbs, as in "I *am* going."

● *Questions and Negatives* ●   There are also predictable sequences in the child's developing use of questions and negatives. In each case, the child seems to go through periods when he creates types of sentences that he has not heard adults use, but that are consistent with the particular set of rules he is using. For example, in the development of questions there is a point at which the child can put a *Wh*- word ("who," "what," "when," "where," "why") at the front end of a sentence, but doesn't yet put the auxiliary verb in the right place, as in "Where you are going now?" Similarly, in the development of negatives, children go through a stage in which they put in *not* or *n't* or *no* but omit the auxiliary verb, as in "I not crying."

● *Overregularization* ●   Another intriguing phenomenon is **overregularization**, or overgeneralization. No language is perfectly regular; every language includes some irregularly conjugated verbs or unusual forms of plurals. What 3- to 4-year-olds do is apply the basic rule to all these irregular instances, thus making the language more regular than it really is (Maratsos, 2000). In English, this is especially clear in children's creation of past tenses such as "wented," "blowed," and "sitted" or plurals such as "teeths" and "blockses" (Fenson et al., 1994).

Such overregularizations illustrate yet again that language development is a rule-governed process that cannot be explained by imitation theories. Children show that they are using rules when they create word forms (such as "wented") they have not heard. Clearly, children cannot have learned these words by imitation. Instead, their presence in children's speech suggests that children actively infer and use language rules.

● *Complex Sentences* ●   After children have figured out inflections and the basic sentence forms using negatives and questions, they soon begin to create remarkably complex sentences, using a conjunction such as "and" or "but" to combine two ideas or using embedded clauses. Here are some examples from children aged 30 to 48 months (de Villiers & de Villiers, 1992, p. 379):

> I didn't catch it but Teddy did!
>
> I'm gonna sit on the one you're sitting on.
>
> Where did you say you put my doll?
>
> Those are punk rockers, aren't they?

When you remember that only about 18 months earlier these children were using sentences little more complex than "See doggie," you can appreciate how far they have come in a short time.

Phonological Awareness

Certain aspects of early childhood language development, such as rate of vocabulary growth, predict how easily a child will learn to read and write when she enters school (Wood & Terrell, 1998). However, one specific component of early childhood language development, phonological awareness, seems to be especially important. **Phonological awareness** is a child's sensitivity to the sound patterns that are specific to the language being acquired. It also includes the child's knowledge of that particular language's system for representing sounds with letters. Researchers measure English-speaking children's phonological awareness with questions like these: "What would *bat* be if you took away the *b*? What would *bat* be if you took away the *b* and put *r* there instead?"

A child doesn't have to acquire phonological awareness in early childhood. It can be learned in elementary school through formal instruction (Ball, 1997; Bus & van IJzendoorn, 1999). However, numerous studies have shown that the greater a child's phonological awareness *before* he enters school, the faster he learns to read (Christensen, 1997; Gilbertson & Bramlett, 1998; Schatschneider, Francis, Foorman, Fletcher, & Mehta, 1999; Wood & Terrell, 1998). In addition, phonological awareness in the early childhood years is related to rate of literacy learning in languages as varied as English, Punjabi, and Chinese (Chiappe & Siegel, 1999; Ho & Bryant, 1997; Huang & Hanley, 1997; McBride-Chang & Ho, 2000).

Phonological awareness appears to develop primarily through word play. For example, among English-speaking children, learning and reciting nursery rhymes contributes to phonological awareness (Bryant, MacLean, & Bradley, 1990; Bryant, MacLean, Bradley, & Crossland, 1990; Layton, Deeny, Tall, & Upton, 1996). For

overregularization attachment of regular inflections to irregular words such as the substitution of *goed* for *went*

phonological awareness children's understanding of the sound patterns of the language they are acquiring

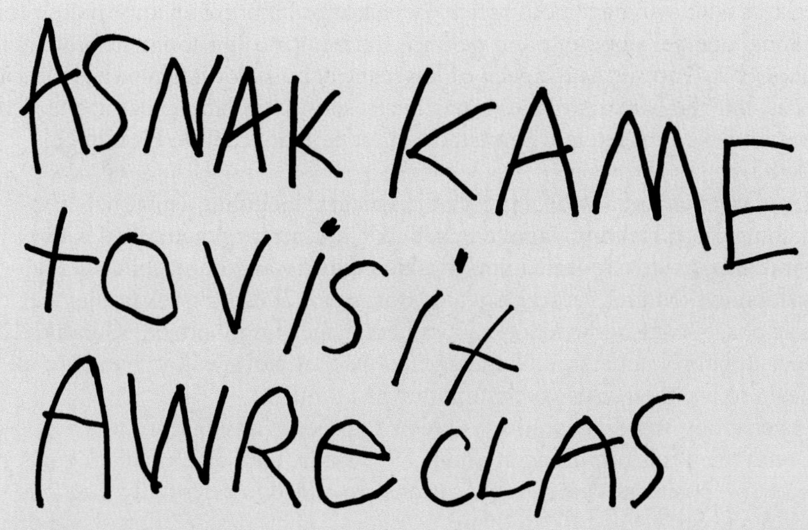

ASNAK KAME to visit AWRe CLAS

FIGURE 6.5

Translation: *A snake came to visit our class.*
A 5-year-old used a strategy called "invented spelling" to write this sentence about a snake's visit (hopefully accompanied by an animal handler!) to her kindergarten class. Invented spelling requires a high level of phonological awareness. Research suggests that children who have well-developed phonological awareness skills by the time they reach kindergarten learn to read more quickly. (Courtesy of Jerry and Denise Boyd. Used with permission.)

Japanese children, a game called *shiritori*, in which one person says a word and another comes up with a word that begins with its ending sound, helps children develop these skills (Norboru, 1997; Serpell & Hatano, 1997). Educators have also found that using such games to teach phonological awareness skills to preschoolers is just as effective as more formal methods such as flash cards and worksheets (Brennan & Ireson, 1997). *Shared*, or *dialogic, reading* has also been found to contribute to growth in phonological awareness (Burgess, 1997).

Preschoolers with good phonological awareness skills—those who have learned a few basic sound-letter connections informally, from their parents or from educational TV programs or videos—often use a strategy called **invented spelling** when they attempt to write (see Figure 6.5). In spite of the many errors they make, children who use invented spelling strategies before receiving school-based instruction in reading and writing are more likely to become good spellers and readers later in childhood (McBride-Chang, 1998). Thus, the evidence suggests that one of the best ways parents and preschool teachers can help young children prepare for formal instruction in reading is to engage them in activities that encourage word play and invented spelling.

Individual and Cross-Linguistic Variations

Longitudinal studies suggest that individual rates of language development vary greatly. Some children begin using individual words at 8 months, others do not do so until 18 months; some do not use two-word sentences until they are 3 years old or more (e.g., Blake, 1994; Bloom, 1991; Brown, 1973). Cross-cultural studies have produced similar findings (e.g., Fenson et al., 1994).

invented spelling a strategy young children with good phonological awareness skills use when they write

The timing of complex speech predicts later intelligence test scores only for those few late talkers who also have poor receptive language. This group appears to remain behind in language development and perhaps in cognitive development more generally (Bates, 1993). Variations in speed of language acquisition seem to have some genetic basis, but they are also at least partly a response to differences in the richness of the child's language environment (Mather & Black, 1984; Plomin & DeFries, 1985).

Studies of speakers of a wide variety of languages, including Turkish, Serbo-Croatian, Hungarian, Hebrew, Japanese, a New Guinean language called Kaluli, German, and Italian, have revealed important similarities in young children's language development (Maitel, Dromi, Sagi, & Bornstein, 2000). For example, the prelinguistic phase seems to be identical in all language communities. All babies coo, then babble; all babies understand language before they can speak it; babies in all cultures begin to use their first words at about 12 months.

Moreover, a one-word phase always seems to precede a two-word phase in every language, with the latter beginning at about 18 months. Likewise, in all languages studied so far, prepositions describing locations are added in essentially the same order. Children learn words for "in," "on," "under," and "beside" first. Then they learn the words for "front" and "back" (Slobin, 1985b). Finally, children everywhere seem to pay more attention to the ends of words than the beginnings, so they learn suffixes before they learn prefixes.

However, the specific word order used in early sentences is not the same for all children in all languages. In some languages, a noun/verb sequence is fairly common; in others, a verb/noun sequence may be heard. In addition, children learn particular inflections in different orders in various languages. Interestingly, Japanese children begin very early to use a special kind of verbal marker, called a *pragmatic marker*, that tells something about feeling or context. For instance, in Japanese, the word *yo* is used at the end of a sentence when the speaker is experiencing some resistance from the listener; the word *ne* is used when the speaker expects approval or agreement. Japanese children begin to use these markers very early, much earlier than children whose languages contain inflections.

Most strikingly, children learning some languages appear not to go through a simple two-word sentence stage in which the sentences contain no inflections. Children learning Turkish, for example, use essentially the full set of noun and verb inflections by age 2 and never go through a stage of using uninflected words. The Turkish-speaking child's language is simple, but it is rarely ungrammatical from the adult's point of view (Aksu-Koc & Slobin, 1985).

Before going on

- Describe children's first sentences.

- What happens during the grammar explosion?

- What is phonological awareness, and why is it important?

- Describe individual and cross-cultural differences in language development.

Differences in Intelligence

Psychologists have constructed intelligence tests that can be used beginning in early childhood and that are correlated both with later test scores and with important variables such as school performance. However, the widespread use of these tests has led to an ongoing debate about the origins of score differences and the degree to which they can be modified.

Measuring Intelligence

An important assumption in studying differences in intelligence is that these differences can be measured. Thus, it's important to understand something about the tests psychologists use to measure intelligence as well as the meaning and stability of the scores the tests generate.

● ***The First Tests*** ● The first modern intelligence test was published in 1905 by two Frenchmen, Alfred Binet and Theodore Simon (Binet & Simon, 1905). From the beginning, the test had a practical purpose—to identify children who might have difficulty in school. For this reason, the tasks Binet and Simon devised for the test were very much like some school tasks, including measures of vocabulary, comprehension of facts and relationships, and mathematical and verbal reasoning. For example, could the child describe the difference between wood and glass? Could the young child identify his nose, his ear, his head? Could he tell which of two weights was heavier?

Lewis Terman and his associates at Stanford University modified and extended many of Binet's original tasks when they translated and revised the test for use in the United States (Terman, 1916; Terman & Merrill, 1937). The Stanford-Binet, the name by which the test is still known, initially described a child's performance in terms of a score called an **intelligence quotient**, later shortened to **IQ**. This score was computed by comparing the child's chronological age (in years and months) with his mental age, defined as the level of questions he could answer correctly. For example, a child who could solve the problems for a 6-year-old but not those for a 7-year-old would have a mental age of 6. The formula used to calculate the IQ was

mental age/chronological age $\times$ *100 = IQ*

This formula results in an IQ above 100 for children whose mental age is higher than their chronological age and an IQ below 100 for children whose mental age is below their chronological age.

This system for calculating IQ is no longer used. Instead, IQ scores for the Stanford-Binet and all other intelligence tests are now based on a direct comparison of a child's performance with the average performance of a large group of other children of the same age. But the scoring is arranged so that an IQ of 100 is still average.

As you can see in Figure 6.6 (page 170), about two-thirds of all children achieve scores between 85 and 115; roughly 96% of scores fall between 70 and 130. Children who score above 130 are often called *gifted*; those who score below 70 are normally referred to as *retarded*, although this label should not be applied unless the child also has problems with "adaptive behavior," such as an inability to dress or feed himself, a problem getting along with others, or a significant problem adapting to the demands of a regular school classroom. Some children with IQ scores in this low range are able to function in a regular schoolroom and should not be labeled retarded.

intelligence quotient (IQ) the ratio of mental age to chronological age; also, a general term for any kind of score derived from an intelligence test

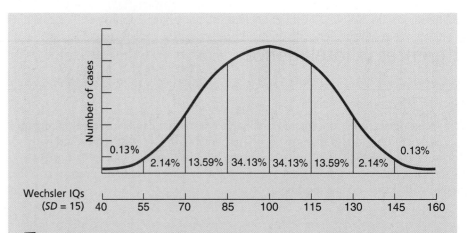

FIGURE 6.6

IQ scores form what mathematicians call a normal distribution—the famous "bell curve" you may have heard about. The two sides of a normal distribution curve are mirror images of each other. Thus, 34% of children score between 85 and 100, and another 34% score between 100 and 115. Likewise, 13% score between 70 and 85 and another 13% between 115 and 130. A few other human characteristics, such as height, are normally distributed as well.

● ***Modern Intelligence Tests*** ● The test used most frequently by psychologists today is the third revision of the Wechsler Intelligence Scales for Children, called the WISC-III, the most recent version of a test originally developed by David Wechsler. On all the WISC tests, the child is tested with ten different types of problems, each ranging from very easy to very hard, that are divided into two subgroups. The *verbal scale* includes tasks measuring vocabulary, understanding of similarities between objects, and general knowledge about the world. The other subgroup, called the *performance scale*, involves nonverbal tasks such as arranging pictures in an order that tells a story or copying a pattern using a set of colored blocks. Many psychologists find this distinction between verbal and performance tests helpful, because significant differences in a child's skills may indicate particular kinds of learning problems.

● ***Stability and Predictive Value of IQ Scores*** ● The correlation between a child's test score and her current or future grades in school is about .50–.60 (Brody, 1992; Carver, 1990; Neisser et al., 1996). This is a strong, but by no means perfect, correlation. It indicates that on the whole, children with high IQ scores will be among the high achievers in school, and those who score low will be among the low achievers. But success in school also depends on many factors other than IQ, including motivation, interest, and persistence. Because of this, some children with high IQ scores don't shine in school, while some lower-IQ children do.

The relationship between school performance and IQ scores holds within each social class and racial group in the United States, as well as in other countries and cultures. Among both poor and the middle class, and among African Americans and Hispanic Americans as well as whites, children with higher IQs are most likely to get good grades, complete high school, and go on to college (Brody, 1992). Such findings have led a number of theorists to argue that

Critical Thinking

In your opinion, how does having a higher IQ make a child more resilient? For example, in what specific ways might the life of a brighter child living in a slum be different from the life of a less-bright child in the same environment?

intelligence adds to the child's resilience—a concept you read about in Chapter 1. Numerous studies show that poor children—whether they are white, Hispanic, African American, or from another minority group—are far more likely to develop the kind of self-confidence and personal competence it takes to move out of poverty if they have higher IQs (Luthar & Zigler, 1992; Masten & Coatsworth, 1998; Werner & Smith, 1992).

At the other end of the scale, low intelligence is associated with a number of negative long-term outcomes, including delinquency in adolescence, adult illiteracy, and criminal behavior in adulthood (Baydar, Brooks-Gunn, & Furstenberg, 1993; Stattin & Klackenberg-Larsson, 1993). This is not to say that all lower-IQ individuals are illiterate or criminals—that is clearly not the case. But low IQ makes a child more vulnerable, just as high IQ increases the child's resilience.

IQ scores are also quite stable. If two tests are given a few months or a few years apart, the scores are likely to be very similar. The correlations between IQ scores from adjacent years in middle childhood, for example, are typically in the range of .80 (Honzik, 1986). Yet this high level of predictability masks an interesting fact: Many children show quite wide fluctuations in their scores. In fact, about half of all children show noticeable changes from one testing to another and over time (McCall, 1993). Some show steadily rising scores, and some have declining ones; some show a peak in middle childhood and then a decline in adolescence. In rare cases, the shifts may cover a range as large as 40 points.

Such wide fluctuations are more common in young children. The general rule of thumb is that the older the child, the more stable the IQ score—although even in older children, scores may still fluctuate in response to major stresses such as parental divorce, a change of schools, or the birth of a sibling.

● *Limitations of IQ Tests* ●   Before moving on to the question of the possible origins of differences in IQ, it is important to emphasize a few key limitations of IQ tests and the scores derived from them. IQ tests do not measure underlying competence. An IQ score cannot tell you (or a teacher, or anyone else) that your child has some specific, fixed, underlying capacity. Traditional IQ tests also do not measure a whole host of skills that are likely to be highly significant for getting along in the world. Originally, IQ tests were designed to measure only the specific range of skills that are needed for success in school. This they do quite well. What they do *not* do is indicate anything about a particular person's creativity, insight, street-smarts, ability to read social cues, or understanding of spatial relationships (Gardner, 1983; Sternberg & Wagner, 1993).

Origins of Individual Differences in Intelligence

You will not be surprised to discover that arguments about the origins of individual differences in IQ nearly always boil down to a dispute about nature versus nurture.

● *Evidence for Heredity* ●   Both twin studies and studies of adopted children show strong hereditary influences on IQ, as you already know from the Research Report in Chapter 3. Identical twins are more like each other in IQ than are fraternal twins, and the IQs of adopted children are better predicted from the IQs of their natural parents than from those of their adoptive parents (Brody, 1992; Loehlin, Horn, & Willerman, 1994; Scarr, Weinberg, & Waldman, 1993). These are precisely the findings researchers would expect if a strong genetic element were at work.

● *Evidence for Environment* ●   Adoption studies also provide some strong support for an environmental influence on IQ scores, because the IQ scores of adopted children are clearly affected by the environment in which they have grown up. The clearest evidence for this comes from a study of 38 French children, all adopted in infancy (Capron & Duyme, 1989). Roughly half the children had been born to better-educated parents from a higher social class, while the other half had been born to working-class or poverty-level parents. Some of the children in each group had then been adopted by parents in a higher social class, while the others grew up in poorer families. The effect of rearing conditions was evident in that the children reared in upper-class homes had IQs 15–16 points higher than those reared in lower-class families, regardless of the social class level or education of the birth parents. A genetic effect was evident in that the children born to upper-class parents had higher IQs than those from lower-class families, no matter what kind of environment they were reared in.

When developmentalists observe how individual families interact with their infants or young children and then follow the children over time to see which ones later have high or low IQs, they begin to get some sense of the kinds of specific family interactions that foster higher scores. For one thing, parents of higher-IQ children provide them with an interesting and complex physical environment, including play materials that are appropriate for the child's age and developmental level (Bradley et al., 1989; Pianta & Egeland, 1994). They also respond warmly and appropriately to the child's behavior, smiling when the child smiles, answering the child's questions, and in myriad ways reacting to the child's cues (Barnard et al., 1989; Lewis, 1993).

Parents of higher-IQ children also talk to them often, using language that is descriptively rich and accurate (Hart & Risley, 1995; Sigman et al., 1988). And when they play with or interact with their children, they operate in what Vygotsky referred to as the *zone of proximal development* (described in Chapter 2), aiming their conversation, their questions, and their assistance at a level that is just above the level the children could manage on their own, thus helping the children to master new skills (Landry et al., 1996).

In addition, parents that appear to foster intellectual development try to avoid being excessively restrictive, punitive, or controlling, instead giving children room to explore, and even opportunities to make mistakes (Bradley et al., 1989; Olson, Bates, & Kaskie, 1992). In a similar vein, these parents ask questions rather than giving commands (Hart & Risley, 1995). Most also expect their children to do well and to develop rapidly. They emphasize and press for school achievement (Entwisle & Alexander, 1990).

Nevertheless, developmentalists can't be sure that these environmental characteristics are causally important, because parents provide both the genes and the environment. Perhaps these are simply the environmental features provided by brighter parents, and it is the genes and not the environment that cause the higher IQs in their children. However, the research on adopted children's IQs cited earlier suggests that these aspects of environment have a very real impact on children's intellectual development beyond whatever hereditary influences may affect them.

Home environments and family interactions are not the only sources of environmental influence. Programs like Head Start are based squarely on the assumption that it is possible to modify the trajectory of a child's intellectual development, especially if the intervention occurs early enough (Ramey & Ramey, 1998) (see Development in the Information Age). Children in enriched preschool programs normally show a gain of about 10 IQ points while enrolled in them, but this IQ gain typically fades and then disappears within the first few years of school (Zigler & Styfco, 1993).

However, on other kinds of measures, a residual effect of enriched preschool expeiences can clearly be seen some years later. Children who go through Head Start or other quality preschool experience are less likely to be placed in special education classes, less likely to repeat a grade, and more likely to graduate from high school (Barnett, 1995; Darlington, 1991). They also have better health, better immunization rates, and better school adjustment than their peers (Zigler & Styfco, 1993). One very long-term longitudinal study even suggested that the impact of enriched programs may last well into adulthood. This study found that young adults who had attended a particularly good experimental preschool program, the Perry Preschool

Children who attend enrichment programs like this Head Start program typically do not show lasting gains in IQ, but they are more likely to succeed in school. (*Photo:* Paul Conklin, PhotoEdit)

DEVELOPMENT in the Information Age

Computers and Early Childhood Learning

Chapter 4 explored the issue of videos for babies and pointed out that they serve to introduce infants to a culturally important medium but do not necessarily enhance cognitive development. A similar question can be asked about the trend toward increasing computer use by 2- to 6-year-olds: Is the computer an effective medium for teaching young children intellectual skills? If so, then preschool programs such as Head Start might be more effective if computer access were part of the curriculum.

Computer programs have been used to teach pre-reading and mathematics skills to preschoolers from a variety of backgrounds (Boone, Higgins, Notari, & Stump, 1996; Elliot & Hall, 1997). Playing computer games also appears to improve children's fine-motor skills and reaction times (Yuji, 1996). Further, children who have access to computers at home during early childhood are more successful in the early school years (Weinberger, 1996).

However, important questions remain to be answered. First, computers are a great deal more expensive than traditional materials, so it's important to examine their effectiveness as compared to other media. Comparison studies have often shown no differences between the skills of computer-trained children and those of peers who were taught with less expensive media, unless those learning with computers spent a significant amount of time using the educational software (Johnston, 1996). Second, preschoolers who spend a lot of time using a computer at home or at school learn to use software more quickly than other children, but they do not learn the material presented in the software any more rapidly or with any greater degree of accuracy (Yuji, 1996). Third, home studies show that parents who make computers available to young children also provide them with a lot of books and educational toys. They also have more knowledge about early childhood development than parents who do not provide computers. Thus, it is impossible

to say whether the home computer has any independent effect on young children's acquisition of intellectual skills (Weinberger, 1996). Finally, most of the research on computer learning in early childhood has involved 5- to 6-year-old kindergarteners. Results of these studies may not be applicable to 2- to 4-year-olds.

Early childhood educators view the computer as a means of providing children with additional learning opportunities rather than as a replacement for traditional activities (Driscoll & Nagel, 1999). They point out that preschoolers can probably learn a great deal from well-designed educational software, but they still need to play with other children. They also benefit from three-dimensional physical interactions, such as playing with blocks, sand, and fingerpaints. In addition, an interactive computer storybook may be both fun and educational for a child, but it can't replace the human interaction that takes place when a parent or teacher reads a story to a child.

Project in Milwaukee, had higher rates of high school graduation, lower rates of criminal behavior, lower rates of unemployment, and a lower probability of being on welfare than did their peers who had not attended such a preschool (Barnett, 1993).

When the enrichment program is begun in infancy rather than at age 3 or 4, even IQ scores remain elevated after the intervention has ended (Ramey & Ramey, 1998). One very well-designed and meticulously reported infancy intervention was called the Abecedarian project (Campbell & Ramey, 1994; Ramey, 1993; Ramey & Campbell, 1987). Infants from poverty-level families whose mothers had low IQs were randomly assigned either to a special day-care program or to a control group that received nutritional supplements and medical care but no special enriched day care. The special day-care program began when the infants were 6–12 weeks old and lasted until they began kindergarten.

Figure 6.7 (page 174) graphs the average IQ scores of the children in each of these two groups from age 2 to age 12. You can see that the IQs of the children who had been enrolled in the special program were higher at every age. Fully 44% of the control group children had IQ scores classified as borderline or retarded (scores below 85), compared with only 12.8% of the children who had been in the special program. In addition, the enriched day-care group had significantly higher scores on both reading and mathematics tests at age 12 and were only half as likely to have repeated a grade (Ramey, 1992, 1993).

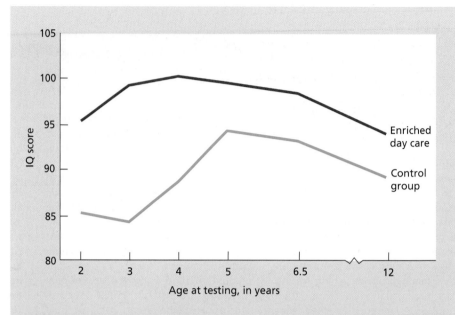

Figure 6.7

In Ramey's study, children from poverty-level families were randomly assigned in infancy to an experimental group that received special day care or to a control group, with the intervention lasting until age 5. At kindergarten, both groups entered public school. The difference in IQ between the experimental and control groups remained statistically significant even at age 12, seven years after the intervention had ended. (*Source:* Ramey & Campbell, 1987, Figure 3, p. 135, with additional data from Ramey, 1993, Figure 2, p. 29.)

● ***Combining the Information*** ● Virtually all psychologists would agree that heredity is a highly important influence on IQ scores. Studies around the world consistently yield estimates that roughly half the variation in IQ within a given population is due to heredity (Neisser et al., 1996; Plomin & Rende, 1991; Rogers, Rowe, & May, 1994). The remaining half is clearly due to environment or to interactions between environment and heredity.

One useful way to think about this interaction is to use the concept of **reaction range**, a range between some upper and lower boundary of functioning established by one's genetic heritage; exactly where a child will fall within those boundaries is determined by environment. Some developmental psychologists estimate that the reaction range for IQ is about 20–25 points (Weinberg, 1989). That is, given a specific genetic heritage, a child's actual IQ test performance may vary as much as 20 or 25 points, depending on the richness or poverty of the environment in which he grows up. When the child's environment is changed for the better, the child moves closer to the upper end of his reaction range. When the environment becomes worse, the child's effective intellectual performance falls toward the lower end of his reaction range. Thus, even though intelligence as measured on an IQ test is highly heritable and falls within the reaction range, the absolute IQ score is determined by environment.

reaction range a range between upper and lower boundaries for traits such as intelligence, which is established by one's genes; one's environment determines where, within those limits, one will be

Racial Differences in Intelligence Test Scores

There appear to be a number of consistent racial differences in IQ test scores and other measures of intellectual performance. For instance, Chinese and Japanese children consistently demonstrate higher performance on achievement tests—particularly math and science tests (Geary, Bow-Thomas, Fan, & Siegler, 1993; Stevenson et al., 1990; Sue & Okazaki, 1990). But the finding that has been most troublesome for researchers and theorists is that in the United States, African American children consistently score lower than white children on measures of IQ. This difference, which is on the order of 12 IQ points, is not found on infant tests of intelligence or on measures of infant habituation rate, but it becomes apparent by the time children are 2 or 3 years old (Brody, 1992; Fagan & Singer, 1983; Peoples, Fagan, & Drotar, 1995). There is some indication that the size of the difference between African American and white children has been declining in the past several decades and may now be less than 10 points, but a noticeable difference persists (Neisser et al., 1996).

Critical Thinking

How does the knowledge that the average IQ scores of African Americans and whites are different affect your own racial attitudes? Do you think psychologists should refrain from discussing such differences to avoid contributing to racial prejudices?

While granting that IQ is highly heritable, many developmentalists point out that the 10- or 12-point difference between average African American and white IQ scores falls well within the presumed reaction range of IQ. They emphasize that the environments in which African American and white children are typically reared differ sufficiently to account for the average difference in score (Brody, 1992). Specifically, African American children in the United States are more likely to be born with low birth weight, to suffer from poor nutrition, and to have high blood levels of lead and are less likely to be read to or to receive a wide range of intellectual stimulation. And each of these environmental characteristics is known to be linked to lower IQ scores.

Some of the most convincing research supporting such an environmental explanation comes from mixed-race adoption studies (Scarr & Weinberg, 1983; Weinberg, Scarr, & Waldman, 1992). For example, researchers have found that African American children adopted at an early age into white middle-class families scored only slightly lower on IQ tests than did white children adopted into the same families. Findings like these persuade many psychologists that the observed IQ score difference between African American and white children primarily reflects the fact that IQ tests, and U.S. schools, are designed by the majority culture to promote a particular form of intellectual activity and that many African American or other minority families rear their children in ways that do not promote or emphasize this particular set of skills.

Another recent entry into the debate on racial differences in IQ scores is the finding that, during the 19th and 20th centuries, average IQ scores increased in every racial group throughout the industrialized world. This phenomenon is known as the *Flynn effect*, because it was discovered by psychologist James Flynn (Flynn, 1999). Flynn's analyses of IQ data over several generations suggest that individuals of average IQ born in the late 19th century would be mentally retarded by today's standards. If IQ is largely genetic, Flynn argues, there should be a great deal of stability in any racial group's average score. Because IQ scores have changed so much in a relatively short period of time, Flynn suggests that cultural changes explain the effect that bears his name. Similarly, Flynn suggests that his cross-generational studies demonstrate that cultural factors are a likely explanation for cross-racial differences as well. He points out that theorists from a variety of fields—from anthropology to medicine—have posited causes for cross-generational gains in IQ such as improved nutrition, greater access to media, and universal literacy. Flynn suggests that all of these factors vary across racial as well as generational groups.

Flynn further points out that many theorists have neglected to consider cultural beliefs in their search for a hereditary basis for intelligence. For example, some psychologists have argued that the differences between Asian and American children in performance on mathematics achievement tests result not from genetic differences in capacity but from differences in cultural beliefs (Stevenson & Lee, 1990). Specifically, Asian societies place little or no value on inborn talent. Instead, they believe that hard work can modify whatever talents a person was born with. Consequently, Asian parents and teachers require students to expend a great deal of effort trying to improve themselves intellectually and do not resort to ability-based explanations of failure. This means that an individual child does not simply accept academic failure as a sign of intellectual deficit but is encouraged by adults to keep on trying. As a result, Asian children spend more time on homework and other academic activities than do children in other cultures.

In contrast, U.S. schools emphasize ability through the routine use of IQ tests to place students in high-, average-, or low-ability classes. This approach reflects American society's greater acceptance of the idea that people are limited by the amount of ability they possess and that it is unfair to ask them to do more than tests suggest they are capable of. It is likely that these complex cultural variables affect children's environments in ways that lead to differences in IQ and achievement test scores (Chang & Murray, 1995; Schneider, Hieshima, Lee, & Plank, 1994; Stevenson & Lee, 1990; Stigler, Lee, & Stevenson, 1987).

Of course, the fact that racial differences in IQ or achievement test performance may be explained by appealing to the concept of reaction range and to cultural beliefs does not make the differences disappear, nor does it make them trivial. Moreover, it's important to remember that there is the same amount of variation in IQ scores in all groups; there are many highly gifted African American children, just as there are many mentally retarded white children. Finally, the benefits of having a high IQ, as well as the risks associated with low IQ, are the same in every racial group (see No Easy Answers).

MAKE THE CONNECTION

In which of Bronfenbrenner's contexts (see Chapter 2, pages 45–47) would you find cultural beliefs about inborn ability? How might these beliefs be manifested in each of the other contexts, and how might they ultimately influence an individual child's development?

No Easy Answers

To Test or Not to Test?

One of the questions that students often ask at this point is, given all the factors that can affect a test score, is it worth bothering with IQ tests at all? The answer is yes: As long as the tests are used properly, intelligence testing can be very beneficial to children.

IQ tests are important tools for identifying children who have special educational needs, such as those who suffer from mental retardation. There are other methods for selecting children for special programs, such as teacher recommendations, but none of the alternatives is as reliable or as valid as an IQ test for measuring that set of cognitive abilities that are demanded by school. Even

when a child's physical characteristics can be used to make a general diagnosis of mental retardation, as in cases of Down syndrome, an intelligence test can reveal to what degree the child is affected. This is important, because effective educational interventions are based on an understanding of how an individual's disability has affected the capacity to learn. Thus, IQ tests are a critical tool in the development of individual educational plans for children with disabilities.

More controversial is routine testing of young children who have no disabilities. Most testing experts agree that using IQ tests to classify normal young children is of little value because their test scores tend to be far less reliable than those of older children. Moreover,

labels based on IQ testing at an early age may be detrimental to young children's future development. Test-based labels may lead teachers and parents to make inappropriate assumptions about children's ability to learn. For example, parents of a high-IQ preschooler may expect her to act like a miniature adult, while the family of a young child whose IQ score is average may limit her opportunities to learn because they are afraid she will fail.

In summary, comprehensive intelligence testing with individual tests can be beneficial to any child who is known to have or suspected of having a disability of any kind. However, labeling nondisabled young children on the basis of IQ scores should be avoided.

Before going on

- Briefly describe the history, usefulness, and limitations of IQ tests.

- What kinds of evidence support the nature and nurture explanations for differences in IQ?

- What theories and evidence have been offered in support of genetic and cultural explanations of racial differences in IQ scores?

A Final Word

Regardless of their IQ scores, all children make tremendous intellectual strides during the early childhood years. By the end of this period, they have attained linguistic fluency. Moreover, they understand a great deal about how others think, and their physical competency far exceeds that of infants. As a result, they function far more independently than when they were toddlers.

Summary

Physical Changes

- Physical development is slower from age 2 to age 6 than it is in infancy, but it nevertheless progresses steadily. Motor skills continue to improve gradually, with marked improvement in large-muscle skills (running, jumping, galloping) and slower advances in small-muscle (fine-motor) skills.

- Significant changes in brain lateralization occur in early childhood. Handedness is weakly related to brain lateralization, but the association between the two is poorly understood.

- Slower rates of growth contribute to declines in appetite. Stress is a factor in early childhood illnesses such as colds and flu.

- Children between the ages of 2 and 9 are more likely to be abused or neglected than are infants or older children. Certain characteristics of both children and parents increase the risk of abuse. Long-term consequences of abuse can include a variety of emotional problems.

Cognitive Changes

- Piaget marked the beginning of the preoperational period at about 18–24 months, at the point when the child begins to use mental symbols. Despite this advance, the preschool child still lacks many sophisticated cognitive skills. In Piaget's view, such children are still egocentric, lack understanding of conservation, and are often fooled by appearances.

- Research challenging Piaget's findings makes it clear that young children are less egocentric than Piaget thought. By age 4, they can distinguish between appearance and reality in a variety of tasks.

- By the end of early childhood, children have a well-developed theory of mind. They understand that other people's actions are based on their thoughts and beliefs.

- Information-processing theory explains early childhood cognitive development in terms of limitations on young children's memory systems. Vygotsky's socio-cultural theory asserts that children's thinking is shaped by social interaction through the medium of language.

Changes in Language

- Language develops at a rapid pace from age 2 to age 4, beginning with simple two-word sentences.

- During the grammar explosion (ages 3 to 4), children make large advances in grammatical fluency.

- Development of an awareness of the sound patterns of a particular language during early childhood is important in learning to read during the school years. Children seem to acquire this skill through word play.

- There are individual differences in the rate of language development. Cross-linguistic studies have shown both similarities and differences in language development among children in different groups.

Differences in Intelligence

- Scores on early childhood intelligence tests are predictive of later school performance and are at least moderately consistent over time.

- Differences in IQ have been attributed to both heredity and environment. Twin and adoption studies make it clear that at least half the variation in IQ scores is due to genetic differences; the remainder is attributable to environment and the interaction of heredity and environment.

- Several kinds of racial differences in IQ or other test scores have been found consistently. Such differences seem most appropriately attributed to environmental variation, rather than to genetics.

Key Terms

conservation (p. 158)

corpus callosum (p. 152)

egocentrism (p. 158)

false belief principle (p. 159)

handedness (p. 152)

hippocampus (p. 152)

inflections (p. 164)

intelligence quotient (IQ) (p. 169)

invented spelling (p. 167)

lateralization (p. 152)

metacognition (p. 162)

metamemory (p. 162)

operational efficiency (p. 162)

overregularization (p. 166)

phonological awareness (p. 166)

preoperational stage (p. 156)

reaction range (p. 174)

short-term storage space (STSS) (p. 162)

theory of mind (p. 160)

CHAPTER 7

Social and Personality Development in Early Childhood

©1998 Aaron Haupt, Stock Boston

If you asked a random sample of adults to tell you the most important characteristics of children between the ages of 2 and 6, the first thing on the list would probably be their rapidly changing social abilities during these years. Nay-saying, oppositional toddlers who spend most of their play time alone become skilled, cooperative playmates by age 5 or 6. Certainly, the huge improvements in language skills are a crucial ingredient in this transition. But the most obvious thing about 5-year-olds is how socially "grown up" they seem compared to toddlers.

This chapter will introduce you to two very different theoretical approaches to understanding social and personality development during the early childhood years. You will also learn about preschoolers' relationships with parents and peers. You will read about important changes in personality, self-concept, and gender understanding that take place during this period. Finally, you will become familiar with how a variety of contexts influence young children's development. As you read, keep the following questions in mind:

- How do the psychoanalytic and social-cognitive perspectives differ in their explanations of social and personality development during early childhood?

- In what ways do family relationships change during the early childhood period?

- What does research reveal about the effects of various family structures and divorce?

- How do preschoolers relate to peers?

- What important changes in personality and self-concept happen during early childhood?

- How does the child's understanding of gender and gender roles develop?

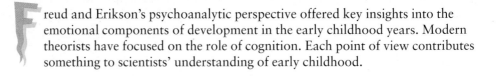

Theories of Social and Personality Development

Freud and Erikson's psychoanalytic perspective offered key insights into the emotional components of development in the early childhood years. Modern theorists have focused on the role of cognition. Each point of view contributes something to scientists' understanding of early childhood.

Psychoanalytic Perspectives

If you go back and look at Table 2.2 (page 28), you'll see that Freud described two stages during these preschool years, each characterized by a different focus of the libido's energy. The first of these, the *anal stage,* Freud thought was dominant between roughly ages 1 and 3. Freud thought toilet training interfered with toddlers' need to experience control over anal functions. Thus, training methods that were either too permissive or too strict, he believed, would lead to problems in personality development. The *phallic stage* occurs between ages 3 and 6. It is during this stage, Freud thought, that the Oedipus or the Electra complex arises, resulting in identification with the same-sex parent. Consequently, healthy personality development, he believed, required the presence of both parents in the home. Moreover, Freud suggested that, for successful resolution of the Oedipus or Electra Complex, the relationships between the child and each parent had to be warm and loving.

Erikson placed the emphasis somewhat differently. Both of the stages he identified in the preschool period (see Table 2.3, page 29) are triggered by children's growing physical, cognitive, and social skills. The stage Erikson called *autonomy versus shame and doubt,* for example, is centered around the toddler's new mobility and the accompanying desire for autonomy. The stage of *initiative versus guilt* is ushered in by new cognitive skills, particularly the preschooler's ability to plan, which accentuates his wish to take the initiative.

Both theorists believed that the key to healthy development during this period is striking a balance between the child's emerging skills and desire for autonomy and the parents' need to protect the child and control the child's behavior. Thus, the parents' task changes rather dramatically after infancy. In the early months of life, the parents' primary task is to provide enough warmth, predictability, and responsiveness to foster a secure attachment and to support basic physiological needs. But once the child becomes physically, linguistically, and cognitively more independent, the need to control becomes a central aspect of the parents' task. Too much control and the child will not have sufficient opportunity to explore; too little control and the child will become unmanageable and fail to learn the social skills he will need to get along with peers as well as adults.

Neither Freud nor Erikson talked much about the role of the child's peers in development, but a number of other theorists have emphasized the vital significance of such encounters. Hartup suggests that each child needs experience in different kinds of relationships (Hartup, 1996). First, each child needs an attachment to someone who has greater knowledge and social power, such as a parent, a teacher, or even an older sibling. Such relationships are complementary rather than reciprocal. The bond may be extremely powerful in both directions, but the actual behaviors the two individuals show toward each other are not the same. For example, a parent makes a sandwich for a child's lunch far more often than the reverse.

Second, children need reciprocal relationships with others, such as same-age peers or near-age siblings, whose knowledge and social power are equal to their own. In reciprocal relationships, partners demonstrate the same behavior toward each other and often work together to accomplish a task. Thus, two children may work together to make sandwiches for lunch.

Hartup's point is that these two kinds of relationships serve different functions for the child, and a child needs both in order to develop effective social skills. Attachment relationships are necessary to provide the child with protection and security. In these relationships, children create basic internal working models and learn fundamental social skills. But in reciprocal relationships—in friendships and in peer groups—children practice social behavior and acquire those social skills that can only be learned in a relationship between equals: cooperation, competition, and intimacy.

Social-Cognitive Perspectives

The emphasis on peer relations proposed by Hartup and others has been important in turning developmentalists' attention toward the contribution of cognitive skills to changes in social and personality development. In contrast to the psychoanalytic tradition, **social-cognitive theory** assumes that social and emotional changes in the child are the result of, or at least are facilitated by, the enormous growth in cognitive abilities that happens during the preschool years (Macrae & Bodenhausen, 2000). Over the past three decades, psychologists have devoted a great deal of theoretical and empirical attention to determining just how the two domains are connected.

According to Freud, young children need strong attachments to both mother and father to successfully resolve the conflicts of the phallic stage. (*Photo:* Will Faller)

social-cognitive theory the theoretical perspective that asserts that social and personality development in early childhood are related to improvements in the cognitive domain

● *Person Perception* ●   Preschoolers' emerging capacity for forming meaningful categories manifests itself in the social domain as a set of ideas and behaviors psychologists call **person perception,** or the ability to classify others. For example, by kindergarten age, children make judgments very similar to those of adults when asked to identify the most intelligent child in their class or play group (Droege & Stipek, 1993). Moreover, they describe their peers in terms of traits such as "grumpy" and "mean" (Yuill, 1997). They also make statements about other people's patterns of behavior—"Grandma always lets me pick the cereal at the grocery store." They use these observations to classify others into groups such as "people I like" and "people I don't like."

However, young children's observations and categorizations of people are far less consistent than those of older children. A playmate they judge to be "nice" one day may be referred to as "mean" the next. Developmentalists have found that young children's judgments about others are inconsistent because they tend to base them on their most recent interactions with those individuals (Ruble & Dweck, 1995). In other words, a 4-year-old girl describes one of her playmates as "nice" on Monday because she shares a cookie, but as "mean" on Tuesday because she refuses to share a candy bar. Or, the child declares "I don't like Grandma any more because she made me go to bed early."

Preschoolers also categorize others on the basis of observable characteristics such as age, gender, and race. They talk about "big kids" (school-age children) and "little kids" (their agemates), and they seem to know that they fit in best with the latter. Self-segregation by gender— a topic you'll read more about later in the chapter—begins as early as age 2. Likewise, young children sometimes segregate themselves according to race (see The Real World).

> *Critical Thinking*
>
> Think of as many explanations as you can for the fact that children begin to prefer to play with same-sex peers as early as age 3 or 4.

● *Understanding Rule Categories* ●   According to social-cognitive theorists, young children also use classification skills to take another important step in social development when they begin to understand the difference between *social conventions* and *moral rules* (Turiel, 1983). A social convention is a rule that serves to regulate behavior but has no moral implications. For example, in the United States, shaking hands with others when you meet them is a social convention. Moral rules are regulations based on an individual's or society's fundamental sense of right and wrong. Most of us would feel differently about eliminating laws against stealing than we would about switching from driving on the right to the left side of the street, because laws against stealing are based on a moral principle—we believe it is morally wrong for one person to take another's property.

Researchers have found that children begin to respond differently to violations of social conventions and moral rules between 2 and 3 (Smetana, Schlagman, & Adams, 1993). For example, they view taking another child's toy without permission as a more serious violation of rules than forgetting to say "thank you." They also say, just as adults would in response to similar questions, that stealing and physical violence are wrong, even if their particular family or preschool has no explicit rule against them. This kind of understanding seems to develop both as a consequence of preschoolers' increasing capacity for classification and as a result of adults' tendency to emphasize moral transgressions more than social-convention violations when punishing children (Nucci & Smetana, 1996).

● *Understanding Others' Intentions* ●   Would you feel differently about a person who deliberately smashed your car's windshield with a baseball bat than you would about someone else who accidentally broke it while washing your car for you?

person perception the ability to classify others according to categories such as age, gender, and race

TEACHING
The Real World

Racism in the Preschool Classroom

The preschool classroom or day-care center is often the only setting in which children of different races come together. Consequently, these classrooms are likely to be important to the development of racial attitudes. Preschool teachers, then, need to be aware of how such attitudes are formed.

Research suggests that, once young children form race schemas, they use them to make judgments about others. These early judgments probably reflect young children's egocentric thinking. Essentially, children view those like themselves as desirable companions and those who are unlike them—in gender, race, and other categorical variables—as undesirable (Doyle & Aboud, 1995). Thus, like the understanding of race itself, race-based playmate preferences probably result from immature cognitive structures rather than true racism.

Of course, cognitive development doesn't happen in a social vacuum, and by age 5, most white children in English-speaking countries have acquired an understanding of their culture's racial stereotypes and prejudices (Bigler & Liben, 1993). Likewise, African American, Hispanic American, and Native American children become sensitive very early in life to the fact that people of their race are viewed negatively by many whites. White preschool teachers may not notice race-based behavior in their classrooms, but research suggests that minority children report a significant number of such events to their parents (Bernhard, Lefebvre, Kilbride, Chud, & Lange, 1998).

Psychologists speculate that the combination of immature cognitive development, acquisition of cultural stereotypes, and preschool teachers' insensitivity to racial incidents may foster racist attitudes. The key to preventing racial awareness from developing into racism, they say, is for preschool teachers to discuss race

openly and to make conscious efforts to help children acquire non-prejudiced attitudes (Cushner, McClelland, & Safford, 1993). For example, they can make young children aware of historical realities such as slavery, race segregation, and minority groups' efforts to achieve equal rights. Teachers can also assign children of different races to do projects together. In addition, they can make children aware of each others' strengths as individuals, since both children and adults seem to perceive individual differences only within their own racial group (Ostrom, Carpenter, Sedikides, & Li, 1993).

Ideally, all children should learn to evaluate their own and others' behavior according to individual criteria rather than group membership, and minority children need to be especially encouraged to view their race positively. Preschool teachers are in a position to provide young children with a significant push toward these important goals.

Chances are you would be far more forgiving of the person who unintentionally broke your windshield, because we tend to base our judgments of others' behavior and our responses to them on what we perceive to be their intentions. Working from his assumptions about young children's egocentrism, Piaget suggested that young children are incapable of such discriminations.

However, more recent research has demonstrated that young children do understand intentions to some degree. For one thing, it's quite common for preschoolers to say "It was an accident . . . I didn't mean to do it" when they are punished. Such protests suggest that children understand that intentional wrongdoing is punished more severely than unintentional transgressions of the rules.

Several studies suggest that children can make judgments about actors' intentions both when faced with abstract problems and when personally motivated by a desire to avoid punishment. For example, in a classic study, 3-year-olds listened to stories about children playing ball (Nelson, 1980). Pictures were used to convey information about intentions (see Figure 7.1, page 184). The children were more likely to label as "bad" or "naughty" the child who intended to harm a playmate than the child who accidentally hit another child in the head with the ball. However, the children's judgments were also influenced by outcomes. In other words, they were more likely to say a child who wanted to hurt his playmate was "good" if he failed to hit the child with the ball. These results suggest that children know more about intentions than Piaget thought, but they are still limited in their ability to base judgments entirely on intentions.

Figure 7.1

Pictures like these have been used to assess young children's understanding of an actor's intentions.

Before going on

- How do the theories of Freud, Erikson, and modern theorists differ in their emphasis on children's families and peers?

- What are the findings of social-cognitive theorists with respect to preschoolers' skills in person perception, understanding of rules, and understanding of others' intentions?

Family Relationships

espite changing views concerning the various influences on early childhood development, psychologists agree that family relationships constitute one of the most, if not the most, influential factors in early childhood development. These relationships reflect both continuity and change, in that the preschooler is no less attached to her family than the infant but, at the same time, is struggling to establish independence.

Attachment

You'll remember from Chapter 5 that by 12 months of age, a baby has normally established a clear attachment to at least one caregiver. By age 2 or 3, the attachment is just as strong, but many attachment behaviors have become less visible. Three-year-olds still want to sit on Mom's or Dad's lap; they are still likely to seek some closeness when Mom returns from an absence. But when she is not afraid or under stress, the 3-year-old is able to wander farther and farther from her safe base without apparent distress. She can also deal with her potential anxiety due to separation by creating shared plans with the parents. For example, a parent might say "I'll be home after your naptime," to which the child may respond "Can we watch a movie then?" (Crittenden, 1992).

Attachment quality also predicts behavior during the preschool years. Children who are securely attached to parents experience fewer behavior problems. Specifically, those who are insecurely attached display more anger and aggression toward both peers and adults in social settings such as day care and preschool (DeMulder, Denham, Schmidt, & Mitchell, 2000).

For most children, the attachment relationship, whether secure or not, seems to change at about age 4. Bowlby described this new stage, or level, as a *goal-corrected partnership*. Just as the first attachment probably requires the baby to understand that his mother will continue to exist when she isn't there, so the preschooler grasps that the *relationship* continues to exist even when the partners are apart. Also at about age 4, the child's internal model of attachment appears to generalize. Bowlby argued that the child's model becomes less a specific property of an individual relationship and more a general property of all the child's social relationships. Thus, it's not surprising that 4- and 5-year-olds who are securely attached to their parents are more likely than their insecurely attached peers to have positive relationships with their preschool teachers (DeMulder et al., 2000).

At the same time, advances in the internal working model lead to new conflicts. In contrast to infants, 2-year-olds realize that they are independent contributors to the parent-child relationship. This heightened sense of autonomy brings them into more and more situations in which parents want one thing and children another. However, contrary to popular stereotypes, 2-year-olds actually comply with parents' requests more often than not. They are more likely to comply with safety requests ("Don't touch that, it's hot!") or with prohibitions about care of objects ("Don't tear up the book") than they are with requests to delay ("I can't talk to you now, I'm on the phone") or with instructions about self-care ("Please wash your hands now"). On the whole, however, children of this age comply fairly readily (Gralinski & Kopp, 1993). When they resist, it is most likely to be passive resistance—simply not doing what is asked rather than saying "no."

Parenting Styles

Of course, families vary in their responses to preschoolers' increasing demands for independence. Psychologists have struggled over the years to identify the best ways of describing the many dimensions along which families may vary. At present, the most fruitful conceptualization is one offered by developmentalist Diana Baumrind, who focuses on four aspects of family functioning: (1) warmth or nurturance; (2) clarity and consistency of rules; (3) level of expectations, which she describes in terms of "maturity demands"; and (4) communication between parent and child (Baumrind, 1972).

Off he goes, into greater independence. A child this age, especially one with secure attachment, is far more confident about being at a distance from his safe base. (*Photo:* Corbis Digital Stock)

MAKE THE CONNECTION

What effect do you think a child's increasingly complex theory of mind (see Chapter 6) has on the child's relationship with her parents?

Each of these four dimensions has been independently shown to be related to various child behaviors. Children with nurturant and warm parents are more securely attached in the first 2 years of life than those with more rejecting parents; they also have higher self-esteem and are more empathetic, more altruistic, and more responsive to others' hurts or distress; they have higher IQs, are more compliant in preschool and elementary school, do better in school, and are less likely to show delinquent behavior in adolescence or criminal behavior in adulthood (Maccoby, 1980; Maughan, Pickles, & Quinton, 1995; Simons, Robertson, & Downs, 1989; Stormshak et al., 2000).

High levels of affection can even buffer a child against the negative effects of otherwise disadvantageous environments. Several studies of children and teens growing up in poor, tough neighborhoods show that parental warmth is associated with both social and academic competence (Masten & Coatsworth, 1998). In contrast, parental hostility is linked to declining school performance and higher risk of delinquency among poor children and adolescents (Melby & Conger, 1996).

The degree and clarity of the parents' control over the child are also significant. Parents with clear rules, consistently applied, have children who are much less likely to be defiant or noncompliant. Such children are also more competent and sure of themselves and less aggressive (Kurdek & Fine, 1994; Patterson, 1980).

Equally important is the form of control the parents use. The most optimal outcomes for the child occur when the parents are not overly restrictive, explain things to the child, and avoid the use of physical punishments. Children whose parents have high expectations (high "maturity demands" in Baumrind's language) also fare better. Such children have higher self-esteem and show more generosity and altruism toward others.

Finally, open and regular communication between parent and child has been linked to more positive outcomes. Listening to the child is as important as talking to him. Ideally, parents need to convey to the child that what the child has to say is worth listening to, that his ideas are important and should be considered in family decisions. Children of such parents have been found to be more emotionally and socially mature (Baumrind, 1971; Bell & Bell, 1982).

While each of these characteristics of families may be significant individually, they do not occur in isolation but in combinations and patterns. In her early research, Baumrind identified three patterns, or styles, of parenting (Baumrind, 1967). The **permissive parenting style** is high in nurturance but low in maturity demands, control, and communication. The **authoritarian parenting style** is high in control and maturity demands but low in nurturance and communication. The **authoritative parenting style** is high in all four dimensions.

Eleanor Maccoby and John Martin have proposed a variation of Baumrind's category system, shown in Figure 7.2 (Maccoby & Martin, 1983). They categorize families on two dimensions: the degree of demand or control, and the amount of acceptance versus rejection. The intersection of these two dimensions creates four types, three of which correspond quite closely to Baumrind's authoritarian, authoritative, and permissive types. Maccoby and Martin's conceptualization adds a fourth type, the **uninvolved parenting style**.

● **The Authoritarian Type** ●   Children growing up in authoritarian families—with high levels of demand and control but relatively low levels of warmth and communication—do less well in school, have lower self-esteem, and are typically less skilled with peers than are children from other types of families. Some of these children appear subdued; others may show high aggressiveness or other indications of being out of control. These effects are not restricted to preschool-aged children. In a series of large studies of high school students, including longitudinal studies of more than 6,000 teens, developmentalists found that teenagers from authoritarian families had poorer grades in school and more negative self-concepts than did teenagers from

permissive parenting style a style of parenting that is high in nurturance and low in maturity demands, control, and communication

authoritarian parenting style a style of parenting that is low in nurturance and communication, but high in control and maturity demands

authoritative parenting style a style of parenting that is high in nurturance, maturity demands, control, and communication

uninvolved parenting style a style of parenting that is low in nurturance, maturity demands, control, and communication

authoritative families (Dornbusch, Ritter, Liederman, Roberts, & Fraleigh, 1987; Lamborn, Mounts, Steinberg, & Dornbusch, 1991; Steinberg, Darling, Fletcher, Brown, & Dornbusch, 1995; Steinberg, Lamborn, Dornbusch, & Darling, 1992; Steinberg, Lamborn, Darling, Mounts, & Dornbusch, 1994).

● *The Permissive Type* ●   Children growing up with indulgent or permissive parents also show some negative outcomes. Researchers have found that these children do slightly worse in school during adolescence and are likely to be both more aggressive (particularly if the parents are specifically permissive toward aggressiveness) and somewhat immature in their behavior with peers and in school. They are less likely to take responsibility and are less independent.

● *The Authoritative Type* ●   The most consistently positive outcomes have been associated with an authoritative pattern in which the parents are high in both control and acceptance—setting clear limits but also responding to the child's individual needs. Children reared in such families typically show higher self-esteem and are more independent, but are also more likely to comply with parental requests and may show more altruistic behavior as well. They are self-confident and achievement-oriented in school and get better grades than do children whose parents have other parenting styles (Crockenberg & Litman, 1990; Dornbusch et al., 1987; Steinberg, Elmen, & Mounts, 1989).

● *The Uninvolved Type* ●   The most consistently negative outcomes are associated with the fourth pattern, the uninvolved or neglecting parenting style. You may remember from the discussion of secure and insecure attachments in Chapter 5 that one of the family characteristics often found in infants rated as insecure/avoidant is the "psychological unavailability" of the mother. The mother may be depressed or may be overwhelmed by other problems in her life and may simply have not made any deep emotional connection with the child. Likewise, a parent may be distracted from parenting by more attractive activities. Whatever the reason, such children continue to show disturbances in their social relationships for many years. In adolescence, for example, youngsters from neglecting families are more impulsive and antisocial, less competent with their peers, and much less achievement oriented in school (Block, 1971; Lamborn et al., 1991; Pulkkinen, 1982).

● *Effects of Parenting Styles* ●   Figure 7.3 illustrates the contrasting outcomes in the longitudinal study of adolescents you read about a few paragraphs back; it graphs variations in grade point average as a function of family style. In a longitudinal analysis, these same researchers found that students who described their parents as most authoritative at the beginning of the study showed more improvement in academic competence and self-reliance and the smallest increases in psychological symptoms and delinquent behavior over the succeeding 2 years. So these effects persist.

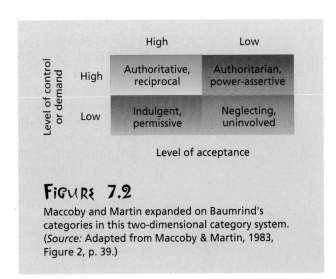

FIGURE 7.2

Maccoby and Martin expanded on Baumrind's categories in this two-dimensional category system. (*Source:* Adapted from Maccoby & Martin, 1983, Figure 2, p. 39.)

Critical Thinking

Why do you think children of permissive parents are less independent than those from authoritative families?

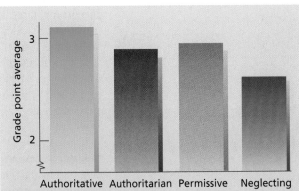

FIGURE 7.3

Grades varied with parenting style in Steinberg and Dornbusch's study. (*Source:* Steinberg et al., 1994, from Table 5, p. 762.)

However, the effects of the family system are more complex than the figure shows. For example, authoritative parents are much more likely to be involved with their child's school, attending school functions and talking to teachers, and this involvement seems to play a crucial role in their children's better school performance. When an authoritative parent is not involved with the school, the academic outcome for the student is not so clearly positive. Similarly, a teenager whose parent is highly involved with the school but is not authoritative shows a less optimal outcome. It is the combination of authoritativeness and school involvement that is associated with the best results (Steinberg et al., 1992).

Another set of complexities is evident in the interaction between parenting style and child temperament. For example, authoritative parents often use **inductive discipline,** a discipline strategy in which parents explain to children why a punished behavior is wrong (Hoffman, 1970). Inductive discipline helps most preschoolers gain control of their behavior and learn to look at situations from perspectives other than their own. Likewise, the majority of preschool-aged children of parents who respond to demonstrations of poor self-control, such as temper tantrums, by asserting their social and physical power—as often happens when parents physically punish children—have poorer self-control than preschoolers whose parents use inductive discipline (Kochanska, 1997b; Kochanska, Murray, Jacques, Koenig, & Vandegeest, 1996).

However, research on inductive discipline suggests that it is not equally effective for all children. Those who have difficult temperaments or who are physically active and who seem to enjoy risk-taking—such as children who like to climb on top of furniture and jump off—seem to have a greater need for firm discipline and to benefit less from inductive discipline than do their peers whose temperamental make-up is different (Kochanska, 1997a). In fact, assumptions about the superiority of inductive discipline, as well as authoritative parenting in general, have been criticized by developmentalists who claim that correlations between discipline strategy and child behavior may arise simply because parents adapt their techniques to their children's behavior. Thus, parents of poorly behaved children may be more punitive or authoritarian because they have discovered that this is the kind of parenting their children need.

Ethnicity, Socio-Economic Status, and Parenting Styles

Ethnicity and socio-economic variables also interact with parenting styles. In an important, large-scale, cross-sectional study involving roughly 10,000 9th- through 12th-grade students representing four ethnic groups (white, African American, Hispanic, and Asian), each student answered questions about the acceptance, control, and autonomy they received from their parents (Steinberg, Mounts, Lamborn, & Dornbusch, 1991). When an adolescent described his family as above the average on all three dimensions, the family was classed as authoritative. Figure 7.4 shows the percentages of families that were classed in this way in the four ethnic groups, broken down further by the social class and intactness of the family.

You can see that the authoritative pattern was most common among white families and least common among Asian Americans, but in each ethnic group, authoritative parenting was more common among the middle class and (with one exception) more common among intact families than among single-parent or step-parent families. Furthermore, these researchers found some relationship between authoritative parenting and positive outcomes in all ethnic groups. In all four groups, for example, teenagers from authoritative families showed more self-reliance and less delinquency than did those from nonauthoritative families. However, this study, like others, found strong links between authoritative parenting style and positive outcomes only for whites and Hispanics. For Asian Americans and African Americans, the researchers

inductive discipline a discipline strategy in which parents explain to children why a punished behavior is wrong

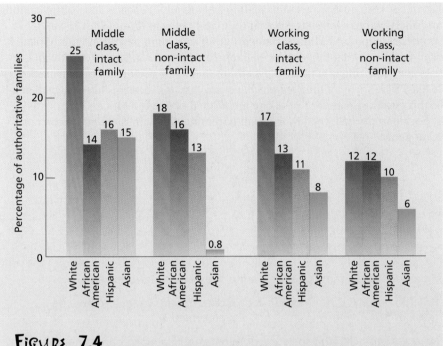

FIGURE 7.4

As this figure suggests, authoritative parenting is more common among middle-class parents as well as in intact families (in which the child lives with both natural parents) of all ethnicities. (*Source:* Steinberg et al., 1991.)

found stronger connections between authoritarian style and variables such as school performance and social competence.

Studies in which children provide information about their parents' style as well as those in which researchers conduct direct observation of parents have consistently found that, in general, Asian American parents display an authoritarian style (Chao, 1994; Wang & Phinney, 1998). The finding that Asian American children score higher than their white counterparts on almost all measures of cognitive competence argues against the assumption that authoritative parenting is best. In fact, developmentalists have found a link between Asian American children's achievement and authoritarian parenting—that is, parents who have the most authoritarian parenting style have the highest-scoring children (Wang & Phinney, 1998).

However, the key variable in these findings may not be ethnicity. Because the growth in Asian immigration to the United States is a fairly recent phenomenon, many parents in these studies were newcomers to the country. Thus, Asian American parents may be authoritarian in response to living in an environment that is different from the one in which they grew up, not because they are Asian. Authoritarian parenting may help them achieve two important goals: to help their children succeed economically and to enable them to maintain a sense of ethnic identity. Evidence supporting this interpretation also comes from studies of Russian families who have recently emigrated to Israel and North African families living in France (Camilleri & Malewska-Peyre, 1997; Roer-Strier & Rivlis, 1998).

The same link between parenting goals and parenting style may help explain the greater incidence of authoritarian behavior on the part of African American parents. Specifically, African American parents are keenly aware of the degree to which social forces such as racism may impede their children's achievement of educational, economic, and social success. Consequently, they may adopt an authoritarian style because they believe it will enhance their children's potential for success. In fact, the correlation between authoritarian parenting and variables such as self-control among African American children suggests that they may be right (Baumrind, 1980).

Another reason that authoritarian parenting may be more common in African American families is that they are more likely to be poor. As Figure 7.4 shows, authoritative parenting is generally less common among poor parents than among middle-class parents in all four major U.S. ethnic groups. It seems likely that the reason for this pattern is similar to the one mentioned above for African Americans—that is, poor parents believe authoritarian parenting will help their children attain important goals.

Before going on

- How does attachment change during the early childhood years?

- How do parents differ in their approaches to parenting, and how do these differences affect children's development?

- How are ethnicity and socio-economic status related to parenting style?

Family Structure and Divorce

o better understand human development, it is important to examine how the structure of children's families may influence their development.

Family Structure

Despite increases in the number of single-parent households, the two-parent family continues to be the dominant structure in the United States. In 1970, almost 95% of children lived in such families, but by the late 1990s, about 70% of children were living in two-parent homes (U.S. Bureau of the Census, 1998). Still, the proportion of single-parent families in the United States far exceeds that in other industrialized countries. For example, in Korea, Japan, and other Asian nations, only 4–8% of children live with a single parent (Martin, 1995). In Australia, the United Kingdom, and Sweden, single-parent families represent about 15% of all households with children (Burns, 1992).

● ***Diversity in Two-Parent and Single-Parent Families*** ● The two-parent family, though still the most common living arrangement for children in the United States, is far more diverse than in the past or in other industrialized nations. Only about half of all children in the United States live with both their biological parents (Hernandez, 1997). From 20% to 30% of two-parent families were created when a divorced or never-married single parent married another single parent or a nonparent (Ganong & Coleman, 1994). Thus, many children in two-parent households have experienced single-parenting at one time or another while growing up.

However, it's important to keep in mind that any set of statistics is like a snapshot of a single moment in time, which fails to capture the number of changes in family structure many children experience across their early years. For example, in some two-parent households, the "parents" are actually the child's grandparents. In most cases, custodial grandparents are caring for the children of a daughter who has some kind of significant problem such as criminal behavior or substance abuse (Jendrek, 1993). These children are likely to have experienced a variety of living arrangements before coming to live with their grandparents. Likewise, many married parents once were single parents who had relationships with one or more live-in partners.

Single-parent households are diverse as well. In contrast to stereotypes, some single parents are very financially secure. In fact, the proportion of births to single mothers is increasing most rapidly among middle-class professional women who have actively decided to become single parents (Ingrassia, 1993). Other single parents, especially unmarried teenagers, are likely to live with their own parents (Jorgenson, 1993). Consequently, single-parent households are no more alike than are two-parent households.

● *Family Structure and Ethnicity* ● Looking at family structure across ethnic groups further illustrates family diversity in the United States. You can get some feeling for the degree of variation from Figure 7.5 (page 192). The figure graphs estimates of the percentages of five different family types among white, African American, and Hispanic 13-year-olds in the United States, based on a nationally representative sample of over 21,000 children (Lee, Burkham, Zimiles, & Ladewski, 1994).

You can see that single-parent families are far more common among African Americans than among other groups. The reasons for this finding are complex. Differences in birth and marriage rates are the statistical explanation. About 26% of white, 41% of Hispanic, and 70% of African American infants are born to unmarried women annually in the United States (U.S. Bureau of the Census, 1998). By the way, it is a myth that extremely high rates of pregnancy among African American teenagers are responsible for this difference. For all racial groups, the majority of births to unmarried women occur when the women are over 20 (89% for white women, 83% for Hispanic Americans, 77% for African Americans) (U.S. Bureau of the Census, 1998).

Second, although many African American single mothers eventually marry, African American adults, whether parents or not, are less likely to marry. Approximately 37% of African American adults have never been married. Among whites, only 18% have remained single throughout their adult lives (U.S. Bureau of the Census, 1998).

Of course, statistics can't explain why African American families are more likely to be headed by single women than those of other groups. Sociologists speculate that lack of economic opportunities for African American men render them less able to take on family responsibilities (Cherlin, 1992). Others add that African American grandparents and other relatives traditionally help support single mothers. As a result, single parents may feel less social and economic pressure to marry.

● *Family Structure Effects* ● The broadest statement psychologists can make about the effects of family structure is that, at least in the United States, research suggests that the optimum situation for children appears to be one that includes two natural parents. Never-married mothers, divorced mothers or fathers who have not remarried, and step-parents are frequently linked to less positive outcomes. Factors

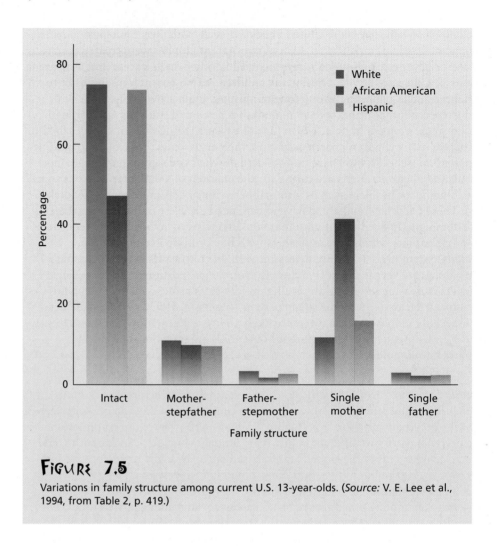

FIGURE 7.5

Variations in family structure among current U.S. 13-year-olds. (*Source:* V. E. Lee et al., 1994, from Table 2, p. 419.)

associated with single-parenthood, such as poverty, may help explain its negative effects on development. Still, the differences between children who never experience single-parenting and those who do are too large to be completely explained by other variables. This means that at least part of the difference is connected to the family structure itself. Thus, it's important to know just what the differences are.

Children growing up in single-parent families are about twice as likely to drop out of high school, twice as likely to have a child before age 20, and less likely to have a steady job in their late teens or early 20s (McLanahan & Sandefur, 1994). Children of adolescent mothers are particularly at risk. Differences between children of teenagers and those whose mothers are older are evident in early childhood. Preschoolers whose mothers are single teenagers display less advanced cognitive and social development than their peers (Coley & Chase-Lansdale, 1998).

● ***Other Types of Family Structures*** ● In contrast to the amount of research comparing two-parent and single-parent families, there are relatively few studies of the effects of other kinds of family structures. For example, research on custodial grandparenting tends to focus on the effects of the parenting experience on aging adults. Consequently, researchers know that grandparents' responses to children's problems are quite similar to those of parents (Daly & Glenwick, 2000). However, the stresses of parenting combined with the physical effects of aging are likely to cause older adults to feel more anxious and depressed than younger adults in similar situations (Burton, 1992; Jendrek, 1993). Thus, developmentalists know something about how parenting affects older adults but very little about how children raised by grandparents fare.

Similarly, concerns about children's sex-role identity and sexual orientation have dominated research on gay and lesbian parenting (Bailey, Brobow, Wolfe, & Mikach, 1995). Studies have generally shown that children raised by gay and lesbian parents develop sex-role identities in the same way as children of heterosexual parents. They are also just as likely to be heterosexual (Golombok & Tasker, 1996).

To help answer general questions about cognitive and social development among the children of gay and lesbian parents, researchers have conducted comprehensive reviews of the small number of studies that have been done. Such reviews have examined a wide variety of studies of gay and lesbian parenting, including case studies, correlational studies, and comparisons of children in gay and lesbian families to those being raised by heterosexual parents. These reviews have typically found that the majority of studies suggest that children raised by gay and lesbian parents do not differ from those raised by heterosexuals (Fitzgerald, 1999; Patterson, 1997). However, most of the gay and lesbian participants in these studies have been raising their own biological children, who were conceived while the parents were involved in heterosexual relationships. Very few studies have involved children who have been raised exclusively by openly gay or lesbian parents, and fewer still have compared children of gay or lesbian parents with partners to those raised by single gays or lesbians.

One recent study involved 80 school-aged children who had been conceived by artificial insemination (Chan, Raboy, & Patterson, 1998). Researchers compared these children across four types of family structures: lesbian couples, single lesbian mothers, heterosexual couples, and single heterosexual mothers. The study found no differences in either cognitive or social development among them. However, they did find that the same variables—parenting stress, parental conflict, parental affection—predicted developmental outcomes in all four groups. These findings, much like those of research contrasting two-parent and single-parent families, suggest that children's development depends more on how parents interact with them than on any particular family configuration.

Divorce

There can be little doubt that divorce is traumatic for children. It's important to note, however, that some of the negative effects of divorce are due to factors that were present *before* the divorce, such as difficult temperament in the child or excessive marital conflict between the parents (Cherlin, Chase-Lansdale, & McRae, 1998). It's also important to keep in mind that divorce is not a single variable; children are probably affected by a multitude of divorce-related factors—parental conflict, poverty, disruptions of daily routine, and so on (Hetherington, Bridges, & Insabella, 1998). For this reason, children whose parents separate or who stay in conflict-ridden marriages may experience many of the same effects as children whose parents actually divorce (Ingoldsby, Shaw, Owens, & Winslow, 1999).

In the first few years after a divorce, children typically show declines in school performance and show more aggressive, defiant, negative, or depressed behavior (Furstenberg & Cherlin, 1991; Hetherington & Clingempeel, 1992; Morrison & Cherlin, 1995; Pagani, Boulerice, Tremblay, & Vitaro, 1998). By adolescence, the children of divorced parents are more likely than their peers to become sexually active at an early age, to experiment with drugs and alcohol, and to engage in criminal behavior (Kurtz & Tremblay, 1995; Wallerstein & Lewis, 1998). Children living in step-parent families also have higher rates of delinquency, more behavior problems in school, and lower grades than do those in intact families (Lee et al., 1994; Pagani et al., 1997).

The negative effects of divorce seem to persist for many years. For example, children whose parents divorce have a higher risk of mental health problems in adulthood (Chase-Lansdale, Cherlin, & Kiernan, 1995; Cherlin, Chase-Lansdale, & McRae, 1998; Wallerstein & Lewis, 1998). Many young adults whose parents are

Many single parents manage to overcome substantial obstacles to give their children the support and supervision they need. (*Photos:* Cindy Charles, PhotoEdit; John Fortunato, Tony Stone Images)

divorced lack the financial resources and emotional support necessary to succeed in college, and a majority report that they struggle with fears of intimacy in relationships (Wallerstein & Lewis, 1998). Not surprisingly, adults whose parents divorced are themselves more likely to divorce.

As a general rule, these negative effects are more pronounced for boys than for girls. However, some researchers have found that the effects are delayed in girls, making it more difficult to associate the effects with the divorce. Consequently, longitudinal studies often find that girls show equal or even greater negative effects (Amato, 1993; Hetherington, 1991a, 1991b). Age differences in the severity of the reaction have been found in some studies but not others. For example, one longitudinal study found that the effects of divorce were most severe in a group of 12-year-olds who experienced parental divorce in early childhood rather than during their school years (Pagani et al., 1997).

Ethnicity, incidentally, does not appear to be a causal factor here. Yes, a larger percentage of African American children grow up in single-parent families. But the same negative outcomes occur in white single-parent families, and the same positive outcomes are found in two-parent minority families. For example, the school dropout rate for a white child from a single-parent family is higher than the dropout rate for a Hispanic American or African American child reared in a two-parent family (McLanahan & Sandefur, 1994).

Understanding the Effects of Family Structure and Divorce

How are we to understand these various findings? First, single parenthood or divorce reduces the financial and emotional resources available to support the child. With only one parent, the household typically has only one income and only one adult to respond to the child's emotional needs. Data from the United States indicate that a woman's income drops an average of 40–50% after a divorce (Smock, 1993). Remarriage does indeed add a second adult to the family system, which alleviates these problems to some degree, but it adds others (Hetherington et al., 1999).

Second, any family transition involves upheaval. Both adults and children adapt slowly and with difficulty to the subtraction or addition of new adults to the family system (Hetherington & Stanley-Hagan, 1995). The period of maximum disruption appears to last several years, during which the parents often find it difficult to monitor their children and maintain control over them.

Perhaps most importantly, single-parenthood, divorce, and step-parenthood all increase the likelihood that the family climate or style will shift away from authoritative parenting. This shift is not uncommon in the first few years after a divorce, when the custodial parent (usually the mother) is distracted or depressed and less able to manage warm control; it occurs in step-families as well, where rates of authoritative parenting are lower than in intact families.

Remember, authoritarian or neglectful parenting is linked to poor outcomes whether it is triggered by a divorce, a stressful remarriage, the father's loss of a job, or any other stress (Goldberg, 1990). Ultimately, it is the parenting style, rather than any particular type of disruption, that is significant for the child (see No Easy Answers). After all, three-quarters of children reared in single-parent or step-parent families finish high school, and roughly half of those high school graduates go on to attend college (McLanahan & Sandefur, 1994).

Many families construct a social network called an **extended family,** a family structure that includes parents, grandparents, aunts, uncles, cousins, and so on. Extended families seem to serve a protective function for children who are growing up in single-parent homes (Wilson, 1995). Grandmothers, for

extended family a social network of grandparents, aunts, uncles, cousins, and so on

Critical Thinking

How important was your own extended family to you and your parent(s) during your early childhood years?

No Easy Answers

When Divorce Is Unavoidable

Most parents know that divorce is traumatic for children and do their best to avoid it. However, as we all know, there are situations in which there is no alternative. In such cases, parents often turn to counselors and psychologists for advice on how to prevent the negative effects of divorce. Like so many other important challenges, helping a child overcome the trauma of divorce is not one for which there is a simple, or even a complex, formula parents can follow.

It's important for divorcing parents to realize that they cannot eliminate all the short-term disruptive effects of this event on children. However, there are some specific things they can do that are likely to soften or lessen the effects:

- *Try to keep the number of separate changes the child has to cope with to a minimum.* If at all possible, keep the children in the same school or day-care setting and in the same house or apartment.

- *If the children are teenagers, consider having each child live with the parent of the same gender.* The data are not totally consistent, but it looks as if this may be a less stressful arrangement (Lee et al., 1994).

- *The custodial parent should help children stay in touch with the noncustodial parent.* Likewise, the noncustodial parent should maintain as much contact as possible with the children, calling and seeing them regularly, attending school functions, and so on.

- *Keep the open conflict to a minimum.* Most of all, try not to fight in front of the children. Open conflict has negative effects on children whether the parents are divorced or not (Amato, 1993; Coiro, 1995; Insabella, 1995). Thus, divorce is not the only culprit; divorce combined with open conflict between the adults has worse effects.

- *Parents should not use the children as go-betweens or talk disparagingly about their ex-spouses to them.* Children who feel caught in the middle between the two parents are more likely to show various kinds of negative symptoms, such as depression or behavior problems (Buchanan, Maccoby, & Dornbusch, 1991).

- *Divorced parents should not expect their children to provide them with emotional support.* Parents should maintain their own network of support, and use that network liberally. They should stay in touch with friends, seek out others in the same situation, join a support group.

In the midst of the emotional upheaval that accompanies divorce, these are not easy prescriptions to follow. However, if divorcing parents are able to do so, their children will probably suffer less.

example, appear to be important sources of emotional warmth for the children of teenaged mothers (Coley & Chase-Lansdale, 1998). Further, extended family members often help single and divorced mothers with financial and emotional support as well as with child care. In the United States, such networks are more common among minorities than among whites (Harrison, Wilson, Pine, Chan, & Buriel, 1990).

Before going on

- How is family structure related to children's development?

- How does divorce affect children's behavior in early childhood and in later years?

- What are some possible reasons for the relationship between family structure and development?

Peer Relationships

The child's family experience is undeniably a central influence on emerging personality and social relationships, particularly in early childhood when a good portion of the time is still spent with parents and siblings. But over the years from 2 to 6, relationships with nonsibling peers become increasingly important.

Relating to Peers through Play

At every age, children are likely to spend at least some of their time playing alone—a pattern known as *solitary play.* However, children first begin to show some positive interest in playing with others as early as 6 months of age. If you place two babies that age on the floor facing each other, they will look at each other, touch, pull each other's hair, imitate each other's actions, and smile at each other.

By 14–18 months, two or more children play together with toys—sometimes cooperating, but more often simply playing side by side with different toys. Developmentalists refer to this as *parallel play.* Toddlers this age express interest in one another and gaze at or make noises at one another. However, it isn't until around 18 months that children engage in *associative play.* In associative play, toddlers pursue their own activities but also engage in spontaneous, though short-lived, social interactions. For example, one toddler may put down a toy to spend a few minutes chasing another, or one may imitate another's action with a toy.

By 3 or 4, children begin to engage in *cooperative play,* a pattern in which several children work together to accomplish a goal. Cooperative play can be either constructive or symbolic. A group of children may cooperate to build a city out of blocks, or they may assign roles such as "mommy," "daddy," and "baby" to one another to play house.

As you learned in Chapter 6, play is related to cognitive development. Play is also related to the development of **social skills,** a set of behaviors that usually lead to being accepted as a play partner or friend by others. For example, many researchers have focused on the social skill of *group entry.* Children who are skilled in group entry spend time observing others to find out what they're doing and then try to become a part of it. Children who have poor group-entry skills try to gain acceptance through aggressive behavior or by interrupting the group. Developmentalists have found that children with poor group-entry skills are often rejected by peers (Fantuzzo, Coolahan, & Mendez, 1998). Peer rejection, in turn, is an important factor in future social development.

According to recent studies, there appear to be sex differences in the reasons for and consequences of poor group-entry skills. For example, one study found that 3-year-old girls with poorly developed group-entry skills spent more time in parallel play than in cooperative play (Sims, Hutchins, & Taylor, 1997). In contrast, girls with better group-entry skills engaged in more cooperative than parallel play. Thus, the unskilled 3-year-old girls' patterns of play placed them at risk for future developmental problems, because age-appropriate play experience in the preschool years is related to social development later in childhood (Howes & Matheson, 1992; Maguire & Dunn, 1997).

The same study found that 3-year-old boys with poor group-entry skills tended to be aggressive and were often actively rejected by peers. They typically responded to rejection by becoming even more aggressive and disruptive (Sims, Hutchins, & Taylor, 1997). Thus, the boys in this study seemed to be caught in a cycle: Aggressive

social skills a set of behaviors that usually lead to being accepted as a play partner or friend by peers

behavior led to peer rejection, which, in turn, led to more aggression. This pattern may place boys at risk for developing an internal working model of relationships that includes aggressive behavior and, as a result, lead them to routinely respond aggressively to others in social situations.

Because of the risks associated with poor social skills, developmentalists have turned their attention to social-skills training as a preventive measure. For example, in one study, socially withdrawn 4- and 5-year-olds were taught specific verbal phrases to use when trying to gain acceptance by a group of peers (Doctoroff, 1997). In addition, their socially accepted peers were taught to remind the trained children to use their new skills. For the most part, social-skills interventions like this one lead to immediate gains in social acceptance. However, the degree to which early childhood social-skills training can prevent later social difficulties is unknown at present.

Aggression

Aggressive interactions are common during the early childhood period. The most common definition of **aggression** is behavior apparently intended to injure another person or damage an object. The emphasis on intentionality helps separate true aggression from rough-and-tumble play in which children sometimes accidentally hurt one another. Every young child shows at least some aggressive behavior, but the form and frequency of aggression changes over the preschool years, as you can see in the summary in Table 7.1.

When 2- or 3-year-old children are upset or frustrated, they are most likely to throw things or hit each other. As their verbal skills improve, however, they shift away from such overt physical aggression toward greater use of verbal aggression, such as taunting or name calling, just as their defiance of their parents shifts from physical to verbal strategies.

The decline in physical aggression over these years also undoubtedly reflects the preschooler's declining egocentrism and increasing understanding of other children's thoughts and feelings. Yet another factor in the decline of physical aggression is the emergence of *dominance hierarchies*. As early as age 3 or 4, groups of children arrange themselves in well-understood *pecking orders* of leaders and followers (Strayer, 1980). They know who will win a fight and who will lose one, which children they dare attack and which ones they must submit to—knowledge that serves to reduce the actual amount of physical aggression.

Developmentalists distinguish between true aggression (intentional harm) and the accidental injuries that often occur during normal rough-and-tumble play. (*Photo:* Myrleen Ferguson, PhotoEdit)

ᴛABLE 7.1   Changes in the Form and Frequency of Aggression from Age 2 to Age 8

	2- to 4-Year-Olds	4- to 8-Year-Olds
Physical aggression	At its peak	Declines
Verbal aggression	Relatively rare at 2; increases as child's verbal skills improve	Dominant form of aggression
Goal of aggression	Mostly instrumental	Mostly hostile
Occasion for aggression	Most often after conflicts with parents	Most often after conflicts with peers

(*Sources:* Cummings, Hollenbeck, Iannotti, Radke-Yarrow, & Zahn-Waxler, 1986; Goodenough, 1931; Hartup, 1974.)

aggression behavior intended to harm another person or an object

A second change in the quality of aggression during the preschool years is a shift from *instrumental aggression* to *hostile aggression*. **Instrumental aggression** is aimed at gaining or damaging some object; the purpose of **hostile aggression** is to hurt another person or gain an advantage. Thus, when 3-year-old Sarah pushes aside her playmate Lucetta in the sandbox and grabs Lucetta's bucket, she is showing instrumental aggression. When Lucetta in turn gets angry at Sarah and calls her a dummy, she is displaying hostile aggression.

Critical Thinking

Think about the groups you belong to. Do they have clear dominance hierarchies? Now imagine a group of adults coming together for the first time. Within a few weeks, a pecking order will emerge. What might determine that order? How might a dominant person establish dominance?

Psychologists have suggested several key factors in aggressive behavior. For example, one early group of American psychologists argued that aggression is always preceded by frustration, and that frustration is always followed by aggression (Dollard, Doob, Miller, Mowrer, & Sears, 1939). The frustration-aggression hypothesis turned out to be too broadly stated; not all frustration leads to aggression, but frustration does make aggression more likely. Toddlers and preschoolers are often frustrated—because they cannot always do what they want, and because they cannot express their needs clearly—and they often express that frustration through aggression. As the child acquires greater ability to communicate, plan, and organize her activities, her frustration level declines, and overt aggression drops.

Other developmentalists argue that reinforcement and modeling are important, For instance, when Sarah pushes Lucetta away and grabs her toy, Sarah is reinforced for her aggression because she gets the toy. This straightforward effect of reinforcement clearly plays a vital role in children's development of aggressive patterns of behavior. Moreover, when parents give in to their young child's tantrums or aggression, they are reinforcing the very behavior they deplore, and they thereby help to establish a long-lasting pattern of aggression and defiance.

Modeling, too, plays a key role in children's learning of aggressive behaviors. In a classic series of studies, psychologist Albert Bandura found that children learn specific forms of aggression, such as hitting, by watching other people perform them (Bandura, Ross, & Ross, 1961, 1963). Clearly, entertainment media offer children many opportunities to observe aggressive behavior, but real-life aggressive models may be more influential. For example, children learn that aggression is an acceptable way of solving problems by watching their parents, siblings, and others behave aggressively. Indeed, parents who consistently use physical punishment have children who are more aggressive than do parents who do not model aggression in this way (Eron, Huesmann, & Zelli, 1991). When children have many different aggressive models, especially if those aggressive models appear to be rewarded for their aggression, then it should not be surprising that they learn aggressive behavior. Certainly, many inner-city neighborhoods in the United States offer such models.

Whatever the cause, most children become less aggressive during the preschool years. There are a few children, however, whose aggressive behavior pattern in early childhood becomes quite literally a way of life, a finding that has been supported by cross-cultural research (Hart, Olsen, Robinson, & Mandleco, 1997; Henry, Caspi, Moffitt, & Silva, 1996; Newman, Caspi, Moffitt, & Silva, 1997). Researchers have searched for causes of this kind of aggression, which some psychologists refer to as *trait aggression,* to distinguish it from developmentally normal forms of aggression.

Some psychologists looking for a genetic basis for trait aggression have produced some supportive data (Plomin, 1990). Others suggest that trait aggression is associated with being raised in an aggressive environment, such as an abusive family (Dodge, 1993). Family factors other than abuse, such as lack of affection and the use

instrumental aggression aggression used to gain or damage an object

hostile aggression aggression used to hurt another person or gain an advantage

of coercive discipline techniques, also appear to be related to trait aggression, especially in boys (McFayden-Ketchumm, Bates, Dodge, & Pettit, 1996).

Still other developmentalists have discovered evidence that aggressive children may shape their environments in order to gain continuing reinforcement for their behavior. For example, aggressive boys as young as 4 years old tend to prefer other aggressive boys as playmates and to form stable peer groups. Boys in these groups develop their own patterns of interaction and reward each other with social approval for aggressive acts (Farver, 1996). This pattern of association among aggressive boys continues through middle childhood and adolescence.

Finally, social-cognitivists have produced a large body of research suggesting that highly aggressive children lag behind their peers in understanding others' intentions (Crick & Dodge, 1994). Research demonstrating that teaching aggressive children how to think about others' intentions reduces aggressive behavior also supports this conclusion (Crick & Dodge, 1996). Specifically, these studies suggest that aggressive school-aged children seem to reason more like 2- to 3-year-olds about intentions. For example, they are likely to perceive a playground incident (say, one child accidentally tripping another during a soccer game) as an intentional act that requires retaliation. Training, which also includes anger management techniques, helps aggressive school-aged children acquire an understanding of others' intentions that most children learn between the ages of 3 and 5. Thus, trait aggression may originate in some kind of deviation from the typical social-cognitive developmental path during the early childhood period.

Prosocial Behavior and Friendships

At the other end of the spectrum of peer relationships is a set of behaviors psychologists call **prosocial behavior.** Like aggression, prosocial behavior is intentional and voluntary, but its purpose is to help another person in some way (Eisenberg, 1992). In everyday language, such behavior is called *altruism,* and it changes with age, just as other aspects of peer behavior change.

● *Development of Prosocial Behavior* ●   Altruistic behaviors first become evident in children of about 2 or 3—at about the same time as real interest in playing with other children arises. They will offer to help another child who is hurt, share a toy, or try to comfort another person (Marcus, 1986; Zahn-Waxler & Radke-Yarrow, 1982; Zahn-Waxler et al., 1992). As you read in Chapter 6, children this young are only beginning to understand that others feel differently than they do—but they obviously understand enough about the emotions of others to respond in supportive and sympathetic ways when they see other children or adults hurt or sad.

Beyond these early years, changes in prosocial behavior show a mixed pattern. Some kinds of prosocial behavior, such as taking turns, seem to increase with age. If you give children an opportunity to donate some treat to another child who is described as needy, older children donate more than younger children do. Helpfulness, too, seems to increase with age, through adolescence. But not all prosocial behaviors show this pattern. Comforting another child, for example, seems to be more common among preschoolers and children in early elementary grades than among older children (Eisenberg, 1992).

Children vary a lot in the amount of altruistic behavior they show, and young children who show relatively more empathy and altruism are also those who regulate their own emotions well. They show positive emotions readily and negative emotions less often (Eisenberg et al., 1996b). These variations among children's level of empathy or altruism seem to be related to specific kinds of child-rearing. In addition, longitudinal studies indicate that children who display higher levels of prosocial behavior in the preschool years continue to demonstrate higher levels of such behavior in adulthood (Eisenberg et al., 1999).

prosocial behavior behavior intended to help another person

● **Parental Influences on Prosocial Behavior** ●   Research suggests that parental behavior contributes to the development of prosocial behavior (Eisenberg, 1992). Specifically, parents of altruistic children create a loving and warm family climate. If such warmth is combined with clear explanations and rules about what to do as well as what not to do, the children are even more likely to behave altruistically. Such parents also often explain the consequences of the child's action in terms of its effects on others—for example, "If you hit Susan, it will hurt her." Stating rules or guidelines positively rather than negatively also appears to be important; for example, "It's always good to be helpful to other people" is more effective guidance than "Don't be so selfish!"

Providing prosocial *attributions*—positive statements about the underlying cause for helpful behavior—also helps. For example, a parent might praise a child by saying "You're such a helpful child!" or "You certainly do a lot of nice things for other people." Having heard such statements often during early childhood helps children incorporate them into their self-concepts later in childhood. In this way, parents may help create a generalized, internalized pattern of altruistic behavior in the child.

Parents of altruistic children also look for opportunities for them to do helpful things. For example, they allow children to help cook, take care of pets, make toys to give away, teach younger siblings, and so forth. Finally, parental modeling of thoughtful and generous behavior—that is, parents demonstrating consistency between what they say and what they do—is another contributing factor.

● **Friendships** ●   Beginning at about 18 months, a few toddlers show early hints of playmate preferences or individual friendships (Howes, 1983, 1987). However, by age 3, about 20% of children have a stable playmate. By 4, more than half spend 30% or more of their time with one other child (Hinde, Titmus, Easton, & Tamplin, 1985). Thus, one important change in social behavior during early childhood is the formation of stable friendships.

To be sure, these early peer interactions are still quite primitive. However, it is noteworthy that preschool friend pairs nonetheless show more mutual liking, more reciprocity, more extended interactions, more positive and less negative behavior, and more supportiveness in a novel situation than do nonfriend pairs at this same age—all signs that these relationships are more than merely passing fancies. Moreover, having had a friend in early childhood is related to social competence during the elementary school years (Maguire & Dunn, 1997).

Before going on

● What are the various kinds of play observed among preschoolers?

● What is the difference between instrumental aggression and hostile aggression, and which is more prevalent in early childhood?

● How does prosocial behavior change during early childhood, and how can parents and teachers encourage its development?

● What are the characteristic patterns of friendship found in younger and older preschoolers?

Personality and Self-Concept

As young children gain more understanding of the social environment, their temperaments ripen into true personalities. At the same time, their self-concepts become more complex, allowing them to exercise greater control over their own behavior.

From Temperament to Personality

As you learned in Chapter 5, a child's temperament—whether he is "easy," "difficult," or "inhibited"—is reasonably stable over infancy, toddlerhood, and later ages (Novosad & Thoman, 1999; Ruben, Nelson, Hastings, & Asendorpt, 1999). By preschool, a link between difficultness of temperament and both concurrent and future behavior problems becomes evident: 3- or 4-year-olds with difficult temperaments are more likely to show heightened aggressiveness, delinquency, or other forms of behavior problems in school, as teenagers, and as adults (Bates, 1989; Caspi, Henry, McGee, Moffitt, & Silva, 1995; Chess & Thomas, 1984). Likewise, shy preschoolers are at risk of developing emotional difficulties later in childhood (Sanson et al., 1996; Schwartz, Snidman, & Kagan, 1996).

You should also remember from Chapter 5 that psychologists distinguish between temperament and personality, and most believe that inborn infant temperament constitutes the foundation of personality in later childhood and adulthood. It seems likely that the processes through which temperament becomes modified into personality begin during the early childhood years. For example, preschoolers with difficult temperaments learn that the behaviors associated with difficultness, such as complaining, often result in peer rejection. As a result, many of them change their behavior to gain social acceptance. Thus, personality represents the combination of the temperament with which children are probably born and the knowledge they gain about temperament-related behavior during childhood (McCrae, Costa, Ostendord, & Angleitner, 2000; Svrakic, Svrakic, & Cloninger, 1996). As a result, correlations between infant temperament and later measures of personality, though still strong, tend to decline over childhood and adolescence (Shaw, Ryst, & Steiner, 1996).

The transition from temperament to personality is also influenced by parental responses to the young child's temperament. If the parents reject the difficult or shy child, the child is likely to emerge from the preschool years with a personality that puts him at risk for developing serious problems in social relationships, and he may suffer from cognitive deficits as well (Bates, 1989; Fagot & Gauvain, 1997; Fish, Stifter, & Belsky, 1991).

Critical Thinking

If parents received a description of their child's temperament at birth (sort of like the owner's manual you get with new appliances), do you think it would help them be better parents? Conversely, do you think it would cause them to be overly tolerant of temperamental characteristics that might need to be modified for the child's own benefit, such as irritability?

Self-Concept

The 18- to 24-month-old is beginning to develop categorical and emotional selves. Between 2 and 6, the child continues to develop these two aspects of the self and adds to them a *social self*. Familiarity with the dimensions of preschoolers' self-concepts helps parents, teachers, and others better understand many aspects of their social behavior.

● ***The Categorical Self*** ●   By the end of the preschool period, a child can give you quite a full description of herself on a whole range of dimensions. Still, these early self-concepts remain highly concrete. The self-concept of a preschool child tends to focus on her own visible characteristics—whether she's a boy or girl, what she looks like, what or whom she plays with, where she lives, what she is good at—rather than on more enduring inner qualities.

As you learned earlier in this chapter, categories are also important in young children's perceptions of others—big kids, little kids, boys, girls, and so on. Preschoolers prefer playmates of their own age and gender. Consequently, the categorical self seems to be as much an internal working model for social relationships as for the self.

● ***The Emotional Self*** ●   Development of the emotional self during the early childhood years centers on the acquisition of emotional control. Recent research has shown that the degree to which young children can control emotion-related behavior, such as finding a way to cheer themselves up when they are sad, is linked to important variables later in life. For instance, self-control in early childhood is related to children's ability to obey moral rules and to think about right and wrong during the school years (Kochanska, Murray, & Coy, 1997).

The process of acquiring emotional control is one in which control shifts slowly from the parents to the child. Here again, the child's temperament is a factor. For example, preschoolers who have consistently exhibited difficult behavior since infancy are more likely to have self-control problems in early childhood (Schmitz et al., 1999). Similarly, preschoolers who were born prematurely or who were delayed in language development in the second year of life experience more difficulties with self-control during early childhood (Carson, Klee, & Perry, 1998; Schothorst & van Engeland, 1996).

However, parents' age-based expectations and parenting behaviors are also important. For instance, most parents know it is unreasonable to expect toddlers to wait for long periods of time, so they provide external control by, for example, reminding toddlers of prohibitions and repeating requests. Over the years from 3 to 6, children gradually internalize parental standards and expectations and take on more of the control task for themselves. For example, if you were to observe parents and children in a doctor's waiting room, you would see that parents of bored toddlers often physically direct and redirect their behavior. A parent of a 2-year-old might be seen taking the child onto his lap and reading to her. In contrast, you would notice that older preschoolers look for things to do on their own. They are more likely to find a book or magazine that looks interesting and ask a parent to read it to them or look at it by themselves. In response to such evidences of emotional maturity, parents expect more control from older preschoolers and use verbal instructions, rather than physical control, to help them manage their behavior.

● ***The Social Self*** ●   Another facet of the child's emerging sense of self is an increasing awareness of herself as a player in the social game. By age 2, the toddler has already learned a variety of social "scripts"—routines of play or interaction with others. The toddler now begins to develop some implicit understanding of her own roles in these scripts (Case, 1991). So she may begin to think of herself as a "helper" in some situations, or as "the boss" when she is telling some other child what to do.

You can see this clearly in children's sociodramatic play, as they begin to take explicit roles: "I'll be the daddy and you be the mommy," or "I'm the boss." As part of the same process, the young child also gradually understands her place in the network of family roles. She has sisters, brothers, father, mother, and so forth.

Moreover, role scripts help young children become more independent. For example, assuming the "student" role provides a preschooler with a prescription for appropriate behavior in the school situation. Students listen when the teacher speaks to the class, get out materials and put them away at certain times, help their classmates in various ways, and so on. Once a preschooler is familiar with and adopts the student role, he can follow the role script and is no longer dependent on the teacher to tell him what to do every minute of the day.

Before going on

- Is temperament stable in early childhood? If not, how does it change?
- What changes take place in the young child's categorical, emotional, and social selves during the preschool years?

The Gender Concept and Sex Roles

One of the most fascinating aspects of the preschool child's emerging sense of self is the development of a sense of gender. The child has several related tasks. On the cognitive side, she must learn the nature of the gender category itself—that boyness or girlness is permanent and unchanged by such things as modifications in clothing or hair length. This understanding is usually called the **gender concept.** On the social side, she has to learn what behaviors go with being a boy or a girl; that is, she must learn the **sex role** appropriate for her gender.

Explaining Gender Concept and Sex-Role Development

As you remember from Chapter 2, Freud suggested that 3- to 6-year-olds overcome the anxiety they feel about their desires for the opposite-sex parent (the Oedipus or Electra conflict) through identification with the same-sex parent. In order to identify with the parent, the child must learn and conform to his or her sex-role concepts. Thus, according to Freud, children learn both the gender concept and sex roles through the process of identification.

The difficulty with Freud's theory is that toddlers seem to understand far more about the gender concept and sex roles than the theory would predict. For example, many 18-month-olds accurately label themselves and others as boys or girls. Likewise, clearly sex-typed behavior appears long before age 4 or 5, when psychoanalytic theories claim identification occurs.

gender concept understanding of gender, gender-related behavior, and sex roles

sex roles behavior expected for males and females in a given culture

Social learning theorists have emphasized the role of parents in shaping children's sex-role behavior and attitudes (Bandura, 1977a; Mischel, 1966, 1970). This notion has been far better supported by research than have Freud's ideas. Parents do seem to reinforce sex-typed activities in children as young as 18 months, not only by buying different kinds of toys for boys and girls, but by responding more positively when their sons play with blocks or trucks or when their daughters play with dolls (Fagot & Hagan, 1991; Lytton & Romney, 1991). Such differential reinforcement is particularly clear with boys, especially from fathers (Siegal, 1987). Some evidence also suggests that toddlers whose parents are more consistent in rewarding sex-typed toy choice or play behavior and whose mothers favor traditional family sex roles learn accurate gender labels earlier than do toddlers whose parents are less focused on the gender-appropriateness of the child's play (Fagot & Leinbach, 1989; Fagot, Leinbach, & O'Boyle, 1992).

Still, helpful as it is, a social-learning explanation is probably not sufficient. In particular, parents differentially reinforce boys' and girls' behavior less than you'd expect, and probably not enough to account for the very early and robust discrimination children seem to make on the basis of gender. Even young children whose parents seem to treat their sons and daughters in highly similar ways nonetheless learn gender labels and prefer same-sex playmates.

A third alternative, social-cognitive theory, suggests that children's understanding of gender is linked to gender-related behavior. For example, one such view, based strongly on Piagetian theory, is Lawrence Kohlberg's suggestion that the crucial aspect of the process is the child's understanding of the gender concept (Kohlberg, 1966; Kohlberg & Ullian, 1974). Once the child realizes that he is a boy or she is a girl forever, he or she becomes highly motivated to learn how to behave in the way that is expected or appropriate for that gender. Specifically, Kohlberg's **gender constancy theory** predicts that systematic same-sex imitation will become evident only after the child has shown full gender constancy. **Gender constancy** is the understanding that gender is an innate characteristic that can't be changed. Most studies designed to test this hypothesis have supported Kohlberg. Children do seem to become much more sensitive to same-sex models after they understand gender constancy (Frey & Ruble, 1992). Kohlberg's theory allows developmentalists to make highly reliable predictions about the development of children's knowledge about gender and sex roles.

However, gender constancy theory is less accurate in predicting behavior. Specifically, it can't explain the obvious fact that children show clearly different sex-role behavior, such as toy preferences, long before they have achieved full understanding of the gender concept. A newer social-cognitive theory derived from the information-processing approach is usually called *gender schema theory* (Martin, 1991; Martin & Halverson, 1981). This approach includes many of Kohlberg's ideas about how gender constancy develops, but it does a better job of predicting behavior.

You'll remember from Chapter 6 that a great deal of *schematic* learning happens in early childhood. A schema is a mental pattern or model that is used to process information. Just as the self-concept can be thought of as a schema, so the child's understanding of gender can be seen in the same way. According to **gender schema theory,** the gender schema begins to develop as soon as the child notices the differences between male and female, knows his own gender, and can label the two groups with some consistency—all of which happens by age 2 or 3. Perhaps because gender is clearly an either/or category, children seem to understand very early that this is a key distinction, so the category serves as a kind of magnet for new information. Once the child has established even a primitive gender schema, a great many experiences can be assimilated to it. Thus, as soon as this schema begins to be formed, children may begin to show preference for same-sex playmates or for gender-stereotyped activities (Martin & Little, 1990).

Preschoolers first learn some broad distinctions about what kinds of activities or behavior "go with" each gender, both by observing other children and through the

gender constancy theory Kohlberg's assertion that children must understand that gender is a permanent characteristic before they can adopt appropriate sex roles

gender constancy the understanding that gender is a component of the self that is not altered by external appearance

gender schema theory an information-processing approach to gender concept development that asserts that people use a schema for each gender to process information about themselves and others

reinforcements they receive from parents. They also learn a few gender *scripts*—whole sequences of events that are normally associated with a given gender, such as "fixing dinner" or "building with tools"—just as they learn other social scripts at about this age (Levy & Fivush, 1993). Then, between age 4 and age 6, the child learns a more subtle and complex set of associations for his own gender—what children of his own gender like and don't like, how they play, how they talk, what kinds of people they associate with. Only between ages of 8 and 10 does the child develop an equivalently complex view of the opposite gender (Martin, Wood, & Little, 1990).

The key difference between this theory and Kohlberg's gender constancy theory is that gender schema theory asserts that the child need not understand that gender is permanent to form an initial gender schema. When they do begin to understand gender constancy, at about 5 or 6, children develop a more elaborate rule, or schema, of "what people who are like me do" and treat this rule the same way they treat other rules—as an absolute. Later, the child's application of the gender rule becomes more flexible. She knows, for example, that most boys don't play with dolls, but that they can do so if they like.

The Gender Concept

Children seem to develop gender constancy in three steps. First comes **gender identity,** which is simply a child's ability to label his or her own sex correctly and to identify other people as men or women, boys or girls. By 9–12 months, babies already treat male and female faces as if they were different categories (Fagot & Leinbach, 1993). Within the next year, they begin to learn the verbal labels that go with these categories. By age 2, most children correctly label themselves as boys or girls and, within 6–12 months, most can correctly label others as well.

Accurate labeling, though, does not signify complete understanding. The second step is **gender stability,** which is the understanding that you stay the same gender throughout life. Researchers have measured this by asking children such questions as "When you were a little baby, were you a little girl or a little boy?" or "When you grow up, will you be a mommy or a daddy?" Most children understand the stability of gender by about age 4 (Slaby & Frey, 1975) (see Figure 7.6, page 206).

The final step is the development of true gender constancy, the recognition that someone stays the same gender even though he may appear to change by wearing different clothes or changing his hair length. For example, boys don't change into girls by wearing dresses. It may seem odd that a child who understands that he will stay the same gender throughout life (gender stability) can nonetheless be confused about the effect of changes in dress or appearance on gender. But numerous studies, including studies of children growing up in other cultures such as Kenya, Nepal, Belize, and Samoa, show that children go through this sequence (Munroe, Shimmin, & Munroe, 1984).

The underlying logic of this sequence may be a bit clearer if you think of a parallel between gender constancy and the concept of conservation. Conservation involves recognition that an object remains the same in some fundamental way even though it changes externally. Gender constancy is thus a kind of "conservation of gender," and is not typically understood until about 5 or 6, when children understand other conservations (Marcus & Overton, 1978).

Sex-Role Knowledge

Figuring out your gender and understanding that it stays constant are only part of the story. Learning what goes with being a boy or a girl in a given culture is also a vital part of the child's task. Researchers have studied this in two ways—by asking children what boys and girls (or men and women) like to do and what they are like (which is an inquiry about gender stereotypes), and by asking children if it is okay for

gender identity the ability to correctly label oneself and others as male or female

gender stability the understanding that gender is a stable, life-long characteristic

FIGURE 7.6

In describing this self-portrait, the 5-year-old artist said, "This is how I will look when I get married to a boy. I am under a rainbow, so beautiful with a bride hat, a belt, and a purse." The girl knows she will always be female and associates gender with externals such as clothing (gender stability). She is also already quite knowledgeable about gender role expectations. (Courtesy of Jerry and Denise Boyd. Used with permission.)

boys to play with dolls or girls to climb trees or to do equivalent cross-sex things (an inquiry about roles).

In every culture, adults have clear sex-role stereotypes. Indeed, the content of those stereotypes is remarkably similar in cultures around the world. Psychologists who have studied gender stereotypes in many different countries, including non-Western countries such as Thailand, Pakistan, and Nigeria, find that the most clearly stereotyped traits are weakness, gentleness, appreciativeness, and soft-heartedness for women, and aggression, strength, cruelty, and coarseness for men (Williams & Best, 1990). In most cultures, men are also seen as competent, skillful, assertive, and able to get things done, while women are seen as warm and expressive, tactful, quiet, gentle, aware of others' feelings, and lacking in competence, independence, and logic (Williams & Best, 1990).

Studies of children show that these stereotyped ideas develop early. It would not be uncommon to hear a 3-year-old in the United States say "Mommies use the stove, and daddies use the grill." A 4-year-old might define gender roles in terms of competencies: "Daddies are better at fixing things, but mommies are better at tying bows and decorating." Even 2-year-olds in the United States already associate certain tasks and possessions with men and women, such as vacuum cleaners and food with women and cars and tools with men. By age 3 or 4, children can assign stereotypic occupations, toys, and activities to each gender. By age 5, children begin to associate certain personality traits, such as assertiveness and nurturance, with males or females (Martin, 1993; Serbin, Powlishta, & Gulko, 1993).

Studies of children's ideas about how men and women (or boys and girls) ought to behave add an interesting further element. For example, in an early study, a psychologist told a story to children aged 4–9 about a little boy named George who liked to play with dolls (Damon, 1977). George's parents told him that only little girls play with dolls; little boys shouldn't. The children were then asked questions about the story, such as "Why do people tell George not to play with dolls?" or "Is there a rule that boys shouldn't play with dolls?"

Four-year-olds in this study thought it was okay for George to play with dolls. There was no rule against it and he should do it if he wanted to. Six-year-olds, in contrast, thought it was wrong for George to play with dolls. By about age 9, children had differentiated between what boys and girls usually do, and what is "wrong." One boy said, for example, that breaking windows was wrong and bad, but that playing with dolls was not bad in the same way: "Breaking windows you're not supposed to do. And if you play with dolls, well you can, but boys usually don't."

What this study appeared to reveal is that the 5- to 6-year-old, having figured out that gender is permanent, is searching for a rule about how boys and girls behave (Martin & Halverson, 1981). The child picks up information from watching adults, from television, from listening to the labels that are attached to different activities (e.g., "Boys don't cry"). Initially, children treat these as absolute, moral rules. Later, they understand that these are social conventions; at this point, sex-role concepts become more flexible and stereotyping declines somewhat (Katz & Ksansnak, 1994).

Sex-Typed Behavior

The final element in the development of sex roles is the actual behavior children show with those of the same and the opposite sex. An unexpected finding is that **sex-typed behavior,** or different patterns of behavior among girls and boys, develops earlier than ideas about sex roles. By 18–24 months, children begin to show some preference for sex-stereotyped toys, such as dolls for girls or trucks or building blocks for boys, which is some months before they can consistently identify their own gender (O'Brien, 1992). By age 3, children begin to show a preference for same-sex friends and are much more sociable with playmates of the same sex—at a time when they do not yet have a concept of gender stability (Maccoby, 1988, 1990; Maccoby & Jacklin, 1987) (see Figure 7.7, page 208).

Not only are preschoolers' friendships and peer interactions increasingly sex-segregated, it is also clear that boy-boy interactions and girl-girl interactions differ in quality, even in these early years. One important part of same-sex interactions seems to involve instruction and modeling of sex-appropriate behavior. In other words, older boys teach younger boys how to be "masculine," and older girls teach younger girls how to be "feminine" (Danby & Baker, 1998).

However, these "lessons" in sex-typed behavior are fairly subtle. Eleanor Maccoby, one of the leading theorists in this area, describes the girls' pattern as an *enabling style* (Maccoby, 1990). Enabling includes such behaviors as supporting the friend, expressing agreement, and making suggestions. All these behaviors tend to foster a greater equality and intimacy in the relationship and keep the interaction going. In contrast, boys are more likely to show what Maccoby calls a *constricting, or restrictive, style.* "A restrictive style is one that tends to derail the interaction—to

As their gender concept develops, children change their views about whether it is acceptable for boys to play with dolls or for girls to play sports such as baseball. (*Photos:* Mary Kay Denny, PhotoEdit; SUNSTAR/Photo Researchers, Inc.)

sex-typed behavior different patterns of behavior exhibited by boys and girls

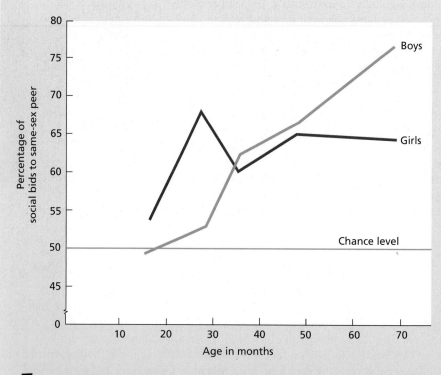

FIGURE 7.7

In one study of playmate preferences, researchers counted how often preschool children played with same-sex or opposite-sex playmates. Children as young as $2\frac{1}{2}$ already showed at least some preference for same-sex playmates. (*Source:* La Freniere, Strayer, & Gauthier, 1984, Figure 1, p. 1961. Copyright by the Society for Research in Child Development, Inc.)

inhibit the partner or cause the partner to withdraw, thus shortening the interaction or bringing it to an end" (1990, p. 517). Contradicting, interrupting, boasting, and other forms of self-display are all aspects of this style.

These two patterns begin to be visible in the preschool years. For example, beginning as early as age 3, boys and girls use quite different strategies in their attempts to influence each other's behavior (Maccoby, 1990). Girls generally ask questions or make requests; boys are much more likely to make demands or phrase things using imperatives ("Give me that!"). The really intriguing finding is that even at this early age, boys simply don't respond to the girls' enabling style. Thus, playing with boys yields little positive reinforcement for girls, and they begin to avoid such interactions and band together.

Another kind of learning opportunity happens when children exhibit **cross-gender behavior,** behavior that is atypical in their culture for their gender. For example, *tomboyishness,* girls' preference for activities that are more typical for boys, is a kind of cross-gender behavior. Generally, tomboyishness is tolerated by adults and peers (Sandnabba & Ahlberg, 1999). Not surprisingly, then, cross-gender behavior is far more common among girls than boys (Etaugh & Liss, 1992). Tomboyishness does not appear to interfere with the development of a "feminine" personality in adulthood, and it may allow girls to acquire positive characteristics such as assertiveness (Burn, O'Neil, & Nederend, 1996).

Critical Thinking

What do you think happens when opposite-sex adults interact in some nonromantic encounter? Is the interaction style some combination of enabling and constricting, or does one style dominate?

cross-gender behavior behavior that is atypical for one's own sex but typical for the opposite sex

Play may provide children with opportunities to learn about gender-role expectations.
(*Photos:* Harry Wilks, Stock Boston; Sue Ann Miller, Tony Stone)

In contrast, both peers and adults actively discourage boys from engaging in cross-gender behavior. Specifically, boys who play with dolls or behave in an effeminate manner are likely to elicit expressions of disapproval, or even ridicule, from children, parents, and teachers (Martin, 1990). Many adults' reactions to boys' cross-gender behavior appear to be related to the fear that it may lead to homosexuality (Sandnabba & Ahlberg, 1999) (see the Research Report).

However, it cannot be assumed that the prevalence of sex-typed play among boys is strictly the result of adult and peer influence. For one thing, sex-typed play preferences appear earlier and are more consistent in male infants, which suggests that they begin to develop before environmental forces have had much chance to influence them (Blakemore, LaRue, & Olejnik, 1979). Further, by age 3, boys are likely to show an actual aversion to girls' activities, for example, by saying "yuck" when experimenters offer them toys like dolls (Bussey & Bandura, 1992). In addition, boys may prefer the company of a girl who is a tomboy to a boy who engages in cross-gender activity (Alexander & Hines, 1994). Finally, researchers have found that it is very difficult to change boys' play preferences with modeling and reinforcement (Paley, 1986; Weisner & Wilson-Mitchell, 1990). These findings suggest that, at least for boys, sex-typed behavior is part of a complex process of identity development and not just the result of cultural modeling and reinforcement.

Before going on

- How do the major theoretical orientations explain gender concept and sex-role development?

- Describe the development of gender identity, gender stability, and gender constancy.

- What are the characteristics of young children's sex-role knowledge?

- How is the behavior of young children sex-typed?

Research Report

The Significance of Early Childhood Cross-Gender Behavior

You may be wondering if there is any link between early childhood cross-gender behavior and homosexuality. To find out, developmentalists would need to collect longitudinal data. In other words, they would have to follow the development of young children who exhibit cross-gender behavior into adolescence and adulthood in order to determine how many, if any, of them were homosexual. To date, no such data exist, but several researchers have carried out retrospective studies in which they questioned adults about their memories of childhood experiences. A comprehensive statistical review of these studies found that a majority of homosexual men and women recalled having engaged in cross-gender activities in early childhood (Bailey & Zucker, 1995).

However, it is important to know that many heterosexual adults, especially women, also recall early childhood cross-gender experiences. In fact, in one study involving female college students in the United States, half the participants reported having been tomboys in early and middle childhood (Burn et al., 1996). Since the prevalence of lesbianism among American women is between 2% and 3%, it is clear that the proportion of women who recall cross-gender experiences far exceeds the proportion of lesbians in the adult female population.

On the other hand, based on these retrospective studies, many psychologists believe that cross-gender behavior of an extreme nature—such as a child's consistently expressing a desire to be the opposite gender over a long period of time—is probably related to the development of a homosexual orientation in both males and females (Zuger, 1990). Moreover, at least one study found that

the reports of homosexual men and their mothers agreed with respect to memories of early cross-gender behavior (Bailey, Nothnagel, & Wolfe, 1995). Once again, though, the correlation is far from perfect. Many heterosexual men recall having expressed such desires in early childhood, and most homosexual men have never experienced a desire to be female (Phillips & Over, 1992).

Moreover, adults' memories for childhood events are known to be faulty and influenced by their current schemas (Bahrick, Hall, & Berger, 1996). Thus, homosexual adults (and their parents) may recall more cross-gender behavior because, when they reflect on how personal childhood experiences relate to sexual orientation, cross-gender episodes stand out for them to a greater degree than for adults who are heterosexual. In summary, parents should probably refrain from reading too much significance into early childhood cross-gender behavior.

A Final Word

It should be clear to you after reading this chapter that the cognitive advances of the 2- to 6-year-old period have important implications for personality and social development. Relations with family and peers, as well as the child's understanding of herself, are different in early childhood than they were in infancy because the child can now use symbols to communicate and think. At the same time, the child's widening and changing social world allows her to gain knowledge and skills, both social and cognitive, from others.

However, the universal aspects of development during this period are intertwined with individual factors. Some children experience stresses during early childhood, such as changes in family structure, that others do not. As a result, developmental outcomes can vary among children. In fact, if you compare early childhood to infant development, you might conclude that, as development becomes more complex, it also becomes more vulnerable to environmental forces, a pattern that will become increasingly evident in later periods.

Summary

Theories of Social and Personality Development

- Freud and Erikson each described two stages of personality development during the preschool years, the anal and phallic stages in Freud's theory, and stages in which autonomy and initiative are developed in Erikson's theory. Both theories, but especially Freud's, place primary importance on the parent-child relationship. More recent psychoanalytic approaches emphasize the importance of relationships with peers and siblings.

- Social-cognitive theorists assert that advances in social and personality development are associated with cognitive development. Three topics of interest to such theorists are person perception, understanding of others' intentions, and understanding of different kinds of rules.

Family Relationships

- The young child's attachment to the parent(s) remains strong, but except in stressful situations, attachment behaviors become less visible as the child gets older. Preschoolers refuse or defy parental influence attempts more than infants do. Outright defiance, however, declines from age 2 to age 6. Both these changes are clearly linked to the child's language and cognitive gains.

- Authoritative parenting, which combines warmth, clear rules, and communication with high maturity demands, is associated with the most positive outcomes for children. Authoritarian parenting has some negative effects on development. However, permissive and uninvolved parenting seem to be the least positive styles.

- Ethnicity and socio-economic class are linked to parenting style. Asian American and African American parents are more authoritarian than those in other ethnic groups, and poor parents in all ethnic groups tend to be authoritarian. Studies of parenting style and developmental outcomes in ethnic groups suggest that, in some situations, authoritative parenting may not be the best style.

Family Structure and Divorce

- Family structure affects early childhood social and personality development. Data from U.S. studies suggest that any family structure other than one that includes two biological parents is linked to more negative outcomes.

- Following a divorce, children typically show disrupted behavior for several years. Parenting styles also change, becoming less authoritative. However, many effects of divorce on children are associated with problems that existed before the marriage ended.

- To understand the influence of family structure on development, a number of variables, such as poverty, associated with differences in family structure must be taken into account. However, these variables alone are insufficient to explain differences in children that are correlated with variations in family make-up.

Peer Relationships

- Play with peers is evident before age 2 and becomes increasingly important through the preschool years.

- Physical aggression toward peers increases and then declines during these years, while verbal aggression increases among older preschoolers. Some children develop a pattern of aggressive behavior that continues to cause problems for them throughout childhood and adolescence.

- Children as young as 2 show prosocial behavior toward others, and this behavior seems to become more common as the child's ability to take another's perspective increases. Stable friendships develop between children in this age range.

Personality and Self-Concept

- During early childhood, children's temperaments are modified by social experiences both within and outside of the family to form their personalities.

- The preschooler continues to define himself along a series of objective dimensions but does not yet have a global sense of self. Children make major strides in self-control and in their understanding of their own social roles in the preschool years, as parents gradually turn over the job of control to the child.

The Gender Concept and Sex Roles

- Neither Freud's nor Erikson's explanations of gender development has received much support from researchers. Social learning explanations are more persuasive but ignore the role of cognitive development. Social-cognitive theories explain and predict gender-related understanding and behavior better than psychoanalytic or learning theories.

- Between ages 2 and 6, most children move through a series of steps in their understanding of gender constancy: first, labeling their own and others' gender; then, understanding the stability of gender; and, finally, comprehending the constancy of gender at about age 5 or 6.

● Beginning at about age 2, children begin to learn what is appropriate behavior for their gender. By age 5 or 6, most children have developed fairly rigid rules about what boys or girls are supposed to do and be.

● Children display sex-typed behavior as early as 18–24 months of age. Some theorists think children play in gender-segregated groups because same-sex peers help them learn about sex-appropriate behavior.

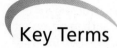

Key Terms

aggression (p. 197)

authoritarian parenting style (p. 186)

authoritative parenting style (p. 186)

cross-gender behavior (p. 209)

extended family (p. 194)

gender concept (p. 203)

gender constancy (p. 204)

gender constancy theory (p. 204)

gender identity (p. 205)

gender schema theory (p. 204)

gender stability (p. 205)

hostile aggression (p. 198)

inductive discipline (p. 188)

instrumental aggression (p. 198)

permissive parenting style (p. 186)

person perception (p. 182)

prosocial behavior (p. 199)

sex roles (p. 203)

sex-typed behavior (p. 207)

social skills (p. 196)

social-cognitive theory (p. 181)

uninvolved parenting style (p. 186)

"Deadbeat Dads": Irresponsible Parents or Political Scapegoats?

Developmental psychologists and policy makers alike have traditionally focused on the mother-child relationship. In recent years, however, attention has turned to the contributions fathers make to children's development. Fathers have received greater attention in recent years because their involvement in family life has declined all over the world as a consequence of urbanization, increased employment of women outside the home, rising rates of divorce and out-of-wedlock births, and declining adherence to traditional cultural and religious values (Engle & Breaux, 1998). Thus, developmentalists have begun to examine the effects of this growing phenomenon.

In general, research has shown that involvement of their father in their lives is associated with a number of benefits for children (Lamb, 1997). For example, low-income African American children who have strong attachments to and regular contact with their fathers have been found to exhibit dramatically lower rates of early sexual activity and depression (Furstenberg & Harris, 1992). They are also more likely to be employed or enrolled in college as young adults. Thus, a number of policy initiatives to increase fathers' involvement in families have been implemented by governments around the world, but such policies have been especially common in the United States (Engle & Breaux, 1998). For the most part, these policies have emphasized the father's economic contribution to the family.

Welfare Reform and Child Support

In 1992 and 1996, the U.S. Congress enacted sweeping changes in welfare eligibility rules. For example, with few exceptions, residents of the United States can no longer receive welfare payments for more than a total of 5 years. In addition to setting limits on welfare eligibility and providing support for the transition to work, both sets of legislation included provisions for improving enforcement of child support orders. Because the overwhelming majority of single parents on welfare are women, politicians often use the catchphrase "deadbeat dads" to signify parents who fail to meet their child support obligations.

Over the course of the welfare reform debate, deadbeat dads have been blamed for a large proportion of welfare spending in the United States. In fact, politicians of both major political parties have consistently cited $34 billion as the annual cost of caring for children abandoned by deadbeat dads, although researchers have had difficulty finding an empirical basis for this assertion (Sorensen, 1997). The image created by the political rhetoric is of irresponsible men who impregnate woman and then expect taxpayers to support these women and children. Politicians assert that to right this wrong governments need to devote more resources to tracking down deadbeat dads and making them pay.

Finding Deadbeat Dads and Making Them Pay

Policies aimed at tracking down deadbeat dads enjoy wide public support, and they have proliferated at both the federal and state levels in recent years. They have also been supported by many developmentalists, because research has demonstrated that fathers' involvement in their children's lives increases when they keep up with child support obligations (Yoshikawa, 1999), and that children whose noncustodial parents are more involved with them have fewer developmental problems and score higher on achievement tests. One consequence of these policies has been that the FBI now investigates child support cases, because it is a federal crime to move from one state to another to avoid complying with a child support order. Another consequence is that, in many states, noncustodial parents can lose their driver's license and even professional credentials, such as a license to practice medicine, when they fail to pay child support (Gledhill, 1997).

However, deadbeat dads aren't the only targets of child support enforcement efforts. These policies are also aimed at forcing custodial mothers to cooperate with government officials. For example, women who receive welfare payments or financial support for

(*Photo:* © Bob Daemmrich, Stock Boston)

(*Photo:* David Young-Wolff, PhotoEdit)

making the transition from welfare to work must identify their children's fathers to government officials and help law enforcement officers find them. If women claim they do not know who their children's fathers are, they must identify all their sexual partners and submit themselves and their children to DNA testing (Monson, 1997). They must also cooperate in obtaining court orders compelling their sexual partners to obtain DNA testing. The penalty for failing to cooperate is denial of benefits.

The general public has also been enlisted in efforts to find deadbeat dads. Numerous Internet sites—some operated by law enforcement agencies and others by private concerns—contain lists of the names of alleged deadbeat dads, as well as addresses, last known location, and amount of support owed. (See, for example, www.scattorneygeneral.com and www.mbisoftware.com/deadbeat-dads.) Many sites include photos, and some offer rewards for "tips" regarding the whereabouts of deadbeat dads.

Criticisms of Deadbeat Dad Policies

One important criticism of deadbeat dad policies concerns the rhetoric itself. The term "deadbeat dad" unnecessarily denigrates fathers and men in general, some critics say. Further, many claim that the assumption that the father is more able than the mother to provide for the child financially is sexist and does not match the realities of many child support cases. Critics point to two facts as proof that courts are already biased against fathers, without the additional effects of a politically inspired public frenzy over deadbeat dads: First, only about 10% of divorced fathers gain custody of their children (Fathers' Rights Coalition, 1999).

Second, less than 30% of custodial fathers who go to court win child support awards from their children's mothers, whereas more than 80% of custodial mothers succeed in obtaining child support orders against their children's fathers (Fathers' Rights Coalition, 1999).

Critics of deadbeat dad policies also say that these policies involve invasions of privacy that Americans would not tolerate under other circumstances. For example, in some states, an alleged deadbeat dad's financial records (bank statements, tax returns, etc.) can be examined by state officials without his consent or knowledge (Archer, 1999). Critics also point out that the ways in which child support orders are handled in the court system actually undermine attainment of their goals. For example, an alleged deadbeat dad can lose his driver's and professional licenses simply for failing to appear in court when ordered. If he loses his professional license as a result of missing the court date, his ability to pay child support will be severely reduced. And even if he retains his license, to make the court date, the father has to take time off from work, which usually results in a loss of income—which, in turn, reduces his ability to pay child support.

It is the ability to pay, according to both fathers' rights organizations and empirical research, that lies at the heart of the child support issue. In spite of the stereotype created by political rhetoric, most noncustodial fathers consistently meet their child support obligations as long as they are financially able to do so (Meyer & Bartfield, 1998). However, research has shown that child support awards given to custodial mothers by judges in the United States often far exceed what a noncustodial father can realistically pay. Fathers are far less likely to pay child support when the amount of the award exceeds 35% of their gross income (Meyer & Bartfield, 1996). Awards are also highly inconsistent. Two noncustodial fathers with the same income may be ordered to pay very different amounts of support. Moreover, surveys have demonstrated that even minimal acceptable levels of support established in state guidelines exceed what most Americans think is fair (Coleman, Ganong, Killian, & McDaniel, 1999).

Even when an initial award is reasonable, noncustodial fathers who lose their jobs or suffer other kinds of financial setbacks rarely succeed in obtaining even temporary court-ordered reductions in the amount of child support they must pay. Courts also frequently fail to realize that fathers' financial difficulties may be the result of substance abuse problems or mental illness (Dion, Braver, Wolchik, & Sandler, 1997). To make matters worse, to petition a court for a reduction, the father must be able to afford to hire an attorney to represent him. In addition, noncustodial fathers are not entitled to a reduction in child support when their children's mothers marry or obtain employment. In fact, in many cases, a custodial mother's standard of living is much higher than that of the noncustodial father, yet the father must continue to pay the same amount of support. Thus, it is not surprising that noncustodial fathers report that financial matters are the biggest source of stress in their lives (Lawson & Thompson, 1996).

Alternatives to Deadbeat Dad Policies

Critics of deadbeat dad policies say that one essential step in improving child support compliance in the United States is to reform the judicial process. First, standards should be set for child support awards so that there is more consistency among cases. Second, legislation that contains more specific criteria for changing child support levels and that takes both noncustodial and custodial parents' current economic circumstances into account is needed. Third, joint custody should be considered more often; fathers who share custody with their

(*Photo:* © Bob Daemmrich, Stock Boston)

children's mothers are more likely to be involved in their children's daily lives and to pay child support (Arditti, 1991).

In addition to judicial reforms, many observers suggest that the issue of child support be embedded in a broader approach to increasing father involvement, one that recognizes that a father's contribution to his children goes far beyond the money he provides for them. Indeed, some critics suggest that the grief and despair many fathers experience when they lose daily contact with their children because of separation or divorce have been completely ignored in the debate over deadbeat dad policies (Knox, 1998). Policy makers also need to increase efforts to reduce the number of out-of-wedlock births, because never-married fathers are far less likely than divorced fathers to make support payments (Caputo, 1996).

The challenge for developmental psychologists is to develop a research base on fathering comparable to the research base they already have on mothering. Researchers need to know exactly what a father's unique contributions are and how fathers' interactions with children bring about those effects. Such research can be the basis for policy initiatives that will increase overall father involvement, across all types of family structures, as well as payment of child support by divorced and never-married fathers.

What Is the Situation in Your State?

Federal welfare reform legislation in 1992 and 1996 required every state to take steps to improve enforcement of child support orders. The states have complied in a variety of ways. As mentioned, several states revoke the driver's and professional licenses of deadbeat dads. However, the federal legislation requires states to make efforts to locate deadbeat dads as well as to establish penalties for nonpayment. Thus, officials in every state have produced some kind of systematic plan for finding them. Because the deadbeat dad issue has been so prominent in recent years, you should be able to find out information about your state's policies.

Your Turn

- What are the penalties in your state for nonpayment of child support?

- What efforts have been made by officials in your state to locate deadbeat dads?

- Can an alleged deadbeat dad or a noncustodial father who is seeking a reduction in child support award represent himself in court in your state? If not, are there agencies that provide low-cost legal assistance to such men?

- Does your state have policies requiring custodial mothers to cooperate in identifying their children's fathers?

- Do welfare statistics in your state indicate that deadbeat dad policies have reduced the welfare rolls?

- Do you agree with your state's current approach to the deadbeat dad issue? Why or why not?

CHAPTER

Physical and Cognitive Development in Middle Childhood

© Jose Azel, Woodfin Camp and Associates

Throughout the industrialized world, as well as in most developing areas, the years of middle childhood are devoted to formal education.

Indeed, the first day of school is considered to be one of the most important transition points in a child's life. In the United States, parents mark the occasion in a variety of ways—with new clothes, fresh school supplies, and carefully selected backpacks and lunch boxes. Some families take pictures of their children's first ride on the schoolbus or first classroom. All of these ways of recognizing this important milestone say to children that this day is unique, and they begin to think of themselves as "big kids" who are engaged in the serious business of going to school, rather than "little kids" who spend most of their time playing.

As important as middle childhood is, however, researchers often pay little attention to these years, as if they were somehow insignificant. Far less research has been done on children in this age group than on either preschoolers or adolescents. Yet it is clear that major cognitive advances occur between the ages of 6 and 12 and that patterns and habits established during this time will affect not only adolescent experience, but also adulthood.

In this chapter, we will explore the many physical changes, including those in the brain, that happen between 6 and 12. You will also learn how children's linguistic abilities expand significantly during these years, and how children acquire the developmental foundation of adult logic and memory. We will examine the influence of formal education on a variety of developmental processes and explore some factors that shape academic achievement. As you read the chapter, keep the following questions in mind:

- How are sex differences in physical activities linked to the development of various body systems in middle childhood? How does the brain change during these years?

- What are the milestones in the development of linguistic, cognitive, and memory skills that mark the 6- to 12-year-old period?

- How does schooling influence development?

- What kinds of individual and group differences are related to development and school achievement?

Physical Changes

 lthough they are more difficult to observe directly, the physical changes of middle childhood are just as impressive as those of early childhood.

Growth and Motor Development

Between 6 and 12, children grow 2–3 inches and add about 6 pounds each year. Large-muscle coordination continues to improve, and children become increasingly adept at skills like bike riding; both strength and speed also increase. Hand-eye coor-

When school-aged boys and girls participate in co-ed sports, boys' superior speed and strength is balanced by girls' advantage in coordination.
(*Photo:* Cindy Charles, PhotoEdit)

dination improves as well (Thomas, Yan, & Stelmach, 2000). As a result, school-aged children perform more skillfully in activities requiring coordination of vision with body movements, such as shooting a basketball or playing a musical instrument.

Perhaps even more significant is the school-aged child's improving fine-motor coordination. Improvements in fine-motor coordination make writing possible, as well as the playing of most musical instruments, drawing, cutting, and many other tasks and activities. Such accomplished uses of the hands are made possible by maturation of the wrist, which, as you may recall from earlier chapters, occurs more rapidly in girls than in boys (Tanner, 1990).

Girls in this age range are ahead of boys in their overall rate of growth as well. By 12, girls have attained about 94% of their adult height, while boys have reached only 84% of theirs (Tanner, 1990). Girls also have slightly more body fat and slightly less muscle tissue than boys. Sex differences in skeletal and muscular maturation cause girls to be better coordinated but slower and somewhat weaker than boys. Thus, girls outperform boys in activities requiring coordinated movement, and boys do better when strength and speed are advantages. Still, the overall sex differences in joint maturation, strength, and speed are small at this age.

The Brain and Nervous System

Two major growth spurts happen in the brain during middle childhood (Spreen, Risser, & Edgell, 1995). In most healthy children, the first takes place between ages 6 and 8, and the second between ages 10 and 12. Both spurts involve development of new synapses as well as increases in the thickness of the cerebral cortex.

The primary sites of brain growth during the first spurt are the sensory and motor areas. Growth in these areas may be linked to the striking improvements in fine-motor skills and eye-hand coordination that usually occur between 6 and 8. During the second spurt of brain growth, the frontal lobes of the cerebral cortex become the focus of developmental processes (Van der Molen & Molenaar, 1994). Predictably, the areas of the brain that govern logic and planning, two cognitive functions that improve dramatically during this period, are located primarily in the frontal lobes.

Myelinization also continues through middle childhood. Of particular importance is the continued myelinization of the reticular formation and of the nerves that link the reticular formation to the frontal lobes. These connections are essential if the child is to be able to take full advantage of improvements in frontal lobe functions because, as you may recall, the reticular formation controls attention. It is well documented that the ability to control attention increases significantly during middle childhood (Lin, Hsiao & Chen, 1999).

It seems likely that myelinization allows the linkages between the frontal lobes and the reticular formation to work together so that 6- to 12-year-olds are able to develop a particular kind of concentration called *selective attention*. **Selective attention** is the ability to focus cognitive activity on the important elements of a problem or situation. For example, suppose your psychology instructor, who usually copies tests on white paper, gives you a test printed on blue paper. You won't spend a lot of time thinking about why the test is blue instead of white; this is an irrelevant detail. Instead, your selective attention skills will prompt you to ignore the color of the paper and focus on the test questions. In contrast, some younger elementary school children might be so distracted by the unusual color of the test paper that their test performance would be affected. As the nerves connecting the reticular formation and the

Critical Thinking

Think about how you're using selective attention skills as you read this book. What distractions are you screening out?

selective attention the ability to focus cognitive activity on the important elements of a problem or situation

frontal lobes become more fully myelinated between ages 6 and 12, children begin to function more like adults in the presence of such distractions.

The neurons of the **association areas**—parts of the brain where sensory, motor, and intellectual functions are linked—are myelinized to some degree by the time children enter middle childhood. However, from 6 to 12, the nerve cells in these areas achieve nearly complete myelinization. Neuroscientists believe that this advance in the myelinization process contributes to increases in information-processing speed. For example, suppose you were to ask a 6-year-old and a 12-year-old to identify pictures of common items—a bicycle, an apple, a desk, a dog—as rapidly as possible. Both children would know the items' names, but the 12-year-old would be able to produce the names of the items much more rapidly than the 6-year-old. Such increases in processing speed probably contribute to improvements in memory function, which you'll read about later in the chapter (Kail, 1990).

Another important advance in middle childhood occurs in the right cerebral hemisphere, with the lateralization of **spatial perception,** the ability to identify and act on relationships between objects in space. For example, when you imagine how a room would look with a different arrangement of furniture, you are using spatial perception. Perception of objects such as faces actually lateralizes before age 6. However, complex spatial perception, such as map-reading, isn't strongly lateralized until about age 8.

A behavioral test of the lateralization of spatial perception often used by neuroscientists involves **relative right-left orientation,** the ability to identify right and left from multiple perspectives. Such a test usually shows that most children younger than 8 know the difference between their own right and left. Typically, though, only children older than 8 understand the difference between statements like "It's on *your* right" and "It's on *my* right." Lateralization of spatial perception may also be related to the increased efficiency with which older children learn math concepts and problem-solving strategies. In addition, it is somewhat correlated to performance on Piaget's conservation tasks (Van der Molen & Molenaar, 1994).

However, the development of spatial perception is more than just a physiological process. Developmentalists know this because this function lateralizes much more slowly in blind children than in those who have sight. Thus, it appears that visual experience plays an important role in this aspect of brain development.

Furthermore, some researchers propose that differences in visual experiences explain sex differences in spatial perception and the related function of **spatial cognition,** the ability to infer rules from and make predictions about the movement of objects in space. For example, when you are driving on a two-lane road, and you make a judgment about whether you have enough room to pass a car ahead of you, you are using spatial cognition. From an early age, boys score much higher than girls, on average, on such spatial tasks (Halpern, 1986; Voyer, Voyer, & Bryden, 1995). Some researchers suggest that boys' play preferences, such as their greater interest in constructive activities such as building with blocks, help them develop more acute spatial perception and cognition (see Development in the Information Age).

Health and Wellness

Generally speaking, most school-aged children are very healthy. However, they continue to benefit from regular medical care. For one thing, there are a few important immunizations that are usually administered during this period (Umetsu, 1998). In addition, some school-aged children have undiagnosed health problems. For example, about 10% of U.S. elementary school children have difficulty sleeping (Owens, Spirito, McGuinn, & Nobile, 2000). In most cases, parents of 6- to 12-year-olds are unaware of such problems until a physician or nurse specifically asks a child about sleep patterns as part of a routine check-up.

Following motor vehicle accidents, bicycle mishaps are the most frequent cause of injuries to school-aged children in the United States (National Center for Injury Prevention and Control, 2000). In fact, 80% of bicycle-related head injuries involve

association areas parts of the brain where sensory, motor, and intellectual functions are linked

spatial perception the ability to identify and act on relationships between objects in space

relative right-left orientation the ability to identify right and left from multiple perspectives

spatial cognition the ability to infer rules from and make predictions about the movement of objects in space

The Effects of Video Games

In the United States, families with children spend more money on video games than on any other kind of entertainment (Interactive Digital Software Association, 1998). Anthropologists propose that video games are one of the many tools industrialized societies use to teach children the technological and intellectual skills they need as adults (Greenfield, 1994). Several studies suggest that playing video games fosters good spatial perception skills (Greenfield, Brannon, &

(*Photo:* Ken Lax, Photo Researchers)

Lohr, 1994). Spatial perception is related to math achievement, a highly valued set of skills in the industrial world. So, the anthropological explanation for the proliferation of video-game playing in technological societies seems to make sense,

Despite the positive effects of video games on cognitive development, research examining the impact of these games on social and emotional development suggests that developmentalists should be cautious about recommending using video games to enhance spatial perception skills. The linked themes of aggression and power predominate among video games; more than 75% of them involve violence. Further, video-game players, 70–80% of whom are male, overwhelmingly prefer violent games to any other type (Funk & Buchman, 1999)

Researchers have found that playing violent video games leads to immediate increases in aggressive behavior and is associated with long-term increases in such behavior among children who have always been more aggressive than others their age (Anderson &

Dill, 2000). In addition, children who play violent video games for 90 minutes or more per day experience higher levels of anxiety and are less able to tolerate frustration than peers (Mediascope, 1999). Indeed, even short-term exposure to violent video games in laboratory settings appears to increase research participants' general level of emotional hostility (Anderson & Dill, 2000).

Violent video games also appear to be part of an overall pattern linking preferences for violent stimuli to aggressive behavior. The more violent television programs children watch, the more violent video games they prefer, and the more aggressively they behave toward peers (Mediascope, 1999). This finding holds for both boys and girls; most girls aren't interested in violent games, but those who are tend to be more physically aggressive than average. Consequently, parents who notice that aggressive and violent themes characterize most of their children's leisure-time interests as well as their interactions with peers should worry about their children playing video games (Funk, Buchman, Myers, & Jenks, 2000).

---

children. Research suggests that wearing a helmet while riding reduces the chances of head injury by more than 85%. Consequently, many cities and states have enacted laws requiring both children and adults to wear helmets when riding bikes.

Aside from accidents, the most significant health risk of the middle childhood period is obesity. Estimates of the prevalence of obesity vary. During the mid-1990s, the most recent period for which reliable figures are available in the United States, approximately 11% of children and adolescents were obese (National Center for Health Statistics [NCHS], 1996). Several studies indicate that the incidence of obesity is increasing (NCHS, 2000). Moreover, obesity is a significant health problem throughout the industrialized world. For example, researchers in Italy found that 23.4% of the boys and 12.7% of the girls in a sample of 10-year-olds were obese (Maffeis, Schutz, Piccoli, Gonfiantini, & Pinelli, 1993).

Obesity is most often defined as a body weight that is 20% or more above the normal weight for a particular height, but recently health care providers have begun using a measure called the *body mass index (BMI)* that estimates a child's proportion of body fat (NCHS, 2000). Using the BMI allows health care providers to more easily distinguish between children who seem to be overweight because they are very muscular and those who are actually obese.

obesity body weight that is 20% or more above the normal weight for height, or, a body mass index higher than most children of similar age

The older a child gets without losing weight, the more likely the child is to remain obese into the adult years (NCHS, 2000). Only a fifth of overweight babies become overweight adults, but half of those who were overweight in elementary school continue to be overweight in adulthood (Serdula et al., 1993). In addition, more than half of obese children have one or more risk factors, such as elevated levels of cholesterol or high blood pressure, that predispose them to heart disease later in life (National Center for Chronic Disease Prevention and Health Promotion [NCCDPHP], 2000).

As you might suspect, overeating or eating too much of the wrong foods causes obesity in children just as it does in adults (NCCDPHP, 2000). However, both twin and adoption studies suggest that obesity probably results from an interaction between a genetic predisposition for obesity and environmental factors that promote overeating or low levels of activity (Stunkard, Harris, Pedersen, & McClearn, 1990). Whatever the genetic contribution might be, public health officials contend that a cultural pattern of decreases in physical activity and increases in the consumption of high-calorie convenience foods has led to the current epidemic of obesity among both children and adults in the United States (NCCDPHP, 2000).

It's important to keep in mind, though, that weight-loss diets for children can be fairly risky. Because they are still growing, the nutritional needs of obese children differ from those of obese adults (Tershakovec & Stallings, 1998). Consequently, obese children require special diets developed and supervised by nutritional experts. Moreover, increasing the amount of exercise children get is just as important as changing their eating habits (NCCDPHP, 2000).

Fear of developing an unattractive body may become a significant problem for some children. Serious eating disorders (which you'll read about in detail in Chapter 10) don't become common until well into adolescence. However, most 6- to 12-year-olds are quite knowledgeable about weight-loss diets and products (Kostanski & Gullone, 1999). Moreover, research suggests that children as young as 7 years of age sometimes express dissatisfaction with their weight or physical appearance, and some begin dieting as early as age 9 (Kostanski & Gullone, 1999; NCHS, 1996; Nutter, 1997). In addition, weight concerns increase among both boys and girls across the 6- to 12-year-old period (Gardner, Friedman, & Jackson, 1999).

It is important to help children develop good eating habits without overemphasizing physical appearance to the extent that children develop patterns of dieting that can threaten their later mental and physical health. Moreover, one way parents can definitely make a difference for all children, regardless of their weight, is to encourage them to be physically active. Simply limiting the time children may spend on television, computers, and video games may lead to increases in physical activity. Public health officials also suggest that school-based nutrition education and exercise programs can help prevent both obesity and eating disorders (NCHS, 1996).

An overweight child not only has different kinds of encounters with his peers, he is also more likely to be fat as an adult, with accompanying increased health risks. (*Photo:* Tony Freeman, PhotoEdit)

Before going on

- Describe the physical growth of 6- to 12-year-olds.

- List the changes in brain growth, myelinization, and lateralization that happen between 6 and 12.

- What are the two most important health hazards for 6- to 12-year-olds?

Cognitive Changes

long with impressive gains in physical development, children acquire some of the important hallmarks of mature thinking between ages 6 and 12.

Language

By age 5 or 6, virtually all children have mastered the basic grammar and pronunciation of their first language, but children of this age still have a fair distance to go before reaching adult levels of fluency. During middle childhood, children become skilled at managing the finer points of grammar (Prat-Sala, Shillcock, & Sorace, 2000; Ragnarsdottir, Simonsen, & Plunkett, 1999). For example, by the end of middle childhood, most children understand various ways of saying something about the past, such as "I went," "I was going," "I have gone," "I had gone," "I had been going," and so on. Moreover, they correctly use such tenses in their own speech.

Across the middle childhood years, children also learn how to maintain the topic of conversation, how to create unambiguous sentences, and how to speak politely or persuasively (Anglin, 1993).

Between 6 and 12, children also continue to add new vocabulary at a fairly astonishing rate of from 5,000 to 10,000 words per year. This estimate comes from several careful studies by developmental psychologist Jeremy Anglin, who estimates children's total vocabularies by testing them on a sample of words drawn at random from a large dictionary (Anglin, 1993, 1995). Figure 8.1 shows Anglin's estimates for first, third, and fifth grade. Anglin finds that the largest gain between third and fifth grades occurs in knowledge of the type of words he calls *derived words*—words that have a basic root to which some prefix or suffix is added, such as "happily" or "unwanted."

Anglin argues that at age 8 or 9, the child shifts to a new level of understanding of the structure of language, figuring out relationships between whole categories of words, such as between adjectives and adverbs ("happy" and "happily," "sad" and "sadly"), between adjectives and nouns ("happy" and "happiness"), and the like. Once he grasps these relationships, the child can understand and create a whole class of new words, and his vocabulary thereafter increases rapidly.

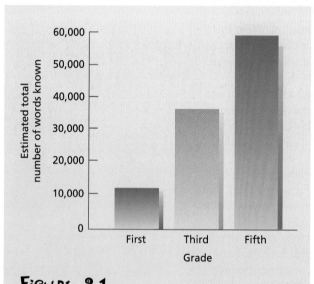

FIGURE 8.1

Anglin's estimates of the total vocabulary of first-, third-, and fifth-graders. (*Source:* Anglin, 1995, from Figure 6, p. 7.)

Piaget's Concrete Operational Stage

From Piaget's perspective, a great leap forward occurs when the school-aged child discovers or develops a set of immensely powerful schemes that Piaget called *concrete operations*. By **concrete operations**, Piaget meant mental processes such as reversibility, addition, subtraction, multiplication, division, and serial ordering. Each of these is a kind of general rule about objects and their relationships. The school-aged child understands the rule that adding makes something more and subtracting makes it less; she understands that objects can belong to more than one category at once and that categories have logical relationships.

concrete operations a set of mental schemes, including reversibility, addition, subtraction, multiplication, division, and serial ordering, that enable children to understand relations among objects

Of all the operations, Piaget thought the most critical was *reversibility*—the understanding that both physical actions and mental operations can be reversed. The clay sausage in a conservation experiment can be made back into a ball; the water can be poured back into the shorter, wider glass. This understanding of the basic reversibility of actions lies behind many of the gains made during the middle childhood period. For example, if a child has mastered reversibility, then knowing that A is larger than B also tells him that B is smaller than A. The ability to understand hierarchies of classes (such as Fido, spaniel, dog, and animal) also rests on this ability to move both ways in thinking about relationships.

Piaget also proposed that during this stage the child develops the ability to use **inductive logic.** She can go from her own experience to a general principle. For example, she can move from the observation that when a toy is added to a set of toys, it has one more than it did before, to a general principle that adding always makes more.

Elementary school children are fairly good observational scientists, and they enjoy cataloging, counting species of trees or birds, or figuring out the nesting habits of guinea pigs. But they are not yet good at **deductive logic** based on hypothetical premises, which requires starting with a general principle and then predicting some outcome or observation— like going from a theory to a hypothesis. For example, in the composition in Figure 8.2 (page 224), a fifth-grader responded to the question "What would you do if you were President of the United States?" Responding to such a question requires deductive, not inductive, logic; this kind of task is difficult for 6- to 12-year-olds because they must imagine things they have not experienced. The concrete operations child is good at dealing with things she can see and manipulate or can imagine seeing or manipulating—that is, she is good with *concrete* things; she does not do well with manipulating ideas or possibilities. Thus, as the composition illustrates, children respond to deductive problems by generating ideas that are essentially copies of the things they know about in the concrete world.

Critical Thinking

Make a brief list of the things you would do if you were President of the United States. How do your ideas differ from those in the fifth-grader's composition in Figure 8.2? How does your thinking demonstrate more mature deductive logic?

Direct Tests of Piaget's View

Piaget understood that it took children some years to apply their new cognitive skills to all kinds of problems, a phenomenon he called *horizontal decalage*. (The French word *decalage* means "a shift.")

● *Horizontal Decalage* ● Researchers have generally found that Piaget was right in his assertion that concrete operational schemes are acquired gradually across the 6- to 12-year-old period. Studies of conservation, for example, consistently show that children grasp conservation of mass or substance by about age 7. That is, they understand that the amount of clay is the same whether it is in a pancake or a ball or some other shape. They generally understand conservation of weight at about age 8, but they don't understand conservation of volume until age 11 (Tomlinson-Keasey, Eisert, Kahle, Hardy-Brown, & Keasey, 1979).

Studies of classification skills show that at about age 7 or 8 the child first grasps the principle of **class inclusion,** the understanding that subordinate classes are included in larger, superordinate classes. Bananas are included in the class of fruit, and fruit is included in the class of food, and so forth. Preschool children understand that bananas are also fruit, but they do not yet fully understand the relationship between the classes.

inductive logic a type of reasoning in which general principles are inferred from specific experiences

deductive logic a type of reasoning based on hypothetical premises that requires predicting a specific outcome from a general principle

class inclusion the understanding that subordinate classes are included in larger, superordinate classes

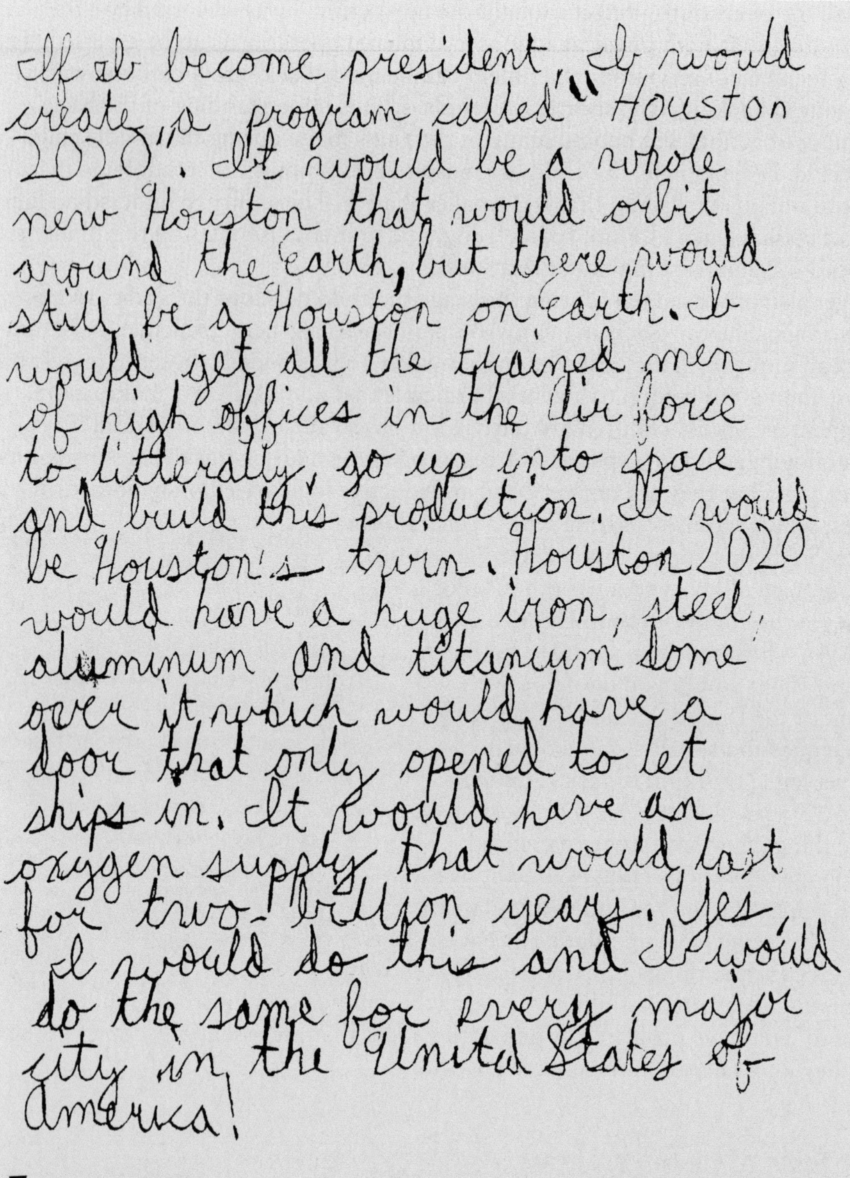

> If I become president, I would create a program called "Houston 2020". It would be a whole new Houston that would orbit around the Earth, but there would still be a Houston on Earth. I would get all the trained men of high offices in the Air force to litterally go up into space and build this production. It would be Houston's twin. Houston 2020 would have a huge iron, steel, aluminum, and titanium dome over it, which would have a door that only opened to let ships in. It would have an oxygen supply that would last for two-billion years. Yes I would do this and I would do the same for every major city in the United States of America!

FIGURE 8.2

This 5th-grader's composition illustrates the difficulty school-aged children have with deductive logic. His response to a hypothetical premise is to reinvent the world as he knows it through his own experiences or through stories about real people, places, and things. True deductive logic goes beyond what is already known. (Courtesy of Jerry and Denise Boyd. Used with permission.)

A good illustration of all these changes comes from an early longitudinal study of concrete operations tasks conducted by Carol Tomlinson-Keasey and her colleagues (Tomlinson-Keasey et al., 1979). They followed a group of 38 children from kindergarten through third grade, testing them with five traditional concrete operations tasks each year: conservation of mass, conservation of weight, conservation of volume, class inclusion, and hierarchical classification. You can see from Figure 8.3 that the children got better at all five tasks over the 3-year period, with a spurt between the end of kindergarten and the beginning of first grade (at about the age Piaget thought that concrete operations really arose) and another spurt during second grade.

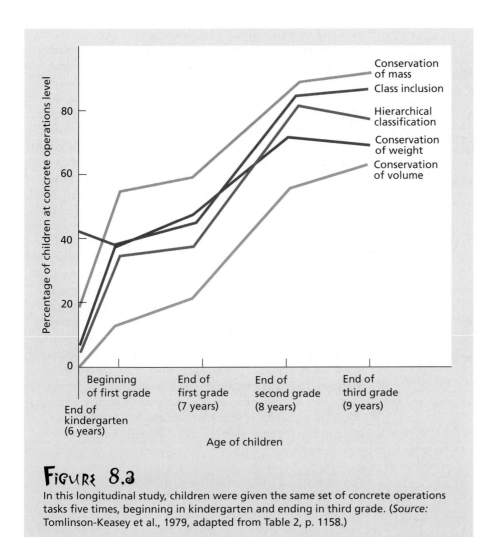

FIGURE 8.3

In this longitudinal study, children were given the same set of concrete operations tasks five times, beginning in kindergarten and ending in third grade. (*Source:* Tomlinson-Keasey et al., 1979, adapted from Table 2, p. 1158.)

● **Concrete Operations as Rules for Problem-Solving** ●   Other psychologists have conceptualized performance on concrete operational tasks in terms of rules for problem-solving. For example, Robert Siegler's approach is a kind of cross between Piagetian theory and information-processing theory. He argues that cognitive development consists in acquiring a set of basic rules that are then applied to a broader and broader range of problems on the basis of experience. There are no stages, only sequences. Siegler proposes that problem-solving rules emerge from experience— from repeated trial and error and experimentation (Siegler, 1994).

Some of Siegler's own early work on the development of rules illustrates how they may be acquired (Siegler, 1976, 1978, 1981). In one test, Siegler used a balance scale with a series of pegs on either side of the center, like the one in Figure 8.4 (page 226). The child is asked to predict which way the balance will fall, depending on the location and number of disk-shaped weights placed on the pegs. A complete solution requires the child to take into account both the number of disks on each side, and the specific location of the disks.

Children do not develop such a complete solution immediately. Instead, Siegler suggests that they develop four rules, in this order: Rule I is basically a preoperational rule, taking into account only one dimension, the number of weights. Children using this rule will predict that the side with more disks will go down, no matter which peg they are placed on. Rule II is a transitional rule. The child still judges on the basis of number, except when the same number of weights appear on each side; in that case the child takes distance from the fulcrum into account. Rule III is basically a

Experience with a teeter-totter, like this boy is getting, may be one source of knowledge about how balance scales work. (*Photo:* Myrleen Ferguson, PhotoEdit)

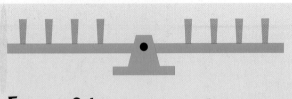

FiGURE 8.4

This balance scale is similar to what Siegler used in his experiments.

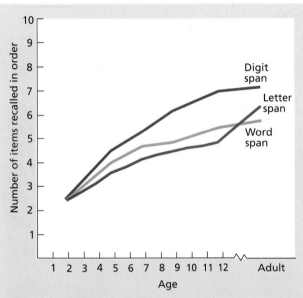

FiGURE 8.5

Psychologists measure basic memory capacity by asking participants to listen to a list of numbers, letters, or words, and then to repeat back the list in order. This figure shows the number of such items children of various ages are able to remember and report accurately. (*Source:* Dempster, 1981, from Figures 1, 2, and 3, pp. 66, 67, 68.)

concrete operational rule; the child tries to take both distance and weight into account simultaneously, except that when the information is conflicting (such as when the side with weights closer to the fulcrum has more weights), the child simply guesses. Rule IV involves the understanding of the actual formula for calculating the combined effect of weight and distance for each side of the balance.

Siegler has found that virtually all children perform on this and similar tasks as if they were following one or another of these rules, and that the rules seem to develop in the given order. Very young children behave as if they don't have a rule (they guess or behave randomly); when they do seem to begin using a rule, it is always Rule I that comes first. But progression from one rule to the next depends heavily on experience. If children are given practice with the balance scale so that they can make predictions and then check which way the balance actually falls, many rapidly develop the next rules in the sequence.

Thus, Siegler is attempting to describe a logical sequence children follow, not unlike the basic sequence of stages that Piaget describes—but Siegler's research shows that a particular child's position in the sequence depends not so much on age as on the child's specific experience with a given set of material. In Piaget's terminology, this is rather like saying that when accommodation of some scheme occurs, it always occurs in a particular sequence, but the rate at which the child moves through that sequence depends on experience.

Advances in Information-Processing Skills

As they progress through the middle childhood years, children are able to remember longer and longer lists of numbers, letters, or words, as illustrated in Figure 8.5. In fact, children's memories function so well that their testimony about events they have witnessed is usually accurate enough to be regarded as reliable in judicial proceedings. Investigations of improvements in information-processing skills such as memory provide developmentalists with a way of looking at cognitive development that is distinct from Piaget's theory.

● *Processing Efficiency* ●   Processing efficiency, the ability to make efficient use of short-term memory capacity, increases steadily with age, a change that most developmentalists now see as the basis for cognitive development (Case, 1985; Halford, Maybery, O'Hare, & Grant, 1994; Kuhn, 1992). The best evidence that cognitive processing becomes more efficient is that it gets steadily faster with age. Robert Kail has found virtually the same exponential increase in processing speed with age for a wide variety of tasks, including perceptual-motor tasks such as tapping in response to a stimulus (for example, pressing a button when you hear a buzzer) and cognitive tasks such as mental addition (Kail, 1991; Kail & Hall, 1994). He has found virtually identical patterns of speed increases in studies in Korea and in the United States, which adds cross-cultural validity to the argument.

● *Automaticity* ●   One of the most important ways in which processing efficiency grows in middle childhood is through the acquisition of **automaticity,** or the ability to recall information from long-term memory without using short-term memory capac-

processing efficiency the ability to make efficient use of short-term memory capacity

automaticity the ability to recall information from long-term memory without using short-term memory capacity

ity. For example, when children can respond "49" to the question "How much is 7 times 7?" without thinking about it, they have achieved automaticity with respect to that particular piece of information.

Automaticity is critical to efficient information-processing because it frees up short-term memory space for more complex processing. Thus, the child who knows "7 times 7" automatically can use that fact in a complex multiplication or division problem without giving up any of the short-term memory space he is using to solve the problem. As a result, he is better able to concentrate on the "big picture" instead of expending effort trying to recall a simple multiplication fact. Not surprisingly, researchers have found that elementary school children who have *automatized* basic math facts in this way learn complex computational skills more rapidly (Jensen & Whang, 1994).

Automaticity is achieved primarily through practice. For example, when babies first learn to walk, they must focus all their mental effort on the act of walking. After a few weeks of practice, walking becomes automatic, and they can think about chasing the family cat or retrieving a ball that has rolled away. Likewise, adults can think about the grocery list while driving to the supermarket, because driving skills and the routes they routinely use to get from place to place are automatized. Thus, automaticity is important to information-processing throughout the lifespan. It is in middle childhood, however, when children seem to begin automatizing large quantities of information and skills at a fairly rapid rate.

Unless they are rank novices, these school-aged chess players will remember a series of chess moves or an arrangement of chess pieces far better than adults who don't play chess. (*Photo:* Elena Rooraid, PhotoEdit)

● ***Executive and Strategic Processes*** ●   If you tried to recall a list of everyday items (chair, pencil, spaghetti, tree . . .), you might consciously consider the various alternative strategies for remembering and then select the best one. You could also explain some things about how your mind works, such as which kinds of mental tasks you find most difficult. These are examples of *metacognition*—knowing about knowing or thinking about thinking—a set of skills first mentioned in Chapter 6. Metacognition is part of a large group of skills known as **executive processes**—information-processing skills that allow a person to devise and carry out alternative strategies for remembering and solving problems. Executive processes are based on a basic understanding of how the mind works. Such skills improve a great deal during middle childhood. For example, 10-year-olds are more likely than 8-year-olds to understand that attending to a story requires effort (Parault & Schwanenflugel, 2000).

One of the advantages of having good metacognitive and executive processing skills is that they help the individual devise methods for remembering information, or **memory strategies**. Although many people possess their own unique methods for remembering, Table 8.1 (page 228) lists a few common memory strategies. For the most part, these memory techniques first appear between the ages of 6 and 12.

● ***Expertise*** ●   There is a great deal of research showing that the amount of knowledge a person possesses makes a huge difference in how efficiently her information-processing system works. Children and adults who know a lot about a topic (dinosaurs, baseball cards, mathematics, or whatever it may be) categorize information about that topic in highly complex and hierarchical ways. They are also better at remembering and logically analyzing new information on that topic (Ni, 1998).

Even typical age differences in strategy use or memory ability disappear when the younger group has more expertise than the older. For example, psychologist Michelene Chi, in her now-classic early study, showed that expert chess players could remember the placement of chess pieces on a board much more quickly and accurately than novice chess players, even when the expert chess players were children and the novices were adults (Chi, 1978).

However, using advanced information-processing skills in their areas of expertise doesn't seem to help children's general memory and reasoning abilities (Ericsson &

executive processes information-processing skills that involve devising and carrying out strategies for remembering and solving problems

memory strategies learned methods for remembering information

TABLE 8.1   Some Common Information-Processing Strategies Used in Remembering

Strategy	Description
Rehearsal	Either mental or vocal repetition; may occur in children as young as 2 years under some conditions, and is common in older children and adults
Organization	Grouping ideas, objects, or words into clusters to help in remembering them, such as "all animals," or "the ingredients in the lasagna recipe," or "the chess pieces involved in the move called *castling*." This strategy is more easily applied to something a person has experience with or particular knowledge about. Two-year-olds use primitive clustering strategies.
Elaboration	Finding shared meaning or a common referent for two or more things that need to be remembered
Mnemonic	A device to assist memory; the phrase for the notes of the lines on the musical staff ("Every Good Boy Does Fine") is a mnemonic.
Systematic Searching	"Scanning" one's memory for the whole domain in which a piece of information might be found. Three- and 4-year-old children can begin to do this when they search for actual objects in the real world, but they are not good at doing this in memory. So search strategies may first be learned in the external world and then applied to inner searches.

(*Source:* Flavell, 1985.)

Crutcher, 1990). For this reason, many information-processing psychologists now believe that an individual's information-processing skills may depend entirely on the quantity and quality of relevant information stored in long-term memory. Thus, they say, to be able to learn scientific reasoning skills, for example, children must first acquire a body of knowledge about scientific topics (Zimmerman, 2000). To paraphrase developmental psychologist John Flavell, expertise makes any of us, including children, look very smart; lack of expertise makes us look very dumb (Flavell, 1985).

Before going on

- Describe vocabulary growth and other advances in language that happen during the middle childhood years.

- What cognitive advantages do children gain as they move through Piaget's concrete operational stage?

- What is horizontal decalage, and how does Siegler explain concrete operational thinking?

- Explain the contributions of processing efficiency, automaticity, metacognition and strategic processes, and expertise to the development of information-processing skills.

Schooling

s you learned at the beginning of this chapter, children all over the world begin school at age 6 or 7. Thus, an examination of the influence of this near-universal experience is important to understanding middle childhood.

Literacy

In the industrialized world, *literacy,* the ability to read and write, is the focus of education in the 6- to 12-year-old period. As you learned in Chapter 6, the skills children bring to school from their early childhood experiences may influence early reading as much as formal instruction (Crone & Whitehurst, 1999). Especially significant among these skills is the set known as *phonological awareness.* Across the early elementary years, phonological awareness skills continue to increase (Shu, Anderson, & Wu, 2000). Thus, children who lack such expertise at the start of school are likely to fall behind unless some systematic effort is made by teachers to provide them with a base of phonological knowledge (Torgesen et al., 1999). However, all beginning readers, both those who have high levels of phonological awareness and those who know less about sounds and symbols, seem to benefit from specific instruction in sound-letter correspondences (Adams & Henry, 1997).

Critical Thinking

How do you think your elementary school experiences affected the rest of your life?

It also appears that beginning readers gain a significant advantage when they achieve automaticity with respect to identifying sound-symbol connections (Samuels & Flor, 1997). Thus, they need plenty of opportunities to practice translating written language into spoken words. For this reason, reading experts suggest that reading out loud is critical to success in the early years (Adams, 1990).

Once children have learned the basic reading process, learning about meaningful word parts, such as prefixes and suffixes, helps them become more efficient readers and better understand what they read (Adams & Henry, 1997). At the same time, instruction in comprehension strategies, such as identifying the purpose of a particular text, also helps (Pressley & Wharton-McDonald, 1997). Of course, all along the way, children need to be exposed to good literature, both in their own reading and in what teachers and parents read to them.

Some of the strategies used to teach reading also help children learn writing, the other component of literacy. For example, instruction in sound-symbol connections helps children learn to spell as well as to read. Of course, good writing is far more than just spelling; it requires instruction and practice, just as reading does. Specifically, children need to learn about writing techniques such as outlining and paragraph development to become good writers. They also need to learn about language mechanics, such as grammar and appropriate uses of words, as well as how to edit their own and others' written work (Graham & Harris, 1997).

Despite educators' best efforts, many children fall behind their classmates in literacy during the early school years. In general, reading researchers have found that poor readers have problems with sound-letter combinations (Gonzalez & Valle, 2000; Mayringer & Wimmer, 2000). Thus, many children who have reading difficulties benefit from highly specific phonics approaches that provide a great deal of practice in translating letters into sounds and vice versa (Berninger et al., 1999).

However, curriculum flexibility is also important in programs for poor readers. Some do not improve when exposed to phonics approaches. In fact, programs that combine sound-letter and comprehension training, such as the Reading Recovery program, have proven to be highly successful in helping poor readers catch up, especially when the programs are implemented in the early elementary years (Klein & Swartz, 1996). Consequently, teachers need to be able to assess the effectiveness of whatever approach they are using and change it to fit the needs of individual students.

Schooling and Cognitive Development

Studies across a variety of cultures—in Mexico, Peru, Colombia, Liberia, Zambia, Nigeria, Uganda, Hong Kong, and many other countries—have led to the conclusion that school experiences are indeed linked to the emergence of some advanced cognitive skills. For example, children who do not attend school proceed through Piaget's concrete operational stage at a much slower rate (Mishra, 1997). It's important to note, too, that most of these studies compared children who differed only in schooling; the children were of the same ethnicity and were similar in socio-economic status.

You might think that rate of cognitive development doesn't matter, so long as everyone gets to the same place developmentally. However, longitudinal studies show that the rate of progression through the concrete operational stage predicts how well children will reason in adolescence and adulthood (Bradmetz, 1999). Thus, the cognitive-developmental advantage a 6- to 12-year-old gains by attending school is one that probably lasts a lifetime.

Unschooled children are also less proficient at generalizing a learned concept or principle to some new setting. A good illustration comes from studies of South American street vendors, most of whom are of elementary school age. These children can carry out monetary calculations with lightning speed and impressive accuracy, yet they have trouble translating their mental calculations into written mathematical problems (Schliemann, Carraher, & Ceci, 1997). It seems that the "language" of mathematics children learn in school helps them acquire number knowledge in a far more abstract way than children whose calculation skills come exclusively from a practical context. Thus, attending school helps children learn to think—precisely what it is intended to do.

Children's experiences in school are similar the world over. The similarities help explain why cognitive-developmental research involving 6- to 12-year-olds yields pretty much the same results in all cultures where children attend school. (*Photos:* A. Ramey, Woodfin Camp and Associates; Tim Davis, Photo Researchers; S. Noorani, Woodfin Camp and Associates)

Measuring and Predicting Achievement

One type of test used in schools is an achievement test, a type of test with which nearly all of you have doubtless had personal experience. **Achievement tests** are designed to assess specific information learned in school, using items like those in Table 8.2. Scores are based on comparison of an individual child's performance to those of other children in the same grade across the country.

Critics of achievement tests point out that although educators and parents may think of achievement tests as indicators of what children learn in school, they are actually very similar to IQ tests. For example, suppose an achievement test contains the math problem "4×4." A bright child who hasn't yet learned multiplication may reason his way to the correct answer of 16. Another child may answer correctly because she has learned it in school. Still another may know the answer because he learned to multiply from his parents. Thus, critics suggest that comprehensive portfolios of children's school work may be better indicators of actual school learning than standardized achievement tests (Neill, 1998).

achievement test a test designed to assess specific information learned in school

TABLE 8.2   Some Sample Items from a Fourth-Grade Achievement Test

Vocabulary	Reference Skills	Mathematics Computation		
jolly old man	Which of these words	79	149	62
1. angry	would be first in ABC	$+14$	-87	$\times 3$
2. fat	order?			
3. merry	1. pair	*Mathematics*		
4. sorry	2. point	What does the 3 in 13		
	3. paint	stand for?		
Language Expression	4. polish	1. 3 ones		
Who wants ____ books?		2. 13 ones		
1. that	*Spelling*	3. 3 tens		
2. these	Jason took the *cleanest*	4. 13 tens		
3. them	glass.			
4. this	right ____ wrong ____			

(*Source:* From *Comprehensive Tests of Basic Skills,* Form S. Reprinted by permission of the publisher, CTB/McGraw-Hill, Del Monte Research Park, Monterey, CA 93940. Copyright © 1973 by McGraw-Hill, Inc. All rights reserved. Printed in the USA.)

Most U.S. schools also require students to take IQ tests at various points in their educational careers. These tests are usually paper-and-pencil multiple-choice tests that can be given to large numbers of children at the same time. Some critics of routine IQ testing say that such tests aren't as accurate as the individual tests you read about in Chapter 6. Others object to the use of IQ tests because they often result in misclassifications of children in minority groups (see No Easy Answers). Nevertheless, IQ tests are often used to group children for instruction because they are strongly correlated with achievement test scores.

Some developmentalists say that the problem with relying on IQ tests to predict achievement is that they fail to provide a complete picture of mental abilities. For example, psychologist Howard Gardner proposed a theory of *multiple intelligences* (Gardner, 1983). This theory claims there are eight types of intelligence:

- *Linguistic*—the ability to use language effectively. People who are good writers or speakers, who learn languages easily, or who possess a lot of knowledge about language possess greater than average linguistic intelligence.

- *Logical/mathematical*—facility with numbers and logical problem-solving. Logical/mathematical intelligence enables individuals to learn math and to generate logical solutions to various kinds of problems.

- *Musical*—the ability to appreciate and produce music. Musicians, singers, composers, and conductors possess musical intelligence.

- *Spatial*—the ability to appreciate spatial relationships. Spatial intelligence is involved in the production and appreciation of works of art such as paintings and sculptures.

- *Bodily kinesthetic*—the ability to move in a coordinated way, combined with a sense of one's body in space. Professional athletes and top-notch amateur ones must possess high levels of this kind of intelligence.

- *Naturalist*—the ability to make fine discriminations among the flora and fauna of the natural world or the patterns and designs of human artifacts.

- *Interpersonal*—sensitivity to the behavior, moods, and needs of others. "Helping" professionals—counselors, social workers, ministers, and the like—usually need to have relatively high levels of interpersonal intelligence.

No Easy Answers

IQ Testing in the Schools

Although IQ tests are frequently used in U.S. schools, they are very controversial. Everyone agrees that these tests have legitimate uses. For example, if a child is having difficulty learning to read, an IQ test can help determine the source of the problem. The arguments about IQ tests center on whether they ought to be used routinely to group elementary school children for instruction. Several strong reasons are usually given against such use.

First, as you may remember from earlier discussions, IQ tests do not measure all the facets of a child's functioning that may be relevant. For example, clinicians have found that some children with IQs below 70, who would be considered retarded if the score alone were used for classification, nonetheless have sufficient social skills to enable them to function well in a regular classroom. If only the IQ score were used, some retarded children would be incorrectly placed in special classes. Second, there is the problem of the self-fulfilling prophecy that an IQ test score may establish. Because many parents and teachers still believe that IQ scores are a permanent feature of a child, once a child

is labeled as "having" a particular IQ, that label tends to be difficult to remove. Psychologist Robert Rosenthal, in a series of famous studies, has shown that a teacher's belief about a given student's ability and potential has a small but significant effect on her behavior toward that student and on the student's eventual achievement (Rosenthal, 1994).

Another negative argument is that tests are biased so that some groups of children are more likely to score high or low, even though their underlying ability is the same. For example, the tests may contain items that are not equally familiar to minorities and whites; taking such tests and doing well may also require certain test-taking skills, motivations, or attitudes less common among some minority children, especially African American children (Kaplan, 1985; Reynolds & Brown, 1984).

There is no quick or easy solution to this dilemma. It is certainly true that schools in the United States reflect the dominant middle-class white culture, with all of its values and assumptions. But it is also true that succeeding in these schools is essential if a child is to acquire the basic skills needed to cope

with the complexities of life in an industrialized country. For a host of reasons, including poorer prenatal care, greater poverty rates, and different familial patterns, more African American children appear to need special classes in order to acquire the skills they lack.

Yet it is also true that placing a child in a special class may create a self-fulfilling prophecy. Expectations are typically lower in such classes, so the children—who were already learning slowly—are challenged even less and so proceed even more slowly. However, to offer no special help to children who come to school lacking the skills needed to succeed seems equally unacceptable to many observers. Likewise, some bright children may benefit from acceleration. Thus, many developmentalists have concluded that IQ tests are more reliable and valid for grouping children than other alternatives such as teacher rating scales (Alvidrez & Weinstein, 1999). However, most developmentalists caution against using a single IQ test as the sole basis for a placement decision, especially in the early elementary grades, when IQ test scores are not as reliable as they are later in childhood and in adolescence.

- *Intrapersonal*—the ability to understand oneself. People who are good at identifying their own strengths and choosing goals accordingly have high levels of intrapersonal intelligence.

Gardner's theory is based on observations of people with brain damage, mental retardation, and other severe mental handicaps. He points out that brain damage usually causes disruption of functioning in very specific mental abilities rather than a general decline in intelligence. He also notes that many individuals with mental deficits have remarkable talents. For example, some are gifted in music, while others can perform complex mathematical computations without using a calculator or pencil and paper. However, critics claim that Gardner's view, although intuitively appealing, has little empirical support (Aiken, 1997).

Robert Sternberg's *triarchic theory of intelligence* proposes three components of human intelligence (Sternberg, 1988). *Contextual intelligence* has to do with knowing the right behavior for a specific situation. For example, the South American street children you read about earlier (who are good at doing practical calculations but perform poorly on more abstract math problems) are highly "intelligent" in their daily context. However, in the school context, they appear to lack intellectual ability.

Experiential intelligence, according to Sternberg, is measured by IQ tests. It involves learning to give specific responses without thinking about them. For example, you can probably respond without thinking to the question "How much is 7 times 7?" IQ tests contain many such questions.

Componential intelligence is a person's ability to come up with effective strategies. To Sternberg, this is the most important component of intelligence. He claims that intelligence tests put more emphasis on "correctness" of answers than on the quality of the strategies people use to arrive at them.

In general, Sternberg says, IQ tests measure how familiar a child is with "school" culture. Thus, children whose cultural background does not include formal schooling perform poorly because they are unfamiliar with the context of the test. Unfortunately, their poor performance is often mistakenly interpreted to mean that they lack intelligence. Sternberg believes that intelligence tests should measure all three components of intelligence, and he has produced some research evidence suggesting that testing procedures based on his theory yield better performance predictions than conventional IQ tests (Sternberg, Wagner, Williams, & Horvath, 1995).

Both Gardner's and Sternberg's theories have become important in helping educators understand the weaknesses of IQ tests. Moreover, psychologist Daniel Goleman's theory of *emotional intelligence* has also added to scientists' understanding of intelligence and achievement (Goleman, 1995). Emotional intelligence has three components: awareness of one's own emotions, the ability to express one's emotions appropriately, and the capacity to channel emotions into the pursuit of worthwhile goals. Without emotional intelligence, Goleman claims, it is impossible to achieve one's intellectual potential. Indeed, research on the relationship between self-control (the third component of emotional intelligence) in early childhood and achievement in adolescence suggests that Goleman's view is correct. Children's ability to exercise control over their emotions in early childhood is strongly related to measures of academic achievement in high school (Shoda, Mischel, & Peake, 1990).

School Quality, Parent Involvement, and Homeschooling

Several factors shape achievement, but the quality of the school a child attends, along with the degree to which his or her parents are involved in the school, are among the most important. Some parents believe they can provide their children with a better education by teaching them at home.

● *Effective Schools* ●   Researchers interested in possible effects of good and poor schools have most often approached the problem by identifying unusually *effective* schools (Good & Weinstein, 1986; Reynolds, 1992; Rutter, 1983). In this research, an effective school is defined as one in which pupils show one or more of the following characteristics at higher rates than would be predicted, given the kind of families or neighborhoods the pupils come from:

● High scores on standardized tests
● Good school attendance
● Low rates of disruptive classroom behavior and delinquency
● A high rate of later college attendance
● High self-esteem

One of the characteristics of academically successful children is that their parents supervise their homework, as this father is doing. (*Photo:* Stone)

Some schools seem to achieve these good outcomes year after year, so the effect is not just chance variation. When these successful schools are compared with others in similar neighborhoods that have less impressive track records, certain common themes emerge. Interestingly, the characteristics of effective schools are similar to those of the authoritative parenting style. For example, effective schools have clear goals and rules, good control, good communication, and high nurturance. The same seems to be true of effective teachers: It is the "authoritative" teachers whose students do best academically. Such teachers have high expectations for their students and make sure that virtually all the students in their classes complete the year's normal work (MacIver, Reuman, & Main, 1995).

But as with any system, the quality of the whole school is more than the sum of the qualities of the teachers or classrooms. Each school also has an overall climate, or *ethos*, that affects its students. The most positive school climate is created when the principal provides clear and strong leadership, is dedicated to effective teaching, and gives concrete assistance to such teaching and when goals are widely shared.

● *Parent Involvement* ● In high-quality schools, a large proportion of parents typically participate in school activities. When parents come to parent-teacher conferences, attend school events, and get involved in supervising children's homework, children are more strongly motivated, feel more competent, and adapt better to school. They learn to read more readily, get better grades through elementary school, and stay in school for more years (Brody, Stoneman, & Flor, 1995; Grolnick & Slowiaczek, 1994; Reynolds & Bezruczko, 1993). The effects of parent involvement are similar for both poor and middle-class children, which indicates that the effect is not just a social class difference in disguise (Luster & McAdoo, 1996; Pianta, Steinberg, & Rollins, 1995; Reynolds & Bezruczko, 1993).

● *Homeschooling* ● Concerns about school philosophy, safety, and quality have led a growing number of parents in the United States to educate their children at home. In 1965, there were only about 2,500 homeschooled children in the United States, but by the end of the 20th century, there were nearly 2 million (Ray, 1999). Homeschooling movements are beginning to appear in other nations as well.

Most parents homeschool because they believe the dominant culture and its educational institutions are hostile to their religious beliefs. For example, many homeschooling parents don't want their children to learn about evolution or other ideas they feel will undermine the religious values they want their children to learn. Some want to protect their children from negative peer influences or school-based crime.

A few parents who have children with disabilities prefer teaching them at home to having them receive special-education services from local schools. The one-on-one teaching these children get at home often helps them achieve more than their disabled peers in public schools (Ensign, 1998). In addition, children with disabilities who are homeschooled don't have to deal with teasing from peers.

Research on homeschooling is sparse. Homeschooling advocates point to a small number of studies showing that homeschooled children are socially competent and emotionally well-adjusted and score above average on standardized achievement tests (Ray, 1999). However, opponents of homeschooling, a group that includes most professional educators, claim that comparisons of homeschooling and public education are misleading. They point out that researchers have studied only homeschooled children whose families volunteer to participate in research studies. In contrast, most public school achievement test data are based on representative samples or on populations of entire schools.

Before going on

- List the components of good literacy instruction.

- How do schooled and unschooled children differ in cognitive development?

- Describe the purpose and content of standardized achievement tests.

- What are the characteristics of effective schools, how does parent involvement affect children's academic achievement, and what are the issues surrounding homeschooling?

Individual and Group Differences

There are a number of individual and group variables that are associated with school performance. Various disabilities and attention problems are correlated with achievement in some way, as are language proficiency, sex, race, and culture.

Learning Disabilities

Some children are born with or develop differences that may significantly interfere with their education unless they receive some kind of special instruction (see Table 8.3, page 236). In the United States, 12–13% of all school children receive such services (National Center for Education Statistics [NCES], 2000; U.S. Department of Education, 1996). The categories listed in Table 8.3 are defined by law, and public schools are legally obligated to provide special education services for all children who qualify.

The largest group served by U.S. special educators have some kind of **learning disability,** or difficulty in mastering a specific academic skill—most often reading—despite possessing normal intelligence and no physical or sensory handicaps. When reading is the problem skill, the term **dyslexia** is often used (even though, technically speaking, *dyslexia* refers to a total absence of reading). Most children with reading disabilities can read, but not as well as others their age. Moreover, it appears that their skill deficits are specific to reading—such as an inability to automatize sound-letter correspondences—rather than the result of a general cognitive dysfunction (Wimmer, Mayringer, & Landerl, 1998).

How common such learning disabilities may be is still a matter of considerable dispute. Some experts in the field argue that up to 80% of all children classified by school systems as learning disabled are misclassified. They claim that only about 5 out of every 1,000 children have genuine neurologically based learning disabilities (Farnham-Diggory, 1992). The remainder who are so classified are more appropriately called *slow learners,* or are suffering from some other problem, perhaps temporary emotional distress or poor teaching.

Practically speaking, however, the term *learning disability* is used very broadly within school systems (at least within the United States) to label a grab-bag of children

learning disability a disorder in which a child has difficulty mastering a specific academic skill, even though she possesses normal intelligence and no physical or sensory handicaps

dyslexia problems in reading or the inability to read

TABLE 8.3   Disabilities for Which U.S. Children Receive Special Education Services

Disability Category	Percentage of Special Education Students in the Category	Description of Disability
Learning Disability	51%	Achievement 2 or more years behind expectations based on intelligence tests
		Example: A fourth-grader with an average IQ who is reading at a first-grade level
Communication Disorder in Speech or Language	21%	A disorder of speech or language that affects a child's education; can be a problem with speech or an impairment in the comprehension or use of any aspect of language
		Example: A first-grader who makes errors in pronunciation like those of a 4-year-old and can't connect sounds and symbols
Mental Retardation	12%	IQ significantly below average intelligence, together with impairments in adaptive functions
		Example: A school-aged child with an IQ lower than 70 who is not fully toilet-trained and who needs special instruction in both academic and self-care skills
Serious Emotional Disturbance	8%	An emotional or behavior disorder that interferes with a child's education
		Example: A child whose severe temper tantrums cause him to be removed from the classroom every day
Other Health Impairments	2.2%	A health problem that interferes with a child's education
		Example: A child with severe asthma who misses several weeks of school each year
Multiple Disabilities	2%	Need for special instruction and ongoing support in two or more areas to benefit from education
		Example: A child with cerebral palsy who is also deaf, who thus requires both physical and instructional adaptations
Hearing Impairment	1.3%	A hearing problem that interferes with a child's education
		Example: A child who needs a sign-language interpreter in the classroom
Orthopedic Impairment	1.2%	An orthopedic handicap that requires special adaptations
		Example: A child in a wheelchair who needs a special physical education class
Visual Impairment	0.5%	Impaired visual acuity or a limited field of vision that interferes with education
		Example: A blind child who needs training in the use of Braille to read and write

(*Sources:* Kirk, Gallagher, & Anastasiow, 1993; U.S. Department of Education, 1996.)

who have unexpected or otherwise unexplainable difficulty with school work. Nearly 6% of all children in the United States are currently labeled in this way (NCES, 1998).

Explanations of the problem are just as subject to disagreement as its definitions. One difficulty is that children labeled as learning disabled rarely show any signs of major brain damage on any standard neurological tests. So, if a learning disability results from a neurological problem, the neurological problem must be a subtle one. Some researchers have suggested that a large number of small abnormalities may develop in the brain during prenatal life, such as some irregularity of neuron arrangement, or clumps of immature brain cells, or scars, or congenital tumors. The growing brain compensates for these problems by "rewiring" around the problem areas. These rewirings, in turn, may scramble normal information-processing pathways just enough to make reading or calculation or some other specific task very difficult (Farnham-Diggory, 1992). Other experts argue that there may not be any underlying neurological problem at all. Instead, children with learning disabilities (especially reading disabilities) may simply have a more general problem with understanding the sound and structure of language (Torgesen et al., 1999). There is also some evidence that learning disabilities, especially dyslexia, may have a genetic basis (Gallagher, Frith, & Snowling, 2000).

These disagreements about both definition and explanation are (understandably) reflected in confusion at the practical level. Children are labeled as learning disabled and assigned to special classes, but a program that works well for one child may not work at all for another. One type of intervention that shows promise is an approach called *reciprocal teaching*. In reciprocal teaching programs, children with learning disabilities work in pairs or groups. Each child takes a turn summarizing and explaining material to be learned to the others in the group. A number of studies have found that, after participating in reciprocal teaching, children with learning disabilities improved in summarization skills and memory strategies (e.g., Lederer, 2000).

Motivating such children to try harder is also likely to be important in helping them overcome their difficulties. Compared to children with other types of disabilities, those with learning disabilities are more likely to believe that increased effort will not necessarily lead to success (Kunnen & Steenbeek, 1999). Still, many children with learning disabilities overcome their difficulties by adulthood, as demonstrated by the growing number of them who are enrolled in college (Horn & Bertold, 1999; Rojewski, 1999).

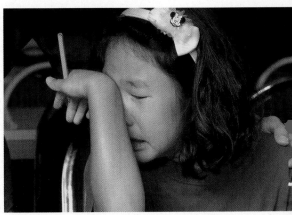

School can be a discouraging and frustrating place for a child with a learning disability. (*Photo: Michael Newman, PhotoEdit*)

Attention-Deficit Hyperactivity Disorder

Some children experience learning difficulties that don't seem to fit the typical special education categories. For example, 3–5% of U.S. school children have a mental disorder called **attention-deficit hyperactivity disorder (ADHD)**. Children with ADHD are more physically active and/or less attentive than their peers. These characteristics often lead to both academic and behavioral problems in school.

Application of the special education classification to an ADHD child depends on how the disorder has affected his education and how it is being treated. For example, a child whose ADHD has caused him to fall more than 2 years behind other children in his grade will be classified as learning disabled. The point is that ADHD is not itself a legally recognized special-education category in the United States. Rather, it is a mental disorder that may cause a child to develop school problems that are so severe that he qualifies for services under one of the legally defined categories.

The cause of ADHD is unknown. However, some developmentalists suggest that children with ADHD are neurologically different from their peers. Specifically, some have asserted that children with ADHD have functional deficits in the right hemisphere of the brain (Sandson, Bachna, & Morin, 2000). Indeed, some type of biological factor does seem to be involved, as children who were born at 24–31 weeks of gestation are four to six times as likely to suffer from the symptoms of ADHD than their peers who were full-term infants (Barlow & Lewandowski, 2000). Other developmentalists hypothesize that children with ADHD require more sensory stimulation than their peers; thus, they move around more in order to get the stimulation they need (Antrop, Roeyers, Van Oost, & Buysse, 2000).

attention-deficit hyperactivity disorder (ADHD) a mental disorder that causes children to have difficulty attending to and completing tasks

Cultural factors may also be important in ADHD, as the disorder is extremely rare outside of the United States. Critics of using medication to control ADHD symptoms suggest that this cross-national difference is the result of overuse of the diagnosis in the United States. However, some developmentalists assert that educators and mental health professionals in other nations have failed to recognize the degree to which ADHD may be prevalent in their children (Overmeyer & Taylor, 1999). Others suggest that there is a real cross-cultural difference in the incidence of ADHD. For example, a study comparing African American and South African 6-year-olds who were similar in family structure and socio-economic status found that a larger proportion of African American children, especially boys, scored higher on scales measuring hyperactivity (Barbarin, 1999).

Psychologists are fairly sure that diet, environmental toxins, or brain damage is not the cause of ADHD, despite what some promoters of "cures" claim (Spreen, Risser, & Edgell, 1995). At present, most experts believe that each individual case of ADHD is caused by a complex interaction of factors that are unique to the specific child. These factors may include genetics, temperament, parenting styles, peer relations, the type and quality of school a child attends, and stressors in the child's life such as poverty, family instability, and parental mental illness.

On many kinds of attention tasks, ADHD children do not differ at all from normal children. They seem to vary from their normal peers in activity level, the ability to sustain attention (especially with boring and repetitive tasks), and the ability to control impulses. However, the degree of hyperactivity ADHD children exhibit is unrelated to their performance on attention tasks. That is, a child can be very physically active and still be good at controlling his attention. Likewise, a child can be very calm yet have little ability to sustain attention. For this reason, there are now two types of ADHD: (1) the hyperactive/impulsive type, in which a high activity level is the main problem; and (2) the inattentive type, in which an inability to sustain attention is the major difficulty (APA, 1994).

Most children with ADHD are successful in learning academic skills (Chadwick et al., 1999). However, their hyperactivity and/or inattentiveness often cause other kinds of problems. For one thing, children with both types of ADHD usually produce school work that is messy and filled with errors, causing them to get poor grades (Cahn et al., 1996). They may be disruptive in class and are often rejected by other children.

By the time their children are diagnosed with ADHD, usually upon entering school, many parents have lost confidence in their ability to control them (Barkley, 1990). Some cope with their difficult child by being extremely permissive. Others use commands and threats—"Go clean your room right now or I'll whip you with a belt." Thus, parent training can be useful in helping parents cope with children who have ADHD.

The goal of such parenting programs is to help parents regain a sense of control (Barkley, 1990). For example, experts recommend that teachers provide parents with daily reports of their children's work in the various school subjects—language, math, social studies, and so on. Parents can then use the information to enforce a standing rule that the child must have completed all school work before watching television or doing other desired activities. Such approaches, when applied consistently, can help parents of children with ADHD manage their children's difficulties, as well as their own emotional reactions, more effectively.

Many children with ADHD take stimulant medications, such as methylphenidate (Ritalin). About 70% of those who do are calmer and can concentrate better. However, some studies show that many children's "response to the medication" may actually be due to changes in expectations on the part of their teachers and parents—sort of a self-fulfilling prophecy (Spreen, Risser, & Edgell, 1995). In addition, studies suggest that the concentration skills of children with ADHD can be improved with training. For example, one study found that the attention skills of a group of children with ADHD were similar to those of a control group of children without attention difficulties following an intensive 18-week training program (Semrud-Clikeman et al., 1999).

It's also important to note that medication doesn't always improve the grades of children with ADHD. For the most part, it seems that stimulant medications reduce such children's activity levels, help them control their impulses, and somewhat improve their social behavior. These effects usually result in improvements in classroom behavior and peer acceptance. Medications such as methylphenidate have the greatest effect on school grades among children whose ADHD symptoms are so severe that they interfere with actual learning (Spreen, Risser, & Edgell, 1995). For this reason, the use of stimulant medications for children who have mild or moderate ADHD symptoms is controversial.

Second-Language Learners

Worldwide patterns of population growth and movement have led to tremendous increases in the number of children who attend school in the United States, Canada, Great Britain, and Australia whose first language is not English. About two-thirds of these children speak English well enough to function in school, but the rest essentially do not speak English. Educators in English-speaking countries use the term *limited English proficient (LEP)* to refer to non–English-speaking children—either immigrant children or native-born children.

Although schools in other countries serve such populations as well, this phenomenon seems to be far more pervasive in the United States and other English-speaking nations. For example, near the end of the 20th century, 46% of all U.S. classrooms had at least one LEP student (NCES, 1997). In California, Florida, Illinois, New Jersey, New York, and Texas, more than 75% of schools offer special programs for LEP students. Most such students live in large cities. For example, more than 100 languages are spoken by school children in New York City, Chicago, Los Angeles, and the suburbs of Washington, DC. Educators in these cities face a particularly difficult task in dealing not only with the large number of LEP children, but also with the staggering number of languages they and their parents speak.

Some LEP children, mostly those whose first language is Spanish, participate in **bilingual education,** in which instruction is given in two languages (NCES, 1997). Such programs have been developed for Spanish-speaking children because they constitute by far the largest group of LEP students in U.S. schools. Other English-speaking countries offer bilingual education to children from large non–English-speaking groups as well. For example, schools in Canada have provided both English- and French-speaking students in Quebec, a province whose residents primarily speak French, with bilingual education for decades.

However, bilingual education is logistically impossible for most school districts that include LEP children. For one thing, if a school system has only a handful of students who speak a particular language, it is not financially feasible to establish a separate curriculum for them. In addition, it may be impossible to find bilingual teachers for children whose language is spoken by very few people outside of their country of origin. For these reasons, about 76% of LEP 6- to 12-year-olds in the United States are enrolled in **English-as-a-second-language (ESL) programs** (NCES, 1997). In ESL programs, children spend part of the day in classes to learn English and part in academic classes that are conducted entirely in English.

Research has shown that no particular approach to second-language learners is more successful than any other (Mohanty & Perregaux, 1997). There is some indication that programs that include a home-based component, such as those that encourage parents to learn the new language along with their children, may be especially effective (Koskinen et al., 2000). But it seems that any structured program, whether bilingual education or ESL, fosters higher achievement among non–English-speaking children than simply integrating them into English-only classes, an approach called *submersion.* Although most children in submersion programs eventually catch up to their English-speaking peers, many educators believe that instruction that supports

MAKE THE CONNECTION

*N*ow that you know more about learning disabilities, look back at Chapter 3 and review the prenatal factors, such as maternal smoking, that increase the likelihood that a child will suffer from such problems.

bilingual education an approach to second-language education in which children receive instruction in two different languages

English-as-a-second-language (ESL) program an approach to second-language education in which children attend English classes for part of the day and receive most of their academic instruction in English

children's home language and culture as well as their English-language skills enhances their overall development (Cushner, McClelland, & Safford, 1992).

With respect to achievement, LEP students' performance in school is very similar to that of English-speaking children (NCES, 1997). In fact, in U.S. schools, native-born English-speaking children are more likely to fail one or more grades than children whose home language is either Asian or European. Spanish-speaking children fail in U.S. schools at about the same rate as English speakers. Thus, there is no evidence that a child who enters school with limited English skills has any greater risk of failure than native-born students.

A cautionary note is necessary, however: An LEP student does not have an increased risk of failure as long as the school provides some kind of transition to English-only instruction and school officials take care to administer all standardized tests in the language with which the child is most familiar (Cushner, McClelland, & Safford, 1992). Providing a transition to English-only instruction is necessary to optimize the LEP child's potential for achievement. Testing children in their native languages ensures that non–English-speaking children will not be misclassified as mentally retarded or learning disabled because of their limited English skills. Beyond these requirements, LEP students represent no particular burden to U.S. schools. Moreover, in all likelihood, their presence enriches the educational experience of children whose first language is English.

Sex Differences in Achievement

Comparisons of total IQ test scores for boys and girls do not reveal consistent differences. It is only when the total scores are broken down into several separate skills that some patterns of sex differences emerge. On average, studies in the United States show that girls do slightly better on verbal tasks and at arithmetic computation and that boys do slightly better at numerical reasoning. For example, more boys than girls test as gifted in mathematics (Benbow, 1988; Lubinski & Benbow, 1992).

Where might such differences come from? The explanatory options should be familiar by now. As you learned earlier in this chapter, brain processes that underlie spatial perception and cognition are often argued to be the cause of sex differences in math achievement. To date, however, neurological research has failed to find sex differences in brain function large enough to explain sex differences in math achievement (Spreen, Risser, & Edgell, 1995).

So far, environmental explanations have proven to be more useful than biological theories in discussions of the sex differences in mathematical or verbal reasoning. Especially in the case of mathematics, there is considerable evidence that girls' and boys' skills are systematically shaped by a series of environmental factors.

For one thing, both teachers and parents seem to believe that boys have more math ability than girls (Jussim & Eccles, 1992; Tiedemann, 2000). Thus, they are more likely to attribute a girl's success in mathematics to effort or good teaching; poor performance by a girl is attributed to lack of ability. In contrast, teachers and parents attribute a boy's success to ability and his failure to lack of application (Jussim & Eccles, 1992). Moreover, children appear to internalize these beliefs, which, in turn, influence their interest in taking math courses and their beliefs about their likelihood of achieving success in math (Eccles, Jacobs, & Harold, 1990). The cumulative effect of these differences in expectations and treatment show up in high school, when sex differences on standardized math tests usually become evident. In part, then, the sex differences in math achievement test scores appear to be perpetuated by subtle family and school influences on children's attitudes.

Racial Differences in Achievement

In the United States, there are racial group differences in achievement test scores similar to the differences in IQ test scores you read about in Chapters 2 and 6. Most developmentalists believe that the same factors the contribute to IQ score differences—

TEACHING The Real World

Dialects at School

A *dialect* is a distinct pattern of phonology (speech sounds), syntax (word order), semantics (word meanings), and pragmatics (social rules for using language) that is specific to a regional, social, or subcultural group. For example, English is written and spoken differently in Great Britain than in the United States. However, the differences between British and American English are so small that we can easily read each other's literature. Moreover, once we adjust to accent differences, we can easily converse.

The term *Standard American English (SAE)* refers to written English and to dialects that are very similar to written English. For a long time, SAE was thought of as correct, while the *vernaculars*, or everyday dialects, of many groups were characterized as incorrect. Teachers viewed correction of the spoken and written language of children who belonged to these groups as an important instructional goal. Today, regional and ethnic dialects are no longer thought of as wrong. However, educators recognize that children whose home vernaculars are closest to SAE have an advantage in school, because SAE is the language of both the classroom and textbooks. As a result, many have looked for ways to encourage children to become fluent in SAE without making them feel that their home vernacular is inferior or wrong.

African American Vernacular English (AAVE), also known as *Black English* and *Ebonics,* is a dialect spoken by many African Americans. It has been at the center of recent debates over the role of dialects in education. Many schools use teaching strategies that build on children's knowledge of AAVE to help them become more skilled in the use of SAE. For example, some teachers put up posters in their classrooms that remind students of AAVE-SAE translations, such as "I had went = I had gone" (Delpit, 1990). In some schools, African American children study the history of the dialect and its relationship to the West African cultures from which many slaves were taken centuries ago. In others, children learn about other dialects, such as Australian English, along with AAVE and SAE (Wolfram, Schilling-Estes, & Hazen, 1996).

The use of AAVE in schools, even as a means of teaching SAE, is controversial, however. Some Americans still regard AAVE as an inferior form of English that has no place in formal education (Wolfram, 1990). In addition, some African Americans believe that reinforcing children's use of the dialect will make it more difficult for them to succeed in a culture dominated by SAE (Fillmore, 1997). They point out that not all African American children speak AAVE, and those who don't shouldn't be forced to learn it strictly on the basis of their race. Some critics have been persuaded to support teaching strategies that involve AAVE, however, after learning that children's reading and writing skills have improved in schools where such strategies have been tried (Council of the Great City Schools, 1997).

---

economic status, access to prenatal care, family stability, and so on—also produce racial differences in measures of school performance such as grades and achievement test scores. Aside from these factors, researchers have identified psychological and cultural variables that may help explain why some groups of children appear to do better in school than others (see The Real World).

For example, psychologists have learned that children who use an **analytical style** define learning goals and follow a set of orderly steps to reach them. These children are well organized, are good at learning details, and think of information in terms of "right" and "wrong." Other children use a **relational style.** These children focus attention on "the big picture" instead of on individual bits of information.

For example, Ayana, who has an analytical style, and Richard, who uses a relational style, both listen carefully to their fourth-grade teacher give instructions for a complicated project. Ayana lists every detail of the teacher's instructions and how many points each part is worth. In contrast, Richard writes down his general impression of each part of the project.

In working on the project, Ayana concentrates her effort on the parts that are worth the most points. Richard pays more attention to the aspects of the project he finds interesting. When it is finished, Ayana's project conforms more exactly to the teacher's instructions than Richard's does, and she receives a higher grade. Ayana's way of approaching school work—her cognitive style—better fits school expectations, giving her an advantage over Richard. In addition, Ayana's way of learning

analytical style a tendency to focus on the details of a task

relational style a tendency to ignore the details of a task in order to focus on the "big picture"

helps her get high scores on achievement tests, which require detailed knowledge of specific information and skills.

Racial groups in the United States differ in the percentages of children who use each style. A higher percentage of Asian American and European American students are analyticals. In contrast, a higher percentage of African American, Hispanic American, and Native American children are relationals. Thus, achievement test scores and school grade differences among these groups may be due to the different percentages of analyticals and relationals (Serpell & Hatano, 1997).

Achievement differences may also be due to philosophical beliefs that characterize some racial and ethnic groups in the United States. For example, American culture tends to be *individualistic*. In other words, it emphasizes the achievements of individuals and encourages competition rather than cooperation. However, some U.S. subcultures place more emphasis on interdependence, an outlook that sociologists and anthropologists usually refer to as *collectivist* (Serpell & Hatano, 1997). In Hawaii, educators tried changing their curriculum and teaching methods to better fit with the collectivist emphasis of Native Hawaiian children and families. The new approach involved more group work and cooperation among students, and it apparently helped children learn more (Cushner, McClellan, & Safford, 1992). The success of such interventions suggests that educational practices in the United States may be well adapted to some groups but not others, thereby producing differences in achievement between groups for whom the educational system is a good cultural "fit" and those for whom it is not.

Feelings of hopelessness on the part of some disadvantaged students may also be a factor. For example, some African American students in the United States, discouraged by racism and lack of opportunity, believe that they won't be able to succeed economically no matter how much they learn in school (Ogbu, 1990). Educators believe schools can affect these students' beliefs by making sure textbooks and other materials accurately reflect the contributions of African Americans to American culture (Cushner, McClelland, & Safford, 1992).

> *Critical Thinking*
>
> How would you characterize your own cognitive style? Do you think you are an analytical or a relational type?

Cross-Cultural Differences in Achievement

In recent years, differences in math and science achievement between Asian children and North American children have been the focus of study and debate. Over a 20-year period, studies have repeatedly shown that U.S. school children are significantly behind their peers in other industrialized nations (Caslyn, Gonzales, & Frase, 1999). Developmentalists speculate that the differences result from variations in both cultural beliefs and teaching methods.

With respect to cultural beliefs, developmentalists have found that North American parents and teachers emphasize innate ability, which they assume to be unchangeable, more than effort. For Asians, the emphasis is just the opposite: They believe that people can become more capable by working harder (Serpell & Hatano, 1997). Because of these differences in beliefs, this theory claims, Asian parents and teachers have higher expectations for children and are better at finding ways to motivate them to do school work.

However, teaching methods in the two cultures also vary. For example, in one important set of studies, educational psychologists James Stigler and Harold Stevenson observed teaching strategies in 120 classrooms in Japan, Taiwan, and the United States, and they are convinced that Asian teachers have devised particularly effective modes of teaching mathematics and science (Stevenson, 1994; Stigler & Stevenson, 1991).

Japanese and Chinese teachers approach mathematics and science by crafting a series of "master lessons," each organized around a single theme or idea, and each involving specific forms of student participation. These lessons are like good stories, with a beginning, a middle, and an end. In U.S. classrooms, by contrast, it is extremely uncommon for teachers to spend 30 or 60 minutes on a single coherent math or science lesson involving the whole class of children and a single topic. Instead, teachers shift often from one topic to another during a single math or science "lesson." They might do a brief bit on addition, then talk about measurement, then about telling time, and finally back to addition. Stigler and Stevenson also found striking differences in the amount of time teachers actually spend leading instruction for the whole class. In the U.S. classrooms they observed, this occurred only 49% of the time; group instruction occurred 74% of the time in Japan and 91% in Taiwan.

Asian and North American math instruction also differs in the emphasis on *computational fluency,* the degree to which an individual can automatically produce solutions to simple calculation problems. A number of mathematicians and professors of mathematics have claimed that math instruction in the United States has been influenced more by "fads" than by a sound understanding of the role of computational fluency in mathematical problem-solving (Murray, 1998). They point out that research has demonstrated that computational fluency is related both to calculation skills and to facility in solving word problems (Geary et al., 1999; Kail & Hall, 1999).

Another difference between U.S. and Asian schools, especially at the elementary level, involves the use of rewards. Because of the influence of Skinner's operant conditioning theory on education in the United States, teachers commonly use material rewards, such as stickers, to motivate children. Such rewards may be effective when they are unexpected and tied to high standards (Deci, Koestner, & Ryan, 1999; Eisenberger, Pierce, & Cameron, 1999). Giving a surprise sticker to the only child in a class who gets a grade of 100% on a spelling test is an example of this approach to using rewards. However, when teachers use such rewards to try to motivate children to do routine tasks, such as turning in homework, they clearly undermine both children's intrinsic motivation and interest in the tasks to which the rewards are linked (Deci, Koestner, & Ryan, 1999).

In response to these criticisms, many educators say that achievement differences between North American and Asian students have been exaggerated to make U.S. schools look worse than they actually are (Berliner & Biddle, 1997). Moreover, more than 70% of American parents give grades of A or B to the nation's public schools (ABC News, 2000). Educators and parents alike often claim that Asian schools teach students to value conformity, while American schools place more emphasis on creativity. Indeed, some Asian educators agree that their schools have sacrificed creativity in order to attain high achievement test scores (Hatano, 1990).

Before going on

- Describe the controversy surrounding the term "learning disability."

- How does attention-deficit hyperactivity disorder affect a child's development?

- What is the difference between a bilingual and an ESL program? Is one approach more effective than the other?

- How do developmentalists explain sex differences in math achievement?

- What are some possible reasons for racial differences in school performance?

- What kinds of cultural factors affect math and science achievement?

A Final Word

The beginning of formal schooling leads to remarkable changes in a child's cognitive development. Even for children with many years of day-care or preschool experience, kindergarten or first grade represents a major change in expectations and demands; children must begin to learn all the specific competencies and roles that are necessary to succeed in the culture. Important maturational changes enable children to benefit from educational experiences, but the experiences in turn seem to speed up the intellectual maturation process in 6- to 12-year-olds. Moreover, the cognitive-developmental events of middle childhood lay the foundation for more advanced thinking in adolescence and adulthood. Thus, with respect to cognitive development, formal schooling during the middle childhood years may be the single most important event of the entire human lifespan.

Summary

Physical Changes

- Physical development from 6 to 12 is steady and slow. Sex differences in bone and skeletal maturation may lead boys and girls to pursue different activities.

- Major brain growth spurts occur in 6- to 8-year-olds and in 10- to 12-year-olds. Neurological development leads to improvements in selective attention, information-processing speed, and spatial perception.

- School-aged children require regular medical check-ups. Accidental injuries and obesity are the most prevalent health problems of this age group.

Cognitive Changes

- Language development continues in middle childhood with vocabulary growth, improvements in grammar, and understanding of the social uses of language.

- Piaget proposed that a major change in the child's thinking occurs at about age 6, when the child begins to understand powerful operations such as reversibility, addition, and serial ordering. The child also learns to use inductive logic, but does not yet use deductive logic.

- Research on this period confirms many of Piaget's descriptions of sequences of development but calls into question Piaget's basic concept of stages. The "operations" he observed may actually be rules for solving specific types of problems.

- Most information-processing theorists conclude that there are no age-related changes in children's information-processing capacity, but there are clearly improvements in speed and efficiency.

Schooling

- To become literate, children need specific instruction in sound-symbol correspondences, word parts, and other aspects of written language. They also need to be exposed to good literature and to have lots of opportunities to practice their reading and writing skills.

- School has a significant effect in fostering the 6- to 12-year-old's shift to a more abstract or strategic form of thinking. Children who lack school experience show less skill of this type.

- Children's school progress is assessed with both IQ tests and achievement tests. Both types of tests may ignore important aspects of intellectual functioning.

- Successful or effective schools have many of the same qualities seen in authoritative families: clear rules, good control, good communication, and nurturance. Parent involvement is also important. Some parents choose to educate their children at home, but opponents say that there is insufficient research on the cognitive and social effects of homeschooling.

Individual and Group Differences

- Roughly 12–13% of U.S. school children receive special education services; most of these are classified as learning disabled.

- Many children with attention-deficit hyperactivity disorder have problems in school but do not fit well into traditional special education categories.
- Children with limited English perform as well as English-speaking peers when they receive specific kinds of support in school.
- There are no sex differences in overall IQ scores, but boys typically do better on tests of advanced mathematical ability. Girls do somewhat better on verbal tasks.

There is as yet no clear agreement on how to explain such differences.
- Although poverty and other social factors may play a role, racial differences in achievement may also result from differences in learning styles, philosophy, or in attitudes toward school.
- Differences in both cultural beliefs and teaching practices are probably responsible for cross-cultural variations in math and science achievement.

Key Terms

achievement test (p. 230)

analytical style (p. 241)

association areas (p. 219)

attention-deficit hyperactivity disorder (p. 237)

automaticity (p. 226)

bilingual education (p. 239)

class inclusion (p. 223)

concrete operations (p. 222)

deductive logic (p. 223)

dyslexia (p. 235)

English-as-a-second-language (ESL) program (p. 239)

executive processes (p. 227)

inductive logic (p. 223)

learning disability (p. 235)

memory strategies (p. 227)

obesity (p. 220)

processing efficiency (p. 226)

relational style (p. 241)

relative right-left orientation (p. 219)

selective attention (p. 218)

spatial cognition (p. 219)

spatial perception (p. 219)

CHAPTER
9

Social and Personality Development in Middle Childhood

John Collett, Stock Boston

★One mother who also happened to be a student in a developmental psychology graduate program had gotten into the habit of trying out research tasks on her 7-year-old daughter, Allison, before using them in actual research. One morning, she asked the girl what she wanted to wear to school. Allison answered, "Do you really want to know, or is this just another one of your studies?" Like most 6- to 12-year-olds, Allison wanted her mother to think of her as an individual, not just another 7-year-old. Children of this age are beginning to realize that they are unique, and they want their uniqueness to be recognized by parents and others.

At the same time, children of this age want to fit into the social world in a meaningful way. Every culture in the world has a *society of childhood,* in which children make up their own social rules that differ from those of adult society. For example, in most U.S. school lunchrooms, food trading is common. A child who refuses to trade may be seen as "stuck-up." But adults who try to talk co-workers into trading lunches are likely to be thought of as pushy or somewhat odd. Such comparisons show that children practice social competence by making up their own social rules rather than simply copying those that exist in the adult world. Creating and enforcing such rules helps children learn to look at things from other people's points of view and to cooperate.

In this chapter, you will read more about the psychoanalytic and social-cognitive approaches to social and personality development. You will also learn about the three dimensions of moral development—emotions, reasoning, and behavior—that are the focus of theory and research. As in earlier chapters covering social and personality development, we will explore social relations, personality, and self-concept. We will also discuss how variables such as after-school care, poverty, and television influence the 6- to 12-year-old's development. As you read, keep the following questions in mind:

● What major points do psychoanalytic and social-cognitive theorists make about social and personality development in middle childhood? How do the major theories explain the three dimensions of moral development?

● How do 6- to 12-year-olds relate to parents, siblings, and peers?

● How do personality and self-concept change in middle childhood?

● What are the characteristics of school-aged children who care for themselves after school or who live in poverty? How does television influence development?

Theories of Social and Personality Development

As you should remember from previous chapters, psychoanalytic theorists explain social and emotional development in terms of a struggle between internal drives and cultural demands. You should also recall that social-cognitive theorists have a very different view: The child's growing understanding of the world provides the impetus for social and emotional development.

Psychoanalytic Perspectives

Freud believed that children between age 6 and age 12 repress sexual desires in order to concentrate on developing friendships with members of the same sex and learning academic and social skills. Freud called this period of development the **latency stage** (see Table 2.2). From Freud's perspective, the important thing about school-aged children's social behavior is their preference for same-sex friends. To Freud, establishing relationships with same-sex peers allows 6- to 12-year-old boys and girls to affirm and expand the sex-role identities they began to develop in the phallic stage through identification with the same-sex parent. Freud claimed that, by avoiding children of the other sex, school-aged children eliminate the stress of sexual attraction. This helps them concentrate on sex-role identity development.

According to Erikson, children between 6 and 12 face a psychosocial crisis that he called the **industry versus inferiority stage,** during which they develop a sense of their own competence through the achievement of culturally defined learning goals (see Table 2.3). The psychosocial task of the 6- to 12-year-old is development of industry, or the willingness to work to accomplish goals. To develop industry, the child must be able to achieve the goals her culture sets for all children her age. In most countries, 6- to 12-year-olds must learn to read and write. If they fail to do so, Erikson's view claims they will enter adolescence and adulthood with feelings of inferiority.

Research suggests that Erikson was right about the link between school experiences and an emerging sense of competence. It seems that most 6- to 12-year-olds gradually develop a view of their own competence as they succeed or fail at academic tasks such as reading and arithmetic (Chapman & Tunmer, 1997; Skaalvik & Valas, 1999). Thus, their self-assessments and actual achievements are strongly correlated; that is, those who are most successful judge themselves to be highly competent, while those who have difficulty perceive themselves as less competent.

MAKE THE CONNECTION

Chapter 7 pointed out that information-processing theorists claim that preschoolers develop networks of knowledge, called gender schemas, about their own and the opposite sex. Information-processing theorists think that 6- to 12-year-olds expand on and fill in the gaps in these gender schemas. How is Freud's idea about the importance of the latency stage and its connection to the phallic stage similar to gender-schema theory?

Critical Thinking

Think back to your own elementary school experiences. Do you think you gained a sense of industry or inferiority from them? How did they affect your subsequent development?

Social-Cognitive Perspectives

As you read in Chapter 8, the school-aged child can understand conservation in part because he can ignore the appearance of change and focus on the underlying continuity. Similarly, a number of early ground-breaking social-cognitive studies demonstrated that the child of this age looks beyond appearances and searches for deeper consistencies that will help him to interpret both his own and other people's behavior.

Like their understanding of the physical world, 6- to 12-year-olds' descriptions of other people move from the concrete to the abstract. If you ask a 6- or 7-year-old to describe others, he will focus almost exclusively on external features—what the person looks like, where he lives, what he does. This description by a 7-year-old boy, taken from a classic study of social-cognitive development, is typical:

> He is very tall. He has dark brown hair, he goes to our school. I don't think he has any brothers or sisters. He is in our class. Today he has a dark orange [sweater] and gray trousers and brown shoes. (Livesley & Bromley, 1973, p. 213)

latency stage the fourth of Freud's psychosexual stages, during which 6- to 12-year-olds' libido is dormant while they establish relationships with same-sex peers

industry versus inferiority stage the fourth of Erikson's psychosocial stages, during which children develop a sense of their own competence through mastery of culturally defined learning tasks

When young children do use internal or evaluative terms to describe people, they are likely to use quite global ones, such as "nice" or "mean," "good" or "bad." Further, young children do not seem to see these qualities as lasting or general traits of the individual, applicable in all situations or over time (Rholes & Ruble, 1984). In other words, the 6- or 7-year-old has not yet developed a concept that might be called "conservation of personality."

Beginning at about age 7 or 8, a rather dramatic shift occurs in children's descriptions of others. The child begins to focus more on the inner traits or qualities of another person and to assume that those traits will be visible in many situations (Gnepp & Chilamkurti, 1988). Children this age still describe others' physical features, but their descriptions are now used as examples of more general points about internal qualities. You can see the change when you compare the 7-year-old's description given above with this description by a child nearly 10 years old:

> He smells very much and is very nasty. He has no sense of humour and is very dull. He is always fighting and he is cruel. He does silly things and is very stupid. He has brown hair and cruel eyes. He is sulky and 11 years old and has lots of sisters. I think he is the most horrible boy in the class. He has a croaky voice and always chews his pencil and picks his teeth and I think he is disgusting. (Livesley & Bromley, 1973, p. 217)

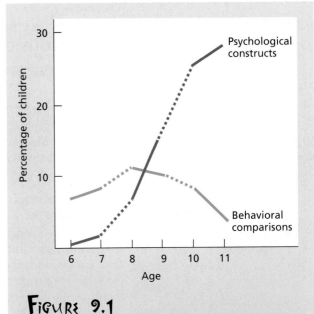

Figure 9.1

These data from Barenboim's study show the change in children's descriptions of their peers during the years of middle childhood. The solid lines represent longitudinal data, the dashed lines cross-sectional comparisons. (*Source:* Barenboim, 1981, Figure 1, p.134.)

This description still includes many external physical features but goes beyond such concrete surface qualities to the level of personality traits, such as lack of humor and cruelty.

The movement from externals to internals in descriptions of others is well documented by research. For example, in one important early study, researchers asked 6-, 8-, and 10-year-olds to describe three other children; a year later, they asked them to do the same thing again (Barenboim, 1981). Figure 9.1 shows the results for two of the categories used in the study's data analysis. A *behavioral comparison* was any description that involved comparing a child's behaviors or physical features with those of another child or with a norm—for example, "Billy runs a lot faster than Jason," or "She draws the best in our whole class." Any statement that involved some internal personality trait was refered to as a *psychological construct*, such as "Sarah is so kind," or "He's a real stubborn idiot!" You can see that behavioral comparisons peaked at around age 8 but psychological constructs increased steadily throughout middle childhood.

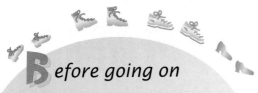

Before going on

- How do Freud and Erikson characterize social and personality development in 6- to 12-year-olds?

- In what ways do children's descriptions of others change in middle childhood?

Dimensions of Moral Development

One of parents' and teachers' greatest concerns is helping children learn to be good people, to do the "right" thing according to the standards and values of their culture. Moral development is very complex. To understand it fully, we must take into account psychoanalytic, cognitive-developmental, and learning theories.

Moral Emotions

According to Freud, the child learns moral rules by identifying with the same-sex parent during the phallic stage (ages 3–6). In other words, boys learn moral rules from their fathers, and girls learn them from their mothers. The rules a child learns from the same-sex parent form the child's *superego,* or internal moral judge. Thus, Freud's theory claims that, by 6, a child has learned all she will ever know about moral rules.

According to Freud, the superego has two parts: a *conscience* and an *ego ideal.* The **conscience** is a list of things that "good boys" and "good girls" don't do, such as telling lies. The **ego ideal** is a list of things that "good boys" and "good girls" do, such as obeying parents. When a child disobeys her conscience, she feels guilt. When she fails to live up to the standards set by the ego ideal, she feels shame. Freud believed that the child learns to obey the rules of her conscience and ego ideal to avoid these uncomfortable feelings.

To better understand Freud's idea about how the superego works, think about a hungry 7-year-old at the grocery store. He can figure out how to take a candy bar without anyone noticing. However, his superego classifies this behavior as stealing, and thinking about stealing a candy bar makes him feel guilty. This creates a conflict for him. If he steals the candy, he'll feel guilty. If he doesn't, he'll be hungry. If he has a healthy personality, Freud believed, he will obey his superego even though it will cause him to be hungry.

Erikson's views on moral development are similar to Freud's. However, Erikson believed that children learn moral rules from both parents. Erikson's theory also claims that pride is just as important to moral development as guilt and shame. For example, if the boy decides not to take the candy, he will not only avoid feeling guilty, he will also feel pride in his ability to resist temptation.

During the last decade, there has been a resurgence of interest in moral emotions among developmentalists (Eisenberg, 2000). Research has shown that, as Freud and Erikson predicted, feelings of guilt, shame, and pride develop before age 6 (Fung, 1999; Kochanska, Casey, & Fukumoto, 1995). Researchers infer that children are experiencing shame when they try to hide an act they know to be wrong. During the 6- to 12-year-old period, most children define "shame" as the emotion people experience when others find out that they have done something wrong (Levorato & Donati, 1999). Adolescents' understanding of shame, predictably, is more complex. They tell researchers that people experience shame when they fail to live up to their own standards of behavior as well as when their wrongdoing is exposed to others.

Connections between moral emotions and moral behavior may depend on cognitive development (Hoffman, 1988). Early in middle childhood, children connect

Critical Thinking

Think about your own conscience and ego ideal. What kinds of prohibitions are contained in your conscience? How do you feel when you violate them? What are the standards of your ego ideal? Under what circumstances do you experience shame?

conscience the list of "don'ts" in the superego; violation of any of these rules leads to feelings of guilt

ego ideal the list of "dos" in the superego; failure to live up to any of these leads to feelings of shame

moral feelings with adult observation. They seem to think that they should feel guilty or ashamed only if a parent or teacher sees them commit a violation of a moral rule. Thus, a 7-year-old candy thief is unlikely to feel guilty unless he gets caught in the act. Later, at about 10 or 11, when children better understand moral feelings, they are more likely to make behavioral choices based on how guilty, ashamed, or proud they think they will feel. For example, an older boy who wants candy at the grocery store will be more likely to choose not to take the candy because he knows resisting temptation will make him feel proud of himself.

Moral Reasoning

Moral reasoning is the process of making judgments about the rightness or wrongness of specific acts. As you learned in Chapter 7, children learn to discriminate between intentional and unintentional acts between age 2 and age 6. However, using this understanding to make moral judgments is another matter. Piaget claimed that the ability to use reasoning about intentions to make judgments about the moral dimensions of behavior appears to emerge along with concrete operational reasoning.

● *Piaget's Moral Realism and Moral Relativism* ●   Piaget studied moral development by observing children playing games. As he watched them play, Piaget noticed that younger children seemed to have less understanding of the games' rules. Following up on these observations, Piaget questioned children of different ages about rules. Their answers led him to propose a two-stage theory of moral development (Piaget, 1932).

At the beginning of the middle childhood period, children are in what Piaget termed the **moral realism stage.** They believe that the rules of games can't be changed because they come from authorities, such as parents, government officials, or religious figures. For example, one 6-year-old told Piaget that the game of marbles was invented on Noah's ark. He went on to explain that the rules can't be changed because the "big ones," meaning adults and older children, wouldn't like it (Piaget, 1965, p. 60).

Moral realists also believe that all rule violations eventually result in punishment. For example, Piaget told children a story about a child who fell into a stream when he tried to use a rotten piece of wood as a bridge. Children younger than 8 told him that the child was being punished for something "naughty" he had done in the past.

After age 8, Piaget proposed, children move into the **moral relativism stage,** in which they learn that people can agree to change rules if they want to. They realize that the important thing about a game is that all the players follow the same rules, regardless of what those are. For example, 8- to 12-year-olds know that a group of children playing baseball can decide to give each batter four strikes rather than three. They understand that their agreement doesn't change the game of baseball and that it doesn't apply to other people who play the game. At the same time, children of this age get better at following the rules of games.

Eight- to twelve-year-olds also know that you don't get punished for rule violations unless you get caught. As a result, they view events like the one in which the child fell into the stream as accidents. They understand that accidents are not caused by "naughty" behavior. Children older than 8 also understand the relationship between punishment and intentions. For example, Piaget's research suggests that children over 8 can distinguish between a child who unintentionally left a store without paying for a candy bar and another who deliberately took it. Older children are likely to say that both children should return or pay for the candy, but only the one who intentionally stole it should be punished.

Research supports Piaget's claim that children over 8 give more weight to intentions than consequences when making moral judgments (Zelazo, Helwig, & Lau, 1996). However, although their thinking is more mature than that of preschoolers,

moral realism stage the first of Piaget's stages of moral development, in which children believe rules are inflexible

moral relativism stage the second of Piaget's stages of moral development, in which children understand that many rules can be changed through social agreement

Encouraging Moral Reasoning

In his book *Raising Good Children*, developmental psychologist Thomas Lickona reminds readers that the development of mature moral reasoning takes many years (Lickona, 1983). At the same time, he offers parents and teachers several suggestions that will help them help their 6- to 12-year-olds prepare for movement to more mature levels. Following are some of his suggestions:

- Require kids to give reasons for what they want.
- Play developmentally appropriate games with them.

- Praise them for observing social conventions such as saying "please" and "thank you."
- When punishment is necessary, provide them with an explanation, advice on how to avoid punishment in the future, and a way of repairing any damage their misbehavior has caused.
- Teach them about reciprocity: "We do nice things for you, so you should be willing to help us."
- Give them meaningful chores so they will think of themselves as important family and community members.

- Help and encourage them to base obedience on love and respect rather than fear.
- Teach them religious and philosophical values, including the idea that some actions are right and others are wrong, regardless of circumstances.
- Challenge their egocentrism by asking questions such as, "How would you feel if someone did that to you?" when they violate others' rights.
- Include them in charitable projects, such as food drives, to extend the idea of love and caring beyond their own families.

6- to 12-year-olds' moral reasoning is still highly egocentric. For example, every parent has heard the exclamation "It's not fair!" when a child fails to receive the same treat or privilege as a sibling. It is rare, if not completely unknown, for a 6- to 12-year-old to protest the fairness of receiving something that a sibling didn't. Thus, school-aged children still have a long way to go with respect to mature moral reasoning, and we will return to this topic in the chapters on adolescent development (see The Real World).

● **Kohlberg's Theory of Moral Development** ●   Building on and revising Piaget's ideas, Lawrence Kohlberg pioneered the practice of assessing moral development by presenting a series of dilemmas in story form, each of which highlighted a specific moral issue, such as the value of human life. One of the most famous of these stories is the dilemma of Heinz, a man whose wife is dying of a disease for which a new, expensive medicine has been developed. Heinz, who can't afford the medicine, must choose between stealing it or allowing his wife to die. After hearing this story, the child or young person is asked a series of questions—for example, "Should Heinz have stolen the drug? What if Heinz didn't love his wife, would that change anything?" On the basis of the answers to such questions about moral dilemmas, Kohlberg concluded that moral reasoning develops in six stages.

Because school-aged children seldom exhibit moral reasoning beyond Kohlberg's first stage, you won't read about his stages in detail until Chapter 11. However, at this point, it's important for you to know that Kohlberg and his colleagues carried out a significant number of longitudinal and cross-cultural studies. Taken together, these studies strongly supported the notion that moral reasoning develops in stages, just as both Piaget and Kohlberg believed, and the stages are linked to progression through Piaget's concrete operational and formal operational stages (Colby, Kohlberg, Gibbs, & Lieberman, 1983; Nisan & Kohlberg, 1982; Snarey, Reimer, & Kohlberg, 1985; Walker, 1989).

Moral Behavior

Learning theorist B. F. Skinner proposed that consequences teach children to obey moral rules. According to Skinner, adults reward children with praise for morally acceptable behavior and punish children for morally unacceptable behavior. As a result, acceptable behavior increases and unacceptable behavior decreases as children get older. Consequences certainly do influence children's behavior. However, both praise and punishment are more effective when they are combined with instruction, an approach called *inductive discipline* that you read about in Chapter 7.

Punishment may actually interfere with moral development. For example, if a child's parent spanks him in the grocery store parking lot for having stolen a candy bar, the parent hopes that the spanking will teach the child that stealing is wrong. However, the child may learn only that he can't steal when he's with the parent. Similarly, when punishment is severe or embarrassing, children may be distracted from making the connection between the behavior and the punishment. A child who has stolen candy may be so angry at his parent for embarrassing him with a public spanking that he concentrates all his attention on his anger. As a result, he fails to realize that his choice to steal caused the spanking (Hoffman, 1988).

A parent who uses inductive discipline, on discovering that a 7-year-old had stolen a candy bar, would respond by telling the child privately that it is wrong to take things that don't belong to you, even if you are very hungry. Next, the parent would require the child to correct the wrong done to the store by admitting his crime, apologizing to the cashier or manager, and paying for the candy. Finally, the 7-year-old would probably have to repay his parents in some way if he used their money to pay for the stolen candy. Such a process allows the child to learn both that it is wrong to steal and that, when a moral rule is broken, something must be done to set things right again (Zahn-Waxler, Radke-Yarrow, & King, 1979).

As you may recall from Chapter 2, social-learning theorist Albert Bandura claims that children learn more from observing others than from either rewards or punishments. His theory predicts that, when a child sees someone rewarded for a behavior, she believes that she will also be rewarded if she behaves in the same way. Similarly, when she sees a model punished, she assumes that she will also experience punishment if she imitates the model's behavior (Bandura, 1977a, 1989). For example, a story about a child who was praised by a parent for resisting the temptation to steal may teach the child who hears or reads it that resisting temptation is praiseworthy. Conversely, when a child is exposed to a story about a boy or girl who steals and doesn't get caught, she may learn that it's possible to steal without getting caught.

Before going on

- What do psychoanalytic theorists emphasize in their explanations of moral development in middle childhood?

- How do cognitive-developmental theorists such as Piaget and Kohlberg explain 6- to 12-year-olds' moral development?

- According to learning theorists, what do reinforcement, punishment, and modeling contribute to moral development?

Social Relationships

School-aged children's growing ability to understand others changes their social relationships in important ways. Children continue to be attached to parents, but they are becoming more independent. Relationships with peers become more stable and many ripen into long-term friendships. In fact, the quality of 6- to 12-year-olds' peer relationships shapes their futures in many important ways.

Family Relationships

Middle childhood is a period of increasing independence of child from family. Yet, attachments to parents and relationships with siblings continue to be important.

● *The Child's Understanding of Family Roles and Processes* ●   As social-cognitive theory would predict, school-aged children understand family roles and relationships much better than younger children do. For example, by about age 9, children who live in two-parent homes understand that their parents' roles as parents are distinct from their roles as partners or spouses (Jenkins & Buccioni, 2000). Thus, a 9-year-old is better able than a 5-year-old to understand when divorcing parents say that their love for the child hasn't changed, even though their relationship with each other has ended. Emotionally, the divorce experience may be just as difficult, but school-aged children are more capable of understanding it cognitively.

School-aged children also know that marital conflict often arises when spouses have different goals (Jenkins & Buccioni, 2000). Moreover, while younger children seem to believe that the only solution for marital conflict is for one spouse to give in to the other, school-aged children appear to understand that spouses can compromise.

● *Attachment* ●   It would be a great mistake to assume that, because school-aged children are more independent than they were when younger, the parent-child attachment relationship has weakened. School-aged children continue to use their parents as a safe base; they continue to rely on their presence, support, and affection (Buhrmester, 1992). The quality of a school-aged child's attachment to his parents is also strongly related to his ability to maintain friendships with peers (Lieberman, Doyle, & Markiewicz, 1999). In addition, positive attitudes toward peers are related to quality of attachment in children of this age (Anan & Barnett, 1999).

What does change, though, is the agenda of issues between parent and child. When the child reaches elementary school, disciplinary interactions with parents decline. Key issues now include children's household responsibilities, whether they will receive allowances or be paid for chores, standards for school performance, and the like (Furnham, 1999; Maccoby, 1984): "Is it okay for Joe to stop off at his friend's house after school without asking ahead of time? How far from home may Diana ride her bike?" In many non-Western cultures, parents must also begin to teach children quite specific tasks, such as agricultural work and care of younger children or animals, all of which may be necessary for the survival of the family.

● *Parental Expectations* ●   The parent-child agenda changes because parents of 6- to 12-year-olds recognize their children's growing capacity for **self-regulation,** the ability to conform to parental standards of behavior without direct supervision. Cul-

self-regulation children's ability to conform to parental standards of behavior without direct supervision

tures differ to some degree in the specific age at which they expect this to occur. For example, white and Hispanic parents in the United States differ in their beliefs about the average age at which school-aged children can carry out specific tasks on their own (Savage & Gauvain, 1998). It appears that Hispanic American parents have less confidence in the self-regulatory abilities of younger school-aged children than white parents do. In general, though, most cultures expect 6- to 12-year-olds to be able to supervise their own behavior at least part of the time.

Some studies suggest that there are sex differences in parents' expectations with respect to self-regulatory behavior. For example, mothers make different kinds of demands on boys and girls. They appear to provide both with the same types of guidance, but are more likely to give boys more autonomy over their own behavior than girls. Nevertheless, they are also more likely to hold daughters to a higher standard of accountability for failure than boys (Pomerantz & Ruble, 1998). Developmentalists speculate that this difference may lead to stronger standards of behavior for girls in later developmental periods.

● **Parenting for Self-Regulation** ●   Researchers have learned that there are several parenting variables that contribute to the development of self-regulation. First, the parents' own ability to self-regulate is important, perhaps because they are providing the child with models of good or poor self-regulation (Prinstein & La Greca, 1999). Also, the degree of self-regulation expected by parents influences the child's self-regulatory behavior. Higher expectations, together with parental monitoring to make certain the expectations are met, are associated with greater self-regulatory competence (Rodrigo, Janssens, & Ceballos, 1999).

You should recall that such parental behaviors are associated with the authoritative style of parenting. Longitudinal research has demonstrated that school-aged children whose parents have been consistently authoritative since they were toddlers are the most socially competent (Baumrind, 1991). Children rated "competent" were seen as both assertive and responsible in their relationships; those rated "partially competent" typically lacked one of these skills; those rated "incompetent" showed neither. In Baumrind's (1991) study, the majority of children from authoritative families were rated as fully competent, while most of those from neglecting families were rated as incompetent.

● **Siblings and Only Children** ●   As a general rule, sibling relationships seem to be less central to the lives of children in this age range than relationships with either friends or parents (Buhrmester, 1992). Elementary school children are less likely to turn to a sibling for affection than to parents and are less likely to turn to a brother or sister for companionship or intimacy than they are to a friend.

However, sibling relationships vary enormously. On the basis of direct studies of young children as well as retrospective reports by young adults about their sibling relationships when they were of school age, researchers have identified several patterns, or styles, of sibling relationships (Murphy, 1993; Stewart, Beilfuss, & Verbrugge, 1995):

●   A *caregiver* relationship, in which one sibling serves as a kind of quasi-parent for the other (this pattern seems to be more common between an older sister and a younger brother than for any other combination)

●   A *buddy* relationship, in which both members of the pair try to be like each other and take pleasure in being together

●   A *critical,* or *conflictual,* relationship, which includes teasing, quarreling, and attempts by one sibling to dominate the other

●   A *rival* relationship, which contains many of the same elements as a critical relationship but is also low in any form of friendliness or support

●   A *casual* relationship, in which the siblings have relatively little to do with one another

Rival or critical relationships seem to be more common when siblings differ in age by 4 years or less (Buhrmester & Furman, 1990). Caregiver or buddy relationships appear to be somewhat more common in pairs of sisters. Rivalry seems to be highest in boy-boy pairs (Buhrmester & Furman, 1990; Stewart et al., 1995).

People often speculate that only children, those without siblings, are deprived of an important developmental experience. Until recently, single-child families were fairly unusual. China's policy of encouraging families to have no more than one child has provided developmentalists with a unique opportunity to carry out research involving large numbers of only children. This research suggests that only children are no different from children with siblings in any important way (Wang et al., 2000). Research involving only children in other countries suggests that if any differences do exist, children without siblings seem to have the advantage. Only children tend to have higher achievement test scores, to be more obedient, and to experience better peer relationships than those who have siblings (Doh & Falbo, 1999; Falbo, 1992).

Research suggests that only children are just as well adjusted as those who have siblings. (*Photo:* Michael Newman, PhotoEdit)

Friendships

The biggest shift in relationships during middle childhood is the increasing importance of peers, particularly close friends. Social-cognitive researcher Robert Selman was one of the first to study children's understanding of friendships. He found that if you ask preschoolers and young school-aged children how people make friends, the answer is usually that they "play together" or spend time physically near each other (Damon, 1977, 1983; Selman, 1980).

In the later years of middle childhood, at around age 10, this view of friendship gives way to one in which the key concept seems to be reciprocal trust (Chen, 1997). Older children see friends as special people who possess desired qualities other than mere proximity, who are generous with each other, who help and trust each other, and so on. Figure 9.2 is a 10-year-old boy's definition of a friend. His characteriza-

My definition of a good friend is someone who you can trust, They will never turn their back on you, They will always be there for you. when you are feeling down in the dumps, They'll try to cheer you up, They will never forget about you.   They'll always sit next to you at lunch,

FIGURE 9.2

This essay on friendship written by a 10-year-old illustrates the way older school-aged children think about friends. (Courtesy of Denise Boyd. Used with permission.)

tion of a friend as someone "you can trust," who "will always be there for you when you are feeling down in the dumps" and "always sits by you at lunch," illustrates the older child's understanding of dimensions of friendships such as trust, emotional support, and loyalty.

Evidence of the centrality of friends to social development in middle childhood also comes from studies of children's behavior within friendships. Children are more open and more supportive when with their chums, smiling at, looking at, laughing with, and touching one another more than when they are with nonfriends; they talk more with friends and cooperate and help one another more. Pairs of friends are also more successful than nonfriends are in solving problems or performing some task together. Yet school-aged children are also more critical of friends and have more conflicts with them; they are more polite with strangers (Hartup, 1996). At the same time, when conflicts with friends occur, children are more concerned about resolving them than they are about settling disagreements with nonfriends. Thus, friendship seems to represent an arena in which children can learn how to manage conflicts (Newcomb & Bagwell, 1995).

Critical Thinking

Do you still have any friends from your elementary school years? If not, why do you think those early friendships did not survive? If you do, what do you think differentiates an early friendship that survives from one that does not?

Gender Segregation

Possibly the most striking thing about peer group interactions in the elementary school years is how gender-segregated they are. This pattern seems to occur in every culture in the world and is frequently visible in children as young as 3 or 4. Boys play with boys and girls play with girls, each in their own areas and at their own kinds of games (Cairns & Cairns, 1994; Harkness & Super, 1985). In fact, gender seems to be more important than age, race, or any other categorical variable in 6- to 12-year-olds' selection of friends; in addition, the strength of children's preference for same-sex associates increases substantially across middle childhood (Graham, Cohen, Zbikowski, & Secrist, 1998). Moreover, gender segregation is unrelated to sex differences in parenting, suggesting that it is a feature of 6- to 12-year-olds' social relationships that they construct for reasons of their own (McHale, Crouter, & Tucker, 1999).

Shared interests and activities are a critical part of friendship in the early years of middle childhood. For example, rough-and-tumble play is common in boy-boy interactions but is typically avoided by girls. Thus, based on activity preferences, boys gravitate to other boys in social situations. In so doing, they learn how to socialize with other boys, but acquire few of the skills used by girls in their interactions, skills such as self-disclosure (Phillipsen, 1999). Thus, boys establish stable peer groups with dominance hierarchies that are based on rough-and-tumble play skills (Pellegrini & Smith, 1998). A similar pattern exists for girls: Gender segregation begins with shared activity preferences but leads to the development of social skills that are more useful in interactions with other girls than in interactions with boys.

However, there are some ritualized "boundary violations" between boys' and girls' groups, such as chasing games. For example, in one universal series of interactions, a girl taunts a boy with a statement like "You can't catch me, nyah nyah." Next, a boy chases and catches her, to the delight of both of their fully supportive same-sex peer groups (Thorne, 1986). As soon as the brief cross-gender encounter

In middle childhood, boys play with boys and girls play with girls. In fact, children's play groups are more sex-segregated at this age than at any other. (Photos: Jeffry W. Myers, Stock Boston; Mary Kate Denny, PhotoEdit)

Why do you think competition is such a strong feature of friendship interactions among boys? Do you think this is true in every culture? (*Photo:* Vincent De Witt, Stock Boston)

ends, both girl and boy return to their respective groups. On the whole, however, girls and boys between the ages of 6 and 12 actively avoid interacting with one another and show strong favoritism toward their own gender and negative stereotyping of the opposite gender (Powlishta, 1995).

Gender segregation patterns are even more pronounced in friendships during middle childhood. For example, when researchers ask children to describe the kind of playmate a fictional child would prefer, school-aged children's predictions are largely gender-based (Halle, 1999). Girls' and boys' friendships also differ in quality in intriguing ways. Boys' friendship groups are larger and more accepting of newcomers than are girls'. Boys play more outdoors and roam over a larger area in their play. Girls are more likely to play in pairs or in small, fairly exclusive groups, and they spend more playtime indoors or near home or school (Benenson, 1994; Gottman, 1986).

Sex differences also characterize the interaction between a pair of friends, as you learned in Chapter 7. Boys' friendships appear to be focused more on competition and dominance than are girls' friendships (Maccoby, 1995). In fact, among school-aged boys, researchers see higher levels of competition between pairs of friends than between strangers—the opposite of what is observed among girls. Friendships between girls include more agreement, more compliance, and more self-disclosure than is true between boys. For example, "controlling" speech—a category that includes rejecting comments, ordering, manipulating, challenging, defiance, refutation, or resistance of another's attempts to control—is twice as common among pairs of 7- and 8-year-old male friends as among pairs of female friends of that age (Leaper, 1991). Among the 4- and 5-year-olds in Leaper's study, there were no sex differences in controlling speech, suggesting that these differences in interaction pattern arise during middle childhood.

None of this information should obscure the fact that the interactions of male and female friendship pairs have much in common. For example, collaborative and cooperative exchanges are the most common forms of communication in both boys' and girls' friendships in middle childhood. And it is not necessarily the case that boys' friendships are less important to them than girls' are to them. Nevertheless, it seems clear that there are gender differences in form and style that may well have enduring implications for patterns of friendship over the lifespan.

Furthermore, school-aged children appear to evaluate the role of gender in peer relationships in light of other variables. For example, when asked whether a fictitious boy would prefer to play with a boy who is a stranger or with a girl who has been his friend for a while, most school-aged children say the boy would prefer to play with the friend (Halle, 1999). Such results suggest that, even though gender is clearly important in school-aged children's peer relationships, they are beginning to understand that other factors may be more important. This is yet another example of how children's growing cognitive abilities—specifically, their ability to think about more than one variable at a time—influence their ideas about the social world.

Patterns of Aggression

You may remember from Chapter 7 that physical aggression declines over the preschool years, while verbal aggression increases. In middle childhood, physical aggression becomes even less common as children learn the cultural rules about when it is acceptable to display anger or aggression and how much of a display is acceptable. In most cultures, this means that anger is increasingly disguised and aggression is increasingly controlled as children get older (Underwood, Coie, & Herbsman, 1992).

One interesting exception to this general pattern is that in all-boy pairs or groups, at least in the United States, physical aggression seems to remain both relatively high and constant over the childhood years. Indeed, at every age, boys show more physical aggression and more assertiveness than do girls, both within friendship

TABLE 9.1   Aggressive Behavior in Boys and Girls Aged 4 to 11

	Percentages as Rated by Teachers	
Behavior	**Boys**	**Girls**
Mean to others	21.8	9.6
Physically attacks people	18.1	4.4
Gets in many fights	30.9	9.8
Destroys own things	10.7	2.1
Destroys others' things	10.6	4.4
Threatens to hurt people	13.1	4.0

(*Source:* Offord, Boyle, & Racine, 1991, from Table 2.3, p. 39.)

pairs and in general (Fabes, Knight, & Higgins, 1995). Furthermore, school-aged boys often express approval for the aggressive behavior of peers (Rodkin, Farmer, Pearl, & Van Acker, 2000). Table 9.1 gives some highly representative data from a very large, careful survey in Canada, in which teachers completed checklists describing each child's behavior (Offord, Boyle, & Racine, 1991). It is clear that boys are described as far more aggressive on all of this study's measures of physical aggressiveness.

Results like these have been so clear and so consistent that most psychologists have concluded that boys are simply "more aggressive." But that conclusion may turn out to be wrong. Instead, it begins to look as if girls simply express their aggressiveness in a different way, using what has recently been labeled *relational aggression,* instead of physical aggression. Physical aggression hurts others physically or poses a threat of such damage; **relational aggression** is aimed at damaging the other person's self-esteem or peer relationships, such as by ostracism or threats of ostracism ("I won't invite you to my birthday party if you do that"), cruel gossip, or facial expressions of disdain. Children are genuinely hurt by such indirect aggression, and they are likely to shun others who use this form of aggression a lot (Casas & Mosher, 1995; Cowan & Underwood, 1995; Crick & Grotpeter, 1995; Rys & Bear, 1997).

Girls are much more likely than boys to use relational aggression, especially toward other girls, a difference that begins as early as the preschool years and becomes very marked by the fourth or fifth grade. For example, in one study of nearly 500 children in the third through sixth grades, researchers found that 17.4% of the girls but only 2% of the boys were rated high in relational aggression—almost precisely the reverse of what is observed for physical aggression (Crick & Grotpeter, 1995). Researchers do not yet know whether this difference in form of aggression has some hormonal/biological basis or is learned at an early age, or both. They do know that higher rates of physical aggression in males have been observed in every human society and in all varieties of primates. And scientists know that some link exists between rates of physical aggression and testosterone levels (e.g., Susman et al., 1987). But the origin of girls' apparent propensity toward relational aggression is still an open question.

Retaliatory aggression—aggression to get back at someone who has hurt you—increases among both boys and girls during the 6- to 12-year-old period (Astor, 1994). Its development is related to children's growing understanding of the difference between intentional and accidental actions. For example, if a child drops his pencil in the path of another child who is walking by and that child happens to kick the pencil across the floor, most 8-year-olds can identify this as an accident. Consequently, the child whose pencil was kicked feels no need to get back at the child who did the kicking. However, children over 8 view intentional harm differently. For example, let's say that one child intentionally takes another's pencil off her desk and

relational aggression aggression aimed at damaging another person's self-esteem or peer relationships, such as by ostracism or threats of ostracism, cruel gossiping, or facial expressions of disdain

retaliatory aggression aggression to get back at someone who has hurt you

throws it across the room. Most children over 8 will try to find a way to get back at a child who does something like this. In fact, children who don't try to retaliate in such situations are also more likely to be seen as socially incompetent and to be bullied by their peers in the future (Astor, 1994).

Peers may approve of retaliatory aggression, but most parents and teachers strive to teach children that, like other forms of intentional harm, such behavior is unacceptable. Research suggests that children can learn nonaggressive techniques for managing the kinds of situations that lead to retaliatory aggression. In one program, called PeaceBuilders, psychologists have attempted to change individual behavior by changing a school's overall emotional climate. In this approach, both children and teachers learn to use positive social strategies (Flannery et al., 2000). For example, both are urged to try to praise others more often than they criticize them. Research suggests that when such programs are integrated into students' classes every day for an entire school year or longer, aggression decreases and prosocial behavior increases. Thus, aggressive interactions between elementary school children may be common, but they do not appear to be an inevitable aspect of development.

Social Status

Developmentalists measure popularity and rejection by asking children to list peers they would not like to play with or by observing which children are sought out or avoided on the playground. These techniques allow researchers to group children according to the degree to which they are accepted by peers—a variable often called **social status.** Typically, researchers find three groups: *popular, rejected,* and *neglected.*

Some of the characteristics that differentiate popular children from those in the other two groups are things outside a child's control. In particular, attractive children and physically larger children are more likely to be popular. Conversely being very different from her peers may cause a child to be neglected or rejected. For example, shy children usually have few friends (Fordham & Stevenson-Hinde, 1999). Similarly, highly creative children are often rejected, as are those who have difficulty controlling their emotions (Aranha, 1997; Maszk, Eisenberg, & Guthrie, 1999).

However, children's social behavior seems to be more important than looks or temperament. Most studies show that popular children behave in positive, supporting, nonpunitive, and nonaggressive ways toward most other children. They explain things, take their playmates' wishes into consideration, take turns in conversation, and are able to regulate the expression of their strong emotions. In addition, popular children are usually good at regulating their own emotions and accurately assessing others' feelings (Underwood, 1997).

There are two types of rejected children. *Withdrawn/rejected* children realize that they are disliked by peers (Harrist, Zaia, Bates, Dodge, & Pettit, 1997). After repeated attempts to gain peer acceptance, these children eventually give up and become socially withdrawn. As a result, they often experience feelings of loneliness. *Aggressive/rejected* children are often disruptive and uncooperative and usually believe that their peers like them (Zakriski & Coie, 1996). Many appear to be unable to control the expression of strong feelings (Eisenberg et al., 1995; Pettit, Clawson, Dodge, & Bates, 1996). They interrupt their play partners more often and fail to take turns in a systematic way.

Aggression and disruptive behavior are often linked to rejection and unpopularity among Chinese children, just as they are among American children (Chen, Rubin, & Li, 1995; Chen, Rubin, & Sun, 1992). As you learned in Chapter 7, aggressive behavior persists into adulthood in some individuals. However, research suggests that aggression is most likely to become a stable characteristic among children who are *both* aggressive and rejected by peers (see the Research Report).

Of course, not all aggressive children are rejected. Among girls, aggression, whether physical or relational, seems to lead to peer rejection consistently. Among

social status an individual child's classification as popular, rejected, or neglected

Research Report

Long-Term Consequences of Childhood Aggression and Peer Rejection

As you learned in Chapter 7, early childhood aggression becomes a lifelong pattern of behavior for some children. However, the correlations between childhood aggression and social difficulties in adulthood become even stronger once children reach middle childhood. Here are a few of the relevant research findings:

- Psychologist Leonard Eron, in an important 22-year longitudinal study, found a high level of aggressiveness toward peers at age 8 to be related to criminal behavior at age 30 (Eron, 1987, p. 439).

- In the Concordia Project, in Canada, psychologists studied several thousand boys who were initially identified by their peers in grade 1, 4, or 7 as either highly aggressive, withdrawn, or both (Serbin, Moskowitz, Schwartzman, & Ledingham, 1991). By adulthood, 45.5% of the aggressive men had appeared in court, compared to only 10.8% of the nonaggressive men.

- A longitudinal study of 400 working-class boys in England, which began when they were 8 and continued until they were in their 30s, found that those who were rated by their teachers as most aggressive at ages 8, 10, and 12 were twice as likely as their less aggressive peers to have committed a violent crime by age 32 (20.4% versus 9.8%) (Farrington, 1991).

The risk of future problems may be greatest for boys who are both aggressive and rejected. For example, in one important longitudinal study, psychologist John Coie and his colleagues followed a group of over a thousand children from the third to the tenth grade (Coie, Terry, Lenox, Lochman, & Hyman, 1995). Among boys, those who were both aggressive *and* rejected in third grade were far more likely to show delinquency or other behavior problems in high school than were any other group of boys, including those who were aggressive but were not rejected by peers. Other researchers have produced similar findings with regard to aggressive boys who are either overtly rejected or who have more subtle types of problems maintaining peer relationships (Crick & Ladd, 1993; Woodward & Fergusson, 2000).

Remember, boys who are aggressive are very likely to misunderstand others' intentions and to perceive accidental acts as deliberate (Coie et al., 1999; Zakriski & Coie, 1996). Remember, too, that school-aged children tend to regard peers who do not retaliate against hostile acts as socially incompetent. Thus, psychologically and socially, aggressive/rejected children may be in a sort of double bind. Their immature social-cognitive skills predispose them to believe that others are hostile toward them, and their school-aged peers expect them to retaliate in response to acts of aggression. But because they can't discriminate well between situations that call for retaliation and those that do not, their acts of retaliation lead to rejection rather than peer approval. In this way, psychological factors and the unique social characteristics of middle childhood work together to shape these children's behavior into a consistent pattern. Unfortunately, longitudinal research suggests that, for many of these boys, the pattern continues into adulthood.

---

boys, however, aggression may result in either popularity or rejection (Rodkin et al., 2000; Xie, Cairns, & Cairns, 1999). In fact, aggressiveness seems to be a fairly typical characteristic of popular African American boys.

In addition, irrespective of aggressive boys' general popularity, their close friends tend to be aggressive as well. Furthermore, aggressiveness seems to precede these relationships. In other words, boys who are aggressive seek out boys like themselves as friends, and being friends doesn't seem to make either member of the pair more aggressive (Poulin & Boivin, 2000). Research also suggests that children have more positive attitudes toward aggressive peers whose aggressive acts are seen as mostly retaliatory and toward those who engage in both prosocial and aggressive behavior (Coie & Cillessen, 1993; Newcomb, Bukowski, & Pattee, 1993; Poulin & Boivin, 1999). Social approval may not increase aggressiveness, but it does seem to help maintain it; interventions to reduce aggressive behavior typically have little effect on aggressive boys who are popular (Phillips, Schwean, & Saklofske, 1997).

Neglected children often do quite well in school, but they are more prone to depression and loneliness than are popular children (Cillessen, van IJzendoorn, van Lieshout, & Hartup, 1992; Rubin, Hymel, Mills, & Rose-Krasnor, 1991; Wentzel &

Asher, 1995). This is especially true for girls, who seem to value popularity more than boys do (Oldenburg & Kerns, 1997). Neglect seems to be much less stable over time than rejection, and neglected children sometimes move to the popular category when they become part of a new peer group.

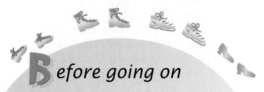

Before going on

● Describe school-aged children's relationships with their parents.

● Describe the 6- to 12-year-old's understanding of friendship.

● What role does gender play in children's social behavior and selection of friends?

● Describe the types of aggression most common in middle childhood.

● How do popular, rejected, and neglected children differ?

Personality and Self-Concept

One key contributor to a school-aged child's social relationships is, of course, her own personality. A child's self-concept also has an impact on her social relationships, and the quality of her relationships contributes to her developing self-perceptions.

The Big Five Personality Traits

You'll recall from Chapter 7 that many developmentalists today think of personality as being built on the foundation of the child's inborn temperament (Rothbart, Ahadi, & Evans, 2000). But just how can researchers describe personality? What are the key dimensions on which personalities differ? Over the past 2 decades, most personality researchers have reached a consensus that adult personality can be adequately described as a set of variations along five major dimensions, often referred to as the **Big Five** (see Table 9.2): *extraversion, agreeableness, conscientiousness, neuroticism,* and *openness/intellect* (Digman, 1990; McCrae & John, 1992). To help you link this list of personality traits to the temperament dimensions described in Chapter 5, Table 9.2 lists some of the possible connections between the two—although these links are still somewhat speculative (e.g., Ahadi & Rothbart, 1994; Digman, 1994).

The Big Five have been found in studies of adults in a variety of countries, including some non-Western cultures (Bond, Nakazato, & Shiraishi, 1975; Borkenau & Ostendorf, 1990). There is also evidence that they are stable traits; among adults, scores on these five personality dimensions have been shown to be stable over periods as long as a decade or more—a point you'll read more about in later chapters.

the Big Five a set of five major dimensions of personality, including extraversion, agreeableness, conscientiousness, neuroticism, and openness/intellect

TABLE 9.2   The Big Five Personality Traits

Trait	Qualities of Individuals Who Show the Trait	Possible Temperament Components
Extraversion	Active, assertive, enthusiastic, outgoing	High activity level; sociability; positive emotionality; talkativeness
Agreeableness	Affectionate, forgiving, generous, kind, sympathetic, trusting	Perhaps high approach/ positive emotionality; perhaps effortful control
Conscientiousness	Efficient, organized, prudent, reliable, responsible	Effortful control/task persistence
Neuroticism (also called emotional instability)	Anxious, self-pitying, tense, touchy, unstable, worrying	Negative emotionality; irritability
Openness/Intellect	Artistic, curious, imaginative, insightful, original, wide interests	Approach; low inhibition

(*Sources:* Ahadi & Rothbart, 1994; John, Caspi, Robins, Moffitt, & Stouthamer-Loeber, 1994, Table 1, p. 161; McCrae & Costa, 1990.)

Research suggests that these five dimensions also describe children's and adolescents' personalities. For example, a large study of children and adolescents in the Netherlands found that the five clearest dimensions characterizing the young participants matched the Big Five very well (van Lieshout & Haselager, 1994). In this sample, agreeableness and neuroticism (emotional instability) were the two clearest dimensions, followed by conscientiousness, extraversion, and openness.

Moreover, in longitudinal studies, school-aged children's scores on these dimensions of personality have been found to strongly predict academic achievement and social skills in adolescence and early adulthood (Shiner, 2000). Measures of personality in middle childhood also predict antisocial behavior, such as stealing, in adolescence and later (see Figure 9.3, page 264) (John et al., 1994; Shiner, 2000). Such longitudinal studies suggest that the Big Five are not only identifiable and stable in middle childhood, but are also extremely important. Thus, personality assessment in middle childhood may be a useful way to identify children who are in need of interventions to prevent delinquency.

The Psychological Self

In earlier chapters, you read about the child's categorical, social, and emotional selves. During middle childhood, an additional component is added to the self-concept—the psychological self. The **psychological self** is a person's understanding of his or her enduring psychological characteristics, such as personality traits. During middle childhood, the psychological self becomes increasingly complex and abstract. For example, a 6-year-old might use simple psychological self-descriptors such as "smart" or "dumb." By 10, a child is more likely to use comparisons in self-descriptions: "I'm smarter than most other kids," or "I'm not as talented in art as my friend" (Rosenberg, 1986; Ruble, 1987).

psychological self an understanding of one's stable, internal traits

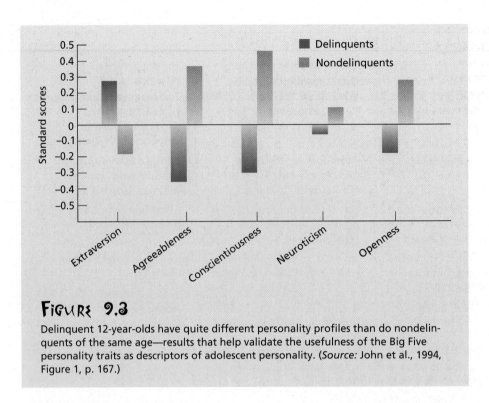

FIGURE 9.3

Delinquent 12-year-olds have quite different personality profiles than do nondelinquents of the same age—results that help validate the usefulness of the Big Five personality traits as descriptors of adolescent personality. (*Source:* John et al., 1994, Figure 1, p. 167.)

This developmental trend was illustrated in the results of an older study of the self-concepts of 9- to 18-year-olds (Montemayor & Eisen, 1977). Children who participated were asked to give 20 answers to the question "Who am I?" The researchers found that the younger children were still using mostly surface qualities to describe themselves, as in this description by a 9-year-old:

> My name is Bruce C. I have brown eyes. I have brown hair. I have brown eyebrows. I am nine years old. I LOVE! Sports. I have seven people in my family. I have great! eye site. I have lots! of friends. I live on 1923 Pinecrest Dr. I am going on 10 in September. I'm a boy. I have a uncle that is almost 7 feet tall. My school is Pinecrest. My teacher is Mrs. V. I play Hockey! I'm almost the smartest boy in the class. I LOVE! food. I love fresh air. I LOVE school. (Montemayor & Eisen, 1977, p. 317)

In contrast, consider the self-description of this 11-year-old girl in the sixth grade:

> My name is A. I'm a human being. I'm a girl. I'm a truthful person. I'm not very pretty. I do so-so in my studies. I'm a very good cellist. I'm a very good pianist. I'm a little bit tall for my age. I like several boys. I like several girls. I'm old-fashioned. I play tennis. I am a very good swimmer. I try to be helpful. I'm always ready to be friends with anybody. Mostly I'm good, but I lose my temper. I'm not well-liked by some girls and boys. I don't know if I'm liked by boys or not. (Montemayor & Eisen, 1977, pp. 317–318)

This girl, like the other 11-year-olds in the study, describes her external qualities, but she also emphasizes psychological factors such as personality traits.

Thus, as a child moves through the concrete operational period, her psychological self becomes more complex, more comparative, less tied to external features, and more centered on feelings and ideas.

Critical Thinking

Take a moment and write down your own 20 answers to the "Who am I?" question. Then compare your answers to the examples given in the text of children's answers. What types of descriptions did you include?

The Valued Self

The self-concept of the 6- to 12-year-old also contains an evaluative aspect. Note, for example, the differences in tone in the two sets of answers to the "Who am I?" question. The 9-year-old makes a lot of positive statements about himself, while the 11-year-old gives a more mixed self-evaluation.

● ***The Nature of Self-Esteem*** ●   A child's evaluative judgments have several interesting features. First of all, over the years of elementary school and high school, children's evaluations of their own abilities become increasingly differentiated, with quite separate judgments about academic or athletic skills, physical appearance, social acceptance, friendships, romantic appeal, and relationships with parents (Harter, 1990; Marsh, Craven, & Debus, 1999). Paradoxically, however, it is when they reach school age—around age 7—that children first develop a global self-evaluation. Seven- and eight-year-olds (but not younger children) readily answer questions about how well they like themselves as people, how happy they are, or how well they like the way they are leading their lives. It is this global evaluation of one's own worth that is usually referred to as **self-esteem,** and it is not merely the sum of all the separate assessments a child makes about his skills in different areas. Instead, each child's level of self-esteem is a product of two internal judgments (Harter, 1987, 1990).

First, as children acquire more sophisticated information-processing skills, they are able to make mental comparisons of their ideal selves and their actual experiences to form experience-based self-esteem judgments. For example, social self-esteem, the assessment of one's own social skills, is higher in popular children than in those who are rejected by their peers (Jackson & Bracken, 1998). However, each component of self-esteem is valued differently by different children. Thus, a child who perceives herself to have poor social skills because she is unpopular may not necessarily have low self-esteem. The degree to which her social self-assessment affects her self-esteem is influenced by how much she values social skills and popularity. In addition, she may see herself as very competent in another area—such as academic skills—that balances her lack of social skills.

The key to self-esteem, then, is the amount of discrepancy between what the child desires and what the child thinks he has achieved. Thus, a child who values sports prowess but who isn't big enough or coordinated enough to be good at sports will have lower self-esteem than will an equally small or uncoordinated child who does not value sports skill so highly. Similarly, being good at something, such as singing or playing chess, won't raise a child's self-esteem unless the child values that particular skill.

The second major influence on a child's self-esteem is the overall support the child feels she is receiving from the important people around her, particularly parents and peers (Franco & Levitt, 1998). Apparently, to develop high self-esteem, children must first acquire the sense that they are liked and accepted in their families, by both parents and siblings. Next, they need to be able to find friends with whom they can develop stable relationships. Since childhood friendships begin with shared interests and activities, children need to be in an environment in which they can find others who like the same things they do and are similarly skilled. Athletic children need other athletic children to associate with; those who are musically inclined need to meet peers who are also musical; and so on.

The separate influences of the perceived discrepancy between the ideal and actual self and the amount of social support are clear in the results of developmental psychologist Susan Harter's research on self-esteem. She asked third-, fourth-, fifth-, and sixth-graders how important it was to them to do well in each of five domains, and how well they thought they actually did in each. The total discrepancy between these sets of judgments constituted the discrepancy score. A high discrepancy score indicates

Hitting a home run will only raise this girl's self-esteem if she places a high value on being good at sports or at baseball specifically. (*Photo:* Don Smetzer, Tony Stone)

self-esteem a global evaluation of one's own worth

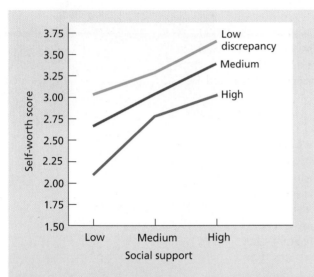

FIGURE 9.4

For these third- and fourth-graders in Harter's studies, self-esteem was about equally influenced by the amount of support the children saw themselves receiving from parents and peers and the degree of discrepancy between the value the children placed on various domains and the skill they thought they had in each of those domains. (*Source:* Harter, 1987, Figure 9.2, p. 227.)

that the child didn't feel he was doing well in areas that mattered to him. The social support score was based on children's replies to a set of questions about whether they thought others (parents and peers) liked them as they were, treated them as a person, or felt that they were important. Figure 9.4 shows the results for the third- and fourth-graders; the findings for the fifth- and sixth-graders are virtually identical to these, and both sets of data support Harter's hypothesis, as does other research, including studies of African American children (Luster & McAdoo, 1995). Note that a low discrepancy score alone does not protect a child completely from low self-esteem if she lacks sufficient social support. Similarly, a loving and accepting family and peer group do not guarantee high self-esteem if the youngster does not feel that she is living up to her own standards.

● ***Consistency of Self-Esteem over Time*** ●   How stable are self-esteem judgments? Is a third-grader with low self-esteem doomed to feel less than worthy for the rest of his life? A number of longitudinal studies of elementary–school-aged children and teenagers show that self-esteem is quite stable in the short term but somewhat less so over periods of several years. The correlation between two self-esteem scores obtained a few months apart is generally about .60. Over several years, this correlation drops to about .40 (Alsaker & Olweus, 1992; Block & Robins, 1993). So, a child with high self-esteem at age 8 or 9 is likely to have high self-esteem at age 10 or 11. But it is also true that self-esteem is subject to a good deal of variation.

● ***Consequences of Variations in Self-Esteem*** ●   Harter and others have found that the child's level of self-esteem is strongly negatively correlated with depression in both middle childhood and adolescence; the lower the self-esteem score, the more depressed the child describes himself to be. The correlations in several of Harter's studies range from −.67 to −.80 which are remarkably strong correlations for research of this type (Harter, 1987; Renouf & Harter, 1990). Bear in mind, though, that this is still correlational evidence. These findings don't prove a causal connection between low self-esteem and depression. More persuasive is Harter's finding from her longitudinal studies that when a child's self-esteem score rises or falls, her depression score falls or rises accordingly.

● ***Origins of Differences in Self-Esteem*** ●   Where do differences in self-esteem come from? There are at least three sources. First, of course, a child's own direct experience with success or failure in various arenas plays an obvious role. In elementary school, children become aware of their relative academic successes; they gain equally direct comparative information when they play sports, take music lessons, or try out for the school play.

Second, the value a child attaches to some skill or quality is obviously affected fairly directly by peers' and parents' attitudes and values. For example, peer (and general cultural) standards for appearance establish benchmarks for all children and teens. A child who is "too tall" or "too fat" or who deviates in some other way from the accepted norms is likely to feel a sense of inadequacy. Similarly, the degree of emphasis parents place on the child's performing well in some domain—whether it is school, athletics, or playing chess—is an important element in the child's formation of aspirations in that area.

Finally, labels and judgments from others play a highly significant role. To a very considerable extent, we come to think of ourselves as others think of us (Cole, 1991). A child who is repeatedly told that she is "smart," "a good athlete," or "pretty" is likely to have higher self-esteem than a child who is told that she is "dumb," "clumsy," or "a late bloomer." A child who brings home a report card with C's and B's on it and hears her parents say, "That's fine, honey. We don't expect you to get all A's" draws conclusions both about the parents' expectations and about their judgments of her abilities.

From all of these sources, the child fashions her ideas (her internal model) about what she should be and what she is. Like the internal model of attachment, self-esteem is not fixed in stone. It is responsive to changes in others' judgments as well as to changes in the child's own experience of success or failure. But once created, the model does tend to persist, both because the child tends to choose experiences that will confirm and support it and because the social environment—including the parents' evaluations of the child—tends to be at least moderately consistent.

Before going on

- List and describe the Big Five personality traits.

- Characterize the psychological self-concepts of 6- to 12-year-olds.

- What is the valued self, and how does it develop?

Influences beyond Family and School

The daily life of the school-aged child is shaped by more than the hours she spends in school. The circumstances in which a child lives also affect her. For example, some parents are at home when children come home from school; others are still at work. A child is also affected by her family's economic circumstances, by the neighborhood she lives in, and by the TV programs she watches.

After-School Care

In the United States, several million children are at home by themselves after school for an hour or more each weekday. They are often referred to as **self-care children.** Self-care arrangements differ so much from child to child that it is impossible to say whether, as a group, self-care children differ from others. For example, some self-care children are home alone but are closely monitored by neighbors or relatives, while others are completely without supervision of any kind (Brandon, 1999). Conse-

self-care children children who are at home by themselves after school for an hour or more each day

quently, the global category "self-care children" isn't very useful in research. To compare self-care children to others and to make predictions, investigators have to focus on variables that may affect self-care—such as the crime rate of the neighborhood in which self-care occurs. Thus, developmentalists have learned that the effects of self-care on a child's development depend on behavioral history, age, gender, the kind of neighborhood the child lives in, and how well parents monitor the child during self-care periods (Posner & Vandell, 1994; Steinberg, 1986).

Research consistently demonstrates that self-care children are more poorly adjusted in terms of both peer relationships and school performance. They tend to be less socially skilled and to have a greater number of behavior problems. However, some of these differences between self-care children and others arises from the effect of self-care on children who already have social and behavioral difficulties before self-care begins. Investigators have found that children who have such problems in the preschool years, before they experience any self-care, are the most negatively affected by the self-care experience (Pettit, Laird, Bates, & Dodge, 1997).

With respect to age, most developmentalists agree that children under the age of 9 or 10 should not care for themselves. In fact, most cities and/or states have laws specifying the age at which a child may be legally left at home alone for long periods of time. In some areas, this age is in the mid-teens. Thus, parents considering self-care should check with local child protective services to find out the specific regulations in their area.

From a developmental perspective, children younger than 9 do not have the cognitive abilities necessary to evaluate risks and deal with emergencies. Children who start self-care in the early elementary years are vulnerable to older self-care children in their neighborhoods who may hurt or even sexually abuse them and more likely to have adjustment difficulties in school (Pettit et al., 1997). High-quality after-school programs can help these younger children attain a higher level of achievement (Peterson, Ewigman, & Kivlahan, 1993; Zigler & Finn-Stevenson, 1993).

Children older than 9 may be cognitively able to manage self-care, but they, too, benefit from participation in well supervised after-school programs. Even part-time participation in supervised activities after school seems to make a difference in the adjustment of self-care children (Pettit et al., 1997). Good programs provide children with opportunities to play, do homework, and get help from adults (Posner & Vandell, 1994).

There are no achievement differences between girls who experience self-care and those who do not. In fact, girls who must engage in self-care because their mothers are working often have more confidence and higher educational goals than girls whose mothers are at home with them after school (Richards & Duckett, 1994; Vandell & Ramanan, 1992; Williams & Radin, 1993). In contrast, boys do better in school if they have a parent at home with them after school. Most developmentalists attribute this finding to the fact that boys tend to have more behavior and learning problems in school on average. Thus, they may have a greater need for the after-school tutoring and individual attention a parent can provide (Hoffman, 1989; Vandell & Ramanan, 1991).

Self-care has the most negative effects for children in low-income neighborhoods with high crime rates (Marshall et al., 1997). Self-care children in such areas may use after-school time to "hang out" with socially deviant peers who may be involved in criminal activity or who have negative attitudes about school. Predictably, then, the positive effects of organized after-school programs on academic achievement are greater for children in low-income neighborhoods (Posner & Vandell, 1994).

Taking everything into consideration, the most important factor in self-care seems to be parental monitoring. Many parents enlist the help of neighbors and relatives to keep an eye on their self-care children. Most require children to call them at work when they get home from school to talk about their school day and get instructions about homework and chores. For example, a working mother might tell a fifth-grader, "By the time I get home at 5:00, you should be finished with your math and spelling. Don't work on your history project until I get home and can help you with it. As soon as you finish your math and spelling, start the dishwasher." Research suggests that children whose periods of self-care are monitored in this way are less likely to experience the potential negative effects of self-care (Galambos & Maggs, 1991).

Poverty

Figure 9.5 shows the percentage of individuals under age 18 who were living in poverty each year from 1959 to 1998. As you can see, the child poverty rate in the United States declined from 22% in 1993 to 18.9% in 1998 (U.S. Bureau of the Census, 1999). However, the child poverty rate in the United States continues to be higher than in any other industrialized country in the world. By way of contrast, the poverty rate for children is roughly 9% in Canada and it is less than 2% in Sweden (McLoyd, 1998).

Child poverty is also unequally distributed across ages, races, and family structures. With respect to age, children under 6 are more likely to live in poverty than those who are older (McLoyd, 1998). In addition, the proportions of African American, Native American, and Hispanic American children living in poverty are more than twice the overall child poverty rate (U.S. Bureau of the Census, 1996). Likewise, children reared by single mothers are far more likely to be living in poverty. Roughly 60% of black and Hispanic children and 40% of white children reared by single mothers in the United States live in poverty (Zill & Nord, 1994). Many single mothers have jobs, but the jobs pay too little to lift the family out of poverty.

● ***The Effects of Poverty on Families and Children*** ●   Among many other things, poverty reduces options for parents. They may not be able to afford prenatal care, so their children are more likely to be born with some sort of disability. When a poor mother works, she is likely to have fewer choices of affordable child care. Her

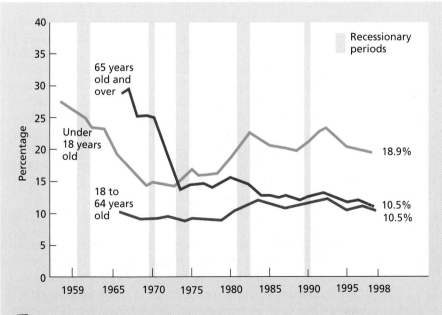

FIGURE 9.5

The graph shows the percentage of people in the United States living in poverty from 1959 to 1998, including children under 18. (*Source:* U.S. Bureau of the Census, 1999.)

children spend more time in poor-quality care and shift more from one care arrangement to another. Poor families also live in smaller and less-than-adequate housing, often in decaying neighborhoods with high rates of violence, and many such families move frequently, which means their children change schools often. The parents are less likely to feel that they have adequate social support, and the children often lack a stable group of playmates (Dodge, Pettit, & Bates, 1994). Parents in these circumstances also tend to be less involved in their children's schools (Griffith, 1998). Overall, the poor live in more chaotic environments, are more highly stressed, and have fewer psychological and social resources than those who are more economically secure (Brooks-Gunn, 1995; McLoyd & Wilson, 1991).

Parents living in poverty in the United States also tend to treat their children differently than do working-class or middle-class parents. They talk to them less, provide fewer age-appropriate toys, spend less time with them in intellectually stimulating activities, explain things less often and less fully, are less warm, and are stricter and more physical in their discipline (Dodge et al., 1994; Sampson & Laub, 1994). Some of this pattern of parental behavior is undoubtedly a response to the extraordinary stresses and special demands of living in poverty—a point buttressed by the repeated observation that parents who are poor but who nonetheless feel that they have enough social support are much less likely to be harshly punitive or unsupportive of their children (Hashima & Amato, 1994; Taylor & Roberts, 1995). To some extent, the stricter discipline and emphasis on obedience of poor parents may be thought of as a logical response to the realities of life in the neighborhoods in which they live.

Some of the differences in child-rearing patterns between poorer and better-off parents may also result from straightforward modeling of the way the parents themselves were reared; some may be a product of ignorance of children's needs. Poor parents with relatively more education, for example, typically talk to their children more, are more responsive, and provide more intellectual stimulation than do equally poor parents with lower levels of education (Kelley, Sanches-Hucles, & Walker, 1993). But whatever the cause, nearly all children reared in poverty experience physical conditions and interactions with their parents that differ from the experiences of better-off children.

Not surprisingly, such children turn out differently. Children from poor environments have higher rates of birth defects and early disabilities, they recover less well from early problems, and they are more often ill and undernourished throughout their childhood years (Klerman, 1991). Typically, they also have lower IQs and move through the sequences of cognitive development more slowly (Brooks-Gunn, 1995). They come to school less ready to learn to read, do consistently less well in school, and are less likely to go on to college (Huston, 1994). As adults, they are more likely to be poor, thus continuing the cycle through another generation. All of these effects are greater for children who have lived continuously in poverty than for children who have experienced some mix of poverty and better economic conditions (Bolger, Patterson, Thompson, & Kupersmidt, 1995; Duncan, Brooks-Gunn, & Klebanov, 1994).

W hen you look at scenes of urban poverty like this, you can see why some refer to such areas as "war zones." (*Photo:* Joseph Nettis, Tony Stone)

● ***The Special Case of Inner-City Poverty*** ● The negative effects of poverty are exacerbated for children growing up in poverty-ravaged urban neighborhoods. They are exposed to street gangs and street violence, to drug pushers, to overcrowded homes, and to abuse. Surveys indicate that nearly half of inner-city elementary and high school students have witnessed at least one violent crime in the past year (Osofsky, 1995). Guns are common in schools as well as on the streets. In one national survey, 22.1% of U.S. high school students reported that they had carried a weapon (gun, knife, or club) sometime in the previous 30 days; 7.9% had carried a gun (Kann et al., 1995).

A growing body of evidence shows that the effect of living in a concentrated pocket of poverty is to intensify all the ill effects of family poverty (Klebanov, Brooks-Gunn, Hofferth, & Duncan, 1995; Kupersmidt, Griesler, DeRosier, Patterson, & Davis, 1995). When the whole neighborhood is poor, parents have fewer other resources to rely on and children have more violent adult models and fewer supportive ones; rates of child abuse rise, along with rates of aggression and delinquency in children (Coulton, Corbin, Su, & Chow, 1995). When the whole neighborhood also lacks what sociologists call connectedness and stability—when the adults do not collaborate to monitor the children and do not provide practical or emotional support to one another—the effects are still worse (Wilson, 1995).

Many children living in such neighborhoods show all the symptoms of post-traumatic stress disorder, including sleep disturbances, irritability, inability to concentrate, and angry outbursts (Garbarino, Dubrow, Kostelny, & Pardo, 1992; Owen, 1998). Many experience flashbacks or intrusive memories of traumatic events. In addition, teachers in urban schools populated mostly by poor children have low expectations for them (McLoyd, 1998). This factor, combined with others—poorer physical health, inconsistent emotional and intellectual support at home, lack of access to learning resources such as books and computers—leads to high rates of school failure (McLoyd, 1998).

● *The Role of Stress and Protective Factors* ●   Of course, most poor children develop along the same lines as their more economically secure peers. To help sort out differences between poor children who do well and those who do not, developmentalists think of poverty in terms of accumulated stresses (McLoyd, 1998). For example, parental alcoholism added to family poverty results in a greater risk of negative developmental outcomes for a child (Malo & Tramblay, 1997). For a child growing up in poverty, perhaps urban poverty especially, the chances of experiencing such multiple stressors are very high indeed.

Studies of resilient and vulnerable children suggest that certain characteristics or circumstances may help protect some children from the detrimental effects of the stressors associated with poverty (Masten & Coatsworth, 1998; Miliotis, Sesma, & Masten, 1999; Schmitt, Sacco, Ramey, Ramey, & Chan, 1999). Among the key protective factors are the following:

- High IQ of the child
- Competent adult parenting, such as an authoritative style (good supervision or monitoring of the child seems especially important)
- Effective schools
- A secure initial attachment of the child to the parent
- A strong community helping network, including friends, family, or neighbors
- Stable parental employment

Thus, the effects of poverty depend on the combined effects of the number of stressors the child must cope with and the range of competencies or advantages the child brings to the situation. Poverty does not guarantee bad outcomes, but it stacks the deck against many children. Moreover, the same kinds of factors interact to affect development in other stressful contexts, as No Easy Answers illustrates.

Television

Another major influence on children, particularly in industrialized countries, is television. Ninety-eight percent of American homes have a TV set. Children between the ages of 2 and 11 spend an average of about 22 hours a week watching television; adolescents spend a bit less (APA, 1993; Fabrikant, 1996). This number has declined,

No Easy Answers

Children and War

Families who live in places like Israel or Bosnia and who want to raise nonviolent children face an especially difficult challenge. For many of them, war is a part of everyday life. Parents can turn off a violent TV program and prohibit their children from watching it again. But Israeli and Palestinian, or Serbian and Bosnian, parents can't simply turn off the long-standing conflicts between their peoples. Instead, they have to find some way of dealing with the realities of war while at the same time encouraging their children to develop peaceful means of solving their personal conflicts.

Like children in violent neighborhoods in the United States, children in countries at war are more aggressive as a group than those who live in more peaceful locations. However, the likelihood that an individual child will engage in violent behavior depends on the same protective and risk factors outlined in the discussion of the effects of poverty (Aptekar & Stocklin, 1997).

In addition, one important factor separates nations at war from neighborhoods with high levels of violence. When nations are at war, the people on each side usually have reasons for continuing to fight, which they believe are important enough to justify war. Research suggests that, if children understand the reasons and goals associated with war, they are less likely to become aggressive. For example, the children of parents who belong to the most extreme groups in Israel, the Hamas on the Palestinian side and the Zionists on the Israeli side, are less likely to be aggressive in their everyday interactions with other children than those of parents who are not deeply committed to either side. However, these children are also more likely than others to become personally involved in the war, even while they are still children (Garbarino, Kostelny, & Dubrow, 1991).

Taken together, research findings suggest that parents in war-torn countries can insulate their children to some degree from the potential developmental effects of their violent surroundings in the same way as parents who live in poor, crime-ridden neighborhoods—with nonabusive, authoritative parenting. Explaining the conflict to children from the differing perspectives of combatant groups may also help. In addition, institutions that care for children whose parents have been killed in a war can protect them against developing emotional problems by making sure each child has an opportunity to develop a close relationship with at least one adult caregiver (Wolff & Fasseha, 1999).

Finally, those of us who live in peaceful circumstances should keep in mind that war is much more than just the political and military events we hear about on the news. It is a context in which ordinary people like ourselves are trying to protect and bring up children.

(*Photo:* © Wesley Bocxe, Photo Researchers)

In the United States, children between 6 and 12 spend more time watching television than they do playing.
(*Photo:* Myrleen Cate, PhotoEdit)

dropping from more than 26 hours a week in 1984, but it is still the case that "by the time American children are 18 years old, they have spent more time watching television than in any other activity except sleep" (Huston, Wright, Rice, Kerkman, & St. Peters, 1990). In the United States, high levels of TV viewing are more common among African American children than among whites or Hispanic Americans, and more common in families in which the parents are less well educated (Anderson, Lorch, Field, Collins, & Nathan, 1986).

Viewing rates are not as high in most other countries, but more than 50% of households in Latin America and in most of Eastern and Western Europe own TV sets, so the influence of television is not limited exclusively to the United States (Comstock, 1991). Of course, television isn't all bad, so it's not surprising that it can have both positive and negative effects on children's development.

● *Positive Educational Effects* ●   Programs specifically designed to be educational or to teach children moral values do indeed have demonstrable positive effects. This is particularly clear among preschoolers, for whom most such programming is designed. For example, children who regularly watch *Sesame Street* develop larger vocabularies than do children who do not watch or who watch less often (Rice, Huston, Truglio, & Wright, 1990). Moreover, those who watch programs that emphasize sharing, kindness, and helpfulness, such as *Mr. Rogers' Neighborhood, Sesame Street,* or even *Lassie,* show more kind and helpful behavior (Murray, 1980).

In addition, children can have learning experiences through TV viewing—such as witnessing the migration of whales—that they could never have otherwise. As you learned in Chapter 8, the advances in information-processing skills that children undergo between 6 and 12 enable them to remember more from such experiences. Moreover, previously acquired knowledge is important to each new learning experience. Thus, television can be an important means by which school-aged children acquire the kinds of expertise that can make them more efficient learners. A child who has seen a TV program about whale migration is likely to get more out of a school science lesson about whales than one who has no relevant knowledge.

● *Negative Effects of Television on Cognitive Skills* ●   Despite the potential positive effects of television on cognitive development, research has demonstrated that heavy TV viewing is associated with lower scores on achievement tests, including measures of such basic skills as reading, arithmetic, and writing. This is particularly clear in the results of an enormous study in California that included more than 500,000 sixth- and twelfth-graders (California Achievement Program, 1980). The researchers found that the more hours of television the students watched, the lower their scores were on standardized tests. This relationship was stronger among children from well-educated families, so it was not due to greater amounts of TV viewing by children in families with lower levels of education. Thus, television can help teach children things they do not already know, but, overall, TV viewing time appears to have a negative effect on school performance.

● *Television and Aggression* ●   By far the largest body of research has focused on the potential impact of television on children's aggressiveness. The level of violence on U.S. television is remarkably high and has remained high over the past two decades, despite many congressional investigations and cries of alarm. In prime-time programs, a violent act occurs 5 or 6 times per hour; in Saturday morning cartoons, the rate is 20 to 25 times per hour. The highest rates of violence are generally found in programs broadcast between 6:00 and 9:00 in the morning and between 2:00 and 5:00 in the afternoon—both times when young children are likely to be watching (Donnerstein, Slaby, & Eron, 1994). Cable television, available in roughly 60% of homes in the United States, adds to this diet of violence. However, does viewing televised violence cause higher rates of aggression or violence in children? Three types of research evidence argue strongly for the existence of a causal link.

First, there have been a few genuinely experimental studies in which one group of children was exposed to a few episodes of moderately violent TV programs while others watched neutral programs. Collectively, these studies show a significant short-term increase in aggression among those who watched the violent programs (Paik & Comstock, 1994). In a recent example of this type of study, a psychologist found that early elementary–school-aged children who were randomly assigned to watch episodes of the popular (and very violent) children's program *The Mighty Morphin Power Rangers* showed seven times as many aggressive acts during subsequent free play with peers as did comparable children who had not just viewed the episodes (Boyatzis, Matillo, Nesbitt, & Cathey, 1995).

A second type of research involves comparing levels of aggression among children who vary in the amount of television they watch in their everyday lives. The

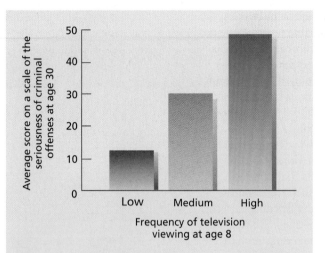

FIGURE 9.6

Eron finds a strong relationship between the amount of television a group of boys watched when they were 8 and the average severity of criminal offenses they had committed by the age of 30. However, this finding alone does not prove there is a causal link between television and later violence. (*Source:* Eron, 1987, Figure 3, p. 440.)

almost universal finding is that those who watch more television are more aggressive than their peers who watch less. Of course, this leaves researchers with a problem of interpretation. In particular, children who already behave aggressively may choose to watch more television and more violent television. And families who watch a great deal of television may also be more likely to use patterns of discipline that foster aggressiveness in the child.

One partial solution to this dilemma is to study children longitudinally. In one important 22-year-long longitudinal study, researchers found that the best predictor of young men's aggressiveness at age 19 was the violence of TV programs they watched when they were 8 (Eron, 1987). When investigators interviewed the men again when they were 30, they found that those who had had higher rates of TV viewing at age 8 were much more likely to have a record of serious criminal behavior in adulthood, a set of results graphed in Figure 9.6. The pattern is the same for women, by the way, but the level of criminal offenses is far lower, just as the level of aggression is lower among girls in childhood.

The results graphed in Figure 9.6 don't prove that the TV viewing contributed in any causal way to the later criminality, because those children who chose to watch a lot of violent television at age 8 may already have been the most violent children. Indeed, the investigators found just such a pattern: 8-year-old boys who watched a lot of violent television were already more aggressive with their peers, indicating that aggressive boys choose to watch more violent television. However, researchers have also found that, among the already aggressive 8-year-olds, those who watched the most television were more delinquent or aggressive as teenagers and as adults (Eron, 1987; Huesmann, Lagerspetz, & Eron, 1984).

Shorter-term longitudinal studies in Poland, Finland, Israel, and Australia show similar links between TV viewing and later high aggression among children (Eron et al., 1991). Collectively, the evidence suggests that the cause-and-effect link goes both ways: "Aggressive children prefer violent television, and the violence on television causes them to be more aggressive" (Eron, 1987, p. 438).

Another research strategy is to examine the conditions surrounding the emergence of a pattern of aggressive behavior in several different countries, to see whether it is possible to identify common antecedents. For example, one researcher looked at changes in homicide rates in the whole population in Canada, and among whites in the United States and South Africa, as a function of the time since television was introduced into each country (Centerwall, 1989, 1992). Television was introduced in both the United States and Canada in about 1950; in South Africa, television became widely available about 25 years later. In each of these three countries, the homicide rate began to rise rapidly 10–15 years after TV viewing became widespread. That is, as soon as the first generation of children who had grown up watching television became adults, homicide rates soared. Moreover, statistical analyses showed that the rise in homicides could not be attributed to urbanization, civil unrest, alcohol use, availability of firearms, or any other social condition that had changed over the same period of time.

Other evidence suggests that repeated viewing of TV violence leads to emotional desensitization regarding violence, to a belief that aggression is a good way to solve problems, and to a reduction in prosocial behavior (Donnerstein et al., 1994). Violent television is clearly not the only, or even the major, cause of aggressiveness among

Critical Thinking

Given all that you have read about television and children's development, how could you as a parent maximize the benefits and limit the negative effects of television? Would you be willing to give up having a television altogether if you thought that was necessary for your child's optimum development?

children or adults. Video games in which children commit violent acts vicariously, through characters whose weapons they choose and actions they direct, are also a concern. But television is a significant influence, both individually and at the broader cultural level.

For parents, the clear message from all the research on television is that it is an educational medium. Children learn from what they watch—vocabulary words, helpful behaviors, dietary preferences, and aggressive behaviors and attitudes. The overall content of television—violence and all—may indeed reflect general cultural values. But families can pick and choose among the various cultural messages by controlling what their children watch on television.

Before going on

- How does self-care affect girls' and boys' development?
- What are the risks associated with growing up in poverty? What types of variables protect children from the effects of poverty?
- How are televised violence and violent behavior related?

A Final Word

The quality of a child's relationships with parents and peers seems to rest, in part, on a basic cognitive understanding of perspective-taking. However, developmentalists have recently come to realize that a great deal of the experience on which the child's cognitive progress is based occurs in social interactions. They have also realized that social relationships are associated with a unique set of demands, both cognitive and emotional, that lead to advances in self-concept and self-esteem. The consequences of many middle childhood milestones appear to last for a lifetime, as the research on peer rejection suggests. Thus, it seems likely that middle childhood is the period during which patterns that were merely trends in early years become developmental trajectories.

Summary

Theories of Social and Personality Development

- Freud claimed that the libido is dormant between ages 6 and 12, a period he called the *latency stage.* Erikson theorized that 6- to 12-year-olds acquire a sense of

industry by achieving educational goals determined by their cultures.

- Between 6 and 12, children's understanding of others' stable, internal traits improves.

Dimensions of Moral Development

- Psychoanalytic theory emphasizes emotions in explaining moral development. Freud and Erikson emphasized guilt, shame, and pride. More recent examinations of moral emotions have focused on delay of gratification and empathy.

- Cognitive-developmental theory focuses on moral reasoning. The theories of Piaget and Kohlberg claim that moral reasoning develops in sequential stages that are correlated with Piaget's cognitive-developmental stages.

- Behavioral theories assert that moral development is a function of reward, punishment, and modeling. Under some conditions, both punishment and modeling may interfere with moral development.

Social Relationships

- Relationships with parents become less overtly affectionate, with fewer attachment behaviors, in middle childhood. The strength of the attachment, however, appears to persist.

- Friendships become stable in middle childhood. Children's selection of friends depends on variables such as trustworthiness as well as overt characteristics such as play preferences and gender.

- Gender segregation of peer groups is at its peak in middle childhood and appears in every culture. Individual friendships also become more common and more enduring; boys' and girls' friendships appear to differ in specific ways.

- Physical aggression declines during middle childhood, although verbal aggression increases. Boys show markedly higher levels of physical and direct verbal aggression, and higher rates of conduct disorders, than girls. Girls show higher rates of relational aggression.

- Rejected children are most strongly characterized by high levels of aggression or bullying and low levels of agree-ableness and helpfulness, but some aggressive children are very popular. Neglected children may suffer depression.

Personality and Self-Concept

- The Big Five personality traits are evident in 6- to 12-year-olds. Variations appear to be related to temperament in infancy and early childhood.

- Between 6 and 12, children construct a psychological self. As a result, their self-descriptions begin to include personality traits, such as intelligence and friendliness, along with physical characteristics.

- Self-esteem appears to be shaped by two factors: the degree of discrepancy a child experiences between goals and achievements, and the degree of perceived social support from peers and parents.

Influences beyond Family and School

- Self-care is associated with several negative effects. Girls, children who live in safe neighborhoods, and children whose parents closely monitor their activities after school are the least likely to be negatively affected by self-care.

- Children who live in poverty are markedly disadvantaged in many ways. They do worse in school and drop out of school at far higher rates. Protective factors, including a secure attachment, higher IQ, authoritative parenting, and effective schools, can counterbalance poverty effects for some children.

- The average American child watches over 3 hours of television per day. Preschoolers can learn vocabulary, prosocial behavior, and other social skills. The more television school children watch, the lower their grades are. Experts agree that watching violence on television increases the level of personal aggression or violence shown by a child.

Key Terms

the Big Five (p. 262)	latency stage (p. 248)	retaliatory aggression (p. 259)
conscience (p. 250)	moral realism stage (p. 251)	self-care children (p. 267)
ego ideal (p. 250)	moral relativism stage (p. 251)	self-esteem (p. 265)
industry versus inferiority stage (p. 248)	psychological self (p. 263)	self-regulation (p. 254)
	relational aggression (p. 259)	social status (p. 260)

CHAPTER

10

Physical and Cognitive Development in Adolescence

Will and Deni McIntyre, Photo Researchers

When people think about adolescence, puberty is usually the first developmental milestone that comes to mind. However, the physical changes of puberty, as dramatic as they are, are only one component of this important period of transition from childhood to adulthood. For example, if you ask an 8-year-old what she wants to be when she grows up, she is likely to give you an answer like "a firefighter" or "a veterinarian." Ask a 15-year-old the same question, and you are likely to hear something like this: "Well, I'm thinking about several things. I know I want to go to college, but I don't know where, and I'm not sure what I want to study." Such differences reflect age-related changes in the overall quality of thought.

The second idea most people have about adolescence is that it is filled with problems. Mention teenagers and many people automatically think of shouting matches between parents and their teenaged children, or of high-risk behaviors such as drug use and unprotected sex. However, such stereotypical images stem from people's tendency to focus on the negative aspects of this period rather than on the enormous strides adolescents take toward maturity.

In this chapter, you will read about these strides as well as about the challenges of adolescence. For example, along with physical maturity come new health risks. You will also learn about advances in the cognitive domain that, by late adolescence, enable teenagers to function almost as well as adults. School experiences are also critical to adolescent development. As you read, keep the following questions in mind:

- How do the reproductive system, the brain, and other body systems change during adolescence?

- What are the major health concerns associated with adolescence?

- What are the characteristics of adolescents who develop substance abuse or mental health problems?

- What kind of thinking becomes possible in Piaget's formal operational stage, and how do adolescents' memory skills differ from those of younger children?

- How do schooling and employment influence adolescent development?

Physical Changes

When we think of the physical changes of adolescence, we usually give the greatest amount of attention to the reproductive system. Reproductive changes are important, as the text will point out. But, momentous changes occur in other systems, and we will discuss those, as well.

The Endocrine and Reproductive Systems

The various **endocrine glands** in the body secrete hormones that govern pubertal growth and physical changes in several ways, as summarized in Table 10.1. The **pituitary gland** triggers the release of hormones from other glands; thus, it is sometimes called the *master gland*. For example, the thyroid gland secretes thyroxine only when it receives a signal in the form of a specific thyroid-stimulating hormone secreted by the pituitary.

The rate of growth is governed largely by thyroid hormone and pituitary growth hormone. Thyroid hormone is secreted in high quantities for the first 2 years of life, after which levels fall and remain steady until adolescence (Tanner, 1990). Secretions from the testes, ovaries, and adrenal gland are also at very low levels in the early years of childhood. This changes at age 7 or 8, when adrenal androgen begins to be secreted—the first signal of the changes of puberty (Shonkoff, 1984).

After the burst of androgen, there is a complex sequence of hormone changes that lasts for several years. The pituitary gland begins secreting increased levels of **gonadotrophic hormones** (two hormones in males, three in females), which are responsible for the development of the sex organs. These hormones also stimulate the testes and ovaries to secrete more of the so-called *sex hormones*—testosterone in boys and a form of estrogen called *estradiol* in girls. Hormonal changes are greater in males than in females. Over the course of puberty, testosterone levels increase 18-fold in boys, while levels of estradiol increase only 8-fold in girls (Biro, Lucky, Huster, & Morrison, 1995; Nottelmann et al., 1987).

The pituitary also secretes two other hormones, *thyroid stimulating hormone* and *general growth hormone;* these, along with adrenal androgen, interact with the specific sex hormones and affect growth. Adrenal androgen, which is chemically very similar to testosterone, plays a particularly important role for girls, triggering the growth spurt and affecting development of pubic hair. For boys, adrenal androgen is less significant, presumably because boys already have so much male hormone in the form of testosterone in their bloodstreams. These hormonal changes trigger two sets

TABLE 10.1   Major Hormones That Contribute to Physical Growth and Development

Gland	Hormone(s)	Aspects of Growth Influenced
Thyroid gland	Thyroxine	Normal brain development and overall rate of growth
Adrenal gland	Adrenal androgen	Some changes at puberty, particularly the development of secondary sex characteristics in girls
Testes (boys)	Testosterone	Crucial in the formation of male genitals prenatally; also triggers the sequence of changes in primary and secondary sex characteristics at puberty in the male
Ovaries (girls)	Estrogen (estradiol)	Development of the menstrual cycle and breasts in girls; has less to do with other secondary sex characteristics than testosterone does for boys
Pituitary gland	General growth hormone, thyroid stimulating hormone, and other activating hormones	Rate of physical maturation; signals other glands to secrete

endocrine glands glands that secrete hormones governing growth and other aspects of physical development

pituitary gland gland that triggers other glands to release hormones

gonadotrophic hormones hormones responsible for the development of the sex organs

of body changes: development of the sex organs, and a much broader set of changes in the brain, bones, muscles, and other body organs.

The most obvious changes of puberty are those associated with sexual maturity. Changes in *primary sex characteristics* include growth of the testes and penis in the male and of the ovaries, uterus, and vagina in the female. Changes in *secondary sex characteristics* include breast development in girls, changing voice pitch and beard growth in boys, and the growth of body hair in both sexes. These physical developments occur in a defined sequence that is customarily divided into five stages, following a system originally suggested by J. M. Tanner (Tanner, 1990). Stage 1 is the preadolescent stage, stage 2 includes the first signs of pubertal change, stages 3 and 4 are the intermediate steps, and stage 5 encompasses the final development of adult characteristics.

● *Sexual Development in Girls* ● Studies of preteens and teens in both Europe and North America show that the various sequential changes are interlocked in a particular pattern in girls, which is shown schematically in the graph on the right in Figure 10.1 (Malina, 1990). The first steps are the early changes in breasts and pubic hair, closely followed by the peak of the growth spurt and by the beginnings of stages 4 and 5, the development of breasts and pubic hair. First menstruation, an event called **menarche** (pronounced men-ARE-kee), typically occurs 2 years after the beginning of other visible changes and is succeeded only by the final stages of breast and pubic hair development. Among girls in industrialized countries today, menarche occurs, on average, between $12\frac{1}{2}$ and $13\frac{1}{2}$; 95% of all girls experience this event between the ages of 11 and 15 (Malina, 1990).

Interestingly, the timing of menarche changed rather dramatically between the mid-19th and the mid-20th centuries. In 1840, the average age of menarche in Western industrialized countries was roughly 17; the average dropped steadily from that time until the 1950s at a rate of about 4 months per decade among European populations, an example of what psychologists call a **secular trend** (Roche, 1979). The change was most likely caused by significant changes in lifestyle and diet, particularly increases in protein and fat intake, along with reductions in physical exercise that resulted in an increase in the proportion of body fat in females. In developing countries, where diets are leaner or even inadequate and children engage in physical labor, menarche still tends to happen in the middle teens rather than in the early teens.

It is possible to become pregnant shortly after menarche, but irregular menstrual cycles are the norm for some time. In as many as three-quarters of the cycles in the first year and half the cycles in the second and third years after menarche, the girl's body produces no ovum (Vihko & Apter, 1980). Full adult fertility thus develops over a period of years. Such irregularity no doubt contributes to the widespread (but false) assumption among younger teenaged girls that they cannot get pregnant.

● *Sexual Development in Boys* ● In boys, as in girls, the peak of the growth spurt typically comes fairly late in the sequence of physical deveopment, as you can see in the graph on the left in Figure 10.1. Studies suggest that, on average, a boy completes stages 2, 3, and 4 of genital development and stages 2 and 3 of pubic hair development before reaching the peak of the growth spurt (Malina, 1990). The development of a beard and the lowering of the voice occur near the end of the sequence. Precisely when in this sequence the boy begins to produce viable sperm is very difficult to determine, although current evidence places this event some time between ages 12 and 14, usually before the boy has reached the peak of the growth spurt (Brooks-Gunn & Reiter, 1990).

Although the order of physical developments in adolescence seems to be highly consistent, there is quite a lot of individual variability. Figure 10.1 depicts the normative, or average, pattern, but individual teenagers often deviate from the norm. For instance, a girl might move through several stages of pubic hair development before

menarche the beginning of menstrual cycles

secular trend the decline in the average age of menarche, along with changes such as an increase in average height for both children and adults, that happened between the mid-18th and mid-19th centuries in Western countries and occurs in developing nations when nutrition and health improve

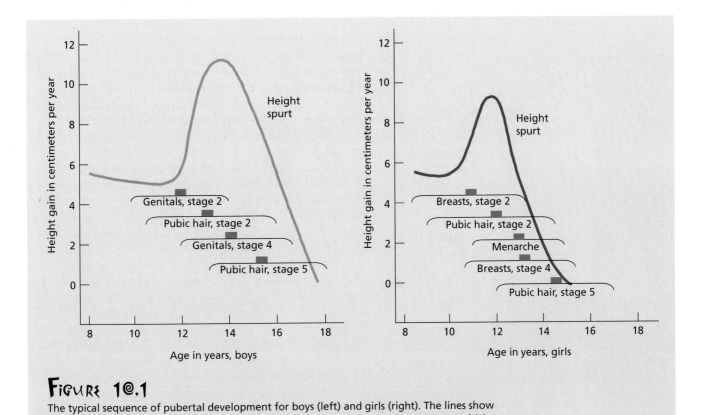

Figure 10.1

The typical sequence of pubertal development for boys (left) and girls (right). The lines show the gains in height at various ages. The colored squares represent the average age at which each physical change occurs; braces show the range of normal times. Note the wide range of normality for all of these changes. Also, note how late in the sequence menarche occurs for girls, and that girls are about 2 years ahead of boys. (Sources: Biro et al., 1995; Chumlea, 1982; Garn, 1980; Malina, 1990; Tanner, 1978.)

experiencing the first clear breast changes, or experience menarche much earlier in the sequence than normal. It is important to keep this variation in mind if you are trying to make a prediction about an individual teenager.

Timing of Puberty

In any random sample of 12- and 13-year-olds, you will find some who are already at stage 5, and others still at stage 1 in the steps of sexual maturation. The accumulated research suggests that each teenager has an internal model, or mental image, of "normal" or "right" timing for puberty (Faust, 1983; Lerner, 1987; Petersen, 1987). Each girl has an internal model about the "right age" to develop breasts or begin menstruation; each boy has an internal model about when it is normal to begin to grow a beard or to reach adult size.

Discrepancies between an adolescent's expectation and what actually happens determine the psychological effect of puberty. Those whose development occurs outside the desired or expected range are likely to think less well of themselves, to be less happy with their bodies and with the process of puberty. They may also display other signs of psychological distress.

In American culture today, most young people seem to share the expectation that pubertal changes will happen sometime between ages 12 and 14. Figure 10.2 (page 282) graphically illustrates the predictions of one model of the effects of pubertal

Girls who develop early report much less positive adolescent experiences and more depression than girls who develop "on time" or later. (*Photo:* David Young-Wolff, PhotoEdit)

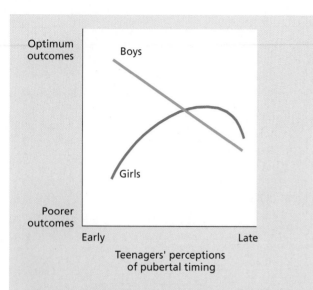

FIGURE 10.2

According to this model of the effects of early and late puberty, optimum outcomes (such as feeling attractive, having a positive body image, performing well in school, and being popular) are more likely for adolescents who perceive their own pubertal changes to be well timed. The best position for girls is to be "on time," whereas for boys the best position is to be "early." For both sexes, however, it is the *perception* of earliness or lateness, and not the actual timing, that is thought to be critical. (*Source:* Adapted from Tobin-Richards, Boxer, & Petersen, 1983, p. 137.)

timing. Note that girls acquire a culturally undesirable body type, an *endomorphic,* or somewhat flabby kind of body, as a result of puberty. Thus, early-developing girls should have more adjustment problems than average- or late-developing girls. Similarly, puberty provides most boys with a culturally admired body type, *mesomorphic,* or lean and muscular body. Thus, early-developing boys should display better psychological and social adjustment than average- or late-developing boys.

Research in the United States generally confirms these predictions. Girls who are early developers (who experience major body changes before age 11 or 12) show consistently more negative body images, such as thinking of themselves as too fat. Such girls are also more likely to get into trouble in school and at home, more likely to get involved with misbehaving peer groups, more likely to engage in delinquent behavior, more likely to be depressed, and more likely to begin smoking in adolescence than are girls who are average or late developers (Alsaker, 1995; Caspi, Lynam, Moffitt, & Silva, 1993; Dick, Rose, Viken, & Kaprio, 2000; Rierdan & Koff, 1993; Silbereisen & Kracke, 1993). Among boys, the earlier their development, the more positive their body image, the better they do in school, the less trouble they get into, and the more friends they have (Duke et al., 1982).

In nearly all studies of adolescent development, earliness or lateness has been defined in terms of the actual physical changes. The evidence is even clearer when researchers have instead asked teenagers about their internal model of the timing of those changes. The link between the internal model and the outcome is especially vivid in a study of ballet dancers by Jeanne Brooks-Gunn (Brooks-Gunn, 1987; Brooks-Gunn & Warren, 1985). She studied 14- to 18-year-old girls, some of whom were serious ballet dancers studying at a national ballet company school. In this group, a very lean, almost prepubescent body is highly desirable. Brooks-Gunn therefore expected that among dancers, those whose pubertal development was very late would actually have a better image of themselves than would those who were on time. And that is exactly what she found. Among the nondancers, menarche at the biologically average time was associated with a better body image than was late menarche, but exactly the reverse was true for the dancers. Thus, as predicted, it is the discrepancy between a teenager's internal model of puberty and the experiential reality that predicts the effects of pubertal timing.

Critical Thinking

Do you remember whether you went through puberty very early, early, "on time," or late? Do you think that perception had any effect on your overall experience of adolescence?

Other Body Systems

Changes in other body systems allow adolescents to acquire new cognitive and motor skills.

● **The Brain** ●   There are two major brain growth spurts in the teenaged years. The first occurs between 13 and 15 (Spreen, Risser, & Edgell, 1995). During this spurt, the cerebral cortex becomes thicker, and the neuronal pathways become more efficient. In addition, more energy is produced and consumed by the brain during this spurt than in the years that precede and follow it (Fischer & Rose, 1994). For the most part, these growth and energy spurts take place in parts of the brain that control spatial perception and motor functions. Consequently, by the mid-teens, adolescents' abilities in these areas far exceed those of school-aged children.

Neuropsychologists Kurt Fischer and Samuel Rose believe that a qualitatively different neural network emerges during the brain growth spurt that occurs between ages 13 and 15, which enables teens to think abstractly and to reflect on their cognitive processes (Fischer & Rose, 1994). As evidence, these researchers cite numerous neurological and psychological studies revealing that major changes in brain organization show up between ages 13 and 15 and that qualitative shifts in cognitive functioning appear after age 15. They claim that the consistency of these research findings is too compelling to ignore.

The second brain growth spurt begins around age 17 and continues into early adulthood (Van der Molen & Molenaar, 1994). This time, the frontal lobes of the cerebral cortex are the focus of development (Davies & Rose, 1999). You may recall that this area of the brain controls logic and planning. Thus, it is not surprising that older teens differ from younger teens in terms of how they deal with problems that require these cognitive functions.

● **The Skeletal System** ●   An adolescent may grow 3–6 inches a year for several years. After the growth spurt, teenagers add height and weight slowly until they reach their adult size. Girls attain most of their height by age 16, while boys continue to grow until they are 18–20 years old (Tanner, 1990).

The shape and proportions of the adolescent's body also go through a series of changes. During the growth spurt, the normal cephalocaudal and proximodistal patterns are reversed. Thus, a teenager's hands and feet are the first body parts to grow to full adult size, followed by the arms and legs; the trunk is usually the slowest part to grow. In fact, a good signal for a parent that a child is entering puberty is a rapid increase in the child's shoe size. Because of this asymmetry in the body parts, adolescents are often stereotyped as awkward or uncoordinated. However, adolescents may look awkward, but they are better coordinated than school-aged children (Malina, 1990).

The skeletal system goes through other changes as it increases in size. For example, during the elementary-school years, the size and shape of a child's jaw change when the permanent teeth come in. In adolescence, both jaws grow forward and the forehead becomes more prominent. This set of changes often gives teenagers' faces (especially boys') an angular, bony appearance.

Joint development enables adolescents to achieve levels of coordination that are close to those of adults. As they do at younger ages, boys continue to lag behind girls. You may remember from earlier chapters that boys' fine-motor skills are poorer than girls' because their wrists develop more slowly. In early adolescence, this sex difference is very large; girls achieve complete development of the wrist by their mid-teens (Tanner, 1990). A similar pattern of sex differences is evident in other joints as well, enabling early-adolescent girls to outperform boys of the same age on a variety of athletic skills that require coordination, such as pitching a softball. However, by the late teens, at age 17 or 18, boys finally catch up with girls in joint development and, on average, gain superiority over them in coordinated movement.

Adolescent girls reach adult height sooner than boys because their bones grow and their joints develop more rapidly. (*Photo*: Elena Rooraid, PhotoEdit)

● **The Muscular System** ●   Muscle fibers also go through a growth spurt at adolescence, becoming thicker and denser, and adolescents become quite a lot stronger in just a few years. Both boys and girls show this increase in strength, but it is much greater in boys. For example, in a cross-sectional study in Canada involving 2,673 children and teenagers, researchers measured strength by having each child hang from a bar, with eyes level with the bar, for as long as possible (Smoll & Schutz, 1990). Between age 9 and age 17, boys increased the average amount of time they could hang by 160%, while girls increased their time by only 37%. By age 17, the boys in this study were three times as strong as the girls. This substantial difference in strength reflects the underlying sex difference in muscle tissue that is accentuated at adolescence: Among adult men, about 40% of total body mass is muscle, compared to only about 24% in adult women.

This sex difference in muscle mass (and accompanying strength) seems to be largely a result of hormone differences. But sex differences in exercise patterns or activities may also be involved. For example, the sex difference in leg strength is much less than in arm strength. Some developmentalists hypothesize that the sex differences result from similar patterns of use of the legs in the sexes (walking, bicycling, and so on) and differential patterns of arm use. Boys are more likely than girls to use their arm muscles in various sports (Tanner, Hughes, & Whitehouse, 1981). Still, there does seem to be a basic hormonal difference as well, because researchers know that even very athletic girls and women are not as strong as very athletic boys and men.

Another major component of the body is fat, most of which is stored immediately under the skin. From birth, girls have slightly more fat tissue than boys do, and this discrepancy becomes gradually more marked during childhood and adolescence. Between ages 13 and 17, the percentage of body weight made up of fat rises from 21% to 24% among girls but drops from 16.1% to 14.0% among boys (Smoll & Schutz, 1990). So, during and after puberty, the proportion of fat rises among girls and declines among boys, while the proportion of weight that is muscle rises in boys and declines in girls.

● **The Heart and Lungs** ● During the teenaged years, the heart and lungs increase considerably in size, and the heart rate drops. Both of these changes are more marked in boys than in girls—another of the factors that make boys' capacity for sustained physical effort greater than that of girls. Before about age 12, boys and girls have similar endurance limits, although even at these earlier ages, when there is a difference, it is usually boys who have greater endurance, because of their lower levels of body fat. After puberty, boys have a clear advantage in endurance as well as in size, strength, and speed (Smoll & Schutz, 1990).

Before going on

● How do patterns of hormone function change at adolescence, and what are the pubertal milestones for girls and boys?

● What are the consequences of early, "on-time," and late puberty for boys and girls?

● How are the brain and other body systems of adolescents different from those of younger children?

Adolescent Health

F or most individuals, adolescence is one of the healthiest periods of life. However, as adolescents gain independence, they encounter numerous health risks.

Health Care Issues

Even though they get sick less often than children and infants, teenagers are frequent visitors to health care facilities. Many adolescents believe themselves to be less healthy than they actually are and may develop physical symptoms in response to perceived parental or peer rejection (Wickrama, Conger, Lorenz, & Elder, 1998). In contrast, teens who perceive their parents to be emotionally supportive think of themselves as healthier and experience fewer physical symptoms than peers whose parents seem to be less supportive (Wickrama, Lorenz, & Conger, 1997).

Teenagers also appear to have what many developmentalists describe as a heightened level of *sensation-seeking,* or a desire to experience increased levels of arousal such as those that accompany fast driving or the "highs" that are associated with drugs. Sensation-seeking leads to recklessness, which, in turn, leads to markedly increased rates of accidents and injuries in this age range. For example, adolescents drive faster and use seat belts less often than adults do (Centers for Disease Control [CDC], 2000). To reduce the number of accidents among teenaged drivers, many states in the United States have enacted laws establishing "graduated" driver's licenses (Cobb, 2000). Sixteen-year-olds can drive in most such states, but they must remain accident- and ticket-free for a certain period of time before they can have privileges such as driving at night.

Risky behaviors may be more common in adolescence than other periods because they help teenagers gain peer acceptance and establish autonomy with respect to parents and other authority figures (Jessor, 1992). In fact, researchers have found that teens who show high rates of reckless behaviors are likely to have been unsuccessful in school or to have experienced early rejection by peers, neglect at home, or some combination of these problems (Robins & McEvoy, 1990). In addition, adolescents who are not involved in extracurricular activities at school or to whom popularity is important are more likely than their peers who value popularity less to engage in risky behavior (Carpenter, 2001; Stein, Roeser, & Markus, 1998).

The messages conveyed in the popular media about sex, violence, and drug and alcohol use may influence teens' risky behavior. In the United States, 13- to 17-year-olds spend more time watching television, listening to music, and playing video games than they do in school (Mediascope Press, 1999a). Surprisingly, though, most teenagers report that their parents have few, if any, rules regarding media use (Mediascope Press, 2000).

Prime-time television programs contain about five sexual incidents per hour, and only 4% of these impart information about the potential consequences of sex (Henry J. Kaiser Family Foundation, 1999). Drugs and alcohol are even more prevalent than sex in the popular media. One survey found that 98% of 200 movies surveyed portrayed characters using some kind of substance, and, in most cases, characters used more than one substance (Mediascope Press, 1999c). Another group of researchers found that 51% of films they surveyed depicted teenagers smoking (Mediascope Press, 1999c). In another 46%, teenagers were shown consuming alcohol, and 3% contained images of teens using illegal drugs. Again, references to the consequences of drug or alcohol use were rare; they occurred in only 13% of films surveyed.

S ensation-seeking and risky behaviors may help teens achieve peer acceptance. Consequently, these behaviors are more likely to happen when adolescents are with peers than when they are alone or with family. (*Photo:* David Young-Wolff, PhotoEdit)

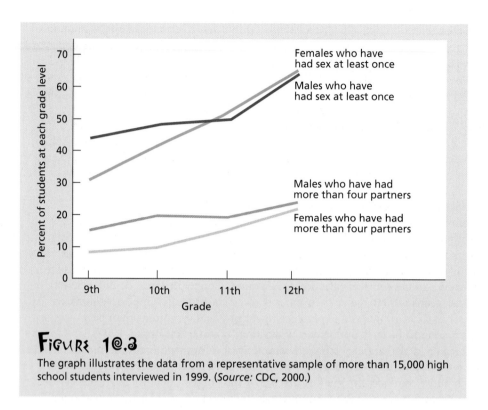

FIGURE 10.3

The graph illustrates the data from a representative sample of more than 15,000 high school students interviewed in 1999. (*Source:* CDC, 2000.)

Sexual Behavior

Figure 10.3 graphs findings from a 1999 national survey of high school students in the United States (CDC, 2000). As you can see, boys were found to be more sexually active than girls. Furthermore, the proportion of sexually experienced teens increased across grades 9 to 12.

Consistent with earlier surveys, sexual experience was found to vary across racial and ethnic groups. About 70% of African American high school students reported having had sexual intercourse at least once in their lives. The rates among Hispanic American and white students were 54% and 45%, respectively. African American students were also more likely than Hispanic American and white teens to have had their first sexual encounter before age 13 (20.5% versus 9.2% and 5.5%, respectively).

There were also age and ethnic differences among students who were currently sexually active—defined as having had sex at least once within 3 months of responding to the survey. For example, roughly 40% of 11th-grade females reported recent sexual activity, while only 24% of 9th-grade females did so. Researchers also found ethnic differences: 53% of African American students reported being currently sexually active, compared to 33% of Hispanic Americans and 36% of whites.

Among students who reported recent sexual activity, only 58% said they had used a condom in their most recent sexual encounter. African Americans were more likely than students in other groups to report having used condoms (70% versus 55% of both Hispanic Americans and whites). Birth control pills were used even less frequently. Only 20% of sexually active females reported being on the pill. In addition, pill usage was far more common among white high school girls (21%) than among their African American or Hispanic American peers (8% in both groups).

Critical Thinking

List all the reasons you can think of to explain why teenagers often do not use contraceptives.

Although sexual activity among boys is somewhat correlated with the amount of testosterone in the blood, social factors are much better predictors than hormones of teenagers' sexual activity (Halpern, Udry, Campbell, & Suchindran, 1993; Udry & Campbell, 1994). In fact, cross-cultural evidence suggests that the same factors are related to sexual behavior even in societies with very low rates of teenaged sexual activity, such as Taiwan (Wang & Chou, 1999). Those who begin sexual activity early are more likely to live in poor neighborhoods in which young people are not well-monitored by adults. They come from poorer families or from families in which sexual activity is condoned and dating rules are lax. They are more likely to use alcohol. Many were abused and/or neglected in early childhood (Herrenkohl, Herrenkohl, Egolf, & Russo, 1998).

Among girls, those who are sexually active are also more likely to have experienced early menarche, to have low interest in school, to have had their first date at a relatively early age, and to have a history of sexual abuse (Billy, Brewster, & Grady, 1994; Hovell et al., 1994; Miller et al., 1998; Small & Luster, 1994). In general, these same factors predict sexual activity among whites, African Americans, and Hispanic Americans. And in every group, the greater the number of risk factors present in the life of an individual teenager, the greater the likelihood that he or she will be sexually active.

Adolescents' moral beliefs and the activites in which they participate also predict their sexual activity. For example, teenagers who believe that premarital sex is morally wrong and who attend religious services frequently are less likely than their peers to become sexually active before reaching adulthood (Miller et al., 1998). Rates of sexual activity are also lower among teens who are involved in sports or other after-school pursuits than they are among their peers who do not participate in such activities (Savage & Holcomb, 1999). Moreover, alcohol use is associated with 25–30% of adolescent sexual encounters; thus, teens who do not use alcohol are less likely to be sexually active than are their peers who drink (CDC, 2000).

Despite their high levels of sexual activity, teenagers know remarkably little about physiology and reproduction. At best, only about half of teenagers can identify the time of greatest fertility in the menstrual cycle (Freeman & Rickels, 1993). Many teens are also woefully ignorant of sexually transmitted diseases and their potential consequences, although about 90% of high school students report having learned about sexually transmitted diseases in school (CDC, 2000; Rosenthal, Lewis, Succop, & Burklow, 1997; Sharma & Sharma, 1997).

Even when they are knowledgeable about STDs, many teens lack the assertiveness necessary to resist sexual pressure from a romantic partner or to discuss condom use. For example, although infection rates have declined in recent years, *chlamydia*, a disease that is preventable through condom use, continues to be the most commonly reported infectious disease in the United States (CDC, 2000). Infection rates are highest among 15- to 19-year-old girls, who account for almost half of all new chlamydia cases each year (CDC, 2000). Public health experts estimate that 75% of females and 50% of males who suffer from chlamydia are symptomless (CDC, 2000). Thus, routine chlamydia screening of asymptomatic, sexually active teens and young adults is critical to reducing the prevalence of this disease. Left untreated, chlamydia can lead to infertility in females and a number of genital and urinary tract disorders in males.

In addition to routine screening, many developmentalists and public health advocates say that more effective sex education programs are needed. Most suggest that programs that include training in social and decision-making skills, as well as information about STDs and pregnancy, are more likely than information-only approaches to reduce the prevalence of sexual activity and to increase the number of teens who protect themselves against disease and pregnancy when they do have sex. However, no clear consensus about the effectiveness of various approaches to sex education has emerged (Hovell et al., 1998).

Many adults object to sex education because they believe it will cause teenagers who are not sexually active to become so. Research suggests that such fears are

Teens who date in early adolescence, as these middle-schoolers may be doing, are more likely to become sexually active while still in school than peers who begin dating later. (*Photo:* David Young-Wolff, PhotoEdit)

unfounded (Berne & Huberman, 1996). There are also debates over the degree to which sex education programs should emphasize abstaining from sex or using contraceptives. Studies examining several types of programs indicate that abstinence-based sex education is most likely to result in delay of first sexual intercourse when it is initiated with younger students—seventh- or eighth-graders—who are not yet sexually active (Olsen, Weed, Nielsen, & Jensen, 1992). Moreover, students who participate in multi-session programs are more likely to remain abstinent than those who are exposed to single-session presentations about abstinence (Postrado & Nicholson, 1992).

Sex education advocates suggest that abstinence and contraceptive education should not be thought of in either/or terms. They point to research that suggests that programs that both encourage abstinence *and* provide basic information about reproduction and contraception appear to influence teen participants both to delay sexual intercourse and to use contraception when they do decide to become sexually active (St. Pierre, Mark, Kaltreider, & Aiken, 1995). Indeed, finding a way to encourage teens to avoid becoming sexually active too early may be critical to influencing contraceptive use. The older teenagers are when they become sexually active, the more likely it is that they will be cognitively capable of weighing the various options and consequences associated with intercourse.

Teenaged Pregnancy

The rate of teenaged pregnancy is higher in the United States than in any other Western industrialized country (Ambuel, 1995; Singh & Darroch, 2000). For example, the overall annual rate is about 50 pregnancies per 1,000 teens in the United States; it is only 4 pregnancies per 1,000 teens in Japan. Ethnic differences exist within the United States as well (U.S. Bureau of the Census, 1998). Births to teenagers represent about a quarter of all births to African American women. Among whites, only 11% of births involve teenaged mothers; among Hispanic women, about 17% of all births are to teenagers.

However, teen pregnancy statistics can be confusing, because they usually refer to all pregnancies among women under age 20. To clarify the extent of the teen pregnancy problem, it is useful to break down the statistics by adolescent subgroups. For example, in the United States, the annual pregnancy rate is 2–3 pregnancies per 1,000 for girls younger than 15; 30 per 1,000 among girls aged 15 to 17; and 170 per 1,000 among girls between 17 and 19 (Federal Interagency Forum on Child and Family Statistics [FIFCFS], 2000; Gullotta, Adams, & Montemayor, 1993). Looking at the numbers this way shows that teen pregnancy is far more frequent among older adolescents and, in fact, is most likely to happen after a girl leaves high school.

However, the age at which an adolescent becomes a parent is only one aspect of the teen pregnancy issue. Birth rates among teenagers have actually dropped in the entire U.S. population since the 1960s, including among 15- to 19-year-olds. What has increased is the rate of births to unmarried teens. During the 1960s, more than 80% of teens who gave birth were married. By contrast, in the late 1990s, only 20% of teenaged mothers were married (Singh & Darroch, 2000).

The proportion of teenaged mothers who eventually marry the baby's father has also declined in recent years, and, again, there are ethnic differences. White teenaged parents are more likely to marry than are African American ones (43% compared to less than 10%) (Gullotta, Adams, & Montemayor, 1993). Moreover, across ethnic groups, only 17% of teen mothers maintain romantic relationships with their babies' fathers beyond the first few months after birth (Gee & Rhodes, 1999).

Whether a girl becomes pregnant during her teenaged years depends on many of the same factors that predict sexual activity in general. The younger a girl is when she becomes sexually active, the more likely she is to become pregnant. Among teenaged girls from poor families, from single-parent families, or from families with relatively uneducated parents, pregnancy rates are higher. Likewise, girls whose mothers

CAREGIVING
The Real World

Crisis Intervention for the Pregnant Teen

A crisis intervention model proposed more than three decades ago continues to be helpful to mental health professionals, teachers, and parents in understanding and dealing with teens in crisis (Caplan, 1964). The first stage in a crisis, called the *initial phase,* is characterized by anxiety and confusion. In fact, any teenager, male or female, who suddenly begins exhibiting such behavior should be suspected of being in some sort of crisis. Thus, the first step in crisis intervention in many teenaged pregnancies often happens when a significant adult in the teenager's life recognizes a change in behavior and questions the girl about it.

Mental health professionals recommend gentle confrontation during this phase (Blau, 1996). For example, a pregnant teenager might be reminded that it isn't possible to keep a pregnancy secret for very long. Pregnant adolescents may be more willing to accept help during the initial phrase than in later stages, but this is clearly not the time to bombard them with questions such as "How are you going to support a baby?

What about school? Are you going to go to college?"

The second stage of a crisis, the *escalation phase,* happens as the teenager begins to try to confront the crisis. In many cases, adolescents in this phase become convinced that they are unable to cope with the situation and may feel too overwhelmed to maintain daily functions such as getting to school and keeping track of homework. Teens in this phase may be responsive to helpers who simplify their decision-making by directly telling them what to do. For example, a pregnant teen's mother may make a doctor's appointment for her and see that she keeps it instead of nagging her to do it herself.

The third stage of a crisis is called the *redefinition phase.* Those who are providing emotional support for the pregnant teen in this stage can help by guiding her through the process of breaking the problem down into small pieces. For the teen who wants to raise her baby, counselors or parents can divide the decisions to be made into financial and educational categories. They can help the teen identify short-term and long-term goals in each category and assist her in finding the answers to important questions. For

example, in the financial category, the girl must find out how much financial support she can expect to receive from the baby's father. With respect to continuing her education, she must determine the available day-care options.

Teens who leave the redefinition phase with a realistic plan of action are typically no longer in a crisis mode. However, teens who fail to redefine their problem appropriately enter the fourth crisis stage, the *dysfunctional phase.* In this stage, either the pregnant adolescent gives up hope, believing there is no solution for her dilemma, or she goes into denial. Teens who see their situation as hopeless may resort to suicide or self-destructive behaviors such as intentionally failing in school. Those in denial may delay seeking medical attention until very late in their pregnancies (Gullotta, Adams, & Montemayor, 1993).

The goal of crisis intervention is to prevent either of the stage-four outcomes. Yet, the entire process probably depends on whether a pregnant teen has a sensitive adult in her life who will recognize the signs of the initial phase— just one more reason why teenagers, who may seem very grown up, still need warm, authoritative parenting.

---

became sexually active at an early age and who bore their first child early are likely to follow a similar path. Peer rejection also increases the likelihood that a girl will become pregnant, especially among girls who are high in aggressiveness (Underwood, Kupersmidt, & Coie, 1996).

In contrast, the likelihood of pregnancy is lower among teenaged girls who do well in school and have strong educational aspirations. Such girls are both less likely to be sexually active at an early age and more likely to use contraception if they are sexually active. Girls who have good communication about sex and contraception with their mothers are also less likely to get pregnant.

When teenaged girls become pregnant, in most cases, they face the most momentous set of decisions they have encountered in their young lives (see The Real World). Just under half of teen pregnancies (48%) across all ethnic groups end in abortion, and about 14% result in miscarriages (Gullotta, Adams, & Montemayor, 1993). Among whites, 7% of teens carry the baby to term and place it for adoption, but only 1% of African American teens relinquish their babies to adoptive families.

The children of teenaged mothers are more likely than children born to older mothers to grow up in poverty, with all the accompanying negative consequences for the child's optimum development (Osofsky, Hann, & Peebles, 1993). However, the children of teenaged mothers whose own parents help with child care, finances, and parenting skills are less likely to suffer such negative effects (Birch, 1998; Uno, Florsheim, & Uchino, 1998). Moreover, social programs that provide teenaged mothers with child care and the support they need to remain in school positively affect both these mothers and their babies. Such programs also improve outcomes for teenaged fathers (Kost, 1997).

Before going on

- How does risky behavior affect adolescent health?
- What are the patterns of adolescent sexual behavior in the United States?
- What are the consequences of teenaged pregnancy, and which teenaged girls are most likely to get pregnant?

Substance Abuse and Mental Health Problems

Despite the stereotype of adolescence as a period of "storm and stress," most teenagers are well adjusted. For a few, however, serious substance abuse or mental health problems arise during this period.

Drugs, Alcohol, and Tobacco

After 2 decades of decline, many types of teenaged drug use are on the rise in the United States. For example, in 1974, about 23% of adolescents reported that they had used marijuana. By 1992, the percentage had fallen to 11.7 (U.S. Bureau of the Census, 1995). In the most recent federal government survey conducted in 1999, 26.7% of high school students reported that they had used marijuana within 3 months of responding to the survey (CDC, 2000).

Alcohol use is also fairly common among teens, at least in the United States. For example, in 1999, 31% of twelfth-graders, 26% of tenth-graders, and 15% of eighth-graders reported that they had engaged in binge drinking (defined as consuming five or more drinks on a single occasion) at least once in the last month (FIFCFS, 2000). Alcohol use is highest among teens in situations where "racial or ethnic minorities live in circumscribed, impoverished areas such as ghettos, barrios, and Indian reservations" (Mitchell et al., 1996, p. 152).

Teenagers who express the most interest in sensation-seeking are those who are most likely to use drugs and consume alcohol (Donohew et al., 1999). Indeed, researchers have found that individual levels of sensation-seeking predict peer associations—that is, teens who are high sensation-seekers choose friends who are similar. Once such groups are formed, sensation-seeking becomes a central feature of their activities. So, for example, if one member tries marijuana or alcohol, others do so as well.

Sensation-seeking also interacts with parenting style to increase the likelihood of drug use. Authoritative parenting seems to provide high sensation-seeking teenagers with protection against their reckless tendencies (Pilgrim, Luo, Urberg, & Fang, 1999). In fact, for African American adolescents, authoritative parenting may entirely negate the potential influence of drug-using peers. Moreover, parents who have realistic perceptions of the prevalence of teenaged drinking are also less likely to have teenaged children who are drinkers. These parents, who are aware of the prevalence of alcohol use among adolescents, try to prevent their children from getting into situations, such as attending unsupervised social events, where drinking is likely to happen (Bogenschneider, Wu, Raffaelli, & Tsay, 1998).

Sensation-seeking seems to be less important in tobacco use. Surveys suggest that, by age 14, 18% of U.S. adolescents are regular smokers, and 40% have tried smoking by that age (Simons-Morton et al., 1999; Thornton, Douglas, & Houghton, 1999). Ethnic groups differ widely in tobacco use. Less than 5% of African American high school seniors smoke daily, compared to about 12% of Hispanic Americans and more than 20% of whites (Hilts, 1995).

Some developmentalists speculate that teenagers begin smoking because they really don't understand its health consequences. Consequently, many anti-smoking campaigns emphasize health risks. However, teenagers seem to be well aware of these risks, including the link between smoking and lung cancer (Taylor et al., 1999). Further, many teens cite moral and ethical reasons for not smoking when asked about it by researchers. Thus, it seems that adolescents are very familiar with all the reasons they shouldn't smoke. So, why do they start smoking if they know they shouldn't?

Peer influences appear to outweigh perceptions of future health risks for many teenagers (Chopak, Vicary, & Crockett, 1998; West, Sweeting, & Ecob, 1999). In fact, some developmentalists advise parents that if their teenaged child's friends smoke, especially close friends with whom the child spends a lot of time, parents should probably assume that their child smokes as well (Urberg, Degirmencioglu, & Pilgrim, 1997). Moreover, the period between ages 15 and 17 seems to be the time during which a teenager is most susceptible to peer influences with regard to smoking (West, Sweeting, & Ecob, 1999). Clearly, then, monitoring the friends of 15- to 17-year-olds and discouraging these teens from associating with smokers may help parents prevent their smoking (Mott, Crowe, Richardson, & Flay, 1999).

Parental influence is important, too—a pattern that is especially clear for mothers and daughters (Kandel & Wu, 1995). When an adult stops smoking, the likelihood that her children will smoke decreases. Thus, another way to prevent teenaged smoking is to encourage parents to give up the habit. In addition, having a family rule against substance use—including drugs, alcohol, and tobacco—has a lot more influence on teenagers' decisions about using such substances than most parents think (Abdelrahman, Rodriguez, Ryan, French, & Weinbaum, 1998; Mott et al., 1999). Similarly, teens who view smoking as morally wrong are less likely to smoke than peers who do not think of smoking as a moral issue (Taylor et al., 1999). Thus, parents who think tobacco use is morally wrong should discuss their beliefs with their children.

Eating Disorders

Eating disorders are among the most significant mental health problems during adolescence. **Bulimia** (sometimes called *bulimia nervosa*) involves an intense concern about weight combined with twice-weekly or more frequent cycles of binge eating

bulimia an eating disorder characterized by binge eating and purging

<W>hen this anorexic 15-year-old looks at herself in the mirror, chances are she sees herself as "too fat," despite being obviously emaciated. (*Photo:* Tony Freeman, PhotoEdit)

followed by purging, through self-induced vomiting, excessive use of laxatives, or excessive exercising (Attie, Brooks-Gunn, & Petersen, 1990). Bulimics are ordinarily not exceptionally thin, but they are obsessed with their weight, feel intense shame about their abnormal behavior, and often experience significant depression. The physical consequences of bulimia include marked tooth decay (from repeated vomiting), stomach irritation, lowered body temperature, disturbances of body chemistry, and loss of hair (Palla & Litt, 1988).

The incidence of bulimia appears to have been increasing in recent decades in many Western countries, particularly among adolescent girls, but firm numbers have been hard to establish. Current estimates are that from 1.0% and 2.8% of adolescent girls and young adult women show the full syndrome of bulimia; as many as 20% of girls in industrialized Western countries show at least some bulimic behaviors, such as occasional purging (Attie & Brooks-Gunn, 1995; Graber, Brooks-Gunn, Paikoff, & Warren, 1994). In contrast, bulimia is unheard of in countries where food is scarce.

Anorexia nervosa is less common but potentially more deadly. It is characterized by extreme dieting, intense fear of gaining weight, and obsessive exercising. In girls or women (who are by far the most common sufferers), the weight loss eventually produces a variety of physical symptoms associated with starvation: sleep disturbance, cessation of menstruation, insensitivity to pain, loss of hair on the head, low blood pressure, a variety of cardiovascular problems, and reduced body temperature. Between 10% to 15% of anorexics literally starve themselves to death; others die because of some type of cardiovascular dysfunction (Deter & Herzog, 1994).

Some theorists have proposed biological causes for eating disorders—for example, some kind of brain dysfunction in the case of bulimics, who often show abnormal brain waves. Others argue for a psychoanalytic explanation, such as a fear of growing up. The most promising explanation, however, may lie in the discrepancy between the young person's internal image of a desirable body and her (or his) perception of her (or his) own body.

This explanation is supported by cross-cultural research demonstrating that adolescents in Western societies, who have the highest rates of eating disorders, are more likely to have negative body images than are adolescents in non-Western societies (Akiba, 1998). In addition, girls who participate in activities such as ballet and gymnastics, in which thinness is highly valued, are at greater risk of developing eating disorders (Picard, 1999; Stoutjesdyk & Jevne, 1993). However, surveys suggest that a fairly large proportion of the general population of teenaged girls in the United States may be at risk. Only 14% of adolescent girls are actually overweight, but 36% believe that they are too fat (CDC, 2000) (see the Research Report).

Some developmentalists suggest that an emphasis on thinness as a characteristic of attractive women, which is common in Western cultures, contributes to the prevalence of eating disorders. However, it is likely that family and individual variables determine the effect of cultural influences on teenagers. For example, one study suggested that mothers' beliefs about the desirability of thinness and their daughters' attractiveness may be just as important in the development of eating disorders as the daughters' own views (Hill & Franklin, 1998). In addition, images of extremely thin models seem to affect only those girls who are already dissatisfied with their bodies (Rabasca, 1999).

It is also important to note that a general tendency toward mental illness may also be a factor in eating disorders. In one longitudinal study, young women who had been anorexic in adolescence (94% of whom had recovered from their eating disorders) were found to be far more likely than the general population to suffer from a

Critical Thinking

If you had the power to change U.S. culture to greatly reduce the rates of bulimia and anorexia, what changes would you want to make? Why and how?

anorexia nervosa an eating disorder characterized by self-starvation

Research Report

An Australian Study Illustrating Sex Differences in Body Image among Adolescents

A study of Australian high school students illustrated that distortions in body image are not restricted to U.S. teenagers and showed how such distortions affect girls' attitudes and behavior (Paxton et al., 1991). A total of 562 Australian teenagers in grades 7–11 reported on their current weight and height and gave their judgment of themselves as either underweight, at a good weight, or overweight. They also responded to questions about the effect that being thinner might have on their lives and described their weight-control behaviors, including dieting and exercise.

Among teenagers whose weight was actually normal for their height, 30.1% of the girls but only 6.8% of the boys described themselves as overweight. Thus, just as research has found in the United States, many of these Australian girls perceived themselves as too fat when they were actually normal. Furthermore, the majority of girls thought that being thinner would make them happier; a few even thought that being thinner would make them more intelligent! Boys, in contrast, thought that being thinner would actually have some negative effects.

Not surprisingly, these differences in the perception of thinness were reflected in dieting behavior in this sample. Twenty-three percent of the girls reported that they went on a crash diet at least occasionally, and 4% said that they did so once or twice a week. The comparable percentages for boys were 9% and 1%, respectively. More girls than boys also reported taking diet pills, using laxatives, and vomiting, although the rates of these behaviors were low for both sexes.

Certainly, having a distorted body image doesn't necessarily mean that a girl will become bulimic or anorexic. However, the potential impact of such distorted thinking on girls' general feelings about themselves and initiation of dangerous practices such crash dieting should be cause for concern.

variety of mental disorders (Nilsson, Gillberg, Gillberg, & Rastam, 1999). *Obsessive-compulsive personality disorder*, a condition characterized by an excessive need for control of the environment, seemed to be especially prevalent in this group. The study's authors further stated that the young women's mental difficulties did not appear to be the result of having previously suffered from an eating disorder. Instead, both the adolescent eating disorders and the women's problems in adulthood seem to have been produced by a consistent tendency toward distorted perceptions.

Depression and Suicide

Epidemiological studies reveal that, at any given time, 5–8% of adolescents are in the midst of an enduring depression. Perhaps twice that many will experience a serious depression at some time in their teenaged years (Compas, Ey, & Grant, 1993; Merikangas & Angst, 1995). Teenaged girls are twice as likely as boys to report feelings of depression, a sex difference that persists throughout adolescence and into adulthood. This sex difference has been found in a number of industrialized countries and across ethnic groups in the United States (Nolen-Hoeksema & Girgus, 1994; Petersen et al., 1993; Roberts & Sobhan, 1992).

The search for developmental pathways leading to adolescent depression begins with the clear finding that children growing up with depressed parents are much more likely to develop depression than are those growing up with nondepressed parents (Merikangas & Angst, 1995). This could indicate that depression is determined to some extent by a genetic factor, a possibility supported by at least a few studies of twins and adopted children (Petersen et al., 1993). Or this link between parental and child depression could be explained in terms of the parenting behaviors of depressed parents, which you read about in earlier chapters. Furthermore, the contributions of a variety of family stressors to adolescent depression are just as clear among children whose parents are not depressed. Any combination of stresses—such as the parents' divorce, the death of a parent or another loved person, the father's loss of job, a move, or a change of schools—increases the likelihood of depression or other kinds of emotional distress in the adolescent (Compas et al., 1993; D'Imperio, Dubow, & Ippolito, 2000).

You'll remember from Chapter 9 that low self-esteem is also part of the equation. Harter's studies reveal that a young person who feels she (or he) does not measure up to her (or his) own standards is much more likely to show symptoms of depression. A great many teenagers are convinced that they do not live up to culturally defined standards of physical appearance. Self-esteem thus drops in early adolescence, and depression rises.

Depression isn't simply an emotional "low" period. It can also hinder academic achievement, because it interferes with memory. For example, depressed adolescents are more likely to remember negative information than positive information (Neshat-Doost, Taghavi, Moradi, Yule, & Dalgleish, 1998). If a teacher says to a depressed adolescent, "You're going to fail algebra unless you start handing in your homework on time," the teenager is likely to remember the part about failing algebra and forget that the teacher also provided a remedy—getting homework done on time. Further, depressed adolescents seem to be less able than their nondepressed peers to store and retrieve verbal information (Horan, Pogge, Borgaro, & Stokes, 1997).

In some teenagers, sadly, the suicidal thoughts that often accompany depression lead to action. Surveys suggest that 20% of high school students in the United States have thought seriously about taking their own lives, and approximately 1 in 13 has actually attempted suicide (National Center for Injury Prevention and Control [NCIPC], 2000). A very small number of teens, about 12 of every 100,000, actually succeed in killing themselves (Blau, 1996). However, public health experts point out that many teenaged deaths, such as those that result from single-car crashes, may be counted as accidents when they are actually suicides (NCIPC, 2000).

Although depression is more common among girls, the likelihood of actually completing a suicide attempt is almost five times as high for adolescent boys. In contrast, suicide attempts are estimated to be three times more common among girls than among boys (Garland & Zigler, 1993). Girls, more often than boys, use methods that are less likely to succeed, such as self-poisoning.

The suicide rate is also nearly twice as high among white teenagers as among all nonwhite adolescents except for Native Americans, who attempt and commit suicide at higher rates than any other group (NCIPC, 2000). The rate among Native Americans teenagers is 26.3 per 100,000 per year, compared with about 20 per 100,000 among white teenaged males. Similarly, Hispanic American youths are more likely to attempt suicide than whites, although their rate of completed suicide is lower (NCIPC, 2000). In addition, teenaged suicide rates are fairly stable in all groups except African American males, among whom the rate more than doubled (from 3.6 to 8.1 per 100,000) during the 1990s (NCIPC, 2000).

It is obviously very difficult to uncover the contributing factors in completed suicides. Nonetheless, it does seem clear that one virtually universal ingredient is some kind of significant psychopathology, including, but not restricted to, depression. Behavior problems such as aggression are also common in the histories of those who complete suicides, as is a family history of psychiatric disorder or suicide or a pattern of drug or alcohol abuse (Garland & Zigler, 1993). In addition, psychologists suggest at least three other contributing factors (Shaffer, Garland, Gould, Fisher, & Trautman, 1988; Swedo et al., 1991):

- *Some triggering stressful event.* Studies of suicides suggest that this triggering event is often a disciplinary crisis with the parents or some rejection or humiliation, such as breaking up with a girlfriend or boyfriend or failing in a valued activity.

- *An altered mental state.* Such a state might be a sense of hopelessness, reduced inhibitions from alcohol consumption, or rage.

- *An opportunity.* A loaded gun in the house or a bottle of sleeping pills in the parents' medicine cabinet creates an opportunity for a teenager to carry out suicidal plans.

Suicide prevention efforts have focused on education—for example, providing training to teachers or to teenagers on how to identify students who are at risk for suicide, in the hope that vulnerable individuals might be reached before they attempt suicide. Special training in coping abilities has also been offered to teenaged students, so that they might be able to find a nonlethal solution to their problems. Unfortunately, most such programs appear to be ineffective in changing teenagers' attitudes or knowledge (Shaffer, Garland, Vieland, Underwood, & Busner, 1991). These discouraging results are not likely to change until psychologists know a great deal more about the developmental pathways that lead to this particular form of psychopathology.

Before going on

- Describe adolescents' patterns of drug, alcohol, and tobacco use.
- What are the characteristics and causes of eating disorders?
- Which adolescents are at greatest risk of depression and suicide?

Changes in Thinking and Memory

At some point in adolescence, most people become capable of several types of thought that appear to be impossible at earlier ages. Piaget was the first psychologist to offer an explanation of this important developmental milestone.

Piaget's Formal Operational Stage

Piaget's observations led him to conclude that this new level of thinking—the **formal operational stage**—emerges fairly rapidly in early adolescence, between roughly age 12 and age 16. During this stage, teenagers learn to reason logically about abstract concepts. Instead of thinking only about real things and actual occurrences, as younger children do, teenagers can think about possible occurrences. Piaget called this kind of thinking hypothetico-deductive reasoning. **Hypothetico-deductive reasoning** is the ability to derive conclusions from hypothetical premises. For example, when a teenager imagines what her life will be like if she goes to college and then compares her imagined future to another possible future that doesn't involve college, she is engaging in hypothetico-deductive reasoning.

The development of hypothetico-deductive reasoning is part of a larger developmental trend, the emergence of the capacity for *deductive reasoning*. Deductive reasoning involves if-then relationships: "If all people are equal, then you and I must be

formal operational stage the fourth of Piaget's stages, during which adolescents learn to reason logically about abstract concepts

hypothetico-deductive reasoning the ability to derive conclusions from hypothetical premises

_High school science classes may be one of the first places where adolescents are required to use deductive logic—a skill Piaget did not think was developed until the period of formal operations. (*Photo:* Bob Daemmrich, Stock Boston)

equal." A great deal of the logic of science is deductive. Scientists begin with a theory and a prediction: "If this theory is correct, then I should observe such and such." Children as young as 4 or 5 can understand some such relationships if the premises given are factually true. But only at adolescence are young people able to understand and use the basic logical relationship implied by if-then statements (Ward & Overton, 1990). Consequently, it isn't surprising that adolescents learn all kinds of scientific processes more easily than elementary school children do.

Similarly, advances in logic enable adolescents to engage in **systematic problem-solving,** a process in which a problem-solver searches for a solution by testing hypotheses about single factors. To study this process, Piaget presented adolescents with complex tasks drawn mostly from the physical sciences. In one of these tasks, the participants were given varying lengths of string and a set of objects of various weights that could be tied to the strings to make a swinging pendulum (Inhelder & Piaget, 1958). They were shown how to start the pendulum by pushing the weight with differing amounts of force and by holding the weight at different heights. The task was to figure out which one factor or combination of factors (length of string, weight of object, force of push, or height of push) determined the *period* of the pendulum, which is the amount of time for one swing. (In case you have forgotten your high school physics, the answer is that only the length of the string affects the period of the pendulum.)

Critical Thinking

Think of a few real-life examples of tasks that demand systematic problem solving.

An adolescent using a formal operational approach is likely to vary just one of the four factors at a time. She may try a heavy object with a short string, then with a medium string, then with a long one. After that, she might try a light object with the three lengths of string. By contrast, the concrete operational thinker (a younger child) will vary the factors in a haphazard way and, thus, never reach a solution.

Direct Tests of Piaget's View

Developmentalist Edith Neimark has summarized the accumulated information on changes in adolescent thinking succinctly:

> An enormous amount of evidence from an assortment of tasks shows that adolescents and adults are capable of feats of reasoning not attained under normal circumstances by [younger] children, and that these abilities develop fairly rapidly during the ages of about 11 to 15. (Neimark, 1982, p. 493)

Some research illustrations will make the change clearer.

In an early cross-sectional study, researchers tested 20 girls in each of four grades (sixth, eighth, tenth, and twelfth) on ten different tasks that required one or more of what Piaget called formal operational skills (Martorano, 1977). Indeed, many of the tasks the researchers used were those Piaget himself had devised. Results of performance on two of these tasks are graphed in Figure 10.4. The pendulum problem is the one described earlier in this section; the balance problem requires a youngster to predict whether two different weights, hung at varying distances on either side of a scale, will balance—a task similar to the balance scale problem Siegler used (recall Figure 8.4). To solve this problem using formal operations, the teenager must consider both weight and distance simultaneously. You can see from Figure 10.4 that older students generally did better, with the biggest improvement in scores between eighth and tenth grades (between ages 13 and 15).

Formal operational reasoning also seems to enable adolescents to understand figurative language, such as metaphors, to a greater degree. For example, one early study found that teenagers were much better than younger children at interpreting

systematic problem-solving the process of finding a solution to a problem by testing single factors

proverbs (Saltz, 1979). Statements such as "People who live in glass houses shouldn't throw stones" are usually interpreted literally by 6- to 11-year-olds. By 12 or 13, most adolescents can easily understand them, even though it isn't until much later that teenagers actually use such expressions in their everyday speech (Gibbs & Beitel, 1995).

In a more practical vein, developmentalists have shown that teenagers' new cognitive abilities alter the ways they make decisions. In one classic study, experimenters asked eighth-, tenth-, and twelfth-grade students to respond to a set of dilemmas that involved a person facing a difficult decision, such as whether to have an operation to repair a facial disfigurement (Lewis, 1981). Forty-two percent of the twelfth-graders, but only 11% of the eighth-graders, mentioned future possibilities in their comments on these dilemmas. For example, in answer to the cosmetic surgery dilemma, a twelfth-grader said,

> Well, you have to look into the different things . . . that might be more important later on in your life. You should think about, will it have any effect on your future and with, maybe, the people you meet. (Lewis, 1981, p. 541)

An eighth-grader, in response to the same dilemma, said,

> The different things I would think about in getting the operation is like if the girls turn you down on a date, or the money, or the kids teasing you at school. (Lewis, 1981, p. 542)

The eighth-grader's answer focused on the here and now, on concrete things. By contrast, the twelfth-grader considered things that might happen in the future.

However, even among twelfth-graders, nearly three-fifths did not show this type of future orientation. And take another look at Figure 10.4: Only about 50–60% of twelfth-graders solved the two formal operations problems, and only 2 of the 20 twelfth-grade participants used formal operational logic on all ten problems. Further, recent studies have found rates of formal operational thinking in high school students that are very similar to those found in studies conducted in the 1960s, 1970s, and 1980s (Bradmetz, 1999). The consistency of such findings over several cohorts of adolescents suggests that Piaget's predictions about adolescents' thinking abilities were overly optimistic—in contrast to his overly pessimistic estimates of young children's abilities, which you read about in earlier chapters.

In adulthood, rates of formal operational thinking increase with education. Generally, the better educated the adult participants in a study of formal operational thinking, the greater the percentage who display this kind of reasoning (Mwamwenda, 1999). Piaget's belief in the universality of formal operations may have resulted from his failure to appreciate the role of education in the development of advanced forms of thought. The current consensus among developmentalists is that all nonretarded teenagers and adults have the capacity for formal operational thinking, but they actually acquire it in response to specific demands, such as those imposed by higher levels of education. Thus, people whose life situations or cultures do not require formal operational thinking do not develop it.

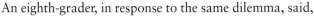

FIGURE 10.4

These are the results from two of the ten different formal operational tasks used in Martorano's cross-sectional study. (*Source:* Martorano, 1977, p. 670. Copyright by the American Psychological Association.)

MAKE THE CONNECTION

In what way might formal operational thinking influence decision-making about risky behavior in adolescence?

Advances in Information-Processing

Adolescents process information faster, use processing resources more efficiently, understand their own memory processes better, and have more knowledge than do elementary school children (Kail, 1990, 1997). As a result, they are much better at using strategies to help themselves remember things and can more easily understand and remember complex information, such as that presented in a textbook.

● *Metacognition, Metamemory, and Strategy Use* ●   By age 14 or 15, the metacognitive and metamemory skills of adolescents far exceed those of younger children. For example, in one classic study, 10- and 14-year-olds were instructed to do a particular activity for exactly 30 minutes (Ceci & Bronfenbrenner, 1985). Experimenters provided them with a clock and instructed them to use it to determine when they should stop. Few of the 10-year-olds periodically checked the time to see if 30 minutes had elapsed, but most of the 14-year-olds did. As a result, less than half of the younger participants succeeded in stopping on time, but more than three-quarters of the teenagers did so.

Another early study of metamemory involved offering fifth-graders, eighth-graders, and college students the opportunity to earn money for remembering words (Cuvo, 1974). Researchers designated the words to be recalled as being worth either 1 cent or 10 cents. Fifth-graders rehearsed 1-cent and 10-cent words equally. In contrast, eighth-graders and college students put more effort into rehearsing the 10-cent words. At the end of the rehearsal period, fifth-graders recalled equal numbers of 1- and 10-cent words, while older participants remembered more 10-cent words. Further, college students outperformed eighth-graders in both rehearsal and recall. This finding suggests that the capacity to apply memory strategies selectively, based on the characteristics of a memory task, appears early in the teenaged years and continues to improve throughout adolescence.

Training studies, in which children and adolescents are taught to use a particular memory strategy, also suggest that metacognitive abilities enable teenagers to benefit more from training than younger children do. For example, researchers taught elementary school students and high school students a strategy for memorizing the manufacturing products associated with different cities (for example, Detroit—automobiles) (Pressley & Dennis-Rounds, 1980). Once participants had learned the strategy and were convinced of its effectiveness, researchers presented them with a similar task, memorizing Latin words and their English translations. Experimenters found that only the high school students made an effort to use the strategy they had just learned to accomplish the new memory task. The elementary school children used the new strategy only when researchers told them to and demonstrated how it could be applied to the new task. High school students' success seemed to be due to their superior ability to recognize the similarity between the two tasks—an aspect of metamemory.

● *Text Learning* ●   Differences between younger children's and adolescents' processing of and memory for text are even more dramatic. In a classic study of text processing, experimenters asked 10-, 13-, 15-, and 18-year-olds to read and summarize a 500-word passage. The researchers hypothesized that participants would use four rules in writing summaries (Brown & Day, 1983). First, they would delete trivial information. Second, their summaries would show categorical organization—that is, they would use terms such as "animals" rather than specific names of animals mentioned in the text. Third, the summaries would use topic sentences from the text. Finally, the participants would invent topic sentences for paragraphs that didn't have them.

The results of the study suggested that participants of all ages used the first rule, because all of the summaries included more general than detailed or trivial information about the passage. However, the 10-year-olds and 13-year-olds used the other rules far less frequently than did the 15- and 18-year-olds. There were also interesting differences between the two older groups. Fifteen-year-olds used categories about as frequently as 18-year-olds did, but the oldest group used topic sentences far more effectively. This pattern of age differences suggests that the ability to summarize a text improves gradually during the second half of adolescence.

Studies of text outlining reveal a similar pattern (Drum, 1985). Both elementary and high school students know that an outline should include the main ideas of a passage along with supporting details. However, research suggests that 17-year-olds generate much more complete outlines than 14-year-olds do. Moreover, 11-year-olds' outlines usually include only a few of the main ideas of a passage and provide little or no supporting details for those main ideas.

Before going on

- What are the characteristics of thought in Piaget's formal operational stage?

- What are some major research findings regarding the formal operational stage?

- List the advances in information-processing capabilities that occur during adolescence.

Schooling

chool experiences are clearly formative in middle childhood, as you'll recall from Chapter 8, but school is no less central a force in the lives of adolescents.

Transition to Secondary School

There are many places in the world, including some in North America, where children attend a lower school for 8 years before moving on to a high school for 4 years. Such an arrangement is known as an *8-4 system*. Because students typically show achievement declines after entering high school, educators have developed two models that include a transitional school—a junior high school, middle school, or intermediate school—between elementary and high school. The junior high system typically includes 6 years of elementary school followed by 3 years of junior high and 3 years of high school. The middle school model includes 5 years of elementary school, 3 years of middle school, and 4 years of high school.

However, neither the junior high nor the middle school approach seems to have solved the transition problem. Students show losses in achievement and in self-esteem across both transition points in the 6-3-3 and 5-3-4 systems. Further, students in both of these systems show greater losses during the transition to high school than those in 8-4 systems (Alspaugh, 1998; Anderman, 1998). Consequently, educators and developmentalists are currently searching for explanations and practical remedies.

One potential explanation for transition-related achievement declines is that students' academic goals change once they enter middle school. Researchers classify

Some developmentalists argue that the transition to middle school or junior high school is difficult for many young adolescents because they are not developmentally ready for the secondary-school model. Children who attend middle and junior high schools where close relationships between teachers and students are encouraged, as they are in elementary school, show smaller declines in achievement and self-esteem.
(*Photo:* Bob Rowan, Progressive Image/CORBIS)

such goals into two very broad categories: *task goals* and *ability goals*. **Task goals** are goals based on personal standards and a desire to become more competent at something. For example, a runner who wants to improve her time in the 100-meter dash has a task goal. An **ability goal** is one that defines success in competitive terms, being better than another person at something. For example, a runner who wants to be the fastest person on her team has an ability goal. Longitudinal research shows that most fifth-graders have task goals, but by the time they have been in sixth grade a few months, most children have shifted to ability goals (Anderman & Anderman, 1999; Anderman & Midgley, 1997).

A student's goal influences his behavior in important ways. Task goals are associated with a greater sense of personal control and more positive attitudes about school (Anderman, 1999). A student who takes a task-goal approach to school work tends to set increasingly higher standards for his performance and attributes success and failure to his own efforts. For example, a task-goal-oriented student is likely to say he received an A in a class because he worked hard or because he wanted to improve his performance.

In contrast, students with ability goals adopt relative standards—that is, they view performance on a given academic task as good as long as it is better than someone else's. Consequently, such students are more strongly influenced by the group with which they identify than by internal standards that define good and bad academic performance. Ability-goal-oriented students are also more likely than others to attribute success and failure to forces outside themselves. For example, such a student might say he got an A in a class because it was easy or because the teacher liked him. Moreover, such students are likely to have a negative view of school (Anderman, 1999).

Because middle schools emphasize ability grouping more than elementary schools, it is likely that many middle school students change their beliefs about their own abilities during these years (Anderman, Maehr, & Midgley, 1999; Roeser & Eccles, 1998). Thus, high-achieving elementary students who maintain their levels of achievement across the sixth-grade transition gain confidence in their abilities (Pajares & Graham, 1999). In contrast, the changes in self-concept experienced by high achievers who fail to meet expectations in middle school as well as average and low-achieving students do probably lead to self-esteem losses for many of them. Once an ability-goal-oriented student adopts the belief that her academic ability is less than adequate, she is likely to stop putting effort into school work. In addition, such students are likely to use ineffective cognitive strategies when attempting to learn academic material (Young, 1997). Consequently, achievement suffers along with self-esteem.

Educators have devised a number of strategies to address this shift in goal structure. One approach is based on research demonstrating that the presence of supportive adults outside a child's family makes the transition easier (Galassi, Gulledge, & Cox, 1997; Wenz-Gross, Siperstein, Untch, & Widaman, 1997). For example, some schools provide students with an adult mentor, either a teacher or a volunteer from the community, to whom they are assigned for a transitional period or throughout the middle school years.

In practice, the characteristics of mentoring programs vary widely (Galassi et al., 1997). Some consist of simply giving sixth-graders the name of a teacher they can consult if they encounter any problems. At the other end of the spectrum, some mentoring programs assign each student to a teacher, who is supposed to monitor several students' daily assignment sheets, homework completion, grades, and even school supplies. The homeroom teacher also maintains communication with each child's parents regarding these factors. If a student isn't doing his math homework or doesn't have any pencils, it is the homeroom teacher's responsibility to tell his parents about the problem. The parents are then responsible for follow-up.

task goals goals based on a desire for self-improvement

ability goals goals based on a desire to be superior to others

Research suggests that programs of this level of intensity are highly successful in improving middle school students' grades (Callahan, Rademacher, & Hildreth, 1998). Their success probably lies in the fact that the homeroom teacher functions very much like an elementary school teacher. This is significant because, despite cultural expectations to the contrary, a sixth-grader is developmentally a child, whether she is in an elementary school or a middle school. Consequently, it isn't surprising that a strategy that makes a middle school more like an elementary school—a school designed for children, not adolescents—is successful. In fact, some observers think that middle schools have failed to meet their goal of easing the transition to high school because they have simply duplicated high school organization and imposed it on students who are not developmentally ready, rather than providing them with a real transition.

One approach aimed at making middle schools truly transitional involves organizing students and teachers into teams. For example, in some schools, sixth, seventh, and eighth grades are physically separated in different wings of the school building. In such schools, each grade is a sort of school-within-a-school. Teachers in each grade-level team work together to balance the demands of different subject-area classes, assess problems of individual students, and devise parent involvement strategies. Preliminary research suggests that the team approach helps to minimize the negative effects of the middle school transition. As a result, it has become the recommended approach of the National Middle School Association in the United States (Loonsbury, 1992).

Regardless of the type of school they attended previously, the early days of high school set a general pattern of success or failure for teenagers that continues into their adult years. For example, teenagers who fail one or more courses in the first year of high school are far less likely than their peers to graduate (Roderick & Camburn, 1999). It appears that minority students have a particularly difficult time recovering from early failure.

However, some psychologists emphasize the positive aspects of transition to high school, claiming that participation in activities that are usually offered only in high school allows students opportunities to develop psychological attributes that can't be acquired elsewhere. To demonstrate the point, a number of research studies had high school students use pagers to signal researchers whenever they were experiencing high levels of intrinsic motivation along with intense mental effort (Larson, 2000). The results showed that students experienced both states in elective classes and during extracurricular activities far more often than in academic classes (Larson, 2000). In other words, a student engaged in an art project or sports practice is more likely to experience this particular combination of states than one who is in a history class. Consequently, educators may be able to ease the transition to high school for many students by offering a wide variety of elective and extracurricular activities and encouraging students to participate.

Critical Thinking

What was your first year of high school like? Did your grades and self-esteem decline? What do you think teachers and administrators could do differently to make the transition easier for students?

Gender, Ethnicity, and Achievement in Science and Math

Girls seem to be at particular risk for achievement losses after the transition to high school. For example, eighth-grade boys outscore girls in science achievement, and the gap widens substantially by the time adolescents reach tenth grade (Burkham, Lee, & Smerdon, 1997). Moreover, research suggests that the gender gap is widest among the most intellectually talented students. It seems that girls' achievement suffers in science learning situations that do not offer hands-on activities. Since high school classes involve many fewer opportunities to engage in these activities than do classes in early grades, developmentalists speculate that girls' achievement could be improved by including more laboratory experiences in high school science classes.

Developmentalists have also found that intellectually talented girls are often discouraged from taking courses and pursuing careers in sciences such as chemistry and physics. Instead, teachers and counselors urge girls who express an interest in science to focus on life sciences such as zoology and botany (Jones & Wheatley, 1990). Girls themselves report more interest and academic confidence in classes on life science than in those on physical sciences (Eccles, Barber, & Jozefowicz, 1998). Thus, it is not surprising that only 8–9% of employed professionals in the physical sciences are women. However, even in the life sciences, women make up only 28% of the professional work force in the United States (National Science Foundation, 1996).

Clearly, cultural attitudes also influence girls' science achievement. For example, girls' and their parents' perceptions of science as a suitable career for females strongly predict girls' success in science courses (Jacobs, Finken, Griffin, & Wright, 1998). Even girls who are very high achievers in high school science have less confidence in their ability to succeed in college science courses and are, thus, less likely to pursue science majors in college (Catsambis, 1995; Guzzetti & Williams, 1996).

The gender gap in mathematics achievement widens in high school as well, although sex differences are smaller today than they were in the 1960s (Hyde, Fennema, & Lamon, 1990). Research suggests that variations in boys' and girls' approaches to problem-solving may be responsible for sex differences in high school. Boys seem to be better at identifying effective strategies for solving the types of problems found on standardized math tests (Gallagher et al., 2000). However, developmentalists still don't know how boys acquire this advantage.

Like their scientifically talented peers, mathematically gifted high school girls have considerably less confidence in their abilities than their male counterparts do, even though the girls typically get better grades (Guzzetti & Williams, 1996; Marsh & Yeung, 1998). Research demonstrates that it is girls' beliefs about their abilities and about the acceptability of success in math for females that shapes their interest in taking higher-level high school and college math courses (Ethington, 1991). Consequently, even though girls get better grades in math than boys do, they are still less likely to take advanced courses such as calculus or to choose careers in math (Davenport et al., 1998). In fact, one survey found that 49% of a group of girls who scored in the top 1% on the mathematics portion of the SAT during their last year of high school were full-time homemakers 11 years after high school graduation, and very few of those who were working were employed in math-related fields (Gohm, Humphreys, & Yao, 1998).

As striking as the gender differences in math are, they pale in comparison to ethnic variations (Davenport et al., 1998). For example, by the last year of high school, only a third of African American and Hispanic American students have completed 2 years of algebra. In contrast, slightly more than half of white students and two-thirds of Asian American students have taken 2 years of algebra. Further, Asian American high school students earn twice as many credits in advanced courses as white students, and three to four times as many as African American and Hispanic American students.

One reason for the ethnic differences is that Asian American and white students are more likely to enter ninth grade with the skills they need to take their first algebra class. More than half of African American and Hispanic American teens are required to take remedial courses before beginning algebra, compared to about one-third of Asian American and white students (Davenport et al., 1998). Observers point out that about the same proportion of high school students across all ethnicities expect to go to college. However, it appears that Asian American and white students are much more likely to enter high school prepared to pursue college-preparatory courses. Many researchers conclude that educators may be encouraging African American and Hispanic American students to attend college without providing them with the necessary skills to attain this goal (Davenport, 1992). Further, recent research suggests that more rigorous transitional classes in eighth and ninth grade might enable greater numbers of African American and Hispanic American students to complete college-preparatory math classes in high school (Gamoran, Porter, Smithson, & White, 1997).

Evidence for this position is drawn from studies involving mathematically talented students. There are large ethnic differences in high school course choices among highly able students—those who score in the top 25% of standardized math achievement tests. One study found that 100% of Asian American and 88% of white high school students scoring at this level were enrolled in advanced mathematics courses. In contrast, only 40% of mathematically talented African American and Hispanic American students were enrolled in such classes (Education Trust, 1996). It may be that high school counselors more often encourage Asian American and white students to take advanced math classes (Davenport, 1992).

Family interactive style predicts academic achievement in high school. Adolescents whose parents display authoritative parenting are more likely than those with authoritarian or permissive parents to achieve academic success in high school. (*Photo:* Will and Deni McIntyre, Photo Researchers)

Dropping Out of High School

The cumulative effect of success over many years of schooling fosters a greater sense of academic confidence among academically successful high school students. Those who achieve, especially those who achieve despite backgrounds that include poverty or other daunting obstacles, are likely to have parents who have high aspirations for them or an authoritative parenting style (Brooks-Gunn, Guo, & Furstenberg, 1993).

Dropping out of high school, like academic success, results from a complex interaction of academic and social variables (Garnier, Stein, & Jacobs, 1997). The proportion of U.S. students who drop out has steadily declined over the past few decades. For example, almost 85% of high school students in the United States receive a diploma (FIFCFS, 2000). Hispanic Americans have the highest drop-out rates at 32%, compared with 16% for African Americans and 10% for whites ("Students cite pregnancies as reason," 1994b).

Despite ethnic differences in drop-out rates, social class is a better predictor of school completion than is ethnicity. Children growing up in poor families—especially poor families with a single parent—are considerably more likely to drop out of high school than are those from more economically advantaged or intact families. When social class is held constant, drop-out rates among African Americans, whites, and Hispanic Americans differ very little (Entwisle, 1990). But because minority teenagers in the United States are so much more likely to come from poor families or from families that do not provide psychological support for academic achievement, they are also more likely to drop out of school. When a teenager's peer group also puts a low value on achievement, as is true in many African American and Hispanic American teen groups in the United States, the risk of dropping out is even higher (Takei & Dubas, 1993) (see No Easy Answers).

Longitudinal studies have found three strong predictors of dropping out: a history of academic failure, a pattern of aggressive behavior, and decisions about risky behavior (Cairns & Cairns, 1994; Garnier, Stein, & Jacobs, 1997; Jimerson, 1999). With respect to risky behavior, decisions about sexual intercourse seem to be especially critical. For girls, giving birth and getting married are strongly linked to dropping out. Another risky behavior, adolescent drug use, is also a strong predictor of dropping out (Garnier, Stein, & Jacobs, 1997). In fact, alcohol and drug use better predict a high school student's grades than do the student's grades in elementary or middle school. Consequently, decisions about such risky behaviors seem to

Reaching the High School Drop-Out

One of the greatest challenges facing educators is how to motivate teenagers who have dropped out of high school to return. One recent educational innovation, the *charter school,* seems to be especially promising with regard to meeting the educational needs of drop-outs. Traditionally, public schools serve a particular geographic area, usually called an "attendance zone." If a family lives in neighborhood A, their children must attend school A. Charter schools offer open enrollment; students from any public school attendance zone can enroll. The schools are funded either by states or by local school districts, based on the number of students they attract. Recent surveys of charter schools reveal that the largest percentage of them, about 40%, are aimed at dropouts (Center for Education Reform, 1999).

YouthBuild/Boston is a good example. Part of a national network of programs,

YouthBuild/Boston offers low-income dropouts an opportunity to achieve three goals. First, students learn marketable construction-related job skills such as carpentry, safety management, and computer-aided drafting. Second, they work toward either a GED or a high school diploma. Third, students work on construction projects that help provide poor families in their neighborhoods with affordable housing.

About 70 17- to 24-year-olds are currently enrolled in YouthBuild/Boston. They spend half their time in academic classes and the other half working at construction sites. Each student has an individualized academic plan, and about a third plan to go on to college.

YouthBuild/Boston also recognizes that drop-outs face a variety of nonacademic obstacles to high school completion. To address students' motivational needs, the program includes counseling, help with goal-setting, and leadership skill development. Students also get

help with material needs such as child care and income assistance through a network of social service providers, to which they are referred by school counselors.

Programs such as YouthBuild/Boston attract large numbers of students and have good attendance rates (Massachusetts Department of Education, 2000). About 30% of enrollees eventually obtain a GED or a high school diploma. Yet, a high proportion of these charter school students drop out. In fact, one of YouthBuild/Boston's program reports indicates that two-thirds of the students in the carpentry skills program dropped out in a single year (YouthBuild/Boston, 2000). Presumably, the same factors that led these youths to drop out of school in the first place continue to be problematic. For this reason, charter schools are continuing to strive to modify their programs to foster higher retention and graduation rates.

be one factor that can cause a teen to deviate from a previously positive developmental pathway.

Peer influence may also be a factor in dropping out. Teens who quit school are likely to have friends who have dropped out or who are contemplating leaving school (Ellenbogen & Chamberland, 1997). Family variables are also linked to dropping out. For example, children whose families move a lot when they are in elementary or middle school are at increased risk for dropping out of high school (Worrell, 1997).

One group of researchers has explored the possibility that, by taking into consideration several relevant factors, a general profile of high school students who are potential drop-outs can be identified. Their research has led to identification of the type of high school student who is likely to drop out: one who is quiet, disengaged, low-achieving, and poorly adjusted (Janosz, Le Blanc, Boulerice, & Tremblay, 2000).

Whatever its cause, dropping out of high school is associated with a number of long-term consequences. For instance, unemployment is higher among adults who dropped out of high school than among those who graduated, and drop-outs who do manage to find jobs earn lower wages than peers who graduate (Crystal, Shae, & Krishnaswami, 1992). Adults who dropped out of high school are also more likely to experience depression (Hagan, 1997). Furthermore, research suggests that staying in school may be an important protective factor for boys who have poor self-regulation skills. When boys who are poor self-regulators stay in school, they appear to be less likely than poor self-regulators who drop out to become involved in criminal activity in early adulthood (Henry et al., 1999).

Working Teens

In the United States, the great majority of high school students have had at least some paid work experience by the time they graduate (Bachman & Schulenberg, 1993). In contrast, teens in other industrialized nations are less likely to be employed, and when they are employed, they work fewer hours (Larson & Verma, 1999). Given the amount of time they devote to employment, and the number of hours they spend watching television, listening to music, and playing video games, it isn't surprising that U.S. teens spend half as much out-of-school time completing school work as do European and Asian high school students. Thus, differences in time allocation may be one reason behind cross-cultural differences in academic achievement.

● *Negative Effects of Employment* ●   Several major studies suggest that the more hours adolescents work, the more negative are the consequences. In the largest single study, researchers accumulated information from more than 70,000 students, seniors in the graduating classes of 1985 through 1989 (Bachman & Schulenberg, 1993). Participants were drawn each year from both private and public schools in every state in the country. Roughly four-fifths of the students worked at least a few hours per week, most of them for pay. Nearly half of the boys (46.5%) and more than a third of the girls (38.4%) worked more than 20 hours per week.

The researchers found that the more hours a student worked, the more he (or she) used drugs (alcohol, cigarettes, marijuana, cocaine), the more aggression he showed toward peers, the more arguments he had with parents, the less sleep he got, the less often he ate breakfast, the less exercise he got, and the less satisfied he was with life. More recent studies have produced similar findings, suggesting that working more than 10–15 hours per week is detrimental to high school students' grades and increases their risk of engaging in a number of risky behaviors (Valois & Dunham, 1998; Valois, Dunham, Jackson, & Waller, 1999).

The second major piece of pessimistic evidence comes from a study of Wisconsin and California teenagers (Steinberg & Dornbusch, 1991; Steinberg, Fegley, & Dornbusch, 1993). This study examined employment information collected in 1987 and 1988 from 5,300 ninth- through twelfth-graders. The researchers found that work has a variety of negative effects on teenagers, including lowering school grades and weakening commitment to school.

Figure 10.5 (page 306) graphs one finding from each of these studies, so you can see the size of the effects. Steinberg and Dornbusch found essentially the same pattern of results for all the ethnic groups in their study and for students from every economic level. So this is a widespread and significant effect.

At this point, some of you are undoubtedly thinking that results like those in Figure 10.5 may not mean that working during the high school years causes the bad effects observed. Instead, students who are least interested in school and who already hang out with others who smoke or drink more may be the same ones who choose to work more. In fact, the results of several studies are consistent with such an interpretation (Bachman & Schulenberg, 1993; Schoenhals, Tienda, & Schneider, 1998). For example, in one study, researchers found that those high school seniors who were getting the best grades and who were planning to go on to college were least likely to work (Bachman & Schulenberg, 1993).

Another potential negative effect of employment is that teenagers may be taken advantage of by employers. Few adolescents or their parents are aware of the legal restrictions on teenaged employment. Table 10.2 (page 306) lists several federal restrictions on adolescent work in the United States, and most states have even stricter laws protecting young workers (U.S. Department of Health and Human Services, 1997). Workplace safety is of particular concern, because about 70 teenagers die each year in work-related accidents in the United States. In addition, more than 70,000 are treated in hospital emergency rooms for injuries suffered on the job.

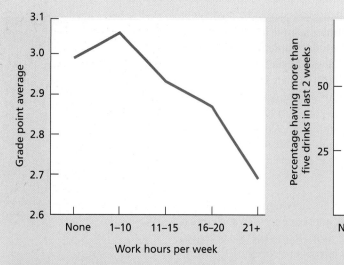

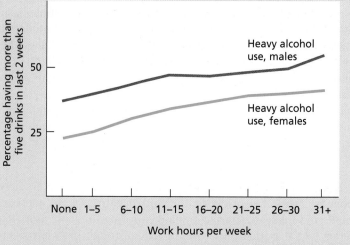

FIGURE 10.5

Evidence for the negative effect of teenage employment: Data on grades come from Steinberg and Dornbusch's study; data on alcohol use come from Bachman and Schulenberg. (*Sources*: Bachman & Schulenberg, 1993, from Figure 1, p. 226; Steinberg & Dornbusch, 1991, from Figure 1, p. 308.)

● **Positive Effects of Employment** ● Some studies suggest that only working on weekdays, not on weekends, has a detrimental effect on high school students' grades (Miller & Pedersen-Randall, 1995). Moreover, studies that consider the quality of the job as well as the number of hours worked find little or no correlation between the number of hours students work and their school grades or risk of problem behavior (Mael, Morath, & McLellan, 1997; McNeal, 1997; Mortimer, Finch, Dennehy, Lee, & Beebe, 1995). It seems that students who have positive work experiences develop increased feelings of competence and efficacy.

TABLE 10.2 Federal Restrictions on Teen Employment in the United States

	Tasks Not Permitted	
Restrictions on Hours	**Workers Younger than 16**	**Workers Younger than 18**
No work before 7 a.m. or after 7. p.m.	Baking or cooking	Driving a motor vehicle or forklift
No work during school hours	Working on a ladder or scaffold	Operating power-driven machinery
No more than 3 hours' work per school day	Warehouse work	Work in any of the following fields or situations: wrecking, demolition, excavation, roofing, mining, logging, sawmills, meat packing, slaughtering
No more than 8 hours' work per weekend day or holiday	Work in construction, building, or manufacturing	
No more than 18 hours' work per week	Loading or unloading trucks, railroad cars, or conveyor belts	Work in radiation-exposed areas or where explosives are used, manufactured, or stored

(*Source:* U.S. Department of Health and Human Services, 1997.)

Studies based on this more complex view of teenagers' employment have also shown that students who seem to benefit from work allocate their time differently than do those who experience negative effects (Schoenhals, Tienda, & Schneider, 1998). Such teens reduce the amount of time they devote to leisure activities, such as television and video games, in order to work. In addition, they continue to spend just as much time studying as they did before they were employed.

Before going on

- How might changes in students' academic goals explain declines in achievement and self-esteem at the middle school transition, and what are the negative and positive aspects of the transition to high school?

- How do male and female students, as well as students in different ethnic and cultural groups, differ with respect to math and science achievement?

- What variables predict the likelihood of dropping out of high school?

- List the negative and positive effects of teenagers' employment.

Most teenagers with jobs have low-level, low-responsibility, low-paying ones. Some psychologists believe that the negative effects of employment in adolescence may be caused by the type of work teens do. (*Photo:* David R. Frazier, Photo Researchers)

A Final Word

Most of us use the word *adolescence* as if it referred to a fairly precise span of years, but the relevant age range is fairly fuzzy. If the hormonal changes of puberty begin at 7 or 8, does this mean that adolescence begins at this age? If a child is still only 10 years old when he enters middle school, is he, then, an adolescent? And what about the clear differences between younger and older adolescents with respect to cognition? Clearly, the term *adolescence* is inadequate to describe this period if the focus is solely on specific developmental changes. Instead, it makes more sense to think of adolescence in cultural terms—as a period of time defined differently by different cultures but marking the transition from childhood to adulthood.

Summary

Physical Changes

- Puberty is triggered by a complex set of hormonal changes, beginning at about age 7 or 8. Very large increases in gonadotrophic hormones are central to the process. In girls, mature sexuality is achieved as early as $12\frac{1}{2}$ or $13\frac{1}{2}$. Sexual maturity is achieved later in boys, with the growth spurt occurring a year or more after the start of genital changes.

- Variations in the rate of pubertal development have some psychological effects. In general, children whose physical development occurs markedly earlier or later than they expect or desire show more negative effects than do those whose development is "on time."
- The brain continues to develop in adolescence. There are two major brain growth spurts: the first between ages 13 and 15, and the second between ages 17 and 19. Puberty is accompanied by a rapid growth spurt in height, and an increase in muscle mass and in fat. Boys add more muscle, and girls more fat.

Adolescent Health

- Adolescents have fewer acute illnesses than younger children but more injuries. In general, they show higher rates of various kinds of risky behavior, including unprotected sex, drug use, and fast driving.
- Sexual activity among teenagers has increased in recent decades in the United States. Roughly half of all U.S. teens have had sexual intercourse by the time they reach their last year of high school.
- Long-term consequences for adolescent girls who bear children are generally negative, although a minority of such girls are able to overcome the disadvantages.

Substance Abuse and Mental Health Problems

- Alcohol and drug use among U.S. teenagers, after declining for several decades, is now on the rise. Those most likely to use or abuse drugs are those who also show other forms of deviant or problem behavior, including poor school achievement.
- Eating disorders such as bulimia and anorexia are more common among teenaged girls than among boys.
- Depression and suicide are other mental health problems that are common during adolescence.

Changes in Thinking and Memory

- Piaget proposed a fourth stage of cognitive development in adolescence. The formal operational stage is characterized by the ability to apply basic cognitive operations to ideas and possibilities, in addition to actual objects.
- Researchers have found clear evidence of such advanced forms of thinking in at least some adolescents. But formal operational thinking is not universal, nor is it consistently used by those who are able to do it.
- Memory function improves in adolescence as teens become more proficient in metacognition, metamemory, and strategy use.

Schooling

- The transition to middle school may be accompanied by changes in children's goal orientation that result in declines in achievement and self-esteem. The high school transition offers many teens more opportunities to pursue special interests and extracurricular activities.
- Female, African American, and Hispanic American high school students score lower on science and math achievement tests and choose to take courses in these disciplines less often than do white and Asian American males. Girls may view success in science and math as unacceptable for women. African American and Hispanic American students may not be getting the preparation they need in middle school for advanced high school math courses.
- Those who succeed academically in high school are typically from authoritative families. Those who drop out are more likely to be poor or to be doing poorly in school.
- Adolescents who work more than 10–15 hours per week get lower grades and engage in more risky behavior than those who work less. Work can be beneficial for students who work only on weekends and have positive work experiences.

Key Terms

ability goals (p. 300)

anorexia nervosa (p. 292)

bulimia (p. 291)

endocrine glands (p. 279)

formal operational stage (p. 295)

gonadotrophic hormones (p. 279)

hypothetico-deductive reasoning (p. 295)

menarche (p. 280)

pituitary gland (p. 279)

secular trend (p. 280)

systematic problem-solving (p. 296)

task goals (p. 300)

CHAPTER

11

Social and Personality Development in Adolescence

Courtesy of Drs. Booker and Madeline Wright. Used with permission.

The change in status from child to adult is considered to be so important that many societies mark its passage with a *rite of passage*, a formal ritual representing an adolescent's initiation into adult culture. In some nonindustrialized societies, young adolescents begin working or sleeping separately from their families for the first time since birth, emphasizing the child's membership in the larger social group (Cohen, 1964). In other cultures, alterations of a teen's physical appearance or trials of endurance play a part in the rite of passage.

In industrialized societies, formal rites of passage are usually confined to specific social, ethnic, or religious groups. For example, the daughters of some wealthy families, such as those in the photograph at the beginning of the chapter, participate in debutante balls that mark their formal entrance into adult society. In many Hispanic communities, a special celebration of a girl's 15th birthday, or *quinceañera,* announces that a girl has reached maturity. Similarly, Jewish boys and girls participate in *bar mitzvah* and *bat mitzvah* ceremonies, and youth in many Christian denominations go through a process called *confirmation.* However, adolescents in industrialized cultures have no universally shared initiation rites. Social scientists speculate that this is one reason why adolescents in such cultures often emphasize their own separation and distinctness, such as by wearing unusual or even outlandish clothing or hairstyles.

Nevertheless, all teens in industrialized countries share many changes in status. The transition from elementary to secondary school is one such change. In the United States, young people can have a driver's license at 16 and can see R-rated movies at 17. At 17 or 18, depending on the state, those who are accused of crimes will be tried in adult rather than juvenile court. At 18, teenagers can vote and enter the military without parental consent.

In this chapter, you will learn about the psychological and social aspects of this important transition. We will begin by examining the process of identity development. In the sections that follow, you will read about changes in adolescents' self-concepts and social relationships. Finally, we will examine the development of moral reasoning. While you read, keep the following questions in mind:

- How do Freud, Erikson, and Marcia view the adolescent years?

- How do teenagers' self-concepts change, and how does personality contribute to development in these years?

- In what ways do adolescents' relationships with parents and peers change?

- How do the views of Kohlberg and his critics differ with respect to moral development?

Theories of Social and Personality Development

As you have learned in earlier chapters, psychoanalytic approaches to social and personality development emphasize conflicts between individual needs and societal demands. Psychoanalytic theories identify and clarify the major themes of social and personality development during adolescence, such as the teenager's acquiring a sense of who she is as an individual. Likewise, cultural perspectives derived from other disciplines can reveal the important role culture plays in the adolescent's transition from child to adult.

Psychoanalytic Perspectives

According to Freud, the post-pubertal years consitute the last stage of personality development; so both adolescents and adults are in what Freud called the **genital stage,** the period during which psychosexual maturity is reached. Freud believed that puberty awakens the sexual drive that has lain dormant during the latency stage. Thus, for Freud, the primary developmental task of the genital stage is to channel the libido into a healthy sexual relationship.

From Freud's cultural perspective, marriage and procreation represented healthy adjustments to the genital stage. However, he believed that fixation at prior stages would undermine an adolescent's or adult's achievement of this goal. Specifically, fixation at the phallic stage could lead to sexual deviance or dysfunction.

Erikson, though not denying the importance of achieving sexual maturity, proposed a somewhat different way of conceptualizing adolescence. In his model, the central crisis of adolescence is **identity versus role confusion.** Erikson argued that the child's early sense of identity comes partly "unglued" in early adolescence because of the combination of rapid body growth and the sexual changes of puberty. Erikson claimed that during this period the adolescent's mind is in a kind of moratorium between childhood and adulthood. The old identity will no longer suffice; a new identity must be forged, one that will equip the young person for the myriad roles of adult life—occupational roles, sexual roles, religious roles, and others.

Confusion about all these role choices is inevitable and leads to a pivotal transition Erikson called the *identity crisis.* The **identity crisis** is a period during which an adolescent is troubled by his lack of an identity. Erikson believed that adolescents' tendency to identify with peer groups was a defense against the emotional turmoil engendered by the identity crisis. In a sense, he claimed, teens protect themselves against the unpleasant emotions of the identity crisis by merging their individual identities with that of a group (Erikson, 1980a). The teenaged group thus forms a base of security from which the young person can move toward a unique solution of the identity crisis. Ultimately, however, each teenager must achieve an integrated view of himself, including his own pattern of beliefs, occupational goals, and relationships.

In the Jewish ceremony called *bar mitzvah* (for boys) or *bat mitzvah* (for girls), 13-year-olds read from the Torah in Hebrew and are admitted to full adult status in the congregation. The Tanzanian boy has had his face painted with white clay as part of an adolescent rite of passage. (*Photos:* Bill Aron, PhotoEdit; The Purcell Team/CORBIS)

Marcia's Theory of Identity Achievement

Nearly all the current work on the formation of adolescent identity has been based on James Marcia's descriptions of *identity statuses,* which are rooted in Erikson's general conceptions of the adolescent identity process (Marcia, 1966, 1980). Following one of Erikson's ideas, Marcia argues that adolescent identity formation has two key parts: a crisis and a commitment. By a *crisis,* Marcia means a period of decision-making when old values and old choices are reexamined. This may occur as a sort of upheaval—the classic notion of a crisis—or it may occur gradually. The outcome of the reevaluation is a *commitment* to some specific role, value, goal, or ideology.

If you put these two elements together, as shown in Figure 11.1 (on p. 312), you can see that four different *identity statuses* are possible.

- **Identity achievement:** The person has been through a crisis and has reached a commitment to ideological, occupational, or other goals.

genital stage in Freud's theory, the period during which people reach psychosexual maturity

identity versus role confusion in Erikson's theory, the stage during which adolescents attain a sense of who they are

identity crisis Erikson's term for the psychological state of emotional turmoil that arises when an adolescent's sense of self becomes "unglued" so that a new, more mature sense of self can be achieved

identity achievement in Marcia's theory, the identity status achieved by a person who has been through a crisis and reached a commitment to ideological or occupational goals

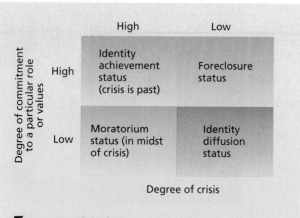

FIGURE 11.1

The four identity statuses proposed by Marcia, based on Erikson's theory. For a fully achieved identity, the young person must have both examined her values or goals and reached a firm commitment. (*Source:* Marcia, 1980.)

- **Moratorium:** A crisis is in progress, but no commitment has yet been made.

- **Foreclosure:** The person has made a commitment without having gone through a crisis. No reassessment of old positions has been made. Instead, the young person has simply accepted a parentally or culturally defined commitment.

- **Identity diffusion:** The young person is not in the midst of a crisis (although there may have been one in the past) and has not made a commitment. Diffusion may thus represent either an early stage in the process (before a crisis) or a failure to reach a commitment after a crisis.

Cross-sectional studies of adolescents and young adults suggest that the whole process of identity formation may occur later than Erikson and Marcia thought. One combined analysis of eight cross-sectional studies revealed that identity achievement occurred most often in college, not during the high school years (Waterman, 1985). Among the participants in these studies, moratorium was relatively uncommon except in the early years of college. So, if most young people go through an identity crisis, the crisis occurs fairly late in adolescence and does not last terribly long. Furthermore, about a third of the young people at every age were in the foreclosure category, which may indicate that many young people simply do not go through a crisis at all, but follow predetermined and well-defined grooves.

As a further caution, it is important to note that all the participants in these studies were either in college or in college-preparatory high school programs. This may give a false impression of the process of identity formation for young people who do not go to college, who do not have the luxury of a long period of questioning but must work out some kind of personal identity while still in their teens.

In addition, cognitive development may be more strongly related to identity formation than either Erikson or Marcia believed. Research suggests that teens who are most advanced in the development of logical thinking and other information-processing skills are also the most likely to have attained Marcia's status of identity achievement (Klaczynski, Fauth, & Swanger, 1998). This may help to explain why the process takes place at somewhat later ages than Erikson's or Marcia's theories predict.

There is also evidence that the quest for personal identity continues throughout the lifespan, with alternating periods of instability and stability. For example, a person's sense of being "young" or "old" and her integration of that idea into a sense of belonging to a particular generation appears to change several times over the course of the adolescent and adult years (Sato, Shimonska, Nakazato, & Kawaai, 1997). Consequently, adolescence may be only one period of identity formation among several.

Other research suggests that males and females experience the adolescent/early adulthood identity crisis differently (Lytle, Bakken, & Romig, 1997; Moretti & Wiebe, 1999). For example, girls seem to fit Erikson's and Marcia's hypotheses about adolescent identity formation better than boys do. They consolidate their identities at a younger age, and they do so by integrating internal beliefs about themselves with information gained through social relationships. Conversely, boys are more likely to delay identity achievement until adulthood and to focus more on internal sources than on social sources of information in the process of identity construction.

Critical Thinking

The implication in Marcia's formulation is that foreclosure is a less developmentally mature status—that one must go through a crisis in order to achieve a mature identity. Does this make sense to you? What is your current identity status? Has it changed much over the past few years?

moratorium in Marcia's theory, the identity status of a person who is in a crisis but who has made no commitment

foreclosure in Marcia's theory, the identity status of a person who has made a commitment without having gone through a crisis; the person has simply accepted a parentally or culturally defined commitment

identity diffusion in Marcia's theory, the identity status of a person who is not in the midst of a crisis and who has made no commitment

Further, teenagers facing extreme stressors, such as life-threatening illnesses, seem to be most optimally adjusted when they adopt the status of foreclosure (Madan-Swain et al., 2000). Accepting others' goals for them, at least temporarily, seems to protect these teens against some of the negative emotional effects of the difficulties they must face. Thus, the idea that progression to identity achievement is the most psychologically healthy response to the identity crisis clearly doesn't apply to some adolescents.

The whole concept of an adolescent identity crisis has also been strongly influenced by current cultural assumptions in Western societies, in which full adult status is postponed for almost a decade after puberty. In such cultures, young people do not normally or necessarily adopt the same roles or occupations as their parents. Indeed, they are encouraged to choose for themselves. These adolescents are faced with what may be a bewildering array of options, a pattern that might well foster the sort of identity crisis Erikson described. In less industrialized cultures, there may well be a shift in identity from that of child to that of adult, but without a crisis of any kind. Further, adolescents' search for identity in other cultures may be better supported by cultural initiation rites that clearly, at least in a symbolic sense, separate childhood from adulthood.

Before going on

- Describe Freud's genital stage and Erikson's stage of identity versus role confusion.

- How does Marcia explain identity development?

Self-Concept and Personality

In Chapter 10, you read that thinking becomes more abstract in adolescence. Thus, you shouldn't be surprised to find that teenagers' self-concepts are a lot more complex than those of younger children.

Self-Understanding

You should remember that, through the elementary school years, the child's self-concept becomes more focused on enduring internal characteristics—the psychological self. This trend continues in adolescence, with self-definition becoming more abstract. You may remember the replies of a 9-year-old and an 11-year-old to the question "Who am I?" in Montemayor and Eisen's study, cited in Chapter 9. Here's a 17-year-old's answer to the same question:

I am a human being. I am a girl. I am an individual. I don't know who I am. I am a Pisces. I am a moody person. I am an indecisive person. I am an ambitious person. I am a very curious person. I am not an individual. I am a loner. I am an American (God help me). I am a Democrat. I am a liberal person. I am a radical. I am a conservative. I am a pseudoliberal. I am an atheist. I am not a classifiable person (i.e., I don't want to be). (Montemayor & Eisen, 1977, p. 318)

Clearly, this girl's self-concept is even less tied to her physical characteristics or even her abilities than are those of younger children. She is describing abstract traits or ideology.

You can see the change very graphically in Figure 11.2, which is based on the answers of all 262 participants in Montemayor and Eisen's study. Each of the answers to the "Who am I?" question was categorized as either a reference to physical properties ("I am tall," "I have blue eyes") or to ideology ("I am a Democrat," "I believe in God"). As you can see, appearance was a highly prominent dimension in the preteen and early teen years but became less dominant in late adolescence, a time when ideology and belief became more important. By late adolescence, most teenagers think of themselves in terms of enduring traits, beliefs, personal philosophy, and moral standards (Damon & Hart, 1988).

At the same time, the adolescent's self-concept becomes more differentiated, as she comes to see herself somewhat differently in each of several roles: as a student, with friends, with parents, and in romantic relationships (Harter & Monsour, 1992). Once these self-concepts are formed, they begin to influence adolescents' behavior. For example, teens whose academic self-concepts are strong take more difficult courses in high school than do teens who believe themselves to be less academically able. Further, they tend to select courses in disciplines in which they believe they have the greatest ability and to avoid courses in perceived areas of weakness (Marsh & Yeung, 1997).

Adolescents' academic self-concepts seem to come both from internal comparisons of their performance to a self-generated ideal and from external comparisons to peer performance (Bong, 1998). It also appears that perceived competency in one domain affects how a teenager feels about his ability in other areas. For example, if a high school student fails a math course, it is likely to affect his self-concept in other disciplines as well as in math. This suggests that teens' self-concepts are hierarchical in nature: Perceived competencies in various domains serve as building blocks for creating a global academic self-concept (Yeung, Chui, & Lau, 1999).

Social self-concepts also predict behavior. For example, a teenager's family self-concept reflects his beliefs about the likelihood of attaining and/or maintaining satisfactory relationships with family members. Developmentalists have found that adolescents who are estranged from their families, such as runaways, perceive themselves to be less competent in the give-and-take of family relations than teens who are close to parents and siblings (Swaim & Bracken, 1997). Indeed, the perceived lack of competency in family relations appears to be distinct from other components of self-concept.

Girls and boys also appear to construct the various components of self-concept somewhat differently. For example, a recent study of teens' evaluations of their own writing abilities found that boys and girls rated themselves as equally capable writers (Pajares & Valiante, 1999). However, the girls scored higher on objective tests of writing ability. In addition, the girls were more likely to describe themselves as being better writers than their peers of both genders. The boys, by contrast, seemed to perceive few ability differences in their peers. In other words, the boys believed they were good writers, but they also thought that their classmates were as good as they were.

Such findings are predictable, given the information in the previous section about girls being influenced by both internal and external comparisons while boys attend more to internal, self-

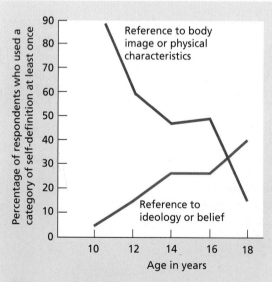

FIGURE 11.2

As they get older, children and adolescents define themselves less and less by what they look like and more and more by what they believe or feel. (*Source:* Montemayor & Eisen, 1977, from Table 1, p. 316.)

defined standards. The findings also raise interesting questions about the degree to which self-concept development is influenced by cultural ideas about sex roles. Perhaps girls pay more attention to their own and others' writing skills because they know that girls are supposed to be better at language skills than boys.

Sex-Role Identity

The links between gender and development in adolescence are partly a result of the physical changes of puberty, are undergirded by each individual teenager's understanding of gender itself, and are influenced by the social environment. For example, in Chapter 10, you learned that early- and late-maturing teens differ in important ways. Also, in contrast to younger children, adolescents understand that sex roles are social conventions, so their attitudes toward them are more flexible (Katz & Ksansnak, 1994). Parental attitudes and parental behavior become increasingly important in shaping teens' ideas about gender and sex roles (Castellino, Lerner, Lerner, & von Eye, 1998; Ex & Janssens, 1998; Jackson & Tein, 1998). In addition, concepts that were largely separate earlier in development, such as beliefs about sex roles and sexuality, seem to become integrated into a conceptual framework that teens use to formulate ideas about the significance of gender in personal identity and social relationships (Mallet, Apostolidis, & Paty, 1997).

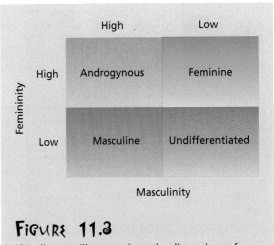

FIGURE 11.3

This diagram illustrates how the dimensions of masculinity and femininity interact to produce four types of sex-role orientation.

By their mid-teens, most adolescents have also largely abandoned the automatic assumption that whatever their own gender does is better or preferable (Powlishta, Serbin, Doyle, & White, 1994). Indeed, a significant minority of teenagers include both masculine and feminine traits in their psychological self-concepts. Developmentalists use the term **sex-role identity** to refer to gender-related aspects of the psychological self.

In the early days of research on sex-role identity, psychologists conceived of masculinity and femininity as polar opposites. A person could be masculine or feminine, but couldn't be both. However, theories first advanced in the 1970s have resulted in a large body of research in support of the notion that masculinity and femininity are dimensions along a continuum and each may be found in varying quantities in the personalities of both men and women (Bem, 1974; Spence & Helmreich, 1978). A male or a female can be high or low on masculinity or femininity, or both. Indeed, if people are categorized as high or low on each of these two dimensions, based on their self-descriptions, four basic sex-role types emerge: *masculine, feminine, androgynous,* and *undifferentiated* (see Figure 11.3).

The masculine and feminine types are the traditional categories; a person in either of these categories sees himself or herself as high in one and low in the other. A "masculine" teenager or adult, according to this view, is thus one who perceives himself (or herself) as having many traditional masculine qualities and few traditional feminine qualities. A feminine teenager or adult shows the reverse pattern. In contrast, androgynous individuals see themselves as having both masculine and feminine traits; undifferentiated individuals describe themselves as lacking both. Several studies show that roughly 25–35% of U.S. junior high and high school students define themselves as androgynous (e.g., Boldizar, 1991; Rose & Montemayor, 1994). More girls than boys seem to show this pattern, and more girls fall into the masculine category than boys in the feminine category.

Self-Esteem

Interestingly, research suggests that either an androgynous or a masculine sex-role identity is associated with higher self-esteem among both boys and girls (Boldizar, 1991; Burnett, Anderson, & Heppner, 1995; Rose & Montemayor, 1994). This finding

sex-role identity the gender-related aspects of the psychological self

Teenaged boys like these may have an easier time achieving high self-esteem than girls of the same age, because both boys and girls seem to place a higher value on certain traditionally "masculine" qualities than on traditionally "feminine" qualities.
(*Photo:* Jeff Greenberg, PhotoEdit)

makes sense in light of the existence of a "masculine bias" in American and other Western societies, which causes both men and women to value traditionally masculine qualities such as independence and competitiveness more than many traditionally female qualities.

If such a bias exists—and there is good reason to think that it does—then the teenaged boy's task is simpler than the teenaged girl's. He can achieve high self-esteem and success with his peers by adopting a traditional masculine sex role. But a girl who adopts a traditional feminine sex role is adopting a less-valued role, with attendant risks of lower self-esteem and a reduced sense of competence (Rose & Montemayor, 1994). Findings like these suggest the possibility that although the creation of rigid rules, or schemas, for sex roles is a normal—even essential—process in young children, a blurring of those rules may be an important process in adolescence, particularly for girls, for whom a more masculine or androgynous self-concept is associated with more positive outcomes.

However, cross-cultural research suggests that adoption of an androgynous or masculine orientation by a girl can lead to lower self-esteem. For example, one study of Israeli girls found that pre-teens who were tomboys and who rated themselves high on masculine personality traits were less popular and had lower self-esteem than their more feminine peers (Lobel, Slone, & Winch, 1997). Consequently, when considering gender roles and sex-role identity, it is important to remember that both are very strongly tied to culture. A particular society may value the masculine role more highly but also actively discourage girls from adopting it. Thus, it may not be universally true that teens who adopt the more highly valued sex-role identity gain self-esteem.

Self-esteem shows other interesting shifts during the teenaged years. The overall trend is a steady rise in self-esteem through the years of adolescence. The average 19- or 20-year-old has a considerably more positive sense of her global self-worth than she did at age 8 or 11 (Diehl, Vicary, & Deike, 1997; Harter, 1990; Wigfield, Eccles, MacIver, Reuman, & Midgley, 1991). However, the rise to higher self-esteem during adolescence is not continuous. At the beginning of adolescence, self-esteem very often drops rather abruptly. In one study, developmentalists followed a group of nearly 600 Hispanic American, African American, and white youngsters over the 2 years from sixth grade to junior high (Seidman, Allen, Aber, Mitchell, & Feinman, 1994). Researchers found a significant average drop in self-esteem over that period, a decline that occurred in each of the three ethnic groups.

To study the relationship of self-esteem to important developmental outcomes, such as school achievement, researchers often divide teens into four groups based on the stability of their self-esteem ratings across adolescence (Diehl, Vicary, & Deike, 1997; Zimmerman, Copeland, Shope, & Dielman, 1997). The largest group, about half in most studies, display consistently high self-esteem throughout adolescence. The self-esteem of those in the second group steadily increases, and the self-esteem ratings of those in the third group are consistently low. Teens in the fourth group enjoy moderate to high self-esteem at the beginning of the period, but it declines steadily as adolescence progresses. One finding of concern is that girls outnumber boys in the third and fourth groups (Zimmerman et al., 1997). In addition, several studies have found that high self-esteem is correlated with positive developmental outcomes. For example, teens with high self-esteem are better able to resist peer pressure and get higher grades in school. You may also remember from Chapter 10 that such teens are less likely to become involved in substance abuse or early sexual intercourse.

Ethnic Identity

ethnic identity a sense of belonging to an ethnic group

Minority teenagers, especially those of color in a predominantly white culture, face the task of creating two identities in adolescence. Like other teens, they must develop a sense of individual identity that they believe sets them apart from others. In addition, they must develop an **ethnic identity** that includes self-identification as a member of their specific group, commitment to that group and its values and attitudes, and some attitudes (positive or negative) about the group to which they belong. Moreover, the process of developing an ethnic identity is often poorly supported by a social environment that is dominated by the concerns of an ethnic majority.

Critical Thinking

How do you think your own ethnicity affects your sense of identity? Do you ever think of yourself as being "bicultural"?

Psychologist Jean Phinney has proposed that in adolescence, the development of a complete ethnic identity moves through three stages (Phinney, 1990; Phinney & Rosenthal, 1992). The first stage is an *unexamined ethnic identity,* equivalent to the identity status Marcia calls foreclosure. For some subgroups in U.S. society, such as African Americans and Native Americans, this unexamined identity typically includes the negative images and stereotypes common in the wider culture. Indeed, it may be especially at adolescence, with the advent of the cognitive ability to reflect and interpret, that the young person becomes keenly aware of how his own group is perceived by the majority. As Spencer and Dornbusch put it, "The young African American may learn as a child that black is beautiful but conclude as an adolescent that white is powerful" (1990, p. 131).

Many minority teenagers initially prefer the dominant white culture or wish they had been born into the majority. An African American journalist who grew up in an urban housing project clearly describes this initial negative feeling:

> If you were black, you didn't quite measure up. . . . For a black kid there was a certain amount of self-doubt. It came at you indirectly. You didn't see any black people on television, you didn't see any black people doing certain things. . . . You don't think it out but you say, "Well, it must mean that white people are better than we are. Smarter, brighter—whatever." (Spencer & Dornbusch, 1990, pp. 131–132)

Not all minority teenagers arrive at such negative views of their own group. Individual youngsters may have very positive ethnic images, conveyed by parents or others around them (see Development in the Information Age). Phinney's point is that this initial ethnic identity is not arrived at independently but comes from outside sources.

Phinney's second stage is the *ethnic identity search,* parallel to the crisis in Marcia's analysis of ego identity. This search is typically triggered by some experience that makes ethnicity relevant—perhaps an example of blatant prejudice or merely the widening experience of high school. At this point, the young person begins to compare his own ethnic group with others, to try to arrive at his own judgments.

This exploration stage is eventually followed by a resolution of the conflicts and contradictions—analogous to Marcia's status of identity achievement. This is often a difficult process. For example, some African American adolescents who wish to try to compete and succeed in the dominant culture may be ostracized by their black friends, who accuse them of "acting white" and betraying their blackness. Hispanic Americans often report similar experiences. Some resolve this by keeping their own ethnic group at arm's length; others deal with it by creating essentially two identities, as expressed by one young Hispanic American interviewed by Phinney:

> Being invited to someone's house, I have to change my ways of how I act at home, because of culture differences. I would have to follow what they do. . . . I am used to it now, switching off between the two. It is not difficult. (Phinney & Rosenthal, 1992, p. 160)

Still others resolve the dilemma by wholeheartedly choosing their own ethnic group's patterns and values, even when that choice may limit their access to the larger culture.

Young people of color often develop two identities: a psychological sense of self and an ethnic identity. Those who succeed at both tasks often think of themselves as "bicultural" and have an easier time relating to peers of the same and other ethnicities. (*Photos:* David Young-Wolff, PhotoEdit; Penny Tweedie, Stone)

The Search for Minority Role Models

Ethnic minority teens have problems when it comes to finding role models that can help with a quest for identity—because ethnic minorities are poorly represented in most media, including television, movies, and video games. For example, in U.S. TV dramas, only 15% of characters are members of ethnic minorities, even though minorities make up about 20% of the U.S. population ("Gerbner tackles 'fairness,' " 1997). Moreover, media portrayals of people of color are often either negative or stereotypical (Graves, 1993).

Given this situation, you might not be surprised to learn that a large majority of respondents to a survey of 4,500

African American boys aged 10 to 18 named a professional athlete when asked to identify a role model outside of their own families (Assibey-Mensah, 1997). The researcher thought that these boys might also name teachers as role models because of their everyday interactions with them. However, not a single one of the boys named a teacher as an important personal role model—which is astounding, considering the number of teens who participated in the study. These findings suggest that professional sports (or mass media) is a more important source of role models for these youths than their real-life experiences with adults. Comparisons of portrayals of teachers to those of athletes in media may help explain why these boys responded as they did.

News reports about public education often characterize schools with large proportions of minority students as failures. The implied image of teachers is that they are ineffective. Fictional teachers are often portrayed as poor, and many popular TV programs geared to young audiences (for example, *South Park* and *The Simpsons*) depict teachers and other school officials as buffoons who are not respected by their students. In contrast, stories about athletes (both fiction and nonfiction) are dominated by themes of fame, wealth, popularity, and achievements such as league championships and record-breaking statistics. Considering the contrast between the two, it isn't surprising that African American boys prefer athletes rather than teachers as role models.

In both cross-sectional and longitudinal studies, Phinney has found that African American teens and young adults do indeed move through these steps or stages toward a clear ethnic identity. The "bicultural" orientation of the last stage has been found to be a consistent characteristic of adolescents and adults who have high self-esteem and enjoy good relations with members of both the dominant culture and their own ethnic group (Yamada & Singelis, 1999). Further, African American teens are more likely than Asian American and white youths to choose friends whose ethnic identity status is similar to their own (Hamm, 2000).

Of course, the search for personal identity is also affected by ethnicity and culture. It is likely that parent-teen conflict is common and even socially acceptable in North American and European families because these individualistic cultures associate separation from parents with psychological and social maturity. As a result, parents in North America and Europe expect to experience these conflicts and endorse adolescents' efforts to demonstrate independence. For example, many American parents think that part-time jobs help teens mature. Thus, if an American parent prohibits a teenager from getting a job, but the adolescent presents a good argument as to why he should be allowed to work, the conflict is seen as a sign of maturity.

In contrast, cultures that emphasize the community rather than the individual view teens' acceptance of family responsibilities as a sign of maturity. A question such as whether a teen should get a job is decided in terms of family needs. If the family needs money, the adolescent might be encouraged to work. However, if the family needs the teenager to care for younger siblings while the parents work, then a part-time job is likely to be forbidden. If the teenager argues about the parents' decision, the conflict is seen as representing immaturity rather than maturity.

Research involving Asian American teenagers helps to illustrate this point. Psychologists have found that first-generation Asian American teens often feel guilty about responding to the individualistic pressures of North American culture. Their feelings of guilt appear to be based on their parents' cultural norms, which hold that the most mature adolescents are those who take a greater role in the family rather than trying to separate from it (Chen, 1999). Thus, for many Asian American adolescents, achievement of personal and ethnic identity involves balancing the individualistic demands of North American culture against the familial obligations of their parents' cultures.

Locus of Control and Other Traits

During adolescence, the Big Five personality traits coalesce with components of teens' understanding of themselves and others to form clusters that can be used to predict variables such as academic achievement and mental illness. One particularly important factor is a social and self-understanding variable known as **locus of control,** a set of beliefs about the causes of events (Rotter, 1990). Locus of control beliefs appear in middle childhood but become stable during the teenaged years, as adolescents' ability to think logically and to engage in complex information-processing improves.

Someone with an *external* locus of control attributes the causes of experiences such as school failure to factors outside himself. For example, an adolescent with an external locus of control might claim that he failed a class because the teacher didn't like him or because the class was too difficult. Someone with an *internal* locus of control views personal variables, such as ability and effort, as responsible for outcomes. A teen who believes either that she failed a class because she lacks ability or that she failed because she didn't try hard enough has an internal locus of control.

There are important correlations between locus of control and behavior (Janssen & Carton, 1999). An external locus of control is associated with procrastination and poor academic performance. In contrast, both teens and adults with an internal locus of control are more likely to complete tasks and to succeed in school.

For most teens who have external locus of control, the trait is balanced by other more positive aspects of personality. However, researchers have found that an external locus of control is sometimes part of a cluster of personality variables that includes low self-esteem, along with the introversion and neuroticism dimensions of the Big Five (Beautrais, Joyce, & Mulder, 1999). (You'll recall that introversion is a preference for solitary rather than social activities; individuals who score high on tests of neuroticism are pessimistic, irritable, and worry a lot.) Developmentalists have found that teens across a variety of cultures who possess this particular combination of characteristics have a very negative outlook on life, resist efforts by parents and friends to help them, and are at greater risk for all kinds of adjustment problems than their peers. For instance, these adolescents are more likely to use *avoidant coping* when they face problems (Gomez, Bounds, Holmberg, Fullarton, & Gomez, 1999; Gomez, Holmberg, Bounds, Fullarton, & Gomez, 1999; Medvedova, 1998). This means that they ignore problems or put off dealing with them. For example, a high school student with these traits who finds out he is failing a class may wait until it is too late to try to do anything about it. However, because he tends to blame others for his problems, he is unlikely to be able to learn from the experience.

Such teens get into these situations over and over again without ever seeming to be able to prevent them or to pull themselves out of trouble in any effective way. As a consequence of their negative outlook combined with their repeated experiences of disappointment and failure, these adolescents are prone to depression (del Barrio, Moreno-Rosset, Lopez-Martinez, & Olmedo, 1997; Ge & Conger, 1999). Once depressed, such teens are likely to attempt suicide (Beautrais, Joyce, & Mulder, 1999). Their emotional difficulties are compounded by the fact that most are rejected by peers (Young & Bradley, 1998).

Teens with these characteristics also seem to be, figuratively speaking, looking at the world through a different lens than their more optimistic peers. For example, they

locus of control a set of beliefs about the causes of events appear to think about themselves and their emotions a great deal more (Yarcheski, Mahon, & Yarcheski, 1998). Girls with this cluster of traits tend to see greater distinctions between male and female roles and personality than other girls do (Wilcox & Francis, 1997). They are also more likely to be intolerant of people whose ethnicity or political beliefs are different from their own (Sotelo & Sangrador, 1997).

The outlook for teens with this set of characteristics is not good. Their beliefs about themselves and the social world are resistant to change and persist into adulthood (Offer, Kaiz, Howard, & Bennett, 1998). In addition, as adults, they continue to be subject to bouts of depression and a variety of occupational and relationship difficulties. Consequently, developmentalists are currently searching for assessment tools and intervention strategies that can be used to identify and help such individuals in middle childhood or early adolescence (Young & Bradley, 1998).

Before going on

- In what ways does self-understanding in adolescence differ from that in childhood?

- What are the sex-role concepts of adolescents?

- How does self-esteem change across the teenaged years?

- How do minority teenagers develop an ethnic identity?

- How does the combination of external locus of control, low self-esteem, introversion, and neuroticism influence an adolescent's development?

Social Relationships

As you can see from the solutions for peer conflicts listed in Table 11.1, adolescents' ideas about other people and their understanding of social situations are more complex than those of children. These advances in interpersonal understanding lead to changes in family and peer relationships.

Relationships with Parents

Teenagers have two, apparently contradictory, tasks in their relationships with their parents: to establish autonomy from them and to maintain a sense of relatedness with them.

● ***Conflicts with Parents*** ●   The rise in conflict between parents and teenagers has been documented by a number of researchers (e.g., Flannery, Montemayor, & Eberly, 1994; Laursen, 1995; Steinberg, 1988). In the great majority of families, there is an increase in mild bickering or conflicts over everyday issues such as chores or personal rights—for example, whether the adolescent should be allowed to wear a bizarre hairstyle or whether and when the teen should be required to do chores. Teenagers

TABLE 11.1   Children's and Adolescent' Comments about How to Solve
Disagreements Between Friends

Age	Comments
5-Year-Olds	• Go away from her and come back later when you're not fighting.
	• Punch her out.
8-Year-Olds	• Around our way the guy who started it just says he's sorry.
	• Well, if you say something and don't really mean it, then you have to mean it when you take it back.
14-Year-Olds	• Sometimes you got to get away for a while. Calm down a bit so you won't be so angry. Then get back and try to talk it out.
	• If you just settle up after a fight that is no good. You gotta really feel that you'd be happy the way things went if you were in your friend's shoes. You can just settle up with someone who is not a friend, but that's not what friendship is really about.
16-Year-Old	• Well, you could talk it out, but it usually fades itself out. It usually takes care of itself. You don't have to explain everything. You do certain things and each of you knows what it means. But if not, then talk it out.

(*Source:* Selman, 1980, pp. 107–113.)

and their parents also often disagree about the age at which certain privileges—such as dating—ought to be granted (Dekovic, Noom, & Meeus, 1997).

Although this increase in discord is widely observed, you should not assume that it signifies a major disruption of the quality of the parent-child relationships. Laurence Steinberg, one of the key researchers on adolescence, estimates that only 5–10% of the families studied in the United States experience a substantial or pervasive deterioration in the quality of parent-child relationship in the years of early adolescence (Steinberg, 1990). Further, parent-teen conflicts appear to cause more distress for parents than for adolescents (Dekovic, 1999).

Individual traits of teenagers themselves may contribute to conflicts with parents. The adolescent's temperament, for example, contributes to the amount of conflict. Those who have been difficult from early childhood are the most likely to experience high degrees of conflict with parents in adolescence (Dekovic, 1999). Teens' pubertal status may be a factor as well. Among girls, conflict seems to rise after menarche (Holmbeck & Hill, 1991). Moreover, as noted earlier, cultural factors affect both the degree of parent-teen conflict and perceptions of its meaning.

● *Attachment* ●   Teenagers' underlying emotional attachment to their parents remains strong on average. Results from a study based on interviews of African American, Hispanic American, and white children aged 7, 10, and 14 help to illustrate this point (Levitt, Guacci-Franco, & Levitt, 1993). Each child was shown a drawing of a set of concentric circles and was asked to write in the middle circle the names of "people who are the most close and important to you—people you love the most and who love you the most." In the next circle outward from the middle, children were asked to write the names of "people who are not quite as close but who are still important—people you really love or like, but not quite as much as the people in the first circle." A third, outermost circle was to contain names of somewhat more distant members of this personal "convoy." The interviewer then asked about the kind of support each listed person provided for the child. Total support was measured by multiplying the number of individuals in each relationship category by

While it is true that the physical changes of puberty are often followed by an increase in the number of conflicts, it is a myth that conflict is the main feature of the parent-adolescent relationship. (*Photo:* Penny Tweedie, Stone)

the number of support functions each provided. Providing support functions included, for example, being "someone you can talk to about problems" and "someone who makes you feel better."

Researchers found that for all three ethnic groups, at all three ages, the names of parents and other close family members were by far the most likely to be written in the inner circle. Even 14-year-olds rarely placed friends in this position. So the parents remain central. At the same time, it is clear from these results that peers become increasingly important as providers of support, as you can see in Figure 11.4, which shows the total amount of support the children and adolescents described from each source. Friends clearly provided more support for the 14-year-olds than for the younger children, a pattern that occurred in all three ethnic groups.

Another large study in the Netherlands suggests that the teenager's bond with her parents may weaken somewhat in the middle of adolescence (ages 15 and 16) and then return to former levels (van Wel, 1994). But virtually all the researchers who have explored this question find that a teenager's sense of well-being or happiness is more strongly correlated with the quality of her attachment to her parents than with the quality of her relationships with peers (e.g., Greenberg, Siegel, & Leitch, 1983; Raja, McGee, & Stanton, 1992). Moreover, research findings regarding the centrality of parent-teen relationships have been consistent across a variety of cultures (Claes, 1998; Okamoto & Uechi, 1999).

Research in several countries has also found that teens who remain closely attached to their parents are the most likely to be academically successful and to enjoy good peer relations (Black & McCartney, 1997; Claes, 1998; Kim, Hetherington, & Reiss, 1999; Mayseless, Wiseman, & Hai, 1998). They are also less likely than less securely attached teens to engage in antisocial behavior (Ma, Shek, Cheung, & Oi Bun Lam, 2000). Further, the quality of attachment in early adolescence predicts drug use in later adolescence and early adulthood (Brook, Whiteman, Finch, & Cohen, 2000). Teens who are close to their parents are less likely to use drugs than peers whose bonds with parents are weaker. Thus, even while teenagers

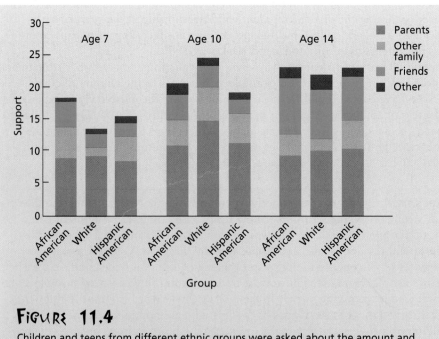

Figure 11.4

Children and teens from different ethnic groups were asked about the amount and type of support they received from various sources. Note that for teens, friends become more significant sources of support, but parents do not become less important. (*Source:* Levitt, Guacci-Franco, & Levitt, 1993, Figure 2, p. 815.)

are becoming more autonomous, they need their parents to provide a psychological safe base.

● **Parenting Styles** ●   For adolescents, as for younger children, authoritative parenting is consistently associated with more positive outcomes. Research suggests that parenting style influences a teen's self-concept and other intrapersonal variables (Dekovic & Meeus, 1997). Internal locus of control, for example, is more common in teens who perceive their parents to be authoritative (McClun & Merrell, 1998). Parental acceptance also appears to be important in teens' development of realistic assessments of their academic abilities (Bornholt & Goodnow, 1999).

Parental involvement in education and extracurricular activities seems to be just as important for teenagers as it is for younger children. For example, lack of parental involvement in school and extracurricular activities is strongly related to conduct problems such as disruptive classroom behavior (Frick, Christian, & Wooton, 1999). In addition, parental involvement in school-based organizations is related to high school students' post-graduation plans (Trusty, 1999). Those whose parents are most involved are the most likely to attend college.

● **Family Structure** ●   Family structure, too, continues to be an important factor in the teenager's life. Adolescents in households including a step-parent are, on average, somewhat less well-adjusted than those who live with two biological parents. These differences are evident even when teens have been living with a step-parent for several years (Hetherington et al., 1999).

However, an interesting exception to the typical pattern of sex differences arises in adolescence. In contrast to younger children, among adolescents, it is girls who show more distress when parents divorce, both when the girl lives with her single mother after the divorce and when there is a stepfather in the household (Amato, 1993; Hetherington & Clingempeel, 1992). Adolescent girls have more trouble interacting with a new stepfather than do their brothers, and they treat him more as an intruder. Girls in this situation are also likely to become depressed and are more likely than boys in the same situation to begin using drugs.

Why this pattern occurs is not so obvious. The adolescent girl may feel displaced from a special position in the family system that she held after her parents' divorce and before the mother's remarriage. In contrast, the teenaged boy may benefit from the addition of the stepfather, because he acquires a male role model. Whatever the explanation, findings like these are reminders that family systems are astonishingly complex.

Relationships with Peers

Despite the importance of family relationships to adolescents, it is an undeniable fact that peer relationships become far more significant in adolescence than they have been at any earlier period, and perhaps than they will be at any time later in life.

● **Friendships** ●   Shared activities and interests continue to be important elements in the selection of friends in adolescence. However, similarity of psychological characteristics and attitudes takes on new significance during the teenaged years. For example, adolescents tend to choose friends who share their beliefs about smoking, drug use, sex, and the importance of academic achievement (Urdan, 1997).

Teens' friendships are increasingly intimate, in the sense that adolescent friends share more and more of their inner feelings and secrets and are more knowledgeable about each other's feelings. Loyalty and faithfulness become more valued characteristics of friendship. However, the ability to display intimacy, loyalty, and faithfulness in the context of a friendship doesn't come automatically with age. In fact, teens vary considerably in these interpersonal skills. The variation may be the result of individual differences in temperament and personality or of teens' experiences with family relationships (Updegraff & Obeidallah, 1999).

Adolescent friendships are also more stable than those of younger children (Degirmencioglu, Urberg, & Tolson, 1998). In one longitudinal study, researchers found that only about 20% of friendships among fourth-graders lasted as long as a year, whereas about 40% of friendships formed by these same youngsters when they were tenth-graders were long-lasting (Cairns & Cairns, 1994). Friendship stability probably increases in adolescence because older teens work harder than younger teens and elementary school children at maintaining positive relationships with friends through negotiation of conflicts (Nagamine, 1999).

In addition, teens often choose friends who are committed to the same activities they are—sports, music, dance, and so on. They tell researchers that maintaining these friendships and continuing in the activities are linked together (Marsh, Craven, & Debus, 1999). In other words, they continue in the activities because their friends do, and they maintain their long-term friendships through continuation of the activities. Such links clearly contribute to friendship stability in adolescence.

Finally, adolescents' reasons for ending friendships reflect the influence of individual differences in rate of development of social skills. For example, a change in identity status from a less mature to a more mature level often leads to acquisition of new friends (Akers, Jones, & Coyl, 1998). Likewise, girls seem to prefer friendships with other girls whose romantic status is the same as their own—that is, girls who have boyfriends prefer female friends who also have boyfriends. In fact, a girl who gets a boyfriend is likely to spend less time with female peers and to end long-standing friendships with girls who haven't yet acquired a romantic partner (Benenson & Benarroch, 1998; Zimmer-Gembeck, 1999). For boys, differences in athletic achievements can lead to the end of previously important friendships.

● *Peer Groups* ●   Like friendships, peer groups become relatively stable in adolescence (Degirmencioglu et al., 1998). Peer group conformity seems to peak at about age 13 or 14 (at about the same time that adolescents show a drop in self-esteem) and then wanes as the teenager begins to arrive at a sense of identity that is more independent of the peer group. However, peer group pressures are less potent and less negative than popular cultural stereotypes might lead you to believe (Berndt, 1992). For one thing, remember that adolescents choose their friends and their crowd. And they are likely to choose to associate with a group that shares their values, attitudes, behaviors, and identity status (Akers et al., 1998; Urberg, Degirmencioglu, & Tolson, 1998). If the discrepancy between their own ideas and those of their friends becomes too great, teens are more likely to switch to a more compatible group of friends than to be persuaded to adopt the first group's values or behaviors. Furthermore, teenagers report that when explicit peer pressure is exerted, it is likely to be pressure toward positive activities, such as school involvement, and away from misconduct.

Only in so-called druggie-tough crowds does there seem to be explicit pressure toward misconduct or law-breaking, and teens who appear to respond to such pressure may be motivated as much by a desire to prove "I'm as tough as you are" as by explicit pressure from peers (Berndt & Keefe, 1995b; Brown, Dolcini, & Leventhal, 1995). Thus, while Erikson appears to have been quite correct in saying that peers are a major force in shaping a child's identity development in adolescence, peer influence is neither all-powerful nor uniformly negative.

● *Changes in Peer Group Structure* ●   The structure of the peer group also changes over the years of adolescence. The classic, widely quoted early study is that of Dunphy (1963) on the formation, dissolution, and interaction of teenaged groups in a high school in Sydney, Australia, between 1958 and 1960. Dunphy identified two important subvarieties of groups. The first type, which he called a **clique,** is made up of four to six young people who appear to be strongly attached to one another. Cliques have strong cohesiveness and high levels of intimate sharing.

In the early years of adolescence, cliques are almost entirely same-sex groups—a holdover from the preadolescent pattern. Gradually, however, the cliques combine into larger sets that Dunphy called **crowds,** which include both males and females. Finally, the crowd breaks down again into heterosexual cliques and then into loose associations of couples. In Dunphy's study, the period during which adolescents socialized in crowds was roughly between 13 and 15—the very years when they display the greatest conformity to peer pressure.

Contemporary researchers on adolescence have changed Dunphy's labels somewhat (Brown, 1990; Brown, Mory, & Kinney, 1994). They use the word *crowd* to refer to the *reputation-based group* with which a young person is identified, either by choice or by peer designation. In U.S. schools, these groups have labels such as "jocks," "brains," "nerds," "dweebs," "punks," "druggies," "toughs," "normals," "populars," "preppies," and "loners." Studies in American junior high and high schools make it clear that teenagers can readily identify each of the major crowds in their school and have quite stereotypical—even caricatured—descriptions of them (e.g., "The partyers goof off a lot more than the jocks do, but they don't come to school stoned like the burnouts do") (Brown et al., 1994, p. 133). Each of these descriptions serves as what Brown calls an *identity prototype:* Labeling others and oneself as belonging to one or more of these groups helps to create or reinforce the adolescent's own identity (Brown et al., 1994). Such labeling also helps the adolescent identify potential friends or foes.

Within any given school, the various crowds are organized into a fairly clear, widely understood pecking order. In U.S. schools, the groups labeled as some variant of "jocks," "populars," or "normals" are typically at the top of the heap, with "brains" somewhere in the middle and "druggies," "loners," and "nerds" at the bottom (Brown et al., 1994).

Through the years of junior high and high school, the social system of crowds becomes increasingly differentiated, with more and more distinct groups. For example, in one midwestern school system, researchers found that junior high students labeled only two major crowds: one small, high-status group (called "trendies" in this school), and the great mass of lower-status students, called "dweebs" (Kinney, 1993). A few years later, the same students named five distinct crowds: three with comparatively high social status and two low-status groups ("grits" and "punkers"). By late high school, these students identified seven or eight crowds, but the crowds now appeared to be less significant in the social organization of the peer group. These observations support other research that finds that mutual friendships and dating pairs are more central to social interactions in later adolescence than are cliques or crowds (Urberg et al., 1995).

Within (and sometimes between) these crowds, Kinney found, adolescents created smaller cliques. These groups, as Dunphy also observed, were almost entirely same-sex in early adolescence. By late adolescence, they had become mixed in gender, often composed of groups of dating couples.

As adolescents age, the structures of their peer groups change. (*Photos:* David Young-Wolff, Stone; Tessa Codrington, Stone)

Critical Thinking

Think back to your own high school years and draw a diagram or map to describe the organization of crowds and cliques. Were those crowds or cliques more or less important in the last few years of high school than they had been earlier?

clique four to six young people who appear to be strongly attached to one another

crowd a combination of cliques, which includes both males and females

● ***Romantic Relationships*** ●   Of all the changes in social relationships in adolescence, perhaps the most profound is the shift from the total dominance of same-sex friendships toward the inclusion of heterosexual relationships. The change happens gradually, but it seems to proceed at a somewhat more rapid pace in girls. At the beginning of adolescence, teens are still fairly rigid about their preferences for same-sex friends (Bukowski, Sippola, & Hoza, 1999). Over the next year or two, they become more open to opposite-sex friendships (Harton & Latane, 1997; Kuttler, LaGreca, & Prinstein, 1999). The skills they gain in relating to opposite-sex peers in such friendships and in mixed-gender groups prepare them for romantic relationships (Feiring, 1999). Thus, although adults often assume that sexual desires are the basis of emergent romantic relationships, it appears that social factors are just as important. In fact, research suggests that social competence in a variety of relationships—with parents, peers, and friends—predicts the ease with which teens move from exclusive same-sex relationships to opposite-sex friendships and romantic relationships (Theriault, 1998).

Despite their social function, these new relationships are nevertheless clearly part of the preparation for assuming a full adult sexual identity. Physical sexuality is part of that role, but so are the skills of personal intimacy with the opposite sex, including flirting, communicating, and reading the social cues used by the other gender. In Western societies, these skills are learned first in larger crowds or cliques and then in dating pairs (Zani, 1993).

By 12 or 13, most adolescents have a basic conception of what it means to be "in love." Interestingly, even though the actual progression toward romantic relationships happens faster for girls, boys report having had the experience of falling in love for the first time at an earlier age. Moreover, by the end of adolescence, it appears that the average boy believes he has been in love several more times than the average girl (Montgomery & Sorel, 1998).

The sense of being in love is an important factor in adolescent dating patterns (Montgomery & Sorel, 1998). In other words, teenagers prefer to date those with whom they believe they are in love, and they view falling out of love as a reason for ending a dating relationship. In addition, for girls (but not for boys), romantic relationships are seen as a context for self-disclosure. Put another way, girls seem to want more psychological intimacy from these early relationships than their partners do (Feiring, 1999).

Early dating and early sexual activity are more common among the poor of every ethnic group and among those who experience relatively early puberty. Religious teachings and individual attitudes about the appropriate age for dating and sexual behavior also make a difference, as does family structure. Girls with parents who are divorced or remarried, for example, report earlier dating and higher levels of sexual experience than do girls from intact families, and those with a strong religious identity report later dating and lower levels of sexuality (Bingham, Miller, & Adams, 1990; Miller & Moore, 1990). But for every group, these are years of experimentation with romantic relationships.

Homosexuality

For the great majority of teens, the pathway through adolescence includes a progression in peer relationships, a movement from unisexual cliques to heterosexual groups and then to heterosexual pairs. For the subgroup of homosexual teens, the process is different. In a study of nearly 35,000 youths in Minnesota public schools, researchers found that about 1% of the adolescent boys and approximately 0.4% of the adolescent girls defined themselves as homosexual, but a much larger number said they were unsure of their sexual orientation (Remafedi, Resnick, Blum, & Harris, 1998). These figures are generally consistent with the data on adults in the United States (Laumann, Gagnon, Michael, & Michaels, 1994).

Several twin studies show that when one identical twin is homosexual, the probability that the other twin will also be homosexual is 50–60%, whereas the concordance rate is only about 20% for fraternal twins and only about 11% among pairs of biologically unrelated boys adopted into the same family (Bailey & Pillard, 1991; Bailey, Pillard, Neale, & Agyei, 1993; Whitam, Diamond, & Martin, 1993). Family studies also suggest that male homosexuality runs in families— that is, the families of most gay men have a higher proportion of homosexual males than do the families of heterosexual men (Bailey et al., 1999). Such findings strengthen the hypothesis that homosexuality has a biological basis (Gladue, 1994; Pillard & Bailey, 1995).

Additional studies suggest that prenatal hormone patterns may also be a causal factor in homosexuality. For example, women whose mothers took the drug diethylstilbestrol (DES, a synthetic estrogen) during pregnancy are more likely to be homosexual as adults than are women who were not exposed to DES in the womb (Meyer-Bahlburg et al., 1995). Moreover, as you learned in Chapter 7, there is some evidence that boys who demonstrate strong cross-sex behavior in early childhood are likely to show homosexual preferences when they reach adolescence. Like the twin and family studies, these results are consistent with the hypothesis that homosexuality is programmed in at birth (Bailey & Zucker, 1995).

Such evidence does not mean that environment plays no role in homosexuality. For example, when one of a pair of identical twins is homosexual, the other twin does *not* share that sexual orientation 40–50% of the time. Something beyond biology must be at work, although developmentalists do not yet know what environmental factors may be involved.

Whatever the cause of variations in sexual orientation, homosexual teenagers are a minority who face high levels of prejudice and stereotyping. Many are verbally attacked or ridiculed; as many as a third are physically assaulted by their peers (Remafedi, Farrow, & Deisher, 1991; Savin-Williams, 1994). For these and other reasons, these young people are at high risk for a variety of problems. For example, homosexual adolescents are more likely than their heterosexual peers to be depressed and to attempt suicide (Remafedi, French, Story, Resnick, & Blum, 1998; Safren & Heimberg, 1999).

Homosexual teenagers must also cope with the decision about whether to "come out" about their homosexuality. Those who do come out are far more likely to tell peers than parents, although telling peers carries some risk. Some research suggests that as many as two-thirds of homosexual youth have not told their parents (Rotheram-Borus, Rosario, & Koopman, 1991).

While homosexual adolescents clearly face unique challenges, they share many of the same concerns as their heterosexual peers. For example, both homosexual and heterosexual girls are more likely than boys to be dissatisfied with their physical appearance (Saewyc, Bearinger, Heinz, Blum, & Resnick, 1998). Consequently, dieting is more common among both homosexual and heterosexual girls than among boys of either sexual orientation. Like their heterosexual counterparts, homosexual male adolescents drink alcohol more often and engage in more risky behavior than do female teenagers.

The same factors predict successful identity and social development in homosexual and heterosexual teens. For example, attachment to parents appears to be just as important for homosexual teens as for their heterosexual peers. In fact, attachment to parents and the maintenance of good relations with them in adolescence seems to help homosexual teens in the coming-out process (Beaty, 1999; Floyd et al., 1999).

There is obviously much that researchers do not know about homosexual adolescents. But it is reasonable to hypothesize that the years of adolescence may be particularly stressful for this subgroup. Like teenagers from ethnic minorities, homosexual teens have an additional task facing them in forming a clear identity.

MAKE THE CONNECTION

Review the concept of reaction range discussed in Chapter 6. How can this view of the interaction of heredity and environment be used to explain the development of homosexuality?

Before going on

● Describe adolescents' family relationships in terms of conflicts, attachment, parenting styles, and family structure.

● What are the characteristics of adolescents' friendships, peer groups, and romantic relationships?

● What are the unique challenges faced by teenagers who are homosexual?

Moral Development

As you read in Chapter 9, theorists representing various orientations think differently about moral development. However, the theorist whose work has had the most powerful impact has been psychologist Lawrence Kohlberg (Colby, Kohlberg, Gibbs, & Lieberman 1983; Kohlberg, 1976, 1981). Moreover, theories of moral reasoning have been important in explanations of adolescent antisocial behavior.

Kohlberg's Theory of Moral Reasoning

You may recall from Chapter 9 that Piaget proposed two stages in the development of moral reasoning. Working from Piaget's basic assumptions, Kohlberg devised a way of measuring moral reasoning based on research participants' responses to moral dilemmas such as the following:

> In Europe, a woman was near death from a special kind of cancer. There was one drug that the doctors thought might save her. It was a form of radium that a druggist in the same town had recently discovered. The drug was expensive to make, but the druggist was charging ten times what the drug cost him to make. He paid $200 for the radium and charged $2000 for a small dose of the drug. The sick woman's husband, Heinz, went to everyone he knew to borrow the money, but he could only get together about $1000. . . . He told the druggist that his wife was dying, and asked him to sell it cheaper or let him pay later. But the druggist said, "No, I discovered the drug and I'm going to make money from it." So Heinz got desperate and broke into the man's store to steal the drug for his wife. (Kohlberg & Elfenbein, 1975, p. 621)

Kohlberg analyzed participants' answers to questions about such dilemmas (for example, "Should Heinz have stolen the drug? Why?") and concluded that there were three levels of moral development, each made up of two substages, as summarized in Table 11.2.

Critical Thinking

How would you respond to the Heinz dilemma? What does your response suggest about your level of moral reasoning?

preconventional morality in Kohlberg's theory, the level of moral reasoning in which judgments are based on authorities outside the self

TABLE 11.2   Kohlberg's Stages of Moral Development

Level	Stages	Description
Level I: Preconventional	Stage 1: Punishment and Obedience Orientation	The child or teenager decides what is wrong on the basis of what is punished. Obedience is valued for its own sake, but the child obeys because the adults have superior power.
	Stage 2: Individualism, Instrumental Purpose, and Exchange	Children and teens follow rules when it is in their immediate interest. What is good is what brings pleasant results.
Level II: Conventional	Stage 3: Mutual Interpersonal Expectations, Relationships, and Interpersonal Conformity	Moral actions are those that live up to the expectations of the family or other significant group. "Being good" becomes important for its own sake.
	Stage 4: Social System and Conscience (Law and Order)	Moral actions are those so defined by larger social groups or the society as a whole. One should fulfill duties one has agreed to and uphold laws, except in extreme cases.
Level III: Postconventional	Stage 5: Social Contract or Utility and Individual Rights	This stage involves acting so as to achieve the "greatest good for the greatest number." The teenager or adult is aware that most values are relative and laws are changeable, although rules should be upheld in order to preserve the social order. Still, there are some basic absolute values, such as the importance of each person's life and liberty.
	Stage 6: Universal Ethical Principles	The small number of adults who reason at Stage 6 develop and follow self-chosen ethical principles in determining what is right. These ethical principles are part of an articulated, integrated, carefully thought-out, and consistently followed system of values and principles.

(*Sources:* Kohlberg, 1976; Lickona, 1978.)

The stages are correlated with age somewhat loosely. Very few children reason beyond stage 1 or 2, and stage 2 and stage 3 reasoning are the most common types found among adolescents (Walker, de Vries, & Trevethan, 1987). Among adults, stages 3 and 4 are the most common (Gibson, 1990). You can see the pattern of age changes in Figure 11.5, which shows the results from Kohlberg's longitudinal study of 58 boys, first interviewed when they were 10 and subsequently followed for more than 20 years (Colby et al., 1983).

At level I, **preconventional morality,** the child's judgments are based on sources of authority who are close by and physically superior—usually the parents. Just as descriptions of others are largely external at this level, so the standards the child uses to judge rightness or wrongness are external rather than internal. In particular, it is the outcome or consequence of an action that determines the rightness or wrongness of the action.

In stage 1 of this level—*the punishment and obedience orientation*—the child relies on the physical consequences of some action to decide whether it is right or wrong. If he is punished, the behavior was wrong; if he is not punished, it was right. He is obedient to adults because they are bigger and stronger.

In stage 2—*individualism, instrumental purpose, and exchange*—the child or adolescent operates on the principle

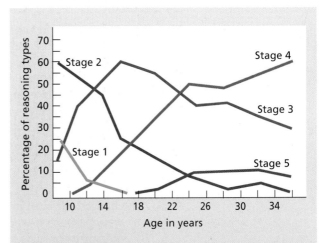

FIGURE 11.5

These findings are from Colby and Kohlberg's long-term longitudinal study of a group of boys who were asked about Kohlberg's moral dilemmas every few years from age 10 through early adulthood. As they got older, the stage or level of their answers changed, with conventional reasoning appearing fairly widely at high school age. Postconventional, or principled, reasoning was not very common at any age. (*Source:* Colby et al., Figure 1, p. 46. © The Society for Research in Child Development.)

that you should do things that are rewarded and avoid things that are punished. For this reason, the stage is sometimes called *naive hedonism.* If it feels good, or brings pleasant results, it is good. Some beginning of concern for other people is apparent during this stage, but only if that concern can be expressed as something that benefits the child or teenager himself as well. So he can enter into agreements such as "If you help me, I'll help you."

To illustrate, here are some responses to variations of the Heinz dilemma, drawn from studies of children and teenagers in a number of different cultures, all of whom were at stage 2:

> He should steal the food for his wife because if she dies he'll have to pay for the funeral, and that costs a lot. [Taiwan]
> [He should steal the drug because] he should protect the life of his wife so he doesn't have to stay alone in life. [Puerto Rico] (Snarey, 1985, p. 221)

At the next major level, the level of **conventional morality,** rules or norms of a group to which the individual belongs become the basis of moral judgments, whether that group is the family, the peer group, a church, or the nation. What the chosen reference group defines as right or good is right or good in the individual's view. Again, very few children exhibit conventional thinking, but many adolescents are capable of this kind of moral reasoning.

Stage 3 (the first stage of level II) is the stage of *mutual interpersonal expectations, relationships, and interpersonal conformity* (sometimes also called the *good boy/nice girl stage*). Regardless of age, individuals who reason at this stage believe that good behavior is what pleases other people. They value trust, loyalty, respect, gratitude, and maintenance of mutual relationships. Andy, a boy Kohlberg interviewed who was at stage 3, said:

> I try to do things for my parents, they've always done things for you. I try to do everything my mother says, I try to please her. Like she wants me to be a doctor and I want to, too, and she's helping me get up there. (Kohlberg, 1964, p. 401)

Another mark of this third stage is that the individual makes judgments based on intentions as well as on outward behavior. If someone "didn't mean to do it," the wrongdoing is seen as less serious than if the person did it "on purpose."

Stage 4, the second stage of the conventional morality level, incorporates the norms of a larger reference group into moral judgments. Kohlberg labeled this the stage of *social system and conscience.* It is also sometimes called the *law-and-order orientation.* People reasoning at this stage focus on doing their duty, respecting authority, following rules and laws. The emphasis is less on what is pleasing to particular people (as in stage 3) and more on adhering to a complex set of regulations. However, the regulations themselves are not questioned, and morality and legality are assumed to be equivalent. Therefore, for a person at stage 4, something that is legal is right, whereas something that is illegal is wrong. Consequently, changes in law can effect changes in the moral views of individuals who reason at stage 4.

The transition to level III, **postconventional morality,** is marked by several changes, the most important of which is a shift in the source of authority. Individuals who reason at level I see authority as totally outside of themselves; at level II, the judgments or rules of external authorities are internalized, but they are not questioned or analyzed; at level III, a new kind of personal authority emerges, in which an individual makes choices and judgments based on self-chosen principles or on principles that are assumed to transcend the needs and concerns of any individual or group. Postconventional thinkers represent only a minority of adults and an even smaller minority of adolescents.

In stage 5 at this level, which Kohlberg called the *social contract orientation,* such self-chosen principles begin to be evident. Rules, laws, and regulations are not seen as irrelevant; they are important ways of ensuring fairness. But people operating at this level also acknowledge that there are times when the rules, laws, and regulations need to be ignored or changed.

conventional morality in Kohlberg's theory, the level of moral reasoning in which judgments are based on rules or norms of a group to which the person belongs

postconventional morality in Kohlberg's theory, the level of moral reasoning in which judgments are based on an integration of individual rights and the needs of society

The American civil rights movement of the 1950s and 1960s is a good example of stage 5 reasoning in action. *Civil disobedience*—deliberately breaking laws that were believed to be immoral—arose as a way of protesting racial segregation. For example, African Americans intentionally took seats in restaurants that were reserved for whites. It is important to note that the practice of civil disobedience does not usually involve avoiding the penalties that accompany criminal behavior. Indeed, some of the most effective and poignant images from that period of U.S. history are photographs of individuals who surrendered and were jailed for breaking segregation laws. This behavior illustrates the stage 5 view that, as a general principle, upholding the law is important, even though a specific law that is deemed to be immoral can, or even should, be broken when breaking it will serve to promote the common good.

In his original writing about moral development, Kohlberg also included a sixth stage, *the universal ethical principles orientation*. People who reason at this level assume personal responsibility for their own actions, based on fundamental and universal principles such as justice and basic respect for persons. Kohlberg eventually concluded that such people are quite rare, but they do represent the logical end point to the sequence of stages.

It is important to understand that what determines the stage or level of a person's moral judgment is not any specific moral choice but the form of reasoning used to justify that choice. For example, either response to Kohlberg's dilemma—that Heinz should steal the drug or that he should not—could be justified with logic at any given stage.

Kohlberg argued that this sequence of reasoning is both universal and hierarchically organized. That is, each stage grows out of the preceding one. Kohlberg did not suggest that all individuals eventually progress through all six stages, or even that each stage is tied to specific ages. But he insisted that the order is invariant and universal. He also believed that the social environment determines how slowly or rapidly individuals move through the stages (see The Real World).

The evidence seems fairly strong that the stages follow one another in the sequence Kohlberg proposed. Long-term longitudinal studies of teenagers and young adults in the United States, Israel, and Turkey show that changes in participants' reasoning nearly always occur in the hypothesized order (Colby et al., 1983; Nisan & Kohlberg, 1982; Snarey, Reimer, & Kohlberg, 1985; Walker, 1989). People do not skip stages, and movement down the sequence rather than up occurs only about 5–7% of the time.

Variations of Kohlberg's dilemmas have been used with children in a wide range of countries, including both Western and non-Western, industrialized and non-industrialized (Snarey, 1985). In every culture, researchers find higher stages of reasoning among older children, but cultures differ in the highest level of reasoning observed. In urban cultures (both Western and non-Western), stage 5 is typically the highest stage observed; in agricultural societies and those in which there is little opportunity for formal education, stage 4 is typically the highest. Collectively, this evidence seems to provide quite strong support for the universality of Kohlberg's stage sequence.

Civil disobedience involves intentionally breaking laws one believes to be immoral. For example, in the early years of the U.S. civil rights movement, African Americans broke laws that excluded them from certain sections of restaurants by "sitting in" at whites-only lunch counters. Practitioners of civil disobedience do not try to evade the consequences of their actions, because they believe in upholding the law as a general principle even though they may view some specific laws as immoral. Thus, the thinking that underlies acts of civil disobedience represents Kohlberg's postconventional level of moral reasoning. (*Photo: Bettmann/CORBIS*)

Causes and Consequences of Moral Development

The most obvious reason for the general correlations between Kohlberg's stages and chronological age is cognitive development. Specifically, it appears that children must have a firm grasp of concrete operational thinking before they can develop or use conventional moral reasoning. Likewise, formal operations appears to be necessary for advancement to the postconventional level.

To be more specific, Kohlberg and many other theorists suggest that the decline of egocentrism that occurs as an individual moves through Piaget's concrete and formal operational stages is the cognitive-developmental variable that matters most in moral reasoning. The idea is that the greater a child's or adolescent's ability to look at a situation from another person's perspective, the more advanced she is likely to be in moral

TEACHING
The Real World

Education for Moral Reasoning

Kohlberg's theory may seem pretty abstract. However, in Kohlberg's own view, the theory had many potential practical implications. The question that interested him was whether children or young people could be taught higher stages of moral reasoning, and, if so, whether such a step up in moral reasoning would change their behavior in school.

One educational application has involved the creation of a "just community" designed to change students' moral

(*Photo:* © Will Hart, PhotoEdit)

behavior as much as their moral reasoning. These experimental programs, typically set up as a "school within a school," operate as a kind of laboratory for moral education (Higgins, 1991; Kohlberg & Higgins, 1987). Kohlberg insisted that the crucial feature of these just communities must be complete democracy: Each teacher and student has one vote, and community issues and problems have to be discussed in open forums. Rules are typically created and discussed at weekly community-wide meetings. In this way, students become responsible for the rules and for one another.

In experimental programs following this model, Kohlberg and his co-workers found that as students reached more sophisticated levels of moral reasoning, their reasoning about responsibility and caring also became more sophisticated. The link between moral reasoning and moral behavior was strengthened as well. For example, stealing and other petty crime virtually disappeared in one school after the students had repeatedly

discussed the problem and finally arrived at a solution that emphasized the fact that stealing damaged the whole community, and thus the whole community had to be responsible (Higgins, 1991).

The effects of just communities make sense when you think about the factors that seem to affect moral behavior. These schools include two elements that tend to support more moral behavior: a sense of personal responsibility, and a group norm of higher moral reasoning and caring. For teenagers, the emotional impact of group pressure may be especially significant, in addition to whatever effect exposure to more mature arguments has (Haan, 1985).

Moral education programs have not proven to be the "quick fix" that many educators hoped for. The gains in moral reasoning are not huge and may not be reflected in increases in moral behavior in the school, unless an effort is made to alter the overall moral atmosphere of the entire school. But these programs do show that provocative and helpful applications of some of the abstract developmental theories are possible.

reasoning. Psychologists use the term **role-taking** to refer to this ability (Selman, 1980). Research has provided strong support for the hypothesized link between role-taking and moral development (Kuhn, Kohlberg, Languer, & Haan, 1977; Walker, 1980).

Nevertheless, cognitive development isn't enough. Kohlberg thought that the development of moral reasoning also required support from the social environment. Specifically, he claimed that in order to foster mature moral reasoning, a child's or teenager's social environment must provide him with opportunities for meaningful, reciprocal dialogue about moral issues.

Longitudinal research relating parenting styles and family climate to levels of moral reasoning suggest that Kohlberg was right (Pratt, Arnold, & Pratt, 1999). Parents' ability to identify, understand, and respond to children's and adolescents' less mature forms of moral reasoning seems to be particularly important to the development of moral reasoning. This ability on the part of parents is important because people of all ages have difficulty understanding and remembering moral arguments that are more advanced than their own level (Narvaez, 1998). Thus, a parent who can express her own moral views in words that reflect her child's level of understanding is more likely to be able to influence the child's moral development.

As an individual's capacity for moral reasoning grows, so does her ability to think logically about issues in other domains. For example, the complexity of an indi-

role-taking the ability to look at a situation from another person's perspective

vidual's political reasoning is very similar to the complexity of her moral reasoning (Raaijmakers, Verbogt, & Vollebergh, 1998). Further, attitudes toward the acceptability of violence also vary with levels of moral reasoning. Individuals at lower levels are more tolerant of violence (Sotelo & Sangrador, 1999).

Perhaps most importantly, teenagers' level of moral reasoning appears to be positively correlated with prosocial behavior and negatively related to antisocial behavior (Schonert-Reichl, 1999). In other words, the highest levels of prosocial behavior are found among teens at the highest levels of moral reasoning (compared to their peers). Alternatively, the highest levels of antisocial behavior are found among adolescents at the lowest levels of moral reasoning.

Criticisms of Kohlberg's Theory

Criticisms of Kohlberg's theory have come from theorists representing different perspectives.

● *Moral Reasoning and Behavior* ●   Although moral reasoning and moral behavior are correlated, the relationship is far from perfect. To explain inconsistencies between reasoning and behavior, learning theorists suggest that moral reasoning is situational rather than developmental. They point to a variety of studies to support this assertion.

First, neither adolescents nor adults reason at the same level in response to every hypothetical dilemma (Rique & Camino, 1997). An individual research participant might reason at the conventional level in response to one dilemma and at the post-conventional level with respect to another. Second, the types of characters in moral dilemmas strongly influence research participants' responses to them, especially when the participants are adolescents. For example, hypothetical dilemmas involving celebrities as characters elicit much lower levels of moral reasoning from teenagers than those involving fictional characters such as Heinz (Einerson, 1998).

In addition, research participants show disparities in levels of moral reasoning in response to hypothetical dilemmas compared to real-life moral issues. For example, Israeli Jewish, Israeli Bedouin, and Palestinian youths living in Israel demonstrate different levels of moral reasoning when responding to hypothetical stories such as the Heinz dilemma than they exhibit in discussing the moral dimensions of the long-standing conflicts among their ethnic groups (Elbedour, Baker, & Charlesworth, 1997). Thus, as learning theorists predict, it appears that situational factors may be more important variables for decisions about actual moral behavior than the level of moral reasoning exhibited in response to hypothetical dilemmas.

● *Moral Reasoning and Emotions* ●   Some theorists criticize Kohlberg's failure to connect moral reasoning to moral emotions. Psychologist Nancy Eisenberg, for example, suggests that *empathy,* the ability to identify with others' emotions, is both a cause and a consequence of moral development (Eisenberg, 2000). Similarly, Eisenberg suggests that a complete explanation of moral development should include age-related and individual variations in the ability to regulate emotions (such as anger) that can motivate antisocial behavior.

Likewise, Carol Gilligan claims that an ethic based on caring for others and on maintaining social relationships may be as important to moral reasoning as ideas about justice. Gilligan's theory argues that there are at least two distinct "moral orientations": justice and care (Gilligan, 1982; Gilligan & Wiggins, 1987). Each has its own central injunction—not to treat others unfairly (justice), and not to turn away from someone in need (caring). Research suggests that adolescents do exhibit a moral orientation based on care and that care-based reasoning about hypothetical moral dilemmas is related to reasoning about real-life dilemmas (Skoe et al., 1999). In response, Kohlberg acknowledged in his later writings that his theory deals specifically with development of reasoning about justice and does not claim to be a comprehensive account of moral development (Kohlberg, Levine, & Hewer, 1983).

Incidents such as the Columbine High School shooting in April, 1999, capture a great deal of public attention and often lead to increased security measures in schools. However, statistically speaking, schools are actually quite safe. Only 1% of all violent deaths among youths in the United States occur in schools (NCIPC, 2000). (*Photo:* AFP/CORBIS)

Possible sex differences in moral reasoning are another focus of Gilligan's theory. According to Gilligan, boys and girls learn both the justice and care orientations, but girls are more likely to operate from the care orientation, whereas boys are more likely to operate from a justice orientation. Because of these differences, girls and boys tend to perceive moral dilemmas quite differently.

Given the emerging evidence on sex differences in styles of interaction and in friendship patterns, Gilligan's hypothesis makes some sense. Perhaps girls, focused more on intimacy in their relationships, judge moral dilemmas by different criteria. But, in fact, research on moral dilemmas has not consistently shown that boys are more likely to use justice reasoning or that girls more often use care reasoning. Several studies of adults do show such a pattern (e.g., Lyons, 1983; Wark & Krebs, 1996). However, studies of children and teenagers generally have not (Jadack, Hyde, Moore, & Keller, 1995; Smetana, Killen, & Turiel, 1991; Walker et al., 1987). Further, recent evidence suggests that such sex differences, if they exist, may be restricted to North American culture (Skoe et al., 1999).

Moral Development and Antisocial Behavior

The consistent finding of low levels of moral reasoning among adolescents who engage in serious forms of antisocial behavior has been of particular interest to developmentalists (Aleixo & Norris, 2000; Gregg, Gibbs, & Basinger, 1994; Smetana, 1990). Delinquency is distinguished from other forms of antisocial behavior, such as bullying, on the basis of actual law-breaking. Thus, the term **delinquency** applies specifically to adolescent behavior that violates the law. Serious forms of delinquency, such as rape and murder, have increased dramatically in the United States in recent years. Attempts to explain this phenomenon have resulted in research that has led to a more comprehensive understanding of youth violence.

Delinquents appear to be behind their peers in moral reasoning because of deficits in role-taking skills. They seem to be unable to look at their crimes from their victims' perspectives or to assess hypothetical crimes from the victims' perspectives. Thus, programs aimed at helping delinquents develop more mature levels of moral reasoning usually focus on heightening their awareness of the victim's point of view. However, few such programs have been successful (Moody, 1997; Putnins, 1997). Consequently, psychologists believe that there is far more to delinquency than just a lack of role-taking and moral reasoning skills.

First, it appears that there are at least two important subvarieties of delinquents, distinguished by the age at which the delinquent behavior begins. Childhood-onset problems are more serious and are more likely to persist into adulthood. Adolescent-onset problems are typically milder and more transitory, apparently more a reflection of peer-group processes or a testing of the limits of authority than a deeply ingrained behavior problem.

The developmental pathway for early-onset delinquency seems to be directed by factors inside the child, such as temperament and personality. In early life, these children throw tantrums and defy parents, they may also develop insecure attachments (Greenberg, Speltz, & DeKlyen, 1993). Once the defiance appears, if the parents are not up to the task of controlling the child, the child's behavior worsens. He may begin to display overt aggression toward others, who then reject him, which aggravates the problem. The seriously aggressive child is pushed in the direction of other children with similar problems, who then become the child's only supportive peer group (Shaw, Kennan, & Vondra, 1994).

By adolescence, these youngsters may exhibit serious disturbances in thinking (Aleixo & Norris, 2000). Most have friends drawn almost exclusively from among other delinquent teens (Tremblay, Masse, Vitaro, & Dobkin, 1995). Of course, this situation is reinforced by frequent rejection by nondelinquent peers (Brendgen, Vitaro, & Bukowski, 1998). Many of these adolescents have parents with histories of

delinquency antisocial behavior that includes law-breaking

No Easy Answers

Preventing Youth Violence

For most delinquent teens, law-breaking is limited to acts of malicious mischief, such as spray-painting obscenities on a wall. Some adolescents, however, engage in antisocial behavior that is far more serious and difficult to understand. For example, in early 1998, Americans were shocked by a tragic episode in which two Arkansas boys, ages 11 and 13, gunned down four of their female classmates and a teacher on the school playground. In 1999, two Colorado high school students shot and killed ten fellow students and one teacher and injured several more. These incidents, along with surveys showing that 20% of all violent crimes in the Unites States are committed by individuals under age 18, have increased public awareness of the growing problem of youth violence (National Center for Injury Prevention and Control [NCIPC], 2000).

Few programs designed to change aggressive and violent behavior in adolescents have been successful. However, as you've read, research suggests that many children who are violent in adolescence began to exhibit this pattern of behavior in the early elementary grades (Moffitt, 1993). Thus, it might seem possible to identify potentially violent children at an early age and place them in programs that would reshape their thinking and behavior so as to prevent them from becoming violent. Recent efforts along these lines suggest that this kind of strategy can be successful. However, as you might imagine, it isn't as easy as it might seem.

A number of psychologists have contributed to the development and evaluation of a program called the Fast Track Project, which involves several hundred aggressive elementary school children in four different U.S. cities (Coie, 1997; Dodge, 1997; McMahon, 1997). The children are divided into experimental and control groups. In special class sessions, children in the experimental group learn how to recognize others' emotions. They also learn strategies for controlling their own feelings, managing aggressive impulses, and solving conflicts with peers.

The teachers of children in the experimental group are trained to use a series of signals to help children maintain control. For example, a red card or a picture of a red traffic light might be used to indicate unacceptable behavior. A yellow card would mean something like "Calm down. You're about to lose control." Parenting classes and support groups help parents learn effective ways of teaching children acceptable behavior, rather than just punishing unacceptable behavior. In addition, parents are encouraged to maintain communication with their children's teachers.

After several years of implementation, the program appears to have produced the following effects among children in the experimental group:

- Better recognition of emotions
- More competence in social relationships
- Lower ratings of aggressiveness by peers
- Lowered risk of being placed in special education classes

In addition, parents of control group children have learned how to use less physical punishment and how to have better control of their children's behavior.

Clearly, this kind of intervention requires a considerable commitment of time and resources. Furthermore, it isn't effective for every child. However, it represents the best option developmentalists have to offer at this point. When balanced against the suffering of the half million or so victims of youth violence each year in the United States, or against the personal consequences of violent behavior for the young perpetrators of these crimes, the costs don't seem quite so extreme.

antisocial behavior as well (Gainey, Catalano, Haggerty, & Hoppe, 1997). Early-onset delinquents are also highly likely to display a whole cluster of other problem behaviors, including drug and alcohol use, truancy or dropping out of school, and early and risky sexual behavior, including having multiple sexual partners (Dishion, French, & Patterson, 1995) (see No Easy Answers).

For young people whose delinquency appears first in adolescence, the pathway is different. They, too, have friends who are delinquents. However, associating with delinquent peers worsens their behavior, while the behavior of early-onset delinquents remains essentially the same, whether they have antisocial friends or are "loners" (Vitaro, Tremblay, Kerr, Pagani, & Bukowski, 1997). Moreover, the antisocial behavior patterns of adolescent-onset delinquents often change as their relationships change (Laird, Pettit, Dodge, & Bates, 1999). Consequently, peer influence seems to be the most important factor in the development of adolescent-onset delinquency.

Parenting style and other relationship variables seem to be additional factors in this type of antisocial behavior. Most of these teens have parents who do not monitor them sufficiently; their individual friendships are not very supportive or intimate; and they are drawn to a clique or crowd that includes some teens who are experimenting with drugs or mild law-breaking. After a period of months of hanging out with such a group of peers, previously nondelinquent adolescents show some increase in risky or antisocial behaviors, such as increased drug-taking (Berndt & Keefe, 1995a; Dishion et al., 1995; Steinberg, Fletcher, & Darling, 1994). However, when parents do provide good monitoring and emotional support, their adolescent child is unlikely to get involved in delinquent acts or drug use even if she hangs around with a tougher crowd or has a close friend who engages in such behavior (Brown & Huang, 1995; Mounts & Steinberg, 1995).

Before going on

- What are the features of moral reasoning at each of Kohlberg's stages?
- What are some important causes and effects in the development of moral reasoning?
- How has Kohlberg's theory been criticized?
- Describe the moral reasoning abilities and other characteristics of delinquents.

A Final Word

A number of experts on adolescence argue that it makes sense to divide the period from age 12 to age 20 into two subperiods, one beginning at 12 or 13, and the other beginning at about 16. The first period, early adolescence, is marked by change in every area of development—physical changes, new educational demands, new social expectations. The young teen's main goal, from a developmental perspective, is to make it through this period without becoming ensnared in one of many possible negative patterns—drug use, delinquency, early sexual activity, and so forth—any of which can derail the identity development process. If she successfully negotiates the early period, a teenager can spend the years of late adolescence developing a unique sense of self along with a plan for fitting into the adult culture. Fortunately, most teens seem to follow just such a pathway, leading to the observation that adolescence is not nearly so disturbing or chaotic a period of development as cultural stereotypes suggest.

Summary

Theories of Social and Personality Development

- According to Freud, adolescents are in the genital stage, a period during which sexual maturity is reached. Erikson viewed adolescence as a period when a person faces a crisis of identity versus role confusion, out of which

the teenager must develop a sense of who he is and where he belongs in his culture

- Building on Erikson's notion of an adolescent identity crisis, Marcia identified four identity statuses. Research suggests that the process of identity formation may take place somewhat later than either Erikson or Marcia believed.

Self-Concept and Personality

- Self-definitions become increasingly abstract at adolescence, with more emphasis on enduring, internal qualities and ideology.

- Teenagers also increasingly define themselves in terms that include both masculine and feminine traits. When both masculinity and femininity are present, the individual is described as androgynous. High levels of androgyny are associated with higher self-esteem in both male and female adolescents.

- Self-esteem drops somewhat at the beginning of adolescence and then rises steadily throughout the teenaged years.

- Young people in clearly identifiable minority groups have the additional task in adolescence of forming an ethnic identity, a process that appears to have several steps analogous to Marcia's model of identity formation.

- Teens who are introverted, neurotic, and pessimistic and who blame their problems on forces outside themselves encounter more difficulties than peers who have a more positive outlook.

Social Relationships

- Adolescent-parent interactions typically become somewhat more conflicted in early adolescence, an effect possibly linked to the physical changes of puberty.

- Strong attachments to parents remain so and are predictive of good peer relations. Authoritative parenting continues to be the optimal style to use with adolescents. The parents' remarriage during a child's adolescence appears to have a more negative effect on girls than on boys.

- Susceptibility to peer-group pressure appears to be at its peak at about age 13 or 14. Reputation-based groups, or *crowds,* as well as smaller groups, called *cliques,* are important parts of adolescent social relationships. By early adolescence, most teens have a concept of being "in love."

- Teens who are homosexual or who are unsure about their sexual orientation face many obstacles in the formation of an identity.

Moral Development

- Kohlberg proposed six stages of moral reasoning, organized into three levels. Preconventional moral reasoning includes reliance on external authority: What is punished is bad, and what feels good is good. Conventional morality is based on rules and norms provided by outside groups, such as the family, church, or society. Postconventional morality is based on self-chosen principles. Research evidence suggests that these levels and stages are loosely correlated with age, develop in a specified order, and appear in this same sequence in all cultures studied so far.

- The acquisition of cognitive role-taking skills is important to moral development, but the social environment is important as well. Specifically, to foster moral reasoning, adults must provide children with opportunities for discussion of moral issues. Moral reasoning and moral behavior are correlated, though the relationship is far from perfect.

- Kohlberg's theory has been criticized by theorists who place more emphasis on learning moral behavior and others who believe that moral reasoning may be based more on emotional factors than on ideas about justice and fairness.

- Delinquent teens are usually found to be far behind their peers in both role-taking and moral reasoning. However, other factors, such as parenting style, may be equally important in delinquency.

Key Terms

clique (p. 325)

conventional morality (p. 330)

crowd (p. 325)

delinquency (p. 334)

ethnic identity (p. 316)

foreclosure (p. 312)

genital stage (p. 311)

identity achievement (p. 311)

identity crisis (p. 311)

identity diffusion (p. 312)

identity versus role confusion (p. 311)

locus of control (p. 319)

moratorium (p. 312)

postconventional morality (p. 330)

preconventional morality (p. 328)

role-taking (p. 332)

sex-role identity (p. 315)

Has Test-Based Reform Improved Schools in the United States?

Over the past 40 years, Americans have become increasingly concerned about the quality of public schools. Politicians and educators have responded to their concerns by proposing many reforms aimed at increasing schools' accountability to the public. The most popular idea among these proposals is based on the assumption that standardized testing can be used both to assess students and to improve school quality. The popularity of this idea has brought about the *test-based school reform movement.*

NAEP Proficiency Levels

Level	Description
Basic	This level denotes partial mastery of prerequisite knowledge and skills that are fundamental for proficient work at each grade.
Proficient	This level represents solid academic performance for each grade assessed. Students reaching this level have demonstrated mastery of challenging subject matter, subject-matter knowledge, application of such knowledge to real-world situations, and analytical skills appropriate to the subject matter.
Advanced	This level signifies superior performance.

(*Source:* National Center for Educational Statistics, 1999.)

High-Stakes Testing

Most historians of education say that the development of the National Assessment of Educational Progress in the 1960s marked the beginning of the test-based school reform movement (Bond, Braskamp, & Roeber, 1996). The NAEP, nicknamed the "Nation's Report Card," is designed to compare what American school children know with what the experts think they should know. At first, NAEP results were reported nationally. American students were described as performing at the advanced, proficient, basic, or below basic level (see the table).

The concept behind the NAEP, that of comparing student achievement to an "ideal" level of achievement, appealed to the public and to many educational policy analysts. Consequently, in the 1970s many states began developing tests similar to the NAEP. By the 1980s, more than half were using them to assess both student learning and school quality.

In 1990, the federal government asked states to voluntarily participate in state-by-state NAEP score reporting. Thirty-seven states agreed to take part. This kind of reporting allowed taxpayers in each state to compare their schools to those in other states. Results were reported in local papers and on TV news programs. The public became accustomed to statements like, "The Nation's Report Card shows that fourth-graders in California are scoring lower than children in most other states on math achievement tests."

NAEP state rankings increased public demand for school accountability. More states moved toward a kind of testing called *high-stakes testing.* The term "high-stakes" refers to the consequences of test performance for students and schools. For example, by the late 1990s, 18 states required students to pass a test to graduate from high school, and many states were using test scores to reward or punish local schools (see Figure 1).

In order to develop tests of this type, standards must be stated in measurable terms. Standards are statements about what knowledge and skills should be taught in schools. For example, a standard might be "All fourth-graders should learn the multiplication tables." A measurable standard would be "Fourth-graders will be able to multiply single-digit numbers with 80% proficiency." By the late 1990s, education agencies across the country were focusing as much attention on the development of standards as on testing programs (Council on Basic Education, 1998).

Criticisms of Test-Based School Reform

Test-based school reform, especially in the form of high-stakes testing, has many critics. Educators claim that state-mandated tests encourage teachers to restrict what they teach to the content of the test (Neill, 2000). This problem is made worse, they say, when penalties are attatched to low scores. A school in danger of losing money or being closed may force students to memorize things they really don't understand just to improve their test scores. Worse yet, in one high-stakes testing state, local school officials have faced criminal charges for deliberately reporting false scores to avoid penalties (Associated Press, 1998).

Teachers also claim that test-based reform has caused a decline in textbook quality (Neill, 1998). State agencies, educators say, force publishers to skimp on quality by demanding that they publish revisions of textbooks to fit state tests within very short periods of time. Despite textbook revisions, many school administrators still feel they need to spend thousands of dollars on materials published by test-preparation entrepreneurs (Associated Press, 1998).

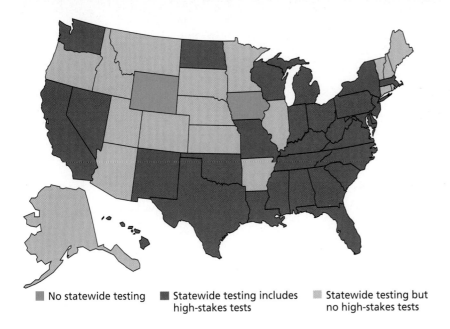

■ No statewide testing ■ Statewide testing includes high-stakes tests ■ Statewide testing but no high-stakes tests

FIGURE 1   States with high-stakes testing, as of 1998. (*Source:* Fairtest, 1998.)

Many testing experts also complain about the quality of the tests currently in use. For one thing, good test development procedures require that standards be written before a test is constructed to measure them. However, critics say that many states pay contractors to develop a test and then create standards to fit the test (Neill, 1998).

Claims of cultural bias have also been made against test-based reform (Neill, 1998). Civil rights organizations say that the knowledge that is tested in most American schools reflects the values and experiences of members of the white, middle-class culture. Further, many states require non–English-speaking children to take tests in English. To date, civil rights groups are unsatisfied with the efforts states have made to reduce bias. Thus,

many have undertaken lawsuits against state education agencies and local schools, and these have yet to be decided.

The Impact of Test-Based Reform

Analyses of standards developed in the last 10 years show that, because of test-based reform, states are moving toward more emphasis on fundamental reading, writing, and mathematics skills (Council on Basic Education, 1998). Moreover, experimental evidence suggests that students try harder (as evidenced by longer and more complex answers to essay questions) and get higher scores on tests when passing tests is tied to outcomes such as high school graduation (DeMars, 2000). As a result, in some areas, high-stakes tests seem to have had a positive impact on

student achievement. Advocates of such testing often point to Texas as an example because of its specific standards and extensive testing program (Council on Basic Education, 1998). The NAEP math scores of Texas school children, especially African American students, have increased a great deal in the past few years.

Despite a few success stories, however, critics argue that the use of high-stakes tests hasn't really improved student achievement, as shown in Figure 2 (Neill, 1998). Nationwide, NAEP scores in all subject areas have remained virtually unchanged during the 40-year history of the test-based reform movement. And students in high-stakes testing states are still more likely to get low scores on the NAEP than students in other states.

Other critics suggest that test-based reform has been most beneficial to students who would have done just as well without it. Research has demonstrated that average and above-average students perform at higher levels on such tests when they are exposed to intensive instruction in test content and test-taking strategies (Fuchs et al., 2000). Low-achieving students, however, seem to benefit very little from such approaches. Furthermore, say critics, despite decades of test-based reform, American public schools continue to turn out thousands of graduates who lack the skills to do college work (Schmidt, 2000).

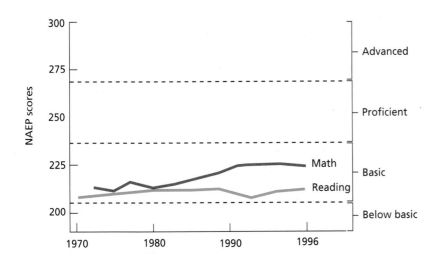

FIGURE 2   NAEP Average Scores

Your Turn

● Talk to public school teachers and administrators about your state's testing program. Do they think test-based reform has improved their schools?

● Check your state education agency's Web site for information on standards and testing.

● Locate newspaper articles that report on what your governor and state legislators think about test-based reform. Do they support a national test?

● Visit www.fairtest.org and www. c-b-e.org to find out how experts on opposite sides of the test-based reform issue rate your state's standards and testing program.

● Go to the Web site of the National Center for Education Statistics at http://www.nces.ed.gov to find out if your state participates in the NAEP.

339

CHAPTER

12

Physical and Cognitive Development in Early Adulthood

Davis Barber, PhotoEdit

You probably know someone like one of the people in the following list. What do all of them have in common?

Cassie, a 22-year-old single mother of a 4-year-old who lives with her parents, works full-time, and attends college classes at night

Joe, a 25-year-old married machinist who attended a trade school after 4 years of military service

Marta, a 27-year-old divorced mother of a preschooler who works as a flight attendant

Devon, a 20-year-old sophomore at a large university who is trying to choose between psychology and music as her major

Renée, a married 30-year-old mother of two school-aged children who has just started college

Marshall, a 33-year-old single man who has been a public school teacher for 10 years

Each member of this diverse group is a young adult. If you think about the people you know who are between the ages of 20 and 40, they probably makeup just as varied a group.

Clearly, young adulthood is the period of life when individuals' developmental pathways begin to diverge significantly. For example, in contrast to younger individuals, the educational experiences of young adults are highly diverse. Some go on to college as soon as they graduate from high school. Others work and attend college part-time. Still others work for a while, or serve in the military, and then further their educations.

Despite these variations, most social science researchers believe that it is still useful to divide the adult years into three roughly equal parts: early adulthood, from 20 to 40; middle adulthood, from 40 to about 65; and late adulthood, from 65 until death. This way of dividing adulthood reflects the fact that optimum physical and cognitive functioning, achieved in the 20s and 30s, begins to wane in some noticeable and measurable ways in the 40s and 50s. Moreover, several important role changes often occur in the early 40s: Children begin to leave home, careers near their peak, and so on.

We will follow the common usage and define "young" or "early" adulthood as the period from age 20 to age 40. In this chapter, you will read about the changes that occur in early adulthood, along with a number of variables that are associated with variation from the "typical" pathway. As you read this chapter, keep the following questions in mind:

- How does physical functioning change in the years from 20 to 40?

- What are the major health issues during early adulthood?

- How do thinking and problem-solving improve in early adulthood?

- How does post-secondary education help shape young adults' development?

Critical Thinking

Before you read the rest of the chapter, think about how you might answer the following questions for yourself: In what ways have your body and mind changed since you were younger? How do you expect them to change as you get older? How has attending college affected your life, and what difference will it make in your future?

Physical Functioning

hen developmentalists study children's development, they are looking at increases or improvements. When developmentalists study adults, especially adults' physical functioning, they begin to ask questions about loss of function, or decline.

Primary and Secondary Aging

Researchers distinguish between two types of aging. The basic, underlying, inevitable aging process is called **primary aging** by most developmentalists. To learn about its effects, they study adults who are disease-free and who have good health practices (Birren & Schroots, 1996).

Secondary aging, in contrast, is the product of environmental influences, health habits, or disease, and is neither inevitable nor experienced by all adults. Research on age differences in health and death rates reveals the expected pattern. For example, 18- to 24-year-olds rarely die from disease (National Center for Health Statistics [NCHS], 1997). However, researchers have found that age interacts with other variables to influence health, a pattern suggesting the influence of secondary aging.

For example, age interacts with social class in a way that is revealed especially clearly in a set of survey data based on questions posed to more than 3,000 adults and analyzed by James House and his colleagues (House, Kessler, & Herzog, 1990; House et al., 1992). Figure 12.1 illustrates the study's results. As you can see, differences among young adults across social class groups are fairly small. However, with increasing age, the differences become much larger.

Similar social class differences in adult health have been found in other industrialized countries, such as Sweden and England, and they occur within ethnic groups in the United States as well as in the overall population (Eames, Ben-Schlomo, & Marmot, 1993; Thorslund & Lundberg, 1994). That is, among African Americans, Hispanic Americans, and Asian Americans, better-educated adults or those with higher incomes have longer life expectancies and better health than do those with less education or lower incomes (Guralnik, Land, Blazer, Fillenbaum, & Branch, 1993).

Social class differences in health may be due to group variations in patterns of primary aging. However, most developmentalists believe they represent secondary aging. In other words, the health differences result from cultural and economic factors such as diet, stress levels, and access to health care that are associated with social class as well as with disease (James, Keenan, & Browning, 1992).

Research also suggests that changes in behavior may prevent or even reverse the effects of aging. Such findings further strengthen the hypothesis that some changes that were formerly thought to be caused by primary aging may turn out to be the result of secondary aging (see No Easy Answers).

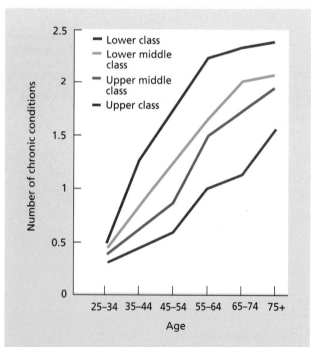

FIGURE 12.1

As people get older, they are more likely to experience some kind of chronic illness, but this change is earlier and more pronounced among poor and working-class adults. (*Source:* House et al., 1990, Figure 1, p. 396.)

primary aging age-related physical changes that have a biological basis and are universally shared and inevitable

secondary aging age-related changes that are due to environmental influences, poor health habits, or disease

No Easy Answers

There Is No Fountain of Youth

Spend a few hours watching television or leafing through magazines, and the advertisements will tell you something very significant about the adult population: Many of us appear to be looking for a quick and easy way to escape the ravages of age. A pill promises to cure a man's baldness. A cream is said to dissolve fat on women's thighs. As appealing as the idea of a fountain of youth is, the truth is that the best way to moderate the effects of primary aging on the body is to follow the hard road of behavioral change. The most significant barriers to remaining youthful are the result of secondary aging and are often preventable. Further, if you develop good habits while you are young, not only will it be easier to maintain those habits, but you will reap benefits over many years.

These are the most important changes you can make:

- *Stop smoking.* If you smoke now, stop. If you don't smoke, don't start.

- *Exercise, exercise, exercise.* Take the stairs instead of the elevator; walk to the grocery store or on other errands; ride a bike to work; get at least 20–30 minutes of vigorous exercise at least three times a week (more than that is even better).

- *Eat a lower-fat diet.* High fat in the diet has been linked to increased risks of both cancer and heart disease, as well as to obesity. The American Heart Association currently recommends that 30% of daily calories come from fat—well below the average American diet. But there is good evidence that a level of 15–20% of calories from fat would be even better. Achieving this level means eating much less meat and dairy products and a lot more vegetables, fruits, grains, and beans. (Goodbye, fast foods!)

- *Get enough calcium.* This is especially important for women, who lose more calcium from their bones than do men, especially after menopause. And once the calcium is lost, it is very hard—perhaps impossible—to regain it. So here is one place where prevention is critical. Weight-bearing exercise helps to retain calcium, but taking calcium supplements from early adulthood is also a good idea.

The Brain and Nervous System

No matter what age an individual is, new synapses are forming, myelinization is occurring, and old connections are dying off. Further, there is recent evidence that, contrary to what neurologists have believed for a long time, some parts of the brain produce new neurons to replace those that die, even in the brains of older adults (Gould, Reeves, Graziano, & Gross, 1999). At some point in development, though, usually in the late teens, developmental processes reach a balance and the brain attains a stable size and weight. Similarly, by early adulthood, most functions have become localized in specific areas of the brain (Gaillard et al., 2000).

Neurologists have found that the pattern of peaks and valleys in the development of brain functions continues into adulthood. In fact, there may be two spurts in brain growth in early adulthood, like those you have read about in earlier chapters. As you may remember from Chapter 10, a major spurt in the growth of the frontal lobes—the area of the brain devoted to logic, planning, and emotional control—begins around age 17. This spurt continues until age 21 or 22 (Spreen, Risser, & Edgell, 1995). Many neuropsychologists believe that this spurt is strongly connected to the increases in the capacity for formal operational thinking and other kinds of abstract reasoning that occur in late adolescence.

In addition to this brain growth spurt between 17 and 21, some neuropsychologists hypothesize that another peak in brain development happens in the mid- to late 20s (Fischer & Rose, 1994). They claim that the cognitive skills that emerge in the middle of the early adulthood period seem to depend on changes in the brain. For example, when you take a multiple-choice test, you need to be able to keep yourself from responding too quickly to the options in order to carefully weigh them all. Neuropsychologists suggest that this kind of *response inhibition* may depend on the ability of the frontal lobes of the brain to regulate the **limbic system,** or the emotional part of the brain. Many scientists

limbic system the part of the brain that regulates emotional responses

believe that the capacity to integrate various brain functions in this way does not become fully developed until early adulthood (Spreen, Risser, & Edgell, 1995).

Still, the gradual loss of speed in virtually every aspect of bodily function appears to be the result of very gradual changes at the neuronal level, particularly the loss of dendrites and a slowing of the "firing rate" of nerves (Birren & Fisher, 1995; Earles & Salthouse, 1995; Salthouse, 1993). As you get older, it takes longer to warm up after you have been very cold, or to cool off after you have been hot. Your reaction time to sudden events slows; you don't respond quite as quickly to a swerving car, for example.

All these functions are tied to particular parts of the nervous system. For example, the hypothalamus regulates body temperature. Declines in reaction times are probably linked to slower communication between the cerebral cortex and the reticular formation. In early adulthood, the nervous system is so redundant—with so many alternative pathways for every signal—that functional changes such as the slowing of neuronal responses have relatively little practical effect on behavior. But over the full sweep of the adult years, the loss of speed becomes very noticeable.

There is considerable controversy about the meaning of sex differences in the adult brain. As you should remember from earlier chapters, the brains of males and females differ to some extent at every age. However, sex differences are even more striking in the adult brain.

For example, the brain contains two types of tissue: *gray matter* and *white matter*. Gray matter is made up of cell bodies and axon terminals (look back at Figure 3.3); white matter contains myelinated axons that connect one neuron to another. Men have a higher proportion of white matter than women do (Gur et al., 1999). In addition, the distributions of gray and white matter differ in the brains of men and women. Men have a lower proportion of white matter in the left brain than in the right brain. In contrast, the proportions of gray matter and white matter in the two hemispheres are equal in women's brains. Such findings have led some neuropsychologists to speculate that men's overall superior spatial perception is associated with sex differences in the distribution of gray and white matter.

There are other sex differences in adult brains. Some listening tasks activate the left hemisphere in men, whereas women respond to them with the right hemisphere (Spreen, Risser, & Edgell, 1995). However, there isn't yet enough consistency across studies to allow neuroscientists to draw definitive conclusions about sex differences in brain function. Moreover, these scientists are still a long way from finding direct links between neurological and behavioral sex differences.

Other Body Systems

Young adults perform better than do the middle-aged or old on virtually every physical measure. Compared to older adults, adults in their 20s and 30s have more muscle tissue; maximum bone calcium; more brain mass; better eyesight, hearing, and sense of smell; greater oxygen capacity; and a more efficient immune system. The young adult is stronger, faster, and better able to recover from exercise or to adapt to changing conditions, such as alterations in temperature or light levels.

● *Declines in Physical Functioning* ●   After this early peak, there is a gradual decline on almost every measure of physical functioning through the years of adulthood. Table 12.1 summarizes these changes. Most of the summary statements in the table are based on both longitudinal and cross-sectional data; many are based on studies in which both experimental and control groups consisted of participants in good health. So developmentalists can be reason-

It's hard to draw a clear line between "early adulthood" and "middle adulthood" because the physical and mental changes are so gradual; even at 30, adults may find that it takes a bit more work to get into or stay in shape than it did at 20. (*Photo:* Charles Gupton, Stock Boston)

TABLE 12.1   A Summary of Age Changes in Physical Functioning

Body Function	Age at Which Change Begins to Be Clear or Measurable	Nature of Change
Vision	Mid-40s	Lens of eye thickens and loses accommodative power, resulting in poorer near vision and more sensitivity to glare
Hearing	50 or 60	Loss of ability to hear very high and very low tones
Smell	About 40	Decline in ability to detect and discriminate among different smells
Taste	None	No apparent loss in taste discrimination ability
Muscles	About 50	Loss of muscle tissue, particularly in "fast twitch" fibers used for bursts of strength or speed
Bones	Mid-30s (women)	Loss of calcium in the bones, called *osteoporosis*; also wear and tear on bone in joints, called *osteoarthritis*, more marked after about 60
Heart and lungs	35 or 40	Most functions (such as aerobic capacity or cardiac output) do not show age changes at rest, but do show age changes during work or exercise
Nervous system	Probably gradual throughout adulthood	Some loss (but not clear how much) of neurons in the brain; gradual reduction in density of dendrites; gradual decline in total brain volume and weight
Immune system	Adolescence	Loss in size of thymus; reduction in number and maturity of T cells; not clear how much of this change is due to stress and how much is primary aging
Reproductive system	Mid-30s (women)	Increased reproductive risk and lowered fertility
	Early 40s (men)	Gradual decline in viable sperm beginning at about age 40; very gradual decline in testosterone from early adulthood
Cellular elasticity	Gradual	Gradual loss of elasticity in most cells, including skin, muscle, tendon, and blood vessel cells; faster deterioration in cells exposed to sunlight
Height	40	Compression of disks in the spine, with resulting loss of height of 1 to 2 inches by age 80
Weight	Nonlinear	In U.S. studies, weight reaches a maximum in middle adulthood and then gradually declines in old age
Skin	40	Increase in wrinkles, as a result of loss of elasticity; oil-secreting glands become less efficient.
Hair	About 50	Becomes thinner and may gray

(*Sources:* Bartoshuk & Weiffenbach, 1990; Blatter et al., 1995; Braveman, 1987; Briggs, 1990; Brock, Guralnik, & Brody, 1990; Doty et al., 1984; Fiatarone & Evans, 1993; Fozard, 1990; Fozard, Metter, & Brant, 1990; Gray, Berlin, McKinlay, & Longcope, 1991; Hallfrisch, Muller, Drinkwater, Tobin, & Adres, 1990; Hayflick, 1994; Ivy, MacLeod, Petit, & Marcus, 1992; Kallman, Plato, & Tobin, 1990; Kline & Scialfa, 1996; Kozma, Stones, & Hannah, 1991; Lakatta, 1990; Lim, Zipursky, Watts, & Pfefferbaum, 1992; McFalls, 1990; Miller, 1990; Mundy, 1994; Scheibel, 1992, 1996; Shock et al., 1984; Weisse, 1992.)

ably confident that most of the age changes listed reflect primary aging and not secondary aging.

The center column of the table lists the approximate age at which the loss or decline reaches the point where it becomes fairly readily apparent. Virtually all these changes begin in early adulthood. But the early losses or declines are not typically noticeable in everyday physical functioning during these years, except when a person is attempting to operate at the absolute edge of physical ability. Among top athletes, for example, the very small losses of speed and strength that occur in the late 20s and 30s are highly significant, often dropping 25-year-olds or 30-year-olds out of the

Research on peak performance in various sports suggests that professional golfers such as Tiger Woods do not perform at peak levels until they are in their early 30s. Considering the degree of success Woods has achieved in his early 20s, what he is likely to accomplish when he reaches his peak may completely alter standards of success in his sport. (*Photo:* Reuters NewMedia Inc./CORBIS)

group of elite athletes (see The Real World, page 348). Nonathletes, though, typically notice little or no drop in everyday physical functioning until middle age.

Another way to think of this change is in terms of a balance between physical demand and physical capacity (Welford, 1993). In early adulthood, almost all of us have ample physical capacity to meet the physical demands we encounter in everyday life. We can read the fine print in the telephone book without bifocals; we can carry heavy boxes or furniture when we move; our immune systems are strong enough to fight off most illnesses, and we recover quickly from sickness. As we move into middle adulthood, the balance sheet changes: We find more and more arenas in which our physical capacities no longer quite meet the demands.

● **Heart and Lungs** ●   The most common measure of overall aerobic fitness is **maximum oxygen uptake (VO_2 max)**, which reflects the ability of the body to take in and transport oxygen to various body organs. When VO_2 max is measured in a person at rest, scientists find only minimal decrements associated with age. But when they measure VO_2 max during exercise (such as during a treadmill test), it shows a systematic decline with age of about 1% per year, beginning between ages 35 and 40 (Goldberg, Dengel, & Hagberg, 1996). Figure 12.2 graphs some typical results from both cross-sectional and longitudinal studies of women. Similar results are found with men (Kozma et al., 1991; Lakatta, 1990). Notice the slight decline in the years of early adulthood, followed by a somewhat more rapid drop in the middle years, a pattern that is highly typical of data on physical changes over adulthood. Similarly, under resting conditions, the quantity of blood flow from the heart (called *cardiac output*) does not decline with age; under exercise or work conditions, however, it declines significantly, dropping 30–40% between age 25 and age 65 (Lakatta, 1990; Rossman, 1980).

One exception to the general statement that heart and lungs do not change with age is found in measurements of blood pressure under resting conditions. You know that when your blood pressure is tested, you are given two numbers. The higher number represents systolic pressure, which is the force of the blood when your heart is contracting. On this measure, age differences are evident even under resting conditions. Systolic pressure is lowest in adults in their 20s and 30s and then rises steadily with age, apparently as a result of loss of elasticity in the blood vessels, a reflection of a much more general loss of elasticity in tissues in all parts of the body.

● **Strength and Speed** ●   The collective effect of changes in muscles and cardiovascular fitness is a general loss of strength and speed with age—not just in top athletes, but in all of us. Figure 12.3 shows both cross-sectional and 9-year longitudinal changes in grip strength in a group of men who participated in the Baltimore Longitudinal Studies of Aging (Kallman et al., 1990). Clearly, strength was at its peak in the men's 20s and early 30s and then declined steadily. Once again, though, such a difference might be the result of the fact that younger adults are more physically active or more likely to be engaged in activities or jobs that demand strength. Arguing against this conclusion, however, are studies of physically active older adults, who also show loss of muscle strength (e.g., Phillips, Bruce, Newton, & Woledge, 1992).

maximum oxygen uptake (VO_2 max) a measure of the body's ability to take in and transport oxygen to various body organs

pelvic inflammatory disease an infection of the female reproductive tract that may result from a sexually transmitted disease and can lead to infertility

● **Reproductive Capacity** ●   In Chapter 3, you read that the risk of miscarriage and other complications of pregnancy is higher in a woman's 30s than in her 20s. An equivalent change occurs in fertility—the ability to conceive—which is at its highest in the late teens and early 20s and drops steadily thereafter (McFalls, 1990; Mosher, 1987; Mosher & Pratt, 1987). Infertility is typically defined as the inability to conceive after 1 or more years of unprotected intercourse. Using this definition, one large U.S. study found that only 7% of women aged 20 to 24 were infertile, compared with 15% of those between 30 and 34, and 28% of those between 35 and 39 (McFalls, 1990). This does not mean, by the way, that 28% of women in their late 30s will be totally unable to conceive; it means that rapid conception is more likely in the early 20s, and that a significant minority of women who postpone childbearing into their late 30s or 40s will not conceive.

The reasons for this decline with age in women's fertility are multiple, including increased problems with ovulation, endometriosis, and a higher probability of having contracted at least one sexually transmitted disease because of more years of potential exposure (Garner, 1995). Sexually transmitted diseases increase the risk of **pelvic inflammatory disease**, which frequently results in a blockage of the fallopian tubes and thus prevents conception.

A man's capacity to impregnate does not appear to change over the years of early adulthood. Male fertility declines somewhat after age 40, but there is no equivalent of menopause among men, who commonly are able to impregnate well into late life. When men in early adulthood have infertility problems—and a significant minority do—it is because their bodies have produced an insufficient number of viable sperm ever since puberty, not because they have lost fertility that they once had. In couples experiencing problems conceiving, the problem is as likely to be with the man as the woman (Davajan & Israel, 1991).

● *Immune System Functioning* ● The two key organs in the immune system are the thymus gland and the bone marrow. Between them, they create two types of cells, B cells and T cells, each of which plays a distinct role. B cells fight against external threats by producing antibodies against such disease organisms as viruses or bacteria; T cells defend against essentially internal threats, such as transplanted tissue, cancer cells, and viruses that live within the body's cells (Kiecolt-Glaser & Glaser, 1995). It is T cells that are most deficient in someone with AIDS and that decline most in number and efficiency with age (Miller, 1996).

Changes in the thymus gland appear to be central to the aging process. This gland is largest in adolescence and declines dramatically thereafter in both size and mass. By age 45 or 50, the thymus has only about 5–10% of the cellular mass it had at puberty (Braveman, 1987; Hausman & Weksler, 1985). This smaller, less functional thymus is less able to turn the immature T cells produced by the bone marrow into fully "adult" cells. As a result, both of the basic protective mechanisms work less efficiently. Adults produce fewer antibodies than do children or teenagers. And T cells partially lose the ability to "recognize" a foreign cell, so that the body may fail to fight off some disease cells

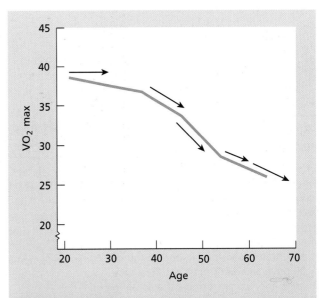

FIGURE 12.2

The continuous line shows VO$_2$ max averages for cross-sectional comparisons; the arrows show changes on the same measure for groups of women studied longitudinally. The two sets of findings match remarkably. Note that the largest drop was between ages 40 and 50. (*Source:* Plowman, Drinkwater, & Horvath, 1979, Figure 1, p. 514.)

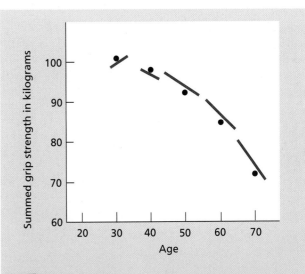

FIGURE 12.3

These data, from the Baltimore Longitudinal Study of Aging, show both cross-sectional data (the dots) and longitudinal data (the lines) for grip strength among men. Once again, there is striking agreement between the two sets of information. (*Source:* Kallman et al., 1990, Figure 2, p. M84.)

AGING

The Real World

Age and Peak Sports Performance

One of the most obvious ways to confirm whether human bodies are at their physical peak in early adulthood is to look at sports performance. Olympic athletes or other top performers in any sport push their bodies to the limit of their abilities. If early adulthood is really the period of peak physical ability, most world-record-holders and top performers should be in their 20s or perhaps early 30s. Another way to approach the same question is to look at the average performance of top athletes in each of several age groups, including those in "master" categories (athletes who are 35 or older). Both types of analysis lead inescapably to the same conclusion: Athletic performance peaks early in life, although the exact timing of the peak varies somewhat from one sport to another.

Swimmers, for example, reach their peak very early—at about age 17 for women and about 19 for men. Golfers peak the latest, at about age 31 (Ericsson,

1990; Schulz & Curnow, 1988; Stones & Kozma, 1996). Runners fall in between, with top performances in their early or middle 20s, although the longer the distance, the later the peak. You can see that pattern in the figure, which represents the average age at which each of a series of top male runners ran his fastest time.

Cross-sectional comparisons of the top performances of competitors of dif-

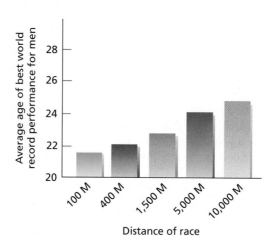

ferent ages lead to the same conclusion. For example, Germany holds national swimming championships each year, giving awards to the top performers in each 5-year age range from 25 through 70. The best times drop steadily with age (Ericsson, 1990).

At the same time, it is also true that older athletes can perform far better than has been commonly thought. World records for master athletes have been repeatedly broken over the past several decades; in many sports, present-day 50-year-olds are performing at higher levels than did Olympic athletes of 100 years ago. The human body, at any age, is more responsive to training than researchers even a decade ago had presumed. But it is still true that for those who achieve and maintain a high level of fitness throughout adult life, peak performance will come in early adulthood (Stones & Kozma, 1996).

(cancer cells, for example). Thus, one of the key physical changes over the years of adulthood is an increasing susceptibility to disease.

But it is not entirely clear whether this susceptibility is due to primary or secondary aging. These changes in the immune system are found in healthy adults, which makes them look like part of primary aging. But there also is growing evidence that the functioning of the immune system is highly responsive to psychological stress and depression (Maier, Watkins, & Fleshner, 1994; Weisse, 1992). College students, for example, show lower levels of one variety of T cells ("natural killer" T cells) during exam periods than at other times (Glaser et al., 1992). And adults who have recently been widowed show a sharp drop in immune system functioning (Irwin & Pike, 1993). Chronic stress, too, has an effect on the immune system, initially stimulating an increase in immune efficiency, followed by a drop (Kiecolt-Glaser et al., 1991).

Collectively, this research points to the possibility that life experiences that demand high levels of change or adaptation will affect immune system functioning. Over a period of years and many stresses, the immune system may become less and less efficient. It may well be that the immune system changes with age in basic ways regardless of the level of stress. But it is also possible that what is thought of as normal aging of the immune system is a response to cumulative stress.

efore going on

- Define primary and secondary aging.

- Why do neuroscientists think there may be a spurt in brain development in the mid-20s?

- Describe the various changes in other body systems that happen in early adulthood.

Health and Wellness

arly adulthood is a relatively healthy period of life, but risky behaviors—having multiple sex partners or engaging in substance use, for example—along with generally poor health habits can be problematic.

Sexually Transmitted Diseases

In contrast to other types of disease, most sexually transmitted diseases (STD)—including gonorrhea, syphilis, genital herpes, and HIV—are more common among young adults than in any other age group (CDC, 1999a, 1999b, 2000a, 2000b). African Americans have particularly high rates of infection. During the late 1990s, 80% of new syphilis cases and 45% of new genital herpes cases in the United States involved African Americans (CDC, 1999b, 2000a). Public health officials attribute racial differences in STD infection rates to poverty, poorer general health and lower resistance to infection among African Americans and other minorities, limited access to STD clinics and other health care facilities, and higher rates of injected drug use (CDC, 2000b).

Sadly, African Americans, who comprise about 15% of the U.S. population, suffer almost half of annual deaths from AIDS (CDC, 1999a). High rates of infection with other STDs are at least partly responsible. Once an individual is infected with any sexually transmitted disease, he or she is more likely than peers to become infected with HIV (CDC, 1998). For example, an individual who has syphilis is three to four times more likely than an uninfected person to acquire HIV from an HIV-positive sex partner or from sharing a hypodermic needle with an HIV-positive drug user (CDC, 1999b). Moreover, the genital secretions of HIV-positive men who are also infected with another STD contain many more active viruses than those of HIV-infected men who have no other sexually transmitted disease (CDC, 1998a). Thus, public health officials point out that one important key to reducing HIV infection rates in African Americans, as well as in other groups, is to reduce overall rates of sexually transmitted diseases.

Like adolescents, many young adults engage in high-risk behaviors that are specifically linked to STDs: having multiple sexual partners, having sex without adequate

Sexually transmitted diseases are one of the most significant health risks of young adulthood. Casual sexual encounters with multiple partners carry with them a higher risk of contracting such diseases than do more careful relationship choices.
(*Photo:* Timothy Shonnard, Stone)

protection, and frequently using drugs or alcohol. However, for most young adults, STDs remain one of the taboo topics. Many young adults are unwilling to insist on the use of condoms; many do not seek medical attention when they develop symptoms and do not inform their partners of potential problems (Lewis, Malow, & Ireland, 1997; Schuster, 1997). And the risks of these behaviors are considerable, especially with the increase in drug-resistant strains of gonorrhea and syphilis. So take note: Safe sex practices—including knowledge of your partner's sexual history—are worth the effort.

Health Habits and Personal Factors

As you might expect, individual health habits, such as exercise, influence health in the early adult years and beyond. Social support networks and attitudes also affect health.

● *Health Habits* ●   The best evidence for the long-term effects of various health habits comes from the Alameda County Study, a major longitudinal epidemiological study conducted in one county in California (Berkman & Breslow, 1983; Breslow & Breslow, 1993; Kaplan, 1992). The study began in 1965, when a random sample of all residents of the county, a total of 6,928 people, completed an extensive questionnaire about many aspects of their lives, including their health habits and their health and disability. These participants were contacted again in 1974 and in 1983, when they again described their health and disability. The researchers also monitored death records and were able to specify the date of death of each of the participants who died between 1965 and 1983. They could then link health practices reported in 1965 to later death, disease, or disability. The researchers initially identified seven good health habits that they thought might be critical: getting physical exercise, not smoking, drinking, over- or undereating, or snacking, eating breakfast, and getting regular sleep.

Data from the first 9 years of the Alameda study show that five of these seven practices were independently related to the risk of death. Only snacking and eating breakfast were unrelated to mortality. When the five strong predictors were combined in the 1974 data, researchers found that, in every age group, those with poorer health habits had a higher risk of mortality. Not surprisingly, poor health habits were also related to disease and disability rates over the 18 years of the study. Those who described poorer health habits in 1965 were more likely to report disability or disease symptoms in 1974 and in 1983 (Breslow & Breslow, 1993; Guralnik & Kaplan, 1989; Strawbridge, Camacho, Cohen, & Kaplan, 1993).

The Alameda study is not the only one to show these connections between health habits and mortality. For example, a 20-year longitudinal study in Sweden confirms the link between physical exercise and lower risk of death (Lissner, Bengtsson, Bjorkelund, & Wedel, 1996). In addition, the Nurses' Health Study, a longitudinal investigation that examined the health behaviors of more than 115,000 nurses in the United States for almost two decades, found that the lower a woman's initial body-mass index (a measure of weight relative to height), the lower her likelihood of death (Manson et al., 1995).

These longitudinal studies suggest that the lifestyle choices of early adulthood have cumulative effects. For example, the effect of a high-cholesterol diet appears to add up over time. However, a radical lowering of fat levels in the diet may reverse the process of cholesterol

Critical Thinking

Think about your own less-than-ideal health habits. What rationalizations do you use to justify them to yourself?

build-up in the blood vessels (Ornish, 1990). Thus, the long-term effects of lifestyle choices made in early adulthood may be either negative or positive. So there is likely to be a payoff for changing your health habits.

● *Social Support* ●   Abundant research shows that adults with adequate *social support* have lower risk of disease, death, and depression than do adults with weaker social networks or less supportive relationships (e.g., Berkman, 1985; Berkman & Breslow, 1983; Cohen, 1991). However, a person's perception of the adequacy of her social contacts and emotional support is more strongly related to physical and emotional health than are the actual number of such contacts (Feld & George, 1994; Sarason, Sarason, & Pierce, 1990). Thus, it is not the objective amount of contact with others that is important, but how that contact is understood or interpreted.

The link between social support and health was revealed in some of the findings from the Alameda study. In this study, the *social network index* reflected an objective measurement: number of contacts with friends and relatives, marital status, church and group membership. Even using this less-than-perfect measure of support, the relationship is vividly clear: Among both men and women in three different age groups (30–49, 50–59, and 60–69), those with the fewest social connections had higher death rates than those with more social connections. Since similar patterns have been found in other countries, including Sweden and Japan, this link between social contact and physical hardiness is not restricted to the United States or to Western cultures (Orth-Gomer, Rosengren, & Wilhelmsen, 1993; Sugisawa, Liang, & Liu, 1994).

The beneficial effect of social support is particularly clear when an individual is under high stress. An excellent example comes from research on depression among women in England (Brown, 1989, 1993; Brown & Harris, 1978). Researchers initially studied 419 women who ranged in age from 18 to 65, gathering information about the number of severely stressful events each woman had experienced in the year prior to the research (such as the death of someone close, a divorce or failed relationship, or the equivalent), about whether they were currently depressed, and about who—if anyone—served as an intimate confidant. The study found that, although stress was more strongly linked to depression than to social support, highly stressed women who had a close confidant, especially if that confidant was a husband or boyfriend, were much less likely to become depressed. That is, the social support of their partner or other confidant buffered them against the negative effects of the stress.

● *A Sense of Control* ●   Another personal characteristic that affects health is an individual's level of what Rodin has called *perceived control* (Rodin, 1990). Psychologist Albert Bandura talks about this same characteristic but refers to it as **self-efficacy**, the belief in one's ability to perform some action or to control one's behavior or environment, to reach some goal or to make something happen (Bandura, 1977b, 1982c, 1986). Such a belief is one aspect of the internal model of the self and is affected by one's experiences with mastering tasks and overcoming obstacles.

A similar idea comes from the work of Martin Seligman, who differentiates between positions of *optimism* and *helplessness* (Seligman, 1991). The pessimist, who feels helpless, believes that misfortune will last a long time, will undermine everything, and is his own fault. The optimist believes that setbacks are temporary and usually caused by circumstances. He is convinced that there is always some solution and that he will be able to work things out. Confronted by defeat, the optimist sees it as a challenge and tries harder, whereas the pessimist gives up. Both Bandura and Seligman propose that self-efficacy or optimism arise in childhood and adolescence, as a result of early experiences of effectiveness, success or failure, and frustration.

Research on the links between a sense of control and health show that those with a more helpless attitude or with a low sense of self-efficacy are more likely to become depressed or physically ill ("Optimism can mean life," 1994a; Seligman, 1991; Syme, 1990). The most striking demonstration of this connection is from a 35-year study of

self-efficacy the belief in one's capacity to cause an intended event to occur or to perform a task

a group of Harvard men who were first interviewed in their freshman years, in 1938–1940. Researchers were able to use material from interviews with these men when they were 25 to assess their degree of pessimism. Their physical health from ages 30 to 60 was then rated by physicians who examined the men every 5 years. Pessimism was not related to health at 30, 35, or 40, but at every assessment from age 45 to age 60, those who had had a more pessimistic approach at age 25 had significantly poorer health, and this was true even after controlling statistically for physical and mental health at 25 (Peterson, Seligman, & Vaillant, 1988).

It is also possible to show that experimentally increasing the sense of control improves an adult's health, even immune function. On this point, there is cross-sectional, longitudinal, and experimental evidence (Welch & West, 1995). In the earliest and best-known study of this kind, researchers found that mortality rates of nursing home residents were lower among those who had been given control over even quite simple aspects of their daily lives, such as whether to have scrambled eggs or omelettes for breakfast or whether to sign up to attend a movie (Rodin & Langer, 1977).

Intimate Partner Abuse

Researchers define **intimate partner abuse** as physical acts or other behavior intended to intimidate or harm an intimate partner. Intimate partners are couples who are dating, cohabiting, engaged, or married, or who were formerly partners. The more common term, *domestic abuse*, refers only to incidents involving individuals who live in the same household.

● *Prevalence* ● Throughout the world, women are more likely to be victimized by intimate partners than men. In the United States, surveys suggest that about 25% of women have been physically abused by a partner, compared to only 8% of men (National Center for Injury Prevention and Control [NCIPC], 2000). However, rates of abuse among women vary significantly around the world, as Figure 12.4 reveals (World Health Organization [WHO], 2000).

Rates vary across ethnic and sexual orientation groups within the United States as well. As many as half of all African American women in the United States have been physically abused by an intimate partner at some time in their adult lives (Wyatt, Axelrod, Chin, Carmona, & Loeb, 2000). Similarly, some studies suggest that Hispanic American women experience partner abuse more frequently than their white counterparts (Duncan, Stayton, & Hall, 1999). Among homosexuals, about 22% of gay men report having been physically abused by a partner (Waldner-Haugrud, Gratch, & Magruder, 1997). By contrast, almost half of lesbians surveyed report that they have been physically assaulted by a partner (Waldner-Haugrud et al., 1997).

● *Causes of Partner Abuse* ● Anthropologists believe that cultural attitudes contribute to rates of abuse (Hicks & Gwynne, 1996). Specifically, in many societies, women are regarded as property, and a man's "right" to beat his partner may be protected by law. In fact, there was a time when, based on English common law traditions, this was true in the United States.

Gender-role prescriptions may also contribute to abuse. For example, rates of abuse are particularly high among Japanese women, over 50% of whom claim to have been victimized (Kozu, 1999). Researchers attribute the prevalence of abuse to the cultural belief that Japanese husbands are absolute authorities over their wives and children. Further, to avoid bringing dishonor on her husband, the Japanese wife is obligated to conceal abusive incidents from those outside the family.

In addition to cultural beliefs, a number of characteristics of abusers and their victims are associated with intimate partner abuse. For example, the same cluster of personality traits contributes to abuse in both heterosexual and homosexual couples

intimate partner abuse physical acts or other behavior intended to intimidate or harm an intimate partner

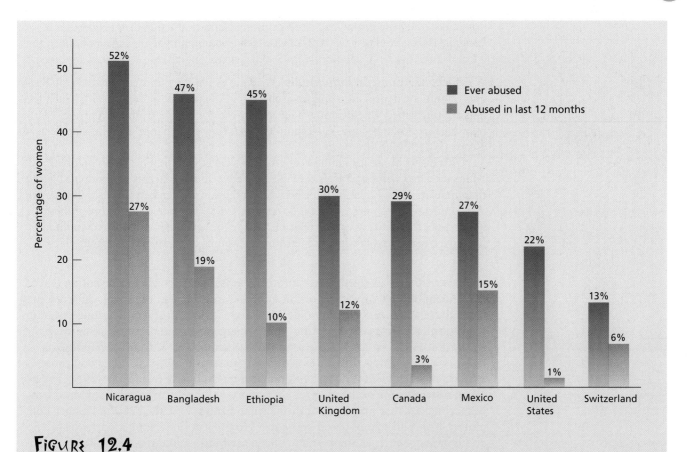

FIGURE 12.4

These data on physical abuse are based on a World Health Organization international survey of medical records. (*Source:* WHO, 2000.)

(Burke & Follingstad, 1999). The cluster includes a tendency toward irrational jealousy, a need for dependency in the partner and control in a relationship, sudden mood swings, and a quick temper (Landolt & Dutton, 1997). Men who are generally more aggressive than others are also more likely than less aggressive men to abuse their partners (Kane, Staiger, & Ricciardelli, 2000). In addition, men who are high school dropouts or who are frequently unemployed abuse their partners more often than other men (Kyriacou et al., 1999).

Abuse victims are more likely to have been abused as children than are their peers who are not involved in abusive relationships (Wyatt et al., 2000). Age is also a factor. Young women between the ages of 16 and 24 are more likely to be abused than those who are older (Buss, 1999; Duncan et al., 1999). This pattern of age differences may result from younger women's lesser ability to function independently from abusive partners. They may lack the education and/or work experience necessary to gain employment. Finally, younger women are more likely to be caring for infants and young children for whom they cannot obtain day care. As a result, many such women remain in abusive relationships, believing they have no other choice (Kaplan & Sadock, 1991).

Alcohol and drug problems are more common among both abusers and victims than among nonabusive partners (Kyriacou et al., 1999; Van Hightower & Gorton, 1998). One extensive study of more than 8,000 intrafamily killings found that, in about half of spousal

Criminologists point out that intimate partner abuse happens most often in the context of arguments over long-standing disagreements that take place when partners are home from work in the evening, on holidays or weekends, and/or have been drinking or using drugs. (*Photo:* Jonathan Nourok, PhotoEdit)

homicides, the perpetrator had been drinking alcohol or using drugs (Dawson & Langan, 1994). Similarly, in 50% of cases, the victim had been using alcohol or drugs.

● ***Effects of Abuse on Individuals*** ● Women who are abused may develop feelings of anxiety, depression, and low self-esteem (Kaplan & Sadock, 1991). Such feelings are intensified when victims believe they cannot escape from the abusive relationship. Some become so despondent that they consider or attempt suicide as an escape (NCIPC, 2000).

Witnessing abuse also influences children's development. One study involving 420 adults who had witnessed physical violence between their parents as children suggested that there are strong relationships between parental violence and a variety of negative developmental outcomes (McNeal & Amato, 1998). For one thing, many of these adults were found to have poor relationships with their own partners and children. Moreover, many had become perpetrators or victims of partner abuse themselves.

● ***Prevention*** ● Vigorous law enforcement is one approach to prevention (Sacco & Kennedy, 1996). Advocates of this approach suggest that the stigma of arrest may force abusers to face the reality that they have a serious problem. Training programs for law enforcement officials and hospital emergency room personnel that teach them to recognize signs of abuse are also essential (Hamberger & Minsky, 2000). As a result of such training, advocates claim, perpetrators may be identified and prosecuted even when victims do not voluntarily report abusive incidents.

A different approach is to provide victims with problem-solving skills and temporary shelters that may prevent their revictimization (NCIPC, 2000). Further, community-wide and school-based approaches to prevention seek to educate the public about intimate partner abuse and to change attitudes about the acceptability of violence in intimate relationships, so that abuse will not happen in the first place.

Sexual Violence

Sexual violence is the use of physical coercion to force a person to engage in a sexual act against his or her will. Engaging in sex with a person who is incapable of understanding what is happening to her, because of a mental disability or a temporary state of consciousness, is also defined as sexual violence. *Rape* is a more specific term that is restricted to forced penetration of either a male or a female victim.

● ***Prevalence*** ● As is true of intimate partner abuse, women are far more likely than men to be sexually victimized. A national survey of women in the United States found that 18% of women had been victims of heterosexual violence at some time in their lives, compared to only 3% of men (NCIPC, 2000). Surveys also indicate that 1–3% of young men have experienced homosexual rape (NCIPC, 2000; Zweig, Barber, & Eccles, 1997).

Most sexual violence occurs in the context of social or romantic relationships. National surveys in the United States indicate that 56% of perpetrators are acquaintances of the victim, and another 26% are intimate partners (NCIPC, 2000). Like sexual violence by males against females, male rape usually involves men who are acquaintances or who are intimate partners (Hodge & Canter, 1998).

Sexual violence rates are quite similar across cultures, with a few rather dramatic exceptions. For example, in an international survey of medical records, 48% of women in Peru were found to have reported being forced into a sexual act during the previous 12 months (WHO, 2000).

Anthropologists hypothesize that rates of sexual violence are similar across nations because there is a prohibition against forced sex in almost all cultures (Hicks

sexual violence the use of physical coercion to force a person to engage in a sexual act against his or her will

& Gwynne, 1996). At the same time, exceptionally high rates, such as those in Peru, are probably the result of a complex set of cultural beliefs. Sexual intercourse, even if it is obtained by force, may be seen as evidence of masculinity, one component of which in many cultures is the right and ability to dominate women. Thus, tolerance of sexual violence may be greater in societies that have a culture of "machismo," as a way of "reminding" men and women of their relative social positions.

● *Causes* ● Some causes of sexual violence are far more subtle than cultural factors. For example, *date rape* is nonconsensual sex that takes place in the context of a date. Men's beliefs about women's sexual behavior—namely, the idea that women say no when they really mean yes—are believed to contribute to date rape.(Christopher, Madura, & Weaver, 1998). Frequently, alcohol and/or drugs, such as the so-called date rape drug Rohypnol, are used by the perpetrator to sedate or to loosen the inhibitions of the victim. Thus, prevention programs urge young women to avoid drinking or using drugs on dates, to confine dating to public places until they know a man very well, and to be as emphatic as possible when discouraging a man's sexual advances.

● *Effects* ● Sexual violence is associated with many of the same psychological effects as intimate partner abuse: depression, low self-esteem, and fear. Moreover, victims of sexual violence can develop post-traumatic stress disorder, and many have difficulties in their sex lives (Kaplan & Sadock, 1991). The effects of male rape are similar, but they may also include fear of developing a homosexual orientation among victims who are heterosexual (Kaplan & Sadock, 1991).

Mental Health Problems

Studies in a number of developed countries show that the risk of virtually every kind of emotional disturbance is higher in early adulthood than in middle age (Kessler, Foster, Webster, & House, 1992; Regier et al., 1988). In fact, survey research suggests that as many as 10% of younger adults, those aged 18 to 24, have seriously considered committing suicide (Brener, Hassan, & Barrios, 1999).

● *Causes of Mental Disorders* ● The most plausible explanation for the differing rates of mental illness between young adults and middle-aged adults is that early adulthood is the period in which adults have both the highest expectations and the highest levels of role conflict and role strain. These are the years when each of us must learn a series of major new roles (spouse, parent, worker). If we fall short of our expectations, emotional difficulties such as anxiety and depression become more likely.

Some people respond very effectively to the challenges of young adulthood, while others do not. For example, the personal factors you read about in an earlier section are important to mental health as well as physical health. However, with respect to mental illness, researchers' attention is becoming more focused on biological causes.

First, mental illnesses tend to run in families, suggesting a genetic factor. In fact, the number of close relatives a person has who suffer from depression or other mood disorders is the best predictor of the likelihood that the individual will develop a mood disorder (Kendler et al., 1995). In addition, an increasing number of studies demonstrate links between mental illnesses and disturbances in specific brain functions (Drevets et al., 1997). Consequently, the current view of most psychologists is that mental disorders result from an interaction of biological and environmental factors.

● *Anxiety, Mood, and Substance Use Disorders* ● The most common mental disorders are those that are associated with fear and anxiety (Kessler et al., 1994). For example, *phobias* are fairly common. A **phobia** is an irrational fear of an object,

phobia an irrational fear of an object, a person, a place, or a situation

a person, a place, or a situation. Most phobias are learned through association of the experience of being in a state of fear with a specific stimulus. For example, a college student who was injured in a car crash may avoid the intersection where the crash occurred, even though doing so adds time and distance to his daily trip from home to campus.

Since phobias are usually learned, therapeutic interventions usually involve some process of *un*learning the association. In fact, many people "cure" their own phobias simply by exposing themselves to the fear-producing stimulus until it no longer induces anxiety. Thus, the student who is phobic about a particular intersection may tell himself that he is being silly and force himself to drive through it repeatedly until the phobic reaction no longer occurs.

After anxiety disorders, problems associated with moods are the most common type of mental difficulty. Depression is the most frequent of these disorders. Rates of depression are higher in early adulthood than in either adolescence or middle age. Thus, paradoxically, the time of life in which people experience their peak of physical and intellectual functioning is also the time when they may be most prone to feelings of sadness. Depression rates may be higher in early adulthood because these are the years when people must create new attachment relationships while at the same time separating from parents (Erikson's task of *intimacy*). Consequently, brief periods during which a person is alone may result in feelings of loneliness and social failure that may lead to depression.

Alcoholism and significant drug addiction also peak between ages 18 and 40, after which they decline gradually. The rates of addiction are higher for men than for women, but the age pattern is very similar in both genders (Anthony & Aboraya, 1992). One large study in the United States found a rate of alcohol abuse or dependence of about 6% among young adults, compared with 4% among the middle aged, and 1.8% for those over 65 (Regier et al., 1988).

Binge drinking (usually defined as consuming five or more drinks on one occasion) is also particularly common among college students in the United States. Although most binge drinkers do not think of themselves as having a problem with alcohol, they clearly display a variety of problem behaviors, including substantially higher rates of unprotected sex, physical injury, driving while intoxicated, and trouble with the police (Wechsler, Davenport, Dowdall, Moeykens, & Castillo, 1994; Wechsler, Dowdall, Maenner, Gledhill-Hoyt, & Lee, 1998). Thus, alarmed by surveys showing that as many as 50% of college students engage in binge drinking, a growing number of colleges and universities are strictly enforcing rules against on-campus substance use (Wechsler et al., 1998). Many also provide students with treatment for alcohol and substance abuse problems.

● ***Personality Disorders*** ●   In a few cases, the stresses of young adulthood, presumably in combination with some type of biological factor, lead to serious disturbances in cognitive, emotional, and social functioning that are not easily treated. For example, a **personality disorder** is an inflexible pattern of behavior that leads to difficulties in social, educational, and occupational functioning. In many cases, the problems that are associated with these disorders appear early in life. However, the behavior pattern is usually not diagnosed as a mental disorder until late adolescence or early adulthood (APA, 1994). The five most common types of personality disorders are listed in Table 12.2.

Some young adults may exhibit behavior that suggests a personality disorder because of stressors such as the break-up of a long-term relationship. For this reason, mental health professionals have to assess an individual's long-term and current levels of functioning in order to diagnose personality disorders. Ethnic and cultural standards of behavior also have to be taken into account, and physical illnesses that can cause abnormal behavior, such as disturbances in the endocrine system, have to be ruled out. Clinicians also have to keep in mind that some of these disorders are closely related, such as the narcissistic and histrionic disorders, and that some individuals suffer from more than one.

personality disorder an inflexible pattern of behavior that leads to difficulty in educational, occupational, and social functioning

TABLE 12.2   Personality Disorders

Type	Characteristics
Antisocial	Difficulty forming emotional attachments; lack of empathy; little regard for the rights of others; self-centered; willingness to violate the law or social rules to achieve a desired objective
Paranoid	Suspicious of others' behavior and motives; emotionally guarded and highly sensitive to minor violations of personal space or perceived rights
Histrionic	Irrational, attention-seeking behavior; inappropriate emotional responses; sexually seductive behavior and clothing
Narcissistic	Exaggerated sense of self-importance; craves attention and approval; exploits others; lack of empathy
Borderline	Unstable moods, relationships; fear of abandonment; tendency to self-injury; highly dependent on others; impulsive and reckless behavior

(*Source:* APA, 1994.)

Generally, to be diagnosed with any of the disorders in Table 12.2, a young adult has to have been exhibiting the associated behavior since mid- or late adolescence. In addition, the person should demonstrate the behavior consistently, across all kinds of situations. For example, a person who steals from an employer but generally respects the property rights of others outside the work environment would probably not be diagnosed with antisocial personality disorder. The individual's functioning at work, at school, or in social relationships also must be impaired to some degree. Psychological tests can be helpful in distinguishing whether an individual simply has a troublesome personality trait, such as suspiciousness, or a genuine mental illness, such as paranoid personality disorder.

Some personality disorders, such as antisocial and borderline disorders, get better on their own as adults gain maturity (APA, 1994). However, most of these disorders remain problematic throughout adult life. In addition, they are not easily treated. In most cases, they do not respond to psychotherapy, because those who suffer from them seem to believe their problems result from others' behavior rather than their own.

● *Schizophrenia* ●   Another type of serious mental illness that is often first diagnosed in early adulthood is **schizophrenia**, a mental disorder characterized by false beliefs known as *delusions* and false sensory experiences called *hallucinations*. For example, a first-year biology student who breaks into a laboratory on his college campus to work on a cure for cancer he has just thought of may suffer from a *delusion of grandeur*. Likewise, a young women who hears voices that guide her behavior is likely to be experiencing hallucinations.

For most schizophrenics, these disturbances of thought become so severe that they can no longer function at work, at school, or in social relationships. In fact, many engage in behavior that endangers themselves or others. For example, a schizophrenic may believe that he can fly and may jump out of an upper-story window. Consequently, schizophrenics are frequently hospitalized. Fortunately, powerful antipsychotic medications can help most schizophrenics regain some degree of normal functioning. Yet, many continue to experience recurring episodes of disturbed thinking even when medication helps them to gain control over their behavior.

schizophrenia a serious mental disorder characterized by disturbances of thought such as delusions and hallucinations

Before going on

- How are age, health habits, and stress related to illness?

- What habits are associated with good health?

- How do social support and a sense of control contribute to good health?

- What are the prevalence rates, causes, and effects of intimate partner abuse?

- What factors are involved in most cases of sexual violence, and what are its effects on victims?

- What are the characteristics of people who suffer from anxiety or mood disorders, substance abuse, personality disorders, or schizophrenia?

Cognitive Changes

Like most aspects of physical functioning, intellectual processes are at their peak in early adulthood. Indeed, it now seems clear that the intellectual peak lasts longer than many early researchers had thought, and that the rate of decline is quite slow.

Current research also makes it clear that the rate and pattern of cognitive decline varies widely—differences that appear to be caused by a variety of environmental and lifestyle factors, as well as by heredity.

Formal Operations and Beyond

As you should recall from Chapter 10, Piaget's formal operational stage emerges in mid- to late adolescence but is not nearly so well developed then as his theory proposed. In fact, it appears that formal operational thinking is more characteristic of adults than of adolescents and is strongly tied to educational experiences. But some theorists dispute Piaget's hypothesis that formal operations is the last stage of cognitive development.

A number of theorists argue that Piaget's concept of formal operations simply doesn't capture many of the kinds of thinking that adults are called on to do. They propose, instead, that new structures, or new stages, of thinking occur in adulthood. One such theorist is Gisela Labouvie-Vief, who argues that formal operational thinking is useful in early adulthood, when the young person has some need to explore or examine many life options (Labouvie-Vief, 1980, 1990). But once an adult has made his initial choices, he no longer has much need for formal operations; instead, he needs thinking skills that are specialized and pragmatic. Adults learn how to solve the problems associated with the particular social roles they occupy, or the particular jobs they hold. In the process, they trade the deductive thoroughness of formal operations for what Labouvie-Vief calls *contextual validity*.

What kind of thinking might this young couple be using to make a budget decision? Pragmatic? Concrete or formal operational? (*Photo:* Diana White, PhotoEdit)

In her view, this trade-off does not reflect a regression or a loss, but rather a necessary structural change.

Labouvie-Vief also makes the point that many young adults begin to turn away from a purely logical, analytic approach, toward a more open, perhaps deeper, mode of understanding that incorporates myth and metaphor and recognizes and accepts paradox and uncertainty. Michael Basseches calls this new adult type of thinking **dialectical thought** (Basseches, 1984, 1989). He suggests that whereas formal operational thought "involves the effort to find fundamental fixed realities—basic elements and immutable laws—[dialectical thought] attempts to describe fundamental processes of change and the dynamic relationships through which this change occurs" (1984, p. 24). According to this view, adults do not give up their ability to use formal reasoning. Instead, they acquire a new ability to deal with the fuzzier problems that make up the majority of the problems of adulthood—problems that do not have a single solution, or in which some critical pieces of information may be missing. Choosing what type of refrigerator to buy might be a decision aided by formal operational thought. But such forms of logical thought may not be helpful in making a decision about whether to adopt a child, or whether to place your aging parent in a nursing home. Basseches argues that such problems demand a different kind of thinking—not a "higher" kind of thinking, but a different one.

Still a third model of "postformal" thinking comes from Patricia Arlin, who argues that Piaget's stage of formal operations is a stage of problem solving (Arlin, 1975, 1989, 1990). Some adults, Arlin proposes, develop a further stage characterized by problem *finding*. This new mode, which includes much of what is normally called *creativity*, is optimal for dealing with problems that have no clear solution or that have multiple solutions. A person operating at this stage is able to generate many possible solutions to ill-defined problems and to see old problems in new ways. Arlin argues that problem finding is a clear stage following formal operations, but that it is achieved by only a small number of adults, such as those involved in advanced science or the arts.

Critical Thinking

List two personal problems you have had to solve in the past six months. What kind of logic or thought process did you use to solve each one? Did your mode of thinking change in response to the nature of the problem?

Many of these new theories of adult cognition are intriguing, but they remain highly speculative, with little empirical evidence to back them up. More generally, psychologists do not yet agree on whether these new types of thinking represent "higher" forms of thought, built on the stages Piaget described, or whether it is more appropriate simply to describe them as different forms of thinking that may or may not emerge in adulthood. What may be most important about such theories is the emphasis on the fact that the normal problems of adult life, with their inconsistencies and complexities, cannot always be addressed fruitfully using formal operational logic. It seems entirely plausible that adults are pushed toward more pragmatic, relativistic forms of thinking and use formal operational thinking only occasionally, if at all. Postformal theorists agree that this change should not be thought of as a loss or a deterioration, but rather as a reasonable adaptation to a different set of cognitive tasks.

Intelligence and Memory

Examination of intelligence and memory in early adulthood suggests that both continuity and change characterize these components of cognitive functioning.

● *IQ Scores* ● IQ scores remain quite stable across middle childhood, adolescence, and early adulthood. For example, a study of Canadian army veterans, tested first when they were in their early 20s and then again in their early 60s, yielded similar

dialectical thought a form of thought involving recognition and acceptance of paradox and uncertainty

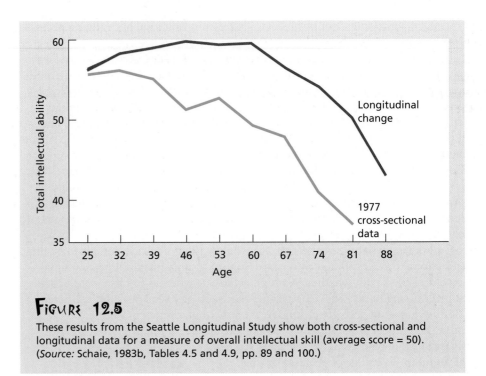

FIGURE 12.5

These results from the Seattle Longitudinal Study show both cross-sectional and longitudinal data for a measure of overall intellectual skill (average score = 50). (*Source:* Schaie, 1983b, Tables 4.5 and 4.9, pp. 89 and 100.)

results; there was a correlation of .78 between verbal IQ scores achieved at the two ages (Gold et al., 1995). Over shorter intervals, the correlations were even higher.

The best single source of evidence on the stability of IQ in adulthood is a remarkable 35-year study by Werner Schaie, referred to as the Seattle Longitudinal Study (1983a, 1989a, 1993, 1994a, 1996; Schaie & Hertzog, 1983). Schaie began in 1956 with a set of cross-sectional samples; the participants in different samples were 7 years apart in age and ranged in age from 25 to 67. All participants took an IQ test at the outset of the study; a subset of the participants in each age group was then followed over 35 years and retested every 7 years. In 1963, another set of cross-sectional samples, covering the same age ranges, was tested, and a subset of these was retested 7, 14, 21, and 28 years later. Further samples were added in 1970, 1977, 1984, and 1991. This remarkable data-collection process enabled Schaie to look at IQ changes over 7-, 14-, 21-, and 28-year intervals for several sets of participants, each from a slightly different cohort. Figure 12.5 graphs one set of cross-sectional comparisons made in 1977 as well as 14-year longitudinal results smoothed over the whole age range. The test involved in this case is a measure of global intelligence on which the average score is set at 50 points (equivalent to an IQ of 100 on most other tests).

You can see that the cross-sectional comparisons show a steady drop in IQ. But the longitudinal evidence suggests that overall intelligence test scores actually rise in early adulthood and then remain quite constant until perhaps age 60, when they begin to decline. Since this pattern has also been found by other researchers (e.g., Sands, Terry, & Meredith, 1989; Siegler, 1983), there is good support for the temptingly optimistic view that intellectual ability remains essentially stable through most of adulthood.

● ***Crystallized and Fluid Intelligence*** ● Looking at different components of intellectual ability gives a clearer picture of change and stability across the adult years. Theorists have suggested several ways to subdivide intellectual tasks. However, the most influential of these theories has been Raymond Cattell and John Horn's distinction between crystallized intelligence and fluid intelligence (Cattell, 1963; Horn, 1982; Horn & Donaldson, 1980).

Crystallized intelligence depends heavily on education and experience. It consists of the set of skills and bits of knowledge that every adult learns as part of growing up in any given culture, such as vocabulary, the ability to read and understand the newspaper, and the ability to evaluate experience. Technical skills you may learn for your job or your life—balancing a checkbook, using a computer, making change, finding the mayonnaise in the grocery store—also represent crystallized intelligence.

Fluid intelligence, in contrast, involves more "basic" abilities—it is the aspect of intelligence that depends more on the efficient functioning of the central nervous system and less on specific experience. A common measure of fluid intelligence is a "letter series test," in which a participant is given a series of letters (for example, A C F J O) and must figure out what letter should go next. This problem demands abstract reasoning rather than reasoning about known or everyday events. Most tests of memory also measure fluid intelligence, as do many tests measuring response speed and those measuring higher-level or abstract mathematical skills. Schaie's results, and the results of many other investigators, suggest that adults maintain crystallized intelligence throughout early and middle adulthood, but that fluid intelligence declines fairly steadily over adulthood, beginning at perhaps age 35 or 40 (Horn & Donaldson, 1980; Schaie, 1994a).

Do results like these mean that developmentalists must revise their generally optimistic conclusions about adult intelligence based on longitudinal studies of total IQ scores? On the face of it, yes: On some kinds of tests, adults appear to show some decline beginning as early as their 40s. But Schaie notes that even the decline in fluid intelligence skills, while statistically significant, may not result in psychologically significant loss until at least late middle age.

Some theorists suggest that psychologically or functionally relevant declines may show up even in early adulthood, when adults are faced with highly complex or difficult tasks—tasks that stretch the individual's skills to the limit—just as significant declines in physical skill show up in early adulthood among top athletes (Baltes, Dittmann-Kohli, & Dixon, 1984, 1986). One of the ironies, then, is that adults whose occupations require them to function regularly at intellectually more taxing levels are likely to become aware of some subtle decline in intellectual skills earlier in adulthood than adults whose life circumstances make less stringent intellectual demands—even though the former individuals may continue to function at very high absolute levels of skill throughout their early and middle years.

So where does this leave us in answering the question about intellectual maintenance or decline over adulthood? It seems safe to conclude, at least tentatively, that intellectual abilities show essentially no decline in early adulthood except at the very top levels of intellectual demand. In middle adulthood, though, declines on fluid intelligence abilities—those tasks that are thought to represent the efficiency of the basic physiological process—become evident (Salthouse, 1991). Indeed, the rate of decline on measures of fluid intelligence closely matches the rate of decline in total brain size, suggesting a possible direct link (Bigler, Johnson, Jackson, & Blatter, 1995).

● **Memory** ● The pattern of results from studies of memory ability generally follows the pattern found in studies of fluid intelligence. Memory skills remain stable during early adulthood, decline somewhat during middle adulthood, and decline more noticeably in late adulthood. For example, measures of short-term memory—recalling something after only a short time, such as a phone number you've just looked up in the phone book—generally show a drop with age.

Age differences become more pronounced for measures of long-term memory—memory for items stored for longer periods, or permanently. Both the process of getting memories into this long-term storage (a process called *encoding* by memory theorists) and the process of retrieving them again seem to be impaired among older adults, as compared to young adults (Salthouse, 1991). With age, memory processes become both slower and less efficient.

crystallized intelligence knowledge and judgment acquired through education and experience

fluid intelligence the aspect of intelligence that reflects fundamental biological processes and does not depend on specific experiences

Before going on

- What are some theoretical proposals regarding a stage of cognitive development beyond Piaget's formal operational stage?

- How do the concepts of crystallized and fluid intelligence help explain age-related changes in IQ scores?

Post-Secondary Education

In today's high-tech, global economy, **post-secondary education**, any formal educational experience that follows high school, has become a necessity for virtually everyone (see Development in the Information Age).

Developmental Impact

There is no longer any doubt about the economic value of post-secondary education, as Figure 12.6 suggests. Further, although some post-secondary education is better than none, people who succeed in completing a degree have a clear income advan-

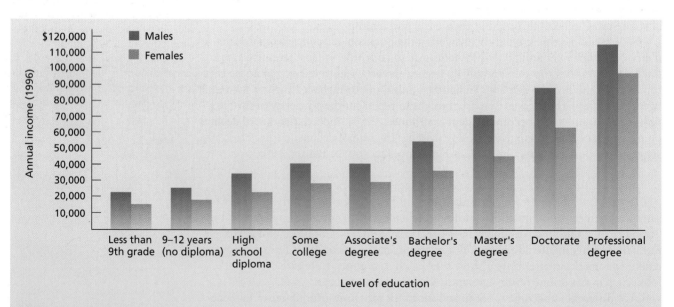

FIGURE 12.6

The association between education and income is clear. The longer a person stays in school, the more she earns. Degree attainment is strongly linked to income as well. The effect of education is similar for men and women, though men earn more at every level. (*Source*: U.S. Bureau of the Census, 1998.)

DEVELOPMENT in the Information Age

Distance Learning

One of the most promising technological innovations in recent years has been the remarkable increase in the availability of opportunities for distance learning. *Distance learning* is any mode of instruction in which teacher and student are at a distance from each other. Information technologies—television, computers, and so on—serve as mediators between the two.

Of course, distance learning in the form of correspondence courses has been around for a long time. Likewise, colleges have offered classes via television for several decades. However, widespread access to the Internet has opened the door to a new era in distance learning. Thanks to the World Wide Web, students can enroll in institutions very far removed from their place of residence. They can also create a flexible schedule for themselves. For example, a student can download a professor's lecture at 4:00 a.m. if that is the hour that suits his particular needs. Thus, it isn't surprising that distance learning college students, especially nontraditional ones, report high levels of satisfaction with Web-based courses (Wernet, Olliges, & Delicath, 2000).

Most distance learning courses and programs are offered by traditional post-secondary institutions. For example, one of the nation's largest community college systems, Dallas Community College (DCC), enrolls more than 10,000 students in distance learning classes each semes-

ter (Carr, 2000). Many are DCC students, but some live very far from Dallas, many in foreign countries, and have discovered DCC's offerings via the Internet. They enroll, pay their tuition and fees, and buy their books via the Net as well.

The potential of the Internet to attract distance learning students and to allow them to register and pay for courses from a distance has led to the creation of new *virtual colleges*, or colleges that offer courses only on the Internet. Some are owned by nonprofit or governmental entities, but many are for-profit businesses. The stimulus for these new institutions is simple: North Americans currently spend more than $200 billion each year on distance learning (Bulkeley, 1998). Thus, traditional colleges and universities see distance learning as an avenue to much-needed additional funds, and entrepreneurs see a potentially profitable market.

However, distance learning students drop out at much higher rates than do on-campus students (Carr, 2000). Most likely, the higher drop-out rate reflects the fact that nontraditional students enroll in distance courses at a higher rate than do traditional students. All the factors that make nontraditional students more likely to withdraw from on-campus courses probably affect their persistence in distance learning courses. In addition, weaker students may need the periodic contact with the instructor and other class members that on-campus courses can provide.

There are other concerns as well. Professors who teach online courses own the copyrights to all original materials they create and upload to their course Web sites. A copyright warning can be included, and professors can protect materials by requiring students to use passwords. Yet, once these documents are on the Net, they become widely accessible. Consequently, many professors shy away from putting time and effort into distance learning courses only to have their work illegally downloaded by others. This leads more institutions to increased use of prepackaged Internet courseware, which, in turn, leads to concerns about course quality and academic freedom.

Distance learning also raises new questions about fraud and cheating (Kennedy, Nowak, Raghuraman, Thomas, & Davis, 2000). If a professor requires distance students to participate in online chats, how does she know if a student has someone substitute for him? Moreover, concerns about fraud make it almost impossible to use conventional tests in online courses unless students can physically come to a testing center. Again, this raises questions about course quality and the equivalence of on-campus and online courses.

Predictions about the potential for distance learning to revolutionize post-secondary education are probably valid. However, like other information-age innovations, there are costs as well as benefits.

---

tage. Interestingly, although there are sex differences in the earnings of men and women at all educational levels, the advantage of post-secondary education seems to be as great for women as for men. (We will return to the issue of sex differences in compensation in Chapter 13.)

College graduates earn more than nongraduates for a variety of reasons (Pascarella & Terenzi, 1991). First, graduates get more promotions and are far less likely than nongraduates to be unemployed for prolonged periods of time. In fact, for minorities, a college education seems to outweigh the potential effects of racial prejudice in hiring decisions. Supervisors prefer minority college graduates to white nongraduates. In addition, college graduates have higher real and perceived status. This means that they are more likely than nongraduates to get high-status managerial, technical, and professional positions, and they are viewed by those who make hiring

post-secondary education any formal educational experience that follows high school

MAKE THE CONNECTION

Review Erikson's stage of industry versus inferiority, discussed in Chapter 9. What would his theory predict about the link between experiences in elementary school and obtaining a college degree?

decisions as more desirable employees than are nongraduates. This finding raises the question of whether college graduates are really different from non-graduates or are simply perceived to be. However, longitudinal evidence suggests that the longer a person remains in college, the better her performance on Piaget's formal operational tasks and other measures of abstract reasoning (Lehman & Nisbett, 1990; Pascarella, 1999).

There is also evidence that, during their years of college enrollment, students' academic and vocational aspirations rise (Pascarella & Terenzi, 1991). For example, a young woman may enter college with the goal of becoming a biology teacher but graduate with the intention of going on to medical school. What seems critical about college to such decisions is that college-level classes allow students to make realistic assessments—for better or worse—of their academic abilities. Thus, another student may intend to be a doctor when he is a freshman but soon conclude that becoming a biology teacher is a more realistic, attainable goal, given his performance in college-level classes.

In addition to cognitive and motivational benefits, going to college provides students with new socialization opportunities. Many students encounter people from racial or ethnic groups other than their own for the first time in college. Advances in moral and social reasoning, as well as increases in the capacity to empathize with others' feelings, are also linked to college attendance (Chickering & Reisser, 1993; Pascarella & Terenzi, 1991). However, the relationships among authoritative parenting, academic performance, and social adjustment you have read about so often in earlier chapters hold true for college students as well (Wintre & Yaffe, 2000). Thus, students' social experiences prior to entering post-secondary education seem to be critical to their ability to benefit fully from the college experience.

College attendance is associated with developmental advances in both the cognitive and social domains. (Photo: Michael Newman, PhotoEdit)

Traditional and Nontraditional Students

Despite the advantages of a college degree, only about one-third of U.S. high school graduates become **traditional post-secondary students** by enrolling in college full-time directly after graduation (Horn & Premo, 1995). Certainly, economic factors are important to this decision; those who can afford to go to college full-time are more likely to do so. However, parental influence seems to be equally important. In a recent survey, researchers asked traditional post-secondary students who were in their first year of college why they had enrolled in college straight out of high school. Almost 40% responded that they enrolled out of a desire to conform to parental expectations (*Chronicle of Higher Education*, 1997).

Many traditional post-secondary students (14–16%) leave college at one time or another during their academic careers. But when they do, most are only temporarily college drop-outs. Thus, traditional post-secondary students have a very high graduation rate: Almost two-thirds obtain a college degree within 5 years (National Center for Educational Statistics [NCES], 1997).

Almost 60% of college students are **nontraditional post-secondary students** (NCES, 1997). Researchers classify students as nontraditional if they (1) delay entering college more than 1 year after high school graduation; (2) are independent from parents; (3) are employed while enrolled; (4) are enrolled part-time; (5) have one or more children; (6) possess a GED rather than a high school diploma; or (7) are single parents.

traditional post-secondary student a student who attends college full-time immediately after graduating from high school

nontraditional post-secondary student a student who either attends college part-time or delays enrollment after high school graduation

Critical Thinking

Suppose a 30-year-old blue-collar worker who is married with two children and who has never been past high school decides to go to college. What obstacles will she have to overcome to succeed in earning a degree? How comfortable would she feel at the institution you are attending?

Clearly, many of these variables apply to traditional students as well. To clarify traditional and nontraditional status, researchers classify students as *minimally*, *moderately*, or *highly* nontraditional, based on the number of these factors present in their lives. As you can see from Figure 12.7, there is a clear association between traditional or nontraditional status and college graduation. The more nontraditional factors a student possesses, the less likely he is to graduate from college.

A majority of traditional post-secondary students are likely to attain their educational objective whether they are pursuing a bachelor's degree, an associate's degree, or a vocational certificate. However, nontraditional post-secondary students are almost twice as likely to complete their program of study when they are pursuing a vocational certificate as when working toward either an associate's or a bachelor's degree (NCES, 1997). About 54% succeed in getting a certificate, but only 26% and 31%, respectively, reach their goals of obtaining associate's or bachelor's degrees. Perhaps this is because nontraditional vocational students set more realistic goals for themselves. Alternatively, vocational programs may do a better job of supporting nontraditional students than academically oriented associate's and bachelor's degree programs.

The issue of support points to another important difference between traditional and nontraditional post-secondary students. Those who go directly from high school to college are concentrated in 4-year institutions, while the majority of nontraditional students attend 2-year colleges (NCES, 1997). Thus, graduation rates may vary across the two groups not only because of variables on which the students themselves differ but also because there are important differences between 2- and 4-year colleges. For example, 4-year institutions are more likely to have counseling centers where students can obtain career guidance and help with personal problems. Likewise, students at 4-year schools, especially those who live on campus, spend more time socializing with one another. Thus, they have a greater opportunity to establish social networks on which they can rely for support in times of difficulty. In contrast, students at 2-year colleges typically do not socialize with or even see one another outside of class. Thus, students in 4-year college settings may be better supported both formally and informally by the institutions they attend.

Fortunately, officials at 2-year colleges have begun to recognize the need for greater student support. Consequently, many are developing innovative programs—such as on-campus child care—based on students' needs. Likewise, officials are attempting to provide greater financial and facility support for student organizations so that students will have more opportunities for social interaction.

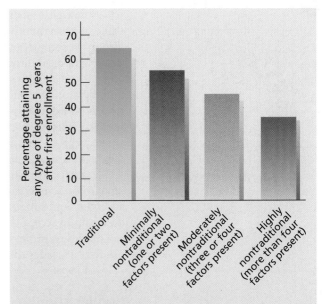

FIGURE 12.7

The greater the number of nontraditional factors present in a student's life, the less likely she is to complete a vocational certificate or college degree. Nontraditional factors include delayed entry into school; being independent from one's family; working full-time and/or attending school part-time; having one or more children; being a single parent; having a GED rather than a high school diploma. (*Source:* NCES, 1997.)

Students with Disabilities

Thanks to a federal law passed by the U.S. Congress in 1990, the Americans with Disabilities Act, many students with disabilities have access to post-secondary education. Colleges are now required to provide them with the same kinds of modifications provided by special education services in the public school system. Thus, blind students are provided with readers and Braille textbooks, hearing-impaired students are accompanied by sign language interpreters when they attend class, and wheelchair-bound students are guaranteed that classroom doors will be wide enough to allow them to enter. Consequently, college enrollment rates of students with disabilities are now very similar to those of their nondisabled peers.

Although it is still too early to draw firm conclusions from research on college students with disabilities, recent studies contain some hints about how such students fare. For example, one reason for recent increases in college enrollment among students with disabilities is their belief that the required instructional modifications make it possible for them to compete academically with other students. One common modification for such students is extended time for taking tests. Research suggests that, with extended time, students with disabilities are able to approach or meet the same standards of academic performance required of other students in college classes (Alster, 1997). Still, students with disabilities usually receive lower course grades than their non-disabled peers (Cosden & McNamara, 1997).

Research also suggests that students with disabilities perceive the college environment to be somewhat inhospitable to them. Although they perceive their peers to be accepting and supportive, many students with disabilities believe that college faculty do not fully accept them (Beilke & Yssel, 1999; Cosden & McNamara, 1997). They say that most professors are willing to comply with classroom modifications but have negative attitudes toward the required modifications and the students themselves.

Gender and the College Experience

A slight majority of college students are female, and women have higher graduation rates than men at all degree levels and in both traditional and nontraditional post-secondary groups (NCES, 1997). Further, females maintain their graduation advantage over males even when they must overcome many obstacles associated with nontraditional status, such as single parenthood (Benshoff & Lewis, 1993).

Paradoxically, women's college entrance examination scores, especially in math, tend to be lower than men's. As a result, more males are admitted to selective universities. In addition, more men are accepted into honors programs. Thus, the different graduation rates of males and females are unlikely to be due to sex differences in intellectual ability. Rather, college men and women differ in attitudes and behavior in ways that significantly affect the likelihood of graduation (Noldon & Sedlacek, 1998).

In contrast to studies of sex bias at lower educational levels, studies in college classrooms have produced mixed results (Brady & Eisler, 1999). Some studies suggest that professors take male students more seriously than female students. Others seem to indicate that women feel less confident and more inhibited in their interactions with college faculty. Yet, the most consistent finding is that there appear to be few, if any, overt indicators of sex bias in college classrooms (Brady & Eisler, 1999). Thus, one reason for the tendency of females to be more successful in college may be that they perceive the post-secondary environment as more intellectually supportive than the institutions they attended when they were younger.

However, intellectually talented women continue to be somewhat reluctant to pursue difficult majors (Jacobs et al., 1998). For the most part, this finding seems to be restricted to women whose talents are in science and mathematics. It seems that many young women, even those who are very capable, have doubts about their ability to succeed in such fields. However, when a wider array of interests and talents is taken into account, there seem to be few consistent sex differences in educational aspirations or academic self-concept among intellectually gifted college students (Achter, Lubinski, Benbow, & Eftekhari-Sanjani, 1999).

When research reveals sex differences in study strategies, they usually favor the females. For example, college women in both the United States and Europe use a greater number of study techniques than do men (Braten & Olaussen, 1998). By contrast, college men are more likely to cheat (Thorpe, Pittenger, & Reed, 1999). Moreover, the kinds of study strategies women use are those that are most likely to lead to long-term retention of information (Pearsall, Skipper, & Mintzes, 1997). Consequently, it isn't surprising that a recent study of gender differences in comprehensive final examination performance among Irish medical school students revealed that women significantly outscored men in several areas (McDonough, Horgan, Codd, & Casey, 2000). In areas in which women did not outscore men, they achieved equally high scores.

Women also appear to adapt easily to the demands of new educational experiences. For example, women outperform men in distance learning classes. They also usually begin with lower levels of computer skills than men. However, when they enroll in classes that require such skills, they learn them very quickly and exhibit levels of performance that equal those of men whose initial skill levels were higher (Clawson & Choate, 1999).

Behaviors outside the classroom may matter as well. For example, binge drinking is more prevalent among college men than women. Similarly, men seem to be more influenced by peer behavior than women do. If a man is with a group of men who are drinking, he is likely to do so as well. Women are more likely to make individual decisions about behaviors such as alcohol use (Senchak, Leonard, & Greene, 1998).

Race and the College Experience

One longitudinal study involving several thousand college students found that most minority groups have lower drop-out rates than whites, even though minority college students typically posses a greater number of nontraditional factors (NCES, 1997). Researchers at the National Center for Educational Statistics found that 17% of Native Americans, 24% of Asian Americans, and 28% of Hispanic Americans, compared to 35% of whites, dropped out and did not return to college during the study's 5-year span. The study also found the drop-out rate of African American students to be 44%.

One approach to explaining the African American students' higher drop-out rates is to determine how they are similar to and different from the students in other groups. For example, African American high school students and beginning college students have educational and career aspirations that are similar to those of students in other groups (Brown, 1997). In addition, their goals seem to be as carefully and realistically formulated as those of students of other races. However, African American students are more likely than students of other races or ethnicities to perceive themselves as not fitting in, not really being a part of the college community (Gossett, Cuyjet, & Cockriel, 1998). In addition, for many African American students, the college campus is the first environment in which they personally experience overt expressions of racism. For example, an African American student may be assumed to be a janitorial employee by a faculty member or fellow student. Thus, African American students often perceive the college environment as hostile and cite personal experiences with overt racism among their reasons for dropping out (Schwitzer, Griffin, Ancie, & Thomas, 1999; Zea, Reisen, Bell, & Caplan, 1997).

A different approach is to find out how African American college students who obtain degrees differ from those who drop out. For example, a strong sense of racial identity is associated with persistence and academic performance in college for African American students (Rowley, 2000; Sellers, Chavous, & Cook 1998). Research also suggests that students who participate in programs aimed at helping minority students stay in college are more likely to graduate and to gain admission to professional and graduate schools than those who do not participate (Hesser, Cregler, & Lewis, 1998).

Researchers have also examined differences between African American students who attend predominantly white colleges and those who enroll in historically black institutions. One advantage of the latter institutions for students may be that most have a larger proportion of black faculty members with whom students can identify and to whom they feel comfortable expressing themselves. In fact, students who attend historically black schools view African American professors very positively and value their relationships with them (Chism & Satcher, 1998).

Interestingly, though, African American females at predominantly white schools appear to have higher levels of self-esteem than peers at historically black institutions

(Poindexter-Cameron & Robinson, 1997). Still, cognitive development across the college years is strongly associated with the racial composition of the college for both male and female African American students. Those who attend historically black colleges show more improvement across a variety of cognitive measures, such as tests of reading comprehension, than do those who attend predominantly white schools (Flowers & Pascarella, 1999).

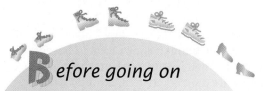

Before going on

- List some of the ways in which college attendance affects individual development.

- How do traditional and nontraditional post-secondary students differ?

- What does research suggest about the experiences of college students with disabilities?

- How is the college experience different for men and women?

- How does race affect the college experiences of African Americans?

A Final Word

Many of us in the youth-oriented culture of the United States think of early adulthood as the easiest or best years of life. Physically, that is certainly true. The body is at its peak in the years from 20 to 40. Any aspect of mental functioning that is based on physiological speed or efficiency is also at its peak. But early adulthood is also a risky period. Rates of STD infection and intimate partner abuse are high during these years. Furthermore, the educational choices young adults make are likely to affect them financially and socially for years to come. Thus, far from being a period of ease, young adulthood is a time during which the opportunities provided by peak physical and intellectual functioning must be balanced against risks and challenges. Consequently, the young adult years, like those of later adulthood, carry with them their own unique sources of stress.

Summary

Physical Functioning

- It is important to distinguish between the unavoidable effects of primary aging and the preventable consequences of secondary aging.

- The brain reaches a stable size and weight in early adulthood. There is strong evidence that at least one spurt in brain development occurs between 17 and 21. Neuropsychologists hypothesize that a second spurt occurs in the mid- to late 20s. Sex differences are apparent in the adult brain, although their significance has yet to be established.

- It is clear that adults are at their peak both physically and cognitively between ages 20 and 40. In these years, a person has more muscle tissue, more calcium in the bones, better sensory acuity, greater aerobic capacity, and a more efficient immune system.

Health and Wellness

- In contrast to other diseases, sexually transmitted diseases are more common among young adults than among older adults.

- The rate of loss of physical and cognitive abilities varies widely across individuals. Some of this difference seems to be explained by varying health habits. Adults with good health habits have lower risk of death and disease at any age.

- Social support and a sense of personal control also affect rates of disease and death, especially in the face of stress.

- Intimate partner abuse is a significant global health problem. Causal factors include cultural beliefs about gender roles, as well as personal variables such as alcohol and drug use.

- Sexual violence usually involves individuals who are acquaintances or intimate partners. Its causes and effects are similar for both heterosexuals and homosexuals.

- Rates of mental illness are higher in early adulthood than in middle adulthood; young adults are more likely to be depressed, anxious, or lonely than are the middle-aged. Early adulthood is the period during which personality disorders and schizophrenia are usually diagnosed.

Cognitive Changes

- There may be a change in cognitive structure in adult life, and theorists have suggested that cognitive development goes beyond Piaget's formal operational stage.

- Some studies of measures of intelligence show a decline with age, but the decline occurs quite late for well-exercised abilities (crystallized abilities) such as recall of vocabulary, everyday memory use, and normal problem solving. A measurable decline occurs earlier for so-called fluid abilities. Memory differences between younger and older adults are usually restricted to tasks involving speed of processing.

Post-Secondary Education

- Post-secondary education has beneficial effects on both cognitive and social development in addition to being associated with higher income.

- Nontraditional post-secondary students are more likely to obtain vocational certificates than bachelor's or associate's degrees.

- There is not yet enough research on students with disabilities to draw firm conclusions about their college experiences, but studies suggest that, with certain accommodations, they can be just as successful in college as students who do not have disabilities.

- Female students seem to have a number of important advantages over male students, including a higher graduation rate. However, many women lack confidence in their academic abilities and are reluctant to enter traditionally male occupations.

- African American students are less likely to complete post-secondary programs than other groups, perhaps because they perceive white-dominated educational environments as hostile.

Key Terms

crystallized intelligence (p. 361)
dialectical thought (p. 359)
fluid intelligence (p. 361)
intimate partner abuse (p. 352)
limbic system (p. 343)
maximum oxygen uptake (VO_2 max) (p. 346)

nontraditional post-secondary student (p. 364)
pelvic inflammatory disease (p. 346)
personality disorder (p. 356)
phobia (p. 355)
post-secondary education (p. 362)

primary aging (p. 342)
schizophrenia (p. 357)
secondary aging (p. 342)
self-efficacy (p. 351)
sexual violence (p. 354)
traditional post-secondary student (p. 364)

Social and Personality Development in Early Adulthood

© Allan Hall Photography. Used with permission

In early adulthood, individuals turn away from the preoccupation with self-definition that is characteristic of adolescence and take on a series of roles that involve new relationships with other people. For example, from their wedding day forward, newlyweds will be known both as individuals and as spouses. The bride is also now a daughter-in-law as well as a daughter; the groom has become a son-in-law in addition to continuing to be his parents' son. It is also likely that the two young adults have already taken on occupational roles, and they may also become parents within a few years.

The timing and content of the various adult roles obviously differ from one culture to another, from one cohort to another, and even from one individual to another. For example, the median age for first marriage among women in the United States rose from 21 in 1970 to 24 in 1988 to 25 in the late 1990s—a very large change in a fairly short span of years (U.S. Bureau of the Census, 1995, 1998). Marriage remains an important milestone of the young adult years, as evidenced by the fact that the percentage of women who have never married drops from 70% among 20-year-old females to 20% among 30-year-old females; the percentage of men who have never married drops from 85% to 30% for the same ages (U.S. Bureau of the Census, 1998). Moreover, the proportion of never-married adults drops below 20% for both males and females during their 30s. In addition, most people become parents for the first time in early adulthood. Thus, regardless of variations in timing, adults' social connections become far more complex between the ages of 20 and 40—through marriage, divorce, parenthood, and career development.

In this chapter you will learn about how these role transitions affect young adults' development. As you read, keep the following questions in mind:

- How do theorists view social and personality development in early adulthood?
- How do young adults go about establishing intimate relationships?
- How do young adults manage the challenges of parenthood and other relationships?
- What factors contribute to career choice, job satisfaction, and sex differences in work patterns?

Theories of Social and Personality Development

Psychoanalytic theories view adult development, like development at younger ages, as a result of a struggle between a person's inner thoughts, feelings, and motives and society's demands. Other perspectives provide different views of this period. Integrating ideas from all of them allows us to better understand early adult development.

Social scientists have not done very well at devising theories to explain lovely romantic moments like these.
(*Photos:* Timothy Shonnard, Stone; David Young-Wolff, PhotoEdit)

Erikson's Stage of Intimacy versus Isolation

For Erikson, the central crisis of early adulthood is **intimacy versus isolation.** The young adult must find a life partner, someone outside her own family with whom she can share her life, or face the prospect of being isolated from society. More specifically, **intimacy** is the capacity to engage in a supportive, affectionate relationship without losing one's own sense of self. Intimate partners can share their views and feelings with each other without fearing that the relationship will end. They can also allow each other some degree of independence without feeling threatened.

As you might suspect, successful resolution of the intimacy versus isolation stage depends on a good resolution of the identity versus role confusion crisis you read about in Chapter 11. Erikson predicted that individuals who reached early adulthood without having established a sense of identity would be incapable of intimacy. That is, such young adults would be, in a sense, predestined to social isolation.

Still, a poor sense of identity is only one barrier to intimacy. Misunderstandings stemming from sex differences in styles of interaction can also get in the way. To women, intimacy is bound up with self-disclosure. Thus, women who are involved with a partner who does not reveal much that is personal perceive the relationship as lacking in intimacy. However, most men don't see self-disclosure as essential to intimacy. Consequently, many men are satisfied with relationships that their female partners see as inadequate.

Though many people involved in intimate relationships wish their relationships were better, most adults succeed in establishing some kind of close relationship. Not everyone marries, of course, but many adults develop affectionate, long-lasting friendships that are significant sources of support for them and may, in some cases, serve the same functions as an intimate life partner. For those who have no such relationships, Erikson's theory seems to be fairly accurate. These individuals experience more loneliness and depression than the average adult and suffer from a variety of mental health problems (Stack, 1998).

Critical Thinking

Have you experienced periods of loneliness? If so, how do you think the state of your love life at the time contributed to your feelings?

intimacy versus isolation Erikson's early adulthood stage, in which an individual must find a life partner or supportive friends in order to avoid social isolation

intimacy the capacity to engage in a supportive, affectionate relationship without losing one's own sense of self

life structure a key concept in Levinson's theory: the underlying pattern or design of a person's life at a given time, which includes roles, relationships, and behavior patterns

Levinson's Life Structures

Levinson's concept of *life structure* represents a different approach to adult development (Levinson, 1978, 1990). A **life structure** includes all the roles an individual occupies, all of his or her relationships, and the conflicts and balance that exist among them. Figure 13.1 illustrates how life structures change over the course of adulthood.

Like Erikson, Levinson theorized that each of these periods presented adults with new developmental tasks and conflicts. He believed that individuals respond psychologically to these tasks and conflicts by creating new life structures. Consequently, adults cycle through periods of stability and instability.

As adults enter a period in which a new life structure is required, there is a period of adjustment, which Levinson called the *novice* phase. In the *mid-era* phase, adults

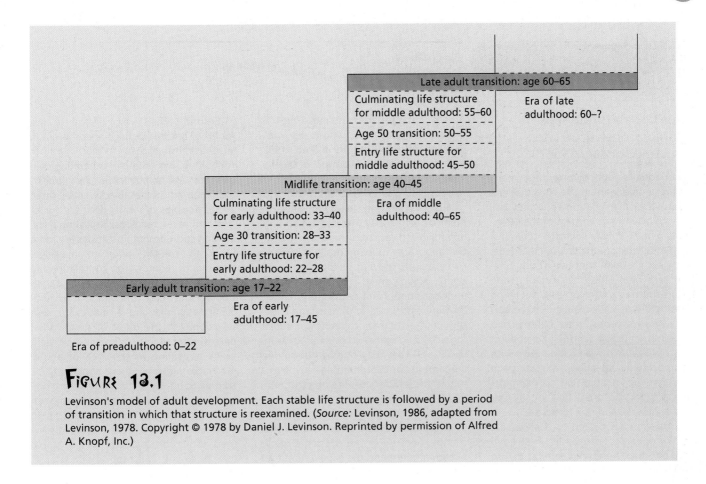

Era of preadulthood: 0–22

FIGURE 13.1

Levinson's model of adult development. Each stable life structure is followed by a period of transition in which that structure is reexamined. (*Source:* Levinson, 1986, adapted from Levinson, 1978. Copyright © 1978 by Daniel J. Levinson. Reprinted by permission of Alfred A. Knopf, Inc.)

become more competent at meeting the new challenges through reassessment and reorganization of the life structure they created during the novice phase. Stability returns in the *culmination* phase, when adults have succeeded in creating a life structure that allows them to manage the demands of the new developmental challenges with more confidence and less distress.

For example, marriage requires a new life structure. Even if the newlyweds have known each other for a very long time or have been living together, they have not known each other in the roles of husband and wife (see No Easy Answers). Moreover, they have never had in-laws. So, young adults who marry acquire a whole new set of relationships. At the same time, they face many new day-to-day, practical issues such as how finances will be managed, how housekeeping chores will be done, and whose family they will visit on which holidays. As Levinson's theory predicts, newlyweds usually go through a period of adjustment, during which they experience more conflict than before the wedding, and after which things are much calmer. The calm comes, as Levinson would put it, when each spouse has achieved a new life structure that is adapted to the demands of marriage.

Both Erikson and Levinson regard formation of an intimate relationship with another adult as a central developmental task of early adulthood. However, neither addresses the process of just how an adult goes about finding a suitable partner. However, other theorists focus specifically on the mating process.

Evolutionary Theory and Mate Selection

As you should remember from Chapter 2, evolutionary explanations of behavior focus on survival value. Heterosexual relationships ensure the survival of the species, of course, because they are the context in which conception takes place. However,

No Easy Answers

Does Cohabitation Help Couples Construct a Life Structure for Marriage?

Given today's high divorce rate, many young people want to be sure that the person they marry is someone they will want to be with for the rest of their lives. Thus, it is relatively common today for couples to live together before marriage. Many such couples conceive of cohabitation as a final "filter," a sort of "test" before marriage: Can we really get along together? Are we sexually compatible? In Levinson's terms, they believe that cohabitation will lessen the likelihood of divorce because it will provide them with an opportunity to build a life structure they can use in adapting to marriage. Interestingly, the great bulk of the evidence shows exactly the opposite.

Studies in the United States, Canada, and European countries such as Sweden all show that those who cohabit before marriage are less satisfied with their subsequent marriages and more likely to divorce than are those who marry without cohabiting (DeMaris & Rao, 1992; Hall & Zhao, 1995; Thomson & Colella, 1992). The most likely explanation of this surprising set of findings is two-fold.

First, cohabiting leads to development of a life structure for cohabiting, not for marriage, because the two relationships are fundamentally different. For example, moving in together is seldom accompanied by the public announcements and celebratory fanfare that are associated with marriage (Lindsay, 2000). Further, cohabiting couples regard their relationships as ambiguous in nature—they may or may not be permanent. In contrast, marriage involves a public declaration of lifelong commitment to another person. Thus, when a cohabiting couple marries, the social and psychological aspects of the relationship change, because of the deepened sense of commitment and the expectation that the relationship is permanent.

Second, adults who choose to live together before marriage are different in key ways from those who marry without cohabiting. For example, cohabiting couples are less *homogamous* (less similar) than married couples (Blackwell & Lichter, 2000). Couples in which partners are of different races, religions, educational levels, and socio-economic statuses are more likely to cohabit prior to marriage. Homogamy contributes to relationship stability. Thus, the difference in marital stability between cohabitants and non-cohabitants may be a matter of self-selection, not the result of some causal process attributable to cohabitation itself.

As appealing as the idea of a trial marriage might be, there appears to be no way to adjust to marriage before one is actually married. The best a couple can do is to examine their relationship in light of what researchers have discovered about the characteristics of stable marriages you will read about later in the chapter.

when choosing a mate, heterosexuals don't simply look for someone of the opposite sex. Instead, mating is a selective process, and evolutionary theorists often cite research on sex differences in mate preferences and mating behavior in support of their views.

Cross-cultural studies conducted over a period of several decades suggest that men prefer physically attractive, younger women, while women look for men whose socio-economic status is higher than their own, who offer earning potential and stability (Buss, 1999). Moreover, in the short run, men appear to be willing to lower their standards when forced to choose between a partner who meets their standards and no partner at all. Thus, availability strongly influences men's selection of short-term mates. In contrast, women seem to have little interest in short-term mating unless it will lead to a beneficial long-term relationship. For example, evolutionary theorists hypothesize that *mate-switching*—using an affair to lead to a long-term relationship with a higher-status man—is an important motive in women's extramarital affairs.

The reason behind men's and women's divergent mating goals are explained by **parental investment theory** (Trivers, 1972). This theory proposes that men value health and availability in their mates and are less selective because their minimum investment in parenting offspring—a single act of sexual intercourse—requires only a few minutes. In contrast, women's minimum investment in childbearing involves nurturing an unborn child in their own bodies for 9 months as well as enduring the potentially physically traumatic experience of giving birth. Given their minimum investments, men seek to maximize the likelihood of survival of the species by maxi-

parental investment theory the theory that sex differences in mate preferences and mating behavior are based on the different amounts of time and effort men and women must invest in child-rearing

mizing the number of their offspring; women seek to minimize them because their investment is so much greater.

Further, evolutionary theorists argue that both men and women realize that a truly adaptive approach to child-rearing requires much more than a minimum investment (Buss, 1999). Human offspring cannot raise themselves. Therefore, men value health and youth in their mates not only because these traits suggest fertility but also because a young, healthy woman is likely to live long enough to raise the children. Moreover, men are willing to abandon their focus on short-term mating in order to gain continuing and exclusive sexual access to a desirable mate through committed, long-term relationships such as marriage. Making such a commitment ensures that any offspring the woman produces will be the man's own and that the children will have a mother to raise them.

Similarly, women realize that to be able to nurture children to adulthood, they must have an economic provider so that they will be able to invest the time needed to raise offspring. Consequently, they look for men who seem to be capable of fulfilling these requirements. Further, women's mating behavior is affected by the higher costs they bear if a selected mate fails to fulfill expectations. Faced with the prospect of having to provide children with both economic support and physical nurturing if a mate fails to "bring home the bacon," women choose mates more carefully and more slowly than men; they prefer not to engage in sexual intercourse until they have tested a man's trustworthiness and reliability (Buss & Schmitt, 1993).

As mentioned above, consistent sex differences in mate preferences and mating behavior have been found across many cultures, and evolutionary theorists suggest that this cross-cultural consistency is strong evidence for a genetic basis for the behavior. However, these claims take us back to the basic nature-versus-nurture arguments we have examined so many times before. Certainly, these sex differences are consistent, but they could be the result of variations in gender roles that are passed on within cultures.

Social Role Theory and Mate Selection

Social role theory provides a different perspective on sex differences in mating (Eagly & Wood, 1999). According to this view, such sex differences are adaptations to gender roles that result from present-day social realities rather than from natural selection pressures that arose in a bygone evolutionary era. Social role theorists point out that gender-based divisions of labor in child-rearing are just as consistent across cultures as sex differences in mating. Men look for women who can perform domestic duties (healthy and young), and women look for men who will be good economic providers (higher socio-economic status and good earning potential).

For example, one team of researchers found that college-educated women with high earning potential prefer to date and marry men whose income potential is higher than their own (Wiederman & Allgeier, 1992). In fact, the more a woman expects to earn herself, the higher are her income requirements in a prospective mate. This study was widely cited by evolutionary theorists as supporting their view that such preferences are genetic and are not influenced by cultural conditions.

However, a different perspective on the same study, proposed by social role theorists, led to a different conclusion (Eagly & Wood, 1999). These theorists suggest that today's high-income women desire to have and raise children almost as much as earlier generations of women. What is different about them, compared to their mothers and grandmothers, is that they want to be able to both pursue a career and raise a family. To meet both goals, most women plan to take time out from their careers to have and raise children (a pattern you will read more about later in this chapter). To be able to do so without lowering their standard of living substantially, these women require a mate who can earn a lot of money. Thus, social role theorists say, such research findings can be explained by social role theory just as well as by evolutionary theory.

social role theory the idea that sex differences in mate preferences and mating behavior are adaptations to gender roles

In addition, social role theorists point out that high-income women desire high-income husbands because members of both sexes prefer mates who are like themselves. People are drawn to those who are of similar age, education, social class, ethnic group membership, religion, attitudes, interests, and temperament. Sociologists refer to this tendency as **assortative mating,** or **homogamy.** Further, partnerships based on homogamy are much more likely to endure than are those in which the partners differ markedly (Murstein, 1986).

In addition to the process of assortative mating, choosing a partner appears to involve some kind of exchange process. Each individual has certain assets to offer to a potential mate. Exchange theorists argue that people try for the best bargain, the best exchange, they can manage (Edwards, 1969). According to this model, women frequently exchange their sexual and domestic services for the economic support offered by a man (Schoen & Wooldredge, 1989). However, social role theorists suggest that, over the past few decades, women have improved their income-producing prospects considerably. As a result, if social role theory is correct, women today should be less concerned about a potential mate's earning potential than women were in the past.

To test this hypothesis, social role theorists reanalyzed a very large set of cross-cultural data, a data set produced and interpreted by evolutionary psychologist David Buss in support of parental investment theory (Buss et al., 1990). In their reanalysis, advocates of social role theory found that both men's and women's mate preferences changed as women gained economic power (Eagly & Wood, 1999): Women's emphasis on potential mates' earning power declined, and men's focus on potential mates' domestics skills decreased.

Before going on

- What did Erikson mean when he described early adulthood as a crisis of intimacy versus isolation?

- What is a life structure? Why and how does it change?

- What types of research findings do evolutionary theorists cite to support their views on mate selection?

- How can social role theory contribute to an understanding of partner selection?

Intimate Relationships

Theories notwithstanding, everyday observations of adults reveal that an intimate relationship forms the secure base from which most young adults move out into the adult world. In many cases, marriage is the context in which such a relationship is created. However, as society has become more tolerant of nonmarital

assortative mating (homogamy) sociologists' term for the tendency to mate with someone who has traits similar to one's own

Internet Relationships

In a survey of 235 Internet users aged 13–74, 93% reported that they had established a personal relationship of some kind on-line (Parks & Roberts, 1998). Most of these relationships were with people of the opposite sex, and one-third had resulted in face-to-face meetings. Internet dating has become so popular that there are Web sites devoted to matching cyber-daters with others with similar interests. One of the most popular of these sites receives more than 3 million "hits" a month (Neville, 1997).

The appeal of Internet dating for many seems to be its capacity to allow individuals to bypass conventional relationship "filters"—physical attractiveness, socio-economic status, and age. Through e-mail, bulletin boards, and chat rooms, cyber-daters can get to know one another psychologically, without the distraction of characteristics that are easily discernible in face-to-face relationships. Cross-cultural research also suggests that interpersonal communica-

tion on the Net is viewed as more pleasurable than in-person communication (Chou, Chou, & Tyang, 1998).

However, some psychologists speculate that, in contrast to conventional dating, Internet relationships may retard development of social skills in young people, because on-line relationships don't allow for the kind of immediate behavioral feedback, such as facial expressions, that face-to-face relationships typically provide (Schnarch, 1997). Further, the more time people spend on the Internet, the less time they spend in other kinds of social interactions where such feedback is available (Kraut et al., 1998).

Another major drawback to Internet dating is the possibility of being deceived. Thus, Internet relationships may be preferable in situations where deception is desirable. For example, adults who want to entice children or teenagers into sexual relationships often use deception. Likewise, married people who want to present themselves to potential partners as single can do so more easily on-line.

Not surprisingly, extramarital affairs that begin or are carried out exclusively on the Internet are a growing phenomenon. In fact, their prevalence has led marital counselors to redefine the word "affair." Historically, an affair has involved sexual contact. But on-line affairs often lack any face-to-face contact, sexual or otherwise. Still, sexual tension and stimulation are typically a large part of on-line affairs. Partners trade pictures, sometimes sexually provocative ones, and engage in flirtatious sexual banter while on-line. Consequently, marital counselors now define an affair as a relationship that involves psychological intimacy, secrecy, and sexual chemistry, in order to help clients understand that marital fidelity involves something more than just sexual monogamy (Glass, 1998).

No doubt the phenomenon of Internet dating will continue to grow. Thus, there is a need for research that will lead to a better understanding of how on-line relationships develop and dissolve as well as how they affect individual development.

relationships—homosexual and lesbian partners, cohabiting heterosexual couples—behavioral scientists have had to expand research on intimacy to include these relationships as well. Further, Internet relationships have added a whole new dimension to courtship and dating (see Development in the Information Age)

Psychological Factors in Intimate Relationships

In predicting the quality of relationships as well as who mates with whom, two psychological factors—attachment and love—seem to be of importance.

● **The Role of Attachment** ● A number of theorists have suggested that internal working models of attachment play an important role in partner selection and relationship formation (e.g., Crowell & Waters, 1995; Feeney, 1994; Fuller & Fincham, 1995; Hazan & Shaver, 1987; Owens et al., 1995; Rothbard & Shaver, 1994). This does not mean that the security of the very first attachment in infancy is invariably carried forward, unaltered. In particular, some adults with insecure attachment histories are able to analyze and accept their childhood relationships and create new internal working models. But whether a young adult's internal working model is the product of redefinition or remains unchanged, it will still affect her expectations for a partner, the sort of partner she chooses, the way she behaves with her partner, and the stability of the relationship.

Research reveals that adults do indeed tend to create internal models of attachment to a prospective spouse that are similar to their attachment to their parents. For example, one study found that nearly two-thirds of a sample of about-to-be-married young people showed the same attachment category (secure, dismissing, or preoccupied) when they described their love relationship as when they described their relationship with their parents (Owens et al., 1995).

However, just what role models of attachment may play in relationship stability or satisfaction is not yet clear from the available evidence. Some studies suggest that any pair including an insecurely attached individual is likely to be less stable and satisfying than are pairs in which both partners are securely attached (Berman, Marcus, & Berman, 1994; Feeney, 1994). But at least one longitudinal study, covering a period of 4 years, indicated that only those pairs with an avoidant man or an ambivalent woman are less stable (Kirkpatrick & Hazan, 1994). It seems highly likely that internal working models of attachment are linked in important ways with relationship processes and success, but developmentalists don't yet understand precisely what the link is.

● **The Role of Love** ● In the Western world, physical attraction and emotional affection are usually the starting points for intimate relationships. In other parts of the world, relationships are often arranged by parents. However, mutual love seems to be important no matter how a relationship begins (Hortacsu, 1999).

The most compelling of theory of romantic love comes from Robert Sternberg, whose approach is much broader than models based on the concept of attachment. Sternberg argues that love has three key components: (1) *intimacy*, which includes feelings that promote closeness and connectedness; (2) *passion*, which includes a feeling of intense longing for union with the other person, including sexual union; and (3) *commitment to a particular other*, often over a long period of time (Sternberg, 1987). When these three components are combined in all possible ways, the result is eight subvarieties of love, as shown in Figure 13.2. Sternberg's theory suggests that the characteristics of the emotional bond that holds a couple together influence the unique pattern of interaction that develops in each intimate relationship.

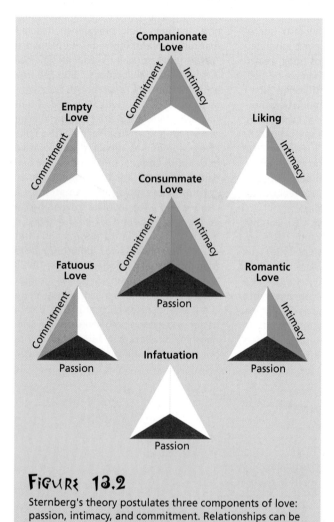

FIGURE 13.2

Sternberg's theory postulates three components of love: passion, intimacy, and commitment. Relationships can be classified according to which of the three components is present.

Partnerships over Time

In one important group of studies, researchers studied 168 couples in their first marriages (Huston & Chorost, 1994; Huston, McHale, & Crouter, 1986; MacDermid, Huston, & McHale, 1990). Each partner was given a lengthy interview within the first 3 months of the marriage, and then again after 1 year. In addition, in the weeks surrounding each of these interviews, each couple was called nine different times and asked to describe in detail what they had done over the previous 24 hours. Thus, these researchers had information not only about feelings and attitudes but about activities. They found that over the first year partners experienced a decrease in satisfaction with both the quantity and the quality of interaction. These couples reported lower levels of love for each other after 1 year, and that was true whether they had had a child or not. Furthermore, their activities had changed. In the early months, they spent a lot more of their leisure time together; after 1 year, when they did things together it was more likely to be "instrumental tasks" (grocery shopping, errands, housework, and the like). They also talked to each other less. Perhaps most importantly, the husbands and wives both described a sizable drop in the frequency of positive interactions, a pattern illustrated in Figure 13.3. In Sternberg's terms, there was a decline in the intimacy aspect of love as well as in the passion aspect.

Such a decline in pleasing behaviors, accompanied by a drop in marital satisfaction, is entirely consistent with the results of research on the sources of stability and instability, satisfaction and dissatisfaction in marriages. In fact, a great deal of what developmentalists know about partnerships in early adulthood comes from studies of the causes of divorce (Gottman, 1994a).

Many powerful influences on marital success are established before a marriage even begins. Each partner brings to the relationship certain skills, resources, and traits that affect the emerging partnership system. The personality characteristics of the partners seem to be especially important (Arrindell & Luteijn, 2000). For example, a high degree of neuroticism in one or both partners usually leads to dissatisfaction and instability in the relationship (Robins et al., 2000). Likewise, attitudes toward divorce affect marital stability. Couples who have tolerant attitudes are less likely to be satisfied with their marriages than those who view divorce as highly undesirable (Amato & Rogers, 1999).

But a marriage or partnership is more than the sum of the characteristics of the two individuals. Equally important for the success of a marriage is the quality of the actual interactions between the couple. And in those interactions, the most crucial feature seems to be simply the relative proportion of "nice" to "nasty" everyday encounters. Couples who will eventually divorce can be identified years ahead of time by looking at the pattern of these positive and negative exchanges (Gottman, 1994a). When negative interactions—criticism, complaints, "yes, but" statements, putdowns, or the like—exceed the positive by too much, divorce becomes far more likely (Gottman, 1994a).

Of course, not all successful marriages are alike. Drawing on a large body of research, psychologists have identified three quite different types of stable or enduring marriages (Gottman, 1994b). **Validating couples** have disagreements, but the disagreements rarely escalate. Partners express mutual respect even when they disagree and listen well to one another. **Volatile couples** squabble a lot, disagree, and don't listen to each other very well when they argue. But they still have more positive than negative encounters and show high levels of laughter and affection. **Avoidant couples**, or "conflict minimizers," don't try to persuade each other—they simply agree to disagree, without apparent rancor, a pattern that is sometimes described as "devitalized."

Similarly, psychologists find two types of unsuccessful marriages. **Hostile/engaged couples**, like volatile couples, have frequent hot arguments, but they lack the balancing effect of humor and affection. **Hostile/detached couples** fight regularly, though the arguments tend to be brief; such couples rarely look at each other, and they also lack affection and support. In both unsuccessful types, the ratio of negative to positive encounters gets out of balance, and the marriage spirals downward toward dissolution.

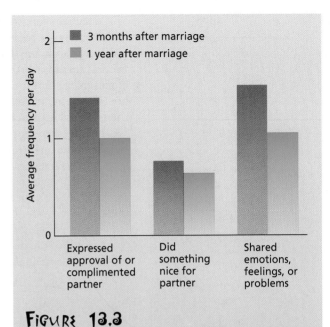

FIGURE 13.3

Most couples become less satisfied with their marriages in their first year together. The reason for such a decline is clear when you look at actual interactions, which become much less positive and supportive. (*Source:* Huston et al., 1986, from Table 7.4, p. 124.)

validating couples couples who express mutual respect even in disagreements and are good listeners

volatile couples couples who argue a lot, don't listen well, but still have more positive than negative interactions

avoidant couples couples who agree to disagree and who minimize conflict by avoiding each other

hostile/engaged couples partners who have frequent arguments that lack the balancing effect of humor and affection

hostile/detached couples couples who fight regularly and rarely look at one another; they also lack affection and support

What can we conclude about causality here? Do couples become unhappy because they are more negative, or are they more negative because they are already unhappy? Both may happen, but it appears that it is more common for couples to become unhappy because they are negative. The best support for this conclusion comes from studies of therapeutic interventions with unhappy couples: Couples who are trained to increase their rate of positive interactions typically show increases in their marital satisfaction (e.g., O'Leary & Smith, 1991).

Finally, there appears to be a parallel between the qualities of a successful marriage and the qualities of a secure attachment. Adults in good marriages have a high level of the same kind of responsiveness to the other's signals that developmentalists see between securely attached infants and their parents. Satisfied partners take turns, read each other's cues, and respond positively. Whatever internal model of attachment each individual may bring to a marriage, the ability of the partners to create such a mutually interlocking and supportive interactive system seems to be critical to the survival of the marriage. Many of the same qualities characterize both homosexual and heterosexual couples (see the Research Report).

Developmental Impact of Intimate Relationships

Married young adults are happier and healthier, live longer, and have lower rates of a variety of psychiatric problems than do young adults without committed partners (Coombs, 1991; Glenn & Weaver, 1988; Lee, Seccombe, & Shehan, 1991; Ross, 1995; Sorlie, Backlund, & Keller, 1995).

At least in U.S. culture, men generally benefit more from marriage than do women on measures of physical and mental health. That is, married men are generally the healthiest and live the longest, while unmarried men are collectively the worst off. The two groups of women fall in between, with married women having a slight advantage over unmarried women. But unmarried women are considerably healthier and happier than are unmarried men.

One explanation of this pattern that has been offered is that some sort of self-selection is occurring. People who are healthy and happy are simply more likely to marry. Logical as it may sound, researchers have found little support for this explanation (Coombs, 1991; Waite, 1995). A second alternative is that married adults follow better health practices. For example, Dutch researchers find that married adults are less likely to smoke or drink to excess, and more likely to exercise than are unmarried adults (Joung, Stronks, van de Mheen, & Mackenbach, 1995).

However, developmentalists argue that it is not marital status per se that is the causal factor, but rather the *quality* of the relationship. For example, researchers in one large-scale study asked unmarried respondents whether they were living with a partner or had a partner who lived in a separate household (Ross, 1995). And each respondent who was in a relationship was asked to say how happy that relationship was. Those whose relationships were very happy were the least likely to report symptoms of depression, while those without a partner or those with unhappy partnerships were most likely to be depressed.

Other research has suggested that the link between relationship quality and an individual's subjective sense of well-being is physiological in nature. An interesting two-phase study of marital quality and health looked for a possible correlation between levels of a stress-related hormone called *cortisol* and the quality of a person's marriage (Kiecolt-Glaser, 2000). Researchers focused on cortisol because it is known to increase when individuals experience negative emotions, and it is one of many stress hormones that are thought to impair immune system functioning. Thus, it may be an important mechanism through which relationship quality affects health.

Investigators measured newlyweds' cortisol levels after they had discussed issues involving conflict, such as in-law relationships or finances. As expected, both husbands' and wives' cortisol levels were somewhat elevated after these discussions. Next, researchers asked couples to tell the story of how they met. As expected, in the

Research Report

Comparing Heterosexual and Homosexual Partnerships

Comparing heterosexual and homosexual partnerships is not as simple as it might seem. For one thing, it's important to compare apples to apples. It would be misleading to claim that heterosexual relationships are more stable on the basis of research comparing married heterosexuals to short-term, "one-night-stand" homosexual partnerships. Consequently, to find out whether relationship characteristics vary across sexual orientation, researchers must limit research samples to couples who are similar in commitment status—that is, to restrict themselves to comparisons of married heterosexuals, long-term cohabiting heterosexuals, and committed, monogamous, homosexual couples. Moreover, research must take into account possible differences between gay and lesbian couples.

Estimates vary, but perhaps 70% of lesbians are in committed relationships, most often monogamous ones. Among gay men, the percentages are somewhat lower. Between 40% and 60% are in long-term committed relationships, but only about a fifth of these relationships are monogamous (compared to roughly three-quarters of heterosexual partnerships) (Blumstein & Schwartz, 1983; Kurdek, 1995b).

A fairly large percentage of married heterosexuals remain together for more than 20 years. When divorce occurs, the average American couple has been married for about 7 years (U.S. Bureau of the Census, 1997). In contrast, very few lesbian relationships endure for 20 years or more; the average length of such partnerships is about 6 years ("National survey results," 1990). Although a large majority of gay men report that they prefer long-term to short-term relationships, such partnerships are less common among them than among either lesbians or heterosexuals (Lever, 1994; "National survey results," 1990).

However, among couples who are committed and monogamous, gay men and lesbians are as likely as heterosexuals to be satisfied with their partner relationships. What does differentiate homosexual from heterosexual unions is the nature of the power relation between the couple. Homosexual couples seem to be more egalitarian than heterosexual couples, with less-specific role prescriptions. It is quite uncommon in homosexual couples for one partner to occupy a "male" role and the other a "female" role. Instead, power and tasks are more equally divided. However, this is more true of lesbian couples—among whom equality of roles is frequently a strong philosophical ideal—than of gay couples (Kurdek, 1995a).

In Chapter 12, you learned that, although rates of partner abuse differ across sexual orientation groups, the same factors contribute to abuse in heterosexual and homosexual couples. Likewise, many of the same variables that affect the success of heterosexual marriages seem to be important in the endurance of homosexual partnerships (Kurdek, 1998). For example, neuroticism in one or both partners is related to relationship quality and length (Kurdek, 1997, 2000). Like married heterosexuals, gay couples experience a drop in their relationship satisfaction in the early months of their partnership (Kurdek & Schmitt, 1986). They argue over similar things, and, like marriages, gay relationships are more likely to last if the two partners share similar backgrounds and are equally committed to the relationship (Krueger-Lebus & Rauchfleisch, 1999; Kurdek, 1997; Peplau, 1991). However, one important difference is that lesbians and gays are more likely to be dependent on a partner as a sole source of social support, because homosexual adults are more likely than heterosexual adults to be isolated from their families of origin (Hill, 1999).

In summary, it would be overstating the case to say that homosexual and heterosexual relationships function in exactly the same ways. The varying degrees of monogamy and the varying lengths of relationships, as well as the different rates of partner abuse, reveal that there are important differences among them. At the same time, however, research suggests that factors related to success or failure are highly consistent across the three types of relationships. Clearly, the most reliable conclusions that can be derived from the current state of research are (1) that homosexual relationships are similar to heterosexual relationships in some ways but differ from them in significant ways, and (2) that a great deal more research is needed to identify the sources of these differences.

majority of both husbands and wives, cortisol levels dropped as they discussed the emotionally neutral topic of relationship history. However, cortisol levels dropped least in participants who were the most emotionally negative (as measured by the number of negative words used in describing their relationships). This component of the study demonstrated a direct link between stress hormones and marital negativity.

In addition, an important sex difference emerged. When couples described negative events in their relationships, wives' cortisol levels increased, while husbands' levels remained constant. This finding suggested that women may be more physiologically sensitive to relationship negativity than men. Thus, these results may help explain why marriage is a more consistently protective factor for men than for women.

Sex differences were also apparent in the study's second phase, during which researchers surveyed participants 8–12 years later to find out if they were still married. Remarkably, the researchers found that the higher the wife's cortisol response to emotional negativity in the first phase, the more likely the couple was to be divorced. Consequently, researchers hypothesized that women's physiological responses to marital quality are an important determinant of relationship stability.

Of course, research findings on the benefits of marriage do not mean that all single adults are unhappy and unhealthy. Many adults are single by preference and have found alternative sources of support. Never-married women, for example, are more likely to maintain very close contact with their parents and siblings, perhaps retaining that central attachment in a less intense form (Allen & Pickett, 1987; Campbell, Connidis, & Davies, 1999). They are also more likely than their married peers to have full-time, continuous careers and to be more successful and better paid as a result (Sorensen, 1983). However, single women are also likely to experience feelings of ambivalence about being single (Lewis & Moon, 1997). Many express feelings of loss or regret related to their unmarried status, while at the same time experiencing high levels of satisfaction with their lives.

Moreover, as you might suspect, there are differences between single adults who have never married and those who are divorced or widowed. Continuous singlehood is associated with greater individual autonomy and capacity for personal growth (Marks & Lambert, 1998). By contrast, the negative effects of the transitional state that accompanies divorce or loss of a spouse seem to hamper the subjective sense of well-being in adults who are single for these reasons.

Divorce

Different ways of computing the U.S. divorce rate can distort our ideas about how frequently divorce happens. The figure usually cited, 50%, is the ratio of divorces to marriages in a given year. In other words, a divorce rate of 50% means that there is one divorce for every two marriages. However, when researchers follow married couples longitudinally, they find that the actual statistical likelihood of divorce in the United States reached a peak of 22% in 1988 and leveled off to 18–20% near the end of the 20th century (Raschke, 1987; U.S. Bureau of the Census, 1997).

● *Psychological Effects* ● At a psychological level, divorce is clearly a major stressor. It is associated with increases in both physical and emotional illness. Recently separated or divorced adults have more automobile accidents, are more likely to commit suicide, lose more days at work because of illness, and are more likely to become depressed (Bloom, White, & Asher, 1979; Menaghan & Lieberman, 1986; Stack, 1992a, 1992b; Stack & Wasserman, 1993). They also report strong feelings of failure and a loss of self-esteem, as well as loneliness (Chase-Lansdale & Hetherington, 1990). These negative effects are strongest in the first months after the separation or divorce, like the effects of parents' divorce on children, which are greatest during the first 12–24 months (Chase-Lansdale & Hetherington, 1990; Kitson, 1992).

Long-term effects vary far more. Some adults seem to grow from the experience of divorce and show better psychological functioning 5 or 10 years later than they had shown before the divorce. Others seem to be worse off psychologically, even 10 years later (Wallerstein, 1986). It appears that those who remarry are likely to be happier than those who remain single—yet another bit of evidence supporting the general conclusion that marriage (or a stable partnership) is linked to better mental and physical health. Yet for those whose second marriage ends in divorce, the negative consequences can be substantial (Spanier & Furstenberg, 1987). At the moment, the most that developmentalists can say is that adults are highly heterogeneous in their responses to divorce. And very little is known about the factors that might predict good or poor long-term reactions, except that those adults with adequate social support are less disrupted in the short term (Chase-Lansdale & Hetherington, 1990).

● **Economic Effects** ●   The psychological effects of divorce are often significantly worsened by serious economic effects, particularly for women. Because most men have had continuous work histories, they commonly leave a marriage with far greater earning power than do women. Women not only typically lack high earning capacity, they also usually retain custody of any children, with attendant costs. Several longitudinal studies in both the United States and European countries show that divorced men generally improve in their economic position, while divorced women are strongly adversely affected, with an average decline of 40–50% of household income (Morgan, 1991; Smock, 1993). Furthermore, this negative economic effect does not disappear quickly—and for some women, it doesn't disappear at all. The most reliable means of economic recovery for divorced women is remarriage, which brings most women back to or above their predivorce economic status. For those women who do not remarry, however, the economic effects tend to persist.

Such a long-term economic loss from divorce is especially likely for working-class women or those with relatively low levels of education. Women who were earning above-average incomes before their divorce are more likely to recover financially, even if they do not remarry (Holden & Smock, 1991).

● **Effects on Life Pathways** ●   For many adults, divorce also affects the sequence and timing of family roles. Even though divorced women with children are less likely to remarry than those who are childless, remarriage expands the number of years of child-rearing for many divorced women (Lampard & Peggs, 1999; Norton, 1983). The total number of years of child-rearing may also be significantly increased for divorced men, especially for those who remarry younger women with young children. One effect of this change in timing is to reduce the number of years a remarried couple may have between the departure of the last child and the time when their elder parents may need economic or physical assistance.

Divorce also brings on a whole new set of roles. For the custodial parent (usually the woman), divorce means taking on parenting roles previously filled by the now-departed spouse. A divorced woman is also likely to take on a greatly expanded job role. Thus, it isn't surprising that divorced women who are custodial mothers experience feelings of anger and frustration for a longer period of time after divorce than do noncustodial fathers (Dreman, Pielberger, & Darzi, 1997).

Remarriage frequently brings with it the remarkably complex role of step-parent. If several sets of children are involved, stages may be added to the standard family role cycle. A woman with children in elementary school may now find herself also the parent of teenagers—a role that demands different skills. Each of these changes seems to be accompanied by a new period of adaptation, often with considerable upheaval. In Levinson's theoretical language, this means divorced and remarried adults have fewer opportunities to create stable life structures and have more periods of transition or crisis. Thus, divorce changes the rhythm of adult life, for good or ill.

Before going on

● In what ways do attachment and love contribute to the formation and stability of relationships?

● How do partnerships change over time?

● How does divorce affect young adults, especially women?

Parenthood and Other Relationships

The second major new role typically acquired in early adulthood is that of parent. The transition into this new role brings with it unique stresses, and, to make matters more complicated, it usually happens at a time when most other social relationships are in transition as well.

Parenthood

Most parents would agree that parenthood is a remarkably mixed emotional experience. On one hand, the desire to become a parent is, for many adults, extremely strong. Thus, fulfilling that desire is an emotional high point for most. On the other hand, parenthood results in a number of stressful changes.

● *The Desire to Become a Parent* ●   In the United States, nine out of every ten women aged 18 to 34 has had or expects to have a child (U.S. Bureau of the Census, 1997). Despite the opportunistic attitude toward mating that evolutionary theory ascribes to men, the percentage of men who feel strongly that they want to become parents and who view parenting as a life-enriching experience is actually greater than the percentage of women who feel this way (Horowitz, McLaughlin, & White, 1998; Muzi, 2000). Furthermore, most expectant fathers become emotionally attached to their unborn children during the third trimester of pregnancy and eagerly anticipate the birth (White, Wilson, Elander, & Persson, 1999).

● *Postpartum Depression* ●   Between 10% and 25% of new mothers experience a severe mood disturbance called *postpartum depression (PPD)*—a disorder found among mothers in Australia, China, Sweden, and Scotland as well as in the United States (Campbell, Cohn, Flanagan, Popper, & Meyers, 1992; Guo, 1993; Lundh & Gyllang, 1993; Webster, Thompson, Mitchell, & Werry, 1994). Women who develop PPD suffer from feelings of sadness for several weeks after the baby's birth. Most cases of PPD persist only a few weeks, but 1–2% of women suffer for a year or more.

Women whose bodies produce unusually high levels of steroid hormones toward the end of pregnancy are more likely to develop postpartum depression (Harris et al., 1994). The disorder is also more common in women whose pregnancies were unplanned, who were anxious about the pregnancy, or whose partner was unsupportive (Campbell et al., 1992; O'Hara, Schlechte, Lewis, & Varner, 1992). The presence of major life stressors during pregnancy or immediately after the baby's birth—such as a move to a new home, the death of someone close, or job loss—also increase the risk of PPD (Swendsen & Mazure, 2000).

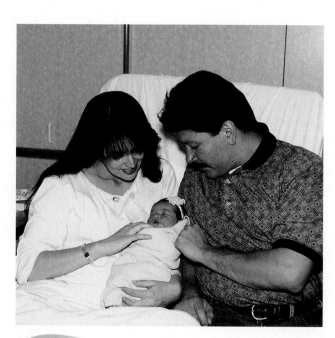

For most couples in long-term relationships, especially those who are married, having a child is an important goal.
(*Photo:* Michael Newman, PhotoEdit)

However, the best predictor of postpartum depression is depression during pregnancy (Da Costa, Larouche, Dritsa, & Brender, 2000). Thus, many cases of PPD can probably be prevented by training health professionals to recognize depression in pregnant women. Similarly, family members of women with absent or unsupportive partners can help them locate agencies that provide material and social support.

● **The Transition Experience** ●   Even when new mothers are emotionally healthy, the transition to parenthood can be very stressful. New parents may argue about child-rearing philosophy as well as how, when, where, and by whom child-care chores should be done (Reichle & Gefke, 1998). Both parents are usually also physically exhausted, perhaps even seriously sleep-deprived, because their newborn keeps them up for much of the night. Predictably, new parents report that they have much less time for each other—less time for conversation, for sex, for simple affection, or even for doing routine chores together (Belsky, Lang, & Rovine, 1985).

Some cultures have developed ritualized rites of passage for this important transition, which can help new parents manage stress. For example, in Hispanic cultures, *la cuarenta* is a period of 40 days following the birth of a child, during which fathers are expected to take on typically feminine tasks such as housework. Extended family members are also expected to help out. Researchers have found that Hispanic couples who observe *la cuarenta* adjust to parenthood more easily than those who do not (Niska, Snyder, & Lia-Hoagberg, 1998).

● **Developmental Impact of Parenthood** ●   Despite its inherent stressfulness, the transition to parenthood is associated with positive behavior change. Sensation-seeking and risky behavior decline considerably when young adults become parents (Arnett, 1998). Despite these positive changes, marital satisfaction tends to decline after the birth of a child. The general pattern is that such satisfaction is at its peak before the birth of the first child, after which it drops and remains at a lower level until the last child leaves home.

In a review of all the research on this point, one psychologist concluded that this curvilinear pattern "is about as close to being certain as anything ever is in the social sciences" (Glenn, 1990, p. 853). Figure 13.4 illustrates the pattern, based on results from an early and widely quoted study (Rollins & Feldman, 1970). The best-documented portion of this curvilinear pattern is the drop in marital satisfaction after the birth of the first child, for which there is both longitudinal and cross-sectional evidence.

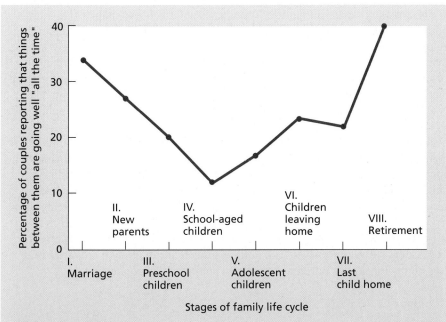

FIGURE 13.4

This pattern of change in marital satisfaction over the stages of the family life cycle is one of the best-documented findings in family sociology research. (*Source:* Rollins & Feldman, 1970, Tables 2 & 3, p. 24. Copyright 1970 by the National Council on Family Relations.)

More recent studies suggest that the decline in marital satisfaction is characteristic of contemporary cohorts of new parents as well, and researchers have found a pattern of marital satisfaction similar to that reported by Rollins and Feldman across a variety of cultures (Ahmad & Najam, 1998; Gloger-Tippelt & Huerkamp, 1998).

A number of variables contribute to just how dissatisfied a couple becomes. One important factor is the division of labor. The more a partner feels that he or she is carrying an unfair proportion of the economic, household, or child-care workload, the greater his or her loss of satisfaction (Wicki, 1999). Support from extended family members is another variable that predicts maintenance or loss of satisfaction (Lee & Keith, 1999).

Some developmentalists suggest that the relative effectiveness of the coping strategies couples use to adjust to their new roles determines how their relationship satisfaction will be affected by the birth of a child (Belsky & Hsieh, 1998). For example, couples who have established effective conflict-resolution strategies before the birth of a child experience less loss of satisfaction (Cox, Paley, Burchinal, & Payne, 1999; Lindahl, Clements, & Markman, 1997). The quality of new parents' attachment to their own parents also predicts how much their relationship satisfaction declines after the birth of a child (Gloger-Tippelt & Huerkamp, 1998). In fact, young adults with anxious or avoidant attachments to their own parents expect the transition to parenthood to be a negative experience more often than do those whose attachments are secure (Rholes, Simpson, Blakely, Lanigan, & Allen, 1997).

It's important to keep in mind, though, that new parents who are married or cohabiting experience a much smaller decline in overall life satisfaction than new single parents, whose lives are far more complicated and stressful (Lee, Law, & Tam, 1999). Likewise, single parents are more likely to suffer from health problems and are less likely to advance to management positions at work (Khlat, Sermet, & Le Pape, 2000; Tharenou, 1999). Instead of focusing on declines in relationship satisfaction, some developmentalists suggest that more attention should be paid to the consistent finding that having a parenting partner—especially one to whom one is married—is a significant protective factor in managing the stressful transition to parenthood.

● *Childlessness* ●   Like parenthood, childlessness affects the shape of an adult's life, both within marriages and in work patterns. Without the presence of children, marital satisfaction fluctuates less over time. As is true of all couples, those who do not have children are likely to experience some drop in satisfaction in the first months and years of marriage. But over the range of adult life, their curve of marital satisfaction is much flatter than the one shown in Figure 13.4 (Houseknecht, 1987; Somers, 1993). Childless couples in their 20s and 30s consistently report higher cohesion in their marriages than do couples with children.

Childlessness also affects the role of worker, especially for women. Childless married women, like unmarried women, are much more likely to have full-time continuous careers. However, a survey involving more than 2,000 participants found that single, childless women had no higher rates of managerial advancement than mothers (Tharenou, 1999). Thus, one of the disadvantages associated with childlessness may be that it is always socially a bit risky to be seen as "different" from others in any important way (Mueller & Yoder, 1999). Tharenou's survey's finding that married fathers whose wives were not employed were more likely to advance than workers of any marital or parental status also supports this conclusion.

Social Networks

Creating a partnership may be the most central task of the process of achieving intimacy, but it is certainly not the only reflection of that basic process. In early adult life, each of us creates a social network made up of family and friends as well as our life partner.

● **Family** ●   If you ask children and adults "Who is the person you don't like to be away from?" or "Who is the person you know will always be there for you?" children and teenagers most often list their parents, while adults most often name their spouses or partners and almost never mention their parents (Hazan, Hutt, Sturgeon, & Bricker, 1991). However, most adults feel emotionally close to their parents and see or talk to them regularly (Campbell, Connidis, & Davies, 1999; Lawton, Silverstein, & Bengtson, 1994).

Critical Thinking

List all the people in your current social network. What is the relative importance of family and friends for you?

A good illustration comes from a relatively old study (Leigh, 1982). Researchers interviewed about 1,300 adults who varied with respect to their stage in the traditional family life cycle. Each adult reported how frequently he or she saw, spoke with, or wrote to parents, brothers and sisters, cousins, and other family members. Figure 13.5 shows the percentage of the young adult respondents who said they had at least monthly contact with their parents, the percentage who had weekly contact with parents, and the percentage who had weekly contact with their siblings. Clearly, some contact is the norm, and frequent contact is common.

Not surprisingly, the amount and kind of contact an adult has with kin is strongly influenced by proximity. Adults who live within 2 hours of their parents and siblings see them far more often than those who live farther away. But distance does not prevent a parent or sibling from being part of an individual adult's social network. These relationships can provide support in times of need, even if physical contact is infrequent.

There are also important cultural differences in young adults' involvement with their families. For example, one study compared the development of social independence among Australian, Canadian, and Japanese children and adults (Takata, 1999). In all three cultures, the sense of being independent from parents and family increased with age. However, Australian and Canadian participants appeared to develop self-perceptions of independence earlier in life. Consequently, Japanese young adults reported a greater sense of connectedness to their families of origin than either Australian or Canadian young adults.

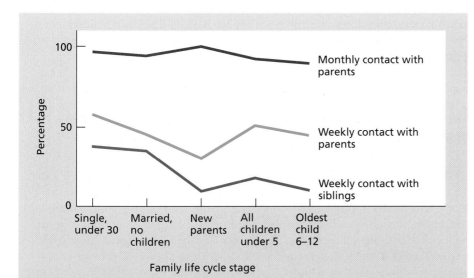

FIGURE 13.5

Despite the process of physical and emotional emancipation that occurs in young adulthood, virtually all adults are in contact with their parents at least monthly. (*Source:* Leigh, 1982, from Table 2, p. 202.)

Although patterns of interaction with family members are similar across U.S. racial groups, Hispanic Americans perceive family ties to be more important than young adults of other races or ethnicities (Schweizer, Schnegg, & Berzborn, 1998). Given a choice, many non-Hispanics de-emphasize kin networks in early adulthood, whereas Hispanic Americans embrace them enthusiastically (Vega, 1990). In the Hispanic American culture, extensive kin networks are the rule rather than the exception, with frequent visiting and exchanges not only between parents, children, and siblings, but with grandparents, cousins, aunts, and uncles (Keefe, 1984). These frequent contacts are not only perceived as enjoyable, they are seen as vital signs of the closeness of kin relationships.

African Americans young adults also tend to value family connections highly, although the reasons are somewhat different. For one thing, African American young adults are less likely to marry than are young adults in other groups, a pattern resulting in part from the high level of unemployment among young African American men (Burgess, 1995). Consequently, more African American young adults live in multigenerational households with their parents, grandparents, or other relatives than do their peers in other groups; many African American households consist of two generations of adult women and one or more children (Hatchett, Cochran, & Jackson, 1991). African American young adults tend to report higher levels of intimacy and warmth in relationships with parents than do whites, Asian Americans, or Hispanic Americans, so it's not surprising that they feel more comfortable living with family than other young adults do (Kane, 1998). Frequent kin contact is also a significant part of the daily life of most African American adults who do not live in extended family households (Hatchett & Jackson, 1993). African Americans also are more likely to form what have been called "pseudo-kin networks," or "fictive" kin relationships—close family-like relationships with neighbors or peers, who provide each other with a wide variety of aid (Taylor, Chatters, Tucker, & Lewis, 1990).

● *Friends* ●   Friends, too, are important members of a social network. We choose our friends as we choose our partners, from among those who are similar to us in education, social class, interests, family background, or family life cycle stage. Cross-sex friendships are more common among adults than they are among 10-year-olds, but they are still outnumbered by same-sex friendships. Young adults' friends are also overwhelmingly drawn from their own age group. Beyond this basic requirement of similarity, close friendship seems to rest on mutual openness and personal disclosure.

Because of the centrality of the task of intimacy in early adulthood, most researchers and theorists assume that young adults have more friends than do middle-aged or older adults. Research has offered some hints of support for this idea, but it has been a difficult assumption to test properly. Developmentalists lack longitudinal data and do not agree on definitions of friendship, which makes combining data across studies very difficult.

● *Sex Differences in Relationship Styles* ●   As in childhood, there are very striking sex differences in both the number and quality of friendships in the social network of young adults. Women have more close friends, and their friendships are more intimate, with more self-disclosure and more exchange of emotional support. Young men's friendships, like those of boys and older men, are more competitive. Male friends are less likely to agree with each other or to ask for or provide emotional support to one another (Dindia & Allen, 1992; Maccoby, 1990). Adult women friends talk to one another; adult men friends do things together.

Whether one sees the female pattern or the male pattern as "better" or "worse" obviously depends on one's gender and point of view. Theorists continue to argue the point (Antonucci, 1994b). Most research shows men to be less satisfied with their friendships than women are (although the sexes are equally satisfied with their family relationships), and women clearly gain in quite specific ways from the buffering effect of their social network. But men also gain from their style of relationship. Women's style, for example, sometimes has the effect of burdening them too much with emotional obligations, whereas men are more able to focus on their work (Antonucci, 1994b). Setting aside value judgments, the important point remains: Men and women appear to create different kinds of relationships, and this difference permeates U.S. culture.

Another facet of this difference is that women most often fill the role of **kin-keeper** (Moen, 1996). They write the letters, make the phone calls, arrange the gatherings of family and friends. (In later stages of adult life, it is also the women who are likely to take on the role of caring for aging parents—a pattern you'll learn more about in Chapter 15.)

Taken together, all this means that women have a much larger "relationship role" than men do. In virtually all cultures, it is part of the female role to be responsible for maintaining the emotional aspects of relationships—with a spouse, with friends, with family, and, of course, with children.

Before going on

● Describe the transition to parenthood and the developmental effects of becoming a parent and remaining childless.

● How are family and friends important to young adults?

The Role of Worker

In addition to the roles of spouse or partner and parent, a large percentage of young adults are simultaneously filling yet another major and relatively new role, that of worker. Most young people need to take on this role to support themselves economically. But that is not the only reason for the centrality of this role. Satisfying work also seems to be an important ingredient in mental health and life satisfaction, for both men and women (Meeus, Dekovic & Iedema, 1997; Tait, Padgett, & Baldwin, 1989). However, before looking at what developmentalists know about career steps and sequences in early adulthood, let's examine how young people choose an occupation.

Choosing an Occupation

As you might imagine, a multitude of factors influence a young person's choice of job or career: family background and values; intelligence and education; gender; and personality (in addition to other factors such as ethnic group, self-concept, and school performance).

kin-keeper a family role, usually occupied by a woman, which includes responsibility for maintaining family and friendship relationships

● **Family Influences** ● Typically, young people tend to choose occupations at the same general social class level as those of their parents—although this is less true today than it was a decade or two ago (Biblarz, Bengtson, & Bucur, 1996). In part, this effect operates through the medium of education. For example, researchers have found that young adults whose parents are college graduates are less likely to enlist in the military than those whose parents have less education (Bachman, Segal, Freedman-Doan, & O'Malley, 2000). Such findings suggest that parents who have higher-than-average levels of education themselves are more likely to encourage their children to go on for further education past high school. Such added education, in turn, makes it more likely that the young person will qualify for middle-class jobs, for which a college education is frequently a required credential.

Families also influence job choices through their value systems. In particular, parents who value academic and professional achievement are far more likely to have children who attend college and choose professional-level jobs. This effect is not just social-class difference in disguise. Among working-class families, it is the children of those who place the strongest emphasis on achievement who are most likely to move up into middle-class jobs (Gustafson & Magnusson, 1991). Further, families whose career aspirations for their children are high tend to produce young adults who are more intrinsically motivated as employees (Cotton, Bynum, & Madhere, 1997).

Similarly, parental moral beliefs influence young adults' willingness to enter various occupations (Bregman & Killen, 1999). For example, young adults whose families believe that drinking alcohol is morally wrong are unlikely to choose alcohol-related occupations such as bartending, waiting tables in a restaurant where liquor is served, or working at a liquor store.

𝒴oung adults who enter military service differ from peers who go to college or into civilian careers. Their parents are less likely to have gone to college and more likely to be poor than parents of young adults who do not go into military service. However, some families encourage their young adult children to join the military in order to have access to the educational opportunities they cannot afford to provide for them and that often accompany military service. (*Photos:* David H. Wells/CORBIS; Stone)

● **Education and Intelligence** ● Education and intelligence also interact very strongly to influence not just the specific job a young person chooses, but also career success over the long haul. You read about some of these links in Chapter 10, but they bear repeating: The higher your intelligence, the more years of education you are likely to complete; the more education you have, the higher the level at which you enter the job market; the higher the level of entry, the further you are likely to go over your lifetime (Brody, 1992; Kamo, Ries, Farmer, Nickinovich, & Borgatta, 1991).

Intelligence has direct effects on job choice and job success as well. Brighter students are more likely to choose technical or professional careers. And highly intelligent workers are more likely to advance, even if they enter the job market at a lower level than those who are less intelligent (Dreher & Bretz, 1991).

● **Gender** ● Specific job choice is also strongly affected by gender. Despite the women's movement, and despite the vast increase in the proportion of women working, it is still true that sex-role definitions designate some jobs as "women's jobs" and some as "men's jobs" (Reskin, 1993). Stereotypically male jobs are more varied, more technical, and higher in both status and income (e.g., doctor, business executive, carpenter). Women's jobs are concentrated in service occupations and are typically lower in status and lower-paid (e.g., teacher, nurse, secretary). One-third of all working women hold clerical jobs; another quarter are in health care, teaching, or domestic service.

Children learn these cultural definitions of "appropriate" jobs for men and women in their early years, just as they learn all the other aspects of sex roles. So it is not surprising that most young women and men choose jobs that fit these sex-role designations. Nonstereotypical job choices are much more common among young people who see themselves as androgynous, or whose parents have unconventional occupations. For instance, young women who choose traditionally masculine careers are more likely to have a mother who has had a long-term career, and are more likely to define themselves either as androgynous or as masculine (Betz & Fitzgerald, 1987; Fitzpatrick & Silverman, 1989).

● **Personality** ● A fourth important influence on job choice is the young adult's personality. John Holland, whose work has been the most influential in this area, proposes six basic personality types, summarized in Table 13.1 (Holland, 1973, 1992). Holland's basic hypothesis is that each of us tends to choose, and be most successful at, an occupation that matches our personality.

Research in non-Western as well as Western cultures, and with African Americans, Hispanic Americans, and Native Americans as well as whites in the United States has generally supported Holland's proposal (e.g., Kahn, Alvi, Shaukat, Hussain, & Baig, 1990; Leong, Austin, Sekaran, & Komarraju, 1998; Tokar, Fischer, & Subich, 1998; Tracey & Rounds, 1993; Upperman & Church, 1995). Ministers, for example, generally score highest on Holland's social scale, engineers highest on the investigative scale, car salespeople on the enterprising scale, and career army officers on the realistic scale.

TABLE 13.1 Holland's Personality Types and Work Preferences

Type	Personality and Work Preferences
Realistic	Aggressive, masculine, physically strong, often with low verbal or interpersonal skills; prefer mechanical activities and tool use, choosing jobs such as mechanic, electrician, or surveyor
Investigative	Oriented toward thinking (particularly abstract thinking), organizing, and planning; prefer ambiguous, challenging tasks, but are low in social skills; are often scientists or engineers
Artistic	Asocial; prefer unstructured, highly individual activity; are often artists
Social	Extraverts; people-oriented, sociable, and need attention; avoid intellectual activity and dislike highly ordered activity; prefer to work with people and choose service jobs like nursing and education
Enterprising	Highly verbal and dominating; enjoy organizing and directing others; are persuasive and strong leaders, often choosing careers in sales
Conventional	Prefer structured activities and subordinate roles; like clear guidelines and see themselves as accurate and precise; may choose occupations such as bookkeeping or filing

(*Source:* Holland, 1973, 1992.)

People whose personalities match their jobs are also more likely to be satisfied with their work. Moreover, obtaining a personality assessment prior to making an occupational choice is associated with greater feelings of confidence about the decision (Francis-Smythe & Smith, 1997).

Jobs over Time

Once the job or career has been chosen, what kinds of experiences do young adults have in their work life? Do they become more or less satisfied with their work over time? Are there clear career steps that might be considered stages?

● *Job Satisfaction* ●   Many studies show that job satisfaction is at its lowest in early adulthood and rises steadily until retirement, a pattern that has been found in repeated surveys of both male and female respondents (Glenn & Weaver, 1985). Researchers know that this is not just a cohort effect, because similar findings have been reported over many years of research, and that it is not entirely culture-specific, since it has been found in many industrialized countries.

But what might cause the pattern? Some research points to the possibility that this pattern is the effect of time on job rather than age (e.g., Bedeian, Ferris, & Kacmar, 1992). Older workers are likely to have had their jobs longer, which may contribute to several sources of satisfaction, including better pay, more job security, and more authority. But there may be some genuine age effects at work, too. The jobs young people hold are likely to be dirtier, physically harder, and less complex and interesting (Spenner, 1988).

However, research also suggests that there are a number of important variables that contribute to job satisfaction in young adults. As with almost every life situation, individual personality traits such as neuroticism affect job satisfaction (Blustein, Phillips, Jobin-Davis, & Finkelberg, 1997; Judge, Bono, & Locke, 2000). In addition, young adults engaged in careers for which they prepared in high school or college have higher levels of satisfaction (Blustein et al., 1997). Race is also related to job satisfaction, with white workers reporting higher levels of satisfaction than minority workers (Weaver & Hinson, 2000).

In addition to personal factors, a number of workplace variables influence job satisfaction. For example, the degree to which a work setting encourages or discourages young employees makes a difference (Blustein et al., 1997). Encouragement may be part of a set of workplace variables that contribute to positive affect, or feelings of emotional contentment, among workers, which, in turn, lead to higher levels of job satisfaction. Research suggests that workers are most satisfied when they experience more pleasant than unpleasant emotions while working (Fisher, 2000).

● *Career Ladders* ●   In most careers, workers tend to move from step to step through a series of milestones that make up a **career ladder**. In academic jobs, the sequence is from instructor to assistant professor to associate professor and then full professor. In an automobile plant, the ladder may go from assembly-line worker to foreman to general foreman to superintendent and on up. In the corporate world, there may be many rungs in a management career ladder.

What kind of progress up the career ladder do young adults typically make? To answer such a question properly, of course, researchers need to conduct longitudinal studies. There have not been many of these, but fortunately there are a few, including a 20-year study of AT&T managers (Bray & Howard, 1983) and a 15-year study of workers in a large manufacturing company (Rosenbaum, 1984). This research suggests several generalizations about the developmental progression of work careers in early adulthood. First, college education makes a very large difference, as you should remember from Chapter 12. Even if the effects of differing intellectual ability are

career ladder the milestones associated with a particular occupation

accounted for, research shows that those with college educations advance further and faster.

Second, early promotion is associated with greater advancement over the long haul. In the manufacturing company that Rosenbaum studied, 83% of those who were promoted within the first year eventually got as far as lower management, while only 33% of those who were first promoted after 3 years of employment got that far.

Third, and perhaps most important, most work advancement occurs early in a career path, after which a plateau is reached. The policy in the manufacturing company that Rosenbaum studied was for all workers—whether they had a college degree or not—to enter at the submanagement level. The first possible promotional step was to the job of foreman; promotion to lower management was the second possible step. The majority of promotions to either position occurred when workers were between the ages of 29 and 34; by age 40, virtually all the promotions that a person was going to receive had already happened. The same pattern is evident in other career paths as well, such as those of accountants and academics, so it is not unique to business career ladders (Spenner, 1988).

Such a pattern may be unique, however, to adults who enter a profession in their 20s and stay in it through most of their adult lives. There are at least a few hints from research with women—whose work histories are frequently much less continuous than men's—that time-in-career rather than age may be the critical variable for the timing of promotions. There may be a window of 10–15 years between the time you enter a profession and the time you reach a plateau. If you begin in your 20s, you are likely to have peaked by your mid-30s. But if you begin when you are 40, you may still have 15 years in which to advance.

● *Another View of Work Sequences* ● Another way to describe the work experience of young adults is in terms of a series of stages, a model proposed originally by Donald Super (Super, 1971, 1986). First comes the *trial stage*, roughly between the ages of 18 and 25, more or less equivalent to the first phase of the young adult period proposed by Levinson (refer back to Figure 13.1). In this stage, the young person must decide on a job or career, and he searches for a fit between his interests and personality and the jobs available. The whole process involves a good deal of trial and error as well as luck or chance. Perhaps because many of the jobs available to those in this age range are not terribly challenging, and because many young adults have not yet found the right fit, job changes are at their peak during this period.

Next comes the *establishment stage* (also called the *stabilization stage*), roughly from age 25 to age 45. Having chosen an occupation, the young person must learn the ropes and begin to move through the early steps in some career ladder as he masters the needed skills, perhaps with a mentor's help. In this period, the worker also focuses on fulfilling whatever aspirations or goals he may have set for himself. In Levinson's terms, he tries to fulfill his dream. The young scientist pushes himself to make an important discovery; the young attorney strives to become a partner; the young business executive tries to move as far up the ladder as he can; the young blue-collar worker may aim for job stability or promotion to foreman. It is in these years that most promotions do in fact occur, although it is also the time when the job plateau is reached.

Sex Differences in Work Patterns

Some of what you have read so far about work patterns is as true for women as it is for men. For example, women's work satisfaction goes up with age (and with job tenure), just as men's does. But women's work experience in early adulthood differs from men's in one strikingly important respect: The great majority of women move in and out of the work force at least once, often many times (Drobnic, Blossfeld, & Rohwer, 1999).

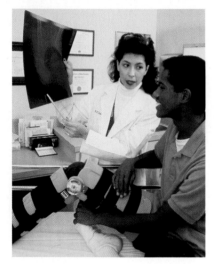

Women are working in larger and larger numbers, but fewer than a third work continuously during the early adult years.
(*Photos:* David Young-Wolff, PhotoEdit; Robert E. Daemmrich, Stone)

MAKE THE CONNECTION

In Chapter 7, you learned about gender schema theory. How would this theory explain women's responses to conflicts between work and family roles?

This pattern has numerous repercussions for women's work roles. For example, women who work continuously have higher salaries and achieve higher levels in their jobs than do those who have moved in and out of employment (Betz, 1984; Van Velsor & O'Rand, 1984). Among women who have not worked continuously, those who worked for several short bursts during their in-and-out stage do better economically than those who were unemployed for a single long stretch, even when the total months or years of employment are the same in the two groups (Gwartney-Gibbs, 1988). Very likely these short bursts of work allow the woman to keep up her work skills, especially if she works at the same type of job each time she reenters the labor market. Part-time work also seems to serve the same function. Clearly, some strategies can help a woman maximize her work success while still allowing her to spend time with her family, but accomplishing both takes a good deal of thought and planning.

Women's work patterns are obviously changing rapidly. For example, researchers found that a large group of female college seniors majoring in business who were interviewed in 1988 expected to work an average of 29.1, years compared to their male peers, who expected to work for 37.7 years (Blau & Ferber, 1991). Only a few years later, a Canadian study found that most of the high school girls the researchers interviewed in the early 1990s expected both to be continuously employed and to have a family in adulthood (Davey, 1998). However, when they were reinterviewed 4 years later, these young women had begun to think about potential conflicts between career and family goals. Most still expected to be continuously employed, but many indicated that they preferred to take time out from their careers to achieve family goals such as raising children. So although the cultural climate has changed drastically with regard to women's work patterns, the essential conflict women feel with regard to work and family, which is the driving force behind discontinuous patterns of employment, continues to be evident in current cohorts.

The evidence on women's patterns of discontinuous employment raises the more general question of how individuals and couples balance the roles of worker and parent and those of worker and spouse. It is an interesting testimony to the strength of cultural gender roles that people have no trouble thinking of a man as simultaneously a worker, a parent, and a spouse, but they think it is problematic for a woman to be all three at once. Women do, in fact, feel more role conflict among these three roles than men do, for several clear reasons (Higgins, Duxbury, & Lee, 1994).

The most obvious reason is that if the hours spent in family work (child care, cleaning, cooking, shopping, etc.) and in paid employment are added together, employed women are working more hours a week than are their husbands or partners, as suggested by Figure 13.6—despite the fact that men whose wives are employed are doing more child care than men in previous generations did (Higgins et al., 1994). Further, unmarried men are as likely as their female counterparts to anticipate the need to balance work and family roles after marriage (Kerpelman & Schvaneveldt, 1999).

However, wives still do roughly twice as much housework (child care, cooking, cleaning, running errands, and so forth) as husbands, even when both work full-time (Blair & Johnson, 1992). African American and Hispanic American men appear to spend slightly more time in household labor than do white men, but the range of variation is not large (Shelton & John, 1993). Thus, although the gap is decreasing, women still devote much more time to family roles than do men.

Women also feel more conflict between family and work roles because of the way sex roles are defined in most cultures. The woman's role is to be relationship-oriented, to care for others, to nurture. To the extent that a woman has internalized that role expectation—and most have—she will define herself, and judge herself, more by how well she performs such caring roles than by how well she performs her job role. Joseph Pleck argues that this means that the boundaries between work and family roles are therefore "asymmetrically permeable" for the two sexes (Pleck, 1977). That is, for a woman, family roles spill over into work life. She not only takes time off from her job when children are born, she stays home with a sick child, takes time off to go to a teacher's conference or a PTA meeting, and thinks about her family tasks during

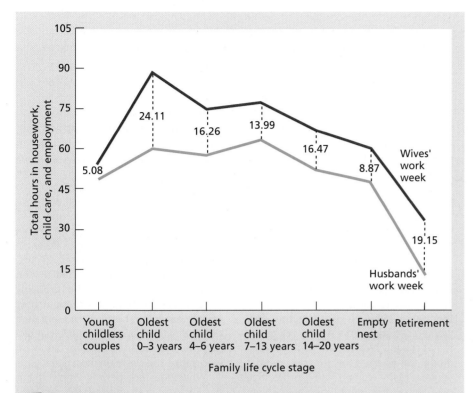

FIGURE 13.6

When both partners work full time, women still do more housework and child care, so their total work week is many hours longer—contributing significantly to women's greater sense of conflict between work and family roles. Note that the gap is greatest right after the birth of the first child—perhaps a time when the man is most likely to be intensely committed to his career. (*Source:* Rexroat & Shehan, 1987, Fig. 1, p. 746.)

her workday. Women view themselves as mothers and wives all day, even when they work. These simultaneous, competing demands are the very definition of role conflict. For men, work and family roles are more sequential than simultaneous. Men view themselves as workers during the day, husbands and fathers when they come home. If the two roles conflict for men, it is more likely to be the work role that spills over into family life than the other way around.

Not all the intersections of family and work roles are problematic for women. For example, working women have more power in their marriages or partnerships than do nonworking women (Blumstein & Schwartz, 1983; Spitze, 1988). The more equal the earnings of the partners, the more equality there is in decision making and in household work. But it remains true that the most striking single fact about work and family roles in this age of high women's employment is that women struggle more than men do to resolve the conflict between the two. It is also clear that this conflict is vastly greater during early adulthood, when children are young and need constant care, than it is in middle or later adult life. In many respects, it is this complex intersection of spousal, parental, and work roles that is the defining feature of early adult life in industrialized societies (see The Real World).

Critical Thinking

What plans do you have to combine work and family? Might your planning, or your thinking, change as a result of what you have read so far?

WORKING The Real World

Strategies for Coping with Conflict between Work and Family Life

Are you overwhelmed by the many competing demands of work and family? Are there some days when you despair? There is no magic formula for eliminating such conflict or distress, but there are some strategies that help. These suggestions are phrased as advice to women, because it is women who experience the greatest role conflict. But men can certainly profit from the same information.

The most helpful strategy overall is something psychologists call *cognitive restructuring*—recasting or reframing the situation for yourself in a way that identifies the positive elements. Cognitive restructuring might include reminding yourself that you had good reasons for choosing to have both a job and a family and recalling other times when you have coped successfully with similar problems (Paden & Buehler, 1995).

A related kind of restructuring involves redefining family roles. In several older studies, psychologists found that women who found ways to redistribute basic household tasks to other family members (husband and children) or who simply gave up doing some tasks, experienced less stress and conflict (Hall, 1972, 1975). You might make a list of all the household chores you and your partner do and go over the list together, eliminating whatever items you can and reassigning the others. Men can clean toilets; clutter can be dealt with less frequently (or not at all!); meals can perhaps be simpler. If economic resources are sufficient, help can also be hired.

You can also redefine the sex roles themselves. Where is it written that only women can stay home with a sick child? It is probably written in your internal model of yourself or in your gender schema. Many women find it difficult to give up such responsibilities, even when they cause severe role conflict, because such nurturing is part of their image of themselves. As one woman whose husband was very involved in the care of their infant said,

> I love seeing the closeness between him and the baby, especially since I didn't have that with my father, but if he does well at his work and his relationship with the baby, what's my special contribution? (Cowan & Cowan, 1987, p. 168)

It may be helpful to try to discover whether the current division of labor in your own household exists because others in the household don't do their share or because of your own inner resistance to changing your view of yourself and your basic contribution to the family unit.

Finally, you may find it helpful to take a class in time management. Research reveals that good planning can, in fact, reduce the sense of strain you feel (Paden & Buehler, 1995). You have probably already heard lots of advice about how to organize things better. Easier said than done! But there are techniques that can help, and many of these are taught in workshops and classes in most cities.

What does not help is simply trying harder to do it all yourself. Women who continue to try to fulfill several roles perfectly report maximum strain and stress. Something has to give, whether it is your standards for housework or your sense of your female role. Combining a number of roles is inherently full of opportunities for conflict. At best, you may manage a delicate balance. At worst, you will find yourself overwhelmed.

Before going on

● What factors influence a person's choice of occupation?

● How do the concepts of job satisfaction and the career ladder contribute to an understanding of how jobs change over time?

● Describe women's patterns of work and how they relate to on-the-job achievement and income. What are the potential conflicts among work and family roles, and how do they differ for men and women?

A Final Word

During the early adult years, people must take on more new roles than at any other age, and there are likely to be more life changes than in any other era. There is also the issue of timing. Being "off time," or out of sequence, in the adoption of any of the major roles of early adult life seems to exact some price. For example, young men and women who become parents in their teens necessarily experience a different life course in the early adult years (Murry, 1997; Nock, 1998). Further, because the descriptions of some adult roles are culturally determined, young adulthood is also the time when we are most defined by external criteria. We measure ourselves against these standards: "Am I a good mother?" and "Will I get a promotion?" Thus, the overarching theme of early adulthood has to do with measuring up to expectations. The challenge is to do so in a way that balances personal needs against social demands.

Summary

Theories of Social and Personality Development

- Erikson proposed that young adults face the crisis of intimacy versus isolation. Those who fail to establish a stable relationship with an intimate partner or a network of friends become socially isolated.

- Levinson hypothesized that adult development involves alternating periods of stability and instability, through which adults construct and refine life structures.

- Evolutionary theories of mate selection suggest that sex differences in mate preferences and mating behavior are the result of natural selection.

- Social role theory emphasize factors such as gender roles, similarity, and economic exchange in explaining sex differences in mating.

Intimate Relationships

- Internal models of attachment are related to assumptions about others and the quality of relationships created in early adulthood. Sternberg's model of love is also influential. He posited three elements: intimacy, passion, and commitment. These three may combine to produce eight varieties of love.

- The quality of a committed partnership—marriage or long-term cohabitation—tends to decline in the first year as the rate of positive interactions drops. Those who enter into a relationship with good resources (education, problem-solving ability, etc.) and who create positive

communication strategies are more likely to enjoy enduring relationships and to avoid divorce or separation.

- Married adults are generally happier and healthier than singles. However, psychologists believe that it is relationship quality, rather than marriage itself, that is associated with both mental and physical health.

- Divorced young adults experience more loneliness and depression, and divorced women are more likely to be poor. Divorce and remarriage may also influence the developmental pathway of early adulthood by increasing the years devoted to child-rearing and complicating family roles.

Parenthood and Other Relationships

- Most men and women want to become parents, because they view raising children as a life-enriching experience.

- The transition to parenthood is stressful and leads to a decline in relationship satisfaction. Factors such as the division of labor between mother and father, individual personality traits, and the availability of help from extended family members contribute to relationship satisfaction.

- Young adults' relationships with their parents tend to be steady and supportive, even if less central than they were at earlier ages. The quality of attachment to parents continues to predict a number of important variables in early adulthood.

- Each young adult creates a network of relationships with friends as well as with a partner and family members.

The Role of Worker

- The specific job or career a young adult chooses is affected by his or her education, intelligence, family background and resources, family values, personality, and gender. The majority of adults choose jobs that fit the cultural norms for their social class and gender. More intelligent young people, and those with more education, are more upwardly mobile.

- Job satisfaction rises steadily throughout early adulthood, in part because the jobs typically available to young adults are less well paid, more repetitive, less creative, and allow the worker very little power or influence. The work role has two stages in early adulthood: a trial stage, in which alternative pathways are explored, and an establishment stage, in which the career path is established.

- For most women, the work role includes an additional "in-and-out" stage, in which periods of focusing on family responsibilities alternate with periods of employment. The more continuous a woman's work history, the more successful she is likely to be at her job.

- When both partners work, the family responsibilities are not equally divided: Women continue to perform more work in the home and feel more role conflict.

Key Terms

assortative mating (homogamy) (p. 376)

avoidant couples (p. 379)

career ladder (p. 392)

hostile/detached couples (p. 379)

hostile/engaged couples (p. 379)

intimacy (p. 372)

intimacy versus isolation (p. 372)

kin-keeper (p. 389)

life structure (p. 372)

parental investment theory (p. 374)

social role theory (p. 375)

validating couples (p. 379)

volatile couples (p. 379)

CHAPTER

14

Physical and Cognitive Development in Middle Adulthood

Kathy Ferguson, PhotoEdit

The great baseball player Satchel Paige, who was still pitching in the major leagues at age 62, once said, "Age is mind over matter. If you don't mind, it doesn't matter."

It's a nice summary of the physical changes of the middle years. Yes, there are changes. Memory does get less efficient in some situations in mid-life; vision and hearing get worse; people slow down slightly and become somewhat weaker. But among adults who are otherwise healthy, the amount of loss is far less than folklore would have us believe. Further, along with obvious losses come important gains. Indeed, although early adulthood may be the physical high point of adulthood, there is a great deal of evidence that middle adulthood is the intellectual and creative peak.

In this chapter you will learn that, with advancing age, the story of human development seems to become more an account of differences than a description of universals. This happens because there are so many factors—behavioral choices, poor health, and so on—that determine the specific developmental pathway an adult follows. Most middle-aged adults are healthy, energetic, and intellectually productive, but others are in decline. Moreover, because developmental psychology has focused more on younger individuals, there simply isn't as much knowledge about universal changes in adulthood. As you read this chapter, keep the following questions in mind:

- How do the nervous system, reproductive system, and other body systems change between age 40 and age 60?

- What are the major issues of physical and mental health in middle adulthood?

- In what ways does cognitive function improve and/or decline?

Physical Changes

For a quick overview of the common physical changes of middle age, take another look at Table 12.1 (page 345), which summarizes most of the evidence. Changes or declines in many physical functions occur very gradually through the 40s and 50s. For a few physical functions, however, change or decline is already substantial in the middle adult years.

The Brain and Nervous System

Relatively little is known about the normal, undamaged brains of middle-aged adults. This is because research has focused on changes associated with trauma and disease rather than changes due to primary aging. However, it is possible to make a few general statements.

After a period of stability across adolescence and the first decade of early adulthood, synaptic density begins to decline around age 30 (Huttenlocher, 1994). The decline continues throughout middle adulthood and the later years and is accompanied by decreases in brain weight. However, it's important to note that new synapses are continuing to form in middle age. Earlier in life, though, new synapses form more rapidly or at the same rate as old connections are lost. In middle age, it appears, more synapses are lost than are formed. The effect of the loss of synaptic density on brain function has yet to be determined.

In addition, developmentalists know that behavioral choices and mental health affect the adult brain. For example, alcoholics and nonalcoholics differ in the distribution of electrical activity in the brain (Duffy, 1994). The brains of depressed and nondepressed adults differ as well. Further, a number of serious mental illnesses, such as schizophrenia, are associated with structural variations in the brain. What researchers don't know yet is whether the brains of alcoholics, depressed persons, or schizophrenics were different from others before the onset of their difficulties. The longitudinal research necessary to answer such questions hasn't yet been done.

Besides studying the effects of trauma and disease, neuropsychologists are also involved in investigating a very important issue in the study of aging—whether declines in cognitive functions are caused by a loss of neurological processing resources. To find out, researchers examine how the brains of young and middle-aged people respond to cognitive tasks. Such studies have produced a rather complex set of findings.

One fairly consistent finding is that cognitive tasks activate a larger area of brain tissue in middle-aged adults than they do in younger adults (Gunter, Jackson, & Mulder, 1998). Of course, neuropsychologists don't know why, but they speculate that cognitive processing in middle-aged adults is less selective than it is in younger adults. It's as if the middle-aged brain has a more difficult time finding just the right neurological tool to carry out a particular function, and so it activates more tools than are necessary. This lack of selectivity could account for differences between age groups in the speed at which cognitive tasks are carried out.

One way of examining this hypothesis is to see if it explains individual differences as well as age variation. Typically, when middle-aged and young adults are compared, the range of individual differences within each age group is far greater than the average difference between the two age groups. Researchers find that in participants in both age groups who perform poorly on tasks such as remembering lists of associated words (*table-chair*) or nonassociated words (*knife-car*), larger areas of the brain are activated than in those who perform well.

In addition, the brains of high performers are more sensitive to different kinds of tasks. For example, recalling nonassociated words requires a larger area of activation (more neurological tools) than recalling associated words, because nonassociated words are more difficult to memorize. The more difficult task activates more of the brain than the easy one does in all adults. But in both young and middle-aged high performers, the difference in brain activation on difficult and easy tasks is much greater.

The brains of middle-aged and younger adults also respond differently to sensory stimuli. For example, patterns of brain waves in different areas vary across age groups when participants are presented with a simple auditory stimulus such as a musical tone (Yordanova, Kolev, & Basar, 1998). Research along this line has suggested that middle-aged adults may have less ability to control attention processes by inhibiting brain responses to irrelevant stimuli (Amenedo & Diaz, 1998, 1999). Their difficulty with attentional control could be another reason for the average difference in processing speed between young and middle-aged adults.

Such findings might lead you to conclude that, in everyday situations requiring intense concentration and rapid judgments, middle-aged adults would perform more poorly than their younger counterparts. Interestingly, though, recent research on lapses of concentration and poor decision-making among drivers shows just the opposite (Dobson, Brown, Ball, Powers, & McFadden, 1999). Younger drivers exhibit more lapses in attention and driving errors than middle-aged drivers. These lapses and errors, combined with younger drivers' greater likelihood of driving after drinking alcohol, help account for the different accident rates of young and middle-aged adults. Such findings, when considered with those on age differences in brain function, illustrate the difficulty researchers face in finding direct relationships between age-related brain differences and cross-age variations in behavior.

The Reproductive System

If you were asked to name a single significant physical change occurring in the years of middle adulthood, chances are you'd say *menopause*—especially if you're a woman. The more general term is the **climacteric**, which refers to the years of middle or late

climacteric the term used to describe the adult period during which reproductive capacity declines or is lost adulthood in both men and women during which reproductive capacity declines or is lost.

● *Male Climacteric* ● In men, the climacteric is extremely gradual, with a slow loss of reproductive capacity, although the rate of change varies widely from one man to the next, and there are documented cases of men in their 90s fathering children. On average, the quantity of viable sperm produced declines slightly, beginning perhaps at about age 40. The testes also shrink very gradually, and the volume of seminal fluid declines after about age 60.

The causal factor is most likely a very slow drop in testosterone levels, beginning in early adulthood and continuing well into old age. There has been some disagreement among researchers about whether such a decline actually occurs; some longitudinal studies among healthy adults have shown no such decline (e.g., Harman & Tsitouras, 1980). But the weight of the evidence seems to point to a small, very gradual, average decline in testosterone over the adult years, with wide variation from one man to the next in normal hormone levels (Tsitouras & Bulat, 1995).

This decline in testosterone is implicated in the gradual loss of muscle tissue (and hence strength) that becomes evident in the middle and later years, as well as in the increased risk of heart disease in middle and old age. It also appears to affect sexual function. In particular, in the middle years, the incidence of impotence begins to increase—although many things other than the slight decline in testosterone contribute to this change, including an increased incidence of poor health, especially heart disease, use of blood pressure medication (and other medications), alcohol abuse, and smoking.

The most complete information about impotence in mid-life comes from a study in Boston involving 1,290 men between the ages of 40 and 90 (Feldman, Goldstein, Hatzichristou, Krane, & McKinlay, 1994). Each man completed a questionnaire about the frequency and duration of his erections and rated himself as having no impotence or minimal, moderate, or complete impotence. Those describing themselves as minimally impotent reported some problems achieving and/or maintaining erections, although most of these men did still have active sex lives. Those describing themselves as moderately impotent had more significant difficulties, but most also reported that they had intercourse at least occasionally. Researchers noted an increase in both categories of impotence during the middle years, a finding replicated in other studies (Keil, Sutherland, Knapp, Waid, & Gazes, 1992). Overall, though, a clear majority of men in the Boston study reported that they were experiencing either no impotence or only a minimal degree of impotence.

● *Menopause* ● Declines in key sex hormones are also clearly implicated in the set of changes in women called **menopause**, which means literally the cessation of the menses. You'll remember from Chapter 10 that secretion of several forms of estrogen by the ovaries increases rapidly during puberty, triggering the onset of menstruation as well as stimulating the development of breasts and secondary sex characteristics. In the adult woman, estrogen levels are high during the first 14 days of the menstrual cycle, stimulating the release of an ovum and the preparation of the uterus for possible implantation. *Progesterone*, which is secreted by the ruptured ovarian follicle from which the ovum emerges, rises during the second half of the menstrual cycle and stimulates the sloughing off of accumulated material in the uterus each month if conception has not occurred.

The average age of menopause for both African American and white American women, and for women in other countries for which data are available, is roughly age 50; anything between age 40 and 60 is considered within the normal range (Bellantoni & Blackman, 1996). About 1 woman in 12 experiences menopause before the age of 40, referred to by physicians as *premature menopause* (Wich & Carnes, 1995).

menopause the cessation of monthly menstrual cycles in middle-aged women

● *Menopausal Phases* ●   Menopause, like puberty, is often thought of as a single event. However, it actually occurs over several years, and researchers generally agree that it consists of three phases. First, during the **premenopausal phase**, estrogen levels begin to fluctuate and decline, typically in the late 30s or early 40s, producing irregular menstrual periods in many women. The ovaries are less sensitive to cyclical hormonal signals, and many women experience *anovulatory cycles*, or cycles in which no ovum is released. Even though no ovum is produced, estrogen levels are high enough in premenopausal women to produce periodic bleeding. However, the lack of ovulation results in a dramatic drop in progesterone. Thus, many experts believe that the menstrual irregularity associated with the premenopausal period is due to progesterone loss rather than estrogen loss (Lee, 1996).

During the **perimenopausal phase**, estrogen levels decrease and women experience more extreme variations in the timing of their menstrual cycles. In addition, about 75% of perimenopausal women experience *hot flashes*, sudden sensations of feeling hot. Of those who have hot flashes, 85% will have them for more than a year; a third or more will have them for 5 years or more (Kletzky & Borenstein, 1987). It is hypothesized that fluctuating levels of estrogen and other hormones cause a woman's blood vessels to expand and contract erratically, thus producing hot flashes (see No Easy Answers).

During a hot flash, the temperature of the skin can rise as much as 1–7 degrees in some parts of the body, although the core body temperature actually drops (Kronenberg, 1994). Hot flashes last, on average, about 3 minutes and may recur as seldom as daily or as often as three times per hour (Bellantoni & Blackman, 1996). Most women learn to manage these brief periods of discomfort if they occur during the day. However, hot flashes frequently disrupt women's sleep. When this happens, it sets in motion a series of changes that are actually due to sleep deprivation rather than menopause. For example, lack of sleep can lead to mental confusion, difficulty with everyday memory tasks, and emotional instability. Thus, perimenopausal women may have the subjective feeling that they are "going crazy" when the real problem is that hot flashes are preventing them from getting enough sleep. The general light-headedness and shakiness that accompany some women's hot flashes can add to this sensation.

Eventually, estrogen and progesterone drop to consistently low levels and menstruation ceases altogether. Once a women has ceased to menstruate for a year, she is in the **postmenopausal phase**. In postmenopausal women, estradiol and estrone, both types of estrogen, drop to about a quarter or less of their premenopausal levels. Progesterone decreases even more, as a result of the cessation of ovulation, although the adrenal glands continue to provide postmenopausal women with some progesterone.

The reduction in estrogen during the perimenopausal and postmenopausal phases also has effects on genital and other tissue. The breasts become less firm, the genitals and the uterus shrink somewhat, and the vagina becomes both shorter and smaller in diameter. The walls of the vagina also become somewhat thinner and less elastic and produce less lubrication during intercourse (McCoy, 1998; Wich & Carnes, 1995).

● *Psychological Effects of Menopause* ●   One other aspect of the climacteric in women deserves some mention. It has been part of folklore for a very long time that menopause involves major emotional upheaval as well as clear physical changes. Women were presumed to be emotionally volatile, angry, depressed, even shrewish during these mid-life years. Studies have shown that, in accordance with this myth, women are likely to view menopausal moods and behavior as being beyond their control (Lawlor & Choi, 1998; Poole, 1998). However, the available evidence contradicts this myth.

Four relevant, well-designed longitudinal studies, three in the United States and one in Sweden, have examined this aspect of menopause. In the largest and most recent of these studies, researchers followed a group of 3,049 women aged 40 to 60

premenopausal phase the stage of menopause during which estrogen levels fall somewhat, menstrual periods are less regular, and anovulatory cycles begin to occur

perimenopausal phase the stage of menopause during which estrogen and progesterone levels are erratic, menstrual cycles may be very irregular, and women begin to experience symptoms such as hot flashes

postmenopausal phase the last stage of menopause; a woman is postmenopausal when she has had no menstrual periods for a year or more

No Easy Answers

The Pros and Cons of Hormone Replacement Therapy

Most of the physical symptoms and effects of menopause—including hot flashes, thinning of the vaginal wall, and loss of vaginal lubrication—can be dramatically reduced by taking estrogen and progesterone. Moreover, hormone replacement is associated with a reduction in mood swings in menopausal women (Klaiber, Broverman, Vogel, Peterson, & Snyder, 1997). However, researchers have found that women are very poorly informed about both menopause itself and the potential risks and benefits of hormone replacement therapy. Apparently, unlike women in nonindustrialized societies, who rely on older women for information, women in the industrialized world rely on drug manufacturers' advertisements on television and in women's magazines for information about menopause (Berg & Lipson, 1999; Clinkingbeard, Minton, Davis, & McDermott, 1999; Whittaker, 1998). Analyses of these sources of information have shown that they contain more misleading than helpful information (Gannon & Stevens, 1998). Thus, a woman who wants to make an informed decision about alternatives for dealing with the effects of menopause has to look beyond these information sources.

Hormone replacement therapy has had a somewhat checkered history. In the 1950s and 1960s, estrogen therapy became extremely common. In some surveys, as many as half of all postmenopausal women in the United States reported using replacement estrogen, many of them over periods of 10 years or more (Stadel & Weiss, 1975). In the 1970s, however, new evidence showed that the risk of endometrial cancer (cancer of the lining of the uterus) increased

threefold to tenfold in women taking replacement estrogen (Nathanson & Lorenz, 1982). Not surprisingly, when this information became public, the use of estrogen therapy dropped dramatically.

The third act in this drama was the discovery that a combination of estrogen and progesterone, at quite low dosages, had the same benefits as estrogen alone and eliminated the increased risk of endometrial cancer. Furthermore, new studies also made clear that the use of replacement estrogen has two additional benefits: It reduces the risk of coronary heart disease by about half, and it significantly retards the bone loss of osteoporosis (Barrett-Connor & Bush, 1991; Ross, Paganini-Hill, Mack, & Henderson, 1987). New research reveals that both of these benefits occur with the newer estrogen-progesterone combinations as well as with estrogen alone (e.g., Cauley et al., 1995; Stampfer et al., 1991; Working Group for the PEPI Trial, 1995).

This sounds almost too good to be true, doesn't it? Why shouldn't every postmenopausal woman be on a program of hormone replacement? There are two counterarguments: First, many women consider the process of aging, including the changes of menopause, to be natural physical processes with which they do not want to tinker. Second, although scientists have evidence that hormone replacement therapy is linked to slightly lower overall cancer risks, some studies have found that it is associated with somewhat higher rates of breast cancer and very slightly higher rates of ovarian cancer (Posthuma, Westendorp, & Vandenbroucke, 1994). When such increases are found—and not every study has found them (e.g., Newcomb et al., 1995)—the increases are not large. In the Nurses' Health Study (which you read about in Chapter 12), researchers found

that for every woman diagnosed with breast cancer who did *not* take replacement hormones, there were roughly 1.4 cases of breast cancer diagnosed among women who did use hormone therapy (Colditz et al., 1995). The equivalent comparison for ovarian cancers, drawn from another study (Rodriguez et al., 1995), was 1.0 case of ovarian cancer in women who did not take hormones and 1.15 cases in women who did.

Added to the debate about whether women should replace hormones or not is a controversy over synthetic and natural hormones. Advocates of natural hormone replacement therapy argue that synthetic estrogen and progesterone contain components that cause a variety of unpleasant side effects and increase the risk of breast and ovarian cancers (Lee, 1996). They claim that natural hormones, those derived from plant sources such as soy and wild yams, are more compatible with the human body and neither create side effects nor increase cancer risk. The research is still limited, but there are a few studies suggesting that natural hormone replacement may be a viable alternative (Lee, 1996).

How can an individual woman add up these various benefits and risks? How does she weigh a halved risk of heart disease against a 40% increased risk of breast cancer? Should she take synthetic or natural hormones? Among other things, a woman should consider not only her present discomfort but her overall risk of heart disease and cancer (heart disease is actually the larger overall risk in the years of middle and late adulthood) including her family history of these diseases. Above all, a woman entering menopause should commit herself to seeking information beyond what can be learned from television and women's magazines.

over a 10-year period (Busch et al., 1994). None of the studies reported any connection between menopausal status and a rise in depression or other psychological symptoms (Busch, Zonderman, & Costa, 1994; Hallstrom & Samuelsson, 1985; Matthews et al., 1990; McKinlay, McKinlay, & Brambilla, 1987). Subsequent studies have produced similar findings (Slaven & Lee, 1998).

What does seem to be associated with moods and social functioning during menopause is, among other things, a woman's overall negativity and number of life stressors before entering menopause (Dennerstein, Lehert, Burger, & Dudley, 1999; Woods & Mitchell, 1997). In other words, a woman's negativity may be attributed to menopause when, in reality, it may be a long-standing component of her personality. Alternatively, she may have a particularly stressful life, and menopausal symptoms are just one more source of difficulty.

Critical Thinking

What is your own view of menopause? How much has your view been influenced by negative stereotypes of menopausal women in the media?

In addition, the actual level of symptoms women experience makes a difference. It isn't surprising that women who are most uncomfortable because of hot flashes and other physical changes, and whose symptoms last the longest, experience the most depression and negative mood. At any rate, research suggests that once they reach the postmenopausal phase, these women's dispositions change.

Cultural factors also influence the menopause experience. In contrast to U.S. culture, there are many societies in which menopause is viewed positively (McMaster, Pitts, & Poyah, 1997). For women in such cultures, pregnancy and childbearing continue to be major threats to health. Thus, with concerns about conception behind them, women in these societies report few menopausal symptoms and generally positive attitudes toward this change. In contrast, women in the United States view menopause as a cardinal sign that one's youth has ended, and they often confuse symptoms of menopause with normal consequences of aging (Jones, 1997). For example, they may think that wrinkled skin is caused by menopause. Thus, research has demonstrated that the more women know about menopause, the less negatively they view it (Hunter & O'Dea, 1999; Liao & Hunter, 1998).

● ***Sexual Activity*** ●   Despite changes in the reproductive system, the great majority of middle-aged adults remain sexually active, although the frequency of sex declines somewhat during these years (Laumann, Gagnon, Michael, & Michaels, 1994; Michael, Gagnon, Laumann, & Kolata, 1994). It is unlikely that this decline during mid-life is due wholly or even largely to drops in sex hormone levels; women do not experience major estrogen declines until their late 40s, but the decline in sexual activity begins much sooner. And the drop in testosterone among men is so gradual and slight during these years that it cannot be the full explanation. An alternative explanation is that the demands of other roles are simply so pressing that middle-aged adults find it hard to find time for sex.

The Skeletal System

Another change that begins to be quite significant in middle adulthood is a loss of calcium from the bones, resulting in reduced bone mass and more brittle and porous bones. This process is called **osteoporosis**. Bone loss begins at about age 30 for both men and women, but in women the process is accelerated by menopause. The major consequence of this loss of bone density is a significantly increased risk of fractures, beginning as early as age 50 for women, much later for men. In the United States, it is estimated that almost one in four women will experience a hip fracture before the age of 80 (Lindsay, 1985). Among older women (and men), such fractures can be a major cause of disability and reduced activity, so osteoporosis is not a trivial change.

In women, it is clear that bone loss is linked quite directly to estrogen and progesterone levels. Researchers know that these hormones fall dramatically after menopause, and it is the timing of menopause rather than age that signals the increase in rate of bone loss. Researchers also know that the rate of bone loss drops

osteoporosis loss of bone mass with age, resulting in more brittle and porous bones

TABLE 14.1   Risk Factors for Osteoporosis

Risk Factor	Explanation
Race	Whites are at higher risk than other races.
Gender	Women have considerably higher risk than men.
Weight	Those who are underweight are at higher risk.
Timing of climacteric	Women who experience early menopause and those who have had their ovaries removed are at higher risk, presumably because their estrogen levels decline at earlier ages.
Family history	Those with a family history of osteoporosis are at higher risk.
Diet	A diet low in calcium during adolescence and early adulthood results in lower peak levels of bone mass, and hence greater risk of falling below critical levels later. Whether there is any benefit in increasing intake of calcium postmenopausally remains in debate. Diets high in either caffeine (especially black coffee) or alcohol are also linked to higher risk.
Exercise	Those with a sedentary lifestyle are at higher risk. Prolonged immobility, such as bed rest, also increases the rate of bone loss. Exercise reduces the rate of bone loss.

(*Sources:* Dalsky et al., 1988; Duursma et al., 1991; Gambert, Schultz, & Hamdy, 1995; Goldberg & Hagberg, 1990; Gordon & Vaughan, 1986; Lindsay, 1985; Morrison et al., 1994; Smith, 1982.)

Any weight-bearing exercise—even walking—will help prevent osteoporosis. (*Photo:* David Madison, Stone)

presbyopia normal loss of visual acuity with aging, especially the ability to focus the eyes on near objects

to premenopausal levels among women who take replacement hormones, all of which makes the link quite clear (Duursma, Raymakers, Boereboom, & Scheven, 1991). While the overall pattern of bone loss seems to be a part of primary aging, the amount of such loss nonetheless varies quite a lot from one individual to another. Table 14.1 lists the known risk factors for osteoporosis.

Aside from taking replacement hormones, women can help prevent osteoporosis by one or both of two strategies. First, they can get enough calcium during early adulthood, so that peak levels of bone mass are as robust as possible. Second, throughout adult life women can get regular exercise, particularly weight-bearing exercise such as walking or strength training. In one study, postmenopausal women who began a program of walking, jogging, or stair climbing for 1 hour three times a week showed an increase in bone mineral content of 5.2% within 9 months, compared with a loss of 1.4% in the nonexercising comparison group (Dalsky et al., 1988). But this benefit faded if the exercise was not maintained. In another study, a group of middle-aged or older women were randomly assigned to a strength-training program consisting of twice-weekly sessions for a year. They showed a gain in bone density over the year, whereas women in a control group without such weight training showed a loss (Nelson et al., 1994).

Vision and Hearing

One of the most noticeable physical changes occurring in the middle years is a loss of visual acuity. Most people find that they need reading glasses or bifocals by the time they are 45 or 50. Two changes in the eyes, collectively called **presbyopia**, are involved. First, the lens of the eye thickens. In a process that begins in childhood but produces noticeable effects only in middle adulthood, layer after layer of slightly pigmented material accumulates on the lens. Because light coming into the eye must pass through this thickened, slightly yellowed material, the total light reaching the retina decreases, which reduces a person's overall sensitivity to light waves, particularly to short wavelengths that are perceived as blue, blue-green, and violet (Fozard, 1990).

Because of this thickening of the lens, it is also harder and harder for the muscles surrounding the eye to change the shape of the lens to adjust the focus. In a young eye, the shape of the lens readily adjusts for distance, so no matter how near or far away some object may be, the light rays passing through the eye converge where they should, on the retina in the back of the eye, giving a sharp image. But as the thickening increases, the elasticity of the lens declines and it can no longer make these fine adjustments. Many images become blurry. In particular, the ability to focus clearly on near objects deteriorates rapidly in the 40s and early 50s. As a result, middle-aged adults often hold books and other items farther and farther away, because only in that way can they get a clear image. Finally, of course, they cannot read print at the distance at which they can focus, and they are forced to wear reading glasses or bifocals. These same changes also affect the ability to adapt quickly to variations in levels of light or glare, such as from passing headlights when driving at night or in the rain. So driving may become more stressful. All in all, these changes in the eyes, which appear to be a genuine part of primary aging, require both physical and psychological adjustment.

The equivalent process in hearing is called **presbycusis**. The auditory nerves and the structures of the inner ear gradually degenerate as a result of basic wear and tear, resulting primarily in losses in the ability to hear sounds of high and very low frequencies. But these changes do not accumulate to the level of significant hearing loss until somewhat later in life than is typical for presbyopia. Hearing loss is quite slow until about age 50, and only a small percentage of middle-aged adults require hearing aids (Fozard, 1990). After age 50 or 55, however, the rate of hearing loss accelerates. Such a pattern of loss also appears to be an aspect of primary aging. But some secondary aging processes are involved as well. In particular, the amount of hearing loss is considerably greater in adults who work or live in very noisy environments—or who listen regularly to very loud music (Baltes, Reese, & Nesselroade, 1977).

By age 45 or 50, nearly everyone needs glasses, especially for reading. (*Photo:* Myrleen Ferguson Cate, PhotoEdit)

Before going on

- What do researchers know about brain function in middle age?
- How does reproductive function change in men and women in middle age?
- What is osteoporosis, and what factors are associated with it?
- How do vision and hearing change in middle ages?

Health and Wellness

No single variable affects the quality of life in middle and late adulthood as much as health. A middle-aged person in good health often functions as well and has as much energy as much younger adults. However, mid-life is the era during which the poor health habits and risky behaviors of earlier years begin to catch up with us.

presbycusis normal loss of hearing with aging, especially of high-frequency tones

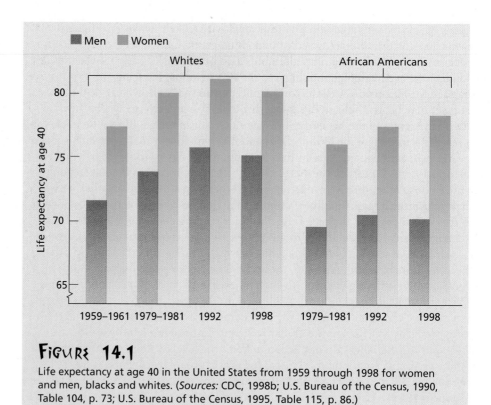

Figure 14.1

Life expectancy at age 40 in the United States from 1959 through 1998 for women and men, blacks and whites. (*Sources:* CDC, 1998b; U.S. Bureau of the Census, 1990, Table 104, p. 73; U.S. Bureau of the Census, 1995, Table 115, p. 86.)

Health Trends at Mid-Life

In general, middle-aged adults report that they experience annoying aches and pains with greater frequency than when they were younger (Helme, 1998). Moreover, many middle-aged adults, especially women, are unhappy with their bodies; most would prefer to be thinner (Allaz, Bernstein, Rouget, Archinard, & Morabia, 1998). In addition, the number of truly healthy adults declines in mid-life. Perhaps half of adults between 40 and 65 have either some diagnosed disease or disability or a significant but undiagnosed problem, such as the early stages of heart disease. Still, 40-year-olds' life expectancy is remarkably high, as you can see from Figure 14.1, and has been rising over the past few decades (Centers for Disease Control [CDC], 1998b; U.S. Bureau of the Census, 1990; U.S. Bureau of the Census, 1995). However, middle-aged adults have more chronic diseases and disabilities such as diabetes and arthritis, than those who are younger (CDC, 1998a; U.S. Bureau of the Census, 1992). Similarly, disease-related death rates increase significantly in middle adulthood, as you can see from Figure 14.2. The two leading causes of death in middle age are heart disease and cancer.

Cardiovascular Disease

The term **cardiovascular disease (CVD)** covers a variety of physical problems, but the key problem is in the arteries. In individuals suffering from CVD, the arteries become clogged with *plaque* (a fibrous or fatty substance), in a process called **atherosclerosis.** Eventually, vital arteries may become completely blocked, producing what laypeople call a heart attack (if the blockage is in the coronary arteries) or a stroke (if the blockage is in the brain). Atherosclerosis is not a normal part of aging. It is a disease, increasingly common with age, but not inevitable.

The rate of CVD has been dropping rapidly in the United States and in most other industrialized countries in recent years. Between 1973 and 1987, for example,

cardiovascular disease (CVD) a set of disease processes in the heart and circulatory system

atherosclerosis narrowing of the arteries caused by deposits of a fatty substance called plaque

it decreased 42% among those under age 55 and dropped by a third for those aged 55 to 84—fairly startling declines that have contributed greatly to the increased life expectancy among today's adults (Davis, Dinse, & Hoel, 1994). During the 1990s, CVD declined another 20% among adults of all ages (U.S. Department of Health and Human Services, 1998b). Yet CVD remains the leading cause of death among adults in the United States and throughout the developed world. In fact, in the United States, heart disease causes more deaths than all other diseases combined (U.S. Department of Health and Human Services, 1998b).

The best information about who is at risk for CVD comes from a number of long-term epidemiological studies, such as the Framingham study or the Nurses' Health Study, in which the health and habits of large numbers of individuals have been tracked over time. In the Framingham study, 5,209 adults were first studied in 1948, when they were aged 30 to 59. Their health (and mortality) has since been assessed repeatedly, which makes it possible to identify characteristics that predict CVD (Anderson, Castelli, & Levy, 1987; Dawber, Kannel, & Lyell, 1963; Garrison, Gold, Wilson, & Kannel, 1993; Kannel & Gordon, 1980). More recent studies continue to suggest the same risk factors (U.S. Department of Health and Human Services, 1998b). The left side of Table 14.2 (page 410) lists the well-established risk factors that emerged from the Framingham study and similar studies, along with a few other risk factors that are more speculative.

Because lists like the one in Table 14.2 have appeared in numerous popular magazines and newspapers, there's not likely to be much that is news here, but there are still a few important points to be made. First, the great majority of Americans have at least one of these risk factors. The Centers for Disease Control found that out of more than 91,000 adults they interviewed in 1992, only 12.6% of men and 17.9% of women between 35 and 49 had none of the controllable risk factors for CVD (smoking, overweight, inactivity, high blood pressure, high cholesterol, and diabetes) (CDC, 1994f). In the 50- to 64-year-old group, even fewer people (9.4% of men and 11.6% of women) showed no risk factors. So, although rates of both smoking and high cholesterol have declined since the significance of these two risk factors became widely publicized, most Americans could still do a much better job of reducing their heart disease risks.

Second, it is important to understand that these risks are cumulative in the same way that the health habits investigated in the Alameda County study seem to be cumulative: The more high-risk behaviors or characteristics you have, the higher your risk of heart disease; the effect is not just additive. For example, high cholesterol is three times more serious in a heavy smoker than in a nonsmoker (Tunstall-Pedoe & Smith, 1990).

Personality may also contribute to heart disease. The **type A personality pattern** was first described by two cardiologists, Meyer Friedman and Ray Rosenman (1974; Rosenman & Friedman, 1983). They were struck by the apparently consistent presence among patients who suffered from heart disease of several other characteristics, including competitive striving for achievement, a sense of time urgency, and hostility or aggressiveness. These people, whom Friedman and Rosenman named type A personalities, were perpetually comparing themselves to others, always wanting to win. They scheduled their lives tightly, timed themselves in routine activities, and often

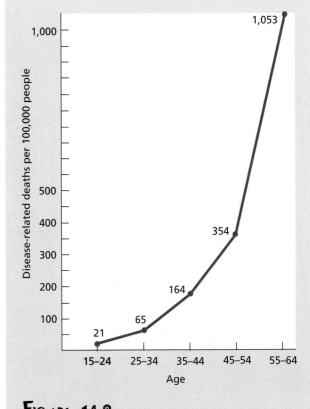

Figure 14.2

In the United States, disease-related deaths become increasingly common during middle adulthood. (*Source*: NCHS, 1997.)

Critical Thinking

How many of the risk factors in Table 14.2 apply to you?

type A personality pattern a personality type associated with greater risk of coronary heart disease; it includes competitive achievement striving, a sense of time urgency, and, sometimes, hostility or aggressiveness

TABLE 14.2 Risk Factors for Heart Disease and Cancer

Risk	Heart Disease	Cancer
Smoking	Major risk; the more you smoke, the greater the risk. Quitting smoking reduces risk.	Substantially increases the risk lung cancer; also implicated in other cancers
Blood pressure	Systolic pressure above 140 or diastolic pressure above 90 linked to higher risk	No known risk
Weight	Some increased risk with any weight above the normal range; risk is greater for those with weight 20% or more above recommended amount.	Being overweight is linked to increased risk of several cancers, including breast cancer, but the risk is smaller than for heart disease.
Cholesterol	Clear risk with elevated levels of low-density lipoproteins	No known risk
Inactivity	Inactive adults have about twice the risk as those who exercise.	Inactivity is associated in some studies with higher rates of colon cancer.
Diet	High-fat, low-fiber diet increases risk; antioxidants such as Vitamin E, Vitamin C, or beta-carotene, may decrease risk.	Results are still unclear; a high-fat diet is linked to risks of some cancers; high-fiber diets appear to be protective for some cancers.
Alcohol	Moderate intake of alcohol, especially wine, linked to decreased CVD risk. Heavy drinking can weaken the heart muscle.	Heavy drinking is associated with cancers of the digestive system.
Heredity	Those with first-degree relatives with CVD have seven to ten times the risk; those who inherit a gene for a particular protein are up to twice as likely to have CVD.	Some genetic component with nearly every cancer

(*Sources:* Centers for Disease Control, 1994f; Gaziano & Hennekens, 1995; Hunter et al., 1996; Lee, Manson, Hennekens, & Paffenbarger, 1993; Manson et al., 1995; Morris, Kritchevsky, & Davis, 1994; Rich-Edwards, Manson, Hennekens, & Buring, 1995; Risch, Jain, Marrett, & Howe, 1994; Rose, 1993; Stampfer et al., 1993; Willett et al., 1992, 1995; Woodward & Tunstall-Pedoe, 1995.)

tried to do such tasks faster each time. They had frequent conflicts with their co-workers and family. Type B people, in contrast, were thought to be less hurried, more laid back, less competitive, and less hostile.

Early research by Friedman and Rosenman suggested that type A behavior was linked to higher levels of cholesterol, and hence to increased risk of CVD, even among people who did not suffer from observable heart disease. Contradictory results from more extensive studies since then, however, have forced some modifications in the original hypothesis (e.g., Miller, Turner, Tindale, Posavac, & Dugoni, 1991; O'Connor, Manson, O'Connor, & Buring, 1995).

For one thing, not all facets of the type A personality, as originally described, seem to be equally significant for CVD. The most consistent link has been found between CVD and hostility; hard-driving competitiveness is less consistently linked to CVD. Time pressure is not consistently related to CVD at all (Friedman, Hawley, & Tucker, 1994; Miller, Smith, Turner, Guijarro, & Hallet, 1996; Siegel, 1992).

What is more, for individuals who are already at high risk of CVD—because of smoking, high blood pressure, or the like—information about levels of hostility does not add to the accuracy of heart disease predictions. That is, if two adults each have high blood pressure and high cholesterol, they are both equally at risk of heart disease, even if one of them also displays high levels of hostility and the other does not. It is only among people who do not show other risk factors that measures of hostility add helpful information to the prediction. The effect is fairly small, but in large samples of otherwise low-risk adults, those who are hostile and competitive are slightly more likely to develop CVD than those who are more easygoing.

Most people who have analyzed this research would now agree that there is some kind of connection between personality and CVD. What is less clear is just which aspect(s) of personality are most strongly predictive. Some research suggests that measures of neuroticism or depression may be even better risk predictors than hostility (e.g., Cramer, 1991).

Cancer

The second leading cause of death in middle and old age (in industrialized countries, at least) is cancer. In middle-aged men, the likelihood of dying of either heart disease or cancer is about equal. Among middle-aged women, though, cancer is considerably more likely to cause death than heart disease.

Like heart disease, cancer does not strike in a totally random fashion. Indeed, as you can see in the right-hand column of Table 14.2, some of the same risk factors are implicated in both diseases. Most of these risk factors are at least partially under your own control. It helps to have established good health habits in early adulthood, but it is also clear from the research that improving your health habits in middle age can reduce your risks of both cancer and heart disease.

The most controversial item listed in Table 14.2 is diet; in particular, scientists debate the role of dietary fat as a potential risk factor. The evidence linking high dietary fat and heart disease is increasingly clear; the data on dietary fat and cancer continue to be very confusing. Some experts estimate that as many as 35% of all cancer deaths can be attributed to diet (Bal & Foerster, 1991); others conclude that the effect is weak at best (e.g., Howe, 1994). This is definitely an area of active research. We can only hope that clearer conclusions—and thus clearer advice—will eventually emerge.

Animal studies demonstrate an obvious causal link between high-fat diets and cancer rates (e.g., Weisburger & Wynder, 1991). Of course, researchers can't experimentally manipulate human diets to find out if a high-fat diet causes cancer in humans. However, some of the strongest evidence for a link between diet and cancer comes from cross-national comparisons.

For example, the typical Japanese diet contains only about 15% fat; the typical U.S. diet is closer to 40% fat. Cancer is much less common in Japan. The possibility of a causal link between dietary fat and cancer is further strengthened by the observation that in those areas in Japan where Western dietary habits have been most extensively adopted, cancer rates have risen to nearer Western levels (Weisburger & Wynder, 1991).

Comparisons of diet and cancer rates in many nations show similar patterns. This is especially clear in results from a study of U.N. data (Kesteloot, Lesaffre, & Joossens, 1991). Researchers obtained two kinds of information for each of 36 countries: (1) the death rates from each of several types of cancer, and (2) the estimated per-person intake of fat from dairy products or lard. (Only dairy fat and lard are included because these are the major sources of saturated fats, thought to be more

The Japanese, whose diet is very low in fat, have lower rates of some kinds of cancer than North Americans and Europeans. (*Photo:* Charles Gupton, Stone)

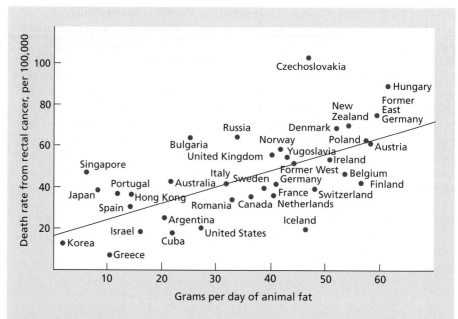

FIGURE 14.3

This figure shows the relationship between deaths from rectal cancer and fat consumption, one of the strongest correlations found in a large set of data relating diet to cancer rates compiled by the United Nations. (*Source:* Kesteloot, Lesaffre, & Joossens, 1991.)

strongly implicated in disease.) Figure 14.3 shows the relationship between deaths from rectal cancer and fat consumption, one of the clearest connections, by country; the average correlation between the two was .64. The average correlations for other types of cancer were .60 for breast cancer in women, .70 for prostate cancer in men, and .43 (in men) and .47 (in women) for colon cancer. For all cancers combined, the correlations were .58 in men and .65 in women.

The relationship among dietary fat, other risk factors, and cancer is obviously complex, and researchers have much yet to learn. For one thing, the typical diets in various countries differ widely in a great many other ways besides fat intake; any one of these differences might affect cancer rates. But cross-national comparisons of this type have generated highly useful hypotheses.

Gender and Health

Figure 14.1 makes it clear that women's life expectancy is greater than men's. But what is not evident is an interesting paradox: Women live longer, but they have more diseases and disabilities. Women are more likely to describe their health as poor, to have more chronic conditions such as arthritis, and to be more limited in their daily activities. Such differences have been found in every country in which the pattern has been studied, including nonindustrialized countries (Rahman, Strauss, Gertler, Ashley, & Fox, 1994).

This difference is already present in early adulthood and grows larger with age. By old age, women are substantially more likely than men to be chronically ill (Guralnik, Land, Blazer, Fillenbaum, & Branch, 1993; Kunkel & Applebaum, 1992). In early adulthood, this gender difference in disease rate can be largely attributed to health problems associated with childbearing. At later ages, the difference cannot be explained in this same way.

Chances are this man will die before his wife does, but she will be more troubled by chronic illnesses in her middle and later years. (*Photo:* Rhoda Sidney, PhotoEdit)

How is it possible that men die younger but are healthier while they are alive? Researchers suggest that the apparent paradox can be resolved by considering sex differences in potentially fatal conditions such as cardiovascular disease (Verbrugge, 1989). In the United States, 233 of every 100,000 men between the ages of 45 and 54 die of heart disease annually, compared with only 81 of every 100,000 women (U.S. Bureau of the Census, 1995). This difference in rates of heart disease diminishes once women are past menopause, although it does not disappear totally even in late old age.

It isn't just that men have higher rates of CVD; they also are more likely to die from the disease once it has been acquired. One reason may be that the heart muscles of women who have CVD seem to be better able to adapt to stresses such as physical exertion (van Doornen, Snieder, & Boomsma, 1998). In addition, once they suffer a heart attack, women recover to a higher level of physical functioning than men do (Bosworth et al., 2000). Sex differences in health habits also seem to contribute to women's greater ability to recover from CVD. For example, women are more likely to get regular checkups and to seek help earlier in an illness than men are (Verbrugge & Wingard, 1987).

By contrast, women are more likely than men to suffer from nonfatal chronic ailments such as arthritis. Because chronic pain is characteristic of arthritis, the activities of women who suffer from it are often limited. Understandably, too, living with chronic pain affects their general sense of well-being.

Socio-Economic Class, Race, and Health

While emphasizing preventive actions such as exercise, developmentalists cannot ignore the importance for health and mental ability in middle adulthood of those familiar demographic variables social class and race. If you look again at Figure 12.1 (page 342), you'll see that social class is a more significant predictor of variations in health in middle age than at any other time of adult life. In middle adulthood, occupational level and education (both of which correlate strongly with socio-economic class) are most predictive of health. Figure 12.1 does not break this pattern down by race, but research suggests that the same link between social class and health is found among Hispanic Americans and African Americans (Chatters, 1991; James, Keenan, & Browning, 1992; Markides & Lee, 1991).

Race is also linked to overall health. For example, African Americans have shorter life expectancies than white Americans, as Figure 14.1 shows. There are also racial differences in incidence of specific diseases. In recent years, public health officials in the United States have begun to study and address these disparities. These efforts have focused on three diseases: cardiovascular disease, diabetes, and cancer.

Although cardiovascular disease (heart attack and stroke) is the leading cause of death in all racial groups, it disables and/or kills a higher proportion of African Americans, Mexican Americans, and Native Americans than of either white or Asian Americans (U.S. Department of Health and Human Services, 1998b). Rates of disease are higher in these groups because they are more likely to possess every risk factor listed in Table 14.2.

Among minority women, the major factor seems to be obesity. More than half of African American and Mexican American women are overweight, compared to 34% of white women (U.S. Department of Health and Human Services, 1998b). Among men, the key risk factor is high blood pressure, or **hypertension** (U.S. Department of Health and Human Services, 1998b). About 25% of white men have elevated blood pressure, compared to 35% of African American men. Mexican American men tend to be more likely than white American men to have hypertension, although precise incidence rates have yet to be determined (U.S. Department of Health and Human Services, 1998b).

The proportion of adults in the United States who suffer from diabetes is growing in all racial groups (U.S. Department of Health and Human Services, 1998c).

hypertension elevated blood pressure

Men and women have equal rates of this disease. However, 10.8% of African Americans, 10.6% of Mexican Americans, and 9% of Native Americans have diabetes, compared to 7.8% of whites. In addition, public health officials estimate that there is at least one undiagnosed case of diabetes for every two individuals who have been diagnosed. Thus, public education about diabetes has become a major health goal in the United States, because the disease can lead to severe complications such as cardiovascular disease, kidney failure, and blindness (CDC, 1998a). Just as they are more likely than whites to have the disease in the first place, minority adults who have been diagnosed with diabetes are more likely than their white counterparts to develop complications (U.S. Department of Health and Human Services, 1998c). Although diabetes itself kills few people, it is the underlying cause of so many other potentially deadly diseases and conditions that death rates among adults who have diabetes are about twice as high at every age as those among individuals who do not have this disease (CDC, 1998a).

Public health officials don't yet have an explanation for racial differences in diabetes rates. However, they hypothesize that complication rates vary because minorities tend to develop the disease earlier in life than whites do (U.S. Department of Health and Human Services, 1998c). Therefore, it affects all of their body systems for a longer period of time. Once diagnosed, minority adults often have less access to regular medical care than whites. However, researchers have found that, even among diabetic whites and African Americans who have the same health insurance benefits and equal access to diabetes care services, African Americans are less likely to seek care for complications at a point when medical intervention can be most effective (U.S. Department of Health and Human Services, 1998c).

For example, because of the disease's effects on the kidneys, some diabetics develop circulation problems in their lower extremities that can cause complications that result in amputation. These problems are evidenced by sores on the feet and legs that do not heal. If diabetics obtain medical intervention when such wounds first appear, the likelihood of amputation can be significantly reduced. Unfortunately, because they delay seeking care, African Americans with diabetes are more likely to have a lower limb amputated than their white counterparts (U.S. Department of Health and Human Services, 1998c). Public health officials do not yet have an explanation for this behavioral difference. However, they agree that educating minority adults who have diabetes about the necessity of obtaining immediate care for any kind of problem is critical to reducing complication rates among them.

African Americans also have higher incidences of most types of cancer and have poorer survival rates once cancer is diagnosed, perhaps because they receive medical care later in the illness (Blakeslee, 1994; Chatters, 1991). For example, African American men have the highest rate of prostate cancer in the world (CDC, 2000). In the United States, 55.5% of white cancer patients survive at least 5 years; among African Americans, the comparable figure is 40.4% (U.S. Bureau of the Census, 1995). Other groups also have higher rates of specific cancers than do white Americans (U.S. Department of Health and Human Services, 1998a). For example, Native American men are more likely than white American men to develop lung cancer or colorectal cancer. In addition, Vietnamese American and Hispanic American women have higher rates of cervical cancer than white women.

The main cause for cross-racial variations in cancer incidence and death rates, according to public health officials, is failure to receive routine cancer screening. Minority men and women are less likely than whites to obtain mammograms, Pap smears, and colorectal examinations. Thus, improving minorities' access to and knowledge about cancer screening services is critical to reducing cancer deaths in these groups (U.S. Department of Health and Human Services, 1998a). Likewise, ensuring that screened adults will have access to follow-up care is another public health goal. Moreover public health officials are concerned that minority cancer rates are likely to increase in the future because the prevalence of tobacco use among minority teens is higher than among white youth and is increasing (CDC, 1998c).

in the Information Age

Is the Internet Addictive?

Although new technologies are usually associated with the young, surveys suggest that middle-aged and even older adults spend more time "surfing the Net" than those who are younger (Hinden, 2000; Miller, 1996). Recently, some mental health professionals have raised concerns about the amount of time some individuals spend on-line. Some claim to have discovered a new disorder they call *Internet Addictive Disorder*, or IAD, (Griffiths, 1999). The criteria for the disorder are the same as for other addictions. Specifically, to be diagnosed with IAD, a person must demonstrate a pattern of Internet use that interferes with normal educational, occupational, and social functioning.

To be sure, there are individuals who spend a great deal of time on-line and who admit that Internet use often interferes with other activities (Brenner, 1997). However, to justify the use of the term *addiction* in relation to a specific activity, the activity itself must have

some addictive power. For example, alcohol induces an altered state of consciousness that users find desirable. The altered state reinforcers the behavior of consuming alcohol. Thus, those who propose that IAD exists are, by implication, saying that the experience of being on-line has the capacity to induce some kind of reinforcing state in users.

Some Internet users report that on-line communication is more pleasurable than face-to-face social encounters (Chou, Chou, & Tyang, 1999). But is this sense of pleasure enough to bring about an addiction, or is socializing on the Internet nothing more than an easy way to escape the usual pressures of social interaction? Similarly, use of on-line pornography for sexual gratification is clearly a problem for some people (Cooper, Putnam, Planchon, & Boies, 1999). However, is it any different from use of conventional sources of pornography such as adult magazines and videos?

In fact, research has suggested that excessive Internet use may be part of a

behavior pattern that is consistent across several media (Greenberg, Lewis, & Dodd, 1999). Those who are "addicted" to the Internet also spend inordinate amounts of time watching television and playing video games. They are also more likely to be addicted to alcohol and other substances.

Thus, rather than being a distinct addictive disorder, what seems more likely is that Internet use is a new means by which people can escape from everyday problems. As such, the Net is no different from books, television, movies, or even drugs. The Net may simply provide people who have some kind of tendency toward a specific addictive problem, with an additional avenue through which to express this tendency. Thus, mental health professionals who oppose the idea of Internet addiction suggest that excessive time on-line either is a symptom of another disorder or may simply reflect fascination with a new medium (Griffiths, 1999; Grohol, 1999).

Mental Health

As you learned in Chapter 12, most types of mental health problems are considerably more common in early adulthood than in the middle years of adult life. However, about two-thirds of adults diagnosed with serious mental disorders in early adulthood continue to have difficulties in middle age (Meeks, 1997). Further, though most addictive disorders begin in adolescence or early adulthood, they frequently go undiagnosed until the middle adulthood years, when they begin to have dramatic effects on health and other areas of functioning that sufferers or their families can no longer deny (see Development in the Information Age).

For example, **alcoholism** is physical and psychological dependence on alcohol. Between 3% and 5% of adult American men are alcoholics. Among American women, the prevalence is lower, about 1%. Alcoholism is more common among the poor of all races. Some studies suggest that African Americans and Native Americans have higher rates of alcoholism than other ethnic groups. Higher rates in these groups may be related to feelings of social and economic powerlessness (Taylor, 2000).

The strongest risk factor for alcoholism in both men and women is a family history of problem drinking (Curran et al., 1999; Sher & Gotham, 1999). This suggests a genetic basis for the disease, and twin studies also suggest that heritability may be a factor, as the concordance rate for alcoholism in identical twins is about 50%

alcoholism physical and psychological dependence on alcohol

(Kendler, Neale, Heath, Kessler, & Eaves, 1994; McGue, Pickens, & Svikis, 1992). However, variables such as socio-economic status, personality, attitudes toward drinking, amount of time spent socializing with drinkers, and cultural attitudes that endorse drinking as a means of dealing with life's problems also contribute to alcoholism (Curran et al., 1999; Pacheco, 1999; Sher & Gotham, 1999).

About one-third of all U.S. families have at least one member who is an alcoholic, and the impact of this disease on a family can be devastating ("Drinking a cause of family problems," 1997). For example, alcoholics' rate of divorce is almost seven times higher than that of nonalcoholics (Sullivan & Thompson, 1994). In addition, alcoholic parents often display negative patterns of interaction with their children (Eiden, Chavez, & Leonard, 1999).

The individual costs of alcoholism are high as well. In one longitudinal study, researchers found that about one-third of participants who had been hospitalized for alcoholism in their late 20s or early 30s were still abusing alcohol 10 years later (Powell et al., 1998). Another third abstained from alcohol, but the remaining third had died—a rather remarkable rate of mortality for such a young group. Of course, age-related mortality patterns suggest that many of these young men died from accidents or homicides, not from the physical effects of alcohol. However, alcohol is frequently a factor in fatal automobile accidents and is often associated with homicide. Alcoholics are also more likely to attempt suicide, both in early adulthood and in middle adulthood (Rossow, Romelsjoe, & Leifman, 1999). Thus, the reason why rates of alcoholism decline from early to middle adulthood may be the extraordinarily high mortality rate of young alcoholics.

Among alcoholics who survive to middle age, the natural declines associated with primary aging interact with the effects of long-term heavy drinking. For example, some parts of the brains of middle-aged alcoholics are smaller and are less responsive to stimuli than the brains of nonalcoholics (Laakso et al., 2000; Polo, Escera, Gual, & Grau, 1999). Functional deficits among alcoholics include problems with memory and language. Cardiovascular disease is more prevalent among alcoholics as well, because long-term exposure to alcohol weakens the muscles of the heart along with the valves and walls of the body's blood vessels. Further, long-term heavy drinking damages the digestive system, impairs the immune system, and contributes to losses in muscle strength (Laso et al., 1999; Tarter et al., 1997). In women, alcoholism is associated with a delay in the course of the phases of menopause (Torgerson, Thomas, Campbell, & Reid, 1997).

The result of this interaction between aging and alcohol abuse is that alcoholics face an increased risk of health problems and death (Dawson, 2000). A longitudinal study involving more than 40,000 males in Norway found that the rate of death prior to age 60 was significantly higher among alcoholics than among nonalcoholics (Rossow & Amundsen, 1997). Not surprising, perhaps, is the finding that alcoholics were three times as likely to die in automobile accidents as their nonalcoholic peers. However, alcoholics were also almost three times as likely to die of heart disease and had twice the rate of deaths from cancer.

Many of the effects of long-term heavy alcohol use are reversible if a person stops drinking. To do so, most alcoholics need help. For example, there is evidence that recovering alcoholics for whom religious faith and participation in a supportive faith community are important are more optimistic about the recovery process and have less anxiety than others (Plante & Pardini, 2000). Thus, some mental health professionals believe that these positive effects of religious faith may increase the likelihood of recovery from alcoholism.

For most alcoholics, a multiple treatment approach is called for (Kaplan & Saddock, 1991). Alcoholics require medical attention to deal with alcohol's physical effects. Medications may be helpful in managing withdrawal from alcohol and depression. In addition, most mental health professionals recommend self-help programs, such as Alcoholics Anonymous, where alcoholics instruct and support each other through the process of recovery.

Before going on

- What are the major trends in health during middle adulthood?
- How does coronary heart disease develop?
- What factors contribute to cancer?
- What are some important differences in the health of middle-aged men and women?
- How are socio-economic status and race related to health in middle adulthood?
- What are some of the consequences of alcoholism for middle-aged adults?

Cognitive Functioning

In the middle adult years, some cognitive abilities improve, while others slow down a bit. Still, many adults have acquired large bodies of knowledge and skill that help them compensate for losses and solve problems within their areas of expertise more efficiently than younger adults do.

A Model of Physical and Cognitive Aging

Many of the various bits and pieces of information you've encountered so far about physical and cognitive changes in adulthood can be combined in a single model, suggested by Nancy Denney and illustrated in Figure 14.4 (Denney 1982, 1984). Denney

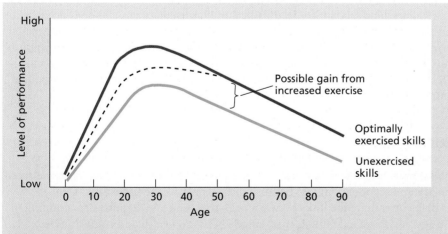

FIGURE 14.4

Denney's model suggests both a basic decay curve and a fairly large gap between actual level of performance on exercised and unexercised abilities. (*Source:* Denney, 1982, 1984.)

proposed that on nearly any measure of physical or cognitive functioning, age-related changes follow a typical curve, like those shown in the figure. But she also argued that the height of this curve varies, depending on the amount an individual exercises some ability or skill. Denney used the word *exercise* very broadly, to refer not only to physical exercise but also to mental exercise and to the extent some specific task may have been performed before. Unexercised abilities generally have a lower peak level of performance; exercised abilities generally have a higher peak.

Many laboratory tests of memory, for example, such as memorizing lists of names, tap unexercised abilities. Everyday memory tasks, such as recalling details from a newspaper column, tap much more exercised abilities. The distinction is somewhat similar to the distinction between crystallized and fluid abilities (see Chapter 12). Most crystallized abilities are at least moderately exercised, whereas many fluid abilities are relatively unexercised. But Denney was making a more general point: Whether abilities are crystallized or fluid, those that are more fully exercised will have a higher peak.

The gap between the curve for unexercised abilities and the curve for maximally exercised abilities represents the degree of improvement that would be possible for any given skill. Any skill that is not fully exercised can be improved if the individual begins to exercise that ability. There is clear evidence, for example, that aerobic capacity (VO_2 max) can be increased at any age if a person begins a program of physical exercise (e.g., Blumenthal et al., 1991; Buchner, Beresford, Larson, LaCroix, & Wagner, 1992). Nonetheless, in Denney's model, the maximum level an adult will be able to achieve, even with optimum exercise, will decline with age, just as performance of top athletes declines, even with optimum training regimens. One implication of this is that young adults are more likely to be able to get away with laziness or poor study habits and still perform well; as adults age, this becomes less and less true, because they are fighting against the basic decay curve of aging.

The dashed line in Figure 14.4 represents a hypothetical curve for a skill that is not optimally exercised but is still used fairly regularly. Many verbal skills fall into this category, as do problem-solving skills. Because skills like these are demanded in a great many jobs, they are well exercised in most adults in their 20s, 30s, 40s, and 50s and are therefore well maintained, creating a flat-topped curve. But if Denney is correct, then at some point even optimum exercise will no longer maintain these abilities at that same level, and some decline will occur.

This model does not take into account all the facts. In particular, Denney's model does not easily handle the wide degree of variation from one individual to the next in the pattern of skill maintenance or decline over age, variation revealed clearly in Schaie's longitudinal study (Schaie, 1990). But what Denney's model does do is emphasize that there is an underlying decay curve. Those in middle adulthood may perform as well or better than the average young adult in arenas in which they regularly exercise their skills. However, with increasing age, this high level of function requires more and more effort, until eventually every adult reaches a point at which even maximum effort will no longer maintain peak function.

Health and Cognitive Functioning

You should remember from Chapter 12 that it is often difficult to separate the effects of primary and secondary aging, because they happen at the same time. Denney's model helps illuminate the links between primary aging and cognitive functioning in middle age. Research examining correlations between health and cognition help developmentalists understand the effects of secondary aging. Specifically, many of the same characteristics that are linked to increased or decreased risk of heart disease and cancer are also linked to the rate of change or the maintenance of intellectual skill in the middle years.

One illustration of this relationship comes from Walter Schaie's analysis of data from the Seattle Longitudinal Study (1983a). He found that those research participants who had some kind of cardiovascular disease (either coronary heart disease or high blood pressure) showed earlier and larger declines on intellectual tests than did those who were disease-free. Other researchers have found similar linkages. Even adults whose blood pressure is controlled by medication seem to show earlier declines (Sands & Meredith, 1992; Schultz, Elias, Robbins, Streeten, & Blakeman, 1986). Schaie cautions against taking these findings too far. The size of the effect is quite small, and it may operate indirectly rather than directly. For example, adults with cardiovascular disease may become physically less active as a response to their disease. The lower level of activity, in turn, may affect the rate of intellectual decline. This raises the possibility that exercise may be one of the critical factors in determining an individual person's overall physical health and cognitive performance during middle adulthood. A growing amount of information confirms such an effect.

One particularly large and well-designed study of the effects of exercise on physical health involved 17,321 Harvard alumni who had been students between 1916 and 1950. In 1962 or 1966, when the men were in their 30s, 40s, or 50s, each man provided detailed information about his daily levels of physical activity (Lee, Hsieh, & Paffenbarger, 1995). (The measures of physical activity were quite detailed. Each man reported how many blocks he normally walked each day, how often he climbed stairs, the amount of time per week he normally engaged in various sports, and so on. All the answers were then converted into estimates of calories expended per week. For example, walking 1 mile on level ground uses roughly 100 calories; climbing one flight of stairs uses about 17.) The researchers tracked all these men until 1988 to identify who had died and of what cause. The link between the level of physical activity and death rates over the succeeding 25 years is shown clearly in Figure 14.5: The more exercise a man reported, the lower his mortality risk.

Researchers were careful to exclude from the study any man who was known to suffer from heart disease or other disease at the onset of the study, in the 1960s. Furthermore, the groups differed *only* in level of energy expenditure; they did not differ in age, or whether they smoked, had high blood pressure, were overweight, or had a family history of early death—which makes the effect of exercise even clearer. To be sure, because the level of exercise was each man's own choice, there may have been

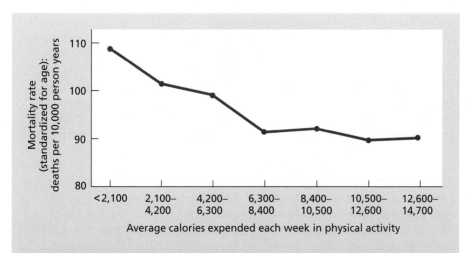

Figure 14.5

Results from the Harvard Alumni Study show clearly that those who are more physically active in middle adulthood have lower risk of mortality over the next decades. (*Source:* Lee et al., 1995, adapted from data from Table 2, p. 1181.)

other differences that separated the various exercise groups that could account for the different death rates. But the pattern, which has been replicated in other groups of both men and women, is so substantial and striking that alternative explanations are hard to come by (e.g., Blair et al., 1995; Lissner, Bengtsson, Bjorkelund, & Wedel, 1996). By far the most likely explanation is that there is a causal connection between longevity and level of physical activity.

Physical exercise also seems to help maintain cognitive abilities in the middle adult years, very likely because it helps to maintain cardiovascular fitness (Rogers, Meyer, & Mortel, 1990). Among physically healthy middle-aged and older adults, those who are more physically active—doing gardening, heavy housework, or aerobic exercise such as walking, running, or swimming—score higher on tests of reasoning, reaction time, and short-term memory (Van Boxtel et al., 1997).

A different approach to studying exercise and cognitive functioning would involve randomly assigning some people to an exercise program and some to a nonexercise control group, and then seeing whether the two groups differed in their cognitive functioning after a period of exercise. The results of the small number of studies of this type have been quite mixed. Every study finds that exercise increases measures of physical functioning, such as VO_2 max, even in very elderly adults. Some—but not all—such studies also show that exercise improves thinking (Hawkins, Kramer, & Capaldi, 1992; Hill, Storandt, & Malley, 1993). Other studies do not come to that conclusion (e.g., Buchner et al., 1992; Emery & Gatz, 1990). In most cases, the experimental exercise program lasts only a few months, and that may not be sufficient to make any difference in mental functioning. Still, because researchers already know that exercise is linked to lower levels of disease and greater longevity, prudence alone would argue for including it in your life.

Changes in Memory and Cognition

When developmentalists study changes in cognitive functioning in middle age, they find almost precisely what Denney's model and Schaie's longitudinal study suggest. That is, lack of mental exercise tends to be correlated with declines in memory and cognitive skills, but major deficits are not found until after age 60 to 65.

● *Memory Function* ● Drawing conclusions about memory function in middle age is difficult, because studies of age differences in adult memory rarely include middle-aged people. Typically, researchers compare very young adults, such as college students, to adults in their 60s and 70s. When the two groups are found to differ, psychologists often infer that middle-aged adults' performance falls somewhere between the two. In other words, they assume that memory function declines steadily, in linear fashion, across the adult years—an assumption that may not be true.

One thing developmentalists do know about memory is that the subjective experience of forgetfulness clearly increases with age. The older we get, the more forgetful we think we are (Commissaris, Ponds, & Jolles, 1998). However, it may be that the memory demands of middle-aged adults' everyday lives are greater than those of young adults. Remember, working memory is limited, and the more you try to remember at one time, the more you will forget.

In addition, increases in the subjective experience of forgetfulness may actually be an aid to metamemory. Not only are middle-aged adults aware of how well or poorly their memories function, they are also very proficient at overcoming perceived memory limitations by using reminders, or *cues*, to help themselves remember information. Thus, the middle-aged person who knows that she may forget where her car is parked makes a point of noting nearby landmarks that will help her remember its location. This may be because middle-aged adults, in contrast to those who are older, continue to have a high sense of self-efficacy with respect to memory (Lineweaver &

MAKE THE CONNECTION

Look back at the information on cross-sectional and longitudinal research designs in Chapter 1. How might cohort differences affect the results of studies comparing cognitive functioning of middle-aged adults to that of both younger and older adults? What kind of design would minimize such cohort effects? If such a study were begun today, how long would it be before researchers could derive useful conclusions from the data?

Hertzog, 1998). In other words, they believe their efforts will make a difference, so they actively work to improve their memories.

Nevertheless, there seem to be some real differences in the memory performance of young and middle-aged adults. For example, visual memory, the ability to remember an object you have seen for just a few seconds, declines in middle age (Fahle & Daum, 1997; Giambra, Arenberg, Zonderman, Kawas, & Costa, 1995). Further, the more complex the visual stimulus and the longer the interval between presentation and recall, the greater the difference. By contrast, memory for auditory stimuli seems to remain stable throughout adulthood.

Performance on more complex memory tasks, such as remembering lists of words and passages of text, also declines with age, but usually not until after about age 55. In contrast, recognition of words and texts appears to remain stable throughout adulthood (Zelinski & Burnight, 1997). Such findings suggest that there are age differences in working memory. Research examining short-term memory capacity at various ages shows that it remains very stable throughout early, middle, and late adulthood. What changes, apparently, is the ability to make efficient use of available capacity (Lincourt, Rybash, & Hoyer, 1998).

● *Semantic and Episodic Memories* ●   Researchers can gain additional insight into age-related memory changes by studying how well young and middle-aged adults encode different kinds of memories. **Episodic memories** are recollections of personal events or episodes. **Semantic memories** represent general knowledge. For example, a person's memories of a vacation in Hawaii are episodic, and her knowledge that Hawaii was the 50th state is semantic.

Researchers find that young and middle-aged adults differ more with respect to new episodic memories than they do with respect to semantic memories (Maylor, 1998; Nilsson, Baeckman, Erngrund, & Nyberg, 1997). For example, a middle-aged person attending a baseball game may forget where he parked his car (episodic memory). However, he is unlikely to forget the basic rules of the game (semantic memory).

Yet, it is too simplistic to say that episodic encoding is better in younger than in older adults. The difference is a bit more complex than that. Research examining the memories of adults for highly memorable episodes, often called *flashbulb memories*, has demonstrated that age has no effect on our ability to recall such events. For example, in one study, researchers asked young, middle-aged, and older adults to recount where they were and what they were doing when they heard about the verdict in the O. J. Simpson trial (Bluck, Levine, & Laulhere, 1999). Respondents of all ages remembered the event with equal clarity. Younger respondents were somewhat more likely to report details. However, other research on such memories suggests that memory for details surrounding such episodes is subject to suggestion and overconfidence (Neisser & Harsch, 1992). So, the younger participants may have thought they remembered details when, in reality, their minds were simply filling in gaps in their memories with assumed details.

● *Practiced and Unpracticed Skills* ●   In general, most adults maintain or even gain in skill on any task that they practice often or that is based on specific learning. For example, verbal abilities increase in middle age (Giambra et al., 1995). It appears that vocabulary—or, more precisely, performance on vocabulary tests—doesn't begin to decline until about age 65.

Similarly, expertise in a particular field helps to compensate for age-related deficits in cognitive functioning (Colonia-Willner, 1999; Tsang, 1999). For example, in one study, researchers examined 17- to 79-year-old participants' ability to recognize melodies performed at varying tempos (Andrews, Dowling, Bartlett, & Halpern, 1998). Some tunes were played very rapidly and then slowed until participants could recognize them. Both age and years of musical training predicted participants' ability to recognize melodies presented in this way, but the relationship between age and recognition was much weaker than the relationship between recognition and musical

episodic memories recollections of personal events

semantic memories general knowledge

training. Other melodies were played too slowly to be recognized at the beginning and then speeded up. Interestingly, only musical training correlated with recognition of tunes played this way; there was no association with age whatsoever.

When researchers examine middle-aged adults' performance on unfamiliar or unpracticed skills, such as a timed arithmetic test or a three-dimensional spatial task, the effects of aging are apparent. In particular, mental processes get steadily slower with age (Salthouse, 1991). Still, longitudinal research suggests that, even in these unfamiliar domains, the actual losses for most adults in this age range are small (Giambra et al., 1995). Major declines seem to happen after about age 60. Such results support conclusions such as that expressed by psychologist Walter Schaie:

> It is my general conclusion that reliably replicable age changes in psychometric abilities of more than trivial magnitude cannot be demonstrated prior to age 60, but that reliable decrements can be shown to have occurred for all abilities by age 74. (Schaie, 1983a, p. 127)

● *New Learning* ●   When it comes to acquiring new knowledge, middle-aged adults seem to be just as capable as younger adults of learning and remembering new information. In fact, middle-aged college students tend to be more academically successful than their younger peers (Burley, Turner, & Vitulli, 1999). Psychologists hypothesize that this difference is due both to motivational differences and the greater amount of background knowledge and experience possessed by older students.

Interestingly, too, surveys suggest that employers believe young adults to be more capable of learning new job skills than those who are older. However, research seems to show that there are few, if any, differences in the rates at which young and middle-aged adults learn new job skills (Forte & Hansvick, 1999). Particularly with regard to computer skills, once the skills have been acquired, there are no age-related differences in performance.

● *Schematic Processing* ●   The literature on memory change with age also offers support for Labouvie-Vief's view that what happens to cognition in adulthood involves not only decline but also changes in emphasis, or structure. Labouvie-Vief, as you may recall from Chapter 12, suggests that middle adults tend to shift away from the logical or formal-operational approach that dominates thinking in adolescence and young adulthood, to a more pragmatic approach aimed at solving everyday problems—a process some developmentalists call *schematic processing* (Labouvie-Vief, 1990). In other words, a middle-aged adult may use schemas to process information that are qualitatively different from those used earlier in life. Such a schematic difference might lead middle-aged adults to pay more attention to overarching themes than to details. In memory, this difference in schematic processing might be reflected in a decline in memory for surface detail, accompanied by an increase in memory for themes and meanings.

A study in which researchers asked adults of various ages to read a story and then to recall it immediately afterward, in writing, yielded support for this hypothesis (Adams, 1991). Younger adults were more likely to report specific events or actions in the story, while middle-aged adults recalled more of the psychological motivations of the characters and offered more interpretations of the story in their recall. What this may mean is that, along with a shift in schematic processing, the encoding process changes as we get older. We may not attempt to encode as much detail, but may store more summarizing information.

Creativity

A somewhat different question about cognitive functioning in the middle years of adulthood—one that may have more direct relevance for one's work life—has to do with creativity and productivity (see The Real World). Some widely quoted early research suggested that peak creativity, like peak physical functioning, occurs in early

Maintaining the Creative "Edge" in Mid-Life and Beyond

In a fascinating set of interviews, a number of highly successful and creative people described how they viewed creativity ("The creators," 2000). Interviewees ranged in age from 50 (musician Bobby McFerrin) to 93 (architect Phillip Johnson). Interestingly, all reported that they viewed themselves as more creative than they had been when they were younger. Their comments suggested that the creative process is a highly individualized intellectual activity. However, what was remarkable was that, by middle age, all had arrived at firm conclusions about what did and did not work for them. So, some part of the maintenance of creativity included acceptance of their own creative idiosyncrasies. Some, for example, expressed the need for external motivation, such as a deadline. Guitarist B. B. King, 74, said, "If you want me to be creative, give me the line to cross and when I have to cross it" (p. 44). Others were more motivated by self-imposed standards than by externals. For example, writer Isabel Allende, 57, reported that she always begins a new work on January 8, because the date is a personally meaningful anniversary for her. Advertising writer Stan Freberg, 73, claimed that when he needs an idea, he takes a shower, because he often gets inspiration while in the shower.

A second theme pervaded these reports. Each creative person, in one way or another, recognized the value of accumulated knowledge and experience. They also tended to acknowledge important sources of this knowledge, such as parents, spouses, and friends. Consequently, these people saw their creative work not only as the product of their own abilities but also as the result of a complex network of influential individuals, life experiences, and their own capacity to reflect on their lives.

We can learn two important things about maintaining creativity and productivity in the middle and late adult years from these extraordinary individuals: First, being consciously aware of one's own creative process—and accepting its boundaries—seems to be critical. Second, some degree of humility, a sense of indebtedness to those who have contributed to and supported one's creative development, appears to be associated with continuing productivity in the middle and late adult years.

---

adulthood (Lehman, 1953). The technique used in this study involved identifying a series of major scientific discoveries of the past several hundred years and finding out how old each scientist was at the time of that discovery. Most were quite young, especially those who worked in more theoretical sciences and in mathematics. The classic example is Einstein, who was 26 when he developed the theory of relativity. These are interesting patterns, but this approach may be going at the question backwards. The alternative is to study scientists or other problem-solvers throughout their working lives and see whether the average person (someone who *isn't* an Einstein) is more productive and creative in early or middle adult life.

More recently, one psychologist has moved a step in this direction by looking at the lifetime creativity and productivity of thousands of notable scientists from the 19th century and earlier (Simonton, 1991, 2000). Simonton identified the age at which these individuals (nearly all men) published their first significant work, their best work, and their last work. In every scientific discipline represented, the thinkers produced their best work at about age 40, on average. But most of them were publishing significant, even outstanding, research through their 40s and into their 50s. In fact, researchers propose that the reason that people tend to do their best work at about 40 is not that the mind works better at that age, but that productivity is at its highest at that time. Chance alone suggests that the best work will come during the time when the most work is being done.

Lifetime creative output of modern-day scientists follows a similar pattern. Mathematicians, psychologists, physicists, and other scientists born in the 20th century have consistently shown their maximum productivity (usually measured by the number of papers published in a single year) when they were about 40. But research quality (as measured by the number of times each research paper is cited by peers) remains high through age 50 or even 60 (Horner, Rushton, & Vernon, 1986; Simonton, 1988).

Among musicians or other artists, peak creativity may occur later or be maintained far longer. For example, in one study, researchers asked judges to rate the aesthetic qualities of musical compositions by the 172 composers whose works are most often performed (Simonton, 1989). Works created late in life ("swan songs") were most likely to be evaluated as masterpieces by the judges.

It is also possible to approach the question of how age is related to creativity or professional effectiveness experimentally. One such study broadened examination of adult creativity beyond the realm of scientific research by focusing on business executives (Streufert, Pogash, Piasecki, & Post, 1990). The researchers created four-person decision-making teams, made up of mid-level managers from state and federal government and private industry. On 15 of the teams, the participants were all between ages 28 and 35. Members of another 15 teams were middle-aged (aged 45 to 55), and another 15 teams included only older adults (aged 65 to 75). Each team was given a wonderfully complex simulated task: They were asked to manage an imaginary developing country called Shamba. They were given packets of information about Shamba ahead of time and could request additional information during their group work, done via a computer—which was of course programmed to make the experience of the different groups as much alike as possible, although the participants did not know that. Every team faced a crisis in Shamba at about the same time in their work.

Researchers recorded all the questions, suggestions, and plans generated by each team, from which they created a series of measures of activity rate, speed of response, depth of analysis, diversity of suggestions, and strategic excellence of each group's performance. The teams of young and middle-aged participants differed significantly on only 3 of the 16 measures: The younger teams did more things (made more decisions and took more actions); they asked for more additional information (often excessively, to the point of creating information overload); they suggested a greater diversity of actions. Middle-aged teams asked for just about the right amount of information—not too much to overload the system, but enough to make good decisions—and used the information effectively. On most of the measures the researchers devised, there were no differences between the young and middle-aged. In contrast, the oldest teams performed less well on virtually every measure. These findings suggest that the ability to apply creative thinking efficiently to complex problems may, indeed, be at its peak in the middle adult years.

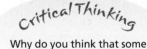

Critical Thinking

Why do you think that some people associate creativity with youth, when there are so many highly creative middle-aged and older adults?

*B*efore going on

- How does Denney's model explain the relationships among exercise, physical health, and cognitive functioning in middle adulthood?

- What does research reveal about the link between health and cognitive functioning?

- Describe differences between young and middle-aged adults in cognition and memory function.

- What does research evidence suggest about age-related changes in creativity?

A Final Word

dults in middle age often feel a sense of being at the height of their powers, of having "learned the ropes" and being able to make things happen. Some talk of an increased sense of the value of accumulated experience. Others speak of seeing their life in a more holistic way, from a larger perspective. Moreover, a greater sense of control and choice also emerges, because at least some of the dominant roles of early adulthood have become considerably less demanding. However, the modest physical and intellectual declines of this period provide many with an accentuated sense of limited time. Consequently, adults in middle age often turn their attention to new challenges and delayed goals.

Summary

Physical Changes

- Brain size diminishes a bit in the middle adult years. Some changes in brain function suggest that middle-aged adults are more subject to distraction. However, middle-aged adults often outperform younger adults on everyday tasks that require concentration and rapid judgments, such as driving.

- The loss of reproductive capacity, called the *climacteric* in both men and women, occurs very gradually in men, but more rapidly in women. Menopause is a three-phase process that results from a series of hormonal changes.

- Bone mass declines significantly beginning at about age 30; accelerated declines in women at menopause are linked to decreased levels of estrogen and progesterone. Faster bone loss occurs in women who experience early menopause, who are underweight, who exercise little, or who have low-calcium diets.

- Thickening of the lens of the eye, with accompanying loss of elasticity, reduces visual acuity noticeably in the 40s or 50s. Hearing loss is more gradual.

Health and Wellness

- The rate of illness and death rises noticeably in middle adulthood. Young adults have more acute illnesses; middle-aged adults have more chronic illnesses. The two major causes of death in middle adulthood are cancer and heart disease.

- Cardiovascular disease is not a normal part of aging; it is a disease, for which there are known risk factors, including smoking, high blood pressure, high blood cholesterol, obesity, and a high-fat diet.

- Cancer, too, has known risk factors, including smoking, obesity, and an inactive lifestyle. The role of a high-fat diet has been debated, but most evidence supports the hypothesis that such a diet contributes to the risk.

- Women tend to live longer than men but are more likely to suffer from chronic illnesses.

- Low-income adults have more chronic illnesses and a higher rate of death than those who are better off economically. African Americans, Hispanic Americans, and Native Americans are more likely to suffer from cardiovascular disease, cancer, and diabetes than whites.

- Middle-aged adults have lower rates of mental health problems of virtually every kind than young adults. Alcoholism usually starts at younger ages but often remains undiagnosed until middle age.

Cognitive Functioning

- Denney's model of aging suggests that exercising either physical or cognitive abilities can improve performance at any age, but the upper limit on improvement declines with increasing age.

- Some studies suggest that differences in health contribute to variations in cognitive functioning among middle-aged adults. Exercise clearly affects the physical health of middle-aged adults, but research is less conclusive with regard to its effects on cognitive functioning.

- Verbal abilities continue to grow in middle age. Some loss of memory speed and skill occurs, but by most measures the loss is quite small until fairly late in the middle adult years. Expertise helps middle-aged adults compensate for losses in processing speed.

- Creative productivity also appears to remain high during middle adulthood, at least for adults in challenging jobs (the category of adults on whom most of this research has focused).

Key Terms

alcoholism (p. 415)

atherosclerosis (p. 408)

cardiovascular disease (CVD) (p. 408)

climacteric (p. 401)

episodic memories (p. 421)

hypertension (p. 413)

menopause (p. 402)

osteoporosis (p. 405)

perimenopausal phase (p. 403)

postmenopausal phase (p. 403)

premenopausal phase (p. 403)

presbycusis (p. 407)

presbyopia (p. 406)

semantic memories (p. 421)

type A personality pattern (p. 409)

CHAPTER

15

Social and Personality Development in Middle Adulthood

Jeff Greenberg, PhotoEdit

When 43-year-old John F. Kennedy was elected to the U.S. presidency in 1960, many of his critics expressed the view that he was too young to be president.

Similarly, in 1980, when Ronald Reagan was elected president at age 68, some thought he was too old to perform effectively. Both views reflect cultural beliefs about the social clock. Middle adulthood is seen as the time when people are best able, developmentally, to manage the weighty demands associated with positions of authority. Thus, those just entering middle adulthood, as Kennedy was in 1960, are thought to be insufficiently mature for such positions, while those who are beyond the middle years, like 68-year-old Reagan, may be seen as no longer sufficiently competent.

Such beliefs and expectations are not entirely unfounded. When middle-aged adults get together with acquaintances, friends, or relatives at events such as high school or family reunions, they find most of their agemates to be in the most powerful positions of their lives. Most have higher incomes than they ever had before or ever will again, and a greater proportion of them hold positions of authority in business, education, and government than was true when they were younger.

The social clock is evident in family relationships as well. The middle-aged cohort of any family tends to have the most responsibility. They are "sandwiched" between adolescent or young adult children and aging parents. When a younger or older family member requires help, the middle-aged members are expected to respond.

What seems most striking about everyday life in middle age, however, is how much less constricting social roles feel. Most middle-aged adults are married, parents, and workers, but by age 40 or 50, these roles have changed in important ways. Children begin to leave home, which dramatically alters and reduces the intensity of the parental role; job promotions have usually reached their limit, so workers have less need to learn new work skills. And when both parenting and work are less demanding, partners can find more time for themselves and for each other. As you read this chapter, keep the following questions in mind:

- How does Erikson view social and personality development in middle adulthood, and what evidence exists to support the "crisis" view of mid-life?

- How do family roles and relationships change in middle adulthood?

- What are the major career issues facing middle-aged adults?

- How do individual personalities and life pathways influence development in middle adulthood?

Theories of Social and Personality Development

ou should remember from Chapter 2 that Erik Erikson viewed middle age as a period when attention turns to creation of a legacy. Adults do this by influencing the lives of those in younger generations. Yet, many have characterized middle age less positively, suggesting that it is a period of intense crisis.

Erikson's Generativity versus Stagnation Stage

Middle-aged adults are in Erikson's **generativity versus stagnation stage.** Their developmental task is to acquire a sense of **generativity,** which involves an interest in establishing and guiding the next generation. Generativity is expressed not only in bearing or rearing one's own children, but through teaching, serving as mentor, or taking on leadership roles in various civic, religious, or charitable organizations. Merely having children is not enough for developing generativity in Erikson's terms. The optimum expression of generativity requires turning outward from a preoccupation with self, a kind of psychological expansion toward caring for others. Those who fail to develop generativity often suffer from a "pervading sense of stagnation and personal impoverishment [and indulge themselves] as if they were their own one and only child" (Erikson, 1963, p. 267).

Research has produced hints of such a developmental stage, but the findings are much less clear than data on changes in earlier years. One hint comes from the Berkeley/Oakland longitudinal studies, which found that assertiveness peaks in the 40s and then drops. The same studies found that a measure of outgoingness also peaked in the 40s among women and then dropped, as did the measure the Berkeley researchers called "cognitively committed," which included aspects of ambition, valuing independence, and valuing intellect. In this sample, then, there were signs of a major change around age 50, after which assertiveness, ambition, and outgoingness seemed to decline.

Erikson's theory also raises questions about the impact of childlessness on adult development. One very interesting analysis comes from a 40-year longitudinal study of a group of inner-city, nondelinquent boys who had originally served as a comparison group in a study of delinquent boys (Snarey, Son, Kuehne, Hauser, & Vaillant, 1987). Of the 343 married men who were still part of this sample in their late 40s, 29 had fathered no children. Researchers found that the way a man had responded earlier to his childlessness was predictive of his psychological health at age 47. At that age, each man was rated on his degree of generativity. A man was considered to be "generative" if he had participated in some kind of mentoring or other teaching or supervising of children or younger adults. Among those with no children, those who were rated as most generative were likely to have responded to their childlessness by finding another child to nurture. They adopted a child, became Big Brothers, or helped with the rearing of someone else's child, such as a niece or nephew. Those childless men rated as nongenerative were more likely to have chosen a pet as a child substitute.

Critical Thinking

Make a list of ways to express generativity other than by bringing up your own children and helping them get a start in life.

Such findings raise the possibility that some aspects of psychological growth in early adulthood may depend on bearing and rearing one's own children or another child who calls forth one's nurturing and caring qualities—just as Erikson proposed. However, critics have suggested that studies of generativity have focused on well-educated, white, middle-aged adults. Researchers who have examined the issue of generativity in other groups have found that generativity is somewhat related to education (McAdams, Hart, & Maruna, 1998). Still, researchers have found consistent patterns of generativity-related behaviors and attitudes among poor as well as middle-class adults and across a variety of ethnic groups (McAdams et al., 1998; Schulz, 1998). Thus, expressions of generativity appear to be normal middle-aged experiences that are relatively independent of ethnicity and economic factors.

generativity versus stagnation stage the seventh of Erikson's stages, in which middle-aged adults find meaning in contributing to the development of younger individuals

generativity a sense that one is making a valuable contribution to society by bringing up children or mentoring younger people in some way

Mid-Life Crisis: Fact or Fiction?

You may recall that the crisis concept is central to Erikson's theory, and a specific mid-life crisis has been part of several other theories as well, including Levinson's. Levinson argued that each person must confront a constellation of difficult tasks at mid-life: accepting of one's own mortality, recognizing new physical limitations and health risks, and adapting to major changes in most roles. Dealing with all these tasks, according to Levinson, is highly likely to exceed an adult's ability to cope, thus creating a crisis.

When developmentalists look at the relevant research evidence, however, they often come to diametrically opposite conclusions. Psychologist David Chiriboga concludes that "there is mounting evidence from research studies that serious mid-life problems are actually experienced by only 2% to 5% of middle agers" (Chiriboga, 1989, p. 117). Another psychologist, Lois Tamir, reading the same evidence, concludes that mid-life is a time of important psychological transition marked with "deep-seated self-doubts or confusion" (Tamir, 1989, p. 161).

There is evidence that the rate of depression peaks among women in their late 30s and early 40s (Anthony & Aboraya, 1992). But even at the peak, the rate is only about 4.5%—hardly evidence of a universal crisis. Other researchers used a mid-life crisis scale, including items about inner turmoil, marital or job dissatisfaction, and a sense of declining power (Costa & McCrae, 1980b; McCrae & Costa, 1984). They compared the responses of over 500 participants in a cross-sectional study of men ranging in age from 35 to 70. They could find no age at which scores on the mid-life crisis scale were significantly high. Others who have devised mid-life crisis scales have arrived at the same conclusion, as have those who have studied responses to stress (e.g., Farrell & Rosenberg, 1981; Pearlin, 1975). Epidemiological studies also do not show any clear rise in mid-life of such likely signs of crisis as divorce, alcoholism, or depression in men (Hunter & Sundel, 1989). And, finally, longitudinal studies do not lend much comfort to mid-life crisis advocates. For example, researchers found no indication that any kind of crisis was common at mid-life among the participants in the Berkeley/Oakland longitudinal study (Haan, 1981b).

There are clearly stresses and tasks that are unique to this period of life. But there is little sign that these stresses and tasks are more likely to overwhelm an adult's coping resources at this age than at any other (Gallagher, 1993).

Role Transitions

The concept of *role* provides a different perspective on adjustment to the various transitions of adulthood. This important idea, which developmentalists borrowed from sociology, has been discussed in several previous chapters. Any social system can be thought of as being made up of interlocking positions (also called *statuses*) such as "employer," "worker," "teacher," "student," "retired person," and "widow." A *role* is the content of a social position—the behaviors and characteristics expected of a person filling that position (Marshall, 1996). Thus, a role is a kind of job description.

Several aspects of the concept of a role are important for an understanding of development. First, roles are at least partially culture- and cohort-specific. "Teacher," for example, may be a different role (a different set of expected behaviors) in one culture than in another, or in the same culture from one time to another.

Second, each of us must occupy multiple roles at the same time, and this inevitably produces frictions of various kinds. For example, a woman can be a member of a profession (say, a psychologist) while simultaneously occupying the roles of wife, mother, stepmother, grandmother, daughter, sister, sister-in-law, aunt, niece, friend, author, board member, singer, and volunteer. There will certainly be times when all these roles don't fit together tidily.

Sociologists use the term **role conflict** to describe any situation in which two or more roles are at least partially incompatible, either because they call for different

role conflict any situation in which two or more roles are at least partially incompatible, either because they call for different behaviors or because their separate demands add up to more hours than there are in the day

TABLE 15.1   Duvall's Stages of the Family Life Cycle

Stage	Description
1	Adult is newly married, with no children; the person assumes the spousal role.
2	First child is born; role of parent is added.
3	Oldest child is between 2 and 6; role of parent changes.
4	Oldest child is in school; parental role changes again.
5	Oldest child is an adolescent; parental role changes again.
6	Oldest child leaves home; parental role involves helping child become independent.
7	All children have left home; sometimes called the postparental stage.
8	One or both spouses has retired; worker role ends.

(*Source:* Duvall, 1962.)

behaviors or because their separate demands add up to more hours than there are in the day. Role conflict happens, for example, when a middle-aged father must choose between helping his aging parents with financial or health problems and attending his teenaged son's football games. A person experiences **role strain** when her own qualities or skills do not measure up to the demands of some role. For example, a 40-year-old worker who is forced to return to college to acquire new skills after a job layoff and who feels anxious about her ability to succeed is experiencing role strain.

The concept of roles can also help explain changes in adult life, because certain roles shift predictably with age. Each age level has accompanying roles. Even more conspicuously, family roles change in predictable ways, and one could argue that adult life marches to the rhythm of these shifts in family roles.

Evelyn Duvall described a sequence of eight family life stages, listed in Table 15.1. Each stage involves either adding or deleting some role or changing the content of a central role (Duvall, 1962). Duvall's idea has served as an organizing model for a great deal of sociological research on adulthood. Instead of comparing adults of different ages, researchers have compared adults in different life-cycle stages, creating a variant of the cross-sectional design. The basic idea, obviously, is that an individual's behavior and attitudes are shaped by the roles he occupies. And since these roles change with age in systematic and predictable ways, adults will also change systematically and predictably. Knowing that a person has a new infant tells you something about his life. If you knew that another person's youngest child had just gone off to college, you would quite correctly infer very different things about her daily existence.

But the idea of family life stages, helpful as it has been, has two major flaws. First, the model totally omits a number of important roles, such as the role of grandparent and that of caregiver to one's own aging parents. The model also does not reflect the years beyond age 65; it is as if the model assumes that no further changes in roles or life patterns occur after retirement. Yet it is increasingly clear that substantial variations in life patterns and roles exist among those over 60. Indeed, gerontologists today customarily divide the later adult years into three periods: the young old (60 to about 75), the old old (from 75 to about 85), and the oldest old (those over 85).

An even more telling problem with Duvall's simple model of family life stages is that in modern industrialized societies, a great many people simply don't move through this sequence of roles in the listed order. Increasing numbers of today's adults do not marry or do not have children; many divorce and move through complex cycles or combinations of family roles.

role strain the strain experienced by an individual whose own qualities or skills do not measure up to the demands of some role

Yet the concept of the family life cycle has important elements that both sociologists and psychologists would like to retain. Although the sequence and timing may vary, the particular family life cycle an individual experiences clearly has an important effect on his or her life pattern (Aldous, 1996). And in any given culture or cohort, some role shifts are likely to be shared, such as retirement in one's 60s in most industrialized countries. One sociologist suggests that the life course should be thought of as containing a number of transitions, defined as "changes in status that are discrete and bounded in duration," such as shifting from being single to being married or from working to being retired (George, 1993, p. 358). Transitions that are highly predictable and widely shared in any given culture or cohort are called *life course markers*. In recent cohorts in industrialized countries, many of the family life transitions that used to be concentrated in early adulthood—such as marriage and first parenthood—have become less predictable, with highly variable timing and sequence. At the same time, some transitions in middle and late adulthood—such as the death of a parent while one is in middle age or voluntary retirement in one's 60s—have become more prevalent and predictable. Sociologists believe that some aspects of Duvall's basic theoretical perspective remain useful, despite the fact that family life stages are not precisely the same for all adults (e.g., Caspi & Elder, 1988). The specific sequence of roles, or the timing of those roles, may change from one cohort to the next, from one culture to the next, or even between different subgroups within a given culture, but dealing with some sequence of roles is the very stuff of adult life.

Before going on

- Briefly describe Erikson's generativity versus stagnation stage and the evidence that supports his theory.

- What does research suggest about the existence of a universal mid-life crisis?

- What do the concepts of role conflict and role strain add to an understanding of middle adulthood?

Changes in Relationships

s suggested previously, family roles are still an important part of life in middle age. However, these roles change significantly during this period of life.

Partnerships

Several lines of evidence suggest that, on average, marital stability and satisfaction increase in mid-life as conflicts over child-rearing and other matters decline (Swensen, Eskew, & Kohlhepp, 1981; Veroff, Douvan, & Kulka, 1981; Wu & Penning, 1997).

Indeed, only a quarter of divorces involve couples over the age of 40 (Uhlenberg, Cooney, & Boyd, 1990). So, despite considerable diversity among mid-life marriages or partnerships, overall, they are less conflicted than those of young adults.

Improvements in marital satisfaction may derive from middle-aged adults' increased sense of control—a kind of marital self-efficacy (Lachman & Weaver, 1998). It is likely that middle-aged partners' identification of successful problem-solving strategies contributes to the sense that they have control over their relationship. Research has provided useful illustrations of this point. For example, researchers typically find that marital problem themes among middle-aged couples are remarkably similar to those of younger adults. Wives complain of an unjust division of labor; husbands express dissatisfaction with limits on their freedom. Yet, relationship stability among middle-aged couples is maintained through the practice of what one researcher called "skilled diplomacy," an approach to solving problems that involves confrontation of the spouse about an issue, followed by a period during which the confronting spouse works to restore harmony (Perho & Korhonen, 1999). Skilled diplomacy is practiced more often by wives than by husbands, but it appears to be an effective technique for marital problem-solving no matter which spouse uses it.

Once the children are grown and gone, many couples find it easier to spend time together—perhaps one of the reasons that marital satisfaction generally rises in middle age. (*Photo:* Jeff Greenberg, PhotoEdit)

Children and Parents

The discussion of the relationship between young adults and their families in Chapter 13 focused almost entirely on connections *up* the chain of family generations—that is, relationships between the young adults and their own middle-aged parents. When looking at family relationships from the perspective of middle age, we have to look in both directions: down the generational chain to relationships with grown children, and up the chain to relationships with aging parents.

One of the striking effects of increased life expectancy in developed countries is that adults are likely to spend many more years focusing on both older and younger generations in their families. For example, in 1800, a woman in the United States could expect both of her parents to be dead by the time she was 37 (Watkins, Menken, & Bongaarts, 1987). In the late 1980s, the average woman could expect to have at least one parent still living until she was in her late 50s, and this pattern will only become more prevalent as life expectancy increases still further.

Each of the positions in a family's generational chain has certain role prescriptions, and people expect to move in an orderly way through those roles (Hagestad, 1986, 1990). In middle adulthood, for current age cohorts at least, the family role involves not only giving assistance in both directions in the generational chain, but also shouldering the primary responsibility for maintaining affectional bonds. These responsibilities produce what is sometimes called the mid-life "squeeze," and those being squeezed form the "sandwich generation."

Such a squeeze was illustrated in the results of interviews with over 13,000 adults in one frequently cited national survey. Among many other things, respondents were asked about the amount of help of various kinds—financial, child care, household assistance, and so forth—they gave to and received from both adult children and aging parents (Bumpass & Aquilino, 1995). The results, graphed in Figure 15.1 (page 434), make it clear that those between ages 40 and 65 give help more than they receive in both directions within the family—to adult children and to aging parents—a pattern confirmed in a variety of other studies, in Canada as well as the United States (e.g., Gallagher, 1994; Hirdes & Strain, 1995).

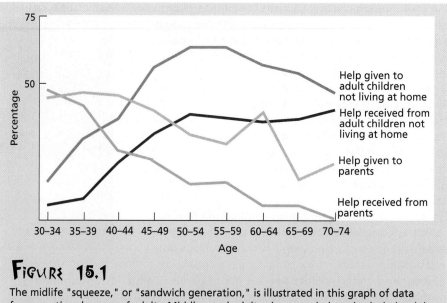

Figure 15.1

The midlife "squeeze," or "sandwich generation," is illustrated in this graph of data from a national survey of adults. Middle-aged adults give more help to both their adult children and their own parents than they receive. (*Source:* Bumpass & Aquilino, 1995, data from Tables 11, 12, 25, and 26.)

Whether most middle-aged adults experience this combination of responsibilities as a burden is not clear from the available information (Bengtson, Rosenthal, & Burton, 1996). Doubtless some do and some do not, depending on the degree of infirmity of the aging parents, the nature of the relationship the middle-aged adult has with those aging parents, and the degree of help required by the young adult children. A 50-year-old whose divorced daughter has returned with young grandchildren to live at home or one who has a parent living nearby and suffering from the early stages of Alzheimer's is far more likely to experience major role strain than is someone of the same age who babysits the grandchildren from time to time and helps her aging parents by doing occasional shopping, snow shoveling, or house-cleaning. But, on average, it is clear that middle adulthood is likely to be a time when more help is given than is received.

A quite different look at patterns of family interaction among middle-aged adults is taken in sociologist Gunhild Hagestad's fascinating three-generation family study (Hagestad, 1984). Hagestad was interested not so much in patterns of aid, but in attempts to influence other generations in the family. Middle-aged adults in this sample of 148 families typically spent more effort trying to influence their children than their parents, but both kinds of effort occurred fairly regularly. Their most successful efforts to influence their aging parents came in the form of practical advice about where to live or how to manage the household and money. Attempts to change their parents' views about social issues or family dynamics largely fell on deaf ears. Influence attempts directed at their young adult children were aimed mostly at shaping the children's transition into key adult roles. So, for example, the older adults talked about educational choices, work, money, and personal lifestyle.

Influence attempts did not radiate exclusively from the middle-aged generation. Both the young adult children and the aging parents in this study tried to influence the middle-aged generation, with varying success. Hagestad found that parents, whatever their age, kept trying to influence their children, and that children, whatever their age, continued to resist such influence and advice. Advice from child to parent was much more likely to be successful. Only about a third of the influence attempts from parents to children were effective, whereas about 70% of the influence attempts in the other direction were received positively.

Hagestad also found that each family seemed to have a particular agenda, or set of themes, that cropped up again and again in their descriptions of interactions across the generations. Some families spent a lot of time talking about money; others never mentioned this subject. Some focused on family dynamics or on health issues. Themes like this were particularly clear in the all-male or all-female lineage. In more than half of the families Hagestad studied, the three generations of women regularly talked about some aspect of interpersonal relationships, particularly family dynamics, while such themes never surfaced in the male lineage. Grandfathers, fathers, and grown sons were more likely to talk about work, education, or money with one another.

Critical Thinking

What do men and women talk about at multigenerational gatherings of your own family?

Other studies of multigenerational families, both in the United States and in Germany, confirm these patterns. When women family members have conflicts, it is most likely to be over how members of the family ought to relate to one another. When fathers, sons, and grandsons have conflicts, they are likely to be about nonfamily issues, such as politics or social issues (e.g., Hagestad, 1985; Lehr, 1982).

Hagestad's research gives a glimpse into the complex workings of family relationships across several generations. But further understanding of family relationships for middle-aged adults can be gained by considering specific aspects of their situation. Research on the "empty nest," on grandparenthood, and on care of aging parents creates a more complete picture of this sandwich generation.

Emptying the Nest

The timing of the "empty nest" stage in the family life cycle obviously depends on a person's (or couple's) age when the last child is born. Women in the cohort born between 1940 and 1949 in the United States had their last child, on average, when they were about 26. If we assume that this last child left home when he or she was 24 or 25, then women in this cohort were roughly 50 when the last child left. Because men are typically somewhat older at marriage, these women's spouses were 53 to 55 when the last child left. Obviously, those who delayed childbearing pushed the empty nest stage to a later age—a pattern more and more typical of today's adults.

Hagestad's work reinforces the obvious fact that the role of parent does not cease when the child leaves home. Support and advice continue to be expected and offered. But the content of the parental role in this "postparental" phase is clearly quite different from what it was when the children were still living at home. The child does not need daily care or supervision. As a result, adults have much more time for their spousal roles, a change that undoubtedly contributes to the higher reported marital satisfaction in this stage of family life.

Folklore in Western cultures predicts that some or even most women become depressed or upset once the "nest" is empty, because they are losing the central role of mother. Of course, it is possible that such a pattern exists in some cultures, but it seems not to be true of U.S. culture, at least not for the great majority of middle-aged women. Suicide rates do go up for women in mid-life, but the rise begins between the ages of 31 and 40, when children are still at home, and then drops for women over 50, which is when the empty nest typically occurs. Similarly, the highest rates of depression among mid-life women appear in the late 30s and early 40s, also before the children have left home. Alcohol abuse also declines among women in their 40s and 50s (U.S. Bureau of the Census, 1984).

More to the point, when women are asked specifically about positive and negative transitions in their lives, those who list the departure of the last child are more

Contrary to popular belief, when this woman's daughter leaves the nest in a few years, it will be a joyful experience. (*Photo:* Courtesy of Drs. Booker and Madeline Wright. Used with permission.)

likely to describe this event as positive rather than negative. In one study of 60 women between the ages of 45 and 60, researchers found that only a third of the participants described any significant transition point when the last child left home (Harris, Ellicott, & Holmes, 1986). Of these, 25% reported that the transition involved a distinct "mellowing," increased marital satisfaction, or increased inner stability; 17% reported that the transition involved an adjustment to the departure of the children. Those few women who do experience some distress in this role transition appear to be those whose sense of self-identity has been heavily focused on the role of mother. In contrast, women in this age range who are in the labor force are much more likely to experience the empty nest as positive.

Grandparenting

Middle-aged adults typically move into several new roles—for example, becoming in-laws as their children marry (see The Real World). In addition, in the United States, about a third of adults become grandparents by their late 40s, and half of women become grandmothers by their early 50s (Bumpass & Aquilino, 1995). As the aver-

PARENTING

The Real World

Me, a Mother-in-Law?

Most middle-aged adults are happy to see their adult children marry and form their own families. However, somewhere in the midst of the excitement a middle-aged woman experiences when an adult child gets married comes the realization that she is going to acquire one of the most maligned social roles there is: that of mother-in-law. Mother-in-law jokes abound in films and TV shows, and relationships between mothers-in-law and their children's spouses are regularly characterized as full of tension and conflict. Typically, it is the relationship between the mother-in-law and the daughter-in-law that is depicted most negatively. Thus, it isn't surprising that most middle-aged women don't look forward to becoming mothers-in-law. But, is the negative stereotyping of mothers-in-law justified?

Research in some societies suggests that the stereotype is somewhat accurate. In these societies, the mother-in-law has a well-defined social role. Newlyweds usually reside with the husband's parents, and the mother-in-law is the supervisor of the young wife and is

responsible for socializing her into the family. In such cultures, wives remain under the authority of their mothers-in-law for many years, usually until the older woman is no longer physically able to fulfill her role's requirements.

Despite the cultural reinforcement of the relationship between mother-in-law and daughter-in-law in traditional societies, these relationships are often high in conflict (Chiapin, DeAraujo, & Wagner, 1998). Most such conflicts involve the husband: The daughter-in-law thinks her husband is too loyal to his mother, or the mother-in-law thinks her son's wife is trying to undermine her relationship with him. Some mothers-in-law go so far as to physically abuse daughters-in-law, and abusive husbands sometimes receive praise from their mothers for keeping young wives in line (Fernandez, 1997).

However, some mothers-in-law may be treated poorly by daughters-in-law. For example, in rural China, a daughter-in-law is expected to care for her elderly mother-in-law. Research suggests that many daughters-in-law fail to live up to this cultural obligation (Yang & Chandler, 1992). This is especially devastating for

the mother-in-law, because, in China, the elderly are completely dependent on their adult children for economic support.

Parallels to these situations exist in more industrialized societies like the United States. Mothers-in-law are perceived as interfering in the marital relationship; daughters-in-law are accused of trying to turn their husbands against their mothers. Consequently, family therapists have devised recommendations to help middle-aged women adjust to the mother-in-law role and to forestall conflict (Greider, 2000). Here are a few such recommendations:

- Don't give unsolicited advice or make unannounced visits.
- When asked for your advice, share your experience in a nonjudgmental way.
- Don't criticize your daughters- or sons-in-law behind their backs.
- Don't insist on being visited every weekend or holiday.
- Respect your children's wishes regarding how grandchildren are to be cared for.

age age of childbearing has risen in recent cohorts, the timing of grandparenthood may shift to a slightly later age, but such a shift would not change the basic fact that this role is normally acquired in middle adulthood.

Most grandparents—92% in one study—express high levels of satisfaction with this role (Peterson, 1999). A majority see or talk to their grandchildren regularly. They may write, call, or visit as often as every couple of weeks, and most describe their relationships as warm and loving. Likewise, many studies have demonstrated the positive impact of warm relationships with grandparents on children's development (Adkins, 1999).

Grandparents seem to be an especially important source of stability in the lives of children of divorced parents. However, court rulings in the United States make it clear that the rights of grandparents are limited by the rights of parents (Jacoby, 2000). In extreme cases, such as when a grandparent is dying or has never been allowed to visit a grandchild, grandparents may sue parents, whether divorced or married, for the right to see their grandchildren. However, courts have ruled that, under most circumstances, denying visitation to a grandparent is within a parent's constitutionally protected right to make decisions about a child's upbringing.

Fortunately, most parents welcome the involvement of their own parents in their children's lives, and surveys suggest that grandparents and grandchildren engage in many of the same activities—watching television, shopping, attending religious services—that parents and children share (Waggoner, 2000). However, while parenthood clearly involves full-time responsibility, there are many degrees of being a grandparent.

Most behavioral scientists place grandparents in one of several categories derived from a study in which researchers interviewed a nationally representative sample of over 500 grandparents (Cherlin & Furstenberg, 1986). Twenty-nine percent of grandparents in the study had **remote relationships;** they saw their grandchildren relatively infrequently and had little direct influence over their grandchildren's lives. The most common reason for this remoteness was physical distance.

By contrast, this statement by one of the grandmothers in the study illustrates a different kind of relationship, for which researchers used the term **companionate relationship:**

> When you have grandchildren, you have more love to spare. Because the discipline goes to the parents and whoever's in charge. But you just have extra love and you will tend to spoil them a little bit. And you know, you give. (Cherlin & Furstenberg, 1986, p. 55)

Just over half of the survey's participants exhibited such attitudes toward their grandchildren and responded that they had very warm, pleasurable relationships with them. Yet these grandparents also said that they were glad they no longer had the day-to-day responsibility. They could love the grandchildren and then send them home.

The third, and least common (16%) type of relationship was exhibited by grandparents who had **involved relationships** with their grandchildren. These grandparents were everyday participants in the rearing of their grandchildren. Some of them lived in three-generation households with one or more children and grandchildren; some had nearly full-time care of the grandchildren. But involved relationships also occurred in some cases in which the grandparent had no daily responsibility for the grandchildren's care but created an unusually close link.

Within American society, involved grandparent care is more common among African Americans than among whites, and more common among poor than among middle-class grandparents. Surveys suggest that the prevalence of custodial grandparenting may be three times as high among African Americans (Tolson & Wilson, 1990). Moreover, about 20% of low-income grandparents have full-time responsibility for a grandchild (Pearson, Hunter, & Cook, 1997). Several studies suggest that, even when they do not have full-time responsibility for grandchildren, African American and Hispanic American grandparents have closer and more frequent contact with their

This girl seems delighted with her grandmother, with whom she seems to have what Cherlin and Furstenberg would call a "companionate" relationship. (*Photo:* Jack Monnier, Stone)

remote relationships relationships in which grandparents do not see their grandchildren often

companionate relationships relationships in which grandparents have frequent contact and warm interactions with grandchildren

involved relationships relationships in which grandparents are directly involved in the everyday care of grandchildren or have close emotional ties with them

grandchildren than white American grandparents do (Bengtson, 1985; Kivett, 1991). However, the incidence of custodial grandparenting has increased in all ethnic and socio-economic groups in recent years. Across groups, about 10% of grandparents have had full-time responsibility for a grandchild for 6 months or longer.

No matter what the family's ethnicity and socio-economic status, full-time grandparent care is especially likely when the grandchild's mother is unmarried. In such cases, the grandmother frequently takes on child-care responsibilities so that her daughter can continue in school or hold down a job. That such assistance is indeed helpful is indicated by the fact that teenaged mothers who have such help from their own mothers complete more years of education and have more successful work careers in adulthood (Taylor, Chatters, Tucker, & Lewis, 1990).

Gender is related to grandparenting as well. Among all ethnic groups, the role of grandmother is likely to be both broader and more intimate than that of grandfather (Hagestad, 1985). In addition, young grandparents, those in their 40s, have less day-to-day contact with grandchildren than those who are older, perhaps because most are still working (Watson, 1997). As a result, they know less about and are less involved in their grandchildren's everyday lives than older grandparents are.

The role of grandparent obviously brings many middle-aged and older adults a good deal of pleasure and satisfaction. However, grandparents who see their grandchildren more often do not describe themselves as happier than those who see theirs less often (Palmore, 1981). Thus, for most adults in middle age, grandparenthood is not central to their lives, to their sense of self, or to their overall morale.

Caring for Aging Parents

Another role that may be added at mid-life, and that *does* have a powerful effect on overall life satisfaction, is that of major caregiver for aging parents (see No Easy Answers). The great majority of adults, in virtually every culture, feel a strong sense of filial responsibility. When their parents need assistance, they endeavor to provide it (Ogawa & Retherford, 1993; Wolfson, Handfield-Jones, Glass, McClaran, & Keyserlingk, 1993). Interestingly, young adults seem to feel a stronger sense of obligation than those who are middle-aged (Stein et al., 1998). This may be because their parents are still healthy and fairly young and they have not yet had to face the prospect of caring for them. In contrast, for middle-aged people, the day-to-day problem of how to care for aging parents is more of a present reality. However, just how many adults actually take on this role is surprisingly unclear.

Daughters, far more than sons, are likely to take on the role of significant caregiver for a disabled or demented parent, as this daughter has done, now that her mother is suffering from Alzheimer's disease. *(Photo: Michael Newman, PhotoEdit)*

Much of the information that developmentalists have comes from studies of elderly adults who are asked about the kind and amount of care they receive from their children. But this information does not reveal much about the typical experience of the middle-aged adult. For example, researchers know that 18% of the elderly people in the United States who have adult children live with one of those children (Crimmins & Ingegneri, 1990; Hoyert, 1991). But because most elders have more than one child, it is not true that 18% of middle-aged children have a parent living with them. Nor is it true that all those home-sharing elders are disabled or in need of regular care. So this kind of study does not show how many of the middle-aged are providing regular or extensive care to an elder parent.

Better information comes from a small number of cross-sectional studies in which representative samples of middle-aged adults have been asked how much and what kind of assistance they provide to their parents (e.g., Rosenthal, Matthews, & Marshall, 1989; Spitze & Logan, 1990). In one such study, researchers interviewed

No Easy Answers

Who Cares for Aging Parents?

One of the most difficult dilemmas of mid-life arises when elderly parents become incapable of caring for themselves. Inevitably, the issue of who will care for them creates conflicts. The financial burden involved in admitting aging parents to nursing homes renders that option impossible for many. Others avoid the nursing home option because they feel a sense of moral obligation to care for their parents directly. Ultimately, even if elders move to long-term care facilities, someone has to take primary responsibility for overseeing their care.

Families typically negotiate the caregiving task along a number of dimensions, including each family member's competing demands and availability of resources. Within a group of siblings, the one most likely to take on the task of caregiving is the one who has no children still at home, is not working, not married, and lives closest to the aging parent (Brody, Litvin, Albert, & Hoffman, 1994; Stoller, Forster, & Duniho, 1992). The child with the strongest attachment to the parent is also most likely to provide help, although distance and time factors often override this effect (Whitbeck, Simons, & Conger, 1991).

Most of these factors combine to make a daughter or daughter-in-law the most likely candidate for the role of caregiver. But it makes a difference whether the frail elder is a mother or a father. Daughters are four times as likely as sons to help an older mother, but only 40% more likely than sons are to help a frail father (Lee, Dwyer, & Coward, 1993). Because women (mothers) live longer than men and are thus more likely to require help, this tendency for children to provide relatively more help to the same-sex parent means that women have a much higher probability of providing such care.

Another factor that increases daughters' involvement in parental care is simple proximity. Perhaps because of greater emotional closeness to their parents or their socialization for the role of kin-keeping, daughters are more likely to live near their parents. And parents, when they approach their later years, are more likely to move to be close to a daughter than to a son.

Yet sons are quite often involved in the care of an elder. If a son is unmarried, he is more likely to take on the caregiving role than is a married sister (Stoller et al., 1992). And if both a son and a daughter are involved, the two often divide the responsibilities, with sons providing more financial assistance or instrumental support (mowing the lawn, home repairs, perhaps shopping) and daughters more often providing help with physical activities of daily living, such as dressing, cleaning, and cooking.

But despite these complexities, the inescapable conclusion is that women are far more likely than men to take on the role of caregiver of an aging parent, just as women are more likely to take on the role of caregiver with children. Whether this will change in the next few decades, as many more middle-aged women enter or remain in the labor force, remains to be seen.

1,200 middle-aged adults in upstate New York. Figure 15.2 (page 440) shows that in this sample, on average, only about 11% of adults between 40 and 65 were providing as much as 3 hours per week of assistance to an older parent—a relatively low level of care. Combining this information with evidence from other similar research gives an estimate that between 10% and 15% of middle-aged adults are providing some kind of regular care for an older parent at any given time (Scharlach & Fredricksen, 1994). But let's be careful about what this number means.

First, studies like these only give information about one point in time, not longitudinal information. So they do not reveal what percentage of adults will take on such a caregiving role at some time in their lives. Several researchers have tried to make such an estimate, but they have used widely varying definitions of "providing care." Research using broader definitions (for example, counting anyone providing any kind of care for a nonresident, seriously ill or disabled relative in the past year) suggests that roughly 40% of middle-aged women will be involved in at least some minimal caregiving in their lifetimes (Himes, 1994).

Using longitudinal data and a much stricter definition of care, other researchers find that about a quarter of women provide significant levels of care to their own parents or parents-in-law at some time in their middle adult years (Robison, Moen, & Dempster-McClain, 1995). Furthermore, the likelihood of such a role rose steadily from one cohort to the next in the 20th century. Only 17% of women born between

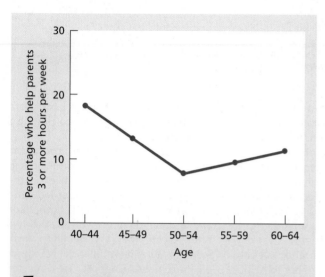

FIGURE 15.2

These cross-sectional data indicate that relatively few middle-aged adults are involved in extensive caregiving for one or both parents at any one time. But such evidence does not indicate what percentage of adults will fill such a role at *some* time in their lives. (*Source:* Spitze & Logan, 1990, from Table 2, p. 189.)

1905 and 1917 were ever major caregivers for a parent, whereas a third of those in the cohort born from 1927 to 1934 took on such a role. As life expectancy continues to rise, the likelihood of caring for an aging parent will rise still further. But even with such increases, it seems clear that while the role of caregiver for an aging parent is a common one in mid-life, it is not a standard experience, even for those in current cohorts. Moreover, future cohorts of elderly are likely to be healthier and more financially secure than today's older adults. Consequently, the experience of caring for an elder may actually become rarer.

Just what impact does caregiving have on the middle-aged adult? In the past decade, there have been hundreds of studies exploring the impact on the caregiver of tending to the daily needs of a parent (or spouse) who is disabled, frail, or demented. In the large majority of studies, the recipient of care has been diagnosed with Alzheimer's disease or some other dementia. Such individuals gradually lose their ability to perform ordinary daily tasks, may ultimately be unable to dress or feed themselves, and may not recognize their caregivers. Providing care for such an individual, especially if the caregiver is also trying to meet the needs of her (or his) own job and family, may drain both energy and finances.

Not surprisingly, such a demanding role takes its toll. The cumulative evidence indicates that such caregivers are more depressed and have lower marital satisfaction than those in comparison groups of similar age and social class (Hoyert & Seltzer, 1992; Jutras & Lavoie, 1995; Schulz, Visintainer, & Williamson, 1990). However, one study comparing African American and white American caregivers found heightened depression only among the white caregivers, an interesting finding that should be investigated further (Haley et al., 1995). Some research also suggests that those who care for demented or frail elders are more often ill themselves or have some reduced efficiency of immune system function (Dura & Kiecolt-Glaser, 1991; Hoyert & Seltzer, 1992; Kiecolt-Glaser et al., 1987). Collectively, these effects are often termed **caregiver burden.**

However, remember that many of these studies involve participants who were recruited from among support groups of families with Alzheimer's patients. It is reasonable to suppose that those who join such support groups may be those for whom caregiving is especially burdensome. Second, although scores on standard scales of depression do indeed rise among those taking on the caregiving role, few of these adults show all the symptoms of a full-scale clinical depression. Third, much less is known about the level of caregiver burden experienced by those who provide relatively low levels of assistance, such as 3 hours per week or less. It seems reasonable to assume that there is a significant difference between daily care for a demented elder and occasional lawn-mowing or shopping assistance. Finally, it is clear that certain factors can significantly lessen the burden, even for those with major caregiving responsibilities. Those who have good support networks (including a supportive spouse), as well as help from other caregivers, experience fewer negative consequences (Brody, Litvin, Hoffman, & Kleban, 1992; Pearlin, Aneshensel, Mullan, & Whitlatch, 1996; Schulz & Williamson, 1991).

For the majority of mid-life adults, the relationship with aging parents is far more positive. Most give more assistance to their parents than they did before, but they also continue to see them regularly for ceremonial and celebratory occasions and to feel affection as well as filial responsibility (Stein et al., 1998). Parents are also symbolically important to middle-aged adults, because as long as they are alive, they occupy the role of elder in the family lineage. When they are gone, each generation moves up a notch in the sequence: Those in the middle generation must come to terms with the fact that they now become the elders and are confronted directly with their own mortality.

caregiver burden a term for the cumulative negative effects of caring for an elderly or disabled person

Friends

The scant research on friendships in middle adulthood suggests that the total number of friendships is lower in these years than in young adulthood. For example, in one small study, researchers interviewed three generations of women in each of 53 families, some white American and some Hispanic American (Levitt, Weber, & Guacci, 1993). Each woman was asked to describe her close relationships. Among both groups, the young adult women had more friends in their social networks than did their middle-aged mothers.

At the same time, there are other bits of research suggesting that mid-life friendships are as intimate and close as those at earlier ages. For example, researchers have analyzed information from the files of 50 participants in the now-familiar Berkeley/Oakland longitudinal study, who had been interviewed or tested repeatedly from adolescence through age 50 (Carstensen, 1992). These analyses revealed that the frequency of interaction with best friends dropped between age 17 and age 50, but that the best-friend relationships remained very close.

These studies suggest that the social network of middle-aged adults is relatively small, although relationships are just as intimate as they were at earlier ages. It may be that the social network shrinks as adults age because there is less need for it. Role conflict and role strain decline significantly in middle age, and the need for emotional support from a social network outside the family seems to decrease accordingly (Due, Holstein, Lund, Modvig, & Avlund, 1999). Yet, because the relationships that do endure are close, the social network is available when needed. Friendship depends less on frequent contact than on a sense that friends are there to provide support as needed. Thus, the nature of friendship itself may be different in middle age.

Before going on

- What contributes to the "mellowing" of marital relationships in middle age?

- What is the family role of middle-aged adults with respect to older and younger generations?

- What is the evidence regarding the existence of an "empty nest syndrome"?

- How does the grandparent role affect middle-aged adults?

- How might caregiver burden affect a middle-aged adult's life?

- How do social networks change during middle adulthood?

Mid-Life Career Issues

Work in mid-life is characterized by two paradoxes: First, work satisfaction is at its peak in these years, despite the fact that most adults receive few work promotions in middle age. Second, the quality of work performance remains high, despite declines in some cognitive or physical skills.

Work Satisfaction

Despite the plateau in promotions that occurs for most adults in the middle years, job satisfaction is typically at its peak, as is a sense of power or job clout. Still, patterns of work and work satisfaction do vary between men and women in middle adulthood.

A cross-sectional study of a nationally representative sample of men suggested that, for them, work satisfaction increases in middle age because the issue of work is less central to their lives (Tamir, 1982). Among young adult men (aged 25 to 39) in this study, job satisfaction was strongly correlated with various measures of personal satisfaction; for the middle-aged men (aged 40-65), it was not. Middle-aged men, in other words, have begun to disengage from their work as a primary source of personal fulfillment or satisfaction, even though they are likely to be more pleased with the work itself.

Whether the same is true of women workers at mid-life is not so clear. For women who begin to work steadily only in their 30s or 40s, the middle adult years may be the time of most rapid work advancement rather than simple maintenance of previous gains. For such women, work satisfaction might have as strong a correlation with overall life satisfaction as it does for young adult men.

Interestingly, though, a shift to full-time employment once the nest is empty is not a very common pattern for women, at least in current cohorts. Longitudinal data from the 10-year Michigan Panel Study of Income Dynamics suggest that most middle-aged women began paid employment while their children were still at home (Moen, 1991). Few began work for the first time after their last child left home. When women did return to full-time work in middle adulthood, the most likely reasons were divorce or widowhood, not the final departure of children.

Moreover, patterns of work satisfaction among middle-aged women may be more complex than those of men. For example, men's satisfaction is generally linked to objective measures of achievement such as promotions and salary history (Allen, Poteet, & Russell, 1998). In contrast, even among very successful women, work satisfaction often depends on how they view the career decisions they made in early adulthood. Many in one study believed that they had given family concerns too high a priority in deciding what kind of career to pursue and claimed that they should have given less primacy to marital and family responsibilities and chosen a different career field (Stewart & Ostrove, 1998). For such women, work satisfaction tends to be low. However, many respond by making mid-life career changes or pursuing additional education.

Cross-gender variations in patterns of work and job satisfaction are accompanied by sex differences in coping style at work (Perho & Korhonen, 1999). Men and women cite the same sources of work dissatisfaction in middle age: time pressure, difficult co-workers, boring tasks, and fear of losing one's job. However, they cope with these challenges differently. Men are more likely to negotiate with supervisors and co-workers directly to effect change. In contrast, women tend to withdraw and to engage in collective complaining with female co-workers. Still, women are better able than men to balance their dissatisfactions with areas of contentment. Consequently, a statement such as "I don't like the boss, but the hours fit my needs" is more likely to come from a woman than a man. Because of their different coping styles, men are more likely to improve their level of satisfaction in situations where change is possible. By contrast, women are probably better able to cope with work settings where they must adjust to dissatisfaction because the situation can't be changed.

Despite their differences, both men and women in mid-life have a greater sense of control over their work lives than younger adults do (Lachman & Weaver, 1998). One reason for the increased feeling of control may be that social-cognitive skills improve from early to middle adulthood (Blanchard-Fields, Chen, Schocke, & Hertzog, 1998; Hess, Bolstad, Woodburn, & Auman, 1999). Middle-aged adults are better than they were when younger at "sizing up" people, relationships, and situations. At the same time, by middle age, they have become proficient at directing their own behavior in ways that allow them to maintain levels of personal satisfaction even in unpleasant circumstances.

Job Performance

In the great majority of occupations, job performance remains high throughout middle adulthood (McEvoy & Cascio, 1989). The few exceptions are those occupations in which physical strength or speedy reaction time is a critical element; some examples are longshoreman, air traffic controller, truck driver, professional athlete, and the like. In these jobs, performance begins to decline at mid-life or earlier, just as you would expect (Sparrow & Davies, 1988). In fact, many adults in such occupations change jobs at mid-life in anticipation of, or because of, such declines. But in most occupations that demand high levels of cognitive skill, performance remains at essentially the same level throughout middle adulthood (Salthouse & Maurer, 1996).

Researchers Paul and Margaret Baltes argue that maintaining high job productivity or performance is possible because adults, faced with small but noticeable erosions of cognitive or physical skill, engage in a process the Balteses call "selective optimization with compensation" (Baltes & Baltes, 1990a). Three subprocesses are involved:

- *Selection.* Workers narrow their range of activities—for example, by focusing on only the most central tasks, delegating more responsibilities to others, or giving up or reducing peripheral job activities.

- *Optimization.* Workers deliberately "exercise" crucial abilities—such as by taking added training or polishing rusty skills—so as to remain as close to maximum skill levels as possible.

- *Compensation.* Workers adopt pragmatic strategies for overcoming specific obstacles—for example, getting stronger glasses or hearing aids, making lists to reduce memory loads, or even carefully emphasizing strengths and minimizing weaknesses when talking to co-workers or bosses.

Researchers have tested this model in a study of 224 working adults aged 40 to 69 (Abraham & Hansson, 1995). Measuring each of the three aspects of the proposed compensatory process as well as job competence, they found that the link between the use of selection, optimization, and compensation on the one hand and the quality of work performance on the other got stronger with increasing age. That is, the older the worker, the more it mattered whether she used helpful compensatory practices. In the older groups (primarily those in their 50s and early 60s), those who used the most selection, optimization, and compensation had the highest work performance. But among the younger workers in this sample (those in their early 40s), the same relationship did not hold. This is obviously only one study, but the results provide some support for the idea that job performance remains high during middle age at least in part because adults take deliberate compensatory actions.

Unemployment and Career Transitions

In today's rapidly changing job market, it is not unusual for men and women to change occupations. However, career transitions can be more difficult in middle age than earlier in adulthood. For one thing, as you learned in Chapter 14, potential employers tend to believe that young adults are more capable of learning a new job than middle-aged applicants, even though research suggests that this generalization is untrue (Forte & Hansvick, 1999). Employers give middle-aged applicants higher ratings on variables such as dependability, but they tend to think that younger applicants will be able to acquire new skills (especially computer skills) more rapidly. Thus, mid-life career changers must often overcome ageism in obtaining new employment.

Career counselors also point out that to understand mid-life career changes, it is useful to categorize workers on the basis of their reasons for changing occupations (Zunker, 1994). They suggest that people change careers for either external or internal reasons and can thus be classified as either *involuntary* or *voluntary* career changers.

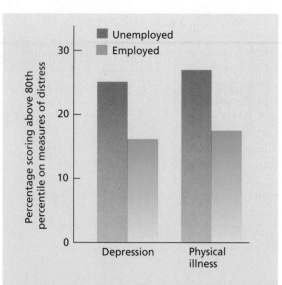

Figure 15.3

Adults who are involuntarily unemployed report more distress on nearly every measure, including both depression and physical illness, as shown by the results of a study in Michigan. (Source: Kessler et al., 1988, from Table 2, p. 74.)

● *Involuntary Career Changers* ●   Involuntary career changers are people who are in transition because of external reasons: Their skills have become obsolete, their jobs have been eliminated through organizational restructuring, or they have been laid off because of shifting economic conditions. They experience heightened levels of anxiety and depression and higher risk of physical illness in the months after the job loss (Kessler, Turner, & House, 1988; Liem & Liem, 1988; Price, 1992). Such effects are not unique to workers in the United States. Similar results have been found in studies in England, Denmark, and other Western developed countries (e.g., Iversen & Sabroe, 1988; Warr, Jackson, & Banks, 1988). You can see an example of this effect in Figure 15.3, which shows results from a study comparing 146 unemployed and 184 employed men and women (Kessler et al., 1988). Interestingly, just as remarriage alleviates many of the stresses associated with divorce, re-employment seems to restore health, emotional stability, and a sense of well-being quite rapidly.

The causal link between job loss and emotional or physical distress is both direct and indirect. The financial strain of job loss is itself a major contributor to heightened levels of anxiety and depression. When job loss does not create significant financial strain—such as when a spouse continues to work at a well-paying job or the family has other resources—the negative effect of job loss is only about half as great (Kessler et al., 1988).

The indirect effects of job loss include changes in family relationships and loss of self-esteem. Most strikingly, marital relationships deteriorate rapidly after one or the other spouse has been laid off. The number of hostile or negative interactions increases, and the number of warm and supportive interactions declines—which means that the crucial ratio of positive to negative interactions spirals downward. Separation and divorce become much more common as a result (Conger, Patterson, & Ge, 1995; Crouter & McHale, 1993; Elder & Caspi, 1988; McLoyd, Jayaratne, Ceballo, & Borquez, 1994).

These negative effects of unemployment are seen in both young and middle-aged adults, but those aged 30 to 60 seem to show the largest effects—the greatest increases in physical illness and the biggest declines in mental health (Warr et al., 1988). This pattern makes some sense in terms of the stages of men's work lives you read about in Chapter 13. During the trial stage, young adults between 18 and 29 may interpret periods of unemployment as a normal part of the trial-and-error process of finding the right job. But workers in the stabilization stage may interpret job loss quite differently—either as a sign of personal failure or as an unrecoverable loss of security. Younger workers are also more likely to be unmarried, with fewer economic responsibilities, and they may be able to return to live with their parents during a period of unemployment. For them, the stress is therefore less pronounced.

The dynamics of job loss appear to be much the same for workers of every racial group. For example, unemployed African American adults, like other unemployed groups, show higher rates of distress and illness and lower levels of life satisfaction (Bowman, 1991). But in the United States and in most European countries, unemployment is considerably more common among African Americans than among whites. As Vonnie McLoyd, who has studied the effects of unemployment on African Americans, observes,

Involuntary career changers must confront a series of stressful situations, such as applying for unemployment benefits. (*Photo:* Rob Crandall, Stock Boston)

Even in the best of times, the official unemployment rate of black workers typically is twice that of white workers. Blacks' increased vulnerability to unemployment is attributable to several factors, including lesser education, lesser skill training, less job seniority, [and] fewer transportable job skills. (1990, p. 316)

What is more, recent changes in the U.S. job market have made this problem worse. There have been heavy job losses in manufacturing and other blue-collar job sectors in which African American men are most likely to be employed. African American women, more often employed in the service sector, have been less severely affected by these changes.

The magnitude of the effect of unemployment may also be larger for African Americans than for white Americans because being unemployed is so often accompanied by a lack of any sense of personal control over the situation. When jobs become increasingly scarce, even hard work and diligence will not necessarily pay off in terms of employment. A sense of victimization is a common result, as is increased ill health and depression. Because many African Americans, confronted with widespread racism or chronic urban poverty, already experience very high levels of stress, unemployment increases the risks proportionately more.

Predictably, the Big Five personality dimensions, especially neuroticism and openness to experience, contribute to mental health during involuntary career transitions across all racial and ethnic groups (Heppner, Fuller, & Multon, 1998). Nevertheless, mental health professionals suggest that the impact of an involuntary career change on an individual's life may be more directly affected by his or her coping skills (Zunker, 1994). For example, the person must be able to assess the situation realistically. If new work skills are needed, then the person must be able to formulate and carry out a plan for obtaining such skills. Researchers have found that mid-life career changers who have good coping skills and use them to manage involuntary transitions are less likely to become depressed (Cook & Heppner, 1997).

As with all types of stress, the effects of unemployment can be partially buffered by having adequate social support (Vinokur & van Ryn, 1993). Further, involuntary career changers benefit from career counseling that addresses both their occupational needs and their psychosocial development (Schadt, 1997). Counselors can help people who are forced to change jobs learn to think of the transition as an opportunity to re-examine goals and priorities—to treat the crisis as an opportunity (Zunker, 1994).

Counselors also urge involuntary career changers to avoid acting impulsively. They suggest viewing the transition as a process of stages that begins with a review of the individual's work history, interests, skills, and values. Based on the information gathered, the career changer should formulate an occupational goal and a plan for obtaining training, if needed. Finally, the person should develop a strategy to reduce the likelihood of another involuntary transition in the future, such as an educational plan for keeping work skills up-to-date.

MAKE THE CONNECTION

How might a middle-aged adult use the post-formal thinking you learned about in Chapter 12 to cope with an involuntary career transition?

● **Voluntary Career Changers** ● Voluntary career changers leave one career to pursue another for a variety of internal reasons (Allen, Dreves, & Ruhe, 1999). For example, they may believe that the new job will be more fulfilling. One pattern occurs when workers look at the next step on the career ladder and decide they don't want to pursue further advancement in their current occupation. For example, both male and female certified public accountants are more likely to leave their profession for this reason than for any other (Greenhaus, Collins, Singh, & Parasuraman, 1997). Others change careers in order be able to express aspects of their personalities that they believe aren't utilized in their present jobs (Young & Rodgers, 1997).

Twin studies suggest that the tendency to change careers voluntarily in adulthood may have a genetic basis (McCall, Cavanaugh, Arvey, & Taubman, 1997). These findings further suggest that such transitions are a by-product of personality. Whatever the reason for the transition, voluntary career changers have a better sense of con-

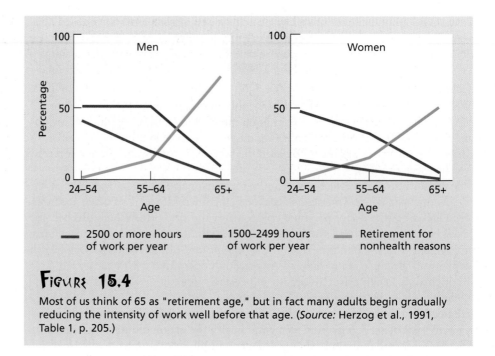

FIGURE 15.4

Most of us think of 65 as "retirement age," but in fact many adults begin gradually reducing the intensity of work well before that age. (*Source:* Herzog et al., 1991, Table 1, p. 205.)

trol over their situation than do people whose job changes are forced on them, but the transition is still stressful. Spouses and family members may not understand why the person wants to change careers. Moreover, changing careers can involve periods of unemployment and, often, a reduction in income. Thus, voluntary career changers manifest many of the same symptoms of anxiety and depression seen in involuntary career changers. Consequently they, too, benefit from social support and career counseling.

Preparing for Retirement

Many middle-aged adults begin to prepare for retirement as early as 15 years before their anticipated retirement date. One aspect of such preparation is a gradual reduction in workload. For example, Figure 15.4 shows the hours worked per year for men and women in a random national sample of 1,339 U.S. adults (Herzog, House, & Morgan, 1991). You can see that the percentage of men and women working very long hours (2,500 hours per year or more, which averages out to 48 hours a week) drops among those aged 55 to 64.

Critical Thinking

Think about the middle-aged people you know. Do any of them seem to be winding down their involvement in work?

As they get nearer to the standard time for retirement, middle-aged adults also increase both formal and informal preparations (Evans, Ekerdt, & Bossé, 1985). They talk with their spouse and with friends or co-workers about retirement options and read more articles about retirement in the popular press. Some also undertake such formal preparations as attending financial planning seminars, determining how much Social Security income they can expect upon retirement, investigating their pension plan at work in more detail, or seeking guidance from a professional retirement planner.

Such preparations are more likely among workers who are looking forward to retirement, who are dissatisfied with their work, or who have a retired friend (Evans et al., 1985). Those who dread retirement do the least planning, but even in this group, the level of informal planning increases as the time of retirement approaches.

However, it may be too early to form conclusions about how people prepare for retirement. After all, the notion of retirement is relatively new and tends to be exclusive to industrialized cultures. Even among the most prosperous nations, the idea of a period of leisure following many years of work did not exist prior to the mid-20th century. Thus, all our notions about preparation for retirement are based on a small number of cohorts, all of whose members were born in the first half of the 20th century. Comparisons of their behavior to that of the current generation of middle-aged adults suggest that ideas about preparing for retirement have changed.

The retirement preparations of the Baby Boom cohort, who are all now middle-aged, are quite different from those of their parents (Monroy, 2000). For one thing, among their parents, retirement planning was primarily a male responsibility. In contrast, Baby Boom women are also doing retirement planning, sometimes together with their husbands, but sometimes independently (Glass & Kilpatrick, 1998). Further, retirement-minded Boomers are largely responsible for the growth of electronic financial services, because of their enthusiastic response to the availability of such services on the Internet.

Most Baby Boomers expect to die in their mid-80s or later but expect to retire fairly early, in their early 60s (Monroy, 2000). This means that their expected length of retirement is far longer than that of earlier generations, 20 years or more. Moreover, Baby Boomers believe that they need higher retirement incomes than their parents. Most have enjoyed a comfortable standard of living, compared to earlier generations, in part because of the proliferation of the two-income family. They expect some decline in income after their retirement, but generally much less change in their standard of living. Further, most do not expect that Social Security payments will be adequate to meet their needs.

Because of their expected length of retirement and income requirements, traditional ideas about preparation for retirement don't seem to fit the Baby Boomers. For example, earlier cohorts tended to put funds they expected to use for retirement into very safe investments (certificates of deposit, government bonds, and the like). However, many Baby Boomers have put their retirement nest eggs into the stock market. Further, they have borrowed rather than saved to achieve their investment objectives. Consequently, financial analysts claim that many individual Boomers may be in precarious situations when they reach retirement age because they are not saving enough money and have substantial debts (Glass & Kilpatrick, 1998; Monroy, 2000). In addition, while their parents' generation tended to think of retirement exclusively in terms of leisure time, most Boomers expect to work at least part-time during their retirement years. In fact, many Boomers look forward to retirement as a time when they can try out occupations that interest them but that they haven't had time to pursue earlier in life.

Because of the retirement wealth many Baby Boomers have accumulated and their intentions to keep working after they retire, economic analysts predict that as a group they are likely to enjoy levels of affluence in retirement that far exceed those of their parents. Further, Boomers are projected to be the healthiest, best-educated, and longest-living retirees in history. Thus, they are likely to substantially change ideas about both preparing for retirement and retirement itself.

One difference between Baby Boomers and earlier cohorts is that more women are involved in retirement planning. (*Photo: Bob Daemmrich, Stock Boston*)

Before going on

- Why are levels of job satisfaction higher among middle-aged workers than among younger workers?

- Describe the job performance strategies used by middle-aged workers.

- What are the factors that contribute to career transitions in mid-life?

- How do Baby Boomers differ from previous cohorts with respect to preparation for retirement?

Individual Differences

There are many individual differences in life experiences during middle adulthood. The pathway an adult follows, or the degree of movement along any one pathway, is affected by a whole range of factors, including individual family history and personality. By mid-life, many people have also encountered specific crises, such as divorce, poor health, early widowhood, or losing a job. As you've learned in earlier chapters, the timing of major life crises and transitions can also make a difference.

Continuity and Change in Personality

Can developmentalists tell what kind of person someone will be in middle adulthood, based on what is known about his childhood, adolescence, or early adult life? As you should remember, the Big Five personality traits are relatively stable across adolescence and adulthood. Similarly, masculinity and androgyny are correlated with self-esteem and social adjustment in adults of all ages (Shimonaka, Nakazato, Kawaai, & Sato, 1997).

Looking at poorly adjusted people as they grow older provides a view of continuity that is different from correlation studies of personality traits. For example, as you know, neuroticism is fairly consistent across ages. In fact, a recent longitudinal study revealed that emotional negativity in adolescence is linked to poor mental health in middle adulthood (Offer, Kaiz, Howard, & Bennett, 1998). In this study, male participants were tested at ages 14, 19, and 48. Researchers found that negative emotional traits in adolescence strongly predicted less-than-optimal mental health status in both early adulthood and middle age.

Despite the evidence for continuity, most people believe that personality changes with age, and most expect themselves to change. In one study, researchers examined 26- to 67-year-olds' current perceptions of their own personalities in terms of the Big Five (Fleeson & Heckhausen, 1997). They also asked them to describe themselves when they were 20 to 25 years old and to speculate about how their personalities might change by the time they reached age 70. Further, they were asked to describe an ideal personality they would like to have. All respondents believed that their personalities had changed since they were younger and that they would change in the future. Their ideas about the kinds of changes that would take place included both gaining and losing some traits. The researchers pointed out that these respondents perceived much more change in personality than is shown by longitudinal studies of the Big Five traits. Apparently, we believe we change much more than we actually do.

Critical Thinking

Has your personality changed since you were younger? In what ways? How do you expect it to change as you get older?

However, there is some evidence of real change in personality in adulthood. For example, most observers agree that during the years from 40 to 65, most adults decline in achievement striving, independence, assertiveness, and individualism, which tend to peak at about mid-life. In fact, several studies suggest that people become more prosocial and less individualistic in middle and late adulthood (e.g., Van Lange, DeBruin, Otten, & Joireman, 1997). Interestingly, though, this change seems to be linked to secure attachment in infancy and childhood, so it has elements of both continuity and change.

Studies of negative and positive emotionality suggest a similar pattern. Even though negative emotionality in early adulthood is moderately to strongly correlated with negative emotionality in middle adulthood, longitudinal studies show that many individuals become *less* negative over time (Helson & Klohnen, 1998). Apparently, then, when researchers consider large groups—which they must to correlate variables such as personality factors—they find that personality is fairly stable over time. However, the correlations can mask a number of individual cases in which there is a great deal of change. Consequently, the best conclusion to draw is that stability is the general pattern, but the increased individual variability in personality that is typically found among middle-aged and older adults suggests that change is clearly possible and may even be common (Nelson & Dannefer, 1992).

Cohort differences must also be kept in mind when interpreting research results. For example, one recent study found that middle-aged women from the Baby Boom generation, most of whom have worked outside the home for a large proportion of their adult lives, may possess characteristics that have not been found in research on earlier cohorts (Stewart & Ostrove, 1998). Historically, researchers consistently found that menopause and the empty nest were the primary landmarks middle-aged women used to characterize their lives. Baby Boom women, however, seem to be more likely to engage in the sort of comprehensive life review that previously was more characteristic of middle-aged men. Physical and family changes appear to continue to be important for these women at mid-life, but career issues and the potential for reshaping their lives as they age seem also to be crucial.

Cross-sectional studies suggest that the mechanism behind personality change in middle adulthood may be an increasing ability to maintain control of one's emotions in a variety of situations (Gross et al., 1997). Supporting this hypothesis is the finding from several cross-sectional studies that introversion, or self-examination, increases slightly over the adult years (e.g., Costa et al., 1986). However, research on introversion is inconsistent. Several studies have found no indication of an increase in introversion in late middle age or among older adults, either in participants' current descriptions of themselves or in their recollections of themselves at earlier ages (Ryff, 1984; Ryff & Heincke, 1983).

Another possible cause of change is growth in personal flexibility. Researchers have examined the tendency of adults to either remain committed to difficult goals or adjust their goals when an objectives seems to be impossible to achieve (Brandtstädter & Baltes-Götz, 1990; Brandtstädter & Greve, 1994). An individual high in **tenacious goal pursuit** would agree with statements like these (Brandtstädter & Baltes-Götz, 1990, p. 216):

> The harder a goal is to achieve, the more desirable it often appears to me.
> Even if everything seems hopeless, I still look for a way to master the situation.

Someone high in **flexible goal adjustment** would agree with the following (pp. 215–216):

> I can adapt quite easily to changes in a situation.
> In general, I'm not upset very long about an opportunity passed up.
> I usually recognize quite easily my own limitations.

Tenacious goal pursuit tends to decrease in middle adulthood, while flexible goal adjustment rises, suggesting a kind of "mellowing" of personality in the middle years.

The Effects of Timing

As in earlier periods, the timing of major life events in middle adulthood affects individual developmental pathways. For example, early menopause seems to be particularly stressful. Women who are peri- or postmenopausal in their late 30s or early 40s manifest negative reactions simply to the word *menopause* (Singer & Hunter, 1999). Many react to discovering that they are menopausal with shock and denial. When they realize that the physical transition is unavoidable, many respond with anger and feel a sense of loss of control. Long-term consequences of early menopause are predicted

tenacious goal pursuit a behavior pattern in which middle-aged adults remain committed to goals that are difficult, and may be impossible, for them to achieve

flexible goal adjustment a behavior pattern in which middle-aged adults adjust goals in order to enhance the likelihood of success

Research suggests that middle-aged women are more resilient than younger women in managing transitions such as divorce. (*Photo:* David Young-Wolff, PhotoEdit)

by a woman's developmental history, material circumstances, and the way in which she fits early menopause into her own autobiography and sense of self.

In another variation on the timing theme, middle-aged adults are likely to feel extra strain, even a sense of failure, if children do not leave home by the time they are about 25 (Hagestad, 1986). Moreover, conflicts between parents and resident adult children are common (Muzi, 2000). Both parents and children feel that they have inadequate privacy. Middle-aged parents' sense of obligation to their children may cause them to feel that they can't pursue their own goals until they have helped their late-blooming children to become self-sufficient. As a child's departure is further and further delayed, frustrations can accumulate.

The percentage of adult children living with their middle-aged parents seems to be increasing. In 1970, only 8% of 25-year-olds lived with their parents. By the 1990s, estimates of the proportion of young adults residing with parents ranged from 12% to 20% (Muzi, 2000; U.S. Bureau of the Census, 1995). Delayed marriage and a rise in the divorce rate probably explain this increase.

Research suggests that, even though conflict occurs, more than half of parents with adult resident children manage to work out good systems for handling the potential stresses and say that they are satisfied with their arrangement (Aquilino & Supple, 1991). In fact, some parents enjoy greater social support from their resident children than from their children who live away from home (Umberson, 1992). But there is little doubt that such an arrangement brings a new set of tasks and roles, and that it is linked to somewhat higher stress levels in many families.

Similarly, adults who become grandparents unusually early seem to be less comfortable with the role (see the Research Report) (Burton & Bengtson, 1985; Troll, 1985; Watson, 1997). Likewise, those whose parents die early find themselves unexpectedly thrust into the role of family "elders" before they are ready for it. As one 40-year-old man whose parents had both just died said, "I'm too young to be next in line!" (Hagestad, 1986).

By contrast, divorce, which is typically an early adulthood event, appears to be less traumatic for middle-aged women than for younger women (Marks & Lambert, 1998). Perhaps the "mellowing" of personality you read about earlier in this chapter renders the middle-aged woman more resilient to such traumatic events. So, timing may be important only when events that are perceived to signal movement into the late adult years—menopause and grandparenthood—occur earlier than expected.

Before going on

- What is the evidence for continuity in personality throughout adulthood?

- What does research suggest about the possibility of adult personality changes?

- In what way does the timing of adult role transitions affect a middle-aged individual's sense of well-being?

Research Report

Early Grandparenthood

Together with increases in pregnancy rates among teenagers, of course, have come increases in the numbers of early grandparents. Although the phenomenon of early grandparenthood is growing among all U.S. ethnic and racial groups, historically it has been most common among African Americans. Thus, the small amount of research on early grandparenting consists primarily of studies of young African American grandparents.

The impact of timing of role changes was vividly illustrated in a study involving 41 African American families in Los Angeles in the mid-1980s; each family included a new mother, a grandmother, and a great-grandmother (Burton & Bengtson, 1985). Each woman was classified as either "early" or "on time" with respect to her particular role. For the grandmothers, being "on time" was defined as becoming a grandmother between the ages of 42 and 57; "early" grandmothers had all acquired the role before they were 38, several of them in their 20s. The large majority of these grandmothers had at least a high school education; few were on welfare. So

these were mostly working-class or middle-class families.

What is striking is how different the experience of grandmotherhood was for those who were early as opposed to those who were on time. Early grandmothers reported far more strain and distress. In part, this occurred because these young grandmothers were still in early adulthood themselves, with all of the role conflict and role overload of that period. Many of these early grandmothers still had young children of their own at home to rear. They were distressed to have the role of grandparent added to the list, especially if they expected to have to take on some of the task of rearing the grandchild.

But the early timing of the role change also seemed to be disturbing in itself. These women associated grandparenthood with being "old," and they did not want to feel old. According to a 28-year-old grandmother,

> I could break my daughter's neck for having this baby. I just got a new boyfriend. Now he will think I'm too old. It was bad enough being a mother so young—now a grandmother too! (Burton & Bengtson, 1985, p. 61)

Another woman who became a grandmother at 27 said, "I'm too young to be a grandmother. You made this baby, you take care of it" (p. 61). Many of these very early grandmothers did end up helping to rear their new grandchildren, but clearly they did so reluctantly. In contrast, women in this study who became grandmothers at the standard time were much more willing to participate in the new child's care and much more pleased about becoming grandmothers.

Many factors are clearly involved here. Very early grandmothers must, of necessity, have been early mothers themselves, and this fact sets them apart from other women in some ways. Further, when grandparents have more material resources than their unmarried children who become parents, the experience of early grandparenting is often mingled with that of parenting a live-in teenaged or young adult mother and her child. In such situations, it is difficult to separate the effects of timing and family stress (Gordon, Chase-Lansdale, Matjasko, & Brooks-Gunn, 1997). But these results are consistent with researchers' general knowledge about the impact of being on-time or off-time in major life transitions.

A Final Word

Middle adulthood is shaped by the various life changes and crises, both standard ones and unanticipated ones, that each adult must confront. The years from 40 to 60 are very different for a divorced woman with few job skills than they are for a woman in an intact marriage who has a successful career. They differ in other ways for a middle-aged man who is laid off from his steady job at age 50 and cannot find other work. Yet, it may well be that what is most significant in shaping the experience of middle adulthood is how an adult copes with such crises, rather than the crises themselves.

Summary

Theories of Social and Personality Development

- Erikson proposed that the primary developmental task of middle adulthood is to acquire a sense of generativity through mentoring younger individuals.

- Many different models of the "mid-life crisis" in middle adulthood have been proposed, but none has been strongly supported by research.

- Sociologists explain adult development in terms of role transitions. Duvall's stage theory of role transitions has provided a framework for research, but it is not comprehensive enough to explain adult development.

Changes in Relationships

- Marital satisfaction is typically higher at mid-life than it is earlier. This higher level of satisfaction appears to be due primarily to a decline in problems and conflicts.

- Middle-aged adults have significant family interactions both up and down the generational chain. The two-way responsibilities can create a mid-life "squeeze" or a "sandwich generation." Middle adults provide more assistance in both directions and attempt to influence both preceding and succeeding generations.

- There is little sign that middle-aged parents experience negative reactions to the "empty nest," when the last child leaves home. On the contrary, the reduction in role demands may contribute to the rise in life satisfaction at this age.

- Most adults become grandparents in middle age. The majority have warm, affectionate relationships with their grandchildren, although there are also many remote relationships. A minority of grandparents are involved in day-to-day care of grandchildren.

- Only a minority of middle-aged adults seem to take on the role of significant caregiver for an aging parent. Those who do report a feeling a considerable burden and suffer increased depression, particularly if the parent being cared for suffers from some form of demen-

tia. Women are two to four times as likely as men to fill the role of caregiver to a frail elder.

- Friendships appear to be somewhat less numerous in middle adulthood, although they appear to be as intimate and central to the individual.

Mid-Life Career Issues

- Job satisfaction is at its peak in middle adulthood, and productivity remains high. But the centrality of the work role appears to wane somewhat, and job satisfaction is less clearly linked to overall life satisfaction than at earlier ages. Research suggests that patterns of work and satisfaction are different for men and women in middle age.

- Levels of job performance in middle adulthood are consistent with those at earlier ages, with the exception of work that involves physical strength or reaction time.

- Involuntary career changes are associated with anxiety and depression. Even many middle-aged adults who make voluntary career transitions experience negative emotions.

- Middle-aged adults prepare for retirement in several ways, not only by specific planning but also by reducing the number of hours they work.

Individual Differences

- The Big Five personality traits and other aspects of personality are correlated across early and middle adulthood. There is evidence for personality change in middle age as well. There are some signs of "mellowing," a lowering of intensity and striving, but middle-aged adults vary more in personality traits than do younger adults.

- Any role change or crisis that is not timed according to expectations for a given cohort or culture is associated with higher levels of stress. Such events include very early grandparenthood, early death of one's parents, and late departure of grown children from the home.

Key Terms

What Types of Couples Should Be Sanctioned by Society?

During the sexual revolution of the 1960s and early 1970s, young adults often referred to marriage as "just a piece of paper." The real bond between intimate partners was psychological, many asserted, and need not be validated by a government license. This view became the driving force behind a movement away from marriage and toward cohabitation. At the same time, gay rights advocates began to suggest that, if being a couple is essentially a psychological union, then sexual orientation should be irrelevant. That is, they argued, homosexuals are capable of establishing the same kinds of interpersonal relationships as heterosexuals. Therefore, heterosexual unions should not be seen as superior in any way simply because they are legally sanctioned by society.

Behavioral scientists are interested in the question of how and to what degree the legal status of a relationship alters its impact on partners' interactions with each other and on their individual development. One interesting point is that changing ideas about relationships, instead of causing marriage to disappear, have led to an increase in the number of legal options available to intimate partners. Thus, it seems that both heterosexual and homosexual couples, rather than regarding a license as "just a piece of paper," continue to want to have their relationships recognized by society in some official way. This common motivation to enter into legally sanctioned relationships has led to a number of changes in social policy.

Marriage and Divorce Reform

The institution of marriage is currently undergoing a wave of reforms, the first of which stems from the right-to-marry movement among homosexuals. In the United States, the federal government and more than 30 states have passed legislation limiting marriage to heterosexual couples, in response to widespread public opposition to homosexual marriage (Public Agenda, Inc., 1999). By contrast, in Denmark and the Netherlands, marriage has been expanded to include homosexual couples—although gay and lesbian couples are less likely than heterosexual couples to enter into legal relationships, even when they have full marital rights (Associated Press, 2000; Halvorsen, 1998; Luetzen, 1998).

Another set of marriage reforms is aimed at reducing divorce. For example, in many states and in Canada, efforts are underway to require couples to undergo premarital counseling.

Reforms of marriage laws have included a number of provisions, such as mandatory premarital counseling, aimed at reducing the divorce rate. (*Photo:* Michael Newman, PhotoEdit)

Advocates of mandatory premarital counseling cite research suggesting that couples who go through premarital counseling experience higher levels of marital satisfaction and are less likely to divorce (e.g., Sayers, Kohn, & Heavey, 1998; Schumm, Resnick, Silliman, & Bell, 1998). Opponents of such requirements point to studies that indicate that couples who go through premarital counseling are no less likely to divorce than others (e.g., Sullivan & Bradbury, 1997). Moreover, couples who participate in premarital counseling are typically more religious than couples who don't go through counseling—and religion itself is a factor that predisposes against divorce. Thus, opponents claim, positive effects associated with premarital counseling are actually self-selection effects: Those who are least likely to divorce are the most likely to obtain premarital counseling.

Similarly, proposed changes in divorce laws include one requiring a couple to undergo marriage counseling before they can divorce. Most studies suggest thet marital therapy usually results in short-term improvements in relationship quality. However, findings regarding long-term effectiveness of

Legislators in the United States have responded to the demands of gay rights advocates to expand marriage to include homosexual couples by creating *registered domestic partnerships* and *civil unions*. (*Photo:* Jonathan Nourok, Stone)

therapy in preventing divorce are inconsistent (Bodenmann, Widmer, & Cina, 1999; Christensen & Heavey, 1999).

Some reformers in the United States and Canada are seeking the establishment of an entirely new legal institution, known as *covenant marriage,* that places strict limits on divorce. In 1999, the state of Louisiana became the first in the United States to pass covenant marriage legislation. Couples in Louisiana who apply for marriage licenses must specify whether theirs will be traditional or a covenant marriage. Those who choose covenant marriage cannot divorce unless one spouse can prove in court that the other has been sexually unfaithful, is addicted to drugs or alcohol, or has been convicted of a felony. Otherwise, the couple can never divorce, even through mutual agreement.

Advocates believe that covenant marriage will enhance couples' level of commitment to the relationship. Although they may be right, it seems likely that couples who are the most committed to each other prior to marriage will choose covenant rather than traditional marriage. Therefore, any difference in commitment level would be attributable to self-selection rather than to the differing effects of traditional and covenant marriage.

Registered Domestic Partnerships and Civil Unions

Numerous jurisdictions have enacted laws that allow both opposite-sex and same-sex couples to enter into *registered domestic partnerships.* Some jurisdictions, including a number of states and cities in the United States, require employers to provide the same benefits to domestic partners that are available to married employees' spouses. In most cases, however, domestic partners have fewer rights, privileges, and legal obligations to each other (such as joint responsibility for debts) than do spouses.

The *civil union* is a newer type of relationship, created specifically to answer homosexual couples' demands for rights equivalent to those of married heterosexuals. In 2000, the first civil union legislation was passed in the state of Vermont. The only legal difference between a civil union and a marriage is that the latter is restricted to male-female couples. Civil unions differ from domestic partnerships in that couples in civil unions have the same rights and obligations as those who are married.

The prevalence of legal relationships among homosexuals may increase in the future, as societal views of homosexuality and the meaning of marriage continue to change. (*Photos:* A. Ramey, Stock Boston; Michelle Bridwell, PhotoEdit)

	Heterosexual couples	Gay couples	Lesbian couples
No legal status (cohabitation)	Cohabiting heterosexuals	Cohabiting gays	Cohabiting lesbians
Registered domestic partnership	Heterosexual partners	Gay partners	Lesbian partners
Civil union	N/A	Gay civil unions	Lesbian civil unions
Marriage	Heterosexual spouses	Gay spouses	Lesbian spouses
Covenant marriage	Heterosexual covenant spouses	N/A	N/A

FIGURE 1

To answer questions about the impact of legal status on relationships and on individual development and about the interaction between legal status and sexual orientation, each group in the grid would have to be compared to every other group.

Further, those who decide to end their relationships must do so in family court, adhering to the same set of rules that apply to divorce, although the term *dissolution* is used rather than divorce.

Typically, opposition to domestic partnership and civil union legislation comes from religious groups, such as the Roman Catholic church, which believe that homosexuality is immoral (Tettamanzi, 1998). Proponents argue that homosexual couples who want to legally affirm their relationships should be able to do so irrespective of others' views of the morality of their sexual orientation. Advocates also suggest that homosexuals need a legal means by which to make health insurance and other employee benefits available to their partners. Similarly, in the absence of a legal relationship, homosexuals have no right to authorize or terminate medical treatment for an ailing or injured partner.

The Impact of Legal Status on Relationships and Individuals

Because the number of legal options available to couples is growing, researchers interested in the effects of legal status on intimate partners' relation-ships and individual development are faced with a much more complex task than when a "couple" was a man and a woman who were either married or living together (see Figure 1) Thus, examination of the cor-relations among relationship legal status, sexual orientation, relation-ship quality, and individual develop-ment is likely to become an active area of research over the next sev-eral decades. To be most useful, such research would have to take into account other variables, including the partners' cultural backgrounds, their personalities, their ages, whether they have children, and so on. Preferably, too, the various groups should be studied longitudinally. The most researchers can say at this point is that there are qualitative differences between legally married and cohabiting heterosexuals (see Chapter 13). Likewise, despite some similarities, there are a few important differences between hetero-sexual and homosexual relationships (see Chapter 13). Thus, both legal status and sexual orientation seem to matter in rela-tionships, but as yet there is no reliable evidence about how the two factors might interact.

Your Turn

- What marriage and divorce reform efforts are currently underway in your state?

- What do your classmates and friends think about the idea of covenant marriage?

- Consult a gay-rights Web site (such as www.gay-civil-unions.com) to find out if there is a right-to-marry movement in your state. If so, how much support does the movement have in your state legislature and among the citizens of your state?

- Find out whether your city and/or state has a domestic partnership law. If so, does the law guarantee employer benefits such as health insurance coverage to domestic partners?

- Interview a marriage therapist. What does this professional think about the effects of legal status on partners' commitment to one another, the quality of their relationship, and their development as individuals?

CHAPTER

16

Physical and Cognitive Development in Late Adulthood

R. W. Jones/CORBIS

In an earlier edition of this book, Helen Bee wrote about her 81-year-old father's tendency to use the term "my brains" to refer to a notebook in which he kept information such as frequently used phone numbers, appointments, birthdays, and the like. He developed this behavior in response to his self-observed increasing forgetfulness, and the substitute "brains" enabled him to get through each day without having to rely on his own brain. As this anecdote illustrates, for many older adults, the experience of aging is a process of learning to offset weaknesses, such as increasing forgetfulness, with strengths, such as practicality and inventiveness.

As the example of Helen Bee's father illustrates, older adults often find ingenious ways of managing age-related changes. Thus, one of the most striking characteristics of old age is the degree to which the experience of growing old varies from one individual to another. In this chapter, we will examine this variability along with changes that appear to affect almost everyone. As you read, keep the following questions in mind:

- How variable are the elderly?

- What physical changes are associated with late adulthood, how do theorists explain them, and how do they affect the lives of older adults?

- What are the major mental health concerns of late adulthood?

- How does aging affect memory, and what theories have psychologists formed regarding the development of wisdom and creativity in old age?

Variability in Late Adulthood

The scientific study of aging is known as **gerontology.** For many years, gerontologists thought about old age almost exclusively in terms of decline and loss. However, perspectives on the later years are rapidly changing, and late adulthood is now thought of as a period of tremendous individual variability rather than one of universal decline (Weaver, 1999).

Characteristics of the Elderly Population

Stereotypes of the elderly abound—they are the stuff of jokes and fairy tales, and today they are reinforced in the media. But real people often belie the stereotypes.

Life Expectancy You might be surprised to learn that life expectancy increases as adults get older. For example, in the United States, the average 65-year-old man lives to about age 80, but once a man reaches 80, he is likely to live to be 90 (Federal Interagency Forum on Aging-Related Statistics [FIFARS], 2000). Life expectancy among women is even longer. The average 65-year-old woman lives to the age of 85, and the average 85-year-old woman can expect to live to over 90. Because of this sex difference in life expectancy, there are more elderly women than men. Life expectancy varies by racial group as well. In general, 65- to 74-year-old white Americans have longer life expectancies than African Americans in this age group, perhaps because of different rates of cancer and other diseases you learned about in Chapter 14. However, by age 75, the life expectancies of white American and African American elders are essentially equivalent (FIFARS, 2000).

gerontology the scientific study of aging

457

No Easy Answers

The Coming Demographic Crisis

Every industrialized nation in the world will face a demographic crisis in the near future. Within the next decade, the elderly population will increase dramatically. As a result, there will be fewer young and middle-aged adult workers for every retired person (Century Foundation, 1998). Consequently, governments may lack sufficient tax revenues to pay for the many benefits they have guaranteed to senior citizens.

With respect to pension plans, such as the Social Security system in the United States, there are really only two options: decreasing benefits to recipients or increasing taxes on workers. Moreover, economic analysts report that neither option alone will solve the problem. Any workable solution must include both reducing the financial burden of elderly entitlements and generating additional revenues.

Unfortunately, polls suggest that the public is opposed to both options (Public Agenda, Inc., 1999). Voters in the United States overwhelmingly oppose reducing benefits for the current cohort of retired people and are only slightly less opposed to reducing benefits for future retirees. At the same time, most workers

believe that their Social Security taxes are already too high but do not want the government to use other funds, such as those generated by income taxes, to pay for Social Security benefits. Moreover, U.S. workers blame the problem on government mismanagement rather than on the mathematical inevitabilities of the demographic crisis. Consequently, lawmakers face a dilemma: A solution must be found, or governments may go bankrupt trying to fulfill their obligations to future elderly citizens. However, any solution politicians impose on voters is likely to be unpopular.

(*Photo:* Mark Richards, PhotoEdit)

For these reasons, policy makers are looking for ways to make elderly entitlement reform more palatable to voters. For example, one proposal involves workers' taking responsibility for their own retirement income by directing how their Social Security taxes are to be invested. The appeal of this option is that it offers workers more autonomy. However, unlike the current system, it would not include a guaranteed retirement income. Those who invest wisely will enjoy a comfortable retirement; those who are less astute may be left with little or nothing.

Surveys suggest the public seems to want both autonomy over retirement investments and a guaranteed income (Public Agenda, Inc., 1999). They would like to be able to invest their own Social Security taxes *and* retain the present system. Clearly, U.S. voters seem to be reluctant to acknowledge that it is impossible to create a system that offers benefits without costs. As a result, workers in the United States are likely to end up with a solution that is imposed on them by legislators rather than one that represents a public consensus.

● **Subgroups** ● Gerontologists point out that there are important differences among the *young old* (aged 60–75), the *old old* (aged 75–85), and the *oldest old* (aged 85 and over). The oldest old are the fastest-growing segment of the population in the United States, which means that terms such as *octogenarian* (a person in his or her 80s) and *centenarian* (a person over 100 years of age) will be used far more often than in the past. From 1960 to 1994, the over-65 population in the United States doubled, while the over-85 population tripled (FIFARS, 2000). By contrast, the overall U.S. population grew only 45% during the same period. Moreover, demographers project that the over-85 population in the United States will exceed 19 million by 2050. Furthermore, every industrialized country in the world is experiencing this same kind of growth in the elderly population (Century Foundation, 1998).

The oldest old are more likely to suffer from significant physical and mental impairments than are the young old or old old. Consequently, the increase in their numbers means that the population of **frail elderly,** older adults who cannot care for themselves, is also likely to grow significantly. Consequently, demographers and economists have become concerned about the ability of young and middle-aged adults to support the growing number of elderly (see No Easy Answers).

frail elderly older adults whose physical and/or mental impairments are so extensive that they cannot care for themselves

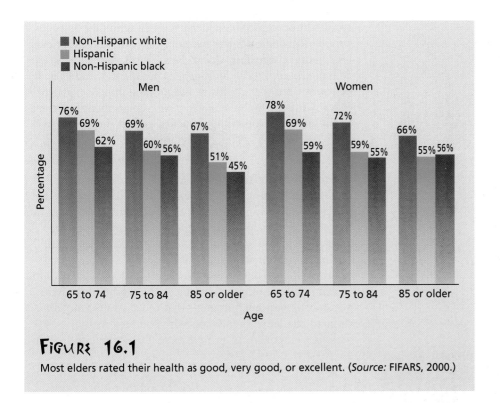

FIGURE 16.1

Most elders rated their health as good, very good, or excellent. (*Source:* FIFARS, 2000.)

● *Health* ● As Figure 16.1 indicates, a majority of older adults across all three age subgroups regard their health as good (FIFARS, 2000). These data contradict stereotypes of old age as a period of illness. However, the proportions of elderly with good health are a great deal lower than the equivalent proportions for young and middle-aged adults. Thus, as you might suspect, health is the single largest factor determining the trajectory of an adult's physical or mental status over the years beyond age 65. As you read more about the prevalence of disability and disease among older adults, keep Figure 16.1 in mind. You will see that these data are a testimony to the emotional resilience of older adults, a majority of whom are able to maintain an optimistic view of themselves and their lives in the face of growing physical challenges.

Those who are already suffering from one or more chronic diseases at 65 show far more rapid declines than do those who begin late adulthood with no disease symptoms. In part, of course, this is an effect of the disease processes themselves. Cardiovascular disease results, among other things, in restricted blood flow to many organs, including the brain, with predictable effects on an adult's ability to learn or remember. Analyses from the Seattle Longitudinal Study show that adults with this disease show earlier declines in all mental abilities (Schaie, 1996). And, of course, those suffering from the early stages of Alzheimer's disease or another disease that causes dementia will experience far more rapid declines in mental abilities than will those who do not have such diseases.

● *Cognitive Functioning* ● Researchers found a great deal of variability in a 7-year longitudinal study of the cognitive abilities of 102 older adults, first tested when they were between ages 62 and 86 (Willis, Jay, Diehl, & Marsiske, 1992). Over the ensuing 7 years, when most of the participants shifted from being young old to being old old, 62% of the group either remained at their original level of competence or showed improvement in competence on everyday intellectual tasks, while the remaining 38% showed decline (Willis et al., 1992). These results are supported by the graph in Figure 16.2 (page 460), which illustrates that a majority of elderly adults, even among those who are over 85, do not suffer from cognitive impairments.

Gerontologists have also learned that hormone replacement therapy contributes to variations in cognitive functioning among postmenopausal women. Longitudinal

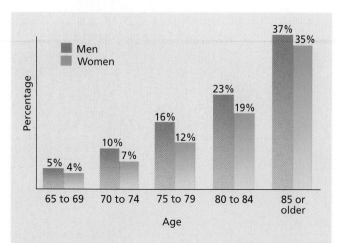

FIGURE 16.2

The graph represents the percentages of young old, old old, and oldest old adults in the United States who have cognitive impairments. (*Source:* FIFARS, 2000.)

Use it or lose it? These men keep their minds sharp by playing games that require complex memory and strategy skills. (*Photo:* A. Ramey, PhotoEdit)

studies have found that elderly women who take estrogen supplements enjoy better memory function and experience less mental confusion (Costa, Reus, Wolkowitz, Manfredi, & Lieberman, 1999). Similarly, experimental studies have demonstrated that cognitive functioning improves when older women who have never taken replacement hormones begin taking estrogen supplements, even if they do so in their 70s (Duka, Tasker, & McGowan, 2000).

● **Mental Exercise** ● Can mental exercise improve mental functioning, just as physical exercise improves physical functioning? Studies with rats show that older rats placed in very rich, interesting environments experience growth in brain tissue, whereas rats placed in neutral or boring environments experience a decrease in brain mass (Cotman & Neeper, 1996). Neurophysiologists involved in this animal research are convinced that something analogous occurs among humans—that older adults who continue to challenge themselves with complex mental activities can delay, or even reverse, the normal decline in brain mass that is part of primary aging.

Correlational evidence supports this argument. For example, in one study, researchers found that older adults who played bridge regularly had higher scores on tests of both memory and reasoning than did non–bridge players. The two groups did not differ in education, health, exercise levels, or life satisfaction or on measures of physical and cognitive functioning that have little relationship to bridge playing, such as reaction time and vocabulary size (Clarkson-Smith & Hartley, 1990).

The difficulties inherent in this research are obvious: Most strikingly, such research suffers from a serious self-selection problem. People who strive to remain mentally active are doubtless different to begin with from those who make less effort. And teasing out the unique effect of mental activity from the role of education, social class, and health is clearly very difficult. But it seems reasonable that some—perhaps significant—enhancement or better maintenance of intellectual skills results from an "engaged" and intellectually active lifestyle (Gold et al., 1995).

● **Limitations on Activities** ● Gerontologists generally define a *disability* as a limitation in an individual's ability to perform certain roles and tasks, particularly self-help tasks and other chores of daily living (Jette, 1996). Daily living tasks are grouped into two categories: **Activities of daily living,** or **ADLs,** include bathing, dressing, using the toilet, and so forth. **Instrumental activities of daily living,** or **IADLs,** include doing housework, cooking, and managing money.

Figure 16.3 gives a sense of how many Medicare recipients in the United States (generally individuals over age 65) have difficulty performing such tasks (FIFARS, 2000). As you can see, a significant proportion of elders have at least some degree of disability. However, the proportions have declined in recent years, and the majority of elderly adults have no difficulty performing ADLs or IADLs.

As you might expect, proportions of older adults with disabilities rise with age. Roughly half of those over 85 report at least some level of difficulty performing some

activities of daily living (ADLs) self-help tasks such as bathing, dressing, and using the toilet

instrumental activities of daily living (IADLs) more complex daily living tasks such as doing housework, cooking, and managing money

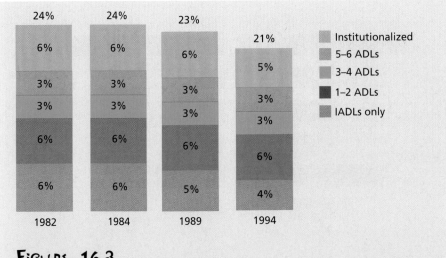

FIGURE 16.3

The graphs show the proportions of chronically disabled Medicare recipients from 1982 to 1994 who had limitations on one or more activities of daily living (ADLs, which are self-care tasks such as bathing) and on instrumental activities of daily living (IADLs, which are more complex tasks such as cooking and money management). (*Source:* FIFARS, 2000.)

basic daily life activities (Jette, 1996). But this means that half of these oldest old do *not* have such problems. To be sure, surveys generally exclude adults who are living in institutions, the vast majority of whom are severely disabled, according to the usual definition. And, of course, many of those with significant disability die before age 85, leaving only the healthiest still surviving among the oldest old. Still, it is important to understand that among the oldest old who live outside of nursing homes, the proportion who have some disability is nowhere near 100%. Even more encouraging is the finding that the rate of disability among the old old and the oldest old has been declining slowly but steadily in the past few decades in the United States, perhaps because of better health care or better health habits (Kolata, 1996).

As you can see from Figure 16.4 (page 462), the physical problems or diseases that are most likely to contribute to some functional disability in late adulthood are arthritis and hypertension. Not everyone with these problems is disabled. But the risk of some kind of functional disability is two to three times higher among elders who suffer from these diseases than among those who do not (Verbrugge, Lepkowski, & Konkol, 1991). As the figure also indicates, except for hypertension among women, the prevalence of these conditions and diseases increased from 1984 to 1995. These increases are most likely the result of population growth among the oldest old, who are more likely than the young old and the old old to be in ill health.

You can also see from Figure 16.4 that women are considerably more likely than men to suffer from arthritis, so they are also more often limited in their ability to carry out the various movements and tasks necessary for independent life (Brock, Guralnik, & Brody,1990). Since women are more likely to be widowed and thus to lack a partner who can assist with these daily living tasks, it is not surprising that more women than men live with their children or in nursing homes.

● ***Racial and Ethnic Differences*** ●   Among ethnic minorities, as among white Americans, individual variability in old age is the rule rather than the exception. Certainly, averages in life expectancy and disabling conditions such as heart disease differ across groups. For example, the prevalence of arthritis among elderly white Americans is about 58%, whereas 50% of Hispanic Americans and 67% of African

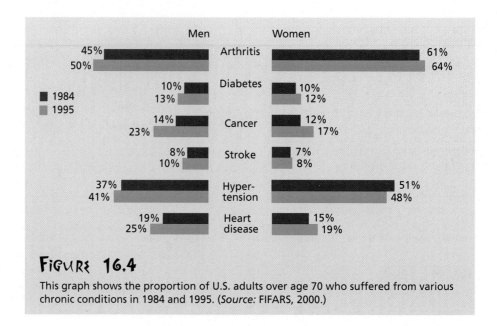

FIGURE 16.4

This graph shows the proportion of U.S. adults over age 70 who suffered from various chronic conditions in 1984 and 1995. (*Source:* FIFARS, 2000.)

Americans have this potentially disabling condition (FIFARS, 2000). Nevertheless, as Figure 16.1 showed, a majority of elders across these three ethnic groups rate their health as good to excellent. (The one exception is African American men over age 85.)

Moreover, everything you have learned so far about the correlations between health habits and health status in adulthood are just as applicable to minorities as to whites. Thus, improved diet, increased physical activity, and participation in treatment programs for debilitating chronic ailments can potentially benefit elders of any race or ethnic group.

Longevity

Part of the shift in thinking about old age is evident in the fact that gerontologists have begun to devote a great deal of attention to studying why some people live to the age of 100 and beyond. By this time, you've learned enough about development to predict that, like most other developmental variables, longevity appears to result from interactions among heredity, environment, and behavioral choices.

● *The Maximum Lifespan* ●   For humans, the maximum lifespan seems to be about 110 or 120 years, although relatively few people attain the status of centenarian (see the Research Report). For turtles, the lifespan is far longer, and for chickens, far less. Such differences among species have persuaded some biologists that there may be some universal genetic process that limits lifespan (e.g., Hayflick, 1977, 1987).

Advocates of this view support their argument with research demonstrating that cells taken from the embryos of different species and placed in nutrient solution double only a fixed number of times, after which the cell colony degenerates. Human embryo cells double about 50 times; those from the Galapagos tortoise double roughly 100 times; chicken cells double only about 25 times. Furthermore, cells taken from human adults double only about 20 times, as if they had already "used up" some of their genetic capacity. The theoretical proposal that emerges from such observations is that each species is subject to a time limit, known as the **Hayflick limit** (because it was proposed by biologist Leonard Hayflick), beyond which cells simply lose their capacity to replicate themselves (Norwood, Smith, & Stein, 1990).

The genetic limits argument has been strengthened by the recent discovery that each chromosome in the human body (and presumably in other species, too) has, at

Hayflick limit the theoretical proposal that each species is subject to a genetically programmed time limit after which cells no longer have any capacity to replicate themselves accurately

Research Report

The New England Centenarian Study

You might be surprised to learn that throughout the industrialized world, the subgroup of the elderly who are 100 years old or older is growing at a more rapid rate than any other segment of the population (Perls, Silver, & Lauerman, 1998). At the beginning of the 20th century, there was only 1 centenarian for every 100,000 people in the United States. By the end of the century, the rate was 1 centenarian per 10,000 people, or a total of about 50,000 individuals over the age of 100. Demographers project that by 2010, the centenarian population will quadruple, reaching more than 200,000. Similar increases are projected to happen every decade, which will result in a centenarian population of over 1,000,000 persons by the middle of the 21st century—more than 90% of whom will be female.

Many researchers have turned their attention to the over-100 group to discover the causes of extreme longevity. Among the most important of these studies is the New England Centenarian Study, which is currently underway at Harvard Medical School. This study has made a number of interesting findings.

For one thing, researchers have found that reports of specific geographic loca-tions where many people are said to live to the age of 150 are either complete fab-rications or gross exaggerations. For example, several years ago a TV commer-cial advertising a certain brand of yogurt claimed that Russians who live in the Cau-casus remain healthy into their mid-100s because of the amount of yogurt they consume. After thorough investigation, researchers determined that the group cited did include many individuals who were old, but their cultural traditions involved assuming the identities of their ancestors and adding the age at death of these forebears to their own ages (Perls, 1999). Thus, their self-reported ages were far older than their actual chronological ages. Still, researchers continue to investi-gate any region where large numbers of people live to be 100 to determine if these places have any characteristics that foster longevity. For example, researchers are currently focusing on a region that extends from Minnesota to Nova Scotia because a remarkable number of cente-narians live there.

It turns out that the oldest docu-mented person in recorded history was 122 years old at her death in 1997. Fam-ily studies suggest that longevity tends to run in families; that is, centenarians are more likely than others to have par-ents and siblings who survived past the age of 100. Surprisingly, most centenari-ans have large numbers of siblings. For example, researchers compared a cur-rent group of centenarians to members of the same cohort who died in their 70s during the late 1960s. They found that the centenarians averaged 4.5 siblings, whereas those who died in their 70s averaged only 3.2 brothers and sisters. Researchers hypothesize that the greater number of siblings may reflect a genetic predisposition to better general health, but as yet little or no evidence exists to support this notion.

Interesting, too, is the association between late motherhood and cente-narian status. Among the 100-year-old women in the New England Centenarian Study, 20% gave birth to a child after age 40. In contrast, only 5% of members of their cohort who died in their 70s delivered a child in middle age. Researchers hypothesize an association between longevity and general health or between longevity and late menopause to be responsible for this correlation. However, evidence has yet to confirm either view.

Whatever the cause of extreme longevity, the increasing number of cen-tenarians is likely to change develop-mentalists' understanding of old age. Perhaps future lifespan development textbooks will include chapters specifi-cally devoted to these super-elders.

its tip, a string of repetitive DNA called a **telomere** (Angier, 1992; Campisi, Dimri, & Hara, 1996). Among other functions, telomeres appear to serve as a kind of time-keeping mechanism for the organism. Researchers have found that the number of telomeres is reduced slightly each time a cell divides, so that the number remaining in a 70-year-old is much lower than what is found in a child. This raises the possibility that there may be a crucial minimum number of telomeres; when the total falls below that number, then disease or death comes fairly quickly.

● *Individual Heredity* ●   Whatever the maximum possible human lifespan, it is clear that there is a large range of individual differences in how long people live. Some general tendency to "live long and prosper" (to quote Mr. Spock from *Star Trek*) is clearly inherited. Identical twins are more similar in length of life than are fraternal twins, and adults whose parents and grandparents were long-lived are also more likely to live longer (Plomin & McClearn, 1990).

telomere string of repetitive DNA at the tip of each chromosome in the body that appears to serve as a kind of timekeeping mechanism

Twin studies in Sweden showed that identical twins have more similar illness rates than do fraternal twins (Pedersen & Harris, 1990). Similarly, for the Harvard men in the Grant study sample, there was a small but significant correlation between the longevity and health of each man's parents and grandparents. Only about a quarter of those whose oldest grandparent had lived past 90 had any kind of chronic illness at age 65, compared with nearly 70% of those whose oldest grandparent had died at 78 or younger (Vaillant, 1991).

Critical Thinking

How many people in your family have lived past the age of 80? Did those who died younger do so because of a controllable lifestyle factor, such as smoking?

● ***Health Habits*** ●   The same health habits that are important predictors of longevity and health in early adulthood continue to be significant predictors in late adulthood. For example, a 17-year follow-up of participants in the Alameda County epidemiological study who were 60 or over at the start of the study showed that smoking, low levels of physical activity, and being significantly underweight or overweight were linked to increased risk of death over the succeeding 17 years (Kaplan, 1992). Many other large epidemiological studies confirm such connections (e.g., Brody, 1996; Paffenbarger, Hyde, Wing, & Hsieh, 1987).

Perhaps the most crucial variable is physical exercise, which has been clearly linked not only to greater longevity but also to lower rates of diseases such as heart disease, cancer, osteoporosis, diabetes, gastrointestinal problems, and arthritis (Brody, 1995; Deeg, Kardaun, & Fozard, 1996). Good evidence on this point comes from a longitudinal study of nearly 7,000 participants who were all 70 or older when they were first tested in 1984 (Wolinsky, Stump, & Clark, 1995). They were then retested every 2 years until 1990. Those who reported in 1984 that they had a regular exercise routine or walked a mile or more at least once a week maintained better physical functioning over the succeeding years, were less likely to die, and were less likely to be in a nursing home by 1990. These outcomes remained likely even when the variations in health in 1984 were factored out—that is, it isn't just that healthy adults are more likely to exercise, but exercise keeps people healthier.

This point is reinforced by studies in which older adults have been assigned randomly to exercise and nonexercise groups (e.g., Blumenthal et al., 1991). In these studies, too, those who exercised had better scores on various measures of physical functioning. One such experiment with a group of adults who were all over age 80, found that muscular strength increased and motor skills improved after only 12 weeks of exercise (Carmeli, Reznick, Coleman, & Carmeli, 2000).

Physical exercise also seems to help maintain higher levels of cognitive performance among the elderly (Albert et al., 1995). Studies with rats, for example, show that older rats who exercise regularly on treadmills have higher levels of a nerve growth factor that keeps neurons healthy (Cotman & Neeper, 1996). Studies of humans, naturally enough, provide less direct evidence, but nonetheless point in the same direction. Some particularly clear evidence comes from a study in which researchers followed a group of 85 men from age 65 through age 69. All the men were well-educated and were in good health at the start of the study, with no symptoms of heart disease or dementia (Rogers, Meyer, & Mortel, 1990). In the succeeding 4 years, a third of the men chose to continue working, mostly at fairly high-level jobs. Another third retired but remained physically active, while the remaining third retired and became physically (and mentally) inactive. The inactive participants

There are many ways to maintain physical fitness in old age. In China, elderly people often can be found practicing Tai Chi in the early morning.

(*Photo:* A. Ramey, Stock Boston)

showed progressive declines on a measure of blood flow to the brain and performed significantly less well than either the active retired men or the still-working men on a battery of cognitive tests.

If anything, physical exercise seems to be even more important in the later years than at earlier ages. For example, one investigation used medical records and self-reports of exercise to examine the degree to which physical activity influenced height loss in the elderly (Sagiv, Vogelaere, Soudry, & Shrsam, 2000). They found that study participants who had exercised regularly lost significantly less height over a 30-year period than those who had not exercised. Further, exercise after age 40 seemed to be especially important in preventing height loss.

Some authors have suggested that as much as half of the decline in various aspects of physical (and perhaps cognitive) functioning in late adulthood could be prevented through improved lifestyle, particularly exercise. Yet less than a fifth of older adults in the United States exercise regularly (McAuley, 1993; Wolinsky et al., 1995). People give many reasons for not exercising, including poor health, arthritic pain, time demands of caring for an ailing spouse, culturally based assumptions about appropriate behavior for older persons, embarrassment about exposing an aging body to others in an exercise program, lack of fitness facilities or lack of transportation to such facilities, fears of various kinds, and plain lethargy.

Before going on

- In what ways do older adults vary across age groups and individually?

- What are the factors that contribute to longevity?

Physical Changes

Despite variability in health and functioning among the elderly, there are several changes in physical functioning that characterize the late adult years for almost everyone.

The Brain and Nervous System

If you look back at Table 12.1 (p. 345), you'll see four main changes in the brain during the adult years: a reduction of brain weight, a loss of gray matter, a decline in the density of dendrites, and slower synaptic speed. The most central of these changes is the loss of dendritic density. You'll remember from Chapter 4 that dendrites are "pruned" during the first few years after birth, so that redundant or unused pathways are eliminated. The loss of dendrites in middle and late adulthood does not seem to be the same type of pruning. Rather, it appears to be a decrease in useful dendritic connections.

However, research suggests that experience as well as aging is involved in the loss of dendritic density. Neurologists have found that, across the years from 60 to 90, adults with higher levels of education show significantly less atrophy of the cerebral cortex than those who have fewer years of schooling (Coffey, Saxton, Ratcliff, Bryan, & Lucke, 1999). Moreover, the brains of well and poorly educated elderly adults do not differ in areas that are less involved in academic learning than the cerebral cortex is. This finding suggests that education itself is the cause of the reduced atrophying of the cerebral cortex rather than some general factor, such as socio-economic status, that is coincidentally related to education.

Dendritic loss also results in a gradual slowing of synaptic speed, with a consequent increase in reaction time for many everyday tasks. Neural pathways are redundant enough that it is nearly always possible for a nerve impulse to move from neuron A to neuron B, or from neuron A to some muscle cell. Neurologists usually refer to this redundancy as **synaptic plasticity.** But with the increasing loss of dendrites, the shortest route may be lost, so plasticity decreases and reaction time increases.

One final change in the nervous system, about which physiologists disagree, is the loss of neurons themselves. For many years, it was believed that an adult lost 100,000 neurons every day. It now appears that this conclusion, like many such conclusions about primary aging, was based on cross-sectional comparisons that included many older adults who had diseases known to affect brain composition and functioning. Researchers have not yet reached a consensus on just how much loss occurs among healthy aging adults, but most agree that 100,000 neurons per day is a considerable overestimation (e.g., Ivy, MacLeod, Petit, & Marcus, 1992; Scheibel, 1996).

In addition, current estimates are that the brain has perhaps 1 trillion neurons (Morgan, 1992). A loss of 100,000 per day, even if it began at birth and lasted for a lifespan of 100 years, would only be about 4 billion neurons, leaving the vast majority (over 99%) still intact. It is only when the brain loses a significant amount of interconnectivity, which occurs as dendrites decrease in number, that "computational power" declines and symptoms of old age appear (Scheibel, 1992, p. 168). In addition, as you learned in Chapter 12, scientists have only recently discovered that new neurons are produced in some parts of the brain even in adulthood, although the effect of this neuron regeneration is not yet known (Gould, Reeves, Graziano, & Gross, 1999).

The Senses and Other Body Systems

In Chapter 14, you read about declines in sensory and other physical functions that occur in middle age. Such deficits become larger in late adulthood, and several more serious threats to the health of these systems arise.

● *Vision* ●   In addition to presbyopia (farsightedness), late adulthood can bring other vision defects due to body changes. For example, blood flow to the eye decreases (perhaps as a side effect of atherosclerosis), which results in an enlarged "blind spot" on the retina and thus a reduced field of vision. The pupil does not widen or narrow as much or as quickly as it previously did, which means that the older adult has more difficulty seeing at night and responding to rapid changes in brightness (Kline & Scialfa, 1996).

synaptic plasticity the redundancy in the nervous system that ensures that it is nearly always possible for a nerve impulse to move from one neuron to another or from a neuron to another type of cell (e.g., a muscle cell)

1992). Similarly, they seem to be less able to judge the speed of oncoming traffic when trying to execute turns and carry out other driving maneuvers (Keskinen, Ota, & Katila, 1998). And the general increase in reaction time affects elders' ability to switch attention from one thing to the next or to react quickly and appropriately when a vehicle or obstacle appears unexpectedly.

Changes in temperature sensitivity, together with general slowing, lead to increases in accidental burns. For example, the elderly are more likely to burn themselves when they mistakenly pick up a hot pan while cooking. The neurological message "Put down this pan because it's going to burn your skin" moves from the hand to the brain almost instantaneously in a young or middle-aged adult. Among older adults, however, a greater amount of heat is required to initiate the message, the message itself travels to the brain more slowly, and the response from the brain that signals the hand to let go of the pan travels more slowly as well. Consequently, burns are far more common in late adulthood than earlier.

This older man has bought himself a very sporty car and doubtless thinks of himself as still a skillful driver. But it is nonetheless true that many of the physical changes associated with aging will make it harder for him to respond quickly, to see clearly in glare, and to adapt rapidly to changing driving conditions. (*Photo:* Tom Prettyman, PhotoEdit)

● ***Sleeping and Eating Patterns*** ●   Another common effect of physical change is a shift in sleep patterns in old age, which occurs among both healthy and less healthy elders. Adults older than 65 typically wake up more frequently in the night and show decreases in rapid eye movement (REM) sleep, the lighter sleep state in which dreaming occurs. Older adults are also more likely to wake early in the morning and go to bed early at night. They become "morning people" instead of "night people" (Hoch, Buysse, Monk, & Reynolds, 1992; Richardson, 1990). And because their night sleep is more often interrupted, older adults also nap more during the day in order to accumulate the needed amount of sleep. These changes in sleep and activity patterns are presumed to be related to changes in nervous system functioning.

The ability of the brain to regulate appetite also changes with advancing age. When you eat, your blood sugar rises, resulting in a chemical message to the brain that creates a sensation called **satiety,** the sense of being full. The feeling of satiety continues until your blood sugar drops, at which time another chemical message is sent to the brain that causes you to feel hunger. In older adults, the satiety part of the pattern seems to be impaired (Keene, Hope, Rogers, & Elliman, 1998). As a result, older adults may feel hungry all the time and may overeat. To compensate, they come to rely more on habits such as taking their meals at certain times and eating the same foods every day. Thus, they may seem to be unnecessarily rigid to those who are younger when, in reality, their adherence to a particular eating regime is simply a (perhaps unconscious) way of coping with a physiological change.

● ***Motor Functions*** ●   The various physical changes associated with aging also combine to produce a reduction in stamina, dexterity, and balance. The loss of stamina clearly arises in large part from the changes in the cardiovascular system, as well as from changes in muscles. Dexterity is lost primarily as a result of arthritic changes in the joints.

Another significant change, one with particularly clear practical ramifications, is a gradual loss of the sense of balance (Guralnik et al., 1994; Simoneau & Liebowitz, 1996; Slobounov, Moss, Slobounova, & Newell, 1998). Older adults, who may be quite mobile in their home environments, are likely to have greater difficulty handling an uneven sidewalk or adapting their bodies to a swaying bus. Such situations require the ability to adjust rapidly to changing body cues and the muscular strength to maintain body position, both of which decline in old age. So

satiety the feeling of fullness that follows a meal

older adults fall more often. About one-quarter of the young old and more than a third of the old old interviewed for one study reported having fallen in the previous year (Hornbrook, Stevens, & Wingfield, 1994). Because of osteoporosis, such falls more often result in a fracture in old age, which can be a very serious health complication for an older adult.

Older adults also have more problems with fine-motor movements (Smith et al., 1999). Such losses are small and gradual with respect to well-practiced skills such as handwriting. However, research suggests that some fine-motor activities, especially those that require learning a new pattern of movement, may be extremely difficult for elderly people. For example, older adults take far longer than young and middle-aged adults do to learn complex computer mouse skills such as clicking and dragging objects across the screen (Smith, Sharit, & Czaja, 1999).

Critical Thinking

How might age-related changes in facial muscles contribute to stereotypes about "grumpiness" in the elderly?

● *Sexual Activity* ● Another behavior that is affected by the cumulative physical changes of aging is sexual behavior. You read in Chapter 14 that the frequency of sexual activity declines gradually in middle adulthood. Both cross-sectional and longitudinal data suggest that this trend continues in late adulthood (Marsiglio & Donnelly, 1991; Palmore, 1981).

The decline in the frequency of sexual activity in late adulthood doubtless has many causes (National Institute on Aging [NIA], 2000b). The continuing decline in testosterone levels among men clearly plays some role. The state of one's overall health plays an increasingly larger role with advancing age. For example, blood pressure medication sometimes produces impotence as a side effect; chronic pain may also affect sexual desire. Stereotypes that portray old age as an essentially asexual period of life may also have some effect.

Despite declining frequency, though, more than 70% of adults continue to be sexually active in old age (Bartlik & Goldstein, 2000). Moreover, the physiological capacity to respond to sexual stimulation, unlike other aspects of functioning, appears not to diminish with age. Indeed, some studies suggest that older adults, especially women, are more sexually adventurous; that is, they appear to be more willing to engage in sexual experimentation than young and middle-aged adults (Purnine & Carey, 1998).

Before going on

● How does the brain change in late adulthood?

● What changes happen in other body systems of older adults?

● How do theories explain biological aging?

● What are the behavioral effects of changes in the various body systems of older adults?

Institutionalization among the Elderly

Research results such as those graphed in Figures 16.3 and 16.4 suggest that the average older adult will spend at least a few years with some kind of disability or chronic disease. How often do such problems require nursing home care? There are several answers to that question, depending on what statistics you look at.

One frequently quoted statistic is that only 4% of all adults over 65 in the United States are in any kind of institutional care (FIFARS, 2000). More older women than men are in nursing homes, and about 25% of the oldest old are in nursing homes. Still, these numbers may be lower than you would have guessed.

A second important piece of information is the estimate that the average 65-year-old man in the United States can expect to spend about 5 months in such an institution before he dies. The average woman can expect to spend 16 to 17 months (Manton, Stallard, & Liu, 1993). But neither of these statistics answers what is perhaps the most important question: What is the probability that

any given 65-year-old will spend time in a nursing home or other institution? In the United States, that probability is about 40% (Belgrave, Wykle, & Choi, 1993; Kane & Kane, 1990). That is, roughly 40% of current older adults can expect to spend at least some time in a nursing home before death. Considering these several pieces of data together, it looks as if some kind of institutional care during late adulthood is common but by no means universal, and that such care is most often fairly brief. Only a quarter of those over 65 can expect to spend as long as a year in a nursing home.

The actual experiences of those in nursing homes paint both rosy and gloomy pictures. It is true that placement in a nursing home is often followed by death within a relatively short time. But it is *not* true that nursing home care necessarily shortens a person's life. Only when an older adult has been placed in an institution (or any other living situation) involuntarily is there evidence that the move itself is a causal factor in rapid decline and death. Involuntarily institutionalized elders show much higher death rates in the ensuing months and

years than do equivalently disabled elders who remain at home, although even this effect is not inevitable (Lawton, 1985, 1990). When the institution itself offers residents high levels of warmth, individuation, and opportunity for choice and control, even an involuntary move need not accelerate the process of physical or mental decline (Fields, 1992).

Nursing homes have a bad reputation—and, unfortunately, in the past some of that reputation was deserved. Only as research has revealed more about the needs and abilities of the elderly has institutional care for this group improved. Given that the number of elderly in the United States is increasing, it's important that those currently caring for the elderly and those who are getting older themselves have a realistic view of the likelihood of entering an institution and how being in an institution affects the elderly. The public must demand that institutional care for the elderly meet high standards and take more varied forms, so that, should some kind of institutional care become necessary (as well it might), the elders involved have the best possible experience.

Mental Health

The best-known mental health problems of old age are the **dementias,** a group of neurological disorders involving problems with memory and thinking that affect an individual's emotional, social, and physical functioning. Dementia is the leading cause of institutionalization of the elderly in the United States (FIFARS, 2000) (see The Real World). However, depression is also a concern in the late adult years.

Alzheimer's Disease and Other Dementias

Alzheimer's disease (technically known as *dementia of the Alzheimer's type*) is a very severe form of dementia. The early stages of Alzheimer's disease usually become evident very slowly, beginning with subtle memory difficulties, repetitive conversation,

dementia a neurological disorder involving problems with memory and thinking that affect an individual's emotional, social, and physical functioning

Alzheimer's disease a very severe form of dementia, the cause of which is unknown

and disorientation in unfamiliar settings. Then, memory for recent events begins to go. Memory for long-ago events or for well-rehearsed daily routines is often retained until late in the illness, presumably because these memories can be accessed through many alternative neural pathways. Eventually, however, an individual with Alzheimer's disease may fail to recognize family members and may be unable to remember the names of common objects or how to perform such routine activities as brushing her teeth or dressing.

Those afflicted with Alzheimer's suffer declines in the ability to communicate and to carry out daily self-care routines. The changes in appetite regulation you read about earlier in this chapter are particularly problematic for those with Alzheimer's, because they can't rely on habit to regulate their eating behavior, as healthy older people do. Left to their own devices, Alzheimer's victims may consume as many as three or four complete meals at one sitting without realizing how much they have eaten. Consequently, their eating behavior must be closely supervised.

Some Alzheimer's patients also have angry outbursts. Others exhibit an increased level of dependency and clinginess toward family or friends (Raskind & Peskind, 1992). In addition, research suggests that the incidence of depression among elders with Alzheimer's disease may be as high as 40% (Harwood et al., 2000).

● ***Causes of Alzheimer's Disease*** ● Clearly, scientists do not yet fully understand the normal aging processes, which makes it extremely difficult to determine the causes of Alzheimer's disease. To be useful, research must compare healthy older adults with healthy younger adults as well as comparing elderly individuals with and without the disease. Such studies produce complex patterns of results that are often difficult to interpret. For example, one recent study found that the immune system is somehow involved in both normal aging and in the development of Alzheimer's disease, but activation of the immune system causes different changes in the blood chemistry of elderly adults with and without Alzheimer's (Maes et al., 1999).

Genetic factors seem to be important in some, but not all, cases of Alzheimer's. Researchers have now found three separate genes that appear to be implicated. The most common of these is a gene on chromosome 19 that controls production of a particular protein (Rose, 1995). When errors in the production of this protein occur, the dendrites and axons of neurons in the brain become tangled and, as a result, do not function as efficiently.

Genes found on chromosome 21 may also be involved in Alzheimer's disease. You should recall from Chapter 3 that trisomy 21, or the presence of three copies of chromosome 21, causes Down syndrome. Alzheimer's disease is more prevalent among adults with Down syndrome than among other groups. In fact, as many as 40% of 30- to 39-year-olds with Down syndrome may also suffer from Alzheimer's disease (Holland, Hon, Huppert, Stevens, & Watson, 1998). Scientists speculate that the development of Alzheimer's disease follows a similar pattern for adults with Down syndrome and normal adults; the process is simply accelerated among those with trisomy 21. Thus, the incidence of the disease reaches 40–50% in the fourth decade of life among Down syndrome victims but does not reach this level until the eighth or ninth decade among normal individuals.

Brain-imaging studies show that patterns of neurological activity may also be genetically linked to Alzheimer's disease. Many relatives of Alzheimer's victims show patterns of neurological activity that differ from those of adults who have no Alzheimer's sufferers in their families (Ponomareva, Fokin, Selesneva, & Voskresen-skaea, 1998). Neurologists are currently investigating the degree to which brain-imaging techniques, such as CT scans, may be used to predict future onset of Alzheimer's disease among middle-aged adults who have family histories of the disease.

Even in families with very high prevalences of Alzheimer's disease, ages of onset are highly variable. In one family study, age of onset ranged from 44 to 67 years (Axelman, Basun, & Lannfelt, 1998). Moreover, there were wide variations in the

in the Information Age

Computers and Dementia

Computers are becoming increasingly important in the treatment of various neurological disorders affecting the elderly. For example, neuropsychologists use computers to test stroke and dementia victims to determine how their cognitive functioning has been affected. Computerization of standard neuropsychological tests allows psychologists to tailor the presentation of test stimuli more precisely to an individual examinee (McKitrick, Friedman, Thompson, Gray, & Yesavage, 1997).

For example, a common assessment task involves presenting test-takers with a series of digits and asking them to add the numbers two at a time. A computer can present a sample problem to determine how long an individual examinee takes to respond. After making that determination, the computer can then present problems at a rate that will allow the examinee sufficient time to respond. Certainly, human examiners can do the same thing, but they are less precise.

Neuropsychologists also use computers in rehabilitation programs. For example, many stroke victims have prob-

(*Photo:* Bob Daemmrich, Stock Boston)

lems with comprehending speech and/or speaking themselves. Researchers have found that computerized speech rehabilitation programs are highly effective at improving the language skills of such people (Katz & Wertz, 1997; Waller, Dennis, Brodie, & Cairns, 1998).

Dementia sufferers benefit from computerized rehabilitation as well. For example, one such program trains those with Alzheimer's and other types of dementia to remember routes from one place to another by guiding them through a virtual apartment. Neuropsychologists report that practicing route-learning in the virtual environment improves these patients' ability to remember such routes in their own living environments (Schreiber, Lutz, Schweizer, Kalveram, & Jaencke, 1998; Schreiber, Schweizer, Lutz, Kalveram, & Jaencke, 1999).

---

severity of the disease's behavioral effects and in the length of time the victims lived once they developed Alzheimer's.

● ***Other Types of Dementia*** ● Strictly speaking, dementia is a symptom and not a disease, and neurological research indicates that Alzheimer's and non-Alzheimer's dementias involve very different disease processes (Fokin, Ponomareva, Androsova, & Gavrilova, 1997). For example, signs of dementia frequently appear after a person suffers multiple small strokes; in this case, the condition is called **multi-infarct dementia.** The brain damage caused by such strokes is irreversible. However, in contrast to most cases of Alzheimer's disease, various forms of therapy—occupational, recreational, and physical—can improve victims' functioning (see Development in the Information Age).

In addition, dementia can be caused by depression, metabolic disturbances, drug intoxication, Parkinson's disease, hypothyroidism, multiple blows to the head (frequent among boxers), a single head trauma, some kinds of tumors, Vitamin B_{12} deficiency, anemia, or alcohol abuse (Anthony & Aboraya, 1992). Clearly, many of these causes are treatable; indeed, roughly 10% of all patients who are evaluated for dementia turn out to have some reversible problem. So, when an older person shows signs of dementia, it is critical to arrange for a careful diagnosis.

● ***Incidence of Alzheimer's and Other Dementias*** ● Evidence from research in China, Sweden, France, Great Britain, Italy, the United States, Canada, and Japan, as

multi-infarct dementia a form of dementia caused by one or more strokes

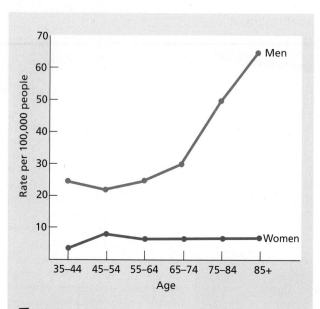

FIGURE 16.6

The data on which this figure is based indicate that suicide rates increase substantially in old age among men but remain fairly stable among women. (*Sources:* NCHS, 1999; U.S. Bureau of the Census, 1997.)

well as studies involving several U.S. ethnic groups, shows that somewhere between 2% and 8% of all adults over age 65 show significant symptoms of some kind of dementia, and that about half of them have Alzheimer's disease (Corrada, Brookmeyer, & Kawas, 1995; Gurland et al., 1999; Rockwood & Stadnyk, 1994). Experts also agree that the rates of all kinds of dementias, including Alzheimer's disease, rise rapidly among people in their 70s and 80s. For example, a large, careful study in Canada showed that 11.1% of adults over 75 and 26.0% of those over 85 suffered from moderate to severe symptoms of dementia (Rockwood & Stadnyk, 1994).

Depression

The earliest studies of age differences in depression suggested that older adults were at higher risk for this disorder than any other age group, which contributed to a widespread cultural stereotype of the inevitably depressed elder. Certainly, suicide statistics suggest that depression increases in old age (see Figure 16.6). However, the full story on depression in late adulthood is complex.

● *Diagnosis, Definitions, and Prevalence* ● Ageism can influence the diagnosis of depression in the elderly. Signs of depression in older adults may be dismissed as old-age "grumpiness" by family members (NIA, 2000a). Alternatively, as noted earlier, depression may be mistaken for dementia because it can cause confusion and memory loss.

Furthermore, standard questionnaires used to assess depression usually include questions about physical symptoms that commonly accompany that disorder, such as loss of appetite, sleep disturbances, and lack of energy. Older adults are more likely to report such symptoms no matter what their emotional state, and so are more likely to wind up with high scores on these standardized depression scales. As a result, elders may be diagnosed with depression when they are not actually depressed.

It is also important to distinguish between depressed mood and full-fledged clinical depression. The latter involves problems (e.g., feelings of hopelessness, insomnia, lack of appetite, loss of interest in social activities) that are of long duration and are severe enough to interfere with a person's ability to carry out normal activities (APA, 1994). By contrast, chronic depressed mood among the elderly, known as **geriatric dysthymia,** typically does not progress to clinical depression and has been found to be related to life stresses (Kocsis, 1998).

Estimates of the prevalence of depression depend on how it is defined. Studies by researchers who define depression as the presence of any kind of depressive symptom suggest that as many as a quarter of the old old and the oldest old suffer from depression, a higher proportion than in any other adult group (FIFARS, 2000). However, researchers using stricter definitions often find that the reporting of depressive symptoms by elderly adults declines slightly after age 75 and that only 4% of those older than that are depressed (Forsell & Winblad, 1999). Moreover, evidence suggests that true clinical depression is, if anything, less common among older adults than among younger adults, while dysthymia increases somewhat in frequency in late old age (Beekman, Copeland, & Prince, 1999; Gatz, Kasl-Godley, & Karel, 1996).

● *Risk Factors* ● The risk factors for depression and dysthymia among the elderly are not difficult to identify: inadequate social support, inadequate income, emotional loss (such as following the deaths of spouse, family, or friends) and nagging health

geriatric dysthymia chronic depressed mood in older adults

problems. However, the strongest predictor appears to be health status. Across all ethnic and socio-economic groups, the more disabling conditions older adults have, the more depressive symptoms they have (Black, Markides, & Miller, 1998; Curyto, Chapleski, & Lichtenberg, 1999; FIFARS, 2000; Lam, Pacala, & Smith, 1997; Okwumabua, Baker, Wong, & Pilgram, 1997).

Gender is also a risk factor; depressed women outnumber men two to one among the elderly, just as they do at younger ages (FIFARS, 2000; Forsell & Winblad, 1999). However, sorting out the causes of this difference is difficult. For one thing, women appear to be more resilient in response to many life stressors. The death of a spouse, for example, is more likely to lead to depression in a man than in a woman (Byrne & Raphael, 1999; Chen et al., 1999). Such findings suggest that depression in women may more often be the result of an accumulation of everyday stresses, while traumatic events are more likely to bring on feelings of depression in men. Another possible explanation is that women are more willing to seek help for depression and, as a result, are more often diagnosed.

There is also a fair amount of consistency in findings that elders living in poverty are at higher risk for depression than others (Beekman et al., 1999). Education is also independently related to depression; that is, poorly educated older adults are more likely to be depressed (Gallagher-Thompson, Tazeau, & Basilio, 1997; Miech & Shanahan, 2000). The association between education and depression exists among elderly adults at all levels of income and in all racial and ethnic groups.

● *Ethnic and Cultural Differences* ●   Poverty and education account for only some of the ethnic differences in depression among older adults. Other differences are explained by health status. That is, on average, minorities have poorer health than whites in the United States; so, on average, most minority groups have higher rates of depression.

For example, the prevalence of depressive symptoms in elderly Native Americans may be as high as 20% (Curyto et al., 1999). You may remember from Chapter 14 that Native Americans suffer from chronic illnesses at higher rates than white Americans. Moreover, among depressed Native Americans, those with the greatest number of physical limitations are the most depressed (Curyto et al., 1999).

The rate of depression among Chinese American and Mexican American elders may also be near 20% (Black et al., 1998; Lam et al., 1997). There is an association between health and depression in these groups, just as there is in others. However, researchers point out that in addition, many older Chinese Americans and Mexican Americans are recent immigrants to the United States and have poor English skills. These factors may help explain their higher incidence of depression, because length of time in the United States and knowledge of English are negatively associated with depression in these groups (Black et al., 1999; Lam et al., 1997). This means that the longer older Chinese Americans and Mexican Americans have been in the United States, and the better integrated they are into the society, the less likely they are to be depressed.

Isolated symptoms of depression, such as insomnia and poor appetite, have sometimes been found to occur more often in elderly African Americans than in those in other minority groups or in white Americans (Blazer, Landerman, Hays, Simonsick, & Saunders, 1998; Foley, Monjan, Izmirlian, Hays, & Blazer, 1999). But the entire cluster of depressive symptoms appears to occur much less often in African Americans, even those who are the least healthy (Leo et al., 1997). For example, a study of several thousand men admitted to veterans' hospitals revealed that African Americans were half as likely as whites to be depressed (Kales, Blow, Bingham, Copeland, & Mellow, 2000). Furthermore, a study in which researchers reviewed the medical records of several hundred African American and white American patients produced similar findings (Leo et al., 1997). However, in both studies, researchers found that elderly African Americans were more likely than elderly white Americans

A frican American elders may be less likely to be depressed than their peers in other ethnic groups because they may treat sad feelings as a spiritual issue rather than a mental health problem.
(*Photo:* Catherine Karnow, Woodfin Camp and Associates)

to suffer from schizophrenia. In addition, among those older African Americans who are depressed, the tendency toward suicidal thoughts may be greater than it is among depressed older white Americans (Leo et al, 1997).

Researchers often attribute low rates of depression in African Americans to underdiagnosis. They hypothesize that African Americans' lack of access to mental health services, reluctance to seek help, and unwillingness to take antidepressant medications contribute to underdiagnosis (Blazer, Hybels, Simonsick, & Hanlon, 2000; Steffens, Artigues, Ornstein, & Krishnan, 1997). However, some developmentalists take issue with this view. These critics point to cultural differences between African Americans and other groups. Specifically, African Americans are more likely to view feelings of sadness as a spiritual issue rather than a mental health problem. Research examining the association between depression and religious beliefs and activities has shown that the tendency to turn to faith and the church for support in times of emotional difficulty is much more prevalent among African Americans than among white Americans (Husaini, Blasi, & Miller, 1999; Steffens et al., 1997). In fact, research demonstrates that religious faith and practice are associated with lower incidences of long-term depression in most ethnic groups, no matter what religion is considered (Braam, Beekman, Deeg, Smit, & van Tilburg, 1997; Idler & Kasl, 1997; Meisenhelder & Chandler, 2000; Musick, Koenig, Hays, & Cohen, 1998; Tapanya, Nicki, & Jarusawad, 1997). And, as you will learn in Chapter 17, these effects are a result of the way elders think about their lives in religious terms, rather than being due to self-selection or the social support provided to elders by religious institutions.

● **Suicide** ● Despite higher rates of depression among women and some minority groups in the United States, elderly white men are more likely to commit suicide than any other group (National Center for Health Statistics, 1999). Thus, white males are largely responsible for the dramatic increase with age in male suicide illustrated in Figure 16.6. However, the overall age-related pattern of sex differences indicated by the figure exists among minority groups as well (U.S. Bureau of the Census, 1994).

The reasons for this dramatic sex difference are not entirely clear. It's important to note, though, that suicide at all ages is predicted by the same factors: a sense of hopelessness, unemployment, psychological disorders, alcoholism, social isolation, and poor physical health (Beck, Brown, Berchick, Stewart, & Steer, 1990; Kaplan & Sadock, 1991). Some theorists believe that elderly men are at higher risk for suicide, even though elderly women are more often depressed, because men are more likely than women to have several of these risk factors in combination (Kaplan & Sadock, 1991).

In addition, loss of economic status through retirement may be more troubling for men than for women in present cohorts of the elderly, because traditional socialization patterns may have led men to equate earnings with self-worth (Mooney, Knox, & Schacht, 2000). Similarly, declining health may cause an elderly man to view himself as a burden on others. The death of a spouse may also be a factor in many male suicides because, as you will learn in Chapter 18, men do not adjust as well as women do to the death of a spouse (Stroebe & Stroebe, 1993). Finally, as is true of younger people, older women attempt suicide more often than older men do, but the men complete the act more often, mostly because they are more likely than women to choose violent methods such as firearms.

● **Therapy and Medication** ● Therapies for depression are the same for older adults as for those who are younger. Psychotherapy is often recommended, especially interventions that help sufferers develop optimistic thought patterns (NIA, 2000a).

However, as with younger adults, therapy appears to be most effective when combined with antidepressant medications ("Depressed elderly," 1999).

Longitudinal studies suggest that the use of antidepressant medications increases rather dramatically with age. One study involving more than 4,000 elderly white and African Americans tracked their medication use for 10 years, beginning in the mid-1980s. At the beginning of the study, approximately 5% of white Americans and 2% of African Americans were taking antidepressant medicines. Remarkably, by 1996, 14% of white participants and 5% of the African Americans were taking such medications (Blazer et al., 2000).

Experts point out that appropriate use of antidepressant medications among the elderly is critical. For one thing, antidepressants may reduce the effectiveness of the life-sustaining drugs some older adults take (NIA, 2000a). In addition, antidepressants are linked to an increased incidence of falls among the institutionalized elderly. One study found a remarkable 80% increase in falls in a group of more than 2,000 nursing home residents who began taking antidepressants (Bender, 1999).

● **Prevention** ●   Given that poor overall health status predicts depression in the elderly, one important aspect of preventing depression is to help older adults improve their health. For example, arthritis limits the activities of more elders than any other chronic condition (FIFARS, 2000). There are many new and effective treatments for arthritis, of which older adults may be unaware. So, one indirect way of preventing depression is to educate older adults and their health care providers about such treatments and to encourage the elders to get help.

Social involvement may also be important in preventing depression in the elderly. For example, in one study, researchers in Mexico examined how participation in activities with children, such as attending children's plays or helping plan children's parties, might affect nursing home residents' emotions (Saavedra, Ramirez, & Contreras, 1997). Researchers found that such activities significantly improved participants' emotional states. So, periodic involvement with children might be an effective way to prevent depression in institutionalized elders.

In addition, research on the connection between religion and depression suggests that caretakers can help elders avoid depression by supporting their spiritual needs. Many older adults need help getting to religious services; those who live in institutions may need to have services brought to them. Declines in vision may mean that an elderly person can no longer read religious books and may deeply appreciate having someone read to him or provide him with recordings. Helping elders maintain religious faith and practice in these ways may be an important key to reducing depression rates.

Interacting with children may help prevent depression in late adulthood. (*Photo:* Alvin Smith)

Before going on

● What is Alzheimer's disease, and how does it differ from other dementias?

● What does research suggest about depression among older adults?

Cognitive Changes

mong the young old (aged 65–75), cognitive changes are still fairly small, and these older adults show little or no average decline on a few measures, such as vocabulary knowledge. But the old old and the oldest old show average declines on virtually all measures of intellectual skill, with the largest declines evident on any measures that involve speed or unexercised abilities (Cunningham & Haman, 1992; Giambra, Arenberg, Zonderman, Kawas, & Costa, 1995). Recall Schaie's comment, quoted in Chapter 14, that "reliable decrement can be shown to have occurred for all abilities by age 74" (Schaie, 1983a, p. 127). By the 80s, the declines are substantial on most abilities (Schaie, 1993).

Memory

As you learned in Chapter 14, forgetfulness becomes more frequent with age (Ponds, Commissaris, & Jolles, 1997). However, it's important to remember that the same basic rules seem to apply to memory processes among both older and younger adults. For both groups, for example, recognition is easier than recall, and tasks that require speed are more difficult. Further, metamemory and metacognition skills are just as important to memory function in old age as they are earlier in life (Olin & Zelinski, 1997).

● ***Short-Term Memory Function*** ● One area in which researchers see significant late adulthood changes is in short-term, or working, memory capacity (Jenkins, Myerson, Hale, & Fry, 1999). You should remember from earlier chapters that there is a limitation on the number of items a person can retain in her memory at once. The more pieces of information she has to handle, the more she forgets, and the poorer her performance on memory and other kinds of cognitive tasks. Thus, the more any given cognitive task makes demands on working memory, the larger the decline with age.

A good illustration comes from a study involving a familiar, everyday task—remembering telephone numbers (West & Crook, 1990). Participants were shown a series of seven-digit or ten-digit telephone numbers on a computer screen, one at a time. The participant said each number as it appeared; then the number disappeared from the screen and the participant had to dial the number she had just seen on a push-button phone attached to the computer. On some trials, the participants got a busy signal when they first dialed and then had to dial the number over again. Figure 16.7 shows the relationship between age and the correct recall of the phone numbers under these four conditions.

Notice that there is essentially no decline with age in immediate recall of a normal seven-digit telephone number (the equivalent of what you do when you look a number up in the phone book, say it to yourself as you read it, and then dial it immediately). When the length of the number increases to the ten-digits used for long-distance numbers, however, a decline with age becomes evident, beginning at

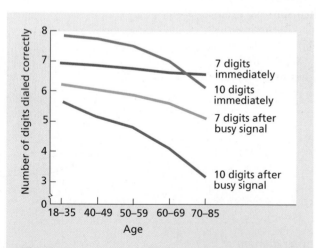

FIGURE 16.7

The graph shows the results from West and Crook's study of memory for telephone numbers. Notice that there is no loss of memory in middle adulthood for the most common condition: a seven-digit number dialed immediately. But if the number of digits increases, or if you have to remember the number a bit longer, some decline in memory begins around age 50 or 60. (*Source:* West & Crook, 1990, from Table 3, page 524.)

about age 60. And with even a brief delay between saying the number and dialing it, the decline occurs earlier.

However, patterns of age differences are not identical for all memory tasks. For example, older adults outperform younger adults on *prospective* memory tasks (Rendell & Thomson, 1999). Prospective tasks require participants to remember an event into the future. For example, researchers might instruct participants to make a phone call at a certain time every day for 2 weeks. Memory researchers have found that the elderly generally outperform young and middle-aged adults on such tasks.

● *Strategy Learning* ● A study of older adults in Germany provides a good example of research findings on strategy learning and memory in older adults (Baltes & Kliegl, 1992; Kliegl, Smith, & Baltes, 1990). Researchers tested 18 college students and 19 old, but physically healthy, adults who ranged in age from 65 to 80, with an average age of 71.7 years. Participants were shown sets of pictures of 30 familiar buildings in Berlin and asked to use the pictures to create associations that would help them remember a list of 30 words. For example, a castle might be paired with the word "bicycle." A typical association would be to imagine someone riding a bicycle in front of a castle. The pictures in each set were displayed for different amounts of time, ranging from 20 seconds each to 1 second each. After participants attempted to learn each list of words, the experimenters asked what images they had used and suggested possible improvements. Training sessions were interspersed with test sessions to check on the participants' progress.

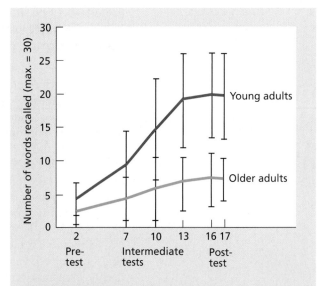

FIGURE 16.8

These results from Kliegl's study show that older adults can learn complex information-processing skills and improve their performance after training, but they don't gain as much as younger adults do. However, this study also suggested that, given enough time, older adults can learn new strategies. (*Source:* Kliegl et al., 1990, adapted from Figure 2, p. 899.)

Figure 16.8 shows the results for pictures and words presented at 5-second intervals. You can see that the older adults showed improvement after training, but their performance was poorer than that of younger adults. These findings suggest that the learning process simply takes longer for older adults—longer to create the mental image, and longer to link that image up with the word in the list. However, when allowed more time to associate each picture and word, older adults' performance was more similar to that of younger participants.

● *Everyday Memory* ● One common argument from those who take a more optimistic view of the effects of aging on cognitive functioning is that older adults may be able to remember just as well as younger adults, but they are simply less motivated to memorize lists of unrelated words given to them by researchers in a laboratory. However, on virtually all everyday tasks—remembering the main points of a story or a newspaper article; recalling movies, conversations, grocery lists, or recipes; recalling the information from a medicine label; remembering whether they did something ("Did I turn off the stove before I left the house?"); or remembering where they heard something (called *source memory*)—older adults perform less well than younger adults (Brown, Jones, & Davis, 1995; Light, 1991; Mäntylä, 1994; Maylor, 1993; Salthouse, 1991; Verhaeghen & Marcoen, 1993; Verhaeghen, Marcoen, & Goossens, 1993). These results have been found in longitudinal as well as cross-sectional studies, particularly after age 70 (Arenberg, 1983; Hultsch, Hertzog, Small, McDonald-Miszczak, & Dixon, 1992; Zelinski, Gilewski, & Schaie, 1993).

Still, task-specific knowledge seems to make a difference among the elderly. For example, older adults who have larger vocabularies outperform peers who know fewer words on tasks involving rapid recognition of words (Kitzan, Ferraro, Petros,

& Ludorf, 1999). Researchers know that prior knowledge is the critical factor in such findings, because elders with large vocabularies perform just as poorly as their less knowledgeable peers on tasks involving nonsense words.

● *Preliminary Explanations* ● How do researchers account for these changes in memory? Extensive statistical analyses of memory function suggest that only a few variables may account for all of the age differences in memory so far identified (Salthouse, 1998; Salthouse & Czaja, 2000; Verhaeghen & Salthouse, 1997). However, exactly what those variables are remains unclear.

One likely candidate appears to be the speed of the whole memory process. Older adults take longer to register some new piece of information, encode it, and retrieve it. Some of the clearest evidence of the important role of speed in memory decline in old age comes from an extensive series of studies by Timothy Salthouse (e.g., Salthouse, 1991, 1993, 1996).

Salthouse has tested both basic reaction speed and memory or other cognitive skills in adults of various ages. According to him, a very large portion of the age decline in memory can be accounted for simply by slower reaction times in older adults. He is convinced that the loss of speed occurs at the level of the central nervous system and not in the peripheral nerves. So physiological changes in neurons and the accompanying loss of nerve conductance speed may be the root causes of these changes in memory.

Virtually all experts now agree with Salthouse that loss of speed is a key aspect of the process of memory decline, and studies have shown that quantitative losses in speed of information-processing very strongly predict qualitative changes in memory function (Byrne, 1998; Maylor, Vousden, & Brown, 1999). But most also believe that speed is not the entire explanation. There appear to be other factors as well, such as changes in attention strategies that lead to less effective processing of information (Gottlob & Madden, 1999).

Wisdom and Creativity

Theorists who study cognition in older adults have also recently begun to ask whether elders might have some advantages over the young because of their accumulation of knowledge and skills. In other words, older adults might be more wise. Researchers have not yet agreed on a common definition of wisdom, but most authors emphasize that it goes beyond mere accumulations of facts. **Wisdom** reflects understanding of "universal truths" or basic laws or patterns; it is knowledge that is blended with values and meaning systems; it is knowledge based on the understanding that clarity is not always possible, that unpredictability and uncertainty are part of life (Baltes & Smith, 1990; Baltes, Smith, & Staudinger, 1992; Baltes, Staudinger, Maercker, & Smith, 1995; Csikszentmihalyi & Rathunde, 1990; Sternberg, 1990a).

You may be wondering how researchers measure wisdom. The leading researcher in this field, Paul Baltes, has devised one useful technique (Baltes & Staudinger, 2000). Baltes presents research participants with stories about fictional characters who are trying to make some major life decision. For example, one dilemma Baltes has used involves a 15-year-old girl who wants to get married. Participants' responses to the stories are judged according to five criteria Baltes hypothesizes to be central to

Critical Thinking

Make a list of the people you think of as wise. How old are they? Is old age necessary for wisdom? If not, how do you think wisdom is acquired?

wisdom a hypothesized cognitive characteristic of older adults that includes accumulated knowledge and the ability to apply that knowledge to practical problems of living

wisdom as it relates to solving practical life problems: factual knowledge, procedural knowledge, understanding of relevance of context, understanding of relevance of values, and recognition that it is impossible to know in advance how any decision will ultimately affect one's life. A person would be judged to be low in wisdom if her response to the 15-year-old's desire to marry were something like "A 15-year-old getting married? That's stupid. I would tell the girl to forget about it until she's older." The answer of a person judged to be high in wisdom would be more complex. A wise person might point out that "There are circumstances when marriage at such a young age might be a good decision. Is she motivated by a desire to make a home for a child she is expecting? Also, the girl might come from a culture where marriage at 15 is quite common. You have to consider people's motivations and their backgrounds to understand their decisions. You also have to know how the person involved views the situation to be able to give advice."

Seeking advice from an elder who is presumed to be wise is one way young adults act on the belief that those who are older have accumulated knowledge and information that can benefit them. (Photo: Vincent DeWitt, Stock Boston)

Virtually all theorists who have written about wisdom assume that it is more likely to be found in the middle-aged and the elderly. However, Baltes has found that younger adults perform as well as older adults in response to the fictional dilemma task. In fact, Baltes has found that, rather than age, intelligence and professional experience are correlated with responses to the dilemma task. So, Baltes's research seems to suggest that the popular idea that age and wisdom are associated is probably not true. Wisdom does not appear to be a characteristic of the elderly that distinguishes them from other subgroups of adults.

Critics have suggested that Baltes is simply measuring general cognitive ability rather than what is usually thought of as wisdom. Nevertheless, Baltes's research has produced an important finding about wisdom and old age: In contrast to performance on information-processing tasks such as memorizing nonsense words, performance on wisdom tasks does not decline with age (Baltes & Staudinger, 2000). Moreover, the speed of accessing wisdom-related knowledge remains constant across adulthood, unlike speed of information processing in other domains. In addition, other researchers (e.g., Orwoll & Perlmutter, 1990) have found that those older adults singled out by their peers as wise are more likely to rank high in what Erikson called ego integrity and are more likely to show concern for humanity as a whole.

Enhanced creativity may also be an element of cognition in older adults. As you learned in Chapter 14, some highly creative individuals, especially composers and artists, reach their peak in late adulthood. To describe the potential for creative work in the later years, a leading gerontologist, Gene Cohen, has developed a four-stage theory of mid- to late-life creativity (Cohen, 2000). Cohen believes that these phases apply to ordinary people who are more creative than others in their everyday lives as well as to "professional creators" such as composers and artists.

Cohen proposes that at around age 50, creative individuals enter a *reevaluation phase*, during which they reflect on past accomplishments and formulate new goals. The reevaluation process, along with an increasing sense of time limitations, leads to an intensification of the desire to create and produce. During the next stage, the *liberation phase*, individuals in their 60s become freer to create, because most have retired from everyday work. Most are also more tolerant of their own failures, and thus are willing to take risks that they would not have taken at earlier ages. In the *summing-up phase*, creative people in their 70s have a desire to knit their accomplishments together into a cohesive, meaningful story. They begin to view their early accomplishments in terms of how those accomplishments prefigured later achievements. Finally, in the *encore phase*, during the 80s and beyond, there is a desire to complete unfinished works or to fulfill desires that have been put aside in the past.

MAKE THE CONNECTION

Look back at the discussion of theories of postformal operational thought in Chapter 12. How would these theories explain abrupt opinion change in the elderly?

Before going on

● Describe memory differences that distinguish older and younger adults, and suggest some possible explanations for these age differences.

● What do theory and research on wisdom and creativity reveal about cognitive functioning in late adulthood?

A Final Word

It is impossible to overemphasize just how much variation there is in the quality of individuals' physical and intellectual functioning after age 65. Even among the old old and the oldest old, there are enormous differences. In addition, every longitudinal study of the elderly has found at least a few participants who show no decline at all in their mental abilities. What all this suggests is the intriguing possibility that decline may be the typical, but not the invariable, accompaniment of aging. If that is true, it holds out the hope that an understanding of what allows the elderly to maintain their skills in the last years of life may lead to an increase in the number of adults who are able to keep all their mental and physical abilities until very near death. That is a hope well worth pursuing with vigorous research.

Summary

Variability in Late Adulthood

● Developmentalists group the elderly into three subgroups: the young old (60–75), the old old (75–85), and the oldest old (85 and older). The oldest old are the fastest-growing group of the elderly in the United States. There are vast individual differences in the timing and pace of all the physical and mental changes associated with aging.

● Heredity, overall health, current and prior health habits (particularly exercise), and availability of adequate social support all influence functioning and longevity. Skills that are not used regularly show more rapid decline.

Physical Changes

● Changes in the brain associated with aging include, most centrally, a loss of dendritic density of neurons, which has the effect of slowing reaction time for almost all tasks.

● Older adults have more difficulty adapting to darkness and light. Loss of hearing is more common and more noticeable after 65 than at earlier ages; many older adults experience loss of hearing for high sounds, some loss of ability to discriminate words, and greater difficulty hearing under noisy conditions. Taste discrimination remains largely unchanged with age, but ability to discriminate smells declines substantially in late adulthood.

- Theories of biological aging emphasize the possible existence of genetic limiting mechanisms and/or the cumulative effects of malfunctions within cells.
- General slowing alters behavior in old age and makes tasks such as driving more dangerous. Older adults also change their sleeping and eating patterns. Motor abilities decline, causing more accidents due to falls. Sexual activity also decreases in frequency, although most older adults continue to be sexually active.

Mental Health

- Dementia is rare before late adulthood, becoming steadily more common with advancing age. The most common cause of dementia is Alzheimer's disease. Its causes are not fully understood, but several specific genetic patterns clearly contribute.

- Mild or moderate depression appears to rise in frequency after age 70 or 75. Serious clinical depression, however, appears not to become more common in old age. Ethnic groups vary in rates of depression, with older African Americans being the least likely to be depressed.

Cognitive Changes

- The elderly experience difficulties in a variety of mental processes, which appear to reflect both the general slowing in the nervous system and perhaps a loss of working-memory capacity.
- Wisdom and creativity may be important aspects of cognitive functioning in old age.

Key Terms

activities of daily living (ADLs) (p. 460)

Alzheimer's disease (p. 473)

cross-linking (p. 469)

dementia (p. 473)

frail elderly (p. 458)

free radicals (p. 469)

geriatric dysthymia (p. 476)

gerontology (p. 457)

Hayflick limit (p. 462)

instrumental activities of daily living (IADLs) (p. 460)

multi-infarct dementia (p. 475)

programmed senescence theory (p. 468)

satiety (p. 471)

senescence (p. 468)

synaptic plasticity (p. 466)

telomere (p. 463)

terminal drop hypothesis (p. 470)

tinnitus (p. 467)

wisdom (p. 482)

CHAPTER 17

Social and Personality Development in Late Adulthood

Frank Siteman, Stone

In an autobiography written when he was in his late 60s, comedian Groucho Marx, who died at 87, said "Age is not a particularly interesting subject. Anyone can get old.

All you have to do is live long enough" (Marx, 1987). Marx's observation implies that there is little value in regarding the attainment of old age as the only thing about oneself that is interesting or remarkable. Indeed, an important part of maintaining a sense of self in late adulthood is recognizing whatever it is about one's life that could not have been done by anyone else. But maintaining a sense of personal uniqueness can be especially challenging for older adults, who are often stereotyped by others as sick, disabled, or incompetent.

As you learned in Chapter 16, the biological clock ticks far more loudly in late adulthood. But the experiences of these years, as in every period of life, extend far beyond the physical domain. Indeed, as you will learn in this chapter, changes in roles and relationships are perhaps just as significant as physical ones. And for many older adults, these changes are not perceived as losses but as opportunities to create new roles and to make old age a time of personal and social gains. As you read this chapter, keep the following questions in mind:

- How do theorists describe the important aspects of social and personality development in late life?
- What factors predict successful aging, and how does religious coping affect older adults' physical and mental health?
- In what ways do social relationships change in late adulthood?
- How do retirement and continued work affect the lives of older adults?

Theories of Social and Personality Development

If the social and personality changes of young adulthood can be described as "individuation" and those of middle adulthood can be described (more tentatively) as "mellowing," how might the changes of late adulthood be described? Several theorists have hypothesized specific forms of change, but there is little agreement among them and very little information supporting any of their theories.

Erikson's Stage of Ego Integrity versus Despair

Erikson termed the last of his eight life crises the **ego integrity versus despair stage**. He thought that the task of achieving **ego integrity**, the sense that one has lived a useful life, began in middle adulthood but was most central in late adulthood. To achieve ego integrity, the older adult must come to terms with who she is and has been, how her life has been lived, the choices that she made, the opportunities gained and lost. The process also involves coming to terms with death and accepting its imminence. Erikson hypothesized that failure to achieve ego integrity in late adulthood would result in feelings of hopelessness and despair because there would be too little time to make changes before death.

Developmentalists have essentially no longitudinal or even cross-sectional data to suggest whether older adults are more likely than younger or middle-aged adults

ego integrity versus despair stage the last of Erikson's psychosocial stages, in which older adults must achieve a sense of satisfaction with their lives

ego integrity the feeling that one's life has been worthwhile

to achieve such self-acceptance. What they have instead are a few bits of information suggesting that adults become more reflective and somewhat more philosophical in orientation as they move through the late adulthood years (Prager, 1998). Moreover, those who use their growing capacity for philosophical reflection to achieve a degree of self-satisfaction are less fearful of death. There is also some evidence that older adults are more likely than young and middle-aged adults to respond to thwarted personal goals with feelings of sadness—a hint that the kind of despair Erikson talked about may be more common in old age than earlier in life (Levine & Bluck, 1997).

One aspect of Erikson's theory that has received a great deal of attention from researchers is the notion that the process of **reminiscence**, thinking about the past, is a necessary and healthy part of achieving ego integrity, and thus an important aspect of old age and preparation for death. However, few developmentalists today would say that the only, or even the most important, purpose of these processes is to help an individual prepare for death. Instead, recent research has examined the link between reminiscence and health.

First, it's important to note that adults of all ages engage in reminiscence. In fact, young adults reminisce more often than middle-aged or older adults (Parker, 1999). Moreover, the emotional effects of reminiscence are correlated with age. For younger adults, reminiscence often evokes negative emotions, whereas it is generally a positive activity for elders.

Developmentalists hypothesize that young and older adults feel differently about reminiscence because they use it for different purposes (Webster & McCall, 1999). Young adults often use reminiscence to search for tried and true methods of solving problems ("How did I handle this the last time it happened?"). For older adults, reminiscence is more often seen as a way of communicating their experiences to younger individuals. In fact, elders who do not have this intergenerational view of reminiscence do not engage in reminiscence as much as peers who do (Muthesius, 1997).

Research suggesting that reminiscence is a positive emotional experience for older adults has led to the development of a wide variety of interventions for use with these adults. Experimental studies comparing reminiscence therapy to other approaches has shown that structured reminiscence increases life satisfaction among nursing home residents (Cook, 1998). In addition, structured reminiscence therapy has been found to be helpful in treating depression in elderly adults (Watt & Cappeliez, 2000). Developmentalists have found that, in general, elders are eager to participate in reminiscence interventions (Atkinson, Kim, Ruelas, & Lin, 1999). In fact, it may be this very eagerness that accounts for the positive effects observed with many of these programs. And as compelling as these research results may seem, they don't indicate whether Erikson was right about the *necessity* of reminiscence in old age.

Activity Theory and Disengagement Theory

Another theoretical perspective on old age focuses on the question of whether it is normal, necessary, or healthy for older adults to remain active as long as possible, or whether the more typical and healthy pattern is some kind of gradual turning inward. The perspective typically referred to as **activity theory**, argues that the psychologically and physically healthiest response to old age is to maintain the greatest possible level of activity and involvement in the greatest possible number of roles.

Activity theorists often cite research demonstrating that the most active older adults report slightly greater satisfaction with themselves or their lives, are healthiest, and have the highest morale (Adelmann, 1994; Bryant & Rakowski, 1992; George, 1996; McIntosh & Danigelis, 1995). The effect is not large, but its direction is consistently positive: More social involvement is linked to better outcomes, even among elders who suffer from disabilities such as arthritis, for whom active social participation may be physically painful (Zimmer, Hickey, & Searle, 1995). Yet, it is also true

reminiscence reflecting on past experience

activity theory the idea that it is normal and healthy for older adults to try to remain as active as possible for as long as possible

disengagement theory the theory that it is normal and healthy for older adults to scale down their social lives and to separate themselves from others to a certain degree that every in-depth study of lifestyles of older adults identifies at least a few who lead socially isolated lives but remain contented, sometimes because they are engaged in an all-consuming hobby (e.g., Maas & Kuypers, 1974; Rubinstein, 1986).

An alternative theory on social and personality development in old age is disengagement theory, first proposed as a formulation of the central psychological process for older adults (Cumming, 1975; Cumming & Henry, 1961). In its current form, **disengagement theory** proposes that aging has three aspects:

Shrinkage of life space: As people age, they interact with fewer and fewer others and fill fewer and fewer roles.

Increased individuality: In the roles and relationships that remain, the older individual is much less governed by strict rules or expectations.

Acceptance of these changes: The healthy older adult actively disengages from roles and relationships, turning increasingly inward and away from interactions with others.

Some older adults are quite content with solitary lives, but disengagement from social contacts is neither a typical nor an optimal choice for most elders. (*Photo:* Frank Siteman, Stone)

The first two of these aspects seem largely beyond dispute. What has been controversial about disengagement theory is the third aspect. Advocates argue that the normal and healthy response to the shrinkage of roles and relationships is for the older adult to step back still further, to stop seeking new roles, to spend more time alone, to turn inward. In essence, they proposed a kind of personality change, not just a decline in involvement.

Clearly, it is possible to choose a highly disengaged lifestyle in late adulthood and to find satisfaction in it. But such disengagement is neither normal for the majority of older adults nor necessary for overall mental health in the later years. For most elders, some level of social involvement is both a sign—and probably a cause—of higher morale and lower levels of depression and other psychiatric symptoms. Roles and relationships may rule our lives less in late adulthood than at earlier ages, but they still seem to be essential ingredients for emotional balance, at least for most of us.

Critical Thinking

Think about the oldest person in your family. Which do you think describes him or her better— activity theory or disengagement theory?

Before going on

- Does research support the existence of Erikson's stage of ego integrity versus despair?

- What are the main ideas of activity theory and disengagement theory?

Individual Differences

Individual differences continue to make substantial contributions to the experiences of older men and women. In fact, research suggests that differences in a variety of behaviors are related to overall quality of life as well as to longevity. Similarly, individual differences in reliance on religious beliefs and institutions as sources of support are also correlated with well-being in late adulthood.

The Successful Aging Paradigm

In recent years, one of the dominant themes in gerontology literature has been the concept of successful aging. As defined by authors John Rowe and Robert Kahn, **successful aging** has three components: good physical health, retention of cognitive abilities, and continuing engagement in social and productive activities (Rowe & Kahn, 1997, 1998). An additional aspect of successful aging is an individual's subjective sense of life satisfaction. The idea of successful aging is part of the overall trend in gerontology (which you read about in Chapter 16) toward viewing old age in terms of variability rather than universal decline. In addition, the concept attempts to integrate physical, social, and personality development in order to create a comprehensive picture of what it means to age successfully.

The three dimensions of successful aging described by Rowe and Kahn are, of course, not entirely independent. For example, good health makes it more likely that an older adult will retain her mental abilities, and better mental functioning enables her to remain socially active. The concept of successful aging is referred to as a *paradigm* because it presents patterns for or examples of such aging. Rather than stating a theory of development, the paradigm of successful aging offers a way of thinking about late adulthood and about how earlier decisions and patterns of behavior contribute to quality of life at later ages.

● *Staying Healthy and Able* ● By now, you should be familiar with the factors that predict health and physical functioning across the lifespan: diet, exercise, avoidance of tobacco, and so on. In a sense, older people reap the consequences of the behavioral choices they made when younger. However, there are also aspects to staying healthy and able that most of us never face until old age.

For example, when an older adult suffers a stroke or fractures a bone, his willingness to engage in the sometimes painful process of rehabilitation significantly affects his degree of recovery. Researchers have found that older adults vary considerably in their willingness to comply with physicians and therapists who supervise their rehabilitations after such events. In both the United States and Japan, an individual's willingness to adopt recovery goals suggested by rehabilitation professionals is related to recovery prospects (Ushikubo, 1998). Those who believe they can reach the suggested goals appear to be the most willing to do the work required for optimal recovery of functioning. Not surprisingly, these individuals gain the most from rehabilitation. So, life-long health habits contribute to successful aging, but individuals' responses to the health crises of old age also matter.

● *Retaining Cognitive Abilities* ● The degree to which elders maintain cognitive functioning seems to be linked to education. As you learned in Chapter 16, those who are the best educated show the least cognitive decline. Moreover, researchers

successful aging the term gerontologists use to describe maintaining one's physical health, mental abilities, social competence, and overall satisfaction with one's life as one ages

who have examined correlations between cognitive functioning and the other two dimensions of successful aging—physical health and social engagement—have found that verbal intelligence and education are related to both (Jorm et al., 1998). Cross-cultural research has found relationships among cognitive functioning, health, and social involvement in Taiwanese and North American elders, as well as in both Mexican Americans and white Americans (Hazuda, Wood, Lichtenstein, & Espino, 1998; Ofstedal, Zimmer, & Lin, 1999).

In addition to education, the complexity of the cognitive challenges older adults are willing to take on also influences their cognitive functioning. For example, older adults are sometimes reluctant to use new technologies such as automatic teller machines (Echt, Morrell, & Park, 1998). Psychologists suggest that self-stereotyping contributes to this reluctance; older people may believe that they can't learn as well as younger people can, and so they stick to established routines. However, neuropsychologists suggest that such avoidance of learning may actually contribute to cognitive decline (Volz, 2000). New learning, these scientists hypothesize, helps to establish new connections between neurons, connections that may protect the aging brain against deterioration. Thus, what might be called *cognitive adventurousness*, a willingness to learn new things, appears to be a key component of successful aging.

● *Social Engagement* ●   Social connectedness and participation in productive activities are clearly important to successful aging. For example, nursing home residents report greater satisfaction with their lives when they have frequent contact with family and friends (Guse & Masesar, 1999). Similarly, among elders with disabilities, frequency of contact with family and friends is associated with reduced feelings of loneliness (Bondevik & Skogstad, 1998).

However, social support does not mean dependence on others. In fact, rehabilitation professionals have found that elderly adults who expect to have someone help them with daily living activities are less likely to recover fully from strokes or other potentially debilitating medical conditions than peers who have no one to help them (Ushikubo, 1998). Moreover, one study of recovering cardiac patients found that social support contributed to mental well-being but was negatively correlated with physical recovery, especially among women (Bosworth et al., 2000).

Research on dependency suggests that the past thinking of behavioral scientists about the role of social support may have been too simplistic. It seems that social support contributes to successful aging because it provides opportunities for older adults to *give* support as well as to receive it. For example, research involving elderly Mexican immigrants to the United States suggests that those who have better functional integration into a community—that is, those who are fulfilling some kind of purposeful role—exhibit higher levels of physical and emotional functioning than those who are socially isolated (Hazuda et al., 1998).

Similarly, researchers studying Japanese elders found that a majority of them say that helping others contributes to their own health and personal sense of well-being (Krause, Ingersoll-Dayton, Liang, & Sugisawa, 1999). In addition, researchers have found that elderly residents of Israeli *kibbutzim* (collective communities) display exceptionally high levels of functioning compared to Israeli elders who do not live in *kibbutzum* (Leviatan, 1999). The key to this successful aging, developmentalists believe, is that the social structure of the kibbutz offers older adults many opportunities to occupy meaningful roles, to remain socially connected to peers, and to contribute to the development of younger community members.

Of course, you might argue that elders who are the healthiest are naturally going to be the best able to make a social contribution. However, developmentalists have found correlations between feeling useful and having a sense of well-being even among older adults who are very unhealthy. For example, researchers who have asked U.S. nursing home residents to rate various quality-of-life factors have found that they often give high ratings to "opportunities to help others" (Guse & Masesar,

For some elders, remaining productive means venturing into new hobbies such as painting, sculpting, or other artistic pursuits. (*Photo:* Stacy Pick, Stock Boston)

1999). Thus, even when elderly adults have significant disabilities, many are still oriented toward helping others and feel more satisfied with their lives when they can do so.

● *Productivity* ●   Contributing to a social network may be one important way of remaining productive, especially for older adults who are retired. **Volunteerism**, performing unpaid work for altruistic reasons, has been linked to successful aging. Remarkably, a California study involving nearly 2,000 older adults found that mortality rates were 60% lower among volunteers than among nonvolunteers (Oman, Thoresen, & McMahon, 1999). Studies have also shown that volunteerism improves older adults' overall life satisfaction (Glass & Jolly, 1997). Moreover, volunteers appear to be healthier than nonvolunteers (Krause et al., 1999). As noted earlier, however, selection effects may account for some of these observed effects—that is, the healthiest elders may volunteer the most.

Surveys suggest that 10–30% of older adults are involved in volunteer activities (Federal Interagency Forum on Aging-Related Statistics [FIFARS], 2000; Oman et al., 1999). Furthermore, surveys of school volunteer programs in the United States have shown that older adults contribute more to such programs than adults in any other age group (Strom & Strom, 1999). So, it seems that the volunteer activities of older adults have the potential to benefit society as well as their own physical and mental health (Warburton, Le Brocque, & Rosenman, 1998).

Some older adults remain productive by venturing into new pursuits, such as taking music lessons, attending college classes, or learning to paint or sculpt. Researchers conducting a study of 36 artists over age 60 asked them to explain how artistic productivity contributed to their successful aging (Fisher & Specht, 1999). Their responses contained several themes: producing art gave them a purpose in life, opportunities to interact with like-minded peers, and a sense of competence. These responses are perhaps not surprising, and they probably vary little from those that might be offered by younger artists. However, the older artists also claimed that creating art helped them stay healthy. Thus, creative productivity may help older adults maintain an optimistic outlook, which, as you have learned, contributes to physical health.

MAKE THE CONNECTION

Look back at the discussions of post-secondary education in Chapter 12 and career selection in Chapter 13. Formulate a model that explains how the experiences of early adulthood contribute to successful aging.

● *Life Satisfaction* ●   *Life satisfaction*, or a sense of personal well-being, is also an important component of successful aging. Many of the factors that predict life satisfaction are very similar to the variables that you have already learned are predictive of successful aging. For example, one characteristic linking successful aging to life satisfaction is a sense of control, which you read about in Chapter 12 (Rodin, 1986). Even life events that could be highly stressful, such as financial problems, may have little negative effect if the individual feels he has some choice (Krause, Jay, & Liang, 1991). Thus, involuntary retirement or involuntary institutionalization typically has negative effects, whereas planned and chosen retirement or a voluntary move to a nursing home does not.

What is critical to life satisfaction in almost all cases is an individual's perception of her own situation, which seems to be more important than objective measures. Perceived adequacy of social support and perceived adequacy of income are critical. Moreover, self-ratings of health, rather than objective measures of health, may be the most significant predictors of life satisfaction and morale (Draper, Gething, Fethney, & Winfield, 1999).

Research also suggests that social comparisons—how well an older adult thinks he is doing compared to others his age—are just as important to these perceptions as the older adult's awareness of the changes he has undergone since his younger years

volunteerism performance of unpaid work for altruistic motives

(Robinson-Whelen & Kiecolt-Glaser, 1997). A majority of older adults, no matter what their personal circumstances, believe that most others their age are worse off than they are (Heckhausen & Brim, 1997). Developmentalists speculate that the tendency to see others as having more problems is an important self-protective psychological device employed by those who are aging successfully.

● *Criticisms of the Successful Aging Paradigm* ●   Critics of the successful aging paradigm suggest that the concept can be misleading. For one thing, they say, the paradigm has the potential to become a new kind of ageist stereotype, one that portrays older adults who suffer from disabilities as incompetent (Scheidt, Humpherys, & Yorgason, 1999). Such critics point out that, for many elderly adults, no amount of optimism, willingness to rehabilitate, social support, or involvement in intellectually demanding activities can moderate their physical limitations. For example, studies of performance on reading comprehension tests that compared university professors over age 70 and graduate students show that some degree of age-based cognitive decline can be expected, even among very bright, highly experienced, and productive adults (Christensen, Henderson, Griffiths, & Levings, 1997). Thus, these critics claim, the danger of the successful aging paradigm is that it can give the erroneous impression that all the effects of aging are under one's control.

Another danger, some critics say, in shifting the focus of gerontology research from disease and decline to quality of life is that medical research still has enormous potential for discovering cures for many of the diseases of old age (Portnoi, 1999). Critics fear that emphasis on successful aging may cause public and institutional support for disease-related research to decline. These critics point out that there is good reason to believe that many conditions that are now thought to be part of "normal" aging are actually disease processes for which medical science can find effective treatments (Portnoi, 1999).

Nevertheless, critics concede that the successful aging paradigm has broadened gerontologists' approaches to studying old age. Thus, they agree that its influence has been largely positive. Still, keeping their criticisms in mind can help balance the optimism of the successful aging paradigm against the realities of life in late adulthood and the need to continue to encourage researchers to search for treatments for age-related diseases such as Alzheimer's.

Religious Coping

Religion appears to be one factor contributing to individual differences in life satisfaction. Psychologists use the term **religious coping** to refer to the tendency to turn to religious beliefs and institutions in times of stress or trouble. People of all ages use religious coping. However, many developmentalists suggest that religious coping may be particularly important in the later years because of the high number of life stressors—including deaths of loved ones, chronic illnesses, and declining sensory abilities. And elders themselves often cite religious coping as their primary means of managing stress (Barusch, 1999).

● *Racial and Sex Differences* ●   As you learned in Chapter 16, the tendency to turn to religion for comfort is stronger among African Americans than among other racial or ethnic groups. For example, research suggests that participation in church social activities is linked to higher reported levels of well-being among older African Americans more than among older white Americans (Bryant & Rakowski, 1992; Husaini, Blasi, & Miller, 1999; Walls & Zarit, 1991). Further, the negative correlation between church involvement and depressive feelings is stronger for elderly African American cancer sufferers than for their white counterparts (Musick, Koenig, Hays, & Cohen, 1998).

religious coping the tendency to turn to religious beliefs and institutions for support in times of difficulty

Strong religious beliefs appear to be positively associated with elders' health and well-being. (*Photo:* Francoise de Mulder/CORBIS)

In addition, some studies suggest that women make more use of religious coping than men do (e.g., Coke, 1992). Most developmentalists attribute this finding to sex differences in social behavior that are observed across the lifespan. However, it's important to keep in mind that, even though the frequency with which religious coping is used may differ according to race and gender, its effects seem to be similar in all racial and ethnic groups and for both women and men. These effects can be best examined by separating the psychological and social components of religious coping.

● *Religious Beliefs* ●   The psychological component of religious coping involves people's beliefs and attitudes. A number of investigators have examined links between religious beliefs and various measures of well-being among the elderly. Typically, researchers distinguish between positive and negative religious coping (Pargament, Smith, Koenig, & Perez, 1998). *Positive religious coping* involves a reliance on the belief that there is a divine purpose in one's difficulties and that one can trust in the divine purpose even when circumstances are grim. *Negative religious coping* is manifested by abandoning or doubting one's religious beliefs because of adversity, believing that one's problems are divine punishment, or attributing adverse events to an evil, all-powerful being. As you might suspect, researchers have found that elders who use positive religious coping are both physically and mentally healthier than those who use negative religious coping or no religious coping at all (Meisenhelder & Chandler, 2000; Pargament, Koenig, & Perez, 2000).

Of course, positive religious coping may be the result of good health rather than the cause of it. But some indication of the direction of causality can be gained from longitudinal studies. In one investigation, researchers in the Netherlands periodically studied symptoms of depression in a group of older adults over a year (Braam, Beekman, Deeg, Smit, & van Tilburg, 1997). Interestingly, they found that depressive symptoms occurred just as often in participants for whom religious beliefs were an important component of coping as they did in other participants. However, religious participants recovered from their depressive symptoms more rapidly and completely than did the participants for whom religious faith was less important. These results suggest that positive religious coping may indeed be a cause of better mental health.

Correlations between religious coping and anxiety have also been found. Elders who place a great deal of emphasis on religious faith worry much less than those who do not (Tapanya, Nicki, & Jarusawad, 1997). Moreover, associations between religious faith and physical and mental health have been found among older adults of diverse faiths—Christians, Buddhists, Moslems, Hindus, and Sikhs—and from a variety of cultures and ethnic groups (Krause et al., 1999; Mehta, 1999; Meisenhelder & Chandler, 2000; Tapanya et al., 1997).

The positive effects of religious coping seem to arise from its influence on how elders think about their lives. For example, older adults who rate their religious beliefs as highly important to them are more likely than others to think that their lives serve an important purpose (Gerwood, LeBlanc, & Piazza, 1998). In addition, religious faith seems to provide older adults with a theme that integrates the various periods of their lives (Mehta, 1999). As a result, religious elders are more likely than their nonreligious peers to view old age as a chapter in an ongoing story rather than as primarily a period of loss of capacities. Further, among low-income elders, divine power is viewed as a resource on which those who have little social power in the material world can rely (Barusch, 1999).

Critical Thinking

Do the people you know who use religious coping do so positively or negatively? How do you think their use of such coping affects these individuals' attitudes and behavior?

● *Attendance at Religious Services* ●   The social aspect of religious coping most often examined by researchers is attendance at religious services. Research suggests that adults who regularly attend such services are healthier than their nonattending peers (Idler & Kasl, 1997a). Once again, selection effects are possible. However, longitudinal studies suggest that patterns of attendance, as well as the association between attendance and health, change little when elders become ill or disabled (Idler & Kasl, 1997b).

In addition, attendance at religious services is linked to health habits. For example, African American elders with hypertension who attend church regularly are more likely than those who attend intermittently to comply with medical advice regarding blood pressure medication; also, the average blood pressure readings of the regular attendees are lower (Koenig et al., 1998). Researchers don't know why, but one explanation might be that church attendance provides opportunities for interaction with peers who suffer from the same disorder. In the context of such interactions, African American elders may receive encouragement to persevere against such chronic ailments as hypertension by complying with medical advice.

Longitudinal studies also suggest that the mortality rate is lower among religious participants. In one study, researchers examined the association between religious attendance and mortality in nearly 2,000 older adults over a 5-year period (Oman & Reed, 1998). Researchers compared participants who were associated with other kinds of organizations to those who were involved with religious institutions. They found that the mortality rate during the 5-year period was lower among the religious older adults, even when the amount of organizational involvement and the size of the organizational social networks were the same as for the nonreligious older adults (Oman & Reed, 1998).

Elders themselves cite a number of reasons for the benefits of religious involvement. For example, many say that religious institutions provide them with opportunities to help others (Krause et al., 1999). Intergenerational involvement is another aspect of religious participation often mentioned by older adults. For many, religious institutions provide a structure within which they can pass on their knowledge and beliefs to younger individuals (Mehta, 1999).

● *Alternative Explanations* ●   As noted throughout this discussion, researchers must always consider selection effects when examining links between variables such as religious coping and health. There are other possible confounding factors as well. For example, religious and nonreligious elders may differ in personality traits. It seems likely that those with higher levels of extraversion would be the most comfortable in religious social environments—and scientists know that extraversion is correlated with successful aging. Thus, the connection between religious coping and health in old age may be a manifestation of personality rather than an independent effect of religion.

In addition, research on the association between religious faith and health focuses on the personal relevance of spirituality rather than on intellectual acceptance of a set of doctrines. So, it may be the intensity and the personal nature of these beliefs, rather than the fact that they have a religious focus, that are responsible for the correlations. In addition, in most research studies, the participants have had longstanding belief and attendance patterns. Thus, these elders may persist in religious faith and involvement, even when they are ill or disabled, because it helps them achieve a sense of continuity of identity. That is, religious involvement may allow an older adult to feel that, despite physical losses, she is still the same person. So, it may be that the sense of personal integration that religion provides is responsible for the correlations. Whatever the reasons, the research evidence suggests that supporting the spiritual needs of the elderly may be just as important to maintaining their health and functioning as meeting their physical and material needs.

Before going on

● Describe the successful aging paradigm, noting the ways in which it is manifested in the lives of older adults.

● How does religious coping influence physical and mental health in late adulthood?

Social Relationships

The social roles older adults occupy are usually different from those they held at younger ages. In addition, both consistency and change characterize social relationships during this period.

Social Roles

Clearly, role changes are inevitable in old age, and physical and cognitive changes are responsible for many of them. Some, however, are the result of ageism. Appearance cues—wrinkles and gray hair and the like—are often the basis for judgments about the competence of those who are older (Hummert, Garstka, & Shaner, 1997). The older people look, the more negatively others stereotype them, and negative stereotypes are more often applied to older women than to older men. Consequently, older adults may be unjustly forced out of roles by younger adults.

Surprisingly, though, elderly adults are just as likely as their younger peers to hold ageist stereotypes. In fact, some data suggest that older adults are actually *more* likely than younger adults to be prejudiced against their elderly peers (Hummert, Garstka, & Shaner, 1997). Thus, an older adult's beliefs about his own competence or attractiveness may be as important to his decisions about role transitions as the prejudices of others.

Moreover, sociologists point out that the roles that older adults do retain have far less content—that is, far fewer duties or expectations (Rosow, 1985). For example, most older adults continue to occupy the role of parent, but this role typically becomes far less demanding. Unless she had children very late in life, or her children encountered unusual difficulties in getting established in their own lives, by the time an individual reaches age 65, her last child is long since fully independent. Similarly, in other arenas, elders may occupy roles that have titles, but fewer duties. A retired university professor, for instance, may have the title of Emeritus Professor, a position that carries a few benefits but essentially no obligations. In other organizations, an older individual may be given the title of Honorary Chairman.

In a practical sense, the decline in role content means that the daily routines of many older adults are no longer structured by specific roles. But is this good or bad?

Some developmentalists see this loss of role definition as carrying with it a significant risk of isolation or alienation. Others see distinct advantages to this "roleless" time in late life. One such advantage is a greater "license for eccentricity" (Bond & Coleman, 1990, p. 78). Because they do not have to fit into the sometimes tight confines of role expectations, older adults feel far freer to express their own individuality—in dress, language, and personal preferences. This change may begin even earlier than late adulthood; the gradual assertion of individuality seems to be characteristic of middle adulthood for many. But certainly older adults benefit from a kind of institutionalized acceptance of eccentricity.

Living Arrangements

As you learned in the Research Report in Chapter 16, only about 4% of elders over age 65 reside in nursing homes (FIFARS, 2000). Of those who are not institutionalized, most live alone. This is quite different from the most common living arrangement of middle adulthood, when the majority of adults live with a spouse or partner. In late adulthood, that arrangement becomes much less common.

Figure 17.1 shows the marital status of the young old, old old, and oldest old in the United States in 1998. Because men typically marry younger women and because women live longer than men, a man can normally expect to have a spouse or intimate partner until he dies. The normal expectation for a woman is that she will eventually be without such a partner, often for many years. Clearly, the percentages in Figure 17.1 support these expectations, and it is hard to exaggerate the importance of that difference for the experience of late adulthood for men and women.

The difference is also clearly reflected in Figure 17.2 (page 498), which shows the living arrangements of noninstitutionalized elders in the United States. As you can see, older women are more likely to live alone than older men. This pattern is typical in other industrialized countries as well.

In the United States and in many other Western industrialized countries, living alone is not only the most common but also the most desired living arrangement among unmarried elders, even among those whose health has declined. A particularly intriguing

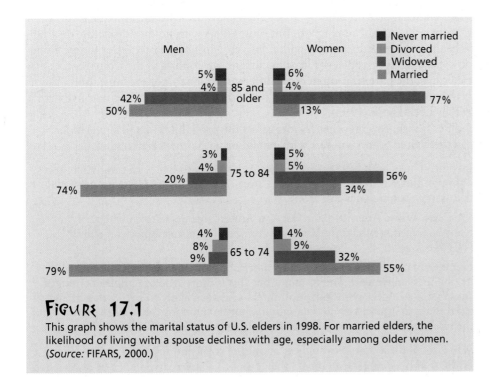

FIGURE 17.1

This graph shows the marital status of U.S. elders in 1998. For married elders, the likelihood of living with a spouse declines with age, especially among older women. (*Source:* FIFARS, 2000.)

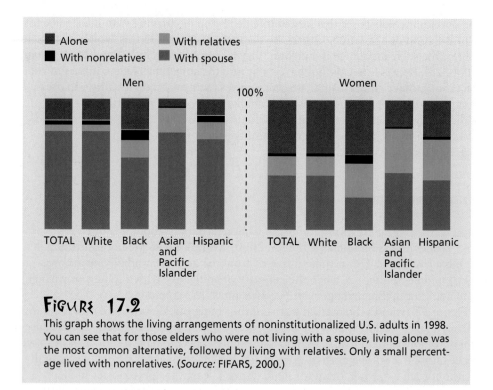

FIGURE 17.2

This graph shows the living arrangements of noninstitutionalized U.S. adults in 1998. You can see that for those elders who were not living with a spouse, living alone was the most common alternative, followed by living with relatives. Only a small percentage lived with nonrelatives. (*Source:* FIFARS, 2000.)

set of data comes from a study in which researchers interviewed more than 2,000 unmarried men and women over 70 (Worobey & Angel, 1990). Each of the participants was contacted twice, once in 1984 and once in 1986, so it was possible for investigators to look at changes in living arrangements for those whose health stayed the same, improved, or declined. Of those who lived alone at the start of the study and whose health declined over the next 2 years, 81% of the men and 76% of the women still lived alone.

That does not mean that health has no impact on living arrangements. In the United States, older adults with significant health problems are more likely to live with their children or with other relatives than are those who are more healthy (Choi, 1991; Stinner, Byun, & Paita, 1990). But most elders with mild or moderate disabilities or health problems do not live with relatives. Most appear to prefer to live alone and do so as long as possible—at least in current age cohorts in the United States. In other cultures, the pattern is often quite different. In Japan, for example, only 7% of adults over 60 live alone, and only 29% live with a spouse only. Over half live with a child (Tsuya & Martin, 1992).

Besides health, several other factors affect the probability that a single older adult in the United States will live with a child or with other relatives:

● Income. Those with lower incomes are more likely to live with family members, although this difference is not large (Choi, 1991). Many elders with marginal or below-poverty incomes live alone.

● Ethnicity. White American and African American elders are considerably more likely to live alone than are Hispanic American or Asian American elders (FIFARS, 2000).

● Number of daughters and sons. The more children an elder has, the more likely he or she is to live with one of them, but this is more true of daughters than of sons. That is, elders with more daughters are more likely to live with a grown child than are those with few daughters, but having more sons does not increase the likelihood of living with an adult child (Soldo, Wolf, & Agree, 1990).

What do all these statistics suggest about the roles and relationships of older adults? First and foremost, of course, they point to a sharp divergence of experience for men and women in the later years. They also indicate that developmentalists need

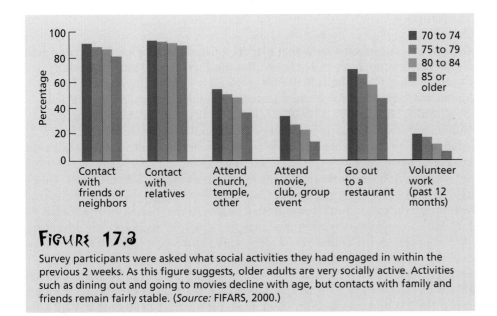

FIGURE 17.3

Survey participants were asked what social activities they had engaged in within the previous 2 weeks. As this figure suggests, older adults are very socially active. Activities such as dining out and going to movies decline with age, but contacts with family and friends remain fairly stable. (*Source:* FIFARS, 2000.)

to look beyond the spousal or partnership relationship if they are to understand the patterns of social interactions that are central to the aging individual.

As you can see from Figure 17.3, older adults in the United States are very socially active. The greatest proportion of their social activities involve contacts with family and friends. For widowed or unmarried elders, relationships with adult children and other family members may become more central in late adulthood than they were in earlier years. But an elder who is no longer able to live alone may be reluctant to live with an adult child with whom she has long-standing disagreements or whom she does not trust (see The Real World).

Elder Abuse

One extreme manifestation of conflict and strain between elders and their children is physical abuse of elders. Such abuse has received a great deal of media coverage in recent years, but it is not especially common; current estimates are that only about 3% of U.S. elders are physically abused (Bengtson, Rosenthal, & Burton, 1996). Physical abuse is most likely to be directed at elders who have some type of dementia, and abuse by spouses is twice as likely as abuse by children (Pillemer & Finkelhor, 1988).

Researchers have identified several risk factors for elder abuse, including mental illness or alcoholism in the abuser, financial dependency of the abuser on the victim, social isolation, and external stresses (Pillemer & Suitor, 1990, 1992). A likely victim of abuse is an elderly widow sharing her household with a dependent son who has a mental disorder or a drug or alcohol problem; the mother is typically too dependent on her son to kick him out and too ashamed of the abuse to tell others about it (Bengtson et al., 1996). Abuse is also more likely when the elder with dementia is physically violent and when a husband has physically abused his wife throughout their adult lives and simply continues to do so in old age.

Other forms of elder abuse may be far more subtle, including financial exploitation or failure to provide needed aid. The existence of such destructive forms of interaction is a clear reminder that older adults' relationships with their kin are not all sweetness and light. But it is also important to remember that these highly negative patterns are the exception rather than the rule. For most elders, relationships with children and other kin may be a mixture of positive and negative, but the scale most often tips toward the positive.

Affection between married partners and pleasure in each other's company clearly do not disappear in old age. (*Photo:* Jeffry Myers, Stock Boston)

Partnerships

Cross-sectional comparisons show that marital satisfaction is higher in the late adult years than when children are still at home. But this high marital satisfaction may have a somewhat different basis than that of the early years of marriage. In late adulthood, marriages tend to be based less on passion and mutual disclosure and more on loyalty, familiarity, and mutual investment in the relationship (Bengtson, Rosenthal, & Burton, 1990). In Sternberg's terms (look back at Figure 13.2, page 378), late adult marriages are more likely to reflect companionate love than romantic or even consummate love.

Of course, this does not mean that the marriages of older adults are necessarily devitalized or neutral. That may well be true of some marriages, but there is evidence to the contrary for many. You'll recall from Chapter 16 that the majority of older adult couples are still sexually active and may be somewhat more sexually adventurous than younger adults. Collectively, older couples also report higher levels of pleasure and lower levels of conflict in their relationships than do middle-aged couples. When older couples do have conflicts, they resolve them in more affectionate and less negative ways (Carstensen, Gottman, & Levenson, 1995; Levenson, Carstensen, & Gottman, 1993). Older couples also spend more time with each other than with family or friends, and although much of this time is spent in passive or basic maintenance activities—watching TV, doing housework, running errands—it is also true that those married elders who spend more time with their spouses report high levels of happiness (Larson, Mannell, & Zuzanek, 1986).

Further evidence of the deep bond that continues to exist in late-life marriages is the remarkable degree of care and assistance older spouses give each other when one or the other is disabled. For married elders with some kind of disability, by far the largest source of assistance is the spouse, not children or friends. Many husbands and wives continue to care for spouses who are ill or who suffer from dementia for very long periods of time. And even when both spouses suffer from significant disabilities, they nonetheless continue to care for each other "until death do us part." Marriages may thus be less romantic or less emotionally intense in late adulthood than they were in earlier years, but they are typically satisfying and highly committed.

Researchers have found similar characteristics and effects in long-term gay and lesbian relationships (Grossman, Daugelli, & Hershberger, 2000). Like heterosexuals, elderly homosexuals who have a long-term partner typically identify the partner as their most important source of emotional support. In addition, those who live with a partner report less loneliness and better physical and mental health.

It is the loss of the marriage or partnership relationship through the death of the spouse or partner that alters this pattern for so many older adults. The gender difference in marital status among elders illustrated in Figure 17.1 is further increased by a higher rate of remarriage for men than for women, a pattern found among both the widowed and the divorced at every age. Twenty percent of single men over 65 remarry, compared with only 2% of women. Older unmarried men are also more likely to date and more likely to live with someone (Bulcroft & Bulcroft, 1991). By contrast, research suggests that widows have little interest in dating or remarriage (Talbott, 1998). Despite older women's reluctance to remarry, studies of the emotional impact of remarriage in late adulthood suggest that both men and women benefit emotionally (Winter, Lawton, Casten, & Sando, 2000). When researchers examine self-ratings of life satisfaction, elderly newlyweds rate their personal happiness more highly than do either long-married or single peers.

Married older adults, like married adults of any age, have certain distinct advantages: They have higher life satisfaction, better health, and lower rates of institutionalization. Such differential advantages are generally greater for married older men than for married older women (again, this is also true among younger adults). This difference might be interpreted as indicating that marriage affords more benefits to men than to women or that men rely more on their marriage relationship for social support and are thus more affected by its loss. Whatever the explanation, it seems clear that, for older women, marital status is less strongly connected to health or life satisfaction, but still strongly connected to financial security.

Family Relationships

Folklore and descriptions of late adulthood in the popular press suggest that family, particularly children and grandchildren, form the core of the social life of older adults, perhaps especially those who are widowed. Older adults do describe intergenerational bonds as strong and important; most report a significant sense of family solidarity and support (Bengtson et al., 1996). These bonds are reflected, among other things, in regular contact between elders and family members.

Elderly newlyweds report higher levels of personal happiness than either long-married or single peers. (*Photo: David Young-Wolff, PhotoEdit*)

● *Contacts with Adult Children* ●   In one national sample of over 11,000 adults aged 65 and older, 63% reported that they saw at least one of their children once a week or more often; another 16% saw a child one to three times a month, and only 20% saw their children as rarely as once a month or less (Crimmins & Ingegneri, 1990). Regular contact is made easier by the fact that even in the highly mobile U.S. society, three-quarters of elders live within an hour's travel of at least one of their children. Very similar figures are reported by researchers in other developed countries such as England, so this pattern is not unique to the United States (Jerrome, 1990).

Part of the regular contact between elders and their adult children, of course, involves giving aid to or receiving it from the elder person—a pattern you learned about in Chapter 15. Most of the time, when older adults need help that cannot be provided by a spouse, it is provided by other family members, principally children. One representative set of data comes from the National Survey of Families and Households, which used a large national sample of more than 1,500 U.S. adults over 65 who had at least one living child. In this group, 52% were receiving some household help and 21% were receiving some financial help from at least one child (Hoyert, 1991).

However, relationships between older parents and their adult children cannot be reduced simply to the exchange of aid. A great deal of the interaction is social as well as functional, and the great majority of older adults describe their relationships with their adult children in positive terms. Most see their children not only out of a sense of obligation or duty but because they take pleasure in such contact, and a very large percentage describe at least one child as a confidant (Connidis & Davies, 1992).

● *Effects of Relationships with Adult Children* ●   Some studies indicate that when relationships between elders and adult children are warm and close, they are more important to elders' sense of well-being than any other kind of social relationship (Pinquart & Soerensen, 2000). By contrast, other researchers have found that elders who see their children more often or report more positive interactions with their children do not describe themselves as happier or healthier overall than do those who have less frequent or less positive relationships with their children (e.g., Mullins & Mushel, 1992). Moreover, such results have been obtained in very different cultural settings, for example in India and among Mexican Americans (Lawrence, Bennett, & Markides, 1992; Venkatraman, 1995). In all these studies, the older adults reported regular contact with their children and said that they enjoyed it, but these relationships did not seem to enhance happiness or health. Moreover, research has

Most elders enjoy maintaining relationships with younger family members. However, research suggests that such connections are not essential to life satisfaction in old age. (*Photo:* Michael Newman, PhotoEdit)

shown that childless elders are just as happy and well adjusted as those who have children (Connidis & McMullin, 1993). Many developmentalists have concluded that good relationships and regular contact with adult children can add to an elderly adult's quality of life, but are not necessary for it.

One possible explanation for this inconsistency in findings is that the relationship with one's children is still governed by role prescriptions, even in old age. It may be friendly, but it is not chosen in the same way that a relationship with a friend is. With your friend, you feel free to be yourself and feel accepted as who you are. With your children, you may feel the need to live up to their demands and expectations.

Several studies support this explanation. For instance, one researcher interviewed 55 older widows at length about their relationships with their children (Talbott, 1990). These women said many positive things about those relationships, but they described certain negatives as well: Some felt neglected by their children, some felt unappreciated, and some were afraid of bothering or burdening their children.

● **Grandchildren and Siblings** ●   As you learned in Chapter 15, interactions between grandchildren and middle-aged grandparents are beneficial to both. However, in late adulthood, contact between grandchildren and grandparents declines as the grandchildren become adults themselves (Silverstein & Long, 1998). Thus, grandchildren are rarely part of an elderly adult's close family network.

Interestingly, though, it appears that relationships with siblings may become more important in late adulthood, especially after both parents have died (Bedford, 1995; Gold, 1996). Siblings seldom provide much practical assistance to one another in old age, but they can and often do serve two other important functions. First, siblings can provide a unique kind of emotional support for one another, based on shared reminiscences and companionship. Once parents are gone, no one else knows all the old stories, all the family jokes, the names and history of former friends and neighbors. Second, many elders see their siblings as a kind of "insurance policy" in old age, a source of support of last resort (Connidis, 1994).

Friendships

Because older adults' friends generally come from the same cohort and have been their friends for a number of years, they can provide the same sense of generational solidarity that siblings may provide. The small amount of research on late-life friendships supports the hypothesis that the number of friendships may diminish gradually from age 65 onward (e.g., Blieszner & Adams, 1992; Levitt, Weber, & Guacci, 1993). However, friendships gain importance in the lives of elders, even as they diminish in number.

Critical Thinking

Why do you think most older adults' friends are long-standing ones? What social or psychological barriers might there be to creating new friendships in old age?

Mounting evidence suggests that contact with friends has a significant impact on overall life satisfaction, on self-esteem, and on the amount of loneliness reported by older adults (Antonucci, 1990; Hartup & Stevens, 1999; Jerrome, 1990). Moreover, for those elders whose families are unavailable, friendships seem to provide an equally effective support network (Takahashi, Tamura, & Tokoro, 1997). This is particularly true of unmarried elders, but is at least somewhat true for married ones as well.

Friends meet different kinds of needs for older adults than do family members. For one thing, relationships with friends are likely to be more reciprocal or equitable, and developmentalists know that equitable relationships are more valued and less stressful. Friends provide companionship, opportunities for laughter, and shared activities. In one Canadian study, for example, friends were second only to spouses as sources of companionship among those over 65 (Connidis & Davies, 1992). Friends may also provide assistance with daily tasks, such as shopping or housework, although they typically provide less help of this kind than do family members.

Friends seem to play an important role in late adulthood, perhaps because they share the same background and memories—like favorite old tunes and dances. (*Photo:* Michael L. Abramson, Woodfin Camp and Associates)

Gender and Racial Differences in Social Networks

As at earlier ages, women and men in late adulthood appear to form different kinds of social networks, with men's friendships involving less disclosure and less intimacy than women's. In addition, older women's networks tend to be larger and closer than those of older men. Developmentalists attribute these findings to a continuation of a pattern evident across most of the lifespan (Barker, Morrow, & Mitteness, 1998). Thus, if you think back on what you learned about sex differences in the chapters on childhood, adolescence, early adulthood, and middle adulthood, sex differences in late adulthood social networks should not be surprising.

However, it would be a mistake to assume that, because men have smaller social networks, their relationships are unimportant to them. Some developmentalists suggest that research on social networks may be biased in such a way that women will always be found to have stronger networks. This bias, critics say, originates from the fact that research emphasizes shared activities and frequency of contact more than the quality of the relationships. Indeed, when quality of relationships is considered, research shows that men's social networks are just as important to them and provide them with the same kinds of emotional support as women's networks do, even though men's networks tend to be smaller (Riggs, 1997).

African Americans tend to have warmer relationships with their siblings and to live with their children more often than white Americans do. In addition, they show two other distinctive patterns in their social networks. They create strong relationships with "fictive kin," a type of relationship you first learned about in Chapter 13. In African American groups, friends often acquire the status of a close sibling, aunt, uncle, or grandparent. Such fictive kin may be important sources of both emotional and instrumental support among elders of all ethnic groups, but the pattern is particularly prevalent among African Americans (Johnson & Barer, 1990; MacRae, 1992).

Other ethnic groups, including Hispanic Americans and Asian Americans, are also often found to have more extensive social networks than white Americans. However, the correlations between social networks and various measures of well-being seem to be similar across these groups (Barker et al., 1998; Baxter et al., 1998; Takahashi et al., 1997). Moreover, most studies suggest that the quality of the social network, not just its size, is important. Thus, as the earlier discussion of successful aging suggested, the number of contacts with family and friends, together with the quality of interactions with them, are important predictors of elders' well-being.

Before going on

● How do social roles change in late adulthood?

● What are the living arrangements of most elderly people in the United States and other industrialized countries?

● How do intimate partnerships contribute to development in late adulthood?

● What is the significance for older adults of family relationships?

● How do friends affect elders' life satisfaction?

● What are some gender and ethnic differences in older adults' social networks?

Career Issues in Late Life

A remarkable capacity for adaptation marks the transition from work to retirement. Although this transition certainly brings the loss of a major role, virtually all the folklore about the negative effects of this particular role loss turns out to be wrong, at least for current older cohorts in developed countries. Developmentalists' knowledge about the process of retirement has been greatly enhanced by a series of excellent longitudinal studies, each following a group of men or women from before retirement into the years past retirement. In one particularly helpful analysis, Erdman Palmore and his colleagues combined the results of seven such studies, yielding a sample of over 7,000 adults, each interviewed at least twice and often many more times than that (Palmore, Burchett, Fillenbaum, George, & Wallman, 1985). Although these data are not completely current, they comprise by far the most comprehensive set of longitudinal data available.

Timing of Retirement

One inaccurate bit of folklore is that 65 is the normal age of retirement. As recently as 1970, 65 was indeed the most common age of retirement for men in the United States. One reason for the uniformity was that many employers forced all workers to retire at 65. However, during the 1980s, age-discrimination legislation outlawed mandatory retirement in the United States (Mooney, Knox, & Schacht, 2000).

Knowing that there is a ban on mandatory retirement might lead you to believe that people are continuing to work to more advanced ages. However, the trend is quite the opposite. In recent decades, both in the United States and in most industrialized countries, the average age of retirement has been declining. One reason for this trend is that many government agencies and private businesses now offer older workers financial incentives ("golden handshakes") to retire. For example, in many countries, 60 is currently the pensionable age; in many others, such as the United States, 65 is the age at which a worker can begin to receive a full pension, although a reduced pension may be drawn earlier (Inkeles & Usui, 1989).

Some European countries are trying to reverse the trend toward younger retirement by gradually raising the age of eligibility for public pensions. A similar change has been proposed in the United States, and such public policy changes may affect individual retirement decisions in the future. But in the United States currently, the most common age at retirement for men is 62; only about 40% of men between ages 62 and 64 and 25% of men between 65 and 69 are still in the work force (Quadagno & Hardy, 1996). A similar shift toward leaving the labor force earlier has also occurred for women. Still, as you learned in Chapter 15, a majority of the current cohort of middle-aged adults (the Baby Boomers) expect to work at least part-time during retirement, so these figures are likely to change in the future.

Critical Thinking

Think about your own attitudes toward retirement. Do you expect this life change to be positive and enjoyable, or do you anticipate it with dread or some anxiety? What do you think has shaped your attitudes?

Reasons for Retirement

Research suggests that financial incentives are only one reason for retiring. Studies point to a collection of "pushes" and "pulls" that combine to influence each person's decision to retire (Kohli, 1994; Quadagno & Hardy, 1996).

● **Age** ● Age itself is obviously an important ingredient in the retirement equation. Internal models play an important role here. If a person's "expected life history" includes retirement at age 62 or 65, he will be strongly inclined to retire at that age, regardless of other factors.

● **Health** ● Poor health provides a particularly strong push toward early retirement (Schulz, 1995). Poor health lowers the average age of retirement by 1–3 years, an effect seen among Hispanic Americans and African Americans as well as among white Americans, and in countries other than the United States (Hayward, Friedman, & Chen, 1996; McDonald & Wanner, 1990; Sammartino, 1987; Stanford, Happersett, Morton, Molgaard, & Peddecord, 1991). However, among those who retire at 65 or later, health is a less powerful factor, presumably because most of these later retirees are in good health.

● **Family Considerations** ● Family composition is important in the decision to retire. Those who are still supporting minor children retire later than do those in the postparental stage. Thus, men and women who bear their children very late, those who acquire a second and younger family in a second marriage, and those rearing grandchildren are likely to continue to work until these children have left home.

● **Financial Support** ● Equally important in the timing of retirement is the availability of adequate financial support for retirement. Those who anticipate receiving pension support in addition to Social Security or who have personal savings to draw on retire earlier than do those who have no such financial backup.

Anticipated pension and health frequently work in opposite directions, because many working-class men and women who have worked in unskilled jobs can expect little supplementary retirement income and are in poor health. In general, working-class adults retire earlier than do middle-class and upper-class adults, often as a result of ill health and social norms, but many poor and working-class adults continue to work well past the normal retirement age in order to supplement their incomes.

On the other end of the social class scale, health and the adequacy of pensions work against each other in the opposite way. Adults in higher socio-economic groups generally have both better health and better pensions; they also tend to have more interesting jobs. The three factors combine to produce somewhat later retirement for this group.

● *Work Characteristics* ● Those who like their work and are highly committed to it, including many self-employed adults, retire later—often quite a lot later—than do those who are less gratified by their work. Those in challenging and interesting jobs are likely to postpone retirement until they are pushed by ill health or attracted by some extra financial inducement. For them, availability of a normal pension is less of an influence (Hayward & Hardy, 1985).

A quite different kind of work influence occurred in the 1990s in occupations or industries in which the work force suffered major "downsizing." A great many workers, blue collar and white collar alike, were pushed to accept early retirement, as their employers offered them special incentives (Hardy & Quadagno, 1995).

● *Sex Differences* ● None of the reasons for retirement, except age, is as significant for women as for men (Palmore et al., 1985). Women retire at about the same age as men do, on average, but retirement benefits, health, or job characteristics do not predict just when they will retire. The most reliable predictor of retirement for a woman is whether her husband has retired (Weaver, 1994). An opposing force that tends to keep women in the labor force is the lure of higher earnings that will augment future Social Security benefits—a factor that may be especially important for current cohorts of women nearing retirement, many of whom entered the labor force only in middle adulthood.

By contrast, the factors that lead to positive views of retirement are very similar for men and women. For example, one study found that health was the most important predictor of quality of life in retirement for both sexes (Quick & Moen, 1998). However, extensive pre-retirement planning seemed to be more important for men. Moreover, almost all of the study's male participants had worked continuously until retirement. Among the retired women, though, some had worked continuously, but others had spent a significant number of years in the home or in part-time employment. The researchers found that those who had worked continuously expressed more satisfaction with the quality of their retirement.

Effects of Retirement

There are a number of shifts that take place at retirement, some positive and some negative. But, overall, retirement seems to have positive effects on the lives of older adults.

● *Income* ● One potentially significant change at retirement affects income. In the United States, retired adults have five potential sources of income: government pensions, such as Social Security; other pensions, such as those offered through an employer or the military; earnings from continued work; income from savings or other assets; and, for those living below the poverty line, public assistance, including food stamps and Supplemental Security Income. For most elderly in the United States, Social Security is the largest source of income (FIFARS, 2000).

Of course, statistics on income sources indicate nothing about changes in income level after retirement. Here again, Palmore's longitudinal data can be helpful. These data suggest that incomes decline roughly 25% after retirement. But this figure paints a misleadingly negative picture of the actual financial status of retired persons.

In the United States, as in many developed countries, many retired adults own their own homes and thus have no mortgage payments, and their children are self-reliant. Furthermore, retirees are eligible for Medicare as well as for many special Senior Citizen benefits. When these factors are taken into consideration, on average, retired adults in the United States, Australia, and most European countries have incomes that are 85–100% of pre-retirement levels (Smeeding, 1990).

● **Poverty** ●   It used to be that post-retirement income losses resulted in high poverty rates among the elderly. However, over the past several decades, poverty rates among the elderly have declined substantially. In 1959, 35% of adults over 65 in the United States were living below the poverty line. In 1998, slightly more than 11% were at that low economic level (FIFARS, 2000).

A variety of factors are responsible for declining poverty rates among the elderly. For one thing, significant improvements in Social Security benefits in the United States (and equivalent improvements in many other countries), including regular cost-of-living increases, have meant that the relative financial position of the elderly has improved more than that of any other age group in the population. Moreover, more elderly adults are high school or college graduates than ever before. In 1950, only 18% of adults over 65 were high school graduates, compared to two-thirds of the over-65 population in 1998 (FIFARS, 2000). Thus, most elderly adults today had better jobs and earned a great deal more money before retirement than did members of previous cohorts. As a result, today's elders have more savings and better retirement benefits.

However, low rates of poverty in the total elderly population obscure much higher rates in various subgroups. For example, Figure 17.4 shows declines in the elderly poverty rates of various ethnic groups in the United States from 1979 to 1989. Although rates declined in all groups over this 10-year period, large disparities across groups remained. From 1989 to 1999, rates continued to decline in all groups, but the same cross-group pattern of variations in poverty rates continued (FIFARS, 2000).

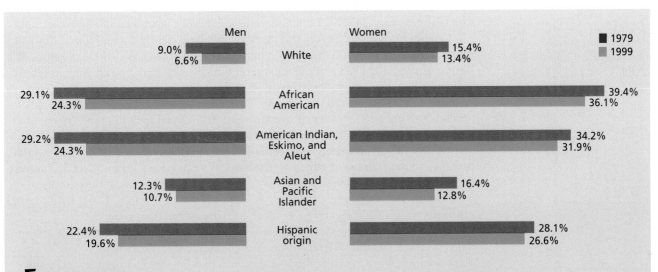

FIGURE 17.4

This graph illustrates how emphasis on declining poverty rates among the elderly can obscure important variations across groups. As the figure shows, poverty rates declined among all ethnic groups of the elderly in the United States from 1980 to 1990 (U.S. Bureau of the Census, 1995). However, the figure also shows that there were large disparities in poverty rates among groups. Although rates have declined even more since 1990, the same patterns of poverty continue.

Ethnic group differences in poverty are, no doubt, related to differences in educational attainment. Among older adults in the United States today, nearly three-quarters of whites and about two-thirds of Asian Americans are high school graduates. So, it is perhaps not surprising that these two groups have the lowest poverty rates. By contrast, less than half of elders in other ethnic or racial groups graduated from high school. Consequently, the employment histories of these groups are different, leading to income disparities in retirement. However, in future cohorts of retirees, these disparities are likely to diminish because of greatly increased rates of high school graduation and college attendance among younger minorities (U.S. Bureau of the Census, 1995).

Similarly, single older adults continue to be more likely to be poor than their married peers, and among older singles, women are more likely to be poor than men (16% versus 9%, respectively) (FIFARS, 2000). Varying poverty rates for single men and women in old age arise from a number of differences in adult life experiences. Current cohorts of older women are much less likely than their male peers to have had paid employment, are less likely to have earned retirement benefits even if they did work, and generally worked for lower wages (Hardy & Hazelrigg, 1993). As a result, many older widows rely entirely on Social Security income. Women in younger cohorts are more likely to have been employed and to have participated in a retirement plan, but, as you learned in earlier chapters, gender differences in work patterns still exist. Thus, there are likely to be gender differences in poverty rates in future cohorts of retirees, though these will probably shrink a bit.

● *Health, Attitudes, and Emotions* ● Longitudinal studies indicate quite clearly that health simply does not change, for better or worse, because of retirement. When ill health accompanies retirement, the causal sequence is nearly always that the individual retired because of poor health. Among those in good health at retirement age, retirement itself has little or no effect on health status over the succeeding years (Palmore et al., 1985). This clear set of research results is interesting because it suggests that retirement is not a highly stressful life change for the vast majority of adults.

Similarly, the bulk of the evidence suggests that retirement has essentially no impact on overall life satisfaction or subjective well-being. Longitudinal studies that have included measures of such attitudes show little difference in scores before and after retirement, and those recently retired show little sign of any increase in depression (Palmore et al., 1985). For most, retirement is not perceived as a stressor at all.

One set of data that makes this point particularly clearly comes from a study of a group of more than 1,500 men over a period of years (Bossé, Aldwin, Levenson, & Workman-Daniels, 1991). In the most recent interviews, participants were asked to indicate which of 31 possibly stressful life events they had experienced in the past year and to rate the overall stressfulness of each of these events. Retirement was ranked 30th out of 31 in overall stressfulness, below even such items as "move to a less desirable residence" or "decrease in responsibilities or hours at work or where you volunteer." Of those who had retired in the previous year, seven out of ten said that they found retirement either not stressful at all or only a little stressful. Among the 30% of retired men in this study who did list some problems with retirement, poor health and poor family finances were the most likely causes. Those with marital problems were also likely to report more daily hassles in their retired lives.

Other evidence suggests that those who respond least well to retirement are those who had the least control over the decision. For example, those who go into retirement because of a late-career job loss show declines in physical and mental health (Gallo, Bradley, Siegel, & Kasl, 2000). Similarly, those who are forced to retire by poor health typically adjust more poorly to retirement (Hardy & Quadagno, 1995). Even workers who accept special early retirement offers from their employers are likely to report lower satisfaction and higher levels of stress than do those who feel they had more control over the retirement decision (Herzog, House, & Morgan, 1991). Retirement is also likely to be more stressful for those whose economic situation is poor, or for those who must simultaneously cope with both retirement and other major life changes, such as widowhood (Stull & Hatch, 1984). But for those for whom retirement is anticipated and on time, this role loss is not stressful.

It appears that what predicts life satisfaction in late adulthood is not whether a person has retired but whether he was satisfied with life in earlier adulthood. We take ourselves with us through the years: Grumpy, negative young people tend to be grumpy, negative old people, and satisfied young adults find satisfaction in retirement as well. The consistency of this finding is quite striking and provides very good support for continuity theories of adulthood. Work does shape daily life for 40 years or more of adulthood, but a person's happiness or unhappiness with life, her growth or stagnation, seems less a function of the specifics of the work experience than a function of the attitudes and qualities she brings to the process.

● *Mobility* ●   For many adults, retirement brings an increase in choices about where to live. When your job or your spouse's job no longer ties you to a specific place, you can choose to move to sunnier climes or to live nearer one of your children. Surprisingly, however, most retirees stay fairly close to the place they have called home for many years (Burkhauser, Butrica, & Wasylenko, 1995; De Jong, Wilmoth, Angel, & Cornwell, 1995).

Charles Longino, who has been one of the most diligent investigators of residential moves among the elderly, suggests that elderly adults make three types of moves (Jackson, Longino, Zimmerman, & Bradsher, 1991; Litwak & Longino, 1987; Longino, 1990; Longino, Jackson, Zimmerman, & Bradsher, 1991). The first type, which he calls an amenity move, is the one most of us probably think of when we think of older adults changing residences. If an older adult makes such a move, it is almost always right around the time of retirement. Most typically, an **amenity move** is in a direction away from the older person's children, frequently to a warmer climate. Florida, California, and Arizona are the most popular destinations for amenity moves in the United States. In Canada, amenity moves are most often westward, particularly to British Columbia; in Britain, the equivalent move is to the seaside.

Those who make amenity moves are likely to be still married and relatively healthy and to have adequate or good retirement income (De Jong et al., 1995; Hazelrigg & Hardy, 1995). Often the relocating couple has vacationed in the new location; many have planned the move carefully over a number of years (Cuba & Longino, 1991). Most report higher levels of life satisfaction or morale after such a move, although some move back to where they came from because they find themselves too isolated from family and friends.

Another pattern of amenity move is to move seasonally rather than making a permanent move to a new locations. Some elders, often called "snowbirds," spend the winter months in sunnier areas and the summer months at home, nearer their families. One survey of older retired residents of Minnesota found that 9% followed such a pattern (Hogan & Steinnes, 1994).

The second type of move, which Longino calls **compensatory (kinship) migration,** occurs when the older adult—most often, a widow living alone—develops such a level of chronic disability that she has serious difficulty managing an independent household. When a move of this type occurs, it is nearly always a shift to be closer to a daughter, son, or some other relative who can provide regular assistance. In some cases, this means moving in with that daughter or son, but often the move is to an apartment or house nearby or into a retirement community in which the individual can live independently but has supportive services available. The final type of move in late adulthood is what Longino calls **institutional migration,** to nursing home care (see No Easy Answers).

E lders who have moved to resort communities specifically designed for retired people have made what social scientists call an amenity move. (*Photo:* Frank Fournier, Woodfin Camp and Associates)

amenity move post-retirement move away from kin to a location that has some desirable feature, such as year-round warm weather

compensatory (kinship) migration a move to a location near family or friends that happens when an elder requires frequent help because of a disability or disease

institutional migration a move to an institution such as a nursing home that is necessitated by a disability

No Easy Answers

Deciding on Nursing Home Care

In Chapter 16 you read about the numbers of older adults living in nursing homes and other institutions. Who are those institutionalized elders? And how do they and their families decide that a nursing home is the best form of care?

One reason the decision to place an elderly parent or relative in a nursing home is so difficult is that nursing home care is widely perceived as impersonal care that deprives elders of dignity and personal control (Biedenharn & Normoyle, 1991). The economics of nursing home care also make it unattractive for many older adults. Such care now costs thousands of dollars per month, costs not covered by Medicare or most health insurance plans. A stay of as long as a year is likely to exhaust the disposable assets of the majority of older adults. To be eligible for Medicaid coverage for such care, a person must first use all of his own disposable assets, which may leave a surviving spouse in very difficult financial straits. Many states now have laws that permit ownership of certain assets, such as a home, to be transferred to a surviving spouse, so that this asset need not be disposed of before the part-

ner in the nursing home is eligible for Medicaid—an alternative that leaves the surviving spouse in somewhat better financial condition. But the spouse may still suffer significant impoverishment.

Not surprisingly, the likelihood of nursing home placement varies considerably from one cultural subgroup to another. Studies in the United States, Canada, and European countries show that the most likely candidate for institutional care is an unmarried white woman over the age of 75 with few or no children (in particular, with no daughters), significant disability or dementia, and few economic resources (Carrière & Pelletier, 1995; Montgomery & Kosloski, 1994; Steinbach, 1992; Wolinsky, Calahan, Fitzgerald, & Johnson, 1993). Married elders are about half as likely as unmarried ones to spend any time in a nursing home, and those with at least one daughter are about one-quarter as likely (Freedman, 1996). Nursing home care is especially likely if the elder is no longer able to use the toilet without help or to feed herself, although even among those who are disabled to this extent, home care rather than institutional care is still the most common arrangement.

The problem for individual families is balancing the older adult's need for

independence and control against the needs of younger family members who have lives of their own to lead. What often tips the balance, one way or the other, is whether any family member is able or willing to provide assistance, and whether other community services are available. For some families, Meals on Wheels, visiting nurses, adult day-care services, and other help may make it possible to continue to care for a frail or demented elder at home. An intermediate alternative, which is becoming more available, is some kind of "supportive housing," where the older person can have an individual apartment and thus live independently but has nursing and meal services available in the building or complex (Pynoos & Golant, 1996).

Certainly, if average nursing home care were of much higher quality than it is now, with built-in opportunities for personal control, challenging activities, and first-rate medical care, and if such care were covered by Medicare or other national health insurance, choosing such an option might be less difficult. But until that better day arrives, the choice of nursing home care—for oneself or for an aging parent—is likely to continue to be wrenching and painful.

Of course, very few older adults actually move three times. Longino's point is that these are three very different kinds of moves, made by quite different subsets of the population of elderly, and at different times in the late adult years. Amenity moves usually occur early, kinship or compensatory migration is likely to occur in middle to late old age, and institutional migration clearly occurs late in life. Only the first of these types of moves reflects the increase in options that may result from retirement.

Choosing Not to Retire

A significant number of adults continue working past the typical retirement age. About 47% of men and 37% of women over age 65 are employed in the United States (FIFARS, 2000). This subgroup actually includes two types of people: (1) those who have never retired from their long-time occupations and (2) those who retired from their regular occupations and ventured into new lines of work, often part-time.

● **Continuing in a Life-Long Occupation** ●   Developmentalists know almost nothing about women who choose not to retire, but they do know something about men who shun retirement. Some are men with very limited education, poor retirement benefits, and thus very low incomes. Many of these men continue working out of economic necessity.

A larger fraction of those who shun retirement are highly educated, healthy, highly work-committed professionals, whose wives often are also still working (Parnes & Sommers, 1994). Many of them have been highly work-committed all their adult lives. For example, men in the National Longitudinal Surveys sample, a group that has been studied over a period of 25 years, were asked in their 50s whether they would continue working if they suddenly found themselves with enough money to live comfortably. Those who said they would continue working are much more likely to shun retirement and to be still working in their 70s and 80s (Parnes & Sommers, 1994). For these men, work continues to provide more satisfaction than they expect retirement to offer.

● **Learning New Job Skills** ●   Perhaps the greatest obstacle to employment for older adults is that many potential employers express concerns about older adults' ability to learn new job skills (Forte & Hansvick, 1999). However, studies of age differences in learning demonstrate that the learning process itself does not change with age. The same factors—interest, anxiety, motivation, quality of instruction, self-efficacy, and so on—predict learning success in both older and younger adults (Chasseigne, Grau, Mullet, & Cama, 1999; Gardiner, Luszcz, & Bryan, 1997; Mead & Fisk, 1998; Plaud, Plaud, & von Duvillard, 1999; Truluck & Courtenay, 1999). Thus, it seems reasonable that many aspects of effective training programs designed for younger workers, such as financial incentives for accomplishment of training goals, should also apply to older employees.

Moreover, an extensive body of research shows that, with appropriately paced training, older adults can significantly improve their performance on many cognitive tasks that are relevant to the workplace (Baltes & Kliegl, 1992; Dittmann-Kohli, Lachman, Kliegl, & Baltes, 1991; Kliegl, Smith, & Baltes, 1989, 1990; Verhaeghen, Marcoen, & Goossens, 1992). Pacing is important, because these studies do suggest that learning new skills sometimes takes longer for older adults. However, even training in the use of new technologies usually results in similar or identical skill levels among younger and older adults (see Development in the Information Age).

About 47% of older men and 37% of older women in the United States are employed (FIFARS, 2000). Further, a fairly high proportion of middle-aged people say they plan to work at least part-time after retirement. Consequently, employers are eager to learn how to best train older workers. (*Photos:* Don Smetzer, Stone; David Weintraub, Stock Boston)

● **Workplace Functioning** ●   With respect to aspects of job functioning other than learning of new skills, supervisors typically give older adults higher ratings than younger adults (Forte & Hansvick, 1999). For example, they view older employees as more reliable. In addition, managers typically report that although younger workers produce a greater quantity of work, the quality of older employees' work is better (Rao & Rao, 1997). Consequently, many employers view older adults as desirable employees.

Research suggests that older adults respond to computer training very much the way younger adults do. Most get over any anxieties they have about using computers after receiving training. In addition, they can become equally as proficient as younger adults, although they may require slower-paced training. (*Photo:* Barbara Alper, Stock Boston)

Development in the Information Age

Older Adults in the Technological Workplace

Computer skills are now required for most jobs, including many held by older adults. As a result, computer and software makers are producing and funding training programs and research aimed at promoting computer use and computer skills among the elderly ("Microsoft senior initiative," 1998).

Older adults are somewhat more anxious about learning computer skills than those who are younger (Czaja & Sharit, 1998). However, knowledge and training reduce their anxiety, often to levels that are comparable to those of young and middle-aged adults (Dyck, Gee, & Smither, 1998; Ellis & Allaire, 1999). Moreover, among elders, anxiety does

not appear to interfere with skill learning (Laguna & Babcock, 1997).

Productivity studies suggest that older workers can be just as productive as younger employees in jobs involving computer usage. In fact, at least one study found that workers over the age of 60 made fewer data-entry mistakes (Czaja, Sharit, Nair, & Rubert, 1998). The study's authors suggested that employers can expect an equal amount of work output from older and younger computer workers because older employees' lower error rate compensates for their slower speed.

Older adults seem to benefit most from training that is specially designed to take into account their motor difficulties and slower speed of cognitive processing. In some cases, training programs

have been specifically tailored to the different needs of the young old and the old old (Mead & Fisk, 1998). For example, researchers used repetition strategies to train young old and old old adults to use automated teller machines (ATMs). They found that both groups benefited more from action training than from verbal explanations of how to use the machine. However, the old old group made more errors and required more repetitions of the various steps involved in ATM use. Studies involving other kinds of technology skills have also shown that the old old take longer to learn new skills than the young old (Echt et al., 1998). However, ultimately, the old old seem to be no less able to learn new skills than young old, middle-aged, and young adults.

Before going on

- At what age do most men and women retire in the United States?
- What are the factors that influence the decision to retire?
- How does retirement affect income, health, attitudes, emotions, and mobility?
- What does research suggest about the decision not to retire?

A Final Word

Two things stand out in looking at social and personality development in late adulthood. First, there is a great deal of continuity in relationships from earlier periods of life. Those who have many friends and extensive social networks in early and middle adulthood are likely to continue to maintain such networks in late adulthood (Hansson & Carpenter, 1994; McCrae & Costa, 1990). In contrast, those who are more solitary or introverted are likely to persist in that pattern.

The second striking observation is that this continuity occurs despite significant attrition in the older adult's social contacts. The majority of older women are widowed; both older men and women lose friends and siblings to death. Yet most older adults adapt to these changes remarkably well and continue to maintain active social contacts throughout the remainder of their lives. They see friends and family and continue to attend church or participate in other organizations. The limiting condition for social activity in late adulthood is far more likely to be one's own physical disability than the death of a partner or friends. This persistence of social contacts in old age speaks not only to the continuing importance of such interactions for adults' sense of connection and well-being, but also to the robust capacity for adaptation that people exhibit even late in life.

Summary

Theories of Social and Personality Development

- Erikson's concept of ego integrity has been influential, but research does not indicate that the development of ego integrity is necessary to adjustment in old age. The notion of reminiscence has been helpful in researchers' attempts to understand development in late adulthood. However, research does not provide strong support for the hypothesis that reminiscence is necessary to successful aging.

- Similarly, disengagement has been found not to be essential in old age; high life satisfaction and good mental health are found most often among elders who disengage the least.

Individual Differences

- Successful aging is defined as maintenance of health along with cognitive and social functioning. Productivity and life satisfaction are also elements of successful aging.

- Religious coping has psychological and social components. It is associated with a lower mortality rate as well as with better physical and mental health.

Social Relationships

- Late adulthood is a time when people discard some roles. Remaining roles also have less content. Having fewer roles may offer greater license for individuality.

- Among unmarried elders in the United States, living alone is the most common and preferred living arrangement. Elderly Hispanic Americans and Asian Americans are more likely to live with relatives than elders in other groups.

- Marriages in late adulthood are, on average, highly satisfying for both spouses, who exhibit strong loyalty and mutual affection. If one spouse is disabled, the healthier spouse is likely to provide care. Married elders, as a group, are somewhat healthier and more satisfied with their lives than are single elders; this difference is larger among men than women.

- The majority of elders have at least one living child, and most take pleasure in seeing their children regularly. There is some indication that relationships with siblings may become more significant in late adulthood than at earlier ages.

- Degree of contact with friends is correlated with overall life satisfaction among older adults.

- Women in this age group continue to have larger social networks than men do, and African Americans tend to have larger social networks than white Americans.

Career Issues in Late Life

- The typical age of retirement is closer to 62 than 65 in the United States and in most Western developed countries.

- Time of retirement is affected by health, family responsibilities, adequacy of anticipated pension income, and satisfaction with one's job.

- Income typically decreases with retirement, but income adequacy does not decline very much. Among elders, women and minorities are most likely to live in poverty.

- Retirement appears not to be a stressful life change for the great majority of people. It is not the cause of deterioration in physical or mental health. The minority of older adults who find retirement stressful are likely to be those who feel they have least control over the decision to retire.

● Those who choose not to retire do so for economic reasons or because of particularly strong commitments to work. Research indicates that older adults can learn new job skills but may do so at slower rates than younger workers.

Key Terms

activity theory (p. 488)

amenity move (p. 509)

compensatory (kinship) migration (p. 509)

disengagement theory (p. 489)

ego integrity (p. 487)

ego integrity versus despair stage (p. 487)

institutional migration (p. 509)

religious coping (p. 493)

reminiscence (p. 488)

successful aging (p. 490)

volunteerism (p. 492)

CHAPTER
18

Death, Dying, and Bereavement

John Eastcott/Yva Momatiuk, Stock Boston

We began our study of the human lifespan with an examination of birth and went on to consider a multitude of changes in the physical, cognitive, and social domains from infancy to late adulthood. Now we turn to the end of life. A particularly eloquent expression of the inevitability of death came from Stewart Alsop, a writer who kept a diary of the last years of his life, as he was dying of leukemia. In one of the very late entries in this journal, he said, "A dying man needs to die as a sleepy man needs to sleep, and there comes a time when it is wrong, as well as useless, to resist" (Alsop, 1973, p. 299). Alsop's statement calls to mind one of the important individual variables you have read about often in earlier chapters—the timing of a universal developmental event in a particular individual's life.

Like Alsop, many people contract fatal diseases and consciously face the inevitability of impending death for a period of months or years. Sometimes an unexpected event—perhaps an accident or a crime—ends a child's or young adult's life prematurely. For most of us, though, death comes in late adulthood and results from the subtle interplay between primary and secondary aging. Consequently, a good deal of what you will learn about dying and death will concern older adults. But the story must begin earlier, with an examination of people's understanding of and attitudes toward dying and death.

In this chapter you will learn about the physical, psychological, and social aspects of death. You will also learn how children's and teens' understanding of death differs from that of adults. The chapter also discusses individuals' responses to their own impending deaths and to the deaths of loved ones. As you read, keep the following questions in mind:

- What are three definitions of death, and how does where a person dies affect the experience of dying?
- How does the meaning of death change over the lifespan?
- How did Elizabeth Kübler-Ross and her critics think about the process of dying?
- In what ways do people experience the psychological process of grieving?
- How do psychoanalytic and attachment theorists explain grieving, and what theories do their critics propose?

The Experience of Death

Most of us use the word *death* as if it described a simple phenomenon. You are either alive or dead. But, in fact, death is a process as well as a state, and physicians have different labels for different aspects of this process. Moreover, for both the deceased and the bereaved, the experience of death is shaped by the circumstances surrounding the end of life.

Death Itself

The term **clinical death** refers to the few minutes after the heart has stopped pumping, when breathing has stopped and there is no evident brain function, but during which resuscitation is still possible. Heart attack patients are sometimes brought back from clinical death; presumably those who report near-death experiences were in a state of clinical death.

Brain death describes a state in which the person no longer has reflexes or any response to vigorous external stimuli and no electrical activity in the brain. When the cortex, but not the brain stem, is affected, the person may still be able to breathe without assistance and may survive for long periods in a vegetative state or on life-support systems. When the brain stem is also dead, no body functioning can occur independently, and the individual is said to be legally dead (Detchant, 1995). Brain death most often occurs after a period of 8–10 minutes of clinical death, but there are cases in which brain death has occurred because of brain injury, as in an auto accident, and other body functions can still be maintained artificially. In such cases, other body organs, such as the heart and kidneys, can be used for organ donation, as long as they are removed without delay.

Social death occurs at the point when the deceased person is treated like a corpse by others; for instance, someone may close the eyes or sign a death certificate. Once social death has been acknowledged, family and friends must begin to deal with the loss.

Where Death Occurs

In the United States and in other industrialized countries, the great majority of adults die in hospitals, rather than at home or even in nursing homes. Naturally, there is a great deal of variation, depending on such factors as age and type of disease or injury. Among the old old, for example, death in a nursing home is quite common. Among younger adults, in contrast, hospital death is the norm. Similarly, adults with progressive diseases, such as cancer or AIDS, are typically in and out of the hospital for months or years before death; at the other end of the continuum are many who are hospitalized with an acute problem, such as a heart attack or pneumonia, and who die soon thereafter, having had no prior hospitalization. In between fall those who may have experienced several different types of care in their final weeks or months, including hospitalization, home health care, and nursing home care. Despite such diversity, it is still true that the majority of deaths, particularly among the elderly, are preceded by some weeks of hospitalization (Merrill & Mor, 1993; Shapiro, 1983).

In recent years, however, an alternative form of terminal care that has become common is **hospice care,** an approach to caring for the dying that emphasizes individual and family control of the process. The hospice movement was given a boost by the writings of Elisabeth Kübler-Ross, who emphasized the importance of a "good death," or a "death with dignity," in which the patient and the patient's family have more control over the entire process (Kübler-Ross, 1974). Many health care professionals, particularly in England and the United States, believe that such a good death is more likely if the dying person remains at home, or in a homelike setting in which contact with family and other friends can be part of daily experience.

Hospice care emerged in England in the late 1960s and in the United States in the early 1970s (Mor, 1987). By 1982, the idea had gained so much support in the United States that Congress was persuaded to add hospice care to the list of benefits paid for by Medicare. There are now more than 1,500 hospice programs in the United States, serving thousands of terminally ill patients and their families.

The philosophy that underlies this alternative approach to the dying patient has several aspects (Bass, 1985):

clinical death a period during which vital signs are absent but resuscitation is still possible

brain death absence of vital signs, including brain activity; resuscitation is no longer possible

social death the point at which family members and medical personnel treat the deceased person as a corpse

hospice care an approach to care for the terminally ill that emphasizes individual and family control of the process of dying

- Death should be viewed as normal, not to be avoided but to be faced and accepted.

- The patient and family should be encouraged to prepare for the death by examining their feelings, planning for after the death, and talking openly about the death.

- The family should be involved in the patient's care as much as is physically possible, not only because this gives the patient the emotional support of loved ones, but because it allows each family member to come to some resolution of her or his relationship with the dying person.

- Control over the patient's care should be in the hands of the patient and the family. They decide what types of medical treatment they will ask for or accept; they decide whether the patient will remain at home or be hospitalized.

- Medical care should be primarily **palliative care** rather than curative. The emphasis is on controlling pain and maximizing comfort, not on invasive or life-prolonging measures.

Three somewhat different types of hospice programs have been developed following these general guidelines. The most common hospice programs are home-based programs, in which one family caregiver—most frequently, the dying person's spouse—provides constant care for the dying person with the support and assistance of specially trained nurses or other staff who visit regularly, provide medication, and help the family deal psychologically with the impending death. A second type of program is the special hospice center, where a small number of patients in the last stages of a terminal disease are cared for in a homelike setting. Finally, hospital-based hospice programs provide palliative care according to the basic hospice philosophy, with daily involvement of family members in the patient's care. It is interesting that these three options parallel so closely the basic birth options now available: home delivery, birthing centers, and hospital-based birthing rooms. The fourth choice, both at birth and at death, is traditional hospital care.

Critical Thinking

Given what you have just read and your own philosophical assumptions, do you think you would choose hospice care for yourself or urge it on a spouse or parent in the last stages of a terminal illness? Why or why not?

The choice of traditional hospital care versus hospice care is most often made on philosophical rather than medical grounds. But it is still worth asking how the two types of care compare in terms of patients' and caregivers' experiences. Two large comparison studies suggest that the differences are small, although the results indicate that patients and caregivers may prefer hospice care slightly more.

The National Hospice Study analyzed the experiences of 1,754 terminally ill cancer patients who were treated in 40 different hospices and 14 conventional hospitals (Greer et al., 1986; Mor, Greer, & Kastenbaum, 1988). Half of the hospice programs were home-based, half were hospital-based. The patients were not assigned randomly to hospice or conventional hospital care, but chose their own form of care.

In comparing the two forms of care, the researchers looked at the patient's reported pain and satisfaction with care and at the main caregiver's quality of life and satisfaction. What is remarkable is how similar the experiences of the hospital patients and those of the hospice patients were. There were no differences in patients' reported pain, length of survival, or satisfaction with care. The major finding of the study was that family members were most satisfied with hospital-based hospice care, while those whose loved one chose home-based hospice care reported feeling a greater sense of burden.

In a smaller study, researchers assigned participants randomly to either hospice care or normal hospital care (Kane, Klein, Bernstein, Rothenberg, & Wales, 1985; Kane, Wales, Bernstein, Leibowitz, & Kaplan, 1984). The hospice care in this case was a combination of home-based and hospital-based. Most hospice patients remained at

palliative care a form of care for the terminally ill that focuses on relieving patients' pain, rather than curing their diseases

home but spent brief periods in the hospital's hospice ward, either when the family needed a break or when the patient's care become too complex to be handled at home. As in the National Hospice Study, investigators found no differences between these two groups in reports of pain or in length of survival. But they did find that patients in the hospice group were more consistently satisfied with the quality of care they received and with their degree of control over their own care. Similarly, the family members in the hospice group in Kane's study were more satisfied with their own involvement with the patient's care and had lower levels of anxiety than did family members in the hospital-treatment group.

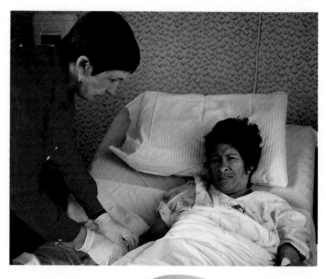

This woman, who is dying of cancer, has chosen to stay at home during her last months, supported by regular visits from hospice nurses. (*Photo:* Bill Aron, PhotoEdit)

Taken together, these two studies, as well as more recent research, suggest that based on purely objective measures, such as control of pain or survival duration, these two types of terminal care do not differ in effectiveness (Bretscher et al., 1999). Where differences exist, it is on measures of attitudes or feelings. On some—but not all—of such measures, those in hospice care and their families are slightly more satisfied. In addition, terminally ill patients who are cared for at home through hospice arrangements are admitted to the hospital less often in the last 6 months of life than those who do not receive home-based care (Stewart, Pearson, Luke, & Horowitz, 1998). Thus, the economic costs of death are reduced by hospice care. At the same time, both studies make it clear that home-based hospice care is a considerable burden, especially on the central caregiver, who may spend as many as 19 hours a day in physical care.

However, both patients and caregivers express concerns about hospice care. For example, both sometimes have more faith in hospital personnel when it comes to providing pain relief. Consequently, patients and their caregivers want assurances that the medical care they will receive in a hospice arrangement will be equivalent in quality to that of a hospital (Vachon, 1998).

In addition, hospice care providers must recognize that caregivers have needs as well. In fact, caring for a dying loved one, particularly someone with dementia, induces a grief response (Lindgren, Connelly, & Gaspar, 1999; Rudd, Viney, & Preston, 1999). Consequently, another important element of hospice care is grief support for the primary caregiver, support that includes both psychosocial and educational components (Meredith & Rassa, 1999; Murphy, Hanrahan, & Luchins, 1997). Similarly, hospice care providers themselves also often require support services because of the emotional strain involved in caring for patients who are terminally ill.

Before going on

- Define clinical death, brain death, and social death.

- How do hospice and hospital care differ with respect to their effects on terminally ill patients?

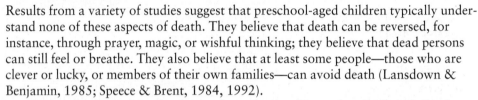

The Meaning of Death across the Lifespan

s an adult, you understand that death is irreversible, that it comes to everyone, and that it means a cessation of all function. But do children and teenagers understand these aspects of death? And what does death mean to adults of different ages?

Children's and Adolescents' Understanding of Death

These children being comforted by an adult at a loved one's grave are likely to have far more mature concepts of death than others their age who have not encountered death firsthand. (*Photo:* Lawrence Migdale, Stone)

Results from a variety of studies suggest that preschool-aged children typically understand none of these aspects of death. They believe that death can be reversed, for instance, through prayer, magic, or wishful thinking; they believe that dead persons can still feel or breathe. They also believe that at least some people—those who are clever or lucky, or members of their own families—can avoid death (Lansdown & Benjamin, 1985; Speece & Brent, 1984, 1992).

By the time they start school, just about the time Piaget described as the beginning of concrete operations, most children seem to understand both the permanence and the universality of death. This understanding is clear from children's own comments. In one study, children were told a story about two children who used to go into a candy store kept by an old lady who had recently died (Lansdown & Benjamin, 1985). After they heard the story, the participants were asked some questions about the old lady, and about what it meant that she was dead.

> A 5-year-old: "Someone came into the shop to kill her. She'll see them again and she'll die again. She can try to get up."
> A 7-year-old: "They never come alive again. You can't move because your heart has stopped. People wish you can come alive but you can't. Children can't die because they start at one and go to 100."
> A 9-year-old: "Their heart can't take it any longer and they die. Babies can die of cancer, kidney problems. Heaven is much nicer than down here." (Lansdown & Benjamin, 1985, p. 20)

The first of these children did not yet understand the permanence of death; the second did not understand its universality; but the third seems to have grasped all three. Some investigators have found that children who understand conservation are also more likely to understand the permanence and universality of death, but not everyone has found such a link (Speece & Brent, 1984). Instead, as is true of so many other milestones of this age range, the child's specific experience seems to make a good deal of difference. Four- and five-year-olds who have had direct experience with the death of a family member are more likely to understand the permanence of death than are those who have had no such personal experience (Stambrook & Parker, 1987).

Adolescents understand the finality of death better than children do. Moreover, in an abstract sense, they understand that death is inevitable. However, psychologist David Elkind proposed that, as teens enter Piaget's formal operational stage, they construct a set of beliefs he called the **personal fable**, a hypothetical life story that tends to portray adolescents' future lives in overly optimistic terms (Elkind, 1967). Elkind claimed that the personal fable leads most teens to believe that death will not happen to them because they do not imagine it happening. Thus, Elkind and others believe that the personal fable contributes to the frequency of teenagers' potentially fatal risky behaviors—fast driving, drug use, and so on—which you read about in Chapter 10 (Arnett, 1990).

personal fable a hypothetical life story created for himself or herself by an adolescent

Similarly, unrealistic beliefs about personal death appear to contribute to adolescent suicide. Typically, teens who attempt suicide claim to understand that death is final, but many tell researchers and counselors that the purpose of their suicidal behavior was to achieve a temporary escape from a stressful personal problem (Blau, 1996). Further, researchers have found that some teenagers who attempt suicide believe that death is a pleasurable experience for most people who die (Gothelf et al., 1998). Certainly, such distorted beliefs may be the result of the powerful emotions that lead teens to attempt suicide, rather than the product of adolescent thinking. However, suicidal adults typically think of death, even when it is desired, as painful and unpleasant. So, there may be a developmental difference between suicidal adolescents' and suicidal adults' understanding of death.

Like those of children, adolescents' ideas about death are affected by their personal experiences. Experiencing the death of a family member or friend, especially someone who is near the teenager's own age, tends to shake an adolescent's confidence in her own immortality. In fact, research suggests that the loss of someone close, such as a sibling, may lead an adolescent to critically re-examine her ideas about death—both as a general concept and as something that is inevitable for herself (Batten & Oltjenbruns, 1999).

The Meaning of Death for Adults

Adults' ideas about death vary with age. Death seems remote to most young adults. The notion of personal mortality is a more common focus of thought in middle age, and by the later years, the idea of death becomes very personally relevant for most adults.

● **Early Adulthood** ● In recent years, research examining young adults' views on death has been guided by a theoretical concept similar to the personal fable. Psychologists point out that young adults have a sense of **unique invulnerability**—a belief that bad things, including death, happen to others but not to themselves. Although young adults are more realistic about personal mortality than adolescents are, researchers find that many believe that they possess unique personal characteristics that somehow protect them against death. For example, researchers often ask participants of various ages to use life-expectancy statistics and risk-factor self-ratings to predict the age at which they will die. Such studies usually find that young adults overestimate their own life expectancy (Snyder, 1997). Moreover, young adults are more likely than those who are middle-aged or older to show increased fear of death following open discussions of the process of dying (Abengozar, Bueno, & Vega, 1999).

Here again, actual experience with death makes a difference. For example, nursing students display less fear of death than college students pursuing other careers, and their anxieties about death lessen with each additional year of training (Sharma, Monsen, & Gary, 1997). Moreover, the sudden loss of a loved one appears to shake a young adult's belief in unique invulnerability and, as a result, is often more traumatic for younger than for older adults. In fact, such losses frequently lead to suicidal thoughts in young adults. Young adults who have recently lost a loved one in an accident or to a homicide or suicide are about five times as likely to formulate a suicide plan as young adults who have not had such a loss, although most never follow through with their plans (Prigerson et al., 1999).

Analyses of public reactions to the deaths of relatively young celebrities, such as Princess Diana and John F. Kennedy, Jr., provide additional insight into young adults' ideas about death. As you may have noticed, perceptions of these public figures often change dramatically after their deaths, and they are given heroic status (Bourreille, 1999). Psychologists hypothesize that such early deaths challenge young people's beliefs in unique invulnerability and, therefore, provoke defensive reactions that cause them to place those who die young in a special category. In other words, to

unique invulnerability the belief that bad things, including death, only happen to others

After the death of John F. Kennedy, Jr., members of the public left thousands of flowers and gifts in front of his Manhattan apartment building in a spontaneous gesture of grief. Based on analyses of such responses to the deaths of public figures, some developmentalists believe that young adults idealize celebrities who die in early adulthood in order to avoid confronting their own mortality.
(*Photo:* Richard Lord, PhotoEdit)

maintain belief in their own unique invulnerability, young people must come up with reasons why death came early to John F. Kennedy, Jr. but will not happen to them. As a result, they elevate such figures to near-sainthood.

● **Middle and Late Adulthood** ● In middle and late adulthood, an understanding of death goes well beyond the simple acceptance of finality, inevitability, and universality. A death changes the roles and relationships of everyone else in a family. For example, when an elder dies, everyone else in that particular lineage "moves up" in the generational system. As you learned in Chapter 15, the death of a parent can be particularly unsettling for a middle-aged adult if the adult does not yet consider himself ready to assume the elder role.

An individual's death also affects the roles of people beyond the family, such as younger adults in a business organization, who then can take on new and perhaps more significant roles. Retirement serves some of the same function, as an older adult steps aside for a younger one. But death brings many permanent changes in families and social systems.

At an individual level, the prospect of death may shape one's view of time (Kalish, 1985). In middle age, most people exhibit a shift in their thinking about time, thinking less about "time since birth" and being more aware of "time till death," a transition clearly reflected in the comment of this middle-aged adult:

> Before I was 35, the future just stretched forth. There would be time to do and see and carry out all the plans I had. . . . Now I keep thinking, will I have time enough to finish off some of the things I want to do? (Neugarten, 1970, p. 78)

Such an "awareness of finitude" is not a part of every middle-aged or older adult's view of death (Marshall, 1975). One study of a group of adults aged 72 and older found that only about half thought in terms of "time remaining" (Keith, 1981/1982). Interestingly, those who did think of death in these terms had less fear of death than did those who thought of their lives as "time lived." Other research confirms this: Middle-aged and older adults who continue to be preoccupied with the past are more likely to be fearful and anxious about death (Pollack, 1979/1980).

Critical Thinking

When you think of your own age, do you think of time since birth, or time till death, or both? If you think in terms of time till death, can you remember when you switched to this view?

● **Death as Loss** ● The most pervasive meaning of death for adults of all ages is loss. Which of the many potential losses is feared or dreaded the most seems to change with age. Young adults are more concerned about loss of opportunity to experience things and about the loss of family relationships; older adults worry more about the loss of time to complete inner work. Such differences are evident in the results of a study in which researchers interviewed roughly 400 adults, equally divided into four ethnic groups: African American, Japanese American, Mexican American, and white American (Kalish & Reynolds, 1976). Among many other questions, researchers asked, "If you were told that you had a terminal disease and 6 months to live, how would you want to spend your time until you died?" Think about this question for a moment yourself. Then look at Table 18.1, which shows both the ethnic differences and the age differences in responses to this question.

You can see that the only sizable ethnic difference was that Mexican Americans were the most likely to say that they would increase the time they spent with family or other loved ones. Age differences were more substantial. Younger adults were

TABLE 18.1   Responses to Hypothetical Impending Death (percentages)

	Ethnic Group				Age Group		
	African American	Japanese American	Mexican American	White American	20–39	40–59	60+
Make a marked change in lifestyle (e.g., travel, have new experiences)	16	24	11	17	24	15	9
Center on inner life (e.g., read, contemplate, pray)	26	20	24	12	14	14	37
Focus concern on others; be with loved ones	14	15	38	23	29	25	12
Attempt to complete projects, tie up loose ends	6	8	13	6	11	10	3
No change in lifestyle	31	25	12	36	17	29	31

(*Source:* Kalish & Reynolds, 1976, p. 205, Item 037.)

more likely to say that they would seek out new experiences; older adults were considerably more likely to say that they would turn inward—an interesting piece of support for disengagement theory.

Fear of Death

Researchers have typically tried to measure fear of death with questionnaires. For example, one strategy is to ask participants to indicate, on a 5-point scale, how disturbed or anxious they feel when thinking about various aspects of death or dying, such as "the shortness of life" or "never thinking or experiencing anything again" or "your lack of control over the process of dying" (Lester, 1990). Another approach asks participants to respond to statements such as "I fear dying a painful death" or "Coffins make me anxious" or "I am worried about what happens to us after we die" (Thorson & Powell, 1992).

● *Fear of Death across Adulthood* ●   Although you might think that those closest to death would fear it the most, research suggests that middle-aged adults are most fearful of death. For young adults, the sense of unique invulnerability probably prevents intense fears of death. In middle-age, though, belief in one's own immortality begins to break down, resulting in increasing anxiety about the end of life. However, by late life, the inevitability of death has been accepted, and anxieties are focused on how death will actually come about.

The difference between the middle-aged and the aged is especially clear from a study in which researchers interviewed a sample of adults, aged 45 to 74, chosen to represent the population of Los Angeles (Bengtson, Cuellar, & Ragan, 1977). Figure 18.1 (page 524) shows the percentages of people in each age group who said they were "very afraid" or "somewhat afraid" of death. The fact that the shape of the curve is so remarkably similar for all three ethnic groups makes the results even more persuasive. And although these are cross-sectional results, similar patterns have emerged

MAKE THE CONNECTION

Look back at the discussion of disengagement theory in Chapter 17. Based on this chapter's discussion of the meanings of death for adults, do you think that Cumming and Henry were correct about disengagement being a natural process toward the end of life? Or did they perhaps place it too early in late adulthood and apply it too sweepingly? Explain.

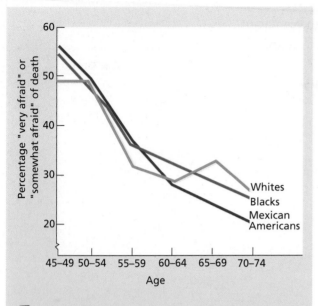

FIGURE 18.1

The remarkable similarity in the pattern of results for these three ethnic groups lends support to the generalization that older adults are less afraid of death than are the middle-aged. (*Source:* Bengtson et al., 1977, Figure 1, p. 80.)

from cross-sectional comparisons done in the 1960s and the 1980s, which makes the conclusion that much more credible (e.g., Gesser, Wong, & Reker, 1987/1988).

However, older adults do not become less preoccupied with death. On the contrary, the elderly think and talk more about death than do those at any other age. Predictably, these discussions lead to less fear and anxiety about death among older adults (Abengozar et al., 1999). Thus, to an older person, death is highly important, but it is apparently not as frightening as it was at mid-life. Older adults are more likely to fear the period of uncertainty before death than they are to fear death itself (Sullivan, Ormel, Kempen, & Tymstra, 1998). They are anxious about where they may die, who will care for them until they do, and whether they will be able to cope with the pain and loss of control and independence that may be part of the last months or years of life (Marshall & Levy, 1990).

● **Religious Beliefs** ● Researchers typically find that adults who are deeply religious or who go to church regularly are less afraid of death than are those who describe themselves as less religious or who participate less regularly in religious activities (Kalish, 1985; Thorson & Powell, 1990). In some instances, however, researchers have found that both those who are deeply religious and those who are totally irreligious report less fear of death. Thus, the most fearful may be those who are uncertain about or uncommitted to any religious or philosophical tradition.

Religious beliefs may moderate fears of death because religious people tend to view death as a transition from one form of life to another, from physical life to some kind of immortality. In the United States, roughly 70% of the population believes in some kind of life after death (Klenow & Bolin, 1989/1990). Such a belief is more common among women than among men, and more common among Catholics and Protestants than among Jews, but there is no age difference. Twenty-year-olds are just as likely to report such a belief as are those over 60.

In addition to framing death as a transition rather than an end, religious beliefs provide adults with death stories that help them cope with both their own deaths and those of loved ones (Winter, 1999). For example, Jewish scriptures, the Christian Bible, and the Moslem Quran all contain many stories that convey the idea that death comes when one's purpose in life has been fulfilled. Many such stories also teach that each individual life is part of a larger, multi-generational story. In this larger context, death is portrayed as a necessary part of the transfer of responsibility from one generation to another. This kind of philosophical approach to death leads believers to focus on the contributions to family and community that they have made during their lives rather than on the losses they will experience at their deaths.

● **Personal Worth** ● Feelings about death are also linked to one's sense of personal worth or competence. Adults who feel that they have achieved the goals they set out to achieve, or who believe that they have become the person they wanted to be, are less anxious about death than are those who are disappointed in themselves (Neimeyer & Chapman, 1980/1981). Adults who believe that their lives have had some purpose or meaning also appear to be less fearful of death, as do those who have some sense of personal competence (Durlak, 1972; Pollack, 1979/1980).

Such findings suggest the possibility that adults who have successfully completed the major tasks of adult life, who have adequately fulfilled the demands of the roles they occupied, and who have developed inwardly are able to face death with greater equanimity. Adults who have not been able to resolve the various tasks and dilemmas of adulthood face their late adult years more anxiously, even with what Erikson described as despair. Fear of death may be merely one facet of such despair.

Preparation for Death

Preparation for death occurs on a number of levels (see No Easy Answers). At a practical level, a person can obtain life insurance or make out a will. Such preparations become more common as people enter late adulthood and become more accepting of the inevitability of death. Thus, older adults are more likely than younger ones to have completed a will and to have made arrangements for their own funeral or burial (Kalish & Reynolds, 1976).

At a somewhat deeper level, adults may prepare for death through some process of reminiscence. Deeper still, there may be unconscious changes that occur in the years just before death, which might be thought of as a type of preparation. You read

Saying Goodbye

The Kaliai, a small Melanesian society in Papua New Guinea, believe that all deaths are caused by a person or spirit whom the dying person has offended in some way (Counts, 1976/1977). Any person who feels that he is near death moves from his house into a temporary shelter, where he attempts to appease whichever person or spirit he thinks he may have offended. He also attempts to thwart death through the use of various medicines and cures. When death becomes imminent, family members and friends return items borrowed from the dying person and pay debts they owe him. Likewise, the dying person returns borrowed items and repays debts owed to family and friends. The Kaliai believe that this process of bringing relationships into balance prepares the dying person for an afterlife in which he will become a powerful superhuman being.

But how do you say goodbye to a dying loved one, or how does a dying person say goodbye to loved ones, in a culture where discussions of death are largely taboo? Research suggests that in the United States, even physicians who routinely treat terminally ill patients are reluctant to state directly that a patient is

going to die (Lutfey & Maynard, 1998). Moreover, the sufferer and her loved ones may avoid discussions of death because admitting that death is approaching may be seen as rejection of the possibility of recovery. Family members may believe that discussing death will undermine the terminally ill patient's optimism and ability to fight the disease. Likewise, those who are dying may not want to make their loved ones feel bad. Still, most people in these situations feel that they must balance the need for closure against fears of fostering pessimism. Consequently, many terminally ill adults and their families create indirect methods of saying farewell.

A study in Australia gives a glimpse of the variety of such goodbyes devised by the dying (Kellehear & Lewin, 1988/1989). Researchers interviewed 90 terminally ill cancer patients, all of whom expected to die within a year. Most had known of their cancer diagnosis for at least a year prior to the interview but had only recently been given a short-term prognosis. As part of the interview, these 90 people were asked if they had already said farewell to anyone, and to describe any plans they had for future farewells. To whom did they want to say goodbye, and how would they say it?

About a fifth of these people planned no farewells. Another three-fifths thought it was important to say goodbye, but wanted to put it off until very near the end so as to distress family and friends as little as possible. They hoped that there would then be time for a few final words with spouses, children, and close friends. The remaining fifth began their farewells much earlier and used many different avenues. In a particularly touching farewell gesture, one woman who had two grown daughters but no grandchildren knitted a set of baby clothes for each daughter, for the grandchildren she would never see.

Kellehear and Lewin make the important point that such farewells are a kind of gift. They signal that the dying person feels that someone is worthy of a last goodbye. Such farewells may also represent a balancing of the relationship slate just as important as the balancing of material possessions is among the Kaliai.

Farewells also may allow the dying person to disengage more readily when death comes closer, and to warn others that death is indeed approaching. Hearing someone say farewell may thus help the living to begin a kind of anticipatory grieving, and in this way prepare better for the loss.

about the physical and mental changes associated with terminal drop in Chapter 16. Research has pointed to the possibility that there may be terminal psychological changes as well.

For example, in a still influential study, researchers studied a group of older adults longitudinally, interviewing and testing each participant regularly over a period of 3 years (Lieberman, 1965; Lieberman & Coplan, 1970). After the testing, investigators kept track of the participants and noted when they died. They were able to identify one group of 40 participants who had all died within 1 year of the end of the interviewing and to compare them with another group of 40, matched to the first group by age, sex, and marital status, who had survived at least 3 years after the end of the testing. By comparing the psychological test scores obtained by those in these two groups during the course of the 3 years of testing, researchers could detect changes that occurred near death.

The study's results revealed that those nearer death not only showed terminal drop on tests of memory and learning, they also became less emotional, introspective, and aggressive or assertive and more conventional, docile, dependent, and warm. In those near death, all these characteristics increased over the 3 years of interviewing, a pattern that did not occur among those of the same age who were further from death. Thus, conventional, docile, dependent, and nonintrospective adults did not die sooner; rather, these qualities became accentuated in those who were close to death.

This is only a single study. As always in such cases, it's important to be careful about drawing sweeping conclusions from limited evidence. But the results are intriguing and suggestive. They paint a picture of a kind of psychological preparation for death—conscious or unconscious—in which an individual "gives up the fight," becomes less active physically and psychologically. Thus, near death, individuals do not necessarily become less involved with other people, but they do seem to show some kind of disengagement.

Before going on

- What are the characteristics of children's and adolescents' ideas about death?
- How do young, middle-aged, and older adults think about death?
- What factors are related to fear of death in adults?
- How do adults prepare for death?

The Process of Dying

lisabeth Kübler-Ross is a Swiss-American psychiatrist who has studied the experiences of the dying and their loved ones. In the 1960s, Kübler-Ross formulated a model that asserted that those who are dying go through a series of psychological stages. These stages of dying, which were formulated on the basis of interviews with approximately 200 adults who were dying of cancer, continue to be highly influential, although Kübler-Ross's model has many critics. In addition, research suggests that individual differences affect the process of dying in important ways.

Kübler-Ross's Stages of Dying

In Kübler-Ross's early writings, she proposed that those who know they are dying move through a series of steps, or stages, arriving finally at the stage she called *acceptance.* Kübler-Ross's ideas and her terminology are still widely used. In fact, surveys of death education programs suggest that Kübler-Ross's model is the only systematic approach to the dying process to which health professionals-in-training are exposed (Downe-Wamboldt & Tamlyn, 1997). Thus, you should at least be familiar with the stages she proposed.

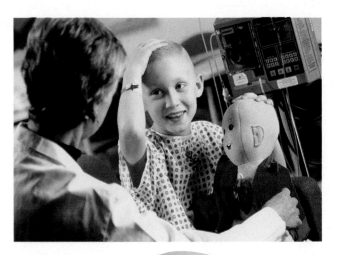

Children use some of the same defenses to deal with impending death as adults. Young cancer patients may deny or bargain—for instance, "If I take my medicine I'll be able to go back to school in the fall." (*Photo: Zigy Kaluzny, Stone*)

Kübler-Ross's model predicts that most people who are confronted with a terminal diagnosis react with some variant of "Not me!" "It must be a mistake," "I'll get another opinion," or "I don't feel sick." All of these are forms of *denial,* a psychological defense that may be highly useful in the early hours and days after such a diagnosis. Denial of this kind may be helpful in insulating a person's emotions from the trauma of hearing such news. Keeping emotions in check in this way may help an individual formulate a rational plan of action based on "what if it's true?" Having a plan of action may help moderate the effects of acknowledging the reality of the diagnosis. Kübler-Ross thought that these extreme forms of denial would fade within a few days, to be replaced by *anger.*

The model further suggests that anger among the dying expresses itself in thoughts like "It's not fair!" but a dying person may also express anger toward God, the doctor who made the diagnosis, nurses or family members. The anger seems to be a response not only to the diagnosis itself but also to the sense of loss of control and helplessness that many patients feel in impersonal medical settings.

Bargaining follows anger in the Kübler-Ross model. This is a form of defense in which the patient tries to make "deals" with doctors, nurses, family, or God: "If I do everything you tell me, then I'll live till spring." Kübler-Ross gave a particularly compelling example of this defense reaction: A patient with terminal cancer wanted to live long enough to attend the wedding of her eldest son. The hospital staff, to help her try to reach this goal, taught her self-hypnosis to deal with her pain and she was able to attend the wedding. Kübler-Ross reported, "I will never forget the moment when she returned to the hospital. She looked tired and somewhat exhausted and—before I could say hello—said, 'Now don't forget, I have another son!'" (1969, p. 83).

Bargaining may be successful as a defense for a while, but the model predicts that, eventually, bargaining breaks down in the face of signs of declining health. At this point, Kübler-Ross's theory predicts, the patient enters the stage of *depression.* According to Kübler-Ross, depression, or despair, is a necessary preparation for the final stage of *acceptance.* In order to reach acceptance, the dying person must grieve for all that will be lost with death.

Criticisms and Alternative Views

Kübler-Ross's model has provided a common language for those who work with dying patients, and her highly compassionate descriptions have, without doubt, sensitized health care workers and families to the complexities of the process of dying. At some moments, what the patient needs is cheering up; at other moments, he simply needs someone to listen to him. There are times to hold his hand quietly and times to provide encouragement or hope. Many new programs for terminally ill patients are clearly outgrowths of this greater sensitivity to the dying process.

These are all worthwhile changes. But Kübler-Ross's basic thesis—that the dying process necessarily involves these specific five stages, in this specific order—has been widely criticized, for several good reasons.

● *Methodological Problems* ● Kübler-Ross's hypothesized sequence was initially based on clinical observation of 200 patients, and she did not provide information about how frequently she talked to them or over how long a period she continued to assess them. She also did not report the ages of the patients she studied, although it is clear that many were middle-aged or young adults, for whom a terminal illness was obviously "off time." Nearly all were apparently cancer patients. Would the same processes be evident in those dying of other diseases, for which it is much less common to have a specific diagnosis or a short-term prognosis? In other words, Kübler-Ross's observations might be correct, but only for a small subset of dying individuals.

● *Cultural Specificity* ● A related question has to do with whether reactions to dying are culture-specific or universal. Kübler-Ross wrote as if the five stages of dying were universal human processes. But most social scientists agree that reactions to dying are strongly culturally conditioned.

For example, you have already read about the influence of religious beliefs on adults' ideas about death. Believing that death is a transition to immortality implies that one should face death with a sense of joy. Exhibitions of denial, anger, and bargaining may seem to indicate a lack of faith and, as a result, may be actively avoided by dying people who are religious. Thus, Kübler-Ross's model may fail to predict reactions to impending death by the religious.

Like religion, cultural traditions can also affect the individual process of dying. For example, in some Native American cultures, death is to be faced and accepted with composure. Because it is part of nature's cycle, it is not to be feared or fought (DeSpelder & Strickland, 1983). And, in Mexican culture, death is seen as a mirror of the person's life. Thus, your way of dying tells much about what kind of person you have been. Furthermore, in Mexican culture, death is discussed frequently, even celebrated in a national feast day, the Day of the Dead (DeSpelder & Strickland, 1983). Would it be reasonable to expect denial, anger, bargaining, and so on, in the context of such cultural expectations?

● *The Stage Concept* ● The most potent criticism of Kübler-Ross's model, however, centers on the issue of stages. Many clinicians and researchers who have attempted to study the process systematically have found that not all dying patients exhibit these five emotions, let alone in a specific order. Of the five, only depression seems to be common among Western patients. Further, neither Kübler-Ross's acceptance nor Cumming and Henry's disengagement (discussed in Chapter 17) appears to be a common end point of the dying process (Baugher, Burger, Smith, & Wallston, 1989/1990). Some patients display acceptance, others remain as active and engaged as possible right up to the end. Edwin Shneidman (1980, 1983), a major theorist and clinician in the field of **thanatology** (the scientific study of death and dying), puts it this way:

> I reject the notion that human beings, as they die, are somehow marched in lock step through a series of stages of the dying process. On the contrary, in working with dying persons, I see a wide [array] of human feelings and emotions, of various human needs, and a broad selection of psychological defenses and maneuvers—a few of these in some people, dozens in others—experienced in an impressive variety of ways. (1980, p. 110)

thanatology the scientific study of death and dying

Instead of stages, Shneidman suggests that the dying process has many "themes" that can appear, disappear, and reappear in any one patient in the process of dealing with death. These themes include terror, pervasive uncertainty, fantasies of being rescued, incredulity, feelings of unfairness, a concern with reputation after death, fear of pain, and so forth.

Another alternative to Kübler-Ross's model is a "task-based" approach suggested by Charles Corr (1991/1992). In his view, coping with dying is like coping with any other problem or dilemma: You need to take care of certain specific tasks. He suggests four such tasks for the dying person:

- Satisfying bodily needs and minimizing physical stress
- Maximizing psychological security, autonomy, and richness of life
- Sustaining and enhancing significant interpersonal attachments
- Identifying, developing, or reaffirming sources of spiritual energy, and thereby fostering hope

Corr does not deny the importance of the various emotional themes described by Shneidman. Rather, he argues that for health professionals who deal with dying individuals, it is more helpful to think in terms of the patient's tasks, because the dying person may need help in performing some or all of them.

Whichever model one uses, what is clear is that there are no common patterns that typify most or all reactions to impending death. Common themes exist, but they are blended together in quite different patterns by each person who faces this last task.

Responses to Impending Death

Individual variations in responding to imminent death have themselves been the subject of a good deal of research interest in the past few decades. The question that researchers have begun to ask is whether specific variations in patients' emotional responses to impending death have any effect at all on the physical process of dying.

The majority of research on individual adaptations to dying involves studies of patients with terminal cancer. Not only is cancer a clear diagnosis, but many forms of it progress quite rapidly, and the patient usually knows when her chances of survival are low. By contrast, heart disease, which is the leading cause of death in middle and old age in industrialized countries, may be present for a long period without the patient knowing that she has the disease. Also, the prognosis with this disease is highly variable. Researchers simply do not know whether any of the conclusions drawn from studies of cancer patients can be applied to adults dying less rapidly or less predictably. Still, the research is quite fascinating.

The most influential research on responses to impending death has been the work of Steven Greer and his colleagues (Greer, 1991; Greer, Morris, & Pettingale, 1979; Pettingale, Morris, Greer, & Haybittle, 1985). They followed a group of 62 women diagnosed in the 1970s with early stages of breast cancer. Three months after the original diagnosis, each woman was interviewed at some length and her reaction to the diagnosis and to her treatment was classed in one of five groups:

- *Denial (positive avoidance)*. Person rejects evidence about diagnosis; insists that surgery was just precautionary
- *Fighting spirit*. Person maintains an optimistic attitude and searches for more information about the disease. These patients often see their disease as a challenge, and plan to fight it with every method available.
- *Stoic acceptance (fatalism)*. Person acknowledges the diagnosis but makes no effort to seek any further information; or, person ignores the diagnosis and carries on normal life as much as possible
- *Helplessness/hopelessness*. Person acts overwhelmed by diagnosis; sees herself as dying or gravely ill and as devoid of hope

- *Anxious preoccupation.* Women in this category had originally been included in the helplessness group, but they were separated out later. The category includes those whose response to the diagnosis is strong and persistent anxiety. If they seek information, they interpret it pessimistically; they monitor their body sensations carefully, interpreting each ache or pain as a possible recurrence.

Greer then checked on the survival rates of these five groups after 5, 10, and 15 years. Table 18.2 shows the 15-year survival rates. Only 35% of those whose initial reaction had been either denial or fighting spirit had died of cancer 15 years later, compared with 76% of those whose initial reaction had been stoic acceptance, anxious preoccupation, or helplessness/hopelessness. Because those in the five groups did not differ initially in the stage of their disease or in their treatment, these results support the hypothesis that psychological responses contribute to disease progress—just as coping strategies more generally affect the likelihood of disease in the first place.

Similar results have emerged from studies of patients with melanoma (a form of skin cancer) as well as other cancers and from several studies of AIDS patients (Reed, Kemeny, Taylor, Wang, & Visscher, 1994; Solano et al., 1993; Temoshok, 1987). And at least one study of coronary bypass patients showed that men who had a more optimistic attitude before the surgery recovered more quickly in the 6 months after surgery and returned more fully to their presurgery pattern of life (Scheier et al., 1989). In general, individuals who report less hostility, who express more stoic acceptance and more helplessness, and who fail to express negative feelings die sooner (O'Leary, 1990). Those who struggle the most, who fight the hardest, who express their anger and hostility openly, and who also find some sources of joy in their lives live longer. In some ways, the data suggest that "good patients"—those who are obedient and who do not question or fight with their doctors or make life difficult for those around them—are in fact likely to die sooner. Difficult patients, who question and challenge those around them, last longer.

Furthermore, a few studies have linked these psychological differences to immune system functioning. A particular subset of immune cells, called NK cells and thought to form an important defense against cancer, have been found in lower counts among patients who report less distress and who seem better adjusted to their illness (O'Leary, 1990). And one study of AIDS patients showed that T-cell counts declined more rapidly among those who responded to their disease with repression (similar to the stoic acceptance or helplessness groups in the Greer study), while those who showed a fighting spirit had slower loss of T cells (Solano et al., 1993).

Despite the consistency of these results, two important cautions are in order before you leap to the conclusion that a fighting spirit is the optimum response to any disease. First, some careful studies find no link between depression, stoic acceptance, or helplessness and more rapid death from cancer (e.g., Cassileth, Walsh, & Lusk,

TABLE 18.2 15-Year Outcomes among Women Cancer Patients

Psychological Attitude 3 Months after Surgery	Outcome 15 Years Later			
	Alive and Well	Died from Cancer	Died from Other Causes	Total
Denial	5	5	0	10
Fighting spirit	4	2	4	10
Stoic acceptance	6	24	3	33
Anxious preoccupation	0	3	0	3
Helplessness/hopelessness	1	5	0	6
Total	16	39	7	62

(*Source:* Greer, 1991, from Table 1, p. 45.)

1988; Richardson, Zarnegar, Bisno, & Levine, 1990). Second, it is not clear that the same psychological response is necessarily appropriate for every disease. Consider heart disease, for example. There is a certain irony in the fact that many of the responses to cancer that appear to be optimum could be considered as reflections of a type A personality. Because having a type A personality constitutes a risk factor for heart disease, a "fighting spirit" response to a diagnosis of advanced heart disease might not be the most desirable. The growing body of research on responses to diseases does confirm, though, that there are connections between psychological defenses or ways of coping and physical functioning, even in the last stages of life.

Another important ingredient in an individual's response to imminent death is the amount of social support he has. Those with positive and supportive relationships describe lower levels of pain and less depression during their final months of illness (Carey, 1974; Hinton, 1975). Such well-supported patients also live longer. For example, both African American and white American heart attack patients who live alone are more likely to have a second heart attack than are those who live with someone else. Similarly, those with significant levels of atherosclerosis live longer if they have a confidant than if they do not (Case, Moss, Case, McDermott, & Eberly, 1992; Williams, 1992).

This link between social support and length of survival has also been found in experimental studies in which patients with equivalent diagnoses and equivalent medical care have been randomly assigned either to an experimental group in which they participate in regular support group sessions or to a control group in which they have no such support system. In one study of a group of 86 women with metastatic breast cancer (that is, cancer that had spread beyond the original site), researchers found that the average length of survival was 36.6 months for those who had access to the support group compared with 18.9 months for those in the control group (Spiegel, Bloom, Kraemer, & Gottheil, 1989). Thus, just as social support helps to buffer children and adults from some of the negative effects of many kinds of nonlethal stress, so it seems to perform a similar function for those facing death.

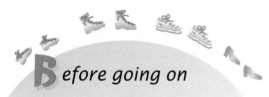

Before going on

- Describe Kübler-Ross's stages of dying.

- What are some other views of the process of dying?

- How do people vary in the ways they adapt to impending death?

The Experience of Grieving

In virtually every culture, the immediate response to a death is some kind of funeral ritual. However, a death ritual is only the first step in the process of **grieving**—the emotional response to a death—which may take months or years to complete.

grieving the emotional response to a death

Each culture has its own death rituals. The customarily quiet graveside service in the United States would seem strange to people in many other societies. (*Photos:* Michael Weisbrot and family, Stock Boston; A. Ramey, Stock Boston)

Psychosocial Functions of Death Rituals

Funerals, wakes, and other death rituals help family members and friends manage their grief by giving them a specific set of roles to play. Like all roles, these include both expected behaviors and prohibited or discouraged behaviors. The content of these roles differs markedly from one culture to the next, but their clarity in most cases provides a shape to the days or weeks immediately following the death of a loved person. In American culture, the rituals prescribe what one should wear, who should be called, who should be fed, what demeanor one should show, and far more. Depending on one's ethnic or religious background, one may gather family and friends for a wake or to "sit shiva," a traditional Jewish 7-day period of mourning during which family members stay in the same home and formally mourn a deceased loved one. One may be expected to respond stoically or to wail and tear one's hair. Friends and acquaintances, too, have guiding rules, at least for those first few days. They may bring food, write letters of condolence, offer help, and attend wakes and funerals.

Death rituals also bring family members together as no other occasion does (with the possible exception of weddings). Frequently, cousins and other distant relatives see one another for the first time in many years at funerals. Such occasions typically inspire shared reminiscences and renew family relationships that have been inactive for a long time. In this way, death rituals can strengthen family ties, clarify the new lines of influence or authority within a family, and "pass the torch" in some way to the next generation. Likewise, funerals help establish deaths as shared milestones for family members—"that was before Grandpa died" or "the last time I saw her was at Grandpa's funeral." A death can become an important organizer of experience that separates the past from the present. Dividing time in this way seems to help survivors cope with grief (Katz & Bartone, 1998).

Death rituals are also designed to help the survivors understand the meaning of death itself, in part by emphasizing the meaning of the life of the person who has died. It is not accidental that most death rituals include testimonials, biographies, and witnessing. By telling the story of a person's life and describing that life's value and meaning, others can more readily accept the person's death.

Finally, death rituals may give some transcendent meaning to death itself by placing it in a philosophical or religious context. In this way, they provide comfort to the bereaved by offering answers to that inevitable question "Why?"

Critical Thinking

Do the various funerals or death rituals you have participated in seem to have served the purposes described in the text?

The Process of Grieving

The ritual of a funeral, in whatever form it occurs, can provide structure and comfort in the days immediately following a death. But what happens when that structure is gone? How do people handle the sense of loss? Answering that question requires a look at a number of factors associated with grief.

● *Age of the Bereaved* ●   Children express feelings of grief very much the way teens and adults do. Like adults, children demonstrate grief through sad facial expressions, crying, loss of appetite, and age-appropriate displays of anger such as

DEVELOPMENT in the Information Age

"Copycat" Suicides

In Shakespeare's *Romeo and Juliet*, the teenaged hero takes his own life because he believes that his beloved has already done so. When Juliet revives and discovers Romeo's body, she commits suicide as well. Many believe that Shakespeare's characterization is a realistic portrayal of an emotionally distressed adolescent's typical reaction to suicide—imitation, or a "copycat" suicide. Based on this belief, many observers have raised concerns about the potential effects of emotion-provoking suicide stories in both fiction and the news media (Samaritans, 1998).

In general, research suggests that concerns about fictional suicides are unfounded. For example, a few years ago, the British public responded with outrage to a TV program that depicted a 15-year-old girl's attempted suicide with a drug overdose. These concerns were based on the fear that teenaged viewers who were experiencing emotional problems might be likely to imitate the character's behavior. Yet, surveys that followed the airing of the program found no increase in frequency of suicide attempts among teenagers. Moreover, few of those who did attempt suicide had seen the program (Simkin, Hawton, Whitehead, Fagg, & Eagle, 1995). Follow-up studies of other suicide-related programs on television have produced similar findings.

News accounts of suicides are a different matter. However, news stories about suicides influence adults' behavior more often than that of teens. Research suggests that, when the news media present sensational coverage of a particular mode of suicide, the number of people who attempt and complete suicides using that method increases. The number of individuals who attempted suicide by setting themselves ablaze, for instance, increased dramatically in Great Britain after several news programs carried reports, including graphic film footage, of a single self-immolation suicide (Ashton & Donnan, 1981). Likewise, suicide attempts involving throwing oneself in front of a sub-way train became so frequent in Vienna after sensational news reports of such incidents that members of the press agreed among themselves to no longer report them (Sonneck, Etzersdorfer, & Nagel-Kuess, 1992).

Despite inconsistencies in research examining the phenomenon of copycat suicide, mental health professionals believe that fictional or journalistic accounts of suicide may influence behavior in individual cases. They suggest that a 15-year-old girl who has already been thinking about taking a drug overdose may become more likely to do so after viewing a television program in which a character carries out a similar suicide plan. Similarly, an individual who wants to add drama to a planned suicide attempt may be inspired by news reports of an unusual method of suicide. Thus, mental health professionals warn that news and entertainment media should avoid romanticizing and sensationalizing suicide (Samaritans, 1998).

---

temper tantrums (Oatley & Jenkins, 1996). Funerals seem to serve the same adaptive function for children as for adults, and most children resolve their feelings of grief within the first year after the loss. In addition, knowing that a loved one or even a pet is ill and in danger of death helps children cope with the loss in advance, just as it does for those who are older (Jarolmen, 1998).

Although the behavioral aspects of adolescents' grief responses vary little from those of adults, teens may be more likely to experience prolonged grief than children or adults. One study found that more than 20% of a group of high school students who had a friend killed in an accident continued to experience intense feelings of grief 9 months after the death (Dyregrov, Gjestad, Bie Wikander, & Vigerust, 1999). Other research suggests that adolescent girls whose mothers have died run a particularly high risk of developing long-term, grief-related problems (Lenhardt & McCourt, 2000). Teenagers may also be more likely than adults to experience grief responses to the deaths of celebrities or to idealize peers' suicides (see Development in the Information Age).

Adolescents' grief responses are probably related to their general cognitive characteristics. You should remember from Chapters 10 and 11 that adolescents often judge the real world by idealized images. Consequently, a teenager may become caught up in fantasizing about how the world would be different if a friend or loved one had not died. In addition, prolonged grieving among adolescents may be rooted in their tendency to engage in "what if" thinking. This kind of thinking may lead teens to believe that they could have prevented the death and, thus, cause them to develop irrational guilt feelings (Cunningham, 1996).

● *Mode of Death* ● How an individual dies also contributes to the grief process of those who are in mourning. For example, widows who have cared for spouses during a period of illness prior to death are less likely to become depressed after the death than those whose spouses die suddenly (Carnelley, Wortman, & Kessler, 1999). Grief-related depression seems to emerge during the spouse's illness rather than after the death. The spouse's death is thought of as an escape from suffering for the one who dies and a release from grieving for the caregiver. Similarly, a death that has intrinsic meaning, such as that of a young soldier who dies defending his country, is not necessarily easier to cope with but does provide the bereaved with a sense that the death has not been without purpose (Malkinson & Bar-Tur, 1999). Consequently, mourners have a built-in cognitive coping device—a rational explanation for the death—that allows them to greive but also protects them from long-term depression.

However, sudden and violent deaths evoke more intense grief responses. One study found that 36% of widows and widowers whose spouses had died in accidents or by suicide were suffering from post-traumatic stress symptoms (e.g., nightmares) 2 months after the death, compared to only 10% of widows and widowers whose spouses had died of natural causes (Zisook, Chentsova-Dutton, & Shuchter, 1998). Moreover, almost all of those whose spouses had died unnaturally and who had PTSD symptoms were also depressed.

Furthermore, suicide is associated with a unique pattern of responses among survivors (Bailley, Kral, & Dunham, 1999). In general, family and close friends of someone who commits suicide experience feelings of rejection and anger. Moreover, their grief over the loss of the loved one is complicated by the feeling that they could or should have done something to prevent the suicide. They are also less likely to discuss the loss with other family members or with friends because of their sense that a suicide in the family is a source of shame. For these reasons, suicide survivors may be more likely than others who have lost loved ones to experience long-term negative effects.

Widowhood

The relationship between the deceased and those who are in mourning also affects the grieving process. For example, bereaved parents often report that their health is poorer than before a child's death, and many continue to experience intense feelings of sadness for several years (Arbuckle & De Vries, 1995; Malkinson & Bar-Tur, 1999) (see The Real World). As a general rule, the most difficult death to recover from is that of a spouse.

● *Widowhood and Physical Health* ● The experience of widowhood (a term that applies to both men and women) appears to have both immediate and longer-term effects on the immune system (Beem et al., 1999; Gallagher-Thompson, Futterman, Farberow, Thompson, & Peterson, 1993; Irwin & Pike, 1993). In one Norwegian study, researchers measured immune functioning in widows twice, shortly after their husbands' deaths and 1 year later (Lindstrom, 1997). Investigators found that the widows' immune systems were suppressed somewhat immediately after the death but had returned to normal a year later, in most cases.

CAREGIVING
The Real World

When an Infant Dies

Many parents grieving for a lost infant do not receive adequate support from either their social networks or health professionals (Vaeisaenen, 1998). It is important for those who are in a position to support grieving parents to understand that the grief that follows the death of an infant is no less intense than any other kind of bereavement. In fact, it may be more complex.

When an older child dies, parents have a relationship history and an intimate knowledge of the child's personality on which to build reminiscences. Such cognitive devices help them reorganize their attachment to the lost child so that they are able to release the child psychologically. But with an infant, there is little or no relationship history to draw on. The parents, of course, feel deep emotions of attachment, but the cognitive elements that help parents cope with the loss of a child are absent. For these reasons, bereaved parents of a dead infant often have a greater need for support from family, friends, and health

professionals than even they themselves realize (Vaeisaenen, 1998).

Well-intentioned friends or family may pressure the couple to cope with their loss by simply replacing the infant with another one. However, research suggests that starting another pregnancy soon after the loss of an infant doesn't necessarily end either a mother's or a father's grief, although it does tend to protect both against long-term negative effects such as depression (Franche & Bulow, 1999). Moreover, parents may fear that a subsequent child will also die in infancy and may try to avoid becoming emotionally attached to a newborn (Wong, 1993). This could have adverse effects on the whole family.

Health professionals have compiled a few guidelines that can be useful to family members or friends in supporting parents who have lost an infant (Wong, 1993):

- Don't try to force bereaved parents to talk about their grief or the infant if they don't want to.
- Always refer to the deceased infant by name.

- Express your own feelings of loss for the infant, if they are sincere.
- Follow the parents' lead in engaging in reminiscences about the baby's looks or personality.
- Discourage the parents from resorting to drugs or alcohol to manage grief.
- Assure grieving parents that their responses are normal and that it will take time to resolve the emotions associated with losing an infant.
- Don't pressure the parents to "replace" the baby with another one.
- Don't offer rationalizations (e.g., "Your baby's an angel now") that may offend the parents.
- Do offer support for the parents' own rationalizations.
- Be aware that the infant's siblings, even those who are very young, are likely to experience some degree of grief.

Similarly, a study comparing widows to married women in the Netherlands found that widows' immune responses continued to differ from those of married participants 7 months after the spouses' deaths (Beem et al., 1999). Interestingly, 7 months after the spouses' deaths, psychological differences (such as feelings of sadness) between the two groups had disappeared, though the immune function differences persisted. Thus, the bereaved may continue to suffer at a biochemical level even after obvious signs of grieving have subsided. Moreover, the association between death of a spouse and ensuing illness in a surviving partner may be the result of the effects of grief on the body's defenses against disease agents such as viruses and bacteria.

● **Widowhood and Mental Health** ●   In the year following bereavement, the incidence of depression among widows and widowers rises substantially, though rates of death and disease rise only slightly (Reich, Zautra, & Guarnaccia, 1989; Stroebe & Stroebe, 1993). In one important longitudinal study, researchers repeatedly interviewed a sample of 3,000 adults, all age 55 or older at the beginning of the study (Norris & Murrell, 1990). Forty-eight of these adults were widowed during the

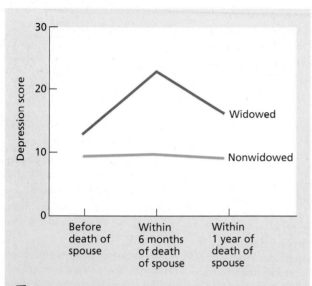

FIGURE 18.2

Those about to be widowed are more depressed than their age-mates who are not, and they also show a distinct increase in depression in the months immediately after the spouse's death. (*Source:* Norris & Murrell, 1990, from Table 1, p. 432.)

$2\frac{1}{2}$ years of the study, which allowed investigators to look at depression and health status before and immediately after bereavement. They found no differences in physical health between widowed and nonwidowed participants, but they did note a rise in depression among the widowed immediately following the loss and then a decline within a year after bereavement, a set of results illustrated in Figure 18.2.

However, other researchers have found that older adults whose spouses have died differ in mental health for several years following the death from peers whose spouses are still alive (Bennett, 1997). So, it appears that declines in physical and mental health follow bereavement fairly consistently, but how long such effects last may be highly variable. Several factors contribute to this variability.

One such factor is mental health history. Older adults who enter widowhood with a history of depression are more likely to experience depression after the death of their spouse (Zisook, Paulus, Shuchter, & Judd 1997). Lack of social support, both actual and perceived, also contributes to variability in depression among widows and widowers (Reed, 1998; Tomita et al., 1997). Moreover, the quality of the relationship of the widow or widower to the deceased spouse is related to depressive symptoms. Perhaps surprisingly, relationships characterized by emotional distance and conflict are *more* likely to lead to depression than those that were warm (van Doorn, Kasl, Beery, Jacobs, & Prigerson, 1998).

Economic changes accompany the loss of a spouse and add to the overall stress involved in the transition to widowhood. Women typically suffer greater economic losses after the death of a spouse than men do, usually because they lose their husbands' income or pension (Zick & Holden, 2000). However, the household incomes of both widows and widowers are lower than those of married elders (Federal Interagency Forum on Aging-Related Statistics, [FIFARS], 2000). Thus, the degree to which an individual's economic status changes as a result of a spouse's death is probably another factor that contributes to individual differences in the long-term effects of bereavement.

● **Pathological Grief** ● Some psychologists argue that **pathological grief**, depression-like symptoms following death of a loved one, should be thought of as a separate disorder from depression (Stroebe et al., 2000). They suggest that individuals who continue to experience grief symptoms such as loss of appetite more than 2 months following loss of a loved one may be developing pathological grief.

Diagnosis and treatment of pathological grief may be important for preventing problems in both mental and physical health among widows and widowers. Researchers have found that survivors whose grief symptoms continue for 6 months or longer are more likely to suffer long-term depression as well as physical ailments such as cancer and heart disease (Prigerson et al., 1997). Moreover, they continue to show important differences in physical and mental functioning for up to 2 years after their spouse's death.

However, it's important to keep in mind that many aspects of grief are culturally determined. Beliefs about how long mourning should last and how the bereaved should behave vary widely from one culture to another (Braun & Nichols, 1997; Rubin & Schechter, 1997). For example, Orthodox Jewish men traditionally do not shave or trim their beards for 30 days after the death of a family member. Furthermore, mourning traditions among Orthodox Jews require abstaining from entertainment such as attending the theater or seeing movies for an entire year after the death of someone close (Bial, 1971).

pathological grief symptoms of depression brought on by death of a loved one

Since inattention to grooming and lack of interest in social activities are also sometimes signs of depression, observers who are unfamiliar with Orthodox Jewish mourning practices might conclude that those who follow them are exhibiting patho-logical rather than normal grieving. Thus, mental health professionals are advised to learn about an individual's cultural beliefs before forming conclusions about grief-related behavior. Likewise, friends, neighbors, and co-workers of someone who is mourning the death of a spouse or other close family member should also be careful to interpret any grief-related behaviors within the context of the person's cultural background.

● *Sex Differences* ●   The death of a spouse appears to be a more negative experi-ence for men than for women, despite the fact that there seem to be no sex differences in the actual grieving process following such a loss (Quigley & Schatz, 1999). The risk of death from either natural causes or suicide in the months immediately after widowhood is significantly greater among men than among women (Stroebe & Stroebe, 1993). Depression and suicidal thoughts are also more common in widowers than in widows (Byrne & Raphael, 1999; Chen et al., 1999). Further, men seem to have a more difficult time than women do in returning to the levels of emotional functioning they exhibited before the spouse's death (van Grootheest, Beekman, van Groenou, & Deeg, 1999).

These differences are most often interpreted as yet another sign of the impor-tance of social support. Social activities are very important in the lives of widows. In contrast, researchers have found that widowers withdraw from social activities to a far greater degree than widows do in the months immediately following bereavement (Bennett, 1998).

However, some developmentalists have suggested that activities-oriented studies have led to a stereotype that characterizes widowers as lonely and isolated. In fact, research involving in-depth examinations of widowers' friendships, rather than of just their social activities, suggests that social relationships are very important in the lives of men who have lost a spouse (Riggs, 1997). Thus, differences in social involve-ment may be part of the explanation for sex differences in health and depressions fol-lowing the death of a spouse, but they do not appear to tell the whole story.

The results of a carefully designed longitudinal study of Australian widowers and married men over age 65 suggest that alcohol use may play a role in the greater prevalence of depression among widowers (Byrne, Raphael, & Arnold, 1999). Researchers found that more than twice as many widowers as married men (19% versus 8%) consumed five or more alcoholic drinks per day. Although alcohol may temporarily relieve unpleasant feelings of grief, it is a central nervous system depres-sant, and prolonged heavy drinking can lead to depression.

● *Preventing Long-Term Problems* ●   Some research suggests that the "talk-it-out" approach to managing grief can be helpful in preventing grief-related depres-sion, especially when feelings are shared with others who have had similar experiences, in the context of a support group (Francis, 1997). Research also indi-cates that developing a coherent personal narrative of the events surrounding the spouse's death helps widows and widowers manage grief (van den Hoonaard, 1999). Participating in support groups, or even jointly recalling relevant events with close family members, can facilitate the formation of such stories.

Clearly, this kind of psychosocial management of grief requires time. Mental health professionals advise employers that providing bereaved employees (especially those whose spouses have died) with sufficient time off to grieve may be critical to their physical and mental health. In the long run, illness and depression among bereaved workers who return to their jobs too soon may be more costly to employers than providing additional time off (Eyetsemitan, 1998).

Before going on

- How do funerals and ceremonies help survivors cope with grief?
- How do the age of the bereaved and the mode of death affect the grieving process?
- How does grief affect the physical and mental health of widows and widowers?

Theoretical Perspectives on Grieving

There are a number of ways of looking at the emotion of grief, but the two that have had the greatest influence on the way psychologists think about grief are Freud's psychoanalytic theory and Bowlby's attachment theory.

Freud's Psychoanalytic Theory

From the psychoanalytic perspective, the death of a loved one is an emotional trauma. As with any trauma, the ego, or mind, tries to insulate itself from the unpleasant emotions such losses induce through the use of defense mechanisms, including denial and repression. However, Freud believed that defense mechanisms were only temporary devices for dealing with negative emotions. Eventually, he thought, the individual must examine the emotions and their source directly. Otherwise, such emotions lead to the development of physical symptoms and, perhaps, mental illnesses.

Freud's view has been very influential in grief counseling and in popular notions about the necessity of "working through" grief in order to avoid its long-term negative effects. It is generally accepted that bereaved individuals need to talk openly about their loss. Thus, grief counselors often recommend that friends of a bereaved person encourage the person to cry or express grief in other ways.

Psychoanalytically based grief therapy for children often emphasizes the use of defense mechanisms other than denial and repression to cope with grief. Following this approach, therapists sometimes encourage children to express their feelings through art. The idea is that this kind of defense mechanism, known as *sublimation*, will lead to better health outcomes than avoidance of emotions through more negative defense mechanisms (Glazer, 1998). Similarly, some therapists advocate encouraging children to use another defense mechanism, *identification*, to manage their grief. This goal can be accomplished by having the child watch popular films depicting children's grief, such as *The Lion King*, discuss the young characters' feelings, and compare the characters' emotions to their own (Sedney, 1999).

In addition, the psychoanalytic perspective has shaped grief research by characterizing the loss of a loved one as a trauma. An important concept in such research is that the more traumatic the death, the more likely it is to be followed by physical or mental problems. In fact, researchers have found that people who lose loved ones in sudden, tragic ways, such as to a drunk-driving accident or a murder, are more likely to display symptoms of post-traumatic stress disorder (Murphy et al., 1999; Sprang & McNeil, 1998).

Bowlby's Attachment Theory

John Bowlby and other attachment theorists argue that intense grief reactions are likely to occur at the loss of any person to whom one is attached, whether a partner, a parent, or a child (Bowlby, 1980; Sanders, 1989). Moreover, their theories predict that the quality of attachment to the loved one should be related in some way to the experience of grief. Research seems to confirm this aspect of their view. The stronger the attachment between a mourner and a lost loved one, the deeper and more prolonged the grief response (van Doorn et al., 1998). By contrast, the death of someone who is part of one's social network but not an intimate confidant or an attachment figure is less likely to trigger an intense emotional reaction (Murrell & Himmelfarb, 1989).

Bowlby proposed four stages of grief, and Catherine Sanders, another attachment theorist, has proposed five stages, but as you can see in Table 18.3, the two systems

TABLE 18.3   Stages of Grief

Stage	Bowlby's Label	Sanders's Label	General Description
1	Numbness	Shock	Characteristic of the first few days after the death of the loved one, and occasionally longer; mourner experiences disbelief, confusion, restlessness, feelings of unreality, a sense of helplessness
2	Yearning	Awareness	The bereaved person tries to recover the lost person; may actively search, or wander as if searching; may report that he sees the dead person; mourner feels full of anger, anxiety, guilt, fear, frustration; may sleep poorly and weep often.
3	Disorganization and despair	Conservation/ withdrawal	Searching ceases and the loss is accepted, but acceptance of loss brings depression and despair, or a sense of helplessness; this stage is often accompanied by great fatigue and a desire to sleep all the time.
4	Reorganization	Healing and renewal	Sanders views this as two periods, Bowlby as only one. Both see this as the period when the individual takes control again. Some forgetting occurs and some sense of hope emerges, along with increased energy, better health, better sleep patterns, and reduced depression.

(*Sources:* Bowlby, 1980; Sanders, 1989.)

overlap a great deal. In the first period, that of shock or numbness, people say things that reveal their state of mind:

> "I feel so vague. I can't keep my mind on anything for very long." (Bowlby, 1980, p. 47)
>
> "I'm afraid I'm losing my mind. I can't seem to think clearly." (Bowlby, 1980, p. 48)
>
> "It was so strange. I was putting on my makeup, combing my hair, and all the time it was as if I were standing by the door watching myself go through these motions." (Sanders, 1989, p. 56).

In the stage of awareness of loss, or yearning, when anger is a common ingredient, people say things such as "His boss should have known better than to ask him to work so hard." Bowlby also suggested that this period is equivalent to what is observed in young children who have been temporarily separated from their closest attachment figures and who go from room to room in search of this favored person. Adults who are widowed do some of the same searching—sometimes physically, sometimes mentally.

In the stage of disorganization and despair, the restlessness of the previous period disappears and is replaced by a great lethargy. One 45-year-old whose child had just died described her feelings:

> I can't understand the way I feel. Up to now, I had been feeling restless. I couldn't sleep. I paced and ranted. Now, I have an opposite reaction. I sleep a lot. I feel fatigued and worn out. I don't even want to see the friends who have kept me going. I sit and stare, too exhausted to move. . . . Just when I thought I should be feeling better, I am feeling worse. (Sanders, 1989, p. 73)

Finally, the resolution of the grieving process comes in Bowlby's stage of reorganization. Sanders hypothesized that this stage comprises two separate periods: healing and renewal. The outcome, from both Bowlby's and Sanders's perspectives, is that the grieving person begins to be able to maintain control. Sleep patterns return to normal, and a more optimistic outlook is typical.

These descriptions of the grieving process are highly evocative and can be useful in counseling grieving individuals. Discussion of the stages helps those who are grieving communicate with therapists about how they are feeling and describe the kinds of symptoms they are experiencing. Stage approaches also help survivors realize that their emotions and physical symptoms are normal and that the grieving process is complex.

However, as with the concept of stages of dying, there are two important questions about these proposed stages of grieving: (1) Do they really occur in fixed stages? (2) Does everyone feel all these feelings, in whatever sequence? The answer to both questions, as you'll see, seems to be no.

Critical Thinking

Think about a loss in your own life. (Even losing a pet causes grief.) Do Bowlby's and Sanders's stages seem to fit your experience?

Alternative Perspectives

A growing set of "revisionist" views of grieving give a rather different picture from that of either Freud or the attachment theorists. First, research suggests that, contrary to psychoanalytic hypotheses, avoiding expressions of grief neither prolongs the experience of grief nor leads inevitably to physical or mental health problems. In fact, at least one study suggests that bereaved individuals who avoid talking about the deceased or their feelings of loss actually experience milder grief and are less likely to suffer long-term effects (Bonanno, Znoj, Siddique, & Horowitz, 1999).

Second, many researchers and theorists find that grieving simply does not occur in fixed stages, with everyone following the same pattern (Wortman & Silver, 1990).

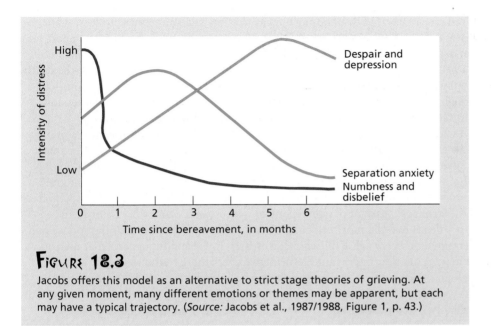

FIGURE 18.3

Jacobs offers this model as an alternative to strict stage theories of grieving. At any given moment, many different emotions or themes may be apparent, but each may have a typical trajectory. (*Source:* Jacobs et al., 1987/1988, Figure 1, p. 43.)

There may be common themes, such as anger, guilt, depression, and restlessness, but these do not seem to appear in a fixed order.

One compromise model suggests that each of the key themes in the grieving process may have a likely trajectory, as suggested in Figure 18.3 (Jacobs et al., 1987/1988). For example, numbness may be most prominent in the days immediately following the loved one's death. After a few months, the grieving person may feel numb at times, but depression may be a more dominant theme. The basic idea, obviously, is that many themes are present at the same time, but that one or another may dominate, in an approximate sequence. Thus, it may well be that disbelief is highest immediately after the death, and that depression peaks some months later—which makes the process look stagelike, although in fact both elements are present throughout. Some bereaved people might move more quickly and others more slowly through these various emotions.

In contrast, other revisionist theorists and researchers contend that for some adults, grieving simply does not include all these elements. Psychologists Camille Wortman and Roxane Silver have amassed an impressive amount of evidence to support such a view (Wortman & Silver, 1989, 1990, 1992; Wortman, Silver, & Kessler, 1993). They dispute the traditional view of grieving expressed in both Freud's and Bowlby's theories. First, Wortman and Silver do not agree that distress is an inevitable response to loss. Second, their research challenges the notion that failure to experience distress is a sign that the individual has not grieved "properly."

Based on their findings, Wortman and Silver conclude that there are at least four distinct patterns of grieving (Wortman & Silver, 1990):

- *Normal*. The person feels great distress immediately following the loss, with relatively rapid recovery.
- *Chronic*. The person's distress continues at a high level over several years.
- *Delayed*. The grieving person feels little distress in the first few months but high levels of distress some months or years later.
- *Absent*. The person feels no notable level of distress either immediately or at any later time.

Contrary to the predictions of stage theories of grief, it turns out that the pattern of absent grief is remarkably common. In Wortman and Silver's own first study, 26% of bereaved participants showed essentially no distress, either immediately after the death or several years later, a pattern confirmed in other research (Levy, Martinkowski, & Derby, 1994; Wortman & Silver, 1990). The least common pattern is delayed grief. Only 1–5% of adults appear to show such a response to loss, while as many as a third show chronic grief. Thus, Wortman and Silver find little support for either aspect of the traditional view: High levels of distress are neither an inevitable nor a necessary aspect of the grieving process. Many adults seem to handle the death of a spouse, a child, or a parent without significant psychological dislocation—although it remains true that on average, bereaved persons have more depression, less life satisfaction, and a greater risk of illness than the nonbereaved.

As yet, developmentalists know relatively little about the characteristics of individuals who react to bereavement in the very different ways outlined by Wortman and Silver, although their research gives a few hints (Wortman et al., 1993). In their studies, widows who had had the best marriages showed the most persistent grief reactions. More surprisingly, Wortman and Silver found that those widows who had had the strongest sense of personal control, self-esteem, or mastery prior to the spouse's death had the most difficulty after his death, as if the loss of the spouse had undermined this very sense of control. Research in Germany suggests that neuroticism may be another important factor; researchers there found that widows who were high in neuroticism before bereavement showed stronger and more persistent negative effects after the deaths of their spouses (Stroebe & Stroebe, 1993).

Finally, it's important not to lose sight of the fact that loss can also lead to growth. Indeed, the majority of widows say not only that they changed as a result of their husbands' deaths, but that the change was toward greater independence and greater skill (Wortman & Silver, 1990). Like all crises and all major life changes, bereavement can be an opportunity as well as, or instead of, a disabling experience. Which way a person responds is likely to depend very heavily on the patterns established from early childhood: in temperament or personality, in internal working models of attachment and self, in intellectual skills, and in social networks. Ultimately, we respond to death—our own or someone else's—as we have responded to life.

Before going on

- How does Freud's psychoanalytic theory view grief?

- What do Bowlby and Sanders suggest about the connection between attachment and grief, and what stages of grieving have they proposed?

- How have more recent theorists criticized the psychoanalytic and attachment theories of the grief process, and what alternative perspectives do they propose?

A Final Word

The last of life's milestones, death, provides an opportunity to look back at the major themes we identified at the beginning of our examination of the human lifespan. First, the relationship between attachment and the grief process provides a good example of continuity in development. Second, individual differences are as evident in the experiences of dying and grief as they are in infant temperament or children's IQ scores. Likewise, gender and cultural differences are as evident in views of death and the experience of grief as they are in other areas of development.

Death and grieving, like all else in life, have basic rhythms, like the beat of a song. Every individual song—every death and every reaction to a death—follows that beat, and so sounds somewhat like all the others. But each individual song has a melody that is different from the rest—different notes and different relations among the notes. The sound of the song—how we face our own deaths and the deaths of our loved ones—depends on all the factors you have read about throughout this book.

Summary

The Experience of Death

- *Death* is a somewhat nonspecific term. Medical personnel refer to *clinical death* and *brain death*; *social death* occurs when the deceased person is treated like a corpse by those around the person.

- The great majority of adults in industrialized countries die in hospitals. Hospice care emphasizes patient and family control of the dying process and palliative care rather than curative treatment. Some studies suggest that patients and families are slightly more satisfied with hospice care than hospital care, but hospice care is also highly burdensome for the caregiver.

The Meaning of Death across the Lifespan

- Until about age 6 or 7, children do not understand that death is permanent and inevitable and involves loss of function. Teens understand the physical aspects of death much better than children do, but they sometimes have distorted ideas about it, especially their own mortality.

- Many young adults believe they possess unique characteristics that protect them from death. For middle-aged and older adults, death has many possible meanings: a signal of changes in family roles, a transition to another state (such as a life after death), and a loss of opportunity and relationships. Awareness of death may also help a person organize her remaining time.

- Fear of death appears to peak in mid-life, after which it drops rather sharply. Older adults talk more about death but are less afraid of it. Deeply religious adults are typically less afraid of death.

- Many adults prepare for death in practical ways, such as by buying life insurance or writing a will. Reminiscence may also serve as preparation. There are also some signs of deeper personality changes immediately before death, including more dependence and docility and less emotionality and assertiveness.

The Process of Dying

- Kübler-Ross suggested five stages of dying: denial, anger, bargaining, depression, and acceptance. Research fails to support the hypothesis that all dying adults go through all five stages or that the stages necessarily occur in this order. The emotion most commonly observed is depression.

- Critics of Kübler-Ross suggest that her findings may be culture-specific. They also argue that the process of dying is less stagelike than her theory claims.

- Research with cancer and AIDS patients suggests that those who are most pessimistic and docile in response to diagnosis and treatment have shorter life expectancies. Those who fight hardest, and even display anger, live longer. Dying adults who have better social support, either from family and friends or through specially created support groups, also live longer than those who lack such support.

The Experience of Grieving

- Funerals and other rituals after death serve important functions, including defining roles for the bereaved, bringing family together, and giving meaning to the deceased's life and death.

- Grief responses depend on a number of variables. The age of the bereaved and the mode of death shape the grief process.

- In general, the death of a spouse evokes the most intense and long-lasting grief. Widows and widowers show high levels of illness and death in the months immediately after the death of a spouse, perhaps as a result of the effects of grief on the immune system. Widowers appear to have a more difficult time managing grief than widows.

Theoretical Perspectives on Grieving

- Freud's psychoanalytic theory emphasizes loss as an emotional trauma, the effects of defense mechanisms, and the need to work through feelings of grief.
- Bowlby's attachment theory views grief as a natural response to the loss of an attachment figure. Attach-ment theorists suggest that the grief process involves several stages.
- Alternative views suggest that neither Freud's nor Bowlby's theory accurately characterizes the grief experience. Responses are more individual than either theory might suggest.

Key Terms

brain death (p. 517)

clinical death (p. 517)

grieving (p. 531)

hospice care (p. 517)

palliative care (p. 518)

pathological grief (p. 536)

personal fable (p. 520)

social death (p. 517)

thanatology (p. 528)

unique invulnerability
  (p. 521)

Do People Have a Right to Die?

One element of having greater control over the process of dying might be the ability to choose the timing of death—a highly controversial topic. Today, most medical ethicists distinguish between two forms of *euthanasia* (also known as "mercy killing"). *Passive euthanasia* occurs when a person (typically, a physician) hastens a death by not using life support systems or medication that would prolong the life or by withdrawing life support or other treatment that may be keeping a patient alive. *Active euthanasia* (also called *assisted suicide*) occurs when a physician or other individual (at a patient's request) hastens the patient's death by active means, such as by administering a fatal dose of a drug.

Living Wills

There is little controversy about passive euthanasia. Most people agree that individuals should be able to determine the degree to which life-support technology will be used to delay their own deaths. Thus, an increasing number of adults have made *living wills* specifying that life-support systems or resuscitation should not be used in case of their clinical death or near death. Such living wills essentially ask physicians to participate in passive euthanasia.

However, it turns out that living wills are often not followed, both because health care professionals who treat a patient in an emergency may not know of the living will and because many physicians find it extremely difficult to "give up," not to use the full array of treatments available to them to prolong a life. Many other physicians, particularly those who have treated a patient over many years, are entirely comfortable urging patients or family members to discontinue some life-prolonging treatment, thus hastening the patient's death.

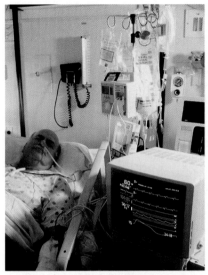

Many hospitals now specifically ask terminal patients during the admission process how they want to be treated in the event that they become mentally incapacitated. (*Photo:* Blair Seitz, Photo Researchers)

Consequently, several states have passed legislation designed to ensure compliance with living wills. Some laws require hospitals to ask all those who are admitted whether they have made such a document. In other states, laws specifically limit the applicability of living wills (which are often vague about which specific technologies can and can't be used) to practices such as tube feeding.

The Assisted Suicide Debate

By contrast, assisted suicide (or any other form of active euthanasia) is far less common and much more controversial. The debate over physician-assisted suicide has been brought to public attention in the United States by the actions of Dr. Jack Kevorkian, a physician who has helped several terminally ill or severely handicapped individuals end their own lives. In the United States at present, the legal status of active euthanasia is tangled. Explicit attempts to legalize assisted suicide through voters' initiatives have been defeated in several states; one such referendum passed in Oregon in 1994, but its implementation was delayed by court action until 1997. Many other state legislatures have explicitly banned assisted suicide, and, in a unanimous ruling in 1997, the U.S. Supreme Court upheld such laws.

The only place in the world where assisted suicide is fully and explicitly legal is in the Netherlands. A law passed in 2001 legalized the long-standing Dutch custom of providing terminally ill patients with lethal doses of pain-killing drugs ("Dutch senate OKs doctor-assisted suicide," 2001). Individuals who wish to die must be terminally ill and have no hope of recovery, and must obtain the approval of two physicians. Children under 12 are prohibited from requesting to die, and those between 12 and 15 must have parental consent. The parents of a 16- or 17-year-old must be

In 1999, Dr. Jack Kevorkian, who lost his license to practice medicine several years earlier, was convicted of murder by a Michigan jury. He is currently in prison. (*Photo:* AFP/CORBIS)

notified of the child's request but do not have the right to prevent the assisted suicide from being carried out.

Many of those who oppose active euthanasia believe that each individual life is sacred. Therefore, they believe, decisions about when to end life should be subject only to divine authority. These critics also view assisted suicide as just another form of suicide—a practice they consider to be immoral.

Other opponents argue against active euthanasia on the grounds that it might be extremely difficult to set limits on the process, even with strict guidelines—a position often labeled "the slippery slope argument" (Twycross, 1996). Advocates for the disabled have been particularly vocal in putting forward this point of view. They claim that once assisted suicide becomes widely viewed as morally acceptable, society may come to the point where those who are infirm or severely disabled will be subtly (or not so subtly) encouraged to end their own lives in order to relieve others of the burden of their care. Such critics even fear that things might reach a point where physicians administer fatal drugs without the patient's consent.

A third argument against any form of active euthanasia is that modern pain management techniques allow even those with extremely painful terminal illnesses to be comfortable in the last days or weeks of their lives. Thus, it is not necessary to hasten death in order to prevent pain. Some physicians also believe that the availability of assisted suicide may cause insurance companies and hospitals to fail to make patients aware of the wide array of pain management techniques because the deaths of these patients will save them money. Similarly, some social workers have pointed out that when patients who have considered assisted suicide learn

about social and medical resources that are available to help them cope, they often change their minds (Hornik, 1998).

For these reasons as well as the personal religious beliefs of some, about three-quarters of a sample of 3,000 oncologists (physicians who specialize in treating cancer) in a survey carried out by the National Institutes of Health were found to oppose active euthanasia of any kind (Emanuel et al., 2000). Instead, they advocate palliative-care education for all physicians to make them aware of the benefits of hospice care as well as the most effective ways of relieving patients' pain. They also suggest that physicians treating terminal patients engage their patients in frank discussions about pain relief as early in the course of their illness as possible. Through such discussions, doctors and patients can decide together what pain relief measures will be taken.

Studies involving patients who refuse treatments such as chemotherapy suggest that such individuals often want to live as long as possible. However, they do not want to go through the difficulties associated with the treatments (Abrams, 1998). Such findings suggest that observers should be cautious about jumping to the conclusion that a person who doesn't want medical treatment is also interested in hastening death.

Opponents of assisted suicide also question terminally ill patients' psychological fitness for making the decision to end their lives. Some fear that such patients may be depressed and that a request to hasten death is really no different from any other kind of suicide attempt. In other words, it is an act born of emotional despair, not rationality. The distinction is important, they say, because the philosophical rationale of assisted suicide laws is that choosing to die involves a rational decision-making process.

To address this concern, assisted suicide legislation, including the Oregon law, typically includes a mandatory waiting period between a request for death and the fulfillment of the request. During the waiting period, a psychiatrist or psychologist is supposed to assess the mental state of the patient to determine whether he or she is competent to make the life-ending decision.

However, mental health professionals generally lack confidence in their ability to make such judgments

(Fenn & Ganzini, 1999). Many believe that such an assessment is possible only when a practitioner has known the patient for a long period of time. Moreover, there is a possibility that a professional's own opinion about the moral acceptability of assisted suicide will influence the assessment of mental competency in such cases. To address these issues, the American Psychological Association and other interested organizations are attempting to develop guidelines and standards to be used in such assessments (Werth, 2000).

Those who favor assisted suicide legislation note that modern medical technology has increasingly made it possible to prolong life well past the point at which death, in earlier decades, would naturally have occurred. Further, proponents of assisted suicide argue that many terminal patients are unable to carry out their own suicides, and therefore require the help of a physician. However, opponents counter that asking another person to help with a suicide is a far cry from giving a person "death with dignity." As one German physician who opposes assisted suicide expressed it, "Everyone has the right to a dignified death, but nobody has the right to be killed" (Cohen, 2001).

Your Turn

- Find out from a local medical society whether hospitals and physicians in your area generally honor living wills. Does your state require medical personnel to ask all hospitalized people whether they have a living will?

- The medical society should also be able to tell you whether your state allows family members to authorize health professionals to terminate aspects of care such as tube feeding in cases where a terminally ill or seriously injured individual can't speak for himself.

- Has anyone in your state ever been prosecuted for helping a dying person hasten death? If so, what were the circumstances and outcome of the case(s)?

- Are there efforts underway in your state to legalize assisted suicide? If so, what do opinion polls suggest about voter support for such laws?

Pro-life groups oppose physician-assisted suicide as well as abortion. (*Photo:* Robert Kusel, Stone)

Glossary

ability goals   goals based on a desire to be superior to others (p. 300)

accommodation   changing a scheme as a result of some new information (p. 39)

achievement test   a test designed to assess specific information learned in school (p. 230)

activities of daily living (ADLs)   self-help tasks such as bathing, dressing, and using the toilet (p. 460)

activity theory   the idea that it is normal and healthy for older adults to try to remain as active as possible for as long as possible (p. 488)

adaptive reflexes   reflexes such as sucking that help newborns survive; some adaptive reflexes persist throughout life (p. 92)

affectional bond   the emotional tie to an infant experienced by a parent (p. 123)

ageism   a prejudicial view of older adults that characterizes them in negative ways (p. 11)

aggression   behavior intended to harm another person or an object (p. 197)

alcoholism   physical and psychological dependence on alcohol (p. 415)

Alzheimer's disease   a very severe form of dementia, the cause of which is unknown (p. 473)

amenity move   post-retirement move away from kin to a location that has some desirable feature, such as year-round warm weather (p. 509)

amnion   fluid-filled sac in which the fetus floats until just before it is born (p. 62)

analytical style   a tendency to focus on the details of a task (p. 241)

anorexia nervosa   an eating disorder characterized by self-starvation (p. 292)

anoxia   oxygen deprivation experienced by a fetus during labor and/or delivery (p. 80)

assimilation   the process of using a scheme to make sense of an event or experience (p. 39)

association areas   parts of the brain where sensory, motor, and intellectual functions are linked (p. 219)

assortative mating (homogamy)   sociologists' term for the tendency to mate with someone who has traits similar to one's own (p. 376)

atherosclerosis   narrowing of the arteries caused by deposits of a fatty substance called plaque (p. 408)

attachment   the emotional tie to a parent experienced by an infant, from which the child derives security (p. 123)

attachment theory   the view that the ability and need to form an attachment relationship early in life are genetic characteristics of all human beings (p. 123)

attention-deficit hyperactivity disorder (ADHD)   a mental disorder that causes children to have difficulty attending to and completing tasks (p. 237)

atypical development   development that deviates from the typical developmental pathway in a way that is harmful to the individual (p. 14)

authoritarian parenting style   a style of parenting that is low in nurturance and communication, but high in control and maturity demands (p. 186)

authoritative parenting style   a style of parenting that is high in nurturance, maturity demands, control, and communication (p. 186)

automaticity   the ability to recall information from long-term memory without using short-term memory capacity (p. 226)

avoidant couples   couples who agree to disagree and who minimize conflict by avoiding each other (p. 379)

behavior genetics   the study of the role of heredity in individual differences (p. 44)

behaviorism   the view that defines development in terms of behavior changes caused by environmental influences (p. 6)

the Big Five   a set of five major dimensions of personality, including extraversion, agreeableness, conscientiousness, neuroticism, and openness/intellect (p. 262)

bilingual education   an approach to second-language education in which children receive instruction in two different languages (p. 239)

brain death   absence of vital signs, including brain activity; resuscitation is no longer possible (p. 517)

bulimia   an eating disorder characterized by binge eating and purging (p. 291)

cardiovascular disease (CVD)   a set of disease processes in the heart and circulatory system (p. 408)

career ladder   the milestones associated with a particular occupation (p. 392)

caregiver burden   a term for the cumulative negative effects of caring for an elderly or disabled person (p. 440)

case study   an in-depth examination of a single individual (p. 18)

cephalocaudal pattern   growth that proceeds from the head downward (p. 62)

chromosomes   strings of genetic material in the nuclei of cells (p. 54)

class inclusion   the understanding that subordinate classes are included in larger, superordinate classes (p. 223)

classical conditioning   learning that results from the association of stimuli (p. 33)

climacteric   the term used to describe the adult period during which reproductive capacity declines or is lost (p. 401)

clinical death   a period during which vital signs are absent but resuscitation is still possible (p. 517)

clique   four to six young people who appear to be strongly attached to one another (p. 325)

cognitive theories   theories that emphasize mental processes in development, such as logic and memory (p. 37)

cohort   a group of individuals who share the same historical experiences at the same times in their lives (p. 12)

colic   an infant behavior pattern involving intense daily bouts of crying, totaling 3 or more hours a day (p. 94)

companionate relationships   relationships in which grandparents have frequent contact and warm interactions with grandchildren (p. 437)

compensatory (kinship) migration   a move to a location near family or friends that happens when an elder requires frequent help because of a disability or disease (p. 509)

concrete operations   a set of mental schemes, including reversibility, addition, subtraction, multiplication, division, and serial ordering, that enable children to understand relations among objects (p. 222)

conscience   the list of "don'ts" in the superego; violation of any of these rules leads to feelings of guilt (p. 250)

conservation   the understanding that matter can change in appearance without changing in quantity (p. 158)

control group   the group in an experiment that receives either no special treatment or a neutral treatment (p. 19)

conventional morality   in Kohlberg's theory, the level of moral reasoning in which judgments are based on rules or norms of a group to which the person belongs (p. 330)

corpus callosum   the membrane that connects the right and left hemispheres of the cerebral cortex (p. 152)

correlation   a relationship between two variables that can be expressed as a number ranging from -1.00 to +1.00 (p. 19)

critical period   a specific period in development when an organism is especially sensitive to the presence (or absence) of some particular kind of experience (p. 13)

cross-gender behavior   behavior that is atypical for one's own sex but typical for the opposite sex (p. 209)

cross-linking   the formation of undesirable bonds between proteins or fats (p. 469)

cross-modal perception   transfer of information from one sense to another, as when an infant can recognize by feel a toy he has seen but never felt before (p. 102)

cross-sectional design   a research design in which groups of different ages are compared (p. 16)

crowd   a combination of cliques, which includes both males and females (p. 325)

crystallized intelligence   knowledge and judgment acquired through education and experience (p. 361)

deductive logic   a type of reasoning based on hypothetical premises that requires predicting a specific outcome from a general principle (p. 223)

defense mechanisms   strategies for reducing anxiety, such as repression, denial, or projection, proposed by Freud (p. 26)

deferred imitation   imitation by an infant of an action seen earlier (p. 104)

delinquency   antisocial behavior that includes law-breaking (p. 334)

dementia   a neurological disorder involving problems with memory and thinking that affect an individual's emotional, social, and physical functioning (p. 473)

deoxyribonucleic acid (DNA)   chemical material that makes up chromosomes and genes (p. 54)

dependent variable   the characteristic or behavior that is expected to be affected by the independent variable (p. 20)

developmental psychology   the scientific study of age-related changes in behavior, thinking, emotion, and personality (p. 3)

dialectical thought   a form of thought involving recognition and acceptance of paradox and uncertainty (p. 359)

disengagement theory   the theory that it is normal and healthy for older adults to scale down their social lives and to separate themselves from others to a certain degree (p. 488)

dishabituation   learning to respond to a familiar stimulus as if it were new (p. 106)

dominant-recessive pattern   pattern of inheritance in which a single dominant gene influences a person's phenotype but two recessive genes are necessary to produce an associated trait (p. 56)

dyslexia   problems in reading or the inability to read (p. 235)

ecological theory   Bronfenbrenner's theory that explains development in terms of relationships between individuals and their environments, or interconnected *contexts* (p. 44)

ego   according to Freud, the thinking element of personality (p. 26)

ego ideal   the list of "dos" in the superego; failure to live up to any of these leads to feelings of shame (p. 250)

ego integrity   the feeling that one's life has been worthwhile (p. 487)

ego integrity versus despair stage   the last of Erikson's psychosocial stages, in which older adults must achieve a sense of satisfaction with their lives (p. 487)

egocentrism   the young child's belief that everyone sees and experiences the world the way she does (p. 158)

embryonic stage   the second stage of prenatal development, from week 2 through week 8, during which the embryo's organ systems form (p. 64)

endocrine glands   glands that secrete hormones governing growth and other aspects of physical development (p. 279)

English-as-a-second-language (ESL) program   an approach to second-language education in which children attend English classes for part of the day and receive most of their academic instruction in English (p. 239)

episodic memories   recollections of personal events (p. 421)

equilibration   the process of balancing assimilation and accommodation to create schemes that fit the environment (p. 39)

ethnic identity   a sense of belonging to an ethnic group (p. 316)

ethnography   a detailed description of a single culture or context (p. 20)

ethology   a perspective on development that emphasizes genetically determined survival behaviors presumed to have evolved through natural selection (p. 43)

executive processes   information-processing skills that involve devising and carrying out strategies for remembering and solving problems (p. 227)

experiment   a study that tests a causal hypothesis (p. 19)

experimental group   the group in an experiment that receives the treatment the experimenter thinks will produce a particular effect (p. 19)

expressive language   the ability to produce spoken language (p. 110)

extended family   a social network of grandparents, aunts, uncles, cousins, and so on (p. 194)

extinction   the gradual elimination of a behavior through repeated nonreinforcement (p. 34)

false belief principle   an understanding that enables a child to look at a situation from another person's point of view and determine what kind of information will cause that person to have a false belief (p. 159)

fetal stage   the third stage of prenatal development, from week 9 to birth, during which growth and organ refinement take place (p. 64)

flexible goal adjustment   a behavior pattern in which middle-aged adults adjust goals in order to enhance the likelihood of success (p. 449)

fluid intelligence   the aspect of intelligence that reflects fundamental biological processes and does not depend on specific experiences (p. 361)

foreclosure   in Marcia's theory, the identity status of a person who has made a commitment without having gone through a crisis; the person has simply accepted a parentally or culturally defined commitment (p. 312)

formal operational stage   the fourth of Piaget's stages, during which adolescents learn to reason logically about abstract concepts (p. 295)

frail elderly   older adults whose physical and/or mental impairments are so extensive that they cannot care for themselves (p. 458)

free radicals   molecules or atoms that possess an unpaired electron (p. 469)

gametes   cells that unite at conception (ova in females; sperm in males) (p. 54)

gender concept   understanding of gender, gender-related behavior, and sex roles (p. 203)

gender constancy   the understanding that gender is a component of the self that is not altered by external appearance (p. 204)

gender constancy theory   Kohlberg's assertion that children must understand that gender is a permanent characteristic before they can adopt appropriate sex roles (p. 204)

gender identity   the ability to correctly label oneself and others as male or female (p. 205)

gender schema theory   an information-processing approach to gender concept development that asserts that people use a schema for each gender to process information about themselves and others (p. 204)

gender stability   the understanding that gender is a stable, life-long characteristic (p. 205)

generativity   a sense that one is making a valuable contribution to society by bringing up children or mentoring younger people in some way (p. 429)

generativity versus stagnation stage   the seventh of Erikson's stages, in which middle-aged adults find meaning in contributing to the development of younger individuals (p. 429)

genes   pieces of genetic material that control or influence traits (p. 54)

genital stage   in Freud's theory, the period during which people reach psychosexual maturity (p. 311)

genotype   the unique genetic blueprint of each individual (p. 56)

geriatric dysthymia   chronic depressed mood in older adults (p. 476)

germinal stage   the first stage of prenatal development, beginning at conception and ending at implantation (approximately 2 weeks) (p. 62)

gerontology   the scientific study of aging (p. 457)

glial cells   specialized cells in the brain that support neurons (p. 64)

gonadotrophic hormones   hormones responsible for the development of the sex organs (p. 279)

gonads   sex glands (ovaries in females; testes in males) (p. 64)

goodness-of-fit   the degree to which an infant's temperament is adaptable to his or her environment, and vice versa (p. 135)

grieving   the emotional response to a death (p. 531)

habituate   to decrease one's attention because a stimulus has become familiar (p. 101)

handedness   a strong preference for using one hand or the other that develops between 3 and 5 years of age (p. 152)

Hayflick limit   the theoretical proposal that each species is subject to a genetically programmed time limit after which cells no longer have any capacity to replicate themselves accurately (p. 462)

hippocampus   a brain structure that is important in learning (p. 152)

holophrases   "phrases" or "sentences" consisting of words and gestures, used by infants in the 2nd year of life (p. 111)

hospice care   an approach to care for the terminally ill that emphasizes individual and family control of the process of dying (p. 517)

hostile aggression   aggression used to hurt another person or gain an advantage (p. 198)

hostile/detached couples   couples who fight regularly and rarely look at one another; they also lack affection and support (p. 379)

hostile/engaged couples   partners who have frequent arguments that lack the balancing effect of humor and affection (p. 379)

hypertension   elevated blood pressure (p. 413)

hypothetico-deductive reasoning   the ability to derive conclusions from hypothetical premises (p. 295)

id   in Freud's theory, the part of the personality that comprises a person's basic sexual and aggressive impulses; it contains the libido and motivates a person to seek pleasure and avoid pain (p. 26)

identity achievement   in Marcia's theory, the identity status achieved by a person who has been through a crisis and reached a commitment to ideological or occupational goals (p. 311)

identity crisis   Erikson's term for the psychological state of emotional turmoil that arises when an adolescent's sense of self becomes "unglued" so that a new, more mature sense of self can be achieved (p. 311)

identity diffusion in Marcia's theory, the identity status of a person who is not in the midst of a crisis and who has made no commitment (p. 312)

identity versus role confusion in Erikson's theory, the stage during which adolescents attain a sense of who they are (p. 311)

independent variable the presumed causal element in an experiment (p. 20)

inductive discipline a discipline strategy in which parents explain to children why a punished behavior is wrong (p. 188)

inductive logic a type of reasoning in which general principles are inferred from specific experiences (p. 223)

industry versus inferiority stage the fourth of Erikson's psychosocial stages, during which children develop a sense of their own competence through mastery of culturally defined learning tasks (p. 248)

inflections grammatical markers attached to words to indicate tense, gender, number, and the like, such as the use of the ending *-ed* to mark the past tense of a verb in English (p. 164)

information-processing theory a theoretical perspective that uses the computer as a model to explain how the mind manages information (p. 39)

insecure/ambivalent attachment a pattern of attachment in which the infant shows little exploratory behavior, is greatly upset when separated from the mother, and is not reassured by her return or efforts to comfort him (p. 128)

insecure/avoidant attachment a pattern of attachment in which an infant avoids contact with the parent and shows no preference for the parent over other people (p. 128)

insecure/disorganized attachment a pattern of attachment in which an infant seems confused or apprehensive and shows contradictory behavior, such as moving toward the mother while looking away from her (p. 128)

institutional migration a move to an institution such as a nursing home that is necessitated by a disability (p. 509)

instrumental activities of daily living (IADLs) more complex daily living tasks such as doing housework, cooking, and managing money (p. 460)

instrumental aggression aggression used to gain or damage an object (p. 198)

intelligence quotient (IQ) the ratio of mental age to chronological age; also, a general term for any kind of score derived from an intelligence test (p. 169)

intersensory integration coordination of information from two or more senses, such as knowing which mouth movements go with which sounds (p. 101)

intimacy the capacity to engage in a supportive, affectionate relationship without losing one's own sense of self (p. 372)

intimacy versus isolation Erikson's early adulthood stage, in which an individual must find a life partner or supportive friends in order to avoid social isolation (p. 372)

intimate partner abuse physical acts or other behavior intended to intimidate or harm an intimate partner (p. 352)

invented spelling a strategy young children with good phonological awareness skills use when they write (p. 167)

involved relationships relationships in which grandparents are directly involved in the everyday care of grandchildren or have close emotional ties with them (p. 437)

kin-keeper a family role, usually occupied by a woman, which includes responsibility for maintaining family and friendship relationships (p. 389)

language acquisition device (LAD) an innate language processor, theorized by Chomsky, that contains the basic grammatical structure of all human language (p. 108)

latency stage the fourth of Freud's psychosexual stages, during which 6- to 12-year-olds' libido is dormant while they establish relationships with same-sex peers (p. 248)

lateralization the process through which brain functions are divided between the two hemispheres of the cerebral cortex (p. 152)

learning disability a disorder in which a child has difficulty mastering a specific academic skill, even though she possesses normal intelligence and no physical or sensory handicaps (p. 235)

learning theories theories that assert that development results from an accumulation of experiences (p. 33)

libido in Freud's theory, an instinctual drive for physical pleasure present at birth and forming the motivating force behind virtually all human behavior (p. 25)

life structure a key concept in Levinson's theory: the underlying pattern or design of a person's life at a given time, which includes roles, relationships, and behavior patterns (p. 372)

lifespan perspective the current view of developmentalists that changes happen throughout the entire human lifespan and that changes must be interpreted in light of the culture and context in which they occur; thus, interdisciplinary research is critical to understanding human development (p. 14)

limbic system the part of the brain that regulates emotional responses (p. 343)

locus of control a set of beliefs about the causes of events (p. 319)

longitudinal design a research design in which people in a single group are studied at different times in their lives (p. 16)

low birth weight (LBW) newborn weight below 5.5 pounds (p. 82)

maturation the gradual unfolding of genetically programmed sequential patterns of change (p. 6)

maximum oxygen uptake (VO_2 max) a measure of the body's ability to take in and transport oxygen to various body organs (p. 346)

memory strategies learned methods for remembering information (p. 227)

menarche the beginning of menstrual cycles (p. 280)

menopause the cessation of monthly menstrual cycles in middle-aged women (p. 402)

metacognition knowledge about how the mind thinks and the ability to control and reflect on one's own thought processes (p. 162)

metamemory knowledge about how memory works and the ability to control and reflect on one's own memory function (p. 162)

moral realism stage the first of Piaget's stages of moral development, in which children believe rules are inflexible (p. 251)

moral relativism stage   the second of Piaget's stages of moral development, in which children understand that many rules can be changed through social agreement (p. 251)

moratorium   in Marcia's theory, the identity status of a person who is in a crisis but who has made no commitment (p. 312)

multi-factorial inheritance   inheritance affected by both genes and the environment (p. 59)

multi-infarct dementia   a form of dementia caused by one or more strokes (p. 475)

myelinization   a process in the development of neurons in which sheaths of a substance called myelin gradually cover individual axons and electrically insulate them from one another, which improves the conductivity of the nerve (p. 92)

naming explosion   a period between 16 and 24 months of age when most children rapidly begin to add new words to their vocabularies (p. 111)

nativism   the view that human beings possess unique genetic traits that will be manifested in all members of the species, regardless of differences in environments (p. 43)

naturalistic observation   the process of studying people in their normal environments (p. 18)

nature-nurture controversy   the debate about the relative contributions of biological process and experiential factors to development (p. 9)

neonate   term for babies between birth and 1 month of age (p. 82)

neo-Piagetian theory   an approach that uses information-processing principles to explain the developmental stages identified by Piaget (p. 40)

neurons   specialized cells of the nervous system (p. 64)

niche-picking   the process of selecting experiences on the basis of temperament (p. 133)

nontraditional post-secondary student   a student who either attends college part-time or delays enrollment after high school graduation (p. 364)

norms   average ages at which developmental milestones are reached (p. 5)

obesity   body weight that is 20% or more above the normal weight for height, or, a body mass index higher than most children of similar age (p. 220)

object permanence   the understanding that objects continue to exist when they can't be seen (p. 103)

objective (categorical) self   the toddler's understanding that she or he is defined by various categories such as gender or qualities such as shyness (p. 135)

observational learning, or **modeling**   learning that results from seeing a model reinforced or punished for a behavior (p. 34)

operant conditioning   learning to repeat or stop behaviors because of their consequences (p. 33)

operational efficiency   a neo-Piagetian term that refers to the maximum number of schemes that can be processed in working memory at one time (p. 162)

organogenesis   process of organ development (p. 64)

osteoporosis   loss of bone mass with age, resulting in more brittle and porous bones (p. 405)

overregularization   attachment of regular inflections to irregular words such as the substitution of *goed* for *went* (p. 166)

palliative care   a form of care for the terminally ill that focuses on relieving patients' pain, rather than curing their diseases (p. 518)

parental investment theory   the theory that sex differences in mate preferences and mating behavior are based on the different amounts of time and effort men and women must invest in child-rearing (p. 374)

pathological grief   symptoms of depression brought on by death of a loved one (p. 536)

pelvic inflammatory disease   an infection of the female reproductive tract that may result from a sexually transmitted disease and can lead to infertility (p. 346)

perimenopausal phase   the stage of menopause during which estrogen and progesterone levels are erratic, menstrual cycles may be very irregular, and women begin to experience symptoms such as hot flashes (p. 403)

permissive parenting style   a style of parenting that is high in nurturance and low in maturity demands, control, and communication (p. 186)

person perception   the ability to classify others according to categories such as age, gender, and race (p. 182)

personal fable   a hypothetical life story created for himself or herself by an adolescent (p. 520)

personality   a pattern of responding to people and objects in the environment (p. 131)

personality disorder   an inflexible pattern of behavior that leads to difficulty in educational, occupational, and social functioning (p. 356)

phenotype   an individual's particular set of observed characteristics (p. 56)

phobia   an irrational fear of an object, a person, a place, or a situation (p. 355)

phonological awareness   children's understanding of the sound patterns of the language they are acquiring (p. 166)

pituitary gland   gland that triggers other glands to release hormones (p. 279)

placenta   specialized organ that allows substances to be transferred from mother to embryo and from embryo to mother, without their blood mixing (p. 62)

polygenic inheritance   pattern of inheritance in which many genes influence a trait (p. 57)

postconventional morality   in Kohlberg's theory, the level of moral reasoning in which judgments are based on an integration of individual rights and the needs of society (p. 330)

postmenopausal phase   the last stage of menopause; a woman is postmenopausal when she has had no menstrual periods for a year or more (p. 403)

post-secondary education   any formal educational experience that follows high school (p. 363)

preconventional morality   in Kohlberg's theory, the level of moral reasoning in which judgments are based on authorities outside the self (p. 328)

premenopausal phase   the stage of menopause during which estrogen levels fall somewhat, menstrual periods are less regular, and anovulatory cycles begin to occur (p. 403)

preoperational stage   Piaget's second stage of cognitive development, during which children become proficient in the use of symbols in thinking and communicating but still have difficulty thinking logically (p. 156)

presbycusis   normal loss of hearing with aging, especially of high-frequency tones (p. 407)

presbyopia   normal loss of visual acuity with aging, especially the ability to focus the eyes on near objects (p. 406)

primary aging   age-related physical changes that have a biological basis and are universally shared and inevitable (p. 342)

primitive reflexes   reflexes controlled by primitive parts of the brain; these reflexes disappear by about 6 months of age (p. 92)

processing efficiency   the ability to make efficient use of short-term memory capacity (p. 226)

programmed senescence theory   the view that age-related declines are the result of species-specific genes for aging (p. 468)

prosocial behavior   behavior intended to help another person (p. 199)

proximodistal pattern   growth that proceeds from the middle of the body outward (p. 62)

psychoanalytic theories   theories proposing that developmental change happens because of the influence of internal drives and emotions on behavior (p. 25)

psychological self   an understanding of one's stable, internal traits (p. 263)

psychosexual stages   Freud's five stages of personality development through which children move in a fixed sequence determined by maturation; the libido is centered in a different body part in each stage (p. 27)

psychosocial stages   Erikson's eight stages, or crises, of personality development in which inner instincts interact with outer cultural and social demands to shape personality (p. 28)

punishment   anything that follows a behavior and causes it to stop (p. 33)

reaction range   a range between upper and lower boundaries for traits such as intelligence, which is established by one's genes; one's environment determines where, within those limits, one will be (p. 174)

reactive attachment disorder   a disorder that appears to prevent a child from forming close social relationships (p. 124)

receptive language   the ability to understand spoken language (p. 109)

reinforcement   anything that follows a behavior and causes it to be repeated (p. 33)

relational aggression   aggression aimed at damaging another person's self-esteem or peer relationships, such as by ostracism or threats of ostracism, cruel gossiping, or facial expressions of disdain (p. 259)

relational style   a tendency to ignore the details of a task in order to focus on the "big picture" (p. 241)

relative right-left orientation   the ability to identify right and left from multiple perspectives (p. 219)

religious coping   the tendency to turn to religious beliefs and institutions for support in times of difficulty (p. 493)

reminiscence   reflecting on past experience (p. 488)

remote relationships   relationships in which grandparents do not see their grandchildren often (p. 437)

research ethics   the guidelines researchers follow to protect the rights of animals used in research and humans who participate in studies (p. 21)

retaliatory aggression   aggression to get back at someone who has hurt you (p. 259)

reticular formation   the part of the brain that regulates attention (p. 92)

role conflict   any situation in which two or more roles are at least partially incompatible, either because they call for different behaviors or because their separate demands add up to more hours than there are in the day (p. 430)

role strain   the strain experienced by an individual whose own qualities or skills do not measure up to the demands of some role (p. 431)

role-taking   the ability to look at a situation from another person's perspective (p. 332)

satiety   the feeling of fullness that follows a meal (p. 471)

schematic learning   organization of experiences into expectancies, called schemas, which enable infants to distinguish between familiar and unfamiliar stimuli (p. 106)

scheme   in Piaget's theory, an internal cognitive structure that provides an individual with a procedure to use in a specific circumstance (p. 39)

schizophrenia   a serious mental disorder characterized by disturbances of thought such as delusions and hallucinations (p. 357)

secondary aging   age-related changes that are due to environmental influences, poor health habits, or disease (p. 342)

secular trend   the decline in the average age of menarche, along with changes such as an increase in average height for both children and adults, that happened between the mid-18th and mid-19th centuries in Western countries and occurs in developing nations when nutrition and health improve (p. 280)

secure attachment   a pattern of attachment in which an infant readily separates from the parent, seeks proximity when stressed, and uses the parent as a safe base for exploration (p. 128)

selective attention   the ability to focus cognitive activity on the important elements of a problem or situation (p. 218)

self-care children   children who are at home by themselves after school for an hour or more each day (p. 267)

self-efficacy   the belief in one's capacity to cause an intended event to occur or to perform a task (p. 351)

self-esteem   a global evaluation of one's own worth (p. 265)

self-regulation   children's ability to conform to parental standards of behavior without direct supervision (p. 254)

semantic memories   general knowledge (p. 421)

senescence   physical changes and declines associated with aging (p. 468)

sensitive period a span of months or years during which a child may be particularly responsive to specific forms of experience or particularly influenced by their absence (p. 13)

sensorimotor stage Piaget's first stage of development, in which infants use information from their senses and motor actions to learn about the world (p. 102)

separation anxiety expressions of discomfort, such as crying, when separated from an attachment figure (p. 127)

sequential design a research design that combines cross-sectional and longitudinal examinations of development (p. 16)

sex roles behavior expected for males and females in a given culture (p. 203)

sex-role identity the gender-related aspects of the psychological self (p. 315)

sex-typed behavior different patterns of behavior exhibited by boys and girls (p. 207)

sex-typing the manifestation or adoption of culturally defined sex-appropriate behavior (p. 144)

sexual violence the use of physical coercion to force a person to engage in a sexual act against his or her will (p. 354)

shaping the reinforcement of intermediate steps until an individual learns a complex behavior (p. 34)

short-term storage space (STSS) neo-Piagetian theorist Robbie Case's term for the working memory (p. 162)

social clock a set of age norms that defines a sequence of life experiences that is considered normal in a given culture and that all individuals in that culture are expected to follow (p. 11)

social death the point at which family members and medical personnel treat the deceased person as a corpse (p. 517)

social referencing an infant's use of others' facial expressions as a guide to his or her own emotions (p. 127)

social role theory the idea that sex differences in mate preferences and mating behavior are adaptations to gender roles (p. 375)

social skills a set of behaviors that usually lead to being accepted as a play partner or friend by peers (p. 196)

social status an individual child's classification as popular, rejected, or neglected (p. 260)

social-cognitive theory the theoretical perspective that asserts that social and personality development in early childhood are related to improvements in the cognitive domain (p. 181)

sociobiology the study of society using the methods and concepts of biology; when used by developmentalists, an approach that emphasizes genes that aid group survival (p. 44)

socio-cultural theory Vygotsky's view that complex forms of thinking have their origins in social interactions rather than in an individual's private explorations (p. 44)

spatial cognition the ability to infer rules from and make predictions about the movement of objects in space (p. 219)

spatial perception the ability to identify and act on relationships between objects in space (p. 219)

states of consciousness different states of sleep and wakefulness in infants (p. 93)

stranger anxiety expressions of discomfort, such as clinging to the mother in the presence of strangers (p. 127)

subjective self an infant's awareness that she or he is a separate person who endures through time and space and can act on the environment (p. 135)

successful aging the term gerontologists use to describe maintaining one's physical health, mental abilities, social competence, and overall satisfaction with one's life as one ages (p. 490)

sudden infant death syndrome (SIDS) the sudden and unexpected death of an apparently healthy infant (p. 98)

superego Freud's term for the part of personality that is the moral judge (p. 26)

synapses connections between neurons (p. 91)

synaptic plasticity the redundancy in the nervous system that ensures that it is nearly always possible for a nerve impulse to move from one neuron to another or from a neuron to another type of cell (e.g., a muscle cell) (p. 466)

synchrony a mutual, interlocking pattern of attachment behaviors shared by a parent and child (p. 125)

systematic problem-solving the process of finding a solution to a problem by testing single factors (p. 296)

task goals goals based on a desire for self-improvement (p. 300)

telomere string of repetitive DNA at the tip of each chromosome in the body that appears to serve as a kind of timekeeping mechanism (p. 463)

temperament inborn predispositions such as activity level that form the foundations of personality (p. 131)

tenacious goal pursuit a behavior pattern in which middle-aged adults remain committed to goals that are difficult, and may be impossible, for them to achieve (p. 449)

teratogens substances such as viruses and drugs that can cause birth defects (p. 70)

terminal drop hypothesis the hypothesis that mental and physical functioning decline drastically only in the few years immediately preceding death (p. 470)

thanatology the scientific study of death and dying (p. 528)

theory of mind a set of ideas constructed by a child or adult to explain other people's ideas, beliefs, desires, and behavior (p. 160)

tinnitus persistent ringing in the ears (p. 467)

traditional post-secondary student a student who attends college full-time immediately after graduating from high school (p. 364)

type A personality pattern a personality type associated with greater risk of coronary heart disease; it includes competitive achievement striving, a sense of time urgency, and, sometimes, hostility or aggressiveness (p. 409)

umbilical cord organ that connects the embryo to the placenta (p. 62)

uninvolved parenting style a style of parenting that is low in nurturance, maturity demands, control, and communication (p. 186)

unique invulnerability the belief that bad things, including death, only happen to others (p. 521)

validating couples   couples who express mutual respect even in disagreements and are good listeners (p. 379)

viability   ability of the fetus to survive outside the womb (p. 65)

visual acuity   the ability to see details at a distance (p. 93)

volatile couples   couples who argue a lot, don't listen well, but still have more positive than negative interactions (p. 379)

volunteerism   performance of unpaid work for altruistic motives (p. 492)

wisdom   a hypothesized cognitive characteristic of older adults that includes accumulated knowledge and the ability to apply that knowledge to practical problems of living (p. 482)

zygote   single cell created when sperm and ovum unite (p. 54)

References

ABC News. (2000, August 22). Poll: Americans like public school. [Online report]. Retrieved August 23, 2000 from the World Wide Web: http://www.abcnews.com

Abdelrahman, A., Rodriguez, G., Ryan, J., French, J., & Weinbaum, D. (1998). The epidemiology of substance use among middle school students: The impact of school, familial, community and individual risk factors. *Journal of Child & Adolescent Substance Abuse, 8,* 55–75.

Abengozar, C., Bueno, B., & Vega, J. (1999). Intervention on attitudes toward death along the life span. *Educational Gerontology, 25,* 435–447.

Abraham, J. D., & Hansson, R. O. (1995). Successful aging at work: An applied study of selection, optimization, and compensation through impression management. *Journals of Gerontology: Psychological Sciences, 50B,* P94–P103.

Abrams, R. (1998). Physician-assisted suicide and euthanasia's impact on the frail elderly: Something to think about. *Journal of Long Term Home Health Care: The Pride Institute Journal, 17,* 19–27.

Abrams, E. J., Matheson, P. B., Thomas, P. A., Thea, D. M., Krasinski, K., Lambert, G., Shaffer, N., Bamji, M., Hutson, D., Grimm, K., Kaul, A., Bateman, D., Rogers, M., & New York City Perinatal HIV Transmission Collaborative Study Group (1995). Neonatal predictors of infection status and early death among 332 infants at risk of HIV-1 infection monitored prospectively from birth. *Pediatrics, 96,* 451–458.

Accardo, P., Tomazic, T., Fete, T., Heaney, M., Lindsay, R., & Whitman, B. (1997). Maternally reported fetal activity levels and developmental diagnoses. *Clinical Pediatrics, 36,* 279–283.

Achter, J., Lubinski, D., Benbow, C., & Eftekhari-Sanjani, H. (1999). Assessing vocational preferences among gifted adolescents adds incremental validity to abilities: A discriminant analysis of educational outcomes over a 10-year interval. *Journal of Educational Psychology, 91,* 777–786.

Adams, C. (1991). Qualitative age differences in memory for text: A life-span developmental perspective. *Psychology and Aging, 6,* 323–336.

Adams, M. J. (1990). *Beginning to read: Thinking and learning about print.* Cambridge, MA: The MIT Press.

Adams, M., & Henry, M. (1997). Myths and realities about words and literacy. *School Psychology Review, 26,* 425–436.

Adelmann, P. K. (1994). Multiple roles and physical health among older adults: Gender and ethnic comparisons. *Research on Aging, 16,* 142–166.

Adesman, A. R. (1996). Fragile X syndrome. In A. J. Capute & P. J. Accardo (Eds.), *Developmental disabilities in infancy and childhood* (2nd ed.). Vol. II. *The spectrum of developmental disabilities* (pp. 255–269). Baltimore: Paul H. Brookes.

Adkins, V. (1999). Grandparents as a national asset: A brief note. *Activities, Adaptation, & Aging, 24,* 13–18.

Ahadi, S. A., & Rothbart, M. K. (1994). Temperament, development, and the big five. In C. F. Halverson, Jr., G. A. Kohnstamm, & R. P. Martin (Eds.), *The developing structure of temperament and personality from infancy to adulthood* (pp. 189–207). Hillsdale, NJ: Erlbaum.

Ahlsten, G., Cnattingius, S., & Lindmark, G. (1993). Cessation of smoking during pregnancy improves foetal growth and reduces infant morbidity in the neonatal period: A population-based prospective study. *Acta Paediatrica, 82,* 177–182.

Ahmad, G., & Najam, N. (1998). A study of marital adjustment during first transition to parenthood. *Journal of Behavioural Sciences, 9,* 67–86.

Aiken, L. (1997). *Psychological testing and assessment* (9th ed.). Boston: Allyn & Bacon.

Ainsworth, M. D. S. (1989). Attachments beyond infancy. *American Psychologist, 44,* 709–716.

Ainsworth, M. D. S., Blehar, M., Waters, E., & Wall, S. (1978). *Patterns of attachment.* Hillsdale, NJ: Erlbaum.

Ainsworth, M. D. S., & Marvin, R. S. (1995). On the shaping of attachment theory and research: An interview with Mary D. S. Ainsworth (Fall 1994). *Monographs of the Society for Research in Child Development, 60* (244, Nos. 2–3), 3–21.

Akers, J., Jones, R., & Coyl, D. (1998). Adolescent friendship pairs: Similarities in identity status development, behaviors, attitudes, and interests. *Journal of Adolescent Research, 13,* 178–201.

Akiba, D. (1998). Cultural variations in body esteem: How young adults in Iran and the United States view their own appearances. *The Journal of Social Psychology, 138,* 539–540.

Aksu-Koc, A. A., & Slobin, D. I. (1985). The acquisition of Turkish. In D. I. Slobin (Ed.), *The crosslinguistic study of language acquisition: Vol. 1. The data* (pp. 839–878). Hillsdale, NJ: Erlbaum.

Albert, M. S., Jones, K., Savage, C. R., Berkman, L., Seeman, T., Blazer, D., & Rowe, J. W. (1995). Predictors of cognitive change in older persons: MacArthur studies of successful aging. *Psychology and Aging, 10,* 578–589.

Aldous, J. (1996). *Family careers: Rethinking the developmental perspective.* Thousand Oaks, CA: Sage.

Aldous, J., & Klein, D. M. (1991). Sentiment and services: Models of intergenerational relationships in mid-life. *Journal of Marriage and the Family, 53,* 595–608.

Aleixo, P., & Norris, C. (2000). Personality and moral reasoning in young offenders. *Personality & Individual Differences, 28,* 609–623.

Alexander, G., & Hines, M. (1994). Gender labels and play styles: Their relative contribution to children's selection of playmates: *Child Development, 65,* 869–879.

Allaz, A., Bernstein, M., Rouget, P., Archinard, M., & Morabia, A. (1998). Body weight preoccupation in middle-aged and ageing women: A general population survey. *International Journal of Eating Disorders, 23,* 287–294.

Allen, C., & Kisilevsky, B. (1999). Fetal behavior in diabetic and nondiabetic pregnant women: An exploratory study. *Developmental Psychobiology, 35,* 69–80.

Allen, K. R., & Pickett, R. S. (1987). Forgotten streams in the family life course: Utilization of qualitative retrospective interviews in the analysis of lifelong single women's family careers. *Journal of Marriage and the Family, 49,* 517–526.

Allen, T., Poteet, M., & Russell, J. (1998). Attitudes of managers who are more or less career plateaued. *Career Development Quarterly, 47,* 159–172.

Allen, W., Dreves, R., & Ruhe, J. (1999). Reasons why college-educated women change employment. *Journal of Business & Psychology, 14,* 77–93.

The Alpha-Tocopherol Beta Carotene Cancer Prevention Study Group (1994). The effect of vitamin E and beta carotene on the incidence of lung cancer and other cancers in male smokers. *New England Journal of Medicine, 330,* 1029–1035.

Alsaker, F. D. (1995). Timing of puberty and reactions to pubertal change. In M. Rutter (Ed.), *Psychosocial disturbances in young people: Challenges for prevention* (pp. 37–82). Cambridge, England: Cambridge University Press.

Alsaker, F. D., & Olweus, D. (1992). Stability of global self-evaluations in early adolescence: A cohort longitudinal study. *Journal of Research on Adolescence, 2,* 123–145.

Alsop, S. (1973). *Stay of execution.* New York: Lippincott.

Alspaugh, J. (1998). Achievement loss associated with the transition to middle school and high school. *Journal of Educational Research, 92,* 20–25.

Alster, E. (1997). The effects of extended time on algebra test scores for college students with and without learning disabilities. *Journal of Learning Disabilities, 30,* 222–227.

Alvidrez, J., & Weinstein, R. (1999). Early teacher perceptions and later student academic achievement. *Journal of Educational Psychology, 91,* 731–746.

Amato, P. R. (1993). Children's adjustment to divorce: Theories, hypotheses, and empirical support. *Journal of Marriage and the Family, 55,* 23–38.

Amato, P., & Rogers, S. (1999). Do attitudes toward divorce affect marital quality? *Journal of Family Issues, 20,* 69–86.

Amato, S. (1998). Human genetics and dysmorphy. In R. Behrman & R. Kliegman (Eds.), *Nelson essentials of pediatrics* (3rd ed., pp. 129–146). Philadelphia: W. B. Saunders.

Ambuel, B. (1995). Adolescents, unintended pregnancy, and abortion: The struggle for a compassionate social policy. *Current Directions in Psychological Science, 4,* 1–5.

Amenedo, E., & Diaz, F. (1998). Aging-related changes in processing of non-target and target stimuli during an auditory oddball task. *Biological Psychology, 48,* 235–267.

Amenedo, E., & Diaz, F. (1999). Aging-related changes in the processing of attended and unattended standard stimuli. *Neuroreport: For Rapid Communication of Neuroscience Research, 10,* 2383–2388.

American Association of Family Physicians. (1998). *Epilepsy and pregnancy: What you should know.* [Online patient brochure]. Retrieved March 6, 2001 from the World Wide Web: http://www.aafp.org/afp/971015ap/971015c.html

American Medical Association. (1990). Legal interventions during pregnancy: Court-ordered medical treatments and legal penalties for potentially harmful behavior by pregnant women. *Journal of the American Medical Association, 264,* 2663–2667.

American Psychiatric Association (1994). *Diagnostic and statistical manual of mental disorders* (4th ed.). Washington, DC: American Psychiatric Association.

American Psychological Association (1993). *Violence and youth: Psychology's response: Vol. 1. Summary report of the American Psychological Association Commission on Violence and Youth.* Washington, DC: American Psychological Association.

American Psychological Association Commission on Ethnic Minority Recruitment, Retention, and Training in Psychology. (1997). *Visions & Transformations: Final Report.* Washington DC: Author.

Amott, T., & Matthaei, J. (1991). *Race, gender, and work: A multicultural economic history of women in the United States.* Boston: South End Press.

Anan, R., & Barnett, D. (1999). Perceived social support mediates between prior attachment and subsequent adjustment: A study of urban African American children. *Developmental Psychology, 35,* 1210–1222.

Anderman, E. (1998). The middle school experience: Effects on the math and science achievement of adolescents with LD. *Journal of Learning Disabilities, 31,* 128–138.

Anderman, E., Maehr, M., & Midgley, C. (1999). Declining motivation after the transition to middle school: Schools can make a difference. *Journal of Research & Development in Education, 32,* 131–147.

Anderman, E., & Midgley, C. (1997). Changes in achievement goal orientations, perceived academic competence, and grades across the transition to middle-level schools. *Contemporary Educational Psychology, 22,* 269–298.

Anderman, L. (1999). Classroom goal orientation, school belonging and social goals as predictors of students' positive and negative affect following the transition to middle school. *Journal of Research & Development in Education, 32,* 89–103.

Anderman, L., & Anderman, E. (1999). Social predictors of changes in students' achievement goal orientations. *Contemporary Educational Psychology, 24,* 21–37.

Anderson, C., & Dill, K. (2000). Video games and aggressive thoughts, feelings, and behavior in the laboratory and in life. *Journal of Personality and Social Psychology, 78,* 772–790.

Anderson, D. R., Lorch, E. P., Field, D. E., Collins, P. A., & Nathan, J. G. (1986). Television viewing at home: Age trends in visual attention and time with TV. *Child Development, 57,* 1024–1033.

Anderson, H., & Sommerfelt, K. (1999). Infant temperamental factors of problem behavior and IQ at age 5 years: Interactional effects of biological and social risk factors. *Child Study Journal, 29,* 207–226.

Anderson, K. M., Castelli, W. P., & Levy, D. (1987). Cholesterol and mortality: 30 years of follow-up from the Framingham study. *Journal of the American Medical Association, 257,* 2176–2180.

Anderson, R. (1998). Examining language loss in bilingual children. *Electronic Multicultural Journal of Communication Disorders, 1.*

Andersson, B. (1989). Effects of public day-care: A longitudinal study. *Child Development, 60,* 857–886.

Andersson, B. (1992). Effects of day-care on cognitive and socioemotional competence of thirteen-year-old Swedish schoolchildren. *Child Development, 63,* 20–36.

Andersson, N., Sonnander, K., & Sommerfelt, K. (1998). Gender and its contribution to the prediction of cognitive abilities at 5 years. *Scandinavian Journal of Psychology, 39,* 257–274.

Andrews, M., Dowling, W., Bartlett, J., & Halpern, A. (1998). Identification of speeded and slowed familiar melodies by younger, middle-aged, and older musicians and nonmusicians. *Psychology & Aging, 13,* 462–471.

Angier, N. (June 9, 1992). Clue to longevity found at chromosome tip. *New York Times,* pp. B5, B9.

Anglin, J. M. (1993). Vocabulary development: A morphological analysis. *Monographs of the Society for Research in Child Development, 58* (Serial No. 238).

Anglin, J. M. (1995, March). *Word learning and the growth of potentially knowable vocabulary.* Paper presented at the biennial meetings of the Society for Research in Child Development, Indianapolis, IN.

Anisfeld, M. (1991). Neonatal imitation. *Developmental Review, 11,* 60–97.

Annunziato, P. W., & Frenkel, L. M. (1993). The epidemiology of pediatric HIV-1 infection. *Pediatric Annals, 22,* 401–405.

Anthony, J. C., & Aboraya, A. (1992). The epidemiology of selected mental disorders in later life. In J. E. Birren, R. B. Sloane, & G. D. Cohen (Eds.), *Handbook of mental health and aging* (2nd ed.) (pp. 28–73). San Diego, CA: Academic Press.

Antonucci, T. C. (1990). Social supports and social relationships. In R. H. Binstock & L. K. George (Eds.), *Handbook of aging and the social sciences* (3rd ed.) (pp. 205–226). San Diego, CA: Academic Press.

Antonucci, T. C. (1991). Attachment, social support, and coping with negative life events in mature adulthood. In E. M. Cummings, A. L. Greene, & K. H. Karraker (Eds.), *Life-span developmental psychology: Perspectives on stress and coping* (pp. 261–276). Hillsdale, NJ: Erlbaum.

Antonucci, T. C. (1994). A life-span view of women's social relations. In B. F. Turner & L. E. Troll (Eds.), *Women growing older: Psychological perspectives* (pp. 239–269). Thousand Oaks, CA: Sage.

Antrop, I., Roeyers, H., Van Oost, P., & Buysse, A. (2000). Stimulation seeking and hyperactivity in children with ADHD. *Journal of Child Psychology, Psychiatry & Allied Disciplines, 41,* 225–231.

Apgar, V. A. (1953). A proposal for a new method of evaluation of the newborn infant. *Current Research in Anesthesia and Analgesia, 32,* 260–267.

Aptekar, L., & Stocklin, D. (1997). Children in particularly difficult circumstances. In J. Berry, P. Dasen, & T. Saraswathi (Eds.), *Handbook of cross-cultural psychology. Vol. 2: Basic processes and human development* (2nd ed.). Boston: Allyn & Bacon.

Aquilino, W. S., & Supple, K. R. (1991). Parent-child relations and parent's satisfaction with living arrangements when adult children live at home. *Journal of Marriage and the Family, 53,* 13–27.

Aranha, M. (1997). Creativity in students and its relation to intelligence and peer perception. *Revista Interamericana de Psicologia, 31,* 309–313.

Arbuckle, N. W., & De Vries, B. (1995). The long-term effects of later life spousal and parental bereavement on personal functioning. *The Gerontologist, 35,* 637–647.

Archer, S. (1999, April 12). Crackdown on delinquent parents. Retrieved December 6, 1999 from the World Wide Web: www.WorldNetDaily.com

Arditti, J. (1991). Child support noncompliance and divorced fathers: Rethinking the role of paternal involvement. *Journal of Divorce and Remarriage, 14,* 107–120.

Arenberg, D. (1983). Memory and learning do decline late in life. In J. E. Birren, J. M. A. Munnichs, H. Thomae, & M. Marios (Eds.), *Aging: A challenge to science and society: Vol. 3. Behavioral sciences and conclusions* (pp. 312–322). New York: Oxford University Press.

Arlin, P. K. (1975). Cognitive development in adulthood: A fifth stage? *Developmental Psychology, 11,* 602–606.

Arlin, P. K. (1989). Problem solving and problem finding in young artists and young scientists. In M. L. Commons, J. D. Sinnott, F. A. Richards, & C. Armon (Eds.), *Adult Development: Vol. 1. Comparisons and applications of developmental models* (pp. 197–216). New York: Praeger.

Arlin, P. K. (1990). Wisdom: The art of problem finding. In R. J. Sternberg (Ed.), *Wisdom. Its nature, origins, and development* (pp. 230–243). New York: Cambridge University Press.

Arnett, J. (1990). Contraceptive use, sensation seeking, and adolescent egocentrism. *Journal of Youth and Adolescence, 19,* 171–180.

Arnett, J. (1998). Risk behavior and family role transitions during the twenties. *Journal of Youth & Adolescence, 27,* 301–320.

Arrindell, W., & Luteijn, F. (2000). Similarity between intimate partners for personality traits as related to individual levels of satisfaction with life. *Personality & Individual Differences, 28,* 629–637.

Asendorpf, J. B., Warkentin, V., & Baudonnière, P. (1996). Self-awareness and other-awareness. II: Mirror self-recognition, social contingency awareness, and synchronic imitation. *Developmental Psychology, 32,* 313–321.

Ashton, J., & Donnan, S. (1981). Suicide by burning as an epidemic phenomenon: An analysis of 82 deaths and inquests in England and Wales in 1978–1979. *Psychological Medicine, 11,* 735–739.

Assibey-Mensah, G. (1997). Role models and youth development: Evidence and lessons from the perceptions of African-American male youth. *Western Journal of Black Studies, 21,* 242–252.

Associated Press. (1996, July 17). Carolina ruling favors unborn; court describes fetus as a person. *Washington Times,* p. A1.

Associated Press. (1998, October 12). TAAS preparation is big business.

Associated Press. (1998, October 27). More subpoenas issued in TAAS inquiry.

Associated Press. (2000, September 18). Netherlands' homosexuals get right to "marry" legally. *Washington Times/National Edition,* p. 24.

Astington, J., & Jenkins, J. (1999). A longitudinal study of the relation between language and theory-of-mind development. *Developmental Psychology, 35,* 1311–1320.

Astington, J. W., & Gopnik, A. (1991). Theoretical explanations of children's understanding of the mind. In G. E. Butterworth, P. L. Harris, A. M. Leslie, & H. M. Wellman (Eds.), *Perspectives on the child's theory of mind* (pp. 7–31). New York: Oxford University Press.

Astington, J. W., & Jenkins, J. M. (1995, March). *Language and theory of mind: A theoretical review and a longitudinal study.* Paper presented at the biennial meetings of the Society for Research in Child Development, Indianapolis, IN.

Astor, R. (1994). Children's moral reasoning about family and peer violence: The role of provocation and retribution. *Child Development, 65,* 1054–1067.

Atkinson, D., Kim, A., Ruelas, S., & Lin, A. (1999). Ethnicity and attitudes toward facilitated reminiscence. *Journal of Mental Health Counseling, 21,* 66–81.

Attie, I., Brooks-Gunn, J., & Petersen, A. (1990). A developmental perspective on eating disorders and eating problems. In M. Lewis & S. M. Miller (Eds.), *Handbook of developmental psychopathology* (pp. 409–420). New York: Plenum.

Avis, J., & Harris, P. L. (1991). Belief-desire reasoning among Baka children: Evidence for a universal conception of mind. *Child Development, 62,* 460–467.

Axelman, K., Basun, H., & Lannfelt, L. (1998). Wide range of disease onset in a family with Alzheimer disease and a His163Tyr mutation in the presenilin-1 gene. *Archives of Neurology, 55,* 698–702.

Bachman, J., Segal, D., Freedman-Doan, P., & O'Malley, P. (2000). Who chooses military service? Correlates of propensity and enlistment in the U. S. Armed Forces. *Military Psychology, 12,* 1–30.

Bachman, J. G., & Schulenberg, J. (1993). How part-time work intensity relates to drug use, problem behavior, time use, and satisfaction among high school seniors: Are these consequences or merely correlates? *Developmental Psychology, 29,* 220–235.

Bachrach, C. A. (1980). Childlessness and social isolation among the elderly. *Journal of Marriage and the Family, 42,* 627–638.

Baddeley, A. (1998). *Human memory: Theory and practice* (Rev. ed.) Boston: Allyn & Bacon.

Bahrick, H., Hall, L., & Berger, S. (1996). Accuracy and distortion in memory for high school grades. *Psychological Science,* 265–271.

Bahrick, L., & Lickliter, R. (2000). Intersensory redundancy guides attentional selectivity and perceptual learning in infancy. *Developmental Psychology, 36,* 190–201.

Bailey, J., Brobow, D., Wolfe, M., & Mikach, S. (1995). Sexual orientation of adult sons of gay fathers. *Developmental Psychology, 31,* 124–129.

Bailey, J., Nothnagel, J., & Wolfe, M. (1995). Retrospectively measured individual differences in childhood sex-typed behavior among gay men: Correspondence between self- and maternal reports. *Archives of Sexual Behavior, 24,* 613–622.

Bailey, J., Pillard, R., Dawood, K., Miller, M., Farrer, L., Trivedi, S., & Murphy, R. (1999). A family history study of male sexual orientation using three independent samples. *Behavior Genetics, 29,* 7986.

Bailey, J. M., & Pillard, R. C. (1991). A genetic study of male sexual orientation. *Archives of General Psychiatry, 48,* 1089–1096.

Bailey, J. M., Pillard, R. C., Neale, M. C., & Agyei, Y. (1993). Heritable factors influence sexual orientation in women. *Archives of General Psychiatry, 50,* 217–223.

Bailey, J. M., & Zucker, K. J. (1995). Childhood sex-typed behavior and sexual orientation: A conceptual analysis and quantitative review. *Developmental Psychology, 31,* 43–55.

Baillargeon, R. (1987). Object permanence in very young infants. *Developmental Psychology, 23,* 655–664.

Baillargeon, R. (1994). How do infants learn about the physical world? *Current Directions in Psychological Science, 3,* 133–140.

Baillargeon, R., & DeVos, J. (1991). Object permanence in young infants: Further evidence. *Child Development, 62,* 1227–1246.

Baillargeon, R., Spelke, E. S., & Wasserman, S. (1985). Object permanence in five-month-old infants. *Cognition, 20,* 191–208.

Bailley, S., Kral, M., & Dunham, K. (1999). Survivors of suicide do grieve differently: Empirical support for a common sense proposition. *Suicide and Life-Threatening Behavior, 29,* 256–271.

Baird, P. A., Sadovnick, A. D., & Yee, I. M. L. (1991). Maternal age and birth defects: A population study. *Lancet, 337,* 527–530.

Bakermans-Kranenburg, M., Juffer, F., & van IJzendoorn, M. (1998). Interventions with video feedback and attachment discussions: Does the type of maternal insecurity make a difference? *Infant Mental Health Journal, 19,* 202–219.

Baker-Ward, L. (1995, March). *Children's reports of a minor medical emergency procedure.* Paper presented at the biennial meetings of the Society for Research in Child Development, Indianapolis, IN.

Baker-Ward, L., Gordon, B. N., Ornstein, P. A., Larus, D. M., & Clubb, P. A. (1993). Young children's long-term retention of a pediatric examination. *Child Development, 64,* 1519–1533.

Bal, D., & Foerster, S. B. (1991). Changing the American diet. *Cancer, 67,* 2671–2680.

Balaban, M. T. (1995). Affective influences on startle in five-month-old infants: Reactions to facial expressions of emotion. *Child Development, 66,* 28–36.

Baldwin, D. A. (1995, March). *Understanding relations between constraints and a socio-pragmatic account of meaning acquisition.* Paper presented at the biennial meetings of the Society for Research in Child Development, Indianapolis, IN.

Ball, E. (1997). Phonological awareness: Implications for whole language and emergent literacy programs. *Topics in Language Disorders, 17,* 14–26.

Baltes, P., & Staudinger, U. (2000). Wisdom: A metaheuristic (pragmatic) to orchestrate mind and virtue toward excellence. *American Psychologist, 55,* 122–136.

Baltes, P. B., & Baltes, M. M. (1990). Psychological perspectives on successful aging: The model of selective optimization with compensation. In P. B. Baltes & M. M. Baltes (Eds.), *Successful aging* (pp. 1–34). Cambridge, England: Cambridge University Press.

Baltes, P. B., Dittmann-Kohli, F., & Dixon, R. A. (1984). New perspectives on the development of intelligence in adulthood: Toward a dual-process conception and a model of selective optimization with compensation. In P. B. Baltes & O. G. Brim, Jr. (Eds.), *Life-span development and behavior* (pp. 34–77). New York: Academic Press.

Baltes, P. B., Dittmann-Kohli, F., & Dixon, R. A. (1986). Multidisciplinary propositions on the development of intelligence during adulthood and old age. In A. B. Sørensen, F. E. Weinert, & L. R. Sherrod (Eds.), *Human development and the life course: Multidisciplinary perspectives* (pp. 467–508). Hillsdale, NJ: Erlbaum.

Baltes, P. B., & Kliegl, R. (1992). Further testing of limits of cognitive plasticity: Negative age differences in a mnemonic skill are robust. *Developmental Psychology, 28,* 121–125.

Baltes, P. B., Reese, H. W., & Lipsitt, L. P. (1980). Life-span developmental psychology. *Annual Review of Psychology, 31,* 65–10.

Baltes, P. B., Reese, H. W., & Nesselroade, J. R. (1977). *Life-span developmental psychology: Introduction to research methods.* Monterey, CA: Books/Cole.

Baltes, P. B., & Smith, J. (1990). Toward a psychology of wisdom and its ontogenesis. In R. J. Sternberg (Ed.), *Wisdom. Its nature, origins, and development* (pp. 87–120). Cambridge, England: Cambridge University Press.

Baltes, P. B., Smith, J., & Staudinger, U. M. (1992). Wisdom and successful aging. In T. B. Sonderegger (Ed.), *Nebraska Symposium on Motivation, 1991* (pp. 123–168). Lincoln: University of Nebraska Press.

Baltes, P. B., Staudinger, U. M., Maercker, A., & Smith, J. (1995). People nominated as wise: A comparative study of wisdom-related knowledge. *Psychology and Aging, 10,* 155–166.

Bambang, S., Spencer, N., Logan, S., & Gill, L. (2000). Cause-specific perinatal death rates, birth weight and deprivation in the West Midlands, 1991–1993. *Child: Care, Health & Development, 26,* 73–82.

Bamford, F. N., Bannister, R. P., Benjamin, C. M., Hillier, V. F., Ward, B. S., & Moore, W. M. O. (1990). Sleep in the first year of life. *Developmental Medicine and Child Neurology, 32,* 718–724.

Bandura, A. (1977a). *Social learning theory.* Englewood Cliffs, NJ: Prentice-Hall.

Bandura, A. (1977b). Self-efficacy: Toward a unifying theory of behavioral change. *Psychological Review, 84,* 91–125.

Bandura, A. (1982a). The psychology of chance encounters and life paths. *American Psychologist, 37,* 747–755.

Bandura, A. (1982b). Self-efficacy mechanism in human agency. *American Psychologist, 37,* 122–147.

Bandura, A. (1986). *Social foundations of thought and action: A social cognitive theory.* Englewood Cliffs, NJ: Prentice-Hall.

Bandura, A. (1989). Social cognitive theory. *Annals of Child Development, 6,* 1–60.

Bandura, A., Ross, D., & Ross, S. A. (1961). Transmission of aggression through imitation of aggressive models. *Journal of Abnormal and Social Psychology, 63,* 575–582.

Bandura, A., Ross, D., & Ross, S. A. (1963). Imitation of film-mediated aggressive models. *Journal of Abnormal and Social Psychology, 66,* 3–11.

Barak, A. (1999). Psychological applications on the Internet: A discipline on the threshold of a new millennium. *Applied & Preventive Psychology, 8,* 231–245.

Barbarin, O. (1999). Social risks and psychological adjustment: A comparison of African American and South African children. *Child Development, 70,* 1348–1359.

Barenboim, C. (1981). The development of person perception in childhood and adolescence: From behavioral comparisons to psychological constructs to psychological comparisons. *Child Development, 52,* 129–144.

Barker, J., Morrow, J., & Mitteness, L. (1998). Gender, informal social support networks, and elderly urban African Americans. *Journal of Aging Studies, 12,* 199–222.

Barkley, R. (1990). *Attention-deficit hyperactivity disorder.* New York: Guilford Press.

Barlow, J., & Lewandowski, L. (2000, August). *Ten-year longitudinal study of preterm infants: Outcomes and predictors.* Paper presented at the annual meeting of the American Psychological Association, Washington, DC.

Barnard, K. E., Hammond, M. A., Booth, C. L., Bee, H. L., Mitchell, S. K., & Spieker, S. J. (1989). Measurement and meaning of parent-child interaction. In J. J. Morrison, C. Lord, & D. P. Keating (Eds.), *Applied developmental psychology* (Vol. 3) (pp. 40–81). San Diego, CA: Academic Press.

Barnett, W. S. (1993). Benefit-cost analysis of preschool education: Findings from a 25-year follow-up. *American Journal of Orthopsychiatry, 63,* 500–508.

Barnett, W. S. (1995). Long-term effects of early childhood programs on cognitive and school outcomes. *The Future of Children, 5* (3), 25–50.

Barrett-Connor, E., & Bush, T. L. (1991). Estrogen and coronary heart disease in women. *Journal of the American Medical Association, 265,* 1861–1867.

Bartel-Sheehan, K., & Grubbs-Hoy, M. (1999). Flaming, complaining, abstaining: How online users respond to privacy concerns. *Journal of Advertising, 28,* 37–51.

Bartlik, B., & Goldstein, M. (2000, June). Maintaining sexual health after menopause. *Psychiatric Services Journal, 51,* 751–753.

Bartoshuk, L. M., & Weiffenbach, J. M. (1990). Chemical senses and aging. In E. L. Schneider & J. W. Rowe (Eds.), *Handbook of the biology of aging* (3rd ed.) (pp. 429–444). San Diego, CA: Academic Press.

Barusch, A. (1999). Religion, adversity and age: Religious experiences of low-income elderly women. *Journal of Sociology & Social Welfare, 26,* 125–142.

Basavappa, S., Rao, S., & Harish, B. (1996). Expert system for dementia/depression diagnosis. *NIMHANS Journal, 14,* 99–106.

Bass, D. M. (1985). The hospice ideology and success of hospice care. *Research on Aging, 7,* 307–328.

Basseches, M. (1984). *Dialectical thinking and adult development.* Norwood, NJ: Ablex.

Basseches, M. (1989). Dialectical thinking as an organized whole: Comments on Irwin and Kramer. In M. L. Commons, J. D. Sinnott, F. A. Richards, & C. Armon (Eds.), *Adult development: Vol. 1. Comparisons and applications of developmental models* (pp. 161–178). New York: Praeger.

Bates, E. (1993). Commentary: Comprehension and production in early language development. *Monographs of the Society for Research in Child Development, 58* (3–4, Serial No. 233), 222–242.

Bates, E., O'Connell, B., & Shore, C. (1987). Language and communication in infancy. In J. D. Osofsky (Ed.), *Handbook of infant development* (2nd ed.) (pp. 149–203). New York: Wiley.

Bates, J. E. (1989). Applications of temperament concepts. In G. A. Kohnstamm, J. E. Bates, & M. K. Rothbart (Eds.), *Temperament in childhood* (pp. 321–356). Chichester, England: Wiley.

Bates, J. E., Marvinney, D., Kelly, T., Dodge, K. A., Bennett, D. S., & Pettit, G. S. (1994). Child-care history and kindergarten adjustment. *Developmental Psychology, 30,* 690–700.

Batten, M., & Oltjenbruns, K. (1999). Adolescent sibling bereavement as a catalyst for spiritual development: A model for understanding. *Death Studies, 23,* 529–546.

Bauer, P., Schwade, J., Wewerka, S., & Delaney, K. (1999). Planning ahead: Goal-directed problem solving by 2-year-olds. *Developmental Psychology, 35,* 1321–1337.

Baugher, R. J., Burger, C., Smith, R., & Wallston, K. (1989/1990). A comparison of terminally ill persons at various time periods to death. *Omega, 20,* 103–115.

Bauminger, N., & Kasari, C. (1999). Brief report: Theory of mind in high-functioning children with autism. *Journal of Autism & Developmental Disorders, 29,* 81–86.

Baumrind, D. (1967). Child care practices anteceding three patterns of preschool behavior. *Genetic Psychology Monographs, 75,* 43–88.

Baumrind, D. (1971). Current patterns of parental authority. *Developmental Psychology Monograph, 4* (1, Part 2).

Baumrind, D. (1972). Socialization and instrumental competence in young children. In W. W. Hartup (Ed.), *The young child: Reviews of research* (Vol. 2) (pp. 202–224). Washington, DC: National Association for the Education of Young Children.

Baumrind, D. (1980). New directions in socialization research. *American Psychologist, 35,* 639-652.

Baumrind, D. (1991). Effective parenting during the early adolescent transition. In P. A. Cowan & M. Hetherington (Eds.), *Family transitions* (pp. 111–163). Hillsdale, NJ: Erlbaum.

Baxter, J., Shetterly, S., Eby, C., Mason, L., Cortese, C., & Hamman, R. (1998). Social network factors associated with perceived quality of life: The San Luis Valley Health and Aging Study. *Journal of Aging & Health, 10,* 287–310.

Baydar, N., & Brooks-Gunn, J. (1991). Effects of maternal employment and child-care arrangements on preschoolers' cognitive and behavioral outcomes: Evidence from the children of the National Longitudinal Survey of Youth. *Developmental Psychology, 27,* 932–945.

Baydar, N., Brooks-Gunn, J., & Furstenberg, F. F. (1993). Early warning signs of functional illiteracy: Predictors in childhood and adolescence. *Child Development, 64,* 815–829.

Bayley, N. (1969). *Bayley scales of infant development.* New York: Psychological Corporation.

Beaty, L. (1999). Identity development of homosexual youth and parental and familial influences on the coming out process. *Adolescence, 34,* 597–601.

Beautrais, A., Joyce, P., & Mulder, R. (1999). Personality traits and cognitive styles as risk factors for serious suicide attempts among young people. *Suicide & Life-Threatening Behavior, 29,* 37–47.

Beck, A., Brown, G., Berchick, R., Stewart, B., & Steer, R. (1990). Relationship between hopelessness and ultimate suicide: A replication with psychiatric outpatients. *American Journal of Psychiatry, 147,* 190–195.

Bedeian, A. G., Ferris, G. R., & Kacmar, K. M. (1992). Age, tenure, and job satisfaction: A tale of two perspectives. *Journal of Vocational Behavior, 40,* 33–48.

Bedford, V. (1995). Sibling relationships in middle and old age. In R. Blieszner & V. H. Bedford (Eds.), *Handbook of aging and the family.* Westport, CT: Greenwood Press.

Bee, H. L., Barnard, K. E., Eyres, S. J., Gray, C. A., Hammond, M. A., Spietz, A. L., Snyder, C., & Clark, B. (1982). Prediction of IQ and language skill from perinatal status, child performance, family characteristics, and mother-infant interaction. *Child Development, 53,* 1135–1156.

Beekman, A., Copeland, J., & Prince, M. (1999). Review of community prevalence of depression in later life. *British Journal of Psychiatry, 174,* 307–311.

Beem, E., Hooijkaas, H., Cleriren, M., Schut, H., Garssen, B., Croon, M., Jabaaij, L., Goodkin, K., Wind, H., & de Vries, M. (1999). The immunological and psychological effects of bereavement: Does grief counseling really make a difference? A pilot study. *Psychiatry Research, 85,* 81–93.

Beilke, J., & Yssel, N. (1999). The chilly climate for students with disabilities in higher education. *College Student Journal, 33,* 364–371.

Belgrave, L. L., Wykle, M. L., & Choi, J. M. (1993). Health, double jeopardy, and culture: The use of institutionalization by African-Americans. *The Gerontologist, 33,* 379–385.

Bell, L. G., & Bell, D. C. (1982). Family climate and the role of the female adolescent: Determinants of adolescent functioning. *Family Relations, 31,* 519–527.

Bellantoni, M. F., & Blackman, M. R. (1996). Menopause and its consequences. In E. L. Schneider & J. W. Rowe (Eds.), *Handbook of the biology of aging* (4th ed.) (pp. 415–430). San Diego, CA: Academic Press.

Belsky, J. (1985). Prepared statement on the effects of day care. In Select Committee on Children, Youth, and Families, House of Representatives, 98th Congress, Second Session, *Improving child care services: What can be done?* Washington, DC: U.S. Government Printing Office.

Belsky, J. (1992). Consequences of child care for children's development: A deconstructionist view. In A. Booth (Ed.), *Child care in the 1990s: Trends and consequences* (pp. 83–94). Hillsdale, NJ: Erlbaum.

Belsky, J., & Hsieh, K. (1998). Patterns of marital change during the early childhood years: Parent personality, coparenting, and division-of-labor correlates. *Journal of Family Psychology, 12,* 511–528.

Belsky, J., Hsieh, K., & Crnic, K. (1996). Infant positive and negative emotionality: One dimension or two? *Developmental Psychology, 32,* 289–298.

Belsky, J., Lang, M. E., & Rovine, M. (1985). Stability and change in marriage across the transition to parenthood: A second study. *Journal of Marriage and the Family, 47,* 855–865.

Belsky, J., & Rovine, M. (1988). Nonmaternal care in the first year of life and the security of infant-parent attachment. *Child Development, 59,* 157–167.

Bem, S. L. (1974). The measurement of psychological androgyny. *Journal of Consulting and Clinical Psychology, 42,* 155–162.

Bender, B. G., Harmon, R. J., Linden, M. G., & Robinson, A. (1995). Psychosocial adaptation of 39 adolescents with sex chromosome abnormalities. *Pediatrics, 96,* 302–308.

Bender, K. (1999). Assessing antidepressant safety in the elderly. *Psychiatric Times, 16.* [Online archives]. Retrieved February 7, 2001 from the World Wide Web: http://www.mhsource.com/pt/p990151.html

Bendersky, M., & Lewis, M. (1994). Environmental risk, biological risk, and developmental outcome. *Developmental Psychology, 30,* 484–494.

Benenson, J. F. (1994). Ages four to six years: Changes in the structures of play networks of girls and boys. *Merrill-Palmer Quarterly, 40,* 478–487.

Benenson, J., & Benarroch, D. (1998). Gender differences in responses to friends' hypothetical greater success. *Journal of Early Adolescence, 18,* 192–208.

Bengtson, V. L. (1985). Diversity and symbolism in grandparent roles. In V. L. Bengtson & J. F. Robertson (Eds.), *Grandparenthood* (pp. 11–26). Beverly Hills, CA: Sage.

Bengtson, V. L., Cuellar, J. B., & Ragan, P. K. (1977). Stratum contrasts and similarities in attitudes toward death. *Journal of Gerontology, 32,* 76–88.

Bengtson, V., Rosenthal, C., & Burton, L. (1990). Families and aging: Diversity and heterogeneity. In R. H. Binstock & L. K. George (Eds.), *Handbook of aging and the social sciences* (3rd ed.) (pp. 263–287). San Diego, CA: Academic Press.

Bengtson, V., Rosenthal, C., & Burton, L. (1996). Paradoxes of families and aging. In R. H. Binstock & L. K. George (Eds.), *Handbook of aging and the social sciences* (4th ed.) (pp. 253–282). San Diego, CA: Academic Press.

Bennett, M. (1997). A longitudinal study of wellbeing in widowed women. *International Journal of Geriatric Psychiatry, 12,* 61–66.

Bennett, M. (1998). Longitudinal changes in mental and physical health among elderly, recently widowed men. *Mortality, 3,* 265–273.

Benoit, D., & Parker, K. C. H. (1994). Stability and transmission of attachment across three generations. *Child Development, 65,* 1444–1456.

Benshoff, J., & Lewis, H. (1993). *Nontraditional College Students.* (ERIC Digest No. ED 34 7483 92)

Berg, J., & Lipson, J. (1999). Information sources, menopause beliefs, and health complaints of midlife Filipinas. *Health, 20,* 81–92.

Berg, S. (1996). Aging, behavior, and terminal decline. In J. E. Birren & K. W. Schaie (Eds.), *Handbook of the psychology of aging* (4th ed.) (pp. 323–337). San Diego, CA: Academic Press.

Bergeman, C. S., Chipuer, H. M., Plomin, R., Pedersen, N. L., McClearn, G. E., Nesselroade, J. R., Costa, P. T., & McCrae, R. R. (1993). Genetic and environmental effects on openness to experience, agreeableness, and conscientiousness: An adoption/twin study. *Journal of Personality, 61,* 159–179.

Bergeson, T., & Trehub, S. (1999). Mothers' singing to infants and preschool children. *Infant Behavior & Development, 22,* 53–64.

Berkman, L. F. (1985). The relationship of social networks and social support to morbidity and mortality. In S. Coen & S. L. Syme (Eds.), *Social support and health* (pp. 241–262). Orlando, FL: Academic Press.

Berkman, L. F., & Breslow, L. (1983). *Health and ways of living: The Alameda County Study.* New York: Oxford University Press.

Berkowitz, G. S., Skovron, M. L., Lapinski, R. H., & Berkowitz, R. L. (1990). Delayed childbearing and the outcome of pregnancy. *New England Journal of Medicine, 322,* 659–664.

Berliner, D., & Biddle, B. (1997). *The manufactured crisis: Myths, fraud, and the attack on America's public schools.* New York: Addison-Wesley.

Berman, W. H., Marcus, L., & Berman, E. R. (1994). Attachment in marital relations. In M. B. Sperling & W. H. Berman (Eds.), *Attachment in adults: Clinical and developmental perspectives* (pp. 204–231). New York: Guilford Press.

Berndt, T. J. (1992). Friendship and friends' influence in adolescence. *Current Directions in Psychological Science, 1,* 156–159.

Berndt, T. J., & Keefe, K. (1995a). Friends' influence on adolescents' adjustment to school. *Child Development, 66,* 1312–1329.

Berndt, T. J., & Keefe, K. (1995b, March). *Friends' influence on school adjustment: A motivational analysis.* Paper presented at the biennial meetings of the Society for Research in Child Development, Indianapolis, IN.

Berne, L., & Huberman, B. (1996, February). Sexuality education works: Here's proof. *Education Digest,* 25–29.

Bernhard, J., Lefebvre, M., Kilbride, K., Chud, G., & Lange, R. (1998). Troubled relationships in early childhood education: Parent-teacher interactions in ethnoculturally diverse child care settings. *Early Education & Development, 9,* 5–28.

Berninger, V., Abbott, R., Zook, D., Ogier, S., et al. (1999). Early intervention for reading disabilities: Teaching the alphabet principle in a connectionist framework. *Journal of Learning Disabilities, 32,* 491–503.

Bertenthal, B. I., & Campos, J. J. (1987). New directions in the study of early experience. *Child Development, 58,* 560–567.

Betancourt, H., & Lopez, S. R. (1993). The study of culture, ethnicity, and race in American psychology. *American Psychologist, 48,* 629–637.

Betancourt, L., Fischer, R., Gianetta, J., Malmud, E., Brodsky, N. & Hurt, H. (1999). Problem-solving ability of inner-city children with and without in utero cocaine exposure. *Journal of Developmental Disabilities, 20,* 418–424.

Betz, E. L. (1984). A study of career patterns of women college graduates. *Journal of Vocational Behavior, 24,* 249–263.

Betz, N. E., & Fitzgerald, L. F. (1987). *The career psychology of women.* Orlando, FL: Academic Press.

Bhatt, R. S., & Rovee-Collier, C. (1996). Infants' forgetting of correlated attributes and object recognition. *Child Development, 67,* 172–187.

Bial, M. (1971). *Liberal Judaism at home.* New York: Union of American Hebrew Congregations.

Bialystok, E. (1997). Effects of bilingualism and biliteracy on children's emerging concepts of print. *Developmental Psychology, 33.*

Bialystok, E., & Majumder, S. (1998). The relationship between bilingualism and the development of cognitive processes in problem solving. *Applied Psycholinguistics, 19,* 69–85.

Bialystok, E., Shenfield, T., & Codd, J. (2000). Languages, scripts, and the environment: Factors in developing concepts of print. *Developmental Psychology, 36,* 66–76.

Bianchi, A. (1993, January–February). Older drivers: The good, the bad, and the iffy. *Harvard Magazine,* pp. 12–13.

Biblarz, T. J., Bengtson, V. L., & Bucur, A. (1996). Social mobility across three generations. *Journal of Marriage and the Family, 58,* 188–200.

Biedenharn, P. J., & Normoyle, J. B. (1991). Elderly community residents' reactions to the nursing home: An analysis of nursing home-related beliefs. *The Gerontologist, 31,* 107–115.

Bigelow, K., & Lutzker, J. (1998). Using video to teach planned activities to parents reported for child abuse. *Child & Family Behavior Therapy, 20,* 1–14.

Bigler, E. D., Johnson, S. C., Jackson, C., & Blatter, D. D. (1995). Aging, brain size, and IQ. *Intelligence, 21,* 109–119.

Bigler, R., & Liben, S. (1993). The role of attitudes and interventions in gender-schematic processing. *Child Development, 61,* 1440–1452.

Billy, J. O. G., Brewster, K. L., & Grady, W. R. (1994). Contextual effects on the sexual behavior of adolescent women. *Journal of Marriage and the Family, 56,* 387–404.

Binet, A., & Simon, T. (1905). Méthodes nouvelles pour le diagnostic du niveau intellectuel des anormaux [New methods for diagnosing the intellectual level of the abnormal]. *L'Anée Psychologique, 11,* 191–244.

Bingham, C. R., Miller, B. C., & Adams, G. R. (1990). Correlates of age at first sexual intercourse in a national sample of young women. *Journal of Adolescent Research, 5,* 18–33.

Birch, D. (1998). The adolescent parent: A fifteen-year longitudinal study of school-age mothers and their children. *International Journal of Adolescent Medicine & Health, 19,* 141–153.

Birch, E., Garfield, S., Hoffman, D., Uauy, R., & Birch, D. (2000). A randomized controlled trial of early dietary supply of longchain polyunsaturated fatty acids and mental development in term infants. *Developmental Medicine & Child Neurology, 42,* 174–181.

Biringen, Z. (2000). Emotional availability: Conceptualization and research findings. *American Journal of Orthopsychiatry, 70,* 104–114.

Biro, F. M., Lucky, A. W., Huster, G. A., & Morrison, J. A. (1995). Pubertal staging in boys. *Journal of Pediatrics, 127,* 100–102.

Birren, J. E., & Fisher, L. M. (1995). Aging and speed of behavior: Possible consequences for psychological functioning. *Annual Review of Psychology, 56,* 329–353.

Birren, J. E., & Schroots, J. J. F. (1996). History, concepts, and theory in the psychology of aging. In J. R. Birren & K. W. Schaie (Eds.), *Handbook of the psychology of aging* (4th ed.) (pp. 3–23). San Diego, CA: Academic Press.

Biswas, M. K., & Craigo, S. D. (1994). The course and conduct of normal labor and delivery. In A. H. DeCherney & M. L. Pernoll (Eds.), *Current obstetric and gynecologic diagnosis & treatment* (pp. 202–227). Norwalk, CT: Appleton & Lange.

Bittner, S., & Newberger, E. (1981). Pediatric understanding of child abuse and neglect. *Pediatric Review, 2,* 198.

Black, D., & Moyer, T. (1998). Clinical features and psychiatric comorbidity of subjects with pathological gambling behavior. *Psychiatric Services, 49,* 1434–1439.

Black, K., & McCartney, K. (1997). Adolescent females' security with parents predicts the quality of peer interactions. *Social Development, 6,* 91–110.

Black, K. A., & McCartney, K. (1995, March). *Associations between adolescent attachment to parents and peer interactions.* Paper presented at the biennial meetings of the Society for Research in Child Development, Indianapolis, IN.

Black, S., Markides, K., & Miller, T. (1998). Correlates of depressive symptomatology among older community-dwelling Mexican Americans: The hispanic EPESE. *Journals of Gerontology: Series B: Psychological Sciences & Social Sciences, 53B,* S198–S208.

Blackman, J. A. (1990). Update on AIDS, CMV, and herpes in young children: Health, developmental, and educational issues. In M. Wolraich & D. K. Routh (Eds.), *Advances in developmental and behavioral pediatrics* (Vol. 9) (pp. 33–58). London: Jessica Kingsley Publishers.

Blackwell, D., & Lichter, D. (2000). Mate selection among married and cohabiting couples. *Journal of Family Issues, 21,* 275–302.

Blair, S. L., & Johnson, M. P. (1992). Wives' perceptions of the fairness of the division of household labor: The intersection of housework and ideology. *Journal of Marriage and the Family, 54,* 570–581.

Blair, S. N., Kohl, H. W., III, Barlow, C. E., Paffenbarger, R. S., Gibbons, L. W., & Macera, C. A. (1995). Changes in physical fitness and all-cause mortality. *Journal of the American Medical Association, 273,* 1093–1098.

Blake, I. K. (1994). Language development and socialization in young African-American children. In P. M. Greenfield & R. R. Cocking (Eds.), *Cross-cultural roots of minority child development* (pp. 167–195). Hillsdale, NJ: Erlbaum.

Blakemore, J., LaRue, A., Olejnik, A. (1979). Sex-appropriate toy preference and the ability to conceptualize toys as sex-role related. *Developmental Psychology, 15,* 339–340.

Blakeslee, S. (April 13, 1994). A genetic factor may help to explain variations in lung cancer rates. *New York Times,* p. B10.

Blanchard-Fields, F., Chen, Y., Schocke, M., & Hertzog, C. (1998). Evidence for content-specificity of causal attributions across the adult life span. *Aging, Neuropsychology, & Cognition, 5,* 241–263.

Blaszczynski, A. (1999). Pathological gambling and obsessive-compulsive spectrum disorders. *Psychological Reports, 84,* 107–113.

Blatter, D. D., Bigler, E. D., Gale, S. D., Johnson, S. C., Anderson, C. V., Burnett, B. M., Parker, N., Kurth, S., & Horn, S. (1995). Quantitative volumetric analysis of brain MR: Normative database spanning five decades (16–65). *American Journal of Neuroradiology, 16,* 241–251.

Blau, F. D., & Ferber, M. A. (1991). Career plans and expectations of young women and men: The earnings gap and labor force participation. *The Journal of Human Resources, 26,* 581–607.

Blau, G. (1996). Adolescent depression and suicide. In G. Blau & T. Gullotta (Eds.), *Adolescent dysfunctional behavior: Causes, interventions, and prevention* (pp. 187–205). Newbury Park, CA: Sage.

Blazer, D., Hybels, C., Simonsick, E., & Hanlon, J. (2000). Marked differences in antidepressant use by race in an elderly community sample: 1986–1996. *American Journal of Psychiatry, 157,* 1089–1094.

Blazer, D., Landerman, L., Hays, J., Simonsick, E., & Saunders, W. (1998). Symptoms of depression among community-dwelling elderly African American and White older adults. *Psychological Medicine, 28,* 1311–1320.

Blieszner, R., & Adams, R. G. (1992). *Adult friendship.* Newbury Park, CA: Sage.

Block, J. (1971). *Lives through time.* Berkeley, CA: Bancroft.

Block, J., & Robins, R. W. (1993). A longitudinal study of consistency and change in self-esteem from early adolescence to early adulthood. *Child Development, 64,* 909–923.

Bloom, B. L., White, S. W., & Asher, S. J. (1979). Marital disruption as a stressful life event. In C. Levinger & O. C. Moles (Eds.), *Divorce and separation: Context, causes, and consequences* (pp. 184–200). New York: Basic Books.

Bloom, L. (1973). *One word at a time.* The Hague: Mouton.

Bloom, L. (1991). *Language development from two to three.* Cambridge, England: Cambridge University Press.

Bloom, L. (1993). *The transition from infancy to language: Acquiring the power of expression.* Cambridge, England: Cambridge University Press.

Bluck, S., Levine, L., & Laulhere, T. (1999). Autobiographical remembering and hypermnesia: A comparison of older and younger adults. *Psychology & Aging, 14,* 671–682.

Blumberg, J. B. (1996). Status and functional impact of nutrition in older adults. In E. L. Schneider & J. W. Rowe (Eds.), *Handbook of the biology of aging* (4th ed.) (pp. 393–414). San Diego, CA: Academic Press.

Blumenthal, J. A., Emery, C. F., Madden, D. J., Schniebolk, S., Walsh-Riddle, M., George, L. K., McKee, D. C., Higginbotham, M. B., Cobb, R. R., & Coleman, R. E. (1991). Long-term effects of exercise on physiological functioning in older men and women. *Journals of Gerontology: Psychological Sciences, 46,* P352–361.

Blumstein, P., & Schwartz, P. (1983). *American couples.* New York: Morrow.

Blustein, D., Phillips, S., Jobin-Davis, K., & Finkelberg, S. (1997). A theory-building investigation of the school-to-work transition. *Counseling Psychology, 25,* 364–402.

Bodenmann, G., Widmer, K., & Cina, A. (1999). The Couples Coping Enhancement Training (CCET): Subjective appraisal of changes within 6 months. *Verhaltenstherapie, 9,* 87–94.

Bogenschneider, K., Wu, M., Raffaelli, M., & Tsay, J. (1998). "Other teens drink, but not my kid": Does parental awareness of adolescent alcohol use protect adolescents from risky consequences? *Journal of Marriage & the Family, 60,* 356–373.

Bohman, M., & Sigvardsson, S. (1990). Outcome in adoption: Lessons from longitudinal studies. In D. M. Brodzinsky (Ed.), *The psychology of adoption* (pp. 93–106). New York: Oxford University Press.

Boldizar, J. (1991). Assessing sex-typing and androgyny in children. *Developmental Psychology, 27,* 506–535.

Bolger, K. E., Patterson, C. J., Thompson, W. W., & Kupersmidt, J. B. (1995). Psychosocial adjustment among children experiencing persistent and intermittent family economic hardship. *Child Development, 66,* 1107–1129.

Bonanno, G., Znoj, H., Siddique, H., & Horowitz, M. (1999). Verbal-autonomic dissociation and adaptation to midlife conjugal loss: A follow-up at 25 months. *Cognitive Therapy & Research, 23,* 605–624.

Bond, J., & Coleman, P. (Eds.). (1990). *Aging in society.* London: Sage.

Bond, L., Braskamp, D., & Roeber, E. (1996). *The status report of the assessment programs in the United States.* Oakbrook, IL: North Central Regional Educational Laboratory. ERIC Document No. ED 401 333.

Bond, M. H., Nakazato, H., & Shiraishi, D. (1975). Universality and distinctiveness in dimensions of Japanese person perception. *Journal of Cross-Cultural Psychology, 6,* 346–357.

Bondevik, M., & Skogstad, A. (1998). The oldest old, ADL, social network, and loneliness. *Western Journal of Nursing Research, 20,* 325–343.

Bong, M. (1998). Tests of the internal/external frames of reference model with subject-specific academic self-efficacy and frame-specific academic self-concepts. *Journal of Educational Psychology, 90,* 102–110.

Boone, R., Higgins, K., Notari, A., & Stump, C. (1996). Hypermedia pre-reading lessons: Learner-centered software for kindergarten. *Journal of Computing in Childhood Education, 7,* 39–70.

Borkenau, P., & Ostendorf, F. (1990). Comparing exploratory and confirmatory factor analysis: A study on the five-factor model of personality. *Personality and Individual Differences, 11,* 515–524.

Bornholt, L., & Goodnow, J. (1999). Cross-generation perceptions of academic competence: Parental expectations and adolescent self-disclosure. *Journal of Adolescent Research, 14,* 427–447.

Bornstein, M. H. (1992). Perception across the life span. In M. H. Bornstein & M. E. Lamb (Eds.), *Developmental psychology: An advanced textbook* (3rd ed.) (pp. 155–210). Hillsdale, NJ: Erlbaum.

Bosch, L., & Sebastian-Galles, N. (1997). Native-language recognition abilities in 4-month-old infants from monolingual and bilingual environments. *Cognition, 65,* 33–69.

Bossé, R., Aldwin, C. M., Levenson, M. R., & Workman-Daniels, K. (1991). How stressful is retirement? Findings from the normative aging study. *Journals of Gerontology: Psychological Sciences, 46,* P9–14.

Bosworth, H., Siegler, I., Brummett, B., Barefoot, J., Williams, R., Clapp-Channing, N., & Mark, D. (2000, August). *Health-related quality of life in a coronary artery sample.* Paper presented at the annual meeting of the American Psychological Association. Washington, DC.

Botwinick, J., & Storandt, M. (1974). *Memory, related functions and age.* Springfield, IL: Charles C. Thomas.

Bouchard, T. J., Jr., & McGue, M. (1981). Familial studies of intelligence: A review. *Science, 212,* 1055–1059.

Bourreille, C. (1999). Diana/Diana. *Cahiers Jungiens de Psychanalyse, 96,* 75–76.

Bowlby, J. (1969). *Attachment and loss: Vol. 1. Attachment.* New York: Basic Books.

Bowlby, J. (1973). *Attachment and loss: Vol. 2. Separation, anxiety, and anger.* New York: Basic Books.

Bowlby, J. (1980). *Attachment and loss: Vol. 3. Loss, sadness, and depression.* New York: Basic Books.

Bowlby, J. (1988a). Developmental psychiatry comes of age. *American Journal of Psychiatry, 145,* 1–10.

Bowlby, J. (1988b). *A secure base.* New York: Basic Books.

Bowler, D., Briskman, J., & Grice, S. (1999). Experimenter effects on children's understanding of false drawings and false beliefs. *Journal of Genetic Psychology, 160,* 443–460.

Bowman, P. J. (1991). Joblessness. In J. J. Jackson (Ed.), *Life in black America* (pp. 156–178). Newbury Park, CA: Sage.

Boyatzis, C. J., Matillo, G., Nesbitt, K., & Cathey, G. (1995, March). *Effects of "The Mighty Morphin Power Rangers" on children's aggression and prosocial behavior.* Paper presented at the biennial meetings of the Society for Research in Child Development, Indianapolis, IN.

Braam, A., Beekman, A., Deeg, D., Smit, J., & van Tilburg, W. (1997). Religiosity as a protective or prognostic factor of depression in later life: Results from a community survey in the Netherlands. *Longitudinal Aging Study, 96,* 199–205.

Bradley, R. H., Caldwell, B. M., Rock, S. L., Barnard, K. E., Gray, C., Hammond, M. A., Mitchell, S., Siegel, L., Ramey, C. D., Gottfried, A. W., & Johnson, D. L. (1989). Home environment and cognitive development in the first 3 years of life: A collaborative study involving six sites and three ethnic groups in North America. *Developmental Psychology, 25,* 217–235.

Bradmetz, J. (1999). Precursors of formal thought: A longitudinal study. *British Journal of Developmental Psychology, 17,* 61–81.

Brady, K., & Eisler, R. (1999). Sex and gender in the college classroom: A quantitative analysis of faculty-student interactions and perceptions. *Journal of Educational Psychology, 91,* 124–145.

Brand, A., & Brinich, P. (1999). Behavior problems and mental health contacts in adopted, foster, and nonadopted children. *Journal of Child Psychology & Psychiatry & Allied Disciplines, 40,* 1221–1229.

Brandon, P. (1999). Determinants of self-care arrangements among school-age children. *Children & Youth Services Review, 21,* 497–520.

Brandtstädter, J., & Baltes-Götz, B. (1990). Personal control over development and quality of life perspectives in adulthood. In P. Baltes & M. M. Baltes (Eds.), *Successful aging* (pp. 197–224). Cambridge, England: Cambridge University Press.

Brandtstädter, J., & Greve, W. (1994). The aging self: Stabilizing and protective processes. *Developmental Review, 14,* 52–80.

Braten, I., & Olaussen, B. (1998). The learning and study strategies of Norwegian first-year college students. *Learning & Individual Differences, 10,* 309–327.

Braun, K., & Nichols, R. (1997). Death and dying in four Asian American cultures: A descriptive study. *Death Studies, 21,* 327–359.

Braveman, N. S. (1987). Immunity and aging immunologic and behavioral perspectives. In M. W. Riley, J. D. Matarazzo, & A. Baum (Eds.), *Perspectives in behavioral medicine: The aging dimension* (pp. 94–124). Hillsdale, NJ: Erlbaum.

Bray, D. W., & Howard, A. (1983). The AT&T longitudinal studies of managers. In K. W. Schaie (Ed.), *Longitudinal studies of adult psychological development* (pp. 266–312). New York: Guilford Press.

Brazelton, T. B. (1984). *Neonatal Behavioral Assessment Scale.* Philadelphia: Lippincott.

Bregman, G., & Killen, M. (1999). Adolescents' and young adults' reasoning about career choice and the role of parental influence. *Journal of Research on Adolescence, 9,* 253–275.

Brendgen, M., Vitaro, F., & Bukowski, W. (1998). Affiliation with delinquent friends: Contributions of parents, self-esteem, delinquent behavior, and rejection by peers. *Journal of Early Adolescence, 18,* 244–265.

Brener, N., Hassan, S., & Barrios, L. (1999). Suicidal ideation among college students in the United States. *Journal of Consulting & Clinical Psychology, 67,* 1004–1008.

Brennan, F., & Ireson, J. (1997). Training phonological awareness: A study to evaluate the effects of a program of metalinguistic games in kindergarten. *Reading & Writing, 9,* 241–263.

Brenner, V. (1997). Psychology of computer use: XLVII. Parameters of Internet use. *Psychological Reports, 80,* 879–882.

Breslau, N., & Chilcoat, H. (2000). Psychiatric sequelae of low birth weight at 11 years of age. *Biological Psychiatry, 47,* 1005–1011.

Breslau, N., DelDotto, J. E., Brown, G. G., Kumar, S., Ezhuthachan, S., Hufnagle, K. G., & Peterson, E. L. (1994). A gradient relationship between low birth weight and IQ at age 6 years. *Archives of Pediatric and Adolescent Medicine, 2148,* 377–383.

Breslow, L., & Breslow, N. (1993). Health practices and disability: Some evidence from Alameda County. *Preventive Medicine, 22,* 86–95.

Bretscher, M., Rummans, T., Sloan, J., Kaur, J., Bartlett, A., Borkenhagen, L., & Loprinzi, C. (1999). Quality of life in hospice patients: A pilot study. *Psychosomatics, 40,* 309–313.

Briggs, R. (1990). Biological aging. In J. Bond & P. Coleman (Eds.), *Aging in society* (pp. 48–61). London: Sage.

Brock, D. B., Guralnik, J. M., & Brody, J. A. (1990). Demography and the epidemiology of aging in the United States. In E. L. Schneider & J. W. Rowe (Eds.), *Handbook of the biology of aging* (3rd ed.) (pp. 3–23). San Diego, CA: Academic Press.

Brockington, I. (1996). *Motherhood and mental health.* Oxford, England: Oxford University Press.

Brody, E. M., Litvin, S. J., Albert, S. M., & Hoffman, C. J. (1994). Marital status of daughters and patterns of parent care. *Journals of Gerontology: Social Sciences, 49,* S95–103.

Brody, E. M., Litvin, S. J., Hoffman, C., & Kleban, M. H. (1992). Differential effects of daughters' marital status on their parent care experiences. *The Gerontologist, 32,* 58–67.

Brody, G. H., Stoneman, Z., & Flor, D. (1995). Linking family processes and academic competence among rural African American youths. *Journal of Marriage and the Family, 47,* 567–579.

Brody, J. E. (April 20, 1994). Making a strong case for antioxidants. *New York Times,* p. B9.

Brody, J. E. (October 4, 1995). Personal health. *New York Times,* p. B7.

Brody, J. E. (February 28, 1996). Good habits outweigh genes as key to a healthy old age. *New York Times,* p. B9.

Brody, N. (1992). *Intelligence* (2nd ed.). San Diego, CA: Academic Press.

Bronfenbrenner, U. (1979). *The ecology of human development.* Cambridge, MA: Harvard University Press.

Bronfenbrenner, U. (1989). Ecological systems theory. *Annals of Child Development, 6,* 187–249.

Bronfenbrenner, U. (1993). The ecology of cognitive development: Research models and fugitive findings. In R. H. Wozniak and K. W. Fischer (Eds.), *Development in context: Acting and thinking in specific environments.* Hillsdale, NJ: Erlbaum.

Brook, J., Whiteman, M., Finch, S., & Cohen, P. (2000). Longitudinally foretelling drug use in the late twenties: Adolescent personality and social-environmental antecedents. *Journal of Genetic Psychology, 161,* 37–51.

Brooks-Gunn, J. (1987). Pubertal processes and girls' psychological adaptation. In R. M. Lerner & T. T. Foch (Eds.), *Biological-psychosocial interactions in early adolescence* (pp. 123–154). Hillsdale, NJ: Erlbaum.

Brooks-Gunn, J. (1995). Children in families in communities: Risk and intervention in the Bronfenbrenner tradition. In P. Moen, G. H. Elder, Jr., & K. Lüscher (Eds.), *Examining lives in context: Perspectives on the ecology of human development* (pp. 467–519). Washington, DC: American Psychological Association.

Brooks-Gunn, J., Guo, G., & Furstenberg, F. F., Jr. (1993). Who drops out of and who continues beyond high school? A 20-year follow-up of black urban youth. *Journal of Research on Adolescence, 3,* 271–294.

Brooks-Gunn, J., Klebanov, P., Liaw, F., & Spiler, D. (1993). Enhancing the development of low birthweight, premature infants: Changes in cognition and behavior over the first three years. *Child Development, 64,* 736–753.

Brooks-Gunn, J., & Reiter, E. O. (1990). The role of pubertal processes. In S. S. Feldman & G. R. Elliott (Eds.), *At the threshold: The developing adolescent* (pp. 16–53). Cambridge, MA: Harvard University Press.

Brooks-Gunn, J., & Warren, M. P. (1985). The effects of delayed menarche in different contexts: Dance and nondance students. *Journal of Youth and Adolescence, 13,* 285–300.

Brown, A., & Day, J. (1983). Macrorules for summarizing text: The development of expertise. *Journal of Verbal Learning and Verbal Behavior, 22,* 1–14.

Brown, A. S., Jones, E. M., & Davis, T. L. (1995). Age differences in conversational source monitoring. *Psychology and Aging, 10,* 111–122.

Brown, B. B. (1990). Peer groups and peer cultures. In S. S. Feldman & G. R. Elliott (Eds.), *At the threshold: The developing adolescent* (pp. 171–196). Cambridge, MA: Harvard University Press.

Brown, B. B., Dolcini, M. M., & Leventhal, A. (1995, March). *The emergence of peer crowds: Friend or foe to adolescent health?* Paper presented at the biennial meetings of the Society for Research in Child Development, Indianapolis, IN.

Brown, B. B., & Huang, B. (1995). Examining parenting practices in different peer contexts: Implications for adolescent trajectories. In L. J. Crockett & A. C. Crouter (Eds.), *Pathways through adolescence* (pp. 151–174). Mahwah, NJ: Erlbaum.

Brown, B. B., Mory, M. S., & Kinney, D. (1994). Casting adolescent crowds in a relational perspective: Caricature, channel, and context. In R. Montemayor, G. R. Adams, & T. P. Gullotta (Eds.), *Personal relationships during adolescence* (pp. 123–167). Thousand Oaks, CA: Sage.

Brown, C. (1997). Sex differences in the career development of urban African American adolescents. *Journal of Career Development, 23,* 295–304.

Brown, G., & Dixson, A. (2000). The development of behavioral sex differences in infant rhesus macaques. *Primates, 41,* 63–77.

Brown, G. W. (1989). Life events and measurement. In G. W. Brown & T. O. Harris (Eds.), *Life events and illness* (pp. 3–45). New York: Guilford Press.

Brown, G. W. (1993). Life events and affective disorder: Replications and limitations. *Psychosomatic Medicine, 55,* 248–259.

Brown, G. W., & Harris, T. (1978). *Social origins of depression.* New York: Free Press.

Brown, J., Bakeman, R., Coles, C., Sexson, W., & Demi, A. (1998). Maternal drug use during pregnancy: Are preterm and full-term infants affected differently? *Developmental Psychology, 34,* 540–554.

Brown, L., Karrison, T., & Cibils, L. A. (1994). Mode of delivery and perinatal results in breech presentation. *American Journal of Obstetrics and Gynecology, 171,* 28–34.

Brown, R. (1973). *A first language: The early stages.* Cambridge, MA: Harvard University Press.

Brownell, C. A. (1990). Peer social skills in toddlers: Competencies and constraints illustrated by same-age and mixed-age interaction. *Child Development, 61,* 836–848.

Brubaker, T. H. (1990). Families in later life: A burgeoning research area. *Journal of Marriage and the Family, 52,* 959–981.

Bruck, M., Ceci, S. J., Francoeur, E., & Barr, R. (1995). "I hardly cried when I got my shot!" Influencing children's reports about a visit to their pediatrician. *Child Development, 66,* 193–208.

Bruer, J. (1999). *The myth of the first three years.* New York: Free Press.

Bruni, F. (April 3, 1996). A historic shift. Federal ruling allows doctors to prescribe drugs to end life. *New York Times,* pp. A1, C18.

Bryant, P., MacLean, M., & Bradley, L. (1990). Rhyme, language, and children's reading. *Applied Psycholinguistics, 11,* 237–252.

Bryant, P. E., MacLean, M., Bradley, L. L., & Crossland, J. (1990). Rhyme and alliteration, phoneme detection, and learning to read. *Developmental Psychology, 26,* 429–438.

Bryant, S., & Rakowski, W. (1992). Predictors of mortality among elderly African-Americans. *Research on Aging, 14,* 50–67.

Buchanan, C. M., Maccoby, E. E., & Dornbusch, S. M. (1991). Caught between parents: Adolescents' experience in divorced homes. *Child Development, 62,* 1008–1029.

Buchner, D. M., Beresford, S. A. A., Larson, E. B., LaCroix, A. Z., & Wagner, E. H. (1992). Effects of physical activity on health status in older adults II: Intervention studies. *Annual Review of Public Health, 13,* 469–488.

Buhrmester, D. (1992). The developmental courses of sibling and peer relationships. In F. Boer & J. Dunn (Eds.), *Children's sibling relationships: Developmental and clinical issues.* Hillsdale, NJ: Erlbaum.

Buhrmester, D., & Furman, W. (1990). Perceptions of sibling relationships during middle childhood and adolescence. *Child Development, 61,* 1387–1398.

Bukowski, W., Sippola, L., & Hoza, B. (1999). Same and other: Interdependency between participation in same- and other-sex friendships. *Journal of Youth & Adolescence, 28,* 439–459.

Bulcroft, R. A., & Bulcroft, K. A. (1991). The nature and functions of dating in later life. *Research on Aging, 13,* 244–260.

Bulkeley, W. (1998, September 16). Education: Kaplan plans a law school via the Web. *Wall Street Journal,* B1.

Bullock, M., & Lütkenhaus, P. (1990). Who am I? Self-understanding in toddlers. *Merrill-Palmer Quarterly, 36,* 217–238.

Bumpass, L. L., & Aquilino, W. S. (1995). *A social map of midlife: Family and work over the middle life course.* Report of the MacArthur Foundation research network on successful midlife development, Vero Beach, FL.

Burgess, N. J. (1995). Looking back, looking forward: African American families in sociohistorical perspective. In B. B. Ingoldsby & S. Smith (Eds.), *Families in multicultural perspective* (pp. 321–334). New York: Guilford Press.

Burgess, S. (1997). The role of shared reading in the development of phonological awareness: A longitudinal study of middle to upper class children. *Early Child Development & Care, 127/128,* 191–199.

Buriel, R., Perez, W., DeMent, T., Chavez, D., & Moran, V. (1998). The relationship of language brokering to academic performance, biculturalism, and self-efficacy among Latino adolescents. *Hispanic Journal of Behavioral Sciences, 20,* 283–297.

Burke, L., & Follingstad, D. (1999). Violence in lesbian and gay relationships: Theory, prevalence, and correlational factors. *Clinical Psychology Review, 19,* 487–512.

Burkham, D., Lee, V., & Smerdon, B. (1997). Gender and science learning early in high school: Subject matter and laboratory experiences. *American Educational Research Journal, 34,* 297–332.

Burkhauser, R. V., Butrica, B. A., & Wasylenko, M. J. (1995). Mobility patterns of older home owners. *Research on Aging, 17,* 363–384.

Burley, R., Turner, L., & Vitulli, W. (1999). The relationship between goal orientation and age among adolescents and adults. *Journal of Genetic Psychology, 160,* 84–88.

Burn, S., O'Neil, A., & Nederend, S. (1996). Childhood tomboyishness and adult androgeny. *Sex Roles, 34,* 419–428.

Burnett, J. W., Anderson, W. P., & Heppner, P. P. (1995). Gender roles and self-esteem: A consideration of environmental factors. *Journal of Counseling and Development, 73,* 323–326.

Burns, A. (1992). Mother-headed families: An international perspective and the case of Australia. *Social Policy Report, Society for Research in Child Development, 6,* 1–22.

Burton, L. (1992). Black grandparents rearing children of drug-addicted parents: Stressors, outcomes, and social service needs. *Gerontologist, 31,* 744–751.

Burton, L. M., & Bengtson, V. L. (1985). Black grandmothers: Issues of timing and continuity of roles. In V. L. Bengtson & J. F. Robertson (Eds.), *Grandparenthood* (pp. 61–78). Beverly Hills, CA: Sage.

Bus, A., & van IJzendoorn, M. (1999). Phonological awareness and early reading: A meta-analysis of experimental training studies. *Journal of Educational Psychology, 91,* 403–414.

Busch, C. M., Zonderman, A. B., & Costa, P. T., Jr. (1994). Menopausal transition and psychological distress in a nationally representative sample: Is menopause associated with psychological distress? *Journal of Aging and Health, 6,* 209–228.

Buss, A. (1989). Temperaments as personality traits. In G. A. Kohnstamm, J. E. Bates, & M. K. Rothbart (Eds.), *Temperament in childhood* (pp. 49–58). Chichester, England: Wiley.

Buss, A. H., & Plomin, R. (1984). *Temperament: Early developing personality traits.* Hillsdale, NJ: Erlbaum.

Buss, A. H., & Plomin, R. (1986). The EAS approach to temperament. In R. Plomin & J. Dunn (Eds.), *The study of temperament: Changes, continuities and challenges* (pp. 67–80). Hillsdale, NJ: Erlbaum.

Buss, D. (1999). *Evolutionary psychology.* Boston: Allyn & Bacon.

Buss, D., Abbott, M., Algleitner, A., Ahserian, A., Biaggio, A., et al. (1990). International preferences in selecting mates: A study of 37 cultures. *Journal of Cross-Cultural Psychology, 21,* 5–47.

Buss, D., & Schmitt, D. (1993). Sexual strategies theory: An evolutionary perspective on human mating. *Psychological Review, 100,* 204–232.

Bussey, K., Bandura, A. (1992). Self-regulation mechanisms governing gender development. *Child Development, 63,* 1236–1250.

Butler, R. N. (1963). The life review: An interpretation of reminiscence in the aged. *Psychiatry, 256,* 65–76.

Byrne, G., & Raphael, B. (1999). Depressive symptoms and depressive episodes in recently widowed older men. *International Psychogeriatrics, 11,* 67–74.

Byrne, G., Raphael, G., & Arnold, E. (1999). Alcohol consumption and psychological distress in recently widowed older men. *Australian & New Zealand Journal of Psychiatry, 33,* 740–747.

Byrne, M. (1998). Taking a computational approach to aging: The SPAN theory of working memory. *Psychology & Aging, 13,* 309–322.

Cahn, D., Marcotte, A., Stern, R., Arruda, J., Akshoomoff, N., & Leshko, I. (1966). The Boston Qualitative Scoring System for the Rey-Osterrieth Complex Figure: A study of children with attention deficit hyperactivity disorder. *Clinical Neuropsychologist, 10,* 397–406.

Cairns, R. B., & Cairns, B. D. (1994). *Lifelines and risks: Pathways of youth in our time.* Cambridge, England: Cambridge University Press.

California Achievement Program (1980). *Student achievement in California schools: 1979–1980 annual report: Television and student achievement.* Sacramento: California State Department of Education.

Callaghan, T. (1999). Early understanding and production of graphic symbols. *Child Development, 70,* 1314–1324.

Callahan, K., Rademacher, J., & Hildreth, B. (1998). The effect of parent participation in strategies to improve the homework performance of students who are at risk. *Remedial & Special Education, 19,* 131–141.

Camilleri, C., & Malewska-Peyre, H. (1997). Socialization and identity strategies. In J. Berry, P. Dasen, & T. Saraswathi (Eds.), *Handbook of cross-cultural psychology. Vol. 2: Basic processes and human development.* Boston: Allyn & Bacon.

Campbell, F. A., & Ramey, C. T. (1994). Effects of early intervention on intellectual and academic achievement: A follow-up study of children from low-income families. *Child Development, 65,* 684–698.

Campbell, L., Connidis, I., & Davies, L. (1999). Sibling ties in later life: A social network analysis. *Journal of Family Issues, 20,* 114–148.

Campbell, S. B., Cohn, J. F., Flanagan, C., Popper, S., & Meyers, T. (1992). Course and correlates of postpartum depression during the transition to parenthood. *Development and Psychopathology, 4,* 29–47.

Campisi, J., Dimri, G., & Hara, E. (1996). Control of replicative senescence. In E. L. Schneider & J. W. Rowe (Eds.), *Handbook of the biology of aging* (4th ed.) (pp. 121–149). San Diego, CA: Academic Press.

Caplan, G. (1964). *Principles of preventive psychiatry.* New York: Basic Books.

Capron, C., & Duyme, M. (1989). Assessment of effects of socio-economic status on IQ in a full cross-fostering study. *Nature, 340,* 552–554.

Capute, A. J., Palmer, F. B., Shapiro, B. K., Wachtel, R. C., Ross, A., & Accardo, P. J. (1984). Primitive reflex profile: A quantification of primitive reflexes in infancy. *Developmental Medicine and Child Neurology, 26*, 375–383.

Caputo, R. (1996). The effects of race and marital status on child support and work effort. *Journal of Sociology & Social Welfare, 23*, 51–68.

Carey, R. G. (1974). Living until death: A program of service and research for the terminally ill. *Hospital Progress*. (Reprinted in E. Kübler-Ross [Ed.], *Death. The final stage of growth*. Englewood Cliffs, NJ: Prentice-Hall, 1975.)

Carlson, E. A., & Sroufe, L. A. (1995). Contribution of attachment theory to developmental psychopathology. In D. Cicchetti & D. J. Conen (Eds.), *Developmental psychopathology: Vol. 1. Theory and methods* (pp. 581–617). New York: Wiley.

Carmeli, E., Reznick, A., Coleman, R., & Carmeli, V. (2000). Muscle strength and mass of lower extremities in relation to functional abilities in elderly adults. *Gerontology, 46*, 249–257.

Carnelley, K., Wortman, C., & Kessler, R. (1999). The impact of widowhood on depression: Findings from a prospective survey. *Psychological Medicine, 29*, 1111–1123.

Caron, A. J., & Caron, R. F. (1981). Processing of relational information as an index of infant risk. In S. Friedman & M. Sigman (Eds.), *Preterm birth and psychological development* (pp. 219–240). New York: Academic Press.

Carpenter, S. (2001). Teens' risky behavior is about more than race and family resources. *APA Monitor, 32*, 22–23.

Carr, S. (2000). As distance education comes of age, the challenge is keeping the students. *Chronicle of Higher Education, 46*, A39–A41.

Carrière, Y., & Pelletier, L. (1995). Factors underlying the institutionalization of elderly persons in Canada. *Journals of Gerontology: Social Sciences, 50B*, S164–S172.

Carson, D., Klee, T. & Perry, C. (1998). Comparisons of children with delayed and normal language at 24 months of age on measures of behavioral difficulties, social and cognitive development. *Infant Mental Health Journal, 19*, 59–75.

Carstensen, L. L. (1992). Social and emotional patterns in adulthood: Support for socioemotional selectivity theory. *Psychology and Aging, 7*, 331–338.

Carstensen, L. L., Gottman, J. M., & Levenson, R. W. (1995). Emotional behavior in long-term marriage. *Psychology and Aging, 10*, 149–149.

Carver, R. P. (1990). Intelligence and reading ability in grades 2–12. *Intelligence, 14*, 449–455.

Casas, J. F., & Mosher, M. (1995, March). *Relational and overt aggression in preschool: "You can't come to my birthday party unless..."* Paper presented at the biennial meeting of the Society for Research in Child Development, Indianapolis, IN.

Casasola, M., & Cohen, L. (2000). Infants' association of linguistic labels with causal actions. *Developmental Psychology, 36*, 155–168.

Case, R. (1985). *Intellectual development: Birth to adulthood*. New York: Academic Press.

Case, R. (1991). Stages in the development of the young child's first sense of self. *Developmental Review, 11*, 210–230.

Case, R. (1992). *The mind's staircase: Exploring thought and knowledge*. Hillsdale, NJ: Erlbaum.

Case, R. (1997). The development of conceptual structures. In B. Damon (General Ed.) and D. Kuhn & R. S. Siegler (Series Eds.), *Handbook of child psychology: Vol. 2. Cognitive, language, and perceptual development*. New York: Wiley.

Case, R. B., Moss, A. J., Case, N., McDermott, M., & Eberly, S. (1992). Living alone after myocardial infarction: Impact on prognosis. *Journal of the American Medical Association, 267*, 515–519.

Casey, M. B., Nuttall, R., Pezaris, E., & Benbow, C. P. (1995). Influence of spatial ability on gender differences in mathematics college entrance test scores across diverse samples. *Developmental Psychology, 31*, 697–705.

Caslyn, C., Gonzales, P., & Frase, M. (1999). *Highlights from the Third International Mathematics and Science Study*. Washington, DC: National Center for Educational Statistics.

Caspi, A. (2000). The child is father of the man: Personality continuities from childhood to adulthood. *Journal of Personality & Social Psychology, 78*, 158–172.

Caspi, A., & Elder, G. H., Jr. (1988). Childhood precursors of the life course: Early personality and life disorganization. In E. M. Hether-

ington, R. M. Lerner, & M. Perlmutter (Eds.), *Child development in life-span perspective* (pp. 115–142). Hillsdale, NJ: Erlbaum.

Caspi, A., Elder, G. H., Jr., & Bem, D. J. (1987). Moving against the world: Life-course patterns of explosive children. *Developmental Psychology, 23*, 308–313.

Caspi, A., Elder, G. H., Jr., & Bem, D. J. (1988). Moving away from the world: Life-course patterns of shy children. *Developmental Psychology, 24*, 824–831.

Caspi, A., Henry, B., McGee, R. O., Moffitt, T. E., & Silva, P. A. (1995). Temperamental origins of child and adolescent behavior problems: From age three to age fifteen. *Child Development, 66*, 55–68.

Caspi, A., Lynam, D., Moffitt, T. E., & Silva, P. A. (1993). Unraveling girls' delinquency: Biological, dispositional, and contextual contributions to adolescent misbehavior. *Developmental Psychology, 29*, 19–30.

Cassidy, J., & Berlin, L. J. (1994). The insecure/ambivalent pattern of attachment: Theory and research. *Child Development, 65*, 971–991.

Cassileth, B. R., Walsh, W. P., & Lusk, E. J. (1988). Psychosocial correlates of cancer survival: A subsequent report 3 to 8 years after cancer diagnosis. *Journal of Clinical Oncology, 6*, 1753–1759.

Castellino, D., Lerner, J., Lerner, R., & von Eye, A. (1998). Maternal employment and education: Predictors of young adolescent career trajectories. *Applied Developmental Science, 2*, 114–126.

Castle, J., Groothues, C., Bredenkamp, D., Beckett, C., et al. (1999). Effects of qualities of early institutional care on cognitive attainment. *American Journal of Orthopsychiatry, 69*, 424–437.

Cate, R. M., & Lloyd, S. A. (1992). *Courtship*. Newbury Park, CA: Sage.

Catsambis, S. (1995). Gender, race, ethnicity, and science education in the middle grades. *Journal of Research in Science Teaching, 32*, 243–257.

Cattell, R. B. (1963). Theory of fluid and crystallized intelligence: A critical experiment. *Journal of Educational Psychology, 54*, 1–22.

Caughy, M. O., DiPietro, J. A., & Strobino, D. M. (1994). Day-care participation as a protective factor in the cognitive development of low-income children. *Child Development, 65*, 457–471.

Cauley, J. A., Seeley, D. G., Ensrud, K., Ettinger, B., Black, D., & Cummings, S. R. (1995). Estrogen replacement therapy and fractures in older women. *Annals of Internal Medicine, 122*, 9–16.

Ceci, S., & Bronfenbrenner, U. (1985). "Don't forget to take the cupcakes out of the oven": Prospective memory, strategic time-monitoring, and context. *Child Development, 56*, 152–164.

Ceci, S. J., & Bruck, M. (1993). Suggestibility of the child witness: A historical review and synthesis. *Psychological Bulletin, 113*, 403–439.

Cederblad, M., Hook, B., Irhammar, M., & Mercke, A. (1999). Mental health in international adoptees as teenagers and young adults: An epidemiological study. *Journal of Child Psychology & Psychiatry & Allied Disciplines, 40*, 1239–1248.

Center for Education Reform. (1999). *Charter schools*. Washington, DC: [Online brochure]. Retrieved February 29, 2000 from the World Wide Web: www.edreform.com

Centers for Disease Control. (1994). Prevalence of adults with no known major risk factors for coronary heart disease—behavioral risk factor surveillance system, 1992. *Morbidity and Mortality Weekly Report, 43*, 61–69.

Centers for Disease Control. (1996, October 18). Population-based prevalence of perinatal exposure to cocaine—Georgia, 1994. *Morbidity & Mortality Weekly Report, 45*, 887.

Centers for Disease Control. (1998a). *National Diabetes Fact Sheet*. [Online report]. Retrieved October 11, 2000 from the World Wide Web: http://www.cdc.gov

Centers for Disease Control. (1998b). *The role of STD detection and treatment in HIV prevention*. [Online report]. Retrieved September 1, 2000 from the World Wide Web: http://www.cdc.gov

Centers for Disease Control. (1998c). Single-year U.S. mortality rates. *National Vital Statistics Reports, 47*, 10, Table 3.

Centers for Disease Control. (1998d). Tobacco use among U.S. racial/ethnic minority groups, African Americans, American Indians and Alaska Natives, Asian Americans and Pacific Islanders, Hispanics: A report of the Surgeon General (Executive Summary). *Morbidity & Mortality Weekly Report, 47*, 1–16.

Centers for Disease Control. (1999a). AIDS Surveillance Report. *Morbidity and Mortality Weekly Report, 11.*

Centers for Disease Control. (1999b). *Syphilis fact sheet.* [Online report]. Retrieved September 1, 2000 from the World Wide Web: http://www.cdc.gov

Centers for Disease Control. (2000a). *The burden of prostate cancer.* [Online at-a-glance factsheet]. Retrieved October 4, 2000 from the World Wide Web: http://www.cdc.gov

Centers for Disease Control. (2000b). *Some facts about genital herpes.* [Online report]. Retrieved September 1, 2000 from the World Wide Web: http://www.cdc.gov

Centers for Disease Control. (2000c). *STD facts: Gonorrhea.* [Online report]. Retrieved September 1, 2000 from the World Wide Web: http://www.cdc.gov

Centers for Disease Control. (2000d). Youth risk behavior surveillance—United States, 1999. *Morbidity and Mortality Weekly Report, 49, 1–96.*

Centers for Disease Control. National Immunization Program. (1999, April 2). Achievements in public health, 1900–1999: Impact of vaccines universally recommended for children. *Morbidity & Mortality Weekly Report, 48* (12), 243–248.

Centers for Disease Control. National Immunization Program. (2000, January 21). 2000 childhood immunization schedule. *Morbidity and Mortality Weekly Report, 49,* 35–38.

Centerwall, B. S. (1989). Exposure to television as a cause of violence. In G. Comstock (Ed.), *Public communication and behavior* (pp. 1–58). San Diego, CA: Academic Press.

Centerwall, B. S. (1992). Television and violence. The scale of the problem and where to go from here. *Journal of the American Medical Association, 267*(22), 3059–3063.

Century Foundation. (1998). *Social security reform: A Century Foundation guide to the issues.* [Online version]. Retrieved February 22, 2001 from the World Wide Web: www.tcf.org/publications/Basics

Cernoch, J. M., & Porter, R. H. (1985). Recognition of maternal axillary odors by infants. *Child Development, 56,* 1593–1598.

Chadwick, O., Taylor, E., Taylor, A., Heptinstall, E. et al., (1999). Hyperactivity and reading disability: A longitudinal study of the nature of the association. *Journal of Child Psychology & Psychiatry, 40,* 1039–1050.

Chan, R., Raboy, B., & Patterson, C. (1998). Psychosocial adjustment among children conceived via donor insemination by lesbian and heterosexual mothers. *Child Development, 69,* 443–457.

Chang, L., & Murray, A. (1995, March). *Math performance of 5- and 6-year-olds in Taiwan and the U.S.: Maternal beliefs, expectations, and tutorial assistance.* Paper presented at the biennial meetings of the Society for Research in Child Development, Indianapolis, IN.

Chao, R. (1994). Beyond parental control and authoritarian parenting style: Understanding Chinese parenting through the cultural notion of training. *Child Development, 65,* 1111–1119.

Chapman, J., & Tunmer, W. (1997). A longitudinal study of beginning reading achievement and reading self-concept. *British Journal of Educational Psychology, 67,* 279–291.

Charlesworth, W. R. (1992). Darwin and developmental psychology: Past and present. *Developmental Psychology, 28,* 5–16.

Chase-Lansdale, P. L., Cherlin, A. J., & Kiernan, K. E. (1995). The long-term effects of parental divorce on the mental health of young adults: A developmental perspective. *Child Development, 66,* 1614–1634.

Chase-Lansdale, P. L., & Hetherington, E. M. (1990). The impact of divorce on life-span development: Short and long term effects. In P. B. Baltes, D. L. Featherman, & R. M. Lerner (Eds.), *Life-span development and behavior* (Vol. 10) (pp. 107–151). Hillsdale, NJ: Erlbaum.

Chasseigne, G., Grau, S., Mullet, E., & Cama, V. (1999). How well do elderly people cope with uncertainty in a learning task? *Acta Psychologica, 103,* 229–238.

Chatlos, J. (1997). Substance use and abuse and the impact on academic difficulties. *Child & Adolescent Clinics of North America, 6,* 545–568.

Chatters, L. M. (1991). Physical health. In J. S. Jackson (Ed.), *Life in black America* (pp. 199–220). Newbury Park, CA: Sage.

Chen, J., Bierhals, A., Prigerson, H., Kasl, S., Mazure, C., & Jacobs, S. (1999). Gender differences in the effects of bereavement-related psychological distress in health outcomes. *Psychological Medicine, 29,* 367–380.

Chen, S. (1997). Child's understanding of secret and friendship development. *Psychological Science (China), 20,* 565–545.

Chen, X., Rubin, K. H., & Li, Z. (1995). Social functioning and adjustment in Chinese children: A longitudinal study. *Developmental Psychology, 31,* 531–539.

Chen, X., Rubin, K. H., & Sun, Y. (1992). Social reputation and peer relationships in Chinese and Canadian children: A cross-cultural study. *Child Development, 63,* 1336–1343.

Chen, Z. (1999). Ethnic similarities and differences in the association of emotional autonomy and adolescent outcomes: Comparing Euro-American and Asian-American adolescents. *Psychological Reports, 84,* 501–516.

Chen-Hafteck, L. (1997). Music and language development in early childhood: Integrating past research in the two domains. *Early Child Development & Care, 130,* 85–97.

Cherlin, A. (1992). *Marriage, divorce, remarriage,* Cambridge, MA: Harvard University Press.

Cherlin, A., Chase-Lansdale, P., & McRae, C. (1998). Effects of parental divorce on mental health throughout the life course. *American Sociological Review, 63,* 239–249.

Cherlin, A., & Furstenberg, F. F. (1986). *The new American grandparent.* New York: Basic Books.

Cherlin, A. J. (1992). Infant care and full-time employment. In A. Booth (Ed.), *Child care in the 1990s: Trends and consequences* (pp. 209–214). Hillsdale, NJ: Erlbaum.

Chess, S., & Thomas, A. (1984). *Origins and evolution of behavior disorders: Infancy to early adult life.* New York: Brunner/Mazel.

Chi, M. T. (1978). Knowledge structure and memory development. In R. S. Siegler (Ed.), *Children's thinking: What develops?* (pp. 73–96). Hillsdale, NJ: Erlbaum.

Chiapin, G., DeAraujo, G., & Wagner, A. (1998). Mother-in-law and daughter-in-law: How is the relationship between these two women? *Psicologia: Reflexao e Critica, 11,* 541–550.

Chiappe, P., & Siegel, L. (1999). Phonological awareness and reading acquisition in English- and Punjabi-speaking Canadian children. *Journal of Educational Psychology, 91,* 20–28.

Chickering, A., & Reisser, L. (1993). *Education and identity* (2nd ed.). San Francisco: Jossey-Bass.

Chincotta, D., & Underwood, G. (1997). Estimates, language of schooling and bilingual digit span. *European Journal of Cognitive Psychology, 9,* 325–348.

Chiriboga, D. A. (1989). Mental health at the midpoint: Crisis, challenge, or relief? In S. Hunter & M. Sundel (Eds.), *Midlife myths: Issues, findings, and practice implications* (pp. 116–144). Newbury Park, CA: Sage.

Chisholm, J. S. (1989). Biology, culture, and the development of temperament: A Navaho example. In J. K. Nugent, B. M. Lester, & T. B. Brazelton (Eds.), *The cultural context of infancy: Vol. 1. Biology, culture, and infant development.* Norwood, NJ: Ablex.

Chism, M., & Satcher, J. (1998). African American students' perceptions toward faculty at historically Black colleges. *College Student Journal, 32,* 315–320.

Choi, N. G. (1991). Racial differences in the determinants of living arrangements of widowed and divorced elderly women. *The Gerontologist, 31,* 496–504.

Choi, S. (2000). Caregiver input in English and Korean: Use of nouns and verbs in book-reading and toy-play contexts. *Journal of Children's Language, 27,* 69–96.

Chomsky, N. (1959). A review of B. F. Skinner's *Verbal Behavior. Language, 35,* 26–129.

Chopak, J., Vicary, J., & Crockett, L. (1998). Predicting alcohol and tobacco use in a sample of rural adolescents. *American Journal of Health Behavior, 22,* 334–341.

Chou, C., Chou, J., & Tyang, N. (1998, February 18–22). *An exploratory study of Internet addiction, usage, and communication pleasure.* Paper presented at the annual meeting of the Association for Educational Communications and Technology. St. Louis, MO. (ERIC No. ED 416 838).

Christensen, A., & Heavey, C. (1999). Interventions for couples. *Annual Review of Psychology, 50,* 165–190.

Christensen, C. (1997). Onset, rhymes, and phonemes in learning to read. *Scientific Studies of Reading, 1,* 341–358.

Christensen, H., Henderson, A., Griffiths, K., & Levings, C. (1997). Does aging inevitably lead to declines in cognitive performance? A longitudinal study of elite academics. *Personality & Individual Differences, 23,* 67–78.

Christopher, F., Madura, M., & Weaver, L. (1998). Premarital sexual aggressors: A multivariate analysis of social, relational, and individual variables. *Journal of Marriage and the Family, 60,* 56–69.

Chronicle of Higher Education. (1997, August 29). Almanac: Facts about the U.S., each of the 50 states, and D.C. Washington, DC: Author.

Chumlea, W. C. (1982). Physical growth in adolescence. In B. B. Wolman (Ed.), *Handbook of developmental psychology* (pp. 471–485). Englewood Cliffs, NJ: Prentice-Hall.

Church, M., Eldis, F., Blakley, B., & Bawle, E. Hearing, language, speech, vestibular, and dento-facial disorders in fetal alcohol syndrome. *Alcoholism: Clinical & Experimental Research, 21,* 227–237.

Ciancio, D., Sadovsky, A., Malabonga, V., Trueblood, L., et al. (1999). Teaching classification and seriation to preschoolers. *Child Study Journal, 29,* 193–205.

Cicirelli, V. G. (1982). Sibling influence throughout the lifespan. In M. E. Lamb & B. Sutton-Smith (Eds.), *Sibling relationships* (pp. 267–304). Hillsdale, NJ: Erlbaum.

Cicirelli, V. G. (1991). Attachment theory in old age: Protection of the attached figure. In K. Pillemer & K. McCargner (Eds.), *Parent-child relationships throughout life* (pp. 25–42). Hillsdale, NJ: Erlbaum.

Cillessen, A. H. N., van IJzendoorn, H. W., van Lieshout, C. F. M., & Hartup, W. W. (1992). Heterogeneity among peer-rejected boys: Subtypes and stabilities. *Child Development, 63,* 893–905.

Claes, M. (1998). Adolescents' closeness with parents, siblings, and friends in three countries: Canada, Belgium, and Italy. *Journal of Youth & Adolescence, 27,* 165–184.

Clark, S., & Miles, M. (1999). Conflicting responses: The experiences of fathers of infants diagnosed with severe congenital heart disease. *Journal of the Society of Pediatric Nurses, 4,* 7–14.

Clarke-Stewart, A. (1992). Consequences of child care for children's development. In A. Booth (Ed.), *Child care in the 1990s: Trends and consequences* (pp. 63–82). Hillsdale, NJ: Erlbaum.

Clarke-Stewart, K. A., Gruber, C. P., & Fitzgerald, L. M. (1994). *Children at home and in day care.* Hillsdale, NJ: Erlbaum.

Clarkson-Smith, L., & Hartley, A. A. (1990). The game of bridge as an exercise in working memory and reasoning. *Journals of Gerontology: Psychological Sciences, 45,* P233–238.

Clawson, R., & Choate, J. (1999). Explaining participation on a class newsgroup. *Social Science Computer Review, 17,* 455–459.

Clinkingbeard, C., Minton, B., Davis, J., & McDermott, K. (1999). Women's knowledge about menopause, hormone replacement therapy (HRT), and interactions with healthcare providers: An exploratory study. *Journal of Women's Health & Gender-Based Medicine, 8,* 1097–1102.

Cnattingius, S., Berendes, H. W., & Forman, M. R. (1993). Do delayed childbearers face increased risks of adverse pregnancy outcomes after the first birth? *Obstetrics and Gynecology, 81,* 512–516.

Cobb, K. (2000, September 3). Breaking in drivers: Texas could join states restricting teens in effort to lower rate of fatal accidents. *Houston Chronicle,* A1, A20.

Coffey, C., Saxton, J., Ratcliff, G., Bryan, R., & Lucke, J. (1999). Relation of education to brain size in normal aging: Implications for the reserve hypothesis. *Neurology, 53,* 189–196.

Cohen, G. (2000). *The creative age: Awakening human potential in the second half of life.* New York: Avon Books.

Cohen, R. (2000, April 11). Horror expressed in Germany over Dutch euthanasia. *New York Times Online.* Retrieved April 17, 2001 from the World Wide Web: www.nytimes.com

Cohen, S. (1991). Social supports and physical health: Symptoms, health behaviors, and infectious disease. In E. M. Cummings, A. L. Greene, & K. H. Karraker (Eds.), *Life-span developmental psychology: Perspectives on stress and coping* (pp. 213–234). Hillsdale, NJ: Erlbaum.

Cohen, Y. A. (1964). *The transition from childhood to adolescence.* Chicago: Aldine.

Coie, J. (1997, August). *Testing developmental theory of antisocial behavior with outcomes from the Fast Track Prevention Project.*

Paper presented at the annual meeting of the American Psychological Association, Chicago.

Coie, J., Cillessen, A., Dodge, K., Hubbard, J., et al., (1999). It takes two to fight: A test of relational factors and a method for assessing aggressive dyads. *Developmental Psychology, 35,* 1179–1188.

Coie, J., Terry, R., Lenox, K., Lochman, J., & Hyman, C. (1995). Childhood peer rejection and aggression as predictors of stable patterns of adolescent disorder. *Development and Psychopathology, 7,* 697–713.

Coie, J. D., & Cillessen, A. H. N. (1993). Peer rejection: Origins and effects on children's development. *Current Directions in Psychological Science, 2,* 89–92.

Coiro, M. J. (1995, March). *Child behavior problems as a function of marital conflict and parenting.* Paper presented at the biennial meetings of the Society for Research in Child Development, Indianapolis, IN.

Coke, M. (1992). Correlates of life satisfaction among elderly African Americans. *The Journals of Gerontology, 47,* P316–P320.

Colby, A., Kohlberg, L., Gibbs, J., & Lieberman, M. (1983). A longitudinal study of moral judgment. *Monographs of the Society for Research in Child Development, 48*(1–2, Serial No. 200).

Colditz, G. A., Hankinson, S. E., Hunter, D. J., Willett, W. C., Manson, J. E., Stampfer, M. J., Hennekens, C., Rosner, B., & Speizer, F. E. (1995). The use of estrogens and progestins and the risk of breast cancer in postmenopausal women. *New England Journal of Medicine, 332,* 1589–1593.

Cole, D. A. (1991). Change in self-perceived competence as a function of peer and teacher evaluation. *Developmental Psychology, 27,* 682–688.

Cole, E., Zucker, A., & Ostrove, J. (1998). Political participation and feminist consciousness among women activists of the 1960s. *Political Psychology, 19,* 349–371.

Cole, M. (1992). Culture in development. In M. H. Bornstein & M. E. Lamb (Eds.), *Developmental psychology: An advanced textbook* (pp. 731–789). Hillsdale, NJ: Erlbaum.

Coleman, J., Pratt, R., Stoddard, R., Gerstmann, D., & Abel, H. (1997). The effects of the male and female singing and speaking voices on selected physiological and behavioral measures of premature infants in the intensive care unit. *International Journal of Arts Medicine, 5,* 4–11.

Coleman, M., Ganong, L., Killian, T., & McDaniel, A. (1999). Child support obligations: Attitudes and rationale. *Journal of Family Issues, 20,* 46–68.

Coley, R., & Chase-Lansdale, L. (1998). Adolescent pregnancy and parenthood: Recent evidence and future directions. *American Psychologist, 53,* 152–166.

Collaer, M. L., & Hines, M. (1995). Human behavioral sex differences: A role for gonadal hormones during early development? *Psychological Bulletin, 118,* 55–107.

Collet, J. P., Burtin, P., Gillet, J., Bossard, N., Ducruet, T., & Durr, F. (1994). Risk of infectious diseases in children attending different types of day-care setting. Epicreche Research Group. *Respiration, 61,* 16–19.

Colombo, J. (1993). *Infant cognition: Predicting later intellectual functioning.* Newbury Park, CA: Sage.

Colonia-Willner, R. (1999). Investing in practical intelligence: Ageing and cognitive efficiency among executives. *International Journal of Behavioral Development, 23,* 591–614.

Colton, M., Buss, K., Mangelsdorf, S., Brooks, C., Sorenson, D., Stansbury, K., Harris, M., & Gunnar, M. (1992). *Relations between toddler coping strategies, temperament, attachment and adrenocortical stress responses.* Poster presented at the 8th International Conference on Infant Studies, Miami.

Commissaris, C., Ponds, R., & Jolles, J. (1998). Subjective forgetfulness in a normal Dutch population: Possibilities of health education and other interventions. *Patient Education & Counseling, 34,* 25–32.

Committee on Infectious Diseases (1996). Recommended childhood immunization schedule. *Pediatrics, 97,* 143–146.

Compas, B. E., Ey, S., & Grant, K. E. (1993). Taxonomy, assessment, and diagnosis of depression during adolescence. *Psychological Bulletin, 114,* 323–344.

Comstock, G. (1991). *Television and the American child.* San Diego, CA: Academic Press.

Condry, J., & Condry, S. (1976). Sex differences: A study in the eye of the beholder. *Child Development, 47,* 812–819.

Conger, R. D., Patterson, G. R., & Ge, X. (1995). It takes two to replicate: A mediational model for the impact of parents' stress on adolescent adjustment. *Child Development, 66,* 80–97.

Connidis, I. A. (1994). Sibling support in older age. *Journals of Gerontology: Social Sciences, 49,* S309–317.

Connidis, I. A., & Davies, L. (1992). Confidants and companions: Choices in later life. *Journals of Gerontology: Social Sciences, 47,* S115–122.

Connidis, I. A., & McMullin, J. A. (1993). To have or have not: Parent status and the subjective well-being of older men and women. *The Gerontologist, 33,* 630–636.

Connolly, K., & Dalgleish, M. (1989). The emergence of a tool-using skill in infancy. *Developmental Psychology, 25,* 894–912.

Cook, E. (1998). Effects of reminiscence on life satisfaction of elderly female nursing home residents. *Health Care for Women International, 19,* 109–118.

Cook, S., & Heppner, P. (1997). Coping control, problem-solving appraisal, and depressive symptoms during a farm crisis. *Journal of Mental Health Counseling, 19,* 64–77.

Coombs, R. H. (1991). Marital status and personal well-being: A literature review. *Family Relations, 40,* 97–102.

Cooney, T. M. (1994). Young adults' relations with parents: The influence of recent parental divorce. *Journal of Marriage and the Family, 56,* 45–56.

Cooper, A., Putnam, D., Planchon, L., & Boies, S. (1999). Online sexual compulsivity: Getting tangled in the net. *Sexual Addiction & Compulsivity, 6,* 79–104.

Corbet, A., Long, W., Schumacher, R., Gerdes, J., & Cotton, R. (1995). Double-blind developmental evaluation at 1-year corrected age of 597 premature infants with birth weights from 500 to 1350 grams enrolled in three placebo-controlled trials of prophylactic synthetic surfactant. *Journal of Pediatrics, 126,* S5–12.

Corr, C. A. (1991/1992). A task-based approach to coping with dying. *Omega, 24,* 81–94.

Corrada, M., Brookmeyer, R., & Kawas, C. (1995). Sources of variability in prevalence rates of Alzheimer's disease. *International Journal of Epidemiology, 24,* 1000–1005.

Corso, J. F. (1987). Sensory-perceptual processes and aging. In K. W. Schaie (Ed.), *Annual Review of Gerontology and Geriatrics* (Vol. 7) (pp. 29–56). New York: Springer.

Corwin, J., Loury, M., & Gilbert, A. N. (1995). Workplace, age, and sex as mediators of olfactory function: Data from the National Geographic smell survey. *Journals of Gerontology: Psychological Sciences, 50B,* P179–186.

Cosden, M., & McNamara, J. (1997). Self-concept and perceived social support among college students with and without learning disabilities. *Learning Disability Quarterly, 20,* 2–12.

Cossette, L., Malcuit, G., & Pomerleau, A. (1991). Sex differences in motor activity during early infancy. *Infant Behavior and Development, 14,* 175–186.

Costa, M., Reus, V., Wolkowitz, O., Manfredi, F., & Lieberman, M. (1999). Estrogen replacement therapy and cognitive decline in memory-impaired post-menopausal women. *Biological Psychiatry, 46,* 182–188.

Costa, P. T., & McCrae, R. R. (1980a). Influence of extraversion and neuroticism on subjective well-being: Happy and unhappy people. *Journal of Personality and Social Psychology, 38,* 668–678.

Costa, P. T., Jr., & McCrae, R. R. (1980b). Still stable after all these years: Personality as a key to some issues in adulthood and old age. In P. B. Baltes & O. G. Brim, Jr. (Eds.), *Life-span development and behavior* (pp. 65–102). New York: Academic Press.

Costa, P. T., Jr., & McCrae, R. R. (1988). Personality in adulthood: A six-year longitudinal study of self-reports and spouse ratings on the NEO personality inventory. *Journal of Personality and Social Psychology, 54,* 853–863.

Costa, P. T., Jr., & McCrae, R. R. (1994a). Set like plaster? Evidence for the stability of adult personality. In T. F. Hetherton & J. L. Weinberger (Eds.), *Can personality change?* (pp. 21–40). Washington, DC: American Psychological Association.

Costa, P. T., Jr., & McCrae, R. R. (1994b). Stability and change in personality from adolescence through adulthood. In C. F. Halverson, Jr., G. A. Kohnstamm, & R. P. Martin (Eds.), *The developing structure of temperament and personality from infancy to adulthood* (pp. 139–150). Hillsdale, NJ: Erlbaum.

Costa, P. T., Jr., McCrae, R. R., Zonderman, A. B., Barbano, H. E., Lebowitz, B., & Larson, D. M. (1986). Cross-sectional studies of personality in a national sample: 2. Stability in neuroticism, extraversion, and openness. *Psychology and Aging, 1,* 144–149.

Cotman, C. W., & Neeper, S. (1996). Activity-dependent plasticity and the aging brain. In E. L. Schneider & J. W. Rowe (Eds.), *Handbook of the biology of aging* (4th ed.) (pp. 284–299). San Diego, CA: Academic Press.

Cotton, L., Bynum, D., & Madhere, S. (1997). Socialization forces and the stability of work values from late adolescence to early adulthood. *Psychological Reports, 80,* 115–124.

Coulton, C. J., Korbin, J. E., Su, M., & Chow, J. (1995). Community level factors and child maltreatment rates. *Child Development, 66,* 1262–1276.

Council of the Great City Schools. (1997). Standard English Proficiency Program: A program in the Oakland Unified School District to facilitate standard English proficiency and self-esteem. In *What Works in Urban Education: Achievement.* [Online brochure]. Retrieved January 15, 2001 from the World Wide Web: www.cgcs.org/services/whatworks/achievement/p27.htm

Council on Basic Education. (1998). *Quality counts.* [Online report]. Retrieved October 21, 1998 from the World Wide Web: http://www.c-b-e.org

Counts, D. R. (1976/1977). The good death in Kaliai: Preparation for death in western New Britain. *Omega, 7,* 367–372.

Court curbs drug tests during pregnancy. (2001, March 22). *New York Times Online.* Retrieved April 4, 2001 from the World Wide Web: www.nytimes.com/2001/03/22/politics/22SCOT.html

Cowan, B. R., & Underwood, M. K. (1995, March). *Sugar and spice and everything nice? A developmental investigation of social aggression among girls.* Paper presented at the biennial meetings of the Society for Research in Child Development, Indianapolis, IN.

Cowan, C. P., & Cowan, P. A. (1987). Men's involvement in parenthood: Identifying the antecedents and understanding the barriers. In P. W. Berman & F. A. Pedersen (Eds.), *Men's transitions to parenthood: Longitudinal studies of early family experience* (pp. 145–174). Hillsdale, NJ: Erlbaum.

Cox, M., Paley, B., Burchinal, M., & Payne, C. (1999). Marital perceptions and interactions across the transition to parenthood. *Journal of Marriage & the Family, 61,* 611–625.

Cramer, D. (1991). Type A behavior pattern, extraversion, neuroticism and psychological distress. *British Journal of Medical Psychology, 64,* 73–83.

Cramer, P. (2000). Defense mechanisms in psychology today. *American Psychologist, 55,* 637–646.

Crawley, A., Anderson, D., Wilder, A., Williams, M., & Santomero, A. (1999). Effects of repeated exposures to a single episode of the television program *Blue's Clues* on the viewing behaviors and comprehension of preschool children. *Educational Psychology, 91,* 630–638.

The creators. (2000, March/April). *Modern Maturity,* pp. 38–44.

Crick, N., & Dodge, K. (1994). A review and reformulation of social information processing mechanisms in children's social adjustment. *Psychological Bulletin, 115,* 74–101.

Crick, N., & Dodge, K. (1996). Social information-processing mechanisms in reactive and proactive aggression. *Child Development, 67,* 993–1002.

Crick, N., & Ladd, G. (1993). Children's perceptions of their peer experiences: Attributions, loneliness, social anxiety, and social avoidance. *Developmental Psychology, 29,* 244–254.

Crick, N. R., & Grotpeter, J. K. (1995). Relational aggression, gender, and social-psychological adjustment. *Child Development, 66,* 710–722.

Crimmins, E. M., & Ingegneri, D. G. (1990). Interaction and living arrangements of older parents and their children. *Research on Aging, 12,* 3–35.

Crittenden, P. M. (1992). Quality of attachment in the preschool years. *Development and Psychopathology, 4,* 209–241.

Crittenden, P. M., Partridge, M. F., & Claussen, A. H. (1991). Family patterns of relationship in normative and dysfunctional families. *Development and Psychopathology, 3,* 491–512.

Crockenberg, S., & Litman, C. (1990). Autonomy as competence in 2-year-olds: Maternal correlates of child defiance, compliance, and self-assertion. *Developmental Psychology, 26,* 961–971.

Crone, D., & Whitehurst, G. (1999). Age and schooling effects on emergent literacy and early reading skills. *Journal of Educational Psychology, 91*, 594–603.

Crouter, A. C., & McHale, S. M. (1993). Familial economic circumstances: Implications for adjustment and development in early adolescence. In R. M. Lerner (Ed.), *Early adolescence. Perspectives on research, policy, and intervention* (pp. 71–91). Hillsdale, NJ: Erlbaum.

Crowell, J. A., & Feldman, S. S. (1988). Mothers' internal models of relationships and children's behavioral and developmental status: A study of mother-child interaction. *Child Development, 50*, 1273–1285.

Crowell, J. A., & Waters, E. (1995, March). *Is the parent-child relationship a prototype of later love relationships? Studies of attachment and working models of attachment.* Paper presented at the biennial meeting of the Society for Research in Child Development, Indianapolis, IN.

Crowley, S. (2000). Snoops finding new ways to breach medical files. *AARP Bulletin, 413*, 24–26.

Crystal, S., Shae, D., & Krishnaswami, S. (1992). Educational attainment, occupational history, and stratification: Determinants of later-life economic outcomes. *Journals of Gerontology: Social Sciences, 47*, S213–221.

Csikszentmihalyi, M., & Rathunde, K. (1990). The psychology of wisdom: An evolutionary interpretation. In R. Sternberg (Ed.), *Wisdom: Its nature, origins, and development* (pp. 25–51). Cambridge, England: Cambridge University Press.

Cuba, L., & Longino, C. F., Jr. (1991). Regional retirement migration: The case of Cape Cod. *Journals of Gerontology: Social Sciences, 46*, S33–42.

Culp, A., Culp, R., Blankemeyer, M., & Passmark, L. (1998). Parent Education Home Visitation Program: Adolescent and nonadolescent mother comparison after six months of intervention. *Infant Mental Health Journal, 19*, 111–123.

Cumming, E. (1975). Engagement with an old theory. *International Journal of Aging and Human Development, 6*, 187–191.

Cumming, E., & Henry, W. E. (1961). *Growing old.* New York: Basic Books.

Cummings, E. M., & Davies, P. T. (1994). Maternal depression and child development. *Journal of Child Psychology and Psychiatry, 35*, 73–112.

Cummings, E. M., Hollenbeck, B., Iannotti, R., Radke-Yarrow, M., & Zahn-Waxler, C. (1986). Early organization of altruism and aggression: Developmental patterns and individual differences. In C. Zahn-Waxler, E. M. Cummings, & R. Iannotti (Eds.), *Altruism and aggression* (pp. 165–188). Cambridge, England: Cambridge University Press.

Cunningham, A. S., Jelliffe, D. B., & Jelliffe, E. F. P. (1991). Breast-feeding and health in the 1980s: A global epidemiologic review. *Journal of Pediatrics, 118*, 659–666.

Cunningham, L. (1996). *Grief and the adolescent.* Newhall, CA: TeenAge Grief, Inc.

Cunningham, W. R., & Haman, K. L. (1992). Intellectual functioning in relation to mental health. In J. E. Birren, R. B. Sloane, & G. D. Cohen (Eds.), *Handbook of mental health and aging* (2nd ed.) (pp. 340–355). San Diego, CA: Academic Press.

Curran, G., Stoltenberg, S., Hill, E., Mudd, S., Blow, F., & Zucker, R. (1999). Gender differences in the relationship among SES, family history of alcohol disorders and alcohol dependence. *Journal of Studies on Alcohol, 60*, 825–832.

Curyto, K., Chapleski, E., & Lichtenberg, P. (1999). Prediction of the presence and stability of depression in the Great Lakes Native American elderly. *Journal of Mental Health & Aging, 5*, 323–340.

Cushner, K., McClelland, A., & Safford, P. (1992). *Human diversity in education.* New York: McGraw-Hill.

Cushner, K., McClelland, A., & Safford, P. (1993). *Human diversity in education.* New York: McGraw-Hill.

Cuvo, A. (1974). Incentive level influence on overt rehearsal and free recall as a function of age. *Journal of Experimental Child Psychology, 18*, 167–181.

Czaja, S., & Sharit, J. (1998). Age differences in attitudes toward computers. *Journals of Gerontology: Series B: Psychological Sciences & Social Sciences, 53B*, P329–P340.

Czaja, S., Sharit, J., Nair, S., & Rubert, M. (1998). Understanding sources of user variability in computer-based data entry performance. *Behaviour & Information Technology, 17*, 282–293.

D'Alton, M. E., & DeCherney, A. H. (1993). Prenatal diagnosis. *New England Journal of Medicine, 328*, 114–118.

Da Costa, D., Larouche, J., Dritsa, M., & Brender, W. (2000). Psychosocial correlates of prepartum and postpartum depressed mood. *Journal of Affective Disorders, 59*, 31–40.

Daly, L. E., Kirke, P. N., Molloy, A., Weir, D. G., & Scott, J. M. (1995). Folate levels and neural tube defects: Implications for prevention. *Journal of the American Medical Association, 274*, 1698–1702.

Daly, M., & Wilson, M. (1996). Violence against stepchildren. *Current Directions in Psychological Science, 5*, 77–81.

Daly, S., & Glenwick, D. (2000). Personal adjustment and perceptions of grandchild behavior in custodial grandmothers. *Journal of Clinical Child Psychology, 29*, 108–118.

Damon, W. (1977). *The social world of the child.* San Francisco: Jossey-Bass.

Damon, W. (1983). The nature of social-cognitive change in the developing child. In W. F. Overton (Ed.), *The relationship between social and cognitive development* (pp. 103–142). Hillsdale, NJ: Erlbaum.

Damon, W., & Hart, D. (1988). *Self understanding in childhood and adolescence.* New York: Cambridge University Press.

Danby, S., & Baker, C. (1998). How to be masculine in the block area. *Childhood: A Global Journal of Child Research, 5*, 151–175.

Darlington, R. B. (1991). The long-term effects of model preschool programs. In L. Okagaki & R. J. Sternberg (Eds.), *Directors of development* (pp. 203–215). Hillsdale, NJ: Erlbaum.

Darrow, C. (1922). *Crime: Its causes and treatment.* New York: Thomas Y. Crowell.

Davajan, V., & Israel, R. (1991). Diagnosis and medical treatment of infertility. In A. L. Stanton & C. Dunkel-Schetter (Eds.), *Infertility: Perspectives from stress and coping research* (pp. 17–28). New York: Plenum.

Davenport, E. (1992). *The making of minority scientists and engineers.* Invited address presented at the annual meeting of the American Educational Research Association, San Francisco, CA.

Davenport, E., Davison, M., Kuang, H., Ding, S., Kim, S., & Kwak, N. (1998). High school mathematics course-taking by gender and ethnicity. *American Educational Research Journal, 35*, 497–514.

Davey, F. (1998). Young women's expected and preferred patterns of employment and child care. *Sex Roles, 38*, 95–102.

Davidson, B., Balswick, J., & Halverson, C. (1983). Affective self-disclosure and marital adjustment: A test of equity theory. *Journal of Marriage and the Family, 45*, 93–103.

Davidson, R. (1994). Temperament, affective style, and frontal lobe asymmetry. In G. Dawson & K. Fischer (Eds.), *Human behavior and the developing brain.* New York: Guilford Press.

Davies, G. M. (1993). Children's memory for other people: An integrative review. In C. A. Nelson (Ed.), *The Minnesota Symposia on Child Psychology* (Vol. 26) (pp. 123–157). Hillsdale, NJ: Erlbaum.

Davies, P., & Rose, J. (1999). Assessment of cognitive development in adolescents by means of neuropsychological tasks. *Developmental Neuropsychology, 15*, 227–248.

Davis, D. L., Dinse, G. E., & Hoel, D. G. (1994). Decreasing cardiovascular disease and increasing cancer among whites in the United States from 1973 through 1987. *Journal of the American Medical Association, 271*, 431–437.

Dawber, T. R., Kannel, W. B., & Lyell, L. P. (1963). An approach to longitudinal studies in a community: The Framingham study. *Annals of the New York Academy of Science, 107*, 539–556.

Dawson, D. (2000). Alcohol consumption, alcohol dependence, and all-cause mortality. *Alcoholism: Clinical & Experimental Research, 24*, 72–81.

Dawson, D. A. (1991). Family structure and children's health and well-being: Data from the 1988 National Health Interview Survey on child health. *Journal of Marriage and the Family, 53*, 573–584.

Dawson, J., & Langan, P. (1994). *Murder in families.* Washington, DC: U.S. Department of Justice.

DeAngelis, T. (1997). When children don't bond with parents. *Monitor of the American Psychological Association, 28*, (6) 10–12.

DeCasper, A. J., Lecanuet, J., Busnel, M., Granier-Deferre, C., & Maugeais, R. (1994). Fetal reactions to recurrent maternal speech. *Infant Behavior and Development, 17*, 159–164.

DeCasper, A. J., & Spence, M. J. (1986). Prenatal maternal speech influences newborns' perception of speech sounds. *Infant Behavior and Development, 9,* 133–150.

Deci, E., Koestner, R., & Ryan, R. (1999). *A meta-analytic review of experiments examining the effects of extrinsic rewards on intrinsic motivation.* Psychological Bulletin, 125, 627–668.

Deeg, D. J. H., Kardaun, W. P. F., & Fozard, J. L. (1996). Health, behavior, and aging. In J. E. Birren & K. W. Schaie (Eds.), *Handbook of the psychology of aging* (4th ed.) (pp. 129–149). San Diego, CA: Academic Press.

Degirmencioglu, S., Urberg, K., & Tolson, J. (1998). Adolescent friendship networks: Continuity and change over the school year. *Merrill-Palmer Quarterly, 44,* 313–337.

de Graaf, C., Polet, P., & van Staveren, W. A. (1994). Sensory perception and pleasantness of food flavors in elderly subjects. *Journals of Gerontology: Psychological Sciences, 49,* P93–99.

de Haan, M., Luciana, M., Maslone, S. M., Matheny, L. S., & Richards, M. L. M. (1994). Development, plasticity, and risk: Commentary on Huttenlocher, Pollit and Gorman, and Gottesman and Goldsmith. In C. A. Nelson (Ed.), *The Minnesota Symposia on Child Psychology* (Vol. 27) (pp. 161–178). Hillsdale, NJ: Erlbaum.

De Jong, G. F., Wilmoth, J. M., Angel, J. L., & Cornwell, G. T. (1995). Motives and the geographic mobility of very old Americans. *Journals of Gerontology: Social Sciences, 50B,* S395–404.

Dekovic, M. (1999). Parent-adolescent conflict: Possible determinants and consequences. *International Journal of Behavioral Development, 23,* 977–1000.

Dekovic, M., & Meeus, W. (1997). Peer relations in adolescence: Effects of parenting and adolescents' self-concept. *Journal of Adolescence, 20,* 163–176.

Dekovic, M., Noom, M., & Meeus, W. (1997). Expectations regarding development during adolescence: Parental and adolescent perceptions. *Journal of Youth & Adolescence, 26,* 253–272.

de Lacoste, M., Horvath, D., & Woodward, J. (1991). Possible sex differences in the developing human fetal brain. *Journal of Clinical and Experimental Neuropsychology, 13,* 831.

del Barrio, V., Moreno-Rosset, C., Lopez-Martinez, R., & Olmedo, M. (1997). Anxiety, depression and personality structure. *Personality & Individual Differences, 23,* 327–335.

DeLoache, J. S. (1995). Early understanding and use of symbols: The model model. *Current Directions in Psychological Science, 4,* 109–113.

Delpit, L. (1990). Language diversity and learning. In S. Hynds & D. Rubin (Eds.), *Perspectives on talk and learning* (pp. 247–266). Urbana, IL: National Council on Teacher Education.

DeMaris, A., & Rao, K. V. (1992). Premarital cohabitation and subsequent marital stability in the United States: A reassessment. *Journal of Marriage and the Family, 54,* 178–190.

DeMars, C. (2000). Test stakes and item format interactions. *Applied Measurement in Education, 13,* 55–77.

DeMeis, D. K., Hock, E., & McBride, S. L. (1986). The balance of employment and motherhood: Longitudinal study of mothers' feelings about separation from their first-born infants. *Developmental Psychology, 22,* 627–632.

DeMulder, E., Denham, S., Schmidt, M., & Mitchell, J. (2000). Q-sort assessment of attachment security during the preschool years: Links from home to school. *Developmental Psycholgy, 36,* 274–282.

Dennerstein, L., Lehert, P., Burger, H., & Dudley, E. (1999). Mood and the menopausal transition. *Journal of Nervous & Mental Disease, 187,* 685–691.

Denney, N. W. (1982). Aging and cognitive changes. In B. B. Wolman (Ed.), *Handbook of developmental psychology* (pp. 807–827). Englewood Cliffs, NJ: Prentice-Hall.

Denney, N. W. (1984). Model of cognitive development across the life span. *Developmental Review, 4,* 171–191.

Dennis, W. (1960). Causes of retardation among institutional children: Iran. *Journal of Genetic Psychology, 96,* 47–59.

Den Ouden, L., Rijken, M., Brand, R., Verloove-Vanhorick, S. P., & Ruys, J. H. (1991). Is it correct to correct? Developmental milestones in 555 "normal" preterm infants compared with term infants. *Journal of Pediatrics, 118,* 399–404.

Depressed elderly react best to a mix of drugs and psychotherapy. (1999, March). *APA Monitor Online* [Archives]. Retrieved February 7, 2001 from the World Wide Web: www.apa.org/monitor/mar99/depress.html

DeSpelder, L. A., & Strickland, A. L. (1983). *The last dance: Encountering death and dying.* Palo Alto, CA: Mayfield.

Dessens, A., Cohen-Kettenis, P., Mellenbergh, G., van de Poll, N., Koppe, J., & Boer, K. (1999). Prenatal exposure to anticonvulsants and psychosexual development. *Archives of Sexual Behavior, 28,* 31–44.

Detchant, Lord Walton. (1995). Dilemmas of life and death: Part one. *Journal of the Royal Society of Medicine, 88*(311–315).

Deter, H., & Herzog, W. (1994). Anorexia nervosa in a long-term perspective: Results of the Heidelberg-Mannheim study. *Psychosomatic Medicine, 56,* 20–27.

de Villiers, P. A., & de Villiers, J. G. (1992). Language development. In M. H. Bornstein & M. E. Lamb (Eds.), *Developmental psychology: An advanced textbook* (3rd ed.) (pp. 337–418). Hillsdale, NJ: Erlbaum.

Dgnelie, G., Zorge, I., & McDonald, T. (2000). Lutein improves visual function in some patients with retinal degeneration: A pilot study via the Internet. *Journal of the American Optometric Association, 71,* 147–164.

The Diagram Group (1977). *Child's body.* New York: Paddington.

Diamond, A. (1991). Neuropsychological insights into the meaning of object concept development. In S. Carey & R. Gelman (Eds.), *The epigenesis of mind: Essays on biology and cognition* (pp. 67–110). Hillsdale, NJ: Erlbaum.

Dick, D., Rose, R., Viken, R., & Kaprio, J. (2000). Pubertal timing and substance use: Associations between and within families across late adolescence. *Developmental Psychology, 36,* 180–189.

Diehl, L., Vicary, J., & Deike, R. (1997). Longitudinal trajectories of self-esteem from early to middle adolescence and related psychosocial variables among rural adolescents. *Journal of Research on Adolescence, 7,* 393–411.

Diener, E. (1984). Subjective well-being. *Psychological Bulletin, 95,* 542–575.

Digman, J. M. (1990). Personality structure: Emergence of the five-factor model. *Annual Review of Psychology, 41,* 417–440.

D'Imperio, R., Dubow, E., & Ippolito, M. (2000). Resilient and stress-affected adolescents in an urban setting. *Journal of Clinical Child Psychology, 29,* 129–142.

Dindia, K., & Allen, M. (1992). Sex differences in self-disclosure: A meta-analysis. *Psychological Bulletin, 112,* 106–124.

Dion, M., Braver, S., Wolchik, S., & Sandler, I. (1997). Alcohol abuse and psychopathic deviance in noncustodial parents as predictors of child support payment and visitation. *American Journal of Orthopsychiatry, 67,* 70–79.

DiPietro, J., Hodgson, D., Costigan, K., Hilton, S., & Johnson, T. (1996). Fetal neurobehavioral development. *Child Development, 67,* 2553–2567.

DiPietro, J., Hodgson, D., Costigan, K., & Johnson, T. (1996). Fetal antecedents of infant temperament. *Child Development, 67,* 2568–2583.

Dishion, T. J., French, D. C., & Patterson, G. R. (1995). The development and ecology of antisocial behavior. In D. Cicchetti & D. J. Cohen (Eds.), *Developmental psychopathology: Vol. 2. Risk, disorder, and adaptation* (pp. 421–471). New York: Wiley.

Dishion, T. J., Patterson, G. R., Stoolmiller, M., & Skinner, M. L. (1991). Family, school, and behavioral antecedents to early adolescent involvement with antisocial peers. *Developmental Psychology, 27,* 172–180.

Dittmann-Kohli, F., Lachman, M. E., Kliegl, R., & Baltes, P. B. (1991). Effects of cognitive training and testing on intellectual efficacy beliefs in elderly adults. *The Journals of Gerontology: Psychological Sciences, 46,* P162–164.

Dobson, A., Brown, W., Ball, J., Powers, J., & McFadden, M. (1999). Women drivers' behaviour, socio-demographic characteristics and accidents. *Accident Analysis & Prevention, 31,* 525–535.

Dockett, S., & Smith, I. (1995, March). *Children's theories of mind and their involvement in complex shared pretense.* Paper presented at the biennial meetings of the Society for Research in Child Development, Indianapolis, IN.

Doctoroff, S. (1997). Sociodramatic script training and peer role prompting: Two tactics to promote and sociodramatic play and peer interaction. *Early Child Development & Care, 136,* 27–43.

Dodge, K. (1993). Social-cognitive mechanisms in the development of conduct disorder and depression. *Annual Review of Psychology, 44,* 559–584.

Dodge, K. (1997, April). *Testing developmental theory through prevention trials.* Paper presented at the biennial meeting of the Society for Research on Child Development. Washington, DC.

Dodge, K. A., Pettit, G. S., & Bates, J. E. (1994). Socialization mediators of the relation between socioeconomic status and child conduct problems. *Child Development, 65,* 649–665.

Doh, H., & Falbo, T. (1999). Social competence, maternal attentiveness, and overprotectiveness: Only children in Korea. *International Journal of Behavioral Development, 23,* 149–162.

Dollard, J., Doob, L. W., Miller, N. E., Mowrer, O. H., & Sears, R. R. (1939). *Frustration and aggression.* New Haven, CT: Yale University Press.

Donnerstein, E., Slaby, R. G., & Eron, L. D. (1994). The mass media and youth aggression. In L. D. Eron, J. H. Gentry, & P. Schlegel (Eds.), *Reason to hope: A psychosocial perspective on violence and youth* (pp. 219–250). Washington, DC: American Psychological Association.

Donohew, R., Hoyle, R., Clayton, R., Skinner, W., Colon, S., & Rice, R. (1999). Sensation seeking and drug use by adolescents and their friends: Models for marijuana and alcohol. *Journal of Studies on Alcohol, 60,* 622–631.

Dornbusch, S. M., Ritter, P. L., Liederman, P. H., Roberts, D. F., & Fraleigh, M. J. (1987). The relation of parenting style to adolescent school performance. *Child Development, 58,* 1244–1257.

Doty, R. L., Shaman, P., Appelbaum, S. L., Bigerson, R., Sikorski, L., & Rosenberg, L. (1984). Smell identification ability: Changes with age. *Science, 226,* 1441–1443.

Downe-Wamboldt, B., & Tamlyn, D. (1997). An international survey of death education trends in faculties of nursing and medicine. *Death Studies, 21,* 177–188.

Doyle, A. B., & Aboud, F. E. (1995). A longitudinal study of white children's racial prejudice as a social-cognitive development. *Merrill-Palmer Quarterly, 41,* 209–228.

Draper, B., Gething, L., Fethney, J., & Winfield, S. (1999). The Senior Psychiatrist Survey III: Attitudes towards personal ageing, life experiences and psychiatric practice. *Australian & New Zealand Journal of Psychiatry, 33,* 717–722.

Dreher, G. F., & Bretz, R. D., Jr. (1991). Cognitive ability and career attainment: Moderating effects of early career success. *Journal of Applied Psychology, 76,* 392–397.

Dreman, S., Pielberger, C., & Darzi, O. (1997). The relation of state-anger to self-esteem, perceptions of family structure and attributions of responsibility for divorce of custodial mothers in the stabilization phase of the divorce process. *Journal of Divorce & Remarriage, 28,* 157–170.

Drevets, W., Price, J., Simpson, J., Todd, R., Reich, T., Vannier, M., & Raichle, M. (1997). Subgenual prefrontal cortex abnormalities in mood disorders. *Nature, 386,* 824–827.

Drinking a cause of family problems for 3 of 10 Americans. (1997, September 27). *Gallup Poll Archives,* 1–6.

Driscoll, A., & Nagel, N. (1999). *Early childhood education: Birth–8.* Needham Heights, MA: Allyn & Bacon.

Drobnic, S., Blossfeld, H., & Rohwer, G. (1999). Dynamics of women's employment patterns over the family life course: A comparison of the United States and Germany. *Journal of Marriage & the Family, 61,* 133–146.

Droege, K., & Stipek, D. (1993). Children's use of dispositions to predict classmates' behavior. *Developmental Psychology, 29,* 646–654.

Drum, P. (1985). Retention of text information by grade, ability and study. *Discourse Processes, 8,* 21–52.

Due, P., Holstein, B., Lund, R., Modvig, J., & Avlund, K. (1999). Social relations: Network, support and relational strain. *Social Science & Medicine, 48,* 661–673.

Duffy, F. (1994). The role of quantified electroencephalography in psychological research. In K. Fischer & G. Dawson (Eds.), *Human behavior and the developing brain* (pp. 93–136). New York: Guilford Press.

Duka, T., Tasker, R., & McGowan, J. (2000). The effects of 3-week estrogen hormone replacement on cognition in elderly healthy females. *Psychopharmacology, 149,* 129–139.

Duke, P. M., Carlsmith, J. M., Jennings, D., Martin, J. A., Dornbusch, S. M., Gross, R. T., & Siegel-Gorelick, B. (1982). Educational correlates of early and late sexual maturation in adolescence. *Journal of Pediatrics, 100,* 633–637.

Duncan, G. J., Brooks-Gunn, J., & Klebanov, P. K. (1994). Economic deprivation and early childhood development. *Child Development, 65,* 296–318.

Duncan, M., Stayton, C., & Hall, C. (1999). Police reports on domestic incidents involving intimate partners: Injuries and medical help-seeking. *Women & Health, 30,* 1–13.

Dunn, J. (1994). Experience and understanding of emotions, relationships, and membership in a particular culture. In P. Ekman & R. J. Davidson (Eds.), *The nature of emotion: Fundamental questions* (pp. 352–355). New York: Oxford University Press.

Dunphy, D. C. (1963). The social structure of urban adolescent peer groups. *Sociometry, 26,* 230–246.

Dura, J. R., & Kiecolt-Glaser, J. K. (1991). Family transitions, stress, and health. In P. A. Cowan & M. Hetherington (Eds.), *Family transitions* (pp. 59–76). Hillsdale, NJ: Erlbaum.

Durlak, J. A. (1972). Relationship between attitudes toward life and death among elderly women. *Developmental Psychology, 8,* 146.

Dutch Senate OKs doctor-assisted suicide. (2001, April 11). *Houston Chronicle,* p. 16A.

Duursma, S. A., Raymakers, J. A., Boereboom, F. T. J., & Scheven, B. A. A. (1991). Estrogen and bone metabolism. *Obstetrical and Gynecological Survey, 47,* 38–44.

Duvall, E. M. (1962). *Family development.* New York: Lippincott.

Dyck, J., Gee, N., & Smither, J. (1998). The changing construct of computer anxiety for younger and older adults. *Computers in Human Behavior, 14,* 61–77.

Dykstra, P. A. (1995). Loneliness among the never and formerly married: The importance of supportive friendships and a desire for independence. *Journals of Gerontology: Social Sciences, 50B,* S321–329.

Dyregrov, A., Gjestad, R., Bie Wikander, A., & Vigerust, S. (1999). Reactions following the sudden death of a classmate. *Scandinavian Journal of Psychology, 40,* 167–176.

Eagly, A., & Wood, W. (1999). The origins of sex differences in human behavior: Evolved dispositions versus social roles. *American Psychologist, 54,* 408–423.

Eames, M., Ben-Schlomo, Y., & Marmot, M. G. (1993). Social deprivation and premature mortality: Regional comparison across England. *British Medical Journal, 307,* 1097–1102.

Earles, J. L., & Salthouse, T. A. (1995). Interrelations of age, health, and speed. *Journals of Gerontology: Psychological Sciences, 50B,* P33–41.

Eccles, J., Barber, B., & Jozefowicz, D. (1998). Linking gender to educational, occupational, and recreational choices: Applying the Eccles et al. model of achievement-related choices. In W. B. Swann, Jr., J. H. Langlois, & L. A. Gibert (Eds.), *Sexism and stereotypes in modern society: The gender science of Janet Spence* (pp. 153–192). Washington, DC: APA Press.

Eccles, J., Jacobs, J., & Harold, R. (1990). Gender role stereotypes, expectancy effects, and parents' socialization of gender differences. *Journal of Social Issues, 46,* 183–201.

Echt, K., Morrell, R., & Park, D. (1998). Effects of age and training formats on basic computer skill acquisition in older adults. *Educational Gerontology, 24,* 3–25.

Education Trust. (1996). *Education watch: The 1996 Education Trust state and national data book.* Washington, DC: Author.

Edwards, J. N. (1969). Familial behavior as social exchange. *Journal of Marriage and the Family, 31,* 518–526.

Eichorn, D. H., Clausen, J. A., Haan, N., Honzik, M. P., & Mussen, P. H. (Eds.). (1981). *Present and past in middle life.* New York: Academic Press.

Eiden, R., Chavez, F., & Leonard, K. (1999). Parent-infant interactions among families with alcoholic fathers. *Development & Psychopathology, 11,* 745–762.

Einerson, M. (1998). Fame, fortune, and failure: Young girls' moral language surrounding popular culture. *Youth & Society, 30,* 241–257.

Eisenberg, N. (1992). *The caring child.* Cambridge, MA: Harvard University Press.

Eisenberg, N. (2000). Emotion, regulation, and moral development. *Annual Review of Psychology, 51,* 665–697.

Eisenberg, N., Fabes, R. A., Murphy, B., Karbon, M., Smith, M., & Maszk, P. (1996b). The relations of children's dispositional empathy-related responding to their emotionality, regulation, and social functioning. *Developmental Psychology, 32,* 195–209.

Eisenberg, N., Fabes, R. A., Murphy, B., Maszk, P., Smith, M., & Karbon, M. (1995). The role of emotionality and regulation in children's social functioning: A longitudinal study. *Child Development, 66*, 1360–1384.

Eisenberg, N., Guthrie, I., Murphy, B., Shepard, S., et al. (1999). Consistency and development of prosocial dispositions: A longitudinal study. *Child Development, 70*, 1360–1372.

Eisenberger, R., Pierce, W., & Cameron, J. (1999). Effects of reward on intrinsic motivation-negative, neutral, and positive: Comment on Deci, Koestner, and Ryan. *Psychological Bulletin, 125*, 677–691.

Elbedour, S., Baker, A., & Charlesworth, W. (1997). The impact of political violence on moral reasoning in children. *Child Abuse & Neglect, 21*, 1053–1066.

Elder, G. H., Jr. (1974). *Children of the Great Depression.* Chicago: University of Chicago Press.

Elder, G. H., Jr. (1978). Family history and the life course. In T. Hareven (Ed.), *Transitions: The family and the life course in historical perspective* (pp. 17–64). New York: Academic Press.

Elder, G. H., Jr. (1979). Historical change in life patterns and personality. In P. B. Baltes & J. O. G. Brim (Eds.), *Life-span development and behavior* (Vol. 2) (pp. 117–159). New York: Academic Press.

Elder, G. H., Jr., & Caspi, A. (1988). Economic stress in lives: Developmental perspectives. *Journal of Social Issues, 44*, 25–45.

Elder, G. H., Jr., Liker, J. K., & Cross, C. E. (1984). Parent-child behavior in the Great Depression: Life course and intergenerational influences. In P. B. Baltes & O. G. Brim, Jr. (Eds.), *Life-span development and behavior* (Vol 6) (pp. 111–159). New York: Academic Press.

Elkind, D. (1967). Egocentrism in adolescence. *Child Development, 38*, 1025–1033.

Ellenbogen, S., & Chamberland, C. (1997). The peer relations of dropouts: A comparative study of at-risk and not at-risk youths. *Journal of Adolescence, 20*, 355–367.

Elliot, A., & Hall, N. (1997). The impact of self-regulatory teaching strategies on "at-risk" preschoolers' mathematical learning in a computer-mediated environment. *Journal of Computing in Childhood Education, 8*, 187–198.

Ellis R., & Allaire, J. (1999). Modeling computer interest in older adults: The role of age, education, computer knowledge, and computer anxiety. *Human Factors, 41*, 345–355.

Emanuel, E., Fairclough, D., Clarridge, B., Blum, D., Bruera, E., Penley, W., Schnipper, L., & Mayer, R. (2000). Attitudes and practices of U. S. oncologists regarding euthanasia and physician-assisted suicide. *Annals of Internal Medicine, 133*, 527–532.

Emde, R. N. (1992). Individual meaning and increasing complexity: Contributions of Sigmund Freud and Rene Spitz to developmental psychology. *Developmental Psychology, 28*, 347–359.

Emde, R. N., Plomin, R., Robinson, J., Corley, R., DeFries, J., Fulker, D. W., Reznick, J. S., Campos, J., Kagan, J., & Zahn-Waxler, C. (1992). Temperament, emotion, and cognition at fourteen months: The MacArthur longitudinal twin study. *Child Development, 63*, 1437–1455.

Emery, C. F., & Gatz, M. (1990). Psychological and cognitive effects of an exercise program for community-residing older adults. *The Gerontologist, 30*, 184–192.

Emery, R., & Laumann-Billings, L. (1998). An overview of the nature, causes, and consequences of abusive family relationships: Toward differentiating maltreatment and violence. *American Psychologist, 53*, 121–135.

Engle, P., & Breaux, C. (1998). Fathers' involvement with children: Perspectives from developing countries. *Society for Research in Child Development Social Policy Report, 12*, 1–21

Ensign, J. (1998). *Defying the stereotypes of special education: Homeschool students.* Paper presented at the annual meeting of the American Education Research Association, San Diego, CA.

Entwisle, D. R. (1990). Schools and the adolescent. In S. S. Feldman & G. R. Elliott (Eds.), *At the threshold: The developing adolescent* (pp. 197–224). Cambridge, MA: Harvard University Press.

Entwisle, D. R., & Alexander, K. L. (1990). Beginning school math competence: Minority and majority comparisons. *Child Development, 61*, 454–471.

Ericsson, K. A. (1990). Peak performance and age: An examination of peak performance in sports. In P. Baltes & M. M. Baltes (Eds.), *Suc-cessful aging* (pp. 164–196). Cambridge, MA: Cambridge University Press.

Ericsson, K. A., & Crutcher, R. J. (1990). The nature of exceptional performance. In P. B. Baltes, D. L. Featherman, & R. M. Lerner (Eds.), *Life-span development and behavior* (Vol. 10) (pp. 188–218). Hillsdale, NJ: Erlbaum.

Erikson, E. H. (1950). *Childhood and society.* New York: Norton.

Erikson, E. H. (1959). *Identity and the life cycle.* New York: Norton (reissued, 1980).

Erikson, E. H. (1963). *Childhood and society* (2nd ed.). New York: Norton.

Erikson, E. H. (1980a). *Identity and the life cycle.* New York: Norton. (originally published 1959)

Erikson, E. H. (1980b). Themes of adulthood in the Freud-Jung correspondence. In N. J. Smelser & E. Erikson (Eds.), *Themes of work and love in adulthood* (pp. 43–76). Cambridge, MA: Harvard University Press.

Erikson, E. H. (1982). *The life cycle completed.* New York: Norton.

Erikson, E. H., Erikson, J. M., & Kivnick, H. Q. (1986). *Vital involvement in old age.* New York: Norton.

Eron, L. D. (1987). The development of aggressive behavior from the perspective of a developing behaviorism. *American Psychologist, 42*, 435–442.

Eron, L. D., Huesmann, L. R., & Zelli, A. (1991). The role of parental variables in the learning of aggression. In D. J. Pepler & K. H. Rubin (Eds.), *The development and treatment of childhood aggression* (pp. 169–188). Hillsdale, NJ: Erlbaum.

Eskes, T. K. A. B. (1992). Home deliveries in the Netherlands-perinatal mortality and morbidity. *International Journal of Gynecology and Obstetrics, 38*, 161–169.

Etaugh, C., & Liss, M. (1992). Home, school, and playroom: Training grounds for adult gender roles. *Sex Roles, 26*, 129–147.

Ethington, C. (1991). A test of a model of achievement behaviors. *American Educational Research Journal, 28*, 155–172.

Eugster, A., & Vingerhoets, A. (1999). Psychological aspects of in vitro fertilization: A review. *Social Science & Medicine, 48*, 575–589.

Evans, D. A., Funkenstein, H. H., Albert, M. S., Scherr, P. A., Cook, N. R., Chown, M. J., Hebert, L. E., Hennekens, C. H., & Taylor, J. O. (1989). Prevalence of Alzheimer's disease in a community population of older persons. *Journal of the American Medical Association, 262*, 2551–2556.

Evans, L., Ekerdt, D. J., & Bossé, R. (1985). Proximity to retirement and anticipatory involvement: Findings from the Normative Aging Study. *Journal of Gerontology, 40*, 368–374.

Evans, R. I. (1969). *Dialogue with Erik Erikson.* New York: Dutton.

Ex, C., & Janssens, J. (1998). Maternal influences on daughters' gender role attitudes. *Sex Roles, 38*, 171–186.

Eyetsemitan, F. (1998). Stifled grief in the workplace. *Death Studies, 22*, 469–479.

Eysenck, H. J. (1985). *Decline and fall of the Freudian empire.* London: Penguin Books.

Eysenck, H. J., & Wilson, G. D. (1973). *The experimental study of Freudian theories.* London: Methuen.

Fabes, R. A., Knight, G. P., & Higgins, D. A. (1995, March). *Gender differences in aggression: A meta-analytic reexamination of time and age effects.* Paper presented at the biennial meetings of the Society for Research in Child Development, Indianapolis, IN.

Fabrikant, G. (1996, April 8). The young and restless audience: Computers and videos cut into children's time for watching TV and ads. *New York Times*, p. C1.

Fagan, J. F., & Singer, L. T. (1983). Infant recognition memory as a measure of intelligence. In L. P. Lipsett (Ed.), *Advances in infancy research* (Vol. 2) (pp. 31–78). Norwood, NJ: Ablex.

Fagard, J., & Jacquet, A. (1989). Onset of bimanual coordination and symmetry versus asymmetry of movement. *Infant Behavior and Development, 12*, 229–235.

Fagot, B. I., & Hagan, R. (1991). Observations of parent reactions to sex-stereotyped behaviors: Age and sex effects. *Child Development, 62*, 617–628.

Fagot, B. I., & Leinbach, M. D. (1989). The young child's gender schema: Environmental input, internal organization. *Child Development, 60*, 663–672.

Fagot, B. I., & Leinbach, M. D. (1993). Gender-role development in young children: From discrimination to labeling. *Developmental Review, 13,* 205–224.

Fagot, B. I., Leinbach, M. D., & O'Boyle, C. (1992). Gender labeling, gender stereotyping, and parenting behaviors. *Developmental Psychology, 28,* 225–230.

Fahle, M., & Daum, I. (1997). Visual learning and memory as functions of age. *Neuropsychologia, 35,* 1583–1589.

Fahrenfort, J., Jacobs, E., Miedema, S., & Schweizer, A. (1996). Signs of emotional disturbance three years after early hospitalization. *Journal of Pediatric Psychology, 21,* 353–366.

Falbo, T. (1992). Social norms and one-child family: Clinical and policy limitations. In F. Boer & J. Dunn (Eds.), Children's sibling relationships (pp. 71–82). Hillsdale, NJ: Erlbaum.

Fantuzzo, J., Coolahan, K., & Mendez, J. (1998). Contextually relevant validation of peer play constructs with African American Head Start children: Penn Interactive Peer Play Scale. *Early Childhood Research Quarterly, 13,* 411–431.

Farnham-Diggory, S. (1992). *The learning-disabled child.* Cambridge, MA: Harvard University Press.

Farrell, M. P., & Rosenberg, S. D. (1981). *Men at midlife.* Boston: Auburn House.

Farrington, D. P. (1991). Childhood aggression and adult violence: Early precursors and later life outcomes. In D. J. Pepler & K. H. Rubin (Eds.), *The development and treatment of childhood aggression* (pp. 5–30). Hillsdale, NJ: Erlbaum.

Farver, J. (1996). Aggressive behavior in preschoolers' social networks: Do birds of a feather flock together? *Early Childhood Research Quarterly, 11,* 333–350.

Fathers' Rights Coalition. (1999). Statistics on a fatherless America. [Online brochure]. Retrieved December 6, 1999 from the World Wide Web: www.fathersrc.com

Faust, M. S. (1983). Alternative constructions of adolescent growth. In J. Brooks-Gunn & A. C. Petersen (Eds.), *Girls at puberty: Biological and psychosocial perspectives* (pp. 105–126). New York: Plenum.

Federal Interagency Forum on Aging-Related Statistics (FIFARS). (2000). *Older Americans 2000: Key indicators of well-being.* Retrieved February 7, 2001 from the World Wide Web: http://www.agingstats.gov/chartbook2000

Federal Interagency Forum on Child and Family Statistics (FIFCFS). (2000). *America's children: Key national indicators of well-being 2000.* Washington, DC: Author.

Feeney, J. A. (1994). Attachment style, communication patterns, and satisfaction across the life cycle of marriage. *Personal Relationships, 1,* 333–348.

Feiring, C. (1999). Other-sex friendship networks and the development of romantic relationships in adolescence. *Journal of Youth & Adolescence, 28,* 495–512.

Feld, S., & George, L. K. (1994). Moderating effects of prior social resources on the hospitalizations of elders who become widowed. *Aging and Health, 6,* 275–295.

Feldman, H. A., Goldstein, I., Hatzichristou, D. G., Krane, R. J., & McKinlay, J. B. (1994). Impotence and its medical and psychosocial correlates: Results of the Massachusetts male aging study. *The Journal of Urology, 151,* 54–61.

Feldman, R., Weller, A., Leckman, J., Kuint, J., & Eidelman, A. (1999). The nature of the mother's tie to her infant: Maternal bonding under conditions of proximity, separation, and potential loss. *Journal of Child Psychology & Psychiatry & Allied Disciplines, 40,* 929–939.

Fenn, D., & Ganzini, L. (1999). Attitudes of Oregon psychologists toward physician-assisted suicide and the Oregon Death With Dignity Act. *Professional Psychology: Research and Practice, 30,* 235–244.

Fenson, L., Dale, P. S., Reznick, J. S., Bates, E., Thal, D. J., & Pethick, S. J. (1994). Variability in early communicative development. *Monographs of the Society for Research in Child Development, 59*(5, Serial No. 242).

Fergusson, D. M., Horwood, L. J., & Lynskey, M. T. (1993). Maternal smoking before and after pregnancy: Effects on behavioral outcomes in middle childhood. *Pediatrics, 92,* 815–822.

Fernald, A., & Kuhl, P. (1987). Acoustic determinants of infant preference for motherese speech. *Infant Behavior and Development, 10,* 279–293.

Fernandez, M. (1997). Domestic violence by extended family members in India. *Journal of Interpersonal Violence, 12,* 433–455.

Fiatarone, M. A., & Evans, W. J. (1993). The etiology and reversibility of muscle dysfunction in the aged. *The Journals of Gerontology, 48*(Special Issue), 77–83.

Field, T. (1995). Psychologically depressed parents. In M. H. Bornstein (Ed.), *Handbook of parenting: Vol. 4. Applied and practical parenting* (pp. 85–99). Mahwah, NJ: Erlbaum.

Field, T. M. (1991). Quality infant day-care and grade school behavior and performance. *Child Development, 62,* 863–870.

Fields, R. B. (1992). Psychosocial response to environment change. In V. B. Van Hasselt & M. Hersen (Eds.), *Handbook of social development: A lifespan perspective* (pp. 503–544). New York: Plenum.

Fillmore, C. (1997). *A linguist looks at the Ebonics debate.* Washington, DC: Center for Applied Linguistics.

Filsinger, E. E., & Thoma, S. J. (1988). Behavioral antecedents of relationship stability and adjustment: A five-year longitudinal study. *Journal of Marriage and the Family, 50,* 785–795.

Fischer, K., & Rose, S. (1994). Dynamic development of coordination of components in brain and behavior: A framework for theory and research. In K. Fischer & G. Dawson (Eds.), *Human behavior and the developing brain* (pp. 3–66). New York: Guilford Press.

Fischer, K. W., & Bidell, T. (1991). Constraining nativist inferences about cognitive capacities. In S. Carey & R. Gelman (Eds.), *The epigenesis of mind: Essays on biology and cognition* (pp. 199–236). Hillsdale, NJ: Erlbaum.

Fish, M., Stifter, C. A., & Belsky, J. (1991). Conditions of continuity and discontinuity in infant negative emotionality: Newborn to five months. *Child Development, 62,* 1525–1537.

Fisher, B., & Specht, D. (1999). Successful aging and creativity in later life. *Journal of Aging Studies, 13,* 457–472.

Fisher, C. (2000). Mood and emotions while working: Missing pieces of job satisfaction? *Journal of Organizational Behavior, 21,* 185–202.

Fitzgerald, B. (1999). Children of lesbian and gay parents: A review of the literature. *Marriage & Family Review, 29,* 57–75.

Fitzpatrick, J. L., & Silverman, T. (1989). Women's selection of careers in engineering: Do traditional-nontraditional differences still exist? *Journal of Vocational Behavior, 34,* 266–278.

Flannery, D., Vazsonyi, A., Embry, D., Powell, K., Atha, H., Vesterdal, W., & Shenyang, G. (2000, August). *Longitudinal effectiveness of the PeaceBuilders' universal school-based violence prevention program.* Paper presented at the annual meeting of the American Psychological Association, Washington, DC.

Flannery, D. J., Montemayor, R., & Eberly, M. B. (1994). The influence of parent negative emotional expression on adolescents' perceptions of their relationships with their parents. *Personal Relationships, 1,* 259–274.

Flavell, J. H. (1985). *Cognitive development* (2nd ed.). Englewood Cliffs, NJ: Prentice-Hall.

Flavell, J. H. (1986). The development of children's knowledge about the appearance-reality distinction. *American Psychologist, 41,* 418–425.

Flavell, J. H. (1993). Young children's understanding of thinking and consciousness. *Current Directions in Psychological Science, 2,* 40–43.

Flavell, J. H., Everett, B. A., Croft, K., & Flavell, E. R. (1981). Young children's knowledge about visual perception: Further evidence for the Level 1–Level 2 distinction. *Developmental Psychology, 17,* 99–103.

Flavell, J. H., Green, F. L., & Flavell, E. R. (1989). Young children's ability to differentiate appearance-reality and level 2 perspectives in the tactile modality. *Child Development, 60,* 201–213.

Flavell, J. H., Green, F. L., & Flavell, E. R. (1990). Developmental changes in young children's knowledge about the mind. *Cognitive Development, 5,* 1–27.

Flavell, J. H., Green, F. L., Wahl, K. E., & Flavell, E. R. (1987). The effects of question clarification and memory aids on young children's performance on appearance-reality tasks. *Cognitive Development, 2,* 127–144.

Flavell, J. H., Zhang, X.-D., Zou, H., Dong, Q., & Qi, S. (1983). A comparison of the appearance-reality distinction in the People's Republic of China and the United States. *Cognitive Psychology, 15,* 459–466.

Fleeson, W., & Heckhausen, J. (1997). More or less "me" in past, present, and future: Perceived lifetime personality during adulthood. *Psychology & Aging, 12,* 125–136.

Fletcher-Finn, C., & Suddendorf, T. (1996). Do computers affect "the mind"? *Journal of Educational Computing Research, 15,* 97–112.

Fletcher-Finn, C., & Suddendorf, T. (1997). Computers and "the mind": An intervention study. *Journal of Educational Computing Research, 17,* 103–108.

Flowers, L., & Pascarella, E. (1999). Cognitive effects of college racial composition on African American students after 3 years of college. *Journal of College Student Development, 40,* 669–677.

Floyd, F., Stein, T., Harter, K., Allison, A., et al. (1999). Gay, lesbian, and bisexual youths: Separation-individuation, parental attitudes, identity consolidation, and well-being. *Journal of Youth & Adolescence, 28,* 705–717.

Floyd, R. L., Rimer, B. K., Giovino, G. A., Mullen, P. D., & Sullivan, S. E. (1993). A review of smoking in pregnancy: Effects on pregnancy outcomes and cessation efforts. *Annual Review of Public Health, 14,* 379–411.

Flynn, J. (1999). Searching for justice: The discovery of IQ gains over time. *American Psychologist, 54,* 5–20.

Fokin, V., Ponomareva, N., Androsova, L., & Gavrilova, S. (1997). Interhemispheric asymmetry and neuroimmune modulation in normal aging and Alzheimer's dementias. *Human Physiology, 23,* 284–288.

Foley, D., Monjan, A., Izmirlian, G., Hays, J., & Blazer, D. (1999). Incidence and remission of insomnia among elderly adults in a biracial cohort. *Sleep, 22* (Supplement 2), S373–S378.

Folk, K. F., & Yi, Y. (1994). Piecing together child care with multiple arrangements: Crazy quilt or preferred pattern for employed parents of preschool children? *Journal of Marriage and the Family, 56,* 669–680.

Folven, R. J., & Bonvillian, J. D. (1991). The transition from nonreferential to referential language in children acquiring American Sign Language. *Developmental Psychology, 27,* 806–816.

Fordham, K., & Stevenson-Hinde, J. (1999). Shyness, friendship quality, and adjustment during middle childhood. *Journal of Child Psychology & Psychiatry & Allied Disciplines, 40,* 757–768.

Forsell, Y., & Winblad, B. (1999). Incidence of major depression in a very elderly population. *Journal of Geriatric Psychiatry, 14,* 368–372.

Forte, C., & Hansvick, C. (1999). Applicant age as a subjective employability factor: A study of workers over and under age fifty. *Journal of Employment Counseling, 36,* 24–34.

Fourn, L., Ducic, S., & Seguin, L. (1999). Smoking and intrauterine growth retardation in the Republic of Benin. *Journal of Epidemiology & Community Health, 53,* 432–433.

Fox, N. A., Kimmerly, N. L., & Schafer, W. D. (1991). Attachment to mother/attachment to father: A meta-analysis. *Child Development, 62,* 210–225.

Fozard, J. L. (1990). Vision and hearing in aging. In J. E. Birren & K. W. Schaie (Eds.), *Handbook of the psychology of aging* (3rd ed.) (pp. 150–171). San Diego, CA: Academic Press.

Fozard, J. L., Metter, E. J., & Brant, L. J. (1990). Next steps in describing aging and disease in longitudinal studies. *Journals of Gerontology: Psychological Sciences, 45,* P116–127.

Franche, R., & Bulow, C. (1999). The impact of a subsequent pregnancy on grief and emotional adjustment following a perinatal loss. *Infant Mental Health Journal, 20,* 175–187.

Francis, L. (1997). Ideology and interpersonal emotion management: Redefining identity in two support groups. *Social Psychology Quarterly, 60,* 153–171.

Francis, P. L., Self, P. A., & Horowitz, F. D. (1987). The behavioral assessment of the neonate: An overview. In J. D. Osofsky (Ed.), *Handbook of infant development* (2nd ed.) (pp. 723–779). New York: Wiley-Interscience.

Francis-Smythe, J., & Smith, P. (1997). The psychological impact of assessment in a development center. *Human Relations, 50,* 149–167.

Franco, N., & Levitt, M. (1998). The social ecology of middle childhood: Family support, friendship quality, and self-esteem. *Family Relations: Interdisciplinary Journal of Applied Family Studies, 47,* 315–321.

Fraser, A. M., Brockert, J. E., & Ward, R. H. (1995). Association of young maternal age with adverse reproductive outcomes. *New England Journal of Medicine, 332,* 1113–1117.

Freedman, D. G. (1979). Ethnic differences in babies. *Human Nature, 2,* 36–43.

Freedman, V. A. (1996). Family structure and the risk of nursing home admission. *Journals of Gerontology: Social Sciences, 51B,* S61–69.

Freeman, E. W., & Rickels, K. (1993). *Early childbearing: Perspectives of black adolescents on pregnancy, abortion, and contraception.* Newbury Park, CA: Sage.

Frey, K. S., & Ruble, D. N. (1992). Gender constancy and the "cost" of sex-typed behavior: A test of the conflict hypothesis. *Developmental Psychology, 28,* 714–721.

Frick, P., Christian, R., & Wooton, J. (1999). Age trends in association between parenting practices and conduct problems. *Behavior Modification, 23,* 106–128.

Friedman, H. S., Hawley, P. H., & Tucker, J. S. (1994). Personality, health, and longevity. *Current Directions in Psychological Science, 3,* 37–41.

Friedman, M., & Rosenman, R. H. (1974). *Type A behavior and your heart.* New York: Knopf.

Fuchs, L., Fuchs, D., Karns, K., Hamlett, C., Dutka, S., & Katsaroff, M. (2000). The importance of providing background information on the structure and scoring of performance assessments. *Applied Measurement in Education, 13,* 134.

Fuller, T. L., & Fincham, F. D. (1995). Attachment style in married couples: Relation to current marital functioning, stability over time, and method of assessment. *Personal Relationships, 2,* 17–34.

Fung, H. (1999). Becoming a moral child: The socialization of shame among young Chinese children. *Ethos, 27,* 180–209.

Funk, J., & Buchman, D. (1999). Playing violent video and computer games and adolescent self-concept. *Journal of Communication, 46,* 19–32.

Funk, J., Buchman, D., Myers, B., & Jenks, J. (2000, August). *Asking the right questions in research on violent electronic games.* Paper presented at the annual meeting of the American Psychological Association, Washington, DC.

Furnham, A. (1999). Economic socialization: A study of adults' perceptions and uses of allowances (pocket money) to educate children. *British Journal of Developmental Psychology, 17,* 585–604.

Furstenberg, F., & Harris, J. (1992). When fathers matter/why fathers matter: the impact of paternal involvement on the offspring of adolescent mothers. In R. Lerman & T. Ooms (Eds.), *Young unwed fathers.* Philadelphia: Temple University Press.

Furstenberg, F. F., Jr., & Cherlin, A. J. (1991). *Divided families: What happens to children when parents part.* Cambridge, MA: Harvard University Press.

Gaillard, W., Hertz-Pannier, L., Mott, S., Barnett, A., LeBihan, D., & Theodore, W. (2000). Functional anatomy of cognitive development: fMRI of verbal fluency in children and adults. *Neurology, 54,* 180–185.

Gainey, R., Catalano, R., Haggerty, K., & Hoppe, M. (1997). Deviance among the children of heroin addicts in treatment: Impact of parents and peers. *Deviant Behavior, 18,* 143–159.

Galambos, N., & Maggs, J. (1991). Out-of-school care of young adolescents and self-reported behavior. *Developmental Psychology, 27,* 644–655.

Galanter, M., Keller, D., & Dermatis, H. (1997). Using the Internet for clinical training: A course on network therapy for substance abuse. *Psychiatric Services, 48,* 999–1000, 1008.

Galassi, J., Gulledge, S., & Cox, N. (1997). Middle school advisories: Retrospect and prospect. *Review of Educational Research, 67,* 301–338.

Gallagher, A., De Lisi, R., Holst, P., McGillicuddy-De Lisi, A., et al. (2000). Gender differences in advanced mathematical problem solving. *Journal of Experimental Child Psychology, 75,* 165–190.

Gallagher, A., Frith, U., & Snowling, M. (2000). Precursors of literacy delay among children at genetic risk of dyslexia. *Journal of Child Psychology & Psychiatry & Allied Disciplines, 41,* 202–213.

Gallagher, S. K. (1994). Doing their share: Comparing patterns of help given by older and younger adults. *Journal of Marriage and the Family, 56,* 567–578.

Gallagher, W. (1993, May). Midlife myths. *The Atlantic Monthly,* pp. 51–68.

Gallagher-Thompson, D., Futterman, A., Farberow, N., Thompson, L. W., & Peterson, J. (1993). The impact of spousal bereavement on older widows and widowers. In M. S. Stroebe, W. Stroebe, & R. O. Hansson (Eds.), *Handbook of bereavement: Theory, research, and intervention* (pp. 227–239). Cambridge, England: Cambridge University Press.

Gallagher-Thompson, D., Tazeau, Y., & Basilio L. (1997). The relationships of dimensions of acculturation to self-reported depression in older Mexican-American women. *Journal of Clinical Geropsychology, 3*, 123–137.

Gallo, W., Bradley, E., Siegel, M., & Kasl, S. (2000). Health effects of involuntary job loss among older workers: Findings from the health and retirement survey. Journals of Gerontology: Series B: *Psychological Sciences & Social Sciences, 55B*, S131–S140.

Gambert, S. R., Schultz, B. M., & Hamdy, R. C. (1995). Osteoporosis: Clinical features, prevention, and treatment. *Endocrinology and Metabolism Clinics of North America, 24*, 317–371.

Gamoran, A., Porter, A., Smithson, J., & White, P. (1997). Upgrading high school mathematics instruction: Improving learning opportunities for low-achieving, low-income youth. *Educational Evaluation & Policy Analysis, 19*, 325–338.

Gannon, L., & Stevens, J. (1998). Portraits of menopause in the mass media. *Women & Health, 27*, 1–15.

Ganong, L., & Coleman, M. (1994). *Remarried family relationships.* Thousand Oaks, CA: Sage Publications.

Garbarino, J., Dubrow, N., Kostelny, K., & Pardo, C. (1992). *Children in danger: Coping with the consequences of community violence:* San Francisco: Jossey-Bass.

Garbarino, J., Kostelny, K., & Dubrow, N. (1991). *No place to be a child: Growing up in a war zone.* Lexington, MA: Lexington Books.

Garbarino, J., & Sherman, D. (1980). High-risk neighborhoods and high-risk families: The human ecology of child maltreatment. *Child Development, 51*, 188–198.

Gardiner, M., Luszcz, M., & Bryan, J. (1997). The manipulation and measurement of task-specific memory self-efficacy in younger and older adults. *International Journal of Behavioral Development, 21*, 209–227.

Gardner, H. (1983). *Frames of mind: The theory of multiple intelligence.* New York: Basic Books.

Gardner, R., Friedman, B., & Jackson, N. (1999). Body size estimations, body dissatisfaction, and ideal size preferences in children six through thirteen. *Journal of Youth & Adolescence, 28*, 603–618.

Garland, A. F., & Zigler, E. (1993). Adolescent suicide prevention: Current research and social policy implications. *American Psychologist, 48*, 169–182.

Garmezy, N. (1993). Vulnerability and resilience. In D. C. Funder, R. D. Parke, C. Tomlinson-Keasey, & K. Widaman (Eds.), *Studying lives through time: Personality and development* (pp. 377–398). Washington, DC: American Psychological Association.

Garmezy, N., & Rutter, M. (Eds.). (1983). *Stress, coping, and development in children.* New York: McGraw-Hill.

Garn, S. M. (1980). Continuities and change in maturational timing. In O. G. Brim, Jr. & J. Kagan (Eds.), *Constancy and change in human development* (pp. 113–162). Cambridge, MA: Harvard University Press.

Garner, C. (1995). Infertility. In C. I. Fogel & N. F. Woods (Eds.), *Women's health care* (pp. 611–628). Thousand Oaks, CA: Sage.

Garnier, H., Stein, J., & Jacobs, J. (1997). The process of dropping out of high school: A 19-year perspective. *American Educational Research Journal, 34*, 395–419.

Garrison, R. J., Gold, R. S., Wilson, P. W. F., & Kannel, W. B. (1993). Educational attainment and coronary heart disease risk: The Framingham offspring study. *Preventive Medicine, 22*, 54–64.

Gatz, M., Kasl-Godley, J. E., & Karel, M. J. (1996). Aging and mental disorders. In J. E. Birren & K. W. Schaie (Eds.), *Handbook of the psychology of aging* (4th ed.) (pp. 365–381). San Diego, CA: Academic Press.

Gaziano, J. M., & Hennekens, C. H. (1995). Dietary fat and risk of prostate cancer. *Journal of the National Cancer Institute, 87*, 1427–1428.

Ge, X., & Conger, R. (1999). Adjustment problems and emerging personality characteristics from early to late adolescence. *American Journal of Community Psychology, 27*, 429–459.

Geary, D., Lin, F., Chen, G., Saults, S., et al. (1999). Contributions of computational fluency to cross-national differences in arithmetical reasoning abilities. *Journal of Educational Psychology, 91*, 716–719.

Geary, D. C., Bow-Thomas, C. C., Fan, L., & Siegler, R. S. (1993). Even before formal instruction, Chinese children outperform American children in mental addition. *Cognitive Development, 8*, 517–529.

Gee, C., & Rhodes, J. (1999). Postpartum transitions in adolescent mothers' romantic and maternal relationships. *Merrill-Palmer Quarterly, 45*, 512–532.

Gelman, R. (1972). Logical capacity of very young children: Number invariance rules. *Child Development, 43*, 75–90.

Gentner, D. (1982). Why nouns are learned before verbs: Linguistic relativity versus natural partitioning. In S. A. Kuczaj, II (Ed.), *Language development: Vol. 2. Language, thought, and culture* (pp. 301–334). Hillsdale, NJ: Erlbaum.

George, L. K. (1990). Social structure, social processes, and social-psychological states. In R. H. Binstock & L. K. George (Eds.), *Handbook of aging and the social sciences* (3rd ed.) (pp. 186–204). San Diego, CA: Academic Press.

George, L. K. (1993). Sociological perspectives on life transitions. *Annual Review of Sociology, 19*, 353–373.

Georgieff, M. K. (1994). Nutritional deficiencies as developmental risk factors: Commentary on Pollitt and Gorman. In C. A. Nelson (Ed.), *The Minnesota Symposia on Child Development* (Vol. 27) (pp. 145–159). Hillsdale, NJ: Erlbaum.

Gerbner tackles "fairness." (1997, February 24). *Electronic Media.* Retrieved January 15, 2001 from the World Wide Web: www.mediascope.org/pubs/ibriefs/dft.html

Gerhardstein, P., Liu, J., & Rovee-Collier, C. (1998). Perceptual constraints on infant memory retrieval. *Journal of Experimental Child Psychology, 69*, 109–131.

Gerwood, J., LeBlanc, M., & Piazza, N. (1998). The Purpose-in-Life Test and religious denomination: Protestant and Catholic scores in an elderly population. *Journal of Clinical Psychology, 54*, 49–53.

Gesell, A. (1925). *The mental growth of the preschool child.* New York: Macmillan.

Gesser, G., Wong, P. T. P., & Reker, G. T. (1987/1988). Death attitudes across the life-span: The development and validation of the death attitude profile (DAP). *Omega, 18*, 113–128.

Giambra, L. M., Arenberg, D., Zonderman, A. B., Kawas, C., & Costa, P. T., Jr. (1995). Adult life span changes in immediate visual memory and verbal intelligence. *Psychology and Aging, 10*, 123–139.

Gibbs, R., & Beitel, D. (1995). What proverb understanding reveals about how people think. *Psychological Bulletin, 118*, 133–154.

Gibson, D. M. (1986). Interaction and well-being in old age: Is it quantity or quality that counts? *International Journal of Aging and Human Development, 24*, 29–40.

Gibson, D. R. (1990). Relation of socioeconomic status to logical and sociomoral judgment of middle-aged men. *Psychology and Aging, 5*, 510–513.

Gilbertson, M., & Bramlett, R. (1998). Phonological awareness screening to identify at-risk readers: Implications for practitioners. *Language, Speech, & Hearing Services in Schools, 29*, 109–116.

Gilligan, C. (1982). *In a different voice: Psychological theory and women's development.* Cambridge, MA: Harvard University Press.

Gilligan, C., & Wiggins, G. (1987). The origins of morality in early childhood relationships. In J. Kagan & S. Lamb (Eds.), *The emergence of morality in young children* (pp. 277–307). Chicago: University of Chicago Press.

Gilman, E. A., Cheng, K. K., Winter, H. R., & Scragg, R. (1995). Trends in rates and seasonal distribution of sudden infant deaths in England and Wales, 1988–1992. *British Medical Journal, 30*, 631–632.

Gladue, B. A. (1994). The biopsychology of sexual orientation. *Current Directions in Psychological Science, 3*, 150–154.

Glaser, D. (2000). Child abuse and neglect and the brain-a review. *Journal of Child Psychology & Psychiatry & Allied Disciplines, 41*, 97–116.

Glaser, R., Kiecolt-Glaser, J. K., Bonneau, R. H., Malarkey, W., Kennedy, S., & Hughes, J. (1992). Stress-induced modulation of the immune response to recombinant hepatitis B vaccine. *Psychosomatic Medicine, 54*, 22–29.

Glass, J., & Jolly, G. (1997). Satisfaction in later life among women 60 or over. *Educational Gerontology, 23,* 297–314.

Glass, J., & Kilpatrick, B. (1998). Gender comparisons of baby boomers and financial preparation for retirement. *Educational Gerontology, 24,* 719–745.

Glass, S. (1998). Shared vows. *Psychology Today, 31,* 34.

Glazer, H. (1998). Expressions of children's grief: A qualitative study. *International Journal of Play Therapy, 7,* 51–65.

Gledhill, L., (1997, March 18). Deadbeat dads. Missouri Digital News. Retrieved December 6, 1999 from the World Wide Web: www.mdn.com

Gleitman, L. R., & Gleitman, H. (1992). A picture is worth a thousand words, but that's the problem: The role of syntax in vocabulary acquisition. *Current Directions in Psychological Science, 1,* 31–35.

Glenn, N. D. (1990). Quantitative research on marital quality in the 1980s: A critical review. *Journal of Marriage and the Family, 52,* 818–831.

Glenn, N. D., & Weaver, C. N. (1985). Age, cohort, and reported job satisfaction in the United States. In A. S. Blau (Ed.), *Current perspectives on aging and the life cycle. A research annual: Vol. 1. Work, retirement and social policy* (pp. 89–110). Greenwich, CT.

Glenn, N. D., & Weaver, C. N. (1988). The changing relationship of marital status to reported happiness. *Journal of Marriage and the Family, 50,* 317–324.

Gloger-Tippelt, G., & Huerkamp, M. (1998). Relationship change at the transition to parenthood and security of infant-mother attachment. *International Journal of Behavioral Development, 23,* 633–655.

Gnepp, J., & Chilamkurti, C. (1988). Children's use of personality attributions to predict other people's emotional and behavioral reactions. *Child Development, 50,* 743–754.

Goetting, A. (1986). The developmental tasks of siblingship over the life cycle. *Journal of Marriage and the Family, 48,* 703–714.

Gohm, C., Humphreys, L., & Yao, G. (1998). Underachievement among spatially gifted students. *American Educational Research Journal, 35,* 515–531.

Gold, D. (1996). Continuities and discontinuities in sibling relationships across the life span. In V. I. Bengtson (Ed.), *Adulthood and aging: Research on continuities and discontinuities.* New York: Springer.

Gold, D. P., Andres, D., Etezadi, J., Arbuckle, T., Schwartzman, A., & Chaikelson, J. (1995). Structural equation model of intellectual change and continuity and predictors of intelligence in older men. *Psychology and Aging, 10,* 294–303.

Gold, D. T. (1990). Late-life sibling relationships: Does race affect typological distribution? *The Gerontologist, 30,* 741–748.

Goldberg, A. P., Dengel, D. R., & Hagberg, J. M. (1996). Exercise physiology and aging. In E. L. Schneider & J. W. Rowe (Eds.), *Handbook of the biology of aging* (4th ed.) (pp. 331–354). San Diego, CA: Academic Press.

Goldberg, A. P., & Hagberg, J. M. (1990). Physical exercise in the elderly. In E. R. Schneider & J. W. Rowe (Eds.), *Handbook of the biology of aging* (3rd ed.) (pp. 407–428). San Diego, CA: Academic Press.

Goldberg, W. A. (1990). Marital quality, parental personality, and spousal agreement about perceptions and expectations for children. *Merrill-Palmer Quarterly, 36,* 531–556.

Goldfield, B. A., & Reznick, J. S. (1990). Early lexical acquisition: Rate, content, and the vocabulary spurt. *Journal of Child Language, 17,* 171–183.

Goldsmith, H., & Alansky, J. (1987). Maternal and infant temperamental predictors of attachment: A meta-analytic review. *Journal of Consulting and Clinical Psychology, 55,* 805–806.

Goldsmith, H. H., Buss, K. A., & Lemery, K. S. (1995, March). *Toddler and childhood temperament: Expanded content, stronger genetic evidence, new evidence for the importance of environment.* Paper presented at the biennial meetings of the Society for Research in Child Development, Indianapolis, IN.

Goleman, D. (1995). *Emotional intelligence.* New York: Bantam.

Golombok, S., & Fivush, R. (1994). *Gender development.* Cambridge, England: Cambridge University Press.

Golombok, S., & Tasker, F. (1996). Do parents influence the sexual orientation of their children? Findings from a longitudinal study of lesbian families. *Developmental Psychology, 32,* 3–11.

Gomez, R., Bounds, J., Holmberg, K., Fullarton, C., & Gomez, A. (1999). Effects of neuroticism and avoidant coping style on maladjustment during early adolescence. *Personality & Individual Differences, 26,* 305–319.

Gomez, R., Holmberg, K., Bounds, J., Fullarton, C., & Gomez, A. (1999). Neuroticism and extraversion as predictors of coping styles during early adolescence. *Personality & Individual Differences, 27,* 3–17.

Gonzalez, J., & Valle, I. (2000). Word identification and reading disorders in the Spanish language. *Journal of Learning Disabilities, 33,* 44–60.

Good, T. L., & Weinstein, R. S. (1986). Schools make a difference: Evidence, criticisms, and new directions. *American Psychologist, 41,* 1090–1097.

Goodenough, F. L. (1931). *Anger in young children.* Minneapolis: University of Minnesota Press.

Goodsitt, J. V., Morse, P. A., Ver Hoeve, J. N., & Cowan, N. (1984). Infant speech recognition in multisyllabic contexts. *Child Development, 55,* 903–910.

Goossens, R., & van IJzendoorn, M. (1990). Quality of infants' attachments to professional caregivers: Relation to infant-parent attachment and day-care characteristics. *Child Development, 61,* 832–837.

Gopnik, A., & Astington, J. W. (1988). Children's understanding of representational change and its relation to the understanding of false belief and the appearance-reality distinction. *Child Development, 59,* 26–37.

Gopnik, A., & Wellman, H. M. (1994). The theory theory. In L. A. Hirschfeld & S. A. Gelman (Eds.), *Mapping the mind* (pp. 257–293). Cambridge, England: Cambridge University Press.

Gordon, G. S., & Vaughan, C. (1986). Calcium and osteoporosis. *Journal of Nutrition, 116,* 319–322.

Gordon, R., Chase-Lansdale, P., Matjasko, J., & Brooks-Gunn, J. (1997). Young mothers living with grandmothers and living apart: How neighborhood and household contexts relate to multigenerational coresidence in African American families. *Applied Developmental Science, 1,* 89–106.

Goss, R., & Klass, D. (1997). Tibetan Buddhism and the resolution of grief: The Bard-thodo for the dying and the grieving. *Death Studies, 21,* 377–395.

Gossett, B., Cuyjet, M., & Cockriel, I. (1998). African Americans' perception of marginality in the campus culture. *College Student Journal, 32,* 22–32.

Gothelf, D., Apter, A., Brand-Gothelf, A., Offer, N., Ofek, H., Tyano, S., & Pfeffer, C. (1998). Death concepts in suicidal adolescents. *Journal of the American Academy of Child & Adolescent Psychiatry, 37,* 1279–1286.

Gottlob, L., & Madden, D. (1999). Age differences in the strategic allocation of visual attention. *Journals of Gerontology: Series B: Psychological Sciences & Social Sciences, 54B,* P165–P172.

Gottman, J. M. (1986). The world of coordinated play: Same- and cross-sex friendship in young children. In J. M. Gottman & J. G. Parker (Eds.), *Conversations of friends: Speculations on affective development* (pp. 139–191). Cambridge, England: Cambridge University Press.

Gottman, J. M. (1994a). *What predicts divorce? The relationship between marital processes and marital outcomes.* Hillsdale, NJ: Erlbaum.

Gottman, J. M. (1994b). *Why marriages succeed or fail.* New York: Simon & Schuster.

Gould, E., Reeves, A., Graziano, M., & Gross, C. (1999). Neurogenesis in the neocortex of adult primates. *Science, 286,* 548–552.

Graber, J. A., Brooks-Gunn, J., Paikoff, R. L., & Warren, M. P. (1994). Prediction of eating problems: An 8-year study of adolescent girls. *Developmental Psychology, 30,* 823–834.

Graham, J., Cohen, R., Zbikowski, S., & Secrist, M. (1998). A longitudinal investigation of race and sex as factors in children's classroom friendship choices. *Child Study Journal, 28,* 245–266.

Graham, S., & Harris, K. (1997). It can be taught, but it does not develop naturally: Myths and realities in writing instruction. *School Psychology Review, 26,* 414–424.

Gralinski, J. H., & Kopp, C. B. (1993). Everyday rules for behavior: Mothers' requests to young children. *Developmental Psychology, 29,* 573–584.

Graves, S. (1993). Television, the portrayal of African Americans, and the development of children's attitudes. In G. L. Berry & J. K. Asamen (Eds.), *Children and television: Images in a changing sociocultural world.* Newbury Park, CA: Sage.

Gray, A., Berlin, J. A., McKinlay, J. B., & Longcope, C. (1991). An examination of research design effects on the association of testosterone and male aging: Results of a meta-analysis. *Journal of Clinical Epidemiology, 44,* 671–684.

Greenberg, J., Lewis, S., & Dodd, D. (1999). Overlapping addictions and self-esteem among college men and women. *Addictive Behaviors, 24,* 565–571.

Greenberg, M. T., Siegel, J. M., & Leitch, C. J. (1983). The nature and importance of attachment relationships to parents and peers during adolescence. *Journal of Youth and Adolescence, 12,* 373–386.

Greenberg, M. T., Speltz, M. L., & DeKlyen, M. (1993). The role of attachment in the early development of disruptive behavior problems. *Development and Psychopathology, 5,* 191–213.

Greenberger, E., & Goldberg, W. A. (1989). Work, parenting, and the socialization of children. *Developmental Psychology, 25,* 22–35.

Greenfield, P. (1994). Video games as cultural artifacts. *Journal of Applied Developmental Psychology, 15,* 3–12.

Greenfield, P., Brannon, C., & Lohr, D. (1994). Two-dimensional representation of movement through three-dimensional space: The role of video game expertise. *Journal of Applied Developmental Psychology, 15,* 87–104.

Greenhaus, J., Collins, K., Singh, R., & Parasuraman, S. (1997). Work and family influences on departure from public accounting. *Journal of Vocational Behavior, 50,* 249–270.

Greenough, W. T., Black, J. E., & Wallace, C. S. (1987). Experience and brain development. *Child Development, 58,* 539–559.

Greer, D. S., Mor, V., Morris, J. N., Sherwood, S., Kidder, D., & Birnbaum, H. (1986). An alternative in terminal care: Results of the National Hospice Study. *Journal of Chronic Diseases, 39,* 9–26.

Greer, S. (1991). Psychological response to cancer and survival. *Psychological Medicine, 21,* 43–49.

Greer, S., Morris, T., & Pettingale, K. W. (1979). Psychological response to breast cancer: Effect on outcome. *Lancet,* 785–787.

Gregg, V., Gibbs, J. C., & Basinger, K. S. (1994). Patterns of developmental delay in moral judgment by male and female delinquents. *Merrill-Palmer Quarterly, 40,* 538–553.

Greider, L. (2000, March/April). How not to be a monster-in-law. *Modern Maturity, 43,* (2), 56–59, 81.

Griffith, J. (1998). The relation of school structure and social environment to parent involvement in elementary schools. *Elementary School Journal, 99,* 53–80.

Griffiths, M. (1999). Internet addiction: Fact or fiction? *Psychologist, 12,* 246–250.

Grohol, J. (1999). *Internet Addiction Guide.* [Online brochure]. Retrieved February 3, 2000 from the World Wide Web: http://www.psychcentral.com/netaddiction

Grolnick, W. S., & Slowiaczek, M. L. (1994). Parents' involvement in children's schooling: A multidimensional conceptualization and motivational model. *Child Development, 65,* 237–252.

Groome, L., Mooney, D., Holland, S., Smith, L., Atterbury, J., & Dykman, R. (1999). Behavioral state affects heart rate response to low-intensity sound in human fetuses. *Early Human Development, 54,* 39–54.

Gross, J., Carstensen, L., Pasupathi, M., Tsai, J., Gostestam-Skorpen, C., & Hsu, A. (1997). Emotion and aging: Experience, expression, and control. *Psychology & Aging, 12,* 590–599.

Grossman, A., Daugelli, A., & Hershberger, S. (2000). Social support networks of lesbian, gay, and bisexual adults 60 years of age and older. *Journals of Gerontology: Series B: Psychological Sciences & Social Sciences, 55B,* P171–P179.

Grossmann, K., Grossmann, K. E., Spangler, G., Suess, G., & Unzner, L. (1985). Maternal sensitivity and newborns' orientation responses as related to quality of attachment in northern Germany. *Monographs of the Society of Research in Child Development, 50*(1–2, Serial No. 209), 233–256.

Grouios, G., Sakadami, N., Poderi, A., & Alevriadou, A. (1999). Excess of non-right-handedness among individuals with intellectual disability: Experimental evidence and possible explanations. *Journal of Intellectual Disability Research, 43,* 306–313.

Guerin, D. W., & Gottfried, A. W. (1994a). Developmental stability and change in parent reports of temperament: A ten-year longitudinal investigation from infancy through preadolescence. *Merrill-Palmer Quarterly, 40,* 334–355.

Guerin, D. W., & Gottfried, A. W. (1994b). Temperamental consequences of infant difficultness. *Infant Behavior and Development, 17,* 413–421.

Guesry, P. (1998). The role of nutrition in brain development. *Preventive Medicine, 27,* 189–194.

Gullotta, T., Adams, G., & Montemayor, R. (1993). *Adolescent sexuality.* Newbury Park, CA: Sage.

Gunnar, M. R. (1994). Psychoendocrine studies of temperament and stress in early childhood: Expanding current models. In J. E. Bates & T. D. Wachs (Eds.), *Temperament: Individual differences at the interface of biology and behavior* (pp. 175–198). Washington, DC: American Psychological Association.

Gunter, T., Jackson, J., & Mulder, G. (1998). Priming and aging: An electrophysiological investigation of N400 and recall. *Brain & Language, 65,* 333–355.

Guo, S. F. (1993). Postpartum depression. *Chung-Hua Fu Chan Ko Tsa Chi, 28,* 532–533, 569.

Gur, R. C., Turetsky, B., Matsui, M., Yan, M., Bilker, W., Hughett, P., & Gur, R. E. (1999). Sex differences in brain gray and white matter in healthy young adults: Correlations with cognitive performance. *Journal of Neuroscience, 19,* 4065–4072.

Guralnik, J. M., & Kaplan, G. A. (1989). Predictors of healthy aging: Prospective evidence from the Alameda County Study. *American Journal of Public Health, 79,* 703–708.

Guralnik, J. M., Land, K. C., Blazer, D., Fillenbaum, G. G., & Branch, L. G. (1993). Educational status and active life expectancy among older blacks and whites. *New England Journal of Medicine, 329,* 110–116.

Guralnik, J. M., & Paul-Brown, D. (1984). Communicative adjustments during behavior-request episodes among children at different developmental levels. *Child Development, 55,* 911–919.

Guralnik, J. M., Simonsick, E. M., Ferrucci, L., Glynn, R. J., Berkman, L. F., Blazer, D. G., Scherr, P. A., & Wallace, R. B. (1994). A short physical performance battery assessing lower extremity function: Association with self-reported disability and prediction of mortality and nursing home admission. *Journals of Gerontology: Medical Sciences, 49,* M85–94.

Gurland, B., Wilder, D., Lantiga, R., Stern, Y., Chen, J., Killeffer, E., & Mayeux, R. (1999). Rates of dementia in three ethnoracial groups. *International Journal of Geriatric Psychiatry, 14,* 481–493.

Guse, L., & Masesar, M. (1999). Quality of life and successful aging in long-term care: Perceptions of residents. *Issues in Mental Health Nursing, 20,* 527–539.

Gustafson, S. B., & Magnusson, D. (1991). *Female life careers: A pattern approach.* Hillsdale, NJ: Erlbaum.

Guthrie, R. (1998). *Even the rat was white* (2nd ed.). Boston: Allyn & Bacon.

Guzzetti, B., & Williams, W. (1996). Gender, text, and discussion: Examining intellectual safety in the science classroom. *Journal of Research in Science Teaching, 33,* 5–20.

Gwartney-Gibbs, P. A. (1988). Women's work experience and the "rusty skills" hypothesis: A reconceptualization and reevaluation of the evidence. In B. A. Gutek, A. H. Stromberg, & L. Larwood (Eds.), *Women and work: An annual review* (Vol. 3) (pp. 169–188). Newbury Park, CA: Sage.

Gzesh, S. M., & Surber, C. F. (1985). Visual perspective-taking skills in children. *Child Development, 56,* 1204–1213.

Haan, N. (1976). "…Change and sameness…" reconsidered. *International Journal of Aging and Human Development, 7,* 59–65.

Haan, N. (1981). Common dimensions of personality development: Early adolescence to middle life. In D. H. Eichorn, J. A. Clausen, N. Haan, M. P.

Haan, N. (1982). The assessment of coping, defense, and stress. In L. Goldberger & S. Breznitz (Eds.), *Handbook of stress: Theoretical and clinical aspects* (pp. 254–269). New York: Free Press.

Haan, N. (1985). Processes of moral development: Cognitive or social disequilibrium? *Developmental Psychology, 21,* 996–1006.

Haan, N., Millsap, R., & Hartka, E. (1986). As time goes by: Change and stability in personality over fifty years. *Psychology and Aging, 1,* 220–232.

Hack, M., Taylor, C. B. H., Klein, N., Eiben, R., Schatschneider, C., & Mercuri-Minich, N. (1994). School-age outcomes in children with birth weights under 750 g. *New England Journal of Medicine, 331,* 753–759.

Hagan, J. (1997). Defiance and despair: Subcultural and structural linkages between delinquency and despair in the life course. *Social Forces, 76,* 119–134.

Hagestad, G. O. (1984). The continuous bond: A dynamic, multigenerational perspective on parent-child relations between adults. In M. Perlmutter (Ed.), *Minnesota Symposia on Child Psychology* (pp. 129–158). Hillsdale, NJ: Erlbaum.

Hagestad, G. O. (1985). Continuity and connectedness. In V. L. Bengtson (Ed.), *Grandparenthood* (pp. 31–38). Beverly Hills, CA: Sage.

Hagestad, G. O. (1986). Dimensions of time and the family. *American Behavioral Scientist, 29,* 679–694.

Hagestad, G. O. (1990). Social perspectives on the life course. In R. H. Binstock & L. K. George (Eds.), *Handbook of aging and the social sciences* (3rd ed.) (pp. 151–168). San Diego, CA: Academic Press.

Haier, R. J., Chueh, D., Touchette, P., Lott, I., Buchsbaum, M. S., MacMillan, D., Sandman, C., LaCasse, L., & Sosa, E. (1995). Brain size and cerebral glucose metabolic rate in nonspecific mental retardation and Down syndrome. *Intelligence, 20,* 191–210.

Haight, W., Wang, X., Fung, H., Williams, K., et al. (1999). Universal, developmental, and variable aspects of young children's play. *Child Development, 70,* 1477–1488.

Haith, M. M. (1980). *Rules that babies look by.* Hillsdale, NJ: Erlbaum.

Hale, S., Fry, A. F., & Jessie, K. A. (1993). Effects of practice on speed of information processing in children and adults: Age sensitivity and age invariance. *Developmental Psychology, 29,* 880–892.

Haley, W. E., West, C. A. C., Wadley, V. G., Ford, G. R., White, F. A., Barrett, J. J., Harrell, L. E., & Roth, D. L. (1995). Psychological, social, and health impact of caregiving: A comparison of black and white dementia family caregivers and noncaregivers. *Psychology and Aging, 10,* 540–552.

Halford, G. S., Maybery, M. T., O'Hare, A. W., & Grant, P. (1994). The development of memory and processing capacity. *Child Development, 65,* 1338–1356.

Halford, W. K., Hahlweg, K., & Dunne, M. (1990). The cross-cultural consistency of marital communication associated with marital distress. *Journal of Marriage and the Family, 52,* 487–500.

Hall, D. R., & Zhao, J. Z. (1995). Cohabitation and divorce in Canada: Testing the selectivity hypothesis. *Journal of Marriage and the Family, 57,* 421–427.

Hall, D. T. (1972). A model of coping with role conflict: The role behavior of college educated women. *Administrative Science Quarterly, 17,* 471–486.

Hall, D. T. (1975). Pressures from work, self, and home in the life stages of married women. *Journal of Vocational Behavior, 6,* 121–132.

Halle, T. (1999). Implicit theories of social interactions: Children's reasoning about the relative importance of gender and friendship in social partner choices. *Merrill-Palmer Quarterly, 45,* 445–467.

Hallfrisch, J., Muller, D., Drinkwater, D., Tobin, J., & Adres, R. (1990). Continuing diet trends in men: The Baltimore Longitudinal Study of Aging. *Journals of Gerontology: Medical Sciences, 45,* M186–191.

Hallstrom, T., & Samuelsson, S. (1985). Mental health in the climacteric: The longitudinal study of women in Gothenburg. *Acta Obstetrics Gynecology Scandanavia, 130*(Suppl), 13–18.

Halpern, C. T., Udry, J. R., Campbell, B., & Suchindran, C. (1993). Testosterone and pubertal development as predictors of sexual activity: A panel analysis of adolescent males. *Psychosomatic Medicine, 55,* 436–447.

Halpern, D. (1997). Sex differences in intelligence: Implications for education. *American Psychologist, 52,* 1091–1102.

Halpern, D. F. (1986). *Sex differences in cognitive abilities.* Hillsdale, NJ: Erlbaum.

Halvorsen, R. (1998). The ambiguity of lesbian and gay marriages: Change and continuity in the symbolic order. *Journal of Homosexuality, 35,* 207–231.

Hamberger, K., & Minsky, D. (2000, August). *Evaluation of domestic violence training programs for health care professionals.* Paper presented at the annual meeting of the American Psychological Association. Washington, DC.

Hamilton, C. E. (1995, March). *Continuity and discontinuity of attachment from infancy through adolescence.* Paper presented at the biennial meetings of the Society for Research in Child Development, Indianapolis, IN.

Hamm, J. (2000). Do birds of a feather flock together? The variable bases for African American, Asian American, and European American adolescents' selection of similar friends. *Developmental Psychology, 36,* 209–219.

Hammond, M., Landry, S., Swank, P., & Smith, K. (2000). Relation of mothers' affective development history and parenting behavior: Effects on infant medical risk. *American Journal of Orthopsychiatry, 70,* 95–103.

Handley-Derry, M., Low, J., Burke, S., Waurick, M., Killen, H., Derrick, E. (1997). Intrapartum fetal asphyxia and the occurrence of minor deficits in 4- to 8-year-old children. *Developmental Medicine & Child Neurology, 39,* 508–514.

Hanna, E., & Meltzoff, A. N. (1993). Peer imitation by toddlers in laboratory, home, and day-care contexts: Implications for social learning and memory. *Developmental Psychology, 29,* 701–710.

Hansson, R. O., & Carpenter, B. N. (1994). *Relationships in old age: Coping with the challenge of transition.* New York: Guilford Press.

Hardy, M. A., & Hazelrigg, L. E. (1993). The gender of poverty in an aging population. *Research on Aging, 15,* 243–278.

Hardy, M. A., & Quadagno, J. (1995). Satisfaction with early retirement: Making choices in the auto industry. *Journals of Gerontology: Social Sciences, 50B,* S217–228.

Harkness, S. (1998). Time for families. *Anthropology Newsletter, 39,* 1, 4.

Harkness, S., & Super, C. M. (1985). The cultural context of gender segregation in children's peer groups. *Child Development, 56,* 219–224.

Harlow, H., & Zimmerman, R. (1959). Affectional responses in the infant monkey. *Science, 130,* 421–432.

Harman, S. M., & Tsitouras, P. D. (1980). Reproductive hormones in aging men: I. Measurement of sex steroids, basal luteinizing hormone, and Leydig cell response to human chorionic gonadotropin. *Journal of Clinical Endocrinology and Metabolism, 51,* 35–40.

Harris, B., Lovett, L., Newcombe, R. G., Read, G. F., Walker, R., & Riad-Fahmy, D. (1994). Maternity blues and major endocrine changes: Cardiff puerperal mood and hormone study II. *British Medical Journal, 308,* 949–953.

Harris, P. L. (1989). *Children and emotion: The development of psychological understanding.* Oxford: Blackwell.

Harris, R. L., Ellicott, A. M., & Holmes, D. S. (1986). The timing of psychosocial transitions and changes in women's lives: An examination of women aged 45 to 60. *Journal of Personality and Social Psychology, 51,* 409–416.

Harrison, A., Wilson, M., Pine, C., Chan, S., & Buriel, R. (1990). Family ecologies of ethnic minority children. *Child Development, 61,* 347–362.

Harrist, A., Zaia, A., Bates, J., Dodge, K., & Pettit, G. (1997). Subtypes of social withdrawal in early childhood: Sociometric status and social-cognitive differences across four years. *Child Development, 68,* 278–294.

Hart, B., & Risley, T. R. (1995). *Meaningful differences in the everyday experience of young American children.* Baltimore: Paul H. Brookes.

Hart, C., Olsen, S., Robinson, C., & Mandleco, B. (1997). The development of social and communicative competence in childhood: Review and a model of personal, familial, and extrafamilial processes. *Communication Yearbook, 20,* 305–373.

Hart, S., Jones, N., Field, T., & Lundy, B. (1999). One-year-old infants of intrusive and withdrawn depressed mothers. *Child Psychiatry & Human Development, 30,* 111–120.

Harter, S. (1987). The determinations and mediational role of global self-worth in children. In N. Eisenberg (Ed.), *Contemporary topics in developmental psychology* (pp. 219–242). New York: Wiley-Interscience.

Harter, S. (1990). Processes underlying adolescent self-concept formation. In R. Montemayor, G. R. Adams, & T. P. Gullotta (Eds.),

From childhood to adolescence: A transitional period? (pp. 205–239). Newbury Park, CA: Sage.

Harter, S., & Monsour, A. (1992). Developmental analysis of conflict caused by opposing attributes in the adolescent self-portrait. *Developmental Psychology, 28,* 251–260.

Harton, H., & Latane, B. (1997). Social influence and adolescent lifestyle attitudes. *Journal of Research on Adolescence, 7,* 197–220.

Hartup, W. W. (1974). Aggression in childhood: Developmental perspectives. *American Psychologist, 29,* 336–341.

Hartup, W. W. (1996). The company they keep: Friendships and their developmental significance. *Child Development, 67,* 1–13.

Harwood, D., Barker, W., Ownby, R., Bravo, M., Aguero, H., & Duara, R. (2000). Depressive symptoms in Alzheimer's disease: An examination among community-dwelling Cuban American patients. *American Journal of Geriatric Psychiatry, 8,* 84–91.

Hashima, P. Y., & Amato, P. R. (1994). Poverty, social support, and parental behavior. *Child Development, 65,* 394–403.

Hatano, G. (1990). Toward the cultural psychology of mathematical cognition: Commentary. In H. Stevenson & S. Lee (Eds.), *Contexts of achievement. Monographs of the Society for Research in Child Development, 55* (12), 108–115, Serial No. 221.

Hatchett, S. J., Cochran, D. L., & Jackson, J. S. (1991). Family life. In J. S. Jackson (Ed.), *Life in black America.* Newbury Park, CA: Sage.

Hatchett, S. J., & Jackson, J. S. (1993). African American extended kin systems: An assessment. In H. P. McAdoo (Ed.), *Family ethnicity: Strength in diversity* (pp. 90–108). Newbury Park, CA: Sage.

Hausman, P. B., & Weksler, M. E. (1985). Changes in the immune response with age. In C. E. Finch & E. L. Schneider (Eds.), *Handbook of the biology of aging* (2nd ed.) (pp. 414–432). New York: Van Nostrand Reinhold.

Haviland, J. M., & Lelwica, M. (1987). The induced affect response: 10-week-old infants' responses to three emotional expressions. *Developmental Psychology, 23,* 97–104.

Hawkins, H. L., Kramer, A. F., & Capaldi, D. (1992). Aging, exercise, and attention. *Psychology and Aging, 7,* 643–653.

Hayflick, L. (1977). The cellular basis for biological aging. In C. E. Finch & L. Hayflick (Eds.), *Handbook of the biology of aging* (pp. 159–186). New York: Van Nostrand Reinhold.

Hayflick, L. (1987). Origins of longevity. In H. R. Warner, R. N. Butler, R. L. Sprott, & E. L. Schneider (Eds.), *Aging: Vol. 31. Modern biological theories of aging* (pp. 21–34). New York: Raven Press.

Hayflick, L. (1994). *How and why we age.* New York: Ballantine Books.

Hayne, H., & Rovee-Collier, C. (1995). The organization of reactivated memory in infancy. *Child Development, 66,* 893–906.

Hayward, M. D., Friedman, S., & Chen, H. (1996). Race inequities in men's retirement. *Journals of Gerontology: Social Sciences, 51B,* S1–10.

Hayward, M. D., & Hardy, M. A. (1985). Early retirement processes among older men: Occupational differences. *Research on Aging, 7,* 491–518.

Hazan, C., Hutt, M., Sturgeon, J., & Bricker, T. (1991, April). *The process of relinquishing parents as attachment figures.* Paper presented at the biennial meetings of the Society for Research in Child Development, Seattle, WA.

Hazan, C., & Shaver, P. (1987). Romantic love conceptualized as an attachment process. *Journal of Personality and Social Psychology, 52,* 511–524.

Hazelrigg, L. E., & Hardy, M. A. (1995). Older adult migration to the sunbelt: Assessing income and related characteristics of recent migrants. *Research on Aging, 17,* 109–234.

Hazuda, H., Wood, R., Lichtenstein, M., & Espino, D. (1998). Sociocultural status, psychosocial factors, and cognitive functional limitation in elderly Mexican Americans: Findings from the San Antonio Longitudinal Study of Aging. *Journal of Gerontological Social Work, 30,* 99–121.

Heaton, T. B., & Pratt, E. L. (1990). The effects of religious homogamy on marital satisfaction and stability. *Journal of Family Issues, 11,* 191–207.

Hebert, L. E., Scherr, P. A., Beckett, L. A., Albert, M. S., Pilgrim, D. M., Chown, M. J., Funkenstein, H. H., & Evans, D. A. (1995). Age-specific incidence of Alzheimer's disease in a community population. *Journal of the American Medical Association, 273,* 1354–1359.

Heckhausen, J., & Brim, O. (1997). Perceived problems for self and others: Self-protection by social downgrading throughout adulthood. *Psychology & Aging, 12,* 610–619.

Heidt-Kozisek, E., Pipp-Siegel, S., Easterbrooks, M., & Harmon, R. (1997). Knowledge of self, mother, and father in preterm and fullterm toddlers. *Infant Behavior & Development, 20,* 311–324.

Heinicke, C., Goorsky, M., Moscov, S., Dudley, K., Gordon, J., Schneider, C., & Guthrie, D. (2000). Relationship-based intervention with at-risk mothers: Factors affecting variations in outcome. *Infant Mental Health Journal, 21,* 133–155.

Hellinghausen, M. (1999, April 29). Miracle birth: Nurses recount unforgettable arrival of the Houston octuplets. *Nurse Week/Health Week.* Retrieved March 6, 2001 from the World Wide Web: http://www.nurseweek.com

Helme, R. (1998). Pain in the elderly. *Australasian Journal on Aging, 17,* 33–35.

Helson, R., & Klohnen, D. (1998). Affective coloring of personality from young adulthood to midlife. *Personality & Social Psychology Bulletin, 24,* 241–252.

Helson, R., Mitchell, V., & Moane, G. (1984). Personality and patterns of adherence and nonadherence to the social clock. *Journal of Personality and Social Psychology, 46,* 1079–1096.

Helson, R., & Moane, G. (1987). Personality change in women from college to midlife. *Journal of Personality and Social Psychology, 53,* 176–186.

Helson, R., & Stewart, A. (1994). Personality change in adulthood. In T. F. Hetherton & J. L. Weinberger (Eds.), *Can personality change?* (pp. 210–225). Washington, DC: American Psychological Association.

Helson, R., & Wink, P. (1992). Personality change in women from the early 40s to the early 50s. *Psychology and Aging, 7,* 46–55.

Henry J. Kaiser Family Foundation. (1999). Sex on TV. Washington, DC: Author.

Henry, B., Caspi, A., Moffitt, T., Harrington, H., et al. (1999). Staying in school protects boys with poor self-regulation in childhood from later crime: A longitudinal study. *International Journal of Behavioral Development, 23,* 1049–1073.

Henry, B., Caspi, A., Moffitt, T., & Silva, P. (1996). Temperamental and familial predictors of violent and nonviolent criminal convictions: Age 3 to age 18. *Developmental Psychology, 32,* 614–623.

Heppner, M., Fuller, B., & Multon, K. (1998). Adults in involuntary career transition: An analysis of the relationship between the psychological and career domains. *Journal of Career Assessment, 6,* 329–346.

Hernandez, D. (1997). Child development and the social demography of childhood. *Child Development, 68,* 149–169.

Hernandez, S., Camacho-Rosales, J., Nieto, A., & Barroso, J. (1997). Cerebral asymmetry and reading performance: Effect of language lateralization and hand preference. *Child Neuropsychology, 3,* 206–225.

Herrenkohl, E., Herrenkohl, R., Egolf, B., & Russo, M. (1998). The relationship between early maltreatment and teenage parenthood. *Journal of Adolescence, 21,* 291–303.

Herzog, A. R., House, J. S., & Morgan, J. N. (1991). Relation of work and retirement to health and well-being in older age. *Psychology and Aging, 6,* 202–211.

Hess, E. H. (1972). "Imprinting" in a natural laboratory. *Scientific American, 227,* 24–31.

Hess, T., Bolstad, C., Woodburn, S., & Auman, C. (1999). Trait diagnosticity versus behavioral consistency as determinants of impression change in adulthood. *Psychology & Aging, 14,* 77–89.

Hesser, A., Cregler, L., & Lewis, L. (1998). Predicting the admission into medical school of African American college students who have participated in summer academic enrichment programs. *Academic Medicine, 73,* 187–191.

Hetherington, E., Bridges, M., & Insabella, G. (1998). What matters? What does not?: Five perspectives on the association between marital transitions and children's adjustment. *American Psychologist, 53,* 167–184.

Hetherington, E., Henderson, S., Reiss, D., Anderson, E., et al. (1999). Adolescent siblings in stepfamilies: Family functioning and adolescent adjustment. *Monographs of the Society for Research in Child Development, 64,* 222.

Hetherington, E. M. (1989). Coping with family transitions: Winners, losers, and survivors. *Child Development, 60*, 1–14.

Hetherington, E. M. (1991a). Presidential address: Families, lies, and videotapes. *Journal of Research on Adolescence, 1*, 323–348.

Hetherington, E. M. (1991b). The role of individual differences and family relationships in children's coping with divorce and remarriage. In P. A. Cowen & M. Hetherington (Eds.), *Family transitions* (pp. 165–194). Hillsdale, NJ: Erlbaum.

Hetherington, E. M., & Clingempeel, W. G. (1992). Coping with marital transitions: A family systems perspective. *Monographs of the Society for Research in Child Development, 57*(2–3, Serial No. 227).

Hetherington, E. M., & Stanley-Hagan, M. M. (1995). Parenting in divorced and remarried families. In M. H. Bornstein (Ed.), *Handbook of parenting: Vol. 3. Status and social conditions of parenting* (pp. 233–254). Mahwah, NJ: Erlbaum.

Hicks, D., & Gwynne, M. (1996). *Cultural anthropology.* New York: HarperCollins.

Higdon, H. (1975). *The crime of the century.* New York: G. P. Putnam's Sons.

Higgins, A. (1991). The just community approach to moral education: Evolution of the idea and recent findings. In W. M. Kurtines & J. L. Gewirtz (Eds.), *Handbook of moral behavior and development: Vol. 3. Application* (pp. 111–141). Hillsdale, NJ: Erlbaum.

Higgins, C., Duxbury, L., & Lee, C. (1994). Impact of life-cycle stage and gender on the ability to balance work and family responsibilities. *Family Relations, 43*, 144–150.

Hightower, E. (1990). Adolescent interpersonal and familial precursors of positive mental health at midlife. *Journal of Youth and Adolescence, 19*, 257–275.

Hill, A., & Franklin, J. (1998). Mothers, daughters, and dieting: Investigating the transmission of weight control. *British Journal of Clinical Psychology, 37*, 3–13.

Hill, C. (1999). Fusion and conflict in lesbian relationships. *Feminism & Psychology, 9*, 179–185.

Hill, M. S. (1988). Marital stability and spouses' shared time: A multidisciplinary hypothesis. *Journal of Family Relations, 9*, 427–451.

Hill, R. D., Storandt, M., & Malley, M. (1993). The impact of long-term exercise training on psychological function in older adults. *Journals of Gerontology: Psychological Sciences, 48*, P12–17.

Hilts, P. J. (1995). Black teen-agers are turning away from smoking, but whites puff on. *New York Times*, April 19, p. B7.

Himes, C. L. (1994). Parental caregiving by adult women. *Research on Aging, 16*, 191–211.

Hinde, R. A., Titmus, G., Easton, D., & Tamplin, A. (1985). Incidence of "friendship" and behavior toward strong associates versus nonassociates in preschoolers. *Child Development, 56*, 234–245.

Hinden, S. (2000). Computer age brings wide new world to golden age. *Washington Post Online.* Retrieved March 19, 2000 from the World Wide Web: www.washingtonpost.com

Hinton, J. (1975). The influence of previous personality on reactions to having terminal cancer. *Omega, 6*, 95–111.

Hirdes, J. P., & Strain, L. A. (1995). The balance of exchange in instrumental support with network members outside the household. *Journals of Gerontology: Social Sciences, 50B*, S134–142.

Ho, C., & Bryant, P. (1997). Learning to read Chinese beyond the logographic phase. *Reading Research Quarterly, 32*, 276–289.

Hobbs, J., & Ferth, P. (1993). *The Bounty pregnancy guide.* New York: Bounty Health Care Publishing.

Hoch, C. C., Buysse, D. J., Monk, T. H., & Reynolds, C. F. I. (1992). Sleep disorders and aging. In J. E. Birren, R. B. Sloane, & G. D. Cohen (Eds.), *Handbook of mental health and aging* (2nd ed.) (pp. 557–582). San Diego, CA: Academic Press.

Hodge, S., & Canter, D. (1998). Victims and perpetrators of male sexual assault. *Journal of Interpersonal Violence, 13*, 222–239.

Hoffman, H. J., & Hillman, L. S. (1992). Epidemiology of the sudden infant death syndrome: Maternal, neonatal, and postneonatal risk factors. *Clinics in Perinatology, 19*(4), 717–737.

Hoffman, L. (1989). Effects of maternal employment in the two-parent family. *American Psychologist, 44*, 283–292.

Hoffman, M. (1970). Moral Development. In P. Mussen (Ed.), *Carmichael's manual of child psychology* (Vol. 2). New York: Wiley.

Hoffman, M. (1988). Moral development. In M. Bornstein & M. Lamb (Eds.), *Developmental psychology: An advanced textbook* (2nd ed.) (pp. 497–548). Hillsdale, NJ: Erlbaum.

Hogan, T. D., & Steinnes, D. N. (1994). Toward an understanding of elderly seasonal migration using origin-based household data. *Research on Aging, 16*, 463–475.

Holden, K. C., & Smock, P. J. (1991). The economic costs of marital dissolution: Why do women bear a disproportionate cost? *Annual Review of Sociology, 17*, 51–78.

Holland, A., Hon, J., Huppert, F., Stevens, F., & Watson, P. (1998). Population-based study of the prevalence and presentation of dementia in adults with Down syndrome. *British Journal of Psychiatry, 172*, 493–498.

Holland, J. L. (1973). *Making vocational choices: A theory of careers.* Englewood Cliffs, NJ: Prentice-Hall.

Holland, J. L. (1992). *Making vocational choices: A theory of vocational personalities and work environments* (2nd ed.). Odessa, FL: Psychological Assessment Resources.

Holmbeck, G. N., & Hill, J. P. (1991). Conflictive engagement, positive affect, and menarche in families with seventh-grade girls. *Child Development, 62*, 1030–1048.

Holmes, E. R., & Holmes, L. D. (1995). *Other cultures, elder years* (2nd ed.). Thousand Oaks, CA: Sage.

Honzik, M. P. (1986). The role of the family in the development of mental abilities: A 50-year study. In N. Datan, A. L. Greene, & H. W. Reese (Eds.), *Life-span developmental psychology: Intergenerational relations* (pp. 185–210). Hillsdale, NJ: Erlbaum.

Horan, W., Pogge, D., Borgaro, S., & Stokes, J. (1997). Learning and memory in adolescent psychiatric inpatients with major depression: A normative study of the California Verbal Learning Test. *Archives of Clinical Neuropsychology, 12*, 575–584.

Horn, J. L. (1982). The aging of human abilities. In B. B. Wolman (Ed.), *Handbook of developmental psychology* (pp. 847–870). Englewood Cliffs, NJ: Prentice-Hall.

Horn, J. L., & Donaldson, G. (1980). Cognitive development in adulthood. In O. G. Brim, Jr. & J. Kagan (Eds.), *Constancy and change in human development* (pp. 415–529). Cambridge, MA: Harvard University Press.

Horn, L., & Bertold, J. (1999). *Students with disabilities in post-secondary education: A profile of preparation, participation, and outcomes.* Washington, DC: National Center for Educational Statistics. [Online report]. Retrieved August 23, 2000 from the World Wide Web: http://www.nces.ed.gov

Horn, L., & Premo, M. (1995). *Profile of undergraduates in U. S. postsecondary education institutions.* Washington DC: U. S. Department of Education.

Hornbrook, M. C., Stevens, V. J., & Wingfield, D. J. (1994). Preventing falls among community-dwelling older persons: Results from a randomized trial. *The Gerontologist, 34*, 16–23.

Horner, K. W., Rushton, J. P., & Vernon, P. A. (1986). Relation between aging and research productivity of academic psychologists. *Psychology and Aging, 1*, 319–324.

Hornik, M. (1998). Physician-assisted suicide and euthanasia's impact on the frail elderly: A social worker's response. *Journal of Long Term Home Health Care: The Pride Institute Journal, 17*, 34–41.

Horowitz, A., McLaughlin, J., & White, H. (1998). How the negative and positive aspects of partner relationships affect the mental health of young married people. *Journal of Health & Social Behavior, 39*, 124–136.

Horowitz, F. D. (1990). Developmental models of individual differences. In J. Colombo & J. Fagen (Eds.), *Individual differences in infancy: Reliability, stability, prediction* (pp. 3–18). Hillsdale, NJ: Erlbaum.

Hortacsu, N. (1999). The first year of family- and couple-initiated marriages of a Turkish sample: A longitudinal investigation. *International Journal of Psychology, 34*, 29–41.

House, J. A., Kessler, R. C., & Herzog, A. R. (1990). Age, socioeconomic status, and health. *The Milbank Quarterly, 68*, 383–411.

House, J. S., Kessler, R. C., Herzog, A. R., Mero, R. P., Kinney, A. M., & Breslow, M. J. (1992). Social stratification, age, and health. In K. W. Schaie, D. Blazer, & J. M. House (Eds.), *Aging, health behaviors, and health outcomes* (pp. 1–32). Hillsdale, NJ: Erlbaum.

Houseknecht, S. K. (1987). Voluntary childlessness. In M. B. Sussman & S. K. Steinmetz (Eds.), *Handbook of marriage and the family* (pp. 369–395). New York: Plenum.

Hovell, M., Blumberg, E., Sipan, C., Hofstetter, C., Burkham, S., Atkins, C., & Felice, M. (1998). Skills training for pregnancy and

AIDS prevention in Anglo and Latino youth. *Journal of Adolescent Health, 23,* 139–149.

Hovell, M., Sipan, C., Blumberg, E., Atkins, C., Hofstetter, C. R., & Kreitner, S. (1994). Family influences on Latino and Anglo adolescents' sexual behavior. *Journal of Marriage and the Family, 56,* 973–986.

Howe, G. R. (1994). Dietary fat and breast cancer risks: An epidemiologic perspective. *Cancer, 74*(3 Suppl.), 1078–1084.

Howes, C. (1983). Patterns of friendship. *Child Development, 54,* 1041–1053.

Howes, C. (1987). Social competence with peers in young children: Developmental sequences. *Developmental Review, 7,* 252–272.

Howes, C., & Matheson, C. C. (1992). Sequences in the development of competent play with peers: Social and pretend play. *Developmental Psychology, 28,* 961–974.

Howes, C., Phillips, D. A., & Whitebook, M. (1992). Thresholds of quality: Implications for the social development of children in center-based child care. *Child Development, 63,* 449–460.

Hoyert, D. L. (1991). Financial and household exchanges between generations. *Research on Aging, 13,* 205–225.

Hoyert, D. L., & Seltzer, M. M. (1992). Factors related to the well-being and life activities of family caregivers. *Family Relations, 41,* 74–81.

Huang, H., & Hanley, J. (1997). A longitudinal study of phonological awareness, visual skills, and Chinese reading acquisition among first-graders in Taiwan. *International Journal of Behavioral Development, 20,* 249–268.

Huesmann, L. R., Lagerspetz, K., & Eron, L. D. (1984). Intervening variables in the television violence-aggression relation: Evidence from two countries. *Developmental Psychology, 20,* 746–775.

Hultsch, D. F., Hertzog, C., Small, B. J., McDonald-Miszczak, L., & Dixon, R. A. (1992). Short-term longitudinal change in cognitive performance in later life. *Psychology and Aging, 7,* 571–584.

Hummert, M., Garstka, T., & Shaner, J. (1997). Stereotyping of older adults: The role of target facial cues and perceiver characteristics. *Psychology & Aging, 21,* 107–114.

Humphreys, A., & Smith, P. (1987). Rough and tumble, friendship, and dominance in school children: Evidence for continuity and change with age. *Child Development, 58,* 201–212.

Hunfeld, J., Tempels, A., Passchier, J., Hazebroek, F., et al. (1999). Parental burden and grief one year after the birth of a child with a congenital anomaly. *Journal of Pediatric Psychology, 24,* 515–520.

Hunter, D. J., Spiegelman, D., Adami, H., Beeson, L., van den Brandt, P. A., Folsom, A. R., Fraser, G. E., Goldbohm, A., Graham, S., Howe, G. R., Kushi, L. H., Marshall, J. R., McDermott, A., Miller, A. B., Speizer, F. E., Wolk, A., Yuan, S., & Willett, W. (1996). Cohort studies of fat intake and the risk of breast cancer-a pooled analysis. *New England Journal of Medicine, 334,* 356–361.

Hunter, M., & O'Dea, I. (1999). An evaluation of a health education intervention for mid-aged women: Five-year follow-up of effects upon knowledge, impact of menopause and health. *Patient Education & Counseling, 38,* 249–255.

Hunter, S., & Sundel, M. (1989). *Midlife myths: Issues, findings, and practice implications.* Newbury Park, CA: Sage.

Hurwitz, E., Gunn, W. J., Pinsky, P. F., & Schonberger, L. B. (1991). Risk of respiratory illness associated with day-care attendance: A nationwide study. *Pediatrics, 87,* 62–69.

Husaini, B., Blasi, A., & Miller, O. (1999). Does public and private religiosity have a moderating effect on depression? A bi-racial study of elders in the American South. *International Journal of Aging & Human Development, 48,* 63–72.

Huston, A. C. (1994). Children in poverty: Designing research to affect policy. *Social Policy Report, Society for Research in Child Development, 8*(2), 1–12.

Huston, A. C., Wright, J. C., Rice, M. L., Kerkman, D., & St. Peters, M. (1990). Development of television viewing patterns in early childhood: A longitudinal investigation. *Developmental Psychology, 26,* 409–420.

Huston, T. L., & Chorost, A. F. (1994). Behavioral buffers on the effect of negativity on marital satisfaction: A longitudinal study. *Personal Relationships, 1,* 223–239.

Huston, T. L., McHale, S. M., & Crouter, A. C. (1986). When the honeymoon's over: Changes in the marriage relationship over the first year. In R. Gilmour & S. Duck (Eds.), *The emerging field of personal relationships* (pp. 109–132). Hillsdale, NJ: Erlbaum.

Hutinger, P. (1996). Computer applications in programs for young children with disabilities: Recurring themes. *Focus on Autism & Other Developmental Disabilities, 11,* 105–114.

Hutt, S. J., Lenard, H. G., & Prechtl, H. F. R. (1969). Psychophysiological studies in newborn infants. In L. P. Lipsitt & H. W. Reese (Eds.), *Advances in child development and behavior* (Vol. 4) (pp. 128–173). New York: Academic Press.

Huttenlocher, P. R. (1994). Synaptogenesis, synapse elimination, and neural plasticity in human cerebral cortex. In C. A. Nelson (Ed.), *The Minnesota Symposia on Child Psychology* (Vol. 27) (pp. 35–54). Hillsdale, NJ: Erlbaum.

Hyde, J., Fennema, E., & Lamon, S. (1990). Gender differences in mathematics performance: A meta-analysis. *Psychological Bulletin, 107,* 139–155.

Idler, E., & Kasl, S. (1997a). Religion among disabled and nondisabled persons I: Cross-sectional patterns in health practices, social activities, and well-being. *Journals of Gerontology: Series B: Psychological Sciences & Social Sciences, 52B,* S294–S305.

Idler, E., & Kasl, S. (1997b). Religion among disabled and nondisabled persons II: Attendance at religious services as a predictor of the course of disability. *Journals of Gerontology: Series B: Psychological Sciences & Social Sciences, 52B,* S306–S316.

Ingoldsby, E., Shaw, D., Owens, E., & Winslow, E. (1999). A longitudinal study of interparental conflict, emotional and behavioral reactivity, and preschoolers' adjustment problems among low-income families. *Journal of Abnormal Child Psychology, 27,* 343–356.

Ingram, D. (1981). Early patterns of grammatical development. In R. E. Stark (Ed.), *Language behavior in infancy and early childhood* (pp. 327–358). New York: Elsevier North-Holland.

Ingrassia, M. (1993, August 2). Daughters of Murphy Brown. *Newsweek,* 58–59.

Inhelder, B., & Piaget, J. (1958). *The growth of logical thinking from childhood to adolescence.* New York: Basic Books.

Inkeles, A., & Usui, C. (1989). Retirement patterns in cross-national perspective. In D. I. Kertzer & K. W. Schaie (Eds.), *Age structuring in comparative perspective* (pp. 227–262). Hillsdale, NJ: Erlbaum.

Insabella, G. M. (1995, March). *Varying levels of exposure to marital conflict: Prediction of adolescent adjustment across intact families and stepfamilies.* Paper presented at the biennial meetings of the Society for Research in Child Development, Indianapolis, IN.

Interactive Digital Software Association. (1998). *Deep impact: How does the interactive entertainment industry affect the U.S. economy?* www.idsa.com

Irwin, M., & Pike, J. (1993). Bereavement, depressive symptoms, and immune function. In M. S. Stroebe, W. Stroebe, & R. O. Hansson (Eds.), *Handbook of bereavement: Theory, research, and intervention* (pp. 160–171). Cambridge, England: Cambridge University Press.

Isabella, R. A. (1995). The origins of infant-mother attachment: Maternal behavior and infant development. *Annals of Child Development, 10,* 57–81.

Iversen, L., & Sabroe, S. (1988). Psychological well-being among unemployed and employed people after a company closedown: A longitudinal study. *Journal of Social Issues, 44,* 141–152.

Ivy, G. O., MacLeod, C. M., Petit, T. L., & Marcus, E. J. (1992). A physiological framework for perceptual and cognitive changes in aging. In F. I. M. Craik & T. A. Salthouse (Eds.), *The handbook of aging and cognition* (pp. 273–314). Hillsdale, NJ: Erlbaum.

Izard, C. E., Fantauzzo, C. A., Castle, J. M., Haynes, O. M., Rayias, M. F., & Putnam, P. H. (1995). The ontogeny and significance of infants' facial expressions in the first 9 months of life. *Developmental Psychology, 31,* 997–1013.

Izard, C. E., & Harris, P. (1995). Emotional development and developmental psychopathology. In D. Cicchetti & D. J. Cohen (Eds.), *Developmental psychopathology: Vol. 1. Theory and methods* (pp. 467–503). New York: Wiley.

Jackson, D., & Tein, J. (1998). Adolescents' conceptualization of adult roles: Relationships with age, gender, work goal, and maternal employment. *Sex Roles, 38,* 987–1008.

Jackson, D. J., Longino, C. F., Jr., Zimmerman, R. S., & Bradsher, J. E. (1991). Environmental adjustments to declining functional ability: Residential mobility and living arrangements. *Research on Aging, 13,* 289–309.

Jackson, L., & Bracken, B. (1998). Relationship between students' social status and global and domain-specific self-concepts. *Journal of School Psychology, 36,* 233–246.

Jacobs, J., Finken, L., Griffin, N., & Wright, J. (1998). The career plans of science-talented rural adolescent girls. *American Educational Research Journal, 35,* 681–704.

Jacobs, S. C., Kosten, T. R., Kasl, S. V., Ostfeld, A. M., Berkman, L., & Charpentier, P. (1987/1988). Attachment theory and multiple dimensions of grief. *Omega, 18,* 41–52.

Jacobsen, T., & Hofmann, V. (1997). Children's attachment representations: Longitudinal relations to school behavior, and academic competency in middle childhood and adolescence. *Developmental Psychology, 33,* 703–710.

Jacobsen, T., Husa, M., Fendrich, M., Kruesi, M., & Ziegenhain, U. (1997). Children's ability to delay gratification: Longitudinal relations to mother-child attachment. *Journal of Genetic Psychology, 158,* 411–426.

Jacoby, S. (2000, July/August). The fine art of grandparenting. *AARP Bulletin, 413,* 23.

Jadack, R. A., Hyde, J. S., Moore, C. F., & Keller, M. L. (1995). Moral reasoning about sexually transmitted diseases. *Child Development, 66,* 167–177.

James, S. A., Keenan, N. L., & Browning, S. (1992). Socioeconomic status, health behaviors, and health status among blacks. In K. W. Schaie, D. Blazer, & J. M. House (Eds.), *Aging, health behaviors, and health outcomes* (pp. 39–57). Hillsdale, NJ: Erlbaum.

Janosz, M., Le Blanc, M., Boulerice, B., & Tremblay, R. (2000). Predicting different types of school dropouts: A typological approach with two longitudinal samples. *Journal of Educational Psychology, 92,* 171–190.

Janssen, T., & Carton, J. (1999). The effects of locus of control and task difficulty on procrastination. *Journal of Genetic Psychology, 160,* 436–442.

Jarolmen, J. (1998). A comparison of the grief reaction of children and adults: Focusing on pet loss and bereavement. *Omega: Journal of Death & Dying, 37,* 133–150.

Jendrek, M. (1993). Grandparents who parent their grandchildren: Effects on lifestyle. *Journal of Marriage and the Family, 55,* 609–621.

Jenkins, J. & Buccioni, J. (2000). Children's understanding of marital conflict and the marital relationship. *Journal of Child Psychology & Psychiatry & Allied Disciplines, 41,* 161–168.

Jenkins, J. M., & Astington, J. W. (1996). Cognitive factors and family structure associated with theory of mind development in young children. *Developmental Psychology, 32,* 70–78.

Jenkins, L., Myerson, J., Hale, S., & Fry, A. (1999). Individual and developmental differences in working memory across the life span. *Psychonomic Bulletin & Review, 6,* 28–40.

Jensen, A., & Whang, P. (1994). Speed of accessing arithmetic facts in long-term memory: A comparison of Chinese-American and Anglo-American children. *Contemporary Educational Psychology, 19,* 1–12.

Jerrome, D. (1990). Intimate relationships. In J. Bond & P. Coleman (Eds.), *Aging in society* (pp. 181–208). London: Sage.

Jessor, R. (1992). Risk behavior in adolescence: A psychosocial framework for understanding and action. *Developmental Review, 12,* 374–390.

Jette, A. M. (1996). Disability trends and transitions. In R. H. Binstock & L. K. George (Eds.), *Handbook of aging and the social sciences* (4th ed.) (pp. 94–116). San Diego, CA: Academic Press.

Jimerson, S. (1999). On the failure of failure: Examining the association between early grade retention and educational and employment outcomes during late adolescence. *Journal of School Psychology, 37,* 243–272.

Jindal-Snape, D., Kato, M., & Maekawa, H. (1998). Using self-evaluation procedures to maintain social skills in a child who is blind. *Journal of Visual Impairment & Blindness, 92,* 362–366.

Johansson, B., & Berg, S. (1989). The robustness of the terminal decline phenomenon: Longitudinal data from the digit-span memory test. *Journals of Gerontology: Psychological Sciences, 44,* P184–186.

John, O. P., Caspi, A., Robins, R. W., Moffitt, T. E., & Stouthamer-Loeber, M. (1994). The "little five": Exploring the nomological network of the five-factor model of personality in adolescent boys. *Child Development, 65,* 160–178.

Johnson, C. L. (1982). Sibling solidarity: Its origin and functioning in Italian-American families. *Journal of Marriage and the Family, 44,* 155–167.

Johnson, C. L., & Barer, B. M. (1990). Families and networks among older inner-city blacks. *The Gerontologist, 30,* 726–733.

Johnson, E., & Breslau, N. (2000). Increased risk of learning disabilities in low birth weight boys at age 11 years. *Biological Psychiatry, 47,* 490–500.

Johnson, H., Nusbaum, B., Bejarano, A., & Rosen, T. (1999). An ecological approach to development in children with prenatal drug exposure. *American Journal of Orthopsychiatry, 69,* 448–456.

Johnston, C. (1996). Interactive storybook software: Effects on verbal development in kindergarten children. *Early Child Development & Care, 132,* 33–44.

Jones, J. (1997). Representations of menopause and their health care implications: A qualitative study. *American Journal of Preventive Medicine, 13,* 58–65.

Jones, M. C. (1924). A laboratory study of fear: The case of Peter. *Pedagogical Seminary, 31,* 308–315.

Jones, M., & Wheatley, J. (1990). Gender differences in teacher-student interactions in science classrooms. *Journal of Research in Science Teaching, 27,* 861–874.

Jorgenson, S. (1993). Adolescent pregnancy and parenting. In T. Gullotta, G. Adams, & R. Montemayor (Eds.), *Adolescent sexuality* (pp. 103–140). Thousand Oaks, CA: Sage Publications.

Jorm, A., Christensen, H., Henderson, A., Jacomb, P., Korten, A., & Mackinnon, A. (1998). Factors associated with successful aging. *Journal of Ageing, 17,* 33–37.

Joseph, R. (2000). Fetal brain behavior and cognitive development. *Developmental Review, 20,* 81–98.

Joshi, M. S., & MacLean, M. (1994). Indian and English children's understanding of the distinction between real and apparent emotion. *Child Development, 65,* 1372–1384.

Josse, D., Thibault, H., Bourdais, C., Mirailles, P., Pireyre, E., Surgal, L., Gerboin-Reyrolles, P., & Chauliac, M. (1999). Iron deficiency and psychomotor development in young children in a child health centre: Assessment with revised version of the Brunet-Lezine scale. *Approche Neuropsychologique des Apprentissages chez l'Enfant, 11,* 21–27.

Joung, I. M. A., Stronks, K., van de Mheen, H., & Mackenbach, J. P. (1995). Health behaviours explain part of the differences in self reported health associated with partner/marital status in The Netherlands. *Journal of Epidemiology and Community Health, 49,* 482–488.

Judge, T., Bono, J., & Locke, E. (2000). Personality and job satisfaction: The mediating role of job characteristics. *Journal of Applied Psychology, 85,* 237–249.

Juffer, F., Hoksbergen, R., Riksen-Walraven, J., & Kohnstamm, G. (1997). Early intervention in adoptive families: Supporting maternal sensitive responsiveness, infant-mother attachment, and infant competence. *Journal of Child Psychology & Psychiatry & Allied Disciplines, 38,* 1039–1050.

Juffer, F., & Rosenboom, L., (1997). Infant mother attachment of internationally adopted children in the Netherlands. *International Journal of Behavioral Development, 20,* 93–107.

Jusczyk, P. (1995). Language acquisition: Speech sounds and phonological development. In J. Miler & P. Eimas (Eds.), *Handbook of perception and cognition: Vol. 11. Speech, language, and communication* (pp. 263–301). Orlando, FL: Academic Press.

Jusczyk, P., & Hohne, E. (1997). Infants' memory for spoken words. *Science, 277.*

Jusczyk, P., Houston, D., & Newsome, M. (1999). The beginnings of word segmentation in English-learning infants. *Cognitive Psychology, 39,* 159–207.

Jussim, L., & Eccles, J. (1992). Teacher expectations II: Construction and reflection of student achievement. *Journal of Personality and Social Psychology, 63,* 947–961.

Jutras, S., & Lavoie, J. (1995). Living with an impaired elderly person: The informal caregiver's physical and mental health. *Journal of Aging and Health, 7,* 46–73.

Kagan, J. (1989). *Unstable ideas: Temperament, cognition, and self.* Cambridge, MA: Harvard University Press.

Kagan, J. (1994). *Galen's prophecy.* New York: Basic Books.

Kagan, J., Arcus, D., Snidman, N., Feng, W. Y., Hendler, J., & Greene, S. (1994). Reactivity in infants: A cross-national comparison. *Developmental Psychology, 30,* 342–345.

Kagan, J., Reznick, J. S., & Snidman, N. (1990). The temperamental qualities of inhibition and lack of inhibition. In M. Lewis & S. M. Miller (Eds.), *Handbook of developmental psychopathology* (pp. 219–226). New York: Plenum.

Kagan, J., Snidman, N., & Arcus, D. (1993). On the temperamental categories of inhibited and uninhibited children. In K. H. Rubin & J. B. Asendorpf (Eds.), *Social withdrawal, inhibition, and shyness in childhood* (pp. 19–28). Hillsdale, NJ: Erlbaum.

Kahn, S. B., Alvi, S., Shaukat, N., Hussain, M. A., & Baig, T. (1990). A study of the validity of Holland's theory in a non-Western culture. *Journal of Vocational Behavior, 36,* 132–146.

Kail, R. (1990). *The development of memory in children* (3rd ed.). New York: Freeman.

Kail, R. (1991). Processing time declines exponentially during childhood and adolescence. *Developmental Psychology, 27,* 259–266.

Kail, R. (1997). Processing time, imagery, and spatial memory. *Journal of Experimental Child Psychology, 64,* 67–78.

Kail, R., & Hall, L. (1999). Sources of developmental change in children's word-problem performance. *Journal of Educational Psychology, 91,* 660–668.

Kail, R., & Hall, L. K. (1994). Processing speed, naming speed, and reading. *Developmental Psychology, 30,* 949–954.

Kales, H., Blow, F., Bingham, R., Copeland, L. & Mellow, A. (2000, June). Race and inpatient psychiatric diagnoses among elderly veterans. *Psychiatric Services Journal, 51,* 795–800.

Kalish, R. A. (1985). The social context of death and dying. In R. H. Binstock & E. Shanas (Eds.), *Handbook of aging and the social sciences* (2nd ed.) (pp. 149–170). New York: Van Nostrand Reinhold.

Kalish, R. A., & Reynolds, D. K. (1976). *Death and ethnicity: A psychocultural study.* Los Angeles: University of Southern California Press. (Reprinted 1981, Baywood Publishing Co, Farmingdale, NJ.)

Kallman, D. A., Plato, C. C., & Tobin, J. D. (1990). The role of muscle loss in the age-related decline of grip strength: Cross-sectional and longitudinal perspectives. *Journals of Gerontology: Medical Sciences, 45,* M82–88.

Kamo, Y., Ries, L. M., Farmer, Y. M., Nickinovich, D. G., & Borgatta, E. F. (1991). Status attainment revisited. The National Survey of Families and Households. *Research on Aging, 13,* 124–143.

Kandel, D. B., & Wu, P. (1995). The contributions of mothers and fathers to the intergenerational transmission of cigarette smoking in adolescence. *Journal of Research on Adolescence, 5,* 225–252.

Kane, C. (1998). Differences in family of origin perceptions among African American, Asian American and Hispanic American college students. *Journal of Black Studies, 29,* 93–105.

Kane, R. L., & Kane, R. A. (1990). Health care for older people: Organizational and policy issues. In R. H. Binstock & L. K. George (Eds.), *Handbook of aging and the social sciences* (3rd ed.) (pp. 415–437). San Diego, CA: Academic Press.

Kane, R. L., Klein, S. J., Bernstein, L., Rothenberg, R., & Wales, J. (1985). Hospice role in alleviating the emotional stress of terminal patients and their families. *Medical Care, 23,* 189–197.

Kane, R. L., Wales, J., Bernstein, L., Leibowitz, A., & Kaplan, S. (1984). A randomized controlled trial of hospice care. *Lancet,* 890–894.

Kane, T., Staiger, P., & Ricciardelli, L. (2000). Male domestic violence: Attitudes, aggression and interpersonal dependency. *Journal of Interpersonal Violence, 15,* 16–29.

Kann, L., Warren, C. W., Harris, W. A., Collins, J. L., Douglas, K. A., Collins, M. E., Williams, B. I., Ross, J. G., & Kolbe, L. J. (1995). Youth risk behavior surveillance-United States, 1993. *Morbidity and Mortality Weekly Reports, 44*(SS 1), 1–55.

Kannel, W. B., & Gordon, T. (1980). Cardiovascular risk factors in the aged: The Framingham study. In S. G. Haynes & M. Feinleib (Eds.), *Second conference on the epidemiology of aging.* U.S. Department of Health and Human Services, NIH Publication No. 80–969 (pp. 65–89). Washington, DC: U.S. Government Printing Office.

Kaplan, G. A. (1992). Health and aging in the Alameda County study. In K. W. Schaie, D. Blazer, & J. M. House (Eds.), *Aging, health behaviors, and health outcomes* (pp. 69–88). Hillsdale, NJ: Erlbaum.

Kaplan, H., & Sadock, B. (1991). *Synopsis of psychiatry* (6th ed.). Baltimore, MD: Williams & Wilkins.

Kaplan, R. M. (1985). The controversy related to the use of psychological tests. In B. B. Wolman (Ed.), *Handbook of intelligence: Theories, measurements, and applications* (pp. 465–504). New York: Wiley.

Karmiloff-Smith, A. (1991). Beyond modularity: Innate constraints and developmental change. In S. Carey & R. Gelman (Eds.), *The epigenesis of mind: Essays on biology and cognition* (pp. 171–197). Hillsdale, NJ: Erlbaum.

Karney, B. R., & Bradbury, T. N. (1995). The longitudinal course of marital quality and stability: A review of theory, method, and research. *Psychological Bulletin, 118,* 3–34.

Katz, P., & Bartone, P. (1998). Mourning, ritual and recovery after an airline tragedy. *Omega: Journal of Death & Dying, 36,* 193–200.

Katz, P. A., & Ksansnak, K. R. (1994). Developmental aspects of gender role flexibility and traditionality in middle childhood and adolescence. *Developmental Psychology, 30,* 272–282.

Katz, R., & Wertz, R. (1997). The efficacy of computer-provided reading treatment for chronic aphasic adults. *Journal of Speech & Hearing Research, 40,* 493–507.

Kaufman, M. (1997). The teratogenic effects of alcohol following exposure during pregnancy, and its influence on the chromosome constitution of the pre-ovulatory egg. *Alcohol & Alcoholism, 32,* 113–128.

Kaye, K. L., & Bower, T. G. R. (1994). Learning and intermodal transfer of information in newborns. *Psychological Science, 5,* 286–288.

Keefe, S. E. (1984). Real and ideal extended familism among Mexican Americans and Anglo Americans: On the meaning of "close" family ties. *Human Organization, 43,* 65–70.

Keene, J., Hope, T., Rogers, P., & Elliman, N. (1998). An investigation of satiety in ageing, dementia, and hyperphagia. *International Journal of Eating Disorders, 23,* 409–418.

Keil, J. E., Sutherland, S. E., Knapp, R. G., Waid, L. R., & Gazes, P. C. (1992). Self-reported sexual functioning in elderly blacks and whites. *Journal of Aging and Health, 4,* 112–125.

Keith, P. M. (1981/1982). Perception of time remaining and distance from death. *Omega, 12,* 307–318.

Kellehear, A., & Lewin, T. (1988/1989). Farewells by the dying: A sociological study. *Omega, 19,* 275–292.

Kelley, M. L., Sanches-Hucles, J., & Walker, R. R. (1993). Correlates of disciplinary practices in working- to middle-class African-American mothers. *Merrill-Palmer Quarterly, 39,* 252–264.

Kelly, E. L., & Conley, J. J. (1987). Personality and compatibility: A prospective analysis of marital stability and marital satisfaction. *Journal of Personality and Social Psychology, 52,* 27–40.

Kendall-Tackett, K., Williams, L., & Finkelhor, D. (1993). Impact of sexual abuse on children: A review and synthesis of recent empirical studies. *Psychological Bulletin, 113,* 164–180.

Kendler, K., Kessler, R., Walters, E., MacLean, C., Neale, M., Health, A., & Eaves, L. (1995). Stressful life events, genetic liability, and onset of an episode of major depression in women. *American Journal of Psychiatry, 152,* 833–842.

Kendler, K., Neale, M., Heath, A., Kessler, R., & Eaves, L. (1994). A twin-family study of alcoholism in women. *American Journal of Psychiatry, 49,* 707–715.

Kennedy, K., Nowak, S., Raghuraman, R., Thomas, J., & Davis, S. (2000). Academic dishonesty and distance learning: Student and faculty views. *College Student Journal, 34,* 309–314.

Kercsmar, C. (1998). The respiratory system. In R. Behrman & R. Kliegman (Eds.), *Nelson essentials of pediatrics (third edition).* Philadelphia: W. B. Saunders.

Kerns, K., Don, A., Mateer, C., & Streissguth, A. (1997). Cognitive deficits in nonretarded adults with fetal alcohol syndrome. *Journal of Learning Disabilities, 30,* 685–693.

Kerpelman, J., & Schvaneveldt, P. (1999). Young adults' anticipated identity importance of career, marital, and parental roles: Comparisons of men and women with different role balance orientations. *Sex Roles, 41,* 189–217.

Keskinen, E., Ota, H., & Katila, A. (1998). Older drivers fail in intersections: Speed discrepancies between older and younger male drivers. *Accident Analysis & Prevention, 30,* 323–330.

Kessler, R., McGonagle, K., Zhao, S., Nelson, C., Hughes., M., Eshleman, S., Wittchen, H., & Kendler, K. (1994). Lifetime and 12-month prevalence of DSM-III-R psychiatric disorders in the United States: Results from the National Comorbidity Survey. *American Journal of Psychiatry, 51,* 8–19.

Kessler, R. C., Foster, C., Webster, P. S., & House, J. S. (1992). The relationship between age and depressive symptoms in two national surveys. *Psychology and Aging, 7,* 119–126.

Kessler, R. C., Turner, J. B., & House, J. S. (1988). Effects of unemployment on health in a community survey: Main, modifying, and mediating effects. *Journal of Social Issues, 44,* 69–85.

Kesteloot, H., Lesaffre, E., & Joossens, J. V. (1991). Dairy fat, saturated animal fat, and cancer risk. *Preventive Medicine, 20,* 226–236.

Khlat, M., Sermet, C., & Le Pape, A. (2000). Women's health in relation with their family and work roles: France in the early 1990s. *Social Science & Medicine, 50,* 1807–1825.

Kiecolt-Glaser, J. (2000, August). *Friends, lovers, relaxation, and immunity: How behavior modifies health. Cortisol and the language of love: Text analysis of newlyweds' relationship stories.* Paper presented at the annual meeting of the American Psychological Association. Washington, DC.

Kiecolt-Glaser, J. K., & Glaser, R. (1995). Measurement of immune response. In S. Cohen, R. C. Kessler, & L. U. Gordon (Eds.), *Measuring stress: A guide for health and social scientists* (pp. 213–229). New York: Oxford University Press.

Kiecolt-Glaser, J. K., Glaser, R., Suttleworth, E. E., Dyer, C. S., Ogrocki, P., & Speicher, C. E. (1987). Chronic stress and immunity in family caregivers of Alzheimer's disease patients. *Psychosomatic Medicine, 49,* 523–535.

Kilbride, H., Castor, C., Hoffman, E., & Fuger, K. (2000). Thirty-six month outcome of prenatal cocaine exposure for term or near-term infants: Impact of early case management. *Journal of Developmental Pediatrics, 21,* 19–26.

Kilpatrick, S. J., & Laros, R. K. (1989). Characteristics of normal labor. *Obstetrics and Gynecology, 74,* 85–87.

Kim, J., Hetherington, E., & Reiss, D. (1999). Associations among family relationships, antisocial peers, and adolescents' externalizing behaviors: Gender and family type differences. *Child Development, 70,* 1209–1230.

Kim, S. (1997). Relationships between young children's day care experience and their attachment relationships with parents and socioemotional behavior problems. *Korean Journal of Child Studies, 18,* 5–18.

Kinney, D. A. (1993). From "nerds" to "normals": Adolescent identity recovery within a changing social system. *Sociology of Education, 66,* 21–40.

Kinzl, J., Mangweth, B., Traweger, C., & Biebl, W. (1996). Sexual dysfunction in males: Significance of adverse childhood experiences. *Child Abuse & Neglect, 20,* 759–766.

Kirk, S., Gallagher, J., & Anastasiow, N. (1993). *Educating exceptional children* (7th ed.). Boston: Houghton Mifflin.

Kirkpatrick, L. A., & Hazan, C. (1994). Attachment styles and close relationships: A four-year prospective study. *Personal Relationships, 1,* 123–142.

Kitson, G. C. (1992). *Portrait of divorce: Adjustment to marital breakdown.* New York: Guilford Press.

Kitson, G. C., Babri, K. B., & Roach, M. J. (1985). Who divorces and why. A review. *Journal of Family Issues, 6,* 255–293.

Kitzan, L., Ferraro, F., Petros, T., & Ludorf, M. (1999). The role of vocabulary ability during visual word recognition in younger and older adults. *Journal of General Psychology, 126,* 6–16.

Kivett, V. R. (1991). Centrality of the grandfather role among older rural black and white men. *Journals of Gerontology: Social Sciences, 46,* S250–258.

Klaczynski, P., Fauth, J., & Swanger, A. (1998). Adolescent identity: Rational vs. experiential processing, formal operations, and critical thinking beliefs. *Journal of Youth & Adolescence, 27,* 185–207.

Klahr, D. (1992). Information-processing approaches to cognitive development. In M. H. Bernstein & M. E. Lamb (Eds.), *Developmental psychology: An advanced textbook* (3rd ed.) (pp. 273–335). Hillsdale, NJ: Erlbaum.

Klaiber, E., Broverman, D., Vogel, W., Peterson, L., & Snyder, M. (1997). Relationships of serum estradiol levels, menopausal duration, and mood during hormonal replacement therapy. *Psychoneuroendocrinology, 22,* 549–558.

Klebanov, P. K., Brooks-Gunn, J., Hofferth, S., & Duncan, G. J. (1995, March). *Neighborhood resources, social support and maternal competence.* Paper presented at the biennial meetings of the Society for Research in Child Development, Indianapolis, IN.

Kleemeier, R. W. (1962). Intellectual changes in the senium. *Proceedings of the Social Statistics Section of the American Statistics Association, 1,* 290–295.

Klein, A., & Swartz, S. (1996). *Reading Recovery in California: Program overview.* San Francisco: San Francisco Unified School District.

Klenow, D. J., & Bolin, R. C. (1989/1990). Belief in an afterlife: A national survey. *Omega, 20,* 63–74.

Klerman, L. V. (1991). The health of poor children: Problems and programs. In A. C. Huston (Ed.), *Children in poverty: Child development and public policy* (pp. 136–157). Cambridge, England: Cambridge University Press.

Kletzky, O. A., & Borenstein, R. (1987). Vasomotor instability of the menopause. In D. R. Mishell, Jr. (Ed.), *Menopause: Physiology and pharmacology.* (pp. 53–66). Chicago: Year Book Medical Publishers.

Kliegl, R., Smith, J., & Baltes, P. B. (1989). Testing-the-limits and the study of adult age differences in cognitive plasticity of a mnemonic skill. *Developmental Psychology, 25,* 247–256.

Kliegl, R., Smith, J., & Baltes, P. B. (1990). On the locus and process of magnification of age differences during mnemonic training. *Developmental Psychology, 26,* 894–904.

Kliegman, R. (1998). Fetal and neonatal medicine. In R. Behrman & R. Kliegman (Eds.), *Nelson essentials of pediatrics* (3rd ed., pp. 167–225). Philadelphia: W. B. Saunders.

Kline, D. W., Kline, T. J. B., Fozard, J. L., Kosnik, W., Schieber, F., & Sekuler, R. (1992). Vision, aging, and driving: The problem of older drivers. *Journals of Gerontology: Psychological Sciences, 47,* P27–34.

Kline, D. W., & Scialfa, C. T. (1996). Visual and auditory aging. In J. E. Birren & K. W. Schaie (Eds.), *Handbook of the psychology of aging* (4th ed.) (pp. 181–203). San Diego, CA: Academic Press.

Klonoff-Cohen, H. D., Edelstein, S. L., Lefkowitz, E. S., Srinivasan, I. P., Kaegi, D., Chang, J. C., & Wiley, K. J. (1995). The effect of passive smoking and tobacco exposure through breast milk on sudden infant death syndrome. *Journal of the American Medical Association, 273,* 795–798.

Knox, D. (1998). *The divorced dad's survival book: How to stay connected to your kids.* New York: Insight.

Kochanska, G. (1997a). Multiple pathways to conscience for children with different temperaments: From toddlerhood to age 5. *Developmental Psychology, 33,* 228–240.

Kochanska, G. (1997b). Mutually responsive orientation between mothers and their young: Implications for early socialization. *Child Development, 68,* 94–112.

Kochanska, G., Casey, R., & Fukumoto, A. (1995). Toddlers' sensitivity to standard violations. *Child Development, 66,* 643–656.

Kochanska, G., Murray, K., & Coy, K. (1997). Inhibitory control as a contributor to conscience in childhood: From toddler to early school age. *Child Development, 68,* 263–277.

Kochanska, G., Murray, K., Jacques, T., Koenig, A., Vandegeest, K. (1996). Inhibitory control in young children and its role in emerging internalization. *Child Development, 67,* 490–507.

Kocsis, J. (1998). Geriatric dysthymia. *Journal of Clinical Psychiatry, 59,* 13–15.

Koenig, H., George, L., Hays, J., Larson, D., Cohen, H., & Blazer, D. (1998). The relationship between religious activities and blood pressure in older adults. *International Journal of Psychiatry in Medicine, 28,* 189–213.

Koenig, H. G., Kvale, J. N., & Ferrell, C. (1988). Religion and well-being in later life. *The Gerontologist, 28,* 18–28.

Koeppe, R. (1996). Language differentiation in bilingual children: The development of grammatical and pragmatic competence. *Linguistics, 34,* 927–954.

Kofoed, L., Morgan, T., Buchkowski, J., & Carr, R. (1997). Dissociative experiences scale and MMPI-2 scores in video poker gamblers, other gamblers, and alcoholic controls. *Journal of Nervous & Mental Disease, 185,* 58–60.

Kohlberg, L. (1964). Development of moral character and moral ideology. In M. L. Hoffman & L. W. Hoffman (Eds.), *Review of child development research* (Vol. 1) (pp. 283–332). New York: Russell Sage Foundation.

Kohlberg, L. (1966). A cognitive-developmental analysis of children's sex-role concepts and attitudes. In E. E. Maccoby (Ed.), *The development of sex differences* (pp. 82–172). Stanford, CA: Stanford University Press.

Kohlberg, L. (1976). Moral stages and moralization: The cognitive developmental approach. In T. Lickona (Ed.), *Moral development and behavior: Theory, research, and social issues* (pp. 31–53). New York: Holt.

Kohlberg, L. (1981). *Essays on moral development: Vol. 1. The philosophy of moral development.* New York: Harper & Row.

Kohlberg, L., & Elfenbein, D. (1975). The development of moral judgments concerning capital punishment. *American Journal of Orthopsychiatry, 54,* 614–640.

Kohlberg, L., & Higgins, A. (1987). School democracy and social interaction. In W. M. Kurtines & J. L. Gewirtz (Eds.), *Moral development through social interaction* (pp. 102–130). New York: Wiley-Interscience.

Kohlberg, L., Levine, C., & Hewer, A. (1983). *Moral stages: A current formulation and a response to critics.* Basel, Switzerland: S. Karger.

Kohlberg, L., & Ullian, D. Z. (1974). Stages in the development of psychosexual concepts and attitudes. In R. C. Friedman, R. M. Richart, & R. L. Vande Wiele (Eds.), *Sex differences in behavior* (pp. 209–222). New York: Wiley.

Kohli, M. (1994). Work and retirement: A comparative perspective. In M. W. Riley, R. L. Kahn, & A. Foner (Eds.), *Age and structural lag* (pp. 80–106). New York: Wiley-Interscience.

Kolata, G. (1996). New era of robust elderly belies the fears of scientists. *New York Times,* February 27, pp. A1, B10.

Kolder, V., Gallagher, J., & Parsons, M. (1987). Court-ordered obstetrical interventions. *New England Journal of Medicine, 316,* 1192–1196.

Koskinen, P., Blum, I., Bisson, S., Phillips, S., et al. (2000). Book access, shared reading, and audio models: The effects of supporting the literacy learning of linguistically diverse students in school and at home. *Journal of Educational Psychology, 92,* 23–36.

Kost, K. (1997). The effects of support on the economic well-being of young fathers. *Families in Society, 78,* 370–382.

Kostanski, M., & Gullone, E. (1999). Dieting and body image in the child's world: Conceptualization and behavior. *Journal of Genetic Psychology, 160,* 488–499.

Kozma, A., Stones, M. J., & Hannah, T. E. (1991). Age, activity, and physical performance: An evaluation of performance models. *Psychology and Aging, 6,* 43–49.

Kozu, J. (1999). Domestic violence in Japan. *American Psychologist, 54,* 50–54.

Krause, N., Ingersoll-Dayton, B., Liang, J., & Sugisawa, H. (1999). Religion, social support, and health among the Japanese elderly. *Journal of Health Behavior & Health Education, 40,* 405–421.

Krause, N., Jay, G., & Liang, J. (1991). Financial strain and psychological well-being among the American and Japanese elderly. *Psychology and Aging, 6,* 170–181.

Krause, N., Liang, J., & Keith, V. (1990). Personality, social support, and psychological distress in later life. *Psychology and Aging, 5,* 315–326.

Kraut, R., Patterson, M., Lundmark, V., Kiesler, S., Mukophadhyay, T., & Schertis, W. (1998). Internet paradox: A social technology that reduces social involvement and psychological well-being? *American Psychologist, 53,* 1017–1031.

Kronenberg, F. (1994). Hot flashes: Phenomenology, quality of life, and search for treatment options. *Experimental Gerontology, 29,* 319–336.

Krueger-Lebus, S., & Rauchfleisch, U. (1999). Level of contentment in lesbian partnerships with and without children. *System Familie, 12,* 74–79.

Kübler-Ross, E. (1969). *On death and dying.* New York: Macmillan.

Kübler-Ross, E. (1974). *Questions and answers on death and dying.* New York: Macmillan.

Kuebli, J., Butler, S., & Fivush, R. (1995). Mother-child talk about past emotions: Relationships of maternal language and child gender over time. *Cognition and Emotion, 9,* 265–283.

Kuhn, D. (1992). Cognitive development. In M. H. Bornstein & M. E. Lamb (Eds.), *Developmental psychology: An advanced textbook* (3rd ed.) (pp. 211–272). Hillsdale, NJ: Erlbaum.

Kuhn, D., Kohlberg, L., Languer, J., & Haan, N. (1977). The development of formal operations in logical and moral judgment. *Genetic Psychology Monographs, 95,* 97–188.

Kunkel, S. R., & Applebaum, R. A. (1992). Estimating the prevalence of long-term disability for an aging society. *Journals of Gerontology: Social Sciences, 47,* S253–260.

Kunnen, E., & Steenbeek, H. (1999). Differences in problems of motivation in different special groups. *Child: Care, Health & Development, 25,* 429–446.

Kupersmidt, J. B., Griesler, P. C., DeRosier, M. E., Patterson, C. J., & Davis, P. W. (1995). Childhood aggression and peer relations in the context of family and neighborhood factors. *Child Development, 66,* 360–375.

Kurdek, L. (1997). Relation between neuroticism and dimensions of relationship commitment: evidence from gay, lesbian, and heterosexual couples. *Journal of Family Psychology, 11,* 109–124.

Kurdek, L. (1998). Relationship outcomes and their predictors: longitudinal evidence from heterosexual married, gay cohabiting, and lesbian cohabiting couples. *Journal of Marriage & the Family, 60,* 553–568.

Kurdek, L. (2000). The link between sociotropy/autonomy and dimensions of relationship commitment: Evidence from gay and lesbian couples. *Personal Relationships, 7,* 153–164.

Kurdek, L. A. (1995a). Developmental changes in relationship quality in gay and lesbian cohabiting couples. *Developmental Psychology, 31,* 86–94.

Kurdek, L. A. (1995b). Lesbian and gay couples. In A. R. D'Augelli & C. J. Patterson (Eds.), *Lesbian, gay, and bisexual identities over the lifespan: Psychological perspectives* (pp. 243–261). New York: Oxford University Press.

Kurdek, L. A., & Fine, M. A. (1994). Family acceptance and family control as predictors of adjustment in young adolescents: Linear, curvilinear, or interactive effects? *Child Development, 65,* 1137–1146.

Kurdek, L. A., & Schmitt, J. P. (1986). Early development of relationship quality in heterosexual married, heterosexual cohabiting, gay, and lesbian couples. *Developmental Psychology, 22,* 305–309.

Kuttler, A., LaGreca, A., & Prinstein, M. (1999). Friendship qualities and social-emotional functioning of adolescents with close, cross-sex friendships. *Journal of Research on Adolescence, 9,* 339–366.

Kyriacou, D., Anglin, D., Taliaferro, E., Stone, S., Tubb, T., Linden, J., Muelleman, R., Barton, E., & Kraus, J. (1999). Risk factors for injury to women from domestic violence. *New England Journal of Medicine, 341,* 1892–1898.

Laakso, M., Vaurio, O., Savolainen, L., Repo, E., Soininen, H., Aronen, H., & Tiihonen, J. (2000). A volumetric MRI study of the hippocampus in type 1 and 2 alcoholism. *Behavioral Brain Research, 109,* 177–186.

Labouvie-Vief, G. (1980). Beyond formal operations: Uses and limits of pure logic in life-span development. *Human Development, 23,* 141–161.

Labouvie-Vief, G. (1990). Modes of knowledge and the organization of development. In M. L. Commons, C. Armon, L. Kohlberg, F. A. Richards, T. A. Grotzer, & J. D. Sinnott (Eds.), *Adult development: Vol. 2. Models and methods in the study of adolescent and adult thought* (pp. 43–62). New York: Praeger.

Lachman, M., & Weaver, S. (1998). Sociodemographic variations in the sense of control by domain: Findings from the MacArthur studies of midlife. *Psychology & Aging, 13,* 553–562.

Lafuente, M., Grifol, R., Segarra, J., Soriano, J., Gorba, M., & Montesinos, A. (1997). Effects of the Firstart method of prenatal stimulation on psychomotor development: The first six months. *Pre- & Peri-Natal Psychology Journal, 11,* 151–162.

Laguna, K., & Babcock, R. (1997). Computer anxiety in young and older adults: Implications for human-computer interactions in older populations. *Computers in Human Behavior, 13,* 317–326.

Laird, R., Pettit, G., Dodge, K., & Bates, J. (1999). Best friendships, group relationships, and antisocial behavior in early adolescence. *Journal of Early Adolescence, 19*, 413–437.

Lakatta, E. G. (1990). Heart and circulation. In E. L. Schneider & J. W. Rowe (Eds.), *Handbook of the biology of aging* (3rd ed.) (pp. 181–217). San Diego, CA: Academic Press.

Lam, R., Pacala, J., & Smith, S. (1997). Factors related to depressive symptoms in an elderly Chinese American sample. *Gerontologist, 17*, 57–70.

Lamb, M. (1997). *The role of father in child development* (3rd ed.). New York: Wiley.

Lamb, M. E. (1981). The development of father-infant relationships. In M. E. Lamb (Ed.), *The role of the father in child development* (2nd ed.) (pp. 459–488). New York: Wiley.

Lamb, M. E., Sternberg, K. J., & Prodromidis, M. (1992). Nonmaternal care and the security of infant-mother attachment: A reanalysis of the data. *Infant Behavior and Development, 15*, 71–83.

Lamborn, S. D., Mounts, N. S., Steinberg, L., & Dornbusch, S. M. (1991). Patterns of competence and adjustment among adolescents from authoritative, authoritarian, indulgent, and neglectful families. *Child Development, 62*, 1049–1065.

Lampard, R., & Peggs, K. (1999). Repartnering: The relevance of parenthood and gender to cohabitation and remarriage among the formerly married. *British Journal of Sociology, 50*, 443–465.

Landolt, M., & Dutton, D. (1997). Power and personality: An analysis of gay male intimate abuse. *Sex Roles, 37*, 335–359.

Landry, S. H., Garner, P. W., Swank, P. R., & Baldwin, C. D. (1996). Effects of maternal scaffolding during joint toy play with preterm and full-term infants. *Merrill-Palmer Quarterly, 42*, 177–199.

Langlois, J. H., Ritter, J. M., Casey, R. J., & Sawin, D. B. (1995). Infant attractiveness predicts maternal behaviors and attitudes. *Developmental Psychology, 31*, 464–472.

Langlois, J. H., Ritter, J. M., Roggman, L. A., & Vaughn, L. S. (1991). Facial diversity and infant preferences for attractive faces. *Developmental Psychology, 27*, 79–84.

Langlois, J. H., Roggman, L. A., Casey, R. J., Ritter, J. M., Rieser-Danner, L. A., & Jenkins, V. Y. (1987). Infant preferences for attractive faces: Rudiments of a stereotype? *Developmental Psychology, 23*, 363–369.

Lansdown, R., & Benjamin, G. (1985). The development of the concept of death in children aged 5–9 years. *Child Care, Health and Development, 11*, 13–30.

Larroque, B., & Kaminski, M. (1998). Prenatal alcohol exposure and development at preschool age: Main results of a French study. *Alcoholism: Clinical & Experimental Research, 22*, 295–303.

Larson, J. H., & Holman, T. B. (1994). Premarital predictors of marital quality and stability. *Family Relations, 43*, 223–237.

Larson, R. (2000). Toward a psychology of positive youth development. *American Psychologist, 55*, 170–183.

Larson, R., Mannell, R., & Zuzanek, J. (1986). Daily well-being of older adults with friends and family. *Psychology and Aging, 1*, 117–126.

Larson, R., & Verma, S. (1999). How children and adolescents spend time across the world: Work, play, and developmental opportunities. *Psychological Bulletin, 125*, 701–736.

Laso, F., Iglesias-Osma, C., Ciudad, J., Lopez, A., Pastor, I., & Orfao, A. (1999). Chronic alcoholism is associated with an imbalanced production of the Th-a/Th-2 cytokines by peripheral blood T cells. *Alcoholism: Clinical & Experimental Research, 23*, 1306–1311.

Laumann, E. O., Gagnon, J. H., Michael, R. T., & Michaels, S. (1994). *The social organization of sexuality: Sexual practices in the United States.* Chicago: University of Chicago Press.

Laursen, B. (1995). Conflict and social interaction in adolescent relationships. *Journal of Research on Adolescence, 5*, 55–70.

Lawlor, S., & Choi, P. (1998). The generation gap in menstrual cycle attributions. *British Journal of Health Psychology, 3*, 257–263.

Lawrence, R. H., Bennett, J. M., & Markides, K. S. (1992). Perceived intergenerational solidarity and psychological distress among older Mexican Americans. *Journals of Gerontology: Social Sciences, 47*, S55–65.

Lawson, E., & Thompson, A. (1996). Black men's perceptions of divorce-related stressors and strategies for coping with divorce. *Journal of Family Issues, 17*, 249–273.

Lawton, L., Silverstein, M., & Bengtson, V. (1994). Affection, social contact, and geographic distance between adult children and their parents. *Journal of Marriage and the Family, 56*, 57–68.

Lawton, M. P. (1985). Housing and living environments of older people. In R. H. Binstock & E. Shanas (Eds.), *Aging and the social sciences* (2nd ed.) (pp. 450–478). New York: Van Nostrand Reinhold.

Lawton, M. P. (1990). Residential environment and self-directedness among older people. *American Psychologist, 45*, 638–640.

Layton, L., Deeny, K., Tall, G., & Upton, G. (1996). Researching and promoting phonological awareness in the nursery class. *Journal of Research in Reading, 19*, 1–13.

Leaper, C. (1991). Influence and involvement in children's discourse: Age, gender, and partner effects. *Child Development, 62*, 797–811.

Lederer, J. (2000). Reciprocal teaching of social studies in inclusive elementary classrooms. *Journal of Learning Disabilities, 33*, 91–106.

Lee, G. R. (1988). Marital satisfaction in later life: The effects of nonmarital roles. *Journal of Marriage and the Family, 50*, 775–783.

Lee, G. R., Dwyer, J. W., & Coward, R. T. (1993). Gender differences in parent care: Demographic factors and same-gender preferences. *Journals of Gerontology: Social Sciences, 48*, S9–16.

Lee, G. R., Seccombe, K., & Shehan, C. L. (1991). Marital status and personal happiness: An analysis of trend data. *Journal of Marriage and the Family, 53*, 839–844.

Lee, I., Manson, J. E., Hennekens, C. H., & Paffenbarger, R. S., Jr. (1993). Body weight and mortality: A 27-year follow-up of middle-aged men. *Journal of the American Medical Association, 270*, 2823–2828.

Lee, I.-M., Hsieh, C., & Paffenbarger, R. S. (1995). Exercise intensity and longevity in men. *Journal of the American Medical Association, 273*, 1179–1184.

Lee, J. (1996). *What your doctor may not tell you about menopause.* New York: Warner Books.

Lee, M., Law, C., & Tam, K. (1999). Parenthood and life satisfaction: A comparison of single and dual-parent families in Hong Kong. *International Social Work, 42*, 139–162.

Lee, S. & Keith, P. (1999). The transition to motherhood of Korean women. *Journal of Comparative Family Studies, 30*, 453–470.

Lee, V. E., Burkham, D. T., Zimiles, H., & Ladewski, B. (1994). Family structure and its effect on behavioral and emotional problems in young adolescents. *Journal of Research on Adolescence, 4*, 405–437.

Lehman, D., & Nisbett, R. (1990). A longitudinal study of the effects of undergraduate training on reasoning. *Developmental Psychology, 26*, 952–960.

Lehman, H. C. (1953). *Age and achievement.* Princeton, NJ: Princeton University Press.

Lehr, U. (1982). Hat die Grosfamilie heute noch eine Chance? [Does the extended family have a chance these days?]. *Der Deutsche Artz, 18 Sonderdruck.*

Leichtman, M. D., & Ceci, S. J. (1995). The effects of stereotypes and suggestions on preschoolers' reports. *Developmental Psychology, 31*, 568–578.

Leigh, G. K. (1982). Kinship interaction over the family life span. *Journal of Marriage and the Family, 44*, 197–208.

Lejoyeux, M., Feuche, N., Loi, S., Solomon, J., & Ades, J. (1999). Study of impulse-control disorders among alcohol-dependent patients. *Journal of Clinical Psychiatry, 60*, 302–305.

Lenhardt, A., & McCourt, B. (2000). Adolescent unresolved grief in response to the death of a mother. *Professional School Counseling, 3*, 189–196.

Leo, R., Narayan, D., Sherry, C., Michalek, C., et al. (1997). Geropsychiatric consultation for African-American and Caucasian patients. *General Hospital Psychiatry, 19*, 216–222.

Leong, F., Austin, J., Sekaran, U., & Komarraju, M. (1998). An evaluation of the cross-cultural validity of Holland's theory: Career choices by workers in India. *Journal of Vocational Behavior, 52*, 441–455.

Lerner, R. M. (1987). A life-span perspective for early adolescence. In R. M. Lerner & T. T. Foch (Eds.), *Biological-psychosocial interactions in early adolescence* (pp. 9–34). Hillsdale, NJ: Erlbaum.

Lester, B., Hoffman, J., & Brazelton, T. (1985). The rhythmic structure of mother-infant interactions in term and preterm infants. *Child Development, 56*, 15–27.

Lester, D. (1990). The Collett-Lester fear of death scale: The original version and a revision. *Death Studies, 14,* 451–468.

Levenson, R. W., Carstensen, L. L., & Gottman, J. M. (1993). Long-term marriage: Age, gender, and satisfaction. *Psychology and Aging, 8,* 301–313.

Lever, J. (1994, August 23). The 1994 Advocate survey of sexuality and relationships: The men. *Advocate,* 16–24.

Leviatan, U. (1999). Contribution of social arrangements to the attainment of successful aging: The experience of the Israeli kibbutz. *Journals of Gerontology: Series B: Psychological Sciences & Social Sciences, 54B,* P205–P213.

Levin, J. S., Chatters, L. M., & Taylor, R. J. (1995). Religious effects on health status and life satisfaction among black Americans. *Journals of Gerontology: Social Sciences, 50B,* S154–163.

Levine, L., & Bluck, S. (1997). Experienced and remembered emotional intensity in older adults. *Psychology of Aging, 12,* 514–523.

Levinson, D. J. (1978). *The seasons of a man's life.* New York: Knopf.

Levinson, D. J. (1986). A conception of adult development. *American Psychologist, 41,* 3–13.

Levinson, D. J. (1990). A theory of life structure development in adulthood. In C. N. Alexander & E. J. Langer (Eds.), *Higher stages of human development* (pp. 35–54). New York: Oxford University Press.

Levitt, M. J., Guacci-Franco, N., & Levitt, J. L. (1993). Convoys of social support in childhood and early adolescence: Structure and function. *Developmental Psychology, 29,* 811–818.

Levitt, M. J., Weber, R. A., & Guacci, N. (1993). Convoys of social support: An intergenerational analysis. *Psychology and Aging, 8,* 323–326.

Levorato, M., & Donati, V. (1999). Conceptual and lexical knowledge of shame in Italian children and adolescents. *International Journal of Behavioral Development, 23,* 873–898.

Levy, G. D., & Fivush, R. (1993). Scripts and gender: A new approach for examining gender-role development. *Developmental Review, 13,* 126–146.

Levy, L. H., Martinkowski, K. S., & Derby, J. F. (1994). Differences in patterns of adaptation in conjugal bereavement: Their sources and potential significance. *Omega, 29,* 71–87.

Levy-Shiff, R., Vakil, E., Dimitrovsky, L., Abramovitz, M., Shahar, N., Har-Even, D., Gross, S., Lerman, M., Levy, I., Sirota, L., & Fish, B. (1998). Medical, cognitive, emotional, and behavioral outcomes in school-age children conceived by in-vitro fertilization. *Journal of Clinical Child Psychology, 27,* 320–329.

Lewis, C. C. (1981). How adolescents approach decisions: Changes over grades seven to twelve and policy implications. *Child Development, 52,* 538–544.

Lewis, J., Malow, R., & Ireland, S. (1997). HIV/AIDS in heterosexual college students: A review of a decade of literature. *Journal of American College Health, 45,* 147–158.

Lewis, K., & Moon, S. (1997). Always single and single-again women: A qualitative study. *Journal of Marital & Family Therapy, 23,* 115–134.

Lewis, M. (1990). Social knowledge and social development. *Merrill-Palmer Quarterly, 36,* 93–116.

Lewis, M. (1991). Ways of knowing: Objective self-awareness of consciousness. *Developmental Review, 11,* 231–243.

Lewis, M., Allesandri, S. M., & Sullivan, M. W. (1992). Differences in shame and pride as a function of children's gender and task difficulty. *Child Development, 63,* 630–638.

Lewis, M., & Brooks, J. (1978). Self-knowledge and emotional development. In M. Lewis & L. A. Rosenblum (Eds.), *The development of affect* (pp. 205–226). New York: Plenum.

Lewis, M., Sullivan, M. W., Stanger, C., & Weiss, M. (1989). Self development and self-conscious emotions. *Child Development, 60,* 146–156.

Lewis, M. D. (1993). Early socioemotional predictors of cognitive competence at 4 years. *Developmental Psychology, 29,* 1036–1045.

Lewkowicz, D. J. (1994). Limitations on infants' response to rate-based auditory-visual relations. *Developmental Psychology, 30,* 880–892.

Liao, K., & Hunter, M. (1998). Preparation for menopause: Prospective evaluation of a health education intervention for mid-aged women. *Maturitas, 29,* 215–224.

Lickona, T. (1978). Moral development and moral education. In J. M. Gallagher & J. J. A. Easley (Eds.), *Knowledge and development* (Vol. 2) (pp. 21–74). New York: Plenum.

Lickona, T. (1983). *Raising good children.* New York: Bantam Books.

Lieberman, M., Doyle, A., & Markiewicz, D. (1995, March). *Attachment to mother and father: Links to peer relations in children.* Paper presented at the biennial meetings of the Society for Research in Child Development, Indianapolis, IN.

Lieberman, M., Doyle, A., & Markiewicz, D. (1999). Developmental patterns in security of attachment to mother and father in late childhood and early adolescence: Associations with peer relations. *Child Development, 70,* 202–213.

Lieberman, M. A. (1965). Psychological correlates of impending death: Some preliminary observations. *Journal of Gerontology, 20,* 182–190.

Lieberman, M. A., & Coplan, A. S. (1970). Distance from death as a variable in the study of aging. *Developmental Psychology, 2,* 71–84.

Lieberman, M. A., & Peskin, H. (1992). Adult life crises. In J. E. Birren, R. B. Sloane, & G. D. Cohen (Eds.), *Handbook of mental health and aging* (2nd ed.) (pp. 119–143). San Diego, CA: Academic Press.

Liem, R., & Liem, J. H. (1988). Psychological effects of unemployment on workers and their families. *Journal of Social Issues, 44,* 87–105.

Light, L. L. (1991). Memory and aging: Four hypotheses in search of data. *Annual Review of Psychology, 42,* 333–376.

Lillard, A. (1998). Ethnopsychologies: Cultural variations in theories of mind. *Psychological Bulletin, 123,* 3–32.

Lillard, A. S., & Flavell, J. H. (1992). Young children's understanding of different mental states. *Developmental Psychology, 28,* 626–634.

Lim, K. O., Zipursky, R. B., Watts, M. C., & Pfefferbaum, A. (1992). Decreased gray matter in normal aging: An in vivo magnetic resonance study. *Journals of Gerontology: Biological Sciences, 47,* B26–30.

Lima, S. D., Hale, S., & Myerson, J. (1991). How general is general slowing? Evidence from the lexical domain. *Psychology and Aging, 6,* 416–425.

Lin, C., Hsiao, C., & Chen, W. (1999). Development of sustained attention assessed using the Continuous Performance Test among children 6–15 years of age. *Journal of Abnormal Child Psychology, 27,* 403–412.

Lincourt, A., Rybash, J., & Hoyer, W. (1998). Aging, working memory, and the development of instance-based retrieval. *Brain & Cognition, 37,* 100–102.

Lindahl, K., Clements, M., & Markman, H. (1997). Predicting marital and parent functioning in dyads and triads: A longitudinal investigation of marital processes. *Journal of Family Psychology, 11,* 139–151.

Lindahl, L. & Heimann, M. (1997). Social proximity in early mother-infant interactions: Implications for gender differences? *Early Development & Parenting, 6,* 83–88.

Lindgren, C., Connelly, C., & Gaspar, H. (1999). Grief in spouse and children caregivers of dementia patients. *Western Journal of Nursing Research, 21,* 521–537.

Lindo, G., & Nordholm, L. (1999). Adaptation strategies, well-being, and activities of daily living among people with low vision. *Journal of Visual Impairment & Blindness, 93,* 434–446.

Lindsay, D. S., & Read, J. D. (1994). Psychotherapy and memory of childhood sexual abuse: A cognitive perspective. *Applied Cognitive Psychology, 8,* 281–338.

Lindsay, J. (2000). An ambiguous commitment: Moving in to a cohabiting relationship. *Journal of Family Studies, 6,* 120–134.

Lindsay, R. (1985). The aging skeleton. In M. R. Haug, A. B. Ford, & M. Sheafor (Eds.), *The physical and mental health of aged women* (pp. 65–82). New York: Springer.

Lindstrom, T. (1997). Immunity and somatic health in bereavement. A prospective study of 39 Norwegian widows. *Omega: Journal of Death & Dying, 35,* 231–241.

Lineweaver, T., & Hertzog, C. (1998). Adults' efficacy and control beliefs regarding memory and aging: Separating general from personal beliefs. *Aging, Neuropsychology, & Cognition, 5,* 264–296.

Linney, J. A., & Seidman, E. (1989). The future of schooling. *American Psychologist, 44,* 336–340.

Lissner, L., Bengtsson, C., Björkelund, C., & Wedel, H. (1996). Physical activity levels and changes in relation to longevity: A prospective study of Swedish women. *American Journal of Epidemiology, 143,* 54–62.

Litwak, E., & Longino, C. F., Jr. (1987). Migration patterns among the elderly: A developmental perspective. *The Gerontologist, 27,* 266–272.

Livesley, W. J., & Bromley, D. B. (1973). *Person perception in childhood and adolescence.* London: Wiley.

Livson, N., & Peskin, H. (1981). Psychological health at 40: Prediction from adolescent personality. In D. H. Eichorn, J. A. Clausen, N. Haan, M. P. Honzik, & P. H. Mussen (Eds.), *Present and past in middle life* (pp. 184–194). New York: Academic Press.

Lobel, T., Slone, M., & Winch, G. (1997). Masculinity, popularity, and self-esteem among Israeli preadolescent girls. *Sex Roles, 36,* 395–408.

Loehlin, J. C., Horn, J. M., & Willerman, L. (1994). Differential inheritance of mental abilities in the Texas Adoption Project. *Intelligence, 19,* 325–336.

Longino, C. F., Jr. (1990). Geographical distribution and migration. In R. H. Binstock & L. K. George (Eds.), *Handbook of aging and the social sciences* (3rd ed.) (pp. 45–63). San Diego, CA: Academic Press.

Longino, C. F., Jr., Jackson, D. J., Zimmerman, R. S., & Bradsher, J. E. (1991). The second move: Health and geographic mobility. *Journals of Gerontology: Social Sciences, 46,* S218–224.

Loonsbury, J. (1992). Interdisciplinary instruction: A mandate for the nineties. In J. Loonsbury (Ed.), *Connecting the curriculum through interdisciplinary instruction.* Columbus, OH: National Middle School Association.

Lubinski, D., & Benbow, C. P. (1992). Gender differences in abilities and preferences among the gifted: Implications for the math-science pipeline. *Current Directions in Psychological Science, 1,* 61–66.

Luetzen, K. (1998). Gay and lesbian politics: Assimilation or subversion. A Danish perspective. *Journal of Homosexuality, 35,* 233–243.

Lundh, W., & Gyllang, C. (1993). Use of the Edinburgh Postnatal Depression Scale in some Swedish child health care centres. *Scandinavian Journal of Caring Sciences, 7,* 149–154.

Luster, T., Boger, R., & Hannan, K. (1993). Infant affect and home environment. *Journal of Marriage and the Family, 55,* 651–661.

Luster, T., & McAdoo, H. P. (1995). Factors related to self-esteem among African American youths: A secondary analysis of the High/Scope Perry Preschool data. *Journal of Research on Adolescence, 5,* 451–467.

Luster, T., & McAdoo, H. (1996). Family and child influences on educational attainment: A secondary analysis of the High/Scope Perry Preschool data. *Developmental Psychology, 32,* 26–39.

Lutfey, K., & Maynard, D. (1998). Bad news in oncology: How physician and patient talk about death and dying without using those words. *Social Psychology Quarterly, 61,* 321–341.

Luthar, S. S., & Zigler, E. (1992). Intelligence and social competence among high-risk adolescents. *Development and Psychopathology, 4,* 287–299.

Lyons, N. P. (1983). Two perspectives: On self, relationships, and morality. *Harvard Educational Review, 53,* 125–145.

Lytle, L., Bakken, L., & Romig, C. (1997). Adolescent female identity development. *Sex Roles, 37,* 175–185.

Lytton, H., & Romney, D. M. (1991). Parents' differential socialization of boys and girls: A meta-analysis. *Psychological Bulletin, 109,* 267–296.

Ma, H., Shek, D., Cheung, P., & Oi Bun Lam, C. (2000). Parental, peer and teacher influences on the social behavior of Hong Kong Chinese adolescents. *Journal of Genetic Psychology, 161,* 65–78.

Maas, H. S., & Kuypers, J. A. (1974). *From thirty to seventy.* San Francisco: Jossey-Bass.

Maccoby, E. E. (1980). *Social development: Psychological growth and the parent-child relationship.* New York: Harcourt Brace Jovanovich.

Maccoby, E. E. (1984). Middle childhood in the context of the family. In W. A. Collins (Ed.), *Development during middle childhood: The years from six to twelve* (pp. 184–239). Washington, DC: National Academy Press.

Maccoby, E. E. (1988). Gender as a social category. *Developmental Psychology, 24,* 755–765.

Maccoby, E. E. (1990). Gender and relationships: A developmental account. *American Psychologist, 45,* 513–520.

Maccoby, E. E. (1995). The two sexes and their social systems. In P. Moen, G. H. Elder, Jr., & K. Lüscher (Eds.), *Examining lives in context: Perspectives on the ecology of human development* (pp. 347–364). Washington, DC: American Psychological Association.

Maccoby, E., & Jacklin, C. (1974). *The psychology of sex differences.* Stanford, CA: Stanford University Press.

Maccoby, E. E., & Jacklin, C. N. (1987). Gender segregation in childhood. In H. W. Reese (Ed.), *Advances in child development and behavior* (Vol. 20) (pp. 239–288). Orlando, FL: Academic Press.

Maccoby, E. E., & Martin, J. A. (1983). Socialization in the context of the family: Parent-child interaction. In E. M. Hetherington (Ed.), *Handbook of child psychology: Socialization, personality, and social development* (Vol. 4) (pp. 1–102). New York: Wiley.

MacDermid, S. M., Huston, T. L., & McHale, S. M. (1990). Changes in marriage associated with the transition to parenthood: Individual differences as a function of sex-role attitudes and changes in the division of household labor. *Journal of Marriage and the Family, 52,* 475–486.

MacDorman, M., & Atkinson, J. (1999, July 30). Infant mortality statistics from the 1997 period. Linked birth/infant death data set. *National Vital Statistics Reports, 47,* (23), 1–24.

MacIver, D. J., Reuman, D. A., & Main, S. R. (1995). Social structuring of the school: Studying what is, illuminating what could be. *Annual Review of Psychology, 46,* 375–400.

Macrae, C., & Bodenhausen, G. (2000). Social cognition: Thinking categorically about others. *Annual Review of Psychology, 51,* 93–120.

MacRae, H. (1992). Fictive kin as a component of the social networks of older people. *Research on Aging, 14,* 226–247.

Madan-Swain, A., Brown, R., Foster, M., Verga, R., et al. (2000). Identity in adolescent survivors of childhood cancer. *Journal of Pediatric Psychology, 25,* 105–115.

Madden, D. J. (1992). Four to ten milliseconds per year: Age-related slowing of visual word identification. *Journals of Gerontology: Psychological Sciences, 47,* P59–68.

Madison, C., Johnson, J., Seikel, J., Arnold, M., & Schultheis, L. (1998). Comparative study of the phonology of preschool children prenatally exposed to cocaine and multiple drugs and non-exposed children. *Journal of Communication Disorders, 31,* 231–244.

Mael, F., Morath, R., & McLellan, J. (1997). Dimensions of adolescent employment. *Career Development Quarterly, 45,* 351–368.

Maes, M., DeVos, N., Wauters, A., Demedts, P., Maurits, V., Neels, H., Bosmans, E., Altamura, C., Lin, A., Song, C., Vandenbroucke, M., & Scharpe, S. (1999). Inflammatory markers in younger vs. elderly normal volunteers and in-patients with Alzheimer's disease. *Journal of Psychiatric Research, 33,* 397–405.

Maffeis, C., Schutz, Y., Piccoli, R., Gonfiantini, E., & Pinelli, L. (1993). Prevalence of obesity in children in north-east Italy. *International Journal of Obesity, 14,* 287–294.

Maguire, M., & Dunn, J. (1997). Friendships in early childhood and social understanding. *International Journal of Behavioral Development, 21,* 669–686.

Maier, S. F., Watkins, L. R., & Fleshner, M. (1994). The interface between behavior, brain, and immunity. *American Psychologist, 49,* 1004–1017.

Main, M., & Hesse, E. (1990). Parents' unresolved traumatic experiences are related to infant disorganized attachment status: Is frightened and/or frightening parental behavior the linking mechanism? In M. T. Greenberg, D. Cicchetti, & E. M. Cummings (Eds.), *Attachment in the preschool years: Theory, research, and intervention* (pp. 161–182). Chicago: University of Chicago Press.

Main, M., & Solomon, J. (1990). Procedures for identifying infants as disorganized/disoriented during the Ainsworth Strange Situation. In M. T. Greenberg, D. Cicchetti, & E. M. Cummings (Eds.), *Attachment in the preschool years: Theory, research, and intervention* (pp. 121–160). Chicago: University of Chicago Press.

Mainemer, H., Gilman, L., & Ames, E. (1998). Parenting stress in families adopting children from Romanian orphanages. *Journal of Family Issues, 19,* 164–180.

Maitel, S., Dromi, E., Sagi, A., & Bornstein, M. (2000). The Hebrew Communicative Development Inventory: Language-specific properties and cross-linguistic generalizations. *Journal of Child Language, 27,* 43–67.

Malina, R. M. (1982). Motor development in the early years. In S. G. Moore & C. R. Cooper (Eds.), *The young child: Reviews of research* (Vol. 3) (pp. 211–232). Washington, DC: National Association for the Education of Young Children.

Malina, R. M. (1990). Physical growth and performance during the transition years. In R. Montemayor, G. R. Adams, & T. P. Gullotta (Eds.), *From childhood to adolescence: A transitional period?* (pp. 41–62). Newbury Park, CA: Sage.

Malinosky-Rummell, R., & Hansen, D. (1993). Long-term consequences of childhood physical abuse. *Psychological Bulletin, 114,* 68–79.

Malkinson, R., & Bar-Tur, L., (1999). The aging of grief in Israel: A perspective of bereaved parents. *Death Studies, 23,* 413–431.

Mallet, P., Apostolidis, T., & Paty, B. (1997). The development of gender schemata about heterosexual and homosexual others during adolescence. *Journal of General Psychology, 124,* 91–104.

Malo, J., & Tremblay, R. (1997). The impact of parental alcoholism and maternal social position on boys' school adjustment, pubertal maturation and sexual behavior: A test of two competing hypotheses. *Journal of Child Psychology & Psychiatry & Allied Disciplines, 38,* 187–197.

Mangelsdorf, S., Plunkett, J., Dedrick, C., Berlin, M., Meiseis, S., McHale, J., & Dichtellmiller, M. (1996). Attachment security in very low birthweight infants. *Developmental Psychology, 32,* 914–920.

Manson, J. E., Willett, W. C., Stampfer, M. J., Colditz, G. A., Hunter, D. J., Hankinson, S. E., Hennekens, C. H., & Speizer, F. E. (1995). Body weight and mortality among women. *New England Journal of Medicine, 333,* 677–685.

Manton, K. G., Stallard, E., & Liu, K. (1993). Forecasts of active life expectancy: Policy and fiscal implications. *The Journals of Gerontology, 48* (Special Issue), 11–26.

Mäntylä, T. (1994). Remembering to remember: Adult age differences in prospective memory. *Journals of Gerontology: Psychological Sciences, 49,* P276–282.

Maratsos, M. (2000). More overregularizations after all: New data and discussion on Marcus, Pinker, Ullman, Hollander, Rosen & Xu. *Journal of Child Language, 27,* 183–212.

Marcia, J. E. (1966). Development and validation of ego identity status. *Journal of Personality and Social Psychology, 3,* 551–558.

Marcia, J. E. (1980). Identity in adolescence. In J. Adelson (Ed.), *Handbook of adolescent psychology* (pp. 159–187). New York: Wiley.

Marcovitch, S., Goldberg, S., Gold, A., & Washington, J. (1997). Determinants of behavioural problems in Romanian children adopted in Ontario. *International Journal of Behavioral Development, 20,* 17–31.

Marcus, D. E., & Overton, W. F. (1978). The development of cognitive gender constancy and sex role preferences. *Child Development, 49,* 434–444.

Marcus, R. F. (1986). Naturalistic observation of cooperation, helping, and sharing and their association with empathy and affect. In C. Zahn-Waxler, E. M. Cummings, & R. Iannotti (Eds.), *Altruism and aggression: Biological and social origins* (pp. 256–279). Cambridge, England: Cambridge University Press.

Marean, G. C., Werner, L. A., & Kuhl, P. K. (1992). Vowel categorization by very young infants. *Developmental Psychology, 28,* 396–405.

Margolin, G., & Gordis, E. (2000). The effects of family and community violence on children. *Annual Review of Psychology, 51,* 445–479.

Markides, K. S., & Lee, D. J. (1991). Predictors of health status in middle-aged and older Mexican Americans. *Journals of Gerontology: Social Sciences, 46,* S243–249.

Markides, K. S., & Mindel, C. H. (1987). *Aging and ethnicity.* Newbury Park, CA: Sage.

Markman, E. M. (1992). Constraints on word learning: Speculations about their nature, origins, and domain specificity. In M. R. Gunnar & M. Maratsos (Eds.), *Minnesota Symposia on Child Psychology* (Vol. 25) (pp. 59–101). Hillsdale, NJ: Erlbaum.

Marks, N., & Lamberg, J. (1998). Marital status continuity and change among young and midlife adults. *Journal of Family Issues, 19,* 652–686.

Marsh, H., Craven, R., & Debus, R. (1999). Separation of competency and affect components of multiple dimensions of academic self-concept: A developmental perspective. *Merrill-Palmer Quarterly, 45,* 567–601.

Marsh, H., & Yeung, A. (1997). Coursework selection: Relations to academic self-concept and achievement. *American Educational Research Journal, 34,* 691–720.

Marsh, H., & Yeung, A. (1998). Longitudinal structural equation models of academic self-concept and achievement: Gender differences in the development of math and English constructs. *American Educational Research Journal, 35,* 705–738.

Marshall, N., Coll, C., Marx, F., McCartney, K., Keefe, N., & Ruh, J. (1997). After-school time and children's behavioral adjustment. *Merrill-Palmer Quarterly, 43,* 497–514.

Marshall, V. W. (1975). Age and awareness of finitude in developmental gerontology. *Omega, 6,* 113–129.

Marshall, V. W. (1996). The state of theory in aging and the social sciences. In R. H. Binstock & L. K. George (Eds.), *Handbook of aging and the social sciences* (4th ed.) (pp. 12–30). San Diego, CA: Academic Press.

Marshall, V. W., & Levy, J. A. (1990). Aging and dying. In R. H. Binstock & L. K. George (Eds.), *Handbook of aging and the social sciences* (3rd ed.) (pp. 245–260). San Diego, CA: Academic Press.

Marsiglio, W., & Donnelly, D. (1991). Sexual relations in later life: A national study of married persons. *Journals of Gerontology: Social Sciences, 46,* S338–344.

Martin, C. L. (1991). The role of cognition in understanding gender effects. In H. W. Reese (Ed.), *Advances in child development and behavior* (Vol. 23) (pp. 113–150). San Diego, CA: Academic Press.

Martin, C. L. (1993). New directions for investigating children's gender knowledge. *Developmental Review, 13,* 184–204.

Martin, C. L., & Halverson, C. F., Jr. (1981). A schematic processing model of sex typing and stereotyping in children. *Child Development, 52,* 1119–1134.

Martin, C. L., & Little, J. K. (1990). The relation of gender understanding to children's sex-typed preferences and gender stereotypes. *Child Development, 61,* 1427–1439.

Martin, C. L., Wood, C. H., & Little, J. K. (1990). The development of gender stereotype components. *Child Development, 61,* 1891–1904.

Martin, J. (1995). Birth characteristics for Asian or Pacific Islander subgroups, 1992. *Monthly Vital Statistics Report, 43 (10),* Supplement.

Martin, R., Noyes, J., Wisenbaker, J. & Huttunen, M. (1999). Prediction of early childhood negative emotionality and inhibition from maternal distress during pregnancy. *Merrill-Palmer Quarterly, 45,* 370–391.

Martin, R. P., Wisenbaker, J., & Huttunen, M. (1994). Review of factor analytic studies of temperament measures based on the Thomas-Chess structural model: Implications for the Big Five. In C. F. Halverson, Jr., G. A. Kohnstamm, & R. P. Martin (Eds.), *The developing structure of temperament and personality from infancy to adulthood* (pp. 157–172). Hillsdale, NJ: Erlbaum.

Martorano, S. C. (1977). A developmental analysis of performance on Piaget's formal operations tasks. *Developmental Psychology, 13,* 666–672.

Marx, G. (1987). *Groucho and me.* New York: AMS Press.

Masataka, N. (1999). Preference for infant-directed singing in 2-day-old hearing infants of deaf parents. *Developmental Psychology, 35,* 1001–1005.

Mascolo, M. F., & Fischer, K. W. (1995). Developmental transformations in appraisals for pride, shame, and guilt. In J. P. Tangney & K. W. Fischer (Eds.), *Self-conscious emotions: The psychology of shame, guilt, embarrassment, and pride* (pp. 64–113). New York: Guilford Press.

Maslow, A. H. (1968). *Toward a psychology of being* (2nd ed.). New York: Van Nostrand Reinhold.

Maslow, A. H. (1970a). *Motivation and personality* (2nd ed.). New York: Harper & Row.

Maslow, A. H. (1970b). *Religions, values, and peak-experiences.* New York: Viking. (Original work published 1964.)

Maslow, A. H. (1971). *The farther reaches of human nature.* New York: Viking.

Massachusetts Department of Education. (2000). *Charter school initiative.* [Online report]. Retrieved February 29, 2000 from the World Wide Web: www.doe.mass.edu/cs.www

Masten, A. S., Best, K. M., & Garmezy, N. (1990). Resilience and development: Contributions from the study of children who overcome adversity. *Development and Psychopathology, 2,* 425–444.

Masten, A., & Coatsworth, D. (1998). The development of competence in favorable and unfavorable environments: Lessons from research on successful children. *American Psychologist, 53,* 205–220.

Masur, E., & Rodemaker, J. (1999). Mothers' and infants' spontaneous vocal, verbal, and action imitation during the second year. *Merrill-Palmer Quarterly, 45,* 392–412.

Maszk, P., Eisenberg, N., & Guthrie, I. (1999). Relations of children's social status to their emotionality and regulation: A short-term longitudinal study. *Merrill-Palmer Quarterly, 454,* 468–492.

Mather, P. L., & Black, K. N. (1984). Heredity and environmental influences on preschool twins' language skills. *Developmental Psychology, 20,* 303–308.

Mathew, A., & Cook, M. (1990). The control of reaching movements by young infants. *Child Development, 61,* 1238–1257.

Matthews, K. A., Wing, R. R., Kuller, L. H., Meilahn, E. N., Kelsey, S. F., Costello, E. J., & Caggiula, A. W. (1990). Influences of natural menopause on psychological characteristics and symptoms of middle-aged healthy women. *Journal of Consulting and Clinical Psychology, 58,* 345–351.

Mattson, S., & Riley, E. (1999). Implicit and explicit memory functioning in children with heavy prenatal alcohol exposure. *Journal of the International Neuropsychological Society, 5,* 462–471.

Mattson, S., Riley, E., Gramling, L., Delis, D. & Jones, K. (1998). Neuropsychological comparison of alcohol-exposed children with or without physical features of fetal alcohol syndrome. *Neuropsychology, 12,* 146–153.

Maughan, B., Pickles, A., & Quinton, D. (1995). Parental hostility, childhood behavior, and adult social functioning. In J. McCord (Ed.), *Coercion and punishment in long-term perspectives* (pp. 34–58). Cambridge, England: Cambridge University Press.

Maurer, D., & Maurer, C. (1988). *The world of the newborn.* New York: Basic Books.

Maylor, D., Vousden, J., & Brown, D. (1999). Adult age differences in short-term memory for serial order: Data and a model. *Psychology & Aging, 14,* 572–594.

Maylor, E. (1998). Changes in event-based prospective memory across adulthood. *Aging, Neuropsychology, & Cognition, 5,* 107–128.

Maylor, E. A. (1993). Aging and forgetting in prospective and retrospective memory tasks. *Psychology and Aging, 8,* 420–428.

Mayringer, H., & Wimmer, H. (2000). Pseudoname learning by German-speaking children with dyslexia: Evidence for a phonological learning deficit. *Journal of Experimental Child Psychology, 75,* 116–133.

Mayseless, O., Wiseman, H., & Hai, I. (1998). Adolescents' relationships with father, mother, and same-gender friend. *Journal of Adolescent Research, 13,* 101–123.

McAdams, D., Hart, H., & Maruna, S. (1998). The anatomy of generativity. In D. P. McAdams & E. de St. Aubin (Eds.), *Generativity and adult development: How and why we care about the next generation* (pp. 7–44). Washington, DC: American Psychological Association.

McAllister, D., Kaplan, B., Edworthy, S., Martin, L., et al. (1997). The influence of systemic lupus erythematosus on fetal development: Cognitive, behavioral, and health trends. *Journal of the International Neurological Society, 3,* 370–376.

McAuley, E. (1993). Self-efficacy, physical activity, and aging. In J. R. Kelly (Ed.), *Activity and aging. Staying involved in late life* (pp. 187–205). Newbury Park, CA: Sage.

McAuley, W. J., & Blieszner, R. (1985). Selection of long-term care arrangements by older community residents. *The Gerontologist, 25,* 188–193.

McBride-Chang, C. (1998). The development of invented spelling. *Early Education & Development, 9,* 147–160.

McBride-Chang, C., & Ho, C. (2000). Developmental issues in Chinese children's character acquisition. *Journal of Educational Psychology, 92,* 50–55.

McCall, B., Cavanaugh, M., Arvey, R., & Taubman, P. (1997). Genetic influences on job and occupational switching. *Journal of Vocational Behavior, 50,* 60–77.

McCall, R. B. (1993). Developmental functions for general mental performance. In D. K. Detterman (Ed.), *Current topics in human intel-ligence: Vol. 3. Individual differences and cognition* (pp. 3–30). Norwood, NJ: Ablex.

McCarthy, J., & Hardy, J. (1993). Age at first birth and birth outcomes. *Journal of Research on Adolescence, 3,* 374–392.

McCarton, C., Brooks-Gunn, J., Wallace, I., Bauer, C., Benett, F., Bernbaum, J., Broyles, S., Casey, P., McCormick, M., Scott, D., Tyson, J., Tonascia, J., & Mainhart, C. (1997). Results at age 8 years of early intervention for low-birth-weight premature infants. *Journal of the American Medical Association, 277,* 126–132.

McClun, L., & Merrell, K. (1998). Relationship of perceived parenting styles, locus of control orientation, and self-concept among junior high age students. *Psychology in the Schools, 35,* 381–390.

McClure, E. (2000). A meta-analytic review of sex differences in facial expression processing and their development in infants, children, and adolescents. *Psychological Bulletin, 126,* 242–453.

McCoy, N. (1998). Methodological problems in the study of sexuality and the menopause. *Maturitas, 29,* 51–60.

McCrae, R. R., & Costa, P. T., Jr. (1984). *Emerging lives, enduring dispositions: Personality in adulthood.* Boston: Little, Brown.

McCrae, R. R., & Costa, P. T., Jr. (1987). Validation of the five-factor model of personality across instruments and observers. *Journal of Personality and Social Psychology, 52,* 81–90.

McCrae, R. R., & Costa, P. T., Jr. (1990). *Personality in adulthood.* New York: Guilford Press.

McCrae, R. R., & Costa, P. T., Jr. (1994). The stability of personality: Observations and evaluations. *Current Directions in Psychological Science, 3,* 173–175.

McCrae, R., Costa, P., Ostendorf, F., & Angleitner, A. (2000). Nature over nurture: Temperament, personality, and life span development. *Journal of Personality & Social Psychology, 78,* 173–186.

McCrae, R. R., & John, O. P. (1992). An introduction to the Five-Factor Model and its applications. *Journal of Personality, 60,* 175–215.

McCullough, M. (1998, December 22). Birth of octuplets worries infertility specialists. *Seattle Times.* [Online edition archives]. Retrieved March 6, 2001 from the World Wide Web: http://www.seattletimes.com

McDonald, P. L., & Wanner, R. A. (1990). *Retirement in Canada.* Toronto: Butterworths.

McDonough, C., Horgan, A., Codd, M., & Casey, P. (2000). Gender differences in the results of the final medical examination at University College Dublin. *Medical Education, 34,* 30–34.

McEvoy, G. M., & Cascio, W. F. (1989). Cumulative evidence of the relationship between employee age and job performance. *Journal of Applied Psychology, 74,* 11–17.

McFadden, D. (1998). Sex differences in the auditory system. *Developmental Neuropsychology, 14,* 261–298.

McFalls, J. A., Jr. (1990). The risks of reproductive impairment in the later years of childbearing. *Annual Review of Sociology, 16,* 491–519.

McFayden-Ketchumm, S., Bates, J., Dodge, K., & Pettit, G. (1996). Patterns of change in early childhood aggressive-disruptive behavior: Gender differences in predictions from early coercive and affectionate mother-child interactions. *Child Development, 67,* 2417–2433.

McGue, M., Pickens, R., & Svikis, D. (1992). Sex and age effects on the inheritance of alcohol problems: A twin study. *Journal of Abnormal Psychology, 101,* 3–17.

McHale, S., Crouter, A., & Tucker, C. (1999). Family context and gender role socialization in middle childhood: Comparing girls to boys and sisters to brothers. *Child Development, 70,* 990–1004.

McIntosh, B. R., & Danigelis, N. L. (1995). Race, gender, and the relevance of productive activity for elders' affect. *Journals of Gerontology: Social Sciences, 50B,* S229–239.

McKinlay, J. B., McKinlay, S. M., & Brambilla, D. J. (1987). Health status and utilization behavior associated with menopause. *American Journal of Epidemiology, 125,* 110–121.

McKitrick, L., Friedman, L., Thompson, L., Gray, C., & Yesavage, J. (1997). Feasibility and psychometric description of a paced auditory serial addition task adapted for older adults. *Journal of Clinical Geropsychology, 3,* 57–71.

McLanahan, S., & Sandefur, G. (1994). *Growing up with a single parent: What hurts, what helps.* Cambridge, MA: Harvard University Press.

McLoyd, V. (1998). Socioeconomic disadvantage and child development. *American Psychologist, 53,* 185–204.

McLoyd, V., & Wilson, L. (1991). The strain of living poor: Parenting, social support, and child mental health. In A. C. Huston (Ed.), *Children in poverty: Child development and public policy* (pp. 105–135). Cambridge, England: Cambridge University Press.

McLoyd, V. C. (1990). The impact of economic hardship on black families and children: Psychological distress, parenting, and socioemotional development. *Child Development, 61,* 311–346.

McLoyd, V. C., Jayaratne, T. E., Ceballo, R., & Borquez, J. (1994). Unemployment and work interruption among African American single mothers: Effects on parenting and adolescent socioemotional functioning. *Child Development, 65,* 562–589.

McMahon, R. (1997, April). *Prevention of antisocial behavior: Initial findings from the Fast Track Project.* Symposium presented at the annual meeting of the society for Research in Child Development, Washington, DC.

McMaster, J., Pitts, M., & Poyah, G. (1997). The menopausal experiences of women in a developing country: "There is a time for everything: to be a teenager, a mother and a granny." *Women & Health, 26,* 1–13.

McNeal, C., & Amato, P. (1998). Parents' marital violence: Long-term consequences for children. *Journal of Family Issues, 19,* 123–139.

McNeal, R. (1997). Are students being pulled out of high school? The effect of adolescent employment on dropping out. *Sociology of Education, 70,* 206–220.

Mead, S., & Fisk, A. (1998). Measuring skill acquisition and retention with an ATM simulator: The need for age-specific training. *Human Factors, 40,* 516–523.

Mediascope, Inc. (1999). *The social effects of electronic interactive games: An annotated bibliography.* Studio City, CA: Mediascope Press.

Mediascope Press. (1999a). *Media use in America/Issue Brief Series.* Studio City, CA: Mediascope Inc.

Mediascope Press. (1999b). *Substance use in popular movies and music/Issue Brief Series.* Studio City, CA: Mediascope Inc.

Mediascope Press. (2000). *Teens, sex and the media/Issue Brief Series.* Studio City, CA: Mediascope Inc.

Medvedova, L. (1998). Personality dimensions—"little five"—and their relationships with coping strategies in early adolescence. *Studia Psychologica, 40,* 261–265.

Meeks, S. (1997). Illnesses in late life: Short-term course of mental illness in middle age and late life. *International Psychogeriatrics, 9,* 343–358.

Meeus, W., Dekovic, M., & Iedema, J. (1997). Unemployment and identity in adolescence: A social comparison perspective. *Career Development Quarterly, 45,* 369–380.

Mehta, K. (1997). The impact of religious beliefs and practices on aging: A cross-cultural comparison. *Journal of Aging Studies, 11,* 101–114.

Meisenhelder, J., & Chandler, E. (2000). Faith, prayer, and health outcomes in elderly Native Americans. *Clinical Nursing Research, 9,* 191–203.

Melby, J. N., & Conger, R. D. (1996). Parental behaviors and adolescent academic performance: A longitudinal analysis. *Journal of Research on Adolescence, 6,* 113–137.

Melot, A., & Houde, O. (1998). Categorization and theories of mind: The case of the appearance/reality distinction. *Cahiers de Psychologie Cognitive/Current Psychology of Cognition, 17,* 71–93.

Melson, G., Peet, S., & Sparks, C. (1991). Children's attachments to their pets: Links to socioemotional development. *Children's Environmental Quarterly, 8,* 55–65.

Meltzoff, A. N. (1988). Infant imitation and memory: Nine-month-olds in immediate and deferred tasks. *Child Development, 59,* 217–225.

Meltzoff, A. N. (1995). Understanding the intentions of others: Reenactment of intended acts by 18-month-old children. *Developmental Psychology, 31,* 838–850.

Menaghan, E. G., & Lieberman, M. A. (1986). Changes in depression following divorce: A panel study. *Journal of Marriage and the Family, 48,* 319–328.

Meredith, K., & Rassa, G. (1999). Aligning the levels of awareness with the stages of grieving. *Journal of Cognitive Rehabilitation, 17,* 10–12.

Merikangas, K. R., & Angst, J. (1995). The challenge of depressive disorders in adolescence. In M. Rutter (Ed.), *Psychosocial disturbances in young people: Challenges for prevention* (pp. 131–165). Cambridge, England: Cambridge University Press.

Merrill, D. M., & Mor, V. (1993). Pathways to hospital death among the oldest old. *Journal of Aging and Health, 5,* 516–535.

Meyer, D., & Bartfield, J. (1996). Compliance with child support orders in divorce cases. *Journal of Marriage & the Family, 58,* 201–212.

Meyer, D. & Bartfield, J. (1998). Patterns of child support compliance in Wisconsin. *Journal of Marriage & the Family, 60,* 309–318.

Meyer, G., & Stadler, M. (1999). Criminal behavior associated with pathological gambling. *Journal of Gambling Studies, 15,* 29–43.

Meyer, M. (1998). Perceptual differences in fetal alcohol syndrome affect boys performing a modeling task. *Perceptual & Motor Skills, 87,* 784–786.

Meyer-Bahlburg, H. F. L., Ehrhardt, A. A., Rosen, L. R., Gruen, R. S., Veridiano, N. P., Vann, F. H., & Neuwalder, H. F. (1995). Prenatal estrogens and the development of homosexual orientation. *Developmental Psychology, 31,* 12–21.

Michael, R. T., Gagnon, J. H., Laumann, E. O., & Kolata, G. (1994). *Sex in America.* Boston: Little, Brown.

Microsoft launches Web site for seniors and a major grant to Senior-Net—two more steps toward closing the "digital divide." (1998, October 1.) *Microsoft News.* [Online story]. Retrieved February 16, 2001 from the World Wide Web: http://www.microsoft.com/presspass

Miech, R., & Shanahan, M. (2000). Socioeconomic status and depression over the life course. *Journal of Health & Social Behavior, 41,* 162–176.

Milar, K. (2000). The first generation of women psychologists and the psychology of women. *American Psychologist, 55,* 613–615.

Miliotis, D., Sesma, A., & Masten, A. (1999). Parenting as a protective process for school success in children from homeless families. *Early Education & Development, 10,* 111–133.

Miller, B., Norton, M., Curtis, T., Hill, E., Schvaneveldt, P., & Young, M. (1998). The timing of sexual intercourse among adolescents: Family, peer, and other antecedents: Erratum. *Youth & Society, 29,* 390.

Miller, B. C., & Moore, K. A. (1990). Adolescent sexual behavior, pregnancy, and parenting: Research through the 1980s. *Journal of Marriage and the Family, 52,* 1025–1044.

Miller, K. E., & Pedersen-Randall, P. (1995, March). *Work, farm work, academic achievement and friendship: A comparison of rural and urban 10th, 11th and 12th graders.* Paper presented at the biennial meetings of the Society for Research in Child Development, Indianapolis, IN.

Miller, P., Eisenberg, N., Fabes, R., & Shell, R. (1996). Relations of moral reasoning and vicarious emotion to young children's prosocial behavior toward peers and adults. *Developmental Psychology, 29,* 3–18.

Miller, R. A. (1990). Aging and the immune response. In E. L. Schneider & J. W. Rowe (Eds.), *Handbook of the biology of aging* (3rd ed.) (pp. 157–180). San Diego, CA: Academic Press.

Miller, R. A. (1996). Aging and the immune response. In E. L. Schneider & J. W. Rowe (Eds.), *Handbook of the biology of aging* (4th ed.) (pp. 355–392). San Diego, CA: Academic Press.

Miller, T. (1996, July). Segmenting the Internet. *American Demographics.* Retrieved March 21, 2000 from the World Wide Web: www.americandemographics.com

Miller, T. Q., Smith, T. W., Turner, C. W., Guijarro, M. L., & Hallet, A. J. (1996). A meta-analytic review of research on hostility and physical health. *Psychological Bulletin, 119,* 322–348.

Miller, T. Q., Turner, C. W., Tindale, R. S., Posavac, E. J., & Dugoni, B. L. (1991). Reasons for the trend toward null findings in research on Type A behavior. *Psychological Bulletin, 110,* 469–495.

Mills, D., Coffey-Corina, S., & Neville, H. (1994). Variability in cerebral organization during primary language acquisition. In G. Dawson & K. Fischer (Eds.) *Human behavior and the developing brain.* New York: Guilford Press.

Minty, B. (1999). Outcomes in long-term foster family care. *Journal of Child Psychology & Psychiatry & Allied Disciplines, 40,* 991–999.

Mischel, W. (1966). A social learning view of sex differences in behavior. In E. E. Maccoby (Ed.), *The development of sex differences* (pp. 56–81). Stanford, CA: Stanford University Press.

Mischel, W. (1970). Sex typing and socialization. In P. H. Mussen (Ed.), *Carmichael's manual of child psychology* (Vol. 2) (pp. 3–72). New York: Wiley.

Mishra, R. C. (1997). Cognition and cognitive development. In J. Berry, P. Dasen, & T. Sarswathi (Eds.), *Handbook of cross-cultural psychology* (Vol. 2). Boston: Allyn & Bacon.

Mitchell, C. M., O'Nell, T. D., Beals, J., Dick, R. W., Keane, E., & Manson, S. M. (1996). Dimensionality of alcohol use among American Indian adolescents: Latent structure, construct validity, and implications for developmental research. *Journal of Research on Adolescence, 6*, 151–180.

Mitchell, P. R., & Kent, R. D. (1990). Phonetic variation in multisyllable babbling. *Journal of Child Language, 17*, 247–265.

Mizuta, I., Zahn-Waxler, C., Cole, P., & Hiruma, N. (1996). A cross-cultural study of preschoolers' attachment: Security and sensitivity in Japanese and U.S. dyads. *International Journal of Behavioral Development, 19*, 141–159.

Moehn, D., & Rossetti, L. (1996). The effects of neonatal intensive care on parental emotions and attachment. *Infant-Toddler Intervention, 6*, 229–246.

Moen, P. (1991). Transitions in mid-life: Women's work and family roles in the 1970s. *Journal of Marriage and the Family, 53*, 135–150.

Moen, P. (1996). Gender, age, and the life course. In R. H. Binstock & L. K. George (Eds.), *Handbook of aging and the social sciences* (4th ed.) (pp. 171–187). San Diego, CA: Academic Press.

Moen, P., & Erickson, M. A. (1995). Linked lives: A transgenerational approach to resilience. In P. Moen, G. H. Elder, Jr., & K. Lüscher (Eds.), *Examining lives in context: Perspectives on the ecology of human development* (pp. 169–210). Washington, DC: American Psychological Association.

Moffitt, T. E. (1993). Adolescence-limited and life-course-persistent antisocial behavior: A developmental taxonomy. *Psychology Review, 100*, 674–701.

Mohanty, A. & Perregaux, C. (1997). Language acquisition and bilingualism. In J. Berry, P. Dasen, & T. Saraswath (Eds.), *Handbook of cross-cultural psychology: Vol. 2*. Boston: Allyn & Bacon.

Monroy, T. (2000, March 15). Boomers alter economics. *Interactive Week*. Retrieved March 21, 2000 from the World Wide Web: www.ZDNet.com

Monson, R. (1997). State-ing sex and gender: Collecting information from mothers and fathers in paternity cases. *Gender & Society, 11*, 279–295.

Montemayor, R., & Eisen, M. (1977). The development of self-conceptions from childhood to adolescence. *Developmental Psychology, 13*, 314–319.

Montgomery, M., & Sorel, G. (1998). Love and dating experience in early and middle adolescence: Grade and gender comparisons. *Journal of Adolescence, 21*, 677–689.

Montgomery, R. J. V., & Kosloski, K. (1994). A longitudinal analysis of nursing home placement for dependent elders cared for by spouses vs adult children. *Journals of Gerontology: Social Sciences, 49*, S62–74.

Moody, E. (1997). Lessons from pair counseling with incarcerated juvenile delinquents. *Journal of Addictions & Offender Counseling, 18*, 10–25.

Moon, C., & Fifer, W. P. (1990). Syllables as signals for 2-day-old infants. *Infant Behavior and Development, 13*, 377–390.

Mooney, L., Knox, D., & Schacht, C. (2000a). *Social problems*. Belmont, CA: Wadsworth.

Mooney, L., Knox, D., & Schacht, C. (2000b). *Understanding social problems* (2nd ed.). Thousand Oaks, CA: Wadsworth.

Moore, C., Barresi, J., & Thompson, C. (1998). The cognitive basis of future-oriented prosocial behavior. *Social Development, 7*, 198–218.

Moore, K. L., & Persaud, T. V. N. (1993). *The developing human: Clinically oriented embryology* (5th ed.). Philadelphia: Saunders.

Mor, V. (1987). *Hospice care systems: Structure, process, costs, and outcome*. New York: Springer.

Mor, V., Greer, D. S., & Kastenbaum, R. (Eds.). (1988). *The hospice experiment*. Baltimore, MD: Johns Hopkins University Press.

Moretti, M., & Wiebe, V. (1999). Self-discrepancy in adolescence: Own and parental standpoints on the self. *Merrill-Palmer Quarterly, 45*, 624–649.

Morgan, C., Covington, J., Geisler, M., Polich, J., & Murphy, C. (1997). Olfactory event-related potentials: Older males demonstrate the greatest deficits. *Electroencephalography & Clinical Neurophysiology, 104*, 351–358.

Morgan, D. G. (1992). Neurochemical changes with aging: Predisposition towards age-related mental disorders. In J. E. Birren, R. B. Sloane, & G. D. Cohen (Eds.), *Handbook of mental health and aging* (2nd ed.) (pp. 175–200). San Diego, CA: Academic Press.

Morgan, L. A. (1991). *After marriage ends: Economic consequences for midlife women*. Newbury Park, CA: Sage.

Morris, D. L., Kritchevsky, S. B., & Davis, C. E. (1994). Serum carotenoids and coronary heart disease. The Lipid Research Clinics Coronary Primary Prevention Trial and Follow-up Study. *Journal of the American Medical Association, 272*, 1439–1441.

Morrison, D. R., & Cherlin, A. J. (1995). The divorce process and young children's well-being: A prospective analysis. *Journal of Marriage and the Family, 57*, 800–812.

Morrison, N. A., Qi, J. C., Tokita, A., Kelly, P. J., Crofts, L., Nguyen, T. V., Sambrook, P. N., & Eisman, J. A. (1994). Prediction of bone density from vitamin D receptor alleles. *Nature, 367*, 284–287.

Morrissette, P. (1999). Post-traumatic stress disorder in child sexual abuse: Diagnostic and treatment considerations. *Child & Youth Care Forum, 28*, 205–219.

Morse, P. A., & Cowan, N. (1982). Infant auditory and speech perception. In T. M. Field, A. Houston, H. C. Quay, L. Troll, & G. E. Finley (Eds.), *Review of human development* (pp. 32–61). New York: Wiley.

Mortimer, J. T., Finch, M. D., Dennehy, K., Lee, C., & Beebe, T. (1995, March). *Work experience in adolescence*. Paper presented at the biennial meetings of the Society for Research in Child Development, Indianapolis, IN.

Mosher, W. D. (1987). Infertility: Why business is booming. *American Demography*, June, 42–43.

Mosher, W. D., & Pratt, W. F. (1987). *Fecundity, infertility, and reproductive health in the United States, 1982: Vital Health Statistics, Series 23, No. 14. National Center for Health Statistics, US Public Health Service*. Washington, DC: USGPO.

Mosteller, F. (1995). The Tennessee study of class size in the early school grades. *The Future of Children, 5*(2, Summer/Fall), 113–127.

Mott, J., Crowe, P., Richardson, J., & Flay, B. (1999). After-school supervision and adolescent cigarette smoking: Contributions of the setting and intensity of after-school self-care. *Journal of Behavioral Medicine, 22*, 35–58.

Mounts, N. S., & Steinberg, L. (1995). An ecological analysis of peer influence on adolescent grade point average and drug use. *Developmental Psychology, 31*, 915–922.

Mueller, K., & Yoder, J. (1999). Stigmatization of non-normative family size status. *Sex Roles, 41*, 901–919.

Mullins, L. C., & Mushel, M. (1992). The existence and emotional closeness of relationships with children, friends, and spouses. The effect on loneliness among older persons. *Research on Aging, 14*, 448–470.

Mundy, G. R. (1994). Boning up on genes. *Nature, 367*, 216–217.

Munroe, R. H., Shimmin, H. S., & Munroe, R. L. (1984). Gender understanding and sex role preference in four cultures. *Developmental Psychology, 20*, 673–682.

Murphy, K., Hanrahan, P., & Luchins, D. (1997). A survey of grief and bereavement in nursing homes: The importance of hospice grief and bereavement for the end-stage Alzheimer's disease patient and family. *Journal of the American Geriatrics Society, 45*, 1104–1107.

Murphy, L., & Mitchell, D. (1998, February). When writing helps to heal: E-mail as therapy. *British Journal of Guidance & Counseling, 26*, 21–32.

Murphy, S., Braun, T., Tillery, L., Cain, K., Johnson, L., & Beaton, R. (1999). PTSD among bereaved parents following the violent deaths of their 12- to 28-year-old children: A longitudinal prospective analysis. *Journal of Traumatic Stress, 12*, 273–291.

Murphy, S. O. (1993, April). *The family context and the transition to siblinghood: Strategies parents use to influence sibling-infant relationships*. Paper presented at the biennial meetings of the Society for Research in Child Development, New Orleans, LA.

Murray, B. (1998, June). Dipping math scores heat up debate over math teaching. *APA Monitor, 29,* 34–35.

Murray, J. P. (1980). *Television and youth: 25 years of research and controversy.* Stanford, CA: The Boys Town Center for the Study of Youth Development.

Murray, L., Sinclair, D., Cooper, P., Ducournau, P., et al. (1999). The socioemotional development of 5-year-old children of postnatally depressed mothers. *Journal of Child Psychology & Psychiatry & Allied Disciplines, 40,* 1259–1271.

Murrell, S. A., & Himmelfarb, S. (1989). Effects of attachment bereavement and pre-event conditions on subsequent depressive symptoms in older adults. *Psychology and Aging, 4,* 166–172.

Murrell, S. A., & Norris, F. H. (1991). Differential social support and life change as contributors to the social class-distress relationship in old age. *Psychology and Aging, 6,* 223–231.

Murry, V. (1997). The impact of sexual activity and fertility timing on African American high school graduates' later life experiences. *Families in Society, 78,* 383–392.

Murstein, B. I. (1986). *Paths to marriage.* Beverly Hills, CA: Sage.

Musick, M., Blazer, D., & Hays, J. (2000). Religious activity, alcohol use, and depression in a sample of elderly Baptists. *Research on Aging, 22,* 91–116.

Musick, M., Koenig, H., Hays, J., & Cohen, H. (1998). Religious activity and depression among community-dwelling elderly persons with cancer: The moderating effect of race. *Journals of Gerontology: Series B: Psychological Sciences & Social Sciences, 53B,* S218–S227.

Mutch, L., Leyland, A., & McGee, A. (1993). Patterns of neuropsychological function in a low-birth-weight population. *Developmental Medicine & Child Neurology, 35,* 943–956.

Muthesius, D. (1997). Reminiscence and the relationship between young and old. *Zeitschrift fuer Gerontologie und Geriatrie, 30,* 354–361.

Muzi, M. (2000). *The experience of parenting.* Upper Saddle River, NJ: Prentice Hall.

Mwamwenda, T. (1999). Undergraduate and graduate students' combinatorial reasoning and formal operations. *Journal of Genetic Psychology, 160,* 503–506.

Myers, D. G., & Diener, E. (1995). Who is happy? *Psychological Science, 6,* 10–17.

Myers, G. C. (1990). Demography of aging. In R. H. Binstock & L. K. George (Eds.), *Handbook of aging and the social sciences* (3rd ed.) (pp. 19–44). San Diego, CA: Academic Press.

Nachmias, M. (1993, April). *Maternal personality relations with toddler's attachment classification, use of coping strategies, and adrenocortical stress response.* Paper presented at the biennial meetings of the Society for Research in Child Development, New Orleans, LA.

Nagamine, S. (1999). Interpersonal conflict situations: Adolescents' negotiation processes using an interpersonal negotiation strategy model: Adolescents' relations with their parents and friends. *Japanese Journal of Educational Psychology, 47,* 218–228.

Narvaez, D. (1998). The influence of moral schemas on the reconstruction of moral narratives in eighth graders and college students. *Journal of Educational Psychology, 90,* 13–24.

Nathanson, C. A., & Lorenz, G. (1982). Women and health: The social dimensions of biomedical data. In J. Z. Giele (Ed.), *Women in the middle years* (pp. 37–88). New York: Wiley.

National Abortion and Reproductive Rights Action League. (1997). Limitations on the rights of pregnant women. [NARAL Factsheet]. Retrieved March 5, 2001 from the World Wide Web: http://www.naral.org/publications/facts

National Center for Chronic Disease Prevention and Health Promotion. (2000). Obesity epidemic increases dramatically in the United States. [Online press release]. Retrieved August 23, 2000 from the World Wide Web: http://www.cdc.gov

National Center for Educational Statistics (NCES). (1997a). *Condition of Education/1997.* Washington, DC: U. S. Department of Education.

National Center for Educational Statistics. (1997b). *National Assessment of Educational Progress: 1996 Long-Term Trend Assessment.* Washington, DC: U. S. Department of Education.

National Center for Educational Statistics (NCES). (1997c). *Nontraditional undergraduates.* Washington, DC: Author.

National Center for Educational Statistics. (1998). *Digest of Educational Statistics.* Washington, DC: Author.

National Center for Educational Statistics. (1999). *Guide to the National Assessment of Educational Progress.* [Online Version]. Retrieved February 15, 2001 from the World Wide Web: http://www.nces.ed.gov/nationsreportcard/guide

National Center for Educational Statistics. (2000). How many students with disabilities receive services? [Online Fast Facts]. Retrieved August 23, 2000 from the World Wide Web: http://www.nces.ed.gov

National Center for Health Statistics. (1996). Guidelines for school health programs to promote lifelong healthy eating. *Morbidity and Mortality Weekly Report, 45,* 1–33.

National Center for Health Statistics. (1997). *Vital statistics of the United States.* Washington, DC: U. S. Government Printing Office.

National Center for Health Statistics (NCHS). (1997). *National Vital Statistics Report, 47,* No. 18. Retrieved March 6, 2001 from the World Wide Web: http:www.cdc.gov/nchs/nvs47

National Center for Health Statistics (NCHS). (1999, September 14). Trends in twin and triplet births: 1980–1997. *National Vital Statistics Reports.*

National Center for Health Statistics. (1999). Surveillance for injuries and violence among older adults. *Morbidity and Mortality Weekly Report, 48,* 27–50.

National Center for Health Statistics. (2000). CDC growth charts. [Online report]. Retrieved August 23, 2000 from the World Wide Web: http://www.cdc.gov/nchs

National Center for Injury Prevention and Control (NCIPC). (2000). *Fact book for the year 2000.* Washington, DC: Author.

National Institute of Child Health and Human Development (NICHD) Early Child Care Research Network. (1998). The effects of infant child care on mother-infant attachment security: Results of the NICHD study of early child care. *Child Development, 68,* 860–879.

National Institute of Child Health & Human Development (NICHD) Early Child Care Research Network. (1999). Chronicity of maternal depressive symptoms, maternal sensitivity, and child functioning at 36 months. *Developmental Psychology, 35,* 1297–1310.

National Institute on Aging. (2000a) *Depression: A serious but treatable illness.* [Online "Age Page"]. Retrieved February 7, 2001 from the World Wide Web: http://www.nih.gov/nia

National Institute on Aging (2000b). *Sexuality in later life.* [Online "Age Page"]. Retrieved February 7, 2001 from the World Wide Web: http://www.nih.gov/nia

National Science Foundation. (1996). *Women, minorities, and persons with disabilities in science and engineering.* Washington, DC: Author.

National survey results of gay couples in long-lasting relationships. (1990, May/June). *Partners: Newsletter for Gay and Lesbian couples,* 1–16.

Neill, M. (1998). *High stakes tests do not improve student learning.* [Online report]. Retrieved October 21, 1998 from the World Wide Web: http://www.fairtest.org

Neill, M. (2000). Too much harmful testing? *Educational Measurement: Issues & Practice, 16,* 57–58.

Neimark, E. D. (1982). Adolescent thought: Transition to formal operations. In B. B. Wolman (Ed.), *Handbook of developmental psychology* (pp. 486–502). Englewood Cliffs, NJ: Prentice-Hall.

Neimeyer, R. A., & Chapman, K. M. (1980/1981). Self/ideal discrepancy and fear of death: The test of an existential hypothesis. *Omega, 11,* 233–239.

Neisser, U., Boodoo, G., Bouchard, T. J., Jr., Boykin, A. W., Brody, N., Ceci, S. J., Halpern, D. F., Loehlin, J. C., Perloff, R., Sternberg, R. J., & Urbina, S. (1996). Intelligence: Knowns and unknowns. *American Psychologist, 51,* 77–101.

Neisser, U., & Harsch, N. (1992). Phantom flashbulbs: False recollections of hearing the news about Challenger. In E. Winograd & U. Neisser (Eds.), *Affect and accuracy in recall: Studies of "flashbulb" memories.* (pp. 9–31). New York: Cambridge University Press.

Nelson, E. A., & Dannefer, D. (1992). Aged heterogeneity: Fact or fiction? The fate of diversity in gerontological research. *The Gerontologist, 32,* 17–23.

Nelson, K. (1973). Structure and strategy in learning to talk. *Monographs of the Society for Research in Child Development, 38*(Serial No. 149).

Nelson, M. E., Fiatarone, M. A., Morganti, C. M., Trice, I., Greenberg, R. A., & Evans, W. J. (1994). Effects of high-intensity strength training on multiple risk factors for osteoporotic fractures. *Journal of the American Medical Association, 272,* 1909–1914.

Nelson, S. (1980). Factors influencing young children's use of motives and outcomes as moral criteria. *Child Development, 51,* 823–829.

Neshat-Doost, H., Taghavi, M., Moradi, A., Yule, W., & Dalgleish, T. (1998). Memory for emotional trait adjectives in clinically depressed youth. *Journal of Abnormal Psychology, 107,* 642–650.

Neugarten, B. L. (1970). Dynamics of transition of middle age to old age. *Journal of Geriatric Psychiatry, 4,* 71–87.

Neugarten, B. L. (1979). Time, age, and the life cycle. *American Journal of Psychiatry, 136,* 887–894.

Neugebauer, R., Hoek, H., & Susser, E. (1999). Prenatal exposure to wartime famine and development of antisocial personal disorder in early adulthood. *Journal of the American Medical Association, 282,* 455–462.

Neville, L. (1997, February 10). Heart trouble. *U. S. News and World Report,* pp. 16–17.

Newcomb, A. F., & Bagwell, C. L. (1995). Children's friendship relations: A meta-analytic review. *Psychological Bulletin, 117,* 306–347.

Newcomb, A. F., Bukowski, W. M., & Pattee, L. (1993). Children's peer relations: A meta-analytic review of popular, rejected, neglected, controversial, and average sociometric status. *Psychological Bulletin, 113,* 99–128.

Newcomb, P. A., Longnecker, M. P., Storer, B. E., Mittendorf, R., Baron, J., Clapp, R. W., Bogdan, G., & Willett, W. C. (1995). Long-term hormone replacement therapy and risk of breast cancer in postmenopausal women. *American Journal of Epidemiology, 142,* 788–795.

Newman, D., Caspi, A., Moffitt, T., & Silva, P. (1997). Antecedents of adult interpersonal functioning: Effects of individual differences in age 3 temperament. *Developmental Psychology, 33,* 206–217.

Ni, Y. (1998). Cognitive structure, content knowledge, and classificatory reasoning. *Journal of Genetic Psychology, 159,* 280–296.

Nicholson, J. (1998). Inborn errors of metabolism. In R. Behrman & R. Kliegman (Eds.), *Nelson essentials of pediatrics* (3rd ed., pp. 147–166). Philadelphia: W. B. Saunders.

Nightingale, E. O., & Goodman, M. (1990). *Before birth. Prenatal testing for genetic disease.* Cambridge, MA: Harvard University Press.

Nilsson, E., Gillberg, C., Gillberg, I., & Rastam, M. (1999). Ten-year follow-up of adolescent-onset anorexia nervosa: Personality disorders. *Journal of the American Academy of Child & Adolescent Psychiatry, 38,* 1389–1395.

Nilsson, L., Baeckman, L., Erngrund, K., & Nyberg, L. (1997). The Betula prospective cohort study: Memory, health, and aging. *Aging, Neuropsychology, & Cognition, 4,* 1–32.

Nilsson, L., & Hamberger, L. (1990). *A child is born.* New York: Delacorte.

Nisan, M., & Kohlberg, L. (1982). Universality and variation in moral judgment: A longitudinal and cross-sectional study in Turkey. *Child Development, 53,* 865–876.

Niska, K., Snyder, M., & Lia-Hoagberg, B. (1998). Family ritual facilitates adaptation to parenthood. *Public Health Nursing, 15,* 329–337.

Nock, S. (1998). The consequences of premarital fatherhood. *American Sociological Review, 63,* 250–263.

Noldon, D., & Sedlacek, W. (1998). Gender differences in attitudes, skills, and behaviors among academically talented university freshmen. *Roeper Review, 21,* 106–109.

Nolen-Hoeksema, S., & Girgus, J. S. (1994). The emergence of gender differences in depression during adolescence. *Psychological Bulletin, 115,* 424–443.

Norboru, T. (1997). A developmental study of wordplay in preschool children: The Japanese game of "Shiritori." *Japanese Journal of Developmental Psychology, 8,* 42–52.

Norris, F. H., & Murrell, S. A. (1990). Social support, life events, and stress as modifiers of adjustment to bereavement by older adults. *Psychology and Aging, 5,* 429–436.

Norton, A. J. (1983). Family life cycle: 1980. *Journal of Marriage and the Family, 45,* 267–275.

Norwood, T. H., Smith, J. R., & Stein, G. H. (1990). Aging at the cellular level: The human fibroblastlike cell model. In E. R. Schneider & J. W. Rowe (Eds.), *Handbook of the biology of aging* (3rd ed.) (pp. 131–154). San Diego, CA: Academic Press.

Nottelmann, E. D., Susman, E. J., Blue, J. H., Inoff-Germain, G., Dorn, L. D., Loriaux, D. L., Cutler, G. B., Jr., & Chrousos, G. P. (1987). Gonadal and adrenal hormone correlates of adjustment in early adolescence. In R. M. Lerner & T. T. Foch (Eds.), *Biological-psychosocial interactions in early adolescence* (pp. 303–324). Hillsdale, NJ: Erlbaum.

Novosad, C., & Thoman, E. (1999). Stability of temperament over the childhood years. *American Journal of Orthopsychiatry, 69,* 457–474.

Nowakowski, R. S. (1987). Basic concepts of CNS development. *Child Development, 58,* 568–595.

Nucci, L., & Smetana, J. (1996). Mothers' concepts of young children's areas of personal freedom. *Child Development, 67,* 1870–1886.

Nuland, S. B. (1993). *How we die.* New York: Knopf.

Nutter, J. (1997). Middle school students' attitudes and use of anabolic steroids. *Journal of Strength Conditioning Research, 11,* 35–39.

Oates, J. (1998). Risk factors for infant attrition and low engagement in experiments and free-play. *Infant Behavior & Development, 21,* 55–569.

Oatley, K., & Jenkins, J. (1996). *Understanding emotions.* Cambridge, MA: Blackwell Publishers.

O'Beirne, H., & Moore, C. (1995, March). *Attachment and sexual behavior in adolescence.* Paper presented at the biennial meetings of the Society for Research in Child Development, Indianapolis, IN.

O'Brien, M. (1992). Gender identity and sex roles. In V. B. Van Hasselt & M. Hersen (Eds.), *Handbook of social development: A lifespan perspective* (pp. 325–345). New York: Plenum.

Ochs, E., & Binik, Y. (1998). A sex expert computer system helps couples learn more about their sexual relationship. *Journal of Sex Education & Therapy, 23,* 145–155.

O'Connor, N. J., Manson, J. E., O'Connor, G. T., & Buring, J. E. (1995). Psychosocial risk factors and nonfatal myocardial infarction. *Circulation, 92,* 1458–1464.

O'Connor, T., Bredenkamp, D., & Rutter, M. (1999). Attachment disturbances and disorders in children exposed to early severe deprivation. *Infant Mental Health Journal, 20,* 10–29.

Offer, D., Kaiz, M., Howard, K., & Bennett, E. (1998). Emotional variables in adolescence and their stability and contribution to the mental health of adult men: Implications for early intervention strategies. *Journal of Youth & Adolescence, 27,* 675–690.

Offord, D. R., Boyle, M. H., & Racine, Y. A. (1991). The epidemiology of antisocial behavior in childhood and adolescence. In D. J. Pepler & K. H. Rubin (Eds.), *The development and treatment of childhood aggression* (pp. 31–54). Hillsdale, NJ: Erlbaum.

Ofstedal, M., Zimmer, Z., & Lin, H. (1999). A comparison of correlates of cognitive functioning in older persons in Taiwan and the United States. *Journals of Gerontology: Series B: Psychological Sciences & Social Sciences. 54B,* S291–S301.

Ogawa, N., & Retherford, R. D. (1993). Care of the elderly in Japan: Changing norms and expectations. *Journal of Marriage and the Family, 55,* 585–597.

Ogbu, J. (1990). Cultural models, identity and literacy. In J. W. Stigler, R. A. Shweder, & G. Hendt (Eds.), *Cultural psychology: Essays on comparative human development* (pp. 520–541). Hillsdale, NJ: Erlbaum.

O'Hara, M. W., Schlechte, J. A., Lewis, D. A., & Varner, M. W. (1992). Controlled prospective study of postpartum mood disorders: Psychological, environmental, and hormonal variables. *Journal of Abnormal Psychology, 100,* 63–73.

Ohtsuka, K., Bruton, E., DeLuca, L., & Borg, V. (1997). Sex differences in pathological gambling using gaming machines. *Psychological Reports, 80,* 1051–1057.

Okamoto, K., & Uechi, Y. (1999). Adolescents' relations with parents and friends in the second individuation process. *Japanese Journal of Educational Psychology, 47,* 248–258.

Okwumabua, J., Baker, F., Wong, S., & Pilgram, B. (1997). Characteristics of depressive symptoms in elderly urban and rural African Americans. *Journal of Gerontology, 52A,* M241–M246.

Oldenburg, C., & Kerns, K. (1997). Associations between peer relationships and depressive symptoms: Testing moderator effects of gender and age. *Journal of Early Adolescence, 17,* 319–337.

O'Leary, A. (1990). Stress, emotion, and human immune function. *Psychological Bulletin, 108,* 363–382.

O'Leary, K. D., & Smith, D. A. (1991). Marital interactions. *Annual Review of Psychology, 42,* 191–212.

O'Leary, S., Slep, A. S., & Reid, M. (1999). A longitudinal study of mothers' overreactive discipline and toddlers' externalizing behavior. *Journal of Abnormal Child Psychology, 27,* 331–341.

Olin, J., & Zelinski, E. (1997). Age differences in calibration of comprehension. *Educational Gerontology, 23,* 67–77.

Oller, D., Cobo-Lewis, A., & Eilers, R. (1998). Phonological translation in bilingual and monolingual children. *Applied Psycholinguistics, 19,* 259–278.

Oller, D. K. (1981). Infant vocalizations: Exploration and reflectivity. In R. E. Stark (Ed.), *Language behavior in infancy and early childhood* (pp. 85–104). New York: Elsevier North-Holland.

Olsen, J., Weed, S., Nielsen, A., & Jensen, L. (1992). Student evaluation of sex education programs advocating abstinence. *Adolescence, 27,* 169–380.

Olson, H., Feldman, J., Streissguth, A., Sampson, P., & Bookstein, F. (1998). Neuropsychological deficits in adolescents with fetal alcohol syndrome: Clinical findings. *Alcoholism: Clinical & Experimental Research, 22,* 1998–2012.

Olson, H. C., Sampson, P. D., Barr, H., Streissguth, A. P., & Bookstein, F. L. (1992). Prenatal exposure to alcohol and school problems in late childhood: A longitudinal prospective study. *Development and Psychopathology, 4,* 341–359.

Olson, S. L., Bates, J. E., & Kaskie, B. (1992). Caregiver-infant interaction antecedents of children's school-age cognitive ability. *Merrill-Palmer Quarterly, 38,* 309–330.

Oman, D., & Reed, D. (1998). Religion and mortality among the community-dwelling elderly. *American Journal of Public Health, 88,* 1469–1475.

Oman, D., Thoresen, C., & McMahon, K. (1999). Volunteerism and mortality among the community-dwelling elderly. *Journal of Health Psychology, 4,* 301–316.

O'Neill, D. K., Astington, J. W., & Flavell, J. H. (1992). Young children's understanding of the role that sensory experiences play in knowledge acquisition. *Child Development, 63,* 474–490.

Optimism can mean life for heart patients and pessimism death, study says (1994a, April 16). *New York Times,* p. 12.

Ormel, J., & Rijsdijk, F. (2000). Continuing change in neuroticism during adulthood: Structural modeling of a 16-year, 5-wave community study. *Personality & Individual Differences, 28,* 461–478.

Ornish, D. (1990). *Dr. Dean Ornish's program for reversing heart disease.* New York: Random House.

Ornish, D. (1993). *Eat more, weigh less.* New York: HarperCollins.

Orr, W. C., & Sohal, R. S. (1994). Extension of life-span by overexpression of superoxide dismutase and catalase in *Drosophila melanogaster. Science, 263,* 1128–1130.

Orth-Gomér, K., Rosengren, A., & Wilhelmsen, L. (1993). Lack of social support and incidence of coronary heart disease in middle-aged Swedish men. *Psychosomatic Medicine, 55,* 37–43.

Orwoll, L., & Perlmutter, M. (1990). The study of wise persons: Integrating a personality perspective. In R. J. Sternberg (Ed.), *Wisdom: Its nature, origins, and development* (pp. 160–180). Cambridge, England: Cambridge University Press.

Osofsky, J. D. (1995). The effects of exposure to violence on young children. *American Psychologist, 50,* 782–788.

Osofsky, J. D., Hann, D. M., & Peebles, C. (1993). Adolescent parenthood: Risks and opportunities for mothers and infants. In C. H. Zeanah, Jr. (Ed.), *Handbook of infant mental health* (pp. 106–119). New York: Guilford Press.

Ostoja, E., McCrone, E., Lehn, L., Reed, T., & Sroufe, L. A. (1995, March). *Representations of close relationships in adolescence: Longitudinal antecedents from infancy through childhood.* Paper presented at the biennial meetings of the Society for Research in Child Development, Indianapolis, IN.

Ostrom, T., Carpenter, S., Sedikides, C., & Li, F. (1993). Differential processing of in-group and out-group information. *Journal of Personality & Social Psychology, 64,* 21–34.

Overmeyer, S., & Taylor, E. (1999). Principles of treatment for hyperkinetic disorder: Practice approaches for the U. K. *Journal of Child Psychology & Psychiatry & Allied Disciplines, 40,* 1147–1157.

Owen, P. (1998). Fears of Hispanic and Anglo children: Real-world fears in the 1990s. *Hispanic Journal of Behavioral Sciences, 20,* 483–491.

Owens, G., Crowell, J. A., Pan, H., Treboux, D., O'Connor, E., & Waters, E. (1995). The prototype hypothesis and the origins of attachment working models: Adult relationships with parents and romantic partners. *Monographs of the Society for Research in Child Development, 60*(244, No. 2–3), 216–233.

Owens, J., Spirito, A., McGuinn, M., & Nobile, C. (2000). Sleep habits and sleep disturbance in elementary school-aged children. *Journal of Developmental & Behavioral Pediatrics, 21,* 27–36.

Ozman, H. A., & Craver, S. M. (1986). *Philosophical foundations of education.* Columbus, OH: Merrill.

Paarlberg, K., Vingerhoets, A. J., Passchier, J., Dekker, G., & van Geign, H. (1995). Psychosocial factors and pregnancy outcome: A review with emphasis on methodological issues. *Journal of Psychosomatic Research, 39,* 563–595.

Pacheco, C. (1999). Alcoholism and work: Representations of masculinity. *PSICO, 30,* 185–204.

Paden, S. L., & Buehler, C. (1995). Coping with the dual-income lifestyle. *Journal of Marriage and the Family, 57,* 101–110.

Paffenbarger, R. S., Hyde, R. T., Wing, A. L., & Hsieh, C. (1987). Physical activity, all-cause mortality, and longevity of college alumni. *New England Journal of Medicine, 314,* 605–613.

Pagani, L., Boulerice, B., Tremblay, R., & Vitaro, F. (1997). Behavioural development in children of divorce and remarriage. *Journal of Child Psychology & Psychiatry & Allied Disciplines, 38,* 769–781.

Paik, H., & Comstock, G. (1994). The effects of television violence on antisocial behavior: A meta-analysis. *Communication Research, 21,* 516–546.

Painter, M., & Bergman, I. (1998). Neurology. In R. Behrman & R. Kliegman (Eds.), *Nelson essentials of pediatrics* (3rd ed., pp. 694–745). Philadelphia: W. B. Saunders.

Pajares, F., & Graham, L. (1999). Self-efficacy, motivation constructs, and mathematics performance of entering middle school students. *Contemporary Educational Psychology, 24,* 124–139.

Pajares, F., & Valiante, G. (1999). Grade level and gender differences in the writing self-beliefs of middle school students. *Contemporary Educational Psychology, 24,* 390–405.

Paley, V. (1986). *Mollie is three: Growing up in school.* Chicago: University of Chicago Press.

Palla, B., & Litt, I. R. (1988). Medical complications of eating disorders in adolescents. *Pediatrics, 81,* 613–623.

Palmore, E. (1981). *Social patterns in normal aging: Findings from the Duke Longitudinal Study.* Durham, NC: Duke University Press.

Palmore, E. B. (1990). *Ageism: Negative and positive.* New York: Springer.

Palmore, E. B., Burchett, B. M., Fillenbaum, G. G., George, L. K., & Wallman, L. M. (1985). *Retirement. Causes and consequences.* New York: Springer.

Palmore, E. B., & Cleveland, W. (1976). Aging, terminal decline, and terminal drop. *Journal of Gerontology, 31,* 76–81.

Papousek, H., & Papousek, M. (1991). Innate and cultural guidance of infants' integrative competencies: China, the United States, and Germany. In M. H. Bornstein (Ed.), *Cultural approaches to parenting* (pp. 23–44). Hillsdale, NJ: Erlbaum.

Parault, S., & Schwanenflugel, P. (2000). The development of conceptual categories of attention during the elementary school years. *Journal of Experimental Child Psychology, 75,* 245–262.

Pargament, K., Koenig, H., & Perez, L. (2000). The many methods of religious coping: Development and initial validation of the RCOPE. *Journal of Clinical Psychology, 56,* 519–543.

Pargament, K., Smith, B., Koenig, H., & Perez, L. (1998). Patterns of positive and negative religious coping with major life stressors. *Journal for the Scientific Study of Religion, 37,* 710–724.

Parke, R. D., & Tinsley, B. R. (1981). The father's role in infancy: Determinants of involvement in caregiving and play. In M. E. Lamb

(Ed.), *The role of the father in child development* (2nd ed.) (pp. 429–458). New York: Wiley.

Parker, R. (1999). Reminiscence as continuity: Comparison of young and older adults. *Journal of Clinical Geropsychology, 5,* 147–157.

Parks, M., & Roberts, L. (1998). "Making MOOsic": The development of personal relationships on line and a comparison to their off-line counterparts. *Journal of Social & Personal Relationships, 15,* 517–537.

Parmelee, A. H., Jr., Wenner, W. H., & Schulz, H. R. (1964). Infant sleep patterns from birth to 16 weeks of age. *Journal of Pediatrics, 65,* 576–582.

Parnes, H. S., & Sommers, D. G. (1994). Shunning retirement: Work experience of men in their seventies and early eighties. *Journals of Gerontology: Social Sciences, 49,* S117–124.

Pascarella, E. (1999). The development of critical thinking: Does college make a difference? *Journal of College Student Development, 40,* 562–569.

Pascarella, E., & Terenzi, P. (1991). *How college affects students: Findings and insights from twenty years of research.* San Francisco: Jossey-Bass.

Patterson, C. (1997). Children of lesbian and gay parents. *Advances in Clinical Child Psychology, 19,* 235–282.

Patterson, G. R. (1980). Mothers: The unacknowledged victims. *Monographs of the Society for Research in Child Development, 45*(Serial No. 186).

Patterson, G. R., Capaldi, D., & Bank, L. (1991). An early starter model for predicting delinquency. In D. J. Pepler & K. H. Rubin (Eds.), *The development and treatment of childhood aggression* (pp. 139–168). Hillsdale, NJ: Erlbaum.

Patterson, G. R., DeBarsyshe, B. D., & Ramsey, E. (1989). A developmental perspective on antisocial behavior. *American Psychologist, 44,* 329–335.

Patterson, J. (1998). Expressive vocabulary of bilingual toddlers: Preliminary findings. *Multicultural Electronic Journal of Communication Disorders, 1.* Retrieved April 11, 2001 from the World Wide Web: www.asha.ucf.edu/patterson.html

Pauen, S. (2000). Early differentiation within the animate domain: Are humans something special? *Journal of Experimental Child Psychology, 75,* 134–151.

Paxton, S. J., Wertheim, E. H., Gibbons, K., Szmukler, G. I., Hillier, L., & Petrovich, J. L. (1991). Body image satisfaction, dieting beliefs, and weight loss behaviors in adolescent girls and boys. *Journal of Youth and Adolescence, 20,* 361–379.

Pearlin, L. (1975). Sex roles and depression. In N. Datan & L. H. Ginsberg (Eds.), *Life-span developmental psychology: Normative life crises* (pp. 191–208). New York: Academic Press.

Pearlin, L. I., Aneshensel, C. S., Mullan, J., & Whitlatch, C. J. (1996). Caregiving and its social support. In R. H. Binstock & L. K. George (Eds.), *Handbook of aging and the social sciences* (4th ed.) (pp. 283–302). San Diego, CA: Academic Press.

Pearsall, N., Skipper, J., & Mintzes, J. (1997). Knowledge restructuring in the life sciences: A longitudinal study of conceptual change in biology. *Science Education, 81,* 193–215.

Pearson, J., Hunter, A., & Cook, J. (1997). Grandmother involvement in child caregiving in an urban community. *Gerontologist, 37,* 650–657.

Pease-Alvarez, L. (1993). *Moving in and out of bilingualism: Investigating native language maintenance and shift in Mexican-descent children.* Research Report. Washington, DC: National Council on Bilingual Education.

Pedersen, N. L., & Harris, J. R. (1990). Developmental behavioral genetics and successful aging. In P. B. Baltes & M. M. Baltes (Eds.), *Successful aging* (pp. 359–380). Cambridge, England: Cambridge University Press.

Pederson, D. R., & Moran, G. (1995). A categorical description of infant-mother relationships in the home and its relation to Q-sort measures of infant-mother interaction. *Monographs of the Society for Research in Child Development, 60*(244, Nos. 2–3), 111–132.

Pederson, D., & Moran, G. (1996). Expressions of the attachment relationship outside of the Strange Situation. *Child Development, 67,* 915–927.

Pederson, D. R., Moran, G., Sitko, C., Campbell, K., Ghesquire, K., & Acton, H. (1990). Maternal sensitivity and the security of infant-mother attachment: A Q-sort study. *Child Development, 61,* 1974–1983.

Pedlow, R., Sanson, A., Prior, M., & Oberklaid, F. (1993). Stability of maternally reported temperament from infancy to 8 years. *Developmental Psychology, 29,* 998–1007.

Peigneux, P., & van der Linden, M. (1999). Influence of ageing and educational level on the prevalence of body-part-as-objects in normal subjects. *Journal of Clinical & Experimental Neuropsychology, 21,* 547–552.

Peisner-Feinberg, E. S. (1995, March). *Developmental outcomes and the relationship to quality of child care experiences.* Paper presented at the biennial meetings of the Society for Research in Child Development, Indianapolis, IN.

Pelligrini, A., & Smith, P. (1998). Physical activity play: The nature and function of a neglected aspect of play. *Child Development, 69,* 577–598.

Peoples, C. E., Fagan, J. F., III, & Drotar, D. (1995). The influence of race on 3-year-old children's performance on the Stanford-Binet: Fourth edition. *Intelligence, 21,* 69–82.

Peplau, L. A. (1991). Lesbian and gay relationships. In J. C. Gonsiorek & J. D. Weinrich (Eds.), *Homosexuality: Research implications for public policy* (pp. 177–196). Newbury Park, CA: Sage.

Perho, H., & Korhonen, M. (1999). Coping in work and marriage at the onset of middle age. *Psykologia, 34,* 115–127.

Perls, T. (1999). *The New England Centenarian Study.* Harvard Medical School. [Online article]. Retrieved February 7, 2001 from the World Wide Web: http://www.med.harvard.edu/programs/necs/studies.html

Perls, T., Silver, M., and Lauerman, J. (1998). *Living to 100: Lessons in living to your maximum potential at any age.* Cambridge, MA: Harvard University Press.

Peskin, H., & Livson, N. (1981). Uses of the past in adult psychological health. In D. H. Eichorn, J. A. Clausen, N. Haan, M. P. Honzik, & P. H. Mussen (Eds.), *Present and past in middle life* (pp. 158–194). New York: Academic Press.

Petersen, A. C. (1987). The nature of biological-psychosocial interactions: The sample case of early adolescence. In R. M. Lerner & T. T. Foch (Eds.), *Biological-psychosocial interactions in early adolescence* (pp. 35–62). Hillsdale, NJ: Erlbaum.

Petersen, A. C., Compas, B. E., Brooks-Gunn, J., Stemmler, M., Ey, S., & Grant, K. E. (1993). Depression in adolescence. *American Psychologist, 48,* 155–168.

Peterson, C. (1999). Grandfathers' and grandmothers' satisfaction with the grandparenting role: Seeking new answers to old questions. *International Journal of Aging & Human Development, 49,* 61–78.

Peterson, C. C., & Siegal, M. (1995). Deafness, conversation and theory of mind. *Journal of Child Psychology and Psychiatry, 36,* 459–474.

Peterson, C., & Siegal, M. (1999). Representing inner worlds: Theory of mind in autistic, deaf, and normal hearing children. *Psychological Science, 10,* 126–129.

Peterson, C., Seligman, M. E. P., & Vaillant, G. E. (1988). Pessimistic explanatory style is a risk factor for physical illness: A thirty-five-year longitudinal study. *Journal of Personality and Social Psychology, 55,* 23–27.

Peterson, L., Ewigman, B., & Kivlahan, C. (1993). Judgments regarding appropriate child supervision to prevent injury: The role of environmental risk and child age. *Child Development, 64,* 934–950.

Petitto, L. A. (1988). "Language" in the prelinguistic child. In F. S. Kessell (Ed.), *The development of language and language researchers: Essays in honor of Roger Brown* (pp. 187–222). Hillsdale, NJ: Erlbaum.

Pettingale, K. W., Morris, T., Greer, S., & Haybittle, J. L. (1985). Mental attitudes to cancer: An additional prognostic factor. *Lancet, 85.*

Pettit, G. S., Clawson, M. A., Dodge, K. A., & Bates, J. E. (1996). Stability and change in peer-rejected status: The role of child behavior, parenting, and family ecology. *Merrill-Palmer Quarterly, 42,* 295–318.

Pettit, G., Laird, R., Bates, J., & Dodge, K. (1997). Patterns of after-school care in middle childhood: Risk factors and developmental outcomes. *Merrill-Palmer Quarterly, 43,* 515–538.

Phelps, L., Wallace, N., & Bontrager, A. (1997). Risk factors in early child development: Is prenatal cocaine/polydrug exposure a key variable? *Psychology in the Schools, 34,* 245–252.

Phillips, D., Schwean, V., & Saklofske, D. (1997). Treatment effect of a school-based cognitive-behavioral program for aggressive children. *Canadian Journal of School Psychology, 13,* 60–67.

Phillips, G., & Over, R. (1995). Differences between heterosexual, bisexual, and lesbian women in recalled childhood experiences. *Archives of Sexual Behavior, 24,* 1–20.

Phillips, S. K., Bruce, S. A., Newton, D., & Woledge, R. C. (1992). The weakness of old age is not due to failure of muscle activation. *Journals of Gerontology: Medical Sciences, 47,* M45–49.

Phillipsen, L. (1999). Associations between age, gender, and group acceptance and three components of friendship quality. *Journal of Early Adolescence, 19,* 438–464.

Phinney, J. S. (1990). Ethnic identity in adolescents and adults: Review of research. *Psychological Bulletin, 108,* 499–514.

Phinney, J. S., & Rosenthal, D. A. (1992). Ethnic identity in adolescence: Process, context, and outcome. In G. R. Adams, T. P. Gullotta, & R. Montemayor (Eds.), *Adolescent identity formation* (pp. 145–172). Newbury Park, CA: Sage.

Piaget, J. (1932). *The moral judgment of the child.* New York: Macmillan.

Piaget, J. (1952). *The origins of intelligence in children.* New York: International Universities Press.

Piaget, J. (1954). *The construction of reality in the child.* New York: Basic Books. (Originally published 1937.)

Piaget, J. (1965). *The moral judgment of the child.* New York: Free Press.

Piaget, J. (1970). Piaget's theory. In P. H. Mussen (Ed.), *Carmichael's manual of child psychology* (Vol. 1, 3rd ed.) (pp. 703–732). New York: Wiley.

Piaget, J. (1977). *The development of thought: Equilibration of cognitive structures.* New York: Viking.

Piaget, J., & Inhelder, B. (1959). *La gènese des structures logiques élémentaires: Classifications et sériations [The origin of elementary logical structures: Classification and seriation].* Neuchâtel, Switzerland: Delachaux et Niestlé.

Piaget, J., & Inhelder, B. (1969). *The psychology of the child.* New York: Basic Books.

Pianta, R., Egeland, B., & Erickson, M. F. (1989). The antecedents of maltreatment: Results of the Mother-Child Interaction Research Project. In D. Cicchetti & V. Carlson (Eds.), *Child maltreatment* (pp. 203–253). Cambridge, England: Cambridge University Press.

Pianta, R. C., & Egeland, B. (1994). Predictors of instability in children's mental test performance at 24, 48, and 96 months. *Intelligence, 18,* 145–163.

Pianta, R. C., Steinberg, M. S., & Rollins, K. B. (1995). Teacher-child relationships and deflections in children's classroom adjustment. *Development and Psychopathology, 7,* 295–312.

Picard, C. (1999). The level of competition as a factor for the development of eating disorders in female collegiate athletes. *Journal of Youth and Adolescence, 28,* 583–594.

Pickens, J. (1994). Perception of auditory-visual distance relations by 5-month-old infants. *Developmental Psychology, 30,* 537–544.

Pilgrim, C., Luo, Q., Urberg, K., & Fang, X. (1999). Influence of peers, parents, and individual characteristics on adolescent drug use in two cultures. *Merrill-Palmer Quarterly, 45,* 85–107.

Pillard, R. C., & Bailey, J. M. (1995). A biologic perspective on sexual orientation. *The Psychiatric Clinics of North America, 18*(1), 71–84.

Pillemer, K., & Finkelhor, D. (1988). The prevalence of elder abuse: A random sample survey. *The Gerontologist, 28,* 51–58.

Pillemer, K., & Suitor, J. J. (1990). Prevention of elder abuse. In R. Ammerman & M. Hersen (Eds.), *Treatment of family violence: A sourcebook* (pp. 406–422). New York: Wiley.

Pillemer, K., & Suitor, J. J. (1992). Violence and violent feelings: What causes them among family caregivers? *Journals of Gerontology: Social Sciences, 47,* S165–172.

Pillow, B. (1999). Children's understanding of inferential knowledge. *Journal of Genetic Psychology, 160,* 419–428.

Pinker, S. (1994). *The language instinct: How the mind creates language.* New York: Morrow.

Pinquart, M., & Soerensen, S. (2000). Influences of socioeconomic status, social network, and competence on subjective well-being in later life: A meta-analysis. *Psychology & Aging, 15,* 187–224.

Plante, T., & Pardini, D. (2000, August). *Religious denomination affiliation and psychological health: Results from a substance abuse population.* Paper presented at the annual meeting of the American Psychological Association. Washington, DC.

Plaud, J., Plaud, D., & von Duvillard, S. (1999). Human behavioral momentum in a sample of older adults. Journal of General Psychology, 126, 165–175.

Pleck, J. (1977). The work-family role system. *Social Problems, 24,* 417–427.

Plomin, R. (1990). *Nature and nurture: An introduction to behavior genetics.* Pacific Grove, CA: Brooks/Cole.

Plomin, R., & DeFries, J. C. (1985). *Origins of individual differences in infancy: The Colorado Adoption Project.* Orlando, FL: Academic Press.

Plomin, R., Emde, R. N., Braungart, J. M., Campos, J., Corley, R., Fulker, D. W., Kagan, J., Reznick, J. S., Robinson, J., Zahn-Waxler, C., & DeFries, J. C. (1993). Genetic change and continuity from fourteen to twenty months: The MacArthur longitudinal twin study. *Child Development, 64,* 1354–1376.

Plomin, R., & McClearn, G. E. (1990). Human behavioral genetics of aging. In J. E. Birren & K. W. Schaie (Eds.), *Handbook of the psychology of aging* (3rd ed.) (pp. 67–79). San Diego, CA: Academic Press.

Plomin, R., & Rende, R. (1991). Human behavioral genetics. *Annual Review of Psychology, 42,* 161–190.

Plowman, S. A., Drinkwater, B. L., & Horvath, S. M. (1979). Age and aerobic power in women: A longitudinal study. *Journal of Gerontology, 34,* 512–520.

Poindexter-Cameron, J., & Robinson, T. (1997). Relationships among racial identity attitudes, womanist identity attitudes, and self-esteem in African American college women. *Journal of College Student Development, 38,* 288–296.

Polka, L., & Werker, J. F. (1994). Developmental changes in perception of nonnative vowel contrasts. *Journal of Experimental Psychology: Human Perception and Performance, 20,* 421–435.

Pollack, J. M. (1979/1980). Correlates of death anxiety: A review of empirical studies. *Omega, 10,* 97–121.

Pollitt, E., & Gorman, K. S. (1994). Nutritional deficiencies as developmental risk factors. In C. A. Nelson (Ed.), *The Minnesota Symposia on Child Development* (Vol. 27) (pp. 121–144). Hillsdale, NJ: Erlbaum.

Polo, M., Escera, D., Gual, A., & Grau, C. (1999). Mismatch negativity and auditory sensory memory in chronic alcoholics. *Clinical & Experimental Research, 23,* 1744–1750.

Pomerantz, E., & Ruble, D. (1998). The role of maternal control in the development of sex differences in child self-evaluative factors. *Child Development, 69,* 458–478.

Pomerleau, A., Malcuit, G., Turgeon, L., & Cossette, L. (1997). Effects of labelled gender on vocal communication of young women with 4-month-old infants. *International Journal of Psychology, 32,* 65–72.

Ponds, R., Commissaris, K., & Jolles, J. (1997). Prevalence and covariates of subjective forgetfulness in a normal population in the Netherlands. *International Journal of Aging & Human Development, 45,* 207–221.

Ponomareva, N., Fokin, V., Selesneva, N., & Voskresenskaea, N. (1998). Possible neurophysiological markers of genetic predisposition to Alzheimer's disease. *Dementia & Geriatric Cognitive Disorders, 9,* 267–273.

Ponsonby, A., Dwyer, T., Gibbons, L. E., Cochrane, J. A., & Wang, Y. (1993). Factors potentiating the risk of sudden infant death syndrome associated with the prone position. *New England Journal of Medicine, 329,* 377–382.

Poole, L. (1998). Attributions of responsibility for depression of menopausal women. *TCA Journal, 26,* 115–122.

Porter, R., Making, J., Davis, L., & Christensen, K. (1992). Breast-fed infants respond to olfactory clues from their own mother and unfamiliar lactating females. *Infant Behavior and Development, 15,* 85–93.

Portnoi, V. (1999). Progressing from disease prevention to health promotion. *Journal of the American Medical Association, 282,* 1813.

Posada, G., Gao, Y., Wu, F., Posada, R., Tascon, M., Schöelmerich, A., Sagi, A., Kondo-Ikemura, K., Haaland, W., & Synnevaag, B. (1995). The secure-base phenomenon across cultures: Children's behavior, mothers' preferences, and experts' concepts. *Monographs of the Society for Research in Child Development, 60*(244, Nos. 2–3), 27–48.

Posner, J., & Vandell, D. (1994). Low-income children's after-school care: Are there beneficial effects of after-school programs? *Child Development, 65*, 440–456.

Posthuma, W. F. M., Westendorp, R. G. J., & Vandenbroucke, J. P. (1994). Cardioprotective effect of hormone replacement therapy in postmenopausal women: Is the evidence biased? *British Medical Journal, 308*, 1268–1269.

Postrado, L., & Nicholson, H. (1992). Effectiveness in delaying the initiation of sexual intercourse in girls aged 12–14. *Youth in Society, 23*, 356–379.

Poulin, F., & Boivin, M. (1999). Proactive and reactive aggression and boys' friendship quality in mainstream classrooms. *Journal of Emotional & Behavioral Disorders, 7*, 168–177.

Poulin, F., & Boivin, M. (2000). The role of proactive and reactive aggression in the formation and development of boys' friendships. *Developmental Psychology, 36*, 233–240.

Poulson, C. L., Nunes, L. R. D., & Warren, S. F. (1989). Imitation in infancy: A critical review. In H. W. Reese (Ed.), *Advances in child development and behavior* (Vol. 22) (pp. 272–298). San Diego, CA: Academic Press.

Powell, B., Landon, J., Cantrell, P., Penick, E., Nickel, E., Liskow, B., Coddington, T., Campbell, J., Dale, T., Vance, M., & Rice, A. (1998). Prediction of drinking outcomes for male alcoholics after 10 to 14 years. *Alcoholism: Clinical & Experimental Research, 22*, 559–566.

Powlishta, K. K. (1995). Intergroup processes in childhood: Social categorization and sex role development. *Developmental Psychology, 31*, 781–788.

Powlishta, K. K., Serbin, L. A., Doyle, A., & White, D. R. (1994). Gender, ethnic, and body type biases: The generality of prejudice in childhood. *Developmental Psychologym 30*, 526–536.

Prager, E. (1998). Men and meaning in later life. *Journal of Clinical Geropsychology, 4*, 191–203.

Prat-Sala, M., Shillcock, R., & Sorace, A. (2000). Animacy effects on the production of object-dislocated descriptions by Catalan-speaking children. *Journal of Child Language, 27*, 97–117.

Pratt, M., Arnold, M., & Pratt, A. (1999). Predicting adolescent moral reasoning from family climate: A longitudinal study. *Journal of Early Adolescence, 19*, 148–175.

Prechtl, H. F. R., & Beintema, D. J. (1964). *The neurological examination of the full-term newborn infant: Clinics in Developmental Medicine, 12.* London: Heinemann.

Prentice, A. (1994). Extended breast-feeding and growth in rural China. *Nutrition Reviews, 52*, 144–146.

Pressley, M., & Dennis-Rounds, J. (1980). Transfer of a mnemonic keyword strategy at two age levels. *Journal of Educational Psychology, 72*, 575–582.

Pressley, M., & Wharton-McDonald, R. (1997). Skilled comprehension and its development through instruction. *School Psychology Review, 26*, 448–466.

Pressman, E., DiPietro, J., Costigan, K., Shupe, A., & Johnson, T. (1998). Fetal neurobehavioral development: Associations with socioeconomic class and fetal sex. *Developmental Psychobiology, 33*, 79–91.

Price, R. H. (1992). Psychosocial impact of job loss on individuals and families. *Current Directions in Psychological Science, 1*, 9–11.

Prigerson, H., Bierhals, A., Kasl, S., Reynolds, C., et al. (1997). Traumatic grief as a risk factor for mental and physical morbidity. *American Journal of Psychiatry, 154*, 616–623.

Prigerson, H., Bridge, J., Maciejewski, P., Beery, L., Rosenheck, R., Jacobs, S., Bierhals, A., Kupfer, D., & Brent, D. (1999). Influence of traumatic grief on suicidal ideation among young adults. *American Journal of Psychiatry, 156*, 1994–1995.

Prince, A. (1998). Infectious diseases. In R. Behrman & R. Kliegman (Eds.), *Nelson essentials of pediatrics* (3rd ed., pp. 315–418). Philadelphia: W. B. Saunders.

Prinstein, M., & La Greca, A. (1999). Links between mothers' and children's social competence and associations with maternal adjustment. *Journal of Clinical Child Psychology, 28*, 197–210.

Public Agenda, Inc. (1999). *U.S. public's views on Social Security reform.* [Online report]. Retrieved February 9, 2001 from the World

Wide Web: http://www.publicagenda.org

Public Agenda, Inc. (1999). *Family issues.* [Online report]. Retrieved April 18, 2000 from the World Wide Web: http://www.publicagenda.org

Pujol, J., Deus, J., Losilla, J., & Capdevila, A. (1999). Cerebral lateralization of language in normal left-handed people: Studies by functional MRI. *Neurology, 52*, 1038–1043.

Pulkkinen, L. (1982). Self-control and continuity from childhood to late adolescence. In P. Baltes & O. G. Brim, Jr. (Eds.), *Life span development and behavior* (Vol. 4) (pp. 64–107). New York: Academic Press.

Purnine, D., & Carey, M. (1998). Age and gender differences in sexual behavior preferences: A follow-up report. *Journal of Sex & Marital Therapy, 24*, 93–102.

Putnins, A. (1997). Victim awareness programs for delinquent youths: Effects on moral reasoning maturity. *Adolescence, 32*, 709–714.

Pynoos, H., Steinberg, A., & Wraith, R. (1995). A developmental model of childhood traumatic stress. In D. Cicchetti & D. Cohen (Eds.), *Developmental psychopathology: Vol 2: Risk, disorder, and adaptation.* New York: Wiley.

Pynoos, J., & Golant, S. (1996). Housing and living arrangements for the elderly. In R. H. Binstock & L. K. George (Eds.), *Handbook of aging and the social sciences* (4th ed.) (pp. 303–324). San Diego, CA: Academic Press.

Quadagno, J., & Hardy, M. A. (1996). Work and retirement. In R. H. Binstock & L. K. George (Eds.), *Handbook of aging and the social sciences* (4th ed.) (pp. 325–345). San Diego, CA: Academic Press.

Quick, H., & Moen, P. (1998). Gender, employment and retirement quality: A life course approach to the differential experiences of men and women. *Journal of Occupational Health Psychology, 3*, 44–64.

Quigley, D., & Schatz, M. (1999). Men and women and their responses in spousal bereavement. *Hospice Journal, 14*, 65–78.

Raaijmakers, Q., Verbogt, T., & Vollebergh, W. (1998). Moral reasoning and political beliefs of Dutch adolescents and young adults. *Journal of Social Issues, 54*, 531–546.

Rabasca, L. (1999, October). Ultra-thin magazine models found to have little negative effect on adolescent girls. *APA Monitor Online 30.* Retrieved January 16, 2001 from the World Wide Web: http://www.apa.org/monitor/oct99

Ragnarsdottir, H., Simonsen, H., & Plunkett, K. (1999). The acquisition of past tense morphology in Icelandic and Norwegian children: An experimental study. *Journal of Child Language, 26*, 577–618.

Rahman, O., Strauss, J., Gertler, P., Ashley, D., & Fox, K. (1994). Gender differences in adult health: An international comparison. *The Gerontologist, 34*, 463–469.

Raja, S. N., McGee, R., & Stanton, W. R. (1992). Perceived attachments to parents and peers and psychological well-being in adolescence. *Journal of Youth and Adolescence, 21*, 471–485.

Ramelson, H., Friedman, R., & Ockene, J. (1999). An automated telephone-based smoking cessation education and counseling system. *Patient Education & Counseling, 36*, 131–144.

Ramey, C. T. (1992). High-risk children and IQ: Altering intergenerational patterns. *Intelligence, 16*, 239–256.

Ramey, C. T. (1993). A rejoinder to Spitz's critique of the Abecedarian experiment. *Intelligence, 17*, 25–30.

Ramey, C. T., & Campbell, F. A. (1987). The Carolina Abecedarian Project: An educational experiment concerning human malleability. In J. J. Gallagher & C. T. Ramey (Eds.), *The malleability of children* (pp. 127–140). Baltimore: Paul H. Brookes.

Ramey, C., & Ramey, S. (1998). Early intervention and early experience. *American Psychologist, 53*, 109–120.

Rao G., & Rao, S. (1997). Sector and age differences in productivity. *Social Science International, 13*, 51–56.

Raschke, H. (1987). Divorce. In M. Sussman & S. Steinmetz (Eds.), *Handbook of marriage and the family* (pp. 597–624). New York: Plenum.

Raskind, M. A., & Peskind, E. R. (1992). Alzheimer's disease and other dementing disorders. In J. E. Birren, R. B. Sloane, & G. D. Cohen (Eds.), *Handbook of mental health and aging* (2nd ed.) (pp. 478–515). San Diego, CA: Academic Press.

Ray, B. (1999). *Home schooling on the threshold: A survey of research at the dawn of the new millenium.* Washington, DC: Home Education Research Institute.

Reamer, R., Brady, M., & Hawkins, J. (1998). The effects of video self-modeling on parents' interactions with children with developmental disabilities. *Education & Training in Mental Retardation & Developmental Disabilities, 33,* 131–143.

Reed, G. M., Kemeny, M. E., Taylor, S. E., Wang, H. J., & Visscher, B. R. (1994). Realistic acceptance as a predictor of decreased survival time in gay men with AIDS. *Health Psychology, 13,* 299–307.

Reed, M. (1998). Predicting grief symptomatology among the suddenly bereaved. *Suicide & Life-Threatening Behavior, 28,* 285–301.

Regier, D. A., Boyd, J. H., Burke, J. D., Rae, D. S., Myers, J. K., Kramer, M., Robins, L. N., George, L. K., Karno, M., & Locke, B. Z. (1988). One-month prevalence of mental disorders in the United States. *Archives of General Psychiatry, 45,* 977–986.

Reich, J. W., Zautra, A. J., & Guarnaccia, C. A. (1989). Effects of disability and bereavement on the mental health and recovery of older adults. *Psychology and Aging, 4,* 57–65.

Reichle, B., & Gefke, M. (1998). Justice of conjugal divisions of labor-you can't always get what you want. *Social Justice Research, 11,* 271–287.

Remafedi, G., Farrow, J. A., & Deisher, R. W. (1991). Risk factors for attempted suicide in gay and bisexual youth. *Pediatrics, 87,* 869–875.

Remafedi, G., French, S., Story, M., Resnick, M., & Blum, R. (1998). The relationship between suicide risk and sexual orientation: Results of a population-based study. *American Journal of Public Health, 88,* 57–60.

Remafedi, G., Resnick, M., Blum, R., & Harris, L. (1998). Demography of sexual orientation in adolescents. *Pediatrics, 89,* 714–721.

Rendell, P., & Thomson, D. (1999). Aging and prospective memory: Differences between naturalistic and laboratory tasks. *Journals of Gerontology, 54B,* P256–P269.

Reno, V. P. (1993). The role of pensions in retirement income: Trends and questions. *Social Security Bulletin, 56,* 29–43.

Renouf, A. G., & Harter, S. (1990). Low self-worth and anger as components of the depressive experience in young adolescents. *Development and Psychopathology, 2,* 293–310.

Reskin, B. (1993). Sex segregation in the workplace. *Annual Review of Sociology, 19,* 241–270.

Rexroat, C., & Shehan, C. (1987). The family life cycle and spouses' time in housework. *Journal of Marriage and the Family, 49,* 737–750.

Reynolds, A. J., & Bezruczko, N. (1993). School adjustment of children at risk through fourth grade. *Merrill-Palmer Quarterly, 39,* 457–480.

Reynolds, C. R., & Brown, R. T. (Eds.). (1984). *Perspectives on bias in mental testing.* New York: Plenum.

Reynolds, D. (1992). School effectiveness and school improvement: An updated review of the British literature. In D. Reynolds & P. Cuttance (Eds.), *School effectiveness: Research, policy, and prejudice.* London: Cassell.

Rholes, W. S., & Ruble, D. N. (1984). Children's understanding of dispositional characteristics of others. *Child Development, 55,* 550–560.

Rholes, W., Simpson, J., Blakely, B., Lanigan, L., & Allen, D. (1997). Adult attachment styles, the desire to have children, and working models of parenthood. *Journal of Personality, 65,* 357–385.

Ricci, C. M., Beal, C. R., & Dekle, D. J. (1995, March). *The effect of parent versus unfamiliar interviewers on young witnesses' memory and identification accuracy.* Paper presented at the biennial meetings of the Society for Research in Child Development, Indianapolis, IN.

Rice, M. L., Huston, A. C., Truglio, R., & Wright, J. (1990). Words from "Sesame Street": Learning vocabulary while viewing. *Developmental Psychology, 26,* 421–428.

Richardson, G. S. (1990). Circadian rhythms and aging. In E. R. Scheider & J. W. Rowe (Eds.), *Handbook of the biology of aging* (3rd ed.) (pp. 275–305). San Diego, CA: Academic Press.

Richardson, G., Conroy, M., & Day, N. (1996). Prenatal cocaine exposure: Effects on the development of school-aged children. *Neurotoxicology & Teratology, 18,* 627–634.

Richardson, J. L., Zarnegar, Z., Bisno, B., & Levine, A. (1990). Psychosocial status at initiation of cancer treatment and survival. *Journal of Psychosomatic Research, 34,* 189–201.

Rich-Edwards, J. W., Manson, J. E., Hennekens, C. H., & Buring, J. E. (1995). The primary prevention of coronary heart disease in women. *New England Journal of Medicine, 332,* 1758–1766.

Rierdan, J., & Koff, E. (1993). Developmental variables in relation to depressive symptoms in adolescent girls. *Development and Psychopathology, 5,* 485–496.

Riggs, A. (1997). Men, friends, and widowhood: Towards successful aging. *Australian Journal on Ageing, 16,* 182–185.

Righetti, P. (1996). The emotional experience of the fetus: A preliminary report. *Pre- & Peri-Natal Psychology Journal, 11,* 55–65.

Rique, J., & Camino, C. (1997). Consistency and inconsistency in adolescents' moral reasoning. *International Journal of Behavioral Development, 21,* 813–836.

Risch, H. A., Jain, M., Marrett, L. D., & Howe, G. R. (1994). Dietary fat intake and risk of epithelial ovarian cancer. *Journal of the National Cancer Institute, 86,* 1409–1415.

Roberts, R. E., & Sobhan, M. (1992). Symptoms of depression in adolescence: A comparison of Anglo, African, and Hispanic Americans. *Journal of Youth and Adolescence, 21,* 639–651.

Robins, L. N., & McEvoy, L. (1990). Conduct problems as predictors of substance abuse. In L. N. Robins & M. Rutter (Eds.), *Straight and devious pathways from childhood to adulthood* (pp. 182–204). Cambridge, England: Cambridge University Press.

Robins, R., Caspi, A., & Moffitt, T. (2000). Two personalities, one relationship: Both partners' personality traits shape the quality of their relationship. *Journal of Personality & Social Psychology, 79,* 251–259.

Robinson-Whelen, S., & Kiecolt-Glaser, N. (1997). The importance of social versus temporal comparison appraisals among older adults. *Journal of Applied Social Psychology, 27,* 959–966.

Robison, J., Moen, P., & Dempster-McClain, D. (1995). Women's caregiving: Changing profiles and pathways. *Journals of Gerontology: Social Sciences, 50B,* S362–373.

Roche, A. F. (1979). Secular trends in human growth, maturation, and development. *Monographs of the Society for Research in Child Development, 44*(3–4, Serial No. 179).

Rock, A., Trainor, L., & Addison, T. (1999). Distinctive messages in infant-directed lullabies and play songs. *Developmental Psychology, 35,* 527–534.

Rockwood, K., & Stadnyk, K. (1994). The prevalence of dementia in the elderly: A review. *Canadian Journal of Psychiatry, 29,* 253–257.

Roderick, M., & Camburn, E. (1999). Risk and recovery from course failure in the early years of high school. *American Educational Research Journal, 36,* 303–343.

Rodin, J. (1986). Aging and health: Effects of the sense of control. *Science, 233,* 1271–1275.

Rodin, J. (1990). Control by any other name: Definitions, concepts, and processes. In J. Rodin, C. Schooler, & K. W. Schaie (Eds.), *Self-directedness: Cause and effects throughout the life course* (pp. 1–17). Hillsdale, NJ: Erlbaum.

Rodin, J., & Langer, E. J. (1977). Long-term effects of a control-relevant intervention with the institutionalized aged. *Journal of Personality and Social Psychology, 35,* 897–902.

Rodkin, P., Farmer, T., Pearl, R., & Van Acker, R. (2000). Heterogeneity of popular boys: Antisocial and prosocial configurations. *Developmental Psychology, 36,* 14–24.

Rodrigo, M., Janssens, J., & Ceballos, E. (1999). Do children's perceptions and attributions mediate the effects of mothers' child rearing actions? *Journal of Family Psychology, 13,* 508–522.

Rodriguez, C., Calle, E. E., Coates, R. J., Miracle-McMahil, H. L., Thun, M. J., & Heath, C. W., Jr. (1995). Estrogen replacement therapy and fatal ovarian cancer. *American Journal of Epidemiology, 141,* 828–835.

Roer-Strier, D., & Rivlis, M. (1998). Timetable of psychological and behavioural autonomy expectations among parents from Israel and the former Soviet Union. *International Journal of Psychology, 33,* 123–135.

Roeser, R., & Eccles J. (1998). Adolescents' perceptions of middle school: Relation to longitudinal changes in academic and psychological adjustment. *Journal of Research on Adolescence, 8,* 123–158.

Rogers, C. R. (1961). *On becoming a person.* Boston: Houghton Mifflin.

Rogers, J. L., Rowe, D. C., & May, K. (1994). DF analysis of NLSY IQ/Achievement data: Nonshared environmental influences. *Intelligence, 19,* 157–177.

Rogers, R. L., Meyer, J. S., & Mortel, K. F. (1990). After reaching retirement age physical activity sustains cerebral perfusion and cognition. *Journal of the American Geriatric Society, 38,* 123–128.

Roggman, L. A., Langlois, J. H., Hubbs-Tait, L., & Rieser-Danner, L. A. (1994). Infant day-care, attachment, and the "file drawer problem." *Child Development, 65,* 1429–1443.

Rogoff, B. (1990). *Apprenticeship in thinking: Cognitive development in social contexts.* New York: Oxford University Press.

Rogosch, F., Cicchetti, D., & Aber, J. (1995). The role of child maltreatment in early deviations in cognitive and affective processing abilities and later peer relationship problems. *Development and Psychopathology, 7,* 591–609.

Rojewski, J. (1999). Occupational and educational aspirations and attainment of young adults with and without LD 2 years after high school completion. *Journal of Learning Disabilities, 32,* 533–552.

Rollins, B. C., & Feldman, H. (1970). Marital satisfaction over the family life cycle. *Journal of Marriage and the Family, 32,* 20–27.

Rolls, E. (2000). Memory systems in the brain. *Annual Review of Psychology, 51,* 599–630.

Rose, A. J., & Montemayor, R. (1994). The relationship between gender role orientation and perceived self-competence in male and female adolescents. *Sex Roles, 31,* 579–595.

Rose, D. P. (1993). Diet, hormones, and cancer. *Annual Review of Public Health, 14,* 1–17.

Rose, R. J. (1995). Genes and human behavior. *Annual Review of Psychology, 56,* 625–654.

Rose, S. A., & Feldman, J. F. (1995). Prediction of IQ and specific cognitive abilities at 11 years from infancy measures. *Developmental Psychology, 31,* 685–696.

Rosenbaum, J. E. (1984). *Career mobility in a corporate hierarchy.* New York: Academic Press.

Rosenberg, M. (1986). Self-concept from middle childhood through adolescence. In J. Suls & A. G. Greenwald (Eds.), *Psychological perspectives on the self* (Vol. 3) (pp. 107–136). Hillsdale, NJ: Erlbaum.

Rosenblith, J. F. (1992). *In the beginning* (2nd ed.). Thousand Oaks, CA: Sage.

Rosenman, R. H., & Friedman, M. (1983). Relationship of Type A behavior pattern to coronary heart disease. In H. Selye (Ed.), *Selye's guide to stress research* (Vol. 2) (pp. 47–106). New York: Scientific and Academic Editions.

Rosenthal, C. J., Matthews, S. H., & Marshall, V. W. (1989). Is parent care normative? The experiences of a sample of middle-aged women. *Research on Aging, 11,* 244–260.

Rosenthal, R. (1994). Interpersonal expectancy effects: A 30-year perspective. *Current Directions in Psychological Science, 3,* 176–179.

Rosenthal, S., Lewis, L., Succop, P., & Burklow, K. (1997). Adolescent girls' perceived prevalence of sexually transmitted diseases and condom use. *Journal of Developmental & Behavioral Pediatrics, 18,* 158–161.

Rosow, I. (1985). Status and role change through the life cycle. In R. H. Binstock & E. Shanas (Eds.), *Handbook of aging and the social sciences* (2nd ed.) (pp. 62–93). New York: Van Nostrand Reinhold.

Ross, C. E. (1995). Reconceptualizing marital status as a continuum of social attachment. *Journal of Marriage and the Family, 57,* 129–140.

Ross, R. K., Paganini-Hill, A., Mack, T. M., & Henderson, B. E. (1987). Estrogen use and cardiovascular disease. In D. R. Mishell, Jr. (Ed.), *Menopause: Physiology and pharmacology* (pp. 209–224). Chicago: Year Book Medical Publishers.

Rossi, A. S. (1989). A life-course approach to gender, aging, and intergenerational relations. In K. W. Schaie & C. Schooler (Eds.), *Social structure and aging: Psychological processes* (pp. 207–236). Hillsdale, NJ: Erlbaum.

Rossman, I. (1980). Bodily changes with aging. In E. W. Busse & D. G. Blazer (Eds.), *Handbook of geriatric psychiatry* (pp. 125–146). New York: Van Nostrand Reinhold.

Rossow, I., & Amundsen, A. (1997). Alcohol abuse and mortality: A 40-year prospective study of Norwegian conscripts. *Social Science & Medicine, 44,* 261–267.

Rossow, I., Romelsjoe, A., & Leifman, H. (1999). Alcohol abuse and suicidal behaviour in young and middle aged men: Differentiating between attempted and completed suicide. *Addiction, 94,* 1199–1207.

Rothbard, J. C., & Shaver, P. R. (1994). Continuity of attachment across the life span. In M. B. Sperling & W. H. Berman (Eds.), *Attachment in adults. Clinical and developmental perspectives* (pp. 31–71). New York: Guilford Press.

Rothbart, M., Ahadi, S., & Evans, D. (2000). Temperament and personality: Origins and outcomes. *Journal of Personality & Social Psychology, 78,* 122–135.

Rothbart, M. K., Derryberry, D., & Posner, M. I. (1994). A psychobiological approach to the development of temperament. In J. E. Bates & T. D. Wachs (Eds.), *Temperament. Individual differences at the interface of biology and behavior* (pp. 83–116). Washington, DC: American Psychological Association.

Rotheram-Borus, M. J., Rosario, M., & Koopman, C. (1991). Minority youths at high risk: Gay males and runaways. In M. E. Colten & S. Gore (Eds.), *Adolescent stress: Causes and consequences* (pp. 181–200). New York: Aldine de Gruyter.

Rotter, J. (1990). Internal versus external control of reinforcement: A case history of a variable. *American Psychologist, 45,* 489–493.

Rotter, J. B. (1966). Generalized expectancies for internal versus external control of reinforcement. *Psychological Monographs, 80*(1, Whole No. 609).

Rovee-Collier, C. (1993). The capacity for long-term memory in infancy. *Current Directions in Psychological Science, 2,* 130–135.

Rowe, J., & Kahn, R. (1997). Successful aging. *Gerontologist, 37,* 433–440.

Rowe, J., & Kahn, R. (1998). *Successful aging.* New York: Pantheon.

Rowley, S. (2000). Profiles of African American college students' educational utility and performance: A cluster analysis. *Journal of Black Psychology, 26,* 3–26.

Roy, P., Rutter, M., & Pickles, A. (2000). Institutional care: Risk from family background or pattern of rearing. *Journal of Child Psychology & Psychiatry & Allied Disciplines, 41,* 139–149.

Ruben, K., Nelson, L., Hastings, P., & Asendorpt, J. (1999). The transaction between parents' perception of their children's shyness and their parenting styles. *International Journal of Behavioral Development, 23,* 937–958.

Rubin, K. H., Fein, G. G., & Vandenberg, B. (1983). Play. In E. M. Hetherington (Ed.), *Handbook of child psychology: Socialization, personality, and social development* (Vol. 4) (pp. 693–774). New York: Wiley.

Rubin, K. H., Hymel, S., Mills, R. S. L., & Rose-Krasnor, L. (1991). Conceptualizing different developmental pathways to and from social isolation in childhood. In D. Cicchetti & S. L. Toth (Eds.), *Internalizing and externalizing expressions of dysfunction: Rochester Symposium on Developmental Psychopathology* (Vol. 2) (pp. 91–122). Hillsdale, NJ: Erlbaum.

Rubin, S., & Schechter, N. (1997). Exploring the social construction of bereavement: Perceptions of adjustment and recovery in bereaved men. *American Journal of Orthopsychiatry, 67,* 279–289.

Rubinstein, R. L. (1986). *Singular paths: Old men living alone.* New York: Columbia University Press.

Rubinstein, R. L., Alexander, B. B., Goodman, M., & Luborsky, M. (1991). Key relationships of never married childless older women: A cultural analysis. *Journals of Gerontology: Social Sciences, 46,* S270–277.

Ruble, D. N. (1987). The acquisition of self-knowledge: A self-socialization perspective. In N. Eisenberg (Ed.), *Contemporary topics in developmental psychology* (pp. 243–270). New York: Wiley-Interscience.

Ruble, D., & Dweck, C. (1995). Self-conceptions, person conceptions, and their development. In N. Eisenberg (Ed.), *Social development.* Thousand Oaks, CA: Sage.

Rudd, M., Viney, L., & Preston, C. (1999). The grief experienced by spousal caregivers of dementia patients: The role of place of care of patient and gender of caregiver. *International Journal of Aging & Human Development, 48,* 217–240.

Rutter, M. (1983). School effects on pupil progress: Research findings and policy implications. *Child Development, 54,* 1–29.

Rutter, M. (1987). Continuities and discontinuities from infancy. In J. D. Osofsky (Ed.), *Handbook of infant development* (2nd ed.) (pp. 1256–1296). New York: Wiley-Interscience.

Ryan, C. J., & Kaye, M. (1996). Euthanasia in Australia-the Northern Territory Rights of the Terminally Ill Act. *New England Journal of Medicine, 334,* 326–328.

Ryff, C. (1984). Personality development from the inside: The subjective experience of change in adulthood and aging. In P. B. Baltes & O. G. Brim, Jr. (Eds.), *Life-span development and behavior* (pp. 244–281). Orlando, FL: Academic Press.

Ryff, C., & Heincke, S. G. (1983). The subjective organization of personality in adulthood and aging. *Journal of Personality and Social Psychology, 44,* 807–816.

Rys, G., & Bear, G. (1997). Relational aggression and peer relations: Gender and developmental issues. *Merrill-Palmer Quarterly, 43,* 87–106.

Saavedra, M., Ramirez, A., & Contreras, C. (1997). Interactive interviews between elders and children: A possible procedure for improving affective state in the elderly. *Psiquiatricay Psicologica de America Latina, 43,* 63–66.

Sacco, V., & Kennedy, L. (1996). *The criminal event.* Belmont, CA: Wadsworth.

Sack, W. H., Mason, R., & Higgins, J. E. (1985). The single parent family and abusive child punishment. *American Journal of Orthopsychiatry, 55,* 252–259.

Sadowski, M. (1995). The numbers game yields simplistic answers on the link between spending and outcomes. *Harvard Education Letter, 11(2),* 1–4.

Saewyc, E., Bearinger, L., Heinz, P., Blum, R., & Resnick, M. (1998). Gender differences in health and risk behaviors among bisexual and homosexual adolescents. *Journal of Adolescent Health, 23,* 181–188.

Safren, S., & Heimberg, R. (1999). Depression, hopelessness, suicidality, and related factors in sexual minority and heterosexual adolescents. *Journal of Consulting & Clinical Psychology, 67,* 859–866.

Sagi, A. (1990). Attachment theory and research from a cross-cultural perspective. *Human Development, 33,* 10–22.

Sagi, A., van IJzendoorn, M. H., & Koren-Karie, N. (1991). Primary appraisal of the Strange Situation: A cross-cultural analysis of pre-separation episodes. *Developmental Psychology, 27,* 587–596.

Sagiv, M., Vogelaere, P., Soudry, M., & Shrsam, R. (2000). Role of physical activity training in attenuation of height loss. *Gerontology, 46,* 266–270.

St. James-Roberts, I., Bowyer, J., Varghese, S., & Sawdon, J. (1994). Infant crying patterns in Manila and London. *Child: Care, Health and Development, 20,* 323–337.

St. Pierre, T., Mark, M., Kaltreider, D., & Aikin, K. (1995). A 27-month evaluation of a sexual activity prevention program in boys and girls clubs across the nation. *Family Relations, 44,* 69–77.

Salthouse, T. (1998). Independence of age-related influences on cognitive abilities across the life span. *Developmental Psychology, 34,* 851–864.

Salthouse, T., & Czaja, S. (2000). Structural constraints on process explanations in cognitive aging. *Psychology & Aging, 15,* 44–55.

Salthouse, T. A. (1991). *Theoretical perspectives on cognitive aging.* Hillsdale, NJ: Erlbaum.

Salthouse, T. A. (1993). Speed mediation of adult age differences in cognition. *Developmental Psychology, 29,* 722–738.

Salthouse, T. A. (1996). General and specific speed mediation of adult age differences in memory. *Journals of Gerontology: Psychological Sciences, 51B,* P30–42.

Salthouse, T. A., & Maurer, T. J. (1996). Aging, job performance, and career development. In J. E. Birren & K. W. Schaie (Eds.), *Handbook of the psychology of aging* (4th ed.) (pp. 353–364). San Diego, CA: Academic Press.

Saltz, R. (1979). Children's interpretation of proverbs. *Language Arts, 56,* 508–514.

Samaritans. (1998). *Media guidelines on portrayals of suicide.* [Online booklet]. Retrieved February 16, 2001 from the World Wide Web: http://www.mentalhelp.net/samaritans/medreport.htm

Sammartino, F. J. (1987). The effect of health on retirement. *Social Security Bulletin, 50(2),* 31–47.

Sampson, P., Kerr, B., Olson, H., Streissguth, A., Hunt, E., Barr, H., Bookstein, F., & Thiede, K. (1997). The effects of prenatal alcohol exposure on adolescent cognitive processing: A speed-accuracy tradeoff. *Intelligence, 24,* 329–353.

Sampson, R. J., & Laub, J. H. (1994). Urban poverty and the family context of delinquency: A new look at structure and process in a classic study. *Child Development, 65,* 523–540.

Samuels, S., & Flor, R. (1997). The importance of automaticity for developing expertise in reading. *Reading & Writing Quarterly: Overcoming Learning Difficulties, 13,* 107–121.

Sanders, C. M. (1989). *Grief: The mourning after.* New York: Wiley-Interscience.

Sandman, C., Wadhwa, P., Chicz-DeMet, A., Porto, M., & Garite, T. (1999). Maternal corticotropin-releasing hormone and habituation in the human fetus. *Developmental Psychobiology, 34,* 163–173.

Sandman, C., Wadhwa, P., Hetrick, W., Porto, M., & Peeke, H. (1997). Human fetal heart rate dishabituation between thirty and thirty-two weeks. *Child Development, 68,* 1031–1040.

Sandnabba, N., & Ahlberg, C. (1999). Parents' attitudes and expectations about children's cross-gender behavior. *Sex Roles, 40,* 249–263.

Sands, L. P., & Meredith, W. (1992). Blood pressure and intellectual functioning in late midlife. *Journals of Gerontology: Psychological Sciences, 47,* P81–84.

Sands, L. P., Terry, H., & Meredith, W. (1989). Change and stability in adult intellectual functioning assessed by Wechsler item responses. *Psychology and Aging, 4,* 79–87.

Sandson, T., Bachna, K., & Morin, M. (2000). Right hemisphere dysfunction in ADHD: Visual hemispatial inattention and clinical subtype. *Journal of Learning Disabilities, 33,* 83–90.

Sanson, A., Pedlow, R., Cann, W., Prior, M., et al. (1996). Shyness ratings: Stability and correlates in early childhood. *International Journal of Behavioral Development, 19,* 705–724.

Sarason, B. R., Sarason, I. G., & Pierce, G. R. (1990). Traditional views of social support and their impact on assessment. In B. R. Sarason, I. G. Sarason, & G. R. Pierce (Eds.), *Social support: An interactional view* (pp. 9–25). New York: Wiley.

Sato, S., Shimonska, Y., Nakazato, K., & Kawaai, C. (1997). A life-span developmental study of age identity: Cohort and gender differences. *Japanese Journal of Developmental Psychology, 8,* 88–97.

Saugstad, L. (1997). Optimal foetal growth in the reduction of learning and behavior disorder and prevention of sudden infant death (SIDS) after the first month. *International Journal of Psychophysiology, 27,* 107–121.

Savage, M., & Holcomb, D. (1999). Adolescent female athletes' sexual risk-taking behaviors. *Journal of Youth and Adolescence, 28,* 583–594.

Savage, S., & Gauvain, M. (1998). Parental beliefs and children's everyday planning in European-American and Latino families. *Journal of Applied Developmental Psychology, 19,* 319–340.

Savin-Williams, R. C. (1994). Verbal and physical abuse as stressors in the lives of lesbian, gay male, and bisexual youths: Associations with school problems, running away, substance abuse, prostitution, and suicide. *Journal of Consulting and Clinical Psychology, 62,* 261–269.

Saxon, T., Colombo, J., Robinson, E., & Frick, J. (2000). Dyadic interaction profiles in infancy and preschool intelligence. *Journal of School Psychology, 38,* 9–25.

Sayers, S., Kohn, C., & Heavey, C. (1998). Prevention of marital dysfunction: Behavioral approaches and beyond. *Clinical Psychology Review, 18,* 713–744.

Scarr, S. (1997). Why child care has little impact on most children's development. *Current Directions in Psychological Science, 6,* 143–147.

Scarr, S., & Eisenberg, M. (1993). Child care research: Issues, perspectives, and results. *Annual Review of Psychology, 44,* 613–644.

Scarr, S., & McCartney, K. (1983). How people make their own environments: A theory of genotype/environment effects. *Child Development, 54,* 424–435.

Scarr, S., & Weinberg, R. A. (1983). The Minnesota adoption studies: Genetic differences and malleability. *Child Development, 54,* 260–267.

Scarr, S., Weinberg, R. A., & Waldman, I. D. (1993). IQ correlations in transracial adoptive families. *Intelligence, 17,* 541–555.

Schaal, B., Marlier, L., & Soussignan, R. (1998). Olfactory function in the human fetus: Evidence from selective neonatal responsiveness to the odor of amniotic fluid. *Behavioral Neuroscience, 112,* 1438–1449.

Schadt, D. (1997). The relationship of type to developmental issues of midlife women: Implications for counseling. *Journal of Psychological Type, 43,* 12–21.

Schafer, R. B., & Keith, P. M. (1984). A causal analysis of the relationship between the self-concept and marital quality. *Journal of Marriage and the Family, 46,* 909–914.

Schaffer, H., & Emerson, P. (1964). The development of social attachments in infancy. *Monographs of the Society for Research in Child Development, 29,* 3, Serial No. 94.

Schaie, K. W. (1983). The Seattle longitudinal study: A 21-year exploration of psychometric intelligence in adulthood. In K. W. Schaie (Ed.), *Longitudinal studies of adult psychological development* (pp. 64–135). New York: Guilford Press.

Schaie, K. W. (1989). The hazards of cognitive aging. *The Gerontologist, 29,* 484–493.

Schaie, K. W. (1990). Intellectual development in adulthood. In J. E. Birren & K. W. Schaie (Eds.), *Handbook of the psychology of aging* (3rd ed.) (pp. 291–309). San Diego, CA: Academic Press.

Schaie, K. W. (1993). The Seattle Longitudinal Studies of adult intelligence. *Current Directions in Psychological Science, 2,* 171–175.

Schaie, K. W. (1994). The course of adult intellectual development. *American Psychologist, 49,* 304–313.

Schaie, K. W. (1996). Intellectual development in adulthood. In J. E. Birren & K. W. Schaie (Eds.), *Handbook of the psychology of aging* (4th ed.) (pp. 266–286). San Diego, CA: Academic Press.

Schaie, K. W., & Hertzog, C. (1983). Fourteen-year cohort-sequential analyses of adult intellectual development. *Developmental Psychology, 19,* 531–543.

Schaie, K. W., & Willis, S. L. (1991). Adult personality and psychomotor performance: Cross-sectional and longitudinal analyses. *Journals of Gerontology: Psychological Sciences, 46,* P275–284.

Scharlach, A. E., & Fredricksen, K. I. (1994). Eldercare versus adult care. Does care recipient age make a difference? *Research on Aging, 16,* 43–68.

Schatschneider, C., Francis, D., Foorman, B., Fletcher, J., & Mehta, P. (1999). The dimensionality of phonological awareness: An application of item response theory. *Journal of Educational Psychology, 91,* 439–449.

Scheibel, A. B. (1992). Structural changes in the aging brain. In J. E. Birren, R. B. Sloane, & G. D. Cohen (Eds.), *Handbook of mental health and aging* (2nd ed.) (pp. 147–174). San Diego, CA: Academic Press.

Scheibel, A. B. (1996). Structural and functional changes in the aging brain. In J. E. Birren & K. W. Schaie (Eds.), *Handbook of the psychology of aging* (4th ed.) (pp. 105–128). San Diego, CA: Academic Press.

Scheidt, R., Humpherys, D., & Yorgason, J. (1999). Successful aging: What's not to like? *Journal of Applied Gerontology, 18,* 277–282.

Scheier, M. F., Matthews, K. A., Owens, J. F., Magovern, G. J., Lefebvre, S., Abbott, R. A., & Carver, C. S. (1989). Dispositional optimism and recovery from coronary artery bypass surgery: The beneficial effects on physical and psychological well-being. *Journal of Personality and Social Psychology, 57,* 1024–1040.

Schieber, F. (1992). Aging and the senses. In J. E. Birren, R. B. Sloane, & G. D. Cohen (Eds.), *Handbook of mental health and aging* (2nd ed.) (pp. 252–306). San Diego, CA: Academic Press.

Schieve, L., Peterson, H., Meikle, S., Jeng, G., Danel, I., Burnett, N., & Wilcox, L. (1999). Birth rates and multiple-birth risk using in vitro fertilization. *Journal of the American Medical Association, 282,* 1832–1838.

Schliemann, A., Carraher, D., & Ceci, S. (1997). Everyday cognition. In J. Berry, P. Dasen, & T. Saraswathi (Eds.), *Handbook of cross-cultural psychology. Vol. 2: Basic processes and human development.* Needham Heights, MA: Allyn & Bacon.

Schlyter, S. (1996). Bilingual children's stories: French passé composé/imparfait and their correspondences in Swedish. *Linguistics, 34,* 1059–1085.

Schmidt, P. (2000, January 21). Colleges prepare for the fallout from state testing policies. *Chronicle of Higher Education, 46,* A26–A28.

Schmitt, N., Sacco, J., Ramey, S., Ramey, C., & Chan, D. (1999). Parental employment, school climate, and children's academic and social development. *Journal of Applied Psychology, 84,* 737–753.

Schmitz, S., Fulker, D., Plomin, R., Zahn-Waxler, C., Emde, R., & DeFries, J. (1999). Temperament and problem behavior during early childhood. *International Journal of Behavioral Development, 23,* 333–355.

Schnarch, D. (1997). Sex, intimacy, and the Internet. *Journal of Sex Education & Therapy, 22,* 15–20.

Schneider, B., Hieshima, J. A., Lee, S., & Plank, S. (1994). East-Asian academic success in the United States: Family, school, and community explanations. In P. M. Greenfield & R. R. Cocking (Eds.), *Cross-cultural roots of minority child development* (pp. 323–350). Hillsdale, NJ: Erlbaum.

Schoen, R., & Wooldredge, J. (1989). Marriage choices in North Carolina and Virginia, 1969–71 and 1979–81. *Journal of Marriage and the Family, 51,* 465–481.

Schoendorf, K. C., Hogue, C. J. R., Kleinman, J. C., & Rowley, D. (1992). Mortality among infants of black as compared with white college-educated parents. *New England Journal of Medicine, 326,* 1522–1526.

Schoendorf, K. C., & Kiely, J. L. (1992). Relationship of Sudden Infant Death Syndrome to maternal smoking during and after pregnancy. *Pediatrics, 90,* 905–908.

Schoenhals, M., Tienda, M., & Schneider, B. (1998). The educational and personal consequences of adolescent employment. *Social Forces, 77,* 723–762.

Schonert-Reichl, K. (1999). Relations of peer acceptance, friendship adjustment, and social behavior to moral reasoning during early adolescence. *Journal of Early Adolescence, 19,* 249–279.

Schothorst, P., & van Engeland, H. (1996). Long-term behavioral sequelae of prematurity. *Journal of the American Academy of Child & Adolescent Psychiatry, 35,* 175–183.

Schreiber, M., Lutz, K., Schweizer, A., Kalveram, K., & Jaencke, L., (1998). Development and evaluation of an interactive computer-based training as a rehabilitation tool for dementia. *Psychologische Reitraege, 40,* 85–102.

Schreiber, M., Schweizer, A., Lutz, K., Kalveram, K., & Jaencke, L. (1999). Potential of an interactive computer-based training in the rehabilitation of dementia. An initial study. *Neuropsychological Rehabilitation, 9,* 155–167.

Schuler, M., & Nair, P. (1999). Frequency of maternal cocaine use during pregnancy and infant neurobehavioral outcome. *Journal of Pediatric Psychology, 24,* 511–514.

Schultz, N. R., Jr., Elias, M. F., Robbins, M. A., Streeten, D. H. P., & Blakeman, N. (1986). A longitudinal comparison of hypertensives and normotensives on the Wechsler Adult Intelligence Scale: Initial findings. *Journal of Gerontology, 41,* 169–175.

Schulz, A. (1998). Navajo women and the politics of identities. *Social Problems, 45,* 336–355.

Schulz, J. H. (1995). *The economics of aging* (6th ed.). Westport, CT: Auburn House.

Schulz, R., & Curnow, C. (1988). Peak performance and age among superathletes: Track and field, swimming, baseball, tennis, and golf. *Journals of Gerontology: Psychological Sciences, 43,* P113–120.

Schulz, R., Visintainer, P., & Williamson, G. M. (1990). Psychiatric and physical morbidity effects of caregiving. *Journals of Gerontology: Psychological Sciences, 45,* 181–191.

Schulz, R., & Williamson, G. M. (1991). A 2-year longitudinal study of depression among Alzheimer's caregivers. *Psychology and Aging, 6,* 569–578.

Schumm, W., Resnick, G., Silliman, B., & Bell, D. (1998). Premarital counseling and marital satisfaction among civilian wives of military service members. *Journal of Sex & Marital Therapy, 24,* 21–28.

Schuster, C. (1997). Condom use behavior: An assessment of United States college students' health education needs. *International Quarterly of Community Health Education, 17,* 237–254.

Schwartz, C., Snidman, N., & Kagan, J. (1996). Early childhood temperament as a determinant of externalizing behavior in adolescence. *Development & Psychopathology, 8,* 527–537.

Schwartz, R. M., Anastasia, M. L., Scanlon, J. W., & Kellogg, R. J. (1994). Effect of surfactant on morbidity, mortality, and resource use in newborn infants weighing 500 to 1500 g. *New England Journal of Medicine, 330,* 1476–1480.

Schwebel, D., Rosen, C., & Singer, J. (1999). Preschoolers' pretend play and theory of mind: The role of jointly constructed pretence. *British Journal of Developmental Psychology, 17,* 333–348.

Schweizer, T., Schnegg, M., & Berzborn, S. (1998). Personal networks and social support in a multiethnic community of southern California. *Social Networks, 20,* 1–21.

Schwitzer, A., Griffin, O., Ancie, J., & Thomas, C. (1999). Social adjustment experiences of African American college students. *Journal of Counseling & Development, 77,* 189–197.

Scott, J. (1998). Hematology. In R. Behrman & R. Kliegman (Eds.), *Nelson essentials of pediatrics* (3rd ed., pp. 545–582). Philadelphia: W. B. Saunders.

Sedney, M. (1999). Children's grief narratives in popular films. *Omega: Journal of Death & Dying, 39,* 314–324.

Seidman, E., Allen, L., Aber, J. L., Mitchell, C., & Feinman, J. (1994). The impact of school transitions in early adolescence on the self-sytem and perceived social context of poor urban youth. *Child Development, 65,* 507–522.

Seifer, R., Schiller, M., Sameroff, A. J., Resnick, S., & Riordan, K. (1996). Attachment, maternal sensitivity, and infant temperament during the first year of life. *Developmental Psychology, 32,* 12–25.

Seligman, M. E. P. (1991). *Learned optimism.* New York: Knopf.

Sellers, R., Chavous, T., & Cooke, D. (1998). Racial ideology and racial centrality as predictors of African American college students' academic performance. *Journal of Black Psychology, 24,* 8–27.

Selman, R. L. (1980). *The growth of interpersonal understanding.* New York: Academic Press.

Semrud-Clikeman, M., Nielsen, K., Clinton, A., Sylvester, L., et al. (1999). An intervention approach for children with teacher- and parent-identified attentional difficulties. *Journal of Learning Disabilities, 32,* 581–590.

Senchak, M., Leonard, K., & Greene, B. (1998). Alcohol use among college students as a function of their typical social drinking context. *Psychology of Addictive Behaviors, 12,* 62–70.

Serbin, L., Moskowitz, D. S., Schwartzman, A. E., & Ledingham, J. E. (1991). Aggressive, withdrawn, and aggressive/withdrawn children in adolescence: Into the next generation. In D. J. Pepler & K. H. Rubin (Eds.), *The development and treatment of childhood aggression* (pp. 55–70). Hillsdale, NJ: Erlbaum.

Serbin, L. A., Powlishta, K. K., & Gulko, J. (1993). The development of sex typing in middle childhood. *Monographs of the Society for Research in Child Development, 58* (2, Serial No. 232).

Serdula, M. K., Ivery, D., Coates, R. J., Freedman, D. S., Williamson, D. F., & Byers, T. (1993). Do obese children become obese adults? A review of the literature. *Preventive Medicine, 22,* 167–177.

Serpell, R., & Hatano, G. (1997). Education, schooling, and literacy. In J. Berry, P. Dasen, & T. Saraswathi (Eds.), *Handbook of cross-cultural psychology. Vol. 2: Basic processes and human development.* Needham Heights, MA: Allyn & Bacon.

Shaffer, D., Garland, A., Gould, M., Fisher, P., & Trautman, P. (1988). Preventing teenage suicide: A critical review. *Journal of the American Academy of Child and Adolescent Psychiatry, 27,* 675–687.

Shaffer, D., Garland, A., Vieland, V., Underwood, M., & Busner, C. (1991). The impact of curriculum-based suicide prevention programs for teenagers. *Journal of the American Academy of Child and Adolescent Psychiatry, 30,* 588–596.

Shapiro, E. (1983). Impending death and the use of hospitals by the elderly. *Journal of the American Geriatric Society, 31,* 348–351.

Sharma, S., Monsen, R., & Gary, J. (1997). Comparison of attitudes toward death and dying among nursing majors and other college students. *Omega: Journal of Death & Dying, 34,* 219–232.

Sharma, V., & Sharma, A. (1997). Adolescent boys in Gujrat, India: Their sexual behavior and their knowledge of acquired immunodeficiency syndrome and other sexually transmitted diseases. *Journal of Developmental & Behavioral Pediatrics, 18,* 399–404.

Shaw, D. S., Kennan, K., & Vondra, J. I. (1994). Developmental precursors of externalizing behavior: Ages 1 to 3. *Developmental Psychology, 30,* 355–364.

Shaw, R., Ryst, E., & Steiner, H. (1996). Temperament as a correlate of adolescent defense mechanisms. *Child Psychiatry & Human Development, 27,* 105–114.

Shelton, B. A., & John, D. (1993). Ethnicity, race, and difference: A comparison of White, Black, and Hispanic men's household labor time. In J. C. Hood (Ed.), *Men, work, and family* (pp. 131–150). Newbury Park, CA: Sage.

Sher, K., & Gotham, H. (1999). Pathological alcohol involvement: A developmental disorder of young adulthood. *Development & Psychopathology, 11,* 933–956.

Shimonaka, Y., Nakazato, K., Kawaai, C., & Sato, S. (1997). Androgyny and successful adaptation across the life span among Japanese adults. *Journal of Genetic Psychology, 158,* 389–400.

Shiner, R. (2000). Linking childhood personality with adaptation: Evidence for continuity and change across time into late adolescence. *Journal of Personality & Social Psychology, 78,* 310–325.

Shneidman, E. S. (1980). *Voices of death.* New York: Harper & Row.

Shneidman, E. S. (1983). *Deaths of man.* New York: Jason Aronson.

Shock, N. W., Greulich, R. C., Andres, R., Arenberg, D., Costa, P. T., Jr., Lakatta, E. G., & Tobin, J. D. (1984). *Normal human aging: The Baltimore Longitudinal Study of Aging.* NIH Publication No. 84–2450, U.S. Department of Health and Human Services, National Institute on Aging. Washington, DC: U.S. Government Printing Office.

Shoda, Y., Mischel, W., & Peake, P. (1990). Predicting adolescent cognitive and self-regulatory competencies from preschool delay of gratification. *Developmental Psychology, 26,* 978–986.

Shonkoff, J. P. (1984). The biological substrate and physical health in middle childhood. In W. A. Collins (Ed.), *Development during middle childhood: The years from six to twelve* (pp. 24–69). Washington, DC: National Academy Press.

Shore, C. M. (1995). *Individual differences in language development.* Thousand Oaks, CA: Sage.

Shu, H., Anderson, R., & Wu, N. (2000). Phonetic awareness: Knowledge of orthography-phonology relationships in the character acquisition of Chinese children. *Journal of Educational Psychology, 92,* 56–62.

Sicotte, C., & Stemberger, R. (1999). Do children with PDDNOS have a theory of mind? *Journal of Autism & Developmental Disorders, 29,* 225–233.

Siegal, M. (1987). Are sons and daughters treated more differently by fathers than by mothers? *Developmental Review, 7,* 183–209.

Siegler, I. C. (1983). Psychological aspects of the Duke Longitudinal Studies. In K. W. Schaie (Ed.), *Longitudinal studies of adult psychological development* (pp. 136–190). New York: Guilford Press.

Siegler, I. C., McCarty, S. M., & Logue, P. E. (1982). Wechsler memory scale scores, selective attrition, and distance from death. *Journal of Gerontology, 37,* 176–181.

Siegler, R. S. (1976). Three aspects of cognitive development. *Cognitive Psychology, 8,* 431–520.

Siegler, R. S. (1978). The origins of scientific reasoning. In R. S. Siegler (Ed.), *Children's thinking: What develops?* (pp. 109–150). Hillsdale, NJ: Erlbaum.

Siegler, R. S. (1981). Developmental sequences within and between concepts. *Monographs of the Society for Research in Child Development, 46* (2, Serial No. 189).

Siegler, R. S. (1994). Cognitive variability: A key to understanding cognitive development. *Current Directions in Psychological Science, 3,* 1–5.

Sigman, M., Neumann, C., Carter, E., Cattle, D. J., D'Souza, S., & Bwibo, N. (1988). Home interactions and the development of Embu toddlers in Kenya. *Child Development, 59,* 1251–1261.

Silbereisen, R. K., & Kracke, B. (1993). Variations in maturational timing and adjustment in adolescence. In S. Jackson & H. Rodrigues-Tomé (Eds.), *Adolescence and its social worlds* (pp. 67–94). Hove, England: Erlbaum.

Silverstein, M., & Long, J. (1998). Trajectories of grandparents' perceived solidarity with adult grandchildren: A growth curve analysis over 23 years. *Journal of Marriage & the Family, 60,* 912–923.

Simkin, S., Hawton, K., Whitehead, L., Fagg, J., & Eagle, M. (1995). A study of the effects of television drama portrayal of paracetamol self-poisoning. *British Journal of Psychiatry, 167,* 754–759.

Simoneau, G. G., & Liebowitz, H. W. (1996). Posture, gait, and falls. In J. E. Birren & K. W. Schaie (Eds.), *Handbook of the psychology of aging* (4th ed.) (pp. 204–217). San Diego, CA: Academic Press.

Simons, R. L., Robertson, J. F., & Downs, W. R. (1989). The nature of the association between parental rejection and delinquent behavior. *Journal of Youth and Adolescence, 18,* 297–309.

Simons-Morton, B., Crump, A., Haynie, D., Saylor, K., Eitel, P., & Yu, K. (1999). Psychosocial, school, and parent factors associated with recent smoking among early-adolescent boys and girls. *Preventive Medicine, 28,* 138–148.

Simonton, D. (2000). Creativity: Cognitive, personal, developmental, and social aspects. *American Psychologist, 55,* 151–158.

Simonton, D. K. (1988). Age and outstanding achievement: What do we know after a century of research? *Psychological Bulletin, 104,* 251–267.

Simonton, D. K. (1991). Career landmarks in science: Individual differences and interdisciplinary contrasts. *Developmental Psychology, 27,* 119–130.

Sims, M., Hutchins, T., & Taylor, M. (1997). Conflict as social interaction: Building relationship skills in child care settings. *Child & Youth Care Forum, 26,* 247–260.

Singer, D., & Hunter, M. (1999). The experience of premature menopause: A thematic discourse analysis. *Journal of Reproductive & Infant Psychology, 17,* 63–81.

Singh, S., & Darroch, J. (2000). Adolescent pregnancy and childbearing: Levels and trends in industrialized countries. *Family Planning Perspectives, 32,* 14–23.

Skaalvik, E., & Valas, H. (1999). Relations among achievement, self-concept and motivation in mathematics and language arts: A longitudinal study. *Journal of Experimental Education, 67,* 135–149.

Skinner, B. F. (1953). *Science and human behavior.* New York: Macmillan.

Skinner, B. F. (1980). The experimental analysis of operant behavior: A history. In R. W. Riebes & K. Salzinger (Eds.), *Psychology: Theoretical-historical perspectives.* New York: Academic Press.

Skoe, E., Hansen, K., Morch, W., Bakke, I., Hoffman, T., Larsen, B., & Aasheim, M. (1999). Care-based moral reasoning in Norwegian and Canadian early adolescents: A cross-national comparison. *Journal of Early Adolescence, 19,* 280–291.

Slaby, R. G., & Frey, K. S. (1975). Development of gender constancy and selective attention to same-sex models. *Child Development, 46,* 849–856.

Slater, A. (1995). Individual differences in infancy and later IQ. *Journal of Child Psychology and Psychiatry, 36,* 69–112.

Slaven, L., & Lee, C. (1998). A cross-sectional survey of menopausal status, symptoms and psychological distress in a community sample of Australian women. *Journal of Health Psychology, 3,* 117–123.

Slobin, D. I. (1985). Introduction: Why study acquisition crosslinguistically? In D. I. Slobin (Ed.), *The crosslinguistic study of language acquisition: Vol. 1. The data* (pp. 3–24). Hillsdale, NJ: Erlbaum.

Slobounov, S., Moss, S., Slobounova, E., & Newell, K. (1998). Aging and time to instability in posture. *Journals of Gerontology: Series A: Biological Sciences & Medical Sciences, 53A,* B71–B78.

Small, S. A., & Luster, T. (1994). Adolescent sexual activity: An ecological, risk-factor approach. *Journal of Marriage and the Family, 56,* 181–192.

Smeeding, T. M. (1990). Economic status of the elderly. In R. H. Binstock & L. K. George (Eds.), *Handbook of aging and the social sciences* (3rd ed.) (pp. 362–381). San Diego, CA: Academic Press.

Smetana, J. G. (1990). Morality and conduct disorders. In M. Lewis & S. M. Miller (Eds.), *Handbook of developmental psychopathology* (pp. 157–180). New York: Plenum.

Smetana, J. G., Killen, M., & Turiel, E. (1991). Children's reasoning about interpersonal and moral conflicts. *Child Development, 62,* 629–644.

Smetana, J., Schlagman, N., & Adams, P. (1993). Preschool children's judgments about hypothetical and actual transgressions. *Child Development, 64,* 202–214.

Smith, C., Umberger, G., Manning, E., Sleven, J., Wekstein, D., Schmitt, F., Markesbery, W., & Zhang, Z. (1999). Critical decline in fine motor hand movements in human aging. *Neurology, 53,* 1458–1461.

Smith, E. L. (1982). Exercise for prevention of osteoporosis: A review. *Physician and Sportsmedicine, 10,* 72–83.

Smith, M., Sharit, J., & Czaja, S. (1999). Aging, motor control, and the performance of computer mouse tasks. *Human Factors, 41,* 389–396.

Smith, S., Howard, J., & Monroe, A. (1998). An analysis of child behavior problems in adoptions in difficulty. *Journal of Social Service Research, 24,* 61–84.

Smock, P. J. (1993). The economic costs of marital disruption for young women over the past two decades. *Demography, 30,* 353–371.

Smoll, F. L., & Schutz, R. W. (1990). Quantifying gender differences in physical performance: A developmental perspective. *Developmental Psychology, 26,* 360–369.

Snarey, J. R. (1985). Cross-cultural universality of social-moral development: A critical review of Kohlbergian research. *Psychological Bulletin, 97,* 202–232.

Snarey, J. R., Reimer, J., & Kohlberg, L. (1985). Development of social-moral reasoning among kibbutz adolescents: A longitudinal cross-sectional study. *Developmental Psychology, 21,* 3–17.

Snarey, J., Son, L., Kuehne, V. S., Hauser, S., & Vaillant, G. (1987). The role of parenting in men's psychosocial development: A longitudinal study of early adulthood infertility and midlife generativity. *Developmental Psychology, 23,* 593–603.

Snyder, C. (1997). Unique invulnerability: A classroom demonstration in estimating personal mortality. *Teaching of Psychology, 24,* 197–199.

Soken, N., & Pick. A. (1999). Infants' perception of dynamic affective expressions: Do infants distinguish specific expressions? *Child Development, 70,* 1275–1282.

Solano, L., Costa, M., Salvati, S., Coda, R., Aiuti, F., Mezzaroma, I., & Bertini, M. (1993). Psychosocial factors and clinical evolution in HIV–1 infection: A longitudinal study. *Journal of Psychosomatic Research, 37,* 39–51.

Soldo, B. J., Wolf, D. A., & Agree, E. M. (1990). Family, households, and care arrangements of frail older women: A structural analysis. *Journals of Gerontology: Social Sciences, 45,* S238–249.

Somers, M. D. (1993). A comparison of voluntarily childfree adults and parents. *Journal of Marriage and the Family, 55,* 643–650.

Sonneck, G., Etzersdorfer, E., & Nagel-Kuess, S. (1992). Subway suicide in Vienna (1980–1990): A contribution to the imitation effect in suicidal behavior. In P. Crepet, G. Ferrari, S. Platt, & M. Bellini (Eds.), *Suicidal behavior in Europe: Recent research findings.* Rome: Libbey.

Sophian, C. (1995). Representation and reasoning in early numerical development: Counting, conservation, and comparisons between sets. *Child Development, 66,* 559–577.

Sørensen, A. (1983). Women's employment patterns after marriage. *Journal of Marriage and the Family, 45,* 311–321.

Sorensen, E. (1997). A national profile of nonresident fathers and their ability to pay child support. *Journal of Marriage & the Family, 59,* 785–797.

Sorlie, P. D., Backlund, E., & Keller, J. B. (1995). U.S. mortality by economic, demographic, and social characteristics: The National Longitudinal Mortality Study. *American Journal of Public Health, 85,* 949–956.

Sotelo, M., & Sangrador, J. (1997). Psychological aspects of political tolerance among adolescents. *Psychological Reports, 81,* 1279–1288.

Sotelo, M., & Sangrador, J. (1999). Correlations of self-ratings of attitude towards violent groups with measures of personality, self-esteem, and moral reasoning. *Psychological Reports, 84,* 558–560.

Spanier, G. B., & Furstenberg, F. F., Jr. (1987). Remarriage and reconstituted families. In M. B. Sussman & S. K. Steinmetz (Eds.), *Handbook of marriage and the family* (pp. 419–434). New York: Plenum.

Sparrow, P. R., & Davies, D. R. (1988). Effects of age, tenure, training, and job complexity on technical performance. *Psychology and Aging, 3,* 307–314.

Speece, M. W., & Brent, S. B. (1984). Children's understanding of death: A review of three components of a death concept. *Child Development, 55,* 1671–1686.

Speece, M. W., & Brent, S. B. (1992). The acquisition of a mature understanding of three components of the concept of death. *Death Studies, 16,* 211–229.

Spelke, E. S. (1991). Physical knowledge in infancy: Reflections on Piaget's theory. In S. Carey & R. Gelman (Eds.), *The epigenesis of mind. Essays on biology and cognition* (pp. 133–169). Hillsdale, NJ: Erlbaum.

Spence, J. T., & Helmreich, R. L. (1978). *Masculinity and femininity.* Austin: University of Texas Press.

Spencer, M. B., & Dornbusch, S. M. (1990). Challenges in studying minority youth. In S. S. Feldman & G. R. Elliott (Eds.), *At the threshold: The developing adolescent* (pp. 123–146). Cambridge, MA: Harvard University Press.

Spenner, K. I. (1988). Occupations, work settings and the course of adult development: Tracing the implications of select historical changes. In P. B. Baltes, D. L. Featherman, & R. M. Lerner (Eds.), *Life-span development and behavior* (Vol. 9) (pp. 244–288). Hillsdale, NJ: Erlbaum.

Spiegel, D., Bloom, J. R., Kraemer, H. C., & Gottheil, E. (1989). Effect of psychosocial treatment on survival of patients with metastatic breast cancer. *Lancet* (October 14), 888–901.

Spiers, P. S., & Guntheroth, W. G. (1994). Recommendations to avoid the prone sleeping position and recent statistics for Sudden Infant Death Syndrome in the United States. *Archives of Pediatric and Adolescent Medicine, 148,* 141–146.

Spitze, G. (1988). Women's employment and family relations: A review. *Journal of Marriage and the Family, 50,* 595–618.

Spitze, G., & Logan, J. (1990). More evidence on women (and men) in the middle. *Research on Aging, 12,* 182–198.

Sprang, G., & McNeil, J. (1998). Post-homicide reactions: Grief, mourning and post-traumatic stress disorder following a drunk driving fatality. *Omega: Journal of Death & Dying, 37,* 41–58.

Spreen, O., Risser, A., & Edgell, D. (1995). *Developmental Neuropsychology.* New York: Oxford University Press.

Sroufe, L. A., Carlson, E., & Schulman, S. (1993). Individuals in relationships: Development from infancy through adolescence. In D. C. Funder, R. D. Parke, C. Tomlinson-Keasey, & K. Widaman (Eds.), *Studying lives through time: Personality and development* (pp. 315–342). Washington, DC: American Psychological Association.

Stack, S. (1992a). The effect of divorce on suicide in Finland: A time series analysis. *Journal of Marriage and the Family, 54,* 636–642.

Stack, S. (1992b). The effect of divorce on suicide in Japan: A time series analysis, 1950–1980. *Journal of Marriage and the Family, 54,* 327–334.

Stack, S., & Wasserman, I. (1993). Marital status, alcohol consumption, and suicide: An analysis of national data. *Journal of Marriage and the Family, 55,* 1018–1024.

Stadel, B. V., & Weiss, N. S. (1975). Characteristics of menopausal women: A survey of King and Pierce Counties in Washington, 1973–74. *American Journal of Epidemiology, 102,* 209–216.

Stambrook, M., & Parker, K. C. H. (1987). The development of the concept of death in childhood: A review of the literature. *Merrill-Palmer Quarterly, 33,* 133–158.

Stampfer, M. J., Colditz, G. A., Willett, W. C., Manson, J. E. Rosner, B., Speizer, F. E., & Hennekens, C. H. (1991). Postmenopausal estrogen therapy and cardiovascular disease: Ten-year follow-up from the Nurses' Health Study. *New England Journal of Medicine, 325,* 756–762.

Stampfer, M. J., Hennekins, C. H., Manson, J. E., Colditz, G. A., Rosner, B., & Willett, W. C. (1993). Vitamin E consumption and the risk of coronary disease in women. *New England Journal of Medicine, 328,* 1444–1449.

Stanford, E. P., Happersett, C. J., Morton, D. J., Molgaard, C. A., & Peddecord, K. M. (1991). Early retirement and functional impairment from a multiethnic perspective. *Research on Aging, 13,* 5–38.

Stanton, A. L., & Danoff-Burg, S. (1995). Selected issues in women's reproductive health: Psychological perspectives. In A. L. Stanton & S. J. Gallant (Eds.), *The psychology of women's health* (pp. 216–305). Washington, DC: American Psychological Association.

Starfield, B. (1991). Childhood morbidity: Comparisons, clusters, and trends. *Pediatrics, 88,* 519–526.

Stattin, H., & Klackenberg-Larsson, I. (1993). Early language and intelligence development and their relationship to future criminal behavior. *Journal of Abnormal Psychology, 102,* 369–378.

Steel, Z., & Blaszczynski, A. (1998). Impulsivity, personality disorders and pathological gambling severity. *Addiction, 93,* 895–905.

Steele, J., & Mayes, S. (1995). Handedness and directional asymmetry in the long bones of the human upper limb. *International Journal of Osteoarchaeology, 5,* 39–49.

Steffens, D., Artigues, D., Ornstein, K., & Krishnan, K. (1997). A review of racial differences in geriatric depression: Implications for care and clinical research. *Journal of the National Medical Association, 89,* 731–736.

Stein, C., Wemmerus, V., Ward, M., Gaines, M., Freeberg, A., & Jewell, T. (1998). "Because they're my parents": An intergenerational study of felt obligation and parental caregiving. *Journal of Marriage & the Family, 60,* 611–622.

Stein, K., Roeser, R., & Markus, H. (1998). Self-schemas and possible selves as predictors and outcomes of risky behaviors in adolescents. *Nursing Research, 47,* 96–106.

Steinbach, U. (1992). Social networks, institutionalization, and mortality among elderly people in the United States. *Journals of Gerontology: Social Sciences, 47,* S183–190.

Steinberg, L. (1986). Latchkey children and susceptibility to peer pressure: An ecological analysis. *Developmental Psychology, 22,* 433–439.

Steinberg, L. (1988). Reciprocal relation between parent-child distance and pubertal maturation. *Developmental Psychology, 24,* 122–128.

Steinberg, L. (1990). Autonomy, conflict and harmony in the parent-adolescent relationship. In S. S. Feldman & G. R. Elliott (Eds.), *At the threshold: The developing adolescent* (pp. 255–276). Cambridge, MA: Harvard University Press.

Steinberg, L., Darling, N. E., Fletcher, A. C., Brown, B. B., & Dornbusch, S. M. (1995). Authoritative parenting and adolescent adjustment: An ecological journey. In P. Moen, G. H. Elder, Jr., & K. Lüscher (Eds.), *Examining lives in context: Perspectives on the ecology of human development* (pp. 423–466). Washington, DC: American Psychological Association.

Steinberg, L., & Dornbusch, S. M. (1991). Negative correlates of part-time employment during adolescence: Replication and elaboration. *Developmental Psychology, 27,* 304–313.

Steinberg, L., Elmen, J. D., & Mounts, N. S. (1989). Authoritative parenting, psychosocial maturity, and academic success among adolescents. *Child Development, 60,* 1424–1436.

Steinberg, L., Fegley, S., & Dornbusch, S. M. (1993). Negative impact of part-time work on adolescent adjustment: Evidence from a longitudinal study. *Developmental Psychology, 29,* 171–180.

Steinberg, L., Fletcher, A., & Darling, N. (1994). Parental monitoring and peer influences on adolescent substance use. *Pediatrics, 93,* 1060–1064.

Steinberg, L., Lamborn, S. D., Darling, N., Mounts, N. S., & Dornbusch, S. M. (1994). Over-time changes in adjustment and competence among adolescents from authoritative, authoritarian, indulgent, and neglectful families. *Child Development, 65,* 754–770.

Steinberg, L., Lamborn, S. D., Dornbusch, S. M., & Darling, N. (1992). Impact of parenting practices on adolescent achievement: Authoritative parenting, school involvement, and encouragement to succeed. *Child Development, 63,* 1266–1281.

Steinberg, L., Mounts, N. S., Lamborn, S. D., & Dornbusch, S. D. (1991). Authoritative parenting and adolescent adjustment across varied ecological niches. *Journal of Research on Adolescence, 1,* 19–36.

Sternberg, R. (1988). *The triarchic mind: A new theory of intelligence.* New York: Viking Press.

Sternberg, R. J. (1987). Liking versus loving: A comparative evaluation of theories. *Psychological Bulletin, 102,* 331–345.

Sternberg, R. J. (1990). Wisdom and its relations to intelligence and creativity. In R. J. Sternberg (Ed.), *Wisdom: Its nature, origins, and development* (pp. 142–159). Cambridge, England: Cambridge University Press.

Sternberg, R. J., & Wagner, R. K. (1993). The g-ocentric view of intelligence and job performance is wrong. *Current Directions in Psychological Science, 2,* 1–5.

Sternberg, R., Wagner, R., Williams, W., & Horvath, J. (1995). Testing common sense. *American Psychologist, 50,* 912–927.

Stevens, J., & Choo, K. (1998). Temperature sensitivity of the body surface over the life span. *Somatosensory & Motor Research, 15,* 13–28.

Stevenson, H. (1994). Moving away from stereotypes and preconceptions: Students and their education in East Asia and the United States. In P. M. Greenfield & R. R. Cocking (Eds.), *Cross-cultural roots of minority child development* (pp. 315–322). Hillsdale, NJ: Erlbaum.

Stevenson, H. W., & Lee, S. (1990). Contexts of achievement: A study of American, Chinese, and Japanese children. *Monographs of the Society for Research in Child Development, 55* (1–2, Serial No. 221).

Stevenson, H. W., Lee, S., Chen, C., Lummis, M., Stigler, J., Fan, L., & Ge, F. (1990). Mathematics achievement of children in China and the United States. *Child Development, 61,* 1053–1066.

Steward, M. S. (1993). Understanding children's memories of medical procedures: "He didn't touch me and it didn't hurt!" In C. A. Nelson (Ed.), *The Minnesota Symposia on Child Psychology* (Vol. 26) (pp. 171–225). Hillsdale, NJ: Erlbaum.

Stewart, A., & Ostrove, J. (1998). Women's personality in middle age: Gender, history, and midcourse corrections. *American Psychologist, 53,* 1185–1194.

Stewart, R. B., Beilfuss, M. L., & Verbrugge, K. M. (1995, March). *That was then, this is now: An empirical typology of adult sibling relationships.* Paper presented at the biennial meetings of the Society for Research in Child Development, Indianapolis, IN.

Stewart, S., Pearson, S., Luke, C., & Horowitz, J. (1998). Effects of home-based intervention on unplanned readmissions and out-of-hospital deaths. *Journal of the American Geriatrics Society, 46,* 174–180.

Stigler, J. W., Lee, S., & Stevenson, H. W. (1987). Mathematics classrooms in Japan, Taiwan, and the United States. *Child Development, 58,* 1272–1285.

Stigler, J. W., & Stevenson, H. W. (1991). How Asian teachers polish each lesson to perfection. *American Educator* (Spring), 12–20, 43–47.

Stinner, W. F., Byun, Y., & Paita, L. (1990). Disability and living arrangements among elderly American men. *Research on Aging, 12,* 339–363.

Stipek, D., Gralinski, J., & Kopp, C. (1990). Self-concept development in the toddler years. *Developmental Psychology, 26,* 972–977.

Stockman, K., & Budd, K. (1997). Directions for intervention with adolescent mothers in substitute care. *Families in Society, 78,* 617–623.

Stoller, E. P., Forster, L. E., & Duniho, T. S. (1992). Systems of parent care within sibling networks. *Research on Aging, 14,* 28–49.

Stones, M. J., & Kozma, A. (1996). Activity, exercise, and behavior. In J. E. Birren & K. W. Schaie (Eds.), *Handbook of the psychology of aging* (4th ed.) (pp. 338–352). San Diego, CA: Academic Press.

Stormshak, E., Bierman, K., McMahon, R., Lengua, L., et al. (2000). Parenting practices and child disruptive behavior problems in early elementary school. *Journal of Clinical Child Psychology, 29,* 17–29.

Stoutjesdyk, D., & Jevne, R. (1993). Eating disorders among high performance athletes. *Journal of Youth and Adolescence, 22,* 271–282.

Strawbridge, W. J., Camacho, T. C., Cohen, R. D., & Kaplan, G. A. (1993). Gender differences in factors associated with change in physical functioning in old age: A 6-year longitudinal study. *The Gerontologist, 33,* 603–609.

Strayer, F. F. (1980). Social ecology of the preschool peer group. In A. Collins (Ed.), *Minnesota symposia on child psychology* (Vol. 13) (pp. 165–196). Hillsdale, NJ: Erlbaum.

Streissguth, A. P., Aase, J. M., Clarren, S. K., Randels, S. P., LaDue, R. A., & Smith, D. F. (1991). Fetal alcohol syndrome in adolescents and adults. *Journal of the American Medical Association, 265,* 1961–1967.

Streissguth, A. P., Barr, H. M., & Sampson, P. D. (1990). Moderate prenatal alcohol exposure: Effects on child IQ and learning problems at age $7\frac{1}{2}$ years. *Alcoholism. Clinical and Experimental Research, 14,* 662–669.

Streissguth, A. P., Landesman-Dwyer, S., Martin, J. C., & Smith, D. W. (1980). Teratogenic effects of alcohol in humans and laboratory animals. *Science, 209,* 353–361.

Streufert, S., Pogash, R., Piasecki, M., & Post, G. M. (1990). Age and management team performance. *Psychology and Aging, 5,* 551–559.

Striano, T., & Rochat, P. (1999). Developmental link between dyadic and triadic social competence in infancy. *British Journal of Developmental Psychology, 17,* 551–562.

Stringfield, S., & Teddlie, C. (1991). Observers as predictors of schools' multiyear outlier status on achievement tests. *The Elementary School Journal, 91,* 357–376.

Stroebe, M., van Son, M., Stroebe, W., Kleber, R., Schut, H., & van den Bout, J. (2000). On the classification and diagnosis of pathological grief. *Clinical Psychology Review, 20,* 57–75.

Stroebe, M. S., & Stroebe, W. (1993). The mortality of bereavement: A review. In M. S. Stroebe, W. Stroebe, & R. O. Hansson (Eds.), *Handbook of bereavement: Theory, research, and intervention* (pp. 175–195). Cambridge, England: Cambridge University Press.

Stroebe, W., & Stroebe, M. S. (1993). Determinants of adjustment to bereavement in younger widows and widowers. In M. S. Stroebe, W. Stroebe, & R. O. Hansson (Eds.), *Handbook of bereavement. Theory, research, and intervention* (pp. 208–226). Cambridge, England: Cambridge University Press.

Strom, R., & Strom, S. (1999). Establishing school volunteer programs. *Child & Youth Services, 20,* 175–188.

Students cite pregnancies as a reason to drop out (1994b, September 14). *New York Times,* p. B7.

Stull, D. E., & Hatch, L. R. (1984). Unravelling the effects of multiple life changes. *Research on Aging, 6,* 560–571.

Stunkard, A. J., Harris, J. R., Pedersen, N. L., & McClearn, G. E. (1990). The body-mass index of twins who have been reared apart. *New England Journal of Medicine, 322,* 1483–1487.

Sue, S., & Okazaki, S. (1990). Asian-American educational achievements: A phenomenon in search of an explanation. *American Psychologist, 45,* 913–920.

Sugisawa, H., Liang, J., & Liu, X. (1994). Social networks, social support, and mortality among older people in Japan. *Journals of Gerontology: Social Sciences, 49,* S3–13.

Sulkes, S. (1998). Developmental and behavioral pediatrics. In R. Behrman & R. Kliegman (Eds.), *Nelson essentials of pediatrics* (3rd ed., pp. 1–55). Philadelphia: W. B. Saunders.

Sullivan, K., & Bradbury, T. (1997). Are premarital prevention programs reaching couples at risk for marital dysfunction? *Journal of Consulting & Clinical Psychology, 65,* 24–30.

Sullivan, K., Zaitchik, D., & Tager-Flusberg, H. (1994). Preschoolers can attribute second-order beliefs. *Developmental Psychology, 30,* 395–402.

Sullivan, M., Ormel, J., Kempen, G., & Tymstra, T. (1998). Beliefs concerning death, dying, and hastening death among older, functionally impaired Dutch adults: A one-year longitudinal study. *Journal of the American Geriatrics Society, 46,* 1251–1257.

Sullivan, T., & Thompson, K. (1994). *Social problems.* New York: Macmillan.

Super, D. E. (1971). A theory of vocational development. In H. J. Peters & J. C. Hansen (Eds.), *Vocational guidance and career development* (pp. 111–122). New York: Macmillan.

Super, D. E. (1986). Life career roles: Self-realization in work and leisure. In D. T. H. &. Associates (Eds.), *Career development in organizations* (pp. 95–119). San Francisco: Jossey-Bass.

Susman, E. J., Inoff-Germain, G., Nottelmann, E. D., Loriaux, D. L., Cutler, G. B., Jr., & Chrousos, G. P. (1987). Hormones, emotional dispositions, and aggressive attributes in young adolescents. *Child Development, 58,* 1114–1134.

Susser, E., & Lin, S. (1992). Schizophrenia after prenatal exposure to the Dutch hunger winter of 1944–45. *Archives of General Psychiatry, 49,* 983–988.

Svrakic, N., Svrakic, D., & Cloninger, C. (1996). A general quantitative theory of personality development: Fundamentals of a self-organizing psychobiological complex. *Development & Psychopathology, 8,* 247–272.

Swaim, K., & Bracken, B. (1997). Global and domain-specific self-concepts of a matched sample of adolescent runaways and nonrunaways. *Journal of Clinical Child Psychology, 26,* 397–403.

Swedo, S. E., Rettew, D. C., Kuppenheimer, M., Lum, D., Dolan, S., & Goldberger, E. (1991). Can adolescent suicide attempters be distinguished from at-risk adolescents? *Pediatrics, 88,* 620–629.

Swendsen, J., & Mazure, C. (2000). Life stress as a risk factor for postpartum depression: Current research and methodological issues. *Clinical Psychology, 7,* 17–31.

Swensen, C. H., Eskew, R. W., & Kohlhepp, K. A. (1981). Stage of family life cycle, ego development, and the marriage relationship. *Journal of Marriage and the Family, 43,* 841–853.

Syme, S. L. (1990). Control and health: An epidemiological perspective. In J. Rodin, C. Schooler, & K. W. Schaie (Eds.), *Self directedness: Cause and effects throughout the life course* (pp. 213–229). Hillsdale, NJ: Erlbaum.

Tait, M., Padgett, M. Y., & Baldwin, T. T. (1989). Job and life satisfaction: A reevaluation of the strength of the relationship and gender effects as a function of the date of the study. *Journal of Applied Psychology, 74,* 502–507.

Takahashi, K., Tamura, J., & Tokoro, M. (1997). Patterns of social relationships and psychological well-being among the elderly. *International Journal of Behavioral Development, 21*, 417–430.

Takata, T. (1999). Development process of independent and interdependent self-construal in Japanese culture: Cross-cultural and cross-sectional analyses. *Japanese Journal of Educational Psychology, 47*, 480–489.

Takei, Y., & Dubas, J. S. (1993). Academic achievement among early adolescents: Social and cultural diversity. In R. M. Lerner (Ed.), *Early adolescence: Perspectives on research, policy, and intervention* (pp. 175–190). Hillsdale, NJ: Erlbaum.

Talan, J. (1998, October 28). Possible genetic link found for right-handedness, not for left. *Seattle Times.*

Talbott, M. (1998). Older widows' attitudes towards men and remarriage. *Journal of Aging Studies, 12*, 429–449.

Tamir, L. M. (1982). *Men in their forties: The transition to middle age.* New York: Springer.

Tanner, J. M. (1978). *Fetus into man: Physical growth from conception to maturity.* Cambridge, MA: Harvard University Press.

Tanner, J. (1990). *Fetus into man: Physical growth from conception to maturity.* Cambridge, MA: Harvard University Press.

Tanner, J. M., Hughes, P. C. R., & Whitehouse, R. H. (1981). Radiographically determined widths of bone, muscle and fat in the upper arm and calf from 3–18 years. *Annals of Human Biology, 8*, 495–517.

Tan-Niam, C., Wood, D.,& O'Malley, C. (1998). A cross-cultural perspective on children's theories of mind and social interaction. *Early Child Development & Care, 144*, 55–67.

Tapanya, S., Nicki, R., & Jarusawad, O. (1997). Worry and intrinsic/extrinsic religious orientation among Buddhist (Thai) and Christian (Canadian) elderly persons. *International Journal of Aging and Human Development, 44*, 73–83.

Tardif, T., & Wellman, H. (2000). Acquisition of mental state language in Mandarin- and Cantonese-speaking children. *Developmental Psychology, 36*, 25–43.

Tarter, R., Panzak, G., Switala, J., Lu, S., et al. (1997). Isokinetic muscle strength and its association with neuropsychological capacity in cirrhotic alcoholics. *Alcoholism: Clinical & Experimental Research, 21*, 191–196.

Taylor, J. A., & Danderson, M. (1995). A reexamination of the risk factors for the sudden infant death syndrome. *Journal of Pediatrics, 126*, 887–891.

Taylor, M. (2000). The influence of self-efficacy on alcohol use among American Indians. *Cultural Diversity & Ethnic Minority Psychology, 6*, 152–167.

Taylor, M., Cartwright, B. S., & Carlson, S. M. (1993). A developmental investigation of children's imaginary companions. *Developmental Psychology, 29*, 276–285.

Taylor, P. J., & Kopelman, M. D. (1984). Amnesia for criminal offenses. *Psychological Medicine, 14*, 481–588.

Taylor, R. D., & Roberts, D. (1995). Kinship support and maternal and adolescent well-being in economically disadvantaged African-American families. *Child Development, 66*, 1585–1597.

Taylor, R. J., Chatters, L. M., Tucker, M. B., & Lewis, E. (1990). Developments in research on black families: A decade review. *Journal of Marriage and the Family, 52*, 993–1014.

Taylor, W., Ayars, C., Gladney, A., Peters, R., Roy, J., Prokhorov, A., Chamberlain, R., & Gritz, E. (1999). Beliefs about smoking among adolescents: Gender and ethnic differences. *Journal of Child & Adolescent Substance Abuse, 8*, 37–54.

Temoshok, L. (1987). Personality, coping style, emotion and cancer: Towards an integrative model. *Cancer Surveys, 6*, 545–567.

Terman, L. (1916). *The measurement of intelligence.* Boston: Houghton Mifflin.

Terman, L., & Merrill, M. A. (1937). *Measuring intelligence: A guide to the administration of the new revised Stanford-Binet tests.* Boston: Houghton Mifflin.

Tershakovec, A. & Stallings, V. (1998). Pediatric nutrition and nutritional disorders. In R. Behrman & R. Kliegman (Eds.), *Nelson essentials of pediatrics (third edition).* Philadelphia: W. B. Saunders.

Teti, D. M., Gelfand, D. M., Messinger, D. S., & Isabella, R. (1995). Maternal depression and the quality of early attachment: An examination of infants, preschoolers, and their mothers. *Developmental Psychology, 31*, 364–376.

Tettamanzi, D. (1998, September 30). Anthropological and ethical thoughts on whether domestic partnerships should have same legal status as the family. *L'Osservatore Romano/English Edition,* p. 9.

Thal, D., & Bates, E. (1990). Continuity and variation in early language development. In J. Colombo & J. Fagen (Eds.), *Individual differences in infancy: Reliability, stability, prediction* (pp. 359–385). Hillsdale, NJ: Erlbaum.

Tharenou, P. (1999). Is there a link between family structures and women's and men's managerial career advancement? *Journal of Organizational Behavior, 20*, 837–863.

Tharp, R. G., & Gallimore, R. (1988). *Rousing minds to life.* New York: Cambridge University Press.

Thelen, E. (1995). Motor development: A new synthesis. *American Psychologist, 50*, 79–95.

Thelen, E., & Adolph, K. E. (1992). Arnold L. Gesell: The paradox of nature and nurture. *Developmental Psychology, 28*, 368–380.

Theriault, J. (1998). Assessing intimacy with the best friend and the sexual partner during adolescence: The PAIR-M inventory. *Journal of Psychology, 132*, 493–506.

Thomas, A., & Chess, S. (1977). *Temperament and development.* New York: Brunner/Mazel.

Thomas, J., Yan, J., & Stelmach, G. (2000). Movement substructures change as a function of practice in children and adults. *Journal of Experimental Child Psychology, 75*, 228–244.

Thomas, M. (1996). *Comparing theories of child development* (4th ed.). New York: Norton.

Thomas, R. M. (Ed.). (1990a). *The encyclopedia of human development and education: Theory, research, and studies.* Oxford, England: Pergamon Press.

Thomson, E., & Colella, U. (1992). Cohabitation and marital stability: Quality or commitment? *Journal of Marriage and the Family, 54*, 259–267.

Thorn, A., & Gathercole, S. (1999). Language-specific knowledge and short-term memory in bilingual and non-bilingual children. *Quarterly Journal of Experimental Psychology: Human Experimental Psychology, 52A*, 303–324.

Thorne, B. (1986). Girls and boys together...but mostly apart: Gender arrangements in elementary schools. In W. W. Hartup & Z. Rubin (Eds.), *Relationships and development* (pp. 167–184). Hillsdale, NJ: Erlbaum.

Thornton, W., Douglas, G., & Houghton, S. (1999). Transition through stages of smoking: The effect of gender and self-concept on smoking behavior. (1999). *Journal of Adolescent Health, 25*, 284–289.

Thorpe, M., Pittenger, D., & Reed, B. (1999). Cheating the researcher: A study of the relation between personality measures and self-reported cheating. *College Student Journal, 33*, 49–59.

Thorslund, M., & Lundberg, O. (1994). Health and inequalities among the oldest old. *Journal of Aging and Health, 6*, 51–69.

Thorson, J. A., & Powell, F. C. (1990). Meanings of death and intrinsic religiosity. *Journal of Clinical Psychology, 46*, 379–390.

Thorson, J. A., & Powell, F. C. (1992). A revised death anxiety scale. *Death Studies, 16*, 507–521.

Tice, R. R., & Setlow, R. B. (1985). DNA repair and replication in aging organisms and cells. In C. E. Finch & E. L. Schneider (Eds.), *Handbook of the biology of aging* (2nd ed.) (pp. 173–224). New York: Van Nostrand Reinhold.

Tiedemann, J. (2000). Parents' gender stereotypes and teachers' beliefs as predictors of children's concept of their mathematical ability in elementary school. *Journal of Educational Psychology, 92*, 144–151.

Tobin-Richards, M. H., Boxer, A. M., & Petersen, A. C. (1983). The psychological significance of pubertal change: Sex differences in perceptions of self during early adolescence. In J. Brooks-Gunn & A. C. Petersen (Eds.), *Girls at puberty. Biological and psychosocial perspectives* (pp. 127–154). New York: Plenum.

Todd, L. (1996). A computer-assisted expert system for clinical diagnosis of eating disorders: A potential tool for practitioners. *Professional Psychology: Research & Practice, 27*, 184–187.

Todd, R. D., Swarzenski, B., Rossi, P. G., & Visconti, P. (1995). Structural and functional development of the human brain. In D. Cicchetti & D. J. Cohen (Eds.), *Developmental psychopathology: Vol. 1. Theory and methods* (pp. 161–194). New York: Wiley.

Tokar, D., Fischer, A., & Subich, L. (1998). Personality and vocational behavior: A selective review of the literature, 1993–1997. *Journal of Vocational Behavior, 53,* 115–153.

Tolson, T., & Wilson, M. (1990). The impact of two- and three-generation black family structure on perceived family climate. *Child Development, 61,* 416–428.

Tomblin, J., Smith, E., & Zhang, X. (1997). Epidemiology of specific language impairment: Prenatal and perinatal risk factors. *Journal of Communication Disorders, 30,* 325–344.

Tomita, T., Ohta, Y., Ogawa, K., Sugiyama, H., Kagami, N., & Agari, I. (1997). Grief process and strategies of psychological helping: A review. *Japanese Journal of Counseling Science, 30,* 49–67.

Tomlinson-Keasey, C., Eisert, D. C., Kahle, L. R., Hardy-Brown, K., & Keasey, B. (1979). The structure of concrete operational thought. *Child Development, 50,* 1153–1163.

Torgerson, D., Thomas, R., Campbell, M., & Reid, D. (1997). Alcohol consumption and age of maternal menopause are associated with menopause onset. *Maturitas, 26,* 21–25.

Torgesen, J., Wagner, R., Rashotte, C., Rose, E., et al. (1999). Preventing reading failure in young children with phonological processing disabilities: Group and individual responses to instruction. *Journal of Educational Psychology, 91,* 594–603.

Torrey, E. (1992). *Freudian fraud: The malignant effect of Freud's theory on American thought and culture.* New York: HarperCollins.

Tortora, G., & Grabowski, S. (1993). *Principles of anatomy and physiology.* New York: HarperCollins.

Tracey, T. J., & Rounds, J. (1993). Evaluating Holland's and Gati's vocational-interest models: A structural meta-analysis. *Psychological Bulletin, 113,* 229–246.

Trainor, L., Clark, E., Huntley, A., & Adams, B. (1997). The acoustic basis of preferences for infant-directed singing. *Infant Behavior & Development, 20,* 383–396.

Trehub, S., Hill, D., & Kamenetsky, S. (1997). Parents' sung performances for infants. *Canadian Journal of Experimental Psychology, 51,* 385–396.

Trehub, S., Unyk, A., Kamenetsky, S., Hill, D., et al. (1997). Mothers' and fathers' singing to infants. *Developmental Psychology, 33,* 500–507.

Tremblay, R. E., Masse, L. C., Vitaro, F., & Dobkin, P. L. (1995). The impact of friends' deviant behavior on early onset of delinquency: Longitudinal data from 6 to 13 years of age. *Development and Psychopathology, 7,* 649–667.

Trivers, R. (1972). Parental investment and sexual selection. In B. Campbell (Ed.), *Sexual selection and the descent of man: 1871–1971* (pp. 136–179). Chicago: Aldine.

Troll, L. E. (1985). The contingencies of grandparenting. In V. L. Bengtson & J. F. Robertson (Eds.), *Grandparenthood* (pp. 135–150). Beverly Hills, CA: Sage.

Tronick, E. Z., Morelli, G. A., & Ivey, P. K. (1992). The Efe forager infant and toddler's pattern of social relationships: Multiple and simultaneous. *Developmental Psychology, 28,* 568–577.

Truluck, J., & Courtenay, B. (1999). Learning style preferences among older adults. *Educational Gerontology, 25,* 221–236.

Trusty, J. (1999). Effects of eighth-grade parental involvement on late adolescents' educational expectations. *Journal of Research & Development in Education, 32,* 224–233.

Tsang, P. (1998). Age, attention, expertise, and time-sharing performance. *Psychology & Aging, 13,* 323–347.

Tsitouras, P. D., & Bulat, T. (1995). The aging male reproductive system. *Endocrinology and Metabolism Clinics of North America, 24,* 297–315.

Tsuya, N. O., & Martin, L. G. (1992). Living arrangements of elderly Japanese and attitudes toward inheritance. *Journals of Gerontology: Social Sciences, 47,* S45–54.

Tunstall-Pedoe, H., & Smith, W. C. S. (1990). Cholesterol as a risk factor for coronary heart disease. *British Medical Bulletin, 46,* 1075–1087.

Turiel, E. (1983). *The development of social knowledge: Morality and convention.* New York: Cambridge University Press.

Twycross, R. G. (1996). Euthanasia: Going Dutch? *Journal of the Royal Society of Medicine, 89,* 61–63.

Udry, J. R., & Campbell, B. C. (1994). Getting started on sexual behavior. In A. S. Rossi (Ed.), *Sexuality across the life course* (pp. 187–208). Chicago: University of Chicago Press.

Uecker, A., & Nadel, L. (1996). Spatial locations gone awry: Object and spatial memory deficits in children with fetal alcohol syndrome. *Neuropsychologia, 34,* 209–223.

Uhlenberg, P., Cooney, T., & Boyd, R. (1990). Divorce for women after midlife. *Journals of Gerontology: Social Sciences, 45,* S3–11.

Umberson, D. (1992). Relationships between adult children and their parents: Psychological consequences for both generations. *Journal of Marriage and the Family, 54,* 664–674.

Umetsu, D. (1998). Immunology and allergy. In R. Behrman & R. Kleigman (Eds.), *Nelson essentials of pediatrics* (3rd ed.). Philadelphia: W. B. Saunders.

Underwood, M. (1997). Peer social status and children's understanding of the expression and control of positive and negative emotions. *Merrill-Palmer Quarterly, 43,* 610–634.

Underwood, M. K., Coie, J. D., & Herbsman, C. R. (1992). Display rules for anger and aggression in school-age children. *Child Development, 63,* 366–380.

Underwood, M. K., Kupersmidt, J. B., & Coie, J. D. (1996). Childhood peer sociometric status and aggression as predictors of adolescent childbearing. *Journal of Research on Adolescence, 6,* 201–224.

U.S. Bureau of the Census. (1984). *Statistical Abstract of the United States: 1984.* Washington, DC: U.S. Government Printing Office.

U.S. Bureau of the Census. (1990). *Statistical Abstract of the United States, 1990.* Washington, DC: U.S. Government Printing Office.

U.S. Bureau of the Census. (1992). *Statistical Abstract of the United States: 1992.* Washington, DC: U.S. Government Printing Office.

U.S. Bureau of the Census. (1994). *Statistical Abstract of the United States: 1994.* Washington, DC: U.S. Government Printing Office.

U.S. Bureau of the Census. (1995a). *Sixty-five plus in the United States.* Statistical Brief. Washington, DC: U.S. Government Printing Office.

U.S. Bureau of the Census. (1995b). *Statistical Abstract of the United States: 1995.* Washington, DC: U.S. Government Printing Office.

U.S. Bureau of the Census. (1996). *Statistical Abstract of the United States.* Washington, DC: U.S. Government Printing Office.

U.S. Bureau of the Census. (1997). *Statistical Abstract of the United States.* Washington, DC: U.S. Government Printing Office.

U.S. Bureau of the Census. (1998). *Statistical Abstract of the United States/1998.* Washington, DC: U.S. Government Printing Office.

U.S. Bureau of the Census. (1999). *Current Population Survey: March 1960 to 1999.* Washington, DC: U.S. Government Printing Office.

U.S. Department of Education. (1996). *Annual report to Congress on implementation of IDEA.* Washington, DC: U.S. Government Printing Office.

U.S. Department of Health and Human Services. (1997). *Are you a working teen? What you should know about safety and health on the job.* (Publication No. 97–132) Washington, DC: U.S. Government Printing Office.

U.S. Department of Health and Human Services. (1998a). *National initiative to eliminate racial and ethnic disparities in health: Cancer.* [Online report]. Retrieved October 11, 2000 from the World Wide Web: http:// www.raceandhealth.omhrc.gov

U.S. Department of Health and Human Services. (1998b). *National initiative to eliminate racial and ethnic disparities in health: Cardiovascular disease.* [Online report]. Retrieved October 11, 2000 from the World Wide Web: http:// www.raceandhealth.omhrc.gov

U.S. Department of Health and Human Services. (1998c). *National initiative to eliminate racial and ethnic disparities in health: Diabetes.* [Online report]. Retrieved October 11, 2000 from the World Wide Web: http:// www.raceandhealth.omhrc.gov

Uno, D., Florsheim, P., & Uchino, B. (1998). Psychosocial mechanisms underlying quality of parenting among Mexican-American and White adolescent mothers. *Journal of Youth & Adolescence, 27,* 585–605.

Updegraff, K., & Obeidallah, D. (1999). Young adolescents' patterns of involvement with siblings and friends. *Social Development, 8,* 52–69.

Upperman, P. U., & Church, A. T. (1995). Investigating Holland's typological theory with army occupational specialties. *Journal of Vocational Behavior, 47,* 61–75.

Urban, J., Carlson, E., Egeland, B., & Sroufe, L. A. (1991). Patterns of individual adaptation across childhood. *Development and Psychopathology, 3,* 445–460.

Urberg, K., Degirmencioglu, S., & Pilgrim, C. (1997). Close friend and group influence on adolescent cigarette smoking and alcohol use. *Developmental Psychology, 33*, 834–844.

Urberg, K., Degirmencioglu, S., & Tolson, J. (1998). Adolescent friendship selection and termination: The role of similarity. *Journal of Social & Personal Relationships, 15*, 703–710.

Urberg, K. A., Degirmencioglu, S. M., Tolson, J. M., & Halliday-Scher, K. (1995). The structure of adolescent peer networks. *Developmental Psychology, 31*, 540–547.

Urdan, T. (1997). Examining the relations among early adolescent students' goals and friends' orientation toward effort and achievement in school. *Contemporary Educational Psychology, 22*, 165–191.

Ushikubo, M. (1998). A study of factors facilitating and inhibiting the willingness of the institutionalized disabled elderly for rehabilitation: A United States–Japanese comparison. *Journal of Cross-Cultural Gerontology, 13*, 127–157.

Vachon, M. (1998). Psychosocial needs of patients and families. *Journal of Palliative Care, 14*, 49–56.

Vaeisaenen, L. (1998). Family grief and recovery process when a baby dies. *Psychiatria Fennica, 29*, 163–174.

Vaillant, G. E. (1975). Natural history of male psychological health: III. Empirical dimensions of mental health. *Archives of General Psychiatry, 32*, 420–426.

Vaillant, G. E. (1977). *Adaptation to life: How the best and brightest came of age.* Boston: Little, Brown.

Vaillant, G. E. (1991). The association of ancestral longevity with successful aging. *Journals of Gerontology: Psychological Sciences, 46*, P292–298.

Vaillant, G. E., & Vaillant, C. O. (1990). Natural history of male psychological health: XII. A 45-year study of predictors of successful aging at age 65. *American Journal of Psychiatry, 147*, 31–37.

Valdez-Menchaca, M. C., & Whitehurst, G. J. (1992). Accelerating language development through picture book reading: A systematic extension to Mexican day care. *Developmental Psychology, 28*, 1106–1114.

Valois, R., & Dunham, A. (1998). Association between employment and sexual risk-taking behaviors among public high school adolescents. *Journal of Child & Family Studies, 7*, 147–159.

Valois, R., Dunham, A., Jackson, K., & Waller, J. (1999). Association between employment and substance abuse behaviors among public high school adolescents. *Journal of Adolescent Health, 25*, 256–263.

van Balen, F. (1998). Development of IVF children. *Developmental Review, 18*, 30–46.

Van Boxtel, M., Paas, F., Houx, P., Adam, J., Teeken, J., & Jolles, J. (1997). Aerobic capacity and cognitive performance in a cross-sectional aging study. *Medicine & Science in Sports & Exercise, 29*, 1357–1365.

Vandell, D., & Ramanan, J. (1991). Children of the National Longitudinal Survey of Youth: Choices in after-school care and child development. *Developmental Psychology, 27*, 637–643.

Vandell, D., & Ramanan, J. (1992). Effects of early and recent maternal employment of children from low-income families. *Child Development, 63*, 938–949.

van den Boom, D. (1995). Do first-year intervention effects endure? Follow-up during toddlerhood of a sample of Dutch irritable infants. *Child Development, 66*, 1798–1816.

van den Boom, D. C. (1994). The influence of temperament and mothering on attachment and exploration: An experimental manipulation of sensitive responsiveness among lower-class mothers with irritable infants. *Child Development, 65*, 1457–1477.

van den Hoonaard, D. (1999). "No regrets": Widows' stories about the last days of their husbands' lives. *Journal of Aging Studies, 13*, 59–72.

van der Molen, M., Molenaar, P. (1994). Cognitive psychophysiology: A window to cognitive development and brain maturation. In G. Dawson & K. Fischer (Eds.), *Human behavior and the developing brain* (pp. 456–492). New York: Guilford Press.

Van Doorn, C., Kasl, S., Beery, L., Jacobs, S., & Prigerson, H. (1998). The influence of marital quality and attachment styles on traumatic grief and depressive symptoms. *Journal of Nervous & Mental Disease, 186*, 566–573.

van Doornen, L., Snieder, H., & Boomsma, D. (1998). Serum lipids and cardiovascular reactivity to stress. *Biological Psychology, 47*, 279–297.

van Grootheest, D., Beekman, A., van Groenou, M., & Deeg, D. (1999). Sex differences in depression after widowhood: Do men suffer more? *Social Psychiatry & Psychiatric Epidemiology, 34*, 391–398.

Van Hightower, N., & Gorton, J. (1998). Domestic violence among patients at two rural health care clinics: Prevalence and social correlates. *Public Health Nursing, 15*, 355–362.

van IJzendoorn, M. H. (1995). Adult attachment representations, parental responsiveness, and infant attachment: A meta-analysis on the predictive validity of the Adult Attachment Interview. *Psychological Bulletin, 117*, 387–403.

van IJzendoorn, M. H., Goldberg, S., Kroonenberg, P. M., & Frenkel, O. J. (1992). The relative effects of maternal and child problems on the quality of attachment: A meta-analysis of attachment in clinical samples. *Child Development, 63*, 840–858.

van IJzendoorn, M. H., & Kroonenberg, P. M. (1988). Cross-cultural patterns of attachment: A meta-analysis of the Strange Situation. *Child Development, 59*, 147–156.

Van Lange, P., DeBruin, E., Otten, W., & Joireman, J. (1997). Development of prosocial, individualistic, and competitive orientations: Theory and preliminary evidence. *Journal of Personality & Social Psychology, 73*, 733–746.

van Lieshout, C. F. M., & Haselager, G. J. T. (1994). The big five personality factors in Q-sort descriptions of children and adolescents. In C. F. Halverson, Jr., G. A. Kohnstamm, & R. P. Martin (Eds.), *The developing structure of temperament and personality from infancy to adulthood* (pp. 293–318). Hillsdale, NJ: Erlbaum.

Van Velsor, E., & O'Rand, A. M. (1984). Family life cycle, work career patterns, and women's wages at midlife. *Journal of Marriage and the Family, 46*, 365–373.

van Wel, F. (1994). "I count my parents among my best friends": Youths' bonds with parents and friends in the Netherlands. *Journal of Marriage and the Family, 56*, 835–843.

Vaughn, B., Stevenson-Hinde, J., Waters, E., Kotsaftis, A., Lefever, G., Shouldice, A., Trudel, M., & Belsky, J. (1992). Attachment security and temperament in infancy and early childhood: Some conceptual clarification. *Developmental Psychology, 28*, 463–473.

Vega, W. A. (1990). Hispanic families in the 1980s: A decade of research. *Journal of Marriage and the Family, 52*, 1015–1024.

Velicer, S. F. & Prochaska, J. O. (1999). An expert system intervention for smoking cessation. *Patient Education & Counseling, 36*, 119–129.

Venkatraman, M. M. (1995). A cross-cultural study of the subjective well-being of married elderly persons in the United States and India. *Journals of Gerontology: Social Sciences, 50B*, S35–44.

Verbrugge, L. M. (1984). A health profile of older women with comparisons to older men. *Research on Aging, 6*, 291–322.

Verbrugge, L. M. (1989). Gender, aging, and health. In K. S. Markides (Ed.), *Aging and health* (pp. 23–78). Newbury Park, CA: Sage.

Verbrugge, L. M., Lepkowski, J. M., & Konkol, L. L. (1991). Levels of disability among U.S. adults with arthritis. *Journals of Gerontology: Social Sciences, 46*, S71–83.

Verbrugge, L. M., & Wingard, D. L. (1987). Sex differentials in health and mortality. *Women and Health, 12*, 103–145.

Verhaeghen, P., & Marcoen, A. (1993). Memory aging as a general phenomenon: Episodic recall of older adults is a function of episodic recall of young adults. *Psychology and Aging, 8*, 380–388.

Verhaeghen, P., Marcoen, A., & Goossens, L. (1992). Improving memory performance in the aged through mnemonic training: A meta-analytic study. *Psychology and Aging, 7*, 242–251.

Verhaeghen, P., Marcoen, A., & Goossens, L. (1993). Facts and fiction about memory aging: A quantitative integration of research findings. *Journals of Gerontology: Psychological Sciences, 48*, P157–171.

Verhaeghen, P., & Salthouse, T. (1997). Meta-analyses of age-cognition relations in adulthood: Estimates of linear and nonlinear age effects and structural models. *Psychological Bulletin, 122*, 231–249.

Verhulst, F., & Versluis-Den Bieman, H. (1995). Development course of problem behaviors in adolescent adoptees. *Journal of the American Academy of Child and Adolescent Psychiatry, 34*, 151–159.

Veroff, J., Douvan, E., & Kulka, R. A. (1981). *The inner American: A self-portrait from 1957 to 1976.* New York: Basic Books.

Vihko, R., & Apter, D. (1980). The role of androgens in adolescent cycles. *Journal of Steroid Biochemistry, 12*, 369–373.

Vinokur, A. D., & van Ryn, M. (1993). Social support and undermining in close relationships: Their independent effects on the mental health of unemployed persons. *Journal of Personality and Social Psychology, 65,* 350–359.

Visser, P., & Krosnick, J. (1999). Development of attitude strength over the life cycle: Surge and decline. *Journal of Personality and Social Psychology, 75,* 1389–1410.

Vitaro, F., Tremblay, R., Kerr, M., Pagani, L., & Bukowski, W. (1997). Disruptiveness, friends' characteristics, and delinquency in early adolescence: A test of two competing models of development. *Child Development, 68,* 676–689.

Volz, J. (2000). Successful aging: The second 50. *Monitor, 31,* 24–28.

Voyer, D., Voyer, S., & Bryden, M. P. (1995). Magnitude of sex differences in spatial abilities: A meta-analysis and consideration of critical variables. *Psychological Bulletin, 117,* 250–270.

Vuchinich, S., Bank, L., & Patterson, G. R. (1992). Parenting, peers, and the stability of antisocial behavior in preadolescent boys. *Developmental Psychology, 28,* 510–521.

Vuorenkoski, L., Kuure, O., Moilanen, I., & Peninkilampi, V. (2000). Bilingualism, school achievement, and mental wellbeing: A follow-up study of return migrant children. *Journal of Child Psychology & Psychiatry & Allied Disciplines, 41,* 261–266.

Vygotsky, L. S. (1978). *Mind and society: The development of higher mental processes.* Cambridge, MA: Harvard University Press. (Original works published 1930, 1933, and 1935.)

Waggoner, G. (2000). The new grandparents: What they buy, what they think. *Modern Maturity, 43,* 85, 91.

Waite, L. J. (1995). *Does marriage matter?* Presidential address to the Population Association of America, Chicago.

Walden, T. A. (1991). Infant social referencing. In J. Garber & K. A. Dodge (Eds.), *The development of emotion regulation and dysregulation* (pp. 69–88). Cambridge, England: Cambridge University Press.

Waldner-Haugrud, L., Gratch, L., & Magruder, B. (1997). Victimization and perpetration rates of violence in gay and lesbian relationships: Gender issues explored. *Violence & Victims, 12,* 173–184.

Walker, H., Messinger, D., Fogel, A., & Karns, J. (1992). Social and communicative development in infancy. In V. B. V. Hasselt & M. Hersen (Eds.), *Handbook of social development: A lifespan perspective* (pp. 157–181). New York: Plenum.

Walker, L. (1980). Cognitive and perspective-taking prerequisites for moral development. *Child Development, 51,* 131–139.

Walker, L. J. (1989). A longitudinal study of moral reasoning. *Child Development, 60,* 157–160.

Walker, L. J., de Vries, B., & Trevethan, S. D. (1987). Moral stages and moral orientations in real-life and hypothetical dilemmas. *Child Development, 58,* 842–858.

Walker-Andrews, A., & Kahana-Kalman, R. (1999). The understanding of pretence across the second year of life. *British Journal of Developmental Psychology, 17,* 523–536.

Walker-Andrews, A. S., & Lennon, E. (1991). Infants' discrimination of vocal expressions: Contributions of auditory and visual information. *Infant Behavior and Development, 14,* 131–142.

Waller, A., Dennis, F., Brodie, J., & Cairns, A. (1998). Evaluating the use of TalksBac, a predictive communication device for nonfluent adults with aphasia. *International Journal of Language and Communication Disorders, 33,* 45–70.

Wallerstein, J., & Lewis, J. (1998). The long-term impact of divorce on children: A first report from a 25-year study. *Family & Conciliation Courts Review, 36,* 368–383.

Wallerstein, J. S. (1986). Women after divorce: Preliminary report from a ten-year-follow-up. *American Journal of Orthopsychiatry, 56,* 65–77.

Walls, C. T., & Zarit, S. H. (1991). Informal support from black churches and the well-being of elderly blacks. *The Gerontologist, 31,* 490–495.

Walton, G. E., Bower, N. J. A., & Bower, T. G. R. (1992). Recognition of familiar faces by newborns. *Infant Behavior and Development, 15,* 265–269.

Wang, C., & Chou, P. (1999). Risk factors for adolescent primigravida in Kaohsium county, Taiwan. *American Journal of Preventive Medicine, 17,* 43–47.

Wang, C., & Phinney, J. (1998). Differences in child rearing attitudes between immigrant Chinese mothers and Anglo-American mothers. *Early Development & Parenting, 7,* 181–189.

Wang, D., Kato, N., Inaba, Y., Tango, T., et al. (2000). Physical and personality traits of preschool children in Fuzhou, China: Only child vs. sibling. *Child: Care, Health & Development, 26,* 49–60.

Warburton, J., Le Brocque, R., & Rosenman, L. (1998). Older people the reserve army of volunteers? An analysis of volunteerism among older Australians. *International Journal of Aging & Human Development, 46,* 229–245.

Ward, S. L., & Overton, W. F. (1990). Semantic familiarity, relevance, and the development of deductive reasoning. *Developmental Psychology, 26,* 488–493.

Wark, G. R., & Krebs, D. L. (1996). Gender and dilemma differences in real-life moral judgment. *Developmental Psychology, 32,* 220–230.

Warr, P., Jackson, P., & Banks, M. (1988). Unemployment and mental health: Some British studies. *Journal of Social Issues, 44,* 47–68.

Wartner, U. B., Grossman, K., Fremmer-Bombik, E., & Suess, G. (1994). Attachment patterns at age six in south Germany: Predictability from infancy and implications for preschool behavior. *Child Development, 65,* 1014–1027.

Waterman, A. S. (1985). Identity in the context of adolescent psychology. *New Directions for Child Development, 30,* 5–24.

Waters, E., Treboux, D., Crowell, J., Merrick, S., & Albersheim, L. (1995, March). *From the Strange Situation to the Adult Attachment Interview: A 20-year longitudinal study of attachment security in infancy and early adulthood.* Paper presented at the biennial meetings of the Society for Research in Child Development, Indianapolis, IN.

Watkins, S. C., Menken, J. A., & Bongaarts, J. (1987). Demographic foundations of family change. *American Sociological Review, 52,* 346–358.

Watson, A., Nixon, C., Wilson, A., & Capage, L. (1999). Social interaction skills and theory of mind in young children. *Developmental Psychology, 35,* 386–391.

Watson, J. (1997). Grandmothering across the lifespan. *Journal of Gerontological Social Work, 28,* 45–62.

Watson, J. B. (1913). Psychology as the behaviorist views it. *Psychological Review, 20,* 158–177.

Watson, J. B. (1928). *Psychological care of the infant and child.* New York: Norton.

Watson, J. B. (1930). *Behaviorism.* New York: Norton.

Watson, J. B., & Rayner, R. (1920). Conditioned emotional reactions. *Journal of Experimental Psychology, 3,* 1–14.

Watt, L., & Cappeliez, P. (2000). Integrative and instrumental reminiscence therapies for depression in older adults: Intervention strategies and treatment effectiveness. *Aging & Mental Health, 4,* 166–177.

Waxman, S. R., & Kosowski, T. D. (1990). Nouns mark category relations: Toddlers' and preschoolers' word-learning biases. *Child Development, 61,* 1461–1473.

Weaver, C., & Hinson, S. (2000). Job satisfaction of Asian Americans. *Psychological Reports, 86,* 586–594.

Weaver, D. A. (1994). The work and retirement decisions of older women: A literature review. *Social Security Bulletin, 57,* 3–24.

Weaver, J. (1999). Gerontology education: A new paradigm for the 21st century. *Educational Gerontology, 25,* 479–490.

Weaver, S., Clifford, E., Hay, D., & Robinson, J. (1997). Psychosocial adjustment to unsuccessful IVF and GIFT treatment. *Patient Education & Counseling, 31,* 7–18.

Webster, J., & McCall, M. (1999). Reminiscence functions across adulthood: A replication and extension. *Journal of Adult Development, 6,* 73–85.

Webster, M. L., Thompson, J. M., Mitchell, E. A., & Werry, J. S. (1994). Postnatal depression in a community cohort. *Australian & New Zealand Journal of Psychiatry, 28,* 42–49.

Webster, P. S., & Herzog, A. R. (1995). Effects of parental divorce and memories of family problems on relationships between adult children and their parents. *Journals of Gerontology: Social Sciences, 50B,* S24–34.

Wechsler, D. (1974). *Manual for the Wechsler Intelligence Scale for Children–Revised.* New York: Psychological Corp.

Wechsler, H., Davenport, A., Dowdall, G., Moeykens, B., & Castillo, S. (1994). Health and behavioral consequences of binge drinking in college. *Journal of the American Medical Association, 272,* 1672–1677.

Wechsler, H., Dowdall, G., Maenner, G., Gledhill-Hoyt, J., & Lee, H. (1998). Changes in binge drinking and related problems among American college students between 1993 and 1997. *Journal of American College Health, 47,* 57–68.

Weinberg, A., & Weinberg, L. (1980). *Clarence Darrow: A sentimental rebel.* New York: Putnam's.

Weinberg, R. A. (1989). Intelligence and IQ: Landmark issues and great debates. *American Psychologist, 44,* 98–104.

Weinberg, R. A., Scarr, S., & Waldman, I. D. (1992). The Minnesota transracial adoption study: A follow-up of IQ test performance. *Intelligence, 16,* 117–135.

Weinberger, J. (1996). A longitudinal study of children's early literacy experiences at home and later literacy development at home and school. *Journal of Research in Reading, 19,* 14–24.

Weinstock, L. (1999). Gender differences in the presentation and management of social anxiety disorder. *Journal of Clinical Psychiatry, 60,* 9–13.

Weisburger, J. H., & Wynder, E. L. (1991). Dietary fat intake and cancer. *Hematology/Oncology Clinics of North America, 5,* 7–23.

Weisner, T., & Wilson-Mitchell, J. (1990). Nonconventional family lifestyles and sex typing in six-year olds. *Child Development, 62,* 1915–1933.

Weiss, M. (1998). Conditions of mothering: The bio-politics of falling in love with your child. *Social Science Journal, 35,* 87–105.

Weiss, R. S. (1986). Continuities and transformations in social relationships from childhood to adulthood. In W. W. Hartup & Z. Rubin (Eds.), *On relationships and development* (pp. 95–110). Hillsdale, NJ: Erlbaum.

Weisse, C. S. (1992). Depression and immunocompetence: A review of the literature. *Psychological Bulletin, 111,* 475–489.

Welch, D. C., & West, R. L. (1995). Self-efficacy and mastery: Its application to issues of environmental control, cognition, and aging. *Developmental Review, 15,* 150–171.

Welch-Ross, M. (1997). Mother-child participation in conversation about the past: Relationships to preschoolers' theory of mind. *Developmental Psychology, 33,* 618–629.

Welford, A. T. (1993). The gerontological balance sheet. In J. Cerella, J. Rybash, W. Hoyer, & M. L. Commons (Eds.), *Adult information processing: Limits on loss* (pp. 3–10). San Diego, CA: Academic Press.

Wellman, H. M. (1982). The foundations of knowledge: Concept development in the young child. In S. G. Moore & C. C. Cooper (Eds.), *The young child: Reviews of research* (Vol. 3) (pp. 115–134). Washington, DC: National Association for the Education of Young Children.

Wells, G., Malpass, R., Lindsay, R., Fisher, R., Turtle, J., & Fulero, S. (2000). From the lab to the police station. *American Psychologist, 55,* 581–598.

Wen, S. W., Goldenberg, R. L., Cutter, G. R., Hoffman, H. J., Cliver, S. P., Davis, R. O., & DuBard, M. D. (1990). Smoking, maternal age, fetal growth, and gestational age at delivery. *American Journal of Obstetrics and Gynecology, 162,* 53–58.

Wentzel, K. R., & Asher, S. R. (1995). The academic lives of neglected, rejected, popular, and controversial children. *Child Development, 66,* 754–763.

Wenz-Gross, M., Siperstein, G., Untch, A., & Widaman, K. (1997). Stress, social support, and adjustment of adolescents in middle school. *Journal of Early Adolescence, 17,* 129–151.

Werner, E. E. (1995). Resilience in development. *Current Directions in Psychological Science, 4,* 81–85.

Werner, E. E., & Smith, R. S. (1992). *Overcoming the odds: High risk children from birth to adulthood.* Ithaca, NY: Cornell University Press.

Wernet, S., Olliges, R., & Delicath, T. (2000). Postcourse evaluations of WebCT (web course tools) classes by social work students. *Research on Social Work Practice, 10,* 387–504.

Werth, J. (2000). End-of-life decisions for persons with AIDS. American Psychological Association Public Interest Directorate [Online article]. Retrieved February 20, 2001 from the World Wide Web: http://www.apa.org/pi/aids/werth.html

West, P., Sweeting, H., & Ecob, R. (1999). Family and friends' influences on the uptake of regular smoking from mid-adolescence to early adulthood. *Addiction, 97,* 1397–1411.

West, R. L., & Crook, T. H. (1990). Age differences in everyday memory: Laboratory analogues of telephone number recall. *Psychology and Aging, 5,* 520–529.

Whitam, F. L., Diamond, M., & Martin, J. (1993). Homosexual orientation in twins: A report on 61 pairs and three triplet sets. *Archives of Sexual Behavior, 22,* 187–206.

Whitbeck, L. B., Simons, R. L., & Conger, R. D. (1991). The effects of early family relationships on contemporary relationships and assistance patterns between adult children and their parents. *Journals of Gerontology: Social Sciences, 46,* S330–337.

White, M., Wilson, M., Elander, G., & Persson, B. (1999). The Swedish family: Transition to parenthood. *Scandinavian Journal of Caring Sciences, 13,* 171–176.

White, N., & Cunningham, W. R. (1988). Is terminal drop pervasive or specific? *Journals of Gerontology: Psychological Sciences, 43,* P141–144.

White, W. H. (1992). G. Stanley Hall: From philosophy to developmental psychology. *Developmental Psychology, 28,* 25–34.

Whitehurst, G. J., Arnold, D. S., Epstein, J. N., Angell, A. L., Smith, M., & Fischel, J. E. (1994). A picture book reading intervention in day care and home for children from low-income families. *Developmental Psychology, 30,* 679–689.

Whitehurst, G. J., Falco, F. L., Lonigan, C. J., Fischel, J. E., DeBaryshe, B. D., Valdez-Menchaca, M. C., & Caulfield, M. (1988). Accelerating language development through picture book reading. *Developmental Psychology, 24,* 552–559.

Whitehurst, G. J., Fischel, J. E., Crone, D. A., & Nania, O. (1995, March). *First year outcomes of a clinical trial of an emergent literacy intervention in Head Start homes and classrooms.* Paper presented at the biennial meetings of the Society for Research in Child Development, Indianapolis, IN.

Whiting, B., & Edwards, C. (1988). *Children of different worlds.* Cambridge, MA: Harvard University Press.

Whitney, M. P., & Thoman, E. B. (1994). Sleep in premature and full-term infants from 24-hour home recordings. *Infant Behavior and Development, 17,* 223–234.

Whittaker, R. (1998). Re-framing the representation of women in advertisements for hormone replacement therapy. *Nursing Inquiry, 5,* 77–86.

Wich, B. K., & Carnes, M. (1995). Menopause and the aging female reproductive system. *Endocrinology and Metabolism Clinics of North America, 24,* 273–295.

Wicki, W. (1999). The impact of family resources and satisfaction with division of labour on coping and worries after the birth of the first child. *International Journal of Behavioral Development, 23,* 431–456.

Wickrama, K., Conger, R., Lorenz, F., & Elder, G. (1998). Parental education and adolescent self-reported physical health. *Journal of Marriage & the Family, 60,* 967–978.

Wickrama, K., Lorenz, F., & Conger, R. (1997). Parental support and adolescent physical health status: A latent growth-curve analysis. *Journal of Health & Social Behavior, 38,* 149–163.

Wiederman, M., & Allgeier, E. (1992). Gender differences in mate selection criteria: Sociobiological or socioeconomic explanation? *Ethology and Sociobiology, 13,* 115–124.

Wigfield, A., Eccles, J. S., MacIver, D., Reuman, D. A., & Midgley, C. (1991). Transitions during early adolescence: Changes in children's domain-specific self-perceptions and general self-esteem across the transition to junior high school. *Developmental Psychology, 27,* 552–565.

Wilcox, C., & Francis, L. (1997). The relationship between neuroticism and the perceived social desirability of feminine characteristics among 16–19-year-old females. *Social Behavior & Personality, 25,* 291–294.

Willett, W. C., Hunter, D. J., Stampfer, M. J., Colditz, G., Manson, J. E., Spiegelman, D., Rosner, B., Hennekens, C. H., & Speizer, F. E. (1992). Dietary fat and fiber in relation to risk of breast cancer: An 8-year follow-up. *Journal of the American Medical Association, 268,* 2037–2044.

Willett, W. C., Manson, J. E., Stampfer, M. J., Colditz, G. A., Rosner, B., Speizer, F. E., & Hennekens, C. H. (1995). Weight, weight change, and coronary heart disease in women: Risk within the "normal" weight range. *Journal of the American Medical Association, 273,* 461–465.

Williams, D. R. (1992). Social structure and the health behaviors of blacks. In K. W. Schaie, D. Blazer, & J. S. House (Eds.), *Aging, health behaviors, and health outcomes* (pp. 59–64). Hillsdale, NJ: Erlbaum.

Williams, E., & Radin, N. (1993). Parental involvement, maternal employment, and adolescents' academic achievement: An 11-year follow-up. *American Journal of Orthopsychiatry, 63,* 306–312.

Williams, J. E., & Best, D. L. (1990). *Measuring sex stereotypes: A multination study* (rev. ed.). Newbury Park, CA: Sage.

Willis, S. L. (1996). Everyday problem solving. In J. E. Birren & K. W. Schaie (Eds.), *Handbook of the psychology of aging* (4th ed.) (pp. 287–307). San Diego, CA: Academic Press.

Willis, S. L., Jay, G. M., Diehl, M., & Marsiske, M. (1992). Longitudinal change and prediction of everyday task competence in the elderly. *Research on Aging, 14,* 68–91.

Willits, F. K., & Crider, D. M. (1988). Health rating and life satisfaction in the later middle years. *Journals of Gerontology: Social Sciences, 43,* S172–176.

Wilson, M. R., & Filsinger, E. E. (1986). Religiosity and marital adjustment: Multidimensional interrelationships. *Journal of Marriage and the Family, 48,* 147–151.

Wilson, W. J. (1995). Jobless ghettos and the social outcome of youngsters. In P. Moen, G. H. Elder, Jr., & K. Lüscher (Eds.), *Examining lives in context: Perspectives on the ecology of human development* (pp. 527–543). Washington, DC: American Psychological Association.

Wimmer, H., Mayringer, H., & Landerl, K. (1998). Poor reading: A deficit in skill-automatization or a phonological deficit? *Scientific Studies of Reading, 2,* 321–340.

Wink, P., & Helson, R. (1993). Personality change in women and their partners. *Journal of Personality and Social Psychology, 65,* 597–605.

Winter, L., Lawton, M., Casten, R., & Sando, R. (2000). The relationship between external events and affect states in older people. *International Journal of Aging & Human Development, 50,* 85–96.

Winter, R. (1999). A Biblical and theological view of grief and bereavement. *Journal of Psychology & Christianity, 18,* 367–379.

Wintgens, A., Lepine, S., Lefebvre, F., Glorieux, J., Gauthier, Y., & Robaey, P. (1998). Attachment, self-esteem, and psychomotor development in extremely premature children at preschool age. *Infant Mental Health Journal, 19,* 394–408.

Wintre, M., & Yaffe, M. (2000). First-year students' adjustment to university life as a function of relationships with parents. *Journal of Adolescent Research, 15,* 9–37.

Wolfe, C., Wang, A., & Bergen, D. (1999). Assessing the Winning Teams program of interactive satellite-based training. *Behavior Research Methods, Instruments, & Computers, 31,* 275–280.

Wolff, P., & Fesseha, G. (1999). The orphans of Eritrea: A five-year follow-up study. *Journal of Child Psychology & Psychiatry & Allied Disciplines, 40,* 1231–1237.

Wolfram, W. (1990). *Incorporating dialect study into the language arts class.* (ERIC Clearinghouse on Languages and Linguistics No. ED 318 231)

Wolfram, W., Schilling-Estes, N., & Hazen, K. (1996). *Dialects and the Ocracoke brogue. Eighth-grade curriculum.* Raleigh, NC: North Carolina Language and Life Project.

Wolfson, C., Handfield-Jones, R., Glass, K. C., McClaran, J., & Keyserlingk, E. (1993). Adult children's perceptions of their responsibility to provide care for dependent elderly parents. *The Gerontologist, 33,* 315–323.

Wolinsky, F. D., Calahan, C. M., Fitzgerald, J. F., & Johnson, R. J. (1993). Changes in functional status and the risks of subsequent nursing home placement and death. *Journals of Gerontology: Social Sciences, 48,* S93–101.

Wolinsky, F. D., Stump, T. E., & Clark, D. (1995). Antecedents and consequences of physical activity and exercise among older adults. *The Gerontologist, 35,* 451–462.

Wong, D. (1993). *Whaley & Wong's essentials of pediatric nursing.* St. Louis, MO: Mosby-Yearbook, Inc.

Wood, C., & Terrell, C. (1998). Pre-school phonological awareness and subsequent literacy development. *Educational Psychology, 18,* 253–274.

Woods, N., & Mitchell, E. (1997). Pathways to depressed mood for midlife women: Observations from the Seattle Midlife Women's Health Study. *Research in Nursing & Health, 20,* 119–129.

Woodward, L., & Fergusson, D. (2000). Childhood peer relationship problems and later risks of educational under-achievement and unemployment. *Journal of Child Psychology & Psychiatry & Allied Disciplines, 41,* 191–201.

Woodward, M., & Tunstall-Pedoe, H. (1995). Alcohol consumption, diet, coronary risk factors, and prevalent coronary heart disease in men and women in the Scottish heart health study. *Journal of Epidemiology and Community Health, 49,* 354–362.

The Working Group for the PEPI Trial (1995). Effects of estrogen or estrogen/progestin regimens on heart disease risk factors in postmenopausal women: The Postmenopausal Estrogen/Progestin Interventions (PEPI) Trial. *Journal of the American Medical Association, 273,* 199–208.

World Health Organization. (2000). *Violence against women.* [Online report]. Retrieved September 1, 2000 from the World Wide Web: http://www.who.int

Worobey, J. L., & Angel, R. J. (1990). Functional capacity and living arrangements of unmarried elderly persons. *Journals of Gerontology: Social Sciences, 45,* S95–101.

Worrell, F. (1997). Predicting successful or non-successful at-risk status using demographic risk factors. *High School Journal, 81,* 46–53.

Wortman, C. B., & Silver, R. C. (1989). The myths of coping with loss. *Journal of Consulting and Clinical Psychology, 57,* 349–357.

Wortman, C. B., & Silver, R. C. (1990). Successful mastery of bereavement and widowhood: A life course perspective. In P. B. Baltes & M. M. Baltes (Eds.), *Successful aging: Perspectives from the behavioral sciences* (pp. 225–264). New York: Cambridge University Press.

Wortman, C. B., & Silver, R. C. (1992). Reconsidering assumptions about coping with loss: An overview of current research. In L. Montada, S. Filipp, & M. J. Lerner (Eds.), *Life crises and experiences of loss in adulthood* (pp. 341–365). Hillsdale, NJ: Erlbaum.

Wortman, C. B., Silver, R. C., & Kessler, R. C. (1993). The meaning of loss and adjustment to bereavement. In M. S. Stroebe, W. Stroebe, & R. O. Hansson (Eds.), *Handbook of bereavement* (pp. 349–366). Cambridge, England: Cambridge University Press.

Wright, C., & Birks, E. (2000). Risk factors for failure to thrive: A population-based survey. *Child: Care, Health & Development, 26,* 5–16.

Wright, S., Taylor, D., & Macarthur, J. (2000). Subtractive bilingualism and the survival of the Inuit language: Heritage versus second-language education. *Journal of Educational Psychology, 92,* 63–84.

Wu, Z., & Penning, M. (1997). Marital instability after midlife. *Journal of Family Issues, 18,* 459–478.

Wyatt, G., Axelrod, J., Chin, D., Carmona, J., & Loeb, T. (2000). Examining patterns of vulnerability to domestic violence among African American women. *Violence Against Women, 6,* 495–514.

Xie, H., Cairns, R., & Cairns, B. (1999). Social networks and configurations in inner-city schools: Aggression, popularity, and implications for students with EBD. *Journal of Emotional & Behavioral Disorders, 7,* 147–155.

Yamada, A., & Singelis, T. (1999). Biculturalism and self-construal. *International Journal of Intercultural Relations, 23,* 697–709.

Yang, H., & Chandler, D. (1992). Intergenerational relations: Grievances of the elderly in rural China. *Journal of Comparative Family Studies, 23,* 431–453.

Yarcheski, A., Mahon, N., & Yarcheski, T. (1998). A study of introspectiveness in adolescents and young adults. *Western Journal of Nursing Research, 20,* 312–324.

Yeung, A., Chui, H., & Lau, I. (1999). Hierarchical and multidimensional academic self-concept of commercial students. *Contemporary Educational Psychology, 24,* 376–389.

Yirmiya, N., Eriel, O., Shaked, M., & Solomonica-Levi, D. (1998). Meta-analyses comparing theory of mind abilities of individuals with autism, individuals with mental retardation, and normally developing individuals. *Psychological Bulletin, 124,* 283–307.

Yirmiya, N., & Shulman, C. (1996). Seriation, conservation, and theory of mind abilities in individuals with autism, individuals with mental retardation, and normally developing children. *Child Development, 67,* 2045–2059.

Yirmiya, N., Solomonica-Levi, D., Shulman, C., & Pilowsky, T. (1996). Theory of mind abilities in individuals with autism, Down syndrome, and mental retardation of unknown etiology: The role of age and intelligence. *Journal of Child Psychology & Psychiatry & Allied Disciplines, 37,* 1003–1014.

Yonas, A., & Owsley, C. (1987). Development of visual space perception. In P. Salpatek & L. Cohen (Eds.), *Handbook of infant perception: Vol. 2: From perception to cognition* (pp. 80–122). Orlando, FL: Academic Press.

Yordanova, J., Kolev, V., & Basar, E. (1998). EEG theta and frontal alpha oscillations during auditory processing change with aging. *Electroencephalography & Clinical Neurophysiology: Evoked Potentials, 108,* 497–505.

Yoshikawa, H. (1999). Welfare dynamics, support services, mothers' earnings, and child cognitive development: Implications for contemporary welfare reform. *Child Development, 70,* 779–801

Young, A. (1997). I think, therefore I'm motivated: The relations among cognitive strategy use, motivational orientation and classroom perceptions over time. *Learning & Individual Differences, 9,* 249–283.

Young, J., & Rodgers, R. (1997). A model of radical career change in the context of psychosocial development. *Journal of Career Assessment, 5,* 167–182.

Young, M., & Bradley, M. (1998). Social withdrawal: Self-efficacy, happiness, and popularity in introverted and extroverted adolescents. *Canadian Journal of School Psychology, 14,* 21–35.

Young, S., Fox, N., & Zahn-Waxler, C. (1999). The relations between temperament and empathy in 2-year-olds. *Developmental Psychology, 35,* 1189–1197.

YouthBuild/Boston. (2000). *Program report.* [Online report]. Retrieved February 29, 2000 from the World Wide Web: http://www.doe.mass.edu/cs.www/cs.youthbuild.html

Yuill, N. (1997). English children as personality theorists: Accounts of the modifiability, development, and origin of traits. *Genetic, Social & General Psychology Monographs, 123,* 5–26.

Yuji, H. (1996). Computer games and information-processing skills. *Perceptual & Motor Skills, 83,* 643–647.

Zahn-Waxler, C., & Radke-Yarrow, M. (1982). The development of altruism: Alternative research strategies. In N. Eisenberg (Ed.), *The development of prosocial behavior* (pp. 109–138). New York: Academic Press.

Zahn-Waxler, C., Radke-Yarrow, M., & King, R. (1979). Child rearing and children's prosocial initiations toward victims of distress. *Child Development, 50,* 319–330.

Zahn-Waxler, C., Radke-Yarrow, M., Wagner, E., & Chapman, M. (1992). Development of concern for others. *Developmental Psychology, 28,* 126–136.

Zakriski, A., & Coie, J. (1996). A comparison of aggressive-rejected and nonaggressive-rejected children's interpretation of self-directed and other-directed rejection. *Child Development, 67,* 1048–1070.

Zani, B. (1993). Dating and interpersonal relationships in adolescence. In S. Jackson & H. Rodrigues-Tomé (Eds.), *Adolescence and its social worlds* (pp. 95–119). Hove, England: Erlbaum.

Zea, M., Reisen, C., Bell, C., & Caplan, R. (1997). Predicting intention to remain in college among ethnic minority and nonminority students. *Journal of Social Psychology, 137,* 149–160.

Zelazo, N. A., Zelazo, P. R., Cohen, K. M., & Zelazo, P. D. (1993). Specificity of practice effects on elementary neuromotor patterns. *Developmental Psychology, 29,* 686–691.

Zelazo, P., Helwig, C., & Lau, A. (1996). Intention, act, and outcome in behavioral prediction and moral judgment. *Child Development, 67,* 2478–2492.

Zelinski, E. M., Gilewski, M. J., & Schaie, K. W. (1993). Individual differences in cross-sectional and 3-year longitudinal memory performance across the adult life span. *Psychology and Aging, 8,* 176–186.

Zelinski, E., & Burnight, K. (1997). Sixteen-year longitudinal and time lag changes in memory and cognition in older adults. *Psychology & Aging, 12,* 503–513.

Zick, C., & Holden, K. (2000). An assessment of the wealth holdings of recent widows. *Journal of Gerontology, 55B,* S90–S97.

Zigler, E., & Finn-Stevenson, M. (1993). *Children in a changing world: Developmental and social issues.* Pacific Grove, CA: Brooks/Cole.

Zigler, E., & Hodapp, R. M. (1991). Behavioral functioning in individuals with mental retardation. *Annual Review of Psychology, 42,* 29–50.

Zigler, E., & Styfco, S. J. (1993). Using research and theory to justify and inform Head Start expansion. *Social Policy Report, Society for Research in Child Development, VII*(2), 1–21.

Zill, N., & Nord, C. W. (1994). *Running in place: How American families are faring in a changing economy and an individualistic society.* Washington, DC: Child Trends.

Zimmer, Z., Hickey, T., & Searle, M. S. (1995). Activity participation and well-being among older people with arthritis. *The Gerontologist, 35,* 463–471.

Zimmer-Gembeck, M. (1999). Stability, change and individual differences in involvement with friends and romantic partners among adolescent females. *Journal of Youth & Adolescence, 28,* 419–438.

Zimmerman, C. (2000). The development of scientific reasoning skills. *Developmental Review, 20,* 99–149.

Zimmerman, M., Copeland, L., Shope, J., & Dielman, T. (1997). A longitudinal study of self-esteem: Implications for adolescent development. *Journal of Youth & Adolescence, 26,* 117–141.

Zisook, S., Chentsova-Dutton, Y., & Shuchter, S. (1998). PTSD following bereavement. *Annals of Clinical Psychiatry, 10,* 157–163.

Zisook, S., Paulus, M., Shuchter, S., & Judd, L. (1997). The many faces of depression following spousal bereavement. *Journal of Affective Disorders, 45,* 85–94.

Zoccolillo, M. (1993). Gender and the development of conduct disorder. *Development and Psychopathology, 5,* 65–78.

Zuger, B. (1990). Changing concepts of the etiology of male homosexuality. *Medical Aspects of Human Sexuality, 24,* 73–75.

Zunker, V. (1994). *Career Counseling.* Pacific Grove, CA: Brooks/Cole.

Zweig, J., Barber, M., & Eccles, J. (1997). Sexual coercion and well-being in young adulthood: Comparison by gender and college status. *Journal of Interpersonal Violence, 12,* 291–308.

Name Index

613

Subject Index

AAVE (African American Vernacular
    English), 241
Abecedarian project, 173
Ability goals, 300
Abnormal behavior, 14
Abortion, 61, 86
Abuse. *See also* Sexual violence
    alcohol and, 353
    child, 154–156
    domestic, 352
    of elderly, 499
    of infants, 142–143
    of intimate partner, 352–354
    physical, 353
    prevention of, 155–156, 354
    sexual, 155
    victims of, 353
Acceptance stage, of dying, 527
Accidents
    bicycle, 219–220
    in early childhood, 154
Accommodation, 38
Achievement
    cultural differences in, 242–243
    measuring and predicting, 230–233
    racial differences in, 240–242
    in science and math, 301–303
    self-care children and, 268
    sex differences in, 240
Achievement test, 230
Active euthanasia, 545–546
Active phase of labor, 80
Activities of daily living (ADLs), 460
Activity level, of infant, 132
Activity theory, 488
Adaptive reflex, 92, 113
Addiction. *See also* Alcohol; Drugs
    to drugs, 356
    to Internet, 415
ADHD (attention-deficit hyperactivity
    disorder), 237–239
ADL (activities of daily living), 460
Adolescence
    achievement in science and math in,
      301–303
    antisocial behavior in, 334–336
    attachment in, 321–323
    attachment quality in infancy and,
      129–130
    brain in, 282–283
    changes in thinking and memory in,
      295–299
    depression in, 293–295
    dropping out of school in, 303–304
    drug, alcohol, and tobacco use in,
      290–291
    eating disorders in, 291–293
    endocrine and reproductive systems in,
      279–281
    ethnic identity in, 316–319
    friendships in, 323–324
    grief in, 533
    health in, 285–290
    homosexuality and, 326–327

information-processing in, 297–299
locus of control in, 319–320
moral development in, 328–336
muscular system in, 283–284
peers in, 323–326
physical changes during, 278–284
pregnancy in, 288–290
psychoanalytic perspectives and, 311
schooling in, 299–307
self concept and personality in,
    313–320
self-esteem in, 315–316
sex-role identity and, 315
sexual behavior in, 286–288
skeletal system in, 283
social and personality theories and,
    310–313
social relationships in, 320–327
suicide in, 294–295, 521
timing of puberty in, 281–282
understanding of death in, 520–521
violence in, 335
working during, 305–307
Adoption
    development and, 124
    intelligence and, 171–172
    mixed race, 175
Adrenal androgen, 279
Adulthood. *See also* Early adulthood;
    Late adulthood; Middle adulthood
    lifespan perspective and, 14
    quality of attachment in infancy and,
    130
Affection, 186
Affectional bond, 123
African American Vernacular English
    (AAVE), 241
African Americans. *See* Cultural Differ-
    ences; Racial differences
Afterbirth, 80
After-school care, 267–269
Age
    changes related to, 16–17
    effect on pregnancy of, 74–75
    long-term memory and, 361
    peak sports performance and, 346
    retirement and, 505
Age norms, 11
Ageism, 11
    depression diagnosis and, 476
    employment and, 443
Aggression
    in early childhood, 197–199
    group entry skills and, 196
    hostile, 198
    instrumental, 198
    long-term consequences of childhood,
      261
    in middle childhood, 258–260
    nonparental care and, 140
    physical, 114, 197, 258–259
    reinforcement and modeling in, 198
    relational, 259
    retaliatory, 259

television and, 273–275
trait, 198
verbal, 197
video games and, 220
Aggressive/rejected social status, 260
Aging
    cross-linking in cells and, 469
    Denney's model of physical and cogni-
      tive, 417–418, 420
    dependency and, 491
    free radicals and, 469
    general slowing down in, 470–471
    primary, 342–343
    programmed senescence theory of,
      468–469
    repair of genetic material and, 469
    secondary, 342
    successful, 490–493
    terminal drop hypothesis and, 470
    theories of biological, 468–470
Agreeableness (personality trait),
    262–263
AIDS, 348, 349, 530
Alameda County Study, 350, 351, 464
Alcohol
    abuse and, 353
    abuse of, 435
    in adolescence, 285, 287, 290–291
    grief and, 537
    in pregnancy, 61
    prenatal development and, 72–73
Alcoholics Anonymous, 416
Alcoholism, 356, 415–416
Alpha-fetoprotein, 76
Altruism, 199
Alzheimer's disease, 434, 438, 440, 459
    causes of, 474
    incidence of, 475–476
Ambivalent attachment, 128–129
Amenity move, 509
American Academy of Pediatrics, 99
American Educational Research Associa-
    tion, 21
American Psychological Association, 21,
    546
Americans with Disabilities Act, 365
Amniocentesis, 76, 77
Amnion, 62
Amygdala, 132
Anal stage, 27–28, 180
Analgesics, in labor, 78–79
Analytical style, 241
Androgynous sex-role orientation, 315
Anemia, 97
Anesthesia, in labor, 78–79
Anger, 527
Anorexia nervosa, 292
Anovulatory cycle, 403
Anoxia, 80
Anticonvulsant drugs, prenatal develop-
    ment and, 76
Antioxidants, 469–470
Antisocial behavior, moral development
    and, 334–336